# Apache HTTP Server Documentation Version 2.5

Apache Software Foundation

June 1, 2016

# About The PDF Documentation

Licensed to the Apache Software Foundation (ASF) under one or more contributor license agreements. See the NO-TICE file distributed with this work for additional information regarding copyright ownership. The ASF licenses this file to You under the Apache License, Version 2.0 (the "License"); you may not use this file except in compliance with the License. You may obtain a copy of the License at http://www.apache.org/licenses/LICENSE-2.0

This version of the Apache HTTP Server Documentation is converted from XML source files to LaTeX using XSLT with the help of Apache Ant, Apache XML Xalan, and Apache XML Xerces.

Since the HTML version of the documentation is more commonly checked during development, the PDF version may contain some errors and inconsistencies, especially in formatting. If you have difficulty reading a part of this file, please consult the HTML version of the documentation on the Apache HTTP Server website at http://httpd.apache.org/docs/trunk/

The Apache HTTP Server Documentation is maintained by the Apache HTTP Server Documentation Project. More information is available at http://httpd.apache.org/docs-project/

# Contents

# Chapter 1

# Release Notes

# 1.1   Upgrading to 2.4 from 2.2

In order to assist folks upgrading, we maintain a document describing information critical to existing Apache HTTP Server users. These are intended to be brief notes, and you should be able to find more information in either the New Features (p. 8) document, or in the `src/CHANGES` file. Application and module developers can find a summary of API changes in the API updates (p. 1035) overview.

This document describes changes in server behavior that might require you to change your configuration or how you use the server in order to continue using 2.4 as you are currently using 2.2. To take advantage of new features in 2.4, see the New Features document.

This document describes only the changes from 2.2 to 2.4. If you are upgrading from version 2.0, you should also consult the 2.0 to 2.2 upgrading document.[1]

**See also**

- Overview of new features in Apache HTTP Server 2.4 (p. 8)

## Compile-Time Configuration Changes

The compilation process is very similar to the one used in version 2.2. Your old `configure` command line (as found in `build/config.nice` in the installed server directory) can be used in most cases. There are some changes in the default settings. Some details of changes:

- These modules have been removed: mod_authn_default, mod_authz_default, mod_mem_cache. If you were using mod_mem_cache in 2.2, look at MOD_CACHE_DISK in 2.4.
- All load balancing implementations have been moved to individual, self-contained mod_proxy submodules, e.g. MOD_LBMETHOD_BYBUSYNESS. You might need to build and load any of these that your configuration uses.
- Platform support has been removed for BeOS, TPF, and even older platforms such as A/UX, Next, and Tandem. These were believed to be broken anyway.
- configure: dynamic modules (DSO) are built by default
- configure: By default, only a basic set of modules is loaded. The other LOADMODULE directives are commented out in the configuration file.
- configure: the "most" module set gets built by default
- configure: the "reallyall" module set adds developer modules to the "all" set

## Run-Time Configuration Changes

There have been significant changes in authorization configuration, and other minor configuration changes, that could require changes to your 2.2 configuration files before using them for 2.4.

### Authorization

Any configuration file that uses authorization will likely need changes.

You should review the Authentication, Authorization and Access Control Howto (p. 227) , especially the section Beyond just authorization (p. 227) which explains the new mechanisms for controlling the order in which the authorization directives are applied.

---

[1]http://httpd.apache.org/docs/2.2/upgrading.html

Directives that control how authorization modules respond when they don't match the authenticated user have been removed: This includes AuthzLDAPAuthoritative, AuthzDBDAuthoritative, AuthzDBMAuthoritative, AuthzGroup-FileAuthoritative, AuthzUserAuthoritative, and AuthzOwnerAuthoritative. These directives have been replaced by the more expressive REQUIREANY, REQUIRENONE, and REQUIREALL.

If you use MOD_AUTHZ_DBM, you must port your configuration to use `Require dbm-group ...` in place of `Require group ...`.

**Access control**

In 2.2, access control based on client hostname, IP address, and other characteristics of client requests was done using the directives ORDER, ALLOW, DENY, and SATISFY.

In 2.4, such access control is done in the same way as other authorization checks, using the new module MOD_AUTHZ_HOST. The old access control idioms should be replaced by the new authentication mechanisms, although for compatibility with old configurations, the new module MOD_ACCESS_COMPAT is provided.

**Mixing old and new directives**

> Mixing old directives like ORDER, ALLOW or DENY with new ones like REQUIRE is technically possible but discouraged. MOD_ACCESS_COMPAT was created to support configurations containing only old directives to facilitate the 2.4 upgrade. Please check the examples below to get a better idea about issues that might arise.

Here are some examples of old and new ways to do the same access control.

In this example, all requests are denied.

**2.2 configuration:**

```
Order deny,allow
Deny from all
```

**2.4 configuration:**

```
Require all denied
```

In this example, all requests are allowed.

**2.2 configuration:**

```
Order allow,deny
Allow from all
```

**2.4 configuration:**

```
Require all granted
```

In the following example, all hosts in the example.org domain are allowed access; all other hosts are denied access.

**2.2 configuration:**

```
Order Deny,Allow
Deny from all
Allow from example.org
```

**2.4 configuration:**

```
Require host example.org
```

In the following example, mixing old and new directives leads to unexpected results.

**Mixing old and new directives: NOT WORKING AS EXPECTED**

```
DocumentRoot "/var/www/html"

<Directory "/">
    AllowOverride None
    Order deny,allow
    Deny from all
</Directory>

<Location "/server-status">
    SetHandler server-status
    Require 127.0.0.1
</Location>

access.log - GET /server-status 403 127.0.0.1
error.log - AH01797: client denied by server configuration: /var/www/html/server-status
```

Why httpd denies access to servers-status even if the configuration seems to allow it? Because MOD_ACCESS_COMPAT directives take precedence over the MOD_AUTHZ_HOST one in this configuration merge (p. 35) scenario.

This example conversely works as expected:

**Mixing old and new directives: WORKING AS EXPECTED**

```
DocumentRoot "/var/www/html"

<Directory "/">
    AllowOverride None
    Require all denied
</Directory>

<Location "/server-status">
    SetHandler server-status
    Order deny,allow
    Deny from all
    Allow From 127.0.0.1
</Location>

access.log - GET /server-status 200 127.0.0.1
```

So even if mixing configuration is still possible, please try to avoid it when upgrading: either keep old directives and then migrate to the new ones on a later stage or just migrate everything in bulk.

**Other configuration changes**

Some other small adjustments may be necessary for particular configurations as discussed below.

- MAXREQUESTSPERCHILD has been renamed to MAXCONNECTIONSPERCHILD, describes more accurately what it does. The old name is still supported.

- MAXCLIENTS has been renamed to MAXREQUESTWORKERS, which describes more accurately what it does. For async MPMs, like EVENT, the maximum number of clients is not equivalent than the number of worker threads. The old name is still supported.

- The DEFAULTTYPE directive no longer has any effect, other than to emit a warning if it's used with any value other than `none`. You need to use other configuration settings to replace it in 2.4.

- ALLOWOVERRIDE now defaults to `None`.

- ENABLESENDFILE now defaults to Off.

- FILEETAG now defaults to "MTime Size" (without INode).

- MOD_DAV_FS: The format of the DAVLOCKDB file has changed for systems with inodes. The old DAVLOCKDB file must be deleted on upgrade.

- KEEPALIVE only accepts values of `On` or `Off`. Previously, any value other than "Off" or "0" was treated as "On".

- Directives AcceptMutex, LockFile, RewriteLock, SSLMutex, SSLStaplingMutex, and WatchdogMutexPath have been replaced with a single MUTEX directive. You will need to evaluate any use of these removed directives in your 2.2 configuration to determine if they can just be deleted or will need to be replaced using MUTEX.

- MOD_CACHE: CACHEIGNOREURLSESSIONIDENTIFIERS now does an exact match against the query string instead of a partial match. If your configuration was using partial strings, e.g. using `sessionid` to match `/someapplication/image.gif;jsessionid=123456789`, then you will need to change to the full string `jsessionid`.

- MOD_CACHE: The second parameter to CACHEENABLE only matches forward proxy content if it begins with the correct protocol. In 2.2 and earlier, a parameter of '/' matched all content.

- MOD_LDAP: LDAPTRUSTEDCLIENTCERT is now consistently a per-directory setting only. If you use this directive, review your configuration to make sure it is present in all the necessary directory contexts.

- MOD_FILTER: FILTERPROVIDER syntax has changed and now uses a boolean expression to determine if a filter is applied.

- MOD_INCLUDE:

    - The `#if expr` element now uses the new expression parser (p. 99) . The old syntax can be restored with the new directive SSILEGACYEXPRPARSER.
    - An SSI* config directive in directory scope no longer causes all other per-directory SSI* directives to be reset to their default values.

- MOD_CHARSET_LITE: The `DebugLevel` option has been removed in favour of per-module LOGLEVEL configuration.

- MOD_EXT_FILTER: The `DebugLevel` option has been removed in favour of per-module LOGLEVEL configuration.

- MOD_PROXY_SCGI: The default setting for `PATH_INFO` has changed from httpd 2.2, and some web applications will no longer operate properly with the new `PATH_INFO` setting. The previous setting can be restored by configuring the `proxy-scgi-pathinfo` variable.

- MOD_SSL: CRL based revocation checking now needs to be explicitly configured through SSLCAREVOCATIONCHECK.

- MOD_SUBSTITUTE: The maximum line length is now limited to 1MB.

- MOD_REQTIMEOUT: If the module is loaded, it will now set some default timeouts.

- MOD_DUMPIO: DUMPIOLOGLEVEL is no longer supported. Data is always logged at LOGLEVEL `trace7`.

- On Unix platforms, piped logging commands configured using either ERRORLOG or CUSTOMLOG were invoked using `/bin/sh -c` in 2.2 and earlier. In 2.4 and later, piped logging commands are executed directly. To restore the old behaviour, see the piped logging documentation (p. 56) .

## Misc Changes

- MOD_AUTOINDEX: will now extract titles and display descriptions for .xhtml files, which were previously ignored.

- MOD_SSL: The default format of the *_DN variables has changed. The old format can still be used with the new LegacyDNStringFormat argument to SSLOPTIONS. The SSLv2 protocol is no longer supported. SSLPROXYCHECKPEERCN and SSLPROXYCHECKPEEREXPIRE now default to On, causing proxy requests to HTTPS hosts with bad or outdated certificates to fail with a 502 status code (Bad gateway)

- htpasswd now uses MD5 hash by default on all platforms.

- The NAMEVIRTUALHOST directive no longer has any effect, other than to emit a warning. Any address/port combination appearing in multiple virtual hosts is implicitly treated as a name-based virtual host.

- MOD_DEFLATE will now skip compression if it knows that the size overhead added by the compression is larger than the data to be compressed.

- Multi-language error documents from 2.2.x may not work unless they are adjusted to the new syntax of MOD_INCLUDE's #if expr= element or the directive SSILEGACYEXPRPARSER is enabled for the directory containing the error documents.

- The functionality provided by mod_authn_alias in previous versions (i.e., the AUTHNPROVIDERALIAS directive) has been moved into MOD_AUTHN_CORE.

- MOD_CGID uses the servers TIMEOUT to limit the length of time to wait for CGI output. This timeout can be overridden with CGIDSCRIPTTIMEOUT.

## Third Party Modules

All modules must be recompiled for 2.4 before being loaded.

Many third-party modules designed for version 2.2 will otherwise work unchanged with the Apache HTTP Server version 2.4. Some will require changes; see the API update (p. 1035) overview.

## Common problems when upgrading

- Startup errors:

    - Invalid command 'User', perhaps misspelled or defined by a module not included in the server configuration - load module MOD_UNIXD

    - Invalid command 'Require', perhaps misspelled or defined by a module not included in the server configuration, or Invalid command 'Order', perhaps misspelled or defined by a module not included in the server configuration - load module MOD_ACCESS_COMPAT, or update configuration to 2.4 authorization directives.

    - Ignoring deprecated use of DefaultType in line NN of /path/to/httpd.conf - remove DEFAULTTYPE and replace with other configuration settings.

    - Invalid command 'AddOutputFilterByType', perhaps misspelled or defined by a module not included in the server configuration - ADDOUTPUTFILTER-BYTYPE has moved from the core to mod_filter, which must be loaded.

- Errors serving requests:

    - configuration error: couldn't check user: /path - load module MOD_AUTHN_CORE.

– `.htaccess` files aren't being processed - Check for an appropriate ALLOWOVERRIDE directive; the default changed to `None` in 2.4.

## 1.2 Overview of new features in Apache HTTP Server 2.4

This document describes some of the major changes between the 2.2 and 2.4 versions of the Apache HTTP Server. For new features since version 2.0, see the 2.2 new features (p. 12) document.

### Core Enhancements

**Run-time Loadable MPMs** Multiple MPMs can now be built as loadable modules (p. 90) at compile time. The MPM of choice can be configured at run time via LOADMODULE directive.

**Event MPM** The Event MPM (p. 1001) is no longer experimental but is now fully supported.

**Asynchronous support** Better support for asynchronous read/write for supporting MPMs and platforms.

**Per-module and per-directory LogLevel configuration** The LOGLEVEL can now be configured per module and per directory. New levels `trace1` to `trace8` have been added above the `debug` log level.

**Per-request configuration sections** <IF>, <ELSEIF>, and <ELSE> sections can be used to set the configuration based on per-request criteria.

**General-purpose expression parser** A new expression parser allows to specify complex conditions (p. 99) using a common syntax in directives like SETENVIFEXPR, REWRITECOND, HEADER, <IF>, and others.

**KeepAliveTimeout in milliseconds** It is now possible to specify KEEPALIVETIMEOUT in milliseconds.

**NameVirtualHost directive** No longer needed and is now deprecated.

**Override Configuration** The new ALLOWOVERRIDELIST directive allows more fine grained control which directives are allowed in `.htaccess` files.

**Config file variables** It is now possible to DEFINE variables in the configuration, allowing a clearer representation if the same value is used at many places in the configuration.

**Reduced memory usage** Despite many new features, 2.4.x tends to use less memory than 2.2.x.

### New Modules

MOD_PROXY_FCGI  FastCGI Protocol backend for MOD_PROXY

MOD_PROXY_SCGI  SCGI Protocol backend for MOD_PROXY

MOD_PROXY_EXPRESS  Provides dynamically configured mass reverse proxies for MOD_PROXY

MOD_REMOTEIP  Replaces the apparent client remote IP address and hostname for the request with the IP address list presented by a proxies or a load balancer via the request headers.

MOD_HEARTMONITOR, MOD_LBMETHOD_HEARTBEAT  Allow MOD_PROXY_BALANCER to base loadbalancing decisions on the number of active connections on the backend servers.

MOD_PROXY_HTML  Formerly a third-party module, this supports fixing of HTML links in a reverse proxy situation, where the backend generates URLs that are not valid for the proxy's clients.

MOD_SED  An advanced replacement of MOD_SUBSTITUTE, allows to edit the response body with the full power of sed.

MOD_AUTH_FORM  Enables form-based authentication.

MOD_SESSION  Enables the use of session state for clients, using cookie or database storage.

MOD_ALLOWMETHODS New module to restrict certain HTTP methods without interfering with authentication or authorization.

MOD_LUA Embeds the Lua[2] language into httpd, for configuration and small business logic functions. (Experimental)

MOD_LOG_DEBUG Allows the addition of customizable debug logging at different phases of the request processing.

MOD_BUFFER Provides for buffering the input and output filter stacks

MOD_DATA Convert response body into an RFC2397 data URL

MOD_RATELIMIT Provides Bandwidth Rate Limiting for Clients

MOD_REQUEST Provides Filters to handle and make available HTTP request bodies

MOD_REFLECTOR Provides Reflection of a request body as a response via the output filter stack.

MOD_SLOTMEM_SHM Provides a Slot-based shared memory provider (ala the scoreboard).

MOD_XML2ENC Formerly a third-party module, this supports internationalisation in libxml2-based (markup-aware) filter modules.

MOD_MACRO **(available since 2.4.5)** Provide macros within configuration files.

MOD_PROXY_WSTUNNEL **(available since 2.4.5)** Support web-socket tunnels.

MOD_AUTHNZ_FCGI **(available since 2.4.10)** Enable FastCGI authorizer applications to authenticate and/or authorize clients.

MOD_HTTP2 **(available since 2.4.17)** Support for the HTTP/2 transport layer.

## Module Enhancements

MOD_SSL MOD_SSL can now be configured to use an OCSP server to check the validation status of a client certificate. The default responder is configurable, along with the decision on whether to prefer the responder designated in the client certificate itself.

MOD_SSL now also supports OCSP stapling, where the server pro-actively obtains an OCSP verification of its certificate and transmits that to the client during the handshake.

MOD_SSL can now be configured to share SSL Session data between servers through memcached

EC keys are now supported in addition to RSA and DSA.

Support for TLS-SRP (available in 2.4.4 and later).

MOD_PROXY The PROXYPASS directive is now most optimally configured within a LOCATION or LOCATIONMATCH block, and offers a significant performance advantage over the traditional two-parameter syntax when present in large numbers. The source address used for proxy requests is now configurable. Support for Unix domain sockets to the backend (available in 2.4.7 and later).

MOD_PROXY_BALANCER More runtime configuration changes for BalancerMembers via balancer-manager

Additional BalancerMembers can be added at runtime via balancer-manager

Runtime configuration of a subset of Balancer parameters

BalancerMembers can be set to 'Drain' so that they only respond to existing sticky sessions, allowing them to be taken gracefully offline.

Balancer settings can be persistent after restarts.

---

[2]http://www.lua.org/

MOD_CACHE  The MOD_CACHE CACHE filter can be optionally inserted at a given point in the filter chain to provide fine control over caching.

MOD_CACHE can now cache HEAD requests.

Where possible, MOD_CACHE directives can now be set per directory, instead of per server.

The base URL of cached URLs can be customised, so that a cluster of caches can share the same endpoint URL prefix.

MOD_CACHE is now capable of serving stale cached data when a backend is unavailable (error 5xx).

MOD_CACHE can now insert HIT/MISS/REVALIDATE into an X-Cache header.

MOD_INCLUDE  Support for the 'onerror' attribute within an 'include' element, allowing an error document to be served on error instead of the default error string.

MOD_CGI, MOD_INCLUDE, MOD_ISAPI, ...  Translation of headers to environment variables is more strict than before to mitigate some possible cross-site-scripting attacks via header injection. Headers containing invalid characters (including underscores) are now silently dropped. Environment Variables in Apache (p. 92) has some pointers on how to work around broken legacy clients which require such headers. (This affects all modules which use these environment variables.)

MOD_AUTHZ_CORE **Authorization Logic Containers**  Advanced authorization logic may now be specified using the REQUIRE directive and the related container directives, such as <REQUIREALL>.

MOD_REWRITE  MOD_REWRITE adds the [QSD] (Query String Discard) and [END] flags for REWRITERULE to simplify common rewriting scenarios. Adds the possibility to use complex boolean expressions in REWRITE-COND. Allows the use of SQL queries as REWRITEMAP functions.

MOD_LDAP, MOD_AUTHNZ_LDAP  MOD_AUTHNZ_LDAP adds support for nested groups. MOD_LDAP adds LDAP-CONNECTIONPOOLTTL, LDAPTIMEOUT, and other improvements in the handling of timeouts. This is especially useful for setups where a stateful firewall drops idle connections to the LDAP server. MOD_LDAP adds LDAPLIBRARYDEBUG to log debug information provided by the used LDAP toolkit.

MOD_INFO  MOD_INFO can now dump the pre-parsed configuration to stdout during server startup.

MOD_AUTH_BASIC  New generic mechanism to fake basic authentication (available in 2.4.5 and later).

## Program Enhancements

**fcgistarter**  New FastCGI daemon starter utility

**htcacheclean**  Current cached URLs can now be listed, with optional metadata included. Allow explicit deletion of individual cached URLs from the cache. File sizes can now be rounded up to the given block size, making the size limits map more closely to the real size on disk. Cache size can now be limited by the number of inodes, instead of or in addition to being limited by the size of the files on disk.

**rotatelogs**  May now create a link to the current log file. May now invoke a custom post-rotate script.

**htpasswd, htdbm**  Support for the bcrypt algorithm (available in 2.4.4 and later).

## Documentation

**mod_rewrite**  The MOD_REWRITE documentation has been rearranged and almost completely rewritten, with a focus on examples and common usage, as well as on showing you when other solutions are more appropriate. The Rewrite Guide (p. 146) is now a top-level section with much more detail and better organization.

**mod_ssl**  The MOD_SSL documentation has been greatly enhanced, with more examples at the getting started level, in addition to the previous focus on technical details.

**Caching Guide** The Caching Guide (p. 43) has been rewritten to properly distinguish between the RFC2616 HTTP/1.1 caching features provided by MOD_CACHE, and the generic key/value caching provided by the socache (p. 114) interface, as well as to cover specialised caching provided by mechanisms such as MOD_FILE_CACHE.

## Module Developer Changes

**Check Configuration Hook Added** A new hook, check_config, has been added which runs between the pre_config and open_logs hooks. It also runs before the test_config hook when the -t option is passed to httpd. The check_config hook allows modules to review interdependent configuration directive values and adjust them while messages can still be logged to the console. The user can thus be alerted to misconfiguration problems before the core open_logs hook function redirects console output to the error log.

**Expression Parser Added** We now have a general-purpose expression parser, whose API is exposed in *ap_expr.h*. This is adapted from the expression parser previously implemented in MOD_SSL.

**Authorization Logic Containers** Authorization modules now register as a provider, via ap_register_auth_provider(), to support advanced authorization logic, such as <REQUIREALL>.

**Small-Object Caching Interface** The *ap_socache.h* header exposes a provider-based interface for caching small data objects, based on the previous implementation of the MOD_SSL session cache. Providers using a shared-memory cyclic buffer, disk-based dbm files, and a memcache distributed cache are currently supported.

**Cache Status Hook Added** The MOD_CACHE module now includes a new cache_status hook, which is called when the caching decision becomes known. A default implementation is provided which adds an optional X-Cache and X-Cache-Detail header to the response.

The developer documentation contains a detailed list of API changes (p. 1035) .

## 1.3   Overview of new features in Apache HTTP Server 2.2

This document describes some of the major changes between the 2.0 and 2.2 versions of the Apache HTTP Server. For new features since version 1.3, see the 2.0 new features (p. 15) document.

### Core Enhancements

**Authn/Authz** The bundled authentication and authorization modules have been refactored. The new mod_authn_alias(already removed from 2.3/2.4) module can greatly simplify certain authentication configurations. See module name changes, and the developer changes for more information about how these changes affects users and module writers.

**Caching** MOD_CACHE, MOD_CACHE_DISK, and mod_mem_cache(already removed from 2.3/2.4) have undergone a lot of changes, and are now considered production-quality. htcacheclean has been introduced to clean up MOD_CACHE_DISK setups.

**Configuration** The default configuration layout has been simplified and modularised. Configuration snippets which can be used to enable commonly-used features are now bundled with Apache, and can be easily added to the main server config.

**Graceful stop** The PREFORK, WORKER and EVENT MPMs now allow httpd to be shutdown gracefully via the graceful-stop (p. 29) signal. The GRACEFULSHUTDOWNTIMEOUT directive has been added to specify an optional timeout, after which httpd will terminate regardless of the status of any requests being served.

**Proxying** The new MOD_PROXY_BALANCER module provides load balancing services for MOD_PROXY. The new MOD_PROXY_AJP module adds support for the Apache JServ Protocol version 1.3 used by Apache Tomcat[3].

**Regular Expression Library Updated** Version 5.0 of the Perl Compatible Regular Expression Library[4] (PCRE) is now included. httpd can be configured to use a system installation of PCRE by passing the --with-pcre flag to configure.

**Smart Filtering** MOD_FILTER introduces dynamic configuration to the output filter chain. It enables filters to be conditionally inserted, based on any Request or Response header or environment variable, and dispenses with the more problematic dependencies and ordering problems in the 2.0 architecture.

**Large File Support** httpd is now built with support for files larger than 2GB on modern 32-bit Unix systems. Support for handling >2GB request bodies has also been added.

**Event MPM** The EVENT MPM uses a separate thread to handle Keep Alive requests and accepting connections. Keep Alive requests have traditionally required httpd to dedicate a worker to handle it. This dedicated worker could not be used again until the Keep Alive timeout was reached.

**SQL Database Support** MOD_DBD, together with the apr_dbd framework, brings direct SQL support to modules that need it. Supports connection pooling in threaded MPMs.

### Module Enhancements

**Authn/Authz** Modules in the aaa directory have been renamed and offer better support for digest authentication. For example, mod_auth is now split into MOD_AUTH_BASIC and MOD_AUTHN_FILE; mod_auth_dbm is now called MOD_AUTHN_DBM; mod_access has been renamed MOD_AUTHZ_HOST. There is also a new mod_authn_alias(already removed from 2.3/2.4) module for simplifying certain authentication configurations.

[3]http://tomcat.apache.org/
[4]http://www.pcre.org/

**MOD_AUTHNZ_LDAP** This module is a port of the 2.0 mod_auth_ldap module to the 2.2 Authn/Authz framework. New features include using LDAP attribute values and complicated search filters in the REQUIRE directive.

**MOD_AUTHZ_OWNER** A new module that authorizes access to files based on the owner of the file on the file system

**MOD_VERSION** A new module that allows configuration blocks to be enabled based on the version number of the running server.

**MOD_INFO** Added a new ?config argument which will show the configuration directives as parsed by Apache, including their file name and line number. The module also shows the order of all request hooks and additional build information, similar to httpd -V.

**MOD_SSL** Added a support for RFC 2817[5], which allows connections to upgrade from clear text to TLS encryption.

**MOD_IMAGEMAP** mod_imap has been renamed to MOD_IMAGEMAP to avoid user confusion.

## Program Enhancements

**httpd** A new command line option -M has been added that lists all modules that are loaded based on the current configuration. Unlike the -l option, this list includes DSOs loaded via MOD_SO.

**httxt2dbm** A new program used to generate dbm files from text input, for use in REWRITEMAP with the dbm map type.

## Module Developer Changes

**APR 1.0 API** Apache 2.2 uses the APR 1.0 API. All deprecated functions and symbols have been removed from APR and APR-Util. For details, see the APR Website[6].

**Authn/Authz** The bundled authentication and authorization modules have been renamed along the following lines:

- mod_auth_* -> Modules that implement an HTTP authentication mechanism
- mod_authn_* -> Modules that provide a backend authentication provider
- mod_authz_* -> Modules that implement authorization (or access)
- mod_authnz_* -> Module that implements both authentication & authorization

There is a new authentication backend provider scheme which greatly eases the construction of new authentication backends.

**Connection Error Logging** A new function, ap_log_cerror has been added to log errors that occur with the client's connection. When logged, the message includes the client IP address.

**Test Configuration Hook Added** A new hook, test_config has been added to aid modules that want to execute special code only when the user passes -t to httpd.

**Set Threaded MPM's Stacksize** A new directive, THREADSTACKSIZE has been added to set the stack size on all threaded MPMs. This is required for some third-party modules on platforms with small default thread stack size.

**Protocol handling for output filters** In the past, every filter has been responsible for ensuring that it generates the correct response headers where it affects them. Filters can now delegate common protocol management to MOD_FILTER, using the ap_register_output_filter_protocol or ap_filter_protocol calls.

---

[5]http://www.ietf.org/rfc/rfc2817.txt
[6]http://apr.apache.org/

**Monitor hook added**   Monitor hook enables modules to run regular/scheduled jobs in the parent (root) process.

**Regular expression API changes**   The `pcreposix.h` header is no longer available; it is replaced by the new `ap_regex.h` header. The POSIX.2 `regex.h` implementation exposed by the old header is now available under the `ap_` namespace from `ap_regex.h`. Calls to `regcomp`, `regexec` and so on can be replaced by calls to `ap_regcomp`, `ap_regexec`.

**DBD Framework (SQL Database API)**   With Apache 1.x and 2.0, modules requiring an SQL backend had to take responsibility for managing it themselves. Apart from reinventing the wheel, this can be very inefficient, for example when several modules each maintain their own connections.

Apache 2.1 and later provides the `ap_dbd` API for managing database connections (including optimised strategies for threaded and unthreaded MPMs), while APR 1.2 and later provides the `apr_dbd` API for interacting with the database.

New modules SHOULD now use these APIs for all SQL database operations. Existing applications SHOULD be upgraded to use it where feasible, either transparently or as a recommended option to their users.

# 1.4   Overview of new features in Apache HTTP Server 2.0

This document describes some of the major changes between the 1.3 and 2.0 versions of the Apache HTTP Server.

**See also**

- Upgrading to 2.0 from 1.3 (p. 2)

## Core Enhancements

**Unix Threading**   On Unix systems with POSIX threads support, Apache httpd can now run in a hybrid multiprocess, multithreaded mode. This improves scalability for many, but not all configurations.

**New Build System**   The build system has been rewritten from scratch to be based on autoconf and libtool. This makes Apache httpd's configuration system more similar to that of other packages.

**Multiprotocol Support**   Apache HTTP Server now has some of the infrastructure in place to support serving multiple protocols. MOD_ECHO has been written as an example.

**Better support for non-Unix platforms**   Apache HTTP Server 2.0 is faster and more stable on non-Unix platforms such as BeOS, OS/2, and Windows. With the introduction of platform-specific multi-processing modules (p. 90) (MPMs) and the Apache Portable Runtime (APR), these platforms are now implemented in their native API, avoiding the often buggy and poorly performing POSIX-emulation layers.

**New Apache httpd API**   The API for modules has changed significantly for 2.0. Many of the module-ordering/priority problems from 1.3 should be gone. 2.0 does much of this automatically, and module ordering is now done per-hook to allow more flexibility. Also, new calls have been added that provide additional module capabilities without patching the core Apache HTTP Server.

**IPv6 Support**   On systems where IPv6 is supported by the underlying Apache Portable Runtime library, Apache httpd gets IPv6 listening sockets by default. Additionally, the LISTEN, NAMEVIRTUALHOST, and VIRTUALHOST directives support IPv6 numeric address strings (e.g., "Listen [2001:db8::1]:8080").

**Filtering**   Apache httpd modules may now be written as filters which act on the stream of content as it is delivered to or from the server. This allows, for example, the output of CGI scripts to be parsed for Server Side Include directives using the INCLUDES filter in MOD_INCLUDE. The module MOD_EXT_FILTER allows external programs to act as filters in much the same way that CGI programs can act as handlers.

**Multilanguage Error Responses**   Error response messages to the browser are now provided in several languages, using SSI documents. They may be customized by the administrator to achieve a consistent look and feel.

**Simplified configuration**   Many confusing directives have been simplified. The often confusing Port and BindAddress directives are gone; only the LISTEN directive is used for IP address binding; the SERVERNAME directive specifies the server name and port number only for redirection and vhost recognition.

**Native Windows NT Unicode Support**   Apache httpd 2.0 on Windows NT now uses utf-8 for all filename encodings. These directly translate to the underlying Unicode file system, providing multilanguage support for all Windows NT-based installations, including Windows 2000 and Windows XP. *This support does not extend to Windows 95, 98 or ME, which continue to use the machine's local codepage for filesystem access.*

**Regular Expression Library Updated**   Apache httpd 2.0 includes the Perl Compatible Regular Expression Library[7] (PCRE). All regular expression evaluation now uses the more powerful Perl 5 syntax.

---

[7]http://www.pcre.org/

## Module Enhancements

MOD_SSL  New module in Apache httpd 2.0. This module is an interface to the SSL/TLS encryption protocols provided by OpenSSL.

MOD_DAV  New module in Apache httpd 2.0. This module implements the HTTP Distributed Authoring and Versioning (DAV) specification for posting and maintaining web content.

MOD_DEFLATE  New module in Apache httpd 2.0. This module allows supporting browsers to request that content be compressed before delivery, saving network bandwidth.

**MOD_AUTH_LDAP**  New module in Apache httpd 2.0.41. This module allows an LDAP database to be used to store credentials for HTTP Basic Authentication. A companion module, MOD_LDAP provides connection pooling and results caching.

MOD_AUTH_DIGEST  Includes additional support for session caching across processes using shared memory.

MOD_CHARSET_LITE  New module in Apache httpd 2.0. This experimental module allows for character set translation or recoding.

MOD_FILE_CACHE  New module in Apache httpd 2.0. This module includes the functionality of mod_mmap_static in Apache HTTP Server version 1.3, plus adds further caching abilities.

MOD_HEADERS  This module is much more flexible in Apache httpd 2.0. It can now modify request headers used by MOD_PROXY, and it can conditionally set response headers.

MOD_PROXY  The proxy module has been completely rewritten to take advantage of the new filter infrastructure and to implement a more reliable, HTTP/1.1 compliant proxy. In addition, new <PROXY> configuration sections provide more readable (and internally faster) control of proxied sites; overloaded <Directory "proxy:..."> configuration are not supported. The module is now divided into specific protocol support modules including proxy_connect, proxy_ftp and proxy_http.

MOD_NEGOTIATION  A new FORCELANGUAGEPRIORITY directive can be used to assure that the client receives a single document in all cases, rather than NOT ACCEPTABLE or MULTIPLE CHOICES responses. In addition, the negotiation and MultiViews algorithms have been cleaned up to provide more consistent results and a new form of type map that can include document content is provided.

MOD_AUTOINDEX  Autoindex'ed directory listings can now be configured to use HTML tables for cleaner formatting, and allow finer-grained control of sorting, including version-sorting, and wildcard filtering of the directory listing.

MOD_INCLUDE  New directives allow the default start and end tags for SSI elements to be changed and allow for error and time format configuration to take place in the main configuration file rather than in the SSI document. Results from regular expression parsing and grouping (now based on Perl's regular expression syntax) can be retrieved using MOD_INCLUDE's variables $0 .. $9.

**MOD_AUTH_DBM**  Now supports multiple types of DBM-like databases using the AUTHDBMTYPE directive.

## 1.5 The Apache License, Version 2.0

Apache License
Version 2.0, January 2004
http://www.apache.org/licenses/

TERMS AND CONDITIONS FOR USE, REPRODUCTION, AND DISTRIBUTION

1. **Definitions**

   "License" shall mean the terms and conditions for use, reproduction, and distribution as defined by Sections 1 through 9 of this document.

   "Licensor" shall mean the copyright owner or entity authorized by the copyright owner that is granting the License.

   "Legal Entity" shall mean the union of the acting entity and all other entities that control, are controlled by, or are under common control with that entity. For the purposes of this definition, "control" means (i) the power, direct or indirect, to cause the direction or management of such entity, whether by contract or otherwise, or (ii) ownership of fifty percent (50%) or more of the outstanding shares, or (iii) beneficial ownership of such entity.

   "You" (or "Your") shall mean an individual or Legal Entity exercising permissions granted by this License.

   "Source" form shall mean the preferred form for making modifications, including but not limited to software source code, documentation source, and configuration files.

   "Object" form shall mean any form resulting from mechanical transformation or translation of a Source form, including but not limited to compiled object code, generated documentation, and conversions to other media types.

   "Work" shall mean the work of authorship, whether in Source or Object form, made available under the License, as indicated by a copyright notice that is included in or attached to the work (an example is provided in the Appendix below).

   "Derivative Works" shall mean any work, whether in Source or Object form, that is based on (or derived from) the Work and for which the editorial revisions, annotations, elaborations, or other modifications represent, as a whole, an original work of authorship. For the purposes of this License, Derivative Works shall not include works that remain separable from, or merely link (or bind by name) to the interfaces of, the Work and Derivative Works thereof.

   "Contribution" shall mean any work of authorship, including the original version of the Work and any modifications or additions to that Work or Derivative Works thereof, that is intentionally submitted to Licensor for inclusion in the Work by the copyright owner or by an individual or Legal Entity authorized to submit on behalf of the copyright owner. For the purposes of this definition, "submitted" means any form of electronic, verbal, or written communication sent to the Licensor or its representatives, including but not limited to communication on electronic mailing lists, source code control systems, and issue tracking systems that are managed by, or on behalf of, the Licensor for the purpose of discussing and improving the Work, but excluding communication that is conspicuously marked or otherwise designated in writing by the copyright owner as "Not a Contribution."

   "Contributor" shall mean Licensor and any individual or Legal Entity on behalf of whom a Contribution has been received by Licensor and subsequently incorporated within the Work.

2. **Grant of Copyright License.** Subject to the terms and conditions of this License, each Contributor hereby grants to You a perpetual, worldwide, non-exclusive, no-charge, royalty-free, irrevocable copyright license to reproduce, prepare Derivative Works of, publicly display, publicly perform, sublicense, and distribute the Work and such Derivative Works in Source or Object form.

3. **Grant of Patent License.** Subject to the terms and conditions of this License, each Contributor hereby grants to You a perpetual, worldwide, non-exclusive, no-charge, royalty-free, irrevocable (except as stated in this section)

patent license to make, have made, use, offer to sell, sell, import, and otherwise transfer the Work, where such license applies only to those patent claims licensable by such Contributor that are necessarily infringed by their Contribution(s) alone or by combination of their Contribution(s) with the Work to which such Contribution(s) was submitted. If You institute patent litigation against any entity (including a cross-claim or counterclaim in a lawsuit) alleging that the Work or a Contribution incorporated within the Work constitutes direct or contributory patent infringement, then any patent licenses granted to You under this License for that Work shall terminate as of the date such litigation is filed.

4. **Redistribution.** You may reproduce and distribute copies of the Work or Derivative Works thereof in any medium, with or without modifications, and in Source or Object form, provided that You meet the following conditions:

   (a) You must give any other recipients of the Work or Derivative Works a copy of this License; and

   (b) You must cause any modified files to carry prominent notices stating that You changed the files; and

   (c) You must retain, in the Source form of any Derivative Works that You distribute, all copyright, patent, trademark, and attribution notices from the Source form of the Work, excluding those notices that do not pertain to any part of the Derivative Works; and

   (d) If the Work includes a "NOTICE" text file as part of its distribution, then any Derivative Works that You distribute must include a readable copy of the attribution notices contained within such NOTICE file, excluding those notices that do not pertain to any part of the Derivative Works, in at least one of the following places: within a NOTICE text file distributed as part of the Derivative Works; within the Source form or documentation, if provided along with the Derivative Works; or, within a display generated by the Derivative Works, if and wherever such third-party notices normally appear. The contents of the NOTICE file are for informational purposes only and do not modify the License. You may add Your own attribution notices within Derivative Works that You distribute, alongside or as an addendum to the NOTICE text from the Work, provided that such additional attribution notices cannot be construed as modifying the License.

   You may add Your own copyright statement to Your modifications and may provide additional or different license terms and conditions for use, reproduction, or distribution of Your modifications, or for any such Derivative Works as a whole, provided Your use, reproduction, and distribution of the Work otherwise complies with the conditions stated in this License.

5. **Submission of Contributions.** Unless You explicitly state otherwise, any Contribution intentionally submitted for inclusion in the Work by You to the Licensor shall be under the terms and conditions of this License, without any additional terms or conditions. Notwithstanding the above, nothing herein shall supersede or modify the terms of any separate license agreement you may have executed with Licensor regarding such Contributions.

6. **Trademarks.** This License does not grant permission to use the trade names, trademarks, service marks, or product names of the Licensor, except as required for reasonable and customary use in describing the origin of the Work and reproducing the content of the NOTICE file.

7. **Disclaimer of Warranty.** Unless required by applicable law or agreed to in writing, Licensor provides the Work (and each Contributor provides its Contributions) on an "AS IS" BASIS, WITHOUT WARRANTIES OR CONDITIONS OF ANY KIND, either express or implied, including, without limitation, any warranties or conditions of TITLE, NON-INFRINGEMENT, MERCHANTABILITY, or FITNESS FOR A PARTICULAR PURPOSE. You are solely responsible for determining the appropriateness of using or redistributing the Work and assume any risks associated with Your exercise of permissions under this License.

8. **Limitation of Liability.** In no event and under no legal theory, whether in tort (including negligence), contract, or otherwise, unless required by applicable law (such as deliberate and grossly negligent acts) or agreed to in writing, shall any Contributor be liable to You for damages, including any direct, indirect, special, incidental, or consequential damages of any character arising as a result of this License or out of the use or inability to use the Work (including but not limited to damages for loss of goodwill, work stoppage, computer failure or malfunction, or any and all other commercial damages or losses), even if such Contributor has been advised of the possibility of such damages.

9. **Accepting Warranty or Additional Liability.** While redistributing the Work or Derivative Works thereof, You may choose to offer, and charge a fee for, acceptance of support, warranty, indemnity, or other liability obligations and/or rights consistent with this License. However, in accepting such obligations, You may act only on Your own behalf and on Your sole responsibility, not on behalf of any other Contributor, and only if You agree to indemnify, defend, and hold each Contributor harmless for any liability incurred by, or claims asserted against, such Contributor by reason of your accepting any such warranty or additional liability.

END OF TERMS AND CONDITIONS

APPENDIX: How to apply the Apache License to your work.

To apply the Apache License to your work, attach the following boilerplate notice, with the fields enclosed by brackets "[]" replaced with your own identifying information. (Don't include the brackets!) The text should be enclosed in the appropriate comment syntax for the file format. We also recommend that a file or class name and description of purpose be included on the same "printed page" as the copyright notice for easier identification within third-party archives.

```
Copyright [yyyy] [name of copyright owner]

Licensed under the Apache License, Version 2.0 (the "License");
you may not use this file except in compliance with the License.
You may obtain a copy of the License at

    http://www.apache.org/licenses/LICENSE-2.0

Unless required by applicable law or agreed to in writing, software
distributed under the License is distributed on an "AS IS" BASIS,
WITHOUT WARRANTIES OR CONDITIONS OF ANY KIND, either express or implied.
See the License for the specific language governing permissions and
limitations under the License.
```

# Chapter 2

# Using the Apache HTTP Server

# 2.1  Compiling and Installing

This document covers compilation and installation of the Apache HTTP Server on Unix and Unix-like systems only. For compiling and installation on Windows, see Using Apache HTTP Server with Microsoft Windows (p. 267) and Compiling Apache for Microsoft Windows (p. 275) . For other platforms, see the platform (p. 266) documentation.

Apache httpd uses `libtool` and `autoconf` to create a build environment that looks like many other Open Source projects.

If you are upgrading from one minor version to the next (for example, 2.4.8 to 2.4.9), please skip down to the upgrading section.

**See also**

- Configure the source tree (p. 307)
- Starting Apache httpd (p. 27)
- Stopping and Restarting (p. 29)

## Overview for the impatient

| Download  | `$ lynx http://httpd.apache.org/download.cgi` |
|-----------|-----------------------------------------------|
| Extract   | `$ gzip -d httpd-NN.tar.gz`                    |
|           | `$ tar xvf httpd-NN.tar`                       |
|           | `$ cd httpd-NN`                                |
| Configure | `$ ./configure --prefix=PREFIX`               |
| Compile   | `$ make`                                       |
| Install   | `$ make install`                              |
| Customize | `$ vi PREFIX/conf/httpd.conf`                  |
| Test      | `$ PREFIX/bin/apachectl -k start`              |

*NN* must be replaced with the current version number, and *PREFIX* must be replaced with the filesystem path under which the server should be installed. If *PREFIX* is not specified, it defaults to `/usr/local/apache2`.

Each section of the compilation and installation process is described in more detail below, beginning with the requirements for compiling and installing Apache httpd.

## Requirements

The following requirements exist for building Apache httpd:

**APR and APR-Util** Make sure you have APR and APR-Util already installed on your system. If you don't, or prefer to not use the system-provided versions, download the latest versions of both APR and APR-Util from Apache APR[1], unpack them into `/httpd_source_tree_root/srclib/apr` and /httpd_source_tree_root/`srclib/apr-util` (be sure the directory names do not have version numbers; for example, the APR distribution must be under /httpd_source_tree_root/srclib/apr/) and use `./configure`'s `--with-included-apr` option. On some platforms, you may have to install the corresponding `-dev` packages to allow httpd to build against your installed copy of APR and APR-Util.

**Perl-Compatible Regular Expressions Library (PCRE)** This library is required but not longer bundled with httpd. Download the source code from http://www.pcre.org[2], or install a Port or Package. If your build system can't find the pcre-config script installed by the PCRE build, point to it using the `--with-pcre` parameter. On some platforms, you may have to install the corresponding `-dev` package to allow httpd to build against your installed copy of PCRE.

---

[1]http://apr.apache.org/
[2]http://www.pcre.org/

**Disk Space** Make sure you have at least 50 MB of temporary free disk space available. After installation the server occupies approximately 10 MB of disk space. The actual disk space requirements will vary considerably based on your chosen configuration options, any third-party modules, and, of course, the size of the web site or sites that you have on the server.

**ANSI-C Compiler and Build System** Make sure you have an ANSI-C compiler installed. The GNU C compiler (GCC)[3] from the Free Software Foundation (FSF)[4] is recommended. If you don't have GCC then at least make sure your vendor's compiler is ANSI compliant. In addition, your `PATH` must contain basic build tools such as `make`.

**Accurate time keeping** Elements of the HTTP protocol are expressed as the time of day. So, it's time to investigate setting some time synchronization facility on your system. Usually the `ntpdate` or `xntpd` programs are used for this purpose which are based on the Network Time Protocol (NTP). See the NTP homepage[5] for more details about NTP software and public time servers.

**Perl 5**[6] **[OPTIONAL]** For some of the support scripts like `apxs` or `dbmmanage` (which are written in Perl) the Perl 5 interpreter is required (versions 5.003 or newer are sufficient). If no Perl 5 interpreter is found by the `configure` script, you will not be able to use the affected support scripts. Of course, you will still be able to build and use Apache httpd.

## Download

The Apache HTTP Server can be downloaded from the Apache HTTP Server download site[7], which lists several mirrors. Most users of Apache on unix-like systems will be better off downloading and compiling a source version. The build process (described below) is easy, and it allows you to customize your server to suit your needs. In addition, binary releases are often not up to date with the latest source releases. If you do download a binary, follow the instructions in the `INSTALL.bindist` file inside the distribution.

After downloading, it is important to verify that you have a complete and unmodified version of the Apache HTTP Server. This can be accomplished by testing the downloaded tarball against the PGP signature. Details on how to do this are available on the download page[8] and an extended example is available describing the use of PGP[9].

## Extract

Extracting the source from the Apache HTTP Server tarball is a simple matter of uncompressing, and then untarring:

```
$ gzip -d httpd-NN.tar.gz
$ tar xvf httpd-NN.tar
```

This will create a new directory under the current directory containing the source code for the distribution. You should `cd` into that directory before proceeding with compiling the server.

## Configuring the source tree

The next step is to configure the Apache source tree for your particular platform and personal requirements. This is done using the script `configure` included in the root directory of the distribution. (Developers downloading an

---

[3]http://gcc.gnu.org/
[4]http://www.gnu.org/
[5]http://www.ntp.org
[7]http://httpd.apache.org/download.cgi
[8]http://httpd.apache.org/download.cgi#verify
[9]http://httpd.apache.org/dev/verification.html

unreleased version of the Apache source tree will need to have `autoconf` and `libtool` installed and will need to run `buildconf` before proceeding with the next steps. This is not necessary for official releases.)

To configure the source tree using all the default options, simply type `./configure`. To change the default options, `configure` accepts a variety of variables and command line options.

The most important option is the location `--prefix` where Apache is to be installed later, because Apache has to be configured for this location to work correctly. More fine-tuned control of the location of files is possible with additional configure options (p. 307) .

Also at this point, you can specify which features (p. 307) you want included in Apache by enabling and disabling modules (p. 1101) . Apache comes with a wide range of modules included by default. They will be compiled as shared objects (DSOs) (p. 68) which can be loaded or unloaded at runtime. You can also choose to compile modules statically by using the option `--enable-`*module*`=static`.

Additional modules are enabled using the `--enable-`*module* option, where *module* is the name of the module with the `mod_` string removed and with any underscore converted to a dash. Similarly, you can disable modules with the `--disable-`*module* option. Be careful when using these options, since `configure` cannot warn you if the module you specify does not exist; it will simply ignore the option.

In addition, it is sometimes necessary to provide the `configure` script with extra information about the location of your compiler, libraries, or header files. This is done by passing either environment variables or command line options to `configure`. For more information, see the `configure` manual page. Or invoke `configure` using the `--help` option.

For a short impression of what possibilities you have, here is a typical example which compiles Apache for the installation tree `/sw/pkg/apache` with a particular compiler and flags plus the two additional modules MOD_LDAP and MOD_LUA:

```
$ CC="pgcc" CFLAGS="-O2" \
./configure --prefix=/sw/pkg/apache \
--enable-ldap=shared \
--enable-lua=shared
```

When `configure` is run it will take several minutes to test for the availability of features on your system and build Makefiles which will later be used to compile the server.

Details on all the different `configure` options are available on the `configure` manual page.

## Build

Now you can build the various parts which form the Apache package by simply running the command:

```
$ make
```

Please be patient here, since a base configuration takes several minutes to compile and the time will vary widely depending on your hardware and the number of modules that you have enabled.

## Install

Now it's time to install the package under the configured installation *PREFIX* (see `--prefix` option above) by running:

```
$ make install
```

This step will typically require root privileges, since *PREFIX* is usually a directory with restricted write permissions. If you are upgrading, the installation will not overwrite your configuration files or documents.

### Customize

Next, you can customize your Apache HTTP server by editing the configuration files (p. 32) under *PREFIX*/`conf/`.

```
$ vi PREFIX/conf/httpd.conf
```

Have a look at the Apache manual under *PREFIX*/`docs/manual/` or consult http://httpd.apache.org/docs/trunk/ for the most recent version of this manual and a complete reference of available configuration directives (p. 1106) .

### Test

Now you can start (p. 27) your Apache HTTP server by immediately running:

```
$ PREFIX/bin/apachectl -k start
```

You should then be able to request your first document via the URL `http://localhost/`. The web page you see is located under the DOCUMENTROOT, which will usually be *PREFIX*/`htdocs/`. Then stop (p. 29) the server again by running:

```
$ PREFIX/bin/apachectl -k stop
```

### Upgrading

The first step in upgrading is to read the release announcement and the file `CHANGES` in the source distribution to find any changes that may affect your site. When changing between major releases (for example, from 2.0 to 2.2 or from 2.2 to 2.4), there will likely be major differences in the compile-time and run-time configuration that will require manual adjustments. All modules will also need to be upgraded to accommodate changes in the module API.

Upgrading from one minor version to the next (for example, from 2.2.55 to 2.2.57) is easier. The `make install` process will not overwrite any of your existing documents, log files, or configuration files. In addition, the developers make every effort to avoid incompatible changes in the `configure` options, run-time configuration, or the module API between minor versions. In most cases you should be able to use an identical `configure` command line, an identical configuration file, and all of your modules should continue to work.

To upgrade across minor versions, start by finding the file `config.nice` in the `build` directory of your installed server or at the root of the source tree for your old install. This will contain the exact `configure` command line that you used to configure the source tree. Then to upgrade from one version to the next, you need only copy the `config.nice` file to the source tree of the new version, edit it to make any desired changes, and then run:

```
$ ./config.nice
$ make
$ make install
$ PREFIX/bin/apachectl -k graceful-stop
$ PREFIX/bin/apachectl -k start
```

You should always test any new version in your environment before putting it into production. For example, you can install and run the new version along side the old one by using a different `--prefix` and a different port (by adjusting the LISTEN directive) to test for any incompatibilities before doing the final upgrade.

You can pass additional arguments to `config.nice`, which will be appended to your original `configure` options:

```
$ ./config.nice --prefix=/home/test/apache --with-port=90
```

## Third-party packages

A large number of third parties provide their own packaged distributions of the Apache HTTP Server for installation on particular platforms. This includes the various Linux distributions, various third-party Windows packages, Mac OS X, Solaris, and many more.

Our software license not only permits, but encourages, this kind of redistribution. However, it does result in a situation where the configuration layout and defaults on your installation of the server may differ from what is stated in the documentation. While unfortunate, this situation is not likely to change any time soon.

A description of these third-party distrubutions[10] is maintained in the HTTP Server wiki, and should reflect the current state of these third-party distributions. However, you will need to familiarize yourself with your particular platform's package management and installation procedures.

---

[10]http://wiki.apache.org/httpd/DistrosDefaultLayout

## 2.2   Starting Apache

On Windows, Apache is normally run as a service. For details, see Running Apache as a Service (p. 267) .

On Unix, the `httpd` program is run as a daemon that executes continuously in the background to handle requests. This document describes how to invoke `httpd`.

**See also**

- Stopping and Restarting (p. 29)
- `httpd`
- `apachectl`

### How Apache Starts

If the LISTEN specified in the configuration file is default of 80 (or any other port below 1024), then it is necessary to have root privileges in order to start apache, so that it can bind to this privileged port. Once the server has started and performed a few preliminary activities such as opening its log files, it will launch several *child* processes which do the work of listening for and answering requests from clients. The main `httpd` process continues to run as the root user, but the child processes run as a less privileged user. This is controlled by the selected Multi-Processing Module (p. 90) .

The recommended method of invoking the `httpd` executable is to use the `apachectl` control script. This script sets certain environment variables that are necessary for `httpd` to function correctly under some operating systems, and then invokes the `httpd` binary. `apachectl` will pass through any command line arguments, so any `httpd` options may also be used with `apachectl`. You may also directly edit the `apachectl` script by changing the `HTTPD` variable near the top to specify the correct location of the `httpd` binary and any command-line arguments that you wish to be *always* present.

The first thing that `httpd` does when it is invoked is to locate and read the configuration file (p. 32) `httpd.conf`. The location of this file is set at compile-time, but it is possible to specify its location at run time using the `-f` command-line option as in

```
/usr/local/apache2/bin/apachectl -f
/usr/local/apache2/conf/httpd.conf
```

If all goes well during startup, the server will detach from the terminal and the command prompt will return almost immediately. This indicates that the server is up and running. You can then use your browser to connect to the server and view the test page in the DOCUMENTROOT directory.

### Errors During Start-up

If Apache suffers a fatal problem during startup, it will write a message describing the problem either to the console or to the ERRORLOG before exiting. One of the most common error messages is `"Unable to bind to Port ..."`. This message is usually caused by either:

- Trying to start the server on a privileged port when not logged in as the root user; or
- Trying to start the server when there is another instance of Apache or some other web server already bound to the same Port.

For further trouble-shooting instructions, consult the Apache FAQ[11].

---

[11]http://wiki.apache.org/httpd/FAQ

## Starting at Boot-Time

If you want your server to continue running after a system reboot, you should add a call to `apachectl` to your system startup files (typically `rc.local` or a file in an `rc.N` directory). This will start Apache as root. Before doing this ensure that your server is properly configured for security and access restrictions.

The `apachectl` script is designed to act like a standard SysV init script; it can take the arguments `start`, `restart`, and `stop` and translate them into the appropriate signals to `httpd`. So you can often simply link `apachectl` into the appropriate init directory. But be sure to check the exact requirements of your system.

## Additional Information

Additional information about the command-line options of `httpd` and `apachectl` as well as other support programs included with the server is available on the Server and Supporting Programs (p. 294) page. There is also documentation on all the modules (p. 1101) included with the Apache distribution and the directives (p. 1106) that they provide.

## 2.3 Stopping and Restarting Apache HTTP Server

This document covers stopping and restarting Apache HTTP Server on Unix-like systems. Windows NT, 2000 and XP users should see Running httpd as a Service (p. 267) and Windows 9x and ME users should see Running httpd as a Console Application (p. 267) for information on how to control httpd on those platforms.

**See also**

- httpd
- apachectl
- Starting (p. 27)

### Introduction

In order to stop or restart the Apache HTTP Server, you must send a signal to the running httpd processes. There are two ways to send the signals. First, you can use the unix kill command to directly send signals to the processes. You will notice many httpd executables running on your system, but you should not send signals to any of them except the parent, whose pid is in the PIDFILE. That is to say you shouldn't ever need to send signals to any process except the parent. There are four signals that you can send the parent: TERM, USR1, HUP, and WINCH, which will be described in a moment.

To send a signal to the parent you should issue a command such as:

```
kill -TERM `cat /usr/local/apache2/logs/httpd.pid`
```

The second method of signaling the httpd processes is to use the -k command line options: stop, restart, graceful and graceful-stop, as described below. These are arguments to the httpd binary, but we recommend that you send them using the apachectl control script, which will pass them through to httpd.

After you have signaled httpd, you can read about its progress by issuing:

```
tail -f /usr/local/apache2/logs/error_log
```

Modify those examples to match your SERVERROOT and PIDFILE settings.

### Stop Now

**Signal: TERM** apachectl -k stop

Sending the TERM or stop signal to the parent causes it to immediately attempt to kill off all of its children. It may take it several seconds to complete killing off its children. Then the parent itself exits. Any requests in progress are terminated, and no further requests are served.

### Graceful Restart

**Signal: USR1** apachectl -k graceful

The USR1 or graceful signal causes the parent process to *advise* the children to exit after their current request (or to exit immediately if they're not serving anything). The parent re-reads its configuration files and re-opens its log files. As each child dies off the parent replaces it with a child from the new *generation* of the configuration, which begins serving new requests immediately.

This code is designed to always respect the process control directive of the MPMs, so the number of processes and threads available to serve clients will be maintained at the appropriate values throughout the restart process. Furthermore, it respects STARTSERVERS in the following manner: if after one second at least STARTSERVERS new children have not been created, then create enough to pick up the slack. Hence the code tries to maintain both the number of children appropriate for the current load on the server, and respect your wishes with the STARTSERVERS parameter.

Users of MOD_STATUS will notice that the server statistics are **not** set to zero when a USR1 is sent. The code was written to both minimize the time in which the server is unable to serve new requests (they will be queued up by the operating system, so they're not lost in any event) and to respect your tuning parameters. In order to do this it has to keep the *scoreboard* used to keep track of all children across generations.

The status module will also use a G to indicate those children which are still serving requests started before the graceful restart was given.

At present there is no way for a log rotation script using USR1 to know for certain that all children writing the pre-restart log have finished. We suggest that you use a suitable delay after sending the USR1 signal before you do anything with the old log. For example if most of your hits take less than 10 minutes to complete for users on low bandwidth links then you could wait 15 minutes before doing anything with the old log.

 When you issue a restart, a syntax check is first run, to ensure that there are no errors in the configuration files. If your configuration file has errors in it, you will get an error message about that syntax error, and the server will refuse to restart. This avoids the situation where the server halts and then cannot restart, leaving you with a non-functioning server.

This still will not guarantee that the server will restart correctly. To check the semantics of the configuration files as well as the syntax, you can try starting httpd as a non-root user. If there are no errors it will attempt to open its sockets and logs and fail because it's not root (or because the currently running httpd already has those ports bound). If it fails for any other reason then it's probably a config file error and the error should be fixed before issuing the graceful restart.

## Restart Now

**Signal: HUP** `apachectl -k restart`

Sending the HUP or restart signal to the parent causes it to kill off its children like in TERM, but the parent doesn't exit. It re-reads its configuration files, and re-opens any log files. Then it spawns a new set of children and continues serving hits.

Users of MOD_STATUS will notice that the server statistics are set to zero when a HUP is sent.

 As with a graceful restart, a syntax check is run before the restart is attempted. If your configuration file has errors in it, the restart will not be attempted, and you will receive notification of the syntax error(s).

## Graceful Stop

**Signal: WINCH** `apachectl -k graceful-stop`

The WINCH or graceful-stop signal causes the parent process to *advise* the children to exit after their current request (or to exit immediately if they're not serving anything). The parent will then remove its PIDFILE and cease listening on all ports. The parent will continue to run, and monitor children which are handling requests. Once all children have finalised and exited or the timeout specified by the GRACEFULSHUTDOWNTIMEOUT has been reached, the parent will also exit. If the timeout is reached, any remaining children will be sent the TERM signal to force them to exit.

A TERM signal will immediately terminate the parent process and all children when in the "graceful" state. However as the PIDFILE will have been removed, you will not be able to use apachectl or httpd to send this signal.

The graceful-stop signal allows you to run multiple identically configured instances of httpd at the same time. This is a powerful feature when performing graceful upgrades of httpd, however it can also cause deadlocks and race conditions with some configurations.

Care has been taken to ensure that on-disk files such as lock files (MUTEX) and Unix socket files (SCRIPTSOCK) contain the server PID, and should coexist without problem. However, if a configuration directive, third-party module or persistent CGI utilises any other on-disk lock or state files, care should be taken to ensure that multiple running instances of httpd do not clobber each other's files.

You should also be wary of other potential race conditions, such as using rotatelogs style piped logging. Multiple running instances of rotatelogs attempting to rotate the same logfiles at the same time may destroy each other's logfiles.

## 2.4   Configuration Files

This document describes the files used to configure Apache HTTP Server.

### Main Configuration Files

| Related Modules | Related Directives |
|---|---|
| MOD_MIME | <IFDEFINE> |
| | INCLUDE |
| | TYPESCONFIG |

Apache HTTP Server is configured by placing directives (p. 1106) in plain text configuration files. The main configuration file is usually called `httpd.conf`. The location of this file is set at compile-time, but may be overridden with the `-f` command line flag. In addition, other configuration files may be added using the INCLUDE directive, and wildcards can be used to include many configuration files. Any directive may be placed in any of these configuration files. Changes to the main configuration files are only recognized by httpd when it is started or restarted.

The server also reads a file containing mime document types; the filename is set by the TYPESCONFIG directive, and is `mime.types` by default.

### Syntax of the Configuration Files

httpd configuration files contain one directive per line. The backslash "\" may be used as the last character on a line to indicate that the directive continues onto the next line. There must be no other characters or white space between the backslash and the end of the line.

Arguments to directives are separated by whitespace. If an argument contains spaces, you must enclose that argument in quotes.

Directives in the configuration files are case-insensitive, but arguments to directives are often case sensitive. Lines that begin with the hash character "#" are considered comments, and are ignored. Comments may **not** be included on the same line as a configuration directive. White space occurring before a directive is ignored, so you may indent directives for clarity. Blank lines are also ignored.

The values of variables defined with the DEFINE of or shell environment variables can be used in configuration file lines using the syntax ${VAR}. If "VAR" is the name of a valid variable, the value of that variable is substituted into that spot in the configuration file line, and processing continues as if that text were found directly in the configuration file. Variables defined with DEFINE take precedence over shell environment variables. If the "VAR" variable is not found, the characters ${VAR} are left unchanged, and a warning is logged. Variable names may not contain colon ":" characters, to avoid clashes with REWRITEMAP's syntax.

Only shell environment variables defined before the server is started can be used in expansions. Environment variables defined in the configuration file itself, for example with SETENV, take effect too late to be used for expansions in the configuration file.

The maximum length of a line in normal configuration files, after variable substitution and joining any continued lines, is approximately 16 MiB. In .htaccess files (p. 32) , the maximum length is 8190 characters.

You can check your configuration files for syntax errors without starting the server by using `apachectl configtest` or the `-t` command line option.

You can use MOD_INFO's -DDUMP_CONFIG to dump the configuration with all included files and environment variables resolved and all comments and non-matching <IFDEFINE> and <IFMODULE> sections removed. However, the output does not reflect the merging or overriding that may happen for repeated directives.

## Modules

| Related Modules | Related Directives |
| --- | --- |
| MOD_SO | <IFMODULE> |
| | LOADMODULE |

httpd is a modular server. This implies that only the most basic functionality is included in the core server. Extended features are available through modules (p. 1101) which can be loaded into httpd. By default, a base (p. 376) set of modules is included in the server at compile-time. If the server is compiled to use dynamically loaded (p. 68) modules, then modules can be compiled separately and added at any time using the LOADMODULE directive. Otherwise, httpd must be recompiled to add or remove modules. Configuration directives may be included conditional on a presence of a particular module by enclosing them in an <IFMODULE> block. However, <IFMODULE> blocks are not required, and in some cases may mask the fact that you're missing an important module.

To see which modules are currently compiled into the server, you can use the -l command line option. You can also see what modules are loaded dynamically using the -M command line option.

## Scope of Directives

| Related Modules | Related Directives |
| --- | --- |
| | <DIRECTORY> |
| | <DIRECTORYMATCH> |
| | <FILES> |
| | <FILESMATCH> |
| | <LOCATION> |
| | <LOCATIONMATCH> |
| | <VIRTUALHOST> |

Directives placed in the main configuration files apply to the entire server. If you wish to change the configuration for only a part of the server, you can scope your directives by placing them in <DIRECTORY>, <DIRECTORYMATCH>, <FILES>, <FILESMATCH>, <LOCATION>, and <LOCATIONMATCH> sections. These sections limit the application of the directives which they enclose to particular filesystem locations or URLs. They can also be nested, allowing for very fine grained configuration.

httpd has the capability to serve many different websites simultaneously. This is called Virtual Hosting (p. 124) . Directives can also be scoped by placing them inside <VIRTUALHOST> sections, so that they will only apply to requests for a particular website.

Although most directives can be placed in any of these sections, some directives do not make sense in some contexts. For example, directives controlling process creation can only be placed in the main server context. To find which directives can be placed in which sections, check the Context (p. 377) of the directive. For further information, we provide details on How Directory, Location and Files sections work (p. 35) .

## .htaccess Files

| Related Modules | Related Directives |
| --- | --- |
| | ACCESSFILENAME |
| | ALLOWOVERRIDE |

httpd allows for decentralized management of configuration via special files placed inside the web tree. The special files are usually called .htaccess, but any name can be specified in the ACCESSFILENAME directive. Directives placed in `.htaccess` files apply to the directory where you place the file, and all sub-directories. The `.htaccess` files follow the same syntax as the main configuration files. Since `.htaccess` files are read on every request, changes made in these files take immediate effect.

To find which directives can be placed in `.htaccess` files, check the Context (p. 377) of the directive. The server administrator further controls what directives may be placed in `.htaccess` files by configuring the ALLOWOVERRIDE directive in the main configuration files.

For more information on `.htaccess` files, see the .htaccess tutorial (p. 249) .

## 2.5 Configuration Sections

Directives in the configuration files (p. 32) may apply to the entire server, or they may be restricted to apply only to particular directories, files, hosts, or URLs. This document describes how to use configuration section containers or .htaccess files to change the scope of other configuration directives.

### Types of Configuration Section Containers

| Related Modules | Related Directives |
| --- | --- |
| CORE | <DIRECTORY> |
| MOD_VERSION | <DIRECTORYMATCH> |
| MOD_PROXY | <FILES> |
| | <FILESMATCH> |
| | <IF> |
| | <IFDEFINE> |
| | <IFMODULE> |
| | <IFVERSION> |
| | <LOCATION> |
| | <LOCATIONMATCH> |
| | <PROXY> |
| | <PROXYMATCH> |
| | <VIRTUALHOST> |

There are two basic types of containers. Most containers are evaluated for each request. The enclosed directives are applied only for those requests that match the containers. The <IFDEFINE>, <IFMODULE>, and <IFVERSION> containers, on the other hand, are evaluated only at server startup and restart. If their conditions are true at startup, then the enclosed directives will apply to all requests. If the conditions are not true, the enclosed directives will be ignored.

The <IFDEFINE> directive encloses directives that will only be applied if an appropriate parameter is defined on the httpd command line. For example, with the following configuration, all requests will be redirected to another site only if the server is started using httpd -DClosedForNow:

```
<IfDefine ClosedForNow>
    Redirect "/" "http://otherserver.example.com/"
</IfDefine>
```

The <IFMODULE> directive is very similar, except it encloses directives that will only be applied if a particular module is available in the server. The module must either be statically compiled in the server, or it must be dynamically compiled and its LOADMODULE line must be earlier in the configuration file. This directive should only be used if you need your configuration file to work whether or not certain modules are installed. It should not be used to enclose directives that you want to work all the time, because it can suppress useful error messages about missing modules.

In the following example, the MIMEMAGICFILE directive will be applied only if MOD_MIME_MAGIC is available.

```
<IfModule mod_mime_magic.c>
    MimeMagicFile conf/magic
</IfModule>
```

The <IFVERSION> directive is very similar to <IFDEFINE> and <IFMODULE>, except it encloses directives that will only be applied if a particular version of the server is executing. This module is designed for the use in test suites and large networks which have to deal with different httpd versions and different configurations.

```
<IfVersion >= 2.4>
    # this happens only in versions greater or
    # equal 2.4.0.
</IfVersion>
```

<IFDEFINE>, <IFMODULE>, and the <IFVERSION> can apply negative conditions by preceding their test with
"!". Also, these sections can be nested to achieve more complex restrictions.

## Filesystem, Webspace, and Boolean Expressions

The most commonly used configuration section containers are the ones that change the configuration of particular
places in the filesystem or webspace. First, it is important to understand the difference between the two. The filesystem is the view of your disks as seen by your operating system. For example, in a default install, Apache httpd resides at
/usr/local/apache2 in the Unix filesystem or "c:/Program Files/Apache Group/Apache2" in the
Windows filesystem. (Note that forward slashes should always be used as the path separator in Apache httpd configuration files, even for Windows.) In contrast, the webspace is the view of your site as delivered by the web server and seen
by the client. So the path /dir/ in the webspace corresponds to the path /usr/local/apache2/htdocs/dir/
in the filesystem of a default Apache httpd install on Unix. The webspace need not map directly to the filesystem,
since webpages may be generated dynamically from databases or other locations.

### Filesystem Containers

The <DIRECTORY> and <FILES> directives, along with their regex counterparts, apply directives to parts of the
filesystem. Directives enclosed in a <DIRECTORY> section apply to the named filesystem directory and all subdirectories of that directory (as well as the files in those directories). The same effect can be obtained using .htaccess files
(p. 249) . For example, in the following configuration, directory indexes will be enabled for the /var/web/dir1
directory and all subdirectories.

```
<Directory "/var/web/dir1">
    Options +Indexes
</Directory>
```

Directives enclosed in a <FILES> section apply to any file with the specified name, regardless of what directory it lies
in. So for example, the following configuration directives will, when placed in the main section of the configuration
file, deny access to any file named private.html regardless of where it is found.

```
<Files "private.html">
    Require all denied
</Files>
```

To address files found in a particular part of the filesystem, the <FILES> and <DIRECTORY> sections can be
combined. For example, the following configuration will deny access to /var/web/dir1/private.html,
/var/web/dir1/subdir2/private.html, /var/web/dir1/subdir3/private.html, and any
other instance of private.html found under the /var/web/dir1/ directory.

```
<Directory "/var/web/dir1">
    <Files "private.html">
        Require all denied
    </Files>
</Directory>
```

**Webspace Containers**

The <LOCATION> directive and its regex counterpart, on the other hand, change the configuration for content in the webspace. For example, the following configuration prevents access to any URL-path that begins in /private. In particular, it will apply to requests for `http://yoursite.example.com/private`, `http://yoursite.example.com/private123`, and `http://yoursite.example.com/private/dir/file.html` as well as any other requests starting with the `/private` string.

```
<LocationMatch "^/private">
    Require all denied
</LocationMatch>
```

The <LOCATION> directive need not have anything to do with the filesystem. For example, the following example shows how to map a particular URL to an internal Apache HTTP Server handler provided by MOD_STATUS. No file called `server-status` needs to exist in the filesystem.

```
<Location "/server-status">
    SetHandler server-status
</Location>
```

**Overlapping Webspace**

In order to have two overlapping URLs one has to consider the order in which certain sections or directives are evaluated. For <LOCATION> this would be:

```
<Location "/foo">
</Location>
<Location "/foo/bar">
</Location>
```

<ALIAS>es on the other hand, are mapped vice-versa:

```
Alias "/foo/bar"  "/srv/www/uncommon/bar"
Alias "/foo"      "/srv/www/common/foo"
```

The same is true for the PROXYPASS directives:

```
ProxyPass "/special-area" "http://special.example.com" smax=5 max=10
ProxyPass "/" "balancer://mycluster/" stickysession=JSESSIONID|jsessionid nofailover=
```

**Wildcards and Regular Expressions**

The <DIRECTORY>, <FILES>, and <LOCATION> directives can each use shell-style wildcard characters as in `fnmatch` from the C standard library. The character "*" matches any sequence of characters, "?" matches any single character, and "[*seq*]" matches any character in *seq*. The "/" character will not be matched by any wildcard; it must be specified explicitly.

If even more flexible matching is required, each container has a regular expression (regex) counterpart <DIRECTORY-MATCH>, <FILESMATCH>, and <LOCATIONMATCH> that allow perl-compatible regular expressions to be used in choosing the matches. But see the section below on configuration merging to find out how using regex sections will change how directives are applied.

A non-regex wildcard section that changes the configuration of all user directories could look as follows:

```
<Directory "/home/*/public_html">
    Options Indexes
</Directory>
```

Using regex sections, we can deny access to many types of image files at once:

```
<FilesMatch "\.(?i:gif|jpe?g|png)$">
    Require all denied
</FilesMatch>
```

Regular expressions containing **named groups and backreferences** are added to the environment with the corresponding name in uppercase. This allows elements of filename paths and URLs to be referenced from within expressions (p. 99) and modules like MOD_REWRITE.

```
<DirectoryMatch "^/var/www/combined/(?<SITENAME>[^/]+)">
    require ldap-group cn=%{env:MATCH_SITENAME},ou=combined,o=Example
</DirectoryMatch>
```

**Boolean expressions**

The <IF> directive change the configuration depending on a condition which can be expressed by a boolean expression. For example, the following configuration denies access if the HTTP Referer header does not start with "http://www.example.com/".

```
<If "!(%{HTTP_REFERER} -strmatch 'http://www.example.com/*')">
    Require all denied
</If>
```

**What to use When**

Choosing between filesystem containers and webspace containers is actually quite easy. When applying directives to objects that reside in the filesystem always use <DIRECTORY> or <FILES>. When applying directives to objects that do not reside in the filesystem (such as a webpage generated from a database), use <LOCATION>.

It is important to never use <LOCATION> when trying to restrict access to objects in the filesystem. This is because many different webspace locations (URLs) could map to the same filesystem location, allowing your restrictions to be circumvented. For example, consider the following configuration:

```
<Location "/dir/">
    Require all denied
</Location>
```

This works fine if the request is for http://yoursite.example.com/dir/. But what if you are on a case-insensitive filesystem? Then your restriction could be easily circumvented by requesting http://yoursite.example.com/DIR/. The <DIRECTORY> directive, in contrast, will apply to any content served from that location, regardless of how it is called. (An exception is filesystem links. The same directory can be placed in more than one part of the filesystem using symbolic links. The <DIRECTORY> directive will follow the symbolic link without resetting the pathname. Therefore, for the highest level of security, symbolic links should be disabled with the appropriate OPTIONS directive.)

If you are, perhaps, thinking that none of this applies to you because you use a case-sensitive filesystem, remember that there are many other ways to map multiple webspace locations to the same filesystem location. Therefore you should always use the filesystem containers when you can. There is, however, one exception to this rule. Putting configuration restrictions in a <Location "/"> section is perfectly safe because this section will apply to all requests regardless of the specific URL.

### Nesting of sections

Some section types can be nested inside other section types. On the one hand, <FILES> can be used inside <DIRECTORY>. On the other hand, <IF> can be used inside <DIRECTORY>, <LOCATION>, and <FILES> sections. The regex counterparts of the named section behave identically.

Nested sections are merged after non-nested sections of the same type.

## Virtual Hosts

The <VIRTUALHOST> container encloses directives that apply to specific hosts. This is useful when serving multiple hosts from the same machine with a different configuration for each. For more information, see the Virtual Host Documentation (p. 124).

## Proxy

The <PROXY> and <PROXYMATCH> containers apply enclosed configuration directives only to sites accessed through MOD_PROXY's proxy server that match the specified URL. For example, the following configuration will allow only a subset of clients to access the www.example.com website using the proxy server:

```
<Proxy http://www.example.com/*>
    Require host yournetwork.example.com
</Proxy>
```

## What Directives are Allowed?

To find out what directives are allowed in what types of configuration sections, check the Context (p. 377) of the directive. Everything that is allowed in <DIRECTORY> sections is also syntactically allowed in <DIRECTORYMATCH>, <FILES>, <FILESMATCH>, <LOCATION>, <LOCATIONMATCH>, <PROXY>, and <PROXYMATCH> sections. There are some exceptions, however:

- The ALLOWOVERRIDE directive works only in <DIRECTORY> sections.
- The FollowSymLinks and SymLinksIfOwnerMatch OPTIONS work only in <DIRECTORY> sections or .htaccess files.
- The OPTIONS directive cannot be used in <FILES> and <FILESMATCH> sections.

## How the sections are merged

The configuration sections are applied in a very particular order. Since this can have important effects on how configuration directives are interpreted, it is important to understand how this works.

The order of merging is:

1. <DIRECTORY> (except regular expressions) and .htaccess done simultaneously (with .htaccess, if allowed, overriding <DIRECTORY>)

2. <DIRECTORYMATCH> (and <Directory ~>)

3. <FILES> and <FILESMATCH> done simultaneously

4. <LOCATION> and <LOCATIONMATCH> done simultaneously

5. <IF>

Apart from <DIRECTORY>, each group is processed in the order that they appear in the configuration files. <DIRECTORY> (group 1 above) is processed in the order shortest directory component to longest. So for example, <Directory "/var/web/dir"> will be processed before <Directory "/var/web/dir/subdir">. If multiple <DIRECTORY> sections apply to the same directory they are processed in the configuration file order. Configurations included via the INCLUDE directive will be treated as if they were inside the including file at the location of the INCLUDE directive.

Sections inside <VIRTUALHOST> sections are applied *after* the corresponding sections outside the virtual host definition. This allows virtual hosts to override the main server configuration.

When the request is served by MOD_PROXY, the <PROXY> container takes the place of the <DIRECTORY> container in the processing order.

**Technical Note**

> There is actually a <Location>/<LocationMatch> sequence performed just before the name translation phase (where Aliases and DocumentRoots are used to map URLs to filenames). The results of this sequence are completely thrown away after the translation has completed.

**Relationship between modules and configuration sections**

One question that often arises after reading how configuration sections are merged is related to how and when directives of specific modules like MOD_REWRITE are processed. The answer is not trivial and needs a bit of background. Each httpd module manages its own configuration, and each of its directives in httpd.conf specify one piece of configuration in a particular context. httpd does not execute a command as it is read.

At runtime, the core of httpd iterates over the defined configuration sections in the order described above to determine which ones apply to the current request. When the first section matches, it is considered the current configuration for this request. If a subsequent section matches too, then each module with a directive in either of the sections is given a chance to merge its configuration between the two sections. The result is a third configuration, and the process goes on until all the configuration sections are evaluated.

After the above step, the "real" processing of the HTTP request begins: each module has a chance to run and perform whatever tasks they like. They can retrieve their own final merged configuration from the core of the httpd to determine how they should act.

An example can help to visualize the whole process. The following configuration uses the HEADER directive of MOD_HEADERS to set a specific HTTP header. What value will httpd set in the CustomHeaderName header for a request to /example/index.html ?

```
<Directory "/">
    Header set CustomHeaderName one
    <FilesMatch ".*">
        Header set CustomHeaderName three
    </FilesMatch>
</Directory>

<Directory "/example">
    Header set CustomHeaderName two
```

```
</Directory>
```

- DIRECTORY "/" matches and an initial configuration to set the CustomHeaderName header with the value one is created.
- DIRECTORY "/example" matches, and since MOD_HEADERS specifies in its code to override in case of a merge, a new configuration is created to set the CustomHeaderName header with the value two.
- FILESMATCH ".*" matches and another merge opportunity arises, causing the CustomHeaderName header to be set with the value three.
- Eventually during the next steps of the HTTP request processing MOD_HEADERS will be called and it will receive the configuration to set the CustomHeaderName header with the value three. MOD_HEADERS normally uses this configuration to perfom its job, namely setting the foo header. This does not mean that a module can't perform a more complex action like discarding directives because not needed or deprecated, etc..

This is true for .htaccess too since they have the same priority as DIRECTORY in the merge order. The important concept to understand is that configuration sections like DIRECTORY and FILESMATCH are not comparable to module specific directives like HEADER or REWRITERULE because they operate on different levels.

**Some useful examples**

Below is an artificial example to show the order of merging. Assuming they all apply to the request, the directives in this example will be applied in the order A > B > C > D > E.

```
<Location "/">
    E
</Location>

<Files "f.html">
    D
</Files>

<VirtualHost *>
<Directory "/a/emphasis role="bold"">
    B
</Directory>
</VirtualHost>

<DirectoryMatch "^.*b$">
    C
</DirectoryMatch>

<Directory "/a/b">
    A
</Directory>
```

For a more concrete example, consider the following. Regardless of any access restrictions placed in <DIRECTORY> sections, the <LOCATION> section will be evaluated last and will allow unrestricted access to the server. In other words, order of merging is important, so be careful!

```
<Location "/">
    Require all granted
</Location>
```

```
# Whoops!  This <Directory> section will have no effect
<Directory "/">
    <RequireAll>
        Require all granted
        Require not host badguy.example.com
    </RequireAll>
</Directory>
```

## 2.6   Caching Guide

This document supplements the MOD_CACHE, MOD_CACHE_DISK, MOD_FILE_CACHE and htcacheclean (p. 319) reference documentation. It describes how to use the Apache HTTP Server's caching features to accelerate web and proxy serving, while avoiding common problems and misconfigurations.

### Introduction

The Apache HTTP server offers a range of caching features that are designed to improve the performance of the server in various ways.

**Three-state RFC2616 HTTP caching**   MOD_CACHE and its provider modules MOD_CACHE_DISK provide intelligent, HTTP-aware caching. The content itself is stored in the cache, and mod_cache aims to honor all of the various HTTP headers and options that control the cacheability of content as described in Section 13 of RFC2616[12]. MOD_CACHE is aimed at both simple and complex caching configurations, where you are dealing with proxied content, dynamic local content or have a need to speed up access to local files on a potentially slow disk.

**Two-state key/value shared object caching**   The shared object cache API (p. 114) (socache) and its provider modules provide a server wide key/value based shared object cache. These modules are designed to cache low level data such as SSL sessions and authentication credentials. Backends allow the data to be stored server wide in shared memory, or datacenter wide in a cache such as memcache or distcache.

**Specialized file caching**   MOD_FILE_CACHE offers the ability to pre-load files into memory on server startup, and can improve access times and save file handles on files that are accessed often, as there is no need to go to disk on each request.

To get the most from this document, you should be familiar with the basics of HTTP, and have read the Users' Guides to Mapping URLs to the Filesystem (p. 64) and Content negotiation (p. 78) .

### Three-state RFC2616 HTTP caching

| Related Modules | Related Directives |
| --- | --- |
| MOD_CACHE | CACHEENABLE |
| MOD_CACHE_DISK | CACHEDISABLE |
| | USECANONICALNAME |
| | CACHENEGOTIATEDDOCS |

The HTTP protocol contains built in support for an in-line caching mechanism

described by section 13 of RFC2616[13], and the MOD_CACHE module can be used to take advantage of this.

Unlike a simple two state key/value cache where the content disappears completely when no longer fresh, an HTTP cache includes a mechanism to retain stale content, and to ask the origin server whether this stale content has changed and if not, make it fresh again.

An entry in an HTTP cache exists in one of three states:

**Fresh**   If the content is new enough (younger than its **freshness lifetime**), it is considered **fresh**. An HTTP cache is free to serve fresh content without making any calls to the origin server at all.

---

[12]http://www.w3.org/Protocols/rfc2616/rfc2616-sec13.html
[13]http://www.w3.org/Protocols/rfc2616/rfc2616-sec13.html

**Stale** If the content is too old (older than its **freshness lifetime**), it is considered **stale**. An HTTP cache should contact the origin server and check whether the content is still fresh before serving stale content to a client. The origin server will either respond with replacement content if not still valid, or ideally, the origin server will respond with a code to tell the cache the content is still fresh, without the need to generate or send the content again. The content becomes fresh again and the cycle continues.

The HTTP protocol does allow the cache to serve stale data under certain circumstances, such as when an attempt to freshen the data with an origin server has failed with a 5xx error, or when another request is already in the process of freshening the given entry. In these cases a `Warning` header is added to the response.

**Non Existent** If the cache gets full, it reserves the option to delete content from the cache to make space. Content can be deleted at any time, and can be stale or fresh. The htcacheclean (p. 319) tool can be run on a once off basis, or deployed as a daemon to keep the size of the cache within the given size, or the given number of inodes. The tool attempts to delete stale content before attempting to delete fresh content.

Full details of how HTTP caching works can be found in

Section 13 of RFC2616[14].


**Interaction with the Server**

The MOD_CACHE module hooks into the server in two possible places depending on the value of the CACHEQUICK-HANDLER directive:


**Quick handler phase** This phase happens very early on during the request processing, just after the request has been parsed. If the content is found within the cache, it is served immediately and almost all request processing is bypassed.

In this scenario, the cache behaves as if it has been "bolted on" to the front of the server.

This mode offers the best performance, as the majority of server processing is bypassed. This mode however also bypasses the authentication and authorization phases of server processing, so this mode should be chosen with care when this is important.

Requests with an "Authorization" header (for example, HTTP Basic Authentication) are neither cacheable nor served from the cache when MOD_CACHE is running in this phase.

**Normal handler phase** This phase happens late in the request processing, after all the request phases have completed.

In this scenario, the cache behaves as if it has been "bolted on" to the back of the server.

This mode offers the most flexibility, as the potential exists for caching to occur at a precisely controlled point in the filter chain, and cached content can be filtered or personalized before being sent to the client.


If the URL is not found within the cache, MOD_CACHE will add a filter (p. 110) to the filter stack in order to record the response to the cache, and then stand down, allowing normal request processing to continue. If the content is determined to be cacheable, the content will be saved to the cache for future serving, otherwise the content will be ignored.

If the content found within the cache is stale, the MOD_CACHE module converts the request into a **conditional request**. If the origin server responds with a normal response, the normal response is cached, replacing the content already cached. If the origin server responds with a 304 Not Modified response, the content is marked as fresh again, and the cached content is served by the filter instead of saving it.

---

[14]http://www.w3.org/Protocols/rfc2616/rfc2616-sec13.html

**Improving Cache Hits**

When a virtual host is known by one of many different server aliases, ensuring that USECANONICALNAME is set to On can dramatically improve the ratio of cache hits. This is because the hostname of the virtual-host serving the content is used within the cache key. With the setting set to On virtual-hosts with multiple server names or aliases will not produce differently cached entities, and instead content will be cached as per the canonical hostname.

**Freshness Lifetime**

Well formed content that is intended to be cached should declare an explicit freshness lifetime with the Cache-Control header's max-age or s-maxage fields, or by including an Expires header.

At the same time, the origin server defined freshness lifetime can be overridden by a client when the client presents their own Cache-Control header within the request. In this case, the lowest freshness lifetime between request and response wins.

When this freshness lifetime is missing from the request or the response, a default freshness lifetime is applied. The default freshness lifetime for cached entities is one hour, however this can be easily over-ridden by using the CACHEDEFAULTEXPIRE directive.

If a response does not include an Expires header but does include a Last-Modified header, MOD_CACHE can infer a freshness lifetime based on a heuristic, which can be controlled through the use of the CACHELASTMODIFIEDFACTOR directive.

For local content, or for remote content that does not define its own Expires header, MOD_EXPIRES may be used to fine-tune the freshness lifetime by adding max-age and Expires.

The maximum freshness lifetime may also be controlled by using the CACHEMAXEXPIRE.

**A Brief Guide to Conditional Requests**

When content expires from the cache and becomes stale, rather than pass on the original request, httpd will modify the request to make it conditional instead.

When an ETag header exists in the original cached response, MOD_CACHE will add an If-None-Match header to the request to the origin server. When a Last-Modified header exists in the original cached response, MOD_CACHE will add an If-Modified-Since header to the request to the origin server. Performing either of these actions makes the request **conditional**.

When a conditional request is received by an origin server, the origin server should check whether the ETag or the Last-Modified parameter has changed, as appropriate for the request. If not, the origin should respond with a terse "304 Not Modified" response. This signals to the cache that the stale content is still fresh should be used for subsequent requests until the content's new freshness lifetime is reached again.

If the content has changed, then the content is served as if the request were not conditional to begin with.

Conditional requests offer two benefits. Firstly, when making such a request to the origin server, if the content from the origin matches the content in the cache, this can be determined easily and without the overhead of transferring the entire resource.

Secondly, a well designed origin server will be designed in such a way that conditional requests will be significantly cheaper to produce than a full response. For static files, typically all that is involved is a call to stat() or similar system call, to see if the file has changed in size or modification time. As such, even local content may still be served faster from the cache if it has not changed.

Origin servers should make every effort to support conditional requests as is practical, however if conditional requests are not supported, the origin will respond as if the request was not conditional, and the cache will respond as if the content had changed and save the new content to the cache. In this case, the cache will behave like a simple two state cache, where content is effectively either fresh or deleted.

**What Can be Cached?**

The full definition of which responses can be cached by an HTTP cache is defined in

RFC2616 Section 13.4 Response Cacheability[15], and can be summed up as follows:

1. Caching must be enabled for this URL. See the CACHEENABLE and CACHEDISABLE directives.

2. The response must have a HTTP status code of 200, 203, 300, 301 or 410.

3. The request must be a HTTP GET request.

4. If the response contains an "Authorization:" header, it must also contain an "s-maxage", "must-revalidate" or "public" option in the "Cache-Control:" header, or it won't be cached.

5. If the URL included a query string (e.g. from a HTML form GET method) it will not be cached unless the response specifies an explicit expiration by including an "Expires:" header or the max-age or s-maxage directive of the "Cache-Control:" header, as per RFC2616 sections 13.9 and 13.2.1.

6. If the response has a status of 200 (OK), the response must also include at least one of the "Etag", "Last-Modified" or the "Expires" headers, or the max-age or s-maxage directive of the "Cache-Control:" header, unless the CACHEIGNORENOLASTMOD directive has been used to require otherwise.

7. If the response includes the "private" option in a "Cache-Control:" header, it will not be stored unless the CACHESTOREPRIVATE has been used to require otherwise.

8. Likewise, if the response includes the "no-store" option in a "Cache-Control:" header, it will not be stored unless the CACHESTORENOSTORE has been used.

9. A response will not be stored if it includes a "Vary:" header containing the match-all "*".

**What Should Not be Cached?**

It should be up to the client creating the request, or the origin server constructing the response to decide whether or not the content should be cacheable or not by correctly setting the Cache-Control header, and MOD_CACHE should be left alone to honor the wishes of the client or server as appropriate.

Content that is time sensitive, or which varies depending on the particulars of the request that are not covered by HTTP negotiation, should not be cached. This content should declare itself uncacheable using the Cache-Control header.

If content changes often, expressed by a freshness lifetime of minutes or seconds, the content can still be cached, however it is highly desirable that the origin server supports **conditional requests** correctly to ensure that full responses do not have to be generated on a regular basis.

Content that varies based on client provided request headers can be cached through intelligent use of the Vary response header.

---

[15]http://www.w3.org/Protocols/rfc2616/rfc2616-sec13.html#sec13.4

**Variable/Negotiated Content**

When the origin server is designed to respond with different content based on the value of headers in the request, for example to serve multiple languages at the same URL, HTTP's caching mechanism makes it possible to cache multiple variants of the same page at the same URL.

This is done by the origin server adding a `Vary` header to indicate which headers must be taken into account by a cache when determining whether two variants are different from one another.

If for example, a response is received with a vary header such as;

```
Vary:   negotiate,accept-language,accept-charset
```

MOD_CACHE will only serve the cached content to requesters with accept-language and accept-charset headers matching those of the original request.

Multiple variants of the content can be cached side by side, MOD_CACHE uses the `Vary` header and the corresponding values of the request headers listed by `Vary` to decide on which of many variants to return to the client.

**Caching to Disk**

The MOD_CACHE module relies on specific backend store implementations in order to manage the cache, and for caching to disk MOD_CACHE_DISK is provided to support this.

Typically the module will be configured as so;

```
CacheRoot    "/var/cache/apache/"
CacheEnable disk /
CacheDirLevels 2
CacheDirLength 1
```

Importantly, as the cached files are locally stored, operating system in-memory caching will typically be applied to their access also. So although the files are stored on disk, if they are frequently accessed it is likely the operating system will ensure that they are actually served from memory.

**Understanding the Cache-Store**

To store items in the cache, MOD_CACHE_DISK creates a 22 character hash of the URL being requested. This hash incorporates the hostname, protocol, port, path and any CGI arguments to the URL, as well as elements defined by the Vary header to ensure that multiple URLs do not collide with one another.

Each character may be any one of 64-different characters, which mean that overall there are $64^{22}$ possible hashes. For example, a URL might be hashed to `xyTGxSMO2b68mBCykqkp1w`. This hash is used as a prefix for the naming of the files specific to that URL within the cache, however first it is split up into directories as per the CACHEDIRLEVELS and CACHEDIRLENGTH directives.

CACHEDIRLEVELS specifies how many levels of subdirectory there should be, and CACHEDIRLENGTH specifies how many characters should be in each directory. With the example settings given above, the hash would be turned into a filename prefix as `/var/cache/apache/x/y/TGxSMO2b68mBCykqkp1w`.

The overall aim of this technique is to reduce the number of subdirectories or files that may be in a particular directory, as most file-systems slow down as this number increases. With setting of "1" for CACHEDIRLENGTH there can at most be 64 subdirectories at any particular level. With a setting of 2 there can be 64 * 64 subdirectories, and so on. Unless you have a good reason not to, using a setting of "1" for CACHEDIRLENGTH is recommended.

Setting CACHEDIRLEVELS depends on how many files you anticipate to store in the cache. With the setting of "2" used in the above example, a grand total of 4096 subdirectories can ultimately be created. With 1 million files cached, this works out at roughly 245 cached URLs per directory.

Each URL uses at least two files in the cache-store. Typically there is a ".header" file, which includes meta-information about the URL, such as when it is due to expire and a ".data" file which is a verbatim copy of the content to be served.

In the case of a content negotiated via the "Vary" header, a ".vary" directory will be created for the URL in question. This directory will have multiple ".data" files corresponding to the differently negotiated content.

**Maintaining the Disk Cache**

The MOD_CACHE_DISK module makes no attempt to regulate the amount of disk space used by the cache, although it will gracefully stand down on any disk error and behave as if the cache was never present.

Instead, provided with httpd is the htcacheclean (p. 319) tool which allows you to clean the cache periodically. Determining how frequently to run htcacheclean (p. 319) and what target size to use for the cache is somewhat complex and trial and error may be needed to select optimal values.

htcacheclean (p. 319) has two modes of operation. It can be run as persistent daemon, or periodically from cron. htcacheclean (p. 319) can take up to an hour or more to process very large (tens of gigabytes) caches and if you are running it from cron it is recommended that you determine how long a typical run takes, to avoid running more than one instance at a time.

It is also recommended that an appropriate "nice" level is chosen for htcacheclean so that the tool does not cause excessive disk io while the server is running.

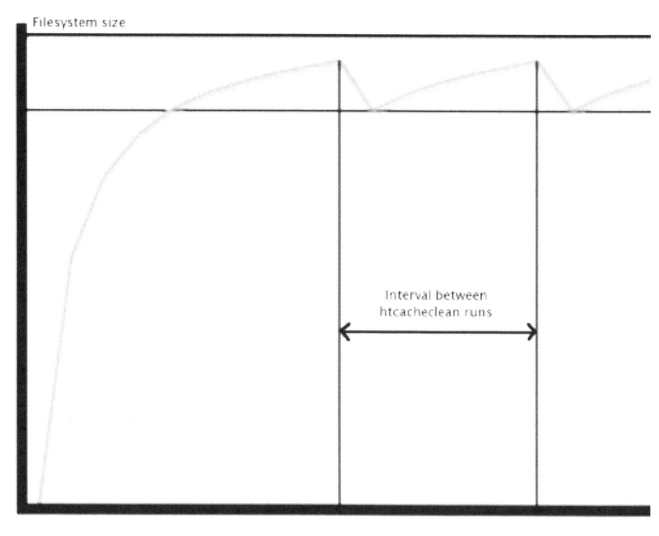

*Figure 1*: Typical cache growth / clean sequence.

Because MOD_CACHE_DISK does not itself pay attention to how much space is used you should ensure that ht-cacheclean (p. 319) is configured to leave enough "grow room" following a clean.

## Two-state Key/Value Shared Object Caching

| Related Modules | Related Directives |
| --- | --- |
| MOD_AUTHN_SOCACHE | AUTHNCACHESOCACHE |
| MOD_SOCACHE_DBM | SSLSESSIONCACHE |
| MOD_SOCACHE_DC | SSLSTAPLINGCACHE |
| MOD_SOCACHE_MEMCACHE | |
| MOD_SOCACHE_SHMCB | |
| MOD_SSL | |

The Apache HTTP server offers a low level shared object cache for caching information such as SSL sessions, or authentication credentials, within the socache (p. 114) interface.

Additional modules are provided for each implementation, offering the following backends:

MOD_SOCACHE_DBM  DBM based shared object cache.

MOD_SOCACHE_DC  Distcache based shared object cache.

MOD_SOCACHE_MEMCACHE  Memcache based shared object cache.

MOD_SOCACHE_SHMCB  Shared memory based shared object cache.

### Caching Authentication Credentials

| Related Modules | Related Directives |
|---|---|
| MOD_AUTHN_SOCACHE | AUTHNCACHESOCACHE |

The MOD_AUTHN_SOCACHE module allows the result of authentication to be cached, relieving load on authentication backends.

### Caching SSL Sessions

| Related Modules | Related Directives |
|---|---|
| MOD_SSL | SSLSESSIONCACHE |
| | SSLSTAPLINGCACHE |

The MOD_SSL module uses the socache interface to provide a session cache and a stapling cache.

## Specialized File Caching

| Related Modules | Related Directives |
|---|---|
| MOD_FILE_CACHE | CACHEFILE |
| | MMAPFILE |

On platforms where a filesystem might be slow, or where file handles are expensive, the option exists to pre-load files into memory on startup.

On systems where opening files is slow, the option exists to open the file on startup and cache the file handle. These options can help on systems where access to static files is slow.

### File-Handle Caching

The act of opening a file can itself be a source of delay, particularly on network filesystems. By maintaining a cache of open file descriptors for commonly served files, httpd can avoid this delay. Currently httpd provides one implementation of File-Handle Caching.

### CacheFile

The most basic form of caching present in httpd is the file-handle caching provided by MOD_FILE_CACHE. Rather than caching file-contents, this cache maintains a table of open file descriptors. Files to be cached in this manner are specified in the configuration file using the CACHEFILE directive.

The CACHEFILE directive instructs httpd to open the file when it is started and to re-use this file-handle for all subsequent access to this file.

```
CacheFile /usr/local/apache2/htdocs/index.html
```

If you intend to cache a large number of files in this manner, you must ensure that your operating system's limit for the number of open files is set appropriately.

Although using CACHEFILE does not cause the file-contents to be cached per-se, it does mean that if the file changes while httpd is running these changes will not be picked up. The file will be consistently served as it was when httpd was started.

If the file is removed while httpd is running, it will continue to maintain an open file descriptor and serve the file as it was when httpd was started. This usually also means that although the file will have been deleted, and not show up on the filesystem, extra free space will not be recovered until httpd is stopped and the file descriptor closed.

### In-Memory Caching

Serving directly from system memory is universally the fastest method of serving content. Reading files from a disk controller or, even worse, from a remote network is orders of magnitude slower. Disk controllers usually involve physical processes, and network access is limited by your available bandwidth. Memory access on the other hand can take mere nano-seconds.

System memory isn't cheap though, byte for byte it's by far the most expensive type of storage and it's important to ensure that it is used efficiently. By caching files in memory you decrease the amount of memory available on the system. As we'll see, in the case of operating system caching, this is not so much of an issue, but when using httpd's own in-memory caching it is important to make sure that you do not allocate too much memory to a cache. Otherwise the system will be forced to swap out memory, which will likely degrade performance.

### Operating System Caching

Almost all modern operating systems cache file-data in memory managed directly by the kernel. This is a powerful feature, and for the most part operating systems get it right. For example, on Linux, let's look at the difference in the time it takes to read a file for the first time and the second time;

```
colm@coroebus:~$ time cat testfile > /dev/null
real    0m0.065s
user    0m0.000s
sys     0m0.001s
colm@coroebus:~$ time cat testfile > /dev/null
real    0m0.003s
user    0m0.003s
sys     0m0.000s
```

Even for this small file, there is a huge difference in the amount of time it takes to read the file. This is because the kernel has cached the file contents in memory.

By ensuring there is "spare" memory on your system, you can ensure that more and more file-contents will be stored in this cache. This can be a very efficient means of in-memory caching, and involves no extra configuration of httpd at all.

Additionally, because the operating system knows when files are deleted or modified, it can automatically remove file contents from the cache when necessary. This is a big advantage over httpd's in-memory caching which has no way of knowing when a file has changed.

Despite the performance and advantages of automatic operating system caching there are some circumstances in which in-memory caching may be better performed by httpd.

**MMapFile Caching**

MOD_FILE_CACHE provides the MMAPFILE directive, which allows you to have httpd map a static file's contents into memory at start time (using the mmap system call). httpd will use the in-memory contents for all subsequent accesses to this file.

```
MMapFile /usr/local/apache2/htdocs/index.html
```

As with the CACHEFILE directive, any changes in these files will not be picked up by httpd after it has started.

The MMAPFILE directive does not keep track of how much memory it allocates, so you must ensure not to over-use the directive. Each httpd child process will replicate this memory, so it is critically important to ensure that the files mapped are not so large as to cause the system to swap memory.

## Security Considerations

**Authorization and Access Control**

Using MOD_CACHE in its default state where CACHEQUICKHANDLER is set to On is very much like having a caching reverse-proxy bolted to the front of the server. Requests will be served by the caching module unless it determines that the origin server should be queried just as an external cache would, and this drastically changes the security model of httpd.

As traversing a filesystem hierarchy to examine potential .htaccess files would be a very expensive operation, partially defeating the point of caching (to speed up requests), MOD_CACHE makes no decision about whether a cached entity is authorised for serving. In other words; if MOD_CACHE has cached some content, it will be served from the cache as long as that content has not expired.

If, for example, your configuration permits access to a resource by IP address you should ensure that this content is not cached. You can do this by using the CACHEDISABLE directive, or MOD_EXPIRES. Left unchecked, MOD_CACHE - very much like a reverse proxy - would cache the content when served and then serve it to any client, on any IP address.

When the CACHEQUICKHANDLER directive is set to Off, the full set of request processing phases are executed and the security model remains unchanged.

**Local exploits**

As requests to end-users can be served from the cache, the cache itself can become a target for those wishing to deface or interfere with content. It is important to bear in mind that the cache must at all times be writable by the user which httpd is running as. This is in stark contrast to the usually recommended situation of maintaining all content unwritable by the Apache user.

If the Apache user is compromised, for example through a flaw in a CGI process, it is possible that the cache may be targeted. When using MOD_CACHE_DISK, it is relatively easy to insert or modify a cached entity.

This presents a somewhat elevated risk in comparison to the other types of attack it is possible to make as the Apache user. If you are using MOD_CACHE_DISK you should bear this in mind - ensure you upgrade httpd when security upgrades are announced and run CGI processes as a non-Apache user using suEXEC (p. 115) if possible.

**Cache Poisoning**

When running httpd as a caching proxy server, there is also the potential for so-called cache poisoning. Cache Poisoning is a broad term for attacks in which an attacker causes the proxy server to retrieve incorrect (and usually undesirable) content from the origin server.

For example if the DNS servers used by your system running httpd are vulnerable to DNS cache poisoning, an attacker may be able to control where httpd connects to when requesting content from the origin server. Another example is so-called HTTP request-smuggling attacks.

This document is not the correct place for an in-depth discussion of HTTP request smuggling (instead, try your favourite search engine) however it is important to be aware that it is possible to make a series of requests, and to exploit a vulnerability on an origin webserver such that the attacker can entirely control the content retrieved by the proxy.

**Denial of Service / Cachebusting**

The Vary mechanism allows multiple variants of the same URL to be cached side by side. Depending on header values provided by the client, the cache will select the correct variant to return to the client. This mechanism can become a problem when an attempt is made to vary on a header that is known to contain a wide range of possible values under normal use, for example the User-Agent header. Depending on the popularity of the particular web site thousands or millions of duplicate cache entries could be created for the same URL, crowding out other entries in the cache.

In other cases, there may be a need to change the URL of a particular resource on every request, usually by adding a "cachebuster" string to the URL. If this content is declared cacheable by a server for a significant freshness lifetime, these entries can crowd out legitimate entries in a cache. While MOD_CACHE provides a CACHEIGNOREURLSESSIONIDENTIFIERS directive, this directive should be used with care to ensure that downstream proxy or browser caches aren't subjected to the same denial of service issue.

## 2.7    Server-Wide Configuration

This document explains some of the directives provided by the CORE server which are used to configure the basic operations of the server.

### Server Identification

| Related Modules | Related Directives |
| --- | --- |
| | SERVERNAME |
| | SERVERADMIN |
| | SERVERSIGNATURE |
| | SERVERTOKENS |
| | USECANONICALNAME |
| | USECANONICALPHYSICALPORT |

The SERVERADMIN and SERVERTOKENS directives control what information about the server will be presented in server-generated documents such as error messages. The SERVERTOKENS directive sets the value of the Server HTTP response header field.

The SERVERNAME, USECANONICALNAME and USECANONICALPHYSICALPORT directives are used by the server to determine how to construct self-referential URLs. For example, when a client requests a directory, but does not include the trailing slash in the directory name, httpd must redirect the client to the full name including the trailing slash so that the client will correctly resolve relative references in the document.

### File Locations

| Related Modules | Related Directives |
| --- | --- |
| | COREDUMPDIRECTORY |
| | DOCUMENTROOT |
| | ERRORLOG |
| | MUTEX |
| | PIDFILE |
| | SCOREBOARDFILE |
| | SERVERROOT |

These directives control the locations of the various files that httpd needs for proper operation. When the pathname used does not begin with a slash (/), the files are located relative to the SERVERROOT. Be careful about locating files in paths which are writable by non-root users. See the security tips (p. 364) documentation for more details.

## Limiting Resource Usage

| Related Modules | Related Directives |
|---|---|
| | LIMITREQUESTBODY |
| | LIMITREQUESTFIELDS |
| | LIMITREQUESTFIELDSIZE |
| | LIMITREQUESTLINE |
| | RLIMITCPU |
| | RLIMITMEM |
| | RLIMITNPROC |
| | THREADSTACKSIZE |

The LIMITREQUEST* directives are used to place limits on the amount of resources httpd will use in reading requests from clients. By limiting these values, some kinds of denial of service attacks can be mitigated.

The RLIMIT* directives are used to limit the amount of resources which can be used by processes forked off from the httpd children. In particular, this will control resources used by CGI scripts and SSI exec commands.

The THREADSTACKSIZE directive is used with some platforms to control the stack size.

## Implementation Choices

| Related Modules | Related Directives |
|---|---|
| | MUTEX |

The MUTEX directive can be used to change the underlying implementation used for mutexes, in order to relieve functional or performance problems with APR's default choice.

# 2.8   Log Files

In order to effectively manage a web server, it is necessary to get feedback about the activity and performance of the server as well as any problems that may be occurring. The Apache HTTP Server provides very comprehensive and flexible logging capabilities. This document describes how to configure its logging capabilities, and how to understand what the logs contain.

## Overview

| Related Modules | Related Directives |
|---|---|
| MOD_LOG_CONFIG | |
| MOD_LOG_FORENSIC | |
| MOD_LOGIO | |
| MOD_CGI | |

The Apache HTTP Server provides a variety of different mechanisms for logging everything that happens on your server, from the initial request, through the URL mapping process, to the final resolution of the connection, including any errors that may have occurred in the process. In addition to this, third-party modules may provide logging capabilities, or inject entries into the existing log files, and applications such as CGI programs, or PHP scripts, or other handlers, may send messages to the server error log.

In this document we discuss the logging modules that are a standard part of the http server.

## Security Warning

Anyone who can write to the directory where Apache httpd is writing a log file can almost certainly gain access to the uid that the server is started as, which is normally root. Do *NOT* give people write access to the directory the logs are stored in without being aware of the consequences; see the security tips (p. 364) document for details.

In addition, log files may contain information supplied directly by the client, without escaping. Therefore, it is possible for malicious clients to insert control-characters in the log files, so care must be taken in dealing with raw logs.

## Error Log

| Related Modules | Related Directives |
|---|---|
| CORE | ERRORLOG |
| | ERRORLOGFORMAT |
| | LOGLEVEL |

The server error log, whose name and location is set by the ERRORLOG directive, is the most important log file. This is the place where Apache httpd will send diagnostic information and record any errors that it encounters in processing requests. It is the first place to look when a problem occurs with starting the server or with the operation of the server, since it will often contain details of what went wrong and how to fix it.

The error log is usually written to a file (typically `error_log` on Unix systems and `error.log` on Windows and OS/2). On Unix systems it is also possible to have the server send errors to `syslog` or pipe them to a program.

The format of the error log is defined by the ERRORLOGFORMAT directive, with which you can customize what values are logged. A default is format defined if you don't specify one. A typical log message follows:

```
[Fri Sep 09 10:42:29.902022 2011] [core:error] [pid 35708:tid
4328636416] [client 72.15.99.187] File does not exist:
/usr/local/apache2/htdocs/favicon.ico
```

The first item in the log entry is the date and time of the message. The next is the module producing the message (core, in this case) and the severity level of that message. This is followed by the process ID and, if appropriate, the thread ID, of the process that experienced the condition. Next, we have the client address that made the request. And finally is the detailed error message, which in this case indicates a request for a file that did not exist.

A very wide variety of different messages can appear in the error log. Most look similar to the example above. The error log will also contain debugging output from CGI scripts. Any information written to stderr by a CGI script will be copied directly to the error log.

Putting a %L token in both the error log and the access log will produce a log entry ID with which you can correlate the entry in the error log with the entry in the access log. If MOD_UNIQUE_ID is loaded, its unique request ID will be used as the log entry ID, too.

During testing, it is often useful to continuously monitor the error log for any problems. On Unix systems, you can accomplish this using:

```
tail -f error_log
```

## Per-module logging

The LOGLEVEL directive allows you to specify a log severity level on a per-module basis. In this way, if you are troubleshooting a problem with just one particular module, you can turn up its logging volume without also getting the details of other modules that you're not interested in. This is particularly useful for modules such as MOD_PROXY or MOD_REWRITE where you want to know details about what it's trying to do.

Do this by specifying the name of the module in your LOGLEVEL directive:

```
LogLevel info rewrite:trace5
```

This sets the main LOGLEVEL to info, but turns it up to trace5 for MOD_REWRITE.

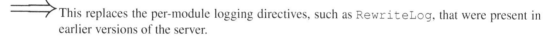 This replaces the per-module logging directives, such as RewriteLog, that were present in earlier versions of the server.

## Access Log

| Related Modules | Related Directives |
| --- | --- |
| MOD_LOG_CONFIG | CUSTOMLOG |
| MOD_SETENVIF | LOGFORMAT |
| | SETENVIF |

The server access log records all requests processed by the server. The location and content of the access log are controlled by the CUSTOMLOG directive. The LOGFORMAT directive can be used to simplify the selection of the contents of the logs. This section describes how to configure the server to record information in the access log.

Of course, storing the information in the access log is only the start of log management. The next step is to analyze this information to produce useful statistics. Log analysis in general is beyond the scope of this document, and not really part of the job of the web server itself. For more information about this topic, and for applications which perform log analysis, check the Open Directory[16].

Various versions of Apache httpd have used other modules and directives to control access logging, including mod_log_referer, mod_log_agent, and the `TransferLog` directive. The CUSTOMLOG directive now subsumes the functionality of all the older directives.

The format of the access log is highly configurable. The format is specified using a format string that looks much like a C-style printf(1) format string. Some examples are presented in the next sections. For a complete list of the possible contents of the format string, see the MOD_LOG_CONFIG format strings (p. 705) .

**Common Log Format**

A typical configuration for the access log might look as follows.

```
LogFormat "%h %l %u %t \"%r\" %>s %b" common
CustomLog "logs/access_log" common
```

This defines the *nickname* common and associates it with a particular log format string. The format string consists of percent directives, each of which tell the server to log a particular piece of information. Literal characters may also be placed in the format string and will be copied directly into the log output. The quote character (") must be escaped by placing a backslash before it to prevent it from being interpreted as the end of the format string. The format string may also contain the special control characters "\n" for new-line and "\t" for tab.

The CUSTOMLOG directive sets up a new log file using the defined *nickname*. The filename for the access log is relative to the SERVERROOT unless it begins with a slash.

The above configuration will write log entries in a format known as the Common Log Format (CLF). This standard format can be produced by many different web servers and read by many log analysis programs. The log file entries produced in CLF will look something like this:

```
127.0.0.1 - frank [10/Oct/2000:13:55:36 -0700] "GET /apache_pb.gif
HTTP/1.0" 200 2326
```

Each part of this log entry is described below.

**127.0.0.1 (%h)** This is the IP address of the client (remote host) which made the request to the server. If HOST-NAMELOOKUPS is set to On, then the server will try to determine the hostname and log it in place of the IP address. However, this configuration is not recommended since it can significantly slow the server. Instead, it is best to use a log post-processor such as `logresolve` to determine the hostnames. The IP address reported here is not necessarily the address of the machine at which the user is sitting. If a proxy server exists between the user and the server, this address will be the address of the proxy, rather than the originating machine.

**- (%l)** The "hyphen" in the output indicates that the requested piece of information is not available. In this case, the information that is not available is the RFC 1413 identity of the client determined by `identd` on the clients machine. This information is highly unreliable and should almost never be used except on tightly controlled internal networks. Apache httpd will not even attempt to determine this information unless IDENTITYCHECK is set to On.

**frank (%u)** This is the userid of the person requesting the document as determined by HTTP authentication. The same value is typically provided to CGI scripts in the REMOTE_USER environment variable. If the status code for the request (see below) is 401, then this value should not be trusted because the user is not yet authenticated. If the document is not password protected, this part will be " - " just like the previous one.

---

[16]http://dmoz.org/Computers/Software/Internet/Site_Management/Log_Analysis/

**[10/Oct/2000:13:55:36 -0700] (%t)** The time that the request was received. The format is:

```
[day/month/year:hour:minute:second zone]
day = 2*digit
month = 3*letter
year = 4*digit
hour = 2*digit
minute = 2*digit
second = 2*digit
zone = ('+' | '-') 4*digit
```

It is possible to have the time displayed in another format by specifying %{format}t in the log format string, where format is either as in strftime(3) from the C standard library, or one of the supported special tokens. For details see the MOD_LOG_CONFIG format strings (p. 705) .

**"GET /apache_pb.gif HTTP/1.0" (\"%r\")** The request line from the client is given in double quotes. The request line contains a great deal of useful information. First, the method used by the client is GET. Second, the client requested the resource /apache_pb.gif, and third, the client used the protocol HTTP/1.0. It is also possible to log one or more parts of the request line independently. For example, the format string "%m %U%q %H" will log the method, path, query-string, and protocol, resulting in exactly the same output as "%r".

**200 (%>s)** This is the status code that the server sends back to the client. This information is very valuable, because it reveals whether the request resulted in a successful response (codes beginning in 2), a redirection (codes beginning in 3), an error caused by the client (codes beginning in 4), or an error in the server (codes beginning in 5). The full list of possible status codes can be found in the HTTP specification[17] (RFC2616 section 10).

**2326 (%b)** The last part indicates the size of the object returned to the client, not including the response headers. If no content was returned to the client, this value will be "-". To log "0" for no content, use %B instead.

**Combined Log Format**

Another commonly used format string is called the Combined Log Format. It can be used as follows.

```
LogFormat "%h %l %u %t \"%r\" %>s %b \"%{Referer}i\" \"%{User-agent}i\"" combined
CustomLog "log/access_log" combined
```

This format is exactly the same as the Common Log Format, with the addition of two more fields. Each of the additional fields uses the percent-directive %{header}i, where *header* can be any HTTP request header. The access log under this format will look like:

```
127.0.0.1 - frank [10/Oct/2000:13:55:36 -0700] "GET /apache_pb.gif
HTTP/1.0" 200 2326 "http://www.example.com/start.html" "Mozilla/4.08
[en] (Win98; I ;Nav)"
```

The additional fields are:

**"http://www.example.com/start.html" (\"%{Referer}i\")** The "Referer" (sic) HTTP request header. This gives the site that the client reports having been referred from. (This should be the page that links to or includes /apache_pb.gif).

**"Mozilla/4.08 [en] (Win98; I ;Nav)" (\"%{User-agent}i\")** The User-Agent HTTP request header. This is the identifying information that the client browser reports about itself.

---

[17]http://www.w3.org/Protocols/rfc2616/rfc2616.txt

**Multiple Access Logs**

Multiple access logs can be created simply by specifying multiple CUSTOMLOG directives in the configuration file. For example, the following directives will create three access logs. The first contains the basic CLF information, while the second and third contain referer and browser information. The last two CUSTOMLOG lines show how to mimic the effects of the ReferLog and AgentLog directives.

```
LogFormat "%h %l %u %t \"%r\" %>s %b" common
CustomLog "logs/access_log" common
CustomLog "logs/referer_log" "%{Referer}i -> %U"
CustomLog "logs/agent_log" "%{User-agent}i"
```

This example also shows that it is not necessary to define a nickname with the LOGFORMAT directive. Instead, the log format can be specified directly in the CUSTOMLOG directive.

**Conditional Logs**

There are times when it is convenient to exclude certain entries from the access logs based on characteristics of the client request. This is easily accomplished with the help of environment variables (p. 92) . First, an environment variable must be set to indicate that the request meets certain conditions. This is usually accomplished with SETENVIF. Then the env= clause of the CUSTOMLOG directive is used to include or exclude requests where the environment variable is set. Some examples:

```
# Mark requests from the loop-back interface
SetEnvIf Remote_Addr "127\.0\.0\.1" dontlog
# Mark requests for the robots.txt file
SetEnvIf Request_URI "^/robots\.txt$" dontlog
# Log what remains
CustomLog "logs/access_log" common env=!dontlog
```

As another example, consider logging requests from english-speakers to one log file, and non-english speakers to a different log file.

```
SetEnvIf Accept-Language "en" english
CustomLog "logs/english_log" common env=english
CustomLog "logs/non_english_log" common env=!english
```

In a caching scenario one would want to know about the efficiency of the cache. A very simple method to find this out would be:

```
SetEnv CACHE_MISS 1
LogFormat "%h %l %u %t "%r " %>s %b %{CACHE_MISS}e" common-cache
CustomLog "logs/access_log" common-cache
```

MOD_CACHE will run before MOD_ENV and, when successful, will deliver the content without it. In that case a cache hit will log –, while a cache miss will log 1.

In addition to the env= syntax, LOGFORMAT supports logging values conditional upon the HTTP response code:

```
LogFormat "%400,501{User-agent}i" browserlog
LogFormat "%!200,304,302{Referer}i" refererlog
```

In the first example, the `User-agent` will be logged if the HTTP status code is 400 or 501. In other cases, a literal "`-`" will be logged instead. Likewise, in the second example, the `Referer` will be logged if the HTTP status code is **not** 200, 204, or 302. (Note the "`!`" before the status codes.

Although we have just shown that conditional logging is very powerful and flexible, it is not the only way to control the contents of the logs. Log files are more useful when they contain a complete record of server activity. It is often easier to simply post-process the log files to remove requests that you do not want to consider.

## Log Rotation

On even a moderately busy server, the quantity of information stored in the log files is very large. The access log file typically grows 1 MB or more per 10,000 requests. It will consequently be necessary to periodically rotate the log files by moving or deleting the existing logs. This cannot be done while the server is running, because Apache httpd will continue writing to the old log file as long as it holds the file open. Instead, the server must be restarted (p. 29) after the log files are moved or deleted so that it will open new log files.

By using a *graceful* restart, the server can be instructed to open new log files without losing any existing or pending connections from clients. However, in order to accomplish this, the server must continue to write to the old log files while it finishes serving old requests. It is therefore necessary to wait for some time after the restart before doing any processing on the log files. A typical scenario that simply rotates the logs and compresses the old logs to save space is:

```
mv access_log access_log.old
mv error_log error_log.old
apachectl graceful
sleep 600
gzip access_log.old error_log.old
```

Another way to perform log rotation is using piped logs as discussed in the next section.

## Piped Logs

Apache httpd is capable of writing error and access log files through a pipe to another process, rather than directly to a file. This capability dramatically increases the flexibility of logging, without adding code to the main server. In order to write logs to a pipe, simply replace the filename with the pipe character "`|`", followed by the name of the executable which should accept log entries on its standard input. The server will start the piped-log process when the server starts, and will restart it if it crashes while the server is running. (This last feature is why we can refer to this technique as "reliable piped logging".)

Piped log processes are spawned by the parent Apache httpd process, and inherit the userid of that process. This means that piped log programs usually run as root. It is therefore very important to keep the programs simple and secure.

One important use of piped logs is to allow log rotation without having to restart the server. The Apache HTTP Server includes a simple program called `rotatelogs` for this purpose. For example, to rotate the logs every 24 hours, you can use:

```
CustomLog "|/usr/local/apache/bin/rotatelogs /var/log/access_log 86400" common
```

Notice that quotes are used to enclose the entire command that will be called for the pipe. Although these examples are for the access log, the same technique can be used for the error log.

As with conditional logging, piped logs are a very powerful tool, but they should not be used where a simpler solution like off-line post-processing is available.

By default the piped log process is spawned without invoking a shell. Use " | $ " instead of " | " to spawn using a shell (usually with /bin/sh -c):

```
# Invoke "rotatelogs" using a shell
CustomLog "|$/usr/local/apache/bin/rotatelogs   /var/log/access_log 86400" common
```

This was the default behaviour for Apache 2.2. Depending on the shell specifics this might lead to an additional shell process for the lifetime of the logging pipe program and signal handling problems during restart. For compatibility reasons with Apache 2.2 the notation " | | " is also supported and equivalent to using " | ".

**Windows note**
>    Note that on Windows, you may run into problems when running many piped log-
>    ger processes, especially when HTTPD is running as a service.  This is caused by
>    running out of desktop heap space.  The desktop heap space given to each ser-
>    vice is specified by the third argument to the SharedSection parameter in the
>    HKEY_LOCAL_MACHINE\System\CurrentControlSet\Control\SessionManager\SubSystems\Windows
>    registry value.**Change this value with care**; the normal caveats for changing the Windows
>    registry apply, but you might also exhaust the desktop heap pool if the number is adjusted too
>    high.

## Virtual Hosts

When running a server with many virtual hosts (p. 124) , there are several options for dealing with log files. First, it is possible to use logs exactly as in a single-host server. Simply by placing the logging directives outside the <VIRTUALHOST> sections in the main server context, it is possible to log all requests in the same access log and error log. This technique does not allow for easy collection of statistics on individual virtual hosts.

If CUSTOMLOG or ERRORLOG directives are placed inside a <VIRTUALHOST> section, all requests or errors for that virtual host will be logged only to the specified file. Any virtual host which does not have logging directives will still have its requests sent to the main server logs. This technique is very useful for a small number of virtual hosts, but if the number of hosts is very large, it can be complicated to manage. In addition, it can often create problems with insufficient file descriptors (p. 144) .

For the access log, there is a very good compromise. By adding information on the virtual host to the log format string, it is possible to log all hosts to the same log, and later split the log into individual files. For example, consider the following directives.

```
LogFormat "%v %l %u %t \"%r\" %>s %b" comonvhost
CustomLog "logs/access_log" comonvhost
```

The %v is used to log the name of the virtual host that is serving the request. Then a program like split-logfile (p. 334) can be used to post-process the access log in order to split it into one file per virtual host.

## Other Log Files

| Related Modules | Related Directives |
|---|---|
| MOD_LOGIO | LOGFORMAT |
| MOD_LOG_CONFIG | BUFFEREDLOGS |
| MOD_LOG_FORENSIC | FORENSICLOG |
| MOD_CGI | PIDFILE |
| | SCRIPTLOG |
| | SCRIPTLOGBUFFER |
| | SCRIPTLOGLENGTH |

**Logging actual bytes sent and received**

MOD_LOGIO adds in two additional LOGFORMAT fields (%I and %O) that log the actual number of bytes received and sent on the network.

**Forensic Logging**

MOD_LOG_FORENSIC provides for forensic logging of client requests. Logging is done before and after processing a request, so the forensic log contains two log lines for each request. The forensic logger is very strict with no customizations. It can be an invaluable debugging and security tool.

**PID File**

On startup, Apache httpd saves the process id of the parent httpd process to the file `logs/httpd.pid`. This filename can be changed with the PIDFILE directive. The process-id is for use by the administrator in restarting and terminating the daemon by sending signals to the parent process; on Windows, use the -k command line option instead. For more information see the Stopping and Restarting (p. 29) page.

**Script Log**

In order to aid in debugging, the SCRIPTLOG directive allows you to record the input to and output from CGI scripts. This should only be used in testing - not for live servers. More information is available in the mod_cgi (p. 580) documentation.

# 2.9  Mapping URLs to Filesystem Locations

This document explains how the Apache HTTP Server uses the URL of a request to determine the filesystem location from which to serve a file.

## Related Modules and Directives

| Related Modules | Related Directives |
|---|---|
| MOD_ACTIONS | ALIAS |
| MOD_ALIAS | ALIASMATCH |
| MOD_AUTOINDEX | CHECKSPELLING |
| MOD_DIR | DIRECTORYINDEX |
| MOD_IMAGEMAP | DOCUMENTROOT |
| MOD_NEGOTIATION | ERRORDOCUMENT |
| MOD_PROXY | OPTIONS |
| MOD_REWRITE | PROXYPASS |
| MOD_SPELING | PROXYPASSREVERSE |
| MOD_USERDIR | PROXYPASSREVERSECOOKIEDOMAIN |
| MOD_VHOST_ALIAS | PROXYPASSREVERSECOOKIEPATH |
|  | REDIRECT |
|  | REDIRECTMATCH |
|  | REWRITECOND |
|  | REWRITERULE |
|  | SCRIPTALIAS |
|  | SCRIPTALIASMATCH |
|  | USERDIR |

## DocumentRoot

In deciding what file to serve for a given request, httpd's default behavior is to take the URL-Path for the request (the part of the URL following the hostname and port) and add it to the end of the DOCUMENTROOT specified in your configuration files. Therefore, the files and directories underneath the DOCUMENTROOT make up the basic document tree which will be visible from the web.

For example, if DOCUMENTROOT were set to `/var/www/html` then a request for `http://www.example.com/fish/guppies.html` would result in the file `/var/www/html/fish/guppies.html` being served to the requesting client.

If a directory is requested (i.e. a path ending with `/`), the file served from that directory is defined by the DIRECTORYINDEX directive. For example, if `DocumentRoot` were set as above, and you were to set:

```
DirectoryIndex index.html index.php
```

Then a request for `http://www.example.com/fish/` will cause httpd to attempt to serve the file `/var/www/html/fish/index.html`. In the event that that file does not exist, it will next attempt to serve the file `/var/www/html/fish/index.php`.

If neither of these files existed, the next step is to attempt to provide a directory index, if MOD_AUTOINDEX is loaded and configured to permit that.

httpd is also capable of Virtual Hosting (p. 124) , where the server receives requests for more than one host. In this case, a different DOCUMENTROOT can be specified for each virtual host, or alternatively, the directives provided by the module MOD_VHOST_ALIAS can be used to dynamically determine the appropriate place from which to serve content based on the requested IP address or hostname.

The DOCUMENTROOT directive is set in your main server configuration file (`httpd.conf`) and, possibly, once per additional Virtual Host (p. 124) you create.

## Files Outside the DocumentRoot

There are frequently circumstances where it is necessary to allow web access to parts of the filesystem that are not strictly underneath the DOCUMENTROOT. httpd offers several different ways to accomplish this. On Unix systems, symbolic links can bring other parts of the filesystem under the DOCUMENTROOT. For security reasons, httpd will follow symbolic links only if the OPTIONS setting for the relevant directory includes `FollowSymLinks` or `SymLinksIfOwnerMatch`.

Alternatively, the ALIAS directive will map any part of the filesystem into the web space. For example, with

```
Alias "/docs" "/var/web"
```

the URL `http://www.example.com/docs/dir/file.html` will be served from `/var/web/dir/file.html`. The SCRIPTALIAS directive works the same way, with the additional effect that all content located at the target path is treated as CGI scripts.

For situations where you require additional flexibility, you can use the ALIASMATCH and SCRIPTALIASMATCH directives to do powerful regular expression based matching and substitution. For example,

```
ScriptAliasMatch "^/~([a-zA-Z0-9]+)/cgi-bin/(.+)"   "/home/$1/cgi-bin/$2"
```

will map a request to `http://example.com/~user/cgi-bin/script.cgi` to the path `/home/user/cgi-bin/script.cgi` and will treat the resulting file as a CGI script.

## User Directories

Traditionally on Unix systems, the home directory of a particular *user* can be referred to as `~user/`. The module MOD_USERDIR extends this idea to the web by allowing files under each user's home directory to be accessed using URLs such as the following.

```
http://www.example.com/~user/file.html
```

For security reasons, it is inappropriate to give direct access to a user's home directory from the web. Therefore, the USERDIR directive specifies a directory underneath the user's home directory where web files are located. Using the default setting of `Userdir public_html`, the above URL maps to a file at a directory like `/home/user/public_html/file.html` where `/home/user/` is the user's home directory as specified in `/etc/passwd`.

There are also several other forms of the `Userdir` directive which you can use on systems where `/etc/passwd` does not contain the location of the home directory.

Some people find the "~" symbol (which is often encoded on the web as `%7e`) to be awkward and prefer to use an alternate string to represent user directories. This functionality is not supported by mod_userdir. However, if users' home directories are structured in a regular way, then it is possible to use the ALIASMATCH directive to achieve the desired effect. For example, to make `http://www.example.com/upages/user/file.html` map to `/home/user/public_html/file.html`, use the following `AliasMatch` directive:

```
AliasMatch "^/upages/([a-zA-Z0-9]+)(/(.*))?$"   "/home/$1/public_html/$3"
```

## URL Redirection

The configuration directives discussed in the above sections tell httpd to get content from a specific place in the filesystem and return it to the client. Sometimes, it is desirable instead to inform the client that the requested content is located at a different URL, and instruct the client to make a new request with the new URL. This is called *redirection* and is implemented by the REDIRECT directive. For example, if the contents of the directory /foo/ under the DOCUMENTROOT are moved to the new directory /bar/, you can instruct clients to request the content at the new location as follows:

```
Redirect permanent "/foo/"   "http://www.example.com/bar/"
```

This will redirect any URL-Path starting in /foo/ to the same URL path on the www.example.com server with /bar/ substituted for /foo/. You can redirect clients to any server, not only the origin server.

httpd also provides a REDIRECTMATCH directive for more complicated rewriting problems. For example, to redirect requests for the site home page to a different site, but leave all other requests alone, use the following configuration:

```
RedirectMatch permanent "^/$"    "http://www.example.com/startpage.html"
```

Alternatively, to temporarily redirect all pages on one site to a particular page on another site, use the following:

```
RedirectMatch temp ".*"  "http://othersite.example.com/startpage.html"
```

## Reverse Proxy

httpd also allows you to bring remote documents into the URL space of the local server. This technique is called *reverse proxying* because the web server acts like a proxy server by fetching the documents from a remote server and returning them to the client. It is different from normal (forward) proxying because, to the client, it appears the documents originate at the reverse proxy server.

In the following example, when clients request documents under the /foo/ directory, the server fetches those documents from the /bar/ directory on internal.example.com and returns them to the client as if they were from the local server.

```
ProxyPass        "/foo/" "http://internal.example.com/bar/"
ProxyPassReverse "/foo/" "http://internal.example.com/bar/"
ProxyPassReverseCookieDomain internal.example.com public.example.com
ProxyPassReverseCookiePath "/foo/" "/bar/"
```

The PROXYPASS configures the server to fetch the appropriate documents, while the PROXYPASSREVERSE directive rewrites redirects originating at internal.example.com so that they target the appropriate directory on the local server. Similarly, the PROXYPASSREVERSECOOKIEDOMAIN and PROXYPASSREVERSECOOKIEPATH rewrite cookies set by the backend server.

It is important to note, however, that links inside the documents will not be rewritten. So any absolute links on internal.example.com will result in the client breaking out of the proxy server and requesting directly from internal.example.com. You can modify these links (and other content) in a page as it is being served to the client using MOD_SUBSTITUTE.

```
Substitute s/internal\.example\.com/www.example.com/i
```

For more sophisticated rewriting of links in HTML and XHTML, the MOD_PROXY_HTML module is also available. It allows you to create maps of URLs that need to be rewritten, so that complex proxying scenarios can be handled.

## Rewriting Engine

When even more powerful substitution is required, the rewriting engine provided by MOD_REWRITE can be useful. The directives provided by this module can use characteristics of the request such as browser type or source IP address in deciding from where to serve content. In addition, mod_rewrite can use external database files or programs to determine how to handle a request. The rewriting engine is capable of performing all three types of mappings discussed above: internal redirects (aliases), external redirects, and proxying. Many practical examples employing mod_rewrite are discussed in the detailed mod_rewrite documentation (p. 146) .

## File Not Found

Inevitably, URLs will be requested for which no matching file can be found in the filesystem. This can happen for several reasons. In some cases, it can be a result of moving documents from one location to another. In this case, it is best to use URL redirection to inform clients of the new location of the resource. In this way, you can assure that old bookmarks and links will continue to work, even though the resource is at a new location.

Another common cause of "File Not Found" errors is accidental mistyping of URLs, either directly in the browser, or in HTML links. httpd provides the module MOD_SPELING (sic) to help with this problem. When this module is activated, it will intercept "File Not Found" errors and look for a resource with a similar filename. If one such file is found, mod_speling will send an HTTP redirect to the client informing it of the correct location. If several "close" files are found, a list of available alternatives will be presented to the client.

An especially useful feature of mod_speling, is that it will compare filenames without respect to case. This can help systems where users are unaware of the case-sensitive nature of URLs and the unix filesystem. But using mod_speling for anything more than the occasional URL correction can place additional load on the server, since each "incorrect" request is followed by a URL redirection and a new request from the client.

MOD_DIR provides FALLBACKRESOURCE, which can be used to map virtual URIs to a real resource, which then serves them. This is a very useful replacement to MOD_REWRITE when implementing a 'front controller'

If all attempts to locate the content fail, httpd returns an error page with HTTP status code 404 (file not found). The appearance of this page is controlled with the ERRORDOCUMENT directive and can be customized in a flexible manner as discussed in the Custom error responses (p. 85) document.

## Other URL Mapping Modules

Other modules available for URL mapping include:

- MOD_ACTIONS - Maps a request to a CGI script based on the request method, or resource MIME type.
- MOD_DIR - Provides basic mapping of a trailing slash into an index file such as `index.html`.
- MOD_IMAGEMAP - Maps a request to a URL based on where a user clicks on an image embedded in a HTML document.
- MOD_NEGOTIATION - Selects an appropriate document based on client preferences such as language or content compression.

# 2.10   Dynamic Shared Object (DSO) Support

The Apache HTTP Server is a modular program where the administrator can choose the functionality to include in the server by selecting a set of modules. Modules will be compiled as Dynamic Shared Objects (DSOs) that exist separately from the main `httpd` binary file. DSO modules may be compiled at the time the server is built, or they may be compiled and added at a later time using the Apache Extension Tool (`apxs`).

Alternatively, the modules can be statically compiled into the `httpd` binary when the server is built.

This document describes how to use DSO modules as well as the theory behind their use.

## Implementation

| Related Modules | Related Directives |
|---|---|
| MOD_SO | LOADMODULE |

The DSO support for loading individual Apache httpd modules is based on a module named MOD_SO which must be statically compiled into the Apache httpd core. It is the only module besides CORE which cannot be put into a DSO itself. Practically all other distributed Apache httpd modules will then be placed into a DSO. After a module is compiled into a DSO named `mod_foo.so` you can use MOD_SO's LOADMODULE directive in your `httpd.conf` file to load this module at server startup or restart.

The DSO builds for individual modules can be disabled via `configure`'s `--enable-mods-static` option as discussed in the install documentation (p. 22) .

To simplify this creation of DSO files for Apache httpd modules (especially for third-party modules) a support program named `apxs` (*APache eXtenSion*) is available. It can be used to build DSO based modules *outside of* the Apache httpd source tree. The idea is simple: When installing Apache HTTP Server the `configure`'s `make install` procedure installs the Apache httpd C header files and puts the platform-dependent compiler and linker flags for building DSO files into the `apxs` program. This way the user can use `apxs` to compile his Apache httpd module sources without the Apache httpd distribution source tree and without having to fiddle with the platform-dependent compiler and linker flags for DSO support.

## Usage Summary

To give you an overview of the DSO features of Apache HTTP Server 2.x, here is a short and concise summary:

1. Build and install a *distributed* Apache httpd module, say `mod_foo.c`, into its own DSO `mod_foo.so`:

```
$ ./configure --prefix=/path/to/install --enable-foo
$ make install
```

2. Configure Apache HTTP Server with all modules enabled. Only a basic set will be loaded during server startup. You can change the set of loaded modules by activating or deactivating the LOADMODULE directives in `httpd.conf`.

```
$ ./configure --enable-mods-shared=all
$ make install
```

3. Some modules are only useful for developers and will not be build. when using the module set *all*. To build all available modules including developer modules use *reallyall*. In addition the LOADMODULE directives for all built modules can be activated via the configure option `--enable-load-all-modules`.

```
$ ./configure --enable-mods-shared=reallyall
--enable-load-all-modules
$ make install
```

4. Build and install a *third-party* Apache httpd module, say `mod_foo.c`, into its own DSO `mod_foo.so` *outside of* the Apache httpd source tree using `apxs`:

```
$ cd /path/to/3rdparty
$ apxs -cia mod_foo.c
```

In all cases, once the shared module is compiled, you must use a LOADMODULE directive in `httpd.conf` to tell Apache httpd to activate the module.

See the apxs documentation (p. 303) for more details.

## Background

On modern Unix derivatives there exists a mechanism called dynamic linking/loading of *Dynamic Shared Objects* (DSO) which provides a way to build a piece of program code in a special format for loading it at run-time into the address space of an executable program.

This loading can usually be done in two ways: automatically by a system program called `ld.so` when an executable program is started or manually from within the executing program via a programmatic system interface to the Unix loader through the system calls `dlopen()`/`dlsym()`.

In the first way the DSO's are usually called *shared libraries* or *DSO libraries* and named `libfoo.so` or `libfoo.so.1.2`. They reside in a system directory (usually `/usr/lib`) and the link to the executable program is established at build-time by specifying `-lfoo` to the linker command. This hard-codes library references into the executable program file so that at start-time the Unix loader is able to locate `libfoo.so` in `/usr/lib`, in paths hard-coded via linker-options like `-R` or in paths configured via the environment variable `LD_LIBRARY_PATH`. It then resolves any (yet unresolved) symbols in the executable program which are available in the DSO.

Symbols in the executable program are usually not referenced by the DSO (because it's a reusable library of general code) and hence no further resolving has to be done. The executable program has no need to do anything on its own to use the symbols from the DSO because the complete resolving is done by the Unix loader. (In fact, the code to invoke `ld.so` is part of the run-time startup code which is linked into every executable program which has been bound non-static). The advantage of dynamic loading of common library code is obvious: the library code needs to be stored only once, in a system library like `libc.so`, saving disk space for every program.

In the second way the DSO's are usually called *shared objects* or *DSO files* and can be named with an arbitrary extension (although the canonical name is `foo.so`). These files usually stay inside a program-specific directory and there is no automatically established link to the executable program where they are used. Instead the executable program manually loads the DSO at run-time into its address space via `dlopen()`. At this time no resolving of symbols from the DSO for the executable program is done. But instead the Unix loader automatically resolves any (yet unresolved) symbols in the DSO from the set of symbols exported by the executable program and its already loaded DSO libraries (especially all symbols from the ubiquitous `libc.so`). This way the DSO gets knowledge of the executable program's symbol set as if it had been statically linked with it in the first place.

Finally, to take advantage of the DSO's API the executable program has to resolve particular symbols from the DSO via `dlsym()` for later use inside dispatch tables *etc.* In other words: The executable program has to manually resolve every symbol it needs to be able to use it. The advantage of such a mechanism is that optional program parts need not be loaded (and thus do not spend memory) until they are needed by the program in question. When required, these program parts can be loaded dynamically to extend the base program's functionality.

Although this DSO mechanism sounds straightforward there is at least one difficult step here: The resolving of symbols from the executable program for the DSO when using a DSO to extend a program (the second way). Why? Because "reverse resolving" DSO symbols from the executable program's symbol set is against the library design (where the library has no knowledge about the programs it is used by) and is neither available under all platforms nor standardized. In practice the executable program's global symbols are often not re-exported and thus not available for use in a DSO. Finding a way to force the linker to export all global symbols is the main problem one has to solve when using DSO for extending a program at run-time.

The shared library approach is the typical one, because it is what the DSO mechanism was designed for, hence it is used for nearly all types of libraries the operating system provides.

## Advantages and Disadvantages

The above DSO based features have the following advantages:

- The server package is more flexible at run-time because the server process can be assembled at run-time via LOADMODULE httpd.conf configuration directives instead of configure options at build-time. For instance, this way one is able to run different server instances (standard & SSL version, minimalistic & dynamic version [mod_perl, mod_php], *etc.*) with only one Apache httpd installation.

- The server package can be easily extended with third-party modules even after installation. This is a great benefit for vendor package maintainers, who can create an Apache httpd core package and additional packages containing extensions like PHP, mod_perl, mod_security, *etc.*

- Easier Apache httpd module prototyping, because with the DSO/apxs pair you can both work outside the Apache httpd source tree and only need an apxs -i command followed by an apachectl restart to bring a new version of your currently developed module into the running Apache HTTP Server.

DSO has the following disadvantages:

- The server is approximately 20% slower at startup time because of the symbol resolving overhead the Unix loader now has to do.

- The server is approximately 5% slower at execution time under some platforms, because position independent code (PIC) sometimes needs complicated assembler tricks for relative addressing, which are not necessarily as fast as absolute addressing.

- Because DSO modules cannot be linked against other DSO-based libraries (ld -lfoo) on all platforms (for instance a.out-based platforms usually don't provide this functionality while ELF-based platforms do) you cannot use the DSO mechanism for all types of modules. Or in other words, modules compiled as DSO files are restricted to only use symbols from the Apache httpd core, from the C library (libc) and all other dynamic or static libraries used by the Apache httpd core, or from static library archives (libfoo.a) containing position independent code. The only chances to use other code is to either make sure the httpd core itself already contains a reference to it or loading the code yourself via dlopen().

# 2.11 HTTP Protocol Compliance

This document describes the mechanism to set a policy for HTTP protocol compliance for a given URL space by the origin servers or applications behind that URL space.

For those who may have received an error message from a rejected policy, and need to know what the policy rejection means and what they might do to fix the error, each policy is described below.

**See also**

- Filters (p. 110)

## Enforcing HTTP Protocol Compliance in Apache 2

| Related Modules | Related Directives |
| --- | --- |
| MOD_POLICY | POLICYCONDITIONAL |
| | POLICYLENGTH |
| | POLICYKEEPALIVE |
| | POLICYTYPE |
| | POLICYVARY |
| | POLICYVALIDATION |
| | POLICYNOCACHE |
| | POLICYMAXAGE |
| | POLICYVERSION |

The HTTP protocol follows the **robustness principle** as described in RFC1122[18], which states **"Be liberal in what you accept, and conservative in what you send"**. As a result of this principle, HTTP clients will compensate for and recover from incorrect or misconfigured responses, or responses that are uncacheable.

As a website is scaled up to face greater and greater traffic loads, suboptimal or misconfigured applications or server configurations can threaten both the stability and scalability of the website, as well as the hosting costs associated with it. A website can also scale up to face greater configuration complexity, and it can be increasingly difficult to detect and keep track of suboptimally configured URL spaces on a given server.

Eventually a point is reached where the principle "conservative in what you send" needs to be enforced by the server administrator.

The MOD_POLICY module provides a set of filters which can be applied to a server, allowing key features of the HTTP protocol to be explicitly tested, and non compliant responses logged as warnings, or rejected outright as an error. Each filter can be applied separately, allowing the administrator to pick and choose which policies should be enforced depending on the circumstances of their environment.

The filters might be placed in testing and staging environments for the benefit of application and website developers, or may be applied to production servers to protect infrastructure from systems outside the administrator's direct control.

---

[18]http://tools.ietf.org/html/rfc1122

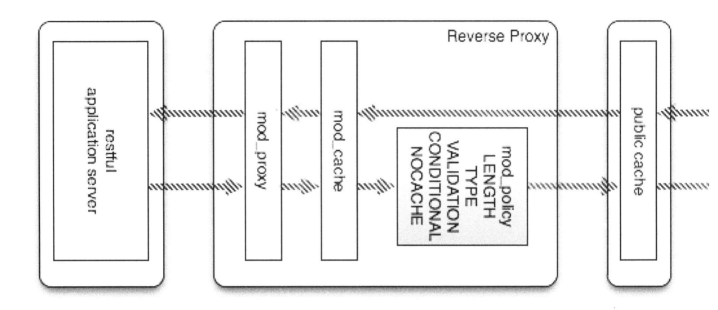

In the above example, an Apache httpd server has been placed between the application server and the internet at large, and configured to cache responses from the application server. The MOD_POLICY filters have been added to enforce support for cacheable content and conditional requests, ensuring that both MOD_CACHE and public caches on the internet are fully able to cache content created by the restful application server efficiently.

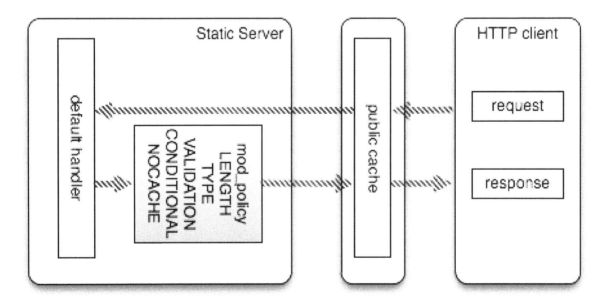

In the above simpler example, a static server serving highly cacheable content has a set of policies applied to ensure that the server configuration conforms to a minimum level of compliance.

## Conditional Request Policy

| Related Modules | Related Directives |
| --- | --- |
| MOD_POLICY | POLICYCONDITIONAL |

This policy will be rejected if the server does not correctly respond to a conditional request with the appropriate status code.

Conditional requests form the mechanism by which an HTTP cache makes stale content fresh again, and particularly for content with short freshness lifetimes, lack of support for conditional requests can add avoidable load to the server.

Most specifically, the existence of any of following headers in the request makes the request conditional:

**If-Match** If the provided ETag in the `If-Match` header does not match the ETag of the response, the server should return `412 Precondition Failed`. Full details of how to handle an `If-Match` header can be found in RFC2616 section 14.24[19].

**If-None-Match** If the provided ETag in the `If-None-Match` header matches the ETag of the response, the server should return either `304 Not Modified` for GET/HEAD requests, or `412 Precondition Failed` for other methods. Full details of how to handle an `If-None-Match` header can be found in RFC2616 section 14.26[20].

**If-Modified-Since** If the provided date in the `If-Modified-Since` header is older than the `Last-Modified` header of the response, the server should return `304 Not Modified`. Full details of how to handle an `If-Modified-Since` header can be found in RFC2616 section 14.25[21].

**If-Unmodified-Since** If the provided date in the `If-Modified-Since` header is newer than the `Last-Modified` header of the response, the server should return `412 Precondition Failed`. Full details of how to handle an `If-Unmodified-Since` header can be found in RFC2616 section 14.28[22].

**If-Range** If the provided ETag or date in the `If-Range` header matches the ETag or Last-Modified of the response, and a valid `Range` is present, the server should return `206 Partial Response`. Full details of how to handle an `If-Range` header can be found in RFC2616 section 14.27[23].

If the response is detected to have been successful (a 2xx response), but was conditional and one of the responses above was expected instead, this policy will be rejected. Responses that indicate a redirect or a failure of some kind (3xx, 4xx, 5xx) will be ignored by this policy.

This policy is implemented by the **POLICY_CONDITIONAL** filter.

## Content-Length Policy

| Related Modules | Related Directives |
| --- | --- |
| MOD_POLICY | POLICYLENGTH |

---

[19] http://www.w3.org/Protocols/rfc2616/rfc2616-sec14.html#sec14.24
[20] http://www.w3.org/Protocols/rfc2616/rfc2616-sec14.html#sec14.26
[21] http://www.w3.org/Protocols/rfc2616/rfc2616-sec14.html#sec14.25
[22] http://www.w3.org/Protocols/rfc2616/rfc2616-sec14.html#sec14.28
[23] http://www.w3.org/Protocols/rfc2616/rfc2616-sec14.html#sec14.27

This policy will be rejected if the server response does not contain an explicit `Content-Length` header.

There are a number of ways of determining the length of a response body, described in full in

RFC2616 section 4.4 Message Length[24].

When the `Content-Length` header is present, the size of the body is declared at the start of the response. If this information is missing, an HTTP cache might choose to ignore the response, as it does not know in advance whether the response will fit within the cache's defined limits.

HTTP/1.1 defines the `Transfer-Encoding` header as an alternative to `Content-Length`, allowing the end of the response to be indicated to the client without the client having to know the length beforehand. However, when HTTP/1.0 requests are processed, and no `Content-Length` is specified, the only mechanism available to the server to indicate the end of the request is to drop the connection. In an environment containing load balancers, this can cause the keepalive mechanism to be bypassed.

If the response is detected to have been successful (a 2xx response), and has a response body (this excludes `204 No Content`), and the `Content-Length` header is missing, this policy will be rejected. Responses that indicate a redirect or a failure of some kind (3xx, 4xx, 5xx) will be ignored by this policy.

 It should be noted that some modules, such as `MOD_PROXY`, add their own `Content-Length` header should the response be small enough for it to have been possible to read the response lacking such a header in one go. This may cause small responses to pass this policy, while larger responses may fail for the same URL.

This policy is implemented by the **POLICY_LENGTH** filter.

## Content-Type Policy

| Related Modules | Related Directives |
| --- | --- |
| MOD_POLICY | POLICYTYPE |

This policy will be rejected if the server response does not contain an explicit and syntactically correct `Content-Type` header that matches the server defined pattern.

The media type of the body is placed in the `Content-Type` header, and the format of the header is described in full in

RFC2616 section 3.7 Media Types[25].

A syntactically valid content type might look as follows:

```
Content-Type:  text/html; charset=iso-8859-1
```

Invalid content types might include:

```
# invalid
Content-Type:  foo
# blank
Content-Type:
```

The server administrator has the option to restrict the policy to one or more specific types, or could specify a general wildcard type such as `*/*`.

This policy is implemented by the **POLICY_TYPE** filter.

---

[24]http://www.w3.org/Protocols/rfc2616/rfc2616-sec4.html#sec4.4
[25]http://www.w3.org/Protocols/rfc2616/rfc2616-sec3.html#sec3.7

## Keepalive Policy

| Related Modules | Related Directives |
|---|---|
| MOD_POLICY | POLICYKEEPALIVE |

This policy will be rejected if the server response does not contain an explicit `Content-Length` header, or a `Transfer-Encoding` of chunked.

There are a number of ways of determining the length of a response body, described in full in

RFC2616 section 4.4 Message Length[26].

When the `Content-Length` header is present, the size of the body is declared at the start of the response. HTTP/1.1 defines the `Transfer-Encoding` header as an alternative to `Content-Length`, allowing the end of the response to be indicated to the client without the client having to know the length beforehand. In the absence of these two mechanisms, the only way for a server to indicate the end of the request is to drop the connection. In an environment containing load balancers, this can cause the keepalive mechanism to be bypassed.

Most specifically, we follow these rules:

**IF** we have not marked this connection as errored;

**and** the client isn't expecting 100-continue

**and** the response status does not require a close;

**and** the response body has a defined length due to the status code being 304 or 204, the request method being HEAD, already having defined Content-Length or Transfer-Encoding: chunked, or the request version being HTTP/1.1 and thus capable of being set as chunked

**THEN** we support keepalive.

> [!] The server may choose to turn off keepalive for various reasons, such as an imminent shutdown, or a Connection: close from the client, or an HTTP/1.0 client request with a response with no `Content-Length`, but for our purposes we only care that keepalive was possible from the application, not that keepalive actually took place.

It should also be noted that the Apache httpd server includes a filter that adds chunked encoding to responses without an explicit content length. This policy catches those cases where this filter is bypassed or not in effect.

This policy is implemented by the **POLICY_KEEPALIVE** filter.

## Freshness Lifetime / Maxage Policy

| Related Modules | Related Directives |
|---|---|
| MOD_POLICY | POLICYMAXAGE |

This policy will be rejected if the server response does not have an explicit **freshness lifetime** at least as long as the server defined limit, or if the freshness lifetime is calculated based on a heuristic.

Full details of how a freshness lifetime is calculated is described in full in

RFC2616 section 13.2 Expiration Model[27].

---

[26]http://www.w3.org/Protocols/rfc2616/rfc2616-sec4.html#sec4.4
[27]http://www.w3.org/Protocols/rfc2616/rfc2616-sec13.html#sec13.2

During the freshness lifetime, a cache does not need to contact the origin server at all, it can simply pass the cached content as is back to the client.

When the freshness lifetime is reached, the cache should contact the origin server in an effort to check whether the content is still fresh, and if not, replace the content.

When the freshness lifetime is too short, it can result in excessive load on the server. In addition, should an outage occur that is as long or longer than the freshness lifetime, all cached content will become stale, which could cause a thundering herd of traffic when the server or network returns.

This policy is implemented by the **POLICY_MAXAGE** filter.

## No Cache Policy

| **Related Modules** | **Related Directives** |
|---|---|
| MOD_POLICY | POLICYNOCACHE |

This policy will be rejected if the server response declares itself uncacheable using either the `Cache-Control` or `Pragma` headers.

Full details of how content may be declared uncacheable is described in full in

RFC2616 section 14.9.1 What is Cacheable[28], and within the definition for the `Pragma` header in

RFC2616 section 14.32 Pragma[29].

Most specifically, should any of the following header combinations exist in the response headers, the response will be rejected:

- `Cache-Control:  no-cache`
- `Cache-Control:  no-store`
- `Cache-Control:  private`
- `Pragma:  no-cache`

When unexpected, uncacheable content may produce unacceptable levels of server load, or may incur significant cost. When this policy is enabled, all server defined uncacheable content will be rejected.

This policy is implemented by the **POLICY_NOCACHE** filter.

## Validation Policy

| **Related Modules** | **Related Directives** |
|---|---|
| MOD_POLICY | POLICYVALIDATION |

This policy will be rejected if the server response does not contain either a syntactically correct `ETag` or `Last-Modified` header.

The `ETag` header is described in full in

RFC2616 section 14.19 Etag[30], and the `Last-Modified` header is described in full in

---

[28]http://www.w3.org/Protocols/rfc2616/rfc2616-sec14.html#sec14.9.1
[29]http://www.w3.org/Protocols/rfc2616/rfc2616-sec14.html#sec14.32
[30]http://www.w3.org/Protocols/rfc2616/rfc2616-sec14.html#sec14.19

RFC2616 section 14.29 Last-Modified[31].

In addition to being checked present, the headers are checked for syntax.

An `ETag` that is not surrounded with quotes, or is not declared `"weak"` by prefixing it with a `"W/"` will cause the policy to be rejected. A `Last-Modified` that is not parsed as a valid date will cause the policy to be rejected.

This policy is implemented by the **POLICY_VALIDATION** filter.

## Vary Header Policy

| Related Modules | Related Directives |
|---|---|
| MOD_POLICY | POLICYVARY |

This policy will be rejected if the server response contains a `Vary` header, and that header in turn contains a header blacklisted by the administrator.

The `Vary` header is described in full in

RFC2616 section 14.44 Vary[32].

Some client provided headers, such as `User-Agent`, can contain thousands or millions of combinations of values over a period of time, and if the response is declared cacheable, a cache might attempt to cache each of these responses separately, filling up the cache and crowding out other entries in the cache. In this scenario, if so configured, the policy will reject the response.

This policy is implemented by the **POLICY_VARY** filter.

## Protocol Version Policy

| Related Modules | Related Directives |
|---|---|
| MOD_POLICY | POLICYVERSION |

This policy will be rejected if the client request was made with a version number lower than the version of HTTP specified.

This policy is typically used with restful applications where control over the type of client is desired. This policy can be used alongside the `POLICY_KEEPALIVE` filter to ensure that HTTP/1.0 clients don't cause keepalive connections to be dropped.

Possible minimum versions that could be specified are:

- `HTTP/1.1`
- `HTTP/1.0`
- `HTTP/0.9`

This policy is implemented by the **POLICY_VERSON** filter.

---

[31]http://www.w3.org/Protocols/rfc2616/rfc2616-sec14.html#sec14.29
[32]http://www.w3.org/Protocols/rfc2616/rfc2616-sec14.html#sec14.44

# 2.12   Content Negotiation

Apache HTTPD supports content negotiation as described in the HTTP/1.1 specification. It can choose the best representation of a resource based on the browser-supplied preferences for media type, languages, character set and encoding. It also implements a couple of features to give more intelligent handling of requests from browsers that send incomplete negotiation information.

Content negotiation is provided by the MOD_NEGOTIATION module, which is compiled in by default.

## About Content Negotiation

A resource may be available in several different representations. For example, it might be available in different languages or different media types, or a combination. One way of selecting the most appropriate choice is to give the user an index page, and let them select. However it is often possible for the server to choose automatically. This works because browsers can send, as part of each request, information about what representations they prefer. For example, a browser could indicate that it would like to see information in French, if possible, else English will do. Browsers indicate their preferences by headers in the request. To request only French representations, the browser would send

```
Accept-Language:  fr
```

Note that this preference will only be applied when there is a choice of representations and they vary by language.

As an example of a more complex request, this browser has been configured to accept French and English, but prefer French, and to accept various media types, preferring HTML over plain text or other text types, and preferring GIF or JPEG over other media types, but also allowing any other media type as a last resort:

```
Accept-Language:  fr; q=1.0, en; q=0.5
Accept:  text/html; q=1.0, text/*; q=0.8, image/gif; q=0.6,
image/jpeg; q=0.6, image/*; q=0.5, */*; q=0.1
```

httpd supports 'server driven' content negotiation, as defined in the HTTP/1.1 specification. It fully supports the Accept, Accept-Language, Accept-Charset and Accept-Encoding request headers. httpd also supports 'transparent' content negotiation, which is an experimental negotiation protocol defined in RFC 2295 and RFC 2296. It does not offer support for 'feature negotiation' as defined in these RFCs.

A **resource** is a conceptual entity identified by a URI (RFC 2396). An HTTP server like Apache HTTP Server provides access to **representations** of the resource(s) within its namespace, with each representation in the form of a sequence of bytes with a defined media type, character set, encoding, etc. Each resource may be associated with zero, one, or more than one representation at any given time. If multiple representations are available, the resource is referred to as **negotiable** and each of its representations is termed a **variant**. The ways in which the variants for a negotiable resource vary are called the **dimensions** of negotiation.

## Negotiation in httpd

In order to negotiate a resource, the server needs to be given information about each of the variants. This is done in one of two ways:

- Using a type map (*i.e.*, a *.var file) which names the files containing the variants explicitly, or
- Using a 'MultiViews' search, where the server does an implicit filename pattern match and chooses from among the results.

**Using a type-map file**

A type map is a document which is associated with the handler named `type-map` (or, for backwards-compatibility with older httpd configurations, the MIME-type `application/x-type-map`). Note that to use this feature, you must have a handler set in the configuration that defines a file suffix as `type-map`; this is best done with

```
AddHandler type-map .var
```

in the server configuration file.

Type map files should have the same name as the resource which they are describing, followed by the extension `.var`. In the examples shown below, the resource is named `foo`, so the type map file is named `foo.var`.

This file should have an entry for each available variant; these entries consist of contiguous HTTP-format header lines. Entries for different variants are separated by blank lines. Blank lines are illegal within an entry. It is conventional to begin a map file with an entry for the combined entity as a whole (although this is not required, and if present will be ignored). An example map file is shown below.

URIs in this file are relative to the location of the type map file. Usually, these files will be located in the same directory as the type map file, but this is not required. You may provide absolute or relative URIs for any file located on the same server as the map file.

```
URI: foo

URI: foo.en.html
Content-type:  text/html
Content-language:  en

URI: foo.fr.de.html
Content-type:  text/html;charset=iso-8859-2
Content-language:  fr, de
```

Note also that a typemap file will take precedence over the filename's extension, even when Multiviews is on. If the variants have different source qualities, that may be indicated by the "qs" parameter to the media type, as in this picture (available as JPEG, GIF, or ASCII-art):

```
URI: foo

URI: foo.jpeg
Content-type:   image/jpeg; qs=0.8

URI: foo.gif
Content-type:   image/gif; qs=0.5

URI: foo.txt
Content-type:   text/plain; qs=0.01
```

qs values can vary in the range 0.000 to 1.000. Note that any variant with a qs value of 0.000 will never be chosen. Variants with no 'qs' parameter value are given a qs factor of 1.0. The qs parameter indicates the relative 'quality' of this variant compared to the other available variants, independent of the client's capabilities. For example, a JPEG file is usually of higher source quality than an ASCII file if it is attempting to represent a photograph. However, if the resource being represented is an original ASCII art, then an ASCII representation would have a higher source quality than a JPEG representation. A qs value is therefore specific to a given variant depending on the nature of the resource it represents.

The full list of headers recognized is available in the mod_negotiation typemap (p. 766) documentation.

**Multiviews**

MultiViews is a per-directory option, meaning it can be set with an OPTIONS directive within a <DIRECTORY>, <LOCATION> or <FILES> section in httpd.conf, or (if ALLOWOVERRIDE is properly set) in .htaccess files. Note that Options All does not set MultiViews; you have to ask for it by name.

The effect of MultiViews is as follows: if the server receives a request for /some/dir/foo, if /some/dir has MultiViews enabled, and /some/dir/foo does *not* exist, then the server reads the directory looking for files named foo.*, and effectively fakes up a type map which names all those files, assigning them the same media types and content-encodings it would have if the client had asked for one of them by name. It then chooses the best match to the client's requirements.

MultiViews may also apply to searches for the file named by the DIRECTORYINDEX directive, if the server is trying to index a directory. If the configuration files specify

```
DirectoryIndex index
```

then the server will arbitrate between index.html and index.html3 if both are present. If neither are present, and index.cgi is there, the server will run it.

If one of the files found when reading the directory does not have an extension recognized by mod_mime to designate its Charset, Content-Type, Language, or Encoding, then the result depends on the setting of the MULTIVIEWSMATCH directive. This directive determines whether handlers, filters, and other extension types can participate in MultiViews negotiation.

## The Negotiation Methods

After httpd has obtained a list of the variants for a given resource, either from a type-map file or from the filenames in the directory, it invokes one of two methods to decide on the 'best' variant to return, if any. It is not necessary to know any of the details of how negotiation actually takes place in order to use httpd's content negotiation features. However the rest of this document explains the methods used for those interested.

There are two negotiation methods:

1. **Server driven negotiation with the httpd algorithm** is used in the normal case. The httpd algorithm is explained in more detail below. When this algorithm is used, httpd can sometimes 'fiddle' the quality factor of a particular dimension to achieve a better result. The ways httpd can fiddle quality factors is explained in more detail below.

2. **Transparent content negotiation** is used when the browser specifically requests this through the mechanism defined in RFC 2295. This negotiation method gives the browser full control over deciding on the 'best' variant, the result is therefore dependent on the specific algorithms used by the browser. As part of the transparent negotiation process, the browser can ask httpd to run the 'remote variant selection algorithm' defined in RFC 2296.

**Dimensions of Negotiation**

| Dimension | Notes |
|---|---|
| Media Type | Browser indicates preferences with the Accept header field. Each item can have an associated quality factor. Variant description can also have a quality factor (the "qs" parameter). |
| Language | Browser indicates preferences with the Accept-Language header field. Each item can have a quality factor. Variants can be associated with none, one or more than one language. |
| Encoding | Browser indicates preference with the Accept-Encoding header field. Each item can have a quality factor. |
| Charset | Browser indicates preference with the Accept-Charset header field. Each item can have a quality factor. Variants can indicate a charset as a parameter of the media type. |

**httpd Negotiation Algorithm**

httpd can use the following algorithm to select the 'best' variant (if any) to return to the browser. This algorithm is not further configurable. It operates as follows:

1. First, for each dimension of the negotiation, check the appropriate *Accept\** header field and assign a quality to each variant. If the *Accept\** header for any dimension implies that this variant is not acceptable, eliminate it. If no variants remain, go to step 4.

2. Select the 'best' variant by a process of elimination. Each of the following tests is applied in order. Any variants not selected at each test are eliminated. After each test, if only one variant remains, select it as the best match and proceed to step 3. If more than one variant remains, move on to the next test.

    (a) Multiply the quality factor from the `Accept` header with the quality-of-source factor for this variants media type, and select the variants with the highest value.

    (b) Select the variants with the highest language quality factor.

    (c) Select the variants with the best language match, using either the order of languages in the `Accept-Language` header (if present), or else the order of languages in the `LanguagePriority` directive (if present).

    (d) Select the variants with the highest 'level' media parameter (used to give the version of text/html media types).

    (e) Select variants with the best charset media parameters, as given on the `Accept-Charset` header line. Charset ISO-8859-1 is acceptable unless explicitly excluded. Variants with a `text/*` media type but not explicitly associated with a particular charset are assumed to be in ISO-8859-1.

    (f) Select those variants which have associated charset media parameters that are *not* ISO-8859-1. If there are no such variants, select all variants instead.

    (g) Select the variants with the best encoding. If there are variants with an encoding that is acceptable to the user-agent, select only these variants. Otherwise if there is a mix of encoded and non-encoded variants, select only the unencoded variants. If either all variants are encoded or all variants are not encoded, select all variants.

    (h) Select the variants with the smallest content length.

    (i) Select the first variant of those remaining. This will be either the first listed in the type-map file, or when variants are read from the directory, the one whose file name comes first when sorted using ASCII code order.

3. The algorithm has now selected one 'best' variant, so return it as the response. The HTTP response header `Vary` is set to indicate the dimensions of negotiation (browsers and caches can use this information when caching the resource). End.

4. To get here means no variant was selected (because none are acceptable to the browser). Return a 406 status (meaning "No acceptable representation") with a response body consisting of an HTML document listing the available variants. Also set the HTTP `Vary` header to indicate the dimensions of variance.

## Fiddling with Quality Values

httpd sometimes changes the quality values from what would be expected by a strict interpretation of the httpd negotiation algorithm above. This is to get a better result from the algorithm for browsers which do not send full or accurate information. Some of the most popular browsers send `Accept` header information which would otherwise result in the selection of the wrong variant in many cases. If a browser sends full and correct information these fiddles will not be applied.

**Media Types and Wildcards**

The `Accept:` request header indicates preferences for media types. It can also include 'wildcard' media types, such as "image/*" or "*/*" where the * matches any string. So a request including:

```
Accept:  image/*, */*
```

would indicate that any type starting "image/" is acceptable, as is any other type. Some browsers routinely send wildcards in addition to explicit types they can handle. For example:

```
Accept:  text/html, text/plain, image/gif, image/jpeg, */*
```

The intention of this is to indicate that the explicitly listed types are preferred, but if a different representation is available, that is ok too. Using explicit quality values, what the browser really wants is something like:

```
Accept:  text/html, text/plain, image/gif, image/jpeg, */*; q=0.01
```

The explicit types have no quality factor, so they default to a preference of 1.0 (the highest). The wildcard */* is given a low preference of 0.01, so other types will only be returned if no variant matches an explicitly listed type.

If the `Accept:` header contains *no* q factors at all, httpd sets the q value of "*/*", if present, to 0.01 to emulate the desired behavior. It also sets the q value of wildcards of the format "type/*" to 0.02 (so these are preferred over matches against "*/*". If any media type on the `Accept:` header contains a q factor, these special values are *not* applied, so requests from browsers which send the explicit information to start with work as expected.

**Language Negotiation Exceptions**

New in httpd 2.0, some exceptions have been added to the negotiation algorithm to allow graceful fallback when language negotiation fails to find a match.

When a client requests a page on your server, but the server cannot find a single page that matches the `Accept-language` sent by the browser, the server will return either a "No Acceptable Variant" or "Multiple Choices" response to the client. To avoid these error messages, it is possible to configure httpd to ignore the `Accept-language` in these cases and provide a document that does not explicitly match the client's request. The FORCELANGUAGEPRIORITY directive can be used to override one or both of these error messages and substitute the servers judgement in the form of the LANGUAGEPRIORITY directive.

The server will also attempt to match language-subsets when no other match can be found. For example, if a client requests documents with the language en-GB for British English, the server is not normally allowed by the HTTP/1.1 standard to match that against a document that is marked as simply en. (Note that it is almost surely a configuration error to include en-GB and not en in the `Accept-Language` header, since it is very unlikely that a reader understands British English, but doesn't understand English in general. Unfortunately, many current clients have default configurations that resemble this.) However, if no other language match is possible and the server is about to return a "No Acceptable Variants" error or fallback to the LANGUAGEPRIORITY, the server will ignore the subset specification and match en-GB against en documents. Implicitly, httpd will add the parent language to the client's acceptable language list with a very low quality value. But note that if the client requests "en-GB; q=0.9, fr; q=0.8", and the server has documents designated "en" and "fr", then the "fr" document will be returned. This is necessary to maintain compliance with the HTTP/1.1 specification and to work effectively with properly configured clients.

In order to support advanced techniques (such as cookies or special URL-paths) to determine the user's preferred language, since httpd 2.0.47 MOD_NEGOTIATION recognizes the environment variable (p. 92) `prefer-language`. If it exists and contains an appropriate language tag, MOD_NEGOTIATION will try to select a matching variant. If there's no such variant, the normal negotiation process applies.

**Example**

```
SetEnvIf Cookie "language=(.+)" prefer-language=$1
Header append Vary cookie
```

## Extensions to Transparent Content Negotiation

httpd extends the transparent content negotiation protocol (RFC 2295) as follows. A new {encoding ..} element is used in variant lists to label variants which are available with a specific content-encoding only. The implementation of the RVSA/1.0 algorithm (RFC 2296) is extended to recognize encoded variants in the list, and to use them as candidate variants whenever their encodings are acceptable according to the Accept-Encoding request header. The RVSA/1.0 implementation does not round computed quality factors to 5 decimal places before choosing the best variant.

## Note on hyperlinks and naming conventions

If you are using language negotiation you can choose between different naming conventions, because files can have more than one extension, and the order of the extensions is normally irrelevant (see the mod_mime (p. 749) documentation for details).

A typical file has a MIME-type extension (*e.g.*, html), maybe an encoding extension (*e.g.*, gz), and of course a language extension (*e.g.*, en) when we have different language variants of this file.

Examples:

- foo.en.html
- foo.html.en
- foo.en.html.gz

Here some more examples of filenames together with valid and invalid hyperlinks:

| Filename | Valid hyperlink | Invalid hyperlink |
|---|---|---|
| *foo.html.en* | foo<br>foo.html | - |
| *foo.en.html* | foo | foo.html |
| *foo.html.en.gz* | foo<br>foo.html | foo.gz<br>foo.html.gz |
| *foo.en.html.gz* | foo | foo.html<br>foo.html.gz<br>foo.gz |
| *foo.gz.html.en* | foo<br>foo.gz<br>foo.gz.html | foo.html |
| *foo.html.gz.en* | foo<br>foo.html<br>foo.html.gz | foo.gz |

Looking at the table above, you will notice that it is always possible to use the name without any extensions in a hyperlink (*e.g.*, foo). The advantage is that you can hide the actual type of a document rsp. file and can change it later, *e.g.*, from html to shtml or cgi without changing any hyperlink references.

If you want to continue to use a MIME-type in your hyperlinks (*e.g.* foo.html) the language extension (including an encoding extension if there is one) must be on the right hand side of the MIME-type extension (*e.g.*, foo.html.en).

**Note on Caching**

When a cache stores a representation, it associates it with the request URL. The next time that URL is requested, the cache can use the stored representation. But, if the resource is negotiable at the server, this might result in only the first requested variant being cached and subsequent cache hits might return the wrong response. To prevent this, httpd normally marks all responses that are returned after content negotiation as non-cacheable by HTTP/1.0 clients. httpd also supports the HTTP/1.1 protocol features to allow caching of negotiated responses.

For requests which come from a HTTP/1.0 compliant client (either a browser or a cache), the directive CACHENE-GOTIATEDDOCS can be used to allow caching of responses which were subject to negotiation. This directive can be given in the server config or virtual host, and takes no arguments. It has no effect on requests from HTTP/1.1 clients.

For HTTP/1.1 clients, httpd sends a `Vary` HTTP response header to indicate the negotiation dimensions for the response. Caches can use this information to determine whether a subsequent request can be served from the local copy. To encourage a cache to use the local copy regardless of the negotiation dimensions, set the `force-no-vary` environment variable (p. 92) .

# 2.13 Custom Error Responses

Although the Apache HTTP Server provides generic error responses in the event of 4xx or 5xx HTTP status codes, these responses are rather stark, uninformative, and can be intimidating to site users. You may wish to provide custom error responses which are either friendlier, or in some language other than English, or perhaps which are styled more in line with your site layout.

Customized error responses can be defined for any HTTP status code designated as an error condition - that is, any 4xx or 5xx status.

Additionally, a set of values are provided, so that the error document can be customized further based on the values of these variables, using Server Side Includes (p. 243) . Or, you can have error conditions handled by a cgi program, or other dynamic handler (PHP, mod_perl, etc) which makes use of these variables.

## Configuration

Custom error documents are configured using the ERRORDOCUMENT directive, which may be used in global, virtualhost, or directory context. It may be used in .htaccess files if ALLOWOVERRIDE is set to FileInfo.

```
ErrorDocument 500 "Sorry, our script crashed. Oh dear"
ErrorDocument 500 /cgi-bin/crash-recover
ErrorDocument 500 http://error.example.com/server_error.html
ErrorDocument 404 /errors/not_found.html
ErrorDocument 401 /subscription/how_to_subscribe.html
```

The syntax of the ErrorDocument directive is:

```
ErrorDocument <3-digit-code> <action>
```

where the action will be treated as:

1. A local URL to redirect to (if the action begins with a "/").

2. An external URL to redirect to (if the action is a valid URL).

3. Text to be displayed (if none of the above). The text must be wrapped in quotes (") if it consists of more than one word.

When redirecting to a local URL, additional environment variables are set so that the response can be further customized. They are not sent to external URLs.

## Available Variables

Redirecting to another URL can be useful, but only if some information can be passed which can then be used to explain or log the error condition more clearly.

To achieve this, when the error redirect is sent, additional environment variables will be set, which will be generated from the headers provided to the original request by prepending 'REDIRECT_' onto the original header name. This provides the error document the context of the original request.

For example, you might receive, in addition to more usual environment variables, the following.

```
REDIRECT_HTTP_ACCEPT=*/*, image/gif, image/jpeg, image/png
REDIRECT_HTTP_USER_AGENT=Mozilla/5.0 Fedora/3.5.8-1.fc12 Firefox/3.5.8
REDIRECT_PATH=.:/bin:/usr/local/bin:/sbin
REDIRECT_QUERY_STRING=
REDIRECT_REMOTE_ADDR=121.345.78.123
REDIRECT_REMOTE_HOST=client.example.com
REDIRECT_SERVER_NAME=www.example.edu
REDIRECT_SERVER_PORT=80
REDIRECT_SERVER_SOFTWARE=Apache/2.2.15
REDIRECT_URL=/cgi-bin/buggy.pl
```

REDIRECT_ environment variables are created from the environment variables which existed prior to the redirect. They are renamed with a REDIRECT_ prefix, *i.e.*, HTTP_USER_AGENT becomes REDIRECT_HTTP_USER_AGENT.

REDIRECT_URL, REDIRECT_STATUS, and REDIRECT_QUERY_STRING are guaranteed to be set, and the other headers will be set only if they existed prior to the error condition.

**None** of these will be set if the ERRORDOCUMENT target is an *external* redirect (anything starting with a scheme name like http:, even if it refers to the same host as the server).

## Customizing Error Responses

If you point your ErrorDocument to some variety of dynamic handler such as a server-side include document, CGI script, or some variety of other handler, you may wish to use the available custom environment variables to customize this response.

If the ErrorDocument specifies a local redirect to a CGI script, the script should include a "Status:" header field in its output in order to ensure the propagation all the way back to the client of the error condition that caused it to be invoked. For instance, a Perl ErrorDocument script might include the following:

```
...
print  "Content-type: text/html\n";
printf "Status: %s Condition Intercepted\n", $ENV{"REDIRECT_STATUS"};
...
```

If the script is dedicated to handling a particular error condition, such as 404NotFound, it can use the specific code and error text instead.

Note that if the response contains Location: header (in order to issue a client-side redirect), the script *must* emit an appropriate Status: header (such as 302Found). Otherwise the Location: header may have no effect.

## Multi Language Custom Error Documents

Provided with your installation of the Apache HTTP Server is a directory of custom error documents translated into 16 different languages. There's also a configuration file in the conf/extra configuration directory that can be included to enable this feature.

In your server configuration file, you'll see a line such as:

```
# Multi-language error messages
#Include conf/extra/httpd-multilang-errordoc.conf
```

Uncommenting this Include line will enable this feature, and provide language-negotiated error messages, based on the language preference set in the client browser.

Additionally, these documents contain various of the REDIRECT_ variables, so that additional information can be provided to the end-user about what happened, and what they can do now.

These documents can be customized to whatever degree you wish to provide more useful information to users about your site, and what they can expect to find there.

MOD_INCLUDE and MOD_NEGOTIATION must be enabled to use this feature.

## 2.14  Binding to Addresses and Ports

Configuring Apache HTTP Server to listen on specific addresses and ports.

**See also**

- Virtual Hosts (p. 124)
- DNS Issues (p. 121)

## Overview

| Related Modules | Related Directives |
|---|---|
| CORE | <VIRTUALHOST> |
| MPM_COMMON | LISTEN |

When httpd starts, it binds to some port and address on the local machine and waits for incoming requests. By default, it listens to all addresses on the machine. However, it may need to be told to listen on specific ports, or only on selected addresses, or a combination of both. This is often combined with the Virtual Host (p. 124) feature, which determines how `httpd` responds to different IP addresses, hostnames and ports.

The LISTEN directive tells the server to accept incoming requests only on the specified port(s) or address-and-port combinations. If only a port number is specified in the LISTEN directive, the server listens to the given port on all interfaces. If an IP address is given as well as a port, the server will listen on the given port and interface. Multiple LISTEN directives may be used to specify a number of addresses and ports to listen on. The server will respond to requests from any of the listed addresses and ports.

For example, to make the server accept connections on both port 80 and port 8000, on all interfaces, use:

```
Listen 80
Listen 8000
```

To make the server accept connections on port 80 for one interface, and port 8000 on another, use

```
Listen 192.0.2.1:80
Listen 192.0.2.5:8000
```

IPv6 addresses must be enclosed in square brackets, as in the following example:

```
Listen [2001:db8::a00:20ff:fea7:ccea]:80
```

! Overlapping LISTEN directives will result in a fatal error which will prevent the server from starting up.

```
(48)Address already in use:  make_sock:  could not bind
to address [::]:80
```

See the discussion in the wiki[a] for further troubleshooting tips.

---

[a]http://wiki.apache.org/httpd/CouldNotBindToAddress

## Special IPv6 Considerations

A growing number of platforms implement IPv6, and APR supports IPv6 on most of these platforms, allowing httpd to allocate IPv6 sockets, and to handle requests sent over IPv6.

One complicating factor for httpd administrators is whether or not an IPv6 socket can handle both IPv4 connections and IPv6 connections. Handling IPv4 connections with an IPv6 socket uses IPv4-mapped IPv6 addresses, which are allowed by default on most platforms, but are disallowed by default on FreeBSD, NetBSD, and OpenBSD, in order to match the system-wide policy on those platforms. On systems where it is disallowed by default, a special `configure` parameter can change this behavior for httpd.

On the other hand, on some platforms, such as Linux and Tru64, the **only** way to handle both IPv6 and IPv4 is to use mapped addresses. If you want `httpd` to handle IPv4 and IPv6 connections with a minimum of sockets, which requires using IPv4-mapped IPv6 addresses, specify the `--enable-v4-mapped configure` option.

`--enable-v4-mapped` is the default on all platforms except FreeBSD, NetBSD, and OpenBSD, so this is probably how your httpd was built.

If you want httpd to handle IPv4 connections only, regardless of what your platform and APR will support, specify an IPv4 address on all LISTEN directives, as in the following examples:

```
Listen 0.0.0.0:80
Listen 192.0.2.1:80
```

If your platform supports it and you want httpd to handle IPv4 and IPv6 connections on separate sockets (i.e., to disable IPv4-mapped addresses), specify the `--disable-v4-mapped configure` option. `--disable-v4-mapped` is the default on FreeBSD, NetBSD, and OpenBSD.

## Specifying the protocol with Listen

The optional second *protocol* argument of LISTEN is not required for most configurations. If not specified, `https` is the default for port 443 and `http` the default for all other ports. The protocol is used to determine which module should handle a request, and to apply protocol specific optimizations with the ACCEPTFILTER directive.

You only need to set the protocol if you are running on non-standard ports. For example, running an `https` site on port 8443:

```
Listen 192.170.2.1:8443 https
```

## How This Works With Virtual Hosts

The LISTEN directive does not implement Virtual Hosts - it only tells the main server what addresses and ports to listen on. If no <VIRTUALHOST> directives are used, the server will behave in the same way for all accepted requests. However, <VIRTUALHOST> can be used to specify a different behavior for one or more of the addresses or ports. To implement a VirtualHost, the server must first be told to listen to the address and port to be used. Then a <VIRTUALHOST> section should be created for the specified address and port to set the behavior of this virtual host. Note that if the <VIRTUALHOST> is set for an address and port that the server is not listening to, it cannot be accessed.

# 2.15 Multi-Processing Modules (MPMs)

This document describes what a Multi-Processing Module is and how they are used by the Apache HTTP Server.

## Introduction

The Apache HTTP Server is designed to be a powerful and flexible web server that can work on a very wide variety of platforms in a range of different environments. Different platforms and different environments often require different features, or may have different ways of implementing the same feature most efficiently. Apache httpd has always accommodated a wide variety of environments through its modular design. This design allows the webmaster to choose which features will be included in the server by selecting which modules to load either at compile-time or at run-time.

Apache HTTP Server 2.0 extends this modular design to the most basic functions of a web server. The server ships with a selection of Multi-Processing Modules (MPMs) which are responsible for binding to network ports on the machine, accepting requests, and dispatching children to handle the requests.

Extending the modular design to this level of the server allows two important benefits:

- Apache httpd can more cleanly and efficiently support a wide variety of operating systems. In particular, the Windows version of the server is now much more efficient, since MPM_WINNT can use native networking features in place of the POSIX layer used in Apache httpd 1.3. This benefit also extends to other operating systems that implement specialized MPMs.

- The server can be better customized for the needs of the particular site. For example, sites that need a great deal of scalability can choose to use a threaded MPM like WORKER or EVENT, while sites requiring stability or compatibility with older software can use a PREFORK.

At the user level, MPMs appear much like other Apache httpd modules. The main difference is that one and only one MPM must be loaded into the server at any time. The list of available MPMs appears on the module index page (p. 1101).

## MPM Defaults

The following table lists the default MPMs for various operating systems. This will be the MPM selected if you do not make another choice at compile-time.

| Netware | MPM_NETWARE |
|---------|-------------|
| OS/2 | MPMT_OS2 |
| Unix | PREFORK, WORKER, or EVENT, depending on platform capabilities |
| Windows | MPM_WINNT |

⟹ Here, 'Unix' is used to mean Unix-like operating systems, such as Linux, BSD, Solaris, Mac OS X, etc.

In the case of Unix, the decision as to which MPM is installed is based on two questions:

1. Does the system support threads?

2. Does the system support thread-safe polling (Specifically, the kqueue and epoll functions)?

If the answer to both questions is 'yes', the default MPM is EVENT.

If The answer to #1 is 'yes', but the answer to #2 is 'no', the default will be WORKER.

If the answer to both questions is 'no', then the default MPM will be PREFORK.

In practical terms, this means that the default will almost always be EVENT, as all modern operating systems support these two features.

## Building an MPM as a static module

MPMs can be built as static modules on all platforms. A single MPM is chosen at build time and linked into the server. The server must be rebuilt in order to change the MPM.

To override the default MPM choice, use the `--with-mpm=`*NAME* option of the `configure` script. *NAME* is the name of the desired MPM.

Once the server has been compiled, it is possible to determine which MPM was chosen by using `./httpd -l`. This command will list every module that is compiled into the server, including the MPM.

## Building an MPM as a DSO module

On Unix and similar platforms, MPMs can be built as DSO modules and dynamically loaded into the server in the same manner as other DSO modules. Building MPMs as DSO modules allows the MPM to be changed by updating the LOADMODULE directive for the MPM instead of by rebuilding the server.

```
LoadModule mpm_prefork_module modules/mod_mpm_prefork.so
```

Attempting to LOADMODULE more than one MPM will result in a startup failure with the following error.

```
AH00534: httpd: Configuration error: More than one MPM loaded.
```

This feature is enabled using the `--enable-mpms-shared` option of the `configure` script. With argument *all*, all possible MPMs for the platform will be installed. Alternately, a list of MPMs can be specified as the argument.

The default MPM, either selected automatically or specified with the `--with-mpm` option of the `configure` script, will be loaded in the generated server configuration file. Edit the LOADMODULE directive to select a different MPM.

## 2.16   Environment Variables in Apache

There are two kinds of environment variables that affect the Apache HTTP Server.

First, there are the environment variables controlled by the underlying operating system. These are set before the server starts. They can be used in expansions in configuration files, and can optionally be passed to CGI scripts and SSI using the PassEnv directive.

Second, the Apache HTTP Server provides a mechanism for storing information in named variables that are also called *environment variables*. This information can be used to control various operations such as logging or access control. The variables are also used as a mechanism to communicate with external programs such as CGI scripts. This document discusses different ways to manipulate and use these variables.

Although these variables are referred to as *environment variables*, they are not the same as the environment variables controlled by the underlying operating system. Instead, these variables are stored and manipulated in an internal Apache structure. They only become actual operating system environment variables when they are provided to CGI scripts and Server Side Include scripts. If you wish to manipulate the operating system environment under which the server itself runs, you must use the standard environment manipulation mechanisms provided by your operating system shell.

## Setting Environment Variables

| Related Modules | Related Directives |
| --- | --- |
| MOD_CACHE | BROWSERMATCH |
| MOD_ENV | BROWSERMATCHNOCASE |
| MOD_REWRITE | PASSENV |
| MOD_SETENVIF | REWRITERULE |
| MOD_UNIQUE_ID | SETENV |
| | SETENVIF |
| | SETENVIFNOCASE |
| | UNSETENV |

### Basic Environment Manipulation

The most basic way to set an environment variable in Apache is using the unconditional SETENV directive. Variables may also be passed from the environment of the shell which started the server using the PASSENV directive.

### Conditional Per-Request Settings

For additional flexibility, the directives provided by MOD_SETENVIF allow environment variables to be set on a per-request basis, conditional on characteristics of particular requests. For example, a variable could be set only when a specific browser (User-Agent) is making a request, or only when a specific Referer [sic] header is found. Even more flexibility is available through the MOD_REWRITE's REWRITERULE which uses the [E=...] option to set environment variables.

### Unique Identifiers

Finally, MOD_UNIQUE_ID sets the environment variable UNIQUE_ID for each request to a value which is guaranteed to be unique across "all" requests under very specific conditions.

**Standard CGI Variables**

In addition to all environment variables set within the Apache configuration and passed from the shell, CGI scripts and SSI pages are provided with a set of environment variables containing meta-information about the request as required by the CGI specification[33].

**Some Caveats**

- It is not possible to override or change the standard CGI variables using the environment manipulation directives.

- When `suexec` is used to launch CGI scripts, the environment will be cleaned down to a set of *safe* variables before CGI scripts are launched. The list of *safe* variables is defined at compile-time in `suexec.c`.

- For portability reasons, the names of environment variables may contain only letters, numbers, and the underscore character. In addition, the first character may not be a number. Characters which do not match this restriction will be replaced by an underscore when passed to CGI scripts and SSI pages.

- A special case are HTTP headers which are passed to CGI scripts and the like via environment variables (see below). They are converted to uppercase and only dashes are replaced with underscores; if the header contains any other (invalid) character, the whole header is silently dropped. See below for a workaround.

- The SETENV directive runs late during request processing meaning that directives such as SETENVIF and REWRITECOND will not see the variables set with it.

- When the server looks up a path via an internal subrequest such as looking for a DIRECTORYINDEX or generating a directory listing with MOD_AUTOINDEX, per-request environment variables are *not* inherited in the subrequest. Additionally, SETENVIF directives are not separately evaluated in the subrequest due to the API phases MOD_SETENVIF takes action in.

## Using Environment Variables

| Related Modules | Related Directives |
|---|---|
| MOD_AUTHZ_HOST | REQUIRE |
| MOD_CGI | CUSTOMLOG |
| MOD_EXT_FILTER | DENY |
| MOD_HEADERS | EXTFILTERDEFINE |
| MOD_INCLUDE | HEADER |
| MOD_LOG_CONFIG | LOGFORMAT |
| MOD_REWRITE | REWRITECOND |
| | REWRITERULE |

**CGI Scripts**

One of the primary uses of environment variables is to communicate information to CGI scripts. As discussed above, the environment passed to CGI scripts includes standard meta-information about the request in addition to any variables set within the Apache configuration. For more details, see the CGI tutorial (p. 236) .

**SSI Pages**

Server-parsed (SSI) documents processed by MOD_INCLUDE's INCLUDES filter can print environment variables using the `echo` element, and can use environment variables in flow control elements to makes parts of a page conditional on

---

[33]http://www.ietf.org/rfc/rfc3875

characteristics of a request. Apache also provides SSI pages with the standard CGI environment variables as discussed above. For more details, see the SSI tutorial (p. 243) .

### Access Control

Access to the server can be controlled based on the value of environment variables using the `allow from env=` and `deny from env=` directives. In combination with SETENVIF, this allows for flexible control of access to the server based on characteristics of the client. For example, you can use these directives to deny access to a particular browser (User-Agent).

### Conditional Logging

Environment variables can be logged in the access log using the LOGFORMAT option `%e`. In addition, the decision on whether or not to log requests can be made based on the status of environment variables using the conditional form of the CUSTOMLOG directive. In combination with SETENVIF this allows for flexible control of which requests are logged. For example, you can choose not to log requests for filenames ending in `gif`, or you can choose to only log requests from clients which are outside your subnet.

### Conditional Response Headers

The HEADER directive can use the presence or absence of an environment variable to determine whether or not a certain HTTP header will be placed in the response to the client. This allows, for example, a certain response header to be sent only if a corresponding header is received in the request from the client.

### External Filter Activation

External filters configured by MOD_EXT_FILTER using the EXTFILTERDEFINE directive can by activated conditional on an environment variable using the `disableenv=` and `enableenv=` options.

### URL Rewriting

The `%{ENV:variable}` form of *TestString* in the REWRITECOND allows MOD_REWRITE's rewrite engine to make decisions conditional on environment variables. Note that the variables accessible in MOD_REWRITE without the ENV: prefix are not actually environment variables. Rather, they are variables special to MOD_REWRITE which cannot be accessed from other modules.

## Special Purpose Environment Variables

Interoperability problems have led to the introduction of mechanisms to modify the way Apache behaves when talking to particular clients. To make these mechanisms as flexible as possible, they are invoked by defining environment variables, typically with BROWSERMATCH, though SETENV and PASSENV could also be used, for example.

### downgrade-1.0

This forces the request to be treated as a HTTP/1.0 request even if it was in a later dialect.

**force-gzip**

If you have the DEFLATE filter activated, this environment variable will ignore the accept-encoding setting of your browser and will send compressed output unconditionally.

**force-no-vary**

This causes any Vary fields to be removed from the response header before it is sent back to the client. Some clients don't interpret this field correctly; setting this variable can work around this problem. Setting this variable also implies **force-response-1.0**.

**force-response-1.0**

This forces an HTTP/1.0 response to clients making an HTTP/1.0 request. It was originally implemented as a result of a problem with AOL's proxies. Some HTTP/1.0 clients may not behave correctly when given an HTTP/1.1 response, and this can be used to interoperate with them.

**gzip-only-text/html**

When set to a value of "1", this variable disables the DEFLATE output filter provided by MOD_DEFLATE for content-types other than text/html. If you'd rather use statically compressed files, MOD_NEGOTIATION evaluates the variable as well (not only for gzip, but for all encodings that differ from "identity").

**no-gzip**

When set, the DEFLATE filter of MOD_DEFLATE will be turned off and MOD_NEGOTIATION will refuse to deliver encoded resources.

**no-cache**

*Available in versions 2.2.12 and later*

When set, MOD_CACHE will not save an otherwise cacheable response. This environment variable does not influence whether a response already in the cache will be served for the current request.

**nokeepalive**

This disables KEEPALIVE when set.

**prefer-language**

This influences MOD_NEGOTIATION's behaviour. If it contains a language tag (such as en, ja or x-klingon), MOD_NEGOTIATION tries to deliver a variant with that language. If there's no such variant, the normal negotiation (p. 78) process applies.

**redirect-carefully**

This forces the server to be more careful when sending a redirect to the client. This is typically used when a client has a known problem handling redirects. This was originally implemented as a result of a problem with Microsoft's WebFolders software which has a problem handling redirects on directory resources via DAV methods.

**suppress-error-charset**

*Available in versions after 2.0.54*

When Apache issues a redirect in response to a client request, the response includes some actual text to be displayed in case the client can't (or doesn't) automatically follow the redirection. Apache ordinarily labels this text according to the character set which it uses, which is ISO-8859-1.

However, if the redirection is to a page that uses a different character set, some broken browser versions will try to use the character set from the redirection text rather than the actual page. This can result in Greek, for instance, being incorrectly rendered.

Setting this environment variable causes Apache to omit the character set for the redirection text, and these broken browsers will then correctly use that of the destination page.

 **Security note**

Sending error pages without a specified character set may allow a cross-site-scripting attack for existing browsers (MSIE) which do not follow the HTTP/1.1 specification and attempt to "guess" the character set from the content. Such browsers can be easily fooled into using the UTF-7 character set, and UTF-7 content from input data (such as the request-URI) will not be escaped by the usual escaping mechanisms designed to prevent cross-site-scripting attacks.

**force-proxy-request-1.0, proxy-nokeepalive, proxy-sendchunked, proxy-sendcl, proxy-chain-auth, proxy-interim-response, proxy-initial-not-pooled**

These directives alter the protocol behavior of MOD_PROXY. See the MOD_PROXY and MOD_PROXY_HTTP documentation for more details.

## Examples

**Passing broken headers to CGI scripts**

Starting with version 2.4, Apache is more strict about how HTTP headers are converted to environment variables in MOD_CGI and other modules: Previously any invalid characters in header names were simply translated to underscores. This allowed for some potential cross-site-scripting attacks via header injection (see Unusual Web Bugs[34], slide 19/20).

If you have to support a client which sends broken headers and which can't be fixed, a simple workaround involving MOD_SETENVIF and MOD_HEADERS allows you to still accept these headers:

```
#
# The following works around a client sending a broken Accept_Encoding
# header.
#
```

---

[34]http://events.ccc.de/congress/2007/Fahrplan/events/2212.en.html

```
SetEnvIfNoCase ^Accept.Encoding$ ^(.*)$ fix_accept_encoding=$1
RequestHeader set Accept-Encoding %{fix_accept_encoding}e env=fix_accept_encoding
```

**Changing protocol behavior with misbehaving clients**

Earlier versions recommended that the following lines be included in httpd.conf to deal with known client problems.
Since the affected clients are no longer seen in the wild, this configuration is likely no-longer necessary.

```
#
# The following directives modify normal HTTP response behavior.
# The first directive disables keepalive for Netscape 2.x and browsers that
# spoof it. There are known problems with these browser implementations.
# The second directive is for Microsoft Internet Explorer 4.0b2
# which has a broken HTTP/1.1 implementation and does not properly
# support keepalive when it is used on 301 or 302 (redirect) responses.
#
BrowserMatch "Mozilla/2" nokeepalive
BrowserMatch "MSIE 4\.0b2;" nokeepalive downgrade-1.0 force-response-1.0

#
# The following directive disables HTTP/1.1 responses to browsers which
# are in violation of the HTTP/1.0 spec by not being able to understand a
# basic 1.1 response.
#
BrowserMatch "RealPlayer 4\.0" force-response-1.0
BrowserMatch "Java/1\.0" force-response-1.0
BrowserMatch "JDK/1\.0" force-response-1.0
```

**Do not log requests for images in the access log**

This example keeps requests for images from appearing in the access log. It can be easily modified to prevent logging
of particular directories, or to prevent logging of requests coming from particular hosts.

```
SetEnvIf Request_URI \.gif image-request
SetEnvIf Request_URI \.jpg image-request
SetEnvIf Request_URI \.png image-request
CustomLog "logs/access_log" common env=!image-request
```

**Prevent "Image Theft"**

This example shows how to keep people not on your server from using images on your server as inline-images on their
pages. This is not a recommended configuration, but it can work in limited circumstances. We assume that all your
images are in a directory called /web/images.

```
SetEnvIf Referer "^http://www\.example\.com/" local_referal
# Allow browsers that do not send Referer info
SetEnvIf Referer "^$" local_referal
<Directory "/web/images">
    Require env local_referal
</Directory>
```

For more information about this technique, see the "Keeping Your Images from Adorning Other Sites[35]" tutorial on ServerWatch.

---

[35]http://www.serverwatch.com/tutorials/article.php/1132731

## 2.17 Expressions in Apache HTTP Server

Historically, there are several syntax variants for expressions used to express a condition in the different modules of the Apache HTTP Server. There is some ongoing effort to only use a single variant, called *ap_expr*, for all configuration directives. This document describes the *ap_expr* expression parser.

The *ap_expr* expression is intended to replace most other expression variants in HTTPD. For example, the deprecated SSLREQUIRE expressions can be replaced by Require expr (p. 519) .

**See also**

- <IF>
- <ELSEIF>
- <ELSE>
- ERRORDOCUMENT
- ALIAS
- SCRIPTALIAS
- REDIRECT
- AUTHBASICFAKE
- AUTHFORMLOGINREQUIREDLOCATION
- AUTHFORMLOGINSUCCESSLOCATION
- AUTHFORMLOGOUTLOCATION
- AUTHNAME
- AUTHTYPE
- REWRITECOND
- SETENVIFEXPR
- HEADER
- REQUESTHEADER
- FILTERPROVIDER
- Require expr (p. 519)
- Require ldap-user (p. 501)
- Require ldap-group (p. 501)
- Require ldap-dn (p. 501)
- Require ldap-attribute (p. 501)
- Require ldap-filter (p. 501)
- Require ldap-search (p. 501)
- Require dbd-group (p. 527)
- Require dbm-group (p. 532)
- Require group (p. 534)
- Require host (p. 536)
- SSLREQUIRE
- LOGMESSAGE
- MOD_INCLUDE

## Grammar in Backus-Naur Form notation

Backus-Naur Form[36] (BNF) is a notation technique for context-free grammars, often used to describe the syntax of languages used in computing. In most cases, expressions are used to express boolean values. For these, the starting point in the BNF is `expr`. However, a few directives like LogMessage accept expressions that evaluate to a string value. For those, the starting point in the BNF is `string`.

```
expr            ::= "true" | "false"
                | "!" expr
                | expr "&&" expr
                | expr "||" expr
                | "(" expr ")"
                | comp

comp            ::= stringcomp
                | integercomp
                | unaryop word
                | word binaryop word
                | word "in" "{" wordlist "}"
                | word "in" listfunction
                | word "=~" regex
                | word "!~" regex


stringcomp  ::= word "==" word
                | word "!=" word
                | word "<"  word
                | word "<=" word
                | word ">"  word
                | word ">=" word

integercomp ::= word "-eq" word | word "eq" word
                | word "-ne" word | word "ne" word
                | word "-lt" word | word "lt" word
                | word "-le" word | word "le" word
                | word "-gt" word | word "gt" word
                | word "-ge" word | word "ge" word

wordlist        ::= word
                | wordlist "," word

word            ::= word "." word
                | digit
                | "'" string "'"
                | """ string """
                | variable
                | rebackref
                | function

string          ::= stringpart
                | string stringpart
```

---

[36]http://en.wikipedia.org/wiki/Backus%E2%80%93Naur_Form

```
stringpart   ::= cstring
                | variable
                | rebackref

cstring      ::= ...
digit        ::= [0-9]+

variable     ::= "%{" varname "}"
                | "%{" funcname ":" funcargs "}"

rebackref    ::= "$" [0-9]

function     ::= funcname "(" wordlist ")"

listfunction ::= listfuncname "(" word ")"
```

## Variables

The expression parser provides a number of variables of the form `%{HTTP_HOST}`. Note that the value of a variable may depend on the phase of the request processing in which it is evaluated. For example, an expression used in an `<If >` directive is evaluated before authentication is done. Therefore, `%{REMOTE_USER}` will not be set in this case.

The following variables provide the values of the named HTTP request headers. The values of other headers can be obtained with the `req` function. Using these variables may cause the header name to be added to the Vary header of the HTTP response, except where otherwise noted for the directive accepting the expression. The `req_novary` function may be used to circumvent this behavior.

| Name |
| --- |
| HTTP_ACCEPT |
| HTTP_COOKIE |
| HTTP_FORWARDED |
| HTTP_HOST |
| HTTP_PROXY_CONNECTION |
| HTTP_REFERER |
| HTTP_USER_AGENT |

Other request related variables

| Name | Description |
| --- | --- |
| REQUEST_METHOD | The HTTP method of the incoming request (e.g. GET) |
| REQUEST_SCHEME | The scheme part of the request's URI |
| REQUEST_URI | The path part of the request's URI |
| DOCUMENT_URI | Same as REQUEST_URI |
| REQUEST_FILENAME | The full local filesystem path to the file or script matching the request, if this has already been determined by the server at the time REQUEST_FILENAME is referenced. Otherwise, such as when used in virtual host context, the same value as REQUEST_URI |
| SCRIPT_FILENAME | Same as REQUEST_FILENAME |
| LAST_MODIFIED | The date and time of last modification of the file in the format 20101231235959, if this has already been determined by the server at the time LAST_MODIFIED is referenced. |
| SCRIPT_USER | The user name of the owner of the script. |
| SCRIPT_GROUP | The group name of the group of the script. |
| PATH_INFO | The trailing path name information, see ACCEPTPATHINFO |

| | |
|---|---|
| QUERY_STRING | The query string of the current request |
| IS_SUBREQ | "true" if the current request is a subrequest, "false" otherwise |
| THE_REQUEST | The complete request line (e.g., "GET /index.html HTTP/1.1") |
| REMOTE_ADDR | The IP address of the remote host |
| REMOTE_HOST | The host name of the remote host |
| REMOTE_USER | The name of the authenticated user, if any (not available during <IF>) |
| REMOTE_IDENT | The user name set by MOD_IDENT |
| SERVER_NAME | The SERVERNAME of the current vhost |
| SERVER_PORT | The server port of the current vhost, see SERVERNAME |
| SERVER_ADMIN | The SERVERADMIN of the current vhost |
| SERVER_PROTOCOL | The protocol used by the request (e.g. HTTP/1.1). In some types of internal subrequests, this variable has the value INCLUDED. |
| SERVER_PROTOCOL_VERSION | A number that encodes the HTTP version of the request: 1000 * major + minor. For example, 1001 corresponds to HTTP/1.1 and 9 corresponds to HTTP/0.9 |
| SERVER_PROTOCOL_VERSION_MAJOR | The major version part of the HTTP version of the request, e.g. 1 for HTTP/1.0 |
| SERVER_PROTOCOL_VERSION_MINOR | The minor version part of the HTTP version of the request, e.g. 0 for HTTP/1.0 |
| DOCUMENT_ROOT | The DOCUMENTROOT of the current vhost |
| AUTH_TYPE | The configured AUTHTYPE (e.g. "basic") |
| CONTENT_TYPE | The content type of the response (not available during <IF>) |
| HANDLER | The name of the handler (p. 108) creating the response |
| HTTP2 | "on" if the request uses http/2, "off" otherwise |
| HTTPS | "on" if the request uses https, "off" otherwise |
| IPV6 | "on" if the connection uses IPv6, "off" otherwise |
| REQUEST_STATUS | The HTTP error status of the request (not available during <IF>) |
| REQUEST_LOG_ID | The error log id of the request (see ERRORLOGFORMAT) |
| CONN_LOG_ID | The error log id of the connection (see ERRORLOGFORMAT) |
| CONN_REMOTE_ADDR | The peer IP address of the connection (see the MOD_REMOTEIP module) |
| CONTEXT_PREFIX | |
| CONTEXT_DOCUMENT_ROOT | |

Misc variables

| Name | Description |
|---|---|
| TIME_YEAR | The current year (e.g. 2010) |
| TIME_MON | The current month (1, ..., 12) |
| TIME_DAY | The current day of the month |
| TIME_HOUR | The hour part of the current time (0, ..., 23) |
| TIME_MIN | The minute part of the current time |
| TIME_SEC | The second part of the current time |
| TIME_WDAY | The day of the week (starting with 0 for Sunday) |
| TIME | The date and time in the format 20101231235959 |
| SERVER_SOFTWARE | The server version string |
| API_VERSION | The date of the API version (module magic number) |

Some modules register additional variables, see e.g. MOD_SSL.

## Binary operators

With the exception of some built-in comparison operators, binary operators have the form
"-[a-zA-Z][a-zA-Z0-9_]+", i.e. a minus and at least two characters. The name is not case
sensitive. Modules may register additional binary operators.

**Comparison operators**

| Name | Alternative | Description |
|------|-------------|-------------|
| == | = | String equality |
| != | | String inequality |
| < | | String less than |
| <= | | String less than or equal |
| > | | String greater than |
| >= | | String greater than or equal |
| =~ | | String matches the regular expression |
| !~ | | String does not match the regular expression |
| -eq | eq | Integer equality |
| -ne | ne | Integer inequality |
| -lt | lt | Integer less than |
| -le | le | Integer less than or equal |
| -gt | gt | Integer greater than |
| -ge | ge | Integer greater than or equal |

**Other binary operators**

| Name | Description |
|------|-------------|
| -ipmatch | IP address matches address/netmask |
| -strmatch | left string matches pattern given by right string (containing wildcards *, ?, []) |
| -strcmatch | same as -strmatch, but case insensitive |
| -fnmatch | same as -strmatch, but slashes are not matched by wildcards |

# Unary operators

Unary operators take one argument and have the form "-[a-zA-Z]", i.e. a minus and one character. The name *is* case sensitive. Modules may register additional unary operators.

| Name | Description | Restricted |
|------|-------------|------------|
| -d | The argument is treated as a filename. True if the file exists and is a directory | yes |
| -e | The argument is treated as a filename. True if the file (or dir or special) exists | yes |
| -f | The argument is treated as a filename. True if the file exists and is regular file | yes |
| -s | The argument is treated as a filename. True if the file exists and is not empty | yes |
| -L | The argument is treated as a filename. True if the file exists and is symlink | yes |
| -h | The argument is treated as a filename.  True if the file exists and is symlink (same as -L) | yes |
| -F | True if string is a valid file, accessible via all the server's currently-configured access controls for that path. This uses an internal subrequest to do the check, so use it with care - it can impact your server's performance! | |
| -U | True if string is a valid URL, accessible via all the server's currently-configured access controls for that path. This uses an internal subrequest to do the check, so use it with care - it can impact your server's performance! | |
| -A | Alias for -U | |
| -n | True if string is not empty | |
| -z | True if string is empty | |
| -T | False if string is empty, "0", "off", "false", or "no" (case insensitive). True otherwise. | |
| -R | Same as "%{REMOTE_ADDR} -ipmatch ...", but more efficient | |

The operators marked as "restricted" are not available in some modules like MOD_INCLUDE.

## Functions

Normal string-valued functions take one string as argument and return a string. Functions names are not case sensitive. Modules may register additional functions.

| Name | Description | Restricted |
|---|---|---|
| `req`, `http` | Get HTTP request header; header names may be added to the Vary header, see below | |
| `req_novary` | Same as `req`, but header names will not be added to the Vary header | |
| `resp` | Get HTTP response header (most response headers will not yet be set during <IF>) | |
| `reqenv` | Lookup request environment variable (as a shortcut, `v` can be used too to access variables) | |
| `osenv` | Lookup operating system environment variable | |
| `note` | Lookup request note | |
| `env` | Return first match of `note`, `reqenv`, `osenv` | |
| `tolower` | Convert string to lower case | |
| `toupper` | Convert string to upper case | |
| `escape` | Escape special characters in %hex encoding | |
| `unescape` | Unescape %hex encoded string, leaving encoded slashes alone; return empty string if %00 is found | |
| `base64` | Encode the string using base64 encoding | |
| `unbase64` | Decode base64 encoded string, return truncated string if 0x00 is found | |
| `md5` | Hash the string using MD5, then encode the hash with hexadecimal encoding | |
| `sha1` | Hash the string using SHA1, then encode the hash with hexadecimal encoding | |
| `file` | Read contents from a file (including line endings, when present) | yes |
| `filemod` | Return last modification time of a file (or 0 if file does not exist or is not regular file) | yes |
| `filesize` | Return size of a file (or 0 if file does not exist or is not regular file) | yes |
| `ldap` | Escape characters as required by LDAP distinguished name escaping (RFC4514) and LDAP filter escaping (RFC4515). | |
| `replace` | replace(string, "from", "to") replaces all occurences of "from" in the string with "to". | |

The functions marked as "restricted" are not available in some modules like MOD_INCLUDE.

When the functions `req` or `http` are used, the header name will automatically be added to the Vary header of the HTTP response, except where otherwise noted for the directive accepting the expression. The `req_novary` function can be used to prevent names from being added to the Vary header.

In addition to string-valued functions, there are also list-valued functions which take one string as argument and return a wordlist, i.e. a list of strings. The wordlist can be used with the special `-in` operator. Functions names are not case sensitive. Modules may register additional functions.

There are no built-in list-valued functions. MOD_SSL provides `PeerExtList`. See the description of SSLREQUIRE for details (but `PeerExtList` is also usable outside of SSLREQUIRE).

## Example expressions

The following examples show how expressions might be used to evaluate requests:

```
# Compare the host name to example.com and redirect to www.example.com if it matches
<If "%{HTTP_HOST} == 'example.com'">
```

```
    Redirect permanent "/" "http://www.example.com/"
</If>

# Force text/plain if requesting a file with the query string contains 'forcetext'
<If "%{QUERY_STRING} =~ /forcetext/">
    ForceType text/plain
</If>

# Only allow access to this content during business hours
<Directory "/foo/bar/business">
    Require expr %{TIME_HOUR} -gt 9 && %{TIME_HOUR} -lt 17
</Directory>

# Check a HTTP header for a list of values
<If "%{HTTP:X-example-header} in { 'foo', 'bar', 'baz' }">
    Header set matched true
</If>

# Check an environment variable for a regular expression, negated.
<If "! reqenv('REDIRECT_FOO') =~ /bar/">
    Header set matched true
</If>

# Check result of URI mapping by running in Directory context with -f
<Directory "/var/www">
    AddEncoding x-gzip gz
<If "-f '%{REQUEST_FILENAME}.unzipme' && ! %{HTTP:Accept-Encoding} =~ /gzip/">
        SetOutputFilter INFLATE
</If>
</Directory>

# Check against the client IP
<If "-R '192.168.1.0/24'">
    Header set matched true
</If>

# Function examples in boolean context
<If "md5('foo') == 'acbd18db4cc2f85cedef654fccc4a4d8'">
  Header set checksum-matched true
</If>
<If "md5('foo') == replace('md5:XXXd18db4cc2f85cedef654fccc4a4d8', 'md5:XXX', 'acb')">
  Header set checksum-matched-2 true
</If>

# Function example in string context
Header set foo-checksum "expr=%{md5:foo}"

# This delays the evaluation of the condition clause compared to <If>
Header always set CustomHeader my-value "expr=%{REQUEST_URI} =~ m#^/special_path.php$#"
```

## Other

| Name | Alternative | Description |
| --- | --- | --- |
| `-in` | `in` | string contained in wordlist |
| `/regexp/` | `m#regexp#` | Regular expression (the second form allows different delimiters than /) |
| `/regexp/i` | `m#regexp#i` | Case insensitive regular expression |
| `$0 ... $9` | | Regular expression backreferences |

### Regular expression backreferences

The strings `$0 ... $9` allow to reference the capture groups from a previously executed, successfully matching regular expressions. They can normally only be used in the same expression as the matching regex, but some modules allow special uses.

## Comparison with SSLRequire

The *ap_expr* syntax is mostly a superset of the syntax of the deprecated SSLREQUIRE directive. The differences are described in SSLREQUIRE's documentation.

## Version History

The `req_novary` function is available for versions 2.4.4 and later.

The `SERVER_PROTOCOL_VERSION`, `SERVER_PROTOCOL_VERSION_MAJOR` and `SERVER_PROTOCOL_VERSION_MINOR` variables are available for versions 2.5.0 and later.

# 2.18   Apache's Handler Use

This document describes the use of Apache's Handlers.

## What is a Handler

| Related Modules | Related Directives |
| --- | --- |
| MOD_ACTIONS | ACTION |
| MOD_ASIS | ADDHANDLER |
| MOD_CGI | REMOVEHANDLER |
| MOD_IMAGEMAP | SETHANDLER |
| MOD_INFO | |
| MOD_MIME | |
| MOD_NEGOTIATION | |
| MOD_STATUS | |

A "handler" is an internal Apache representation of the action to be performed when a file is called. Generally, files have implicit handlers, based on the file type. Normally, all files are simply served by the server, but certain file types are "handled" separately.

Handlers may also be configured explicitly, based on either filename extensions or on location, without relation to file type. This is advantageous both because it is a more elegant solution, and because it also allows for both a type **and** a handler to be associated with a file. (See also Files with Multiple Extensions (p. 749) .)

Handlers can either be built into the server or included in a module, or they can be added with the ACTION directive. The built-in handlers in the standard distribution are as follows:

- **default-handler**: Send the file using the `default_handler()`, which is the handler used by default to handle static content. (core)
- **send-as-is**: Send file with HTTP headers as is. (MOD_ASIS)
- **cgi-script**: Treat the file as a CGI script. (MOD_CGI)
- **imap-file**: Parse as an imagemap rule file. (MOD_IMAGEMAP)
- **server-info**: Get the server's configuration information. (MOD_INFO)
- **server-status**: Get the server's status report. (MOD_STATUS)
- **type-map**: Parse as a type map file for content negotiation. (MOD_NEGOTIATION)

## Examples

### Modifying static content using a CGI script

The following directives will cause requests for files with the `html` extension to trigger the launch of the `footer.pl` CGI script.

```
Action add-footer /cgi-bin/footer.pl
AddHandler add-footer .html
```

Then the CGI script is responsible for sending the originally requested document (pointed to by the `PATH_TRANSLATED` environment variable) and making whatever modifications or additions are desired.

**Files with HTTP headers**

The following directives will enable the `send-as-is` handler, which is used for files which contain their own HTTP headers. All files in the `/web/htdocs/asis/` directory will be processed by the `send-as-is` handler, regardless of their filename extensions.

```
<Directory "/web/htdocs/asis">
    SetHandler send-as-is
</Directory>
```

## Programmer's Note

In order to implement the handler features, an addition has been made to the Apache API (p. 1019) that you may wish to make use of. Specifically, a new record has been added to the `request_rec` structure:

```
char *handler
```

If you wish to have your module engage a handler, you need only to set `r->handler` to the name of the handler at any time prior to the `invoke_handler` stage of the request. Handlers are implemented as they were before, albeit using the handler name instead of a content type. While it is not necessary, the naming convention for handlers is to use a dash-separated word, with no slashes, so as to not invade the media type name-space.

## 2.19   Filters

This document describes the use of filters in Apache.

### Filtering in Apache 2

| Related Modules | Related Directives |
|---|---|
| MOD_FILTER | FILTERCHAIN |
| MOD_DEFLATE | FILTERDECLARE |
| MOD_EXT_FILTER | FILTERPROTOCOL |
| MOD_INCLUDE | FILTERPROVIDER |
| MOD_CHARSET_LITE | ADDINPUTFILTER |
| MOD_REFLECTOR | ADDOUTPUTFILTER |
| MOD_BUFFER | REMOVEINPUTFILTER |
| MOD_DATA | REMOVEOUTPUTFILTER |
| MOD_RATELIMIT | REFLECTORHEADER |
| MOD_REQTIMEOUT | EXTFILTERDEFINE |
| MOD_REQUEST | EXTFILTEROPTIONS |
| MOD_SED | SETINPUTFILTER |
| MOD_SUBSTITUTE | SETOUTPUTFILTER |
| MOD_XML2ENC | |
| MOD_PROXY_HTML | |
| MOD_POLICY | |

The Filter Chain is available in Apache 2.0 and higher, and enables applications to process incoming and outgoing data in a highly flexible and configurable manner, regardless of where the data comes from. We can pre-process incoming data, and post-process outgoing data, at will. This is basically independent of the traditional request processing phases.

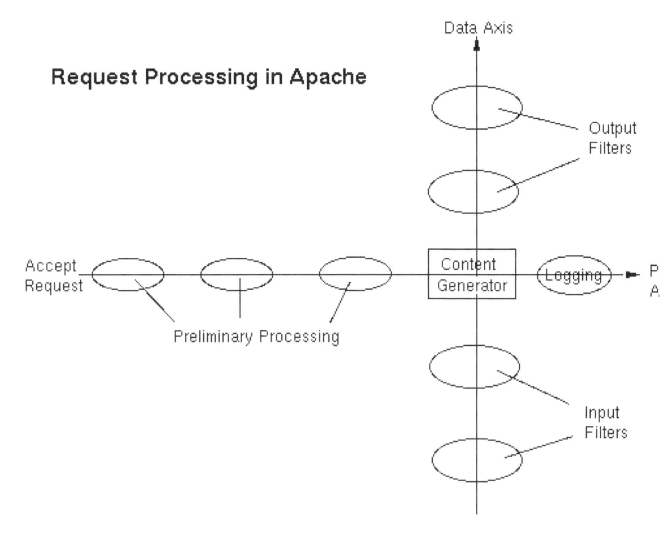

Some examples of filtering in the standard Apache distribution are:

- MOD_INCLUDE, implements server-side includes.
- MOD_SSL, implements SSL encryption (https).
- MOD_DEFLATE, implements compression/decompression on the fly.
- MOD_CHARSET_LITE, transcodes between different character sets.
- MOD_EXT_FILTER, runs an external program as a filter.

Apache also uses a number of filters internally to perform functions like chunking and byte-range handling.

A wider range of applications are implemented by third-party filter modules available from modules.apache.org[37] and elsewhere. A few of these are:

- HTML and XML processing and rewriting
- XSLT transforms and XIncludes
- XML Namespace support

---

[37]http://modules.apache.org/

- File Upload handling and decoding of HTML Forms
- Image processing
- Protection of vulnerable applications such as PHP scripts
- Text search-and-replace editing

**Smart Filtering**

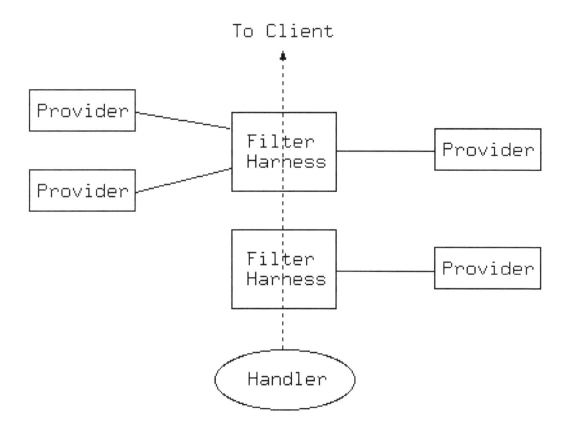

MOD_FILTER, included in Apache 2.1 and later, enables the filter chain to be configured dynamically at run time. So for example you can set up a proxy to rewrite HTML with an HTML filter and JPEG images with a completely separate filter, despite the proxy having no prior information about what the origin server will send. This works by using a filter harness, that dispatches to different providers according to the actual contents at runtime. Any filter may be either inserted directly in the chain and run unconditionally, or used as a provider and inserted dynamically. For example,

- an HTML processing filter will only run if the content is text/html or application/xhtml+xml
- A compression filter will only run if the input is a compressible type and not already compressed
- A charset conversion filter will be inserted if a text document is not already in the desired charset

**Exposing Filters as an HTTP Service**

Filters can be used to process content originating from the client in addition to processing content originating on the server using the MOD_REFLECTOR module.

MOD_REFLECTOR accepts POST requests from clients, and reflects the content request body received within the POST request back in the response, passing through the output filter stack on the way back to the client.

This technique can be used as an alternative to a web service running within an application server stack, where an output filter provides the transformation required on the request body. For example, the MOD_DEFLATE module might be used to provide a general compression service, or an image transformation filter might be turned into an image transformation service.

## Using Filters

There are two ways to use filtering: Simple and Dynamic. In general, you should use one or the other; mixing them can have unexpected consequences (although simple Input filtering can be mixed freely with either simple or dynamic Output filtering).

The Simple Way is the only way to configure input filters, and is sufficient for output filters where you need a static filter chain. Relevant directives are SETINPUTFILTER, SETOUTPUTFILTER, ADDINPUTFILTER, ADDOUTPUTFILTER, REMOVEINPUTFILTER, and REMOVEOUTPUTFILTER.

The Dynamic Way enables both static and flexible, dynamic configuration of output filters, as discussed in the MOD_FILTER page. Relevant directives are FILTERCHAIN, FILTERDECLARE, and FILTERPROVIDER.

One further directive ADDOUTPUTFILTERBYTYPE is still supported, but deprecated. Use dynamic configuration instead.

## 2.20   Shared Object Cache in Apache HTTP Server

The Shared Object Cache provides a means to share simple data across all a server's workers, regardless of thread and process models (p. 90) . It is used where the advantages of sharing data across processes outweigh the performance overhead of inter-process communication.

### Shared Object Cache Providers

The shared object cache as such is an abstraction. Four different modules implement it. To use the cache, one or more of these modules must be present, and configured.

The only configuration required is to select which cache provider to use. This is the responsibility of modules using the cache, and they enable selection using directives such as CACHESOCACHE, AUTHNCACHESOCACHE, SSLSESSIONCACHE, and SSLSTAPLINGCACHE.

Currently available providers are:

**"dbm"** (MOD_SOCACHE_DBM)   This makes use of a DBM hash file.  The choice of underlying DBM used may be configurable if the installed APR version supports multiple DBM implementations.

**"dc"** (MOD_SOCACHE_DC)   This makes use of the distcache[38] distributed session caching libraries.

**"memcache"** (MOD_SOCACHE_MEMCACHE)   This makes use of the memcached[39] high-performance, distributed memory object caching system.

**"shmcb"** (MOD_SOCACHE_SHMCB)   This makes use of a high-performance cyclic buffer inside a shared memory segment.

The API provides the following functions:

**const char \*create(ap_socache_instance_t \*\*instance, const char \*arg, apr_pool_t \*tmp, apr_pool_t \*p);**   Create a session cache based on the given configuration string. The instance pointer returned in the instance paramater will be passed as the first argument to subsequent invocations.

**apr_status_t init(ap_socache_instance_t \*instance, const char \*cname, const struct ap_socache_hints \*hints, server_rec \*s, apr_po** Initialize the cache. The cname must be of maximum length 16 characters, and uniquely identifies the consumer of the cache within the server; using the module name is recommended, e.g. "mod_ssl-sess". This string may be used within a filesystem path so use of only alphanumeric [a-z0-9_-] characters is recommended. If hints is non-NULL, it gives a set of hints for the provider. Return APR error code.

**void destroy(ap_socache_instance_t \*instance, server_rec \*s)**   Destroy a given cache instance object.

**apr_status_t store(ap_socache_instance_t \*instance, server_rec \*s, const unsigned char \*id, unsigned int idlen, apr_time_t expiry,** Store an object in a cache instance.

**apr_status_t retrieve(ap_socache_instance_t \*instance, server_rec \*s, const unsigned char \*id, unsigned int idlen, unsigned char \*** Retrieve a cached object.

**apr_status_t remove(ap_socache_instance_t \*instance, server_rec \*s, const unsigned char \*id, unsigned int idlen, apr_pool_t \*poo** Remove an object from the cache.

**void status(ap_socache_instance_t \*instance, request_rec \*r, int flags)**   Dump the status of a cache instance for mod_status.

**apr_status_t iterate(ap_socache_instance_t \*instance, server_rec \*s, void \*userctx, ap_socache_iterator_t \*iterator, apr_pool_t \*po** Dump all cached objects through an iterator callback.

---

[38]http://distcache.sourceforge.net/
[39]http://memcached.org/

# 2.21 suEXEC Support

The **suEXEC** feature provides users of the Apache HTTP Server the ability to run **CGI** and **SSI** programs under user IDs different from the user ID of the calling web server. Normally, when a CGI or SSI program executes, it runs as the same user who is running the web server.

Used properly, this feature can reduce considerably the security risks involved with allowing users to develop and run private CGI or SSI programs. However, if suEXEC is improperly configured, it can cause any number of problems and possibly create new holes in your computer's security. If you aren't familiar with managing *setuid root* programs and the security issues they present, we highly recommend that you not consider using suEXEC.

## Before we begin

Before jumping head-first into this document, you should be aware that certain assumptions are made about you and the environment in which you will be using suexec.

First, it is assumed that you are using a UNIX derivative operating system that is capable of **setuid** and **setgid** operations. All command examples are given in this regard. Other platforms, if they are capable of supporting suEXEC, may differ in their configuration.

Second, it is assumed you are familiar with some basic concepts of your computer's security and its administration. This involves an understanding of **setuid/setgid** operations and the various effects they may have on your system and its level of security.

Third, it is assumed that you are using an **unmodified** version of suEXEC code. All code for suEXEC has been carefully scrutinized and tested by the developers as well as numerous beta testers. Every precaution has been taken to ensure a simple yet solidly safe base of code. Altering this code can cause unexpected problems and new security risks. It is **highly** recommended you not alter the suEXEC code unless you are well versed in the particulars of security programming and are willing to share your work with the Apache HTTP Server development team for consideration.

Fourth, and last, it has been the decision of the Apache HTTP Server development team to **NOT** make suEXEC part of the default installation of Apache httpd. To this end, suEXEC configuration requires of the administrator careful attention to details. After due consideration has been given to the various settings for suEXEC, the administrator may install suEXEC through normal installation methods. The values for these settings need to be carefully determined and specified by the administrator to properly maintain system security during the use of suEXEC functionality. It is through this detailed process that we hope to limit suEXEC installation only to those who are careful and determined enough to use it.

Still with us? Yes? Good. Let's move on!

## suEXEC Security Model

Before we begin configuring and installing suEXEC, we will first discuss the security model you are about to implement. By doing so, you may better understand what exactly is going on inside suEXEC and what precautions are taken to ensure your system's security.

**suEXEC** is based on a setuid "wrapper" program that is called by the main Apache HTTP Server. This wrapper is called when an HTTP request is made for a CGI or SSI program that the administrator has designated to run as a userid other than that of the main server. When such a request is made, Apache httpd provides the suEXEC wrapper with the program's name and the user and group IDs under which the program is to execute.

The wrapper then employs the following process to determine success or failure – if any one of these conditions fail, the program logs the failure and exits with an error, otherwise it will continue:

1. **Is the user executing this wrapper a valid user of this system?**

   This is to ensure that the user executing the wrapper is truly a user of the system.

2. **Was the wrapper called with the proper number of arguments?**

   The wrapper will only execute if it is given the proper number of arguments. The proper argument format is known to the Apache HTTP Server. If the wrapper is not receiving the proper number of arguments, it is either being hacked, or there is something wrong with the suEXEC portion of your Apache httpd binary.

3. **Is this valid user allowed to run the wrapper?**

   Is this user the user allowed to run this wrapper? Only one user (the Apache user) is allowed to execute this program.

4. **Does the target CGI or SSI program have an unsafe hierarchical reference?**

   Does the target CGI or SSI program's path contain a leading '/' or have a '..' backreference? These are not allowed; the target CGI/SSI program must reside within suEXEC's document root (see `--with-suexec-docroot=DIR` below).

5. **Is the target user name valid?**

   Does the target user exist?

6. **Is the target group name valid?**

   Does the target group exist?

7. **Is the target user *NOT* superuser?**

   suEXEC does not allow `root` to execute CGI/SSI programs.

8. **Is the target userid *ABOVE* the minimum ID number?**

   The minimum user ID number is specified during configuration. This allows you to set the lowest possible userid that will be allowed to execute CGI/SSI programs. This is useful to block out `"system"` accounts.

9. **Is the target group *NOT* the superuser group?**

   Presently, suEXEC does not allow the `root` group to execute CGI/SSI programs.

10. **Is the target groupid *ABOVE* the minimum ID number?**

    The minimum group ID number is specified during configuration. This allows you to set the lowest possible groupid that will be allowed to execute CGI/SSI programs. This is useful to block out `"system"` groups.

11. **Can the wrapper successfully become the target user and group?**

    Here is where the program becomes the target user and group via setuid and setgid calls. The group access list is also initialized with all of the groups of which the user is a member.

12. **Can we change directory to the one in which the target CGI/SSI program resides?**

    If it doesn't exist, it can't very well contain files. If we can't change directory to it, it might as well not exist.

13. **Is the directory within the httpd webspace?**

    If the request is for a regular portion of the server, is the requested directory within suEXEC's document root? If the request is for a UserDir, is the requested directory within the directory configured as suEXEC's userdir (see suEXEC's configuration options)?

14. **Is the directory *NOT* writable by anyone else?**

    We don't want to open up the directory to others; only the owner user may be able to alter this directories contents.

15. **Does the target CGI/SSI program exist?**

    If it doesn't exists, it can't very well be executed.

16. **Is the target CGI/SSI program *NOT* writable by anyone else?**

    We don't want to give anyone other than the owner the ability to change the CGI/SSI program.

17. **Is the target CGI/SSI program *NOT* setuid or setgid?**

    We do not want to execute programs that will then change our UID/GID again.

18. **Is the target user/group the same as the program's user/group?**

    Is the user the owner of the file?

19. **Can we successfully clean the process environment to ensure safe operations?**

    suEXEC cleans the process' environment by establishing a safe execution PATH (defined during configuration), as well as only passing through those variables whose names are listed in the safe environment list (also created during configuration).

20. **Can we successfully become the target CGI/SSI program and execute?**

    Here is where suEXEC ends and the target CGI/SSI program begins.

This is the standard operation of the suEXEC wrapper's security model. It is somewhat stringent and can impose new limitations and guidelines for CGI/SSI design, but it was developed carefully step-by-step with security in mind.

For more information as to how this security model can limit your possibilities in regards to server configuration, as well as what security risks can be avoided with a proper suEXEC setup, see the "Beware the Jabberwock" section of this document.

## Configuring & Installing suEXEC

Here's where we begin the fun.

**suEXEC configuration options**

**`--enable-suexec`** This option enables the suEXEC feature which is never installed or activated by default. At least one `--with-suexec-xxxxx` option has to be provided together with the `--enable-suexec` option to let APACI accept your request for using the suEXEC feature.

**`--enable-suexec-capabilities`** **Linux specific:** Normally, the `suexec` binary is installed "setuid/setgid root", which allows it to run with the full privileges of the root user. If this option is used, the `suexec` binary will instead be installed with only the setuid/setgid "capability" bits set, which is the subset of full root priviliges required for suexec operation. Note that the `suexec` binary may not be able to write to a log file in this mode; it is recommended that the `--with-suexec-syslog --without-suexec-logfile` options are used in conjunction with this mode, so that syslog logging is used instead.

**`--with-suexec-bin=PATH`** The path to the `suexec` binary must be hard-coded in the server for security reasons. Use this option to override the default path. *e.g.* `--with-suexec-bin=/usr/sbin/suexec`

**`--with-suexec-caller=UID`** The username (p. 990) under which httpd normally runs. This is the only user allowed to execute the suEXEC wrapper.

**`--with-suexec-userdir=DIR`** Define to be the subdirectory under users' home directories where suEXEC access should be allowed. All executables under this directory will be executable by suEXEC as the user so they should be "safe" programs. If you are using a "simple" USERDIR directive (ie. one without a "*" in it) this should be set to the same value. suEXEC will not work properly in cases where the USERDIR directive points to a location that is not the same as the user's home directory as referenced in the `passwd` file. Default value is `"public_html"`.

If you have virtual hosts with a different USERDIR for each, you will need to define them to all reside in one parent directory; then name that parent directory here. **If this is not defined properly, "˜userdir" cgi requests will not work!**

**--with-suexec-docroot=*DIR*** Define as the DocumentRoot set for httpd.  This will be the only hierarchy (aside from USERDIRS) that can be used for suEXEC behavior.  The default directory is the `--datadir` value with the suffix `"/htdocs"`, *e.g.* if you configure with `"--datadir=/home/apache"` the directory `"/home/apache/htdocs"` is used as document root for the suEXEC wrapper.

**--with-suexec-uidmin=*UID*** Define this as the lowest UID allowed to be a target user for suEXEC. For most systems, 500 or 100 is common. Default value is 100.

**--with-suexec-gidmin=*GID*** Define this as the lowest GID allowed to be a target group for suEXEC. For most systems, 100 is common and therefore used as default value.

**--with-suexec-logfile=*FILE*** This defines the filename to which all suEXEC transactions and errors are logged (useful for auditing and debugging purposes).  By default the logfile is named `"suexec_log"` and located in your standard logfile directory (`--logfiledir`).

**--with-suexec-syslog** If defined, suexec will log notices and errors to syslog instead of a logfile. This option must be combined with `--without-suexec-logfile`.

**--with-suexec-safepath=*PATH*** Define a safe PATH environment to pass to CGI executables. Default value is `"/usr/local/bin:/usr/bin:/bin"`.

### Compiling and installing the suEXEC wrapper

If you have enabled the suEXEC feature with the `--enable-suexec` option the `suexec` binary (together with httpd itself) is automatically built if you execute the `make` command.

After all components have been built you can execute the command `make install` to install them.  The binary image `suexec` is installed in the directory defined by the `--sbindir` option.  The default location is "/usr/local/apache2/bin/suexec".

Please note that you need *root privileges* for the installation step.  In order for the wrapper to set the user ID, it must be installed as owner `root` and must have the setuserid execution bit set for file modes.

### Setting paranoid permissions

Although the suEXEC wrapper will check to ensure that its caller is the correct user as specified with the `--with-suexec-caller configure` option, there is always the possibility that a system or library call suEXEC uses before this check may be exploitable on your system. To counter this, and because it is best-practise in general, you should use filesystem permissions to ensure that only the group httpd runs as may execute suEXEC.

If for example, your web server is configured to run as:

```
User www
Group webgroup
```

and `suexec` is installed at "/usr/local/apache2/bin/suexec", you should run:

```
chgrp webgroup /usr/local/apache2/bin/suexec
chmod 4750 /usr/local/apache2/bin/suexec
```

This will ensure that only the group httpd runs as can even execute the suEXEC wrapper.

## Enabling & Disabling suEXEC

Upon startup of httpd, it looks for the file `suexec` in the directory defined by the `--sbindir` option (default is "/usr/local/apache/sbin/suexec"). If httpd finds a properly configured suEXEC wrapper, it will print the following message to the error log:

```
[notice] suEXEC mechanism enabled (wrapper: /path/to/suexec)
```

If you don't see this message at server startup, the server is most likely not finding the wrapper program where it expects it, or the executable is not installed *setuid root*.

If you want to enable the suEXEC mechanism for the first time and an Apache HTTP Server is already running you must kill and restart httpd. Restarting it with a simple HUP or USR1 signal will not be enough.

If you want to disable suEXEC you should kill and restart httpd after you have removed the `suexec` file.

## Using suEXEC

Requests for CGI programs will call the suEXEC wrapper only if they are for a virtual host containing a SUEXE-CUSERGROUP directive or if they are processed by MOD_USERDIR.

**Virtual Hosts:**
One way to use the suEXEC wrapper is through the SUEXECUSERGROUP directive in VIRTUALHOST definitions. By setting this directive to values different from the main server user ID, all requests for CGI resources will be executed as the *User* and *Group* defined for that <VIRTUALHOST>. If this directive is not specified for a <VIRTUALHOST> then the main server userid is assumed.

**User directories:**
Requests that are processed by MOD_USERDIR will call the suEXEC wrapper to execute CGI programs under the userid of the requested user directory. The only requirement needed for this feature to work is for CGI execution to be enabled for the user and that the script must meet the scrutiny of the security checks above. See also the `--with-suexec-userdir` compile time option.

## Debugging suEXEC

The suEXEC wrapper will write log information to the file defined with the `--with-suexec-logfile` option as indicated above, or to syslog if `--with-suexec-syslog` is used. If you feel you have configured and installed the wrapper properly, have a look at the log and the error_log for the server to see where you may have gone astray. The output of "`suexec -V`" will show the options used to compile suexec, if using a binary distribution.

## Beware the Jabberwock: Warnings & Examples

**NOTE!** This section may not be complete. For the latest revision of this section of the documentation, see the Online Documentation[40] version.

There are a few points of interest regarding the wrapper that can cause limitations on server setup. Please review these before submitting any "bugs" regarding suEXEC.

- **suEXEC Points Of Interest**

---

[40]http://httpd.apache.org/docs/trunk/suexec.html

- Hierarchy limitations

  For security and efficiency reasons, all suEXEC requests must remain within either a top-level document root for virtual host requests, or one top-level personal document root for userdir requests. For example, if you have four VirtualHosts configured, you would need to structure all of your VHosts' document roots off of one main httpd document hierarchy to take advantage of suEXEC for VirtualHosts. (Example forthcoming.)

- suEXEC's PATH environment variable

  This can be a dangerous thing to change. Make certain every path you include in this define is a **trusted** directory. You don't want to open people up to having someone from across the world running a trojan horse on them.

- Altering the suEXEC code

  Again, this can cause **Big Trouble** if you try this without knowing what you are doing. Stay away from it if at all possible.

# 2.22   Issues Regarding DNS and Apache HTTP Server

This page could be summarized with the statement: don't configure Apache HTTP Server in such a way that it relies on DNS resolution for parsing of the configuration files. If httpd requires DNS resolution to parse the configuration files then your server may be subject to reliability problems (ie. it might not start up), or denial and theft of service attacks (including virtual hosts able to steal hits from other virtual hosts).

## A Simple Example

```
# This is a misconfiguration example, do not use on your server
<VirtualHost www.example.dom>
  ServerAdmin webgirl@example.dom
  DocumentRoot "/www/example"
</VirtualHost>
```

In order for the server to function properly, it absolutely needs to have two pieces of information about each virtual host: the SERVERNAME and at least one IP address that the server will bind and respond to. The above example does not include the IP address, so httpd must use DNS to find the address of www.example.dom. If for some reason DNS is not available at the time your server is parsing its config file, then this virtual host **will not be configured**. It won't be able to respond to any hits to this virtual host.

Suppose that www.example.dom has address 192.0.2.1. Then consider this configuration snippet:

```
# This is a misconfiguration example, do not use on your server
<VirtualHost 192.0.2.1>
  ServerAdmin webgirl@example.dom
  DocumentRoot "/www/example"
</VirtualHost>
```

This time httpd needs to use reverse DNS to find the ServerName for this virtualhost. If that reverse lookup fails then it will partially disable the virtualhost. If the virtual host is name-based then it will effectively be totally disabled, but if it is IP-based then it will mostly work. However, if httpd should ever have to generate a full URL for the server which includes the server name (such as when a Redirect is issued), then it will fail to generate a valid URL.

Here is a snippet that avoids both of these problems:

```
<VirtualHost 192.0.2.1>
  ServerName www.example.dom
  ServerAdmin webgirl@example.dom
  DocumentRoot "/www/example"
</VirtualHost>
```

## Denial of Service

Consider this configuration snippet:

```
<VirtualHost www.example1.dom>
  ServerAdmin webgirl@example1.dom
  DocumentRoot "/www/example1"
</VirtualHost>
<VirtualHost www.example2.dom>
  ServerAdmin webguy@example2.dom
```

```
  DocumentRoot "/www/example2"
</VirtualHost>
```

Suppose that you've assigned 192.0.2.1 to `www.example1.dom` and 192.0.2.2 to `www.example2.dom`. Furthermore, suppose that `example1.dom` has control of their own DNS. With this config you have put `example1.dom` into a position where they can steal all traffic destined to `example2.dom`. To do so, all they have to do is set `www.example1.dom` to 192.0.2.2. Since they control their own DNS you can't stop them from pointing the `www.example1.dom` record wherever they wish.

Requests coming in to 192.0.2.2 (including all those where users typed in URLs of the form `http://www.example2.dom/whatever`) will all be served by the `example1.dom` virtual host. To better understand why this happens requires a more in-depth discussion of how httpd matches up incoming requests with the virtual host that will serve it. A rough document describing this is available (p. 141) .

## The "main server" Address

Name-based virtual host support (p. 125) requires httpd to know the IP address(es) of the host that `httpd` is running on. To get this address it uses either the global SERVERNAME (if present) or calls the C function `gethostname` (which should return the same as typing "hostname" at the command prompt). Then it performs a DNS lookup on this address. At present there is no way to avoid this lookup.

If you fear that this lookup might fail because your DNS server is down then you can insert the hostname in `/etc/hosts` (where you probably already have it so that the machine can boot properly). Then ensure that your machine is configured to use `/etc/hosts` in the event that DNS fails. Depending on what OS you are using this might be accomplished by editing `/etc/resolv.conf`, or maybe `/etc/nsswitch.conf`.

If your server doesn't have to perform DNS for any other reason then you might be able to get away with running httpd with the HOSTRESORDER environment variable set to "local". This all depends on what OS and resolver libraries you are using. It also affects CGIs unless you use MOD_ENV to control the environment. It's best to consult the man pages or FAQs for your OS.

## Tips to Avoid These Problems

- use IP addresses in VIRTUALHOST
- use IP addresses in LISTEN
- ensure all virtual hosts have an explicit SERVERNAME
- create a `<VirtualHost _default_:*>` server that has no pages to serve

# Chapter 3

# Apache Virtual Host documentation

## 3.1  Apache Virtual Host documentation

The term *Virtual Host* refers to the practice of running more than one web site (such as `company1.example.com` and `company2.example.com`) on a single machine. Virtual hosts can be "IP-based (p. 128) ", meaning that you have a different IP address for every web site, or "name-based (p. 125) ", meaning that you have multiple names running on each IP address. The fact that they are running on the same physical server is not apparent to the end user.

Apache was one of the first servers to support IP-based virtual hosts right out of the box. Versions 1.1 and later of Apache support both IP-based and name-based virtual hosts (vhosts). The latter variant of virtual hosts is sometimes also called *host-based* or *non-IP virtual hosts.*

Below is a list of documentation pages which explain all details of virtual host support in Apache HTTP Server:

**See also**

- MOD_VHOST_ALIAS
- Name-based virtual hosts (p. 125)
- IP-based virtual hosts (p. 128)
- Virtual host examples (p. 134)
- File descriptor limits (p. 144)
- Mass virtual hosting (p. 130)
- Details of host matching (p. 141)

### Virtual Host Support

- Name-based Virtual Hosts (p. 125) (More than one web site per IP address)
- IP-based Virtual Hosts (p. 128) (An IP address for each web site)
- Virtual Host examples for common setups (p. 134)
- File Descriptor Limits (p. 144) (or, *Too many log files*)
- Dynamically Configured Mass Virtual Hosting (p. 130)
- In-Depth Discussion of Virtual Host Matching (p. 141)

### Configuration directives

- <VIRTUALHOST>
- SERVERNAME
- SERVERALIAS
- SERVERPATH

If you are trying to debug your virtual host configuration, you may find the Apache -S command line switch useful. That is, type the following command:

```
/usr/local/apache2/bin/httpd -S
```

This command will dump out a description of how Apache parsed the configuration file. Careful examination of the IP addresses and server names may help uncover configuration mistakes. (See the docs for the `httpd` program for other command line options)

# 3.2   Name-based Virtual Host Support

This document describes when and how to use name-based virtual hosts.

**See also**

- IP-based Virtual Host Support (p. 128)
- An In-Depth Discussion of Virtual Host Matching (p. 141)
- Dynamically configured mass virtual hosting (p. 130)
- Virtual Host examples for common setups (p. 134)

## Name-based vs. IP-based Virtual Hosts

IP-based virtual hosts (p. 128) use the IP address of the connection to determine the correct virtual host to serve. Therefore you need to have a separate IP address for each host.

With name-based virtual hosting, the server relies on the client to report the hostname as part of the HTTP headers. Using this technique, many different hosts can share the same IP address.

Name-based virtual hosting is usually simpler, since you need only configure your DNS server to map each hostname to the correct IP address and then configure the Apache HTTP Server to recognize the different hostnames. Name-based virtual hosting also eases the demand for scarce IP addresses. Therefore you should use name-based virtual hosting unless you are using equipment that explicitly demands IP-based hosting. Historical reasons for IP-based virtual hosting based on client support are no longer applicable to a general-purpose web server.

Name-based virtual hosting builds off of the IP-based virtual host selection algorithm, meaning that searches for the proper server name occur only between virtual hosts that have the best IP-based address.

## How the server selects the proper name-based virtual host

It is important to recognize that the first step in name-based virtual host resolution is IP-based resolution. Name-based virtual host resolution only chooses the most appropriate name-based virtual host after narrowing down the candidates to the best IP-based match. Using a wildcard (*) for the IP address in all of the VirtualHost directives makes this IP-based mapping irrelevant.

When a request arrives, the server will find the best (most specific) matching <VIRTUALHOST> argument based on the IP address and port used by the request. If there is more than one virtual host containing this best-match address and port combination, Apache will further compare the SERVERNAME and SERVERALIAS directives to the server name present in the request.

If you omit the SERVERNAME directive from any name-based virtual host, the server will default to a fully qualified domain name (FQDN) derived from the system hostname. This implicitly set server name can lead to counter-intuitive virtual host matching and is discouraged.

### The default name-based vhost for an IP and port combination

If no matching ServerName or ServerAlias is found in the set of virtual hosts containing the most specific matching IP address and port combination, then **the first listed virtual host** that matches that will be used.

## Using Name-based Virtual Hosts

| Related Modules | Related Directives |
| --- | --- |
| CORE | DOCUMENTROOT |
| | SERVERALIAS |
| | SERVERNAME |
| | <VIRTUALHOST> |

The first step is to create a <VIRTUALHOST> block for each different host that you would like to serve. Inside each <VIRTUALHOST> block, you will need at minimum a SERVERNAME directive to designate which host is served and a DOCUMENTROOT directive to show where in the filesystem the content for that host lives.

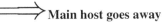**Main host goes away**

Any request that doesn't match an existing <VIRTUALHOST> is handled by the global server configuration, regardless of the hostname or ServerName.

When you add a name-based virtual host to an existing server, and the virtual host arguments match preexisting IP and port combinations, requests will now be handled by an explicit virtual host. In this case, it's usually wise to create a default virtual host with a SERVERNAME matching that of the base server. New domains on the same interface and port, but requiring separate configurations, can then be added as subsequent (non-default) virtual hosts.

**ServerName inheritance**

It is best to always explicitly list a SERVERNAME in every name-based virtual host.

If a VIRTUALHOST doesn't specify a SERVERNAME, a server name will be inherited from the base server configuration. If no server name was specified globally, one is detected at startup through reverse DNS resolution of the first listening address. In either case, this inherited server name will influence name-based virtual host resolution, so it is best to always explicitly list a SERVERNAME in every name-based virtual host.

For example, suppose that you are serving the domain www.example.com and you wish to add the virtual host other.example.com, which points at the same IP address. Then you simply add the following to httpd.conf:

```
<VirtualHost *:80>
    # This first-listed virtual host is also the default for *:80
    ServerName www.example.com
    ServerAlias example.com
    DocumentRoot "/www/domain"
</VirtualHost>

<VirtualHost *:80>
    ServerName other.example.com
    DocumentRoot "/www/otherdomain"
</VirtualHost>
```

You can alternatively specify an explicit IP address in place of the * in <VIRTUALHOST> directives. For example, you might want to do this in order to run some name-based virtual hosts on one IP address, and either IP-based, or another set of name-based virtual hosts on another address.

Many servers want to be accessible by more than one name. This is possible with the SERVERALIAS directive, placed inside the <VIRTUALHOST> section. For example in the first <VIRTUALHOST> block above, the SERVERALIAS directive indicates that the listed names are other names which people can use to see that same web site:

```
ServerAlias example.com *.example.com
```

then requests for all hosts in the `example.com` domain will be served by the `www.example.com` virtual host. The wildcard characters `*` and `?` can be used to match names. Of course, you can't just make up names and place them in SERVERNAME or `ServerAlias`. You must first have your DNS server properly configured to map those names to an IP address associated with your server.

Name-based virtual hosts for the best-matching set of <VIRTUALHOST>s are processed in the order they appear in the configuration. The first matching SERVERNAME or SERVERALIAS is used, with no different precedence for wildcards (nor for ServerName vs. ServerAlias).

The complete list of names in the VIRTUALHOST directive are treated just like a (non wildcard) SERVERALIAS.

Finally, you can fine-tune the configuration of the virtual hosts by placing other directives inside the <VIRTUAL-HOST> containers. Most directives can be placed in these containers and will then change the configuration only of the relevant virtual host. To find out if a particular directive is allowed, check the Context (p. 377) of the directive. Configuration directives set in the *main server context* (outside any <VIRTUALHOST> container) will be used only if they are not overridden by the virtual host settings.

# 3.3   Apache IP-based Virtual Host Support

**See also**

- Name-based Virtual Hosts Support (p. 125)

## What is IP-based virtual hosting

IP-based virtual hosting is a method to apply different directives based on the IP address and port a request is received on. Most commonly, this is used to serve different websites on different ports or interfaces.

In many cases, name-based virtual hosts (p. 125) are more convenient, because they allow many virtual hosts to share a single address/port. See Name-based vs. IP-based Virtual Hosts (p. 125) to help you decide.

## System requirements

As the term *IP-based* indicates, the server **must have a different IP address/port combination for each IP-based virtual host**. This can be achieved by the machine having several physical network connections, or by use of virtual interfaces which are supported by most modern operating systems (see system documentation for details, these are frequently called "ip aliases", and the "ifconfig" command is most commonly used to set them up), and/or using multiple port numbers.

In the terminology of Apache HTTP Server, using a single IP address but multiple TCP ports, is also IP-based virtual hosting.

## How to set up Apache

There are two ways of configuring apache to support multiple hosts. Either by running a separate `httpd` daemon for each hostname, or by running a single daemon which supports all the virtual hosts.

Use multiple daemons when:

- There are security partitioning issues, such as company1 does not want anyone at company2 to be able to read their data except via the web. In this case you would need two daemons, each running with different USER, GROUP, LISTEN, and SERVERROOT settings.
- You can afford the memory and file descriptor requirements of listening to every IP alias on the machine. It's only possible to LISTEN to the "wildcard" address, or to specific addresses. So if you have a need to listen to a specific address for whatever reason, then you will need to listen to all specific addresses. (Although one `httpd` could listen to N-1 of the addresses, and another could listen to the remaining address.)

Use a single daemon when:

- Sharing of the httpd configuration between virtual hosts is acceptable.
- The machine services a large number of requests, and so the performance loss in running separate daemons may be significant.

## Setting up multiple daemons

Create a separate `httpd` installation for each virtual host. For each installation, use the LISTEN directive in the configuration file to select which IP address (or virtual host) that daemon services. e.g.

```
Listen 192.0.2.100:80
```

It is recommended that you use an IP address instead of a hostname (see DNS caveats (p. 121) ).

### Setting up a single daemon with virtual hosts

For this case, a single `httpd` will service requests for the main server and all the virtual hosts. The VIRTUALHOST directive in the configuration file is used to set the values of SERVERADMIN, SERVERNAME, DOCUMENTROOT, ERRORLOG and TRANSFERLOG or CUSTOMLOG configuration directives to different values for each virtual host. e.g.

```
<VirtualHost 172.20.30.40:80>
    ServerAdmin webmaster@www1.example.com
    DocumentRoot "/www/vhosts/www1"
    ServerName www1.example.com
    ErrorLog "/www/logs/www1/error_log"
    CustomLog "/www/logs/www1/access_log" combined
</VirtualHost>

<VirtualHost 172.20.30.50:80>
    ServerAdmin "webmaster@www2.example.org"
    DocumentRoot "/www/vhosts/www2"
    ServerName www2.example.org
    ErrorLog "/www/logs/www2/error_log"
    CustomLog "/www/logs/www2/access_log" combined
</VirtualHost>
```

It is recommended that you use an IP address instead of a hostname in the <VirtualHost> directive (see DNS caveats (p. 121) ).

Specific IP addresses or ports have precedence over their wildcard equivalents, and any virtual host that matches has precedence over the servers base configuration.

Almost **any** configuration directive can be put in the VirtualHost directive, with the exception of directives that control process creation and a few other directives. To find out if a directive can be used in the VirtualHost directive, check the Context (p. 377) using the directive index (p. 1106) .

SUEXECUSERGROUP may be used inside a VirtualHost directive if the suEXEC wrapper (p. 115) is used.

*SECURITY:* When specifying where to write log files, be aware of some security risks which are present if anyone other than the user that starts Apache has write access to the directory where they are written. See the security tips (p. 364) document for details.

# 3.4   Dynamically Configured Mass Virtual Hosting

This document describes how to efficiently serve an arbitrary number of virtual hosts with the Apache HTTP Server. A separate document (p. 162) discusses using MOD_REWRITE to create dynamic mass virtual hosts.

## Motivation

The techniques described here are of interest if your httpd.conf contains many <VirtualHost> sections that are substantially the same, for example:

```
<VirtualHost 111.22.33.44>
    ServerName                 customer-1.example.com
    DocumentRoot        "/www/hosts/customer-1.example.com/docs"
    ScriptAlias  "/cgi-bin/"  "/www/hosts/customer-1.example.com/cgi-bin"
</VirtualHost>

<VirtualHost 111.22.33.44>
    ServerName                 customer-2.example.com
    DocumentRoot        "/www/hosts/customer-2.example.com/docs"
    ScriptAlias  "/cgi-bin/"  "/www/hosts/customer-2.example.com/cgi-bin"
</VirtualHost>

<VirtualHost 111.22.33.44>
    ServerName                 customer-N.example.com
    DocumentRoot        "/www/hosts/customer-N.example.com/docs"
    ScriptAlias  "/cgi-bin/"  "/www/hosts/customer-N.example.com/cgi-bin"
</VirtualHost>
```

We wish to replace these multiple <VirtualHost> blocks with a mechanism that works them out dynamically. This has a number of advantages:

1. Your configuration file is smaller, so Apache starts more quickly and uses less memory. Perhaps more importantly, the smaller configuration is easier to maintain, and leaves less room for errors.

2. Adding virtual hosts is simply a matter of creating the appropriate directories in the filesystem and entries in the DNS - you don't need to reconfigure or restart Apache.

The main disadvantage is that you cannot have a different log file for each virtual host; however, if you have many virtual hosts, doing this can be a bad idea anyway, because of the number of file descriptors needed (p. 144) . It is better to log to a pipe or a fifo (p. 56) , and arrange for the process at the other end to split up the log files into one per virtual host. One example of such a process can be found in the split-logfile (p. 336) utility.

## Overview

A virtual host is defined by two pieces of information: its IP address, and the contents of the Host: header in the HTTP request. The dynamic mass virtual hosting technique used here is based on automatically inserting this information into the pathname of the file that is used to satisfy the request. This can be most easily done by using MOD_VHOST_ALIAS with Apache httpd. Alternatively, mod_rewrite can be used (p. 162) .

Both of these modules are disabled by default; you must enable one of them when configuring and building Apache httpd if you want to use this technique.

A couple of things need to be determined from the request in order to make the dynamic virtual host look like a normal one. The most important is the server name, which is used by the server to generate self-referential URLs etc. It is configured with the ServerName directive, and it is available to CGIs via the SERVER_NAME environment variable. The actual value used at run time is controlled by the UseCanonicalName setting. With UseCanonicalName Off, the server name is taken from the contents of the Host: header in the request. With UseCanonicalName DNS, it is taken from a reverse DNS lookup of the virtual host's IP address. The former setting is used for name-based dynamic virtual hosting, and the latter is used for IP-based hosting. If httpd cannot work out the server name because there is no Host: header, or the DNS lookup fails, then the value configured with ServerName is used instead.

The other thing to determine is the document root (configured with DocumentRoot and available to CGI scripts via the DOCUMENT_ROOT environment variable). In a normal configuration, this is used by the core module when mapping URIs to filenames, but when the server is configured to do dynamic virtual hosting, that job must be taken over by another module (either MOD_VHOST_ALIAS or MOD_REWRITE), which has a different way of doing the mapping. Neither of these modules is responsible for setting the DOCUMENT_ROOT environment variable so if any CGIs or SSI documents make use of it, they will get a misleading value.

## Dynamic Virtual Hosts with mod_vhost_alias

This extract from httpd.conf implements the virtual host arrangement outlined in the Motivation section above using MOD_VHOST_ALIAS.

```
# get the server name from the Host: header
UseCanonicalName Off

# this log format can be split per-virtual-host based on the first field
# using the split-logfile utility.
LogFormat "%V %h %l %u %t \"%r\" %s %b" vcommon
CustomLog "logs/access_log" vcommon

# include the server name in the filenames used to satisfy requests
VirtualDocumentRoot "/www/hosts/%0/docs"
VirtualScriptAlias  "/www/hosts/%0/cgi-bin"
```

This configuration can be changed into an IP-based virtual hosting solution by just turning UseCanonicalName Off into UseCanonicalName DNS. The server name that is inserted into the filename is then derived from the IP address of the virtual host. The variable %0 references the requested servername, as indicated in the Host: header.

See the MOD_VHOST_ALIAS documentation for more usage examples.

## Simplified Dynamic Virtual Hosts

This is an adjustment of the above system, tailored for an ISP's web hosting server. Using %2, we can select substrings of the server name to use in the filename so that, for example, the documents for www.user.example.com are found in /home/user/www. It uses a single cgi-bin directory instead of one per virtual host.

```
UseCanonicalName Off

LogFormat "%V %h %l %u %t \"%r\" %s %b" vcommon
CustomLog "logs/access_log" vcommon

# include part of the server name in the filenames
VirtualDocumentRoot "/home/%2/www"
```

```
# single cgi-bin directory
ScriptAlias  "/cgi-bin/"  "/www/std-cgi/"
```

There are examples of more complicated `VirtualDocumentRoot` settings in the MOD_VHOST_ALIAS documentation.

## Using Multiple Virtual Hosting Systems on the Same Server

With more complicated setups, you can use httpd's normal `<VirtualHost>` directives to control the scope of the various virtual hosting configurations. For example, you could have one IP address for general customers' homepages, and another for commercial customers, with the following setup. This can be combined with conventional `<VirtualHost>` configuration sections, as shown below.

```
UseCanonicalName Off

LogFormat "%V %h %l %u %t \"%r\" %s %b" vcommon

<Directory "/www/commercial">
    Options FollowSymLinks
    AllowOverride All
</Directory>

<Directory "/www/homepages">
    Options FollowSymLinks
    AllowOverride None
</Directory>

<VirtualHost 111.22.33.44>
    ServerName www.commercial.example.com

    CustomLog "logs/access_log.commercial" vcommon

    VirtualDocumentRoot "/www/commercial/%0/docs"
    VirtualScriptAlias  "/www/commercial/%0/cgi-bin"
</VirtualHost>

<VirtualHost 111.22.33.45>
    ServerName www.homepages.example.com

    CustomLog "logs/access_log.homepages" vcommon

    VirtualDocumentRoot "/www/homepages/%0/docs"
    ScriptAlias         "/cgi-bin/" "/www/std-cgi/"
</VirtualHost>
```

⟹ **Note**

> If the first VirtualHost block does *not* include a SERVERNAME directive, the reverse DNS of the relevant IP will be used instead. If this is not the server name you wish to use, a bogus entry (eg. ServerName `none.example.com`) can be added to get around this behaviour.

## More Efficient IP-Based Virtual Hosting

The configuration changes suggested to turn the first example into an IP-based virtual hosting setup result in a rather inefficient setup. A new DNS lookup is required for every request. To avoid this overhead, the filesystem can be arranged to correspond to the IP addresses, instead of to the host names, thereby negating the need for a DNS lookup. Logging will also have to be adjusted to fit this system.

```
# get the server name from the reverse DNS of the IP address
UseCanonicalName DNS

# include the IP address in the logs so they may be split
LogFormat "%A %h %l %u %t \"%r\" %s %b" vcommon
CustomLog "logs/access_log" vcommon

# include the IP address in the filenames
VirtualDocumentRootIP "/www/hosts/%0/docs"
VirtualScriptAliasIP  "/www/hosts/%0/cgi-bin"
```

## Mass virtual hosts with mod_rewrite

Mass virtual hosting may also be accomplished using MOD_REWRITE, either using simple REWRITERULE directives, or using more complicated techniques such as storing the vhost definitions externally and accessing them via REWRITEMAP. These techniques are discussed in the rewrite documentation (p. 162) .

## Mass virtual hosts with mod_macro

Another option for dynamically generated virtual hosts is MOD_MACRO, with which you can create a virtualhost template, and invoke it for multiple hostnames. An example of this is provided in the **Usage** section of the module documentation.

## 3.5    VirtualHost Examples

This document attempts to answer the commonly-asked questions about setting up virtual hosts (p. 124). These scenarios are those involving multiple web sites running on a single server, via name-based (p. 125) or IP-based (p. 128) virtual hosts.

### Running several name-based web sites on a single IP address.

Your server has multiple hostnames that resolve to a single address, and you want to respond differently for `www.example.com` and `www.example.org`.

Note

> Creating virtual host configurations on your Apache server does not magically cause DNS
> entries to be created for those host names. You *must* have the names in DNS, resolving to your
> IP address, or nobody else will be able to see your web site. You can put entries in your `hosts`
> file for local testing, but that will work only from the machine with those `hosts` entries.

```
# Ensure that Apache listens on port 80
Listen 80
<VirtualHost *:80>
    DocumentRoot "/www/example1"
    ServerName www.example.com

    # Other directives here
</VirtualHost>

<VirtualHost *:80>
    DocumentRoot "/www/example2"
    ServerName www.example.org

    # Other directives here
</VirtualHost>
```

The asterisks match all addresses, so the main server serves no requests. Due to the fact that the virtual host with `ServerName www.example.com` is first in the configuration file, it has the highest priority and can be seen as the *default* or *primary* server. That means that if a request is received that does not match one of the specified `ServerName` directives, it will be served by this first `VirtualHost`.

The above configuration is what you will want to use in almost all name-based virtual hosting situations. The only thing that this configuration will not work for, in fact, is when you are serving different content based on differing IP addresses or ports.

Note

> You may replace * with a specific IP address on the system. Such virtual hosts will only be
> used for HTTP requests received on connection to the specified IP address.
> However, it is additionally useful to use * on systems where the IP address is not predictable
> - for example if you have a dynamic IP address with your ISP, and you are using some variety
> of dynamic DNS solution. Since * matches any IP address, this configuration would work
> without changes whenever your IP address changes.

## Name-based hosts on more than one IP address.

Note

Any of the techniques discussed here can be extended to any number of IP addresses.

The server has two IP addresses. On one (172.20.30.40), we will serve the "main" server, server.example.com and on the other (172.20.30.50), we will serve two or more virtual hosts.

```
Listen 80

# This is the "main" server running on 172.20.30.40
ServerName server.example.com
DocumentRoot "/www/mainserver"

<VirtualHost 172.20.30.50>
    DocumentRoot "/www/example1"
    ServerName www.example.com

    # Other directives here ...
</VirtualHost>

<VirtualHost 172.20.30.50>
    DocumentRoot "/www/example2"
    ServerName www.example.org

    # Other directives here ...
</VirtualHost>
```

Any request to an address other than 172.20.30.50 will be served from the main server. A request to 172.20.30.50 with an unknown hostname, or no Host: header, will be served from www.example.com.

## Serving the same content on different IP addresses (such as an internal and external address).

The server machine has two IP addresses (192.168.1.1 and 172.20.30.40). The machine is sitting between an internal (intranet) network and an external (internet) network. Outside of the network, the name server.example.com resolves to the external address (172.20.30.40), but inside the network, that same name resolves to the internal address (192.168.1.1).

The server can be made to respond to internal and external requests with the same content, with just one VirtualHost section.

```
<VirtualHost 192.168.1.1 172.20.30.40>
    DocumentRoot "/www/server1"
    ServerName server.example.com
    ServerAlias server
</VirtualHost>
```

Now requests from both networks will be served from the same VirtualHost.

Note:

On the internal network, one can just use the name server rather than the fully qualified host name server.example.com.

Note also that, in the above example, you can replace the list of IP addresses with *, which will cause the server to respond the same on all addresses.

**Running different sites on different ports.**

You have multiple domains going to the same IP and also want to serve multiple ports. The example below illustrates that the name-matching takes place after the best matching IP address and port combination is determined.

```
Listen 80
Listen 8080

<VirtualHost 172.20.30.40:80>
    ServerName www.example.com
    DocumentRoot "/www/domain-80"
</VirtualHost>

<VirtualHost 172.20.30.40:8080>
    ServerName www.example.com
    DocumentRoot "/www/domain-8080"
</VirtualHost>

<VirtualHost 172.20.30.40:80>
    ServerName www.example.org
    DocumentRoot "/www/otherdomain-80"
</VirtualHost>

<VirtualHost 172.20.30.40:8080>
    ServerName www.example.org
    DocumentRoot "/www/otherdomain-8080"
</VirtualHost>
```

**IP-based virtual hosting**

The server has two IP addresses (`172.20.30.40` and `172.20.30.50`) which resolve to the names `www.example.com` and `www.example.org` respectively.

```
Listen 80

<VirtualHost 172.20.30.40>
    DocumentRoot "/www/example1"
    ServerName www.example.com
</VirtualHost>

<VirtualHost 172.20.30.50>
    DocumentRoot "/www/example2"
    ServerName www.example.org
</VirtualHost>
```

Requests for any address not specified in one of the `<VirtualHost>` directives (such as `localhost`, for example) will go to the main server, if there is one.

**Mixed port-based and ip-based virtual hosts**

The server machine has two IP addresses (`172.20.30.40` and `172.20.30.50`) which resolve to the names `www.example.com` and `www.example.org` respectively. In each case, we want to run hosts on ports 80 and

8080.

```
Listen 172.20.30.40:80
Listen 172.20.30.40:8080
Listen 172.20.30.50:80
Listen 172.20.30.50:8080

<VirtualHost 172.20.30.40:80>
    DocumentRoot "/www/example1-80"
    ServerName www.example.com
</VirtualHost>

<VirtualHost 172.20.30.40:8080>
    DocumentRoot "/www/example1-8080"
    ServerName www.example.com
</VirtualHost>

<VirtualHost 172.20.30.50:80>
    DocumentRoot "/www/example2-80"
    ServerName www.example.org
</VirtualHost>

<VirtualHost 172.20.30.50:8080>
    DocumentRoot "/www/example2-8080"
    ServerName www.example.org
</VirtualHost>
```

## Mixed name-based and IP-based vhosts

Any address mentioned in the argument to a virtualhost that never appears in another virtual host is a strictly IP-based virtual host.

```
Listen 80
<VirtualHost 172.20.30.40>
    DocumentRoot "/www/example1"
    ServerName www.example.com
</VirtualHost>

<VirtualHost 172.20.30.40>
    DocumentRoot "/www/example2"
    ServerName www.example.org
</VirtualHost>

<VirtualHost 172.20.30.40>
    DocumentRoot "/www/example3"
    ServerName www.example.net
</VirtualHost>

# IP-based
<VirtualHost 172.20.30.50>
    DocumentRoot "/www/example4"
    ServerName www.example.edu
```

```
</VirtualHost>

<VirtualHost 172.20.30.60>
    DocumentRoot "/www/example5"
    ServerName www.example.gov
</VirtualHost>
```

## Using `Virtual_host` and mod_proxy together

The following example allows a front-end machine to proxy a virtual host through to a server running on another machine. In the example, a virtual host of the same name is configured on a machine at `192.168.111.2`. The PROXYPRESERVEHOST ON directive is used so that the desired hostname is passed through, in case we are proxying multiple hostnames to a single machine.

```
<VirtualHost *:*>
    ProxyPreserveHost On
    ProxyPass        "/" "http://192.168.111.2/"
    ProxyPassReverse "/" "http://192.168.111.2/"
    ServerName hostname.example.com
</VirtualHost>
```

## Using `_default_` vhosts

### `_default_` vhosts for all ports

Catching *every* request to any unspecified IP address and port, *i.e.*, an address/port combination that is not used for any other virtual host.

```
<VirtualHost _default_:*>
    DocumentRoot "/www/default"
</VirtualHost>
```

Using such a default vhost with a wildcard port effectively prevents any request going to the main server.

A default vhost never serves a request that was sent to an address/port that is used for name-based vhosts. If the request contained an unknown or no `Host:` header it is always served from the primary name-based vhost (the vhost for that address/port appearing first in the configuration file).

You can use ALIASMATCH or REWRITERULE to rewrite any request to a single information page (or script).

### `_default_` vhosts for different ports

Same as setup 1, but the server listens on several ports and we want to use a second `_default_` vhost for port 80.

```
<VirtualHost _default_:80>
    DocumentRoot "/www/default80"
    # ...
</VirtualHost>

<VirtualHost _default_:*>
    DocumentRoot "/www/default"
    # ...
</VirtualHost>
```

The default vhost for port 80 (which *must* appear before any default vhost with a wildcard port) catches all requests that were sent to an unspecified IP address. The main server is never used to serve a request.

### _default_ vhosts for one port

We want to have a default vhost for port 80, but no other default vhosts.

```
<VirtualHost _default_:80>
    DocumentRoot "/www/default"
...
</VirtualHost>
```

A request to an unspecified address on port 80 is served from the default vhost. Any other request to an unspecified address and port is served from the main server.

Any use of * in a virtual host declaration will have higher precedence than _default_.

## Migrating a name-based vhost to an IP-based vhost

The name-based vhost with the hostname www.example.org (from our name-based example, setup 2) should get its own IP address. To avoid problems with name servers or proxies who cached the old IP address for the name-based vhost we want to provide both variants during a migration phase.

The solution is easy, because we can simply add the new IP address (172.20.30.50) to the VirtualHost directive.

```
Listen 80
ServerName www.example.com
DocumentRoot "/www/example1"

<VirtualHost 172.20.30.40 172.20.30.50>
    DocumentRoot "/www/example2"
    ServerName www.example.org
    # ...
</VirtualHost>

<VirtualHost 172.20.30.40>
    DocumentRoot "/www/example3"
    ServerName www.example.net
    ServerAlias *.example.net
    # ...
</VirtualHost>
```

The vhost can now be accessed through the new address (as an IP-based vhost) and through the old address (as a name-based vhost).

## Using the ServerPath directive

We have a server with two name-based vhosts. In order to match the correct virtual host a client must send the correct Host: header. Old HTTP/1.0 clients do not send such a header and Apache has no clue what vhost the client tried to reach (and serves the request from the primary vhost). To provide as much backward compatibility as possible we create a primary vhost which returns a single page containing links with an URL prefix to the name-based virtual hosts.

```
<VirtualHost 172.20.30.40>
    # primary vhost
    DocumentRoot "/www/subdomain"
    RewriteEngine On
    RewriteRule "." "/www/subdomain/index.html"
    # ...
</VirtualHost>

<VirtualHost 172.20.30.40>
    DocumentRoot "/www/subdomain/sub1"
    ServerName www.sub1.domain.tld
    ServerPath /sub1/
    RewriteEngine On
    RewriteRule "^(/sub1/.*)" "/www/subdomain$1"
    # ...
</VirtualHost>

<VirtualHost 172.20.30.40>
    DocumentRoot "/www/subdomain/sub2"
    ServerName www.sub2.domain.tld
    ServerPath /sub2/
    RewriteEngine On
    RewriteRule "^(/sub2/.*)" "/www/subdomain$1"
    # ...
</VirtualHost>
```

Due to the SERVERPATH directive a request to the URL `http://www.sub1.domain.tld/sub1/` is *always* served from the sub1-vhost.
A request to the URL `http://www.sub1.domain.tld/` is only served from the sub1-vhost if the client sent a correct `Host:` header. If no `Host:` header is sent the client gets the information page from the primary host.

Please note that there is one oddity: A request to `http://www.sub2.domain.tld/sub1/` is also served from the sub1-vhost if the client sent no `Host:` header.

The REWRITERULE directives are used to make sure that a client which sent a correct `Host:` header can use both URL variants, *i.e.*, with or without URL prefix.

# 3.6 An In-Depth Discussion of Virtual Host Matching

This document attempts to explain exactly what Apache HTTP Server does when deciding what virtual host to serve a request from.

Most users should read about Name-based vs. IP-based Virtual Hosts (p. 125) to decide which type they want to use, then read more about name-based (p. 125) or IP-based (p. 128) virtualhosts, and then see some examples (p. 134) .

If you want to understand all the details, then you can come back to this page.

**See also**

- IP-based Virtual Host Support (p. 128)
- Name-based Virtual Hosts Support (p. 125)
- Virtual Host examples for common setups (p. 134)
- Dynamically configured mass virtual hosting (p. 130)

## Configuration File

There is a *main server* which consists of all the definitions appearing outside of <VirtualHost> sections.

There are virtual servers, called *vhosts*, which are defined by <VIRTUALHOST> sections.

Each VirtualHost directive includes one or more addresses and optional ports.

Hostnames can be used in place of IP addresses in a virtual host definition, but they are resolved at startup and if any name resolutions fail, those virtual host definitions are ignored. This is, therefore, not recommended.

The address can be specified as *, which will match a request if no other vhost has the explicit address on which the request was received.

The address appearing in the VirtualHost directive can have an optional port. If the port is unspecified, it is treated as a wildcard port, which can also be indicated explicitly using *. The wildcard port matches any port.

(Port numbers specified in the VirtualHost directive do not influence what port numbers Apache will listen on, they only control which VirtualHost will be selected to handle a request. Use the LISTEN directive to control the addresses and ports on which the server listens.)

Collectively the entire set of addresses (including multiple results from DNS lookups) are called the vhost's *address set*.

Apache automatically discriminates on the basis of the HTTP Host header supplied by the client whenever the most specific match for an IP address and port combination is listed in multiple virtual hosts.

The SERVERNAME directive may appear anywhere within the definition of a server. However, each appearance overrides the previous appearance (within that server). If no ServerName is specified, the server attempts to deduce it from the server's IP address.

The first name-based vhost in the configuration file for a given IP:port pair is significant because it is used for all requests received on that address and port for which no other vhost for that IP:port pair has a matching ServerName or ServerAlias. It is also used for all SSL connections if the server does not support Server Name Indication.

The complete list of names in the VirtualHost directive are treated just like a (non wildcard) ServerAlias (but are not overridden by any ServerAlias statement).

For every vhost various default values are set. In particular:

1. If a vhost has no SERVERADMIN, TIMEOUT, KEEPALIVETIMEOUT, KEEPALIVE, MAXKEEPALIV-EREQUESTS, RECEIVEBUFFERSIZE, or SENDBUFFERSIZE directive then the respective value is inherited from the main server. (That is, inherited from whatever the final setting of that value is in the main server.)

2. The "lookup defaults" that define the default directory permissions for a vhost are merged with those of the main server. This includes any per-directory configuration information for any module.

3. The per-server configs for each module from the main server are merged into the vhost server.

Essentially, the main server is treated as "defaults" or a "base" on which to build each vhost. But the positioning of these main server definitions in the config file is largely irrelevant – the entire config of the main server has been parsed when this final merging occurs. So even if a main server definition appears after a vhost definition it might affect the vhost definition.

If the main server has no `ServerName` at this point, then the hostname of the machine that `httpd` is running on is used instead. We will call the *main server address set* those IP addresses returned by a DNS lookup on the `ServerName` of the main server.

For any undefined `ServerName` fields, a name-based vhost defaults to the address given first in the `VirtualHost` statement defining the vhost.

Any vhost that includes the magic `_default_` wildcard is given the same `ServerName` as the main server.

## Virtual Host Matching

The server determines which vhost to use for a request as follows:

### IP address lookup

When the connection is first received on some address and port, the server looks for all the `VirtualHost` definitions that have the same IP address and port.

If there are no exact matches for the address and port, then wildcard (`*`) matches are considered.

If no matches are found, the request is served by the main server.

If there are `VirtualHost` definitions for the IP address, the next step is to decide if we have to deal with an IP-based or a name-based vhost.

### IP-based vhost

If there is exactly one `VirtualHost` directive listing the IP address and port combination that was determined to be the best match, no further actions are performed and the request is served from the matching vhost.

### Name-based vhost

If there are multiple `VirtualHost` directives listing the IP address and port combination that was determined to be the best match, the "list" in the remaining steps refers to the list of vhosts that matched, in the order they were in the configuration file.

If the connection is using SSL, the server supports Server Name Indication, and the SSL client handshake includes the TLS extension with the requested hostname, then that hostname is used below just like the `Host:` header would be used on a non-SSL connection. Otherwise, the first name-based vhost whose address matched is used for SSL connections. This is significant because the vhost determines which certificate the server will use for the connection.

If the request contains a `Host:` header field, the list is searched for the first vhost with a matching `ServerName` or `ServerAlias`, and the request is served from that vhost. A `Host:` header field can contain a port number, but Apache always ignores it and matches against the real port to which the client sent the request.

The first vhost in the config file with the specified IP address has the highest priority and catches any request to an unknown server name, or a request without a `Host:` header field (such as a HTTP/1.0 request).

**Persistent connections**

The *IP lookup* described above is only done *once* for a particular TCP/IP session while the *name lookup* is done on *every* request during a KeepAlive/persistent connection. In other words, a client may request pages from different name-based vhosts during a single persistent connection.

**Absolute URI**

If the URI from the request is an absolute URI, and its hostname and port match the main server or one of the configured virtual hosts *and* match the address and port to which the client sent the request, then the scheme/hostname/port prefix is stripped off and the remaining relative URI is served by the corresponding main server or virtual host. If it does not match, then the URI remains untouched and the request is taken to be a proxy request.

**Observations**

- Name-based virtual hosting is a process applied after the server has selected the best matching IP-based virtual host.

- If you don't care what IP address the client has connected to, use a "*" as the address of every virtual host, and name-based virtual hosting is applied across all configured virtual hosts.

- `ServerName` and `ServerAlias` checks are never performed for an IP-based vhost.

- Only the ordering of name-based vhosts for a specific address set is significant. The one name-based vhosts that comes first in the configuration file has the highest priority for its corresponding address set.

- Any port in the `Host:` header field is never used during the matching process. Apache always uses the real port to which the client sent the request.

- If two vhosts have an address in common, those common addresses act as name-based virtual hosts implicitly. This is new behavior as of 2.3.11.

- The main server is only used to serve a request if the IP address and port number to which the client connected does not match any vhost (including a * vhost). In other words, the main server only catches a request for an unspecified address/port combination (unless there is a _default_ vhost which matches that port).

- You should never specify DNS names in `VirtualHost` directives because it will force your server to rely on DNS to boot. Furthermore it poses a security threat if you do not control the DNS for all the domains listed. There's more information (p. 121) available on this and the next two topics.

- `ServerName` should always be set for each vhost. Otherwise A DNS lookup is required for each vhost.

## Tips

In addition to the tips on the DNS Issues (p. 121) page, here are some further tips:

- Place all main server definitions before any `VirtualHost` definitions. (This is to aid the readability of the configuration – the post-config merging process makes it non-obvious that definitions mixed in around virtual hosts might affect all virtual hosts.)

# 3.7    File Descriptor Limits

When using a large number of Virtual Hosts, Apache may run out of available file descriptors (sometimes called *file handles*) if each Virtual Host specifies different log files. The total number of file descriptors used by Apache is one for each distinct error log file, one for every other log file directive, plus 10-20 for internal use. Unix operating systems limit the number of file descriptors that may be used by a process; the limit is typically 64, and may usually be increased up to a large hard-limit.

Although Apache attempts to increase the limit as required, this may not work if:

1. Your system does not provide the `setrlimit()` system call.

2. The `setrlimit(RLIMIT_NOFILE)` call does not function on your system (such as Solaris 2.3)

3. The number of file descriptors required exceeds the hard limit.

4. Your system imposes other limits on file descriptors, such as a limit on stdio streams only using file descriptors below 256. (Solaris 2)

In the event of problems you can:

- Reduce the number of log files; don't specify log files in the <VIRTUALHOST> sections, but only log to the main log files. (See Splitting up your log files, below, for more information on doing this.)
- If you system falls into 1 or 2 (above), then increase the file descriptor limit before starting Apache, using a script like

```
#!/bin/sh
ulimit -S -n 100
exec httpd
```

## Splitting up your log files

If you want to log multiple virtual hosts to the same log file, you may want to split up the log files afterwards in order to run statistical analysis of the various virtual hosts. This can be accomplished in the following manner.

First, you will need to add the virtual host information to the log entries. This can be done using the LOGFORMAT directive, and the `%v` variable. Add this to the beginning of your log format string:

```
LogFormat "%v %h %l %u %t \"%r\" %>s %b" vhost
CustomLog "logs/multiple_vhost_log" vhost
```

This will create a log file in the common log format, but with the canonical virtual host (whatever appears in the SERVERNAME directive) prepended to each line. (See MOD_LOG_CONFIG for more about customizing your log files.)

When you wish to split your log file into its component parts (one file per virtual host) you can use the program `split-logfile` (p. 336) to accomplish this. You'll find this program in the `support` directory of the Apache distribution.

Run this program with the command:

```
split-logfile < /logs/multiple_vhost_log
```

This program, when run with the name of your vhost log file, will generate one file for each virtual host that appears in your log file. Each file will be called `hostname.log`.

# Chapter 4

# URL Rewriting Guide

# 4.1   Apache mod_rewrite

MOD_REWRITE provides a way to modify incoming URL requests, dynamically, based on regular expression (p. 147) rules. This allows you to map arbitrary URLs onto your internal URL structure in any way you like.

It supports an unlimited number of rules and an unlimited number of attached rule conditions for each rule to provide a really flexible and powerful URL manipulation mechanism. The URL manipulations can depend on various tests: server variables, environment variables, HTTP headers, time stamps, external database lookups, and various other external programs or handlers, can be used to achieve granular URL matching.

Rewrite rules can operate on the full URLs, including the path-info and query string portions, and may be used in per-server context (`httpd.conf`), per-virtualhost context (<VIRTUALHOST> blocks), or per-directory context (`.htaccess` files and <DIRECTORY> blocks). The rewritten result can lead to further rules, internal sub-processing, external request redirection, or proxy passthrough, depending on what flags (p. 178) you attach to the rules.

Since mod_rewrite is so powerful, it can indeed be rather complex. This document supplements the reference documentation (p. 867) , and attempts to allay some of that complexity, and provide highly annotated examples of common scenarios that you may handle with mod_rewrite. But we also attempt to show you when you should not use mod_rewrite, and use other standard Apache features instead, thus avoiding this unnecessary complexity.

- mod_rewrite reference documentation (p. 867)
- Introduction to regular expressions and mod_rewrite (p. 147)
- RewriteRule Flags (p. 178)
- Using RewriteMap (p. 166)
- When **NOT** to use mod_rewrite (p. 175)
- Using mod_rewrite for redirection and remapping of URLs (p. 152)
- Using mod_rewrite to control access (p. 159)
- Dynamic virtual hosts with mod_rewrite (p. 162)
- Dynamic proxying with mod_rewrite (p. 165)
- Advanced techniques (p. 172)
- Technical details (p. 187)

**See also**

- mod_rewrite reference documentation (p. 867)
- Mapping URLs to the Filesystem (p. 64)
- mod_rewrite wiki[1]
- Glossary (p. 1096)

---

[1]http://wiki.apache.org/httpd/Rewrite

# 4.2 Apache mod_rewrite Introduction

This document supplements the MOD_REWRITE reference documentation (p. 867) . It describes the basic concepts necessary for use of MOD_REWRITE. Other documents go into greater detail, but this doc should help the beginner get their feet wet.

**See also**

- Module documentation (p. 867)

- Redirection and remapping (p. 152)

- Controlling access (p. 159)

- Virtual hosts (p. 162)

- Proxying (p. 165)

- Using RewriteMap (p. 166)

- Advanced techniques (p. 172)

- When not to use mod_rewrite (p. 175)

## Introduction

The Apache module MOD_REWRITE is a very powerful and sophisticated module which provides a way to do URL manipulations. With it, you can do nearly all types of URL rewriting that you may need. It is, however, somewhat complex, and may be intimidating to the beginner. There is also a tendency to treat rewrite rules as magic incantation, using them without actually understanding what they do.

This document attempts to give sufficient background so that what follows is understood, rather than just copied blindly.

Remember that many common URL-manipulation tasks don't require the full power and complexity of MOD_REWRITE. For simple tasks, see MOD_ALIAS and the documentation on mapping URLs to the filesystem (p. 64) .

Finally, before proceeding, be sure to configure MOD_REWRITE's log level to one of the trace levels using the LOGLEVEL directive. Although this can give an overwhelming amount of information, it is indispensable in debugging problems with MOD_REWRITE configuration, since it will tell you exactly how each rule is processed.

## Regular Expressions

mod_rewrite uses the Perl Compatible Regular Expression[2] vocabulary. In this document, we do not attempt to provide a detailed reference to regular expressions. For that, we recommend the PCRE man pages[3], the Perl regular expression man page[4], and Mastering Regular Expressions, by Jeffrey Friedl[5].

In this document, we attempt to provide enough of a regex vocabulary to get you started, without being overwhelming, in the hope that REWRITERULEs will be scientific formulae, rather than magical incantations.

---

[2]http://pcre.org/

[3]http://pcre.org/pcre.txt

[4]http://perldoc.perl.org/perlre.html

[5]http://shop.oreilly.com/product/9780596528126.do

**Regex vocabulary**

The following are the minimal building blocks you will need, in order to write regular expressions and REWRITERULEs. They certainly do not represent a complete regular expression vocabulary, but they are a good place to start, and should help you read basic regular expressions, as well as write your own.

| Character | Meaning | Example |
|---|---|---|
| . | Matches any single character | `c.t` will match `cat`, `cot`, `cut`, etc. |
| + | Repeats the previous match one or more times | `a+` matches `a`, `aa`, `aaa`, etc |
| * | Repeats the previous match zero or more times. | `a*` matches all the same things `a+` matches, but will also match an empty string. |
| ? | Makes the match optional. | `colou?r` will match `color` and `colour`. |
| ^ | Called an anchor, matches the beginning of the string | `^a` matches a string that begins with `a` |
| $ | The other anchor, this matches the end of the string. | `a$` matches a string that ends with `a`. |
| ( ) | Groups several characters into a single unit, and captures a match for use in a backreference. | `(ab)+` matches `ababab` - that is, the + applies to the group. For more on back-references see below. |
| [ ] | A character class - matches one of the characters | `c[uoa]t` matches `cut`, `cot` or `cat`. |
| [^ ] | Negative character class - matches any character not specified | `c[^/]t` matches `cat` or `c=t` but not `c/t` |

In MOD_REWRITE the `!` character can be used before a regular expression to negate it. This is, a string will be considered to have matched only if it does not match the rest of the expression.

**Regex Back-Reference Availability**

One important thing here has to be remembered: Whenever you use parentheses in *Pattern* or in one of the *Cond-Pattern*, back-references are internally created which can be used with the strings $N and %N (see below). These are available for creating the *Substitution* parameter of a REWRITERULE or the *TestString* parameter of a REWRITECOND.

Captures in the REWRITERULE patterns are (counterintuitively) available to all preceding REWRITECOND directives, because the REWRITERULE expression is evaluated before the individual conditions.

Figure 1 shows to which locations the back-references are transferred for expansion as well as illustrating the flow of the RewriteRule, RewriteCond matching. In the next chapters, we will be exploring how to use these back-references, so do not fret if it seems a bit alien to you at first.

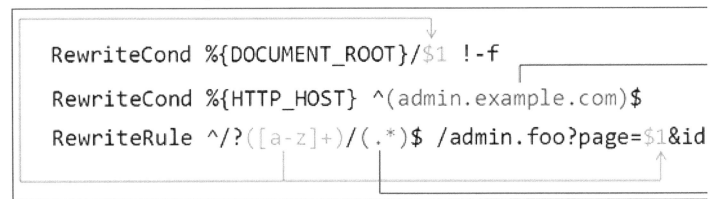

*Figure 1:* The back-reference flow through a rule.
In this example, a request for `/test/1234` would be transformed into `/admin.foo?page=test&id=1234&host=admin.example.com`.

## RewriteRule Basics

A REWRITERULE consists of three arguments separated by spaces. The arguments are

1. *Pattern*: which incoming URLs should be affected by the rule;

2. *Substitution*: where should the matching requests be sent;

3. *[flags]*: options affecting the rewritten request.

The *Pattern* is a regular expression. It is initially (for the first rewrite rule or until a substitution occurs) matched against the URL-path of the incoming request (the part after the hostname but before any question mark indicating the beginning of a query string) or, in per-directory context, against the request's path relative to the directory for which the rule is defined. Once a substitution has occurred, the rules that follow are matched against the substituted value.

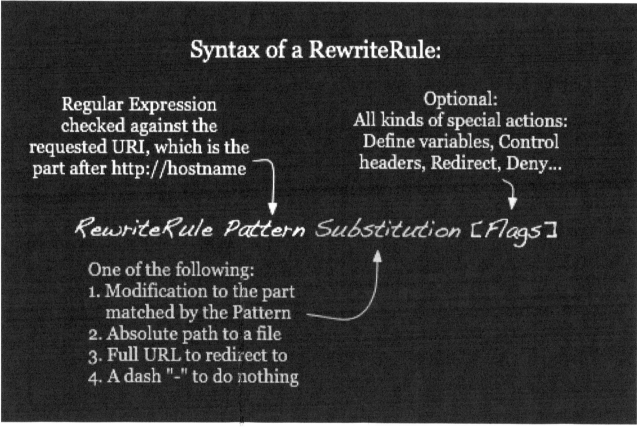

*Figure 2:* Syntax of the RewriteRule directive.

The *Substitution* can itself be one of three things:

**A full filesystem path to a resource** `RewriteRule "^/games" "/usr/local/games/web"`
This maps a request to an arbitrary location on your filesystem, much like the ALIAS directive.

**A web-path to a resource** `RewriteRule "^/foo$" "/bar"`
If DOCUMENTROOT is set to `/usr/local/apache2/htdocs`, then this directive would map requests for `http://example.com/foo` to the path `/usr/local/apache2/htdocs/bar`.

**An absolute URL** `RewriteRule "^/product/view$" "http://site2.example.com/seeproduct.html`
This tells the client to make a new request for the specified URL.

The *Substitution* can also contain *back-references* to parts of the incoming URL-path matched by the *Pattern*. Consider the following:

```
RewriteRule "^/product/(.*)/view$" "/var/web/productdb/$1"
```

The variable `$1` will be replaced with whatever text was matched by the expression inside the parenthesis in the *Pattern*. For example, a request for `http://example.com/product/r14df/view` will be mapped to the path `/var/web/productdb/r14df`.

If there is more than one expression in parenthesis, they are available in order in the variables `$1`, `$2`, `$3`, and so on.

## Rewrite Flags

The behavior of a REWRITERULE can be modified by the application of one or more flags to the end of the rule. For example, the matching behavior of a rule can be made case-insensitive by the application of the `[NC]` flag:

```
RewriteRule "^puppy.html" "smalldog.html" [NC]
```

For more details on the available flags, their meanings, and examples, see the Rewrite Flags (p. 178) document.

## Rewrite Conditions

One or more REWRITECOND directives can be used to restrict the types of requests that will be subject to the following REWRITERULE. The first argument is a variable describing a characteristic of the request, the second argument is a regular expression that must match the variable, and a third optional argument is a list of flags that modify how the match is evaluated.

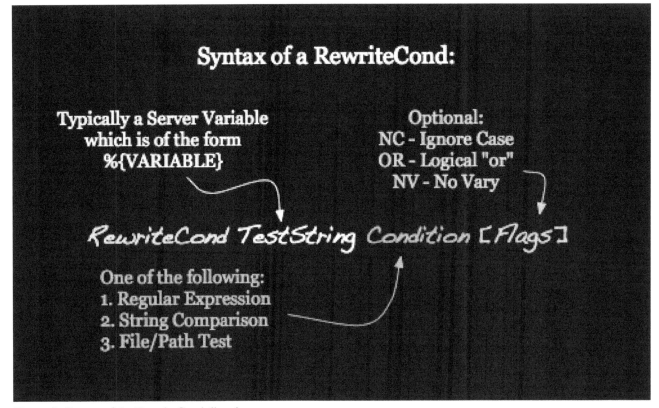

*Figure 3:* Syntax of the RewriteCond directive

For example, to send all requests from a particular IP range to a different server, you could use:

```
RewriteCond "%{REMOTE_ADDR}" "^10\.2\."
RewriteRule "(.*)"              "http://intranet.example.com$1"
```

When more than one REWRITECOND is specified, they must all match for the REWRITERULE to be applied. For example, to deny requests that contain the word "hack" in their query string, unless they also contain a cookie containing the word "go", you could use:

```
RewriteCond "%{QUERY_STRING}" "hack"
RewriteCond "%{HTTP_COOKIE}"  !go
RewriteRule "."               "-"    [F]
```

Notice that the exclamation mark specifies a negative match, so the rule is only applied if the cookie does not contain "go".

Matches in the regular expressions contained in the REWRITECONDs can be used as part of the *Substitution* in the REWRITERULE using the variables %1, %2, etc. For example, this will direct the request to a different directory depending on the hostname used to access the site:

```
RewriteCond "%{HTTP_HOST}" "(.*)"
RewriteRule "^/(.*)"       "/sites/%1/$1"
```

If the request was for http://example.com/foo/bar, then %1 would contain example.com and $1 would contain foo/bar.

## Rewrite maps

The REWRITEMAP directive provides a way to call an external function, so to speak, to do your rewriting for you. This is discussed in greater detail in the RewriteMap supplementary documentation (p. 166) .

## .htaccess files

Rewriting is typically configured in the main server configuration setting (outside any <DIRECTORY> section) or inside <VIRTUALHOST> containers. This is the easiest way to do rewriting and is recommended. It is possible, however, to do rewriting inside <DIRECTORY> sections or .htaccess files (p. 249) at the expense of some additional complexity. This technique is called per-directory rewrites.

The main difference with per-server rewrites is that the path prefix of the directory containing the .htaccess file is stripped before matching in the REWRITERULE. In addition, the REWRITEBASE should be used to assure the request is properly mapped.

# 4.3   Redirecting and Remapping with mod_rewrite

This document supplements the MOD_REWRITE reference documentation (p. 867) . It describes how you can use MOD_REWRITE to redirect and remap request. This includes many examples of common uses of mod_rewrite, including detailed descriptions of how each works.

 Note that many of these examples won't work unchanged in your particular server configuration, so it's important that you understand them, rather than merely cutting and pasting the examples into your configuration.

**See also**

- Module documentation (p. 867)
- mod_rewrite introduction (p. 147)
- Controlling access (p. 159)
- Virtual hosts (p. 162)
- Proxying (p. 165)
- Using RewriteMap (p. 166)
- Advanced techniques (p. 172)
- When not to use mod_rewrite (p. 175)

## From Old to New (internal)

**Description:** Assume we have recently renamed the page `foo.html` to `bar.html` and now want to provide the old URL for backward compatibility. However, we want that users of the old URL even not recognize that the pages was renamed - that is, we don't want the address to change in their browser.

**Solution:** We rewrite the old URL to the new one internally via the following rule:

```
RewriteEngine   on
RewriteRule     "^/foo\.html$"  "/bar.html" [PT]
```

## Rewriting From Old to New (external)

**Description:** Assume again that we have recently renamed the page `foo.html` to `bar.html` and now want to provide the old URL for backward compatibility. But this time we want that the users of the old URL get hinted to the new one, i.e. their browsers Location field should change, too.

**Solution:** We force a HTTP redirect to the new URL which leads to a change of the browsers and thus the users view:

```
RewriteEngine   on
RewriteRule     "^/foo\.html$"  "bar.html"  [R]
```

**Discussion** In this example, as contrasted to the internal example above, we can simply use the Redirect directive. mod_rewrite was used in that earlier example in order to hide the redirect from the client:

```
Redirect "/foo.html" "/bar.html"
```

## Resource Moved to Another Server

**Description:** If a resource has moved to another server, you may wish to have URLs continue to work for a time on the old server while people update their bookmarks.

**Solution:** You can use MOD_REWRITE to redirect these URLs to the new server, but you might also consider using the Redirect or RedirectMatch directive.

```
#With mod_rewrite
RewriteEngine on
RewriteRule   "^/docs/(.+)"  "http://new.example.com/docs/$1"  [R,L]


#With RedirectMatch
RedirectMatch "^/docs/(.*)" "http://new.example.com/docs/$1"


#With Redirect
Redirect "/docs/" "http://new.example.com/docs/"
```

## From Static to Dynamic

**Description:** How can we transform a static page `foo.html` into a dynamic variant `foo.cgi` in a seamless way, i.e. without notice by the browser/user.

**Solution:** We just rewrite the URL to the CGI-script and force the handler to be **cgi-script** so that it is executed as a CGI program. This way a request to `/~quux/foo.html` internally leads to the invocation of `/~quux/foo.cgi`.

```
RewriteEngine  on
RewriteBase    "/~quux/"
RewriteRule    "^foo\.html$"  "foo.cgi"  [H=cgi-script]
```

## Backward Compatibility for file extension change

**Description:** How can we make URLs backward compatible (still existing virtually) after migrating `document.YYYY` to `document.XXXX`, e.g. after translating a bunch of `.html` files to `.php`?

**Solution:** We rewrite the name to its basename and test for existence of the new extension. If it exists, we take that name, else we rewrite the URL to its original state.

```
#   backward compatibility ruleset for
#   rewriting document.html to document.php
#   when and only when document.php exists
<Directory "/var/www/htdocs">
    RewriteEngine on
    RewriteBase   "/var/www/htdocs"

    RewriteCond   "$1.php"        -f
    RewriteCond   "$1.html"       !-f
    RewriteRule   "^(.*).html$"   "$1.php"
</Directory>
```

**Discussion**  This example uses an often-overlooked feature of mod_rewrite, by taking advantage of the order of execution of the ruleset. In particular, mod_rewrite evaluates the left-hand-side of the RewriteRule before it evaluates the RewriteCond directives. Consequently, $1 is already defined by the time the RewriteCond directives are evaluated. This allows us to test for the existence of the original (`document.html`) and target (`document.php`) files using the same base filename.

This ruleset is designed to use in a per-directory context (In a <Directory> block or in a .htaccess file), so that the -f checks are looking at the correct directory path. You may need to set a REWRITEBASE directive to specify the directory base that you're working in.

## Canonical Hostnames

**Description:**  The goal of this rule is to force the use of a particular hostname, in preference to other hostnames which may be used to reach the same site. For example, if you wish to force the use of **www.example.com** instead of **example.com**, you might use a variant of the following recipe.

**Solution:**  The very best way to solve this doesn't involve mod_rewrite at all, but rather uses the REDIRECT directive placed in a virtual host for the non-canonical hostname(s).

```
<VirtualHost *:80>
  ServerName undesired.example.com
  ServerAlias example.com notthis.example.com

  Redirect "/" "http://www.example.com/"
</VirtualHost>

<VirtualHost *:80>
  ServerName www.example.com
</VirtualHost>
```

You can alternatively accomplish this using the <IF> directive: (**2.4 and later**)

```
<If "%{HTTP_HOST} != 'www.example.com'">
    Redirect "/" "http://www.example.com/"
</If>
```

Or, for example, to redirect a portion of your site to HTTPS, you might do the following:

```
<If "%{SERVER_PROTOCOL} != 'HTTPS'">
    Redirect "/admin/" "https://www.example.com/admin/"
</If>
```

If, for whatever reason, you still want to use mod_rewrite - if, for example, you need this to work with a larger set of RewriteRules - you might use one of the recipes below.

For sites running on a port other than 80:

```
RewriteCond "%{HTTP_HOST}"   "!^www\.example\.com" [NC]
RewriteCond "%{HTTP_HOST}"   "!^$"
RewriteCond "%{SERVER_PORT}" "!^80$"
RewriteRule "^/?(.*)"        "http://www.example.com:%{SERVER_PORT}/$1" [L,R,NE]
```

And for a site running on port 80

```
RewriteCond "%{HTTP_HOST}"    "!^www\.example\.com"      [NC]
RewriteCond "%{HTTP_HOST}"    "!^$"
RewriteRule "^/?(.*)"         "http://www.example.com/$1" [L,R,NE]
```

If you wanted to do this generically for all domain names - that is, if you want to redirect **example.com** to **www.example.com** for all possible values of **example.com**, you could use the following recipe:

```
RewriteCond "%{HTTP_HOST}" "!^www\."             [NC]
RewriteCond "%{HTTP_HOST}" "!^$"
RewriteRule "^/?(.*)"      "http://www.%{HTTP_HOST}/$1" [L,R,NE]
```

These rulesets will work either in your main server configuration file, or in a `.htaccess` file placed in the DOCUMENTROOT of the server.

## Search for pages in more than one directory

**Description:** A particular resource might exist in one of several places, and we want to look in those places for the resource when it is requested. Perhaps we've recently rearranged our directory structure, dividing content into several locations.

**Solution:** The following ruleset searches in two directories to find the resource, and, if not finding it in either place, will attempt to just serve it out of the location requested.

```
RewriteEngine on

#   first try to find it in dir1/...
#   ...and if found stop and be happy:
RewriteCond         "%{DOCUMENT_ROOT}/dir1/%{REQUEST_URI}"  -f
RewriteRule "^(.+)" "%{DOCUMENT_ROOT}/dir1/$1"  [L]

#   second try to find it in dir2/...
#   ...and if found stop and be happy:
RewriteCond         "%{DOCUMENT_ROOT}/dir2/%{REQUEST_URI}"  -f
RewriteRule "^(.+)" "%{DOCUMENT_ROOT}/dir2/$1"  [L]

#   else go on for other Alias or ScriptAlias directives,
#   etc.
RewriteRule "^"     "-"                                      [PT]
```

## Redirecting to Geographically Distributed Servers

**Description:** We have numerous mirrors of our website, and want to redirect people to the one that is located in the country where they are located.

**Solution:** Looking at the hostname of the requesting client, we determine which country they are coming from. If we can't do a lookup on their IP address, we fall back to a default server.

We'll use a REWRITEMAP directive to build a list of servers that we wish to use.

```
HostnameLookups on
RewriteEngine on
RewriteMap    multiplex        "txt:/path/to/map.mirrors"
RewriteCond   "%{REMOTE_HOST}" "([a-z]+)$"                      [NC]
RewriteRule   "^/(.*)$"        "${multiplex:%1|http://www.example.com/}$1"  [R,
```

```
## map.mirrors -- Multiplexing Map
de http://www.example.de/
uk http://www.example.uk/
com http://www.example.com/
##EOF##
```

**Discussion**  &#9888;  This ruleset relies on HOSTNAMELOOKUPS being set on, which can be a significant performance hit.

The REWRITECOND directive captures the last portion of the hostname of the requesting client - the country code - and the following RewriteRule uses that value to look up the appropriate mirror host in the map file.

## Canonical URLs

**Description:** On some webservers there is more than one URL for a resource. Usually there are canonical URLs (which are be actually used and distributed) and those which are just shortcuts, internal ones, and so on. Independent of which URL the user supplied with the request, they should finally see the canonical one in their browser address bar.

**Solution:** We do an external HTTP redirect for all non-canonical URLs to fix them in the location view of the Browser and for all subsequent requests. In the example ruleset below we replace /puppies and /canines by the canonical /dogs.

```
RewriteRule    "^/(puppies|canines)/(.*)"    "/dogs/$2"   [R]
```

**Discussion:** This should really be accomplished with Redirect or RedirectMatch directives:

```
RedirectMatch "^/(puppies|canines)/(.*)" "/dogs/$2"
```

## Moved `DocumentRoot`

**Description:** Usually the DOCUMENTROOT of the webserver directly relates to the URL "/". But often this data is not really of top-level priority. For example, you may wish for visitors, on first entering a site, to go to a particular subdirectory /about/. This may be accomplished using the following ruleset:

**Solution:** We redirect the URL / to /about/:

```
RewriteEngine on
RewriteRule    "^/$"  "/about/"   [R]
```

Note that this can also be handled using the REDIRECTMATCH directive:

```
RedirectMatch "^/$" "http://example.com/about/"
```

Note also that the example rewrites only the root URL. That is, it rewrites a request for http://example.com/, but not a request for http://example.com/page.html. If you have in fact changed your document root - that is, if **all** of your content is in fact in that subdirectory, it is greatly preferable to simply change your DOCUMENTROOT directive, or move all of the content up one directory, rather than rewriting URLs.

## Fallback Resource

**Description:** You want a single resource (say, a certain file, like index.php) to handle all requests that come to a particular directory, except those that should go to an existing resource such as an image, or a css file.

**Solution:** As of version 2.2.16, you should use the FALLBACKRESOURCE directive for this:

```
<Directory "/var/www/my_blog">
  FallbackResource index.php
</Directory>
```

However, in earlier versions of Apache, or if your needs are more complicated than this, you can use a variation of the following rewrite set to accomplish the same thing:

```
<Directory "/var/www/my_blog">
  RewriteBase "/my_blog"

  RewriteCond "/var/www/my_blog/%{REQUEST_FILENAME}" !-f
  RewriteCond "/var/www/my_blog/%{REQUEST_FILENAME}" !-d
  RewriteRule "^"                                    "index.php" [PT]
</Directory>
```

If, on the other hand, you wish to pass the requested URI as a query string argument to index.php, you can replace that RewriteRule with:

```
RewriteRule "(.*)" "index.php?$1" [PT,QSA]
```

Note that these rulesets can be used in a .htaccess file, as well as in a <Directory> block.

## Rewrite query string

**Description:** You want to capture a particular value from a query string and either replace it or incorporate it into another component of the URL.

**Solutions:** Many of the solutions in this section will all use the same condition, which leaves the matched value in the %2 backreference. %1 is the beginining of the query string (up to the key of intererest), and %3 is the remainder. This condition is a bit complex for flexibility and to avoid double '&&' in the substitutions.

- This solution removes the matching key and value:

  ```
  # Remove mykey=???
  RewriteCond "%{QUERY_STRING}" "(.*(?:^|&))mykey=([^&]*)&?(.*)&?$"
  RewriteRule "(.*)"            "$1?%1%3"
  ```

- This solution uses the captured value in the URL subsitution, discarding the rest of the original query by appending a '?':

  ```
  # Copy from query string to PATH_INFO
  RewriteCond "%{QUERY_STRING}" "(.*(?:^|&))mykey=([^&]*)&?(.*)&?$"
  RewriteRule "(.*)"            "$1/products/%2/?" [PT]
  ```

- This solution checks the captured value in a subsequent condition:

```
# Capture the value of mykey in the query string
RewriteCond "%{QUERY_STRING}" "(.*(?:^|&))mykey=([^&]*)&?(.*)&?$"
RewriteCond "%2"              !=not-so-secret-value
RewriteRule "(.*)"           "-" [F]
```

- This solution shows the reverse of the previous ones, copying path components (perhaps PATH_INFO) from the URL into the query string.

```
# The desired URL might be /products/kitchen-sink, and the script expects
# /path?products=kitchen-sink.
RewriteRule "^/?path/([^/]+)/([^/]+)" "/path?$1=$2" [PT]
```

## 4.4 Using mod_rewrite to control access

This document supplements the MOD_REWRITE reference documentation (p. 867). It describes how you can use MOD_REWRITE to control access to various resources, and other related techniques. This includes many examples of common uses of mod_rewrite, including detailed descriptions of how each works.

 Note that many of these examples won't work unchanged in your particular server configuration, so it's important that you understand them, rather than merely cutting and pasting the examples into your configuration.

**See also**

- Module documentation (p. 867)
- mod_rewrite introduction (p. 147)
- Redirection and remapping (p. 152)
- Virtual hosts (p. 162)
- Proxying (p. 165)
- Using RewriteMap (p. 166)
- Advanced techniques (p. 172)
- When not to use mod_rewrite (p. 175)

### Forbidding Image "Hotlinking"

**Description:** The following technique forbids the practice of other sites including your images inline in their pages. This practice is often referred to as "hotlinking", and results in your bandwidth being used to serve content for someone else's site.

**Solution:** This technique relies on the value of the HTTP_REFERER variable, which is optional. As such, it's possible for some people to circumvent this limitation. However, most users will experience the failed request, which should, over time, result in the image being removed from that other site.

There are several ways that you can handle this situation.

In this first example, we simply deny the request, if it didn't initiate from a page on our site. For the purpose of this example, we assume that our site is www.example.com.

```
RewriteCond "%{HTTP_REFERER}"  "!^$"
RewriteCond "%{HTTP_REFERER}"  "!www.example.com" [NC]
RewriteRule "\.(gif|jpg|png)$" "-"                [F,NC]
```

In this second example, instead of failing the request, we display an alternate image instead.

```
RewriteCond "%{HTTP_REFERER}"  "!^$"
RewriteCond "%{HTTP_REFERER}"  "!www.example.com"    [NC]
RewriteRule "\.(gif|jpg|png)$" "/images/go-away.png" [R,NC]
```

In the third example, we redirect the request to an image on some other site.

```
RewriteCond "%{HTTP_REFERER}"  "!^$"
RewriteCond "%{HTTP_REFERER}"  "!www.example.com"                    [NC]
RewriteRule "\.(gif|jpg|png)$" "http://other.example.com/image.gif"  [R,NC]
```

Of these techniques, the last two tend to be the most effective in getting people to stop hotlinking your images, because they will simply not see the image that they expected to see.

**Discussion:** If all you wish to do is deny access to the resource, rather than redirecting that request elsewhere, this can be accomplished without the use of mod_rewrite:

```
SetEnvIf Referer example\.com localreferer
<FilesMatch "\.(jpg|png|gif)$">
    Require env localreferer
</FilesMatch>
```

## Blocking of Robots

**Description:** In this recipe, we discuss how to block persistent requests from a particular robot, or user agent.

The standard for robot exclusion defines a file, /robots.txt that specifies those portions of your website where you wish to exclude robots. However, some robots do not honor these files.

Note that there are methods of accomplishing this which do not use mod_rewrite. Note also that any technique that relies on the clients USER_AGENT string can be circumvented very easily, since that string can be changed.

**Solution:** We use a ruleset that specifies the directory to be protected, and the client USER_AGENT that identifies the malicious or persistent robot.

In this example, we are blocking a robot called NameOfBadRobot from a location /secret/files. You may also specify an IP address range, if you are trying to block that user agent only from the particular source.

```
RewriteCond "%{HTTP_USER_AGENT}"   "^NameOfBadRobot"
RewriteCond "%{REMOTE_ADDR}"       "=123\.45\.67\.[8-9]"
RewriteRule "^/secret/files/"      "-"                    [F]
```

**Discussion:** Rather than using mod_rewrite for this, you can accomplish the same end using alternate means, as illustrated here:

```
SetEnvIfNoCase User-Agent ^NameOfBadRobot goaway
<Location "/secret/files">
    <RequireAll>
        Require all granted
        Require not env goaway
    </RequireAll>
</Location>
```

As noted above, this technique is trivial to circumvent, by simply modifying the USER_AGENT request header. If you are experiencing a sustained attack, you should consider blocking it at a higher level, such as at your firewall.

## Denying Hosts in a Blacklist

**Description:** We wish to maintain a blacklist of hosts, rather like hosts.deny, and have those hosts blocked from accessing our server.

**Solution:** `RewriteEngine on`
```
RewriteMap    hosts-deny  "txt:/path/to/hosts.deny"
RewriteCond   "${hosts-deny:%{REMOTE_ADDR}|NOT-FOUND}" "!=NOT-FOUND" [OR]
RewriteCond   "${hosts-deny:%{REMOTE_HOST}|NOT-FOUND}" "!=NOT-FOUND"
RewriteRule   "^"                                       "-"           [F]
```

```
##
## hosts.deny
##
## ATTENTION! This is a map, not a list, even when we treat it as
such.
## mod_rewrite parses it for key/value pairs, so at least a
## dummy value "-" must be present for each entry.
##
193.102.180.41 -
bsdti1.sdm.de -
192.76.162.40 -
```

**Discussion:** The second RewriteCond assumes that you have HostNameLookups turned on, so that client IP addresses will be resolved. If that's not the case, you should drop the second RewriteCond, and drop the [OR] flag from the first RewriteCond.

## Referer-based Deflector

**Description:** Redirect requests based on the Referer from which the request came, with different targets per Referer.

**Solution:** The following ruleset uses a map file to associate each Referer with a redirection target.

```
RewriteMap  deflector "txt:/path/to/deflector.map"

RewriteCond "%{HTTP_REFERER}"                    !=""
RewriteCond "${deflector:%{HTTP_REFERER}}" =-
RewriteRule "^"                                  "%{HTTP_REFERER}" [R,L]

RewriteCond "%{HTTP_REFERER}"                    !=""
RewriteCond "${deflector:%{HTTP_REFERER}|NOT-FOUND}" "!=NOT-FOUND"
RewriteRule "^"                                  "${deflector:%{HTTP_REFERER}}" [R,L]
```

The map file lists redirection targets for each referer, or, if we just wish to redirect back to where they came from, a "-" is placed in the map:

```
##
##  deflector.map
##

http://badguys.example.com/bad/index.html    -
http://badguys.example.com/bad/index2.html   -
http://badguys.example.com/bad/index3.html   http://somewhere.example.com/
```

## 4.5   Dynamic mass virtual hosts with mod_rewrite

This document supplements the MOD_REWRITE reference documentation (p. 867) . It describes how you can use MOD_REWRITE to create dynamically configured virtual hosts.

> ⚠ mod_rewrite is usually not the best way to configure virtual hosts. You should first consider the alternatives (p. 130) before resorting to mod_rewrite. See also the "how to avoid mod_rewrite (p. 175) document.

**See also**

- Module documentation (p. 867)
- mod_rewrite introduction (p. 147)
- Redirection and remapping (p. 152)
- Controlling access (p. 159)
- Proxying (p. 165)
- RewriteMap (p. 166)
- Advanced techniques (p. 172)
- When not to use mod_rewrite (p. 175)

### Virtual Hosts For Arbitrary Hostnames

**Description:** We want to automatically create a virtual host for every hostname which resolves in our domain, without having to create new VirtualHost sections.

In this recipe, we assume that we'll be using the hostname **SITE**.example.com for each user, and serve their content out of /home/**SITE**/www. However, we want www.example.com to be ommitted from this mapping.

**Solution:** `RewriteEngine on`

```
RewriteMap     lowercase int:tolower

RewriteCond    %{HTTP_HOST} !^www\.
RewriteCond    ${lowercase:%{HTTP_HOST}}   ^([^.]+)\.example\.com$
RewriteRule    ^(.*)     /home/%1/www$1
```

**Discussion** ⚠ You will need to take care of the DNS resolution - Apache does not handle name resolution. You'll need either to create CNAME records for each hostname, or a DNS wildcard record. Creating DNS records is beyond the scope of this document.

The internal `tolower` RewriteMap directive is used to ensure that the hostnames being used are all lowercase, so that there is no ambiguity in the directory structure which must be created.

Parentheses used in a REWRITECOND are captured into the backreferences %1, %2, etc, while parentheses used in REWRITERULE are captured into the backreferences $1, $2, etc.

The first `RewriteCond` checks to see if the hostname starts with www., and if it does, the rewriting is skipped.

As with many techniques discussed in this document, mod_rewrite really isn't the best way to accomplish this task. You should, instead, consider using MOD_VHOST_ALIAS instead, as it will much more gracefully handle anything beyond serving static files, such as any dynamic content, and Alias resolution.

## Dynamic Virtual Hosts Using MOD_REWRITE

This extract from `httpd.conf` does the same thing as the first example. The first half is very similar to the corresponding part above, except for some changes, required for backward compatibility and to make the `mod_rewrite` part work properly; the second half configures `mod_rewrite` to do the actual work.

Because `mod_rewrite` runs before other URI translation modules (e.g., `mod_alias`), `mod_rewrite` must be told to explicitly ignore any URLs that would have been handled by those modules. And, because these rules would otherwise bypass any `ScriptAlias` directives, we must have `mod_rewrite` explicitly enact those mappings.

```
# get the server name from the Host: header
UseCanonicalName Off

# splittable logs
LogFormat "%{Host}i %h %l %u %t \"%r\" %s %b" vcommon
CustomLog "logs/access_log" vcommon

<Directory "/www/hosts">
    # ExecCGI is needed here because we can't force
    # CGI execution in the way that ScriptAlias does
    Options FollowSymLinks ExecCGI
</Directory>

RewriteEngine On

# a ServerName derived from a Host: header may be any case at all
RewriteMap  lowercase  "int:tolower"

## deal with normal documents first:
# allow Alias /icons/ to work - repeat for other aliases
RewriteCond  "%{REQUEST_URI}"  "!^/icons/"
# allow CGIs to work
RewriteCond  "%{REQUEST_URI}"  "!^/cgi-bin/"
# do the magic
RewriteRule  "^/(.*)$"          "/www/hosts/${lowercase:%{SERVER_NAME}}/docs/$1"

## and now deal with CGIs - we have to force a handler
RewriteCond  "%{REQUEST_URI}"  "^/cgi-bin/"
RewriteRule  "^/(.*)$"          "/www/hosts/${lowercase:%{SERVER_NAME}}/cgi-bin/$1"
```

## Using a Separate Virtual Host Configuration File

This arrangement uses more advanced MOD_REWRITE features to work out the translation from virtual host to document root, from a separate configuration file. This provides more flexibility, but requires more complicated configuration.

The `vhost.map` file should look something like this:

```
customer-1.example.com /www/customers/1
customer-2.example.com /www/customers/2
# ...
customer-N.example.com /www/customers/N
```

The `httpd.conf` should contain the following:

```
RewriteEngine on

RewriteMap    lowercase   "int:tolower"

# define the map file
RewriteMap    vhost        "txt:/www/conf/vhost.map"

# deal with aliases as above
RewriteCond  "%{REQUEST_URI}"                  "!^/icons/"
RewriteCond  "%{REQUEST_URI}"                  "!^/cgi-bin/"
RewriteCond  "${lowercase:%{SERVER_NAME}}"  "^(.+)$"
# this does the file-based remap
RewriteCond  "${vhost:%1}"                     "^(/.*)$"
RewriteRule  "^/(.*)$"                         "%1/docs/$1"

RewriteCond  "%{REQUEST_URI}"                  "^/cgi-bin/"
RewriteCond  "${lowercase:%{SERVER_NAME}}"  "^(.+)$"
RewriteCond  "${vhost:%1}"                     "^(/.*)$"
RewriteRule  "^/(.*)$"                         "%1/cgi-bin/$1" [H=cgi-script]
```

# 4.6 Using mod_rewrite for Proxying

This document supplements the MOD_REWRITE reference documentation (p. 867) . It describes how to use the RewriteRule's [P] flag to proxy content to another server. A number of recipes are provided that describe common scenarios.

**See also**

- Module documentation (p. 867)
- mod_rewrite introduction (p. 147)
- Redirection and remapping (p. 152)
- Controlling access (p. 159)
- Virtual hosts (p. 162)
- Using RewriteMap (p. 166)
- Advanced techniques (p. 172)
- When not to use mod_rewrite (p. 175)

## Proxying Content with mod_rewrite

**Description:** mod_rewrite provides the [P] flag, which allows URLs to be passed, via mod_proxy, to another server. Two examples are given here. In one example, a URL is passed directly to another server, and served as though it were a local URL. In the other example, we proxy missing content to a back-end server.

**Solution:** To simply map a URL to another server, we use the [P] flag, as follows:

```
RewriteEngine   on
RewriteBase     "/products/"
RewriteRule     "^widget/(.*)$"  "http://product.example.com/widget/$1"  [P]
ProxyPassReverse "/products/widget/" "http://product.example.com/widget/"
```

In the second example, we proxy the request only if we can't find the resource locally. This can be very useful when you're migrating from one server to another, and you're not sure if all the content has been migrated yet.

```
RewriteCond "%{REQUEST_FILENAME}"        !-f
RewriteCond "%{REQUEST_FILENAME}"        !-d
RewriteRule "^/(.*)"                      "http://old.example.com/$1" [P]
ProxyPassReverse "/" "http://old.example.com/"
```

**Discussion:** In each case, we add a PROXYPASSREVERSE directive to ensure that any redirects issued by the backend are correctly passed on to the client.

Consider using either PROXYPASS or PROXYPASSMATCH whenever possible in preference to mod_rewrite.

## 4.7   Using RewriteMap

This document supplements the MOD_REWRITE reference documentation (p. 867) . It describes the use of the REWRITEMAP directive, and provides examples of each of the various REWRITEMAP types.

> ! Note that many of these examples won't work unchanged in your particular server configuration, so it's important that you understand them, rather than merely cutting and pasting the examples into your configuration.

**See also**

### Introduction

The REWRITEMAP directive defines an external function which can be called in the context of REWRITERULE or REWRITECOND directives to perform rewriting that is too complicated, or too specialized to be performed just by regular expressions. The source of this lookup can be any of the types listed in the sections below, and enumerated in the REWRITEMAP reference documentation.

The syntax of the REWRITEMAP directive is as follows:

```
RewriteMap MapName MapType:MapSource
```

The *MapName* is an arbitray name that you assign to the map, and which you will use in directives later on. Arguments are passed to the map via the following syntax:

**${ *MapName* : *LookupKey* }**
**${ *MapName* : *LookupKey* | *DefaultValue* }**

When such a construct occurs, the map *MapName* is consulted and the key *LookupKey* is looked-up. If the key is found, the map-function construct is substituted by *SubstValue*. If the key is not found then it is substituted by *DefaultValue* or by the empty string if no *DefaultValue* was specified.

For example, you can define a REWRITEMAP as:

```
RewriteMap examplemap "txt:/path/to/file/map.txt"
```

You would then be able to use this map in a REWRITERULE as follows:

```
RewriteRule "^/ex/(.*)" "${examplemap:$1}"
```

A default value can be specified in the event that nothing is found in the map:

```
RewriteRule "^/ex/(.*)" "${examplemap:$1|/not_found.html}"
```

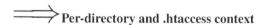 **Per-directory and .htaccess context**

> The REWRITEMAP directive may not be used in <DIRECTORY> sections or .htaccess
> files. You must declare the map in server or virtualhost context. You may use the map, once
> created, in your REWRITERULE and REWRITECOND directives in those scopes. You just can't
> **declare** it in those scopes.

The sections that follow describe the various *MapType*s that may be used, and give examples of each.

## int: Internal Function

When a MapType of int is used, the MapSource is one of the available internal REWRITEMAP functions. Module
authors can provide additional internal functions by registering them with the ap_register_rewrite_mapfunc
API. The functions that are provided by default are:

- **toupper**:
  Converts the key to all upper case.

- **tolower**:
  Converts the key to all lower case.

- **escape**:
  Translates special characters in the key to hex-encodings.

- **unescape**:
  Translates hex-encodings in the key back to special characters.

To use one of these functions, create a REWRITEMAP referencing the int function, and then use that in your
REWRITERULE:

**Redirect a URI to an all-lowercase version of itself**

```
RewriteMap lc int:tolower
RewriteRule "(.*)" "${lc:$1}" [R]
```

> Please note that the example offered here is for illustration purposes only, and is not a recom-
> mendation. If you want to make URLs case-insensitive, consider using MOD_SPELING instead.

## txt: Plain text maps

When a MapType of txt is used, the MapSource is a filesystem path to a plain-text mapping file, containing one
space-separated key/value pair per line. Optionally, a line may contain a comment, starting with a '#' character.

A valid text rewrite map file will have the following syntax:

```
# Comment line
MatchingKey SubstValue
MatchingKey SubstValue # comment
```

When the REWRITEMAP is invoked the argument is looked for in the first argument of a line, and, if found, the substitution value is returned.

For example, we can use a mapfile to translate product names to product IDs for easier-to-remember URLs, using the following recipe:

**Product to ID configuration**

```
RewriteMap product2id "txt:/etc/apache2/productmap.txt"
RewriteRule "^/product/(.*)" "/prods.php?id=${product2id:$1|NOTFOUND}" [PT]
```

We assume here that the `prods.php` script knows what to do when it received an argument of `id=NOTFOUND` when a product is not found in the lookup map.

The file `/etc/apache2/productmap.txt` then contains the following:

```
Product to ID map
##
## productmap.txt - Product to ID map file
##
television 993
stereo 198
fishingrod 043
basketball 418
telephone 328
```

Thus, when `http://example.com/product/television` is requested, the REWRITERULE is applied, and the request is internally mapped to `/prods.php?id=993`.

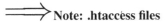

**Note: .htaccess files**

The example given is crafted to be used in server or virtualhost scope. If you're planning to use this in a `.htaccess` file, you'll need to remove the leading slash from the rewrite pattern in order for it to match anything:

```
RewriteRule "^product/(.*)" "/prods.php?id=${product2id:$1|NOTFOUND}" [PT]
```

**Cached lookups**

The looked-up keys are cached by httpd until the `mtime` (modified time) of the mapfile changes, or the httpd server is restarted. This ensures better performance on maps that are called by many requests.

## rnd: Randomized Plain Text

When a MapType of `rnd` is used, the MapSource is a filesystem path to a plain-text mapping file, each line of which contains a key, and one or more values separated by `|`. One of these values will be chosen at random if the key is matched.

For example, you can use the following map file and directives to provide a random load balancing between several back-end servers, via a reverse-proxy. Images are sent to one of the servers in the 'static' pool, while everything else is sent to one of the 'dynamic' pool.

```
Rewrite map file
##
## map.txt -- rewriting map
##
static www1|www2|www3|www4
dynamic www5|www6
```

**Configuration directives**

```
RewriteMap servers "rnd:/path/to/file/map.txt"

RewriteRule "^/(.*\.(png|gif|jpg))" "http://${servers:static}/$1"  [NC,P,L]
RewriteRule "^/(.*)"                 "http://${servers:dynamic}/$1" [P,L]
```

So, when an image is requested and the first of these rules is matched, REWRITEMAP looks up the string static in the map file, which returns one of the specified hostnames at random, which is then used in the REWRITERULE target.

If you wanted to have one of the servers more likely to be chosen (for example, if one of the server has more memory than the others, and so can handle more requests) simply list it more times in the map file.

```
static www1|www1|www2|www3|www4
```

## dbm: DBM Hash File

When a MapType of dbm is used, the MapSource is a filesystem path to a DBM database file containing key/value pairs to be used in the mapping. This works exactly the same way as the txt map, but is much faster, because a DBM is indexed, whereas a text file is not. This allows more rapid access to the desired key.

You may optionally specify a particular dbm type:

```
RewriteMap examplemap "dbm=sdbm:/etc/apache/mapfile.dbm"
```

The type can be sdbm, gdbm, ndbm or db. However, it is recommended that you just use the httxt2dbm (p. 328) utility that is provided with Apache HTTP Server, as it will use the correct DBM library, matching the one that was used when httpd itself was built.

To create a dbm file, first create a text map file as described in the txt section. Then run httxt2dbm:

```
$ httxt2dbm -i mapfile.txt -o mapfile.map
```

You can then reference the resulting file in your REWRITEMAP directive:

```
RewriteMap mapname "dbm:/etc/apache/mapfile.map"
```

> Note that with some dbm types, more than one file is generated, with a common base name. For example, you may have two files named mapfile.map.dir and mapfiile.map.pag. This is normal, and you need only use the base name mapfile.map in your REWRITEMAP directive.

> **Cached lookups**

> The looked-up keys are cached by httpd until the mtime (modified time) of the mapfile changes, or the httpd server is restarted. This ensures better performance on maps that are called by many requests.

## prg: External Rewriting Program

When a MapType of `prg` is used, the MapSource is a filesystem path to an executable program which will providing the mapping behavior. This can be a compiled binary file, or a program in an interpreted language such as Perl or Python.

This program is started once, when the Apache HTTP Server is started, and then communicates with the rewriting engine via `STDIN` and `STDOUT`. That is, for each map function lookup, it expects one argument via `STDIN`, and should return one new-line terminated response string on `STDOUT`. If there is no corresponding lookup value, the map program should return the four-character string `"NULL"` to indicate this.

External rewriting programs are not started if they're defined in a context that does not have REWRITEENGINE set to `on`.

By default, external rewriting programs are run as the user:group who started httpd. This can be changed on UNIX systems by passing user name and group name as third argument to REWRITEMAP in the `username:groupname` format.

This feature utilizes the `rewrite-map` mutex, which is required for reliable communication with the program. The mutex mechanism and lock file can be configured with the MUTEX directive.

A simple example is shown here which will replace all dashes with underscores in a request URI.

**Rewrite configuration**

```
RewriteMap d2u "prg:/www/bin/dash2under.programlisting" apache:apache
RewriteRule "-" "${d2u:%{REQUEST_URI}}"
```

**dash2under.pl**

```
#!/usr/bin/perl
$| = 1; # Turn off I/O buffering
while (<STDIN>) {
    s/-/_/g; # Replace dashes with underscores
    print $_;
}
```

⟹ **Caution!**

- Keep your rewrite map program as simple as possible. If the program hangs, it will cause httpd to wait indefinitely for a response from the map, which will, in turn, cause httpd to stop responding to requests.

- Be sure to turn off buffering in your program. In Perl this is done by the second line in the example script: `$| = 1;` This will of course vary in other languages. Buffered I/O will cause httpd to wait for the output, and so it will hang.

- Remember that there is only one copy of the program, started at server startup. All requests will need to go through this one bottleneck. This can cause significant slowdowns if many requests must go through this process, or if the script itself is very slow.

## dbd or fastdbd: SQL Query

When a MapType of `dbd` or `fastdbd` is used, the MapSource is a SQL SELECT statement that takes a single argument and returns a single value.

MOD_DBD will need to be configured to point at the right database for this statement to be executed.

There are two forms of this MapType. Using a MapType of dbd causes the query to be executed with each map request, while using fastdbd caches the database lookups internally. So, while fastdbd is more efficient, and therefore faster, it won't pick up on changes to the database until the server is restarted.

If a query returns more than one row, a random row from the result set is used.

**Example**

```
RewriteMap myquery "fastdbd:SELECT destination FROM rewrite WHERE source = %s"
```

## Summary

The REWRITEMAP directive can occur more than once. For each mapping-function use one REWRITEMAP directive to declare its rewriting mapfile.

While you cannot **declare** a map in per-directory context (.htaccess files or <DIRECTORY> blocks) it is possible to **use** this map in per-directory context.

# 4.8    Advanced Techniques with mod_rewrite

This document supplements the MOD_REWRITE reference documentation (p. 867) . It provides a few advanced techniques using mod_rewrite.

 Note that many of these examples won't work unchanged in your particular server configuration, so it's important that you understand them, rather than merely cutting and pasting the examples into your configuration.

**See also**

- Module documentation (p. 867)
- mod_rewrite introduction (p. 147)
- Redirection and remapping (p. 152)
- Controlling access (p. 159)
- Virtual hosts (p. 162)
- Proxying (p. 165)
- Using RewriteMap (p. 166)
- When not to use mod_rewrite (p. 175)

## URL-based sharding across multiple backends

**Description:**  A common technique for distributing the burden of server load or storage space is called "sharding". When using this method, a front-end server will use the url to consistently "shard" users or objects to separate backend servers.

**Solution:**  A mapping is maintained, from users to target servers, in external map files. They look like:

```
user1 physical_host_of_user1
user2 physical_host_of_user2
:   :
```

We put this into a `map.users-to-hosts` file. The aim is to map;

```
/u/user1/anypath
```

to

```
http://physical_host_of_user1/u/user/anypath
```

thus every URL path need not be valid on every backend physical host. The following ruleset does this for us with the help of the map files assuming that server0 is a default server which will be used if a user has no entry in the map:

```
RewriteEngine on
RewriteMap     users-to-hosts      "txt:/path/to/map.users-to-hosts"
RewriteRule    "^/u/([^/]+)/?(.*)" "http://${users-to-hosts:$1|server0}/u/$1/$2"
```

See the REWRITEMAP documentation for more discussion of the syntax of this directive.

### On-the-fly Content-Regeneration

**Description:** We wish to dynamically generate content, but store it statically once it is generated. This rule will check for the existence of the static file, and if it's not there, generate it. The static files can be removed periodically, if desired (say, via cron) and will be regenerated on demand.

**Solution:** This is done via the following ruleset:

```
# This example is valid in per-directory context only
RewriteCond "%{REQUEST_URI}"    !-U
RewriteRule "^(.+)\.html$"       "/regenerate_page.cgi"    [PT,L]
```

The -U operator determines whether the test string (in this case, REQUEST_URI) is a valid URL. It does this via a subrequest. In the event that this subrequest fails - that is, the requested resource doesn't exist - this rule invokes the CGI program /regenerate_page.cgi, which generates the requested resource and saves it into the document directory, so that the next time it is requested, a static copy can be served.

In this way, documents that are infrequently updated can be served in static form. if documents need to be refreshed, they can be deleted from the document directory, and they will then be regenerated the next time they are requested.

### Load Balancing

**Description:** We wish to randomly distribute load across several servers using mod_rewrite.

**Solution:** We'll use REWRITEMAP and a list of servers to accomplish this.

```
RewriteEngine on
RewriteMap  lb        "rnd:/path/to/serverlist.txt"
RewriteRule "^/(.*)" "http://${lb:servers}/$1"      [P,L]
```

serverlist.txt will contain a list of the servers:

```
## serverlist.txt
servers one.example.com|two.example.com|three.example.com
```

If you want one particular server to get more of the load than the others, add it more times to the list.

**Discussion** Apache comes with a load-balancing module - MOD_PROXY_BALANCER - which is far more flexible and featureful than anything you can cobble together using mod_rewrite.

### Structured Userdirs

**Description:** Some sites with thousands of users use a structured homedir layout, *i.e.* each home-dir is in a subdirectory which begins (for instance) with the first character of the username. So, /~larry/anypath is /home/**l**/larry/public_html/anypath while /~waldo/anypath is /home/**w**/waldo/public_html/anypath.

**Solution:** We use the following ruleset to expand the tilde URLs into the above layout.

```
RewriteEngine on
RewriteRule   "^/~(([a-z])[a-z0-9]+)(.*)"  "/home/$2/$1/public_html$3"
```

## Redirecting Anchors

**Description:**  By default, redirecting to an HTML anchor doesn't work, because mod_rewrite escapes the # character, turning it into %23. This, in turn, breaks the redirection.

**Solution:**  Use the [NE] flag on the RewriteRule. NE stands for No Escape.

**Discussion:**  This technique will of course also work with other special characters that mod_rewrite, by default, URL-encodes.

## Time-Dependent Rewriting

**Description:**  We wish to use mod_rewrite to serve different content based on the time of day.

**Solution:**  There are a lot of variables named TIME_xxx for rewrite conditions.  In conjunction with the special lexicographic comparison patterns <STRING, >STRING and =STRING we can do time-dependent redirects:

```
RewriteEngine on
RewriteCond    "%{TIME_HOUR}%{TIME_MIN}" >0700
RewriteCond    "%{TIME_HOUR}%{TIME_MIN}" <1900
RewriteRule    "^foo\.html$"             "foo.day.html" [L]
RewriteRule    "^foo\.html$"             "foo.night.html"
```

This provides the content of foo.day.html under the URL foo.html from 07:01-18:59 and at the remaining time the contents of foo.night.html.

 MOD_CACHE, intermediate proxies and browsers may each cache responses and cause the either page to be shown outside of the time-window configured. MOD_EXPIRES may be used to control this effect. You are, of course, much better off simply serving the content dynamically, and customizing it based on the time of day.

## Set Environment Variables Based On URL Parts

**Description:**  At time, we want to maintain some kind of status when we perform a rewrite. For example, you want to make a note that you've done that rewrite, so that you can check later to see if a request can via that rewrite. One way to do this is by setting an environment variable.

**Solution:**  Use the [E] flag to set an environment variable.

```
RewriteEngine on
RewriteRule   "^/horse/(.*)"   "/pony/$1" [E=rewritten:1]
```

Later in your ruleset you might check for this environment variable using a RewriteCond:

```
RewriteCond "%{ENV:rewritten}"  =1
```

Note that environment variables do not survive an external redirect. You might consider using the [CO] flag to set a cookie.

## 4.9   When not to use mod_rewrite

This document supplements the MOD_REWRITE reference documentation (p. 867) . It describes perhaps one of the most important concepts about MOD_REWRITE - namely, when to avoid using it.

MOD_REWRITE should be considered a last resort, when other alternatives are found wanting. Using it when there are simpler alternatives leads to configurations which are confusing, fragile, and hard to maintain. Understanding what other alternatives are available is a very important step towards MOD_REWRITE mastery.

Note that many of these examples won't work unchanged in your particular server configuration, so it's important that you understand them, rather than merely cutting and pasting the examples into your configuration.

The most common situation in which MOD_REWRITE is the right tool is when the very best solution requires access to the server configuration files, and you don't have that access. Some configuration directives are only available in the server configuration file. So if you are in a hosting situation where you only have .htaccess files to work with, you may need to resort to MOD_REWRITE.

**See also**

- Module documentation (p. 867)
- mod_rewrite introduction (p. 147)
- Redirection and remapping (p. 152)
- Controlling access (p. 159)
- Virtual hosts (p. 162)
- Proxying (p. 165)
- Using RewriteMap (p. 166)
- Advanced techniques (p. 172)

### Simple Redirection

MOD_ALIAS provides the REDIRECT and REDIRECTMATCH directives, which provide a means to redirect one URL to another. This kind of simple redirection of one URL, or a class of URLs, to somewhere else, should be accomplished using these directives rather than REWRITERULE. RedirectMatch allows you to include a regular expression in your redirection criteria, providing many of the benefits of using RewriteRule.

A common use for RewriteRule is to redirect an entire class of URLs. For example, all URLs in the /one directory must be redirected to http://one.example.com/, or perhaps all http requests must be redirected to https.

These situations are better handled by the Redirect directive. Remember that Redirect preserves path information. That is to say, a redirect for a URL /one will also redirect all URLs under that, such as /one/two.html and /one/three/four.html.

To redirect URLs under /one to http://one.example.com, do the following:

```
Redirect "/one/" "http://one.example.com/"
```

To redirect one hostname to another, for example example.com to www.example.com, see the Canonical Hostnames (p. 152) recipe.

To redirect http URLs to https, do the following:

```
<VirtualHost *:80>
    ServerName www.example.com
    Redirect "/" "https://www.example.com/"
```

```
</VirtualHost>

<VirtualHost *:443>
    ServerName www.example.com
    # ... SSL configuration goes here
</VirtualHost>
```

The use of `RewriteRule` to perform this task may be appropriate if there are other `RewriteRule` directives in the same scope. This is because, when there are `Redirect` and `RewriteRule` directives in the same scope, the `RewriteRule` directives will run first, regardless of the order of appearance in the configuration file.

In the case of the *http-to-https* redirection, the use of `RewriteRule` would be appropriate if you don't have access to the main server configuration file, and are obliged to perform this task in a `.htaccess` file instead.

## URL Aliasing

The ALIAS directive provides mapping from a URI to a directory - usually a directory outside of your DOCUMEN-TROOT. Although it is possible to perform this mapping with MOD_REWRITE, ALIAS is the preferred method, for reasons of simplicity and performance.

### Using Alias

```
Alias "/cats" "/var/www/virtualhosts/felines/htdocs"
```

The use of MOD_REWRITE to perform this mapping may be appropriate when you do not have access to the server configuration files. Alias may only be used in server or virtualhost context, and not in a `.htaccess` file.

Symbolic links would be another way to accomplish the same thing, if you have `Options FollowSymLinks` enabled on your server.

## Virtual Hosting

Although it is possible to handle virtual hosts with mod_rewrite (p. 162) , it is seldom the right way. Creating individual <VIRTUALHOST> blocks is almost always the right way to go. In the event that you have an enormous number of virtual hosts, consider using MOD_VHOST_ALIAS to create these hosts automatically.

Modules such as MOD_MACRO are also useful for creating a large number of virtual hosts dynamically.

Using MOD_REWRITE for vitualhost creation may be appropriate if you are using a hosting service that does not provide you access to the server configuration files, and you are therefore restricted to configuration using `.htaccess` files.

See the virtual hosts with mod_rewrite (p. 162) document for more details on how you might accomplish this if it still seems like the right approach.

## Simple Proxying

REWRITERULE provides the [P] (p. 178) flag to pass rewritten URIs through MOD_PROXY.

```
RewriteRule "^/?images(.*)" "http://imageserver.local/images$1" [P]
```

However, in many cases, when there is no actual pattern matching needed, as in the example shown above, the PROX-YPASS directive is a better choice. The example here could be rendered as:

```
ProxyPass "/images/" "http://imageserver.local/images/"
```

Note that whether you use REWRITERULE or PROXYPASS, you'll still need to use the PROXYPASSREVERSE directive to catch redirects issued from the back-end server:

```
ProxyPassReverse "/images/" "http://imageserver.local/images/"
```

You may need to use `RewriteRule` instead when there are other `RewriteRule`s in effect in the same scope, as a `RewriteRule` will usually take effect before a `ProxyPass`, and so may preempt what you're trying to accomplish.

## Environment Variable Testing

MOD_REWRITE is frequently used to take a particular action based on the presence or absence of a particular environment variable or request header. This can be done more efficiently using the <IF>.

Consider, for example, the common scenario where REWRITERULE is used to enforce a canonical hostname, such as `www.example.com` instead of `example.com`. This can be done using the <IF> directive, as shown here:

```
<If "req('Host') != 'www.example.com'">
    Redirect "/" "http://www.example.com/"
</If>
```

This technique can be used to take actions based on any request header, response header, or environment variable, replacing MOD_REWRITE in many common scenarios.

See especially the expression evaluation documentation (p. 99) for a overview of what types of expressions you can use in <IF> sections, and in certain other directives.

# 4.10   RewriteRule Flags

This document discusses the flags which are available to the REWRITERULE directive, providing detailed explanations and examples.

**See also**

- Module documentation (p. 867)
- mod_rewrite introduction (p. 147)
- Redirection and remapping (p. 152)
- Controlling access (p. 159)
- Virtual hosts (p. 162)
- Proxying (p. 165)
- Using RewriteMap (p. 166)
- Advanced techniques (p. 172)
- When not to use mod_rewrite (p. 175)

## Introduction

A REWRITERULE can have its behavior modified by one or more flags. Flags are included in square brackets at the end of the rule, and multiple flags are separated by commas.

```
RewriteRule pattern target [Flag1,Flag2,Flag3]
```

Each flag (with a few exceptions) has a short form, such as CO, as well as a longer form, such as cookie. While it is most common to use the short form, it is recommended that you familiarize yourself with the long form, so that you remember what each flag is supposed to do. Some flags take one or more arguments. Flags are not case sensitive.

Flags that alter metadata associated with the request (T=, H=, E=) have no affect in per-directory and htaccess context, when a substitution (other than '-') is performed during the same round of rewrite processing.

Presented here are each of the available flags, along with an example of how you might use them.

## B (escape backreferences)

The [B] flag instructs REWRITERULE to escape non-alphanumeric characters before applying the transformation.

In 2.4.10 and later, you can limit the escaping to specific characters in backreferences by listing them: [B=#?;]. Note: The space character can be used in the list of characters to escape, but it cannot be the last character in the list.

mod_rewrite has to unescape URLs before mapping them, so backreferences are unescaped at the time they are applied. Using the B flag, non-alphanumeric characters in backreferences will be escaped. For example, consider the rule:

```
RewriteRule "^search/(.*)$" "/search.php?term=$1"
```

Given a search term of 'x & y/z', a browser will encode it as 'x%20%26%20y%2Fz', making the request 'search/x%20%26%20y%2Fz'. Without the B flag, this rewrite rule will map to 'search.php?term=x & y/z', which isn't a valid URL, and so would be encoded as search.php?term=x%20&y%2Fz=, which is not what was intended.

With the B flag set on this same rule, the parameters are re-encoded before being passed on to the output URL, resulting in a correct mapping to `/search.php?term=x%20%26%20y%2Fz`.

Note that you may also need to set ALLOWENCODEDSLASHES to On to get this particular example to work, as httpd does not allow encoded slashes in URLs, and returns a 404 if it sees one.

This escaping is particularly necessary in a proxy situation, when the backend may break if presented with an un-escaped URL.

An alternative to this flag is using a REWRITECOND to capture against %{THE_REQUEST} which will capture strings in the encoded form.

## BNP—backrefnoplus (don't escape space to +)

The [BNP] flag instructs REWRITERULE to escape the space character in a backreference to %20 rather than '+'. Useful when the backreference will be used in the path component rather than the query string.

## C—chain

The [C] or [chain] flag indicates that the REWRITERULE is chained to the next rule. That is, if the rule matches, then it is processed as usual and control moves on to the next rule. However, if it does not match, then the next rule, and any other rules that are chained together, are skipped.

## CO—cookie

The [CO], or [cookie] flag, allows you to set a cookie when a particular REWRITERULE matches. The argument consists of three required fields and four optional fields.

The full syntax for the flag, including all attributes, is as follows:

```
[CO=NAME:VALUE:DOMAIN:lifetime:path:secure:httponly]
```

If a literal ':' character is needed in any of the cookie fields, an alternate syntax is available. To opt-in to the alternate syntax, the cookie "Name" should be preceded with a ';' character, and field separators should be specified as ';'.

```
[CO=;NAME;VALUE:MOREVALUE;DOMAIN;lifetime;path;secure;httponly]
```

You must declare a name, a value, and a domain for the cookie to be set.

**Domain** The domain for which you want the cookie to be valid. This may be a hostname, such as `www.example.com`, or it may be a domain, such as `.example.com`. It must be at least two parts separated by a dot. That is, it may not be merely `.com` or `.net`. Cookies of that kind are forbidden by the cookie security model.

You may optionally also set the following values:

**Lifetime** The time for which the cookie will persist, in minutes. A value of 0 indicates that the cookie will persist only for the current browser session. This is the default value if none is specified.

**Path** The path, on the current website, for which the cookie is valid, such as `/customers/` or `/files/download/`. By default, this is set to / - that is, the entire website.

**Secure** If set to `secure`, `true`, or `1`, the cookie will only be permitted to be translated via secure (https) connections.

**httponly** If set to `HttpOnly`, `true`, or `1`, the cookie will have the `HttpOnly` flag set, which means that the cookie is inaccessible to JavaScript code on browsers that support this feature.

Consider this example:

```
RewriteEngine On
RewriteRule   "^/index\.html"   "-" [CO=frontdoor:yes:.example.com:1440:/]
```

In the example give, the rule doesn't rewrite the request. The `"-"` rewrite target tells mod_rewrite to pass the request through unchanged. Instead, it sets a cookie called 'frontdoor' to a value of 'yes'. The cookie is valid for any host in the `.example.com` domain. It is set to expire in 1440 minutes (24 hours) and is returned for all URIs.

## DPI—discardpath

The DPI flag causes the PATH_INFO portion of the rewritten URI to be discarded.

This flag is available in version 2.2.12 and later.

In per-directory context, the URI each REWRITERULE compares against is the concatenation of the current values of the URI and PATH_INFO.

The current URI can be the initial URI as requested by the client, the result of a previous round of mod_rewrite processing, or the result of a prior rule in the current round of mod_rewrite processing.

In contrast, the PATH_INFO that is appended to the URI before each rule reflects only the value of PATH_INFO before this round of mod_rewrite processing. As a consequence, if large portions of the URI are matched and copied into a substitution in multiple REWRITERULE directives, without regard for which parts of the URI came from the current PATH_INFO, the final URI may have multiple copies of PATH_INFO appended to it.

Use this flag on any substitution where the PATH_INFO that resulted from the previous mapping of this request to the filesystem is not of interest. This flag permanently forgets the PATH_INFO established before this round of mod_rewrite processing began. PATH_INFO will not be recalculated until the current round of mod_rewrite processing completes. Subsequent rules during this round of processing will see only the direct result of substitutions, without any PATH_INFO appended.

## E—env

With the [E], or [env] flag, you can set the value of an environment variable. Note that some environment variables may be set after the rule is run, thus unsetting what you have set. See the Environment Variables document (p. 92) for more details on how Environment variables work.

The full syntax for this flag is:

```
[E=VAR:VAL]
[E=!VAR]
```

`VAL` may contain backreferences (`$N` or `%N`) which are expanded.

Using the short form

```
[E=VAR]
```

you can set the environment variable named VAR to an empty value.

The form

```
[E=!VAR]
```

allows to unset a previously set environment variable named VAR.

Environment variables can then be used in a variety of contexts, including CGI programs, other RewriteRule directives, or CustomLog directives.

The following example sets an environment variable called 'image' to a value of '1' if the requested URI is an image file. Then, that environment variable is used to exclude those requests from the access log.

```
RewriteRule "\.(png|gif|jpg)$"    "-" [E=image:1]
CustomLog   "logs/access_log"     combined env=!image
```

Note that this same effect can be obtained using SETENVIF. This technique is offered as an example, not as a recommendation.

## END

Using the [END] flag terminates not only the current round of rewrite processing (like [L]) but also prevents any subsequent rewrite processing from occurring in per-directory (htaccess) context.

This does not apply to new requests resulting from external redirects.

## F—forbidden

Using the [F] flag causes the server to return a 403 Forbidden status code to the client. While the same behavior can be accomplished using the DENY directive, this allows more flexibility in assigning a Forbidden status.

The following rule will forbid .exe files from being downloaded from your server.

```
RewriteRule "\.exe"   "-" [F]
```

This example uses the "-" syntax for the rewrite target, which means that the requested URI is not modified. There's no reason to rewrite to another URI, if you're going to forbid the request.

When using [F], an [L] is implied - that is, the response is returned immediately, and no further rules are evaluated.

## G—gone

The [G] flag forces the server to return a 410 Gone status with the response. This indicates that a resource used to be available, but is no longer available.

As with the [F] flag, you will typically use the "-" syntax for the rewrite target when using the [G] flag:

```
RewriteRule "oldproduct"   "-" [G,NC]
```

When using [G], an [L] is implied - that is, the response is returned immediately, and no further rules are evaluated.

## H—handler

Forces the resulting request to be handled with the specified handler. For example, one might use this to force all files without a file extension to be parsed by the php handler:

```
RewriteRule "!\." "-" [H=application/x-httpd-php]
```

The regular expression above - !\. - will match any request that does not contain the literal . character.

This can be also used to force the handler based on some conditions. For example, the following snippet used in per-server context allows .php files to be *displayed* by mod_php if they are requested with the .phps extension:

```
RewriteRule "^(/source/.+\.php)s$" "$1" [H=application/x-httpd-php-source]
```

The regular expression above - ^(/source/.+\.php)s$ - will match any request that starts with /source/ followed by 1 or n characters followed by .phps literally. The backreference $1 referrers to the captured match within parenthesis of the regular expression.

## L—last

The [L] flag causes MOD_REWRITE to stop processing the rule set. In most contexts, this means that if the rule matches, no further rules will be processed. This corresponds to the last command in Perl, or the break command in C. Use this flag to indicate that the current rule should be applied immediately without considering further rules.

If you are using REWRITERULE in either .htaccess files or in <DIRECTORY> sections, it is important to have some understanding of how the rules are processed. The simplified form of this is that once the rules have been processed, the rewritten request is handed back to the URL parsing engine to do what it may with it. It is possible that as the rewritten request is handled, the .htaccess file or <DIRECTORY> section may be encountered again, and thus the ruleset may be run again from the start. Most commonly this will happen if one of the rules causes a redirect - either internal or external - causing the request process to start over.

It is therefore important, if you are using REWRITERULE directives in one of these contexts, that you take explicit steps to avoid rules looping, and not count solely on the [L] flag to terminate execution of a series of rules, as shown below.

An alternative flag, [END], can be used to terminate not only the current round of rewrite processing but prevent any subsequent rewrite processing from occurring in per-directory (htaccess) context. This does not apply to new requests resulting from external redirects.

The example given here will rewrite any request to index.php, giving the original request as a query string argument to index.php, however, the REWRITECOND ensures that if the request is already for index.php, the REWRITERULE will be skipped.

```
RewriteBase "/"
RewriteCond "%{REQUEST_URI}" !=/index.php
RewriteRule "^(.*)"          "/index.php?req=$1" [L,PT]
```

## N—next

The [N] flag causes the ruleset to start over again from the top, using the result of the ruleset so far as a starting point. Use with extreme caution, as it may result in loop.

The [Next] flag could be used, for example, if you wished to replace a certain string or letter repeatedly in a request. The example shown here will replace A with B everywhere in a request, and will continue doing so until there are no more As to be replaced.

```
RewriteRule "(.*)A(.*)" "$1B$2" [N]
```

You can think of this as a `while` loop: While this pattern still matches (i.e., while the URI still contains an A), perform this substitution (i.e., replace the A with a B).

In 2.5.0 and later, this module returns an error after 10,000 iterations to protect against unintended looping. An alternative maximum number of iterations can be specified by adding to the N flag.

```
# Be willing to replace 1 character in each pass of the loop
RewriteRule "(.+)[><;]$" "$1" [N=32000]
# ... or, give up if after 10 loops
RewriteRule "(.+)[><;]$" "$1" [N=10]
```

## NC—nocase

Use of the [NC] flag causes the REWRITERULE to be matched in a case-insensitive manner. That is, it doesn't care whether letters appear as upper-case or lower-case in the matched URI.

In the example below, any request for an image file will be proxied to your dedicated image server. The match is case-insensitive, so that `.jpg` and `.JPG` files are both acceptable, for example.

```
RewriteRule "(.*\.(jpg|gif|png))$" "http://images.example.com$1" [P,NC]
```

## NE—noescape

By default, special characters, such as `&` and `?`, for example, will be converted to their hexcode equivalent. Using the [NE] flag prevents that from happening.

```
RewriteRule "^/anchor/(.+)" "/bigpage.html#$1" [NE,R]
```

The above example will redirect `/anchor/xyz` to `/bigpage.html#xyz`. Omitting the [NE] will result in the # being converted to its hexcode equivalent, `%23`, which will then result in a 404 Not Found error condition.

## NS—nosubreq

Use of the [NS] flag prevents the rule from being used on subrequests. For example, a page which is included using an SSI (Server Side Include) is a subrequest, and you may want to avoid rewrites happening on those subrequests. Also, when MOD_DIR tries to find out information about possible directory default files (such as `index.html` files), this is an internal subrequest, and you often want to avoid rewrites on such subrequests. On subrequests, it is not always useful, and can even cause errors, if the complete set of rules are applied. Use this flag to exclude problematic rules.

To decide whether or not to use this rule: if you prefix URLs with CGI-scripts, to force them to be processed by the CGI-script, it's likely that you will run into problems (or significant overhead) on sub-requests. In these cases, use this flag.

Images, javascript files, or css files, loaded as part of an HTML page, are not subrequests - the browser requests them as separate HTTP requests.

## P—proxy

Use of the [P] flag causes the request to be handled by MOD_PROXY, and handled via a proxy request. For example, if you wanted all image requests to be handled by a back-end image server, you might do something like the following:

```
RewriteRule "/(.*)\.(jpg|gif|png)$" "http://images.example.com/$1.$2" [P]
```

Use of the [P] flag implies [L] - that is, the request is immediately pushed through the proxy, and any following rules will not be considered.

You must make sure that the substitution string is a valid URI (typically starting with http://*hostname*) which can be handled by the MOD_PROXY. If not, you will get an error from the proxy module. Use this flag to achieve a more powerful implementation of the PROXYPASS directive, to map remote content into the namespace of the local server.

 **Security Warning**

> Take care when constructing the target URL of the rule, considering the security impact from allowing the client influence over the set of URLs to which your server will act as a proxy. Ensure that the scheme and hostname part of the URL is either fixed, or does not allow the client undue influence.

 **Performance warning**

> Using this flag triggers the use of MOD_PROXY, without handling of persistent connections. This means the performance of your proxy will be better if you set it up with PROXYPASS or PROXYPASSMATCH
> This is because this flag triggers the use of the default worker, which does not handle connection pooling.
> Avoid using this flag and prefer those directives, whenever you can.

Note: MOD_PROXY must be enabled in order to use this flag.

## PT—passthrough

The target (or substitution string) in a RewriteRule is assumed to be a file path, by default. The use of the [PT] flag causes it to be treated as a URI instead. That is to say, the use of the [PT] flag causes the result of the REWRITERULE to be passed back through URL mapping, so that location-based mappings, such as ALIAS, REDIRECT, or SCRIPTALIAS, for example, might have a chance to take effect.

If, for example, you have an ALIAS for /icons, and have a REWRITERULE pointing there, you should use the [PT] flag to ensure that the ALIAS is evaluated.

```
Alias "/icons" "/usr/local/apache/icons"
RewriteRule "/pics/(.+)\.jpg$" "/icons/$1.gif" [PT]
```

Omission of the [PT] flag in this case will cause the Alias to be ignored, resulting in a 'File not found' error being returned.

The PT flag implies the L flag: rewriting will be stopped in order to pass the request to the next phase of processing.

Note that the PT flag is implied in per-directory contexts such as <DIRECTORY> sections or in .htaccess files. The only way to circumvent that is to rewrite to -.

## QSA—qsappend

When the replacement URI contains a query string, the default behavior of REWRITERULE is to discard the existing query string, and replace it with the newly generated one. Using the [QSA] flag causes the query strings to be combined.

Consider the following rule:

```
RewriteRule "/pages/(.+)" "/page.php?page=$1" [QSA]
```

With the [QSA] flag, a request for /pages/123?one=two will be mapped to /page.php?page=123&one=two. Without the [QSA] flag, that same request will be mapped to /page.php?page=123 - that is, the existing query string will be discarded.

## QSD—qsdiscard

When the requested URI contains a query string, and the target URI does not, the default behavior of REWRITERULE is to copy that query string to the target URI. Using the [QSD] flag causes the query string to be discarded.

This flag is available in version 2.4.0 and later.

Using [QSD] and [QSA] together will result in [QSD] taking precedence.

If the target URI has a query string, the default behavior will be observed - that is, the original query string will be discarded and replaced with the query string in the RewriteRule target URI.

## QSL—qslast

By default, the first (left-most) question mark in the substitution delimits the path from the query string. Using the [QSL] flag instructs REWRITERULE to instead split the two components using the last (right-most) question mark.

This is useful when mapping to files that have literal question marks in their filename. If no query string is used in the substitution, a question mark can be appended to it in combination with this flag.

This flag is available in version 2.4.19 and later.

## R—redirect

Use of the [R] flag causes a HTTP redirect to be issued to the browser. If a fully-qualified URL is specified (that is, including http://servername/) then a redirect will be issued to that location. Otherwise, the current protocol, servername, and port number will be used to generate the URL sent with the redirect.

*Any* valid HTTP response status code may be specified, using the syntax [R=305], with a 302 status code being used by default if none is specified. The status code specified need not necessarily be a redirect (3xx) status code. However, if a status code is outside the redirect range (300-399) then the substitution string is dropped entirely, and rewriting is stopped as if the L were used.

In addition to response status codes, you may also specify redirect status using their symbolic names: temp (default), permanent, or seeother.

You will almost always want to use [R] in conjunction with [L] (that is, use [R,L]) because on its own, the [R] flag prepends http://thishost[:thisport] to the URI, but then passes this on to the next rule in the ruleset, which can often result in 'Invalid URI in request' warnings.

## S—skip

The [S] flag is used to skip rules that you don't want to run. The syntax of the skip flag is [S=*N*], where *N* signifies the number of rules to skip (provided the REWRITERULE and any preceding REWRITECOND directives match). This can be thought of as a goto statement in your rewrite ruleset. In the following example, we only want to run the REWRITERULE if the requested URI doesn't correspond with an actual file.

```
# Is the request for a non-existent file?
RewriteCond "%{REQUEST_FILENAME}" !-f
RewriteCond "%{REQUEST_FILENAME}" !-d
# If so, skip these two RewriteRules
RewriteRule ".?"                    "-" [S=2]

RewriteRule "(.*\.gif)"            "images.php?$1"
RewriteRule "(.*\.html)"          "docs.php?$1"
```

This technique is useful because a RewriteCond only applies to the RewriteRule immediately following it. Thus, if you want to make a RewriteCond apply to several RewriteRules, one possible technique is to negate those conditions and add a RewriteRule with a [Skip] flag. You can use this to make pseudo if-then-else constructs: The last rule of the then-clause becomes skip=N, where N is the number of rules in the else-clause:

```
# Does the file exist?
RewriteCond "%{REQUEST_FILENAME}" !-f
RewriteCond "%{REQUEST_FILENAME}" !-d
# Create an if-then-else construct by skipping 3 lines if we meant to go to the "else" sta
RewriteRule ".?"                    "-" [S=3]

# IF the file exists, then:
    RewriteRule "(.*\.gif)"  "images.php?$1"
    RewriteRule "(.*\.html)" "docs.php?$1"
    # Skip past the "else" stanza.
    RewriteRule ".?"         "-" [S=1]
# ELSE...
    RewriteRule "(.*)"       "404.php?file=$1"
# END
```

It is probably easier to accomplish this kind of configuration using the <IF>, <ELSEIF>, and <ELSE> directives instead.

## T—type

Sets the MIME type with which the resulting response will be sent. This has the same effect as the ADDTYPE directive.

For example, you might use the following technique to serve Perl source code as plain text, if requested in a particular way:

```
# Serve .pl files as plain text
RewriteRule "\.pl$"  "-" [T=text/plain]
```

Or, perhaps, if you have a camera that produces jpeg images without file extensions, you could force those images to be served with the correct MIME type by virtue of their file names:

```
# Files with 'IMG' in the name are jpg images.
RewriteRule "IMG"  "-" [T=image/jpg]
```

Please note that this is a trivial example, and could be better done using <FILESMATCH> instead. Always consider the alternate solutions to a problem before resorting to rewrite, which will invariably be a less efficient solution than the alternatives.

If used in per-directory context, use only - (dash) as the substitution *for the entire round of mod_rewrite processing*, otherwise the MIME-type set with this flag is lost due to an internal re-processing (including subsequent rounds of mod_rewrite processing). The L flag can be useful in this context to end the *current* round of mod_rewrite processing.

# 4.11 Apache mod_rewrite Technical Details

This document discusses some of the technical details of mod_rewrite and URL matching.

**See also**

- Module documentation (p. 867)
- mod_rewrite introduction (p. 147)
- Redirection and remapping (p. 152)
- Controlling access (p. 159)
- Virtual hosts (p. 162)
- Proxying (p. 165)
- Using RewriteMap (p. 166)
- Advanced techniques (p. 172)
- When not to use mod_rewrite (p. 175)

## API Phases

The Apache HTTP Server handles requests in several phases. At each of these phases, one or more modules may be called upon to handle that portion of the request lifecycle. Phases include things like URL-to-filename translation, authentication, authorization, content, and logging. (This is not an exhaustive list.)

mod_rewrite acts in two of these phases (or "hooks", as they are often called) to influence how URLs may be rewritten.

First, it uses the URL-to-filename translation hook, which occurs after the HTTP request has been read, but before any authorization starts. Secondly, it uses the Fixup hook, which is after the authorization phases, and after per-directory configuration files (`.htaccess` files) have been read, but before the content handler is called.

After a request comes in and a corresponding server or virtual host has been determined, the rewriting engine starts processing any `mod_rewrite` directives appearing in the per-server configuration. (i.e., in the main server configuration file and <VIRTUALHOST> sections.) This happens in the URL-to-filename phase.

A few steps later, once the final data directories have been found, the per-directory configuration directives (`.htaccess` files and <DIRECTORY> blocks) are applied. This happens in the Fixup phase.

In each of these cases, mod_rewrite rewrites the REQUEST_URI either to a new URL, or to a filename.

In per-directory context (i.e., within `.htaccess` files and `Directory` blocks), these rules are being applied after a URL has already been translated to a filename. Because of this, the URL-path that mod_rewrite initially compares REWRITERULE directives against is the full filesystem path to the translated filename with the current directories path (including a trailing slash) removed from the front.

To illustrate: If rules are in /var/www/foo/.htaccess and a request for /foo/bar/baz is being processed, an expression like ^bar/baz$ would match.

If a substitution is made in per-directory context, a new internal subrequest is issued with the new URL, which restarts processing of the request phases. If the substitution is a relative path, the REWRITEBASE directive determines the URL-path prefix prepended to the substitution. In per-directory context, care must be taken to create rules which will eventually (in some future "round" of per-directory rewrite processing) not perform a substitution to avoid looping. (See RewriteLooping[6] for further discussion of this problem.)

Because of this further manipulation of the URL in per-directory context, you'll need to take care to craft your rewrite rules differently in that context. In particular, remember that the leading directory path will be stripped off of the URL that your rewrite rules will see. Consider the examples below for further clarification.

---

[6]http://wiki.apache.org/httpd/RewriteLooping

| Location of rule | Rule |
|---|---|
| VirtualHost section | RewriteRule "^/images/(.+)\.jpg" "/images/$1.gif" |
| .htaccess file in document root | RewriteRule "^images/(.+)\.jpg" "images/$1.gif" |
| .htaccess file in images directory | RewriteRule "^(.+)\.jpg" "$1.gif" |

For even more insight into how mod_rewrite manipulates URLs in different contexts, you should consult the log entries (p. 867) made during rewriting.

## Ruleset Processing

Now when mod_rewrite is triggered in these two API phases, it reads the configured rulesets from its configuration structure (which itself was either created on startup for per-server context or during the directory walk of the Apache kernel for per-directory context). Then the URL rewriting engine is started with the contained ruleset (one or more rules together with their conditions). The operation of the URL rewriting engine itself is exactly the same for both configuration contexts. Only the final result processing is different.

The order of rules in the ruleset is important because the rewriting engine processes them in a special (and not very obvious) order. The rule is this: The rewriting engine loops through the ruleset rule by rule (REWRITERULE directives) and when a particular rule matches it optionally loops through existing corresponding conditions (RewriteCond directives). For historical reasons the conditions are given first, and so the control flow is a little bit long-winded. See Figure 1 for more details.

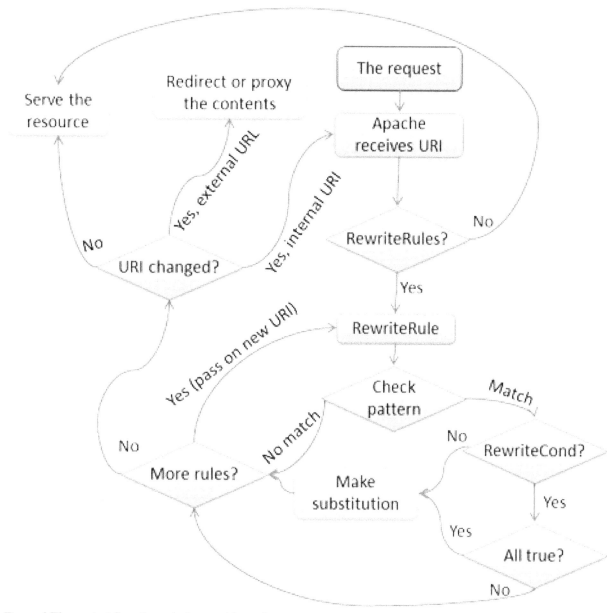

*Figure 1:*The control flow through the rewriting ruleset

First the URL is matched against the *Pattern* of each rule. If it fails, mod_rewrite immediately stops processing this rule, and continues with the next rule. If the *Pattern* matches, mod_rewrite looks for corresponding rule conditions (RewriteCond directives, appearing immediately above the RewriteRule in the configuration). If none are present, it substitutes the URL with a new value, which is constructed from the string *Substitution*, and goes on with its rule-looping. But if conditions exist, it starts an inner loop for processing them in the order that they are listed. For conditions, the logic is different: we don't match a pattern against the current URL. Instead we first create a string *TestString* by expanding variables, back-references, map lookups, *etc.* and then we try to match *CondPattern* against it. If the pattern doesn't match, the complete set of conditions and the corresponding rule fails. If the pattern matches, then the next condition is processed until no more conditions are available. If all conditions match, processing is continued with the substitution of the URL with *Substitution*.

# Chapter 5

# Apache SSL/TLS Encryption

## 5.1    Apache SSL/TLS Encryption

The Apache HTTP Server module MOD_SSL provides an interface to the OpenSSL[1] library, which provides Strong Encryption using the Secure Sockets Layer and Transport Layer Security protocols.

### Documentation

- mod_ssl Configuration How-To (p. 206)
- Introduction To SSL (p. 193)
- Compatibility (p. 202)
- Frequently Asked Questions (p. 212)
- Glossary (p. 1096)

### mod_ssl

Extensive documentation on the directives and environment variables provided by this module is provided in the mod_ssl reference documentation (p. 916) .

---

[1]http://www.openssl.org/

# 5.2 SSL/TLS Strong Encryption: An Introduction

As an introduction this chapter is aimed at readers who are familiar with the Web, HTTP, and Apache, but are not security experts. It is not intended to be a definitive guide to the SSL protocol, nor does it discuss specific techniques for managing certificates in an organization, or the important legal issues of patents and import and export restrictions. Rather, it is intended to provide a common background to MOD_SSL users by pulling together various concepts, definitions, and examples as a starting point for further exploration.

## Cryptographic Techniques

Understanding SSL requires an understanding of cryptographic algorithms, message digest functions (aka. one-way or hash functions), and digital signatures. These techniques are the subject of entire books (see for instance [AC96]) and provide the basis for privacy, integrity, and authentication.

### Cryptographic Algorithms

Suppose Alice wants to send a message to her bank to transfer some money. Alice would like the message to be private, since it will include information such as her account number and transfer amount. One solution is to use a cryptographic algorithm, a technique that would transform her message into an encrypted form, unreadable until it is decrypted. Once in this form, the message can only be decrypted by using a secret key. Without the key the message is useless: good cryptographic algorithms make it so difficult for intruders to decode the original text that it isn't worth their effort.

There are two categories of cryptographic algorithms: conventional and public key.

**Conventional cryptography** also known as symmetric cryptography, requires the sender and receiver to share a key: a secret piece of information that may be used to encrypt or decrypt a message. As long as this key is kept secret, nobody other than the sender or recipient can read the message. If Alice and the bank know a secret key, then they can send each other private messages. The task of sharing a key between sender and recipient before communicating, while also keeping it secret from others, can be problematic.

**Public key cryptography** also known as asymmetric cryptography, solves the key exchange problem by defining an algorithm which uses two keys, each of which may be used to encrypt a message. If one key is used to encrypt a message then the other must be used to decrypt it. This makes it possible to receive secure messages by simply publishing one key (the public key) and keeping the other secret (the private key).

Anyone can encrypt a message using the public key, but only the owner of the private key will be able to read it. In this way, Alice can send private messages to the owner of a key-pair (the bank), by encrypting them using their public key. Only the bank will be able to decrypt them.

### Message Digests

Although Alice may encrypt her message to make it private, there is still a concern that someone might modify her original message or substitute it with a different one, in order to transfer the money to themselves, for instance. One way of guaranteeing the integrity of Alice's message is for her to create a concise summary of her message and send this to the bank as well. Upon receipt of the message, the bank creates its own summary and compares it with the one Alice sent. If the summaries are the same then the message has been received intact.

A summary such as this is called a *message digest*, *one-way function* or *hash function*. Message digests are used to create a short, fixed-length representation of a longer, variable-length message. Digest algorithms are designed to produce a unique digest for each message. Message digests are designed to make it impractically difficult to determine the message from the digest and (in theory) impossible to find two different messages which create the same digest – thus eliminating the possibility of substituting one message for another while maintaining the same digest.

Another challenge that Alice faces is finding a way to send the digest to the bank securely; if the digest is not sent securely, its integrity may be compromised and with it the possibility for the bank to determine the integrity of the original message. Only if the digest is sent securely can the integrity of the associated message be determined.

One way to send the digest securely is to include it in a digital signature.

### Digital Signatures

When Alice sends a message to the bank, the bank needs to ensure that the message is really from her, so an intruder cannot request a transaction involving her account. A *digital signature*, created by Alice and included with the message, serves this purpose.

Digital signatures are created by encrypting a digest of the message and other information (such as a sequence number) with the sender's private key. Though anyone can *decrypt* the signature using the public key, only the sender knows the private key. This means that only the sender can have signed the message. Including the digest in the signature means the signature is only good for that message; it also ensures the integrity of the message since no one can change the digest and still sign it.

To guard against interception and reuse of the signature by an intruder at a later date, the signature contains a unique sequence number. This protects the bank from a fraudulent claim from Alice that she did not send the message – only she could have signed it (non-repudiation).

## Certificates

Although Alice could have sent a private message to the bank, signed it and ensured the integrity of the message, she still needs to be sure that she is really communicating with the bank. This means that she needs to be sure that the public key she is using is part of the bank's key-pair, and not an intruder's. Similarly, the bank needs to verify that the message signature really was signed by the private key that belongs to Alice.

If each party has a certificate which validates the other's identity, confirms the public key and is signed by a trusted agency, then both can be assured that they are communicating with whom they think they are. Such a trusted agency is called a *Certificate Authority* and certificates are used for authentication.

### Certificate Contents

A certificate associates a public key with the real identity of an individual, server, or other entity, known as the subject. As shown in Table 1, information about the subject includes identifying information (the distinguished name) and the public key. It also includes the identification and signature of the Certificate Authority that issued the certificate and the period of time during which the certificate is valid. It may have additional information (or extensions) as well as administrative information for the Certificate Authority's use, such as a serial number.

**Table 1: Certificate Information**

| Subject | Distinguished Name, Public Key |
|---|---|
| **Issuer** | Distinguished Name, Signature |
| **Period of Validity** | Not Before Date, Not After Date |
| **Administrative Information** | Version, Serial Number |
| **Extended Information** | Basic Constraints, Netscape Flags, etc. |

A distinguished name is used to provide an identity in a specific context – for instance, an individual might have a personal certificate as well as one for their identity as an employee. Distinguished names are defined by the X.509 standard [X509], which defines the fields, field names and abbreviations used to refer to the fields (see Table 2).

**Table 2: Distinguished Name Information**

| DN Field | Abbrev. | Description | Example |
|---|---|---|---|
| Common Name | CN | Name being certified | CN=Joe Average |
| Organization or Company | O | Name is associated with this organization | O=Snake Oil, Ltd. |
| Organizational Unit | OU | Name is associated with this organization unit, such as a department | OU=Research Institute |
| City/Locality | L | Name is located in this City | L=Snake City |
| State/Province | ST | Name is located in this State/Province | ST=Desert |
| Country | C | Name is located in this Country (ISO code) | C=XZ |

A Certificate Authority may define a policy specifying which distinguished field names are optional and which are required. It may also place requirements upon the field contents, as may users of certificates. For example, a Netscape browser requires that the Common Name for a certificate representing a server matches a wildcard pattern for the domain name of that server, such as `*.snakeoil.com`.

The binary format of a certificate is defined using the ASN.1 notation [ASN1] [PKCS]. This notation defines how to specify the contents and encoding rules define how this information is translated into binary form. The binary encoding of the certificate is defined using Distinguished Encoding Rules (DER), which are based on the more general Basic Encoding Rules (BER). For those transmissions which cannot handle binary, the binary form may be translated into an ASCII form by using Base64 encoding [MIME]. When placed between begin and end delimiter lines (as below), this encoded version is called a PEM (`"Privacy Enhanced Mail"`) encoded certificate.

### Example of a PEM-encoded certificate (snakeoil.crt)

```
-----BEGIN CERTIFICATE-----
MIIC7jCCAlegAwIBAgIBATANBgkqhkiG9w0BAQQFADCBqTELMAkGA1UEBhMCWFkx
FTATBgNVBAgTDFNuYWtlIERlc2VydDETMBEGA1UEBxMKU25ha2UgVG93bjEXMBUG
A1UEChMOU25ha2UgT2lsLCBMdGQxHjAcBgNVBAsTFUNlcnRpZmljYXRlIEF1dGhv
cml0eTEVMBMGA1UEAxMMU25ha2UgT2lsIENBMR4wHAYJKoZIhvcNAQkBFg9jYUBz
bmFrZW9pbC5kb20wHhcNOTgxMDIxMDg1ODM2WhcNOTkxMDIxMDg1ODM2WjCBpzEL
MAkGA1UEBhMCWFkxFTATBgNVBAgTDFNuYWtlIERlc2VydDETMBEGA1UEBxMKU25h
a2UgVG93bjEXMBUGA1UEChMOU25ha2UgT2lsLCBMdGQxFzAVBgNVBAsTDldlYnNl
cnZlciBUZWFtMRkwFwYDVQQDExB3d3cuc25ha2VvaWwuZG9tMR8wHQYJKoZIhvcN
AQkBFhB3d3dAc25ha2VvaWwuZG9tMIGfMA0GCSqGSIb3DQEBAQUAA4GNADCBiQKB
gQDH9Ge/s2zcH+da+rPTx/DPRp3xGjHZ4GG6pCmvADIEtBtKBFAcZ64n+Dy7Np8b
vKR+yy5DGQiijsH1D/j8HlGE+q4TZ8OFk7BNBFazHxFbYI4OKMiCxdKzdif1yfaa
lWoANFlAzlSdbxeGVHoT0K+gT5w3UxwZKv2DLbCTzLZyPwIDAQABoyYwJDAPBgNV
HRMECDAGAQH/AgEAMBEGCWCGSAGG+EIBAQQEAwIAQDANBgkqhkiG9w0BAQQFAAOB
gQAZUIHAL4D09oE6Lv2k56Gp38OBDuILvwLg1v1KL8mQR+KFjghCrtpqaztZqcDt
2q2QoyulCgSzHbEGmi0EsdkPfg6mp0penssIFePYNI+/8u9HT4LuKMJX15hxBam7
dUHzICxBVC1lnHyYGjDuAMhe3961YAn8bCld1/L4NMGBCQ==
-----END CERTIFICATE-----
```

## Certificate Authorities

By verifying the information in a certificate request before granting the certificate, the Certificate Authority assures itself of the identity of the private key owner of a key-pair. For instance, if Alice requests a personal certificate, the Certificate Authority must first make sure that Alice really is the person the certificate request claims she is.

**Certificate Chains**

A Certificate Authority may also issue a certificate for another Certificate Authority. When examining a certificate, Alice may need to examine the certificate of the issuer, for each parent Certificate Authority, until reaching one which she has confidence in. She may decide to trust only certificates with a limited chain of issuers, to reduce her risk of a "bad" certificate in the chain.

**Creating a Root-Level CA**

As noted earlier, each certificate requires an issuer to assert the validity of the identity of the certificate subject, up to the top-level Certificate Authority (CA). This presents a problem: who can vouch for the certificate of the top-level authority, which has no issuer? In this unique case, the certificate is "self-signed", so the issuer of the certificate is the same as the subject. Browsers are preconfigured to trust well-known certificate authorities, but it is important to exercise extra care in trusting a self-signed certificate. The wide publication of a public key by the root authority reduces the risk in trusting this key – it would be obvious if someone else publicized a key claiming to be the authority.

A number of companies, such as Thawte[2] and VeriSign[3] have established themselves as Certificate Authorities. These companies provide the following services:

- Verifying certificate requests
- Processing certificate requests
- Issuing and managing certificates

It is also possible to create your own Certificate Authority. Although risky in the Internet environment, it may be useful within an Intranet where the organization can easily verify the identities of individuals and servers.

**Certificate Management**

Establishing a Certificate Authority is a responsibility which requires a solid administrative, technical and management framework. Certificate Authorities not only issue certificates, they also manage them – that is, they determine for how long certificates remain valid, they renew them and keep lists of certificates that were issued in the past but are no longer valid (Certificate Revocation Lists, or CRLs).

For example, if Alice is entitled to a certificate as an employee of a company but has now left that company, her certificate may need to be revoked. Because certificates are only issued after the subject's identity has been verified and can then be passed around to all those with whom the subject may communicate, it is impossible to tell from the certificate alone that it has been revoked. Therefore when examining certificates for validity it is necessary to contact the issuing Certificate Authority to check CRLs – this is usually not an automated part of the process.

**Note**

> If you use a Certificate Authority that browsers are not configured to trust by default, it is necessary to load the Certificate Authority certificate into the browser, enabling the browser to validate server certificates signed by that Certificate Authority. Doing so may be dangerous, since once loaded, the browser will accept all certificates signed by that Certificate Authority.

# Secure Sockets Layer (SSL)

The Secure Sockets Layer protocol is a protocol layer which may be placed between a reliable connection-oriented network layer protocol (e.g. TCP/IP) and the application protocol layer (e.g. HTTP). SSL provides for secure communication between client and server by allowing mutual authentication, the use of digital signatures for integrity and encryption for privacy.

[2]http://www.thawte.com/
[3]http://www.verisign.com/

The protocol is designed to support a range of choices for specific algorithms used for cryptography, digests and signatures. This allows algorithm selection for specific servers to be made based on legal, export or other concerns and also enables the protocol to take advantage of new algorithms. Choices are negotiated between client and server when establishing a protocol session.

**Table 4: Versions of the SSL protocol**

| Version | Source | Description |
|---------|--------|-------------|
| SSL v2.0 | Vendor Standard (from Netscape Corp.) | First SSL protocol for which implementations exist |
| SSL v3.0 | Expired Internet Draft (from Netscape Corp.) [SSL3] | Revisions to prevent specific security attacks, add non-RSA ciphers and support for certificate chains |
| TLS v1.0 | Proposed Internet Standard (from IETF) [TLS1] | Revision of SSL 3.0 to update the MAC layer to HMAC, add block padding for block ciphers, message order standardization and more alert messages. |
| TLS v1.1 | Proposed Internet Standard (from IETF) [TLS11] | Update of TLS 1.0 to add protection against Cipher block chaining (CBC) attacks. |
| TLS v1.2 | Proposed Internet Standard (from IETF) [TLS12] | Update of TLS 1.2 deprecating MD5 as hash, and adding incompatibility to SSL so it will never negotiate the use of SSLv2. |

There are a number of versions of the SSL protocol, as shown in Table 4. As noted there, one of the benefits in SSL 3.0 is that it adds support of certificate chain loading. This feature allows a server to pass a server certificate along with issuer certificates to the browser. Chain loading also permits the browser to validate the server certificate, even if Certificate Authority certificates are not installed for the intermediate issuers, since they are included in the certificate chain. SSL 3.0 is the basis for the Transport Layer Security [TLS] protocol standard, currently in development by the Internet Engineering Task Force (IETF).

**Establishing a Session**

The SSL session is established by following a handshake sequence between client and server, as shown in Figure 1. This sequence may vary, depending on whether the server is configured to provide a server certificate or request a client certificate. Although cases exist where additional handshake steps are required for management of cipher information, this article summarizes one common scenario. See the SSL specification for the full range of possibilities.

Note

> Once an SSL session has been established, it may be reused. This avoids the performance penalty of repeating the many steps needed to start a session. To do this, the server assigns each SSL session a unique session identifier which is cached in the server and which the client can use in future connections to reduce the handshake time (until the session identifier expires from the cache of the server).

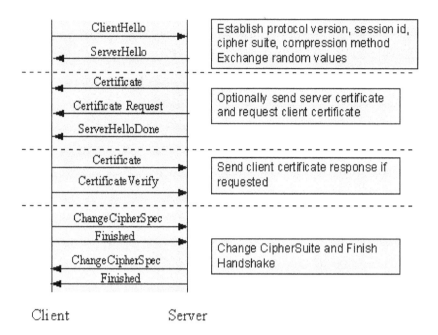

*Figure 1*: Simplified SSL Handshake Sequence

The elements of the handshake sequence, as used by the client and server, are listed below:

1. Negotiate the Cipher Suite to be used during data transfer

2. Establish and share a session key between client and server

3. Optionally authenticate the server to the client

4. Optionally authenticate the client to the server

The first step, Cipher Suite Negotiation, allows the client and server to choose a Cipher Suite supported by both of them. The SSL3.0 protocol specification defines 31 Cipher Suites. A Cipher Suite is defined by the following components:

- Key Exchange Method
- Cipher for Data Transfer
- Message Digest for creating the Message Authentication Code (MAC)

These three elements are described in the sections that follow.

**Key Exchange Method**

The key exchange method defines how the shared secret symmetric cryptography key used for application data transfer will be agreed upon by client and server. SSL 2.0 uses RSA key exchange only, while SSL 3.0 supports a choice of key exchange algorithms including RSA key exchange (when certificates are used), and Diffie-Hellman key exchange (for exchanging keys without certificates, or without prior communication between client and server).

One variable in the choice of key exchange methods is digital signatures – whether or not to use them, and if so, what kind of signatures to use. Signing with a private key provides protection against a man-in-the-middle-attack during the information exchange used to generating the shared key [AC96, p516].

**Cipher for Data Transfer**

SSL uses conventional symmetric cryptography, as described earlier, for encrypting messages in a session. There are nine choices of how to encrypt, including the option not to encrypt:

- No encryption
- Stream Ciphers

    - RC4 with 40-bit keys
    - RC4 with 128-bit keys

- CBC Block Ciphers

    - RC2 with 40 bit key
    - DES with 40 bit key
    - DES with 56 bit key
    - Triple-DES with 168 bit key
    - Idea (128 bit key)
    - Fortezza (96 bit key)

"CBC" refers to Cipher Block Chaining, which means that a portion of the previously encrypted cipher text is used in the encryption of the current block. "DES" refers to the Data Encryption Standard [AC96, ch12], which has a number of variants (including DES40 and 3DES_EDE). "Idea" is currently one of the best and cryptographically strongest algorithms available, and "RC2" is a proprietary algorithm from RSA DSI [AC96, ch13].

**Digest Function**

The choice of digest function determines how a digest is created from a record unit. SSL supports the following:

- No digest (Null choice)
- MD5, a 128-bit hash
- Secure Hash Algorithm (SHA-1), a 160-bit hash

The message digest is used to create a Message Authentication Code (MAC) which is encrypted with the message to verify integrity and to protect against replay attacks.

**Handshake Sequence Protocol**

The handshake sequence uses three protocols:

- The *SSL Handshake Protocol* for performing the client and server SSL session establishment.
- The *SSL Change Cipher Spec Protocol* for actually establishing agreement on the Cipher Suite for the session.
- The *SSL Alert Protocol* for conveying SSL error messages between client and server.

These protocols, as well as application protocol data, are encapsulated in the *SSL Record Protocol*, as shown in Figure 2. An encapsulated protocol is transferred as data by the lower layer protocol, which does not examine the data. The encapsulated protocol has no knowledge of the underlying protocol.

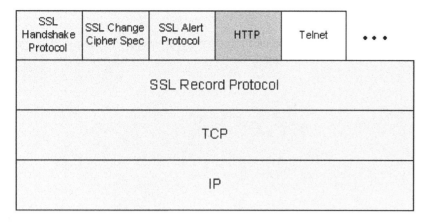

*Figure 2*: SSL Protocol Stack

The encapsulation of SSL control protocols by the record protocol means that if an active session is renegotiated the control protocols will be transmitted securely. If there was no previous session, the Null cipher suite is used, which means there will be no encryption and messages will have no integrity digests, until the session has been established.

**Data Transfer**

The SSL Record Protocol, shown in Figure 3, is used to transfer application and SSL Control data between the client and server, where necessary fragmenting this data into smaller units, or combining multiple higher level protocol data messages into single units. It may compress, attach digest signatures, and encrypt these units before transmitting them using the underlying reliable transport protocol (Note: currently, no major SSL implementations include support for compression).

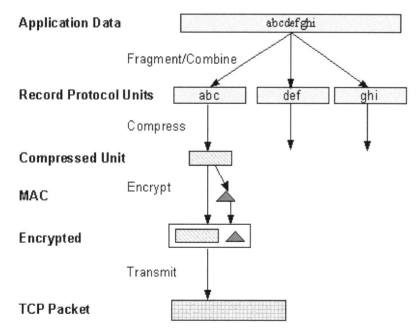

*Figure 3*: SSL Record Protocol

**Securing HTTP Communication**

One common use of SSL is to secure Web HTTP communication between a browser and a webserver. This does not preclude the use of non-secured HTTP - the secure version (called HTTPS) is the same as plain HTTP over SSL, but uses the URL scheme `https` rather than `http`, and a different server port (by default, port 443). This functionality is a large part of what MOD_SSL provides for the Apache webserver.

# References

**[AC96]** Bruce Schneier, *Applied Cryptography*, 2nd Edition, Wiley, 1996. See http://www.counterpane.com/ for various other materials by Bruce Schneier.

**[ASN1]** ITU-T Recommendation X.208, *Specification of Abstract Syntax Notation One (ASN.1)*, last updated 2008. See http://www.itu.int/ITU-T/asn1/.

**[X509]** ITU-T Recommendation X.509, *The Directory - Authentication Framework.* For references, see http://en.wikipedia.org/wiki/X.509.

**[PKCS]** *Public Key Cryptography Standards (PKCS)*, RSA Laboratories Technical Notes, See http://www.rsasecurity.com/rsalabs/pkcs/.

**[MIME]** N. Freed, N. Borenstein, *Multipurpose Internet Mail Extensions (MIME) Part One: Format of Internet Message Bodies*, RFC2045. See for instance http://tools.ietf.org/html/rfc2045.

**[SSL3]** Alan O. Freier, Philip Karlton, Paul C. Kocher, *The SSL Protocol Version 3.0*, 1996. See http://www.netscape.com/eng/ssl3/draft302.txt.

**[TLS1]** Tim Dierks, Christopher Allen, *The TLS Protocol Version 1.0*, 1999. See http://ietf.org/rfc/rfc2246.txt.

**[TLS11]** *The TLS Protocol Version 1.1*, 2006. See http://tools.ietf.org/html/rfc4346.

**[TLS12]** *The TLS Protocol Version 1.2*, 2008. See http://tools.ietf.org/html/rfc5246.

# 5.3   SSL/TLS Strong Encryption: Compatibility

This page covers backwards compatibility between mod_ssl and other SSL solutions. mod_ssl is not the only SSL solution for Apache; four additional products are (or were) also available: Ben Laurie's freely available Apache-SSL[4] (from where mod_ssl were originally derived in 1998), Red Hat's commercial Secure Web Server (which was based on mod_ssl), Covalent's commercial Raven SSL Module (also based on mod_ssl) and finally C2Net's (now Red Hat's) commercial product Stronghold[5] (based on a different evolution branch, named Sioux up to Stronghold 2.x, and based on mod_ssl since Stronghold 3.x).

mod_ssl mostly provides a superset of the functionality of all the other solutions, so it's simple to migrate from one of the older modules to mod_ssl. The configuration directives and environment variable names used by the older SSL solutions vary from those used in mod_ssl; mapping tables are included here to give the equivalents used by mod_ssl.

## Configuration Directives

The mapping between configuration directives used by Apache-SSL 1.x and mod_ssl 2.0.x is given in Table 1. The mapping from Sioux 1.x and Stronghold 2.x is only partial because of special functionality in these interfaces which mod_ssl doesn't provide.

**Table 1: Configuration Directive Mapping**

| Old Directive | mod_ssl Directive | Comment |
|---|---|---|
| **Apache-SSL 1.x & mod_ssl 2.0.x compatibility:** | | |
| SSLEnable | SSLEngine on | compactified |
| SSLDisable | SSLEngine off | compactified |
| SSLLogFile *file* | | Use per-module LOGLEVEL setting instead. |
| SSLRequiredCiphers *spec* | SSLCipherSuite *spec* | renamed |
| SSLRequireCipher *cl* ... | SSLRequire %{SSL_CIPHER} in {"cl", ...} | generalized |
| SSLBanCipher *cl* ... | SSLRequire not (%{SSL_CIPHER} in {"cl", ...}) | generalized |
| SSLFakeBasicAuth | SSLOptions +FakeBasicAuth | merged |
| SSLCacheServerPath *dir* | - | functionality removed |
| SSLCacheServerPort *integer* | - | functionality removed |
| **Apache-SSL 1.x compatibility:** | | |
| SSLExportClientCertificates | SSLOptions +ExportCertData | merged |
| SSLCacheServerRunDir *dir* | - | functionality not supported |
| **Sioux 1.x compatibility:** | | |
| SSL_CertFile *file* | SSLCertificateFile *file* | renamed |
| SSL_KeyFile *file* | SSLCertificateKeyFile *file* | renamed |
| SSL_CipherSuite *arg* | SSLCipherSuite *arg* | renamed |
| SSL_X509VerifyDir *arg* | SSLCACertificatePath *arg* | renamed |
| SSL_Log *file* | – | Use per-module LOGLEVEL setting instead. |
| SSL_Connect *flag* | SSLEngine *flag* | renamed |
| SSL_ClientAuth *arg* | SSLVerifyClient *arg* | renamed |
| SSL_X509VerifyDepth *arg* | SSLVerifyDepth *arg* | renamed |

---

[4] http://www.apache-ssl.org/
[5] http://www.redhat.com/explore/stronghold/

| | | |
|---|---|---|
| `SSL_FetchKeyPhraseFrom` *arg* | - | not directly mappable; use SSLPassPhraseDialog |
| `SSL_SessionDir` *dir* | - | not directly mappable; use SSLSessionCache |
| `SSL_Require` *expr* | - | not directly mappable; use SSLRequire |
| `SSL_CertFileType` *arg* | - | functionality not supported |
| `SSL_KeyFileType` *arg* | - | functionality not supported |
| `SSL_X509VerifyPolicy` *arg* | - | functionality not supported |
| `SSL_LogX509Attributes` *arg* | - | functionality not supported |
| **Stronghold 2.x compatibility:** | | |
| `StrongholdAccelerator` *engine* | `SSLCryptoDevice` *engine* | renamed |
| `StrongholdKey` *dir* | - | functionality not needed |
| `StrongholdLicenseFile` *dir* | - | functionality not needed |
| `SSLFlag` *flag* | `SSLEngine` *flag* | renamed |
| `SSLSessionLockFile` *file* | `SSLMutex` *file* | renamed |
| `SSLCipherList` *spec* | `SSLCipherSuite` *spec* | renamed |
| `RequireSSL` | `SSLRequireSSL` | renamed |
| `SSLErrorFile` *file* | - | functionality not supported |
| `SSLRoot` *dir* | - | functionality not supported |
| `SSL_CertificateLogDir` *dir* | - | functionality not supported |
| `AuthCertDir` *dir* | - | functionality not supported |
| `SSL_Group` *name* | - | functionality not supported |
| `SSLProxyMachineCertPath` *dir* | `SSLProxyMachineCertificatePath` *dir* | renamed |
| `SSLProxyMachineCertFile` *file* | `SSLProxyMachineCertificateFile` *file* | renamed |
| `SSLProxyCipherList` *spec* | `SSLProxyCipherSpec` *spec* | renamed |

## Environment Variables

The mapping between environment variable names used by the older SSL solutions and the names used by mod_ssl is given in Table 2.

**Table 2: Environment Variable Derivation**

| Old Variable | mod_ssl Variable | Comment |
|---|---|---|
| `SSL_PROTOCOL_VERSION` | `SSL_PROTOCOL` | renamed |
| `SSLEAY_VERSION` | `SSL_VERSION_LIBRARY` | renamed |
| `HTTPS_SECRETKEYSIZE` | `SSL_CIPHER_USEKEYSIZE` | renamed |
| `HTTPS_KEYSIZE` | `SSL_CIPHER_ALGKEYSIZE` | renamed |
| `HTTPS_CIPHER` | `SSL_CIPHER` | renamed |
| `HTTPS_EXPORT` | `SSL_CIPHER_EXPORT` | renamed |
| `SSL_SERVER_KEY_SIZE` | `SSL_CIPHER_ALGKEYSIZE` | renamed |
| `SSL_SERVER_CERTIFICATE` | `SSL_SERVER_CERT` | renamed |
| `SSL_SERVER_CERT_START` | `SSL_SERVER_V_START` | renamed |
| `SSL_SERVER_CERT_END` | `SSL_SERVER_V_END` | renamed |
| `SSL_SERVER_CERT_SERIAL` | `SSL_SERVER_M_SERIAL` | renamed |
| `SSL_SERVER_SIGNATURE_ALGORITHM` | `SSL_SERVER_A_SIG` | renamed |
| `SSL_SERVER_DN` | `SSL_SERVER_S_DN` | renamed |
| `SSL_SERVER_CN` | `SSL_SERVER_S_DN_CN` | renamed |
| `SSL_SERVER_EMAIL` | `SSL_SERVER_S_DN_Email` | renamed |
| `SSL_SERVER_O` | `SSL_SERVER_S_DN_O` | renamed |
| `SSL_SERVER_OU` | `SSL_SERVER_S_DN_OU` | renamed |

| | | |
|---|---|---|
| `SSL_SERVER_C` | `SSL_SERVER_S_DN_C` | renamed |
| `SSL_SERVER_SP` | `SSL_SERVER_S_DN_SP` | renamed |
| `SSL_SERVER_L` | `SSL_SERVER_S_DN_L` | renamed |
| `SSL_SERVER_IDN` | `SSL_SERVER_I_DN` | renamed |
| `SSL_SERVER_ICN` | `SSL_SERVER_I_DN_CN` | renamed |
| `SSL_SERVER_IEMAIL` | `SSL_SERVER_I_DN_Email` | renamed |
| `SSL_SERVER_IO` | `SSL_SERVER_I_DN_O` | renamed |
| `SSL_SERVER_IOU` | `SSL_SERVER_I_DN_OU` | renamed |
| `SSL_SERVER_IC` | `SSL_SERVER_I_DN_C` | renamed |
| `SSL_SERVER_ISP` | `SSL_SERVER_I_DN_SP` | renamed |
| `SSL_SERVER_IL` | `SSL_SERVER_I_DN_L` | renamed |
| `SSL_CLIENT_CERTIFICATE` | `SSL_CLIENT_CERT` | renamed |
| `SSL_CLIENT_CERT_START` | `SSL_CLIENT_V_START` | renamed |
| `SSL_CLIENT_CERT_END` | `SSL_CLIENT_V_END` | renamed |
| `SSL_CLIENT_CERT_SERIAL` | `SSL_CLIENT_M_SERIAL` | renamed |
| `SSL_CLIENT_SIGNATURE_ALGORITHM` | `SSL_CLIENT_A_SIG` | renamed |
| `SSL_CLIENT_DN` | `SSL_CLIENT_S_DN` | renamed |
| `SSL_CLIENT_CN` | `SSL_CLIENT_S_DN_CN` | renamed |
| `SSL_CLIENT_EMAIL` | `SSL_CLIENT_S_DN_Email` | renamed |
| `SSL_CLIENT_O` | `SSL_CLIENT_S_DN_O` | renamed |
| `SSL_CLIENT_OU` | `SSL_CLIENT_S_DN_OU` | renamed |
| `SSL_CLIENT_C` | `SSL_CLIENT_S_DN_C` | renamed |
| `SSL_CLIENT_SP` | `SSL_CLIENT_S_DN_SP` | renamed |
| `SSL_CLIENT_L` | `SSL_CLIENT_S_DN_L` | renamed |
| `SSL_CLIENT_IDN` | `SSL_CLIENT_I_DN` | renamed |
| `SSL_CLIENT_ICN` | `SSL_CLIENT_I_DN_CN` | renamed |
| `SSL_CLIENT_IEMAIL` | `SSL_CLIENT_I_DN_Email` | renamed |
| `SSL_CLIENT_IO` | `SSL_CLIENT_I_DN_O` | renamed |
| `SSL_CLIENT_IOU` | `SSL_CLIENT_I_DN_OU` | renamed |
| `SSL_CLIENT_IC` | `SSL_CLIENT_I_DN_C` | renamed |
| `SSL_CLIENT_ISP` | `SSL_CLIENT_I_DN_SP` | renamed |
| `SSL_CLIENT_IL` | `SSL_CLIENT_I_DN_L` | renamed |
| `SSL_EXPORT` | `SSL_CIPHER_EXPORT` | renamed |
| `SSL_KEYSIZE` | `SSL_CIPHER_ALGKEYSIZE` | renamed |
| `SSL_SECKEYSIZE` | `SSL_CIPHER_USEKEYSIZE` | renamed |
| `SSL_SSLEAY_VERSION` | `SSL_VERSION_LIBRARY` | renamed |
| `SSL_STRONG_CRYPTO` | – | Not supported by mod_ssl |
| `SSL_SERVER_KEY_EXP` | – | Not supported by mod_ssl |
| `SSL_SERVER_KEY_ALGORITHM` | – | Not supported by mod_ssl |
| `SSL_SERVER_KEY_SIZE` | – | Not supported by mod_ssl |
| `SSL_SERVER_SESSIONDIR` | – | Not supported by mod_ssl |
| `SSL_SERVER_CERTIFICATELOGDIR` | – | Not supported by mod_ssl |
| `SSL_SERVER_CERTFILE` | – | Not supported by mod_ssl |
| `SSL_SERVER_KEYFILE` | – | Not supported by mod_ssl |
| `SSL_SERVER_KEYFILETYPE` | – | Not supported by mod_ssl |
| `SSL_CLIENT_KEY_EXP` | – | Not supported by mod_ssl |
| `SSL_CLIENT_KEY_ALGORITHM` | – | Not supported by mod_ssl |
| `SSL_CLIENT_KEY_SIZE` | – | Not supported by mod_ssl |

## Custom Log Functions

When mod_ssl is enabled, additional functions exist for the Custom Log Format (p. 705) of `MOD_LOG_CONFIG` as documented in the Reference Chapter. Beside the "`%{varname}x`" eXtension format function which can be used to expand any variables provided by any module, an additional Cryptography "`%{`*name*`}c`" cryptography format function exists for backward compatibility. The currently implemented function calls are listed in Table 3.

**Table 3: Custom Log Cryptography Function**

| Function Call | Description |
|---|---|
| `%...{version}c` | SSL protocol version |
| `%...{cipher}c` | SSL cipher |
| `%...{subjectdn}c` | Client Certificate Subject Distinguished Name |
| `%...{issuerdn}c` | Client Certificate Issuer Distinguished Name |
| `%...{errcode}c` | Certificate Verification Error (numerical) |
| `%...{errstr}c` | Certificate Verification Error (string) |

# 5.4   SSL/TLS Strong Encryption: How-To

This document is intended to get you started, and get a few things working. You are strongly encouraged to read the rest of the SSL documentation, and arrive at a deeper understanding of the material, before progressing to the advanced techniques.

## Basic Configuration Example

Your SSL configuration will need to contain, at minimum, the following directives.

```
Listen 443
<VirtualHost *:443>
    ServerName www.example.com
    SSLEngine on
    SSLCertificateFile "/path/to/www.example.com.cert"
    SSLCertificateKeyFile "/path/to/www.example.com.key"
</VirtualHost>
```

## Cipher Suites and Enforcing Strong Security

- How can I create an SSL server which accepts strong encryption only?
- How can I create an SSL server which accepts all types of ciphers in general, but requires a strong cipher for access to a particular URL?

**How can I create an SSL server which accepts strong encryption only?**

The following enables only the strongest ciphers:

```
SSLCipherSuite HIGH:!aNULL:!MD5
```

While with the following configuration you specify a preference for specific speed-optimized ciphers (which will be selected by mod_ssl, provided that they are supported by the client):

```
SSLCipherSuite RC4-SHA:AES128-SHA:HIGH:!aNULL:!MD5
SSLHonorCipherOrder on
```

**How can I create an SSL server which accepts all types of ciphers in general, but requires a strong ciphers for access to a particular URL?**

Obviously, a server-wide SSLCipherSuite which restricts ciphers to the strong variants, isn't the answer here. However, MOD_SSL can be reconfigured within Location blocks, to give a per-directory solution, and can automatically force a renegotiation of the SSL parameters to meet the new configuration. This can be done as follows:

```
# be liberal in general
SSLCipherSuite ALL:!aNULL:RC4+RSA:+HIGH:+MEDIUM:+LOW:+EXP:+eNULL

<Location "/strong/area">
# but https://hostname/strong/area/ and below
# requires strong ciphers
SSLCipherSuite HIGH:!aNULL:!MD5
</Location>
```

## OCSP Stapling

The Online Certificate Status Protocol (OCSP) is a mechanism for determining whether or not a server certificate has been revoked, and OCSP Stapling is a special form of this in which the server, such as httpd and mod_ssl, maintains current OCSP responses for its certificates and sends them to clients which communicate with the server. Most certificates contain the address of an OCSP responder maintained by the issuing Certificate Authority, and mod_ssl can communicate with that responder to obtain a signed response that can be sent to clients communicating with the server.

Because the client can obtain the certificate revocation status from the server, without requiring an extra connection from the client to the Certificate Authority, OCSP Stapling is the preferred way for the revocation status to be obtained. Other benefits of eliminating the communication between clients and the Certificate Authority are that the client browsing history is not exposed to the Certificate Authority and obtaining status is more reliable by not depending on potentially heavily loaded Certificate Authority servers.

Because the response obtained by the server can be reused for all clients using the same certificate during the time that the response is valid, the overhead for the server is minimal.

Once general SSL support has been configured properly, enabling OCSP Stapling generally requires only very minor modifications to the httpd configuration - the addition of these two directives:

```
SSLUseStapling On
SSLStaplingCache "shmcb:ssl_stapling(32768)"
```

These directives are placed at global scope (i.e., not within a virtual host definition) wherever other global SSL configuration directives are placed, such as in `conf/extra/httpd-ssl.conf` for normal open source builds of httpd, `/etc/apache2/mods-enabled/ssl.conf` for the Ubuntu or Debian-bundled httpd, etc.

This particular SSLSTAPLINGCACHE directive requires MOD_SOCACHE_SHMCB (from the `shmcb` prefix on the directive's argument). This module is usually enabled already for SSLSESSIONCACHE or on behalf of some module other than MOD_SSL. If you enabled an SSL session cache using a mechanism other than MOD_SOCACHE_SHMCB, use that alternative mechanism for SSLSTAPLINGCACHE as well. For example:

```
SSLSessionCache "dbm:ssl_scache"
SSLStaplingCache "dbm:ssl_stapling"
```

You can use the openssl command-line program to verify that an OCSP response is sent by your server:

```
$ openssl s_client -connect www.example.com:443 -status -servername www.example.com
...
OCSP response:
======================================
OCSP Response Data:
    OCSP Response Status: successful (0x0)
    Response Type: Basic OCSP Response
...
    Cert Status: Good
...
```

The following sections highlight the most common situations which require further modification to the configuration. Refer also to the MOD_SSL reference manual.

**If more than a few SSL certificates are used for the server**

OCSP responses are stored in the SSL stapling cache. While the responses are typically a few hundred to a few thousand bytes in size, mod_ssl supports OCSP responses up to around 10K bytes in size. With more than a few certificates, the stapling cache size (32768 bytes in the example above) may need to be increased. Error message AH01929 will be logged in case of an error storing a response.

**If the certificate does not point to an OCSP responder, or if a different address must be used**

Refer to the SSLStaplingForceURL directive.

You can confirm that a server certificate points to an OCSP responder using the openssl command-line program, as follows:

```
$ openssl x509 -in ./www.example.com.crt -text | grep 'OCSP.*http'
OCSP - URI:http://ocsp.example.com
```

If the OCSP URI is provided and the web server can communicate to it directly without using a proxy, no configuration is required. Note that firewall rules that control outbound connections from the web server may need to be adjusted.

If no OCSP URI is provided, contact your Certificate Authority to determine if one is available; if so, configure it with SSLStaplingForceURL in the virtual host that uses the certificate.

**If multiple SSL-enabled virtual hosts are configured and OCSP Stapling should be disabled for some**

Add `SSLUseStapling Off` to the virtual hosts for which OCSP Stapling should be disabled.

**If the OCSP responder is slow or unreliable**

Several directives are available to handle timeouts and errors. Refer to the documentation for the SSLStaplingFakeTryLater, SSLStaplingResponderTimeout, and SSLStaplingReturnResponderErrors directives.

**If mod_ssl logs error AH02217**

```
AH02217: ssl_stapling_init_cert: Can't retrieve issuer certificate!
```

In order to support OCSP Stapling when a particular server certificate is used, the certificate chain for that certificate must be configured. If it was not configured as part of enabling SSL, the AH02217 error will be issued when stapling is enabled, and an OCSP response will not be provided for clients using the certificate.

Refer to the SSLCertificateChainFile and SSLCertificateFile for instructions for configuring the certificate chain.

## Client Authentication and Access Control

- How can I force clients to authenticate using certificates?
- How can I force clients to authenticate using certificates for a particular URL, but still allow arbitrary clients to access the rest of the server?
- How can I allow only clients who have certificates to access a particular URL, but allow all clients to access the rest of the server?

- How can I require HTTPS with strong ciphers, and either basic authentication or client certificates, for access to part of the Intranet website, for clients coming from the Internet?

**How can I force clients to authenticate using certificates?**

When you know all of your users (eg, as is often the case on a corporate Intranet), you can require plain certificate authentication. All you need to do is to create client certificates signed by your own CA certificate (`ca.crt`) and then verify the clients against this certificate.

```
# require a client certificate which has to be directly
# signed by our CA certificate in ca.crt
SSLVerifyClient require
SSLVerifyDepth 1
SSLCACertificateFile "conf/ssl.crt/ca.crt"
```

**How can I force clients to authenticate using certificates for a particular URL, but still allow arbitrary clients to access the rest of the server?**

To force clients to authenticate using certificates for a particular URL, you can use the per-directory reconfiguration features of MOD_SSL:

```
SSLVerifyClient none
SSLCACertificateFile "conf/ssl.crt/ca.crt"

<Location "/secure/area">
SSLVerifyClient require
SSLVerifyDepth 1
</Location>
```

**How can I allow only clients who have certificates to access a particular URL, but allow all clients to access the rest of the server?**

The key to doing this is checking that part of the client certificate matches what you expect. Usually this means checking all or part of the Distinguished Name (DN), to see if it contains some known string. There are two ways to do this, using either MOD_AUTH_BASIC or SSLREQUIRE.

The MOD_AUTH_BASIC method is generally required when the certificates are completely arbitrary, or when their DNs have no common fields (usually the organisation, etc.). In this case, you should establish a password database containing *all* clients allowed, as follows:

```
SSLVerifyClient         none
SSLCACertificateFile "conf/ssl.crt/ca.crt"
SSLCACertificatePath "conf/ssl.crt"

<Directory "/usr/local/apache2/htdocs/secure/area">
    SSLVerifyClient         require
    SSLVerifyDepth          5
    SSLOptions              +FakeBasicAuth
    SSLRequireSSL
    AuthName                "Snake Oil Authentication"
    AuthType                Basic
```

```
    AuthBasicProvider       file
    AuthUserFile            "/usr/local/apache2/conf/httpd.passwd"
    Require                 valid-user
</Directory>
```

The password used in this example is the DES encrypted string "password".  See the SSLOPTIONS docs for more
information.

### httpd.passwd

```
/C=DE/L=Munich/O=Snake Oil, Ltd./OU=Staff/CN=Foo:xxj31ZMTZzkVA
/C=US/L=S.F./O=Snake Oil, Ltd./OU=CA/CN=Bar:xxj31ZMTZzkVA
/C=US/L=L.A./O=Snake Oil, Ltd./OU=Dev/CN=Quux:xxj31ZMTZzkVA
```

When your clients are all part of a common hierarchy, which is encoded into the DN, you can match them more easily
using SSLREQUIRE, as follows:

```
SSLVerifyClient       none
SSLCACertificateFile "conf/ssl.crt/ca.crt"
SSLCACertificatePath "conf/ssl.crt"

<Directory "/usr/local/apache2/htdocs/secure/area">
  SSLVerifyClient       require
  SSLVerifyDepth        5
  SSLOptions            +FakeBasicAuth
  SSLRequireSSL
  SSLRequire            %{SSL_CLIENT_S_DN_O}  eq "Snake Oil, Ltd." \
              and %{SSL_CLIENT_S_DN_OU} in {"Staff", "CA", "Dev"}
</Directory>
```

**How can I require HTTPS with strong ciphers, and either basic authentication or client certificates, for access
to part of the Intranet website, for clients coming from the Internet? I still want to allow plain HTTP access for
clients on the Intranet.**

These examples presume that clients on the Intranet have IPs in the range 192.168.1.0/24, and that the part of the
Intranet website you want to allow internet access to is /usr/local/apache2/htdocs/subarea. This configuration should remain outside of your HTTPS virtual host, so that it applies to both HTTPS and HTTP.

```
SSLCACertificateFile "conf/ssl.crt/company-ca.crt"

<Directory "/usr/local/apache2/htdocs">
    #   Outside the subarea only Intranet access is granted
    Require              ip 192.168.1.0/24
</Directory>

<Directory "/usr/local/apache2/htdocs/subarea">
    #   Inside the subarea any Intranet access is allowed
    #   but from the Internet only HTTPS + Strong-Cipher + Password
    #   or the alternative HTTPS + Strong-Cipher + Client-Certificate

    #   If HTTPS is used, make sure a strong cipher is used.
    #   Additionally allow client certs as alternative to basic auth.
    SSLVerifyClient      optional
```

```
SSLVerifyDepth          1
SSLOptions              +FakeBasicAuth +StrictRequire
SSLRequire              %{SSL_CIPHER_USEKEYSIZE} >= 128

#   Force clients from the Internet to use HTTPS
RewriteEngine           on
RewriteCond             "%{REMOTE_ADDR}"  "!^192\.168\.1\.[0-9]+$"
RewriteCond             "%{HTTPS}"        "!=on"
RewriteRule             "."               "-"                        [F]

#   Allow Network Access and/or Basic Auth
Satisfy                 any

#   Network Access Control
Require                 ip 192.168.1.0/24

#   HTTP Basic Authentication
AuthType                basic
AuthName                "Protected Intranet Area"
AuthBasicProvider       file
AuthUserFile            "conf/protected.passwd"
Require                 valid-user
</Directory>
```

## Logging

MOD_SSL can log extremely verbose debugging information to the error log, when its LOGLEVEL is set to the higher trace levels. On the other hand, on a very busy server, level `info` may already be too much. Remember that you can configure the LOGLEVEL per module to suite your needs.

# 5.5   SSL/TLS Strong Encryption: FAQ

The wise man doesn't give the right answers, he poses the right questions.
*– Claude Levi-Strauss*

## Installation

- Why do I get permission errors related to SSLMutex when I start Apache?
- Why does mod_ssl stop with the error "Failed to generate temporary 512 bit RSA private key" when I start Apache?

**Why do I get permission errors related to SSLMutex when I start Apache?**

Errors such as "`mod_ssl:  Child could not open SSLMutex lockfile /opt/apache/logs/ssl_mutex.18332 (System error follows) [...]  System: Permission denied (errno:  13)`" are usually caused by overly restrictive permissions on the *parent* directories. Make sure that all parent directories (here `/opt`, `/opt/apache` and `/opt/apache/logs`) have the x-bit set for, at minimum, the UID under which Apache's children are running (see the USER directive).

**Why does mod_ssl stop with the error "Failed to generate temporary 512 bit RSA private key" when I start Apache?**

Cryptographic software needs a source of unpredictable data to work correctly. Many open source operating systems provide a "randomness device" that serves this purpose (usually named `/dev/random`). On other systems, applications have to seed the OpenSSL Pseudo Random Number Generator (PRNG) manually with appropriate data before generating keys or performing public key encryption. As of version 0.9.5, the OpenSSL functions that need randomness report an error if the PRNG has not been seeded with at least 128 bits of randomness.

To prevent this error, MOD_SSL has to provide enough entropy to the PRNG to allow it to work correctly. This can be done via the SSLRANDOMSEED directive.

## Configuration

- Is it possible to provide HTTP and HTTPS from the same server?
- Which port does HTTPS use?
- How do I speak HTTPS manually for testing purposes?
- Why does the connection hang when I connect to my SSL-aware Apache server?
- Why do I get "Connection Refused" errors, when trying to access my newly installed Apache+mod_ssl server via HTTPS?
- Why are the SSL_XXX variables not available to my CGI & SSI scripts?
- How can I switch between HTTP and HTTPS in relative hyperlinks?

**Is it possible to provide HTTP and HTTPS from the same server?**

Yes. HTTP and HTTPS use different server ports (HTTP binds to port 80, HTTPS to port 443), so there is no direct conflict between them. You can either run two separate server instances bound to these ports, or use Apache's elegant virtual hosting facility to create two virtual servers, both served by the same instance of Apache - one responding over HTTP to requests on port 80, and the other responding over HTTPS to requests on port 443.

**Which port does HTTPS use?**

You can run HTTPS on any port, but the standards specify port 443, which is where any HTTPS compliant browser will look by default. You can force your browser to look on a different port by specifying it in the URL. For example, if your server is set up to serve pages over HTTPS on port 8080, you can access them at `https://example.com:8080/`

**How do I speak HTTPS manually for testing purposes?**

While you usually just use

```
$ telnet localhost 80
GET / HTTP/1.0
```

for simple testing of Apache via HTTP, it's not so easy for HTTPS because of the SSL protocol between TCP and HTTP. With the help of OpenSSL's `s_client` command, however, you can do a similar check via HTTPS:

```
$ openssl s_client -connect localhost:443 -state -debug
GET / HTTP/1.0
```

Before the actual HTTP response you will receive detailed information about the SSL handshake. For a more general command line client which directly understands both HTTP and HTTPS, can perform GET and POST operations, can use a proxy, supports byte ranges, etc. you should have a look at the nifty cURL[6] tool. Using this, you can check that Apache is responding correctly to requests via HTTP and HTTPS as follows:

```
$ curl http://localhost/
$ curl https://localhost/
```

**Why does the connection hang when I connect to my SSL-aware Apache server?**

This can happen when you try to connect to a HTTPS server (or virtual server) via HTTP (eg, using `http://example.com/` instead of `https://example.com`). It can also happen when trying to connect via HTTPS to a HTTP server (eg, using `https://example.com/` on a server which doesn't support HTTPS, or which supports it on a non-standard port). Make sure that you're connecting to a (virtual) server that supports SSL.

**Why do I get "Connection Refused" messages, when trying to access my newly installed Apache+mod_ssl server via HTTPS?**

This error can be caused by an incorrect configuration. Please make sure that your LISTEN directives match your <VIRTUALHOST> directives. If all else fails, please start afresh, using the default configuration provided by MOD_SSL.

**Why are the SSL_XXX variables not available to my CGI & SSI scripts?**

Please make sure you have "`SSLOptions +StdEnvVars`" enabled for the context of your CGI/SSI requests.

---

[6]http://curl.haxx.se/

**How can I switch between HTTP and HTTPS in relative hyperlinks?**

Usually, to switch between HTTP and HTTPS, you have to use fully-qualified hyperlinks (because you have to change the URL scheme). Using MOD_REWRITE however, you can manipulate relative hyperlinks, to achieve the same effect.

```
RewriteEngine on
RewriteRule   "^/(.*)_SSL$"   "https://%{SERVER_NAME}/$1" [R,L]
RewriteRule   "^/(.*)_NOSSL$" "http://%{SERVER_NAME}/$1"  [R,L]
```

This rewrite ruleset lets you use hyperlinks of the form `<a href="document.html_SSL">`, to switch to HTTPS in a relative link. (Replace SSL with NOSSL to switch to HTTP.)


# Certificates

- What are RSA Private Keys, CSRs and Certificates?

- Is there a difference on startup between a non-SSL-aware Apache and an SSL-aware Apache?

- How do I create a self-signed SSL Certificate for testing purposes?

- How do I create a real SSL Certificate?

- How do I create and use my own Certificate Authority (CA)?

- How can I change the pass-phrase on my private key file?

- How can I get rid of the pass-phrase dialog at Apache startup time?

- How do I verify that a private key matches its Certificate?

- How can I convert a certificate from PEM to DER format?

- Why do browsers complain that they cannot verify my server certificate?


**What are RSA Private Keys, CSRs and Certificates?**

An RSA private key file is a digital file that you can use to decrypt messages sent to you. It has a public component which you distribute (via your Certificate file) which allows people to encrypt those messages to you.

A Certificate Signing Request (CSR) is a digital file which contains your public key and your name. You send the CSR to a Certifying Authority (CA), who will convert it into a real Certificate, by signing it.

A Certificate contains your RSA public key, your name, the name of the CA, and is digitally signed by the CA. Browsers that know the CA can verify the signature on that Certificate, thereby obtaining your RSA public key. That enables them to send messages which only you can decrypt.

See the Introduction (p. 193) chapter for a general description of the SSL protocol.


**Is there a difference on startup between a non-SSL-aware Apache and an SSL-aware Apache?**

Yes. In general, starting Apache with MOD_SSL built-in is just like starting Apache without it. However, if you have a passphrase on your SSL private key file, a startup dialog will pop up which asks you to enter the pass phrase.

Having to manually enter the passphrase when starting the server can be problematic - for example, when starting the server from the system boot scripts. In this case, you can follow the steps below to remove the passphrase from your private key. Bear in mind that doing so brings additional security risks - proceed with caution!

**How do I create a self-signed SSL Certificate for testing purposes?**

1. Make sure OpenSSL is installed and in your PATH.

2. Run the following command, to create server.key and server.crt files:
   ```
   $ openssl req -new -x509 -nodes -out server.crt -keyout server.key
   ```
   These can be used as follows in your httpd.conf file:

   ```
   SSLCertificateFile    /path/to/this/server.crt
   SSLCertificateKeyFile /path/to/this/server.key
   ```

3. It is important that you are aware that this server.key does *not* have any passphrase. To add a passphrase to the key, you should run the following command, and enter & verify the passphrase as requested.
   ```
   $ openssl rsa -des3 -in server.key -out server.key.new
   $ mv server.key.new server.key
   ```
   Please backup the server.key file, and the passphrase you entered, in a secure location.

**How do I create a real SSL Certificate?**

Here is a step-by-step description:

1. Make sure OpenSSL is installed and in your PATH.

2. Create a RSA private key for your Apache server (will be Triple-DES encrypted and PEM formatted):
   ```
   $ openssl genrsa -des3 -out server.key 2048
   ```
   Please backup this server.key file and the pass-phrase you entered in a secure location. You can see the details of this RSA private key by using the command:

   ```
   $ openssl rsa -noout -text -in server.key
   ```
   If necessary, you can also create a decrypted PEM version (not recommended) of this RSA private key with:

   ```
   $ openssl rsa -in server.key -out server.key.unsecure
   ```

3. Create a Certificate Signing Request (CSR) with the server RSA private key (output will be PEM formatted):
   ```
   $ openssl req -new -key server.key -out server.csr
   ```
   Make sure you enter the FQDN ("Fully Qualified Domain Name") of the server when OpenSSL prompts you for the "CommonName", i.e. when you generate a CSR for a website which will be later accessed via https://www.foo.dom/, enter "www.foo.dom" here. You can see the details of this CSR by using

   ```
   $ openssl req -noout -text -in server.csr
   ```

4. You now have to send this Certificate Signing Request (CSR) to a Certifying Authority (CA) to be signed. Once the CSR has been signed, you will have a real Certificate, which can be used by Apache. You can have a CSR signed by a commercial CA, or you can create your own CA to sign it.
   Commercial CAs usually ask you to post the CSR into a web form, pay for the signing, and then send a signed Certificate, which you can store in a server.crt file.

For details on how to create your own CA, and use this to sign a CSR, see below.

Once your CSR has been signed, you can see the details of the Certificate as follows:
```
$ openssl x509 -noout -text -in server.crt
```

5. You should now have two files: `server.key` and `server.crt`. These can be used as follows in your `httpd.conf` file:

```
SSLCertificateFile     /path/to/this/server.crt
SSLCertificateKeyFile /path/to/this/server.key
```

The `server.csr` file is no longer needed.


**How do I create and use my own Certificate Authority (CA)?**

The short answer is to use the `CA.sh` or `CA.pl` script provided by OpenSSL. Unless you have a good reason not to, you should use these for preference. If you cannot, you can create a self-signed certificate as follows:

1. Create a RSA private key for your server (will be Triple-DES encrypted and PEM formatted):
```
$ openssl genrsa -des3 -out server.key 2048
```
Please backup this `server.key` file and the pass-phrase you entered in a secure location. You can see the details of this RSA private key by using the command:
```
$ openssl rsa -noout -text -in server.key
```
If necessary, you can also create a decrypted PEM version (not recommended) of this RSA private key with:
```
$ openssl rsa -in server.key -out server.key.unsecure
```

2. Create a self-signed Certificate (X509 structure) with the RSA key you just created (output will be PEM formatted):
```
$ openssl req -new -x509 -nodes -sha1 -days 365 -key server.key -out
server.crt -extensions usr_cert
```
This signs the server CSR and results in a `server.crt` file.

You can see the details of this Certificate using:
```
$ openssl x509 -noout -text -in server.crt
```


**How can I change the pass-phrase on my private key file?**

You simply have to read it with the old pass-phrase and write it again, specifying the new pass-phrase. You can accomplish this with the following commands:

```
$ openssl rsa -des3 -in server.key -out server.key.new
$ mv server.key.new server.key
```

The first time you're asked for a PEM pass-phrase, you should enter the old pass-phrase. After that, you'll be asked again to enter a pass-phrase - this time, use the new pass-phrase. If you are asked to verify the pass-phrase, you'll need to enter the new pass-phrase a second time.

**How can I get rid of the pass-phrase dialog at Apache startup time?**

The reason this dialog pops up at startup and every re-start is that the RSA private key inside your server.key file is stored in encrypted format for security reasons. The pass-phrase is needed to decrypt this file, so it can be read and parsed. Removing the pass-phrase removes a layer of security from your server - proceed with caution!

1. Remove the encryption from the RSA private key (while keeping a backup copy of the original file):
   ```
   $ cp server.key server.key.org
   $ openssl rsa -in server.key.org -out server.key
   ```

2. Make sure the server.key file is only readable by root:
   ```
   $ chmod 400 server.key
   ```

Now `server.key` contains an unencrypted copy of the key. If you point your server at this file, it will not prompt you for a pass-phrase. HOWEVER, if anyone gets this key they will be able to impersonate you on the net. PLEASE make sure that the permissions on this file are such that only root or the web server user can read it (preferably get your web server to start as root but run as another user, and have the key readable only by root).

As an alternative approach you can use the "`SSLPassPhraseDialog exec:/path/to/program`" facility. Bear in mind that this is neither more nor less secure, of course.

**How do I verify that a private key matches its Certificate?**

A private key contains a series of numbers. Two of these numbers form the "public key", the others are part of the "private key". The "public key" bits are included when you generate a CSR, and subsequently form part of the associated Certificate.

To check that the public key in your Certificate matches the public portion of your private key, you simply need to compare these numbers. To view the Certificate and the key run the commands:

```
$ openssl x509 -noout -text -in server.crt
$ openssl rsa -noout -text -in server.key
```

The 'modulus' and the 'public exponent' portions in the key and the Certificate must match. As the public exponent is usually 65537 and it's difficult to visually check that the long modulus numbers are the same, you can use the following approach:

```
$ openssl x509 -noout -modulus -in server.crt | openssl md5
$ openssl rsa -noout -modulus -in server.key | openssl md5
```

This leaves you with two rather shorter numbers to compare. It is, in theory, possible that these numbers may be the same, without the modulus numbers being the same, but the chances of this are overwhelmingly remote.

Should you wish to check to which key or certificate a particular CSR belongs you can perform the same calculation on the CSR as follows:

```
$ openssl req -noout -modulus -in server.csr | openssl md5
```

**How can I convert a certificate from PEM to DER format?**

The default certificate format for OpenSSL is PEM, which is simply Base64 encoded DER, with header and footer lines. For some applications (e.g. Microsoft Internet Explorer) you need the certificate in plain DER format. You can convert a PEM file `cert.pem` into the corresponding DER file `cert.der` using the following command: `$ openssl x509 -in cert.pem -out cert.der -outform DER`

**Why do browsers complain that they cannot verify my server certificate?**

One reason this might happen is because your server certificate is signed by an intermediate CA. Various CAs, such as Verisign or Thawte, have started signing certificates not with their root certificate but with intermediate certificates.

Intermediate CA certificates lie between the root CA certificate (which is installed in the browsers) and the server certificate (which you installed on the server). In order for the browser to be able to traverse and verify the trust chain from the server certificate to the root certificate it needs need to be given the intermediate certificates. The CAs should be able to provide you such intermediate certificate packages that can be installed on the server.

You need to include those intermediate certificates with the SSLCERTIFICATECHAINFILE directive.

## The SSL Protocol

- Why do I get lots of random SSL protocol errors under heavy server load?
- Why does my webserver have a higher load, now that it serves SSL encrypted traffic?
- Why do HTTPS connections to my server sometimes take up to 30 seconds to establish a connection?
- What SSL Ciphers are supported by mod_ssl?
- Why do I get "no shared cipher" errors, when trying to use Anonymous Diffie-Hellman (ADH) ciphers?
- Why do I get a 'no shared ciphers' error when connecting to my newly installed server?
- Why can't I use SSL with name-based/non-IP-based virtual hosts?
- Is it possible to use Name-Based Virtual Hosting to identify different SSL virtual hosts?
- How do I get SSL compression working?
- When I use Basic Authentication over HTTPS the lock icon in Netscape browsers stays unlocked when the dialog pops up. Does this mean the username/password is being sent unencrypted?
- Why do I get I/O errors when connecting via HTTPS to an Apache+mod_ssl server with Microsoft Internet Explorer (MSIE)?
- How do I enable TLS-SRP?
- Why do I get handshake failures with Java-based clients when using a certificate with more than 1024 bits?

**Why do I get lots of random SSL protocol errors under heavy server load?**

There can be a number of reasons for this, but the main one is problems with the SSL session Cache specified by the SSLSESSIONCACHE directive. The DBM session cache is the most likely source of the problem, so using the SHM session cache (or no cache at all) may help.

**Why does my webserver have a higher load, now that it serves SSL encrypted traffic?**

SSL uses strong cryptographic encryption, which necessitates a lot of number crunching. When you request a webpage via HTTPS, everything (even the images) is encrypted before it is transferred. So increased HTTPS traffic leads to load increases.

**Why do HTTPS connections to my server sometimes take up to 30 seconds to establish a connection?**

This is usually caused by a /dev/random device for SSLRANDOMSEED which blocks the read(2) call until enough entropy is available to service the request. More information is available in the reference manual for the SSLRANDOMSEED directive.

**What SSL Ciphers are supported by mod_ssl?**

Usually, any SSL ciphers supported by the version of OpenSSL in use, are also supported by MOD_SSL. Which ciphers are available can depend on the way you built OpenSSL. Typically, at least the following ciphers are supported:

1. RC4 with SHA1

2. AES with SHA1

3. Triple-DES with SHA1

To determine the actual list of ciphers available, you should run the following:

```
$ openssl ciphers -v
```

**Why do I get "no shared cipher" errors, when trying to use Anonymous Diffie-Hellman (ADH) ciphers?**

By default, OpenSSL does *not* allow ADH ciphers, for security reasons. Please be sure you are aware of the potential side-effects if you choose to enable these ciphers.

In order to use Anonymous Diffie-Hellman (ADH) ciphers, you must build OpenSSL with "-DSSL_ALLOW_ADH", and then add "ADH" into your SSLCipherSuite.

**Why do I get a 'no shared ciphers' error when connecting to my newly installed server?**

Either you have made a mistake with your SSLCipherSuite directive (compare it with the pre-configured example in extra/httpd-ssl.conf) or you chose to use DSA/DH algorithms instead of RSA when you generated your private key and ignored or overlooked the warnings. If you have chosen DSA/DH, then your server cannot communicate using RSA-based SSL ciphers (at least until you configure an additional RSA-based certificate/key pair). Modern browsers like NS or IE can only communicate over SSL using RSA ciphers. The result is the "no shared ciphers" error. To fix this, regenerate your server certificate/key pair, using the RSA algorithm.

**Why can't I use SSL with name-based/non-IP-based virtual hosts?**

The reason is very technical, and a somewhat "chicken and egg" problem. The SSL protocol layer stays below the HTTP protocol layer and encapsulates HTTP. When an SSL connection (HTTPS) is established Apache/mod_ssl has to negotiate the SSL protocol parameters with the client. For this, mod_ssl has to consult the configuration of the virtual server (for instance it has to look for the cipher suite, the server certificate, etc.). But in order to go to the correct virtual server Apache has to know the Host HTTP header field. To do this, the HTTP request header has to be read. This cannot be done before the SSL handshake is finished, but the information is needed in order to complete the SSL handshake phase. See the next question for how to circumvent this issue.

Note that if you have a wildcard SSL certificate, or a certificate that has multiple hostnames on it using subjectAltName fields, you can use SSL on name-based virtual hosts without further workarounds.

**Is it possible to use Name-Based Virtual Hosting to identify different SSL virtual hosts?**

Name-Based Virtual Hosting is a very popular method of identifying different virtual hosts. It allows you to use the same IP address and the same port number for many different sites. When people move on to SSL, it seems natural to assume that the same method can be used to have lots of different SSL virtual hosts on the same server.

It is possible, but only if using a 2.2.12 or later web server, built with 0.9.8j or later OpenSSL. This is because it requires a feature that only the most recent revisions of the SSL specification added, called Server Name Indication (SNI).

Note that if you have a wildcard SSL certificate, or a certificate that has multiple hostnames on it using subjectAltName fields, you can use SSL on name-based virtual hosts without further workarounds.

The reason is that the SSL protocol is a separate layer which encapsulates the HTTP protocol. So the SSL session is a separate transaction, that takes place before the HTTP session has begun. The server receives an SSL request on IP address X and port Y (usually 443). Since the SSL request did not contain any Host: field, the server had no way to decide which SSL virtual host to use. Usually, it just used the first one it found which matched the port and IP address specified.

If you are using a version of the web server and OpenSSL that support SNI, though, and the client's browser also supports SNI, then the hostname is included in the original SSL request, and the web server can select the correct SSL virtual host.

You can, of course, use Name-Based Virtual Hosting to identify many non-SSL virtual hosts (all on port 80, for example) and then have a single SSL virtual host (on port 443). But if you do this, you must make sure to put the non-SSL port number on the NameVirtualHost directive, e.g.

```
NameVirtualHost 192.168.1.1:80
```

Other workaround solutions include:

Using separate IP addresses for different SSL hosts. Using different port numbers for different SSL hosts.


**How do I get SSL compression working?**

Although SSL compression negotiation was defined in the specification of SSLv2 and TLS, it took until May 2004 for RFC 3749 to define DEFLATE as a negotiable standard compression method.

OpenSSL 0.9.8 started to support this by default when compiled with the `zlib` option. If both the client and the server support compression, it will be used. However, most clients still try to initially connect with an SSLv2 Hello. As SSLv2 did not include an array of preferred compression algorithms in its handshake, compression cannot be negotiated with these clients. If the client disables support for SSLv2, either an SSLv3 or TLS Hello may be sent, depending on which SSL library is used, and compression may be set up. You can verify whether clients make use of SSL compression by logging the `%{SSL_COMPRESS_METHOD}x` variable.


**When I use Basic Authentication over HTTPS the lock icon in Netscape browsers stays unlocked when the dialog pops up. Does this mean the username/password is being sent unencrypted?**

No, the username/password is transmitted encrypted. The icon in Netscape browsers is not actually synchronized with the SSL/TLS layer. It only toggles to the locked state when the first part of the actual webpage data is transferred, which may confuse people. The Basic Authentication facility is part of the HTTP layer, which is above the SSL/TLS layer in HTTPS. Before any HTTP data communication takes place in HTTPS, the SSL/TLS layer has already completed its handshake phase, and switched to encrypted communication. So don't be confused by this icon.


**Why do I get I/O errors when connecting via HTTPS to an Apache+mod_ssl server with older versions of Microsoft Internet Explorer (MSIE)?**

The first reason is that the SSL implementation in some MSIE versions has some subtle bugs related to the HTTP keep-alive facility and the SSL close notify alerts on socket connection close. Additionally the interaction between SSL and HTTP/1.1 features are problematic in some MSIE versions. You can work around these problems by forcing

Apache not to use HTTP/1.1, keep-alive connections or send the SSL close notify messages to MSIE clients. This can be done by using the following directive in your SSL-aware virtual host section:

```
SetEnvIf User-Agent "MSIE [2-5]" \
        nokeepalive ssl-unclean-shutdown \
        downgrade-1.0 force-response-1.0
```

Further, some MSIE versions have problems with particular ciphers. Unfortunately, it is not possible to implement a MSIE-specific workaround for this, because the ciphers are needed as early as the SSL handshake phase. So a MSIE-specific SETENVIF won't solve these problems. Instead, you will have to make more drastic adjustments to the global parameters. Before you decide to do this, make sure your clients really have problems. If not, do not make these changes - they will affect *all* your clients, MSIE or otherwise.

**How do I enable TLS-SRP?**

TLS-SRP (Secure Remote Password key exchange for TLS, specified in RFC 5054) can supplement or replace certificates in authenticating an SSL connection. To use TLS-SRP, set the SSLSRPVERIFIERFILE directive to point to an OpenSSL SRP verifier file. To create the verifier file, use the `openssl` tool:

```
openssl srp -srpvfile passwd.srpv -add username
```

After creating this file, specify it in the SSL server configuration:

```
SSLSRPVerifierFile /path/to/passwd.srpv
```

To force clients to use non-certificate TLS-SRP cipher suites, use the following directive:

```
SSLCipherSuite "!DSS:!aRSA:SRP"
```

**Why do I get handshake failures with Java-based clients when using a certificate with more than 1024 bits?**

Beginning with version 2.5.0-dev as of 2013-09-29, MOD_SSL will use DH parameters which include primes with lengths of more than 1024 bits. Java 7 and earlier limit their support for DH prime sizes to a maximum of 1024 bits, however.

If your Java-based client aborts with exceptions such as `java.lang.RuntimeException: Could not generate DH keypair` and `java.security.InvalidAlgorithmParameterException: Prime size must be multiple of 64, and can only range from 512 to 1024 (inclusive)`, and httpd logs `tlsv1 alert internal error` (SSL alert number 80) (at LOGLEVEL info or higher), you can either rearrange mod_ssl's cipher list with SSLCIPHERSUITE (possibly in conjunction with SSLHONORCIPHERORDER), or you can use custom DH parameters with a 1024-bit prime, which will always have precedence over any of the built-in DH parameters.

To generate custom DH parameters, use the `openssl dhparam 1024` command. Alternatively, you can use the following standard 1024-bit DH parameters from RFC 2409[7], section 6.2:

---

[7]http://www.ietf.org/rfc/rfc2409.txt

```
-----BEGIN DH PARAMETERS-----
MIGHAoGBAP//////////yQ/aoiFowjTExmKLgNwc0SkCTgiKZ8x0Agu+pjsTmyJR
Sgh5jjQE3e+VGbPNOkMbMCsKbfJfFDdP4TVtbVHCReSFtXZiXn7G9ExC6aY37WsL
/1y29Aa37e44a/taiZ+lrp8kEXxLH+ZJKGZR7OZTgf//////////AgEC
-----END DH PARAMETERS-----
```

Add the custom parameters including the "BEGIN DH PARAMETERS" and "END DH PARAMETERS" lines to
the end of the first certificate file you have configured using the SSLCERTIFICATEFILE directive.

## mod_ssl Support

- What information resources are available in case of mod_ssl problems?
- What support contacts are available in case of mod_ssl problems?
- What information should I provide when writing a bug report?
- I had a core dump, can you help me?
- How do I get a backtrace, to help find the reason for my core dump?

### What information resources are available in case of mod_ssl problems?

The following information resources are available. In case of problems you should search here first.

**Answers in the User Manual's F.A.Q. List (this)**  http://httpd.apache.org/docs/trunk/ssl/ssl_faq.html[8]
First check the F.A.Q. (this text). If your problem is a common one, it may have been answered several times
before, and been included in this doc.

### What support contacts are available in case of mod_ssl problems?

The following lists all support possibilities for mod_ssl, in order of preference. Please go through these possibilities *in
this order* - don't just pick the one you like the look of.

1. *Send a Problem Report to the Apache httpd Users Support Mailing List*

   users@httpd.apache.org[9]
   This is the second way of submitting your problem report. Again, you must subscribe to the list first, but you
   can then easily discuss your problem with the whole Apache httpd user community.

2. *Write a Problem Report in the Bug Database*

   http://httpd.apache.org/bug_report.html[10]
   This is the last way of submitting your problem report. You should only do this if you've already posted to the
   mailing lists, and had no success. Please follow the instructions on the above page *carefully*.

---

[8]http://httpd.apache.org/docs/trunk/ssl/ssl_faq.html
[9]mailto:users@httpd.apache.org
[10]http://httpd.apache.org/bug_report.html

**What information should I provide when writing a bug report?**

You should always provide at least the following information:

**Apache httpd and OpenSSL version information** The Apache version can be determined by running `httpd -v`. The OpenSSL version can be determined by running `openssl version`. Alternatively, if you have Lynx installed, you can run the command `lynx -mime_header http://localhost/ | grep Server` to gather this information in a single step.

**The details on how you built and installed Apache httpd and OpenSSL** For this you can provide a logfile of your terminal session which shows the configuration and install steps. If this is not possible, you should at least provide the `configure` command line you used.

**In case of core dumps please include a Backtrace** If your Apache httpd dumps its core, please attach a stack-frame "backtrace" (see below for information on how to get this). This information is required in order to find a reason for your core dump.

**A detailed description of your problem** Don't laugh, we really mean it! Many problem reports don't include a description of what the actual problem is. Without this, it's very difficult for anyone to help you. So, it's in your own interest (you want the problem be solved, don't you?) to include as much detail as possible, please. Of course, you should still include all the essentials above too.

**I had a core dump, can you help me?**

In general no, at least not unless you provide more details about the code location where Apache dumped core. What is usually always required in order to help you is a backtrace (see next question). Without this information it is mostly impossible to find the problem and help you in fixing it.

**How do I get a backtrace, to help find the reason for my core dump?**

Following are the steps you will need to complete, to get a backtrace:

1. Make sure you have debugging symbols available, at least in Apache. On platforms where you use GCC/GDB, you will have to build Apache+mod_ssl with "`OPTIM="-g -ggdb3"`" to get this. On other platforms at least "`OPTIM="-g"`" is needed.

2. Start the server and try to reproduce the core-dump. For this you may want to use a directive like "`CoreDumpDirectory /tmp`" to make sure that the core-dump file can be written. This should result in a `/tmp/core` or `/tmp/httpd.core` file. If you don't get one of these, try running your server under a non-root UID. Many modern kernels do not allow a process to dump core after it has done a `setuid()` (unless it does an `exec()`) for security reasons (there can be privileged information left over in memory). If necessary, you can run `/path/to/httpd -X` manually to force Apache to not fork.

3. Analyze the core-dump. For this, run `gdb /path/to/httpd /tmp/httpd.core` or a similar command. In GDB, all you have to do then is to enter `bt`, and voila, you get the backtrace. For other debuggers consult your local debugger manual.

# Chapter 6

# Guides, Tutorials, and HowTos

# 6.1   How-To / Tutorials

## How-To / Tutorials

**Authentication and Authorization** Authentication is any process by which you verify that someone is who they claim they are. Authorization is any process by which someone is allowed to be where they want to go, or to have information that they want to have.

See: Authentication, Authorization (p. 227)

**Access Control** Access control refers to the process of restricting, or granting access to a resource based on arbitrary criteria. There are a variety of different ways that this can be accomplished.

See: Access Control (p. 234)

**Dynamic Content with CGI** The CGI (Common Gateway Interface) defines a way for a web server to interact with external content-generating programs, which are often referred to as CGI programs or CGI scripts. It is a simple way to put dynamic content on your web site. This document will be an introduction to setting up CGI on your Apache web server, and getting started writing CGI programs.

See: CGI: Dynamic Content (p. 236)

**.htaccess files** .htaccess files provide a way to make configuration changes on a per-directory basis. A file, containing one or more configuration directives, is placed in a particular document directory, and the directives apply to that directory, and all subdirectories thereof.

See: .htaccess files (p. 249)

**HTTP/2 with httpd** HTTP/2 is the evolution of the world's most successful application layer protocol, HTTP. It focuses on making more efficient use of network resources without changing the semantics of HTTP. This guide explains how HTTP/2 is implemented in httpd, showing basic configurations tips and best practices.

See: HTTP/2 guide (p. **??**)

**Introduction to Server Side Includes** SSI (Server Side Includes) are directives that are placed in HTML pages, and evaluated on the server while the pages are being served. They let you add dynamically generated content to an existing HTML page, without having to serve the entire page via a CGI program, or other dynamic technology.

See: Server Side Includes (SSI) (p. 243)

**Per-user web directories** On systems with multiple users, each user can be permitted to have a web site in their home directory using the USERDIR directive. Visitors to a URL http://example.com/~username/ will get content out of the home directory of the user "username", out of the subdirectory specified by the USERDIR directive.

See: User web directories (public_html) (p. 258)

**Reverse Proxy guide** Apache httpd has extensive capabilities as a reverse proxy server using the PROXYPASS directive as well as BALANCERMEMBER to create sophisticated reverse proxying implementations which provide for high-availability, load balancing and failover, cloud-based clustering and dynamic on-the-fly reconfiguration.

See: Reverse proxy guide (p. **??**)

## 6.2 Authentication and Authorization

Authentication is any process by which you verify that someone is who they claim they are. Authorization is any process by which someone is allowed to be where they want to go, or to have information that they want to have.

For general access control, see the Access Control How-To (p. 234) .

### Related Modules and Directives

There are three types of modules involved in the authentication and authorization process. You will usually need to choose at least one module from each group.

- Authentication type (see the AUTHTYPE directive)

    - MOD_AUTH_BASIC
    - MOD_AUTH_DIGEST

- Authentication provider (see the AUTHBASICPROVIDER and AUTHDIGESTPROVIDER directives)

    - MOD_AUTHN_ANON
    - MOD_AUTHN_DBD
    - MOD_AUTHN_DBM
    - MOD_AUTHN_FILE
    - MOD_AUTHNZ_LDAP
    - MOD_AUTHN_SOCACHE

- Authorization (see the REQUIRE directive)

    - MOD_AUTHNZ_LDAP
    - MOD_AUTHZ_DBD
    - MOD_AUTHZ_DBM
    - MOD_AUTHZ_GROUPFILE
    - MOD_AUTHZ_HOST
    - MOD_AUTHZ_OWNER
    - MOD_AUTHZ_USER

In addition to these modules, there are also MOD_AUTHN_CORE and MOD_AUTHZ_CORE. These modules implement core directives that are core to all auth modules.

The module MOD_AUTHNZ_LDAP is both an authentication and authorization provider. The module MOD_AUTHZ_HOST provides authorization and access control based on hostname, IP address or characteristics of the request, but is not part of the authentication provider system. For backwards compatibility with the mod_access, there is a new module MOD_ACCESS_COMPAT.

You probably also want to take a look at the Access Control (p. 234) howto, which discusses the various ways to control access to your server.

### Introduction

If you have information on your web site that is sensitive or intended for only a small group of people, the techniques in this article will help you make sure that the people that see those pages are the people that you wanted to see them.

This article covers the "standard" way of protecting parts of your web site that most of you are going to use.

**Note:**

> If your data really needs to be secure, consider using MOD_SSL in addition to any authentication.

## The Prerequisites

The directives discussed in this article will need to go either in your main server configuration file (typically in a <DIRECTORY> section), or in per-directory configuration files (.htaccess files).

If you plan to use .htaccess files, you will need to have a server configuration that permits putting authentication directives in these files. This is done with the ALLOWOVERRIDE directive, which specifies which directives, if any, may be put in per-directory configuration files.

Since we're talking here about authentication, you will need an ALLOWOVERRIDE directive like the following:

```
AllowOverride AuthConfig
```

Or, if you are just going to put the directives directly in your main server configuration file, you will of course need to have write permission to that file.

And you'll need to know a little bit about the directory structure of your server, in order to know where some files are kept. This should not be terribly difficult, and I'll try to make this clear when we come to that point.

You will also need to make sure that the modules MOD_AUTHN_CORE and MOD_AUTHZ_CORE have either been built into the httpd binary or loaded by the httpd.conf configuration file. Both of these modules provide core directives and functionality that are critical to the configuration and use of authentication and authorization in the web server.

## Getting it working

Here's the basics of password protecting a directory on your server.

First, you need to create a password file. Exactly how you do this will vary depending on what authentication provider you have chosen. More on that later. To start with, we'll use a text password file.

This file should be placed somewhere not accessible from the web. This is so that folks cannot download the password file. For example, if your documents are served out of /usr/local/apache/htdocs, you might want to put the password file(s) in /usr/local/apache/passwd.

To create the file, use the htpasswd utility that came with Apache. This will be located in the bin directory of wherever you installed Apache. If you have installed Apache from a third-party package, it may be in your execution path.

To create the file, type:

```
htpasswd -c /usr/local/apache/passwd/passwords rbowen
```

htpasswd will ask you for the password, and then ask you to type it again to confirm it:

```
# htpasswd -c /usr/local/apache/passwd/passwords rbowen
New password: mypassword
Re-type new password: mypassword
Adding password for user rbowen
```

If `htpasswd` is not in your path, of course you'll have to type the full path to the file to get it to run. With a default installation, it's located at `/usr/local/apache2/bin/htpasswd`

Next, you'll need to configure the server to request a password and tell the server which users are allowed access. You can do this either by editing the `httpd.conf` file or using an `.htaccess` file. For example, if you wish to protect the directory `/usr/local/apache/htdocs/secret`, you can use the following directives, either placed in the file `/usr/local/apache/htdocs/secret/.htaccess`, or placed in `httpd.conf` inside a <Directory "/usr/local/apache/htdocs/secret"> section.

```
AuthType Basic
AuthName "Restricted Files"
# (Following line optional)
AuthBasicProvider file
AuthUserFile "/usr/local/apache/passwd/passwords"
Require user rbowen
```

Let's examine each of those directives individually. The AUTHTYPE directive selects that method that is used to authenticate the user. The most common method is `Basic`, and this is the method implemented by MOD_AUTH_BASIC. It is important to be aware, however, that Basic authentication sends the password from the client to the server unencrypted. This method should therefore not be used for highly sensitive data, unless accompanied by MOD_SSL. Apache supports one other authentication method: `AuthType Digest`. This method is implemented by MOD_AUTH_DIGEST and was intended to be more secure. This is no longer the case and the connection should be encrypted with MOD_SSL instead.

The AUTHNAME directive sets the *Realm* to be used in the authentication. The realm serves two major functions. First, the client often presents this information to the user as part of the password dialog box. Second, it is used by the client to determine what password to send for a given authenticated area.

So, for example, once a client has authenticated in the `"Restricted Files"` area, it will automatically retry the same password for any area on the same server that is marked with the `"Restricted Files"` Realm. Therefore, you can prevent a user from being prompted more than once for a password by letting multiple restricted areas share the same realm. Of course, for security reasons, the client will always need to ask again for the password whenever the hostname of the server changes.

The AUTHBASICPROVIDER is, in this case, optional, since `file` is the default value for this directive. You'll need to use this directive if you are choosing a different source for authentication, such as MOD_AUTHN_DBM or MOD_AUTHN_DBD.

The AUTHUSERFILE directive sets the path to the password file that we just created with `htpasswd`. If you have a large number of users, it can be quite slow to search through a plain text file to authenticate the user on each request. Apache also has the ability to store user information in fast database files. The MOD_AUTHN_DBM module provides the AUTHDBMUSERFILE directive. These files can be created and manipulated with the `dbmmanage` and `htdbm` programs. Many other types of authentication options are available from third party modules in the Apache Modules Database[1].

Finally, the REQUIRE directive provides the authorization part of the process by setting the user that is allowed to access this region of the server. In the next section, we discuss various ways to use the REQUIRE directive.

## Letting more than one person in

The directives above only let one person (specifically someone with a username of `rbowen`) into the directory. In most cases, you'll want to let more than one person in. This is where the AUTHGROUPFILE comes in.

---

[1]http://modules.apache.org/

If you want to let more than one person in, you'll need to create a group file that associates group names with a list of users in that group. The format of this file is pretty simple, and you can create it with your favorite editor. The contents of the file will look like this:

```
GroupName:   rbowen dpitts sungo rshersey
```

That's just a list of the members of the group in a long line separated by spaces.

To add a user to your already existing password file, type:

```
htpasswd /usr/local/apache/passwd/passwords dpitts
```

You'll get the same response as before, but it will be appended to the existing file, rather than creating a new file. (It's the -c that makes it create a new password file).

Now, you need to modify your .htaccess file to look like the following:

```
AuthType Basic
AuthName "By Invitation Only"
# Optional line:
AuthBasicProvider file
AuthUserFile "/usr/local/apache/passwd/passwords"
AuthGroupFile "/usr/local/apache/passwd/groups"
Require group GroupName
```

Now, anyone that is listed in the group GroupName, and has an entry in the password file, will be let in, if they type the correct password.

There's another way to let multiple users in that is less specific. Rather than creating a group file, you can just use the following directive:

```
Require valid-user
```

Using that rather than the Require user rbowen line will allow anyone in that is listed in the password file, and who correctly enters their password. You can even emulate the group behavior here, by just keeping a separate password file for each group. The advantage of this approach is that Apache only has to check one file, rather than two. The disadvantage is that you have to maintain a bunch of password files, and remember to reference the right one in the AUTHUSERFILE directive.

## Possible problems

Because of the way that Basic authentication is specified, your username and password must be verified every time you request a document from the server. This is even if you're reloading the same page, and for every image on the page (if they come from a protected directory). As you can imagine, this slows things down a little. The amount that it slows things down is proportional to the size of the password file, because it has to open up that file, and go down the list of users until it gets to your name. And it has to do this every time a page is loaded.

A consequence of this is that there's a practical limit to how many users you can put in one password file. This limit will vary depending on the performance of your particular server machine, but you can expect to see slowdowns once you get above a few hundred entries, and may wish to consider a different authentication method at that time.

## Alternate password storage

Because storing passwords in plain text files has the above problems, you may wish to store your passwords somewhere else, such as in a database.

MOD_AUTHN_DBM and MOD_AUTHN_DBD are two modules which make this possible. Rather than selecting AUTHBASICPROVIDER file, instead you can choose dbm or dbd as your storage format.

To select a dbm file rather than a text file, for example:

```
<Directory "/www/docs/private">
    AuthName "Private"
    AuthType Basic
    AuthBasicProvider dbm
    AuthDBMUserFile "/www/passwords/passwd.dbm"
    Require valid-user
</Directory>
```

Other options are available. Consult the MOD_AUTHN_DBM documentation for more details.

## Using multiple providers

With the introduction of the new provider based authentication and authorization architecture, you are no longer locked into a single authentication or authorization method. In fact any number of the providers can be mixed and matched to provide you with exactly the scheme that meets your needs. In the following example, both the file and LDAP based authentication providers are being used.

```
<Directory "/www/docs/private">
    AuthName "Private"
    AuthType Basic
    AuthBasicProvider file ldap
    AuthUserFile "/usr/local/apache/passwd/passwords"
    AuthLDAPURL ldap://ldaphost/o=yourorg
    Require valid-user
</Directory>
```

In this example the file provider will attempt to authenticate the user first. If it is unable to authenticate the user, the LDAP provider will be called. This allows the scope of authentication to be broadened if your organization implements more than one type of authentication store. Other authentication and authorization scenarios may include mixing one type of authentication with a different type of authorization. For example, authenticating against a password file yet authorizing against an LDAP directory.

Just as multiple authentication providers can be implemented, multiple authorization methods can also be used. In this example both file group authorization as well as LDAP group authorization is being used.

```
<Directory "/www/docs/private">
    AuthName "Private"
    AuthType Basic
    AuthBasicProvider file
    AuthUserFile "/usr/local/apache/passwd/passwords"
    AuthLDAPURL ldap://ldaphost/o=yourorg
    AuthGroupFile "/usr/local/apache/passwd/groups"
    Require group GroupName
    Require ldap-group cn=mygroup,o=yourorg
</Directory>
```

To take authorization a little further, authorization container directives such as <REQUIREALL> and <REQUIRE-ANY> allow logic to be applied so that the order in which authorization is handled can be completely controlled through the configuration. See Authorization Containers (p. 519) for an example of how they may be applied.

## Beyond just authorization

The way that authorization can be applied is now much more flexible than just a single check against a single data store. Ordering, logic and choosing how authorization will be done is now possible.

### Applying logic and ordering

Controlling how and in what order authorization will be applied has been a bit of a mystery in the past. In Apache 2.2 a provider-based authentication mechanism was introduced to decouple the actual authentication process from authorization and supporting functionality. One of the side benefits was that authentication providers could be configured and called in a specific order which didn't depend on the load order of the auth module itself. This same provider based mechanism has been brought forward into authorization as well. What this means is that the REQUIRE directive not only specifies which authorization methods should be used, it also specifies the order in which they are called. Multiple authorization methods are called in the same order in which the REQUIRE directives appear in the configuration.

With the introduction of authorization container directives such as <REQUIREALL> and <REQUIREANY>, the configuration also has control over when the authorization methods are called and what criteria determines when access is granted. See Authorization Containers (p. 519) for an example of how they may be used to express complex authorization logic.

By default all REQUIRE directives are handled as though contained within a <REQUIREANY> container directive. In other words, if any of the specified authorization methods succeed, then authorization is granted.

### Using authorization providers for access control

Authentication by username and password is only part of the story. Frequently you want to let people in based on something other than who they are. Something such as where they are coming from.

The authorization providers `all`, `env`, `host` and `ip` let you allow or deny access based on other host based criteria such as host name or ip address of the machine requesting a document.

The usage of these providers is specified through the REQUIRE directive. This directive registers the authorization providers that will be called during the authorization stage of the request processing. For example:

```
Require ip address
```

where *address* is an IP address (or a partial IP address) or:

```
Require host domain_name
```

where *domain_name* is a fully qualified domain name (or a partial domain name); you may provide multiple addresses or domain names, if desired.

For example, if you have someone spamming your message board, and you want to keep them out, you could do the following:

```
<RequireAll>
    Require all granted
    Require not ip 10.252.46.165
</RequireAll>
```

Visitors coming from that address will not be able to see the content covered by this directive. If, instead, you have a machine name, rather than an IP address, you can use that.

```
<RequireAll>
    Require all granted
    Require not host host.example.com
</RequireAll>
```

And, if you'd like to block access from an entire domain, you can specify just part of an address or domain name:

```
<RequireAll>
    Require all granted
    Require not ip 192.168.205
    Require not host phishers.example.com moreidiots.example
    Require not host ke
</RequireAll>
```

Using <REQUIREALL> with multiple <REQUIRE> directives, each negated with not, will only allow access, if all of negated conditions are true. In other words, access will be blocked, if any of the negated conditions fails.

**Access Control backwards compatibility**

One of the side effects of adopting a provider based mechanism for authentication is that the previous access control directives ORDER, ALLOW, DENY and SATISFY are no longer needed. However to provide backwards compatibility for older configurations, these directives have been moved to the MOD_ACCESS_COMPAT module.

 **Note**

The directives provided by MOD_ACCESS_COMPAT have been deprecated by MOD_AUTHZ_HOST. Mixing old directives like ORDER, ALLOW or DENY with new ones like REQUIRE is technically possible but discouraged. The MOD_ACCESS_COMPAT module was created to support configurations containing only old directives to facilitate the 2.4 upgrade. Please check the upgrading (p. 2) guide for more information.

## Authentication Caching

There may be times when authentication puts an unacceptable load on a provider or on your network. This is most likely to affect users of MOD_AUTHN_DBD (or third-party/custom providers). To deal with this, HTTPD 2.3/2.4 introduces a new caching provider MOD_AUTHN_SOCACHE to cache credentials and reduce the load on the origin provider(s).

This may offer a substantial performance boost to some users.

## More information

You should also read the documentation for MOD_AUTH_BASIC and MOD_AUTHZ_HOST which contain some more information about how this all works. The directive <AUTHNPROVIDERALIAS> can also help in simplifying certain authentication configurations.

The various ciphers supported by Apache for authentication data are explained in Password Encryptions (p. 371) .

And you may want to look at the Access Control (p. 234) howto, which discusses a number of related topics.

# 6.3   Access Control

Access control refers to any means of controlling access to any resource. This is separate from authentication and authorization (p. 227) .

## Related Modules and Directives

Access control can be done by several different modules. The most important of these are MOD_AUTHZ_CORE and MOD_AUTHZ_HOST. Also discussed in this document is access control using MOD_REWRITE.

## Access control by host

If you wish to restrict access to portions of your site based on the host address of your visitors, this is most easily done using MOD_AUTHZ_HOST.

The REQUIRE provides a variety of different ways to allow or deny access to resources. In conjunction with the REQUIREALL, REQUIREANY, and REQUIRENONE directives, these requirements may be combined in arbitrarily complex ways, to enforce whatever your access policy happens to be.

 The ALLOW, DENY, and ORDER directives, provided by MOD_ACCESS_COMPAT, are deprecated and will go away in a future version. You should avoid using them, and avoid outdated
tutorials recommending their use.

The usage of these directives is:

```
Require host address
Require ip ip.address
```

In the first form, *address* is a fully qualified domain name (or a partial domain name); you may provide multiple addresses or domain names, if desired.

In the second form, *ip.address* is an IP address, a partial IP address, a network/netmask pair, or a network/nnn CIDR specification. Either IPv4 or IPv6 addresses may be used.

See the mod_authz_host documentation (p. 536) for further examples of this syntax.

You can insert not to negate a particular requirement. Note, that since a not is a negation of a value, it cannot be used by itself to allow or deny a request, as *not true* does not constitute *false*. Thus, to deny a visit using a negation, the block must have one element that evaluates as true or false. For example, if you have someone spamming your message board, and you want to keep them out, you could do the following:

```
<RequireAll>
    Require all granted
    Require not ip 10.252.46.165
</RequireAll>
```

Visitors coming from that address (10.252.46.165) will not be able to see the content covered by this directive. If, instead, you have a machine name, rather than an IP address, you can use that.

```
Require not host host.example.com
```

And, if you'd like to block access from an entire domain, you can specify just part of an address or domain name:

```
Require not ip 192.168.205
Require not host phishers.example.com moreidiots.example
Require not host gov
```

Use of the REQUIREALL, REQUIREANY, and REQUIRENONE directives may be used to enforce more complex sets of requirements.

## Access control by arbitrary variables

Using the <IF>, you can allow or deny access based on arbitrary environment variables or request header values. For example, to deny access based on user-agent (the browser type) you might do the following:

```
<If "%{HTTP_USER_AGENT} == 'BadBot'">
    Require all denied
</If>
```

Using the REQUIRE expr syntax, this could also be written as:

```
Require expr %{HTTP_USER_AGENT} != 'BadBot'
```

**Warning:**
> Access control by User-Agent is an unreliable technique, since the User-Agent header can be set to anything at all, at the whim of the end user.

See the expressions document (p. 99) for a further discussion of what expression syntaxes and variables are available to you.

## Access control with mod_rewrite

The [F] REWRITERULE flag causes a 403 Forbidden response to be sent. Using this, you can deny access to a resource based on arbitrary criteria.

For example, if you wish to block access to a resource between 8pm and 7am, you can do this using MOD_REWRITE.

```
RewriteEngine On
RewriteCond "%{TIME_HOUR}" ">=20" [OR]
RewriteCond "%{TIME_HOUR}" "<07"
RewriteRule "^/fridge"     "-"          [F]
```

This will return a 403 Forbidden response for any request after 8pm or before 7am. This technique can be used for any criteria that you wish to check. You can also redirect, or otherwise rewrite these requests, if that approach is preferred.

The <IF> directive, added in 2.4, replaces many things that MOD_REWRITE has traditionally been used to do, and you should probably look there first before resorting to mod_rewrite.

## More information

The expression engine (p. 99) gives you a great deal of power to do a variety of things based on arbitrary server variables, and you should consult that document for more detail.

Also, you should read the MOD_AUTHZ_CORE documentation for examples of combining multiple access requirements and specifying how they interact.

See also the Authentication and Authorization (p. 227) howto.

## 6.4   Apache Tutorial: Dynamic Content with CGI

### Introduction

| Related Modules | Related Directives |
| --- | --- |
| MOD_ALIAS | ADDHANDLER |
| MOD_CGI | OPTIONS |
| | SCRIPTALIAS |

The CGI (Common Gateway Interface) defines a way for a web server to interact with external content-generating programs, which are often referred to as CGI programs or CGI scripts. It is the simplest, and most common, way to put dynamic content on your web site. This document will be an introduction to setting up CGI on your Apache web server, and getting started writing CGI programs.

### Configuring Apache to permit CGI

In order to get your CGI programs to work properly, you'll need to have Apache configured to permit CGI execution. There are several ways to do this.

> **!**   Note: If Apache has been built with shared module support you need to ensure that the module is loaded; in your `httpd.conf` you need to make sure the LOADMODULE directive has not been commented out. A correctly configured directive may look like this:
>
> ```
> LoadModule cgi_module modules/mod_cgi.so
> ```

#### ScriptAlias

The SCRIPTALIAS

directive tells Apache that a particular directory is set aside for CGI programs. Apache will assume that every file in this directory is a CGI program, and will attempt to execute it, when that particular resource is requested by a client.

The SCRIPTALIAS directive looks like:

```
ScriptAlias "/cgi-bin/" "/usr/local/apache2/cgi-bin/"
```

The example shown is from your default `httpd.conf` configuration file, if you installed Apache in the default location. The SCRIPTALIAS directive is much like the ALIAS directive, which defines a URL prefix that is to mapped to a particular directory. ALIAS and SCRIPTALIAS are usually used for directories that are outside of the DOCUMENTROOT directory. The difference between ALIAS and SCRIPTALIAS is that SCRIPTALIAS has the added meaning that everything under that URL prefix will be considered a CGI program. So, the example above tells Apache that any request for a resource beginning with `/cgi-bin/` should be served from the directory `/usr/local/apache2/cgi-bin/`, and should be treated as a CGI program.

For example, if the URL `http://www.example.com/cgi-bin/test.pl` is requested, Apache will attempt to execute the file `/usr/local/apache2/cgi-bin/test.pl` and return the output. Of course, the file will have to exist, and be executable, and return output in a particular way, or Apache will return an error message.

#### CGI outside of ScriptAlias directories

CGI programs are often restricted to SCRIPTALIAS'ed directories for security reasons. In this way, administrators can tightly control who is allowed to use CGI programs. However, if the proper security precautions are taken, there is no reason why CGI programs cannot be run from arbitrary directories. For example, you may wish to let users have web content in their home directories with the USERDIR directive. If they want to have their own CGI programs, but don't have access to the main `cgi-bin` directory, they will need to be able to run CGI programs elsewhere.

There are two steps to allowing CGI execution in an arbitrary directory. First, the `cgi-script` handler must be activated using the ADDHANDLER or SETHANDLER directive. Second, ExecCGI must be specified in the OPTIONS directive.

### Explicitly using Options to permit CGI execution

You could explicitly use the OPTIONS directive, inside your main server configuration file, to specify that CGI execution was permitted in a particular directory:

```
<Directory "/usr/local/apache2/htdocs/somedir">
    Options +ExecCGI
</Directory>
```

The above directive tells Apache to permit the execution of CGI files. You will also need to tell the server what files are CGI files. The following ADDHANDLER directive tells the server to treat all files with the `cgi` or `pl` extension as CGI programs:

```
AddHandler cgi-script .cgi .pl
```

### .htaccess files

The `.htaccess` tutorial (p. 249) shows how to activate CGI programs if you do not have access to `httpd.conf`.

### User Directories

To allow CGI program execution for any file ending in `.cgi` in users' directories, you can use the following configuration.

```
<Directory "/home/*/public_html">
    Options +ExecCGI
    AddHandler cgi-script .cgi
</Directory>
```

If you wish designate a `cgi-bin` subdirectory of a user's directory where everything will be treated as a CGI program, you can use the following.

```
<Directory "/home/*/public_html/cgi-bin">
    Options ExecCGI
    SetHandler cgi-script
</Directory>
```

## Writing a CGI program

There are two main differences between "regular" programming, and CGI programming.

First, all output from your CGI program must be preceded by a MIME-type header. This is HTTP header that tells the client what sort of content it is receiving. Most of the time, this will look like:

```
Content-type:  text/html
```

Secondly, your output needs to be in HTML, or some other format that a browser will be able to display. Most of the time, this will be HTML, but occasionally you might write a CGI program that outputs a gif image, or other non-HTML content.

Apart from those two things, writing a CGI program will look a lot like any other program that you might write.

**Your first CGI program**

The following is an example CGI program that prints one line to your browser. Type in the following, save it to a file called `first.pl`, and put it in your `cgi-bin` directory.

```
#!/usr/bin/perl
print "Content-type: text/html\n\n";
print "Hello, World.";
```

Even if you are not familiar with Perl, you should be able to see what is happening here. The first line tells Apache (or whatever shell you happen to be running under) that this program can be executed by feeding the file to the interpreter found at the location `/usr/bin/perl`. The second line prints the content-type declaration we talked about, followed by two carriage-return newline pairs. This puts a blank line after the header, to indicate the end of the HTTP headers, and the beginning of the body. The third line prints the string "Hello, World.". And that's the end of it.

If you open your favorite browser and tell it to get the address

```
http://www.example.com/cgi-bin/first.pl
```

or wherever you put your file, you will see the one line `Hello, World.` appear in your browser window. It's not very exciting, but once you get that working, you'll have a good chance of getting just about anything working.

## But it's still not working!

There are four basic things that you may see in your browser when you try to access your CGI program from the web:

**The output of your CGI program** Great! That means everything worked fine. If the output is correct, but the browser is not processing it correctly, make sure you have the correct `Content-Type` set in your CGI program.

**The source code of your CGI program or a "POST Method Not Allowed" message** That means that you have not properly configured Apache to process your CGI program. Reread the section on configuring Apache and try to find what you missed.

**A message starting with "Forbidden"** That means that there is a permissions problem. Check the Apache error log and the section below on file permissions.

**A message saying "Internal Server Error"** If you check the Apache error log, you will probably find that it says "Premature end of script headers", possibly along with an error message generated by your CGI program. In this case, you will want to check each of the below sections to see what might be preventing your CGI program from emitting the proper HTTP headers.

### File permissions

Remember that the server does not run as you. That is, when the server starts up, it is running with the permissions of an unprivileged user - usually `nobody`, or `www` - and so it will need extra permissions to execute files that are owned by you. Usually, the way to give a file sufficient permissions to be executed by `nobody` is to give everyone execute permission on the file:

```
chmod a+x first.pl
```

Also, if your program reads from, or writes to, any other files, those files will need to have the correct permissions to permit this.

### Path information and environment

When you run a program from your command line, you have certain information that is passed to the shell without you thinking about it. For example, you have a `PATH`, which tells the shell where it can look for files that you reference.

When a program runs through the web server as a CGI program, it may not have the same `PATH`. Any programs that you invoke in your CGI program (like `sendmail`, for example) will need to be specified by a full path, so that the shell can find them when it attempts to execute your CGI program.

A common manifestation of this is the path to the script interpreter (often `perl`) indicated in the first line of your CGI program, which will look something like:

```
#!/usr/bin/perl
```

Make sure that this is in fact the path to the interpreter.

 When editing CGI scripts on Windows, end-of-line characters may be appended to the interpreter path. Ensure that files are then transferred to the server in ASCII mode. Failure to do so may result in "Command not found" warnings from the OS, due to the unrecognized end-of-line character being interpreted as a part of the interpreter filename.

### Missing environment variables

If your CGI program depends on non-standard environment variables, you will need to assure that those variables are passed by Apache.

When you miss HTTP headers from the environment, make sure they are formatted according to RFC 2616[2], section 4.2: Header names must start with a letter, followed only by letters, numbers or hyphen. Any header violating this rule will be dropped silently.

### Program errors

Most of the time when a CGI program fails, it's because of a problem with the program itself. This is particularly true once you get the hang of this CGI stuff, and no longer make the above two mistakes. The first thing to do is to make sure that your program runs from the command line before testing it via the web server. For example, try:

```
cd /usr/local/apache2/cgi-bin
./first.pl
```

---

[2]http://tools.ietf.org/html/rfc2616

(Do not call the `perl` interpreter. The shell and Apache should find the interpreter using the path information on the first line of the script.)

The first thing you see written by your program should be a set of HTTP headers, including the `Content-Type`, followed by a blank line. If you see anything else, Apache will return the `Premature end of script headers` error if you try to run it through the server. See Writing a CGI program above for more details.

### Error logs

The error logs are your friend. Anything that goes wrong generates message in the error log. You should always look there first. If the place where you are hosting your web site does not permit you access to the error log, you should probably host your site somewhere else. Learn to read the error logs, and you'll find that almost all of your problems are quickly identified, and quickly solved.

### Suexec

The suexec (p. 115) support program allows CGI programs to be run under different user permissions, depending on which virtual host or user home directory they are located in. Suexec has very strict permission checking, and any failure in that checking will result in your CGI programs failing with `Premature end of script headers`.

To check if you are using suexec, run `apachectl -V` and check for the location of `SUEXEC_BIN`. If Apache finds an `suexec` binary there on startup, suexec will be activated.

Unless you fully understand suexec, you should not be using it. To disable suexec, simply remove (or rename) the `suexec` binary pointed to by `SUEXEC_BIN` and then restart the server. If, after reading about suexec (p. 115) , you still wish to use it, then run `suexec -V` to find the location of the suexec log file, and use that log file to find what policy you are violating.

## What's going on behind the scenes?

As you become more advanced in CGI programming, it will become useful to understand more about what's happening behind the scenes. Specifically, how the browser and server communicate with one another. Because although it's all very well to write a program that prints "Hello, World.", it's not particularly useful.

### Environment variables

Environment variables are values that float around you as you use your computer. They are useful things like your path (where the computer searches for the actual file implementing a command when you type it), your username, your terminal type, and so on. For a full list of your normal, every day environment variables, type `env` at a command prompt.

During the CGI transaction, the server and the browser also set environment variables, so that they can communicate with one another. These are things like the browser type (Netscape, IE, Lynx), the server type (Apache, IIS, WebSite), the name of the CGI program that is being run, and so on.

These variables are available to the CGI programmer, and are half of the story of the client-server communication. The complete list of required variables is at Common Gateway Interface RFC[3].

This simple Perl CGI program will display all of the environment variables that are being passed around. Two similar programs are included in the `cgi-bin`

---

[3]http://www.ietf.org/rfc/rfc3875

directory of the Apache distribution. Note that some variables are required, while others are optional, so you may see some variables listed that were not in the official list. In addition, Apache provides many different ways for you to add your own environment variables (p. 92) to the basic ones provided by default.

```perl
#!/usr/bin/perl
use strict;
use warnings;

print "Content-type: text/html\n\n";
foreach my $key (keys %ENV) {
    print "$key --> $ENV{$key}<br>";
}
```

**STDIN and STDOUT**

Other communication between the server and the client happens over standard input (STDIN) and standard output (STDOUT). In normal everyday context, STDIN means the keyboard, or a file that a program is given to act on, and STDOUT usually means the console or screen.

When you POST a web form to a CGI program, the data in that form is bundled up into a special format and gets delivered to your CGI program over STDIN. The program then can process that data as though it was coming in from the keyboard, or from a file

The "special format" is very simple. A field name and its value are joined together with an equals (=) sign, and pairs of values are joined together with an ampersand (&). Inconvenient characters like spaces, ampersands, and equals signs, are converted into their hex equivalent so that they don't gum up the works. The whole data string might look something like:

```
name=Rich%20Bowen&city=Lexington&state=KY&sidekick=Squirrel%20Monkey
```

You'll sometimes also see this type of string appended to a URL. When that is done, the server puts that string into the environment variable called QUERY_STRING. That's called a GET request. Your HTML form specifies whether a GET or a POST is used to deliver the data, by setting the METHOD attribute in the FORM tag.

Your program is then responsible for splitting that string up into useful information. Fortunately, there are libraries and modules available to help you process this data, as well as handle other of the aspects of your CGI program.

**CGI modules/libraries**

When you write CGI programs, you should consider using a code library, or module, to do most of the grunt work for you. This leads to fewer errors, and faster development.

If you're writing CGI programs in Perl, modules are available on CPAN[4]. The most popular module for this purpose is CGI.pm. You might also consider CGI::Lite, which implements a minimal set of functionality, which is all you need in most programs.

If you're writing CGI programs in C, there are a variety of options. One of these is the CGIC library, from http://www.boutell.com/cgic/.

---

[4]http://www.cpan.org/

**For more information**

The current CGI specification is available in the Common Gateway Interface RFC[5].

When you post a question about a CGI problem that you're having, whether to a mailing list, or to a newsgroup, make sure you provide enough information about what happened, what you expected to happen, and how what actually happened was different, what server you're running, what language your CGI program was in, and, if possible, the offending code. This will make finding your problem much simpler.

Note that questions about CGI problems should **never** be posted to the Apache bug database unless you are sure you have found a problem in the Apache source code.

---

[5]http://www.ietf.org/rfc/rfc3875

## 6.5 Apache httpd Tutorial: Introduction to Server Side Includes

Server-side includes provide a means to add dynamic content to existing HTML documents.

### Introduction

| Related Modules | Related Directives |
|---|---|
| MOD_INCLUDE | OPTIONS |
| MOD_CGI | XBITHACK |
| MOD_EXPIRES | ADDTYPE |
| | SETOUTPUTFILTER |
| | BROWSERMATCHNOCASE |

This article deals with Server Side Includes, usually called simply SSI. In this article, I'll talk about configuring your server to permit SSI, and introduce some basic SSI techniques for adding dynamic content to your existing HTML pages.

In the latter part of the article, we'll talk about some of the somewhat more advanced things that can be done with SSI, such as conditional statements in your SSI directives.

### What are SSI?

SSI (Server Side Includes) are directives that are placed in HTML pages, and evaluated on the server while the pages are being served. They let you add dynamically generated content to an existing HTML page, without having to serve the entire page via a CGI program, or other dynamic technology.

For example, you might place a directive into an existing HTML page, such as:

```
<!--#echo var="DATE_LOCAL" -->
```

And, when the page is served, this fragment will be evaluated and replaced with its value:

```
Tuesday, 15-Jan-2013 19:28:54 EST
```

The decision of when to use SSI, and when to have your page entirely generated by some program, is usually a matter of how much of the page is static, and how much needs to be recalculated every time the page is served. SSI is a great way to add small pieces of information, such as the current time - shown above. But if a majority of your page is being generated at the time that it is served, you need to look for some other solution.

### Configuring your server to permit SSI

To permit SSI on your server, you must have the following directive either in your `httpd.conf` file, or in a `.htaccess` file:

```
Options +Includes
```

This tells Apache that you want to permit files to be parsed for SSI directives. Note that most configurations contain multiple OPTIONS directives that can override each other. You will probably need to apply the `Options` to the specific directory where you want SSI enabled in order to assure that it gets evaluated last.

Not just any file is parsed for SSI directives. You have to tell Apache which files should be parsed. There are two ways to do this. You can tell Apache to parse any file with a particular file extension, such as .shtml, with the following directives:

```
AddType text/html .shtml
AddOutputFilter INCLUDES .shtml
```

One disadvantage to this approach is that if you wanted to add SSI directives to an existing page, you would have to change the name of that page, and all links to that page, in order to give it a .shtml extension, so that those directives would be executed.

The other method is to use the XBITHACK directive:

```
XBitHack on
```

XBITHACK tells Apache to parse files for SSI directives if they have the execute bit set. So, to add SSI directives to an existing page, rather than having to change the file name, you would just need to make the file executable using chmod.

```
chmod +x pagename.html
```

A brief comment about what not to do. You'll occasionally see people recommending that you just tell Apache to parse all .html files for SSI, so that you don't have to mess with .shtml file names. These folks have perhaps not heard about XBITHACK. The thing to keep in mind is that, by doing this, you're requiring that Apache read through every single file that it sends out to clients, even if they don't contain any SSI directives. This can slow things down quite a bit, and is not a good idea.

Of course, on Windows, there is no such thing as an execute bit to set, so that limits your options a little.

In its default configuration, Apache does not send the last modified date or content length HTTP headers on SSI pages, because these values are difficult to calculate for dynamic content. This can prevent your document from being cached, and result in slower perceived client performance. There are two ways to solve this:

1. Use the XBitHack Full configuration. This tells Apache to determine the last modified date by looking only at the date of the originally requested file, ignoring the modification date of any included files.

2. Use the directives provided by MOD_EXPIRES to set an explicit expiration time on your files, thereby letting browsers and proxies know that it is acceptable to cache them.

## Basic SSI directives

SSI directives have the following syntax:

```
<!--#function attribute=value attribute=value ...   -->
```

It is formatted like an HTML comment, so if you don't have SSI correctly enabled, the browser will ignore it, but it will still be visible in the HTML source. If you have SSI correctly configured, the directive will be replaced with its results.

The function can be one of a number of things, and we'll talk some more about most of these in the next installment of this series. For now, here are some examples of what you can do with SSI

**Today's date**

```
<!--#echo var="DATE_LOCAL" -->
```

The echo function just spits out the value of a variable. There are a number of standard variables, which include the whole set of environment variables that are available to CGI programs. Also, you can define your own variables with the set function.

If you don't like the format in which the date gets printed, you can use the config function, with a timefmt attribute, to modify that formatting.

```
<!--#config timefmt="%A %B %d, %Y" -->
Today is <!--#echo var="DATE_LOCAL" -->
```

**Modification date of the file**

```
This document last modified <!--#flastmod file="index.html" -->
```

This function is also subject to timefmt format configurations.

**Including the results of a CGI program**

This is one of the more common uses of SSI - to output the results of a CGI program, such as everybody's favorite, a "hit counter."

```
<!--#include virtual="/cgi-bin/counter.pl" -->
```

## Additional examples

Following are some specific examples of things you can do in your HTML documents with SSI.

**When was this document modified?**

Earlier, we mentioned that you could use SSI to inform the user when the document was most recently modified. However, the actual method for doing that was left somewhat in question. The following code, placed in your HTML document, will put such a time stamp on your page. Of course, you will have to have SSI correctly enabled, as discussed above.

```
<!--#config timefmt="%A %B %d, %Y" -->
This file last modified <!--#flastmod file="ssi.shtml" -->
```

Of course, you will need to replace the ssi.shtml with the actual name of the file that you're referring to. This can be inconvenient if you're just looking for a generic piece of code that you can paste into any file, so you probably want to use the LAST_MODIFIED variable instead:

```
<!--#config timefmt="%D" -->
This file last modified <!--#echo var="LAST_MODIFIED" -->
```

For more details on the timefmt format, go to your favorite search site and look for strftime. The syntax is the same.

**Including a standard footer**

If you are managing any site that is more than a few pages, you may find that making changes to all those pages can be a real pain, particularly if you are trying to maintain some kind of standard look across all those pages.

Using an include file for a header and/or a footer can reduce the burden of these updates. You just have to make one footer file, and then include it into each page with the `include` SSI command. The `include` function can determine what file to include with either the `file` attribute, or the `virtual` attribute. The `file` attribute is a file path, *relative to the current directory*. That means that it cannot be an absolute file path (starting with /), nor can it contain ../ as part of that path. The `virtual` attribute is probably more useful, and should specify a URL relative to the document being served. It can start with a /, but must be on the same server as the file being served.

```
<!--#include virtual="/footer.html" -->
```

I'll frequently combine the last two things, putting a `LAST_MODIFIED` directive inside a footer file to be included. SSI directives can be contained in the included file, and includes can be nested - that is, the included file can include another file, and so on.

## What else can I config?

In addition to being able to `config` the time format, you can also `config` two other things.

Usually, when something goes wrong with your SSI directive, you get the message

```
[an error occurred while processing this directive]
```

If you want to change that message to something else, you can do so with the `errmsg` attribute to the `config` function:

```
<!--#config errmsg="[It appears that you don't know how to use SSI]"
-->
```

Hopefully, end users will never see this message, because you will have resolved all the problems with your SSI directives before your site goes live. (Right?)

And you can `config` the format in which file sizes are returned with the `sizefmt` attribute. You can specify `bytes` for a full count in bytes, or `abbrev` for an abbreviated number in Kb or Mb, as appropriate.

## Executing commands

I expect that I'll have an article some time in the coming months about using SSI with small CGI programs. For now, here's something else that you can do with the `exec` function. You can actually have SSI execute a command using the shell (`/bin/sh`, to be precise - or the DOS shell, if you're on Win32). The following, for example, will give you a directory listing.

```
<pre>
<!--#exec cmd="ls" -->
</pre>
```

or, on Windows

```
<pre>
<!--#exec cmd="dir" -->
</pre>
```

You might notice some strange formatting with this directive on Windows, because the output from `dir` contains the string "`<dir>`" in it, which confuses browsers.

Note that this feature is exceedingly dangerous, as it will execute whatever code happens to be embedded in the `exec` tag. If you have any situation where users can edit content on your web pages, such as with a "guestbook", for example, make sure that you have this feature disabled. You can allow SSI, but not the `exec` feature, with the `IncludesNOEXEC` argument to the `Options` directive.

## Advanced SSI techniques

In addition to spitting out content, Apache SSI gives you the option of setting variables, and using those variables in comparisons and conditionals.

### Setting variables

Using the `set` directive, you can set variables for later use. We'll need this later in the discussion, so we'll talk about it here. The syntax of this is as follows:

```
<!--#set var="name" value="Rich" -->
```

In addition to merely setting values literally like that, you can use any other variable, including environment variables (p. 92) or the variables discussed above (like `LAST_MODIFIED`, for example) to give values to your variables. You will specify that something is a variable, rather than a literal string, by using the dollar sign ($) before the name of the variable.

```
<!--#set var="modified" value="$LAST_MODIFIED" -->
```

To put a literal dollar sign into the value of your variable, you need to escape the dollar sign with a backslash.

```
<!--#set var="cost" value="\$100" -->
```

Finally, if you want to put a variable in the midst of a longer string, and there's a chance that the name of the variable will run up against some other characters, and thus be confused with those characters, you can place the name of the variable in braces, to remove this confusion. (It's hard to come up with a really good example of this, but hopefully you'll get the point.)

```
<!--#set var="date" value="${DATE_LOCAL}_${DATE_GMT}" -->
```

**Conditional expressions**

Now that we have variables, and are able to set and compare their values, we can use them to express conditionals. This lets SSI be a tiny programming language of sorts. MOD_INCLUDE provides an `if`, `elif`, `else`, `endif` structure for building conditional statements. This allows you to effectively generate multiple logical pages out of one actual page.

The structure of this conditional construct is:

```
<!--#if expr="test_condition" -->
<!--#elif expr="test_condition" -->
<!--#else -->
<!--#endif -->
```

A *test_condition* can be any sort of logical comparison - either comparing values to one another, or testing the "truth" of a particular value. (A given string is true if it is nonempty.) For a full list of the comparison operators available to you, see the MOD_INCLUDE documentation.

For example, if you wish to customize the text on your web page based on the time of day, you could use the following recipe, placed in the HTML page:

```
Good <!--#if expr="%{TIME_HOUR} <12" -->
morning!
<!--#else -->
afternoon!
<!--#endif -->
```

Any other variable (either ones that you define, or normal environment variables) can be used in conditional statements. See Expressions in Apache HTTP Server (p. 99) for more information on the expression evaluation engine.

With Apache's ability to set environment variables with the `SetEnvIf` directives, and other related directives, this functionality can let you do a wide variety of dynamic content on the server side without resorting a full web application.

## Conclusion

SSI is certainly not a replacement for CGI, or other technologies used for generating dynamic web pages. But it is a great way to add small amounts of dynamic content to pages, without doing a lot of extra work.

# 6.6 Apache HTTP Server Tutorial: .htaccess files

.htaccess files provide a way to make configuration changes on a per-directory basis.

### .htaccess files

| Related Modules | Related Directives |
|---|---|
| CORE | ACCESSFILENAME |
| MOD_AUTHN_FILE | ALLOWOVERRIDE |
| MOD_AUTHZ_GROUPFILE | OPTIONS |
| MOD_CGI | ADDHANDLER |
| MOD_INCLUDE | SETHANDLER |
| MOD_MIME | AUTHTYPE |
| | AUTHNAME |
| | AUTHUSERFILE |
| | AUTHGROUPFILE |
| | REQUIRE |

You should avoid using .htaccess files completely if you have access to httpd main server config file. Using .htaccess files slows down your Apache http server. Any directive that you can include in a .htaccess file is better set in a DIRECTORY block, as it will have the same effect with better performance.

### What they are/How to use them

.htaccess files (or "distributed configuration files") provide a way to make configuration changes on a per-directory basis. A file, containing one or more configuration directives, is placed in a particular document directory, and the directives apply to that directory, and all subdirectories thereof.

**Note:**

If you want to call your .htaccess file something else, you can change the name of the file using the ACCESSFILENAME directive. For example, if you would rather call the file .config then you can put the following in your server configuration file:

```
AccessFileName ".config"
```

In general, .htaccess files use the same syntax as the main configuration files (p. 32). What you can put in these files is determined by the ALLOWOVERRIDE directive. This directive specifies, in categories, what directives will be honored if they are found in a .htaccess file. If a directive is permitted in a .htaccess file, the documentation for that directive will contain an Override section, specifying what value must be in ALLOWOVERRIDE in order for that directive to be permitted.

For example, if you look at the documentation for the ADDDEFAULTCHARSET directive, you will find that it is permitted in .htaccess files. (See the Context line in the directive summary.) The Override (p. 377) line reads FileInfo. Thus, you must have at least AllowOverride FileInfo in order for this directive to be honored in .htaccess files.

| **Example:** | |
|---|---|
| Context: (p. 377) | server config, virtual host, directory, .htaccess |
| Override: (p. 377) | FileInfo |

If you are unsure whether a particular directive is permitted in a .htaccess file, look at the documentation for that directive, and check the Context line for ".htaccess".

## When (not) to use .htaccess files

In general, you should only use .htaccess files when you don't have access to the main server configuration file. There is, for example, a common misconception that user authentication should always be done in .htaccess files, and, in more recent years, another misconception that MOD_REWRITE directives must go in .htaccess files. This is simply not the case. You can put user authentication configurations in the main server configuration, and this is, in fact, the preferred way to do things. Likewise, mod_rewrite directives work better, in many respects, in the main server configuration.

.htaccess files should be used in a case where the content providers need to make configuration changes to the server on a per-directory basis, but do not have root access on the server system. In the event that the server administrator is not willing to make frequent configuration changes, it might be desirable to permit individual users to make these changes in .htaccess files for themselves. This is particularly true, for example, in cases where ISPs are hosting multiple user sites on a single machine, and want their users to be able to alter their configuration.

However, in general, use of .htaccess files should be avoided when possible. Any configuration that you would consider putting in a .htaccess file, can just as effectively be made in a <DIRECTORY> section in your main server configuration file.

There are two main reasons to avoid the use of .htaccess files.

The first of these is performance. When ALLOWOVERRIDE is set to allow the use of .htaccess files, httpd will look in every directory for .htaccess files. Thus, permitting .htaccess files causes a performance hit, whether or not you actually even use them! Also, the .htaccess file is loaded every time a document is requested.

Further note that httpd must look for .htaccess files in all higher-level directories, in order to have a full complement of directives that it must apply. (See section on how directives are applied.) Thus, if a file is requested out of a directory /www/htdocs/example, httpd must look for the following files:

```
/.htaccess
/www/.htaccess
/www/htdocs/.htaccess
/www/htdocs/example/.htaccess
```

And so, for each file access out of that directory, there are 4 additional file-system accesses, even if none of those files are present. (Note that this would only be the case if .htaccess files were enabled for /, which is not usually the case.)

In the case of REWRITERULE directives, in .htaccess context these regular expressions must be re-compiled with every request to the directory, whereas in main server configuration context they are compiled once and cached. Additionally, the rules themselves are more complicated, as one must work around the restrictions that come with per-directory context and mod_rewrite. Consult the Rewrite Guide (p. 147) for more detail on this subject.

The second consideration is one of security. You are permitting users to modify server configuration, which may result in changes over which you have no control. Carefully consider whether you want to give your users this privilege. Note also that giving users less privileges than they need will lead to additional technical support requests. Make sure you clearly tell your users what level of privileges you have given them. Specifying exactly what you have set ALLOWOVERRIDE to, and pointing them to the relevant documentation, will save yourself a lot of confusion later.

Note that it is completely equivalent to put a .htaccess file in a directory /www/htdocs/example containing a directive, and to put that same directive in a Directory section <Directory "/www/htdocs/example"> in your main server configuration:

.htaccess file in /www/htdocs/example:

**Contents of .htaccess file in `/www/htdocs/example`**

```
AddType text/example ".exm"
```

**Section from your `httpd.conf` file**

```
<Directory "/www/htdocs/example">
    AddType text/example ".exm"
</Directory>
```

However, putting this configuration in your server configuration file will result in less of a performance hit, as the configuration is loaded once when httpd starts, rather than every time a file is requested.

The use of `.htaccess` files can be disabled completely by setting the ALLOWOVERRIDE directive to `none`:

```
AllowOverride None
```

## How directives are applied

The configuration directives found in a `.htaccess` file are applied to the directory in which the `.htaccess` file is found, and to all subdirectories thereof. However, it is important to also remember that there may have been `.htaccess` files in directories higher up. Directives are applied in the order that they are found. Therefore, a `.htaccess` file in a particular directory may override directives found in `.htaccess` files found higher up in the directory tree. And those, in turn, may have overridden directives found yet higher up, or in the main server configuration file itself.

Example:

In the directory `/www/htdocs/example1` we have a `.htaccess` file containing the following:

```
Options +ExecCGI
```

(Note: you must have "`AllowOverride Options`" in effect to permit the use of the "OPTIONS" directive in `.htaccess` files.)

In the directory `/www/htdocs/example1/example2` we have a `.htaccess` file containing:

```
Options Includes
```

Because of this second `.htaccess` file, in the directory `/www/htdocs/example1/example2`, CGI execution is not permitted, as only `Options Includes` is in effect, which completely overrides any earlier setting that may have been in place.

### Merging of .htaccess with the main configuration files

As discussed in the documentation on Configuration Sections (p. 35), `.htaccess` files can override the <DIRECTORY> sections for the corresponding directory, but will be overridden by other types of configuration sections from the main configuration files. This fact can be used to enforce certain configurations, even in the presence of a liberal ALLOWOVERRIDE setting. For example, to prevent script execution while allowing anything else to be set in `.htaccess` you can use:

```
<Directory "/www/htdocs">
    AllowOverride All
</Directory>

<Location "/">
    Options +IncludesNoExec -ExecCGI
</Location>
```

⟹ This example assumes that your DOCUMENTROOT is /www/htdocs.


## Authentication example

If you jumped directly to this part of the document to find out how to do authentication, it is important to note one thing. There is a common misconception that you are required to use .htaccess files in order to implement password authentication. This is not the case. Putting authentication directives in a <DIRECTORY> section, in your main server configuration file, is the preferred way to implement this, and .htaccess files should be used only if you don't have access to the main server configuration file. See above for a discussion of when you should and should not use .htaccess files.

Having said that, if you still think you need to use a .htaccess file, you may find that a configuration such as what follows may work for you.

.htaccess file contents:

```
AuthType Basic
AuthName "Password Required"
AuthUserFile "/www/passwords/password.file"
AuthGroupFile "/www/passwords/group.file"
Require group admins
```

Note that AllowOverride AuthConfig must be in effect for these directives to have any effect.

Please see the authentication tutorial (p. 227) for a more complete discussion of authentication and authorization.


## Server Side Includes example

Another common use of .htaccess files is to enable Server Side Includes for a particular directory. This may be done with the following configuration directives, placed in a .htaccess file in the desired directory:

```
Options +Includes
AddType text/html "shtml"
AddHandler server-parsed shtml
```

Note that AllowOverride Options and AllowOverride FileInfo must both be in effect for these directives to have any effect.

Please see the SSI tutorial (p. 243) for a more complete discussion of server-side includes.


## Rewrite Rules in .htaccess files

When using REWRITERULE in .htaccess files, be aware that the per-directory context changes things a bit. In particular, rules are taken to be relative to the current directory, rather than being the original requested URI. Consider the following examples:

```
# In httpd.conf
RewriteRule "^/images/(.+)\.jpg" "/images/$1.png"

# In .htaccess in root dir
RewriteRule "^images/(.+)\.jpg" "images/$1.png"

# In .htaccess in images/
RewriteRule "^(.+)\.jpg" "$1.png"
```

In a .htaccess in your document directory, the leading slash is removed from the value supplied to REWRITERULE, and in the images subdirectory, /images/ is removed from it. Thus, your regular expression needs to omit that portion as well.

Consult the mod_rewrite documentation (p. 146) for further details on using mod_rewrite.

## CGI example

Finally, you may wish to use a .htaccess file to permit the execution of CGI programs in a particular directory. This may be implemented with the following configuration:

```
Options +ExecCGI
AddHandler cgi-script "cgi" "pl"
```

Alternately, if you wish to have all files in the given directory be considered to be CGI programs, this may be done with the following configuration:

```
Options +ExecCGI
SetHandler cgi-script
```

Note that AllowOverride Options and AllowOverride FileInfo must both be in effect for these directives to have any effect.

Please see the CGI tutorial (p. 236) for a more complete discussion of CGI programming and configuration.

## Troubleshooting

When you put configuration directives in a .htaccess file, and you don't get the desired effect, there are a number of things that may be going wrong.

Most commonly, the problem is that ALLOWOVERRIDE is not set such that your configuration directives are being honored. Make sure that you don't have a AllowOverride None in effect for the file scope in question. A good test for this is to put garbage in your .htaccess file and reload the page. If a server error is not generated, then you almost certainly have AllowOverride None in effect.

If, on the other hand, you are getting server errors when trying to access documents, check your httpd error log. It will likely tell you that the directive used in your .htaccess file is not permitted.

```
[Fri Sep 17 18:43:16 2010] [alert] [client 192.168.200.51]
/var/www/html/.htaccess:  DirectoryIndex not allowed here
```

This will indicate either that you've used a directive that is never permitted in .htaccess files, or that you simply don't have ALLOWOVERRIDE set to a level sufficient for the directive you've used. Consult the documentation for that particular directive to determine which is the case.

Alternately, it may tell you that you had a syntax error in your usage of the directive itself.

```
[Sat Aug 09 16:22:34 2008] [alert] [client 192.168.200.51]
/var/www/html/.htaccess:  RewriteCond:  bad flag delimiters
```

In this case, the error message should be specific to the particular syntax error that you have committed.

# 6.7 Per-user web directories

On systems with multiple users, each user can be permitted to have a web site in their home directory using the USERDIR directive. Visitors to a URL http://example.com/~username/ will get content out of the home directory of the user "username", out of the subdirectory specified by the USERDIR directive.

Note that, by default, access to these directories is **not** enabled. You can enable access when using USERDIR by uncommenting the line:

```
#Include conf/extra/httpd-userdir.conf
```

in the default config file conf/httpd.conf, and adapting the httpd-userdir.conf file as necessary, or by including the appropriate directives in a <DIRECTORY> block within the main config file.

**See also**

- Mapping URLs to the Filesystem (p. 64)

## Per-user web directories

| Related Modules | Related Directives |
|---|---|
| MOD_USERDIR | USERDIR |
| | DIRECTORYMATCH |
| | ALLOWOVERRIDE |

## Setting the file path with UserDir

The USERDIR directive specifies a directory out of which per-user content is loaded. This directive may take several different forms.

If a path is given which does not start with a leading slash, it is assumed to be a directory path relative to the home directory of the specified user. Given this configuration:

```
UserDir public_html
```

the URL http://example.com/~rbowen/file.html will be translated to the file path /home/rbowen/public_html/file.html

If a path is given starting with a slash, a directory path will be constructed using that path, plus the username specified. Given this configuration:

```
UserDir /var/html
```

the URL http://example.com/~rbowen/file.html will be translated to the file path /var/html/rbowen/file.html

If a path is provided which contains an asterisk (*), a path is used in which the asterisk is replaced with the username. Given this configuration:

```
UserDir /var/www/*/docs
```

the   URL   `http://example.com/~rbowen/file.html`   will   be   translated   to   the   file   path
`/var/www/rbowen/docs/file.html`

Multiple directories or directory paths can also be set.

```
UserDir public_html /var/html
```

For the URL `http://example.com/~rbowen/file.html`, Apache will search for ~rbowen. If it isn't
found, Apache will search for rbowen in `/var/html`. If found, the above URL will then be translated to the file
path `/var/html/rbowen/file.html`

### Redirecting to external URLs

The UserDir directive can be used to redirect user directory requests to external URLs.

```
UserDir http://example.org/users/*/
```

The   above   example   will   redirect   a   request   for   `http://example.com/~bob/abc.html`   to
`http://example.org/users/bob/abc.html`.

### Restricting what users are permitted to use this feature

Using the syntax shown in the UserDir documentation, you can restrict what users are permitted to use this functionality:

```
UserDir disabled root jro fish
```

The configuration above will enable the feature for all users except for those listed in the `disabled` statement. You
can, likewise, disable the feature for all but a few users by using a configuration like the following:

```
UserDir disabled
UserDir enabled rbowen krietz
```

See UserDir documentation for additional examples.

### Enabling a cgi directory for each user

In order to give each user their own cgi-bin directory, you can use a <Directory> directive to make a particular
subdirectory of a user's home directory cgi-enabled.

```
<Directory "/home/*/public_html/cgi-bin/">
    Options ExecCGI
    SetHandler cgi-script
</Directory>
```

Then, presuming that UserDir is set to public_html, a cgi program example.cgi could be loaded from that
directory as:

```
http://example.com/~rbowen/cgi-bin/example.cgi
```

## Allowing users to alter configuration

If you want to allows users to modify the server configuration in their web space, they will need to use `.htaccess` files to make these changes. Ensure that you have set ALLOWOVERRIDE to a value sufficient for the directives that you want to permit the users to modify. See the .htaccess tutorial (p. 249) for additional details on how this works.

## 6.8    Reverse Proxy Guide

In addition to being a "basic" web server, and providing static and dynamic content to end-users, Apache httpd (as well as most other web servers) can also act as a reverse proxy server, also-known-as a "gateway" server.

In such scenarios, httpd itself does not generate or host the data, but rather the content is obtained by one or several backend servers, which normally have no direct connection to the external network. As httpd receives a request from a client, the request itself is *proxied* to one of these backend servers, which then handles the request, generates the content and then sends this content back to httpd, which then generates the actual HTTP response back to the client.

There are numerous reasons for such an implementation, but generally the typical rationales are due to security, high-availability, load-balancing and centralized authentication/authorization. It is critical in these implementations that the layout, design and architecture of the backend infrastructure (those servers which actually handle the requests) are insulated and protected from the outside; as far as the client is concerned, the reverse proxy server *is* the sole source of all content.

A typical implementation is below:

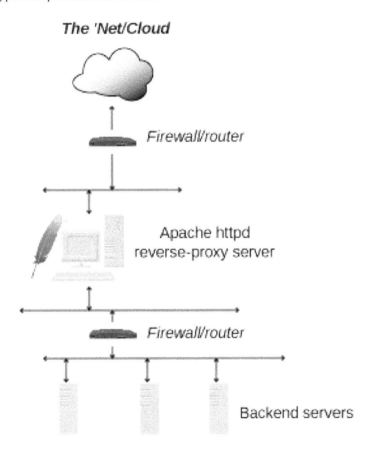

### Reverse Proxy

| **Related Modules** | **Related Directives** |
|---|---|
| MOD_PROXY | PROXYPASS |
| MOD_PROXY_BALANCER | BALANCERMEMBER |
| MOD_PROXY_HCHECK | |

## Simple reverse proxying

The PROXYPASS directive specifies the mapping of incoming requests to the backend server (or a cluster of servers known as a `Balancer` group). The simpliest example proxies all requests ("/") to a single backend:

```
ProxyPass "/"  "http://www.example.com/"
```

To ensure that and `Location:` headers generated from the backend are modified to point to the reverse proxy, instead of back to itself, the PROXYPASSREVERSE directive is most often required:

```
ProxyPass "/"  "http://www.example.com/"
ProxyPassReverse "/"  "http://www.example.com/"
```

Only specific URIs can be proxied, as shown in this example:

```
ProxyPass "/images"  "http://www.example.com/"
ProxyPassReverse "/images"  "http://www.example.com/"
```

In the above, any requests which start with the `/images` path with be proxied to the specified backend, otherwise it will be handled locally.

## Clusters and Balancers

As useful as the above is, it still has the deficiencies that should the (single) backend node go down, or become heavily loaded, that proxying those requests provides no real advantage. What is needed is the ability to define a set or group of backend servers which can handle such requests and for the reverse proxy to load balance and failover among them. This group is sometimes called a *cluster* but Apache httpd's term is a *balancer*. One defines a balancer by leveraging the <PROXY> and BALANCERMEMBER directives as shown:

```
<Proxy balancer://myset>
    BalancerMember http://www2.example.com:8080
    BalancerMember http://www3.example.com:8080
    ProxySet lbmethod=bytraffic
</Proxy>

ProxyPass "/images/"  "balancer://myset/"
ProxyPassReverse "/images/"  "balancer://myset/"
```

The `balancer://` scheme is what tells httpd that we are creating a balancer set, with the name *myset*. It includes 2 backend servers, which httpd calls *BalancerMembers*. In this case, any requests for `/images` will be proxied to *one* of the 2 backends. The PROXYSET directive specifies that the *myset* Balancer use a load balancing algorithm that balances based on I/O bytes.

**Hint**

> *BalancerMembers* are also sometimes referred to as *workers*.

### Balancer and BalancerMember configuration

You can adjust numerous configuration details of the *balancers* and the *workers* via the various parameters defined in PROXYPASS.  For example, assuming we would want `http://www3.example.com:8080` to handle 3x the traffic with a timeout of 1 second, we would adjust the configuration as follows:

```
<Proxy balancer://myset>
    BalancerMember http://www2.example.com:8080
    BalancerMember http://www3.example.com:8080 loadfactor=3 timeout=1
    ProxySet lbmethod=bytraffic
</Proxy>

ProxyPass "/images"  "balancer://myset/"
ProxyPassReverse "/images"  "balancer://myset/"
```

## Failover

You can also fine-tune various failover scenarios, detailing which workers and even which balancers should accessed in such cases.   For example, the below setup implements 2 failover cases:   In the first, `http://hstandby.example.com:8080` is only sent traffic if all other workers in the *myset* balancer are not available.  If that worker itself is not available, only then will the `http://bkup1.example.com:8080` and `http://bkup2.example.com:8080` workers be brought into rotation:

```
<Proxy balancer://myset>
    BalancerMember http://www2.example.com:8080
    BalancerMember http://www3.example.com:8080 loadfactor=3 timeout=1
    BalancerMember http://hstandby.example.com:8080 status=+H
    BalancerMember http://bkup1.example.com:8080 lbset=1
    BalancerMember http://bkup2.example.com:8080 lbset=1
    ProxySet lbmethod=byrequests
</Proxy>

ProxyPass "/images/"  "balancer://myset/"
ProxyPassReverse "/images/"  "balancer://myset/"
```

The magic of this failover setup is setting `http://hstandby.example.com:8080` with the +H status flag, which puts it in *hot standby* mode, and making the 2 `bkup#` servers part of the #1 load balancer set (the default set is 0); for failover, hot standbys (if they exist) are used 1st, when all regular workers are unavailable; load balancer sets are always tried lowest number first.

## Balancer Manager

One of the most unique and useful features of Apache httpd's reverse proxy is the embedded *balancer-manager* application. Similar to MOD_STATUS, *balancer-manager* displays the current working configuration and status of the enabled balancers and workers currently in use. However, not only does it display these parameters, it also allows for dynamic, runtime, on-the-fly reconfiguration of almost all of them, including adding new *BalancerMembers* (workers) to an existing balancer. To enable these capability, the following needs to be added to your configuration:

```
<Location "/balancer-manager">
    SetHandler balancer-manager
    Require host localhost
</Location>
```

**Warning**

Do not enable the *balancer-manager* until you have secured your server (p. 787). In particular, ensure that access to the URL is tightly restricted.

When the reverse proxy server is accessed at that url (eg: `http://rproxy.example.com/balancer-manager/`, you will see a page similar to the below:

# Load Balancer Manager for localhost

Server Version: Apache/2.5.0-dev (Unix) OpenSSL/1.0.2f
Server Built: Feb 9 2016 07:00:20
Balancer changes will NOT be persisted on restart.
Balancers are NOT inherited from main server.
ProxyPass settings are NOT inherited from main server.

**LoadBalancer Status for balancer://demo [p4420eeae_demo]**

| MaxMembers | StickySession | DisableFailover | Timeout | FailoverAttempts | Method | Path | Active |
|---|---|---|---|---|---|---|---|
| 6 [1 Used] | (None) | Off | 0 | 0 | bytraffic | /c/ | Yes |

| Worker URL | Route | RouteRedir | Factor | Set | Status | Elected | Busy | Load | To | From | HC Method | HC Interval | Passes | Fails | HC uri | HC Expr |
|---|---|---|---|---|---|---|---|---|---|---|---|---|---|---|---|---|
| http://www.example.com/ | 1 | 0 | Init Ok | 7 | 0 | 0 | 3.1K | 2.5K | GET | 10 | 1 (0) | 2 (0) | foof2 |

**Health check cond. expressions:**

| Expr name | Expression |
|---|---|
| foof | %{REQUEST_STATUS} =~ /^[234]/ |
| foof2 | hc('body') =~ /domain is established/ |

This form allows the devops admin to adjust various parameters, take workers offline, change load balancing methods and add new works. For example, clicking on the balancer itself, you will get the following page:

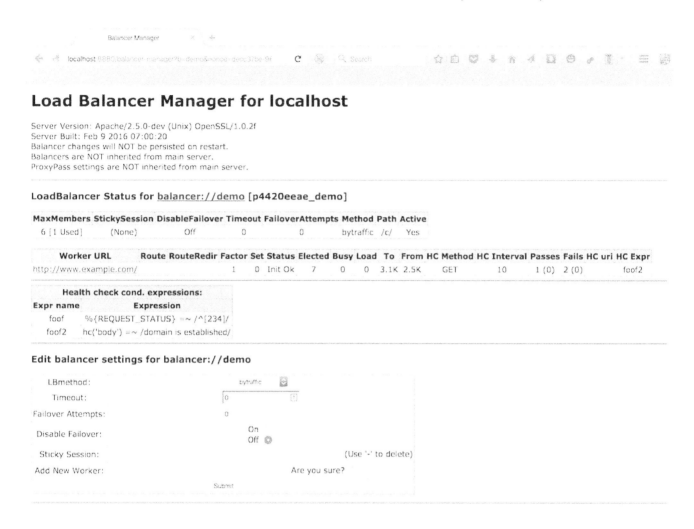

Whereas clicking on a worker, displays this page:

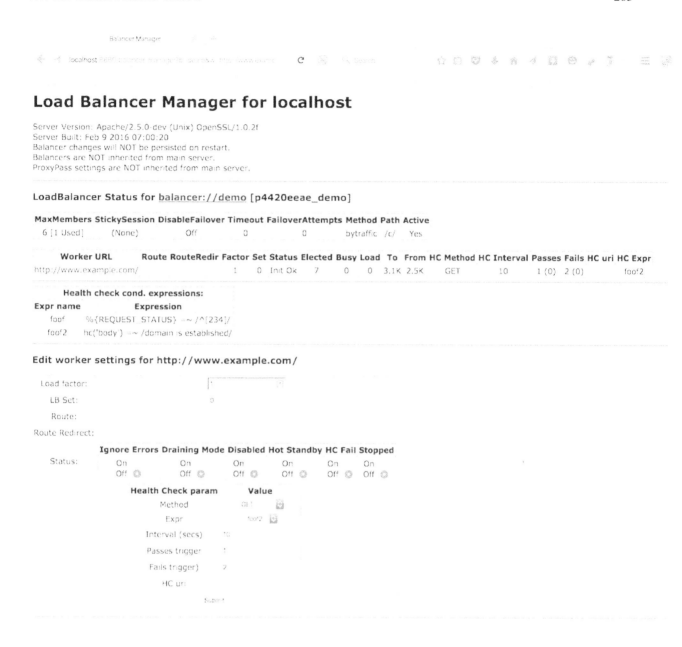

To have these changes persist restarts of the reverse proxy, ensure that BALANCERPERSIST is enabled.

## Dynamic Health Checks

Before httpd proxies a request to a worker, it can *"test"* if that worker is available via setting the `ping` parameter for that worker using PROXYPASS. Oftentimes it is more useful to check the health of the workers *out of band*, in a dynamic fashion. This is achieved in Apache httpd by the MOD_PROXY_HCHECK module.

## BalancerMember status flags

In the *balancer-manager* the current state, or *status*, of a worker is displayed and can be set/reset. The meanings of these statuses are as follows:

| Flag | String | Description |
|------|--------|-------------|
|      | *Ok*   | Worker is available |
|      | *Init* | Worker has been initialized |
| D    | *Dis*  | Worker is disabled and will not accept any requests; will be automatically retried. |
| S    | *Stop* | Worker is administratively stopped; will not accept requests and will not be automatically retried |
| I    | *Ign*  | Worker is in ignore-errors mode and will always be considered available. |
| H    | *Stby* | Worker is in hot-standby mode and will only be used if no other viable workers are available. |
| E    | *Err*  | Worker is in an error state, usually due to failing pre-request check; requests will not be proxied to this worker, but it will be retried depending on the `retry` setting of the worker. |
| N    | *Drn*  | Worker is in drain mode and will only accept existing sticky sessions destined for itself and ignore all other requests. |
| C    | *HcFl* | Worker has failed dynamic health check and will not be used until it passes subsequent health checks. |

# Chapter 7

# Platform-specific Notes

# 7.1   Platform Specific Notes

## Microsoft Windows

**Using Apache**  This document explains how to install, configure and run Apache 2.4 under Microsoft Windows.

> See: Using Apache with Microsoft Windows (p. 267)

**Compiling Apache**  There are many important points before you begin compiling Apache.  This document explain them.

> See: Compiling Apache for Microsoft Windows (p. 275)

## Unix Systems

**RPM Based Systems (Redhat / CentOS / Fedora)**  This document explains how to build, install, and run Apache 2.4 on systems supporting the RPM packaging format.

> See: Using Apache With RPM Based Systems (p. 281)

## Other Platforms

**Novell NetWare**  This document explains how to install, configure and run Apache 2.4 under Novell NetWare 5.1 and above.

> See: Using Apache With Novell NetWare (p. 284)

# 7.2 Using Apache HTTP Server on Microsoft Windows

This document explains how to install, configure and run Apache 2.5 under Microsoft Windows. If you have questions after reviewing the documentation (and any event and error logs), you should consult the peer-supported users' mailing list[1].

This document assumes that you are installing a binary distribution of Apache. If you want to compile Apache yourself (possibly to help with development or tracking down bugs), see Compiling Apache for Microsoft Windows (p. 275) .

## Operating System Requirements

The primary Windows platform for running Apache 2.5 is Windows 2000 or later. Always obtain and install the current service pack to avoid operating system bugs.

$\Longrightarrow$ Apache HTTP Server versions later than 2.2 will not run on any operating system earlier than Windows 2000.

## Downloading Apache for Windows

The Apache HTTP Server Project itself does not provide binary releases of software, only source code. Individual committers *may* provide binary packages as a convenience, but it is not a release deliverable.

If you cannot compile the Apache HTTP Server yourself, you can obtain a binary package from numerous binary distributions available on the Internet.

Popular options for deploying Apache httpd, and, optionally, PHP and MySQL, on Microsoft Windows, include:

- ApacheHaus[2]
- Apache Lounge[3]
- Bitnami WAMP Stack[4]
- WampServer[5]
- XAMPP[6]

## Customizing Apache for Windows

Apache is configured by the files in the `conf` subdirectory. These are the same files used to configure the Unix version, but there are a few different directives for Apache on Windows. See the directive index (p. 1106) for all the available directives.

The main differences in Apache for Windows are:

- Because Apache for Windows is multithreaded, it does not use a separate process for each request, as Apache can on Unix. Instead there are usually only two Apache processes running: a parent process, and a child which handles the requests. Within the child process each request is handled by a separate thread.

  The process management directives are also different:

---

[1] http://httpd.apache.org/userslist.html
[2] http://www.apachehaus.com/cgi-bin/download.plx
[3] http://www.apachelounge.com/download/
[4] http://bitnami.com/stack/wamp
[5] http://www.wampserver.com/
[6] http://www.apachefriends.org/en/xampp.html

MAXCONNECTIONSPERCHILD: Like the Unix directive, this controls how many connections a single child process will serve before exiting. However, unlike on Unix, a replacement process is not instantly available. Use the default `MaxConnectionsPerChild 0`, unless instructed to change the behavior to overcome a memory leak in third party modules or in-process applications.

 **Warning: The server configuration file is reread when a new child process is started. If you have modified `httpd.conf`, the new child may not start or you may receive unexpected results.**

THREADSPERCHILD: This directive is new. It tells the server how many threads it should use. This is the maximum number of connections the server can handle at once, so be sure to set this number high enough for your site if you get a lot of hits. The recommended default is `ThreadsPerChild 150`, but this must be adjusted to reflect the greatest anticipated number of simultaneous connections to accept.

- The directives that accept filenames as arguments must use Windows filenames instead of Unix ones. However, because Apache may interpret backslashes as an "escape character" sequence, you should consistently use forward slashes in path names, not backslashes.

- While filenames are generally case-insensitive on Windows, URLs are still treated internally as case-sensitive before they are mapped to the filesystem. For example, the <LOCATION>, ALIAS, and PROXYPASS directives all use case-sensitive arguments. For this reason, it is particularly important to use the <DIRECTORY> directive when attempting to limit access to content in the filesystem, since this directive applies to any content in a directory, regardless of how it is accessed. If you wish to assure that only lowercase is used in URLs, you can use something like:

```
RewriteEngine On
RewriteMap lowercase "int:tolower"
RewriteCond "%{REQUEST_URI}" "[A-Z]"
RewriteRule "(.*)"            "${lowercase:$1}" [R,L]
```

- When running, Apache needs write access only to the logs directory and any configured cache directory tree. Due to the issue of case insensitive and short 8.3 format names, Apache must validate all path names given. This means that each directory which Apache evaluates, from the drive root up to the directory leaf, must have read, list and traverse directory permissions. If Apache2.5 is installed at C:\Program Files, then the root directory, Program Files and Apache2.5 must all be visible to Apache.

- Apache for Windows contains the ability to load modules at runtime, without recompiling the server. If Apache is compiled normally, it will install a number of optional modules in the \Apache2.5\modules directory. To activate these or other modules, the new LOADMODULE directive must be used. For example, to activate the status module, use the following (in addition to the status-activating directives in `access.conf`):

```
LoadModule status_module "modules/mod_status.so"
```

Information on creating loadable modules (p. 908) is also available.

- Apache can also load ISAPI (Internet Server Application Programming Interface) extensions such as those used by Microsoft IIS and other Windows servers. More information is available (p. 683) . Note that Apache **cannot** load ISAPI Filters, and ISAPI Handlers with some Microsoft feature extensions will not work.

- When running CGI scripts, the method Apache uses to find the interpreter for the script is configurable using the SCRIPTINTERPRETERSOURCE directive.

- Since it is often difficult to manage files with names like `.htaccess` in Windows, you may find it useful to change the name of this per-directory configuration file using the ACCESSFILENAME directive.

- Any errors during Apache startup are logged into the Windows event log when running on Windows NT. This mechanism acts as a backup for those situations where Apache is not yet prepared to use the `error.log` file. You can review the Windows Application Event Log by using the Event Viewer, e.g. Start - Settings - Control Panel - Administrative Tools - Event Viewer.

## Running Apache as a Service

Apache comes with a utility called the Apache Service Monitor. With it you can see and manage the state of all installed Apache services on any machine on your network. To be able to manage an Apache service with the monitor, you have to first install the service (either automatically via the installation or manually).

You can install Apache as a Windows NT service as follows from the command prompt at the Apache `bin` subdirectory:

```
httpd.exe -k install
```

If you need to specify the name of the service you want to install, use the following command. You have to do this if you have several different service installations of Apache on your computer. If you specify a name during the install, you have to also specify it during any other -k operation.

```
httpd.exe -k install -n "MyServiceName"
```

If you need to have specifically named configuration files for different services, you must use this:

```
httpd.exe -k install -n "MyServiceName" -f "c:\files\my.conf"
```

If you use the first command without any special parameters except `-k install`, the service will be called `Apache2.5` and the configuration will be assumed to be `conf\httpd.conf`.

Removing an Apache service is easy. Just use:

```
httpd.exe -k uninstall
```

The specific Apache service to be uninstalled can be specified by using:

```
httpd.exe -k uninstall -n "MyServiceName"
```

Normal starting, restarting and shutting down of an Apache service is usually done via the Apache Service Monitor, by using commands like `NET START Apache2.5` and `NET STOP Apache2.5` or via normal Windows service management. Before starting Apache as a service by any means, you should test the service's configuration file by using:

```
httpd.exe -n "MyServiceName" -t
```

You can control an Apache service by its command line switches, too. To start an installed Apache service you'll use this:

```
httpd.exe -k start -n "MyServiceName"
```

To stop an Apache service via the command line switches, use this:

```
httpd.exe -k stop -n "MyServiceName"
```

or

```
httpd.exe -k shutdown -n "MyServiceName"
```

You can also restart a running service and force it to reread its configuration file by using:

```
httpd.exe -k restart -n "MyServiceName"
```

By default, all Apache services are registered to run as the system user (the `LocalSystem` account).  The `LocalSystem` account has no privileges to your network via any Windows-secured mechanism, including the file system, named pipes, DCOM, or secure RPC. It has, however, wide privileges locally.

> ⚠ **Never grant any network privileges to the `LocalSystem` account!  If you need Apache to be able to access network resources, create a separate account for Apache as noted below.**

It is recommended that users create a separate account for running Apache service(s).  If you have to access network resources via Apache, this is required.

1. Create a normal domain user account, and be sure to memorize its password.

2. Grant the newly-created user a privilege of `Log on as a service` and `Act as part of the operating system`.  On Windows NT 4.0 these privileges are granted via User Manager for Domains, but on Windows 2000 and XP you probably want to use Group Policy for propagating these settings. You can also manually set these via the Local Security Policy MMC snap-in.

3. Confirm that the created account is a member of the Users group.

4. Grant the account read and execute (RX) rights to all document and script folders (`htdocs` and `cgi-bin` for example).

5. Grant the account change (RWXD) rights to the Apache `logs` directory.

6. Grant the account read and execute (RX) rights to the `httpd.exe` binary executable.

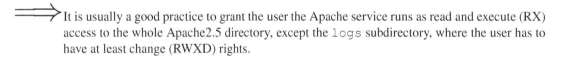
It is usually a good practice to grant the user the Apache service runs as read and execute (RX) access to the whole Apache2.5 directory, except the `logs` subdirectory, where the user has to have at least change (RWXD) rights.

If you allow the account to log in as a user and as a service, then you can log on with that account and test that the account has the privileges to execute the scripts, read the web pages, and that you can start Apache in a console window. If this works, and you have followed the steps above, Apache should execute as a service with no problems.

**Error code 2186** is a good indication that you need to review the "Log On As" configuration for the service, since Apache cannot access a required network resource.  Also, pay close attention to the privileges of the user Apache is configured to run as.

When starting Apache as a service you may encounter an error message from the Windows Service Control Manager. For example, if you try to start Apache by using the Services applet in the Windows Control Panel, you may get the following message:

```
Could not start the Apache2.5 service on \\COMPUTER
Error 1067; The process terminated unexpectedly.
```

You will get this generic error if there is any problem with starting the Apache service. In order to see what is really causing the problem you should follow the instructions for Running Apache for Windows from the Command Prompt.

If you are having problems with the service, it is suggested you follow the instructions below to try starting httpd.exe from a console window, and work out the errors before struggling to start it as a service again.

## Running Apache as a Console Application

Running Apache as a service is usually the recommended way to use it, but it is sometimes easier to work from the command line, especially during initial configuration and testing.

To run Apache from the command line as a console application, use the following command:

```
httpd.exe
```

Apache will execute, and will remain running until it is stopped by pressing Control-C.

You can also run Apache via the shortcut Start Apache in Console placed to `Start Menu --> Programs --> Apache HTTP Server 2.5.xx --> Control Apache Server` during the installation. This will open a console window and start Apache inside it. If you don't have Apache installed as a service, the window will remain visible until you stop Apache by pressing Control-C in the console window where Apache is running in. The server will exit in a few seconds. However, if you do have Apache installed as a service, the shortcut starts the service. If the Apache service is running already, the shortcut doesn't do anything.

If Apache is running as a service, you can tell it to stop by opening another console window and entering:

```
httpd.exe -k shutdown
```

Running as a service should be preferred over running in a console window because this lets Apache end any current operations and clean up gracefully.

But if the server is running in a console window, you can only stop it by pressing Control-C in the same window.

You can also tell Apache to restart. This forces it to reread the configuration file. Any operations in progress are allowed to complete without interruption. To restart Apache, either press Control-Break in the console window you used for starting Apache, or enter

```
httpd.exe -k restart
```

if the server is running as a service.

> Note for people familiar with the Unix version of Apache: these commands provide a Windows equivalent to `kill -TERM` *pid* and `kill -USR1` *pid*. The command line option used, `-k`, was chosen as a reminder of the `kill` command used on Unix.

If the Apache console window closes immediately or unexpectedly after startup, open the Command Prompt from the Start Menu –> Programs. Change to the folder to which you installed Apache, type the command `httpd.exe`, and read the error message. Then change to the logs folder, and review the `error.log` file for configuration mistakes. Assuming httpd was installed into `C:\Program Files\Apache Software Foundation\Apache2.5\`, you can do the following:

```
c:
cd "\Program Files\Apache Software Foundation\Apache2.5\bin"
httpd.exe
```

Then wait for Apache to stop, or press Control-C. Then enter the following:

```
cd ..\logs
more < error.log
```

When working with Apache it is important to know how it will find the configuration file. You can specify a configuration file on the command line in two ways:

- `-f` specifies an absolute or relative path to a particular configuration file:

```
httpd.exe -f "c:\my server files\anotherconfig.conf"
```

or

```
httpd.exe -f files\anotherconfig.conf
```

- `-n` specifies the installed Apache service whose configuration file is to be used:

```
httpd.exe -n "MyServiceName"
```

In both of these cases, the proper SERVERROOT should be set in the configuration file.

If you don't specify a configuration file with `-f` or `-n`, Apache will use the file name compiled into the server, such as `conf\httpd.conf`. This built-in path is relative to the installation directory. You can verify the compiled file name from a value labelled as `SERVER_CONFIG_FILE` when invoking Apache with the `-V` switch, like this:

```
httpd.exe -V
```

Apache will then try to determine its SERVERROOT by trying the following, in this order:

1. A SERVERROOT directive via the `-C` command line switch.

2. The `-d` switch on the command line.

3. Current working directory.

4. A registry entry which was created if you did a binary installation.

5. The server root compiled into the server. This is `/apache` by default, you can verify it by using `httpd.exe -V` and looking for a value labelled as `HTTPD_ROOT`.

If you did not do a binary install, Apache will in some scenarios complain about the missing registry key. This warning can be ignored if the server was otherwise able to find its configuration file.

The value of this key is the SERVERROOT directory which contains the `conf` subdirectory. When Apache starts it reads the `httpd.conf` file from that directory. If this file contains a SERVERROOT directive which contains a different directory from the one obtained from the registry key above, Apache will forget the registry key and use the directory from the configuration file. If you copy the Apache directory or configuration files to a new location it is vital that you update the SERVERROOT directive in the `httpd.conf` file to reflect the new location.

## Testing the Installation

After starting Apache (either in a console window or as a service) it will be listening on port 80 (unless you changed the LISTEN directive in the configuration files or installed Apache only for the current user). To connect to the server and access the default page, launch a browser and enter this URL:

```
http://localhost/
```

Apache should respond with a welcome page and you should see "It Works!". If nothing happens or you get an error, look in the `error.log` file in the `logs` subdirectory. If your host is not connected to the net, or if you have serious problems with your DNS (Domain Name Service) configuration, you may have to use this URL:

```
http://127.0.0.1/
```

If you happen to be running Apache on an alternate port, you need to explicitly put that in the URL:

```
http://127.0.0.1:8080/
```

Once your basic installation is working, you should configure it properly by editing the files in the `conf` subdirectory. Again, if you change the configuration of the Windows NT service for Apache, first attempt to start it from the command line to make sure that the service starts with no errors.

Because Apache **cannot** share the same port with another TCP/IP application, you may need to stop, uninstall or reconfigure certain other services before running Apache. These conflicting services include other WWW servers, some firewall implementations, and even some client applications (such as Skype) which will use port 80 to attempt to bypass firewall issues.

## Configuring Access to Network Resources

Access to files over the network can be specified using two mechanisms provided by Windows:

**Mapped drive letters** e.g., `Alias /images/ Z:/`

**UNC paths** e.g., `Alias /images/ //imagehost/www/images/`

Mapped drive letters allow the administrator to maintain the mapping to a specific machine and path outside of the Apache httpd configuration. However, these mappings are associated only with interactive sessions and are not directly available to Apache httpd when it is started as a service. **Use only UNC paths for network resources in httpd.conf** so that the resources can be accessed consistently regardless of how Apache httpd is started. (Arcane and error prone procedures may work around the restriction on mapped drive letters, but this is not recommended.)

### Example DocumentRoot with UNC path

```
DocumentRoot "//dochost/www/html/"
```

### Example DocumentRoot with IP address in UNC path

```
DocumentRoot "//192.168.1.50/docs/"
```

**Example Alias and corresponding Directory with UNC path**

```
Alias "/images/" "//imagehost/www/images/"

<Directory "//imagehost/www/images/">
#...
<Directory>
```

When running Apache httpd as a service, you must create a separate account in order to access network resources, as described above.

## Windows Tuning

- If more than a few dozen piped loggers are used on an operating system instance, scaling up the "desktop heap" is often necessary. For more detailed information, refer to the piped logging (p. 56) documentation.

# 7.3 Compiling Apache for Microsoft Windows

There are many important points to consider before you begin compiling Apache HTTP Server (httpd). See Using Apache HTTP Server on Microsoft Windows (p. 267) before you begin.

httpd can be built on Windows using a cmake-based build system or with Visual Studio project files maintained by httpd developers. The cmake-based build system directly supports more versions of Visual Studio but currently has considerable functional limitations.

## Building httpd with the included Visual Studio project files

### Requirements

Compiling Apache requires the following environment to be properly installed:

- Disk Space

  Make sure you have at least 200 MB of free disk space available. After installation Apache requires approximately 80 MB of disk space, plus space for log and cache files, which can grow rapidly. The actual disk space requirements will vary considerably based on your chosen configuration and any third-party modules or libraries, especially when OpenSSL is also built. Because many files are text and very easily compressed, NTFS filesystem compression cuts these requirements in half.

- Appropriate Patches

  The httpd binary is built with the help of several patches to third party packages, which ensure the released code is buildable and debuggable. These patches are available and distributed from http://www.apache.org/dist/httpd/binaries/win32/patches_applied/ and are recommended to be applied to obtain identical results as the "official" ASF distributed binaries.

- Microsoft Visual C++ 6.0 (Visual Studio 97) or later.

  Apache can be built using the command line tools, or from within the Visual Studio IDE Workbench. The command line build requires the environment to reflect the `PATH`, `INCLUDE`, `LIB` and other variables that can be configured with the `vcvars32.bat` script.

  > You may want the Visual Studio Processor Pack for your older version of Visual Studio, or a full (not Express) version of newer Visual Studio editions, for the ml.exe assembler. This will allow you to build OpenSSL, if desired, using the more efficient assembly code implementation.

  > Only the Microsoft compiler tool chain is actively supported by the active httpd contributors. Although the project regularly accepts patches to ensure MinGW and other alternative builds work and improve upon them, they are not actively maintained and are often broken in the course of normal development.

- Updated Microsoft Windows Platform SDK, February 2003 or later.

  An appropriate Windows Platform SDK is included by default in the full (not express/lite) versions of Visual C++ 7.1 (Visual Studio 2002) and later, these users can ignore these steps unless explicitly choosing a newer or different version of the Platform SDK.

  To use Visual C++ 6.0 or 7.0 (Studio 2000 .NET), the Platform SDK environment must be prepared using the `setenv.bat` script (installed by the Platform SDK) before starting the command line build or launching the msdev/devenv GUI environment. Installing the Platform SDK for Visual Studio Express versions (2003 and later) should adjust the default environment appropriately.

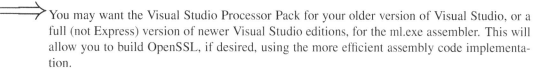

```
"c:\Program Files\Microsoft Visual Studio\VC98\Bin\VCVARS32"
"c:\Program Files\Platform SDK\setenv.bat"
```

- Perl and awk

  Several steps recommended here require a perl interpreter during the build preparation process, but it is otherwise not required.

  To install Apache within the build system, several files are modified using the `awk.exe` utility. awk was chosen since it is a very small download (compared with Perl or WSH/VB) and accomplishes the task of modifying configuration files upon installation. Brian Kernighan's http://www.cs.princeton.edu/~bwk/btl.mirror/ site has a compiled native Win32 binary, http://www.cs.princeton.edu/~bwk/btl.mirror/awk95.exe which you must save with the name `awk.exe` (rather than `awk95.exe`).

  ⟹ If awk.exe is not found, Makefile.win's install target will not perform substitutions in the installed .conf files. You must manually modify the installed .conf files to allow the server to start. Search and replace all `"@token@"` tags as appropriate.

  ⟹ The Visual Studio IDE will only find `awk.exe` from the PATH, or executable path specified in the menu option Tools -> Options -> (Projects ->) Directories. Ensure awk.exe is in your system path.

  ⟹ Also note that if you are using Cygwin tools (http://www.cygwin.com/) the awk utility is named `gawk.exe` and that the file `awk.exe` is really a symlink to the `gawk.exe` file. The Windows command shell does not recognize symlinks, and because of this building InstallBin will fail. A workaround is to delete `awk.exe` from the cygwin installation and copy `gawk.exe` to `awk.exe`. Also note the cygwin/mingw ports of gawk 3.0.x were buggy, please upgrade to 3.1.x before attempting to use any gawk port.

- [Optional] zlib library (for MOD_DEFLATE)

  Zlib must be installed into a `srclib` subdirectory named `zlib`. This must be built in-place. Zlib can be obtained from http://www.zlib.net/ – the MOD_DEFLATE is confirmed to work correctly with version 1.2.3.

  ```
  nmake -f win32\Makefile.msc
  nmake -f win32\Makefile.msc test
  ```

- [Optional] OpenSSL libraries (for MOD_SSL and `ab.exe` with ssl support)

  ⟹ The OpenSSL library is cryptographic software. The country in which you currently reside may have restrictions on the import, possession, use, and/or re-export to another country, of encryption software. BEFORE using any encryption software, please check your country's laws, regulations and policies concerning the import, possession, or use, and re-export of encryption software, to see if this is permitted. See http://www.wassenaar.org/ for more information.

  Configuring and building OpenSSL requires perl to be installed.

  OpenSSL must be installed into a `srclib` subdirectory named `openssl`, obtained from http://www.openssl.org/source/, in order to compile MOD_SSL or the `abs.exe` project, which is ab.c with SSL support enabled. To prepare OpenSSL to be linked to Apache mod_ssl or abs.exe, and disable patent encumbered features in OpenSSL, you might use the following build commands:

  ```
  perl Configure no-rc5 no-idea enable-mdc2 enable-zlib VC-WIN32
  -Ipath/to/srclib/zlib -Lpath/to/srclib/zlib
  ms\do_masm.bat
  nmake -f ms\ntdll.mak
  ```

  ⟹ It is not advisable to use zlib-dynamic, as that transfers the cost of deflating SSL streams to the first request which must load the zlib dll. Note the suggested patch enables the -L flag to work with windows builds, corrects the name of zdll.lib and ensures .pdb files are generated for troubleshooting. If the assembler is not installed, you would add no-asm above and use ms\do_ms.bat instead of the ms\do_masm.bat script.

- [Optional] Database libraries (for MOD_DBD and MOD_AUTHN_DBM)

  The apr-util library exposes dbm (keyed database) and dbd (query oriented database) client functionality to the httpd server and its modules, such as authentication and authorization. The sdbm dbm and odbc dbd providers are compiled unconditionally.

  The dbd support includes the Oracle instantclient package, MySQL, PostgreSQL and sqlite. To build these all, for example, set up the LIB to include the library path, INCLUDE to include the headers path, and PATH to include the dll bin path of all four SDK's, and set the DBD_LIST environment variable to inform the build which client driver SDKs are installed correctly, e.g.;

  ```
  set DBD_LIST=sqlite3 pgsql oracle mysql
  ```

  Similarly, the dbm support can be extended with DBM_LIST to build a Berkeley DB provider (db) and/or gdbm provider, by similarly configuring LIB, INCLUDE and PATH first to ensure the client library libs and headers are available.

  ```
  set DBM_LIST=db gdbm
  ```

  $\Longrightarrow$ Depending on the choice of database distributions, it may be necessary to change the actual link target name (e.g. gdbm.lib vs. libgdb.lib) that are listed in the corresponding .dsp/.mak files within the directories srclib\apr-util\dbd or ...\dbm.

  See the README-win32.txt file for more hints on obtaining the various database driver SDKs.

### Building from Unix sources

The policy of the Apache HTTP Server project is to only release Unix sources. Windows source packages made available for download have been supplied by volunteers and may not be available for every release. You can still build the server on Windows from the Unix source tarball with just a few additional steps.

1. Download and unpack the Unix source tarball for the latest version.

2. Download and unpack the Unix source tarball for latest version of APR, AR-Util and APR-Iconv, place these sources in directories httpd-2.x.x\srclib\apr, httpd-2.x.x\srclib\apr-util and httpd-2.x.x\srclib\apr-iconv

3. Open a Command Prompt and CD to the httpd-2.x.x folder

4. Run the line endings conversion utility at the prompt;

```
perl srclib\apr\build\lineends.pl
```

You can now build the server with the Visual Studio 6.0 development environment using the IDE. Command-Line builds of the server are not possible from Unix sources unless you export .mak files as explained below.

**Command-Line Build**

`Makefile.win` is the top level Apache makefile. To compile Apache on Windows, simply use one of the following commands to build the `release` or `debug` flavor:

```
nmake /f Makefile.win _apacher
nmake /f Makefile.win _apached
```

Either command will compile Apache. The latter will disable optimization of the resulting files, making it easier to single step the code to find bugs and track down problems.

You can add your apr-util dbd and dbm provider choices with the additional make (environment) variables DBD_LIST and DBM_LIST, see the comments about [Optional] Database libraries, above. Review the initial comments in Makefile.win for additional options that can be provided when invoking the build.

**Developer Studio Workspace IDE Build**

Apache can also be compiled using VC++'s Visual Studio development environment. To simplify this process, a Visual Studio workspace, `Apache.dsw`, is provided. This workspace exposes the entire list of working `.dsp` projects that are required for the complete Apache binary release. It includes dependencies between the projects to assure that they are built in the appropriate order.

Open the `Apache.dsw` workspace, and select `InstallBin` (`Release` or `Debug` build, as desired) as the Active Project. `InstallBin` causes all related project to be built, and then invokes `Makefile.win` to move the compiled executables and dlls. You may personalize the `INSTDIR=` choice by changing `InstallBin`'s Settings, General tab, Build command line entry. `INSTDIR` defaults to the `/Apache2` directory. If you only want a test compile (without installing) you may build the `BuildBin` project instead.

The `.dsp` project files are distributed in Visual Studio 6.0 (98) format. Visual C++ 5.0 (97) will recognize them. Visual Studio 2002 (.NET) and later users must convert `Apache.dsw` plus the `.dsp` files into an `Apache.sln` plus `.msproj` files. Be sure you reconvert the `.msproj` file again if its source `.dsp` file changes! This is really trivial, just open `Apache.dsw` in the VC++ 7.0 IDE once again and reconvert.

⟹ There is a flaw in the .vcproj conversion of .dsp files. devenv.exe will mis-parse the /D flag for RC flags containing long quoted /D'efines which contain spaces. The command:

```
perl srclib\apr\build\cvtdsp.pl -2005
```

will convert the /D flags for RC flags to use an alternate, parseable syntax; unfortunately this syntax isn't supported by Visual Studio 97 or its exported .mak files. These /D flags are used to pass the long description of the mod_apachemodule.so files to the shared .rc resource version-identifier build.

Visual Studio 2002 (.NET) and later users should also use the Build menu, Configuration Manager dialog to uncheck both the `Debug` and `Release` Solution modules abs, MOD_DEFLATE and MOD_SSL components, as well as every component starting with `apr_db*`. These modules are built by invoking `nmake`, or the IDE directly with the `BinBuild` target, which builds those modules conditionally if the `srclib` directories `openssl` and/or `zlib` exist, and based on the setting of DBD_LIST and DBM_LIST environment variables.

**Exporting command-line .mak files**

Exported `.mak` files pose a greater hassle, but they are required for Visual C++ 5.0 users to build MOD_SSL, abs (ab with SSL support) and/or MOD_DEFLATE. The .mak files also support a broader range of C++ tool chain distributions, such as Visual Studio Express.

You must first build all projects in order to create all dynamic auto-generated targets, so that dependencies can be parsed correctly. Build the entire project from within the Visual Studio 6.0 (98) IDE, using the `BuildAll` target, then use the Project Menu Export for all makefiles (checking on "with dependencies".) Run the following command to correct absolute paths into relative paths so they will build anywhere:

```
perl srclib\apr\build\fixwin32mak.pl
```

You must type this command from the *top level* directory of the httpd source tree. Every `.mak` and `.dep` project file within the current directory and below will be corrected, and the timestamps adjusted to reflect the `.dsp`.

Always review the generated `.mak` and `.dep` files for Platform SDK or other local, machine specific file paths. The `DevStudio\Common\MSDev98\bin\` (VC6) directory contains a `sysincl.dat` file, which lists all exceptions. Update this file (including both forward and backslashed paths, such as both `sys/time.h` and `sys\time.h`) to ignore such newer dependencies. Including local-install paths in a distributed `.mak` file will cause the build to fail completely.

If you contribute back a patch that revises project files, we must commit project files in Visual Studio 6.0 format. Changes should be simple, with minimal compilation and linkage flags that can be recognized by all Visual Studio environments.

### Installation

Once Apache has been compiled, it needs to be installed in its server root directory. The default is the `\Apache2` directory, of the same drive.

To build and install all the files into the desired folder *dir* automatically, use one of the following `nmake` commands:

```
nmake /f Makefile.win installr INSTDIR=dir
nmake /f Makefile.win installd INSTDIR=dir
```

The *dir* argument to `INSTDIR` provides the installation directory; it can be omitted if Apache is to be installed into `\Apache22` (of the current drive).

### Warning about building Apache from the development tree

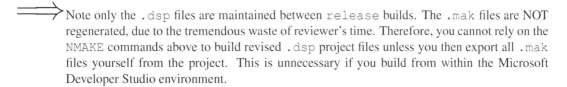 Note only the `.dsp` files are maintained between `release` builds. The `.mak` files are NOT regenerated, due to the tremendous waste of reviewer's time. Therefore, you cannot rely on the NMAKE commands above to build revised `.dsp` project files unless you then export all `.mak` files yourself from the project. This is unnecessary if you build from within the Microsoft Developer Studio environment.

## Building httpd with cmake

The primary documentation for this build mechanism is in the `README.cmake` file in the source distribution. Refer to that file for detailed instructions.

Building httpd with cmake requires building APR and APR-util separately. Refer to their `README.cmake` files for instructions.

The primary limitations of the cmake-based build are inherited from the APR-util project, and are listed below because of their impact on httpd:

- No cmake build for the APR-iconv subproject is available, and the APR-util cmake build cannot consume an existing APR-iconv build. Thus, `MOD_CHARSET_LITE` and possibly some third-party modules cannot be used.

- The cmake build for the APR-util subproject does not support most of the optional DBM and DBD libraries supported by the included Visual Studio project files. This limits the database backends supported by a number of bundled and third-party modules.

# 7.4 Using Apache With RPM Based Systems (Redhat / CentOS / Fedora)

While many distributions make Apache httpd available as operating system supported packages, it can sometimes be desirable to install and use the canonical version of Apache httpd on these systems, replacing the natively provided versions of the packages.

While the Apache httpd project does not currently create binary RPMs for the various distributions out there, it is easy to build your own binary RPMs from the canonical Apache httpd tarball.

This document explains how to build, install, configure and run Apache httpd 2.4 under Unix systems supporting the RPM packaging format.

## Creating a Source RPM

The Apache httpd source tarball can be converted into an SRPM as follows:

```
rpmbuild -ts httpd-2.4.x.tar.bz2
```

## Building RPMs

RPMs can be built directly from the Apache httpd source tarballs using the following command:

```
rpmbuild -tb httpd-2.4.x.tar.bz2
```

Corresponding "-devel" packages will be required to be installed on your build system prior to building the RPMs, the `rpmbuild` command will automatically calculate what RPMs are required and will list any dependencies that are missing on your system. These "-devel" packages will not be required after the build is completed, and can be safely removed.

If successful, the following RPMs will be created:

**httpd-2.4.x-1.i686.rpm** The core server and basic module set.

**httpd-debuginfo-2.4.x-1.i686.rpm** Debugging symbols for the server and all modules.

**httpd-devel-2.4.x-1.i686.rpm** Headers and development files for the server.

**httpd-manual-2.4.x-1.i686.rpm** The webserver manual.

**httpd-tools-2.4.x-1.i686.rpm** Supporting tools for the webserver.

**mod_authnz_ldap-2.4.x-1.i686.rpm** MOD_LDAP and MOD_AUTHNZ_LDAP, with corresponding dependency on openldap.

**mod_lua-2.4.x-1.i686.rpm** MOD_LUA module, with corresponding dependency on lua.

**mod_proxy_html-2.4.x-1.i686.rpm** MOD_PROXY_HTML module, with corresponding dependency on libxml2.

**mod_socache_dc-2.4.x-1.i686.rpm** MOD_SOCACHE_DC module, with corresponding dependency on distcache.

**mod_ssl-2.4.x-1.i686.rpm** MOD_SSL module, with corresponding dependency on openssl.

## Installing the Server

The `httpd` RPM is the only RPM necessary to get a basic server to run. Install it as follows:

```
rpm -U httpd-2.4.x-1.i686.rpm
```

Self contained modules are included with the server. Modules that depend on external libraries are provided as separate RPMs to install if needed.

## Configuring the Default Instance of Apache httpd

The default configuration for the server is installed by default beneath the `/etc/httpd` directory, with logs written by default to `/var/log/httpd`. The environment for the webserver is set by default within the optional `/etc/sysconfig/httpd` file.

Start the server as follows:

```
service httpd restart
```

## Configuring Additional Instances of Apache httpd on the Same Machine

It is possible to configure additional instances of the Apache httpd server running independently alongside each other on the same machine. These instances can have independent configurations, and can potentially run as separate users if so configured.

This was done by making the httpd startup script aware of its own name. This name is then used to find the environment file for the server, and in turn, the server root of the server instance.

To create an additional instance called `httpd-additional`, follow these steps:

- Create a symbolic link to the startup script for the additional server:

```
ln -s /etc/rc.d/init.d/httpd /etc/rc.d/init.d/httpd-additional
chkconfig --add httpd-additional
```

- Create an environment file for the server, using the `/etc/sysconfig/httpd` file as a template:

```
# template from httpd
cp /etc/sysconfig/httpd /etc/sysconfig/httpd-additional
```

```
# blank template
touch /etc/sysconfig/httpd-additional
```

Edit `/etc/sysconfig/httpd-additional` and pass the server root of the new server instance within the `OPTIONS` environment variable.

```
OPTIONS="-d /etc/httpd-additional -f conf/httpd-additional.conf"
```

- Edit the server configuration file `/etc/httpd-additional/conf/httpd-additional.conf` to ensure the correct ports and paths are configured.
- Start the server as follows:

```
service httpd-additional restart
```

- Repeat this process as required for each server instance.

# 7.5   Using Apache With Novell NetWare

This document explains how to install, configure and run Apache 2.0 under Novell NetWare 6.0 and above. If you find any bugs, or wish to contribute in other ways, please use our bug reporting page.[7]

The bug reporting page and dev-httpd mailing list are *not* provided to answer questions about configuration or running Apache. Before you submit a bug report or request, first consult this document, the Frequently Asked Questions[8] page and the other relevant documentation topics. If you still have a question or problem, post it to the novell.devsup.webserver[9] newsgroup, where many Apache users are more than willing to answer new and obscure questions about using Apache on NetWare.

Most of this document assumes that you are installing Apache from a binary distribution. If you want to compile Apache yourself (possibly to help with development, or to track down bugs), see the section on Compiling Apache for NetWare below.

## Requirements

Apache 2.0 is designed to run on NetWare 6.0 service pack 3 and above. If you are running a service pack less than SP3, you must install the latest NetWare Libraries for C (LibC)[10].

NetWare service packs are available here[11].

Apache 2.0 for NetWare can also be run in a NetWare 5.1 environment as long as the latest service pack or the latest version of the NetWare Libraries for C (LibC)[12] has been installed . **WARNING:** Apache 2.0 for NetWare has not been targeted for or tested in this environment.

## Downloading Apache for NetWare

Information on the latest version of Apache can be found on the Apache web server at http://www.apache.org/. This will list the current release, any more recent alpha or beta-test releases, together with details of mirror web and anonymous ftp sites. Binary builds of the latest releases of Apache 2.0 for NetWare can be downloaded from here[13].

## Installing Apache for NetWare

There is no Apache install program for NetWare currently. If you are building Apache 2.0 for NetWare from source, you will need to copy the files over to the server manually.

Follow these steps to install Apache on NetWare from the binary download (assuming you will install to `sys:/apache2`):

- Unzip the binary download file to the root of the `SYS:` volume (may be installed to any volume)
- Edit the `httpd.conf` file setting SERVERROOT and SERVERNAME along with any file path values to reflect your correct server settings
- Add `SYS:/APACHE2` to the search path, for example:

```
SEARCH ADD SYS:\APACHE2
```

---

[7]http://httpd.apache.org/bug_report.html

[8]http://wiki.apache.org/httpd/FAQ

[9]news://developer-forums.novell.com/novell.devsup.webserver

[10]http://developer.novell.com/ndk/libc.htm

[11]http://support.novell.com/misc/patlst.htm#nw

[12]http://developer.novell.com/ndk/libc.htm

[13]http://www.apache.org/dist/httpd/binaries/netware

Follow these steps to install Apache on NetWare manually from your own build source (assuming you will install to `sys:/apache2`):

- Create a directory called `Apache2` on a NetWare volume
- Copy `APACHE2.NLM`, `APRLIB.NLM` to `SYS:/APACHE2`
- Create a directory under `SYS:/APACHE2` called `BIN`
- Copy `HTDIGEST.NLM`, `HTPASSWD.NLM`, `HTDBM.NLM`, `LOGRES.NLM`, `ROTLOGS.NLM` to `SYS:/APACHE2/BIN`
- Create a directory under `SYS:/APACHE2` called `CONF`
- Copy the `HTTPD-STD.CONF` file to the `SYS:/APACHE2/CONF` directory and rename to `HTTPD.CONF`
- Copy the `MIME.TYPES`, `CHARSET.CONV` and `MAGIC` files to `SYS:/APACHE2/CONF` directory
- Copy all files and subdirectories in `\HTTPD-2.0\DOCS\ICONS` to `SYS:/APACHE2/ICONS`
- Copy all files and subdirectories in `\HTTPD-2.0\DOCS\MANUAL` to `SYS:/APACHE2/MANUAL`
- Copy all files and subdirectories in `\HTTPD-2.0\DOCS\ERROR` to `SYS:/APACHE2/ERROR`
- Copy all files and subdirectories in `\HTTPD-2.0\DOCS\DOCROOT` to `SYS:/APACHE2/HTDOCS`
- Create the directory `SYS:/APACHE2/LOGS` on the server
- Create the directory `SYS:/APACHE2/CGI-BIN` on the server
- Create the directory `SYS:/APACHE2/MODULES` and copy all nlm modules into the `modules` directory
- Edit the `HTTPD.CONF` file searching for all `@@Value@@` markers and replacing them with the appropriate setting
- Add `SYS:/APACHE2` to the search path, for example:

```
SEARCH ADD SYS:\APACHE2
```

Apache may be installed to other volumes besides the default `SYS` volume.

During the build process, adding the keyword "install" to the makefile command line will automatically produce a complete distribution package under the subdirectory `DIST`. Install Apache by simply copying the distribution that was produced by the makfiles to the root of a NetWare volume (see: Compiling Apache for NetWare below).

## Running Apache for NetWare

To start Apache just type `apache` at the console. This will load apache in the OS address space. If you prefer to load Apache in a protected address space you may specify the address space with the load statement as follows:

```
load address space = apache2 apache2
```

This will load Apache into an address space called apache2. Running multiple instances of Apache concurrently on NetWare is possible by loading each instance into its own protected address space.

After starting Apache, it will be listening to port 80 (unless you changed the LISTEN directive in the configuration files). To connect to the server and access the default page, launch a browser and enter the server's name or address. This should respond with a welcome page, and a link to the Apache manual. If nothing happens or you get an error, look in the `error_log` file in the `logs` directory.

Once your basic installation is working, you should configure it properly by editing the files in the `conf` directory.

To unload Apache running in the OS address space just type the following at the console:

```
unload apache2
```

or

```
apache2 shutdown
```

If apache is running in a protected address space specify the address space in the unload statement:

```
unload address space = apache2 apache2
```

When working with Apache it is important to know how it will find the configuration files. You can specify a configuration file on the command line in two ways:

- `-f` specifies a path to a particular configuration file

```
apache2 -f "vol:/my server/conf/my.conf"
```

```
apache -f test/test.conf
```

In these cases, the proper SERVERROOT should be set in the configuration file.

If you don't specify a configuration file name with `-f`, Apache will use the file name compiled into the server, usually `conf/httpd.conf`. Invoking Apache with the `-V` switch will display this value labeled as `SERVER_CONFIG_FILE`. Apache will then determine its SERVERROOT by trying the following, in this order:

- A `ServerRoot` directive via a `-C` switch.
- The `-d` switch on the command line.
- Current working directory
- The server root compiled into the server.

The server root compiled into the server is usually `sys:/apache2`. invoking apache with the `-V` switch will display this value labeled as `HTTPD_ROOT`.

Apache 2.0 for NetWare includes a set of command line directives that can be used to modify or display information about the running instance of the web server. These directives are only available while Apache is running. Each of these directives must be preceded by the keyword `APACHE2`.

**RESTART** Instructs Apache to terminate all running worker threads as they become idle, reread the configuration file and restart each worker thread based on the new configuration.

**VERSION** Displays version information about the currently running instance of Apache.

**MODULES** Displays a list of loaded modules both built-in and external.

**DIRECTIVES** Displays a list of all available directives.

**SETTINGS** Enables or disables the thread status display on the console. When enabled, the state of each running threads is displayed on the Apache console screen.

**SHUTDOWN** Terminates the running instance of the Apache web server.

**HELP** Describes each of the runtime directives.

By default these directives are issued against the instance of Apache running in the OS address space. To issue a directive against a specific instance running in a protected address space, include the -p parameter along with the name of the address space. For more information type `"apache2 Help"` on the command line.

## Configuring Apache for NetWare

Apache is configured by reading configuration files usually stored in the `conf` directory. These are the same as files used to configure the Unix version, but there are a few different directives for Apache on NetWare. See the Apache module documentation (p. 1101) for all the available directives.

The main differences in Apache for NetWare are:

- Because Apache for NetWare is multithreaded, it does not use a separate process for each request, as Apache does on some Unix implementations. Instead there are only threads running: a parent thread, and multiple child or worker threads which handle the requests.

  Therefore the "process"-management directives are different:

  MAXCONNECTIONSPERCHILD - Like the Unix directive, this controls how many connections a worker thread will serve before exiting. The recommended default, `MaxConnectionsPerChild 0`, causes the thread to continue servicing request indefinitely. It is recommended on NetWare, unless there is some specific reason, that this directive always remain set to 0.

  STARTTHREADS - This directive tells the server how many threads it should start initially. The recommended default is `StartThreads 50`.

  MINSPARETHREADS - This directive instructs the server to spawn additional worker threads if the number of idle threads ever falls below this value. The recommended default is `MinSpareThreads 10`.

  MAXSPARETHREADS - This directive instructs the server to begin terminating worker threads if the number of idle threads ever exceeds this value. The recommended default is `MaxSpareThreads 100`.

  MAXTHREADS - This directive limits the total number of work threads to a maximum value. The recommended default is `ThreadsPerChild 250`.

  THREADSTACKSIZE - This directive tells the server what size of stack to use for the individual worker thread. The recommended default is `ThreadStackSize 65536`.

- The directives that accept filenames as arguments must use NetWare filenames instead of Unix names. However, because Apache uses Unix-style names internally, forward slashes must be used rather than backslashes. It is recommended that all rooted file paths begin with a volume name. If omitted, Apache will assume the `SYS:` volume which may not be correct.

- Apache for NetWare has the ability to load modules at runtime, without recompiling the server. If Apache is compiled normally, it will install a number of optional modules in the `\Apache2\modules` directory. To activate these, or other modules, the LOADMODULE directive must be used. For example, to active the status module, use the following:

```
LoadModule status_module modules/status.nlm
```

Information on creating loadable modules (p. 908) is also available.

**Additional NetWare specific directives:**

- CGIMAPEXTENSION - This directive maps a CGI file extension to a script interpreter.

- SECURELISTEN - Enables SSL encryption for a specified port.

- NWSSLTRUSTEDCERTS - Adds trusted certificates that are used to create secure connections to proxied servers.

- NWSSLUPGRADEABLE - Allow a connection created on the specified address/port to be upgraded to an SSL connection.

## Compiling Apache for NetWare

Compiling Apache requires MetroWerks CodeWarrior 6.x or higher. Once Apache has been built, it can be installed to the root of any NetWare volume. The default is the `sys:/Apache2` directory.

Before running the server you must fill out the `conf` directory. Copy the file `HTTPD-STD.CONF` from the distribution `conf` directory and rename it to `HTTPD.CONF`. Edit the `HTTPD.CONF` file searching for all `@@Value@@` markers and replacing them with the appropriate setting. Copy over the `conf/magic` and `conf/mime.types` files as well. Alternatively, a complete distribution can be built by including the keyword `install` when invoking the makefiles.

### Requirements:

The following development tools are required to build Apache 2.0 for NetWare:

- Metrowerks CodeWarrior 6.0 or higher with the NetWare PDK 3.0[14] or higher.
- NetWare Libraries for C (LibC)[15]
- LDAP Libraries for C[16]
- ZLIB Compression Library source code[17]
- AWK utility (awk, gawk or similar). AWK can be downloaded from http://developer.novell.com/ndk/apache.htm. The utility must be found in your windows path and must be named `awk.exe`.
- To build using the makefiles, you will need GNU make version 3.78.1 (GMake) available at http://developer.novell.com/ndk/apache.htm.

### Building Apache using the NetWare makefiles:

- Set the environment variable `NOVELLLIBC` to the location of the NetWare Libraries for C SDK, for example:

```
Set NOVELLLIBC=c:\novell\ndk\libc
```

- Set the environment variable `METROWERKS` to the location where you installed the Metrowerks CodeWarrior compiler, for example:

```
Set METROWERKS=C:\Program Files\Metrowerks\CodeWarrior
```

If you installed to the default location `C:\Program Files\Metrowerks\CodeWarrior`, you don't need to set this.

- Set the environment variable `LDAPSDK` to the location where you installed the LDAP Libraries for C, for example:

```
Set LDAPSDK=c:\Novell\NDK\cldapsdk\NetWare\libc
```

- Set the environment variable `ZLIBSDK` to the location where you installed the source code for the ZLib Library, for example:

---

[14] http://developer.novell.com/ndk/cwpdk.htm
[15] http://developer.novell.com/ndk/libc.htm
[16] http://developer.novell.com/ndk/cldap.htm
[17] http://www.gzip.org/zlib/

```
Set ZLIBSDK=D:\NOVELL\zlib
```

- Set the environment variable PCRESDK to the location where you installed the source code for the PCRE Library, for example:

```
Set PCRESDK=D:\NOVELL\pcre
```

- Set the environment variable AP_WORK to the full path of the httpd source code directory.

```
Set AP_WORK=D:\httpd-2.0.x
```

- Set the environment variable APR_WORK to the full path of the apr source code directory. Typically \httpd\srclib\apr but the APR project can be outside of the httpd directory structure.

```
Set APR_WORK=D:\apr-1.x.x
```

- Set the environment variable APU_WORK to the full path of the apr-util source code directory. Typically \httpd\srclib\apr-util but the APR-UTIL project can be outside of the httpd directory structure.

```
Set APU_WORK=D:\apr-util-1.x.x
```

- Make sure that the path to the AWK utility and the GNU make utility (gmake.exe) have been included in the system's PATH environment variable.
- Download the source code and unzip to an appropriate directory on your workstation.
- Change directory to \httpd-2.0 and build the prebuild utilities by running "gmake -f nwgnumakefile prebuild". This target will create the directory \httpd-2.0\nwprebuild and copy each of the utilities to this location that are necessary to complete the following build steps.
- Copy the files \httpd-2.0\nwprebuild\GENCHARS.nlm and \httpd-2.0\nwprebuild\DFTABLES.nlm to the SYS: volume of a NetWare server and run them using the following commands:

```
SYS:\genchars > sys:\test_char.h
SYS:\dftables sys:\chartables.c
```

- Copy the files test_char.h and chartables.c to the directory \httpd-2.0\os\netware on the build machine.
- Change directory to \httpd-2.0 and build Apache by running "gmake -f nwgnumakefile". You can create a distribution directory by adding an install parameter to the command, for example:

```
gmake -f nwgnumakefile install
```

**Additional make options**

- `gmake -f nwgnumakefile` Builds release versions of all of the binaries and copies them to a `\release` destination directory.

- `gmake -f nwgnumakefile DEBUG=1` Builds debug versions of all of the binaries and copies them to a `\debug` destination directory.

- `gmake -f nwgnumakefile install` Creates a complete Apache distribution with binaries, docs and additional support files in a `\dist\Apache2` directory.

- `gmake -f nwgnumakefile prebuild` Builds all of the prebuild utilities and copies them to the `\nwprebuild` directory.

- `gmake -f nwgnumakefile installdev` Same as install but also creates a `\lib` and `\include` directory in the destination directory and copies headers and import files.

- `gmake -f nwgnumakefile clean` Cleans all object files and binaries from the `\release.o` or `\debug.o` build areas depending on whether `DEBUG` has been defined.

- `gmake -f nwgnumakefile clobber_all` Same as clean and also deletes the distribution directory if it exists.

**Additional environment variable options**

- To build all of the experimental modules, set the environment variable `EXPERIMENTAL`:

```
Set EXPERIMENTAL=1
```

- To build Apache using standard BSD style sockets rather than Winsock, set the environment variable `USE_STDSOCKETS`:

```
Set USE_STDSOCKETS=1
```

**Building mod_ssl for the NetWare platform**

By default Apache for NetWare uses the built-in module MOD_NW_SSL to provide SSL services. This module simply enables the native SSL services implemented in NetWare OS to handle all encryption for a given port. Alternatively, mod_ssl can also be used in the same manner as on other platforms.

Before mod_ssl can be built for the NetWare platform, the OpenSSL libraries must be provided. This can be done through the following steps:

- Download the recent OpenSSL 0.9.8 release source code from the OpenSSL Source[18] page (older 0.9.7 versions need to be patched and are therefore not recommended).

- Edit the file `NetWare/set_env.bat` and modify any tools and utilities paths so that they correspond to your build environment.

- From the root of the OpenSSL source directory, run the following scripts:

```
Netware\set_env netware-libc
Netware\build netware-libc
```

---

[18]http://www.openssl.org/source/

For performance reasons you should enable to build with ASM code. Download NASM from the SF site[19]. Then configure OpenSSL to use ASM code:

```
Netware\build netware-libc nw-nasm enable-mdc2 enable-md5
```

Warning: dont use the CodeWarrior Assembler - it produces broken code!

- Before building Apache, set the environment variable OSSLSDK to the full path to the root of the openssl source code directory, and set WITH_MOD_SSL to 1.

```
Set OSSLSDK=d:\openssl-0.9.8x
Set WITH_MOD_SSL=1
```

---

[19]http://nasm.sourceforge.net/

## 7.6   Running a High-Performance Web Server on HPUX

```
Date: Wed, 05 Nov 1997 16:59:34 -0800
From: Rick Jones <raj@cup.hp.com>
Reply-To: raj@cup.hp.com
Organization: Network Performance
Subject: HP-UX tuning tips
```

Here are some tuning tips for HP-UX to add to the tuning page.

For HP-UX 9.X: Upgrade to 10.20
For HP-UX 10.[00—01—10]: Upgrade to 10.20

For HP-UX 10.20:

Install the latest cumulative ARPA Transport Patch. This will allow you to configure the size of the TCP connection lookup hash table. The default is 256 buckets and must be set to a power of two. This is accomplished with adb against the *disc* image of the kernel. The variable name is `tcp_hash_size`. Notice that it's critically important that you use `"W"` to write a 32 bit quantity, not `"w"` to write a 16 bit value when patching the disc image because the `tcp_hash_size` variable is a 32 bit quantity.

How to pick the value? Examine the output of ftp://ftp.cup.hp.com/dist/networking/tools/connhist and see how many total TCP connections exist on the system. You probably want that number divided by the hash table size to be reasonably small, say less than 10. Folks can look at HP's SPECweb96 disclosures for some common settings. These can be found at http://www.specbench.org/. If an HP-UX system was performing at 1000 SPECweb96 connections per second, the `TIME_WAIT` time of 60 seconds would mean 60,000 TCP "connections" being tracked.

Folks can check their listen queue depths with ftp://ftp.cup.hp.com/dist/networking/misc/listenq.

If folks are running Apache on a PA-8000 based system, they should consider "chatr'ing" the Apache executable to have a large page size. This would be `"chatr +pi L <BINARY>"`. The GID of the running executable must have `MLOCK` privileges. `Setprivgrp(1m)` should be consulted for assigning `MLOCK`. The change can be validated by running Glance and examining the memory regions of the server(s) to make sure that they show a non-trivial fraction of the text segment being locked.

If folks are running Apache on MP systems, they might consider writing a small program that uses `mpctl()` to bind processes to processors. A simple `pid % numcpu` algorithm is probably sufficient. This might even go into the source code.

If folks are concerned about the number of `FIN_WAIT_2` connections, they can use nettune to shrink the value of `tcp_keepstart`. However, they should be careful there - certainly do not make it less than oh two to four minutes. If `tcp_hash_size` has been set well, it is probably OK to let the `FIN_WAIT_2`'s take longer to timeout (perhaps even the default two hours) - they will not on average have a big impact on performance.

There are other things that could go into the code base, but that might be left for another email. Feel free to drop me a message if you or others are interested.

sincerely,

rick jones

http://www.netperf.org/netperf/

# Chapter 8

# Apache HTTP Server and Supporting Programs

# 8.1   Server and Supporting Programs

This page documents all the executable programs included with the Apache HTTP Server.

## Index

**httpd**  Apache hypertext transfer protocol server

**apachectl**  Apache HTTP server control interface

**ab**  Apache HTTP server benchmarking tool

**apxs**  APache eXtenSion tool

**configure**  Configure the source tree

**dbmmanage**  Create and update user authentication files in DBM format for basic authentication

**fcgistarter**  Start a FastCGI program

**firehose**  Demultiplex a firehose from MOD_FIREHOSE

**htcacheclean**  Clean up the disk cache

**htdigest**  Create and update user authentication files for digest authentication

**htdbm**  Manipulate DBM password databases.

**htpasswd**  Create and update user authentication files for basic authentication

**httxt2dbm**  Create dbm files for use with RewriteMap

**logresolve**  Resolve hostnames for IP-addresses in Apache logfiles

**log_server_status**  Periodically log the server's status

**rotatelogs**  Rotate Apache logs without having to kill the server

**split-logfile**  Split a multi-vhost logfile into per-host logfiles

**suexec**  Switch User For Exec

## 8.2 httpd - Apache Hypertext Transfer Protocol Server

httpd is the Apache HyperText Transfer Protocol (HTTP) server program. It is designed to be run as a standalone daemon process. When used like this it will create a pool of child processes or threads to handle requests.

In general, httpd should not be invoked directly, but rather should be invoked via apachectl on Unix-based systems or as a service on Windows NT, 2000 and XP (p. 267) and as a console application on Windows 9x and ME (p. 267).

**See also**

- Starting Apache httpd (p. 27)
- Stopping Apache httpd (p. 29)
- Configuration Files (p. 32)
- Platform-specific Documentation (p. 266)
- apachectl

### Synopsis

httpd [ -d *serverroot* ] [ -f *config* ] [ -C *directive* ] [ -c *directive* ] [ -D *parameter* ] [ -e *level* ] [ -E *file* ] [ -k start|restart|graceful|stop|graceful-stop ] [ -R *directory* ] [ -h ] [ -l ] [ -L ] [ -S ] [ -t ] [ -v ] [ -V ] [ -X ] [ -M ] [ -T ]

On Windows systems (p. 267), the following additional arguments are available:

httpd [ -k install|config|uninstall ] [ -n *name* ] [ -w ]

### Options

**-d *serverroot*** Set the initial value for the SERVERROOT directive to *serverroot*. This can be overridden by the ServerRoot directive in the configuration file. The default is /usr/local/apache2.

**-f *config*** Uses the directives in the file *config* on startup. If *config* does not begin with a /, then it is taken to be a path relative to the SERVERROOT. The default is conf/httpd.conf.

**-k start|restart|graceful|stop|graceful-stop** Signals httpd to start, restart, or stop. See Stopping Apache httpd (p. 29) for more information.

**-C *directive*** Process the configuration *directive* before reading config files.

**-c *directive*** Process the configuration *directive* after reading config files.

**-D *parameter*** Sets a configuration *parameter* which can be used with <IFDEFINE> sections in the configuration files to conditionally skip or process commands at server startup and restart. Also can be used to set certain less-common startup parameters including -DNO_DETACH (prevent the parent from forking) and -DFOREGROUND (prevent the parent from calling setsid() et al).

**-e *level*** Sets the LOGLEVEL to *level* during server startup. This is useful for temporarily increasing the verbosity of the error messages to find problems during startup.

**-E *file*** Send error messages during server startup to *file*.

**-h** Output a short summary of available command line options.

**-l** Output a list of modules compiled into the server. This will **not** list dynamically loaded modules included using the LOADMODULE directive.

**-L** Output a list of directives provided by static modules, together with expected arguments and places where the directive is valid. Directives provided by shared modules are not listed.

**-M** Dump a list of loaded Static and Shared Modules.

**-S** Show the settings as parsed from the config file (currently only shows the virtualhost settings).

**-T (Available in 2.3.8 and later)** Skip document root check at startup/restart.

**-t** Run syntax tests for configuration files only. The program immediately exits after these syntax parsing tests with either a return code of 0 (Syntax OK) or return code not equal to 0 (Syntax Error). If -D *DUMP_VHOSTS* is also set, details of the virtual host configuration will be printed. If -D *DUMP_MODULES* is set, all loaded modules will be printed. If -D *DUMP_CERTS* is set and MOD_SSL is used, configured SSL certificates will be printed. If -D *DUMP_CA_CERTS* is set and MOD_SSL is used, configured SSL CA certificates and configured directories containing SSL CA certificates will be printed.

**-v** Print the version of httpd, and then exit.

**-V** Print the version and build parameters of httpd, and then exit.

**-X** Run httpd in debug mode. Only one worker will be started and the server will not detach from the console.

The following arguments are available only on the Windows platform (p. 267) :

**-k install|config|uninstall** Install Apache httpd as a Windows NT service; change startup options for the Apache httpd service; and uninstall the Apache httpd service.

**-n *name*** The *name* of the Apache httpd service to signal.

**-w** Keep the console window open on error so that the error message can be read.

# 8.3 ab - Apache HTTP server benchmarking tool

`ab` is a tool for benchmarking your Apache Hypertext Transfer Protocol (HTTP) server. It is designed to give you an impression of how your current Apache installation performs. This especially shows you how many requests per second your Apache installation is capable of serving.

**See also**

- `httpd`

## Synopsis

**ab** [ **-A** *auth-username:password* ] [ **-b** *windowsize* ] [ **-B** *local-address* ] [ **-c** *concurrency* ] [ **-C** *cookie-name=value* ] [ **-d** ] [ **-e** *csv-file* ] [ **-f** *protocol* ] [ **-g** *gnuplot-file* ] [ **-h** ] [ **-H** *custom-header* ] [ **-i** ] [ **-k** ] [ **-l** ] [ **-m** *HTTP-method* ] [ **-n** *requests* ] [ **-p** *POST-file* ] [ **-P** *proxy-auth-username:password* ] [ **-q** ] [ **-r** ] [ **-s** *timeout* ] [ **-S** ] [ **-t** *timelimit* ] [ **-T** *content-type* ] [ **-u** *PUT-file* ] [ **-v** *verbosity*] [ **-V** ] [ **-w** ] [ **-x** *<table>-attributes* ] [ **-X** *proxy[:port]* ] [ **-y** *<tr>-attributes* ] [ **-z** *<td>-attributes* ] [ **-Z** *ciphersuite* ] [http[s]://]*hostname[:port]/path*

## Options

**-A** *auth-username:password* Supply BASIC Authentication credentials to the server. The username and password are separated by a single : and sent on the wire base64 encoded. The string is sent regardless of whether the server needs it (*i.e.*, has sent an 401 authentication needed).

**-b** *windowsize* Size of TCP send/receive buffer, in bytes.

**-B** *local-address* Address to bind to when making outgoing connections.

**-c** *concurrency* Number of multiple requests to perform at a time. Default is one request at a time.

**-C** *cookie-name=value* Add a `Cookie:` line to the request. The argument is typically in the form of a *name=value* pair. This field is repeatable.

**-d** Do not display the "percentage served within XX [ms] table". (legacy support).

**-e** *csv-file* Write a Comma separated value (CSV) file which contains for each percentage (from 1% to 100%) the time (in milliseconds) it took to serve that percentage of the requests. This is usually more useful than the 'gnuplot' file; as the results are already 'binned'.

**-f** *protocol* Specify SSL/TLS protocol (SSL2, SSL3, TLS1, TLS1.1, TLS1.2, or ALL). TLS1.1 and TLS1.2 support available in 2.4.4 and later.

**-g** *gnuplot-file* Write all measured values out as a 'gnuplot' or TSV (Tab separate values) file. This file can easily be imported into packages like Gnuplot, IDL, Mathematica, Igor or even Excel. The labels are on the first line of the file.

**-h** Display usage information.

**-H** *custom-header* Append extra headers to the request. The argument is typically in the form of a valid header line, containing a colon-separated field-value pair (*i.e.*, `"Accept-Encoding: zip/zop;8bit"`).

**-i** Do `HEAD` requests instead of `GET`.

**-k** Enable the HTTP KeepAlive feature, *i.e.*, perform multiple requests within one HTTP session. Default is no KeepAlive.

**-l** Do not report errors if the length of the responses is not constant. This can be useful for dynamic pages. Available in 2.4.7 and later.

**-m** *HTTP-method* Custom HTTP method for the requests. Available in 2.4.10 and later.

**-n** *requests* Number of requests to perform for the benchmarking session. The default is to just perform a single request which usually leads to non-representative benchmarking results.

**-p** *POST-file* File containing data to POST. Remember to also set -T.

**-P** *proxy-auth-username:password* Supply BASIC Authentication credentials to a proxy en-route. The username and password are separated by a single : and sent on the wire base64 encoded. The string is sent regardless of whether the proxy needs it (*i.e.*, has sent an 407 proxy authentication needed).

**-q** When processing more than 150 requests, ab outputs a progress count on stderr every 10% or 100 requests or so. The -q flag will suppress these messages.

**-r** Don't exit on socket receive errors.

**-s** *timeout* Maximum number of seconds to wait before the socket times out. Default is 30 seconds. Available in 2.4.4 and later.

**-S** Do not display the median and standard deviation values, nor display the warning/error messages when the average and median are more than one or two times the standard deviation apart. And default to the min/avg/max values. (legacy support).

**-t** *timelimit* Maximum number of seconds to spend for benchmarking. This implies a -n 50000 internally. Use this to benchmark the server within a fixed total amount of time. Per default there is no timelimit.

**-T** *content-type* Content-type    header    to    use    for    POST/PUT    data,    eg. application/x-www-form-urlencoded. Default is text/plain.

**-u** *PUT-file* File containing data to PUT. Remember to also set -T.

**-v** *verbosity* Set verbosity level - 4 and above prints information on headers, 3 and above prints response codes (404, 200, etc.), 2 and above prints warnings and info.

**-V** Display version number and exit.

**-w** Print out results in HTML tables. Default table is two columns wide, with a white background.

**-x** *<table>-attributes* String to use as attributes for <table>. Attributes are inserted <table *here* >.

**-X** *proxy[:port]* Use a proxy server for the requests.

**-y** *<tr>-attributes* String to use as attributes for <tr>.

**-z** *<td>-attributes* String to use as attributes for <td>.

**-Z** *ciphersuite* Specify SSL/TLS cipher suite (See openssl ciphers)

## Output

The following list describes the values returned by `ab`:

**Server Software** The value, if any, returned in the *server* HTTP header of the first successful response. This includes all characters in the header from beginning to the point a character with decimal value of 32 (most notably: a space or CR/LF) is detected.

**Server Hostname** The DNS or IP address given on the command line

**Server Port** The port to which ab is connecting. If no port is given on the command line, this will default to 80 for http and 443 for https.

**SSL/TLS Protocol** The protocol parameters negotiated between the client and server. This will only be printed if SSL is used.

**Document Path** The request URI parsed from the command line string.

**Document Length** This is the size in bytes of the first successfully returned document. If the document length changes during testing, the response is considered an error.

**Concurrency Level** The number of concurrent clients used during the test

**Time taken for tests** This is the time taken from the moment the first socket connection is created to the moment the last response is received

**Complete requests** The number of successful responses received

**Failed requests** The number of requests that were considered a failure. If the number is greater than zero, another line will be printed showing the number of requests that failed due to connecting, reading, incorrect content length, or exceptions.

**Write errors** The number of errors that failed during write (broken pipe).

**Non-2xx responses** The number of responses that were not in the 200 series of response codes. If all responses were 200, this field is not printed.

**Keep-Alive requests** The number of connections that resulted in Keep-Alive requests

**Total body sent** If configured to send data as part of the test, this is the total number of bytes sent during the tests. This field is omitted if the test did not include a body to send.

**Total transferred** The total number of bytes received from the server. This number is essentially the number of bytes sent over the wire.

**HTML transferred** The total number of document bytes received from the server. This number excludes bytes received in HTTP headers

**Requests per second** This is the number of requests per second. This value is the result of dividing the number of requests by the total time taken

**Time per request** The average time spent per request. The first value is calculated with the formula `concurrency * timetaken * 1000 / done` while the second value is calculated with the formula `timetaken * 1000 / done`

**Transfer rate** The rate of transfer as calculated by the formula `totalread / 1024 / timetaken`

**Bugs**

There are various statically declared buffers of fixed length. Combined with the lazy parsing of the command line arguments, the response headers from the server and other external inputs, this might bite you.

It does not implement HTTP/1.x fully; only accepts some 'expected' forms of responses. The rather heavy use of `strstr(3)` shows up top in profile, which might indicate a performance problem; *i.e.*, you would measure the `ab` performance rather than the server's.

# 8.4 apachectl - Apache HTTP Server Control Interface

`apachectl` is a front end to the Apache HyperText Transfer Protocol (HTTP) server. It is designed to help the administrator control the functioning of the Apache `httpd` daemon.

The `apachectl` script can operate in two modes. First, it can act as a simple front-end to the `httpd` command that simply sets any necessary environment variables and then invokes `httpd`, passing through any command line arguments. Second, `apachectl` can act as a SysV init script, taking simple one-word arguments like `start`, `restart`, and `stop`, and translating them into appropriate signals to `httpd`.

If your Apache installation uses non-standard paths, you will need to edit the `apachectl` script to set the appropriate paths to the `httpd` binary. You can also specify any necessary `httpd` command line arguments. See the comments in the script for details.

The `apachectl` script returns a 0 exit value on success, and >0 if an error occurs. For more details, view the comments in the script.

**See also**

- Starting Apache (p. 27)
- Stopping Apache (p. 29)
- Configuration Files (p. 32)
- Platform Docs (p. 266)
- `httpd`

## Synopsis

When acting in pass-through mode, `apachectl` can take all the arguments available for the `httpd` binary.

**apachectl** [ *httpd-argument* ]

When acting in SysV init mode, `apachectl` takes simple, one-word commands, defined below.

**apachectl** *command*

## Options

Only the SysV init-style options are defined here. Other arguments are defined on the `httpd` manual page.

**start** Start the Apache `httpd` daemon. Gives an error if it is already running. This is equivalent to `apachectl -k start`.

**stop** Stops the Apache `httpd` daemon. This is equivalent to `apachectl -k stop`.

**restart** Restarts the Apache `httpd` daemon. If the daemon is not running, it is started. This command automatically checks the configuration files as in `configtest` before initiating the restart to make sure the daemon doesn't die. This is equivalent to `apachectl -k restart`.

**fullstatus** Displays a full status report from MOD_STATUS. For this to work, you need to have MOD_STATUS enabled on your server and a text-based browser such as `lynx` available on your system. The URL used to access the status report can be set by editing the STATUSURL variable in the script.

**status** Displays a brief status report. Similar to the `fullstatus` option, except that the list of requests currently being served is omitted.

**graceful** Gracefully restarts the Apache `httpd` daemon. If the daemon is not running, it is started. This differs from a normal restart in that currently open connections are not aborted. A side effect is that old log files will not be closed immediately. This means that if used in a log rotation script, a substantial delay may be necessary to ensure that the old log files are closed before processing them. This command automatically checks the configuration files as in `configtest` before initiating the restart to make sure Apache doesn't die. This is equivalent to `apachectl -k graceful`.

**graceful-stop** Gracefully stops the Apache `httpd` daemon. This differs from a normal stop in that currently open connections are not aborted. A side effect is that old log files will not be closed immediately. This is equivalent to `apachectl -k graceful-stop`.

**configtest** Run a configuration file syntax test. It parses the configuration files and either reports `Syntax Ok` or detailed information about the particular syntax error. This is equivalent to `apachectl -t`.

The following option was available in earlier versions but has been removed.

**startssl** To start `httpd` with SSL support, you should edit your configuration file to include the relevant directives and then use the normal `apachectl start`.

# 8.5 apxs - APache eXtenSion tool

`apxs` is a tool for building and installing extension modules for the Apache HyperText Transfer Protocol (HTTP) server. This is achieved by building a dynamic shared object (DSO) from one or more source or object *files* which then can be loaded into the Apache server under runtime via the LOADMODULE directive from MOD_SO.

So to use this extension mechanism your platform has to support the DSO feature and your Apache `httpd` binary has to be built with the MOD_SO module. The `apxs` tool automatically complains if this is not the case. You can check this yourself by manually running the command

```
$ httpd -l
```

The module MOD_SO should be part of the displayed list. If these requirements are fulfilled you can easily extend your Apache server's functionality by installing your own modules with the DSO mechanism by the help of this `apxs` tool:

```
$ apxs -i -a -c mod_foo.c
gcc -fpic -DSHARED_MODULE -I/path/to/apache/include -c mod_foo.c
ld -Bshareable -o mod_foo.so mod_foo.o
cp mod_foo.so /path/to/apache/modules/mod_foo.so
chmod 755 /path/to/apache/modules/mod_foo.so
[activating module 'foo' in /path/to/apache/etc/httpd.conf]
$ apachectl restart
/path/to/apache/sbin/apachectl restart:  httpd not running, trying to
start
[Tue Mar 31 11:27:55 1998] [debug] mod_so.c(303):  loaded module
foo_module
/path/to/apache/sbin/apachectl restart:  httpd started
$ _
```

The arguments *files* can be any C source file (.c), a object file (.o) or even a library archive (.a). The `apxs` tool automatically recognizes these extensions and automatically used the C source files for compilation while just using the object and archive files for the linking phase. But when using such pre-compiled objects make sure they are compiled for position independent code (PIC) to be able to use them for a dynamically loaded shared object. For instance with GCC you always just have to use `-fpic`. For other C compilers consult its manual page or at watch for the flags `apxs` uses to compile the object files.

For more details about DSO support in Apache read the documentation of MOD_SO or perhaps even read the `src/modules/standard/mod_so.c` source file.

**See also**

- `apachectl`
- `httpd`

## Synopsis

**apxs** -**g** [ -**S** *name=value* ] -**n** *modname*

**apxs** -**q** [ -**v** ] [ -**S** *name=value* ] *query* ...

**apxs** -**c** [ -**S** *name=value* ] [ -**o** *dsofile* ] [ -**I** *incdir* ] [ -**D** *name=value* ] [ -**L** *libdir* ] [ -**l** *libname* ] [ -**Wc,** *compiler-flags* ] [ -**Wl,** *linker-flags* ] *files* ...

**apxs** -**i** [ -**S** *name=value* ] [ -**n** *modname* ] [ -**a** ] [ -**A** ] *dso-file* ...

**apxs** -**e** [ -**S** *name=value* ] [ -**n** *modname* ] [ -**a** ] [ -**A** ] *dso-file* ...

## Options

### Common Options

**-n** *modname* This explicitly sets the module name for the -i (install) and -g (template generation) option. Use this to explicitly specify the module name. For option -g this is required, for option -i the apxs tool tries to determine the name from the source or (as a fallback) at least by guessing it from the filename.

### Query Options

**-q** Performs a query for variables and environment settings used to build httpd. When invoked without *query* parameters, it prints all known variables and their values. The optional -v parameter formats the list output.

Use this to manually determine settings used to build the httpd that will load your module. For instance use

```
INC=-I'apxs -q INCLUDEDIR'
```

inside your own Makefiles if you need manual access to Apache's C header files.

### Configuration Options

**-S** *name=value* This option changes the apxs settings described above.

### Template Generation Options

**-g** This generates a subdirectory *name* (see option -n) and there two files: A sample module source file named mod_*name*.c which can be used as a template for creating your own modules or as a quick start for playing with the apxs mechanism. And a corresponding Makefile for even easier build and installing of this module.

### DSO Compilation Options

**-c** This indicates the compilation operation. It first compiles the C source files (.c) of *files* into corresponding object files (.o) and then builds a dynamically shared object in *dsofile* by linking these object files plus the remaining object files (.o and .a) of *files*. If no -o option is specified the output file is guessed from the first filename in *files* and thus usually defaults to mod_*name*.so.

**-o** *dsofile* Explicitly specifies the filename of the created dynamically shared object. If not specified and the name cannot be guessed from the *files* list, the fallback name mod_unknown.so is used.

**-D** *name=value* This option is directly passed through to the compilation command(s). Use this to add your own defines to the build process.

**-I** *incdir* This option is directly passed through to the compilation command(s). Use this to add your own include directories to search to the build process.

**-L** *libdir* This option is directly passed through to the linker command. Use this to add your own library directories to search to the build process.

**-l** *libname* This option is directly passed through to the linker command. Use this to add your own libraries to search to the build process.

**-Wc,** *compiler-flags* This option passes *compiler-flags* as additional flags to the libtool --mode=compile command. Use this to add local compiler-specific options.

**-Wl,*linker-flags*** This option passes *linker-flags* as additional flags to the `libtool --mode=link` command. Use this to add local linker-specific options.

**-p** This option causes apxs to link against the apr/apr-util libraries. This is useful when compiling helper programs that use the apr/apr-util libraries.

### DSO Installation and Configuration Options

**-i** This indicates the installation operation and installs one or more dynamically shared objects into the server's *modules* directory.

**-a** This activates the module by automatically adding a corresponding LOADMODULE line to Apache's `httpd.conf` configuration file, or by enabling it if it already exists.

**-A** Same as option -a but the created LOADMODULE directive is prefixed with a hash sign (#), *i.e.*, the module is just prepared for later activation but initially disabled.

**-e** This indicates the editing operation, which can be used with the -a and -A options similarly to the -i operation to edit Apache's `httpd.conf` configuration file without attempting to install the module.

## Examples

Assume you have an Apache module named `mod_foo.c` available which should extend Apache's server functionality. To accomplish this you first have to compile the C source into a shared object suitable for loading into the Apache server under runtime via the following command:

```
$ apxs -c mod_foo.c
/path/to/libtool --mode=compile gcc ...  -c mod_foo.c
/path/to/libtool --mode=link gcc ...  -o mod_foo.la mod_foo.slo
$ _
```

Then you have to update the Apache configuration by making sure a LOADMODULE directive is present to load this shared object. To simplify this step apxs provides an automatic way to install the shared object in its "modules" directory and updating the `httpd.conf` file accordingly. This can be achieved by running:

```
$ apxs -i -a mod_foo.la
/path/to/instdso.sh mod_foo.la /path/to/apache/modules
/path/to/libtool --mode=install cp mod_foo.la /path/to/apache/modules
...  chmod 755 /path/to/apache/modules/mod_foo.so
[activating module 'foo' in /path/to/apache/conf/httpd.conf]
$ _
```

This way a line named

```
LoadModule foo_module modules/mod_foo.so
```

is added to the configuration file if still not present. If you want to have this disabled per default use the -A option, *i.e.*

```
$ apxs -i -A mod_foo.c
```

For a quick test of the apxs mechanism you can create a sample Apache module template plus a corresponding Makefile via:

```
$ apxs -g -n foo
Creating [DIR] foo
Creating [FILE] foo/Makefile
Creating [FILE] foo/modules.mk
Creating [FILE] foo/mod_foo.c
Creating [FILE] foo/.deps
$ _
```

Then you can immediately compile this sample module into a shared object and load it into the Apache server:

```
$ cd foo
$ make all reload
apxs -c mod_foo.c
/path/to/libtool --mode=compile gcc ...  -c mod_foo.c
/path/to/libtool --mode=link gcc ...  -o mod_foo.la mod_foo.slo
apxs -i -a -n "foo" mod_foo.la
/path/to/instdso.sh mod_foo.la /path/to/apache/modules
/path/to/libtool --mode=install cp mod_foo.la /path/to/apache/modules
...  chmod 755 /path/to/apache/modules/mod_foo.so
[activating module 'foo' in /path/to/apache/conf/httpd.conf]
apachectl restart
/path/to/apache/sbin/apachectl restart:  httpd not running, trying to
start
[Tue Mar 31 11:27:55 1998] [debug] mod_so.c(303):  loaded module
foo_module
/path/to/apache/sbin/apachectl restart:  httpd started
$ _
```

# 8.6 configure - Configure the source tree

The `configure` script configures the source tree for compiling and installing the Apache HTTP Server on your particular platform. Various options allow the compilation of a server corresponding to your personal requirements.

This script, included in the root directory of the source distribution, is for compilation on Unix and Unix-like systems only. For other platforms, see the platform (p. 266) documentation.

**See also**

- Compiling and Installing (p. 22)

## Synopsis

You should call the `configure` script from within the root directory of the distribution.

**`./configure`** *[OPTION]*... *[VAR=VALUE]*...

To assign environment variables (e.g. `CC`, `CFLAGS` ...), specify them as *VAR=VALUE*. See below for descriptions of some of the useful variables.

## Options

- Configuration options
- Installation directories
- System types
- Optional features
- Options for support programs

**Configuration options**

The following options influence the behavior of `configure` itself.

**-C**

**--config-cache** This is an alias for `--cache-file=config.cache`

**--cache-file=*FILE*** The test results will be cached in file *FILE*. This option is disabled by default.

**-h**

**--help [short|recursive]** Output the help and exit. With the argument `short` only options specific to this package will displayed. The argument `recursive` displays the short help of all the included packages.

**-n**

**--no-create** The `configure` script is run normally but does not create output files. This is useful to check the test results before generating makefiles for compilation.

**-q**

**--quiet** Do not print `checking` ... messages during the configure process.

**--srcdir=*DIR*** Defines directory *DIR* to be the source file directory. Default is the directory where `configure` is located, or the parent directory.

**--silent** Same as `--quiet`

**-V**

**–version** Display copyright information and exit.

### Installation directories

These options define the installation directory. The installation tree depends on the selected layout.

**--prefix=*PREFIX*** Install architecture-independent files in *PREFIX*. By default the installation directory is set to `/usr/local/apache2`.

**--exec-prefix=*EPREFIX*** Install architecture-dependent files in *EPREFIX*. By default the installation directory is set to the *PREFIX* directory.

By default, `make install` will install all the files in `/usr/local/apache2/bin`, `/usr/local/apache2/lib` etc. You can specify an installation prefix other than `/usr/local/apache2` using `--prefix`, for instance `--prefix=$HOME`.

### Define a directory layout

**--enable-layout=*LAYOUT*** Configure the source code and build scripts to assume an installation tree based on the layout *LAYOUT*. This allows you to separately specify the locations for each type of file within the Apache HTTP Server installation. The `config.layout` file contains several example configurations, and you can also create your own custom configuration following the examples. The different layouts in this file are grouped into `<Layout FOO>`...`</Layout>` sections and referred to by name as in `FOO`. The default layout is `Apache`.

### Fine tuning of the installation directories

For better control of the installation directories, use the options below. Please note that the directory defaults are set by `autoconf` and are overwritten by the corresponding layout setting.

**--bindir=*DIR*** Install user executables in *DIR*. The user executables are supporting programs like `htpasswd`, `dbmmanage`, etc. which are useful for site administrators. By default *DIR* is set to *EPREFIX*`/bin`.

**--datadir=*DIR*** Install read-only architecture-independent data in *DIR*. By default `datadir` is set to *PREFIX*`/share`. This option is offered by `autoconf` and currently unused.

**--includedir=*DIR*** Install C header files in *DIR*. By default `includedir` is set to *EPREFIX*`/include`.

**--infodir=*DIR*** Install info documentation in *DIR*. By default `infodir` is set to *PREFIX*`/info`. This option is currently unused.

**--libdir=*DIR*** Install object code libraries in *DIR*. By default `libdir` is set to *EPREFIX*`/lib`.

**--libexecdir=*DIR*** Install the program executables (i.e., shared modules) in *DIR*. By default `libexecdir` is set to *EPREFIX*`/modules`.

**--localstatedir=*DIR*** Install modifiable single-machine data in *DIR*. By default `localstatedir` is set to *PREFIX*`/var`. This option is offered by `autoconf` and currently unused.

**--mandir=*DIR*** Install the man documentation in *DIR*. By default `mandir` is set to *EPREFIX*`/man`.

**--oldincludedir=*DIR*** Install C header files for non-gcc in *DIR*. By default `oldincludedir` is set to `/usr/include`. This option is offered by `autoconf` and currently unused.

**--sbindir=*DIR*** Install the system administrator executables in *DIR*. Those are server programs like `httpd`, `apachectl`, `suexec`, etc. which are necessary to run the Apache HTTP Server. By default `sbindir` is set to *EPREFIX*/`sbin`.

**--sharedstatedir=*DIR*** Install modifiable architecture-independent data in *DIR*. By default `sharedstatedir` is set to *PREFIX*/`com`. This option is offered by `autoconf` and currently unused.

**--sysconfdir=*DIR*** Install read-only single-machine data like the server configuration files `httpd.conf`, `mime.types`, etc. in *DIR*. By default `sysconfdir` is set to *PREFIX*/`conf`.

### System types

These options are used to cross-compile the Apache HTTP Server to run on another system. In normal cases, when building and running the server on the same system, these options are not used.

**--build=*BUILD*** Defines the system type of the system on which the tools are being built. It defaults to the result of the script `config.guess`.

**--host=*HOST*** Defines the system type of the system on which the server will run. *HOST* defaults to *BUILD*.

**--target=*TARGET*** Configure for building compilers for the system type *TARGET*. It defaults to *HOST*. This option is offered by `autoconf` and not necessary for the Apache HTTP Server.

### Optional Features

These options are used to fine tune the features your HTTP server will have.

### General syntax

Generally you can use the following syntax to enable or disable a feature:

**--disable-*FEATURE*** Do not include *FEATURE*. This is the same as --enable-*FEATURE*=no.

**--enable-*FEATURE*[=*ARG*]** Include *FEATURE*. The default value for *ARG* is `yes`.

**--enable-*MODULE*=shared** The corresponding module will be build as DSO module. By default enabled modules are linked dynamically.

**--enable-*MODULE*=static** The corresponding module will be linked statically.

**Note**

> `configure` will not complain about --enable-*foo* even if *foo* doesn't exist, so you need to type carefully.

**Choosing modules to compile**

Most modules are compiled by default and have to be disabled explicitly or by using the keywords `few` or `none` (see `--enable-modules`, `--enable-mods-shared` and `--enable-mods-static` below for further explanation) to be removed.

Other modules are not compiled by default and have to be enabled explicitly or by using the keywords `all` or `reallyall` to be available.

To find out which modules are compiled by default, run `./configure -h` or `./configure --help` and look under `Optional Features`. Suppose you are interested in `mod_example1` and `mod_example2`, and you see this:

```
Optional Features:
  ...
  --disable-example1    example module 1
  --enable-example2     example module 2
  ...
```

Then `mod_example1` is enabled by default, and you would use `--disable-example1` to not compile it. `mod_example2` is disabled by default, and you would use `--enable-example2` to compile it.

**Multi-Processing Modules**

Multi-Processing Modules (p. 90) , or MPMs, implement the basic behavior of the server. A single MPM must be active in order for the server to function. The list of available MPMs appears on the module index page (p. 1101) .

MPMs can be built as DSOs for dynamic loading or statically linked with the server, and are enabled using the following options:

**--with-mpm=MPM** Choose the default MPM for your server. If MPMs are built as DSO modules (see `--enable-mpms-shared`), this directive selects the MPM which will be loaded in the default configuration file. Otherwise, this directive selects the only available MPM, which will be statically linked into the server.

If this option is omitted, the default MPM (p. 90) for your operating system will be used.

**--enable-mpms-shared=*MPM-LIST*** Enable a list of MPMs as dynamic shared modules. One of these modules must be loaded dynamically using the LOADMODULE directive.

*MPM-LIST* is a space-separated list of MPM names enclosed by quotation marks. For example:

```
--enable-mpms-shared='prefork worker'
```

Additionally you can use the special keyword `all`, which will select all MPMs which support dynamic loading on the current platform and build them as DSO modules. For example:

```
--enable-mpms-shared=all
```

**Third-party modules**

To add additional third-party modules use the following options:

**--with-module=***module-type***:***module-file***[,** *module-type***:***module-file***]** Add one or more third-party modules to the list of statically linked modules. The module source file *module-file* will be searched in the modules/*module-type* subdirectory of your Apache HTTP server source tree. If it is not found there configure is considering *module-file* to be an absolute file path and tries to copy the source file into the *module-type* subdirectory. If the subdirectory doesn't exist it will be created and populated with a standard Makefile.in.

This option is useful to add small external modules consisting of one source file. For more complex modules you should read the vendor's documentation.

**Note**

If you want to build a DSO module instead of a statically linked use apxs.

**Cumulative and other options**

**--enable-maintainer-mode** Turn on debugging and compile time warnings and load all compiled modules.

**--enable-mods-shared=***MODULE-LIST* Defines a list of modules to be enabled and build as dynamic shared modules. This mean, these module have to be loaded dynamically by using the LOADMODULE directive.

*MODULE-LIST* is a space separated list of modulenames enclosed by quotation marks. The module names are given without the preceding mod_. For example:

```
--enable-mods-shared='headers rewrite dav'
```

Additionally you can use the special keywords reallyall, all, most, few and none. For example,

```
--enable-mods-shared=most
```

will compile most modules and build them as DSO modules,

```
--enable-mods-shared=few
```

will only compile a very basic set of modules.

The default set is most.

The LOADMODULE directives for the chosen modules will be automatically generated in the main configuration file. By default, all those directives will be commented out except for the modules that are either required or explicitly selected by a configure --enable-foo argument. You can change the set of loaded modules by activating or deactivating the LOADMODULE directives in httpd.conf. In addition the LOADMODULE directives for all built modules can be activated via the configure option --enable-load-all-modules.

**--enable-mods-static=***MODULE-LIST* This option behaves similar to --enable-mods-shared, but will link the given modules statically. This mean, these modules will always be present while running httpd. They need not be loaded with LOADMODULE.

**--enable-modules=***MODULE-LIST* This option behaves like to --enable-mods-shared, and will also link the given modules dynamically. The special keyword none disables the build of all modules.

**--enable-v4-mapped** Allow IPv6 sockets to handle IPv4 connections.

**--with-port=***PORT* This defines the port on which httpd will listen. This port number is used when generating the configuration file httpd.conf. The default is 80.

**--with-program-name** Define an alternative executable name. The default is httpd.

**Optional packages**

These options are used to define optional packages.

**General syntax**

Generally you can use the following syntax to define an optional package:

**--with-*PACKAGE*[=*ARG*]**  Use the package *PACKAGE*. The default value for *ARG* is yes.

**--without-*PACKAGE***  Do not use the package *PACKAGE*. This is the same as --with-*PACKAGE*=no. This
option is provided by autoconf but not very useful for the Apache HTTP Server.

**Specific packages**

**--with-apr=*DIR*|*FILE***  The Apache Portable Runtime (APR) is part of the httpd source distribution and will
automatically be build together with the HTTP server. If you want to use an already installed APR instead you
have to tell configure the path to the apr-config script. You may set the absolute path and name or the
directory to the installed APR. apr-config must exist within this directory or the subdirectory bin.

**--with-apr-util=*DIR*|*FILE***  The Apache Portable Runtime Utilities (APU) are part of the httpd source distri-
bution and will automatically be build together with the HTTP server. If you want to use an already installed
APU instead you have to tell configure the path to the apu-config script. You may set the absolute
path and name or the directory to the installed APU. apu-config must exist within this directory or the
subdirectory bin.

**--with-ssl=*DIR***  If MOD_SSL has been enabled configure searches for an installed OpenSSL. You can set the
directory path to the SSL/TLS toolkit instead.

**--with-z=*DIR***  configure searches automatically for an installed zlib library if your source configuration
requires one (e.g., when MOD_DEFLATE is enabled). You can set the directory path to the compression library
instead.

Several features of the Apache HTTP Server, including MOD_AUTHN_DBM and MOD_REWRITE's DBM
REWRITEMAP use simple key/value databases for quick lookups of information. SDBM is included in the APU,
so this database is always available. If you would like to use other database types, use the following options to enable
them:

**--with-gdbm[=*path*]**  If no *path* is specified, configure will search for the include files and libraries of a GNU
DBM installation in the usual search paths. An explicit *path* will cause configure to look in *path*/lib and
*path*/include for the relevant files. Finally, the *path* may specify specific include and library paths separated
by a colon.

**--with-ndbm[=*path*]**  Like --with-gdbm, but searches for a New DBM installation.

**--with-berkeley-db[=*path*]**  Like --with-gdbm, but searches for a Berkeley DB installation.

Note

> The DBM options are provided by the APU and passed through to its configuration script.
> They are useless when using an already installed APU defined by --with-apr-util.
> You may use more then one DBM implementation together with your HTTP server. The ap-
> propriated DBM type will be configured within the runtime configuration at each time.

**Options for support programs**

**--enable-static-support** Build a statically linked version of the support binaries. This means, a stand-alone executable will be built with all the necessary libraries integrated. Otherwise the support binaries are linked dynamically by default.

**--enable-suexec** Use this option to enable `suexec`, which allows you to set uid and gid for spawned processes. **Do not use this option unless you understand all the security implications of running a suid binary on your server.** Further options to configure `suexec` are described below.

It is possible to create a statically linked binary of a single support program by using the following options:

**--enable-static-ab** Build a statically linked version of `ab`.

**--enable-static-checkgid** Build a statically linked version of `checkgid`.

**--enable-static-htdbm** Build a statically linked version of `htdbm`.

**--enable-static-htdigest** Build a statically linked version of `htdigest`.

**--enable-static-htpasswd** Build a statically linked version of `htpasswd`.

**--enable-static-logresolve** Build a statically linked version of `logresolve`.

**--enable-static-rotatelogs** Build a statically linked version of `rotatelogs`.

**suexec configuration options**

The following options are used to fine tune the behavior of `suexec`. See Configuring and installing suEXEC (p. 335) for further information.

**--with-suexec-bin** This defines the path to `suexec` binary. Default is `--sbindir` (see Fine tuning of installation directories).

**--with-suexec-caller** This defines the user allowed to call `suexec`. It should be the same as the user under which `httpd` normally runs.

**--with-suexec-docroot** This defines the directory tree under which `suexec` access is allowed for executables. Default value is `--datadir/htdocs`.

**--with-suexec-gidmin** Define this as the lowest GID allowed to be a target user for `suexec`. The default value is 100.

**--with-suexec-logfile** This defines the filename of the `suexec` logfile. By default the logfile is named `suexec_log` and located in `--logfiledir`.

**--with-suexec-safepath** Define the value of the environment variable `PATH` to be set for processes started by `suexec`. Default value is `/usr/local/bin:/usr/bin:/bin`.

**--with-suexec-userdir** This defines the subdirectory under the user's directory that contains all executables for which `suexec` access is allowed. This setting is necessary when you want to use `suexec` together with user-specific directories (as provided by MOD_USERDIR). The default is `public_html`.

**--with-suexec-uidmin** Define this as the lowest UID allowed to be a target user for `suexec`. The default value is 100.

**--with-suexec-umask** Set `umask` for processes started by `suexec`. It defaults to your system settings.

## Environment variables

There are some useful environment variables to override the choices made by `configure` or to help it to find libraries and programs with nonstandard names or locations.

**CC** Define the C compiler command to be used for compilation.

**CFLAGS** Set C compiler flags you want to use for compilation.

**CPP** Define the C preprocessor command to be used.

**CPPFLAGS** Set C/C++ preprocessor flags, e.g. `-Iincludedir` if you have headers in a nonstandard directory *includedir*.

**LDFLAGS** Set linker flags, e.g. `-Llibdir` if you have libraries in a nonstandard directory *libdir*.

## 8.7 dbmmanage - Manage user authentication files in DBM format

dbmmanage is used to create and update the DBM format files used to store usernames and password for basic authentication of HTTP users via MOD_AUTHN_DBM. Resources available from the Apache HTTP server can be restricted to just the users listed in the files created by dbmmanage. This program can only be used when the usernames are stored in a DBM file. To use a flat-file database see htpasswd.

Another tool to maintain a DBM password database is htdbm.

This manual page only lists the command line arguments. For details of the directives necessary to configure user authentication in httpd see the httpd manual, which is part of the Apache distribution or can be found at http://httpd.apache.org/.

**See also**

- httpd
- htdbm
- MOD_AUTHN_DBM
- MOD_AUTHZ_DBM

### Synopsis

**dbmmanage** [ *encoding* ] *filename* add|adduser|check|delete|update *username* [ *encpasswd* [ *group*[,*group*...] [ *comment* ] ] ]

**dbmmanage** *filename* view [ *username* ]

**dbmmanage** *filename* import

### Options

**filename** The filename of the DBM format file. Usually without the extension .db, .pag, or .dir.

**username** The user for which the operations are performed. The *username* may not contain a colon (:).

**encpasswd** This is the already encrypted password to use for the update and add commands. You may use a hyphen (−) if you want to get prompted for the password, but fill in the fields afterwards. Additionally when using the update command, a period (.) keeps the original password untouched.

**group** A group, which the user is member of. A groupname may not contain a colon (:). You may use a hyphen (−) if you don't want to assign the user to a group, but fill in the comment field. Additionally when using the update command, a period (.) keeps the original groups untouched.

**comment** This is the place for your opaque comments about the user, like realname, mailaddress or such things. The server will ignore this field.

### Encodings

**−d** crypt encryption (default, except on Win32, Netware)

**−m** MD5 encryption (default on Win32, Netware)

**−s** SHA1 encryption

**−p** plaintext (*not recommended*)

**Commands**

**add** Adds an entry for *username* to *filename* using the encrypted password *encpasswd*.

```
dbmmanage passwords.dat add rbowen foKntnEF3KSXA
```

**adduser** Asks for a password and then adds an entry for *username* to *filename*.

```
dbmmanage passwords.dat adduser krietz
```

**check** Asks for a password and then checks if *username* is in *filename* and if it's password matches the specified one.

```
dbmmanage passwords.dat check rbowen
```

**delete** Deletes the *username* entry from *filename*.

```
dbmmanage passwords.dat delete rbowen
```

**import** Reads *username:password* entries (one per line) from STDIN and adds them to *filename*. The passwords already have to be crypted.

**update** Same as the adduser command, except that it makes sure *username* already exists in *filename*.

```
dbmmanage passwords.dat update rbowen
```

**view** Just displays the contents of the DBM file. If you specify a *username*, it displays the particular record only.

```
dbmmanage passwords.dat view
```

## Bugs

One should be aware that there are a number of different DBM file formats in existence, and with all likelihood, libraries for more than one format may exist on your system. The three primary examples are SDBM, NDBM, the GNU project's GDBM, and Berkeley DB 2. Unfortunately, all these libraries use different file formats, and you must make sure that the file format used by *filename* is the same format that dbmmanage expects to see. dbmmanage currently has no way of determining what type of DBM file it is looking at. If used against the wrong format, will simply return nothing, or may create a different DBM file with a different name, or at worst, it may corrupt the DBM file if you were attempting to write to it.

dbmmanage has a list of DBM format preferences, defined by the @AnyDBM::ISA array near the beginning of the program. Since we prefer the Berkeley DB 2 file format, the order in which dbmmanage will look for system libraries is Berkeley DB 2, then NDBM, then GDBM and then SDBM. The first library found will be the library dbmmanage will attempt to use for all DBM file transactions. This ordering is slightly different than the standard @AnyDBM::ISA ordering in Perl, as well as the ordering used by the simple dbmopen() call in Perl, so if you use any other utilities to manage your DBM files, they must also follow this preference ordering. Similar care must be taken if using programs in other languages, like C, to access these files.

One can usually use the file program supplied with most Unix systems to see what format a DBM file is in.

# 8.8 fcgistarter - Start a FastCGI program

**See also**

- MOD_PROXY_FCGI

## Note

Currently only works on Unix systems.

## Synopsis

**fcgistarter** **-c** *command* **-p** *port* [ **-i** *interface* ] **-N** *num*

## Options

**-c** *command* FastCGI program

**-p** *port* Port which the program will listen on

**-i** *interface* Interface which the program will listen on

**-N** *num* Number of instances of the program

## 8.9   firehose - Demultiplex a firehose stream

firehose demultiplexes the given stream of multiplexed connections, and writes each connection to an individual file.

When writing to files, each connection is placed into a dedicated file named after the UUID of the connection within the stream. Separate files will be created if requests and responses are found in the stream.

If an optional prefix is specified as a parameter, connections that start with the given prefix will be included. The prefix needs to fit completely within the first fragment for a successful match to occur.

**See also**

- MOD_FIREHOSE

### Synopsis

**firehose** [ **-f** *input* ] [ **-o** *output-directory* ] [ **-u** *uuid* ] [ **-h** ] [ **--version** ]
[*prefix1* [...]]

### Options

**--file, -f** *filename* File to read the firehose from. Defaults to stdin.

**--output-directory, -o** *output-directory* Directory to write demultiplexed connections to.

**--uuid, -u** *uuid* The UUID of the connection to demultiplex. Can be specified more than once. If not specified, all UUIDs will be demultiplexed.

**--help, -h** This help text.

**--version** Display the version of the program.

## 8.10   htcacheclean - Clean up the disk cache

htcacheclean is used to keep the size of MOD_CACHE_DISK's storage within a given size limit, or limit on inodes in use. This tool can run either manually or in daemon mode. When running in daemon mode, it sleeps in the background and checks the cache directory at regular intervals for cached content to be removed. You can stop the daemon cleanly by sending it a TERM or INT signal. When run manually, a once off check of the cache directory is made for cached content to be removed. If one or more URLs are specified, each URL will be deleted from the cache, if present.

**See also**

* MOD_CACHE_DISK

### Synopsis

htcacheclean [ -D ] [ -v ] [ -t ] [ -r ] [ -n ] [ -R*round* ] -p*path* [-l*limit*| -L*limit*]

htcacheclean [ -n ] [ -t ] [ -i ] [ -P*pidfile* ] [ -R*round* ] -d*interval* -p*path* [-l*limit*| -L*limit*]

htcacheclean [ -v ] [ -R*round* ] -p*path* [ -a ] [ -A ]

htcacheclean [ -D ] [ -v ] [ -t ] [ -R*round* ] -p*path* *url*

### Options

**-d*interval*** Daemonize and repeat cache cleaning every *interval* minutes. This option is mutually exclusive with the -D, -v and -r options. To shutdown the daemon cleanly, just send it a SIGTERM or SIGINT.

**-D** Do a dry run and don't delete anything. This option is mutually exclusive with the -d option. When doing a dry run and deleting directories with -t, the inodes reported deleted in the stats cannot take into account the directories deleted, and will be marked as an estimate.

**-v** Be verbose and print statistics. This option is mutually exclusive with the -d option.

**-r** Clean thoroughly. This assumes that the Apache web server is not running (otherwise you may get garbage in the cache). This option is mutually exclusive with the -d option and implies the -t option.

**-n** Be nice. This causes slower processing in favour of other processes. htcacheclean will sleep from time to time so that (a) the disk IO will be delayed and (b) the kernel can schedule other processes in the meantime.

**-t** Delete all empty directories. By default only cache files are removed, however with some configurations the large number of directories created may require attention. If your configuration requires a very large number of directories, to the point that inode or file allocation table exhaustion may become an issue, use of this option is advised.

**-p*path*** Specify *path* as the root directory of the disk cache. This should be the same value as specified with the CacheRoot directive.

**-P*pidfile*** Specify *pidfile* as the name of the file to write the process ID to when daemonized.

**-R*round*** Specify *round* as the amount to round sizes up to, to compensate for disk block sizes. Set to the block size of the cache partition.

**-l*limit*** Specify *limit* as the total disk cache size limit. The value is expressed in bytes by default (or attaching B to the number). Attach K for Kbytes or M for MBytes.

**-L***limit* Specify *limit* as the total disk cache inode limit.

**-i** Be intelligent and run only when there was a modification of the disk cache. This option is only possible together with the −d option.

**-a** List the URLs currently stored in the cache. Variants of the same URL will be listed once for each variant.

**-A** List the URLs currently stored in the cache, along with their attributes in the following order: url, header size, body size, status, entity version, date, expiry, request time, response time, body present, head request.

## Deleting a specific URL

If htcacheclean is passed one or more URLs, each URL will be deleted from the cache. If multiple variants of an URL exists, all variants would be deleted.

When a reverse proxied URL is to be deleted, the effective URL is constructed from the **Host** header, the **port**, the **path** and the **query**. Note the '?' in the URL must always be specified explicitly, whether a query string is present or not. For example, an attempt to delete the path **/** from the server **localhost**, the URL to delete would be **http://localhost:80/?**.

## Listing URLs in the Cache

By passing the −a or −A options to htcacheclean, the URLs within the cache will be listed as they are found, one URL per line. The −A option dumps the full cache entry after the URL, with fields in the following order:

**url** The URL of the entry.

**header size** The size of the header in bytes.

**body size** The size of the body in bytes.

**status** Status of the cached response.

**entity version** The number of times this entry has been revalidated without being deleted.

**date** Date of the response.

**expiry** Expiry date of the response.

**request time** Time of the start of the request.

**response time** Time of the end of the request.

**body present** If 0, no body is stored with this request, 1 otherwise.

**head request** If 1, the entry contains a cached HEAD request with no body, 0 otherwise.

## Exit Status

htcacheclean returns a zero status ("true") if all operations were successful, 1 otherwise. If an URL is specified, and the URL was cached and successfully removed, 0 is returned, 2 otherwise. If an error occurred during URL removal, 1 is returned.

## 8.11   htdbm - Manipulate DBM password databases

htdbm is used to manipulate the DBM format files used to store usernames and password for basic authentication of HTTP users via MOD_AUTHN_DBM. See the dbmmanage documentation for more information about these DBM files.

**See also**

- httpd
- dbmmanage
- MOD_AUTHN_DBM

## Synopsis

htdbm [ -T*DBTYPE* ] [ -i ] [ -c ] [ -m | -B | -d | -s | -p ] [ -C *cost* ] [ -t ] [ -v ] *filename username*

htdbm -b [ -T*DBTYPE* ] [ -c ] [ -m | -B | -d | -s | -p ] [ -C *cost* ] [ -t ] [ -v ] *filename username password*

htdbm -n [ -i ] [ -c ] [ -m | -B | -d | -s | -p ] [ -C *cost* ] [ -t ] [ -v ] *username*

htdbm -nb [ -c ] [ -m | -B | -d | -s | -p ] [ -C *cost* ] [ -t ] [ -v ] *username password*

htdbm -v [ -T*DBTYPE* ] [ -i ] [ -c ] [ -m | -B | -d | -s | -p ] [ -C *cost* ] [ -t ] [ -v ] *filename username*

htdbm -vb [ -T*DBTYPE* ] [ -c ] [ -m | -B | -d | -s | -p ] [ -C *cost* ] [ -t ] [ -v ] *filename username password*

htdbm -x [ -T*DBTYPE* ] *filename username*

htdbm -l [ -T*DBTYPE* ]

## Options

**-b** Use batch mode; *i.e.*, get the password from the command line rather than prompting for it. This option should be used with extreme care, since **the password is clearly visible** on the command line. For script use see the -i option.

**-i** Read the password from stdin without verification (for script usage).

**-c** Create the *passwdfile*. If *passwdfile* already exists, it is rewritten and truncated. This option cannot be combined with the -n option.

**-n** Display the results on standard output rather than updating a database. This option changes the syntax of the command line, since the *passwdfile* argument (usually the first one) is omitted. It cannot be combined with the -c option.

**-m** Use MD5 encryption for passwords. On Windows and Netware, this is the default.

**-B** Use bcrypt encryption for passwords. This is currently considered to be very secure.

**-C** This flag is only allowed in combination with -B (bcrypt encryption). It sets the computing time used for the bcrypt algorithm (higher is more secure but slower, default: 5, valid: 4 to 31).

**-d** Use `crypt()` encryption for passwords. The default on all platforms but Windows and Netware. Though possibly supported by `htdbm` on all platforms, it is not supported by the `httpd` server on Windows and Netware. This algorithm is **insecure** by today's standards.

**-s** Use SHA encryption for passwords. Facilitates migration from/to Netscape servers using the LDAP Directory Interchange Format (ldif). This algorithm is **insecure** by today's standards.

**-p** Use plaintext passwords. Though `htdbm` will support creation on all platforms, the `httpd` daemon will only accept plain text passwords on Windows and Netware.

**-l** Print each of the usernames and comments from the database on stdout.

**-v** Verify the username and password. The program will print a message indicating whether the supplied password is valid. If the password is invalid, the program exits with error code 3.

**-x** Delete user. If the username exists in the specified DBM file, it will be deleted.

**-t** Interpret the final parameter as a comment. When this option is specified, an additional string can be appended to the command line; this string will be stored in the "Comment" field of the database, associated with the specified username.

*filename* The filename of the DBM format file. Usually without the extension `.db`, `.pag`, or `.dir`. If `-c` is given, the DBM file is created if it does not already exist, or updated if it does exist.

*username* The username to create or update in *passwdfile*. If *username* does not exist in this file, an entry is added. If it does exist, the password is changed.

*password* The plaintext password to be encrypted and stored in the DBM file. Used only with the `-b` flag.

*-TDBTYPE* Type of DBM file (SDBM, GDBM, DB, or `"default"`).

## Bugs

One should be aware that there are a number of different DBM file formats in existence, and with all likelihood, libraries for more than one format may exist on your system. The three primary examples are SDBM, NDBM, GNU GDBM, and Berkeley/Sleepycat DB 2/3/4. Unfortunately, all these libraries use different file formats, and you must make sure that the file format used by *filename* is the same format that `htdbm` expects to see. `htdbm` currently has no way of determining what type of DBM file it is looking at. If used against the wrong format, will simply return nothing, or may create a different DBM file with a different name, or at worst, it may corrupt the DBM file if you were attempting to write to it.

One can usually use the `file` program supplied with most Unix systems to see what format a DBM file is in.

## Exit Status

`htdbm` returns a zero status (`"true"`) if the username and password have been successfully added or updated in the DBM File. `htdbm` returns 1 if it encounters some problem accessing files, 2 if there was a syntax problem with the command line, 3 if the password was entered interactively and the verification entry didn't match, 4 if its operation was interrupted, 5 if a value is too long (username, filename, password, or final computed record), 6 if the username contains illegal characters (see the Restrictions section), and 7 if the file is not a valid DBM password file.

## Examples

```
htdbm /usr/local/etc/apache/.htdbm-users jsmith
```

Adds or modifies the password for user `jsmith`. The user is prompted for the password. If executed on a Windows system, the password will be encrypted using the modified Apache MD5 algorithm; otherwise, the system's `crypt()` routine will be used. If the file does not exist, `htdbm` will do nothing except return an error.

```
htdbm -c /home/doe/public_html/.htdbm jane
```

Creates a new file and stores a record in it for user `jane`. The user is prompted for the password. If the file exists and cannot be read, or cannot be written, it is not altered and `htdbm` will display a message and return an error status.

```
htdbm -mb /usr/web/.htdbm-all jones Pwd4Steve
```

Encrypts the password from the command line (`Pwd4Steve`) using the MD5 algorithm, and stores it in the specified file.

## Security Considerations

Web password files such as those managed by `htdbm` should *not* be within the Web server's URI space – that is, they should not be fetchable with a browser.

The use of the `-b` option is discouraged, since when it is used the unencrypted password appears on the command line.

When using the `crypt()` algorithm, note that only the first 8 characters of the password are used to form the password. If the supplied password is longer, the extra characters will be silently discarded.

The SHA encryption format does not use salting: for a given password, there is only one encrypted representation. The `crypt()` and MD5 formats permute the representation by prepending a random salt string, to make dictionary attacks against the passwords more difficult.

The SHA and `crypt()` formats are insecure by today's standards.

## Restrictions

On the Windows platform, passwords encrypted with `htdbm` are limited to no more than 255 characters in length. Longer passwords will be truncated to 255 characters.

The MD5 algorithm used by `htdbm` is specific to the Apache software; passwords encrypted using it will not be usable with other Web servers.

Usernames are limited to 255 bytes and may not include the character :.

# 8.12  htdigest - manage user files for digest authentication

`htdigest` is used to create and update the flat-files used to store usernames, realm and password for digest authentication of HTTP users. Resources available from the Apache HTTP server can be restricted to just the users listed in the files created by `htdigest`.

This manual page only lists the command line arguments. For details of the directives necessary to configure digest authentication in `httpd` see the Apache manual, which is part of the Apache distribution or can be found at http://httpd.apache.org/.

**See also**

- `httpd`
- MOD_AUTH_DIGEST

## Synopsis

**htdigest** [ **-c** ] *passwdfile realm username*

## Options

**-c** Create the *passwdfile*. If *passwdfile* already exists, it is deleted first.

**passwdfile** Name of the file to contain the username, realm and password. If -c is given, this file is created if it does not already exist, or deleted and recreated if it does exist.

**realm** The realm name to which the user name belongs. See

http://tools.ietf.org/html/rfc2617#section-3.2.1[1] for more details.

**username** The user name to create or update in *passwdfile*. If *username* does not exist is this file, an entry is added. If it does exist, the password is changed.

## Security Considerations

This program is not safe as a setuid executable. Do *not* make it setuid.

---

[1]http://tools.ietf.org/html/rfc2617#section-3.2.1

## 8.13 htpasswd - Manage user files for basic authentication

htpasswd is used to create and update the flat-files used to store usernames and password for basic authentication of HTTP users. If htpasswd cannot access a file, such as not being able to write to the output file or not being able to read the file in order to update it, it returns an error status and makes no changes.

Resources available from the Apache HTTP server can be restricted to just the users listed in the files created by htpasswd. This program can only manage usernames and passwords stored in a flat-file. It can encrypt and display password information for use in other types of data stores, though. To use a DBM database see dbmmanage or htdbm.

htpasswd encrypts passwords using either bcrypt, a version of MD5 modified for Apache, SHA1, or the system's crypt() routine. Files managed by htpasswd may contain a mixture of different encoding types of passwords; some user records may have bcrypt or MD5-encrypted passwords while others in the same file may have passwords encrypted with crypt().

This manual page only lists the command line arguments. For details of the directives necessary to configure user authentication in httpd see the Apache manual, which is part of the Apache distribution or can be found at http://httpd.apache.org/[2].

**See also**

- httpd
- htdbm
- The scripts in support/SHA1 which come with the distribution.

## Synopsis

**htpasswd** [ **-c** ] [ **-i** ] [ **-m** | **-B** | **-d** | **-s** | **-p** ] [ **-C** *cost* ] [ **-D** ] [ **-v** ] *passwdfile username*

**htpasswd -b** [ **-c** ] [ **-m** | **-B** | **-d** | **-s** | **-p** ] [ **-C** *cost* ] [ **-D** ] [ **-v** ] *passwdfile username password*

**htpasswd -n** [ **-i** ] [ **-m** | **-B** | **-d** | **-s** | **-p** ] [ **-C** *cost* ] *username*

**htpasswd -nb** [ **-m** | **-B** | **-d** | **-s** | **-p** ] [ **-C** *cost* ] *username password*

## Options

**-b** Use batch mode; *i.e.*, get the password from the command line rather than prompting for it. This option should be used with extreme care, since **the password is clearly visible** on the command line. For script use see the -i option.
Available in 2.4.4 and later.

**-i** Read the password from stdin without verification (for script usage).

**-c** Create the *passwdfile*. If *passwdfile* already exists, it is rewritten and truncated. This option cannot be combined with the -n option.

**-n** Display the results on standard output rather than updating a file. This is useful for generating password records acceptable to Apache for inclusion in non-text data stores. This option changes the syntax of the command line, since the *passwdfile* argument (usually the first one) is omitted. It cannot be combined with the -c option.

**-m** Use MD5 encryption for passwords. This is the default (since version 2.2.18).

---

[2]http://httpd.apache.org

**-B** Use bcrypt encryption for passwords. This is currently considered to be very secure.

**-C** This flag is only allowed in combination with -B (bcrypt encryption). It sets the computing time used for the bcrypt algorithm (higher is more secure but slower, default: 5, valid: 4 to 31).

**-d** Use crypt() encryption for passwords. This is not supported by the httpd server on Windows and Netware. This algorithm limits the password length to 8 characters. This algorithm is **insecure** by today's standards. It used to be the default algorithm until version 2.2.17.

**-s** Use SHA encryption for passwords. Facilitates migration from/to Netscape servers using the LDAP Directory Interchange Format (ldif). This algorithm is **insecure** by today's standards.

**-p** Use plaintext passwords. Though htpasswd will support creation on all platforms, the httpd daemon will only accept plain text passwords on Windows and Netware.

**-D** Delete user. If the username exists in the specified htpasswd file, it will be deleted.

**-v** Verify password. Verify that the given password matches the password of the user stored in the specified htpasswd file.
Available in 2.4.5 and later.

***passwdfile*** Name of the file to contain the user name and password. If -c is given, this file is created if it does not already exist, or rewritten and truncated if it does exist.

***username*** The username to create or update in *passwdfile*. If *username* does not exist in this file, an entry is added. If it does exist, the password is changed.

***password*** The plaintext password to be encrypted and stored in the file. Only used with the -b flag.

## Exit Status

htpasswd returns a zero status ("true") if the username and password have been successfully added or updated in the *passwdfile*. htpasswd returns 1 if it encounters some problem accessing files, 2 if there was a syntax problem with the command line, 3 if the password was entered interactively and the verification entry didn't match, 4 if its operation was interrupted, 5 if a value is too long (username, filename, password, or final computed record), 6 if the username contains illegal characters (see the Restrictions section), and 7 if the file is not a valid password file.

## Examples

```
htpasswd /usr/local/etc/apache/.htpasswd-users jsmith
```

Adds or modifies the password for user jsmith. The user is prompted for the password. The password will be encrypted using the modified Apache MD5 algorithm. If the file does not exist, htpasswd will do nothing except return an error.

```
htpasswd -c /home/doe/public_html/.htpasswd jane
```

Creates a new file and stores a record in it for user jane. The user is prompted for the password. If the file exists and cannot be read, or cannot be written, it is not altered and htpasswd will display a message and return an error status.

```
htpasswd -db /usr/web/.htpasswd-all jones Pwd4Steve
```

Encrypts the password from the command line (Pwd4Steve) using the crypt() algorithm, and stores it in the specified file.

## Security Considerations

Web password files such as those managed by `htpasswd` should *not* be within the Web server's URI space – that is, they should not be fetchable with a browser.

This program is not safe as a setuid executable. Do *not* make it setuid.

The use of the `-b` option is discouraged, since when it is used the unencrypted password appears on the command line.

When using the `crypt()` algorithm, note that only the first 8 characters of the password are used to form the password. If the supplied password is longer, the extra characters will be silently discarded.

The SHA encryption format does not use salting: for a given password, there is only one encrypted representation. The `crypt()` and MD5 formats permute the representation by prepending a random salt string, to make dictionary attacks against the passwords more difficult.

The SHA and `crypt()` formats are insecure by today's standards.

## Restrictions

On the Windows platform, passwords encrypted with `htpasswd` are limited to no more than `255` characters in length. Longer passwords will be truncated to 255 characters.

The MD5 algorithm used by `htpasswd` is specific to the Apache software; passwords encrypted using it will not be usable with other Web servers.

Usernames are limited to `255` bytes and may not include the character `:`.

# 8.14   httxt2dbm - Generate dbm files for use with RewriteMap

httxt2dbm is used to generate dbm files from text input, for use in REWRITEMAP with the dbm map type.

If the output file already exists, it will not be truncated. New keys will be added and existing keys will be updated.

**See also**

- httpd
- MOD_REWRITE

## Synopsis

**httxt2dbm** [ **-v** ] [ **-f** *DBM_TYPE* ] **-i** *SOURCE_TXT* **-o** *OUTPUT_DBM*

## Options

**-v** More verbose output

**-f** *DBM_TYPE* Specify the DBM type to be used for the output. If not specified, will use the APR Default. Available types are: GDBM for GDBM files, SDBM for SDBM files, DB for berkeley DB files, NDBM for NDBM files, default for the default DBM type.

**-i** *SOURCE_TXT* Input file from which the dbm is to be created. The file should be formated with one record per line, of the form: key value. See the documentation for REWRITEMAP for further details of this file's format and meaning.

**-o** *OUTPUT_DBM* Name of the output dbm files.

## Examples

```
httxt2dbm -i rewritemap.txt -o rewritemap.dbm
httxt2dbm -f SDBM -i rewritemap.txt -o rewritemap.dbm
```

## 8.15   logresolve - Resolve IP-addresses to hostnames in Apache log files

`logresolve` is a post-processing program to resolve IP-addresses in Apache's access logfiles. To minimize impact on your nameserver, logresolve has its very own internal hash-table cache. This means that each IP number will only be looked up the first time it is found in the log file.

Takes an Apache log file on standard input. The IP addresses must be the first thing on each line and must be separated from the remainder of the line by a space.

### Synopsis

**logresolve** [ **-s** *filename* ] [ **-c** ] < *access_log* > *access_log.new*

### Options

**-s *filename*** Specifies a filename to record statistics.

**-c** This causes `logresolve` to apply some DNS checks: after finding the hostname from the IP address, it looks up the IP addresses for the hostname and checks that one of these matches the original address.

# 8.16   log_server_status - Log periodic status summaries

This perl script is designed to be run at a frequent interval by something like cron. It connects to the server and downloads the status information. It reformats the information to a single line and logs it to a file. Adjust the variables at the top of the script to specify the location of the resulting logfile. MOD_STATUS will need to be loaded and configured in order for this script to do its job.

## Usage

The script contains the following section.

```
my $wherelog = "/usr/local/apache2/logs/";  # Logs will be like "/usr/local/apache2/logs/1
my $server   = "localhost";        # Name of server, could be "www.foo.com"
my $port     = "80";               # Port on server
my $request  = "/server-status/?auto";   # Request to send
```

You'll need to ensure that these variables have the correct values, and you'll need to have the /server-status handler configured at the location specified, and the specified log location needs to be writable by the user which will run the script.

Run the script periodically via cron to produce a daily log file, which can then be used for statistical analysis.

# 8.17 rotatelogs - Piped logging program to rotate Apache logs

`rotatelogs` is a simple program for use in conjunction with Apache's piped logfile feature. It supports rotation based on a time interval or maximum size of the log.

## Synopsis

**rotatelogs** [ **-l** ] [ **-L** *linkname* ] [ **-p** *program* ] [ **-f** ] [ **-D** ] [ **-t** ] [ **-v** ] [ **-e** ] [ **-c** ] [ **-n** *number-of-files* ] *logfile rotationtime*|*filesize*(B|K|M|G) [ *offset* ]

## Options

**-l** Causes the use of local time rather than GMT as the base for the interval or for `strftime(3)` formatting with size-based rotation.

**-L** *linkname* Causes a hard link to be made from the current logfile to the specified link name. This can be used to watch the log continuously across rotations using a command like `tail -F linkname`.

**-p** *program* If given, `rotatelogs` will execute the specified program every time a new log file is opened. The filename of the newly opened file is passed as the first argument to the program. If executing after a rotation, the old log file is passed as the second argument. `rotatelogs` does not wait for the specified program to terminate before continuing to operate, and will not log any error code returned on termination. The spawned program uses the same stdin, stdout, and stderr as rotatelogs itself, and also inherits the environment.

**-f** Causes the logfile to be opened immediately, as soon as `rotatelogs` starts, instead of waiting for the first logfile entry to be read (for non-busy sites, there may be a substantial delay between when the server is started and when the first request is handled, meaning that the associated logfile does not "exist" until then, which causes problems from some automated logging tools)

**-D** Creates the parent directories of the path that the log file will be placed in if they do not already exist. This allows `strftime(3)` formatting to be used in the path and not just the filename.

**-t** Causes the logfile to be truncated instead of rotated. This is useful when a log is processed in real time by a command like tail, and there is no need for archived data. No suffix will be added to the filename, however format strings containing '%' characters will be respected.

**-v** Produce verbose output on STDERR. The output contains the result of the configuration parsing, and all file open and close actions.

**-e** Echo logs through to stdout. Useful when logs need to be further processed in real time by a further tool in the chain.

**-c** Create log file for each interval, even if empty.

**-n** *number-of-files* Use a circular list of filenames without timestamps. With -n 3, the series of log files opened would be "logfile", "logfile.1", "logfile.2", then overwriting "logfile".
Available in 2.4.5 and later.

*logfile* The path plus basename of the logfile. If *logfile* includes any '%' characters, it is treated as a format string for `strftime(3)`. Otherwise, the suffix *.nnnnnnnnnn* is automatically added and is the time in seconds (unless the -t option is used). Both formats compute the start time from the beginning of the current period. For example, if a rotation time of 86400 is specified, the hour, minute, and second fields created from the `strftime(3)` format will all be zero, referring to the beginning of the current 24-hour period (midnight).

When using strftime(3) filename formatting, be sure the log file format has enough granularity to produce a different file name each time the logs are rotated. Otherwise rotation will overwrite the same file instead of starting a new one. For example, if *logfile* was /var/log/errorlog.%Y-%m-%d with log rotation at 5 megabytes, but 5 megabytes was reached twice in the same day, the same log file name would be produced and log rotation would keep writing to the same file.

***rotationtime***  The time between log file rotations in seconds. The rotation occurs at the beginning of this interval. For example, if the rotation time is 3600, the log file will be rotated at the beginning of every hour; if the rotation time is 86400, the log file will be rotated every night at midnight. (If no data is logged during an interval, no file will be created.)

***filesize(B|K|M|G)***  The maximum file size in followed by exactly one of the letters B (Bytes), K (KBytes), M (MBytes) or G (GBytes).

When time and size are specified, the size must be given after the time. Rotation will occur whenever either time or size limits are reached.

***offset***  The number of minutes offset from UTC. If omitted, zero is assumed and UTC is used. For example, to use local time in the zone UTC -5 hours, specify a value of −300 for this argument. In most cases, −1 should be used instead of specifying an offset.

## Examples

```
CustomLog "|bin/rotatelogs /var/log/logfile 86400" common
```

This creates the files /var/log/logfile.nnnn where nnnn is the system time at which the log nominally starts (this time will always be a multiple of the rotation time, so you can synchronize cron scripts with it). At the end of each rotation time (here after 24 hours) a new log is started.

```
CustomLog "|bin/rotatelogs -l /var/log/logfile.%Y.%m.%d 86400" common
```

This creates the files /var/log/logfile.yyyy.mm.dd where yyyy is the year, mm is the month, and dd is the day of the month. Logging will switch to a new file every day at midnight, local time.

```
CustomLog "|bin/rotatelogs /var/log/logfile 5M" common
```

This configuration will rotate the logfile whenever it reaches a size of 5 megabytes.

```
ErrorLog "|bin/rotatelogs /var/log/errorlog.%Y-%m-%d-%H_%M_%S 5M"
```

This configuration will rotate the error logfile whenever it reaches a size of 5 megabytes, and the suffix to the logfile name will be created of the form errorlog.YYYY-mm-dd-HH_MM_SS.

```
CustomLog "|bin/rotatelogs -t /var/log/logfile 86400" common
```

This creates the file /var/log/logfile, truncating the file at startup and then truncating the file once per day. It is expected in this scenario that a separate process (such as tail) would process the file in real time.

## Portability

The following logfile format string substitutions should be supported by all strftime(3) implementations, see the strftime(3) man page for library-specific extensions.

| %A | full weekday name (localized) |
|----|-------------------------------|
| %a | 3-character weekday name (localized) |
| %B | full month name (localized) |
| %b | 3-character month name (localized) |
| %c | date and time (localized) |
| %d | 2-digit day of month |
| %H | 2-digit hour (24 hour clock) |
| %I | 2-digit hour (12 hour clock) |
| %j | 3-digit day of year |
| %M | 2-digit minute |
| %m | 2-digit month |
| %p | am/pm of 12 hour clock (localized) |
| %S | 2-digit second |
| %U | 2-digit week of year (Sunday first day of week) |
| %W | 2-digit week of year (Monday first day of week) |
| %w | 1-digit weekday (Sunday first day of week) |
| %X | time (localized) |
| %x | date (localized) |
| %Y | 4-digit year |
| %y | 2-digit year |
| %Z | time zone name |
| %% | literal '%' |

## 8.18   split-logfile - Split up multi-vhost logfiles

This perl script will take a combined Web server access log file and break its contents into separate files. It assumes that the first field of each line is the virtual host identity, put there using the "%v" variable in LOGFORMAT.

### Usage

Create a log file with virtual host information in it:

```
LogFormat "%v %h %l %u %t \"%r\" %>s %b \"%{Referer}i\" \"%{User-agent}i\"" combined_plus_
CustomLog "logs/access_log" combined_plus_vhost
```

Log files will be created, in the directory where you run the script, for each virtual host name that appears in the combined log file. These logfiles will named after the hostname, with a .log file extension.

The combined log file is read from stdin. Records read will be appended to any existing log files.

```
split-logfile < access_log
```

## 8.19 suexec - Switch user before executing external programs

`suexec` is used by the Apache HTTP Server to switch to another user before executing CGI programs. In order to achieve this, it must run as `root`. Since the HTTP daemon normally doesn't run as `root`, the `suexec` executable needs the setuid bit set and must be owned by `root`. It should never be writable for any other person than `root`.

For further information about the concepts and the security model of suexec please refer to the suexec documentation (http://httpd.apache.org/docs/trunk/suexec.html).

### Synopsis

**suexec -V**

### Options

**-V** If you are `root`, this option displays the compile options of `suexec`. For security reasons all configuration options are changeable only at compile time.

## 8.20   Other Programs

This page used to contain documentation for programs which now have their own docs pages. Please update any links.

```
log_server_status
```

```
split-logfile
```

# Chapter 9

# Apache Miscellaneous Documentation

## 9.1   Apache Miscellaneous Documentation

Below is a list of additional documentation pages that apply to the Apache web server development project.

 **Warning**
The documents below have not been fully updated to take into account changes made in the
2.1 version of the Apache HTTP Server.  Some of the information may still be relevant, but
please use it with care.

**Performance Notes - Apache Tuning (p. 339)**   Notes about how to (run-time and compile-time) configure Apache
for highest performance.  Notes explaining why Apache does some things, and why it doesn't do other things
(which make it slower/faster).

**Performance Scaling (p. 350)**   Some easily accessible configuration and tuning options for Apache httpd 2.2 and 2.4
as well as monitoring tools.

**Security Tips (p. 364)**   Some "do"s - and "don't"s - for keeping your Apache web site secure.

**Relevant Standards (p. 369)**   This document acts as a reference page for most of the relevant standards that Apache
follows.

**Password Encryption Formats (p. 371)**   Discussion of the various ciphers supported by Apache for authentication
purposes.

## 9.2 Apache Performance Tuning

Apache 2.x is a general-purpose webserver, designed to provide a balance of flexibility, portability, and performance. Although it has not been designed specifically to set benchmark records, Apache 2.x is capable of high performance in many real-world situations.

Compared to Apache 1.3, release 2.x contains many additional optimizations to increase throughput and scalability. Most of these improvements are enabled by default. However, there are compile-time and run-time configuration choices that can significantly affect performance. This document describes the options that a server administrator can configure to tune the performance of an Apache 2.x installation. Some of these configuration options enable the httpd to better take advantage of the capabilities of the hardware and OS, while others allow the administrator to trade functionality for speed.

### Hardware and Operating System Issues

The single biggest hardware issue affecting webserver performance is RAM. A webserver should never ever have to swap, as swapping increases the latency of each request beyond a point that users consider "fast enough". This causes users to hit stop and reload, further increasing the load. You can, and should, control the MAXREQUESTWORKERS setting so that your server does not spawn so many children that it starts swapping. The procedure for doing this is simple: determine the size of your average Apache process, by looking at your process list via a tool such as `top`, and divide this into your total available memory, leaving some room for other processes.

Beyond that the rest is mundane: get a fast enough CPU, a fast enough network card, and fast enough disks, where "fast enough" is something that needs to be determined by experimentation.

Operating system choice is largely a matter of local concerns. But some guidelines that have proven generally useful are:

- Run the latest stable release and patch level of the operating system that you choose. Many OS suppliers have introduced significant performance improvements to their TCP stacks and thread libraries in recent years.

- If your OS supports a `sendfile(2)` system call, make sure you install the release and/or patches needed to enable it. (With Linux, for example, this means using Linux 2.4 or later. For early releases of Solaris 8, you may need to apply a patch.) On systems where it is available, `sendfile` enables Apache 2 to deliver static content faster and with lower CPU utilization.

### Run-Time Configuration Issues

| Related Modules | Related Directives |
|---|---|
| MOD_DIR | ALLOWOVERRIDE |
| MPM_COMMON | DIRECTORYINDEX |
| MOD_STATUS | HOSTNAMELOOKUPS |
| | ENABLEMMAP |
| | ENABLESENDFILE |
| | KEEPALIVETIMEOUT |
| | MAXSPARESERVERS |
| | MINSPARESERVERS |
| | OPTIONS |
| | STARTSERVERS |

**HostnameLookups and other DNS considerations**

Prior to Apache 1.3, HOSTNAMELOOKUPS defaulted to On. This adds latency to every request because it requires a DNS lookup to complete before the request is finished. In Apache 1.3 this setting defaults to Off. If you need to have addresses in your log files resolved to hostnames, use the logresolve program that comes with Apache, or one of the numerous log reporting packages which are available.

It is recommended that you do this sort of postprocessing of your log files on some machine other than the production web server machine, in order that this activity not adversely affect server performance.

If you use any ALLOW from domain or DENY from domain directives (i.e., using a hostname, or a domain name, rather than an IP address) then you will pay for two DNS lookups (a reverse, followed by a forward lookup to make sure that the reverse is not being spoofed). For best performance, therefore, use IP addresses, rather than names, when using these directives, if possible.

Note that it's possible to scope the directives, such as within a <Location "/server-status"> section. In this case the DNS lookups are only performed on requests matching the criteria. Here's an example which disables lookups except for .html and .cgi files:

```
HostnameLookups off
<Files ~ "\.(html|cgi)$">
  HostnameLookups on
</Files>
```

But even still, if you just need DNS names in some CGIs you could consider doing the gethostbyname call in the specific CGIs that need it.

**FollowSymLinks and SymLinksIfOwnerMatch**

Wherever in your URL-space you do not have an Options FollowSymLinks, or you do have an Options SymLinksIfOwnerMatch, Apache will need to issue extra system calls to check up on symlinks. (One extra call per filename component.) For example, if you had:

```
DocumentRoot "/www/htdocs"
<Directory "/">
  Options SymLinksIfOwnerMatch
</Directory>
```

and a request is made for the URI /index.html, then Apache will perform lstat(2) on /www, /www/htdocs, and /www/htdocs/index.html. The results of these lstats are never cached, so they will occur on every single request. If you really desire the symlinks security checking, you can do something like this:

```
DocumentRoot "/www/htdocs"
<Directory "/">
  Options FollowSymLinks
</Directory>

<Directory "/www/htdocs">
  Options -FollowSymLinks +SymLinksIfOwnerMatch
</Directory>
```

This at least avoids the extra checks for the DOCUMENTROOT path. Note that you'll need to add similar sections if you have any ALIAS or REWRITERULE paths outside of your document root. For highest performance, and no symlink protection, set FollowSymLinks everywhere, and never set SymLinksIfOwnerMatch.

### AllowOverride

Wherever in your URL-space you allow overrides (typically `.htaccess` files), Apache will attempt to open `.htaccess` for each filename component. For example,

```
DocumentRoot "/www/htdocs"
<Directory "/">
  AllowOverride all
</Directory>
```

and a request is made for the URI `/index.html`. Then Apache will attempt to open `/.htaccess`, `/www/.htaccess`, and `/www/htdocs/.htaccess`. The solutions are similar to the previous case of `Options FollowSymLinks`. For highest performance use `AllowOverride None` everywhere in your filesystem.

### Negotiation

If at all possible, avoid content negotiation if you're really interested in every last ounce of performance. In practice the benefits of negotiation outweigh the performance penalties. There's one case where you can speed up the server. Instead of using a wildcard such as:

```
DirectoryIndex index
```

Use a complete list of options:

```
DirectoryIndex index.cgi index.pl index.shtml index.html
```

where you list the most common choice first.

Also note that explicitly creating a `type-map` file provides better performance than using `MultiViews`, as the necessary information can be determined by reading this single file, rather than having to scan the directory for files.

If your site needs content negotiation, consider using `type-map` files, rather than the `Options MultiViews` directive to accomplish the negotiation. See the Content Negotiation (p. 78) documentation for a full discussion of the methods of negotiation, and instructions for creating `type-map` files.

### Memory-mapping

In situations where Apache 2.x needs to look at the contents of a file being delivered–for example, when doing server-side-include processing–it normally memory-maps the file if the OS supports some form of `mmap(2)`.

On some platforms, this memory-mapping improves performance. However, there are cases where memory-mapping can hurt the performance or even the stability of the httpd:

- On some operating systems, `mmap` does not scale as well as `read(2)` when the number of CPUs increases. On multiprocessor Solaris servers, for example, Apache 2.x sometimes delivers server-parsed files faster when `mmap` is disabled.

- If you memory-map a file located on an NFS-mounted filesystem and a process on another NFS client machine deletes or truncates the file, your process may get a bus error the next time it tries to access the mapped file content.

For installations where either of these factors applies, you should use `EnableMMAP off` to disable the memory-mapping of delivered files. (Note: This directive can be overridden on a per-directory basis.)

**Sendfile**

In situations where Apache 2.x can ignore the contents of the file to be delivered – for example, when serving static file content – it normally uses the kernel sendfile support for the file if the OS supports the `sendfile(2)` operation.

On most platforms, using sendfile improves performance by eliminating separate read and send mechanics. However, there are cases where using sendfile can harm the stability of the httpd:

- Some platforms may have broken sendfile support that the build system did not detect, especially if the binaries were built on another box and moved to such a machine with broken sendfile support.
- With an NFS-mounted filesystem, the kernel may be unable to reliably serve the network file through its own cache.

For installations where either of these factors applies, you should use `EnableSendfile off` to disable sendfile delivery of file contents. (Note: This directive can be overridden on a per-directory basis.)

**Process Creation**

Prior to Apache 1.3 the MINSPARESERVERS, MAXSPARESERVERS, and STARTSERVERS settings all had drastic effects on benchmark results. In particular, Apache required a "ramp-up" period in order to reach a number of children sufficient to serve the load being applied. After the initial spawning of STARTSERVERS children, only one child per second would be created to satisfy the MINSPARESERVERS setting. So a server being accessed by 100 simultaneous clients, using the default STARTSERVERS of 5 would take on the order of 95 seconds to spawn enough children to handle the load. This works fine in practice on real-life servers because they aren't restarted frequently. But it does really poorly on benchmarks which might only run for ten minutes.

The one-per-second rule was implemented in an effort to avoid swamping the machine with the startup of new children. If the machine is busy spawning children, it can't service requests. But it has such a drastic effect on the perceived performance of Apache that it had to be replaced. As of Apache 1.3, the code will relax the one-per-second rule. It will spawn one, wait a second, then spawn two, wait a second, then spawn four, and it will continue exponentially until it is spawning 32 children per second. It will stop whenever it satisfies the MINSPARESERVERS setting.

This appears to be responsive enough that it's almost unnecessary to twiddle the MINSPARESERVERS, MAXSPARE-SERVERS and STARTSERVERS knobs. When more than 4 children are spawned per second, a message will be emitted to the ERRORLOG. If you see a lot of these errors, then consider tuning these settings. Use the MOD_STATUS output as a guide.

Related to process creation is process death induced by the MAXCONNECTIONSPERCHILD setting. By default this is 0, which means that there is no limit to the number of connections handled per child. If your configuration currently has this set to some very low number, such as 30, you may want to bump this up significantly. If you are running SunOS or an old version of Solaris, limit this to 10000 or so because of memory leaks.

When keep-alives are in use, children will be kept busy doing nothing waiting for more requests on the already open connection. The default KEEPALIVETIMEOUT of 5 seconds attempts to minimize this effect. The tradeoff here is between network bandwidth and server resources. In no event should you raise this above about 60 seconds, as most of the benefits are lost[1].

## Compile-Time Configuration Issues

**Choosing an MPM**

Apache 2.x supports pluggable concurrency models, called Multi-Processing Modules (p. 90) (MPMs). When building Apache, you must choose an MPM to use. There are platform-specific MPMs for some platforms: MPM_NETWARE,

---
[1]http://www.hpl.hp.com/techreports/Compaq-DEC/WRL-95-4.html

MPMT_OS2, and MPM_WINNT. For general Unix-type systems, there are several MPMs from which to choose. The choice of MPM can affect the speed and scalability of the httpd:

- The WORKER MPM uses multiple child processes with many threads each. Each thread handles one connection at a time. Worker generally is a good choice for high-traffic servers because it has a smaller memory footprint than the prefork MPM.

- The EVENT MPM is threaded like the Worker MPM, but is designed to allow more requests to be served simultaneously by passing off some processing work to supporting threads, freeing up the main threads to work on new requests.

- The PREFORK MPM uses multiple child processes with one thread each. Each process handles one connection at a time. On many systems, prefork is comparable in speed to worker, but it uses more memory. Prefork's threadless design has advantages over worker in some situations: it can be used with non-thread-safe third-party modules, and it is easier to debug on platforms with poor thread debugging support.

For more information on these and other MPMs, please see the MPM documentation (p. 90) .

## Modules

Since memory usage is such an important consideration in performance, you should attempt to eliminate modules that you are not actually using. If you have built the modules as DSOs (p. 68) , eliminating modules is a simple matter of commenting out the associated LoadModule directive for that module. This allows you to experiment with removing modules and seeing if your site still functions in their absence.

If, on the other hand, you have modules statically linked into your Apache binary, you will need to recompile Apache in order to remove unwanted modules.

An associated question that arises here is, of course, what modules you need, and which ones you don't. The answer here will, of course, vary from one web site to another. However, the *minimal* list of modules which you can get by with tends to include MOD_MIME, MOD_DIR, and MOD_LOG_CONFIG. mod_log_config is, of course, optional, as you can run a web site without log files. This is, however, not recommended.

## Atomic Operations

Some modules, such as MOD_CACHE and recent development builds of the worker MPM, use APR's atomic API. This API provides atomic operations that can be used for lightweight thread synchronization.

By default, APR implements these operations using the most efficient mechanism available on each target OS/CPU platform. Many modern CPUs, for example, have an instruction that does an atomic compare-and-swap (CAS) operation in hardware. On some platforms, however, APR defaults to a slower, mutex-based implementation of the atomic API in order to ensure compatibility with older CPU models that lack such instructions. If you are building Apache for one of these platforms, and you plan to run only on newer CPUs, you can select a faster atomic implementation at build time by configuring Apache with the --enable-nonportable-atomics option:

```
./buildconf
./configure --with-mpm=worker --enable-nonportable-atomics=yes
```

The --enable-nonportable-atomics option is relevant for the following platforms:

- Solaris on SPARC
  By default, APR uses mutex-based atomics on Solaris/SPARC. If you configure with --enable-nonportable-atomics, however, APR generates code that uses a SPARC v8plus opcode for fast hardware compare-and-swap. If you configure Apache with this option, the atomic operations

will be more efficient (allowing for lower CPU utilization and higher concurrency), but the resulting executable
will run only on UltraSPARC chips.

- Linux on x86
  By default, APR uses mutex-based atomics on Linux. If you configure with
  `--enable-nonportable-atomics`, however, APR generates code that uses a 486 opcode for
  fast hardware compare-and-swap. This will result in more efficient atomic operations, but the resulting
  executable will run only on 486 and later chips (and not on 386).

### mod_status and ExtendedStatus On

If you include MOD_STATUS and you also set `ExtendedStatus On` when building and running Apache, then on
every request Apache will perform two calls to `gettimeofday(2)` (or `times(2)` depending on your operating
system), and (pre-1.3) several extra calls to `time(2)`. This is all done so that the status report contains timing
indications. For highest performance, set `ExtendedStatus off` (which is the default).

### accept Serialization - Multiple Sockets

**Warning:**
This section has not been fully updated to take into account changes made in the 2.x version of
the Apache HTTP Server. Some of the information may still be relevant, but please use it with
care.

This discusses a shortcoming in the Unix socket API. Suppose your web server uses multiple LISTEN statements
to listen on either multiple ports or multiple addresses. In order to test each socket to see if a connection is ready,
Apache uses `select(2)`. `select(2)` indicates that a socket has *zero* or *at least one* connection waiting on it.
Apache's model includes multiple children, and all the idle ones test for new connections at the same time. A naive
implementation looks something like this (these examples do not match the code, they're contrived for pedagogical
purposes):

```
for (;;) {
  for (;;) {
    fd_set accept_fds;

    FD_ZERO (&accept_fds);
    for (i = first_socket; i <= last_socket; ++i) {
      FD_SET (i, &accept_fds);
    }
    rc = select (last_socket+1, &accept_fds, NULL, NULL, NULL);
    if (rc < 1) continue;
    new_connection = -1;
    for (i = first_socket; i <= last_socket; ++i) {
      if (FD_ISSET (i, &accept_fds)) {
        new_connection = accept (i, NULL, NULL);
        if (new_connection != -1) break;
      }
    }
    if (new_connection != -1) break;
  }
  process_the(new_connection);
}
```

But this naive implementation has a serious starvation problem. Recall that multiple children execute this loop at the same time, and so multiple children will block at `select` when they are in between requests. All those blocked children will awaken and return from `select` when a single request appears on any socket. (The number of children which awaken varies depending on the operating system and timing issues.) They will all then fall down into the loop and try to `accept` the connection. But only one will succeed (assuming there's still only one connection ready). The rest will be *blocked* in `accept`. This effectively locks those children into serving requests from that one socket and no other sockets, and they'll be stuck there until enough new requests appear on that socket to wake them all up. This starvation problem was first documented in PR#467[2]. There are at least two solutions.

One solution is to make the sockets non-blocking. In this case the `accept` won't block the children, and they will be allowed to continue immediately. But this wastes CPU time. Suppose you have ten idle children in `select`, and one connection arrives. Then nine of those children will wake up, try to `accept` the connection, fail, and loop back into `select`, accomplishing nothing. Meanwhile none of those children are servicing requests that occurred on other sockets until they get back up to the `select` again. Overall this solution does not seem very fruitful unless you have as many idle CPUs (in a multiprocessor box) as you have idle children (not a very likely situation).

Another solution, the one used by Apache, is to serialize entry into the inner loop. The loop looks like this (differences highlighted):

```
for (;;) {
  accept_mutex_on ();
  for (;;) {
    fd_set accept_fds;

    FD_ZERO (&accept_fds);
    for (i = first_socket; i <= last_socket; ++i) {
      FD_SET (i, &accept_fds);
    }
    rc = select (last_socket+1, &accept_fds, NULL, NULL, NULL);
    if (rc < 1) continue;
    new_connection = -1;
    for (i = first_socket; i <= last_socket; ++i) {
      if (FD_ISSET (i, &accept_fds)) {
        new_connection = accept (i, NULL, NULL);
        if (new_connection != -1) break;
      }
    }
    if (new_connection != -1) break;
  }
  accept_mutex_off ();
  process the new_connection;
}
```

The functions `accept_mutex_on` and `accept_mutex_off` implement a mutual exclusion semaphore. Only one child can have the mutex at any time. There are several choices for implementing these mutexes. The choice is defined in `src/conf.h` (pre-1.3) or `src/include/ap_config.h` (1.3 or later). Some architectures do not have any locking choice made, on these architectures it is unsafe to use multiple LISTEN directives.

The MUTEX directive can be used to change the mutex implementation of the `mpm-accept` mutex at run-time. Special considerations for different mutex implementations are documented with that directive.

Another solution that has been considered but never implemented is to partially serialize the loop – that is, let in a certain number of processes. This would only be of interest on multiprocessor boxes where it's possible that multiple

---

[2]http://bugs.apache.org/index/full/467

children could run simultaneously, and the serialization actually doesn't take advantage of the full bandwidth. This is a possible area of future investigation, but priority remains low because highly parallel web servers are not the norm.

Ideally you should run servers without multiple LISTEN statements if you want the highest performance. But read on.

### accept Serialization - Single Socket

The above is fine and dandy for multiple socket servers, but what about single socket servers? In theory they shouldn't experience any of these same problems because all children can just block in `accept(2)` until a connection arrives, and no starvation results. In practice this hides almost the same "spinning" behavior discussed above in the non-blocking solution. The way that most TCP stacks are implemented, the kernel actually wakes up all processes blocked in `accept` when a single connection arrives. One of those processes gets the connection and returns to user-space. The rest spin in the kernel and go back to sleep when they discover there's no connection for them. This spinning is hidden from the user-land code, but it's there nonetheless. This can result in the same load-spiking wasteful behavior that a non-blocking solution to the multiple sockets case can.

For this reason we have found that many architectures behave more "nicely" if we serialize even the single socket case. So this is actually the default in almost all cases. Crude experiments under Linux (2.0.30 on a dual Pentium pro 166 w/128Mb RAM) have shown that the serialization of the single socket case causes less than a 3% decrease in requests per second over unserialized single-socket. But unserialized single-socket showed an extra 100ms latency on each request. This latency is probably a wash on long haul lines, and only an issue on LANs. If you want to override the single socket serialization, you can define `SINGLE_LISTEN_UNSERIALIZED_ACCEPT`, and then single-socket servers will not serialize at all.

### Lingering Close

As discussed in draft-ietf-http-connection-00.txt[3] section 8, in order for an HTTP server to **reliably** implement the protocol, it needs to shut down each direction of the communication independently. (Recall that a TCP connection is bi-directional. Each half is independent of the other.)

When this feature was added to Apache, it caused a flurry of problems on various versions of Unix because of short-sightedness. The TCP specification does not state that the FIN_WAIT_2 state has a timeout, but it doesn't prohibit it. On systems without the timeout, Apache 1.2 induces many sockets stuck forever in the FIN_WAIT_2 state. In many cases this can be avoided by simply upgrading to the latest TCP/IP patches supplied by the vendor. In cases where the vendor has never released patches (*i.e.*, SunOS4 – although folks with a source license can patch it themselves), we have decided to disable this feature.

There are two ways to accomplish this. One is the socket option SO_LINGER. But as fate would have it, this has never been implemented properly in most TCP/IP stacks. Even on those stacks with a proper implementation (*i.e.*, Linux 2.0.31), this method proves to be more expensive (cputime) than the next solution.

For the most part, Apache implements this in a function called `lingering_close` (in `http_main.c`). The function looks roughly like this:

```
void lingering_close (int s)
{
  char junk_buffer[2048];

  /* shutdown the sending side */
  shutdown (s, 1);

  signal (SIGALRM, lingering_death);
  alarm (30);
```

---

[3]http://www.ics.uci.edu/pub/ietf/http/draft-ietf-http-connection-00.txt

```
        for (;;) {
          select (s for reading, 2 second timeout);
          if (error) break;
          if (s is ready for reading) {
            if (read (s, junk_buffer, sizeof (junk_buffer)) <= 0) {
              break;
            }
            /* just toss away whatever is here */
          }
        }

        close (s);
      }
```

This naturally adds some expense at the end of a connection, but it is required for a reliable implementation. As HTTP/1.1 becomes more prevalent, and all connections are persistent, this expense will be amortized over more requests. If you want to play with fire and disable this feature, you can define NO_LINGCLOSE, but this is not recommended at all. In particular, as HTTP/1.1 pipelined persistent connections come into use, lingering_close is an absolute necessity (and pipelined connections are faster[4], so you want to support them).

**Scoreboard File**

Apache's parent and children communicate with each other through something called the scoreboard. Ideally this should be implemented in shared memory. For those operating systems that we either have access to, or have been given detailed ports for, it typically is implemented using shared memory. The rest default to using an on-disk file. The on-disk file is not only slow, but it is unreliable (and less featured). Peruse the src/main/conf.h file for your architecture, and look for either USE_MMAP_SCOREBOARD or USE_SHMGET_SCOREBOARD. Defining one of those two (as well as their companions HAVE_MMAP and HAVE_SHMGET respectively) enables the supplied shared memory code. If your system has another type of shared memory, edit the file src/main/http_main.c and add the hooks necessary to use it in Apache. (Send us back a patch too, please.)

Historical note: The Linux port of Apache didn't start to use shared memory until version 1.2 of Apache. This oversight resulted in really poor and unreliable behavior of earlier versions of Apache on Linux.

**DYNAMIC_MODULE_LIMIT**

If you have no intention of using dynamically loaded modules (you probably don't if you're reading this and tuning your server for every last ounce of performance), then you should add -DDYNAMIC_MODULE_LIMIT=0 when building your server. This will save RAM that's allocated only for supporting dynamically loaded modules.

## Appendix: Detailed Analysis of a Trace

Here is a system call trace of Apache 2.0.38 with the worker MPM on Solaris 8. This trace was collected using:

```
truss -l -p httpd_child_pid.
```

---

[4]http://www.w3.org/Protocols/HTTP/Performance/Pipeline.html

The `-l` option tells truss to log the ID of the LWP (lightweight process–Solaris' form of kernel-level thread) that invokes each system call.

Other systems may have different system call tracing utilities such as `strace`, `ktrace`, or `par`. They all produce similar output.

In this trace, a client has requested a 10KB static file from the httpd. Traces of non-static requests or requests with content negotiation look wildly different (and quite ugly in some cases).

```
/67:    accept(3, 0x00200BEC, 0x00200C0C, 1) (sleeping...)
/67:    accept(3, 0x00200BEC, 0x00200C0C, 1)              = 9
```

In this trace, the listener thread is running within LWP #67.

⟹ Note the lack of `accept(2)` serialization. On this particular platform, the worker MPM uses an unserialized accept by default unless it is listening on multiple ports.

```
/65:    lwp_park(0x00000000, 0)                           = 0
/67:    lwp_unpark(65, 1)                                 = 0
```

Upon accepting the connection, the listener thread wakes up a worker thread to do the request processing. In this trace, the worker thread that handles the request is mapped to LWP #65.

```
/65:    getsockname(9, 0x00200BA4, 0x00200BC4, 1)         = 0
```

In order to implement virtual hosts, Apache needs to know the local socket address used to accept the connection. It is possible to eliminate this call in many situations (such as when there are no virtual hosts, or when LISTEN directives are used which do not have wildcard addresses). But no effort has yet been made to do these optimizations.

```
/65:    brk(0x002170E8)                                   = 0
/65:    brk(0x002190E8)                                   = 0
```

The `brk(2)` calls allocate memory from the heap. It is rare to see these in a system call trace, because the httpd uses custom memory allocators (`apr_pool` and `apr_bucket_alloc`) for most request processing. In this trace, the httpd has just been started, so it must call `malloc(3)` to get the blocks of raw memory with which to create the custom memory allocators.

```
/65:    fcntl(9, F_GETFL, 0x00000000)                     = 2
/65:    fstat64(9, 0xFAF7B818)                            = 0
/65:    getsockopt(9, 65535, 8192, 0xFAF7B918, 0xFAF7B910, 2190656) = 0
/65:    fstat64(9, 0xFAF7B818)                            = 0
/65:    getsockopt(9, 65535, 8192, 0xFAF7B918, 0xFAF7B914, 2190656) = 0
/65:    setsockopt(9, 65535, 8192, 0xFAF7B918, 4, 2190656) = 0
/65:    fcntl(9, F_SETFL, 0x00000082)                     = 0
```

Next, the worker thread puts the connection to the client (file descriptor 9) in non-blocking mode. The `setsockopt(2)` and `getsockopt(2)` calls are a side-effect of how Solaris' libc handles `fcntl(2)` on sockets.

```
/65:    read(9, "G E T   / 1 0 k . h t m".., 8000)    = 97
```

The worker thread reads the request from the client.

```
/65:    stat("/var/httpd/apache/httpd-8999/htdocs/10k.html", 0xFAF7B978) = 0
/65:    open("/var/httpd/apache/httpd-8999/htdocs/10k.html", O_RDONLY) = 10
```

This httpd has been configured with Options FollowSymLinks and AllowOverride None. Thus it doesn't need to lstat(2) each directory in the path leading up to the requested file, nor check for .htaccess files. It simply calls stat(2) to verify that the file: 1) exists, and 2) is a regular file, not a directory.

```
/65:    sendfilev(0, 9, 0x00200F90, 2, 0xFAF7B53C)    = 10269
```

In this example, the httpd is able to send the HTTP response header and the requested file with a single sendfilev(2) system call. Sendfile semantics vary among operating systems. On some other systems, it is necessary to do a write(2) or writev(2) call to send the headers before calling sendfile(2).

```
/65:    write(4, "1 2 7 . 0 . 0 . 1   -  ".., 78)    = 78
```

This write(2) call records the request in the access log. Note that one thing missing from this trace is a time(2) call. Unlike Apache 1.3, Apache 2.x uses gettimeofday(3) to look up the time. On some operating systems, like Linux or Solaris, gettimeofday has an optimized implementation that doesn't require as much overhead as a typical system call.

```
/65:    shutdown(9, 1, 1)                    = 0
/65:    poll(0xFAF7B980, 1, 2000)            = 1
/65:    read(9, 0xFAF7BC20, 512)             = 0
/65:    close(9)                             = 0
```

The worker thread does a lingering close of the connection.

```
/65:    close(10)                            = 0
/65:    lwp_park(0x00000000, 0)      (sleeping...)
```

Finally the worker thread closes the file that it has just delivered and blocks until the listener assigns it another connection.

```
/67:    accept(3, 0x001FEB74, 0x001FEB94, 1) (sleeping...)
```

Meanwhile, the listener thread is able to accept another connection as soon as it has dispatched this connection to a worker thread (subject to some flow-control logic in the worker MPM that throttles the listener if all the available workers are busy). Though it isn't apparent from this trace, the next accept(2) can (and usually does, under high load conditions) occur in parallel with the worker thread's handling of the just-accepted connection.

# 9.3    Performance Scaling

The Performance Tuning page in the Apache 1.3 documentation says:

> "Apache is a general webserver, which is designed to be correct first, and fast second. Even so, its performance is quite satisfactory. Most sites have less than 10Mbits of outgoing bandwidth, which Apache can fill using only a low end Pentium-based webserver."

However, this sentence was written a few years ago, and in the meantime several things have happened. On one hand, web server hardware has become much faster. On the other hand, many sites now are allowed much more than ten megabits per second of outgoing bandwidth. In addition, web applications have become more complex. The classic brochureware site is alive and well, but the web has grown up substantially as a computing application platform and webmasters may find themselves running dynamic content in Perl, PHP or Java, all of which take a toll on performance.

Therefore, in spite of strides forward in machine speed and bandwidth allowances, web server performance and web application performance remain areas of concern. In this documentation several aspects of web server performance will be discussed.

## What Will and Will Not Be Discussed

The session will focus on easily accessible configuration and tuning options for Apache httpd 2.2 and 2.4 as well as monitoring tools. Monitoring tools will allow you to observe your web server to gather information about its performance, or lack thereof. We'll assume that you don't have an unlimited budget for server hardware, so the existing infrastructure will have to do the job. You have no desire to compile your own Apache, or to recompile the operating system kernel. We do assume, though, that you have some familiarity with the Apache httpd configuration file.

## Monitoring Your Server

The first task when sizing or performance-tuning your server is to find out how your system is currently performing. By monitoring your server under real-world load, or artificially generated load, you can extrapolate its behavior under stress, such as when your site is mentioned on Slashdot.

### Monitoring Tools

#### top

The top tool ships with Linux and FreeBSD. Solaris offers `prstat(1)`. It collects a number of statistics for the system and for each running process, then displays them interactively on your terminal. The data displayed is refreshed every second and varies by platform, but typically includes system load average, number of processes and their current states, the percent CPU(s) time spent executing user and system code, and the state of the virtual memory system. The data displayed for each process is typically configurable and includes its process name and ID, priority and nice values, memory footprint, and percentage CPU usage. The following example shows multiple httpd processes (with MPM worker and event) running on an Linux (Xen) system:

```
top - 23:10:58 up 71 days,  6:14,  4 users,  load average: 0.25, 0.53, 0.47
Tasks: 163 total,   1 running, 162 sleeping,   0 stopped,   0 zombie
Cpu(s): 11.6%us,  0.7%sy,  0.0%ni, 87.3%id,  0.4%wa,  0.0%hi,  0.0%si,  0.0%st
Mem:   2621656k total,  2178684k used,   442972k free,   100500k buffers
Swap:  4194296k total,   860584k used,  3333712k free,  1157552k cached

  PID USER      PR  NI  VIRT  RES  SHR S %CPU %MEM    TIME+  COMMAND
16687 example_  20   0 1200m 547m 179m S   45 21.4  1:09.59 httpd-worker
15195 www       20   0  441m  33m 2468 S    0  1.3  0:41.41 httpd-worker
    1 root      20   0 10312  328  308 S    0  0.0  0:33.17 init
    2 root      15  -5     0    0    0 S    0  0.0  0:00.00 kthreadd
    3 root      RT  -5     0    0    0 S    0  0.0  0:00.14 migration/0
    4 root      15  -5     0    0    0 S    0  0.0  0:04.58 ksoftirqd/0
    5 root      RT  -5     0    0    0 S    0  0.0  4:45.89 watchdog/0
    6 root      15  -5     0    0    0 S    0  0.0  1:42.52 events/0
    7 root      15  -5     0    0    0 S    0  0.0  0:00.00 khelper
   19 root      15  -5     0    0    0 S    0  0.0  0:00.00 xenwatch
   20 root      15  -5     0    0    0 S    0  0.0  0:00.00 xenbus
   28 root      RT  -5     0    0    0 S    0  0.0  0:00.14 migration/1
   29 root      15  -5     0    0    0 S    0  0.0  0:00.20 ksoftirqd/1
   30 root      RT  -5     0    0    0 S    0  0.0  0:05.96 watchdog/1
   31 root      15  -5     0    0    0 S    0  0.0  1:18.35 events/1
   32 root      RT  -5     0    0    0 S    0  0.0  0:00.08 migration/2
   33 root      15  -5     0    0    0 S    0  0.0  0:00.18 ksoftirqd/2
   34 root      RT  -5     0    0    0 S    0  0.0  0:06.00 watchdog/2
   35 root      15  -5     0    0    0 S    0  0.0  1:08.39 events/2
   36 root      RT  -5     0    0    0 S    0  0.0  0:00.10 migration/3
   37 root      15  -5     0    0    0 S    0  0.0  0:00.16 ksoftirqd/3
   38 root      RT  -5     0    0    0 S    0  0.0  0:06.08 watchdog/3
   39 root      15  -5     0    0    0 S    0  0.0  1:22.81 events/3
   68 root      15  -5     0    0    0 S    0  0.0  0:06.28 kblockd/0
   69 root      15  -5     0    0    0 S    0  0.0  0:00.04 kblockd/1
   70 root      15  -5     0    0    0 S    0  0.0  0:00.04 kblockd/2
```

Top is a wonderful tool even though it's slightly resource intensive (when running, its own process is usually in the top ten CPU gluttons). It is indispensable in determining the size of a running process, which comes in handy when determining how many server processes you can run on your machine. How to do this is described in sizing MaxClients. Top is, however, an interactive tool and running it continuously has few if any advantages.

**free**

This command is only available on Linux. It shows how much memory and swap space is in use. Linux allocates unused memory as file system cache. The free command shows usage both with and without this cache. The free command can be used to find out how much memory the operating system is using, as described in the paragraph sizing MaxClients. The output of free looks like this:

```
sctemme@brutus:~$ free
            total       used       free     shared    buffers     cached
Mem:      4026028    3901892     124136          0     253144     841044
-/+ buffers/cache:    2807704    1218324
Swap:     3903784      12540    3891244
```

**vmstat**

This command is available on many unix platforms. It displays a large number of operating system metrics. Run without argument, it displays a status line for that moment. When a numeric argument is added, the status is redisplayed at designated intervals. For example, `vmstat 5` causes the information to reappear every five seconds. Vmstat displays the amount of virtual memory in use, how much memory is swapped in and out each second, the number of processes currently running and sleeping, the number of interrupts and context switches per second and the usage percentages of the CPU.

The following is `vmstat` output of an idle server:

```
[sctemme@GayDeceiver sctemme]$ vmstat 5 3
   procs                      memory    swap          io     system          cpu
 r b w    swpd    free    buff cache si so      bi   bo in      cs us  sy id
 0 0 0       0 186252    6688 37516  0   0    12    5 47     311  0   1 99
 0 0 0       0 186244    6696 37516  0   0     0   16 41     314  0   0 100
 0 0 0       0 186236    6704 37516  0   0     0    9 44     314  0   0 100
```

And this is output of a server that is under a load of one hundred simultaneous connections fetching static content:

```
[sctemme@GayDeceiver sctemme]$ vmstat 5 3
   procs                      memory    swap     io        system        cpu
 r b w    swpd    free    buff cache si so     bi bo    in      cs us sy  id
 1 0 1       0 162580    6848 40056  0   0   11  5   150     324  1  1  98
 6 0 1       0 163280    6856 40248  0   0    0 66  6384 1117     42 25  32
11 0 0       0 162780    6864 40436  0   0    0 61  6309 1165     33 28  40
```

The first line gives averages since the last reboot. The subsequent lines give information for five second intervals. The second argument tells vmstat to generate three reports and then exit.

**SE Toolkit**

The SE Toolkit is a system monitoring toolkit for Solaris. Its programming language is based on the C preprocessor and comes with a number of sample scripts. It can use both the command line and the GUI to display information. It can also be programmed to apply rules to the system data. The example script shown in Figure 2, Zoom.se, shows green, orange or red indicators when utilization of various parts of the system rises above certain thresholds. Another included script, Virtual Adrian, applies performance tuning metrics according to.

The SE Toolkit has drifted around for a while and has had several owners since its inception. It seems that it has now found a final home at Sunfreeware.com, where it can be downloaded at no charge. There is a single package for Solaris 8, 9 and 10 on SPARC and x86, and includes source code. SE Toolkit author Richard Pettit has started a new company, Captive Metrics4 that plans to bring to market a multiplatform monitoring tool built on the same principles as SE Toolkit, written in Java.

**DTrace**

Given that DTrace is available for Solaris, FreeBSD and OS X, it might be worth exploring it. There's also mod_dtrace available for httpd.

**mod_status**

The mod_status module gives an overview of the server performance at a given moment. It generates an HTML page with, among others, the number of Apache processes running and how many bytes each has served, and the CPU load caused by httpd and the rest of the system. The Apache Software Foundation uses MOD_STATUS on its own web site[5]. If you put the `ExtendedStatus On` directive in your `httpd.conf`, the MOD_STATUS page will give you more information at the cost of a little extra work per request.

**Web Server Log Files**

Monitoring and analyzing the log files httpd writes is one of the most effective ways to keep track of your server health and performance. Monitoring the error log allows you to detect error conditions, discover attacks and find performance issues. Analyzing the access logs tells you how busy your server is, which resources are the most popular and where your users come from. Historical log file data can give you invaluable insight into trends in access to your server, which allows you to predict when your performance needs will overtake your server capacity.

**Error Log**

The error log will contain messages if the server has reached the maximum number of active processes or the maximum number of concurrently open files. The error log also reflects when processes are being spawned at a higher-than-usual rate in response to a sudden increase in load. When the server starts, the stderr file descriptor is redirected to the error logfile, so any error encountered by httpd after it opens its logfiles will appear in this log. This makes it good practice to review the error log frequently.

Before Apache httpd opens its logfiles, any errors will be written to the stderr stream. If you start httpd manually, this error information will appear on your terminal and you can use it directly to troubleshoot your server. If your httpd is started by a startup script, the destination of early error messages depends on their design. The `/var/log/messages` file is usually a good bet. On Windows, early error messages are written to the Applications Event Log, which can be viewed through the Event Viewer in Administrative Tools.

The Error Log is configured through the ERRORLOG and LOGLEVEL configuration directives. The error log of httpd's main server configuration receives the log messages that pertain to the entire server: startup, shutdown, crashes, excessive process spawns, etc. The ERRORLOG directive can also be used in virtual host containers. The error log of a virtual host receives only log messages specific to that virtual host, such as authentication failures and 'File not Found' errors.

On a server that is visible to the Internet, expect to see a lot of exploit attempt and worm attacks in the error log. A lot of these will be targeted at other server platforms instead of Apache, but the current state of affairs is that attack scripts just throw everything they have at any open port, regardless of which server is actually running or what applications might be installed. You could block these attempts using a firewall or mod_security[6], but this falls outside the scope of this discussion.

The LOGLEVEL directive determines the level of detail included in the logs. There are eight log levels as described here:

---

[5]http://apache.org/server-status
[6]http://www.modsecurity.org/

| Level | Description |
|-------|-------------|
| emerg | Emergencies - system is unusable. |
| alert | Action must be taken immediately. |
| crit | Critical Conditions. |
| error | Error conditions. |
| warn | Warning conditions. |
| notice | Normal but significant condition. |
| info | Informational. |
| debug | Debug-level messages |

The default log level is warn. A production server should not be run on debug, but increasing the level of detail in the error log can be useful during troubleshooting. Starting with 2.3.8 LOGLEVEL can be specified on a per module basis:

```
LogLevel debug mod_ssl:warn
```

This puts all of the server in debug mode, except for MOD_SSL, which tends to be very noisy.

**Access Log**

Apache httpd keeps track of every request it services in its access log file. In addition to the time and nature of a request, httpd can log the client IP address, date and time of the request, the result and a host of other information. The various logging format features are documented in the manual. This file exists by default for the main server and can be configured per virtual host by using the TRANSFERLOG or CUSTOMLOG configuration directive.

The access logs can be analyzed with any of several free and commercially available programs. Popular free analysis packages include Analog and Webalizer. Log analysis should be done offline so the web server machine is not burdened by processing the log files. Most log analysis packages understand the Common Log Format. The fields in the log lines are explained in the following:

```
195.54.228.42 - - [24/Mar/2007:23:05:11 -0400] "GET /sander/feed/ HTTP/1.1" 200 9747
64.34.165.214 - - [24/Mar/2007:23:10:11 -0400] "GET /sander/feed/atom HTTP/1.1" 200 9068
60.28.164.72 - - [24/Mar/2007:23:11:41 -0400] "GET / HTTP/1.0" 200 618
85.140.155.56 - - [24/Mar/2007:23:14:12 -0400] "GET /sander/2006/09/27/44/ HTTP/1.1" 200 14:
85.140.155.56 - - [24/Mar/2007:23:14:15 -0400] "GET /sander/2006/09/21/gore-tax-pollution/ I
74.6.72.187 - - [24/Mar/2007:23:18:11 -0400] "GET /sander/2006/09/27/44/ HTTP/1.0" 200 1417:
74.6.72.229 - - [24/Mar/2007:23:24:22 -0400] "GET /sander/2006/11/21/os-java/ HTTP/1.0" 200
```

| Field | Content | Explanation |
|-------|---------|-------------|
| Client IP | 195.54.228.42 | IP address where the request originated |
| RFC 1413 ident | - | Remote user identity as reported by their identd |
| username | - | Remote username as authenticated by Apache |
| timestamp | [24/Mar/2007:23:05:11 -0400] | Date and time of request |
| Request | "GET /sander/feed/ HTTP/1.1" | Request line |
| Status Code | 200 | Response code |
| Content Bytes | 9747 | Bytes transferred w/o headers |

**Rotating Log Files**

There are several reasons to rotate logfiles. Even though almost no operating systems out there have a hard file size limit of two Gigabytes anymore, log files simply become too large to handle over time. Additionally, any periodic log file analysis should not be performed on files to which the server is actively writing. Periodic logfile rotation helps keep the analysis job manageable, and allows you to keep a closer eye on usage trends.

On unix systems, you can simply rotate logfiles by giving the old file a new name using mv. The server will keep writing to the open file even though it has a new name. When you send a graceful restart signal to the server, it will open a new logfile with the configured name. For example, you could run a script from cron like this:

```
APACHE=/usr/local/apache2
HTTPD=$APACHE/bin/httpd
mv $APACHE/logs/access_log $APACHE/logarchive/access_log-`date +%F`
$HTTPD -k graceful
```

This approach also works on Windows, just not as smoothly. While the httpd process on your Windows server will keep writing to the log file after it has been renamed, the Windows Service that runs Apache can not do a graceful restart. Restarting a Service on Windows means stopping it and then starting it again. The advantage of a graceful restart is that the httpd child processes get to complete responding to their current requests before they exit. Meanwhile, the httpd server becomes immediately available again to serve new requests. The stop-start that the Windows Service has to perform will interrupt any requests currently in progress, and the server is unavailable until it is started again. Plan for this when you decide the timing of your restarts.

A second approach is to use piped logs. From the CUSTOMLOG, TRANSFERLOG or ERRORLOG directives you can send the log data into any program using a pipe character ( | ). For instance:

```
CustomLog "|/usr/local/apache2/bin/rotatelogs /var/log/access_log
86400" common
```

The program on the other end of the pipe will receive the Apache log data on its stdin stream, and can do with this data whatever it wants. The rotatelogs program that comes with Apache seamlessly turns over the log file based on time elapsed or the amount of data written, and leaves the old log files with a timestamp suffix to its name. This method for rotating logfiles works well on unix platforms, but is currently broken on Windows.

**Logging and Performance**

Writing entries to the Apache log files obviously takes some effort, but the information gathered from the logs is so valuable that under normal circumstances logging should not be turned off. For optimal performance, you should put your disk-based site content on a different physical disk than the server log files: the access patterns are very different. Retrieving content from disk is a read operation in a fairly random pattern, and log files are written to disk sequentially.

Do not run a production server with your error LOGLEVEL set to debug. This log level causes a vast amount of information to be written to the error log, including, in the case of SSL access, complete dumps of BIO read and write operations. The performance implications are significant: use the default warn level instead.

If your server has more than one virtual host, you may give each virtual host a separate access logfile. This makes it easier to analyze the logfile later. However, if your server has many virtual hosts, all the open logfiles put a resource burden on your system, and it may be preferable to log to a single file. Use the %v format character at the start of your LOGFORMAT and starting 2.3.8 of your ERRORLOG to make httpd print the hostname of the virtual host that received the request or the error at the beginning of each log line. A simple Perl script can split out the log file after it rotates: one is included with the Apache source under support/split-logfile.

You can use the BUFFEREDLOGS directive to have Apache collect several log lines in memory before writing them to disk. This might yield better performance, but could affect the order in which the server's log is written.

**Generating A Test Load**

It is useful to generate a test load to monitor system performance under realistic operating circumstances. Besides commercial packages such as LoadRunner[7] ,there are a number of freely available tools to generate a test load against your web server.

- Apache ships with a test program called ab, short for Apache Bench. It can generate a web server load by repeatedly asking for the same file in rapid succession. You can specify a number of concurrent connections and have the program run for either a given amount of time or a specified number of requests.
- Another freely available load generator is http load11 . This program works with a URL file and can be compiled with SSL support.
- The Apache Software Foundation offers a tool named flood12 . Flood is a fairly sophisticated program that is configured through an XML file.
- Finally, JMeter13 , a Jakarta subproject, is an all-Java load-testing tool. While early versions of this application were slow and difficult to use, the current version 2.1.1 seems to be versatile and useful.
- ASF external projects, that have proven to be quite good: grinder, httperf, tsung, FunkLoad[8]

When you load-test your web server, please keep in mind that if that server is in production, the test load may negatively affect the server's response. Also, any data traffic you generate may be charged against your monthly traffic allowance.

## Configuring for Performance

**Httpd Configuration**

The Apache 2.2 httpd is by default a pre-forking web server. When the server starts, the parent process spawns a number of child processes that do the actual work of servicing requests. But Apache httpd 2.0 introduced the concept of the Multi-Processing Module (MPM). Developers can write MPMs to suit the process- or threadingarchitecture of their specific operating system. Apache 2 comes with special MPMs for Windows, OS/2, Netware and BeOS. On unix-like platforms, the two most popular MPMs are Prefork and Worker. The Prefork MPM offers the same pre-forking process model that Apache 1.3 uses. The Worker MPM runs a smaller number of child processes, and spawns multiple request handling threads within each child process. In 2.4 MPMs are no longer hard-wired. They too can be exchanged via LOADMODULE. The default MPM in 2.4 is the event MPM.

The maximum number of workers, be they pre-forked child processes or threads within a process, is an indication of how many requests your server can manage concurrently. It is merely a rough estimate because the kernel can queue connection attempts for your web server. When your site becomes busy and the maximum number of workers is running, the machine doesn't hit a hard limit beyond which clients will be denied access. However, once requests start backing up, system performance is likely to degrade.

Finally, if the httpd server in question is not executing any third-party code, via mod_php, mod_perl or similar, we recommend the use of MPM_EVENT. This MPM is ideal for situations where httpd serves as a thin layer between clients and backend servers doing the real job, such as a proxy or cache.

**MaxClients**

The MaxClients directive in your Apache httpd configuration file specifies the maximum number of workers your server can create. It has two related directives, MinSpareServers and MaxSpareServers ,which specify the number of workers Apache keeps waiting in the wings ready to serve requests. The absolute maximum number of processes is configurable through the ServerLimit directive.

---

[7]http://learnloadrunner.com/
[8]http://funkload.nuxeo.org/

**Spinning Threads**

For the prefork MPM of the above directives are all there is to determining the process limit. However, if you are running a threaded MPM the situation is a little more complicated. Threaded MPMs support the `ThreadsPerChild` directive1 . Apache requires that `MaxClients` is evenly divisible by `ThreadsPerChild` .If you set either directive to a number that doesn't meet this requirement, Apache will send a message of complaint to the error log and adjust the `ThreadsPerChild` value downwards until it is an even factor of `MaxClients`.

**Sizing MaxClients**

Optimally, the maximum number of processes should be set so that all the memory on your system is used, but no more. If your system gets so overloaded that it needs to heavily swap core memory out to disk, performance will degrade quickly. The formula for determining MAXCLIENTS is fairly simple:

```
total RAM - RAM for OS - RAM for external programs
MaxClients = -------------------------------------------------
RAM per httpd process
```

The various amounts of memory allocated for the OS, external programs and the httpd processes is best determined by observation: use the top and free commands described above to determine the memory footprint of the OS without the web server running. You can also determine the footprint of a typical web server process from top: most top implementations have a Resident Size (RSS) column and a Shared Memory column.

The difference between these two is the amount of memory per-process. The shared segment really exists only once and is used for the code and libraries loaded and the dynamic inter-process tally, or 'scoreboard,' that Apache keeps. How much memory each process takes for itself depends heavily on the number and kind of modules you use. The best approach to use in determining this need is to generate a typical test load against your web site and see how large the httpd processes become.

The RAM for external programs parameter is intended mostly for CGI programs and scripts that run outside the web server process. However, if you have a Java virtual machine running Tomcat on the same box it will need a significant amount of memory as well. The above assessment should give you an idea how far you can push `MaxClients` ,but it is not an exact science. When in doubt, be conservative and use a low `MaxClients` value. The Linux kernel will put extra memory to good use for caching disk access. On Solaris you need enough available real RAM memory to create any process. If no real memory is available, httpd will start writing 'No space left on device' messages to the error log and be unable to fork additional child processes, so a higher `MaxClients` value may actually be a disadvantage.

**Selecting your MPM**

The prime reason for selecting a threaded MPM is that threads consume fewer system resources than processes, and it takes less effort for the system to switch between threads. This is more true for some operating systems than for others. On systems like Solaris and AIX, manipulating processes is relatively expensive in terms of system resources. On these systems, running a threaded MPM makes sense. On Linux, the threading implementation actually uses one process for each thread. Linux processes are relatively lightweight, but it means that a threaded MPM offers less of a performance advantage than in other environments.

Running a threaded MPM can cause stability problems in some situations For instance, should a child process of a preforked MPM crash, at most one client connection is affected. However, if a threaded child crashes, all the threads in that process disappear, which means all the clients currently being served by that process will see their connection aborted. Additionally, there may be so-called "thread-safety" issues, especially with third-party libraries. In threaded applications, threads may access the same variables indiscriminately, not knowing whether a variable may have been changed by another thread.

This has been a sore point within the PHP community. The PHP processor heavily relies on third-party libraries and cannot guarantee that all of these are thread-safe. The good news is that if you are running Apache on Linux, you can run PHP in the preforked MPM without fear of losing too much performance relative to the threaded option.

### Spinning Locks

Apache httpd maintains an inter-process lock around its network listener. For all practical purposes, this means that only one httpd child process can receive a request at any given time. The other processes are either servicing requests already received or are 'camping out' on the lock, waiting for the network listener to become available. This process is best visualized as a revolving door, with only one process allowed in the door at any time. On a heavily loaded web server with requests arriving constantly, the door spins quickly and requests are accepted at a steady rate. On a lightly loaded web server, the process that currently "holds" the lock may have to stay in the door for a while, during which all the other processes sit idle, waiting to acquire the lock. At this time, the parent process may decide to terminate some children based on its `MaxSpareServers` directive.

### The Thundering Herd

The function of the 'accept mutex' (as this inter-process lock is called) is to keep request reception moving along in an orderly fashion. If the lock is absent, the server may exhibit the Thundering Herd syndrome.

Consider an American Football team poised on the line of scrimmage. If the football players were Apache processes all team members would go for the ball simultaneously at the snap. One process would get it, and all the others would have to lumber back to the line for the next snap. In this metaphor, the accept mutex acts as the quarterback, delivering the connection "ball" to the appropriate player process.

Moving this much information around is obviously a lot of work, and, like a smart person, a smart web server tries to avoid it whenever possible. Hence the revolving door construction. In recent years, many operating systems, including Linux and Solaris, have put code in place to prevent the Thundering Herd syndrome. Apache recognizes this and if you run with just one network listener, meaning one virtual host or just the main server, Apache will refrain from using an accept mutex. If you run with multiple listeners (for instance because you have a virtual host serving SSL requests), it will activate the accept mutex to avoid internal conflicts.

You can manipulate the accept mutex with the `AcceptMutex` directive. Besides turning the accept mutex off, you can select the locking mechanism. Common locking mechanisms include fcntl, System V Semaphores and pthread locking. Not all are available on every platform, and their availability also depends on compile-time settings. The various locking mechanisms may place specific demands on system resources: manipulate them with care.

There is no compelling reason to disable the accept mutex. Apache automatically recognizes the single listener situation described above and knows if it is safe to run without mutex on your platform.

### Tuning the Operating System

People often look for the 'magic tune-up' that will make their system perform four times as fast by tweaking just one little setting. The truth is, present-day UNIX derivatives are pretty well adjusted straight out of the box and there is not a lot that needs to be done to make them perform optimally. However, there are a few things that an administrator can do to improve performance.

### RAM and Swap Space

The usual mantra regarding RAM is "more is better". As discussed above, unused RAM is put to good use as file system cache. The Apache processes get bigger if you load more modules, especially if you use modules that generate dynamic page content within the processes, like PHP and mod_perl. A large configuration file-with many virtual hosts-also tends to inflate the process footprint. Having ample RAM allows you to run Apache with more child processes, which allows the server to process more concurrent requests.

While the various platforms treat their virtual memory in different ways, it is never a good idea to run with less disk-based swap space than RAM. The virtual memory system is designed to provide a fallback for RAM, but when you don't have disk space available and run out of swappable memory, your machine grinds to a halt. This can crash your box, requiring a physical reboot for which your hosting facility may charge you.

Also, such an outage naturally occurs when you least want it: when the world has found your website and is beating a path to your door. If you have enough disk-based swap space available and the machine gets overloaded, it may get very, very slow as the system needs to swap memory pages to disk and back, but when the load decreases the system should recover. Remember, you still have `MaxClients` to keep things in hand.

Most unix-like operating systems use designated disk partitions for swap space. When a system starts up it finds all swap partitions on the disk(s), by partition type or because they are listed in the file `/etc/fstab` ,and automatically enables them. When adding a disk or installing the operating system, be sure to allocate enough swap space to accommodate eventual RAM upgrades. Reassigning disk space on a running system is a cumbersome process.

Plan for available hard drive swap space of at least twice your amount of RAM, perhaps up to four times in situations with frequent peaking loads. Remember to adjust this configuration whenever you upgrade RAM on your system. In a pinch, you can use a regular file as swap space. For instructions on how to do this, see the manual pages for the `mkswap` and `swapon` or `swap` programs.

### ulimit: Files and Processes

Given a machine with plenty of RAM and processor capacity, you can run hundreds of Apache processes if necessary. . . and if your kernel allows it.

Consider a situation in which several hundred web servers are running; if some of these need to spawn CGI processes, the maximum number of processes would occur quickly.

However, you can change this limit with the command

```
ulimit [-H|-S] -u [newvalue]
```

This must be changed before starting the server, since the new value will only be available to the current shell and programs started from it. In newer Linux kernels the default has been raised to 2048. On FreeBSD, the number seems to be the rather unusual 513. In the default user shell on this system, `csh` the equivalent is `limit` and works analogous to the Bourne-like `ulimit` :

```
limit [-h] maxproc [newvalue]
```

Similarly, the kernel may limit the number of open files per process. This is generally not a problem for pre-forked servers, which just handle one request at a time per process. Threaded servers, however, serve many requests per process and much more easily run out of available file descriptors. You can increase the maximum number of open files per process by running the

```
ulimit -n [newvalue]
```

command. Once again, this must be done prior to starting Apache.

**Setting User Limits on System Startup**

Under Linux, you can set the ulimit parameters on bootup by editing the `/etc/security/limits.conf` file. This file allows you to set soft and hard limits on a per-user or per-group basis; the file contains commentary explaining the options. To enable this, make sure that the file `/etc/pam.d/login` contains the line

```
session required /lib/security/pam_limits.so
```

All items can have a 'soft' and a 'hard' limit: the first is the default setting and the second the maximum value for that item.

In FreeBSD's `/etc/login.conf` these resources can be limited or extended system wide, analogously to `limits.conf`. 'Soft' limits can be specified with `-cur` and 'hard' limits with `-max`.

Solaris has a similar mechanism for manipulating limit values at boot time: In `/etc/system` you can set kernel tunables valid for the entire system at boot time. These are the same tunables that can be set with the `mdb` kernel debugger during run time. The soft and hard limit corresponding to ulimit -u can be set via:

```
set rlim_fd_max=65536
set rlim_fd_cur=2048
```

Solaris calculates the maximum number of allowed processes per user (`maxuprc`) based on the total amount available memory on the system (`maxusers`). You can review the numbers with

```
sysdef -i | grep maximum
```

but it is not recommended to change them.

**Turn Off Unused Services and Modules**

Many UNIX and Linux distributions come with a slew of services turned on by default. You probably need few of them. For example, your web server does not need to be running sendmail, nor is it likely to be an NFS server, etc. Turn them off.

On Red Hat Linux, the chkconfig tool will help you do this from the command line. On Solaris systems `svcs` and `svcadm` will show which services are enabled and disable them respectively.

In a similar fashion, cast a critical eye on the Apache modules you load. Most binary distributions of Apache httpd, and pre-installed versions that come with Linux distributions, have their modules enabled through the LOADMODULE directive.

Unused modules may be culled: if you don't rely on their functionality and configuration directives, you can turn them off by commenting out the corresponding LOADMODULE lines. Read the documentation on each module's functionality before deciding whether to keep it enabled. While the performance overhead of an unused module is small, it's also unnecessary.

## Caching Content

Requests for dynamically generated content usually take significantly more resources than requests for static content. Static content consists of simple filespages, images, etc.-on disk that are very efficiently served. Many operating systems also automatically cache the contents of frequently accessed files in memory.

Processing dynamic requests, on the contrary, can be much more involved. Running CGI scripts, handing off requests to an external application server and accessing database content can introduce significant latency and processing load to a busy web server. Under many circumstances, performance can be improved by turning popular dynamic requests into static requests. In this section, two approaches to this will be discussed.

**Making Popular Pages Static**

By pre-rendering the response pages for the most popular queries in your application, you can gain a significant performance improvement without giving up the flexibility of dynamically generated content. For instance, if your application is a flower delivery service, you would probably want to pre-render your catalog pages for red roses during the weeks leading up to Valentine's Day. When the user searches for red roses, they are served the pre-rendered page. Queries for, say, yellow roses will be generated directly from the database. The mod_rewrite module included with Apache is a great tool to implement these substitutions.

**Example: A Statically Rendered Blog**

Blosxom is a lightweight web log package that runs as a CGI. It is written in Perl and uses plain text files for entry input. Besides running as CGI, Blosxom can be run from the command line to pre-render blog pages. Pre-rendering pages to static HTML can yield a significant performance boost in the event that large numbers of people actually start reading your blog.

To run blosxom for static page generation, edit the CGI script according to the documentation. Set the $static dir variable to the DOCUMENTROOT of the web server, and run the script from the command line as follows:

```
$ perl blosxom.cgi -password='whateveryourpassword'
```

This can be run periodically from Cron, after you upload content, etc. To make Apache substitute the statically rendered pages for the dynamic content, we'll use mod_rewrite. This module is included with the Apache source code, but is not compiled by default. It can be built with the server by passing the option --enable-rewrite[=shared] to the configure command. Many binary distributions of Apache come with MOD_REWRITE included. The following is an example of an Apache virtual host that takes advantage of pre-rendered blog pages:

```
Listen *:8001
  <VirtualHost *:8001>
      ServerName blog.sandla.org:8001
      ServerAdmin sander@temme.net
      DocumentRoot "/home/sctemme/inst/blog/httpd/htdocs"
      <Directory "/home/sctemme/inst/blog/httpd/htdocs">
          Options +Indexes
          Require all granted
          RewriteEngine on
          RewriteCond "%{REQUEST_FILENAME}" "!-f"
          RewriteCond "%{REQUEST_FILENAME}" "!-d"
          RewriteRule "^(.*)$"               "/cgi-bin/blosxom.cgi/$1" [L,QSA]
      </Directory>
      RewriteLog "/home/sctemme/inst/blog/httpd/logs/rewrite_log"
      RewriteLogLevel 9
      ErrorLog "/home/sctemme/inst/blog/httpd/logs/error_log"
      LogLevel debug
      CustomLog "/home/sctemme/inst/blog/httpd/logs/access_log" common
      ScriptAlias "/cgi-bin/" "/home/sctemme/inst/blog/bin/"
      <Directory "/home/sctemme/inst/blog/bin">
```

```
        Options +ExecCGI
        Require all granted
    </Directory>
  </VirtualHost>
```

The REWRITECOND and REWRITERULE directives say that, if the requested resource does not exist as a file or a directory, its path is passed to the Blosxom CGI for rendering. Blosxom uses Path Info to specify blog entries and index pages, so this means that if a particular path under Blosxom exists as a static file in the file system, the file is served instead. Any request that isn't pre- rendered is served by the CGI. This means that individual entries, which show the comments, are always served by the CGI which in turn means that your comment spam is always visible. This configuration also hides the Blosxom CGI from the user-visible URL in their Location bar. mod_rewrite is a fantastically powerful and versatile module: investigate it to arrive at a configuration that is best for your situation.

### Caching Content With mod_cache

The mod_cache module provides intelligent caching of HTTP responses: it is aware of the expiration timing and content requirements that are part of the HTTP specification. The mod_cache module caches URL response content. If content sent to the client is considered cacheable, it is saved to disk. Subsequent requests for that URL will be served directly from the cache. The provider module for mod_cache, mod_disk_cache, determines how the cached content is stored on disk. Most server systems will have more disk available than memory, and it's good to note that some operating system kernels cache frequently accessed disk content transparently in memory, so replicating this in the server is not very useful.

To enable efficient content caching and avoid presenting the user with stale or invalid content, the application that generates the actual content has to send the correct response headers. Without headers like `Etag:`, `Last-Modified:` or `Expires:`, MOD_CACHE can not make the right decision on whether to cache the content, serve it from cache or leave it alone. When testing content caching, you may find that you need to modify your application or, if this is impossible, selectively disable caching for URLs that cause problems. The mod_cache modules are not compiled by default, but can be enabled by passing the option `--enable-cache[=shared]` to the configure script. If you use a binary distribution of Apache httpd, or it came with your port or package collection, it may have MOD_CACHE already included.

### Example: wiki.apache.org

The Apache Software Foundation Wiki is served by MoinMoin. MoinMoin is written in Python and runs as a CGI. To date, any attempts to run it under mod_python has been unsuccessful. The CGI proved to place an untenably high load on the server machine, especially when the Wiki was being indexed by search engines like Google. To lighten the load on the server machine, the Apache Infrastructure team turned to mod_cache. It turned out MoinMoin needed a small patch to ensure proper behavior behind the caching server: certain requests can never be cached and the corresponding Python modules were patched to send the proper HTTP response headers. After this modification, the cache in front of the Wiki was enabled with the following configuration snippet in `httpd.conf`:

```
CacheRoot /raid1/cacheroot
CacheEnable disk /
# A page modified 100 minutes ago will expire in 10 minutes
CacheLastModifiedFactor .1
# Always check again after 6 hours
CacheMaxExpire 21600
```

This configuration will try to cache any and all content within its virtual host. It will never cache content for more than six hours (the CACHEMAXEXPIRE directive). If no `Expires:` header is present in the response, MOD_CACHE will compute an expiration period from the Last-Modified: header. The computation using CACHELASTMOD-IFIEDFACTOR is based on the assumption that if a page was recently modified, it is likely to change again in the near future and will have to be re-cached.

Do note that it can pay off to *disable* the ETag: header: For files smaller than 1k the server has to calculate the checksum (usually MD5) and then send out a 304 Not Modified response, which will use up some CPU and still saturate the same amount of network resources for the transfer (one TCP packet). For resources larger than 1k it might prove CPU expensive to calculate the header for each request. Unfortunately there does currently not exist a way to cache these headers.

```
<FilesMatch "\.(jpe?g|png|gif|js|css|x?html|xml)">
    FileETag None
</FilesMatch>
```

This will disable the generation of the ETag: header for most static resources. The server does not calculate these headers for dynamic resources.

## Further Considerations

Armed with the knowledge of how to tune a sytem to deliver the desired the performance, we will soon discover that *one* system might prove a bottleneck. How to make a system fit for growth, or how to put a number of systems into tune will be discussed in PerformanceScalingOut[9].

---

[9]http://wiki.apache.org/httpd/PerformanceScalingOut

# 9.4   Security Tips

Some hints and tips on security issues in setting up a web server. Some of the suggestions will be general, others specific to Apache.

### Keep up to Date

The Apache HTTP Server has a good record for security and a developer community highly concerned about security issues. But it is inevitable that some problems – small or large – will be discovered in software after it is released. For this reason, it is crucial to keep aware of updates to the software. If you have obtained your version of the HTTP Server directly from Apache, we highly recommend you subscribe to the Apache HTTP Server Announcements List[10] where you can keep informed of new releases and security updates. Similar services are available from most third-party distributors of Apache software.

Of course, most times that a web server is compromised, it is not because of problems in the HTTP Server code. Rather, it comes from problems in add-on code, CGI scripts, or the underlying Operating System. You must therefore stay aware of problems and updates with all the software on your system.

### Denial of Service (DoS) attacks

All network servers can be subject to denial of service attacks that attempt to prevent responses to clients by tying up the resources of the server. It is not possible to prevent such attacks entirely, but you can do certain things to mitigate the problems that they create.

Often the most effective anti-DoS tool will be a firewall or other operating-system configurations. For example, most firewalls can be configured to restrict the number of simultaneous connections from any individual IP address or network, thus preventing a range of simple attacks. Of course this is no help against Distributed Denial of Service attacks (DDoS).

There are also certain Apache HTTP Server configuration settings that can help mitigate problems:

- The REQUESTREADTIMEOUT directive allows to limit the time a client may take to send the request.

- The TIMEOUT directive should be lowered on sites that are subject to DoS attacks. Setting this to as low as a few seconds may be appropriate. As TIMEOUT is currently used for several different operations, setting it to a low value introduces problems with long running CGI scripts.

- The KEEPALIVETIMEOUT directive may be also lowered on sites that are subject to DoS attacks. Some sites even turn off the keepalives completely via KEEPALIVE, which has of course other drawbacks on performance.

- The values of various timeout-related directives provided by other modules should be checked.

- The directives LIMITREQUESTBODY, LIMITREQUESTFIELDS, LIMITREQUESTFIELDSIZE, LIMITREQUEST-LINE, and LIMITXMLREQUESTBODY should be carefully configured to limit resource consumption triggered by client input.

- On operating systems that support it, make sure that you use the ACCEPTFILTER directive to offload part of the request processing to the operating system. This is active by default in Apache httpd, but may require reconfiguration of your kernel.

- Tune the MAXREQUESTWORKERS directive to allow the server to handle the maximum number of simultaneous connections without running out of resources. See also the performance tuning documentation (p. 339)

---

[10]http://httpd.apache.org/lists.html#http-announce

- The use of a threaded mpm (p. 90) may allow you to handle more simultaneous connections, thereby mitigating DoS attacks. Further, the EVENT mpm uses asynchronous processing to avoid devoting a thread to each connection. Due to the nature of the OpenSSL library the EVENT mpm is currently incompatible with MOD_SSL and other input filters. In these cases it falls back to the behaviour of the WORKER mpm.

- There are a number of third-party modules available through http://modules.apache.org/ that can restrict certain client behaviors and thereby mitigate DoS problems.

## Permissions on ServerRoot Directories

In typical operation, Apache is started by the root user, and it switches to the user defined by the USER directive to serve hits. As is the case with any command that root executes, you must take care that it is protected from modification by non-root users. Not only must the files themselves be writeable only by root, but so must the directories, and parents of all directories. For example, if you choose to place ServerRoot in /usr/local/apache then it is suggested that you create that directory as root, with commands like these:

```
mkdir /usr/local/apache
cd /usr/local/apache
mkdir bin conf logs
chown 0 .  bin conf logs
chgrp 0 .  bin conf logs
chmod 755 .  bin conf logs
```

It is assumed that /, /usr, and /usr/local are only modifiable by root. When you install the httpd executable, you should ensure that it is similarly protected:

```
cp httpd /usr/local/apache/bin
chown 0 /usr/local/apache/bin/httpd
chgrp 0 /usr/local/apache/bin/httpd
chmod 511 /usr/local/apache/bin/httpd
```

You can create an htdocs subdirectory which is modifiable by other users – since root never executes any files out of there, and shouldn't be creating files in there.

If you allow non-root users to modify any files that root either executes or writes on then you open your system to root compromises. For example, someone could replace the httpd binary so that the next time you start it, it will execute some arbitrary code. If the logs directory is writeable (by a non-root user), someone could replace a log file with a symlink to some other system file, and then root might overwrite that file with arbitrary data. If the log files themselves are writeable (by a non-root user), then someone may be able to overwrite the log itself with bogus data.

## Server Side Includes

Server Side Includes (SSI) present a server administrator with several potential security risks.

The first risk is the increased load on the server. All SSI-enabled files have to be parsed by Apache, whether or not there are any SSI directives included within the files. While this load increase is minor, in a shared server environment it can become significant.

SSI files also pose the same risks that are associated with CGI scripts in general. Using the exec cmd element, SSI-enabled files can execute any CGI script or program under the permissions of the user and group Apache runs as, as configured in httpd.conf.

There are ways to enhance the security of SSI files while still taking advantage of the benefits they provide.

To isolate the damage a wayward SSI file can cause, a server administrator can enable suexec (p. 115) as described in the CGI in General section.

Enabling SSI for files with `.html` or `.htm` extensions can be dangerous. This is especially true in a shared, or high traffic, server environment. SSI-enabled files should have a separate extension, such as the conventional `.shtml`. This helps keep server load at a minimum and allows for easier management of risk.

Another solution is to disable the ability to run scripts and programs from SSI pages. To do this replace `Includes` with `IncludesNOEXEC` in the OPTIONS directive. Note that users may still use `<--#include virtual="..." -->` to execute CGI scripts if these scripts are in directories designated by a SCRIPTALIAS directive.

## CGI in General

First of all, you always have to remember that you must trust the writers of the CGI scripts/programs or your ability to spot potential security holes in CGI, whether they were deliberate or accidental. CGI scripts can run essentially arbitrary commands on your system with the permissions of the web server user and can therefore be extremely dangerous if they are not carefully checked.

All the CGI scripts will run as the same user, so they have potential to conflict (accidentally or deliberately) with other scripts e.g. User A hates User B, so he writes a script to trash User B's CGI database. One program which can be used to allow scripts to run as different users is suEXEC (p. 115) which is included with Apache as of 1.2 and is called from special hooks in the Apache server code. Another popular way of doing this is with CGIWrap[11].

## Non Script Aliased CGI

Allowing users to execute CGI scripts in any directory should only be considered if:

- You trust your users not to write scripts which will deliberately or accidentally expose your system to an attack.

- You consider security at your site to be so feeble in other areas, as to make one more potential hole irrelevant.

- You have no users, and nobody ever visits your server.

## Script Aliased CGI

Limiting CGI to special directories gives the admin control over what goes into those directories. This is inevitably more secure than non script aliased CGI, but only if users with write access to the directories are trusted or the admin is willing to test each new CGI script/program for potential security holes.

Most sites choose this option over the non script aliased CGI approach.

## Other sources of dynamic content

Embedded scripting options which run as part of the server itself, such as `mod_php`, `mod_perl`, `mod_tcl`, and `mod_python`, run under the identity of the server itself (see the USER directive), and therefore scripts executed by these engines potentially can access anything the server user can. Some scripting engines may provide restrictions, but it is better to be safe and assume not.

---

[11]http://cgiwrap.sourceforge.net/

## Dynamic content security

When setting up dynamic content, such as `mod_php`, `mod_perl` or `mod_python`, many security considerations get out of the scope of `httpd` itself, and you need to consult documentation from those modules. For example, PHP lets you setup Safe Mode[12], which is most usually disabled by default. Another example is Suhosin[13], a PHP addon for more security. For more information about those, consult each project documentation.

At the Apache level, a module named mod_security[14] can be seen as a HTTP firewall and, provided you configure it finely enough, can help you enhance your dynamic content security.

## Protecting System Settings

To run a really tight ship, you'll want to stop users from setting up `.htaccess` files which can override security features you've configured. Here's one way to do it.

In the server configuration file, put

```
<Directory "/">
    AllowOverride None
</Directory>
```

This prevents the use of `.htaccess` files in all directories apart from those specifically enabled.

Note that this setting is the default since Apache 2.3.9.

## Protect Server Files by Default

One aspect of Apache which is occasionally misunderstood is the feature of default access. That is, unless you take steps to change it, if the server can find its way to a file through normal URL mapping rules, it can serve it to clients.

For instance, consider the following example:

```
# cd /; ln -s / public_html
Accessing http://localhost/~root/
```

This would allow clients to walk through the entire filesystem. To work around this, add the following block to your server's configuration:

```
<Directory "/">
    Require all denied
</Directory>
```

This will forbid default access to filesystem locations. Add appropriate DIRECTORY blocks to allow access only in those areas you wish. For example,

```
<Directory "/usr/users/*/public_html">
    Require all granted
</Directory>
<Directory "/usr/local/httpd">
    Require all granted
</Directory>
```

---

[12]http://www.php.net/manual/en/ini.sect.safe-mode.php
[13]http://www.hardened-php.net/suhosin/
[14]http://modsecurity.org/

Pay particular attention to the interactions of LOCATION and DIRECTORY directives; for instance, even if `<Directory "/">` denies access, a `<Location "/">` directive might overturn it.

Also be wary of playing games with the USERDIR directive; setting it to something like `./` would have the same effect, for root, as the first example above. We strongly recommend that you include the following line in your server configuration files:

```
UserDir disabled root
```

## Watching Your Logs

To keep up-to-date with what is actually going on against your server you have to check the Log Files (p. 56) . Even though the log files only reports what has already happened, they will give you some understanding of what attacks is thrown against the server and allow you to check if the necessary level of security is present.

A couple of examples:

```
grep -c "/jsp/source.jsp?/jsp/ /jsp/source.jsp??" access_log
grep "client denied" error_log | tail -n 10
```

The first example will list the number of attacks trying to exploit the Apache Tomcat Source.JSP Malformed Request Information Disclosure Vulnerability[15], the second example will list the ten last denied clients, for example:

```
[Thu Jul 11 17:18:39 2002] [error] [client foo.example.com] client
denied by server configuration:  /usr/local/apache/htdocs/.htpasswd
```

As you can see, the log files only report what already has happened, so if the client had been able to access the `.htpasswd` file you would have seen something similar to:

```
foo.example.com - - [12/Jul/2002:01:59:13 +0200] "GET /.htpasswd
HTTP/1.1"
```

in your Access Log (p. 56) . This means you probably commented out the following in your server configuration file:

```
<Files ".ht*">
    Require all denied
</Files>
```

## Merging of configuration sections

The merging of configuration sections is complicated and sometimes directive specific. Always test your changes when creating dependencies on how directives are merged.

For modules that don't implement any merging logic, such as MOD_ACCESS_COMPAT, the behavior in later sections depends on whether the later section has any directives from the module. The configuration is inherited until a change is made, at which point the configuration is *replaced* and not merged.

---

[15]http://online.securityfocus.com/bid/4876/info/

# 9.5 Relevant Standards

This page documents all the relevant standards that the Apache HTTP Server follows, along with brief descriptions.

In addition to the information listed below, the following resources should be consulted:

- http://purl.org/NET/http-errata[16] - HTTP/1.1 Specification Errata
- http://www.rfc-editor.org/errata.php[17] - RFC Errata
- http://ftp.ics.uci.edu/pub/ietf/http/#RFC[18] - A pre-compiled list of HTTP related RFCs

 **Notice**
This document is not yet complete.

## HTTP Recommendations

Regardless of what modules are compiled and used, Apache as a basic web server complies with the following IETF recommendations:

**RFC 1945**[19] **(Informational)** The Hypertext Transfer Protocol (HTTP) is an application-level protocol with the lightness and speed necessary for distributed, collaborative, hypermedia information systems. This documents HTTP/1.0.

**RFC 2616**[20] **(Standards Track)** The Hypertext Transfer Protocol (HTTP) is an application-level protocol for distributed, collaborative, hypermedia information systems. This documents HTTP/1.1.

**RFC 2396**[21] **(Standards Track)** A Uniform Resource Identifier (URI) is a compact string of characters for identifying an abstract or physical resource.

**RFC 4346**[22] **(Standards Track)** The TLS protocol provides communications security over the Internet. It provides encryption, and is designed to prevent eavesdropping, tampering, and message forgery.

## HTML Recommendations

Regarding the Hypertext Markup Language, Apache complies with the following IETF and W3C recommendations:

**RFC 2854**[23] **(Informational)** This document summarizes the history of HTML development, and defines the "text/html" MIME type by pointing to the relevant W3C recommendations.

**HTML 4.01 Specification**[24] **(Errata**[25]**)** This specification defines the HyperText Markup Language (HTML), the publishing language of the World Wide Web. This specification defines HTML 4.01, which is a subversion of HTML 4.

**HTML 3.2 Reference Specification**[26] The HyperText Markup Language (HTML) is a simple markup language used to create hypertext documents that are portable from one platform to another. HTML documents are SGML documents.

**XHTML 1.1 - Module-based XHTML**[27] **(Errata**[28]**)** This Recommendation defines a new XHTML document type that is based upon the module framework and modules defined in Modularization of XHTML.

---

[16]http://purl.org/NET/http-errata
[17]http://www.rfc-editor.org/errata.php
[18]http://ftp.ics.uci.edu/pub/ietf/http/#RFC

**XHTML 1.0 The Extensible HyperText Markup Language (Second Edition)**[29] **(Errata**[30]**)**   This specification defines the Second Edition of XHTML 1.0, a reformulation of HTML 4 as an XML 1.0 application, and three DTDs corresponding to the ones defined by HTML 4.

## Authentication

Concerning the different methods of authentication, Apache follows the following IETF recommendations:

**RFC 2617**[31] **(Standards Track)**   "HTTP/1.0", includes the specification for a Basic Access Authentication scheme.

## Language/Country Codes

The following links document ISO and other language and country code information:

**ISO 639-2**[32]   ISO 639 provides two sets of language codes, one as a two-letter code set (639-1) and another as a three-letter code set (this part of ISO 639) for the representation of names of languages.

**ISO 3166-1**[33]   These pages document the country names (official short names in English) in alphabetical order as given in ISO 3166-1 and the corresponding ISO 3166-1-alpha-2 code elements.

**BCP 47**[34] **(Best Current Practice), RFC 3066**[35]   This document describes a language tag for use in cases where it is desired to indicate the language used in an information object, how to register values for use in this language tag, and a construct for matching such language tags.

**RFC 3282**[36] **(Standards Track)**   This document defines a "Content-language:" header, for use in cases where one desires to indicate the language of something that has RFC 822-like headers, like MIME body parts or Web documents, and an "Accept-Language:" header for use in cases where one wishes to indicate one's preferences with regard to language.

# 9.6 Password Formats

Notes about the password encryption formats generated and understood by Apache.

## Basic Authentication

There are five formats that Apache recognizes for basic-authentication passwords. Note that not all formats work on every platform:

**bcrypt** "$2y$" + the result of the crypt_blowfish algorithm. See the APR source file crypt_blowfish.c[37] for the details of the algorithm.

**MD5** "$apr1$" + the result of an Apache-specific algorithm using an iterated (1,000 times) MD5 digest of various combinations of a random 32-bit salt and the password. See the APR source file apr_md5.c[38] for the details of the algorithm.

**SHA1** "{SHA}" + Base64-encoded SHA-1 digest of the password. Insecure.

**CRYPT** Unix only. Uses the traditional Unix `crypt(3)` function with a randomly-generated 32-bit salt (only 12 bits used) and the first 8 characters of the password. Insecure.

**PLAIN TEXT (i.e. *unencrypted*)** Windows & Netware only. Insecure.

### Generating values with htpasswd

```
bcrypt
$ htpasswd -nbB myName myPassword
myName:$2y$05$c4WoMPo3SXsafkva.HHa6uXQZWr7oboPiC2bT/r7q1BB8I2s0BRqC
```

```
MD5
$ htpasswd -nbm myName myPassword
myName:$apr1$r31.....$HqJZimcKQFAMYayBlzkrA/
```

```
SHA1
$ htpasswd -nbs myName myPassword
myName:{SHA}VBPuJHI7uixaa6LQGWx4s+5GKNE=
```

```
CRYPT
$ htpasswd -nbd myName myPassword
myName:rqXexS6ZhobKA
```

---

[37]http://svn.apache.org/viewvc/apr/apr/trunk/crypto/crypt_blowfish.c?view=markup
[38]http://svn.apache.org/viewvc/apr/apr/trunk/crypto/apr_md5.c?view=markup

**Generating CRYPT and MD5 values with the OpenSSL command-line program**

OpenSSL knows the Apache-specific MD5 algorithm.

```
MD5
$ openssl passwd -apr1 myPassword
$apr1$qHDFfhPC$nITSVHgYbDAK1Y0acGRnY0
```

```
CRYPT
openssl passwd -crypt myPassword
qQ5vTYO3c8dsU
```

**Validating CRYPT or MD5 passwords with the OpenSSL command line program**

The salt for a CRYPT password is the first two characters (converted to a binary value). To validate myPassword against rqXexS6ZhobKA

```
CRYPT
$ openssl passwd -crypt -salt rq myPassword
Warning:  truncating password to 8 characters
rqXexS6ZhobKA
```

Note that using myPasswo instead of myPassword will produce the same result because only the first 8 characters of CRYPT passwords are considered.

The salt for an MD5 password is between $apr1$ and the following $ (as a Base64-encoded binary value - max 8 chars). To validate myPassword against $apr1$r31.....$HqJZimcKQFAMYayBlzkrA/

```
MD5
$ openssl passwd -apr1 -salt r31.....  myPassword
$apr1$r31.....$HqJZimcKQFAMYayBlzkrA/
```

**Database password fields for mod_dbd**

The SHA1 variant is probably the most useful format for DBD authentication. Since the SHA1 and Base64 functions are commonly available, other software can populate a database with encrypted passwords that are usable by Apache basic authentication.

To create Apache SHA1-variant basic-authentication passwords in various languages:

```
PHP
'{SHA}' .  base64_encode(sha1($password, TRUE))
```

```
Java
"{SHA}" + new
sun.misc.BASE64Encoder().encode(java.security.MessageDigest.getInstance("SHA1").digest(passw
```

---

**ColdFusion**
```
"{SHA}" & ToBase64(BinaryDecode(Hash(password, "SHA1"), "Hex"))
```

---

**Ruby**
```
require 'digest/sha1'
require 'base64'
'{SHA}' + Base64.encode64(Digest::SHA1.digest(password))
```

---

**C or C++**
```
Use the APR function:  apr_sha1_base64
```

---

**Python**
```
import base64
import hashlib
"{SHA}" + format(base64.b64encode(hashlib.sha1(password).digest()))
```

---

**PostgreSQL (with the contrib/pgcrypto functions installed)**
```
'{SHA}'||encode(digest(password,'sha1'),'base64')
```

## Digest Authentication

Apache recognizes one format for digest-authentication passwords - the MD5 hash of the string `user:realm:password` as a 32-character string of hexadecimal digits. `realm` is the Authorization Realm argument to the AUTHNAME directive in httpd.conf.

### Database password fields for mod_dbd

Since the MD5 function is commonly available, other software can populate a database with encrypted passwords that are usable by Apache digest authentication.

To create Apache digest-authentication passwords in various languages:

---

**PHP**
```
md5($user . ':'  . $realm . ':'  .$password)
```

---

**Java**
```
byte b[] = java.security.MessageDigest.getInstance("MD5").digest(
(user + ":" + realm + ":" + password ).getBytes());
java.math.BigInteger bi = new java.math.BigInteger(1, b);
String s = bi.toString(16);
while (s.length() < 32)
   s = "0" + s;
// String s is the encrypted password
```

**ColdFusion**
```
LCase(Hash( (user & ":" & realm & ":" & password) , "MD5"))
```

**Ruby**
```
require 'digest/md5'
Digest::MD5.hexdigest(user + ':'  + realm + ':'  + password)
```

**PostgreSQL (with the contrib/pgcrypto functions installed)**
```
encode(digest( user || ':'  || realm || ':'  || password , 'md5'),
'hex')
```

# Chapter 10

# Apache modules

# 10.1   Terms Used to Describe Modules

This document describes the terms that are used to describe each Apache module (p. 1101) .

## Description

A brief description of the purpose of the module.

## Status

This indicates how tightly bound into the Apache Web server the module is; in other words, you may need to recompile the server in order to gain access to the module and its functionality. Possible values for this attribute are:

**MPM** A module with status "MPM" is a Multi-Processing Module (p. 90) . Unlike the other types of modules, Apache must have one and only one MPM in use at any time. This type of module is responsible for basic request handling and dispatching.

**Base** A module labeled as having "Base" status is compiled and loaded into the server by default, and is therefore normally available unless you have taken steps to remove the module from your configuration.

**Extension** A module with "Extension" status is not normally compiled and loaded into the server. To enable the module and its functionality, you may need to change the server build configuration files and re-compile Apache.

**Experimental** "Experimental" status indicates that the module is available as part of the Apache kit, but you are on your own if you try to use it. The module is being documented for completeness, and is not necessarily supported.

**External** Modules which are not included with the base Apache distribution ("third-party modules") may use the "External" status. We are not responsible for, nor do we support such modules.

## Source File

This quite simply lists the name of the source file which contains the code for the module. This is also the name used by the <IFMODULE> directive.

## Module Identifier

This is a string which identifies the module for use in the LOADMODULE directive when dynamically loading modules. In particular, it is the name of the external variable of type module in the source file.

## Compatibility

If the module was not part of the original Apache version 2 distribution, the version in which it was introduced should be listed here. In addition, if the module is limited to particular platforms, the details will be listed here.

## 10.2 Terms Used to Describe Directives

This document describes the terms that are used to describe each Apache configuration directive (p. 1106) .

**See also**

- Configuration files (p. 32)

### Description

A brief description of the purpose of the directive.

### Syntax

This indicates the format of the directive as it would appear in a configuration file. This syntax is extremely directive-specific, and is described in detail in the directive's definition. Generally, the directive name is followed by a series of one or more space-separated arguments. If an argument contains a space, the argument must be enclosed in double quotes. Optional arguments are enclosed in square brackets. Where an argument can take on more than one possible value, the possible values are separated by vertical bars "—". Literal text is presented in the default font, while argument-types for which substitution is necessary are *emphasized*. Directives which can take a variable number of arguments will end in "..." indicating that the last argument is repeated.

Directives use a great number of different argument types. A few common ones are defined below.

***URL*** A complete Uniform Resource Locator including a scheme, hostname, and optional pathname as in `http://www.example.com/path/to/file.html`

***URL-path*** The part of a *url* which follows the scheme and hostname as in `/path/to/file.html`. The *url-path* represents a web-view of a resource, as opposed to a file-system view.

***file-path*** The path to a file in the local file-system beginning with the root directory as in `/usr/local/apache/htdocs/path/to/file.html`. Unless otherwise specified, a *file-path* which does not begin with a slash will be treated as relative to the ServerRoot (p. 380) .

***directory-path*** The path to a directory in the local file-system beginning with the root directory as in `/usr/local/apache/htdocs/path/to/`.

***filename*** The name of a file with no accompanying path information as in `file.html`.

***regex*** A Perl-compatible regular expression. The directive definition will specify what the *regex* is matching against.

***extension*** In general, this is the part of the *filename* which follows the last dot. However, Apache recognizes multiple filename extensions, so if a *filename* contains more than one dot, each dot-separated part of the filename following the first dot is an *extension*. For example, the *filename* `file.html.en` contains two extensions: `.html` and `.en`. For Apache directives, you may specify *extension*s with or without the leading dot. In addition, *extension*s are not case sensitive.

***MIME-type*** A method of describing the format of a file which consists of a major format type and a minor format type, separated by a slash as in `text/html`.

***env-variable*** The name of an environment variable (p. 92) defined in the Apache configuration process. Note this is not necessarily the same as an operating system environment variable. See the environment variable documentation (p. 92) for more details.

## Default

If the directive has a default value (*i.e.*, if you omit it from your configuration entirely, the Apache Web server will behave as though you set it to a particular value), it is described here. If there is no default value, this section should say "*None*". Note that the default listed here is not necessarily the same as the value the directive takes in the default httpd.conf distributed with the server.

## Context

This indicates where in the server's configuration files the directive is legal. It's a comma-separated list of one or more of the following values:

**server config** This means that the directive may be used in the server configuration files (*e.g.*, `httpd.conf`), but **not** within any <VIRTUALHOST> or <DIRECTORY> containers. It is not allowed in `.htaccess` files at all.

**virtual host** This context means that the directive may appear inside <VIRTUALHOST> containers in the server configuration files.

**directory** A directive marked as being valid in this context may be used inside <DIRECTORY>, <LOCATION>, <FILES>, <IF>, and <PROXY> containers in the server configuration files, subject to the restrictions outlined in Configuration Sections (p. 35) .

**.htaccess** If a directive is valid in this context, it means that it can appear inside *per*-directory `.htaccess` files. It may not be processed, though depending upon the overrides currently active.

The directive is *only* allowed within the designated context; if you try to use it elsewhere, you'll get a configuration error that will either prevent the server from handling requests in that context correctly, or will keep the server from operating at all – *i.e.*, the server won't even start.

The valid locations for the directive are actually the result of a Boolean OR of all of the listed contexts. In other words, a directive that is marked as being valid in "`server config, .htaccess`" can be used in the `httpd.conf` file and in `.htaccess` files, but not within any <DIRECTORY> or <VIRTUALHOST> containers.

## Override

This directive attribute indicates which configuration override must be active in order for the directive to be processed when it appears in a `.htaccess` file. If the directive's context doesn't permit it to appear in `.htaccess` files, then no context will be listed.

Overrides are activated by the ALLOWOVERRIDE directive, and apply to a particular scope (such as a directory) and all descendants, unless further modified by other ALLOWOVERRIDE directives at lower levels. The documentation for that directive also lists the possible override names available.

## Status

This indicates how tightly bound into the Apache Web server the directive is; in other words, you may need to recompile the server with an enhanced set of modules in order to gain access to the directive and its functionality. Possible values for this attribute are:

**Core** If a directive is listed as having "Core" status, that means it is part of the innermost portions of the Apache Web server, and is always available.

**MPM** A directive labeled as having "MPM" status is provided by a Multi-Processing Module (p. 90) . This type of directive will be available if and only if you are using one of the MPMs listed on the Module line of the directive definition.

**Base** A directive labeled as having "Base" status is supported by one of the standard Apache modules which is compiled into the server by default, and is therefore normally available unless you've taken steps to remove the module from your configuration.

**Extension** A directive with "Extension" status is provided by one of the modules included with the Apache server kit, but the module isn't normally compiled into the server. To enable the directive and its functionality, you will need to change the server build configuration files and re-compile Apache.

**Experimental** "Experimental" status indicates that the directive is available as part of the Apache kit, but you're on your own if you try to use it. The directive is being documented for completeness, and is not necessarily supported. The module which provides the directive may or may not be compiled in by default; check the top of the page which describes the directive and its module to see if it remarks on the availability.

## Module

This quite simply lists the name of the source module which defines the directive.

## Compatibility

If the directive wasn't part of the original Apache version 2 distribution, the version in which it was introduced should be listed here. In addition, if the directive is available only on certain platforms, it will be noted here.

## 10.3   Apache Module core

| | |
|---|---|
| Description: | Core Apache HTTP Server features that are always available |
| Status: | Core |

**Directives**

- AcceptFilter
- AcceptPathInfo
- AccessFileName
- AddDefaultCharset
- AllowEncodedSlashes
- AllowOverride
- AllowOverrideList
- AsyncFilter
- CGIMapExtension
- CGIPassAuth
- CGIVar
- ContentDigest
- DefaultRuntimeDir
- DefaultType
- Define
- <Directory>
- <DirectoryMatch>
- DocumentRoot
- <Else>
- <ElseIf>
- EnableMMAP
- EnableSendfile
- Error
- ErrorDocument
- ErrorLog
- ErrorLogFormat
- ExtendedStatus
- FileETag
- <Files>
- <FilesMatch>
- ForceType
- GprofDir
- HostnameLookups
- <If>
- <IfDefine>

- <IfModule>
- Include
- IncludeOptional
- KeepAlive
- KeepAliveTimeout
- <Limit>
- <LimitExcept>
- LimitInternalRecursion
- LimitRequestBody
- LimitRequestFields
- LimitRequestFieldSize
- LimitRequestLine
- LimitXMLRequestBody
- <Location>
- <LocationMatch>
- LogLevel
- LogLevelOverride
- MaxKeepAliveRequests
- MaxRangeOverlaps
- MaxRangeReversals
- MaxRanges
- MergeTrailers
- Mutex
- NameVirtualHost
- Options
- Protocol
- Protocols
- ProtocolsHonorOrder
- QualifyRedirectURL
- RegisterHttpMethod
- RLimitCPU
- RLimitMEM
- RLimitNPROC
- ScriptInterpreterSource
- SeeRequestTail
- ServerAdmin
- ServerAlias
- ServerName
- ServerPath
- ServerRoot
- ServerSignature

- ServerTokens
- SetHandler
- SetInputFilter
- SetOutputFilter
- TimeOut
- TraceEnable
- UnDefine
- UseCanonicalName
- UseCanonicalPhysicalPort
- <VirtualHost>
- Warning

## AcceptFilter Directive

| Description: | Configures optimizations for a Protocol's Listener Sockets |
|---|---|
| Syntax: | `AcceptFilter protocol accept_filter` |
| Context: | server config |
| Status: | Core |
| Module: | core |

This directive enables operating system specific optimizations for a listening socket by the PROTOCOL type. The basic premise is for the kernel to not send a socket to the server process until either data is received or an entire HTTP Request is buffered. Only FreeBSD's Accept Filters[1], Linux's more primitive `TCP_DEFER_ACCEPT`, and Windows' optimized AcceptEx() are currently supported.

Using `none` for an argument will disable any accept filters for that protocol. This is useful for protocols that require a server send data first, such as `ftp:` or `nntp:`

```
AcceptFilter nntp none
```

The default protocol names are `https` for port 443 and `http` for all other ports. To specify that another protocol is being used with a listening port, add the *protocol* argument to the LISTEN directive.

The default values on FreeBSD are:

```
AcceptFilter http httpready
AcceptFilter https dataready
```

The `httpready` accept filter buffers entire HTTP requests at the kernel level. Once an entire request is received, the kernel then sends it to the server. See the

accf_http(9)[2] man page for more details. Since HTTPS requests are encrypted, only the accf_data(9)[3] filter is used.

The default values on Linux are:

```
AcceptFilter http data
AcceptFilter https data
```

[1] http://www.freebsd.org/cgi/man.cgi?query=accept_filter&sektion=9
[2] http://www.freebsd.org/cgi/man.cgi?query=accf_http&sektion=9
[3] http://www.freebsd.org/cgi/man.cgi?query=accf_data&sektion=9

Linux's `TCP_DEFER_ACCEPT` does not support buffering http requests. Any value besides `none` will enable `TCP_DEFER_ACCEPT` on that listener. For more details see the Linux

tcp(7)[4] man page.

The default values on Windows are:

```
AcceptFilter http data
AcceptFilter https data
```

Window's mpm_winnt interprets the AcceptFilter to toggle the AcceptEx() API, and does not support http protocol buffering. There are two values which utilize the Windows AcceptEx() API and will recycle network sockets between connections. `data` waits until data has been transmitted as documented above, and the initial data buffer and network endpoint addresses are all retrieved from the single AcceptEx() invocation. `connect` will use the AcceptEx() API, also retrieve the network endpoint addresses, but like `none` the `connect` option does not wait for the initial data transmission.

On Windows, `none` uses accept() rather than AcceptEx() and will not recycle sockets between connections. This is useful for network adapters with broken driver support, as well as some virtual network providers such as vpn drivers, or spam, virus or spyware filters.

**See also**

- PROTOCOL

## AcceptPathInfo Directive

| | |
|---|---|
| Description: | Resources accept trailing pathname information |
| Syntax: | `AcceptPathInfo On|Off|Default` |
| Default: | `AcceptPathInfo Default` |
| Context: | server config, virtual host, directory, .htaccess |
| Override: | FileInfo |
| Status: | Core |
| Module: | core |

This directive controls whether requests that contain trailing pathname information that follows an actual filename (or non-existent file in an existing directory) will be accepted or rejected. The trailing pathname information can be made available to scripts in the `PATH_INFO` environment variable.

For example, assume the location `/test/` points to a directory that contains only the single file `here.html`. Then requests for `/test/here.html/more` and `/test/nothere.html/more` both collect `/more` as `PATH_INFO`.

The three possible arguments for the ACCEPTPATHINFO directive are:

**Off** A request will only be accepted if it maps to a literal path that exists. Therefore a request with trailing pathname information after the true filename such as `/test/here.html/more` in the above example will return a 404 NOT FOUND error.

**On** A request will be accepted if a leading path component maps to a file that exists. The above example `/test/here.html/more` will be accepted if `/test/here.html` maps to a valid file.

**Default** The treatment of requests with trailing pathname information is determined by the handler (p. 108) responsible for the request. The core handler for normal files defaults to rejecting `PATH_INFO` requests. Handlers that serve scripts, such as cgi-script (p. 580) and isapi-handler (p. 683) , generally accept `PATH_INFO` by default.

---

[4]http://homepages.cwi.nl/~aeb/linux/man2html/man7/tcp.7.html

The primary purpose of the `AcceptPathInfo` directive is to allow you to override the handler's choice of accepting or rejecting `PATH_INFO`. This override is required, for example, when you use a filter (p. 110), such as INCLUDES (p. 667), to generate content based on `PATH_INFO`. The core handler would usually reject the request, so you can use the following configuration to enable such a script:

```
<Files "mypaths.shtml">
  Options +Includes
  SetOutputFilter INCLUDES
  AcceptPathInfo On
</Files>
```

## AccessFileName Directive

| | |
|---|---|
| Description: | Name of the distributed configuration file |
| Syntax: | `AccessFileName filename [filename] ...` |
| Default: | `AccessFileName .htaccess` |
| Context: | server config, virtual host |
| Status: | Core |
| Module: | core |

While processing a request, the server looks for the first existing configuration file from this list of names in every directory of the path to the document, if distributed configuration files are enabled for that directory. For example:

```
AccessFileName .acl
```

Before returning the document `/usr/local/web/index.html`, the server will read `/.acl`, `/usr/.acl`, `/usr/local/.acl` and `/usr/local/web/.acl` for directives unless they have been disabled with:

```
<Directory "/">
    AllowOverride None
</Directory>
```

### See also

- ALLOWOVERRIDE
- Configuration Files (p. 32)
- .htaccess Files (p. 249)

## AddDefaultCharset Directive

| | |
|---|---|
| Description: | Default charset parameter to be added when a response content-type is `text/plain` or `text/html` |
| Syntax: | `AddDefaultCharset On\|Off\|charset` |
| Default: | `AddDefaultCharset Off` |
| Context: | server config, virtual host, directory, .htaccess |
| Override: | FileInfo |
| Status: | Core |
| Module: | core |

This directive specifies a default value for the media type charset parameter (the name of a character encoding) to be added to a response if and only if the response's content-type is either `text/plain` or `text/html`. This should override any charset specified in the body of the response via a `META` element, though the exact behavior is often dependent on the user's client configuration. A setting of `AddDefaultCharset Off` disables this functionality. `AddDefaultCharset On` enables a default charset of `iso-8859-1`. Any other value is assumed to be the *charset* to be used, which should be one of the IANA registered charset values[5] for use in Internet media types (MIME types). For example:

```
AddDefaultCharset utf-8
```

ADDDEFAULTCHARSET should only be used when all of the text resources to which it applies are known to be in that character encoding and it is too inconvenient to label their charset individually. One such example is to add the charset parameter to resources containing generated content, such as legacy CGI scripts, that might be vulnerable to cross-site scripting attacks due to user-provided data being included in the output. Note, however, that a better solution is to just fix (or delete) those scripts, since setting a default charset does not protect users that have enabled the "auto-detect character encoding" feature on their browser.

**See also**

- ADDCHARSET

## AllowEncodedSlashes Directive

| | |
|---|---|
| Description: | Determines whether encoded path separators in URLs are allowed to be passed through |
| Syntax: | `AllowEncodedSlashes On|Off|NoDecode` |
| Default: | `AllowEncodedSlashes Off` |
| Context: | server config, virtual host |
| Status: | Core |
| Module: | core |
| Compatibility: | NoDecode option available in 2.3.12 and later. |

The ALLOWENCODEDSLASHES directive allows URLs which contain encoded path separators (`%2F` for `/` and additionally `%5C` for `\` on accordant systems) to be used in the path info.

With the default value, `Off`, such URLs are refused with a 404 (Not found) error.

With the value `On`, such URLs are accepted, and encoded slashes are decoded like all other encoded characters.

With the value `NoDecode`, such URLs are accepted, but encoded slashes are not decoded but left in their encoded state.

Turning ALLOWENCODEDSLASHES `On` is mostly useful when used in conjunction with `PATH_INFO`.

**Note**

> If encoded slashes are needed in path info, use of `NoDecode` is strongly recommended as a security measure. Allowing slashes to be decoded could potentially allow unsafe paths.

**See also**

- ACCEPTPATHINFO

---

[5]http://www.iana.org/assignments/character-sets

## AllowOverride Directive

| | |
|---|---|
| Description: | Types of directives that are allowed in `.htaccess` files |
| Syntax: | `AllowOverride All|None|directive-type [directive-type] ...` |
| Default: | `AllowOverride None (2.3.9 and later), AllowOverride All (2.3.8 and earlier)` |
| Context: | directory |
| Status: | Core |
| Module: | core |

When the server finds an `.htaccess` file (as specified by ACCESSFILENAME), it needs to know which directives declared in that file can override earlier configuration directives.

 **Only available in <Directory> sections**
> ALLOWOVERRIDE is valid only in <DIRECTORY> sections specified without regular expressions, not in <LOCATION>, <DIRECTORYMATCH> or <FILES> sections.

When this directive is set to `None` and ALLOWOVERRIDELIST is set to `None`, .htaccess files are completely ignored. In this case, the server will not even attempt to read `.htaccess` files in the filesystem.

When this directive is set to `All`, then any directive which has the .htaccess Context (p. 377) is allowed in `.htaccess` files.

The *directive-type* can be one of the following groupings of directives.

**AuthConfig** Allow use of the authorization directives (AUTHDBMGROUPFILE, AUTHDBMUSERFILE, AUTH-GROUPFILE, AUTHNAME, AUTHTYPE, AUTHUSERFILE, REQUIRE, *etc.*).

**FileInfo** Allow use of the directives controlling document types (ERRORDOCUMENT, FORCETYPE, LAN-GUAGEPRIORITY, SETHANDLER, SETINPUTFILTER, SETOUTPUTFILTER, and MOD_MIME Add* and Re-move* directives), document meta data (HEADER, REQUESTHEADER, SETENVIF, SETENVIFNOCASE, BROWSERMATCH, COOKIEEXPIRES, COOKIEDOMAIN, COOKIESTYLE, COOKIETRACKING, COOKIEN-AME), MOD_REWRITE directives (REWRITEENGINE, REWRITEOPTIONS, REWRITEBASE, REWRITECOND, REWRITERULE), MOD_ALIAS directives (REDIRECT, REDIRECTTEMP, REDIRECTPERMANENT, REDIRECT-MATCH), and ACTION from MOD_ACTIONS.

**Indexes** Allow use of the directives controlling directory indexing (ADDDESCRIPTION, ADDICON, AD-DICONBYENCODING, ADDICONBYTYPE, DEFAULTICON, DIRECTORYINDEX, FALLBACKRESOURCE, FancyIndexing (p. 542) , HEADERNAME, INDEXIGNORE, INDEXOPTIONS, READMENAME, *etc.*).

**Limit** Allow use of the directives controlling host access (ALLOW, DENY and ORDER).

**Nonfatal=[Override—Unknown—All]** Allow use of AllowOverride option to treat invalid (unrecognized or disal-lowed) directives in .htaccess as nonfatal. Instead of causing an Internal Server Error, disallowed or unrecog-nised directives will be ignored and a warning logged:

- **Nonfatal=Override** treats directives forbidden by AllowOverride as nonfatal.
- **Nonfatal=Unknown** treats unknown directives as nonfatal. This covers typos and directives implemented by a module that's not present.
- **Nonfatal=All** treats both the above as nonfatal.

Note that a syntax error in a valid directive will still cause an Internal Server Error.

 **Security**
> Nonfatal errors may have security implications for .htaccess users. For example, if AllowOver-ride disallows AuthConfig, users' configuration designed to restrict access to a site will be disabled.

**Options[=*Option,...*]** Allow use of the directives controlling specific directory features (OPTIONS and XBITHACK). An equal sign may be given followed by a comma-separated list, without spaces, of options that may be set using the OPTIONS command.

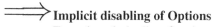**Implicit disabling of Options**

Even though the list of options that may be used in .htaccess files can be limited with this directive, as long as any OPTIONS directive is allowed any other inherited option can be disabled by using the non-relative syntax. In other words, this mechanism cannot force a specific option to remain *set* while allowing any others to be set.

```
AllowOverride Options=Indexes,MultiViews
```

Example:

```
AllowOverride AuthConfig Indexes
```

In the example above, all directives that are neither in the group `AuthConfig` nor `Indexes` cause an internal server error.

For security and performance reasons, do not set `AllowOverride` to anything other than `None` in your `<Directory "/">` block. Instead, find (or create) the `<Directory>` block that refers to the directory where you're actually planning to place a `.htaccess` file.

**See also**

- ACCESSFILENAME
- ALLOWOVERRIDELIST
- Configuration Files (p. 32)
- .htaccess Files (p. 249)

## AllowOverrideList Directive

| | |
|---|---|
| Description: | Individual directives that are allowed in `.htaccess` files |
| Syntax: | `AllowOverrideList None\|directive [directive-type] ...` |
| Default: | `AllowOverrideList None` |
| Context: | directory |
| Status: | Core |
| Module: | core |

When the server finds an `.htaccess` file (as specified by ACCESSFILENAME), it needs to know which directives declared in that file can override earlier configuration directives.

**Only available in <Directory> sections**

ALLOWOVERRIDELIST is valid only in <DIRECTORY> sections specified without regular expressions, not in <LOCATION>, <DIRECTORYMATCH> or <FILES> sections.

When this directive is set to `None` and ALLOWOVERRIDE is set to `None`, then .htaccess files are completely ignored. In this case, the server will not even attempt to read `.htaccess` files in the filesystem.

Example:

```
AllowOverride None
AllowOverrideList Redirect RedirectMatch
```

In the example above, only the `Redirect` and `RedirectMatch` directives are allowed. All others will cause an Internal Server Error.

Example:

```
AllowOverride AuthConfig
AllowOverrideList CookieTracking CookieName
```

In the example above, ALLOWOVERRIDE grants permission to the `AuthConfig` directive grouping and AL-LOWOVERRIDELIST grants permission to only two directives from the `FileInfo` directive grouping. All others will cause an Internal Server Error.

**See also**

- ACCESSFILENAME

- ALLOWOVERRIDE

- Configuration Files (p. 32)

- .htaccess Files (p. 249)

## AsyncFilter Directive

| | |
|---|---|
| Description: | Set the minimum filter type eligible for asynchronous handling |
| Syntax: | `AsyncFilter request|connection|network` |
| Default: | `AsyncFilter request` |
| Context: | server config, virtual host |
| Status: | Core |
| Module: | core |
| Compatibility: | Only available from Apache 2.5.0 and later. |

This directive controls the minimum filter levels that are eligible for asynchronous handling. This may be necessary to support legacy external filters that did not handle meta buckets correctly.

If set to "network", asynchronous handling will be limited to the network filter only. If set to "connection", all connection and network filters will be eligible for asynchronous handling, including MOD_SSL. If set to "request", all filters will be eligible for asynchronous handling.

## CGIMapExtension Directive

| | |
|---|---|
| Description: | Technique for locating the interpreter for CGI scripts |
| Syntax: | `CGIMapExtension cgi-path .extension` |
| Context: | directory, .htaccess |
| Override: | FileInfo |
| Status: | Core |
| Module: | core |
| Compatibility: | NetWare only |

This directive is used to control how Apache httpd finds the interpreter used to run CGI scripts. For example, setting `CGIMapExtension sys:\foo.nlm .foo` will cause all CGI script files with a `.foo` extension to be passed to the FOO interpreter.

## CGIPassAuth Directive

| | |
|---|---|
| Description: | Enables passing HTTP authorization headers to scripts as CGI variables |
| Syntax: | `CGIPassAuth On\|Off` |
| Default: | `CGIPassAuth Off` |
| Context: | directory, .htaccess |
| Override: | AuthConfig |
| Status: | Core |
| Module: | core |
| Compatibility: | Available in Apache HTTP Server 2.4.13 and later |

CGIPASSAUTH allows scripts access to HTTP authorization headers such as `Authorization`, which is required for scripts that implement HTTP Basic authentication. Normally these HTTP headers are hidden from scripts. This is to disallow scripts from seeing user ids and passwords used to access the server when HTTP Basic authentication is enabled in the web server. This directive should be used when scripts are allowed to implement HTTP Basic authentication.

This directive can be used instead of the compile-time setting `SECURITY_HOLE_PASS_AUTHORIZATION` which has been available in previous versions of Apache HTTP Server.

The setting is respected by any modules which use `ap_add_common_vars()`, such as MOD_CGI, MOD_CGID, MOD_PROXY_FCGI, MOD_PROXY_SCGI, and so on. Notably, it affects modules which don't handle the request in the usual sense but still use this API; examples of this are MOD_INCLUDE and MOD_EXT_FILTER. Third-party modules that don't use `ap_add_common_vars()` may choose to respect the setting as well.

## CGIVar Directive

| | |
|---|---|
| Description: | Controls how some CGI variables are set |
| Syntax: | `CGIVar variable rule` |
| Context: | directory, .htaccess |
| Override: | FileInfo |
| Status: | Core |
| Module: | core |
| Compatibility: | Available in Apache HTTP Server 2.4.21 and later |

This directive controls how some CGI variables are set.

**REQUEST_URI** rules:

`original-uri` **(default)** The value is taken from the original request line, and will not reflect internal redirects or subrequests which change the requested resource.

`current-uri` The value reflects the resource currently being processed, which may be different than the original request from the client due to internal redirects or subrequests.

## ContentDigest Directive

| | |
|---|---|
| Description: | Enables the generation of `Content-MD5` HTTP Response headers |
| Syntax: | `ContentDigest On\|Off` |
| Default: | `ContentDigest Off` |
| Context: | server config, virtual host, directory, .htaccess |
| Override: | Options |
| Status: | Core |
| Module: | core |

This directive enables the generation of `Content-MD5` headers as defined in RFC1864 respectively RFC2616.

MD5 is an algorithm for computing a "message digest" (sometimes called "fingerprint") of arbitrary-length data, with a high degree of confidence that any alterations in the data will be reflected in alterations in the message digest.

The `Content-MD5` header provides an end-to-end message integrity check (MIC) of the entity-body. A proxy or client may check this header for detecting accidental modification of the entity-body in transit. Example header:

```
Content-MD5:  AuLb7Dp1rqtRtxz2m9kRpA==
```

Note that this can cause performance problems on your server since the message digest is computed on every request (the values are not cached).

`Content-MD5` is only sent for documents served by the CORE, and not by any module. For example, SSI documents, output from CGI scripts, and byte range responses do not have this header.

## DefaultRuntimeDir Directive

| | |
|---|---|
| Description: | Base directory for the server run-time files |
| Syntax: | `DefaultRuntimeDir directory-path` |
| Default: | `DefaultRuntimeDir DEFAULT_REL_RUNTIMEDIR (logs/)` |
| Context: | server config |
| Status: | Core |
| Module: | core |
| Compatibility: | Available in Apache 2.4.2 and later |

The DEFAULTRUNTIMEDIR directive sets the directory in which the server will create various run-time files (shared memory, locks, etc.). If set as a relative path, the full path will be relative to SERVERROOT.

**Example**

```
DefaultRuntimeDir scratch/
```

The default location of DEFAULTRUNTIMEDIR may be modified by changing the `DEFAULT_REL_RUNTIMEDIR` #define at build time.

Note: SERVERROOT should be specified before this directive is used. Otherwise, the default value of SERVERROOT would be used to set the base directory.

**See also**

- the security tips (p. 364) for information on how to properly set permissions on the SERVERROOT

## DefaultType Directive

| | |
|---|---|
| Description: | This directive has no effect other than to emit warnings if the value is not `none`. In prior versions, DefaultType would specify a default media type to assign to response content for which no other media type configuration could be found. |
| Syntax: | `DefaultType media-type\|none` |
| Default: | `DefaultType none` |
| Context: | server config, virtual host, directory, .htaccess |
| Override: | FileInfo |
| Status: | Core |
| Module: | core |
| Compatibility: | All choices except `none` are DISABLED for 2.3.x and later. |

This directive has been disabled. For backwards compatibility of configuration files, it may be specified with the value `none`, meaning no default media type. For example:

```
DefaultType None
```

`DefaultType None` is only available in httpd-2.2.7 and later.

Use the mime.types configuration file and the ADDTYPE to configure media type assignments via file extensions, or the FORCETYPE directive to configure the media type for specific resources. Otherwise, the server will send the response without a Content-Type header field and the recipient may attempt to guess the media type.

## Define Directive

| | |
|---|---|
| Description: | Define a variable |
| Syntax: | `Define parameter-name [parameter-value]` |
| Context: | server config, virtual host |
| Status: | Core |
| Module: | core |

In its one parameter form, DEFINE is equivalent to passing the `-D` argument to `httpd`. It can be used to toggle the use of <IFDEFINE> sections without needing to alter `-D` arguments in any startup scripts.

In addition to that, if the second parameter is given, a config variable is set to this value. The variable can be used in the configuration using the `${VAR}` syntax. The variable is always globally defined and not limited to the scope of the surrounding config section.

```
<IfDefine TEST>
  Define servername test.example.com
</IfDefine>
<IfDefine !TEST>
  Define servername www.example.com
  Define SSL
</IfDefine>

DocumentRoot "/var/www/${servername}/htdocs"
```

Variable names may not contain colon `":"` characters, to avoid clashes with REWRITEMAP's syntax.

While this directive is supported in virtual host context, the changes it makes are visible to any later configuration directives, beyond any enclosing virtual host

## Directory Directive

| | |
|---|---|
| Description: | Enclose a group of directives that apply only to the named file-system directory, sub-directories, and their contents. |
| Syntax: | `<Directory directory-path> ... </Directory>` |
| Context: | server config, virtual host |
| Status: | Core |
| Module: | core |

<DIRECTORY> and `</Directory>` are used to enclose a group of directives that will apply only to the named directory, sub-directories of that directory, and the files within the respective directories. Any directive that is allowed in a directory context may be used. *Directory-path* is either the full path to a directory, or a wild-card string using Unix shell-style matching. In a wild-card string, `?` matches any single character, and `*` matches any sequences of characters. You may also use `[]` character ranges. None of the wildcards match a '/' character, so `<Directory "/*/public_html">` will not match /home/user/public_html, but `<Directory "/home/*/public_html">` will match. Example:

```
<Directory "/usr/local/httpd/htdocs">
  Options Indexes FollowSymLinks
</Directory>
```

Directory paths *may* be quoted, if you like, however, it *must* be quoted if the path contains spaces. This is because a space would otherwise indicate the end of an argument.

Be careful with the *directory-path* arguments: They have to literally match the filesystem path which Apache httpd uses to access the files. Directives applied to a particular <Directory> will not apply to files accessed from that same directory via a different path, such as via different symbolic links.

Regular expressions can also be used, with the addition of the ~ character. For example:

```
<Directory ~ "^/www/[0-9]{3}">

</Directory>
```

would match directories in /www/ that consisted of three numbers.

If multiple (non-regular expression) <DIRECTORY> sections match the directory (or one of its parents) containing a document, then the directives are applied in the order of shortest match first, interspersed with the directives from the .htaccess files. For example, with

```
<Directory "/">
  AllowOverride None
</Directory>

<Directory "/home">
  AllowOverride FileInfo
</Directory>
```

for access to the document /home/web/dir/doc.html the steps are:

- Apply directive AllowOverride None (disabling .htaccess files).
- Apply directive AllowOverride FileInfo (for directory /home).
- Apply any FileInfo directives in /home/.htaccess, /home/web/.htaccess and /home/web/dir/.htaccess in that order.

Regular expressions are not considered until after all of the normal sections have been applied. Then all of the regular expressions are tested in the order they appeared in the configuration file. For example, with

```
<Directory ~ "abc$">
  # ... directives here ...
</Directory>
```

the regular expression section won't be considered until after all normal <DIRECTORY>s and .htaccess files have been applied. Then the regular expression will match on /home/abc/public_html/abc and the corresponding <DIRECTORY> will be applied.

**Note that the default access for <Directory "/"> is to permit all access. This means that Apache httpd will serve any file mapped from an URL. It is recommended that you change this with a block such as**

```
<Directory "/">
  Require all denied
</Directory>
```

**and then override this for directories you *want* accessible. See the Security Tips (p. 364) page for more details.**

The directory sections occur in the `httpd.conf` file. <DIRECTORY> directives cannot nest, and cannot appear in a <LIMIT> or <LIMITEXCEPT> section.

**See also**

- How <Directory>, <Location> and <Files> sections work (p. 35) for an explanation of how these different sections are combined when a request is received

## DirectoryMatch Directive

| | |
|---|---|
| Description: | Enclose directives that apply to the contents of file-system directories matching a regular expression. |
| Syntax: | `<DirectoryMatch regex> ... </DirectoryMatch>` |
| Context: | server config, virtual host |
| Status: | Core |
| Module: | core |

<DIRECTORYMATCH> and </DirectoryMatch> are used to enclose a group of directives which will apply only to the named directory (and the files within), the same as <DIRECTORY>. However, it takes as an argument a regular expression. For example:

```
<DirectoryMatch "^/www/(.+/)?[0-9]{3}/">
    # ...
</DirectoryMatch>
```

matches directories in `/www/` (or any subdirectory thereof) that consist of three numbers.

**Compatability**

Prior to 2.3.9, this directive implicitly applied to sub-directories (like <DIRECTORY>) and could not match the end of line symbol ($). In 2.3.9 and later, only directories that match the expression are affected by the enclosed directives.

**Trailing Slash**

This directive applies to requests for directories that may or may not end in a trailing slash, so expressions that are anchored to the end of line ($) must be written with care.

From 2.4.8 onwards, named groups and backreferences are captured and written to the environment with the corresponding name prefixed with "MATCH_" and in upper case. This allows elements of paths to be referenced from within expressions (p. 99) and modules like MOD_REWRITE. In order to prevent confusion, numbered (unnamed) backreferences are ignored. Use named groups instead.

```
<DirectoryMatch "^/var/www/combined/(?<sitename>[^/]+)">
    Require ldap-group cn=%{env:MATCH_SITENAME},ou=combined,o=Example
</DirectoryMatch>
```

**See also**

- <DIRECTORY> for a description of how regular expressions are mixed in with normal <DIRECTORY>s
- How <Directory>, <Location> and <Files> sections work (p. 35) for an explanation of how these different sections are combined when a request is received

## DocumentRoot Directive

| | |
|---|---|
| Description: | Directory that forms the main document tree visible from the web |
| Syntax: | `DocumentRoot directory-path` |
| Default: | `DocumentRoot /usr/local/apache/htdocs` |
| Context: | server config, virtual host |
| Status: | Core |
| Module: | core |

This directive sets the directory from which `httpd` will serve files. Unless matched by a directive like ALIAS, the server appends the path from the requested URL to the document root to make the path to the document. Example:

```
DocumentRoot "/usr/web"
```

then an access to `http://my.example.com/index.html` refers to `/usr/web/index.html`. If the *directory-path* is not absolute then it is assumed to be relative to the SERVERROOT.

The DOCUMENTROOT should be specified without a trailing slash.

**See also**

- Mapping URLs to Filesystem Locations (p. 64)

## Else Directive

| | |
|---|---|
| Description: | Contains directives that apply only if the condition of a previous <IF> or <ELSEIF> section is not satisfied by a request at runtime |
| Syntax: | `<Else> ... </Else>` |
| Context: | server config, virtual host, directory, .htaccess |
| Override: | All |
| Status: | Core |
| Module: | core |

The <ELSE> applies the enclosed directives if and only if the most recent <IF> or <ELSEIF> section in the same scope has not been applied. For example: In

```
<If "-z req('Host')">
  # ...
</If>
<Else>
  # ...
</Else>
```

The <IF> would match HTTP/1.0 requests without a *Host:* header and the <ELSE> would match requests with a *Host:* header.

**See also**

- <IF>

- <ELSEIF>

- How <Directory>, <Location>, <Files> sections work (p. 35) for an explanation of how these different sections are combined when a request is received. <IF>, <ELSEIF>, and <ELSE> are applied last.

## ElseIf Directive

| | |
|---|---|
| Description: | Contains directives that apply only if a condition is satisfied by a request at runtime while the condition of a previous <IF> or <ELSEIF> section is not satisfied |
| Syntax: | <ElseIf expression> ... </ElseIf> |
| Context: | server config, virtual host, directory, .htaccess |
| Override: | All |
| Status: | Core |
| Module: | core |

The <ELSEIF> applies the enclosed directives if and only if both the given condition evaluates to true and the most recent <IF> or <ELSEIF> section in the same scope has not been applied. For example: In

```
<If "-R '10.1.0.0/16'">
  #...
</If>
<ElseIf "-R '10.0.0.0/8'">
  #...
</ElseIf>
<Else>
  #...
</Else>
```

The <ELSEIF> would match if the remote address of a request belongs to the subnet 10.0.0.0/8 but not to the subnet 10.1.0.0/16.

**See also**

- Expressions in Apache HTTP Server (p. 99), for a complete reference and more examples.
- <IF>
- <ELSE>
- How <Directory>, <Location>, <Files> sections work (p. 35) for an explanation of how these different sections are combined when a request is received. <IF>, <ELSEIF>, and <ELSE> are applied last.

## EnableMMAP Directive

| | |
|---|---|
| Description: | Use memory-mapping to read files during delivery |
| Syntax: | EnableMMAP On\|Off |
| Default: | EnableMMAP On |
| Context: | server config, virtual host, directory, .htaccess |
| Override: | FileInfo |
| Status: | Core |
| Module: | core |

This directive controls whether the httpd may use memory-mapping if it needs to read the contents of a file during delivery. By default, when the handling of a request requires access to the data within a file – for example, when delivering a server-parsed file using MOD_INCLUDE – Apache httpd memory-maps the file if the OS supports it.

This memory-mapping sometimes yields a performance improvement. But in some environments, it is better to disable the memory-mapping to prevent operational problems:

- On some multiprocessor systems, memory-mapping can reduce the performance of the httpd.
- Deleting or truncating a file while httpd has it memory-mapped can cause httpd to crash with a segmentation fault.

For server configurations that are vulnerable to these problems, you should disable memory-mapping of delivered files by specifying:

```
EnableMMAP Off
```

For NFS mounted files, this feature may be disabled explicitly for the offending files by specifying:

```
<Directory "/path-to-nfs-files">
  EnableMMAP Off
</Directory>
```

## EnableSendfile Directive

| | |
|---|---|
| Description: | Use the kernel sendfile support to deliver files to the client |
| Syntax: | EnableSendfile On\|Off |
| Default: | EnableSendfile Off |
| Context: | server config, virtual host, directory, .htaccess |
| Override: | FileInfo |
| Status: | Core |
| Module: | core |
| Compatibility: | Default changed to Off in version 2.3.9. |

This directive controls whether `httpd` may use the sendfile support from the kernel to transmit file contents to the client. By default, when the handling of a request requires no access to the data within a file – for example, when delivering a static file – Apache httpd uses sendfile to deliver the file contents without ever reading the file if the OS supports it.

This sendfile mechanism avoids separate read and send operations, and buffer allocations. But on some platforms or within some filesystems, it is better to disable this feature to avoid operational problems:

- Some platforms may have broken sendfile support that the build system did not detect, especially if the binaries were built on another box and moved to such a machine with broken sendfile support.
- On Linux the use of sendfile triggers TCP-checksum offloading bugs on certain networking cards when using IPv6.
- On Linux on Itanium, `sendfile` may be unable to handle files over 2GB in size.
- With a network-mounted DOCUMENTROOT (e.g., NFS, SMB, CIFS, FUSE), the kernel may be unable to serve the network file through its own cache.

For server configurations that are not vulnerable to these problems, you may enable this feature by specifying:

```
EnableSendfile On
```

For network mounted files, this feature may be disabled explicitly for the offending files by specifying:

```
<Directory "/path-to-nfs-files">
  EnableSendfile Off
</Directory>
```

Please note that the per-directory and .htaccess configuration of ENABLESENDFILE is not supported by MOD_CACHE_DISK. Only global definition of ENABLESENDFILE is taken into account by the module.

## Error Directive

| | |
|---|---|
| Description: | Abort configuration parsing with a custom error message |
| Syntax: | `Error message` |
| Context: | server config, virtual host, directory, .htaccess |
| Status: | Core |
| Module: | core |
| Compatibility: | 2.3.9 and later |

If an error can be detected within the configuration, this directive can be used to generate a custom error message, and halt configuration parsing. The typical use is for reporting required modules which are missing from the configuration.

```
# Example
# ensure that mod_include is loaded
<IfModule !include_module>
  Error "mod_include is required by mod_foo.  Load it with LoadModule."
</IfModule>

# ensure that exactly one of SSL,NOSSL is defined
<IfDefine SSL>
<IfDefine NOSSL>
  Error "Both SSL and NOSSL are defined.  Define only one of them."
</IfDefine>
</IfDefine>
<IfDefine !SSL>
<IfDefine !NOSSL>
  Error "Either SSL or NOSSL must be defined."
</IfDefine>
</IfDefine>
```

## ErrorDocument Directive

| | |
|---|---|
| Description: | What the server will return to the client in case of an error |
| Syntax: | `ErrorDocument error-code document` |
| Context: | server config, virtual host, directory, .htaccess |
| Override: | FileInfo |
| Status: | Core |
| Module: | core |

In the event of a problem or error, Apache httpd can be configured to do one of four things,

1. output a simple hardcoded error message

2. output a customized message

3. internally redirect to a local *URL-path* to handle the problem/error

4. redirect to an external *URL* to handle the problem/error

The first option is the default, while options 2-4 are configured using the ERRORDOCUMENT directive, which is followed by the HTTP response code and a URL or a message. Apache httpd will sometimes offer additional information regarding the problem/error.

From 2.4.13, expression syntax (p. 99) can be used inside the directive to produce dynamic strings and URLs.

URLs can begin with a slash (/) for local web-paths (relative to the DOCUMENTROOT), or be a full URL which the client can resolve. Alternatively, a message can be provided to be displayed by the browser. Note that deciding whether the parameter is an URL, a path or a message is performed before any expression is parsed. Examples:

```
ErrorDocument 500 http://example.com/cgi-bin/server-error.cgi
ErrorDocument 404 /errors/bad_urls.php
ErrorDocument 401 /subscription_info.html
ErrorDocument 403 "Sorry, can't allow you access today"
ErrorDocument 403 Forbidden!
ErrorDocument 403 /errors/forbidden.py?referrer=%{escape:%{HTTP_REFERER}}
```

Additionally, the special value `default` can be used to specify Apache httpd's simple hardcoded message. While not required under normal circumstances, `default` will restore Apache httpd's simple hardcoded message for configurations that would otherwise inherit an existing ERRORDOCUMENT.

```
ErrorDocument 404 /cgi-bin/bad_urls.pl

<Directory "/web/docs">
  ErrorDocument 404 default
</Directory>
```

Note that when you specify an ERRORDOCUMENT that points to a remote URL (ie. anything with a method such as `http` in front of it), Apache HTTP Server will send a redirect to the client to tell it where to find the document, even if the document ends up being on the same server. This has several implications, the most important being that the client will not receive the original error status code, but instead will receive a redirect status code. This in turn can confuse web robots and other clients which try to determine if a URL is valid using the status code. In addition, if you use a remote URL in an `ErrorDocument 401`, the client will not know to prompt the user for a password since it will not receive the 401 status code. Therefore, **if you use an `ErrorDocument 401` directive, then it must refer to a local document.**

Microsoft Internet Explorer (MSIE) will by default ignore server-generated error messages when they are "too small" and substitute its own "friendly" error messages. The size threshold varies depending on the type of error, but in general, if you make your error document greater than 512 bytes, then MSIE will show the server-generated error rather than masking it. More information is available in Microsoft Knowledge Base article Q294807[6].

Although most error messages can be overridden, there are certain circumstances where the internal messages are used regardless of the setting of ERRORDOCUMENT. In particular, if a malformed request is detected, normal request processing will be immediately halted and the internal error message returned. This is necessary to guard against security problems caused by bad requests.

If you are using mod_proxy, you may wish to enable PROXYERROROVERRIDE so that you can provide custom error messages on behalf of your Origin servers. If you don't enable ProxyErrorOverride, Apache httpd will not generate custom error documents for proxied content.

**See also**

- documentation of customizable responses (p. 85)

---

## ErrorLog Directive

| | |
|---|---|
| Description: | Location where the server will log errors |
| Syntax: | `ErrorLog file-path|syslog[:facility]` |
| Default: | `ErrorLog logs/error_log (Unix) ErrorLog logs/error.log (Windows and OS/2)` |
| Context: | server config, virtual host |
| Status: | Core |
| Module: | core |

The ERRORLOG directive sets the name of the file to which the server will log any errors it encounters. If the *file-path* is not absolute then it is assumed to be relative to the SERVERROOT.

```
ErrorLog "/var/log/httpd/error_log"
```

If the *file-path* begins with a pipe character " | " then it is assumed to be a command to spawn to handle the error log.

```
ErrorLog "|/usr/local/bin/httpd_errors"
```

See the notes on piped logs (p. 56) for more information.

Using `syslog` instead of a filename enables logging via syslogd(8) if the system supports it and if MOD_SYSLOG is loaded. The default is to use syslog facility `local7`, but you can override this by using the `syslog:facility` syntax where *facility* can be one of the names usually documented in syslog(1). The facility is effectively global, and if it is changed in individual virtual hosts, the final facility specified affects the entire server.

```
ErrorLog syslog:user
```

Additional modules can provide their own ErrorLog providers. The syntax is similar to the `syslog` example above.

SECURITY: See the security tips (p. 364) document for details on why your security could be compromised if the directory where log files are stored is writable by anyone other than the user that starts the server.

 **Note**

When entering a file path on non-Unix platforms, care should be taken to make sure that only forward slashes are used even though the platform may allow the use of back slashes. In general it is a good idea to always use forward slashes throughout the configuration files.

**See also**

- LOGLEVEL
- Apache HTTP Server Log Files (p. 56)

## ErrorLogFormat Directive

| | |
|---|---|
| Description: | Format specification for error log entries |
| Syntax: | `ErrorLogFormat [connection|request] format` |
| Context: | server config, virtual host |
| Status: | Core |
| Module: | core |

ERRORLOGFORMAT allows to specify what supplementary information is logged in the error log in addition to the actual log message.

```
#Simple example
ErrorLogFormat "[%t] [%l] [pid %P] %F: %E: [client %a] %M"
```

Specifying `connection` or `request` as first parameter allows to specify additional formats, causing additional information to be logged when the first message is logged for a specific connection or request, respectively. This additional information is only logged once per connection/request. If a connection or request is processed without causing any log message, the additional information is not logged either.

It can happen that some format string items do not produce output. For example, the Referer header is only present if the log message is associated to a request and the log message happens at a time when the Referer header has already been read from the client. If no output is produced, the default behavior is to delete everything from the preceding space character to the next space character. This means the log line is implicitly divided into fields on non-whitespace to whitespace transitions. If a format string item does not produce output, the whole field is omitted. For example, if the remote address %a in the log format [%t] [%l] [%a] %M is not available, the surrounding brackets are not logged either. Space characters can be escaped with a backslash to prevent them from delimiting a field. The combination '%' (percent space) is a zero-width field delimiter that does not produce any output.

The above behavior can be changed by adding modifiers to the format string item. A – (minus) modifier causes a minus to be logged if the respective item does not produce any output. In once-per-connection/request formats, it is also possible to use the + (plus) modifier. If an item with the plus modifier does not produce any output, the whole line is omitted.

A number as modifier can be used to assign a log severity level to a format item. The item will only be logged if the severity of the log message is not higher than the specified log severity level. The number can range from 1 (alert) over 4 (warn) and 7 (debug) to 15 (trace8).

For example, here's what would happen if you added modifiers to the `%{Referer}i` token, which logs the `Referer` request header.

| Modified Token | Meaning |
|---|---|
| %-{Referer}i | Logs a – if `Referer` is not set. |
| %+{Referer}i | Omits the entire line if `Referer` is not set. |
| %4{Referer}i | Logs the `Referer` only if the log message severity is higher than 4. |

Some format string items accept additional parameters in braces.

| FormatString | Description |
|---|---|
| %% | The percent sign |
| %a | Client IP address and port of the request |
| %{c}a | Underlying peer IP address and port of the connection (see the MOD_REMOTEIP module) |
| %A | Local IP-address and port |
| %{name}e | Request environment variable *name* |
| %E | APR/OS error status code and string |
| %F | Source file name and line number of the log call |
| %{name}i | Request header *name* |
| %k | Number of keep-alive requests on this connection |
| %l | Loglevel of the message |
| %L | Log ID of the request |
| %{c}L | Log ID of the connection |
| %{C}L | Log ID of the connection if used in connection scope, empty otherwise |
| %m | Name of the module logging the message |
| %M | The actual log message |
| %{name}n | Request note *name* |
| %P | Process ID of current process |
| %T | Thread ID of current thread |
| %{g}T | System unique thread ID of current thread (the same ID as displayed by e.g. top; currently Linux only) |

| %t | The current time |
|---|---|
| %{u}t | The current time including micro-seconds |
| %{cu}t | The current time in compact ISO 8601 format, including micro-seconds |
| %v | The canonical SERVERNAME of the current server. |
| %V | The server name of the server serving the request according to the USECANONICALNAME setting. |
| \ (backslash space) | Non-field delimiting space |
| % (percent space) | Field delimiter (no output) |

The log ID format %L produces a unique id for a connection or request. This can be used to correlate which log lines belong to the same connection or request, which request happens on which connection. A %L format string is also available in MOD_LOG_CONFIG to allow to correlate access log entries with error log lines. If MOD_UNIQUE_ID is loaded, its unique id will be used as log ID for requests.

```
#Example (default format for threaded MPMs)
ErrorLogFormat "[%{u}t] [%-m:%l] [pid %P:tid %T] %7F: %E: [client\ %a] %M%,\referer\
```

This would result in error messages such as:

```
[Thu May 12 08:28:57.652118 2011] [core:error] [pid 8777:tid
4326490112] [client ::1:58619] File does not exist:
/usr/local/apache2/htdocs/favicon.ico
```

Notice that, as discussed above, some fields are omitted entirely because they are not defined.

```
#Example (similar to the 2.2.x format)
ErrorLogFormat "[%t] [%l] %7F: %E: [client\ %a] %M%,\referer\%{Referer}i"


#Advanced example with request/connection log IDs
ErrorLogFormat "[%{uc}t] [%-m:%-l] [R:%L] [C:%{C}L] %7F: %E: %M"
ErrorLogFormat request "[%{uc}t] [R:%L] Request %k on C:%{c}L pid:%P tid:%T"
ErrorLogFormat request "[%{uc}t] [R:%L] UA:'%+{User-Agent}i'"
ErrorLogFormat request "[%{uc}t] [R:%L] Referer:'%+{Referer}i'"
ErrorLogFormat connection "[%{uc}t] [C:%{c}L] local\ %a remote\ %A"
```

### See also

- ERRORLOG
- LOGLEVEL
- Apache HTTP Server Log Files (p. 56)

## ExtendedStatus Directive

| Description: | Keep track of extended status information for each request |
|---|---|
| Syntax: | ExtendedStatus On\|Off |
| Default: | ExtendedStatus Off[*] |
| Context: | server config |
| Status: | Core |
| Module: | core |

This option tracks additional data per worker about the currently executing request and creates a utilization summary. You can see these variables during runtime by configuring MOD_STATUS. Note that other modules may rely on this scoreboard.

This setting applies to the entire server and cannot be enabled or disabled on a virtualhost-by-virtualhost basis. The collection of extended status information can slow down the server. Also note that this setting cannot be changed during a graceful restart.

> Note that loading MOD_STATUS will change the default behavior to ExtendedStatus On, while other third party modules may do the same. Such modules rely on collecting detailed information about the state of all workers. The default is changed by MOD_STATUS beginning with version 2.3.6. The previous default was always Off.

## FileETag Directive

| | |
|---|---|
| Description: | File attributes used to create the ETag HTTP response header for static files |
| Syntax: | `FileETag component ...` |
| Default: | `FileETag MTime Size` |
| Context: | server config, virtual host, directory, .htaccess |
| Override: | FileInfo |
| Status: | Core |
| Module: | core |
| Compatibility: | The default used to be "INodeMTimeSize" in 2.3.14 and earlier. |

The FILEETAG directive configures the file attributes that are used to create the `ETag` (entity tag) response header field when the document is based on a static file. (The `ETag` value is used in cache management to save network bandwidth.) The FILEETAG directive allows you to choose which of these – if any – should be used. The recognized keywords are:

**INode** The file's i-node number will be included in the calculation

**MTime** The date and time the file was last modified will be included

**Size** The number of bytes in the file will be included

**All** All available fields will be used. This is equivalent to:

```
FileETag INode MTime Size
```

**None** If a document is file-based, no `ETag` field will be included in the response

The `INode`, `MTime`, and `Size` keywords may be prefixed with either + or −, which allow changes to be made to the default setting inherited from a broader scope. Any keyword appearing without such a prefix immediately and completely cancels the inherited setting.

If a directory's configuration includes `FileETagINodeMTimeSize`, and a subdirectory's includes `FileETag-INode`, the setting for that subdirectory (which will be inherited by any sub-subdirectories that don't override it) will be equivalent to `FileETagMTimeSize`.

**Warning**

Do not change the default for directories or locations that have WebDAV enabled and use MOD_DAV_FS as a storage provider. MOD_DAV_FS uses `MTimeSize` as a fixed format for `ETag` comparisons on conditional requests. These conditional requests will break if the `ETag` format is changed via FILEETAG.

**Server Side Includes**

An ETag is not generated for responses parsed by MOD_INCLUDE since the response entity can change without a change of the INode, MTime, or Size of the static file with embedded SSI directives.

## Files Directive

| | |
|---|---|
| Description: | Contains directives that apply to matched filenames |
| Syntax: | `<Files filename> ... </Files>` |
| Context: | server config, virtual host, directory, .htaccess |
| Override: | All |
| Status: | Core |
| Module: | core |

The <FILES> directive limits the scope of the enclosed directives by filename. It is comparable to the <DIRECTORY> and <LOCATION> directives. It should be matched with a </Files> directive. The directives given within this section will be applied to any object with a basename (last component of filename) matching the specified filename. <FILES> sections are processed in the order they appear in the configuration file, after the <DIRECTORY> sections and .htaccess files are read, but before <LOCATION> sections. Note that <FILES> can be nested inside <DIRECTORY> sections to restrict the portion of the filesystem they apply to.

The *filename* argument should include a filename, or a wild-card string, where ? matches any single character, and * matches any sequences of characters.

```
<Files "cat.html">
    # Insert stuff that applies to cat.html here
</Files>

<Files "?at.*">
    # This would apply to cat.html, bat.html, hat.php and so on.
</Files>
```

Regular expressions can also be used, with the addition of the ~ character. For example:

```
<Files ~ "\.(gif|jpe?g|png)$">
    #...
</Files>
```

would match most common Internet graphics formats. <FILESMATCH> is preferred, however.

Note that unlike <DIRECTORY> and <LOCATION> sections, <FILES> sections can be used inside .htaccess files. This allows users to control access to their own files, at a file-by-file level.

**See also**

- How <Directory>, <Location> and <Files> sections work (p. 35) for an explanation of how these different sections are combined when a request is received

## FilesMatch Directive

| | |
|---|---|
| Description: | Contains directives that apply to regular-expression matched filenames |
| Syntax: | `<FilesMatch regex> ... </FilesMatch>` |
| Context: | server config, virtual host, directory, .htaccess |
| Override: | All |
| Status: | Core |
| Module: | core |

The <FILESMATCH> directive limits the scope of the enclosed directives by filename, just as the <FILES> directive does. However, it accepts a regular expression. For example:

```
<FilesMatch ".+\.(gif|jpe?g|png)$">
    # ...
</FilesMatch>
```

would match most common Internet graphics formats.

⟹ The .+ at the start of the regex ensures that files named .png, or .gif, for example, are not matched.

From 2.4.8 onwards, named groups and backreferences are captured and written to the environment with the corresponding name prefixed with "MATCH_" and in upper case. This allows elements of files to be referenced from within expressions (p. 99) and modules like MOD_REWRITE. In order to prevent confusion, numbered (unnamed) backreferences are ignored. Use named groups instead.

```
<FilesMatch "^(?<sitename>[^/]+)">
    require ldap-group cn=%{env:MATCH_SITENAME},ou=combined,o=Example
</FilesMatch>
```

**See also**

- How <Directory>, <Location> and <Files> sections work (p. 35) for an explanation of how these different sections are combined when a request is received

## ForceType Directive

| | |
|---|---|
| Description: | Forces all matching files to be served with the specified media type in the HTTP Content-Type header field |
| Syntax: | ForceType media-type|None |
| Context: | directory, .htaccess |
| Override: | FileInfo |
| Status: | Core |
| Module: | core |

When placed into an .htaccess file or a <DIRECTORY>, or <LOCATION> or <FILES> section, this directive forces all matching files to be served with the content type identification given by *media-type*. For example, if you had a directory full of GIF files, but did not want to label them all with .gif, you might want to use:

```
ForceType image/gif
```

Note that this directive overrides other indirect media type associations defined in mime.types or via the ADDTYPE.

You can also override more general FORCETYPE settings by using the value of None:

```
# force all files to be image/gif:
<Location "/images">
  ForceType image/gif
</Location>

# but normal mime-type associations here:
<Location "/images/mixed">
  ForceType None
</Location>
```

This directive primarily overrides the content types generated for static files served out of the filesystem. For resources other than static files, where the generator of the response typically specifies a Content-Type, this directive has no effect.

**Note**

> If no handler is explicitly set for a request, the specified content type will also be used as the handler name.
>
> When explicit directives such as SETHANDLER or ADDHANDLER do not apply to the current request, the internal handler name normally set by those directives is instead set to the content type specified by this directive.
>
> This is a historical behavior that some third-party modules (such as mod_php) may look for a "synthetic" content type used only to signal the module to take responsibility for the matching request.
>
> Configurations that rely on such "synthetic" types should be avoided. Additionally, configurations that restrict access to SETHANDLER or ADDHANDLER should restrict access to this directive as well.

## GprofDir Directive

| | |
|---|---|
| Description: | Directory to write gmon.out profiling data to. |
| Syntax: | GprofDir /tmp/gprof/\|/tmp/gprof/% |
| Context: | server config, virtual host |
| Status: | Core |
| Module: | core |

When the server has been compiled with gprof profiling support, GPROFDIR causes gmon.out files to be written to the specified directory when the process exits. If the argument ends with a percent symbol ('%'), subdirectories are created for each process id.

This directive currently only works with the PREFORK MPM.

## HostnameLookups Directive

| | |
|---|---|
| Description: | Enables DNS lookups on client IP addresses |
| Syntax: | HostnameLookups On\|Off\|Double |
| Default: | HostnameLookups Off |
| Context: | server config, virtual host, directory |
| Status: | Core |
| Module: | core |

This directive enables DNS lookups so that host names can be logged (and passed to CGIs/SSIs in REMOTE_HOST). The value Double refers to doing double-reverse DNS lookup. That is, after a reverse lookup is performed, a forward lookup is then performed on that result. At least one of the IP addresses in the forward lookup must match the original address. (In "tcpwrappers" terminology this is called PARANOID.)

Regardless of the setting, when MOD_AUTHZ_HOST is used for controlling access by hostname, a double reverse lookup will be performed. This is necessary for security. Note that the result of this double-reverse isn't generally available unless you set HostnameLookups Double. For example, if only HostnameLookups On and a request is made to an object that is protected by hostname restrictions, regardless of whether the double-reverse fails or not, CGIs will still be passed the single-reverse result in REMOTE_HOST.

The default is Off in order to save the network traffic for those sites that don't truly need the reverse lookups done. It is also better for the end users because they don't have to suffer the extra latency that a lookup entails. Heavily loaded sites should leave this directive Off, since DNS lookups can take considerable amounts of time. The utility `logresolve`, compiled by default to the `bin` subdirectory of your installation directory, can be used to look up host names from logged IP addresses offline.

Finally, if you have hostname-based Require directives (p. 536) , a hostname lookup will be performed regardless of the setting of `HostnameLookups`.

## If Directive

| | |
|---|---|
| Description: | Contains directives that apply only if a condition is satisfied by a request at runtime |
| Syntax: | `<If expression> ... </If>` |
| Context: | server config, virtual host, directory, .htaccess |
| Override: | All |
| Status: | Core |
| Module: | core |

The <IF> directive evaluates an expression at runtime, and applies the enclosed directives if and only if the expression evaluates to true. For example:

```
<If "-z req('Host')">
```

would match HTTP/1.0 requests without a *Host:* header. Expressions may contain various shell-like operators for string comparison (==, !=, <, ...), integer comparison (-eq, -ne, ...), and others (-n, -z, -f, ...). It is also possible to use regular expressions,

```
<If "%{QUERY_STRING} =~ /(delete|commit)=.*?elem/">
```

shell-like pattern matches and many other operations. These operations can be done on request headers (`req`), environment variables (`env`), and a large number of other properties. The full documentation is available in Expressions in Apache HTTP Server (p. 99) .

Only directives that support the directory context (p. 377) can be used within this configuration section.

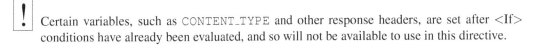

> Certain variables, such as `CONTENT_TYPE` and other response headers, are set after <If> conditions have already been evaluated, and so will not be available to use in this directive.

**See also**

- Expressions in Apache HTTP Server (p. 99) , for a complete reference and more examples.
- <ELSEIF>
- <ELSE>
- How <Directory>, <Location>, <Files> sections work (p. 35) for an explanation of how these different sections are combined when a request is received. <IF>, <ELSEIF>, and <ELSE> are applied last.

## IfDefine Directive

| | |
|---|---|
| Description: | Encloses directives that will be processed only if a test is true at startup |
| Syntax: | `<IfDefine [!]parameter-name> ... </IfDefine>` |
| Context: | server config, virtual host, directory, .htaccess |
| Override: | All |
| Status: | Core |
| Module: | core |

The <IfDefine *test*>...</IfDefine> section is used to mark directives that are conditional. The directives within an <IFDEFINE> section are only processed if the *test* is true. If *test* is false, everything between the start and end markers is ignored.

The *test* in the <IFDEFINE> section directive can be one of two forms:

- *parameter-name*
- ! *parameter-name*

In the former case, the directives between the start and end markers are only processed if the parameter named *parameter-name* is defined. The second format reverses the test, and only processes the directives if *parameter-name* is **not** defined.

The *parameter-name* argument is a define as given on the httpd command line via -D*parameter* at the time the server was started or by the DEFINE directive.

<IFDEFINE> sections are nest-able, which can be used to implement simple multiple-parameter tests. Example:

```
httpd -DReverseProxy -DUseCache -DMemCache ...
```

```
<IfDefine ReverseProxy>
  LoadModule proxy_module    modules/mod_proxy.so
  LoadModule proxy_http_module    modules/mod_proxy_http.so
  <IfDefine UseCache>
    LoadModule cache_module    modules/mod_cache.so
    <IfDefine MemCache>
      LoadModule mem_cache_module    modules/mod_mem_cache.so
    </IfDefine>
    <IfDefine !MemCache>
      LoadModule cache_disk_module    modules/mod_cache_disk.so
    </IfDefine>
  </IfDefine>
</IfDefine>
```

## IfModule Directive

| | |
|---|---|
| Description: | Encloses directives that are processed conditional on the presence or absence of a specific module |
| Syntax: | <IfModule [!]module-file\|module-identifier> ... </IfModule> |
| Context: | server config, virtual host, directory, .htaccess |
| Override: | All |
| Status: | Core |
| Module: | core |

The <IfModule *test*>...</IfModule> section is used to mark directives that are conditional on the presence of a specific module. The directives within an <IFMODULE> section are only processed if the *test* is true. If *test* is false, everything between the start and end markers is ignored.

The *test* in the <IFMODULE> section directive can be one of two forms:

- *module*
- !*module*

In the former case, the directives between the start and end markers are only processed if the module named *module* is included in Apache httpd – either compiled in or dynamically loaded using LOADMODULE. The second format reverses the test, and only processes the directives if *module* is **not** included.

The *module* argument can be either the module identifier or the file name of the module, at the time it was compiled. For example, `rewrite_module` is the identifier and `mod_rewrite.c` is the file name. If a module consists of several source files, use the name of the file containing the string `STANDARD20_MODULE_STUFF`.

<IFMODULE> sections are nest-able, which can be used to implement simple multiple-module tests.

This section should only be used if you need to have one configuration file that works whether or not a specific module is available. In normal operation, directives need not be placed in <IFMODULE> sections.

## Include Directive

| | |
|---|---|
| Description: | Includes other configuration files from within the server configuration files |
| Syntax: | `Include file-path|directory-path|wildcard` |
| Context: | server config, virtual host, directory |
| Status: | Core |
| Module: | core |
| Compatibility: | Directory wildcard matching available in 2.3.6 and later |

This directive allows inclusion of other configuration files from within the server configuration files.

Shell-style (`fnmatch()`) wildcard characters can be used in the filename or directory parts of the path to include several files at once, in alphabetical order. In addition, if INCLUDE points to a directory, rather than a file, Apache httpd will read all files in that directory and any subdirectory. However, including entire directories is not recommended, because it is easy to accidentally leave temporary files in a directory that can cause `httpd` to fail. Instead, we encourage you to use the wildcard syntax shown below, to include files that match a particular pattern, such as *.conf, for example.

The INCLUDE directive will **fail with an error** if a wildcard expression does not match any file. The INCLUDEOP-TIONAL directive can be used if non-matching wildcards should be ignored.

The file path specified may be an absolute path, or may be relative to the SERVERROOT directory.

Examples:

```
Include /usr/local/apache2/conf/ssl.conf
Include /usr/local/apache2/conf/vhosts/*.conf
```

Or, providing paths relative to your SERVERROOT directory:

```
Include conf/ssl.conf
Include conf/vhosts/*.conf
```

Wildcards may be included in the directory or file portion of the path. This example will fail if there is no subdirectory in conf/vhosts that contains at least one *.conf file:

```
Include conf/vhosts/*/*.conf
```

Alternatively, the following command will just be ignored in case of missing files or directories:

```
IncludeOptional conf/vhosts/*/*.conf
```

**See also**

- INCLUDEOPTIONAL
- apachectl

## IncludeOptional Directive

| | |
|---|---|
| Description: | Includes other configuration files from within the server configuration files |
| Syntax: | `IncludeOptional file-path|directory-path|wildcard` |
| Context: | server config, virtual host, directory |
| Status: | Core |
| Module: | core |
| Compatibility: | Available in 2.3.6 and later |

This directive allows inclusion of other configuration files from within the server configuration files. It works identically to the INCLUDE directive, with the exception that if wildcards do not match any file or directory, the INCLUDEOPTIONAL directive will be silently ignored instead of causing an error.

**See also**

- INCLUDE
- apachectl

## KeepAlive Directive

| | |
|---|---|
| Description: | Enables HTTP persistent connections |
| Syntax: | `KeepAlive On|Off` |
| Default: | `KeepAlive On` |
| Context: | server config, virtual host |
| Status: | Core |
| Module: | core |

The Keep-Alive extension to HTTP/1.0 and the persistent connection feature of HTTP/1.1 provide long-lived HTTP sessions which allow multiple requests to be sent over the same TCP connection. In some cases this has been shown to result in an almost 50% speedup in latency times for HTML documents with many images. To enable Keep-Alive connections, set `KeepAlive On`.

For HTTP/1.0 clients, Keep-Alive connections will only be used if they are specifically requested by a client. In addition, a Keep-Alive connection with an HTTP/1.0 client can only be used when the length of the content is known in advance. This implies that dynamic content such as CGI output, SSI pages, and server-generated directory listings will generally not use Keep-Alive connections to HTTP/1.0 clients. For HTTP/1.1 clients, persistent connections are the default unless otherwise specified. If the client requests it, chunked encoding will be used in order to send content of unknown length over persistent connections.

When a client uses a Keep-Alive connection, it will be counted as a single "request" for the MAXCONNECTIONSPERCHILD directive, regardless of how many requests are sent using the connection.

**See also**

- MAXKEEPALIVEREQUESTS

## KeepAliveTimeout Directive

| | |
|---|---|
| Description: | Amount of time the server will wait for subsequent requests on a persistent connection |
| Syntax: | `KeepAliveTimeout num[ms]` |
| Default: | `KeepAliveTimeout 5` |
| Context: | server config, virtual host |
| Status: | Core |
| Module: | core |

The number of seconds Apache httpd will wait for a subsequent request before closing the connection. By adding a postfix of ms the timeout can be also set in milliseconds. Once a request has been received, the timeout value specified by the TIMEOUT directive applies.

Setting KEEPALIVETIMEOUT to a high value may cause performance problems in heavily loaded servers. The higher the timeout, the more server processes will be kept occupied waiting on connections with idle clients.

If KEEPALIVETIMEOUT is **not** set for a name-based virtual host, the value of the first defined virtual host best matching the local IP and port will be used.

## Limit Directive

| | |
|---|---|
| Description: | Restrict enclosed access controls to only certain HTTP methods |
| Syntax: | `<Limit method [method] ...  > ...  </Limit>` |
| Context: | directory, .htaccess |
| Override: | AuthConfig, Limit |
| Status: | Core |
| Module: | core |

Access controls are normally effective for **all** access methods, and this is the usual desired behavior. **In the general case, access control directives should not be placed within a <LIMIT> section.**

The purpose of the <LIMIT> directive is to restrict the effect of the access controls to the nominated HTTP methods. For all other methods, the access restrictions that are enclosed in the <LIMIT> bracket **will have no effect.** The following example applies the access control only to the methods `POST`, `PUT`, and `DELETE`, leaving all other methods unprotected:

```
<Limit POST PUT DELETE>
  Require valid-user
</Limit>
```

The method names listed can be one or more of: `GET`, `POST`, `PUT`, `DELETE`, `CONNECT`, `OPTIONS`, `PATCH`, `PROPFIND`, `PROPPATCH`, `MKCOL`, `COPY`, `MOVE`, `LOCK`, and `UNLOCK`. **The method name is case-sensitive.** If `GET` is used, it will also restrict `HEAD` requests. The `TRACE` method cannot be limited (see TRACEENABLE).

> **!** A <LIMITEXCEPT> section should always be used in preference to a <LIMIT> section when restricting access, since a <LIMITEXCEPT> section provides protection against arbitrary methods.

The <LIMIT> and <LIMITEXCEPT> directives may be nested. In this case, each successive level of <LIMIT> or <LIMITEXCEPT> directives must further restrict the set of methods to which access controls apply.

> **!** When using <LIMIT> or <LIMITEXCEPT> directives with the REQUIRE directive, note that the first REQUIRE to succeed authorizes the request, regardless of the presence of other REQUIRE directives.

For example, given the following configuration, all users will be authorized for POST requests, and the Require group editors directive will be ignored in all cases:

```
<LimitExcept GET>
  Require valid-user
</LimitExcept>
<Limit POST>
  Require group editors
</Limit>
```

## LimitExcept Directive

| | |
|---|---|
| Description: | Restrict access controls to all HTTP methods except the named ones |
| Syntax: | `<LimitExcept method [method] ... > ... </LimitExcept>` |
| Context: | directory, .htaccess |
| Override: | AuthConfig, Limit |
| Status: | Core |
| Module: | core |

<LIMITEXCEPT> and </LimitExcept> are used to enclose a group of access control directives which will then apply to any HTTP access method **not** listed in the arguments; i.e., it is the opposite of a <LIMIT> section and can be used to control both standard and nonstandard/unrecognized methods. See the documentation for <LIMIT> for more details.

For example:

```
<LimitExcept POST GET>
  Require valid-user
</LimitExcept>
```

## LimitInternalRecursion Directive

| | |
|---|---|
| Description: | Determine maximum number of internal redirects and nested subrequests |
| Syntax: | `LimitInternalRecursion number [number]` |
| Default: | `LimitInternalRecursion 10` |
| Context: | server config, virtual host |
| Status: | Core |
| Module: | core |

An internal redirect happens, for example, when using the ACTION directive, which internally redirects the original request to a CGI script. A subrequest is Apache httpd's mechanism to find out what would happen for some URI if it were requested. For example, MOD_DIR uses subrequests to look for the files listed in the DIRECTORYINDEX directive.

LIMITINTERNALRECURSION prevents the server from crashing when entering an infinite loop of internal redirects or subrequests. Such loops are usually caused by misconfigurations.

The directive stores two different limits, which are evaluated on per-request basis. The first *number* is the maximum number of internal redirects that may follow each other. The second *number* determines how deeply subrequests may be nested. If you specify only one *number*, it will be assigned to both limits.

```
LimitInternalRecursion 5
```

## LimitRequestBody Directive

| | |
|---|---|
| Description: | Restricts the total size of the HTTP request body sent from the client |
| Syntax: | `LimitRequestBody bytes` |
| Default: | `LimitRequestBody 0` |
| Context: | server config, virtual host, directory, .htaccess |
| Override: | All |
| Status: | Core |
| Module: | core |

This directive specifies the number of *bytes* from 0 (meaning unlimited) to 2147483647 (2GB) that are allowed in a request body. See the note below for the limited applicability to proxy requests.

The LIMITREQUESTBODY directive allows the user to set a limit on the allowed size of an HTTP request message body within the context in which the directive is given (server, per-directory, per-file or per-location). If the client request exceeds that limit, the server will return an error response instead of servicing the request. The size of a normal request message body will vary greatly depending on the nature of the resource and the methods allowed on that resource. CGI scripts typically use the message body for retrieving form information. Implementations of the PUT method will require a value at least as large as any representation that the server wishes to accept for that resource.

This directive gives the server administrator greater control over abnormal client request behavior, which may be useful for avoiding some forms of denial-of-service attacks.

If, for example, you are permitting file upload to a particular location and wish to limit the size of the uploaded file to 100K, you might use the following directive:

```
LimitRequestBody 102400
```

For a full description of how this directive is interpreted by proxy requests, see the MOD_PROXY documentation.

## LimitRequestFields Directive

| | |
|---|---|
| Description: | Limits the number of HTTP request header fields that will be accepted from the client |
| Syntax: | `LimitRequestFields number` |
| Default: | `LimitRequestFields 100` |
| Context: | server config, virtual host |
| Status: | Core |
| Module: | core |

*Number* is an integer from 0 (meaning unlimited) to 32767. The default value is defined by the compile-time constant DEFAULT_LIMIT_REQUEST_FIELDS (100 as distributed).

The LIMITREQUESTFIELDS directive allows the server administrator to modify the limit on the number of request header fields allowed in an HTTP request. A server needs this value to be larger than the number of fields that a normal client request might include. The number of request header fields used by a client rarely exceeds 20, but this may vary among different client implementations, often depending upon the extent to which a user has configured their browser to support detailed content negotiation. Optional HTTP extensions are often expressed using request header fields.

This directive gives the server administrator greater control over abnormal client request behavior, which may be useful for avoiding some forms of denial-of-service attacks. The value should be increased if normal clients see an error response from the server that indicates too many fields were sent in the request.

For example:

```
LimitRequestFields 50
```

**Warning**

When name-based virtual hosting is used, the value for this directive is taken from the default (first-listed) virtual host for the local IP and port combination.

## LimitRequestFieldSize Directive

| | |
|---|---|
| Description: | Limits the size of the HTTP request header allowed from the client |
| Syntax: | `LimitRequestFieldSize bytes` |
| Default: | `LimitRequestFieldSize 8190` |
| Context: | server config, virtual host |
| Status: | Core |
| Module: | core |

This directive specifies the number of *bytes* that will be allowed in an HTTP request header.

The LIMITREQUESTFIELDSIZE directive allows the server administrator to set the limit on the allowed size of an HTTP request header field. A server needs this value to be large enough to hold any one header field from a normal client request. The size of a normal request header field will vary greatly among different client implementations, often depending upon the extent to which a user has configured their browser to support detailed content negotiation. SPNEGO authentication headers can be up to 12392 bytes.

This directive gives the server administrator greater control over abnormal client request behavior, which may be useful for avoiding some forms of denial-of-service attacks.

For example:

```
LimitRequestFieldSize 4094
```

 Under normal conditions, the value should not be changed from the default.

 **Warning**

When name-based virtual hosting is used, the value for this directive is taken from the default (first-listed) virtual host best matching the current IP address and port combination.

## LimitRequestLine Directive

| | |
|---|---|
| Description: | Limit the size of the HTTP request line that will be accepted from the client |
| Syntax: | `LimitRequestLine bytes` |
| Default: | `LimitRequestLine 8190` |
| Context: | server config, virtual host |
| Status: | Core |
| Module: | core |

This directive sets the number of *bytes* that will be allowed on the HTTP request-line.

The LIMITREQUESTLINE directive allows the server administrator to set the limit on the allowed size of a client's HTTP request-line. Since the request-line consists of the HTTP method, URI, and protocol version, the LIMITRE-QUESTLINE directive places a restriction on the length of a request-URI allowed for a request on the server. A server needs this value to be large enough to hold any of its resource names, including any information that might be passed in the query part of a `GET` request.

This directive gives the server administrator greater control over abnormal client request behavior, which may be useful for avoiding some forms of denial-of-service attacks.

For example:

```
LimitRequestLine 4094
```

Under normal conditions, the value should not be changed from the default.

**! Warning**

When name-based virtual hosting is used, the value for this directive is taken from the default (first-listed) virtual host best matching the current IP address and port combination.

## LimitXMLRequestBody Directive

| | |
|---|---|
| Description: | Limits the size of an XML-based request body |
| Syntax: | `LimitXMLRequestBody bytes` |
| Default: | `LimitXMLRequestBody 1000000` |
| Context: | server config, virtual host, directory, .htaccess |
| Override: | All |
| Status: | Core |
| Module: | core |

Limit (in bytes) on maximum size of an XML-based request body. A value of 0 will disable any checking.

Example:

```
LimitXMLRequestBody 0
```

## Location Directive

| | |
|---|---|
| Description: | Applies the enclosed directives only to matching URLs |
| Syntax: | `<Location URL-path|URL> ... </Location>` |
| Context: | server config, virtual host |
| Status: | Core |
| Module: | core |

The <LOCATION> directive limits the scope of the enclosed directives by URL. It is similar to the <DIRECTORY> directive, and starts a subsection which is terminated with a `</Location>` directive. <LOCATION> sections are processed in the order they appear in the configuration file, after the <DIRECTORY> sections and `.htaccess` files are read, and after the <FILES> sections.

<LOCATION> sections operate completely outside the filesystem. This has several consequences. Most importantly, <LOCATION> directives should not be used to control access to filesystem locations. Since several different URLs may map to the same filesystem location, such access controls may by circumvented.

The enclosed directives will be applied to the request if the path component of the URL meets *any* of the following criteria:

- The specified location matches exactly the path component of the URL.
- The specified location, which ends in a forward slash, is a prefix of the path component of the URL (treated as a context root).
- The specified location, with the addition of a trailing slash, is a prefix of the path component of the URL (also treated as a context root).

In the example below, where no trailing slash is used, requests to /private1, /private1/ and /private1/file.txt will have the enclosed directives applied, but /private1other would not.

```
<Location "/private1">
    #  ...
</Location>
```

In the example below, where a trailing slash is used, requests to /private2/ and /private2/file.txt will have the enclosed directives applied, but /private2 and /private2other would not.

```
<Location "/private2/">
    #  ...
</Location>
```

**When to use <LOCATION>**

Use <LOCATION> to apply directives to content that lives outside the filesystem. For content that lives in the filesystem, use <DIRECTORY> and <FILES>. An exception is <Location "/">, which is an easy way to apply a configuration to the entire server.

For all origin (non-proxy) requests, the URL to be matched is a URL-path of the form /path/. *No scheme, hostname, port, or query string may be included.* For proxy requests, the URL to be matched is of the form scheme://servername/path, and you must include the prefix.

The URL may use wildcards. In a wild-card string, ? matches any single character, and ⋆ matches any sequences of characters. Neither wildcard character matches a / in the URL-path.

Regular expressions can also be used, with the addition of the ˜ character. For example:

```
<Location ˜ "/(extra|special)/data">
    #...
</Location>
```

would match URLs that contained the substring /extra/data or /special/data. The directive <LOCATION-MATCH> behaves identical to the regex version of <LOCATION>, and is preferred, for the simple reason that ˜ is hard to distinguish from – in many fonts.

The <LOCATION> functionality is especially useful when combined with the SETHANDLER directive. For example, to enable status requests but allow them only from browsers at example.com, you might use:

```
<Location "/status">
  SetHandler server-status
  Require host example.com
</Location>
```

**Note about / (slash)**

The slash character has special meaning depending on where in a URL it appears. People may be used to its behavior in the filesystem where multiple adjacent slashes are frequently collapsed to a single slash (*i.e.*, /home///foo is the same as /home/foo). In URL-space this is not necessarily true. The <LOCATIONMATCH> directive and the regex version of <LOCATION> require you to explicitly specify multiple slashes if that is your intention.
For example, <LocationMatch "ˆ/abc"> would match the request URL /abc but not the request URL //abc. The (non-regex) <LOCATION> directive behaves similarly when used for proxy requests. But when (non-regex) <LOCATION> is used for non-proxy requests it will implicitly match multiple slashes with a single slash. For example, if you specify <Location "/abc/def"> and the request is to /abc//def then it will match.

**See also**

- How <Directory>, <Location> and <Files> sections work (p. 35) for an explanation of how these different sections are combined when a request is received.

- LOCATIONMATCH

## LocationMatch Directive

| | |
|---|---|
| Description: | Applies the enclosed directives only to regular-expression matching URLs |
| Syntax: | `<LocationMatch regex> ...  </LocationMatch>` |
| Context: | server config, virtual host |
| Status: | Core |
| Module: | core |

The <LOCATIONMATCH> directive limits the scope of the enclosed directives by URL, in an identical manner to <LOCATION>. However, it takes a regular expression as an argument instead of a simple string. For example:

```
<LocationMatch "/(extra|special)/data">
    # ...
</LocationMatch>
```

would match URLs that contained the substring /extra/data or /special/data.

➡️ If the intent is that a URL **starts with** /extra/data, rather than merely **contains** /extra/data, prefix the regular expression with a ^ to require this.

```
<LocationMatch "^/(extra|special)/data">
```

From 2.4.8 onwards, named groups and backreferences are captured and written to the environment with the corresponding name prefixed with "MATCH_" and in upper case. This allows elements of URLs to be referenced from within expressions (p. 99) and modules like MOD_REWRITE. In order to prevent confusion, numbered (unnamed) backreferences are ignored. Use named groups instead.

```
<LocationMatch "^/combined/(?<sitename>[^/]+)">
    require ldap-group cn=%{env:MATCH_SITENAME},ou=combined,o=Example
</LocationMatch>
```

**See also**

- How <Directory>, <Location> and <Files> sections work (p. 35) for an explanation of how these different sections are combined when a request is received

## LogLevel Directive

| | |
|---|---|
| Description: | Controls the verbosity of the ErrorLog |
| Syntax: | `LogLevel [module:]level [module:level] ...` |
| Default: | `LogLevel warn` |
| Context: | server config, virtual host, directory |
| Status: | Core |
| Module: | core |
| Compatibility: | Per-module and per-directory configuration is available in Apache HTTP Server 2.3.6 and later |

LOGLEVEL adjusts the verbosity of the messages recorded in the error logs (see ERRORLOG directive). The following *level*s are available, in order of decreasing significance:

| Level | Description | Example |
|-------|-------------|---------|
| `emerg` | Emergencies - system is unusable. | "Child cannot open lock file. Exiting" |
| `alert` | Action must be taken immediately. | "getpwuid: couldn't determine user name from uid" |
| `crit` | Critical Conditions. | "socket: Failed to get a socket, exiting child" |
| `error` | Error conditions. | "Premature end of script headers" |
| `warn` | Warning conditions. | "child process 1234 did not exit, sending another SIGHUP" |
| `notice` | Normal but significant condition. | "httpd: caught SIGBUS, attempting to dump core in ..." |
| `info` | Informational. | "Server seems busy, (you may need to increase StartServers, or Min/MaxSpareServers)..." |
| `debug` | Debug-level messages | "Opening config file ..." |
| `trace1` | Trace messages | "proxy: FTP: control connection complete" |
| `trace2` | Trace messages | "proxy: CONNECT: sending the CONNECT request to the remote proxy" |
| `trace3` | Trace messages | "openssl: Handshake: start" |
| `trace4` | Trace messages | "read from buffered SSL brigade, mode 0, 17 bytes" |
| `trace5` | Trace messages | "map lookup FAILED: map=rewritemap key=keyname" |
| `trace6` | Trace messages | "cache lookup FAILED, forcing new map lookup" |
| `trace7` | Trace messages, dumping large amounts of data | "— 0000: 02 23 44 30 13 40 ac 34 df 3d bf 9a 19 49 39 15 —" |
| `trace8` | Trace messages, dumping large amounts of data | "— 0000: 02 23 44 30 13 40 ac 34 df 3d bf 9a 19 49 39 15 —" |

When a particular level is specified, messages from all other levels of higher significance will be reported as well. *E.g.*, when `LogLevel info` is specified, then messages with log levels of `notice` and `warn` will also be posted.

Using a level of at least `crit` is recommended.

For example:

```
LogLevel notice
```

**Note**

When logging to a regular file, messages of the level `notice` cannot be suppressed and thus are always logged. However, this doesn't apply when logging is done using `syslog`.

Specifying a level without a module name will reset the level for all modules to that level. Specifying a level with a module name will set the level for that module only. It is possible to use the module source file name, the module identifier, or the module identifier with the trailing `_module` omitted as module specification. This means the following three specifications are equivalent:

```
LogLevel info ssl:warn
LogLevel info mod_ssl.c:warn
LogLevel info ssl_module:warn
```

It is also possible to change the level per directory:

```
LogLevel info
<Directory "/usr/local/apache/htdocs/app">
  LogLevel debug
</Directory>
```

Per directory loglevel configuration only affects messages that are logged after the request has been parsed and that are associated with the request. Log messages which are associated with the server or the connection are not affected. The latter can be influenced by the LOGLEVEL-OVERRIDE directive, though.

**See also**

- ERRORLOG
- ERRORLOGFORMAT
- LOGLEVELOVERRIDE
- Apache HTTP Server Log Files (p. 56)

## LogLevelOverride Directive

| | |
|---|---|
| Description: | Override the verbosity of the ErrorLog for certain clients |
| Syntax: | `LogLevel ipaddress[/prefixlen] [module:]level [module:level]` `...` |
| Default: | `unset` |
| Context: | server config, virtual host |
| Status: | Core |
| Module: | core |
| Compatibility: | Available in Apache HTTP Server 2.5.0 and later |

LOGLEVELOVERRIDE adjusts the LOGLEVEL for requests coming from certain client IP addresses. This allows to enable verbose logging only for certain test clients. The IP address is checked at a very early state in the connection processing. Therefore, LOGLEVELOVERRIDE allows to change the log level for things like the SSL handshake which happen before a LOGLEVEL directive in an <IF> container would be evaluated.

LOGLEVELOVERRIDE accepts either a single IP-address or a CIDR IP-address/len subnet specification. For the syntax of the loglevel specification, see the LOGLEVEL directive.

For requests that match a LOGLEVELOVERRIDE directive, per-directory specifications of LOGLEVEL are ignored.

Examples:

```
LogLevelOverride 192.0.2.0/24 ssl:trace6
LogLevelOverride 192.0.2.7 ssl:trace8
```

⟹ LOGLEVELOVERRIDE only affects log messages that are associated with the request or the connection. Log messages which are associated with the server are not affected.

**See also**

- LOGLEVEL

## MaxKeepAliveRequests Directive

| | |
|---|---|
| Description: | Number of requests allowed on a persistent connection |
| Syntax: | `MaxKeepAliveRequests number` |
| Default: | `MaxKeepAliveRequests 100` |
| Context: | server config, virtual host |
| Status: | Core |
| Module: | core |

The MAXKEEPALIVEREQUESTS directive limits the number of requests allowed per connection when KEEPALIVE is on. If it is set to 0, unlimited requests will be allowed. We recommend that this setting be kept to a high value for maximum server performance.

For example:

```
MaxKeepAliveRequests 500
```

## MaxRangeOverlaps Directive

| | |
|---|---|
| Description: | Number of overlapping ranges (eg: `100-200,150-300`) allowed before returning the complete resource |
| Syntax: | `MaxRangeOverlaps default | unlimited | none | number-of-ranges` |
| Default: | `MaxRangeOverlaps 20` |
| Context: | server config, virtual host, directory |
| Status: | Core |
| Module: | core |
| Compatibility: | Available in Apache HTTP Server 2.3.15 and later |

The MAXRANGEOVERLAPS directive limits the number of overlapping HTTP ranges the server is willing to return to the client. If more overlapping ranges than permitted are requested, the complete resource is returned instead.

**default** Limits the number of overlapping ranges to a compile-time default of 20.

**none** No overlapping Range headers are allowed.

**unlimited** The server does not limit the number of overlapping ranges it is willing to satisfy.

*number-of-ranges* A positive number representing the maximum number of overlapping ranges the server is willing to satisfy.

## MaxRangeReversals Directive

| | |
|---|---|
| Description: | Number of range reversals (eg: `100-200,50-70`) allowed before returning the complete resource |
| Syntax: | `MaxRangeReversals default | unlimited | none | number-of-ranges` |
| Default: | `MaxRangeReversals 20` |
| Context: | server config, virtual host, directory |
| Status: | Core |
| Module: | core |
| Compatibility: | Available in Apache HTTP Server 2.3.15 and later |

The MAXRANGEREVERSALS directive limits the number of HTTP Range reversals the server is willing to return to the client. If more ranges reversals than permitted are requested, the complete resource is returned instead.

**default** Limits the number of range reversals to a compile-time default of 20.

**none** No Range reversals headers are allowed.

**unlimited** The server does not limit the number of range reversals it is willing to satisfy.

*number-of-ranges* A positive number representing the maximum number of range reversals the server is willing to satisfy.

## MaxRanges Directive

| | |
|---|---|
| Description: | Number of ranges allowed before returning the complete resource |
| Syntax: | `MaxRanges default | unlimited | none | number-of-ranges` |
| Default: | `MaxRanges 200` |
| Context: | server config, virtual host, directory |
| Status: | Core |
| Module: | core |
| Compatibility: | Available in Apache HTTP Server 2.3.15 and later |

The MAXRANGES directive limits the number of HTTP ranges the server is willing to return to the client. If more ranges than permitted are requested, the complete resource is returned instead.

**default** Limits the number of ranges to a compile-time default of 200.

**none** Range headers are ignored.

**unlimited** The server does not limit the number of ranges it is willing to satisfy.

*number-of-ranges* A positive number representing the maximum number of ranges the server is willing to satisfy.

## MergeTrailers Directive

| | |
|---|---|
| Description: | Determines whether trailers are merged into headers |
| Syntax: | `MergeTrailers [on|off]` |
| Default: | `MergeTrailers off` |
| Context: | server config, virtual host |
| Status: | Core |
| Module: | core |
| Compatibility: | 2.4.11 and later |

This directive controls whether HTTP trailers are copied into the internal representation of HTTP headers. This merging occurs when the request body has been completely consumed, long after most header processing would have a chance to examine or modify request headers.

This option is provided for compatibility with releases prior to 2.4.11, where trailers were always merged.

## Mutex Directive

| | |
|---|---|
| Description: | Configures mutex mechanism and lock file directory for all or specified mutexes |
| Syntax: | `Mutex mechanism [default|mutex-name] ...  [OmitPID]` |
| Default: | `Mutex default` |
| Context: | server config |
| Status: | Core |
| Module: | core |
| Compatibility: | Available in Apache HTTP Server 2.3.4 and later |

The MUTEX directive sets the mechanism, and optionally the lock file location, that httpd and modules use to serialize access to resources. Specify `default` as the second argument to change the settings for all mutexes; specify a mutex name (see table below) as the second argument to override defaults only for that mutex.

The MUTEX directive is typically used in the following exceptional situations:

- change the mutex mechanism when the default mechanism selected by APR has a functional or performance problem
- change the directory used by file-based mutexes when the default directory does not support locking

> **Supported modules**
> This directive only configures mutexes which have been registered with the core server using the `ap_mutex_register()` API. All modules bundled with httpd support the MUTEX directive, but third-party modules may not. Consult the documentation of the third-party module, which must indicate the mutex name(s) which can be configured if this directive is supported.

The following mutex *mechanisms* are available:

- `default | yes` This selects the default locking implementation, as determined by APR. The default locking implementation can be displayed by running `httpd` with the `-V` option.

- `none | no` This effectively disables the mutex, and is only allowed for a mutex if the module indicates that it is a valid choice. Consult the module documentation for more information.

- `posixsem` This is a mutex variant based on a Posix semaphore.

**Warning**
The semaphore ownership is not recovered if a thread in the process holding the mutex segfaults, resulting in a hang of the web server.

- `sysvsem` This is a mutex variant based on a SystemV IPC semaphore.

**Warning**
It is possible to "leak" SysV semaphores if processes crash before the semaphore is removed.

**Security**
The semaphore API allows for a denial of service attack by any CGIs running under the same uid as the webserver (*i.e.*, all CGIs, unless you use something like `suexec` or `cgiwrapper`).

- `sem` This selects the "best" available semaphore implementation, choosing between Posix and SystemV IPC semaphores, in that order.

- `pthread` This is a mutex variant based on cross-process Posix thread mutexes.

**Warning**
On most systems, if a child process terminates abnormally while holding a mutex that uses this implementation, the server will deadlock and stop responding to requests. When this occurs, the server will require a manual restart to recover.
Solaris and Linux are notable exceptions as they provide a mechanism which usually allows the mutex to be recovered after a child process terminates abnormally while holding a mutex.
If your system is POSIX compliant or if it implements the `pthread_mutexattr_setrobust_np()` function, you may be able to use the `pthread` option safely.

- `fcntl:/path/to/mutex` This is a mutex variant where a physical (lock-)file and the `fcntl()` function are used as the mutex.

**Warning**
When multiple mutexes based on this mechanism are used within multi-threaded, multi-process environments, deadlock errors (EDEADLK) can be reported for valid mutex operations if `fcntl()` is not thread-aware, such as on Solaris.

- `flock:/path/to/mutex` This is similar to the `fcntl:/path/to/mutex` method with the exception that the `flock()` function is used to provide file locking.

- `file:/path/to/mutex` This selects the "best" available file locking implementation, choosing between `fcntl` and `flock`, in that order.

Most mechanisms are only available on selected platforms, where the underlying platform and APR support it. Mechanisms which aren't available on all platforms are *posixsem, sysvsem, sem, pthread, fcntl, flock,* and *file*.

With the file-based mechanisms *fcntl* and *flock*, the path, if provided, is a directory where the lock file will be created. The default directory is httpd's run-time file directory, DEFAULTRUNTIMEDIR. If a relative path is provided, it is relative to DEFAULTRUNTIMEDIR. Always use a local disk filesystem for `/path/to/mutex` and never a directory residing on a NFS- or AFS-filesystem. The basename of the file will be the mutex type, an optional instance string provided by the module, and unless the `OmitPID` keyword is specified, the process id of the httpd parent process will be appended to make the file name unique, avoiding conflicts when multiple httpd instances share a lock file directory. For example, if the mutex name is `mpm-accept` and the lock file directory is `/var/httpd/locks`, the lock file name for the httpd instance with parent process id 12345 would be `/var/httpd/locks/mpm-accept.12345`.

 **Security**

It is best to *avoid* putting mutex files in a world-writable directory such as `/var/tmp` because someone could create a denial of service attack and prevent the server from starting by creating a lockfile with the same name as the one the server will try to create.

The following table documents the names of mutexes used by httpd and bundled modules.

| Mutex name | Module(s) | Protected resource |
|---|---|---|
| mpm-accept | PREFORK and WORKER MPMs | incoming connections, to avoid the thundering herd problem; for more information, refer to the performance tuning (p. 339) documentation |
| authdigest-client | MOD_AUTH_DIGEST | client list in shared memory |
| authdigest-opaque | MOD_AUTH_DIGEST | counter in shared memory |
| ldap-cache | MOD_LDAP | LDAP result cache |
| rewrite-map | MOD_REWRITE | communication with external mapping programs, to avoid intermixed I/O from multiple requests |
| ssl-cache | MOD_SSL | SSL session cache |
| ssl-stapling | MOD_SSL | OCSP stapling response cache |
| watchdog-callback | MOD_WATCHDOG | callback function of a particular client module |

The `OmitPID` keyword suppresses the addition of the httpd parent process id from the lock file name.

In the following example, the mutex mechanism for the MPM accept mutex will be changed from the compiled-in default to `fcntl`, with the associated lock file created in directory `/var/httpd/locks`. The mutex mechanism for all other mutexes will be changed from the compiled-in default to `sysvsem`.

```
Mutex sysvsem default
Mutex fcntl:/var/httpd/locks mpm-accept
```

## NameVirtualHost Directive

| Description: | DEPRECATED: Designates an IP address for name-virtual hosting |
|---|---|
| Syntax: | `NameVirtualHost addr[:port]` |
| Context: | server config |
| Status: | Core |
| Module: | core |

Prior to 2.3.11, NAMEVIRTUALHOST was required to instruct the server that a particular IP address and port combination was usable as a name-based virtual host. In 2.3.11 and later, any time an IP address and port combination is used in multiple virtual hosts, name-based virtual hosting is automatically enabled for that address.

This directive currently has no effect.

**See also**

- Virtual Hosts documentation (p. 124)

## Options Directive

| | |
|---|---|
| Description: | Configures what features are available in a particular directory |
| Syntax: | `Options [+|-]option [[+|-]option] ...` |
| Default: | `Options FollowSymlinks` |
| Context: | server config, virtual host, directory, .htaccess |
| Override: | Options |
| Status: | Core |
| Module: | core |
| Compatibility: | The default was changed from All to FollowSymlinks in 2.3.11 |

The OPTIONS directive controls which server features are available in a particular directory.

*option* can be set to `None`, in which case none of the extra features are enabled, or one or more of the following:

**All** All options except for `MultiViews`.

**ExecCGI** Execution of CGI scripts using MOD_CGI is permitted.

**FollowSymLinks** The server will follow symbolic links in this directory. This is the default setting.

 Even though the server follows the symlink it does *not* change the pathname used to match against <DIRECTORY> sections.
The `FollowSymLinks` and `SymLinksIfOwnerMatch` OPTIONS work only in <DIRECTORY> sections or `.htaccess` files.
Omitting this option should not be considered a security restriction, since symlink testing is subject to race conditions that make it circumventable.

**Includes** Server-side includes provided by MOD_INCLUDE are permitted.

**IncludesNOEXEC** Server-side includes are permitted, but the `#exec cmd` and `#exec cgi` are disabled. It is still possible to `#include virtual` CGI scripts from SCRIPTALIASed directories.

**Indexes** If a URL which maps to a directory is requested and there is no DIRECTORYINDEX (*e.g.*, `index.html`) in that directory, then MOD_AUTOINDEX will return a formatted listing of the directory.

**MultiViews** Content negotiated (p. 78) "MultiViews" are allowed using MOD_NEGOTIATION.
Note
This option gets ignored if set anywhere other than <DIRECTORY>, as MOD_NEGOTIATION needs real resources to compare against and evaluate from.

**SymLinksIfOwnerMatch** The server will only follow symbolic links for which the target file or directory is owned by the same user id as the link.
Note
The `FollowSymLinks` and `SymLinksIfOwnerMatch` OPTIONS work only in <DIRECTORY> sections or `.htaccess` files.
This option should not be considered a security restriction, since symlink testing is subject to race conditions that make it circumventable.

Normally, if multiple OPTIONS could apply to a directory, then the most specific one is used and others are ignored; the options are not merged. (See how sections are merged (p. 35) .) However if *all* the options on the OPTIONS directive are preceded by a + or − symbol, the options are merged. Any options preceded by a + are added to the options currently in force, and any options preceded by a − are removed from the options currently in force.

Note
Mixing OPTIONS with a + or − with those without is not valid syntax and will be rejected during server startup by the syntax check with an abort.

For example, without any + and − symbols:

```
<Directory "/web/docs">
  Options Indexes FollowSymLinks
</Directory>

<Directory "/web/docs/spec">
  Options Includes
</Directory>
```

then only `Includes` will be set for the `/web/docs/spec` directory. However if the second OPTIONS directive uses the + and − symbols:

```
<Directory "/web/docs">
  Options Indexes FollowSymLinks
</Directory>

<Directory "/web/docs/spec">
  Options +Includes -Indexes
</Directory>
```

then the options `FollowSymLinks` and `Includes` are set for the `/web/docs/spec` directory.

**Note**

> Using `-IncludesNOEXEC` or `-Includes` disables server-side includes completely regardless of the previous setting.

The default in the absence of any other settings is `FollowSymlinks`.

## Protocol Directive

| | |
|---|---|
| Description: | Protocol for a listening socket |
| Syntax: | `Protocol protocol` |
| Context: | server config, virtual host |
| Status: | Core |
| Module: | core |
| Compatibility: | On Windows, only available from Apache 2.3.3 and later. |

This directive specifies the protocol used for a specific listening socket. The protocol is used to determine which module should handle a request and to apply protocol specific optimizations with the ACCEPTFILTER directive.

You only need to set the protocol if you are running on non-standard ports; otherwise, `http` is assumed for port 80 and `https` for port 443.

For example, if you are running `https` on a non-standard port, specify the protocol explicitly:

```
Protocol https
```

You can also specify the protocol using the LISTEN directive.

**See also**

- ACCEPTFILTER
- LISTEN

## Protocols Directive

| | |
|---|---|
| Description: | Protocols available for a server/virtual host |
| Syntax: | `Protocols protocol ...` |
| Default: | `Protocols http/1.1` |
| Context: | server config, virtual host |
| Status: | Core |
| Module: | core |
| Compatibility: | Only available from Apache 2.4.17 and later. |

This directive specifies the list of protocols supported for a server/virtual host. The list determines the allowed protocols a client may negotiate for this server/host.

You need to set protocols if you want to extend the available protocols for a server/host. By default, only the http/1.1 protocol (which includes the compatibility with 1.0 and 0.9 clients) is allowed.

For example, if you want to support HTTP/2 for a server with TLS, specify:

```
Protocols h2 http/1.1
```

Valid protocols are `http/1.1` for http and https connections, `h2` on https connections and `h2c` for http connections. Modules may enable more protocols.

It is safe to specify protocols that are unavailable/disabled. Such protocol names will simply be ignored.

Protocols specified in base servers are inherited for virtual hosts only if the virtual host has no own Protocols directive. Or, the other way around, Protocols directives in virtual hosts replace any such directive in the base server.

**See also**

- PROTOCOLSHONORORDER

## ProtocolsHonorOrder Directive

| | |
|---|---|
| Description: | Determines if order of Protocols determines precedence during negotiation |
| Syntax: | `ProtocolsHonorOrder On\|Off` |
| Default: | `ProtocolsHonorOrder On` |
| Context: | server config, virtual host |
| Status: | Core |
| Module: | core |
| Compatibility: | Only available from Apache 2.4.17 and later. |

This directive specifies if the server should honor the order in which the PROTOCOLS directive lists protocols.

If configured Off, the client supplied list order of protocols has precedence over the order in the server configuration.

With PROTOCOLSHONORORDER set to `on` (default), the client ordering does not matter and only the ordering in the server settings influences the outcome of the protocol negotiation.

**See also**

- PROTOCOLS

## QualifyRedirectURL Directive

| | |
|---|---|
| Description: | Controls whether the REDIRECT_URL environment variable is fully qualified |
| Syntax: | `QualifyRedirectURL ON\|OFF` |
| Default: | `QualifyRedirectURL OFF` |
| Context: | server config, virtual host, directory |
| Override: | FileInfo |
| Status: | Core |
| Module: | core |
| Compatibility: | Directive supported in 2.4.18 and later.  2.4.17 acted as if 'QualifyRedirectURL ON' was configured. |

This directive controls whether the server will ensure that the REDIRECT_URL environment variable is fully qualified. By default, the variable contains the verbatim URL requested by the client, such as "/index.html". With QUAL-IFYREDIRECTURL ON, the same request would result in a value such as "http://www.example.com/index.html".

Even without this directive set, when a request is issued against a fully qualified URL, REDIRECT_URL will remain fully qualified.

## RegisterHttpMethod Directive

| | |
|---|---|
| Description: | Register non-standard HTTP methods |
| Syntax: | `RegisterHttpMethod method [method [...]]` |
| Context: | server config |
| Status: | Core |
| Module: | core |

HTTP Methods that are not conforming to the relvant RFCs are normally rejected by request processing in Apache HTTPD. To avoid this, modules can register non-standard HTTP methods they support. The REGISTERHTTPMETHOD allows to register such methods manually. This can be useful if such methods are forwarded for external processing, e.g. to a CGI script.

## RLimitCPU Directive

| | |
|---|---|
| Description: | Limits the CPU consumption of processes launched by Apache httpd children |
| Syntax: | `RLimitCPU seconds\|max [seconds\|max]` |
| Default: | `Unset; uses operating system defaults` |
| Context: | server config, virtual host, directory, .htaccess |
| Override: | All |
| Status: | Core |
| Module: | core |

Takes 1 or 2 parameters. The first parameter sets the soft resource limit for all processes and the second parameter sets the maximum resource limit. Either parameter can be a number, or `max` to indicate to the server that the limit should be set to the maximum allowed by the operating system configuration. Raising the maximum resource limit requires that the server is running as `root` or in the initial startup phase.

This applies to processes forked from Apache httpd children servicing requests, not the Apache httpd children themselves. This includes CGI scripts and SSI exec commands, but not any processes forked from the Apache httpd parent, such as piped logs.

CPU resource limits are expressed in seconds per process.

**See also**

- RLIMITMEM

- RLimitNPROC

## RLimitMEM Directive

| Description: | Limits the memory consumption of processes launched by Apache httpd children |
|---|---|
| Syntax: | RLimitMEM bytes\|max [bytes\|max] |
| Default: | Unset; uses operating system defaults |
| Context: | server config, virtual host, directory, .htaccess |
| Override: | All |
| Status: | Core |
| Module: | core |

Takes 1 or 2 parameters. The first parameter sets the soft resource limit for all processes and the second parameter sets the maximum resource limit. Either parameter can be a number, or max to indicate to the server that the limit should be set to the maximum allowed by the operating system configuration. Raising the maximum resource limit requires that the server is running as root or in the initial startup phase.

This applies to processes forked from Apache httpd children servicing requests, not the Apache httpd children themselves. This includes CGI scripts and SSI exec commands, but not any processes forked from the Apache httpd parent, such as piped logs.

Memory resource limits are expressed in bytes per process.

**See also**

- RLimitCPU
- RLimitNPROC

## RLimitNPROC Directive

| Description: | Limits the number of processes that can be launched by processes launched by Apache httpd children |
|---|---|
| Syntax: | RLimitNPROC number\|max [number\|max] |
| Default: | Unset; uses operating system defaults |
| Context: | server config, virtual host, directory, .htaccess |
| Override: | All |
| Status: | Core |
| Module: | core |

Takes 1 or 2 parameters. The first parameter sets the soft resource limit for all processes, and the second parameter sets the maximum resource limit. Either parameter can be a number, or max to indicate to the server that the limit should be set to the maximum allowed by the operating system configuration. Raising the maximum resource limit requires that the server is running as root or in the initial startup phase.

This applies to processes forked from Apache httpd children servicing requests, not the Apache httpd children themselves. This includes CGI scripts and SSI exec commands, but not any processes forked from the Apache httpd parent, such as piped logs.

Process limits control the number of processes per user.

**Note**
> If CGI processes are **not** running under user ids other than the web server user id, this directive will limit the number of processes that the server itself can create. Evidence of this situation will be indicated by **cannot fork** messages in the error_log.

**See also**

- RLimitMEM
- RLimitCPU

## ScriptInterpreterSource Directive

| | |
|---|---|
| Description: | Technique for locating the interpreter for CGI scripts |
| Syntax: | `ScriptInterpreterSource Registry｜Registry-Strict｜Script` |
| Default: | `ScriptInterpreterSource Script` |
| Context: | server config, virtual host, directory, .htaccess |
| Override: | FileInfo |
| Status: | Core |
| Module: | core |
| Compatibility: | Win32 only. |

This directive is used to control how Apache httpd finds the interpreter used to run CGI scripts. The default setting is `Script`. This causes Apache httpd to use the interpreter pointed to by the shebang line (first line, starting with `#!`) in the script. On Win32 systems this line usually looks like:

```
#!C:/Perl/bin/perl.exe
```

or, if `perl` is in the `PATH`, simply:

```
#!perl
```

Setting `ScriptInterpreterSource Registry` will cause the Windows Registry tree `HKEY_CLASSES_ROOT` to be searched using the script file extension (e.g., `.pl`) as a search key. The command defined by the registry subkey `Shell\ExecCGI\Command` or, if it does not exist, by the subkey `Shell\Open\Command` is used to open the script file. If the registry keys cannot be found, Apache httpd falls back to the behavior of the `Script` option.

**Security**

Be careful when using `ScriptInterpreterSource Registry` with SCRIPTALIAS'ed directories, because Apache httpd will try to execute **every** file within this directory. The `Registry` setting may cause undesired program calls on files which are typically not executed. For example, the default open command on `.htm` files on most Windows systems will execute Microsoft Internet Explorer, so any HTTP request for an `.htm` file existing within the script directory would start the browser in the background on the server. This is a good way to crash your system within a minute or so.

The option `Registry-Strict` which is new in Apache HTTP Server 2.0 does the same thing as `Registry` but uses only the subkey `Shell\ExecCGI\Command`. The `ExecCGI` key is not a common one. It must be configured manually in the windows registry and hence prevents accidental program calls on your system.

## SeeRequestTail Directive

| | |
|---|---|
| Description: | Determine if mod_status displays the first 63 characters of a request or the last 63, assuming the request itself is greater than 63 chars. |
| Syntax: | `SeeRequestTail On｜Off` |
| Default: | `SeeRequestTail Off` |
| Context: | server config |
| Status: | Core |
| Module: | core |

mod_status with `ExtendedStatus On` displays the actual request being handled. For historical purposes, only 63 characters of the request are actually stored for display purposes. This directive controls whether the 1st 63 characters are stored (the previous behavior and the default) or if the last 63 characters are. This is only applicable, of course, if the length of the request is 64 characters or greater.

If Apache httpd is handling `GET/disk1/storage/apache/htdocs/images/imagestore1/food/apples.jpg` mod_status displays as follows:

| **Off (default)** | GET/disk1/storage/apache/htdocs/images/imagestore1/food/apples |
|---|---|
| **On** | orage/apache/htdocs/images/imagestore1/food/apples.jpgHTTP/1.1 |

## ServerAdmin Directive

| Description: | Email address that the server includes in error messages sent to the client |
|---|---|
| Syntax: | `ServerAdmin email-address|URL` |
| Context: | server config, virtual host |
| Status: | Core |
| Module: | core |

The SERVERADMIN sets the contact address that the server includes in any error messages it returns to the client. If the `httpd` doesn't recognize the supplied argument as an URL, it assumes, that it's an *email-address* and prepends it with `mailto:` in hyperlink targets. However, it's recommended to actually use an email address, since there are a lot of CGI scripts that make that assumption. If you want to use an URL, it should point to another server under your control. Otherwise users may not be able to contact you in case of errors.

It may be worth setting up a dedicated address for this, e.g.

```
ServerAdmin www-admin@foo.example.com
```

as users do not always mention that they are talking about the server!

## ServerAlias Directive

| Description: | Alternate names for a host used when matching requests to name-virtual hosts |
|---|---|
| Syntax: | `ServerAlias hostname [hostname] ...` |
| Context: | virtual host |
| Status: | Core |
| Module: | core |

The SERVERALIAS directive sets the alternate names for a host, for use with name-based virtual hosts (p. 125) . The SERVERALIAS may include wildcards, if appropriate.

```
<VirtualHost *:80>
  ServerName server.example.com
  ServerAlias server server2.example.com server2
  ServerAlias *.example.com
  UseCanonicalName Off
  # ...
</VirtualHost>
```

Name-based virtual hosts for the best-matching set of <VIRTUALHOST>s are processed in the order they appear in the configuration. The first matching SERVERNAME or SERVERALIAS is used, with no different precedence for wildcards (nor for ServerName vs. ServerAlias).

The complete list of names in the VIRTUALHOST directive are treated just like a (non wildcard) SERVERALIAS.

**See also**

- USECANONICALNAME
- Apache HTTP Server Virtual Host documentation (p. 124)

## ServerName Directive

| | |
|---|---|
| Description: | Hostname and port that the server uses to identify itself |
| Syntax: | `ServerName [scheme://]domain-name|ip-address[:port]` |
| Context: | server config, virtual host |
| Status: | Core |
| Module: | core |

The SERVERNAME directive sets the request scheme, hostname and port that the server uses to identify itself.

SERVERNAME is used (possibly in conjunction with SERVERALIAS) to uniquely identify a virtual host, when using name-based virtual hosts (p. 125) .

Additionally, this is used when creating self-referential redirection URLs when USECANONICALNAME is set to a non-default value.

For example, if the name of the machine hosting the web server is `simple.example.com`, but the machine also has the DNS alias `www.example.com` and you wish the web server to be so identified, the following directive should be used:

```
ServerName www.example.com
```

The SERVERNAME directive may appear anywhere within the definition of a server.  However, each appearance overrides the previous appearance (within that server).

If no SERVERNAME is specified, the server attempts to deduce the client visible hostname by first asking the operating system for the system hostname, and if that fails, performing a reverse lookup on an IP address present on the system.

If no port is specified in the SERVERNAME, then the server will use the port from the incoming request. For optimal reliability and predictability, you should specify an explicit hostname and port using the SERVERNAME directive.

If you are using name-based virtual hosts (p. 125) , the SERVERNAME inside a <VIRTUALHOST> section specifies what hostname must appear in the request's `Host:` header to match this virtual host.

Sometimes, the server runs behind a device that processes SSL, such as a reverse proxy, load balancer or SSL offload appliance. When this is the case, specify the `https://` scheme and the port number to which the clients connect in the SERVERNAME directive to make sure that the server generates the correct self-referential URLs.

See the description of the USECANONICALNAME and USECANONICALPHYSICALPORT directives for settings which determine whether self-referential URLs (e.g., by the MOD_DIR module) will refer to the specified port, or to the port number given in the client's request.

 Failure to set SERVERNAME to a name that your server can resolve to an IP address will result in a startup warning. `httpd` will then use whatever hostname it can determine, using the system's `hostname` command. This will almost never be the hostname you actually want.

```
httpd:  Could not reliably determine the server's fully
qualified domain name, using rocinante.local for
ServerName
```

**See also**

- Issues Regarding DNS and Apache HTTP Server (p. 121)
- Apache HTTP Server virtual host documentation (p. 124)
- USECANONICALNAME
- USECANONICALPHYSICALPORT
- SERVERALIAS

## ServerPath Directive

| | |
|---|---|
| Description: | Legacy URL pathname for a name-based virtual host that is accessed by an incompatible browser |
| Syntax: | `ServerPath URL-path` |
| Context: | virtual host |
| Status: | Core |
| Module: | core |

The SERVERPATH directive sets the legacy URL pathname for a host, for use with name-based virtual hosts (p. 124) .

**See also**

- Apache HTTP Server Virtual Host documentation (p. 124)

## ServerRoot Directive

| | |
|---|---|
| Description: | Base directory for the server installation |
| Syntax: | `ServerRoot directory-path` |
| Default: | `ServerRoot /usr/local/apache` |
| Context: | server config |
| Status: | Core |
| Module: | core |

The SERVERROOT directive sets the directory in which the server lives. Typically it will contain the subdirectories `conf/` and `logs/`. Relative paths in other configuration directives (such as INCLUDE or LOADMODULE, for example) are taken as relative to this directory.

```
ServerRoot "/home/httpd"
```

The default location of SERVERROOT may be modified by using the `--prefix` argument to `configure` (p. 307) , and most third-party distributions of the server have a different default location from the one listed above.

**See also**

- the `-d` option to `httpd` (p. 27)
- the security tips (p. 364) for information on how to properly set permissions on the SERVERROOT

## ServerSignature Directive

| | |
|---|---|
| Description: | Configures the footer on server-generated documents |
| Syntax: | `ServerSignature On|Off|EMail` |
| Default: | `ServerSignature Off` |
| Context: | server config, virtual host, directory, .htaccess |
| Override: | All |
| Status: | Core |
| Module: | core |

The SERVERSIGNATURE directive allows the configuration of a trailing footer line under server-generated documents (error messages, MOD_PROXY ftp directory listings, MOD_INFO output, ...). The reason why you would want to enable such a footer line is that in a chain of proxies, the user often has no possibility to tell which of the chained servers actually produced a returned error message.

The Off setting, which is the default, suppresses the footer line (and is therefore compatible with the behavior of Apache-1.2 and below). The On setting simply adds a line with the server version number and SERVERNAME of the serving virtual host, and the EMail setting additionally creates a "mailto:" reference to the SERVERADMIN of the referenced document.

After version 2.0.44, the details of the server version number presented are controlled by the SERVERTOKENS directive.

**See also**

- SERVERTOKENS

## ServerTokens Directive

| | |
|---|---|
| Description: | Configures the Server HTTP response header |
| Syntax: | ServerTokens Major|Minor|Min[imal]|Prod[uctOnly]|OS|Full |
| Default: | ServerTokens Full |
| Context: | server config |
| Status: | Core |
| Module: | core |

This directive controls whether Server response header field which is sent back to clients includes a description of the generic OS-type of the server as well as information about compiled-in modules.

**ServerTokens Full (or not specified)** Server  sends  (*e.g.*):    Server:  Apache/2.4.2 (Unix) PHP/4.2.2 MyMod/1.2

**ServerTokens Prod[uctOnly]** Server sends (*e.g.*): Server:  Apache

**ServerTokens Major** Server sends (*e.g.*): Server:  Apache/2

**ServerTokens Minor** Server sends (*e.g.*): Server:  Apache/2.4

**ServerTokens Min[imal]** Server sends (*e.g.*): Server:  Apache/2.4.2

**ServerTokens OS** Server sends (*e.g.*): Server:  Apache/2.4.2 (Unix)

This setting applies to the entire server, and cannot be enabled or disabled on a virtualhost-by-virtualhost basis.

After version 2.0.44, this directive also controls the information presented by the SERVERSIGNATURE directive.

⟹ Setting SERVERTOKENS to less than minimal is not recommended because it makes it more difficult to debug interoperational problems. Also note that disabling the Server: header does nothing at all to make your server more secure. The idea of "security through obscurity" is a myth and leads to a false sense of safety.

**See also**

- SERVERSIGNATURE

## SetHandler Directive

| | |
|---|---|
| Description: | Forces all matching files to be processed by a handler |
| Syntax: | `SetHandler handler-name|none|expression` |
| Context: | server config, virtual host, directory, .htaccess |
| Override: | FileInfo |
| Status: | Core |
| Module: | core |
| Compatibility: | 2.5 and later |

When placed into an `.htaccess` file or a <DIRECTORY> or <LOCATION> section, this directive forces all matching files to be parsed through the handler (p. 108) given by *handler-name*. For example, if you had a directory you wanted to be parsed entirely as imagemap rule files, regardless of extension, you might put the following into an `.htaccess` file in that directory:

```
SetHandler imap-file
```

Another example: if you wanted to have the server display a status report whenever a URL of `http://servername/status` was called, you might put the following into `httpd.conf`:

```
<Location "/status">
  SetHandler server-status
</Location>
```

You could also use this directive to configure a particular handler for files with a particular file extension. For example:

```
<FilesMatch "\.php$">
    SetHandler application/x-httpd-php
</FilesMatch>
```

String-valued expressions can be used to reference per-request variables, including backreferences to named regular expressions:

```
<LocationMatch ^/app/(?<sub>[^/]+)/>
    SetHandler "proxy:unix:/var/run/app_%{env:MATCH_sub}.sock|fcgi://localhost:8080'
</LocationMatch>
```

You can override an earlier defined SETHANDLER directive by using the value `None`.

 **Note**

> Because SETHANDLER overrides default handlers, normal behavior such as handling of URLs ending in a slash (/) as directories or index files is suppressed.

**See also**

- ADDHANDLER

## SetInputFilter Directive

| | |
|---|---|
| Description: | Sets the filters that will process client requests and POST input |
| Syntax: | `SetInputFilter filter[;filter...]` |
| Context: | server config, virtual host, directory, .htaccess |
| Override: | FileInfo |
| Status: | Core |
| Module: | core |

The SETINPUTFILTER directive sets the filter or filters which will process client requests and POST input when they are received by the server. This is in addition to any filters defined elsewhere, including the ADDINPUTFILTER directive.

If more than one filter is specified, they must be separated by semicolons in the order in which they should process the content.

**See also**

- Filters (p. 110) documentation

## SetOutputFilter Directive

| | |
|---|---|
| Description: | Sets the filters that will process responses from the server |
| Syntax: | `SetOutputFilter filter[;filter...]` |
| Context: | server config, virtual host, directory, .htaccess |
| Override: | FileInfo |
| Status: | Core |
| Module: | core |

The SETOUTPUTFILTER directive sets the filters which will process responses from the server before they are sent to the client. This is in addition to any filters defined elsewhere, including the ADDOUTPUTFILTER directive.

For example, the following configuration will process all files in the `/www/data/` directory for server-side includes.

```
<Directory "/www/data/">
  SetOutputFilter INCLUDES
</Directory>
```

If more than one filter is specified, they must be separated by semicolons in the order in which they should process the content.

**See also**

- Filters (p. 110) documentation

## TimeOut Directive

| | |
|---|---|
| Description: | Amount of time the server will wait for certain events before failing a request |
| Syntax: | `TimeOut seconds` |
| Default: | `TimeOut 60` |
| Context: | server config, virtual host |
| Status: | Core |
| Module: | core |

The TIMEOUT directive defines the length of time Apache httpd will wait for I/O in various circumstances:

- When reading data from the client, the length of time to wait for a TCP packet to arrive if the read buffer is empty.

  For initial data on a new connection, this directive doesn't take effect until after any configured ACCEPTFILTER has passed the new connection to the server.

- When writing data to the client, the length of time to wait for an acknowledgement of a packet if the send buffer is full.

- In MOD_CGI and MOD_CGID, the length of time to wait for output from a CGI script.

- In MOD_EXT_FILTER, the length of time to wait for output from a filtering process.
- In MOD_PROXY, the default timeout value if PROXYTIMEOUT is not configured.

### TraceEnable Directive

| | |
|---|---|
| Description: | Determines the behavior on TRACE requests |
| Syntax: | `TraceEnable [on|off|extended]` |
| Default: | `TraceEnable on` |
| Context: | server config, virtual host |
| Status: | Core |
| Module: | core |

This directive overrides the behavior of TRACE for both the core server and MOD_PROXY. The default TraceEnable on permits TRACE requests per RFC 2616, which disallows any request body to accompany the request. TraceEnable off causes the core server and MOD_PROXY to return a 405 (Method not allowed) error to the client.

Finally, for testing and diagnostic purposes only, request bodies may be allowed using the non-compliant TraceEnable extended directive. The core (as an origin server) will restrict the request body to 64k (plus 8k for chunk headers if Transfer-Encoding: chunked is used). The core will reflect the full headers and all chunk headers with the response body. As a proxy server, the request body is not restricted to 64k.

**Note**

> Despite claims to the contrary, TRACE is not a security vulnerability, and there is no viable reason for it to be disabled. Doing so necessarily makes your server noncompliant.

### UnDefine Directive

| | |
|---|---|
| Description: | Undefine the existence of a variable |
| Syntax: | `UnDefine parameter-name` |
| Context: | server config, virtual host |
| Status: | Core |
| Module: | core |

Undoes the effect of a DEFINE or of passing a -D argument to httpd.

This directive can be used to toggle the use of <IFDEFINE> sections without needing to alter -D arguments in any startup scripts.

While this directive is supported in virtual host context, the changes it makes are visible to any later configuration directives, beyond any enclosing virtual host.

### UseCanonicalName Directive

| | |
|---|---|
| Description: | Configures how the server determines its own name and port |
| Syntax: | `UseCanonicalName On|Off|DNS` |
| Default: | `UseCanonicalName Off` |
| Context: | server config, virtual host, directory |
| Status: | Core |
| Module: | core |

In many situations Apache httpd must construct a *self-referential* URL – that is, a URL that refers back to the same server. With UseCanonicalName On Apache httpd will use the hostname and port specified in the SERVERNAME directive to construct the canonical name for the server. This name is used in all self-referential URLs, and for the values of SERVER_NAME and SERVER_PORT in CGIs.

With `UseCanonicalName Off` Apache httpd will form self-referential URLs using the hostname and port supplied by the client if any are supplied (otherwise it will use the canonical name, as defined above). These values are the same that are used to implement name-based virtual hosts (p. 125) and are available with the same clients. The CGI variables `SERVER_NAME` and `SERVER_PORT` will be constructed from the client supplied values as well.

An example where this may be useful is on an intranet server where you have users connecting to the machine using short names such as `www`. You'll notice that if the users type a shortname and a URL which is a directory, such as `http://www/splat`, *without the trailing slash*, then Apache httpd will redirect them to `http://www.example.com/splat/`. If you have authentication enabled, this will cause the user to have to authenticate twice (once for `www` and once again for `www.example.com` – see the FAQ on this subject for more information[7]). But if USECANONICALNAME is set `Off`, then Apache httpd will redirect to `http://www/splat/`.

There is a third option, `UseCanonicalName DNS`, which is intended for use with mass IP-based virtual hosting to support ancient clients that do not provide a `Host:` header. With this option, Apache httpd does a reverse DNS lookup on the server IP address that the client connected to in order to work out self-referential URLs.

 **Warning**

> If CGIs make assumptions about the values of `SERVER_NAME`, they may be broken by this option. The client is essentially free to give whatever value they want as a hostname. But if the CGI is only using `SERVER_NAME` to construct self-referential URLs, then it should be just fine.

**See also**

- USECANONICALPHYSICALPORT

- SERVERNAME

- LISTEN

### UseCanonicalPhysicalPort Directive

| Description: | Configures how the server determines its own port |
|---|---|
| Syntax: | `UseCanonicalPhysicalPort On|Off` |
| Default: | `UseCanonicalPhysicalPort Off` |
| Context: | server config, virtual host, directory |
| Status: | Core |
| Module: | core |

In many situations Apache httpd must construct a *self-referential* URL – that is, a URL that refers back to the same server. With `UseCanonicalPhysicalPort On`, Apache httpd will, when constructing the canonical port for the server to honor the USECANONICALNAME directive, provide the actual physical port number being used by this request as a potential port. With `UseCanonicalPhysicalPort Off`, Apache httpd will not ever use the actual physical port number, instead relying on all configured information to construct a valid port number.

---

[7]http://wiki.apache.org/httpd/FAQ#Why_does_Apache_ask_for_my_password_twice_before_serving_a_file.3F

⟹ **Note**

The ordering of the lookup when the physical port is used is as follows:

**UseCanonicalName On**    1. Port provided in SERVERNAME

2. Physical port

3. Default port

**UseCanonicalName Off | DNS**    1. Parsed port from Host: header

2. Physical port

3. Port provided in SERVERNAME

4. Default port

With UseCanonicalPhysicalPort Off, the physical ports are removed from the ordering.

**See also**

- USECANONICALNAME
- SERVERNAME
- LISTEN

## VirtualHost Directive

| | |
|---|---|
| Description: | Contains directives that apply only to a specific hostname or IP address |
| Syntax: | <VirtualHost addr[:port] [addr[:port]] ...> ... </VirtualHost> |
| Context: | server config |
| Status: | Core |
| Module: | core |

<VIRTUALHOST> and </VirtualHost> are used to enclose a group of directives that will apply only to a particular virtual host. Any directive that is allowed in a virtual host context may be used. When the server receives a request for a document on a particular virtual host, it uses the configuration directives enclosed in the <VIRTUAL-HOST> section. *Addr* can be any of the following, optionally followed by a colon and a port number (or *):

- The IP address of the virtual host;
- A fully qualified domain name for the IP address of the virtual host (not recommended);
- The character *, which acts as a wildcard and matches any IP address.
- The string _default_, which is an alias for *

```
<VirtualHost 10.1.2.3:80>
  ServerAdmin webmaster@host.example.com
  DocumentRoot "/www/docs/host.example.com"
  ServerName host.example.com
  ErrorLog "logs/host.example.com-error_log"
  TransferLog "logs/host.example.com-access_log"
</VirtualHost>
```

IPv6 addresses must be specified in square brackets because the optional port number could not be determined otherwise. An IPv6 example is shown below:

```
<VirtualHost [2001:db8::a00:20ff:fea7:ccea]:80>
  ServerAdmin webmaster@host.example.com
  DocumentRoot "/www/docs/host.example.com"
  ServerName host.example.com
  ErrorLog "logs/host.example.com-error_log"
  TransferLog "logs/host.example.com-access_log"
</VirtualHost>
```

Each Virtual Host must correspond to a different IP address, different port number, or a different host name for the server, in the former case the server machine must be configured to accept IP packets for multiple addresses. (If the machine does not have multiple network interfaces, then this can be accomplished with the `ifconfig alias` command – if your OS supports it).

**Note**

> The use of <VIRTUALHOST> does **not** affect what addresses Apache httpd listens on. You
> may need to ensure that Apache httpd is listening on the correct addresses using LISTEN.

A SERVERNAME should be specified inside each <VIRTUALHOST> block. If it is absent, the SERVERNAME from the "main" server configuration will be inherited.

When a request is received, the server first maps it to the best matching <VIRTUALHOST> based on the local IP address and port combination only. Non-wildcards have a higher precedence. If no match based on IP and port occurs at all, the "main" server configuration is used.

If multiple virtual hosts contain the best matching IP address and port, the server selects from these virtual hosts the best match based on the requested hostname. If no matching name-based virtual host is found, then the first listed virtual host that matched the IP address will be used. As a consequence, the first listed virtual host for a given IP address and port combination is the default virtual host for that IP and port combination.

**Security**

> See the security tips (p. 364) document for details on why your security could be compromised
> if the directory where log files are stored is writable by anyone other than the user that starts
> the server.

**See also**

- Apache HTTP Server Virtual Host documentation (p. 124)
- Issues Regarding DNS and Apache HTTP Server (p. 121)
- Setting which addresses and ports Apache HTTP Server uses (p. 88)
- How <Directory>, <Location> and <Files> sections work (p. 35) for an explanation of how these different sections are combined when a request is received

## Warning Directive

| | |
|---|---|
| Description: | Warn from configuration parsing with a custom message |
| Syntax: | `Warning message` |
| Context: | server config, virtual host, directory, .htaccess |
| Status: | Core |
| Module: | core |
| Compatibility: | 2.5 and later |

If an issue can be detected from within the configuration, this directive can be used to generate a custom warning message. The configuration parsing is not halted. The typical use is to check whether some user define options are set, and warn if not.

```
# Example
# tell when ReverseProxy is not set
<IfDefine !ReverseProxy>
  Warning "reverse proxy is not started, hope this is okay!"
</IfDefine>

<IfDefine ReverseProxy>
  # define custom proxy configuration
</IfDefine>
```

## 10.4    Apache Module mod_access_compat

| Description: | Group authorizations based on host (name or IP address) |
|---|---|
| Status: | Extension |
| ModuleIdentifier: | access_compat_module |
| SourceFile: | mod_access_compat.c |
| Compatibility: | Available in Apache HTTP Server 2.3 as a compatibility module with previous versions of Apache httpd 2.x. The directives provided by this module have been deprecated by the new authz refactoring. Please see MOD_AUTHZ_HOST |

### Summary

The directives provided by MOD_ACCESS_COMPAT are used in <DIRECTORY>, <FILES>, and <LOCATION> sections as well as .htaccess (p. 380)  files to control access to particular parts of the server. Access can be controlled based on the client hostname, IP address, or other characteristics of the client request, as captured in environment variables (p. 92) . The ALLOW and DENY directives are used to specify which clients are or are not allowed access to the server, while the ORDER directive sets the default access state, and configures how the ALLOW and DENY directives interact with each other.

Both host-based access restrictions and password-based authentication may be implemented simultaneously. In that case, the SATISFY directive is used to determine how the two sets of restrictions interact.

**Note**

The directives provided by MOD_ACCESS_COMPAT have been deprecated by MOD_AUTHZ_HOST. Mixing old directives like ORDER, ALLOW or DENY with new ones like REQUIRE is technically possible but discouraged. This module was created to support configurations containing only old directives to facilitate the 2.4 upgrade. Please check the upgrading (p. 2) guide for more information.

In general, access restriction directives apply to all access methods (GET, PUT, POST, etc). This is the desired behavior in most cases. However, it is possible to restrict some methods, while leaving other methods unrestricted, by enclosing the directives in a <LIMIT> section.

**Merging of configuration sections**

When any directive provided by this module is used in a new configuration section, no directives provided by this module are inherited from previous configuration sections.

### Directives

- Allow
- Deny
- Order
- Satisfy

### See also

- REQUIRE
- MOD_AUTHZ_HOST
- MOD_AUTHZ_CORE

**Allow Directive**

| | |
|---|---|
| Description: | Controls which hosts can access an area of the server |
| Syntax: | `Allow from all|host|env=[!]env-variable [host|env=[!]env-variable]` `...` |
| Context: | directory, .htaccess |
| Override: | Limit |
| Status: | Extension |
| Module: | mod_access_compat |

The ALLOW directive affects which hosts can access an area of the server. Access can be controlled by hostname, IP address, IP address range, or by other characteristics of the client request captured in environment variables.

The first argument to this directive is always `from`. The subsequent arguments can take three different forms. If `Allow from all` is specified, then all hosts are allowed access, subject to the configuration of the DENY and ORDER directives as discussed below. To allow only particular hosts or groups of hosts to access the server, the *host* can be specified in any of the following formats:

**A (partial) domain-name** `Allow from example.org`
> `Allow from .net example.edu`
>
> Hosts whose names match, or end in, this string are allowed access. Only complete components are matched, so the above example will match `foo.example.org` but it will not match `fooexample.org`. This configuration will cause Apache httpd to perform a double DNS lookup on the client IP address, regardless of the setting of the HOSTNAMELOOKUPS directive. It will do a reverse DNS lookup on the IP address to find the associated hostname, and then do a forward lookup on the hostname to assure that it matches the original IP address. Only if the forward and reverse DNS are consistent and the hostname matches will access be allowed.

**A full IP address** `Allow from 10.1.2.3`
> `Allow from 192.168.1.104 192.168.1.205`
>
> An IP address of a host allowed access

**A partial IP address** `Allow from 10.1`
> `Allow from 10 172.20 192.168.2`
>
> The first 1 to 3 bytes of an IP address, for subnet restriction.

**A network/netmask pair** `Allow from 10.1.0.0/255.255.0.0`
> A network a.b.c.d, and a netmask w.x.y.z. For more fine-grained subnet restriction.

**A network/nnn CIDR specification** `Allow from 10.1.0.0/16`
> Similar to the previous case, except the netmask consists of nnn high-order 1 bits.

Note that the last three examples above match exactly the same set of hosts.

IPv6 addresses and IPv6 subnets can be specified as shown below:

```
Allow from 2001:db8::a00:20ff:fea7:ccea
Allow from 2001:db8::a00:20ff:fea7:ccea/10
```

The third format of the arguments to the ALLOW directive allows access to the server to be controlled based on the existence of an environment variable (p. 92) . When `Allow from env=env-variable` is specified, then the request is allowed access if the environment variable *env-variable* exists. When `Allow from env=!env-variable` is specified, then the request is allowed access if the environment variable *env-variable* doesn't exist. The server provides the ability to set environment variables in a flexible way based on characteristics of the client request using the directives provided by MOD_SETENVIF. Therefore, this directive can be used to allow access based on such factors as the clients `User-Agent` (browser type), `Referer`, or other HTTP request header fields.

```
SetEnvIf User-Agent ^KnockKnock/2\.0 let_me_in
<Directory "/docroot">
    Order Deny,Allow
    Deny from all
    Allow from env=let_me_in
</Directory>
```

In this case, browsers with a user-agent string beginning with `KnockKnock/2.0` will be allowed access, and all others will be denied.

 **Merging of configuration sections**

   When any directive provided by this module is used in a new configuration section, no directives provided by this module are inherited from previous configuration sections.

## Deny Directive

| | |
|---|---|
| Description: | Controls which hosts are denied access to the server |
| Syntax: | `Deny from all|host|env=[!]env-variable [host|env=[!]env-variable]` `...` |
| Context: | directory, .htaccess |
| Override: | Limit |
| Status: | Extension |
| Module: | mod_access_compat |

This directive allows access to the server to be restricted based on hostname, IP address, or environment variables. The arguments for the DENY directive are identical to the arguments for the ALLOW directive.

## Order Directive

| | |
|---|---|
| Description: | Controls the default access state and the order in which ALLOW and DENY are evaluated. |
| Syntax: | `Order ordering` |
| Default: | `Order Deny,Allow` |
| Context: | directory, .htaccess |
| Override: | Limit |
| Status: | Extension |
| Module: | mod_access_compat |

The ORDER directive, along with the ALLOW and DENY directives, controls a three-pass access control system. The first pass processes either all ALLOW or all DENY directives, as specified by the ORDER directive. The second pass parses the rest of the directives (DENY or ALLOW). The third pass applies to all requests which do not match either of the first two.

Note that all ALLOW and DENY directives are processed, unlike a typical firewall, where only the first match is used. The last match is effective (also unlike a typical firewall). Additionally, the order in which lines appear in the configuration files is not significant – all ALLOW lines are processed as one group, all DENY lines are considered as another, and the default state is considered by itself.

*Ordering* is one of:

**Allow,Deny** First, all ALLOW directives are evaluated; at least one must match, or the request is rejected. Next, all DENY directives are evaluated. If any matches, the request is rejected. Last, any requests which do not match an ALLOW or a DENY directive are denied by default.

**Deny,Allow** First, all DENY directives are evaluated; if any match, the request is denied **unless** it also matches an ALLOW directive. Any requests which do not match any ALLOW or DENY directives are permitted.

**Mutual-failure** This order has the same effect as `Order Allow,Deny` and is deprecated in its favor.

Keywords may only be separated by a comma; *no whitespace* is allowed between them.

| Match | Allow,Deny result | Deny,Allow result |
|---|---|---|
| **Match Allow only** | Request allowed | Request allowed |
| **Match Deny only** | Request denied | Request denied |
| **No match** | Default to second directive: Denied | Default to second directive: Allowed |
| **Match both Allow & Deny** | Final match controls: Denied | Final match controls: Allowed |

In the following example, all hosts in the example.org domain are allowed access; all other hosts are denied access.

```
Order Deny,Allow
Deny from all
Allow from example.org
```

In the next example, all hosts in the example.org domain are allowed access, except for the hosts which are in the foo.example.org subdomain, who are denied access. All hosts not in the example.org domain are denied access because the default state is to DENY access to the server.

```
Order Allow,Deny
Allow from example.org
Deny from foo.example.org
```

On the other hand, if the ORDER in the last example is changed to `Deny,Allow`, all hosts will be allowed access. This happens because, regardless of the actual ordering of the directives in the configuration file, the `Allow from example.org` will be evaluated last and will override the `Deny from foo.example.org`. All hosts not in the `example.org` domain will also be allowed access because the default state is ALLOW.

The presence of an ORDER directive can affect access to a part of the server even in the absence of accompanying ALLOW and DENY directives because of its effect on the default access state. For example,

```
<Directory "/www">
    Order Allow,Deny
</Directory>
```

will Deny all access to the `/www` directory because the default access state is set to DENY.

The ORDER directive controls the order of access directive processing only within each phase of the server's configuration processing. This implies, for example, that an ALLOW or DENY directive occurring in a <LOCATION> section will always be evaluated after an ALLOW or DENY directive occurring in a <DIRECTORY> section or `.htaccess` file, regardless of the setting of the ORDER directive. For details on the merging of configuration sections, see the documentation on How Directory, Location and Files sections work (p. 35) .

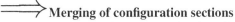**Merging of configuration sections**

When any directive provided by this module is used in a new configuration section, no directives provided by this module are inherited from previous configuration sections.

## Satisfy Directive

| Description: | Interaction between host-level access control and user authentication |
|---|---|
| Syntax: | `Satisfy Any\|All` |
| Default: | `Satisfy All` |
| Context: | directory, .htaccess |
| Override: | AuthConfig |
| Status: | Extension |
| Module: | mod_access_compat |

Access policy if both ALLOW and REQUIRE used. The parameter can be either `All` or `Any`. This directive is only useful if access to a particular area is being restricted by both username/password *and* client host address. In this case the default behavior (`All`) is to require that the client passes the address access restriction *and* enters a valid username and password. With the `Any` option the client will be granted access if they either pass the host restriction or enter a valid username and password. This can be used to password restrict an area, but to let clients from particular addresses in without prompting for a password.

For example, if you wanted to let people on your network have unrestricted access to a portion of your website, but require that people outside of your network provide a password, you could use a configuration similar to the following:

```
Require valid-user
Allow from 192.168.1
Satisfy Any
```

Another frequent use of the SATISFY directive is to relax access restrictions for a subdirectory:

```
<Directory "/var/www/private">
    Require valid-user
</Directory>

<Directory "/var/www/private/public">
    Allow from all
    Satisfy Any
</Directory>
```

In the above example, authentication will be required for the `/var/www/private` directory, but will not be required for the `/var/www/private/public` directory.

Since version 2.0.51 SATISFY directives can be restricted to particular methods by <LIMIT> and <LIMITEXCEPT> sections.

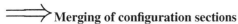**Merging of configuration sections**

> When any directive provided by this module is used in a new configuration section, no directives provided by this module are inherited from previous configuration sections.

**See also**

- ALLOW
- REQUIRE

# 10.5 Apache Module mod_actions

| | |
|---|---|
| Description: | Execute CGI scripts based on media type or request method. |
| Status: | Base |
| ModuleIdentifier: | actions_module |
| SourceFile: | mod_actions.c |

## Summary

This module has two directives. The ACTION directive lets you run CGI scripts whenever a file of a certain MIME content type is requested. The SCRIPT directive lets you run CGI scripts whenever a particular method is used in a request. This makes it much easier to execute scripts that process files.

### Directives

- Action
- Script

### See also

- MOD_CGI
- Dynamic Content with CGI (p. 236)
- Apache httpd's Handler Use (p. 108)

## Action Directive

| | |
|---|---|
| Description: | Activates a CGI script for a particular handler or content-type |
| Syntax: | `Action action-type cgi-script [virtual]` |
| Context: | server config, virtual host, directory, .htaccess |
| Override: | FileInfo |
| Status: | Base |
| Module: | mod_actions |

This directive adds an action, which will activate *cgi-script* when *action-type* is triggered by the request. The *cgi-script* is the URL-path to a resource that has been designated as a CGI script using SCRIPTALIAS or ADDHANDLER. The *action-type* can be either a handler (p. 108) or a MIME content type. It sends the URL and file path of the requested document using the standard CGI PATH_INFO and PATH_TRANSLATED environment variables. The handler used for the particular request is passed using the REDIRECT_HANDLER variable.

### Example: MIME type

```
# Requests for files of a particular MIME content type:
Action image/gif /cgi-bin/images.cgi
```

In this example, requests for files with a MIME content type of `image/gif` will be handled by the specified cgi script `/cgi-bin/images.cgi`.

### Example: File extension

```
# Files of a particular file extension
AddHandler my-file-type .xyz
Action my-file-type /cgi-bin/program.cgi
```

In this example, requests for files with a file extension of `.xyz` are handled by the specified cgi script `/cgi-bin/program.cgi`.

The optional `virtual` modifier turns off the check whether the requested file really exists. This is useful, for example, if you want to use the ACTION directive in virtual locations.

```
<Location "/news">
    SetHandler news-handler
    Action news-handler /cgi-bin/news.cgi virtual
</Location>
```

**See also**

- ADDHANDLER

## Script Directive

| | |
|---|---|
| Description: | Activates a CGI script for a particular request method. |
| Syntax: | `Script method cgi-script` |
| Context: | server config, virtual host, directory |
| Status: | Base |
| Module: | mod_actions |

This directive adds an action, which will activate *cgi-script* when a file is requested using the method of *method*. The *cgi-script* is the URL-path to a resource that has been designated as a CGI script using SCRIPTALIAS or AD-DHANDLER. The URL and file path of the requested document is sent using the standard CGI `PATH_INFO` and `PATH_TRANSLATED` environment variables.

⟹ Any arbitrary method name may be used. **Method names are case-sensitive**, so `Script PUT` and `Script put` have two entirely different effects.

Note that the SCRIPT command defines default actions only. If a CGI script is called, or some other resource that is capable of handling the requested method internally, it will do so. Also note that SCRIPT with a method of `GET` will only be called if there are query arguments present (*e.g.*, foo.html?hi). Otherwise, the request will proceed normally.

```
# All GET requests go here
Script GET /cgi-bin/search

# A CGI PUT handler
Script PUT /~bob/put.cgi
```

# 10.6 Apache Module mod_alias

| Description: | Provides for mapping different parts of the host filesystem in the document tree and for URL redirection |
|---|---|
| Status: | Base |
| ModuleIdentifier: | alias_module |
| SourceFile: | mod_alias.c |

## Summary

The directives contained in this module allow for manipulation and control of URLs as requests arrive at the server. The ALIAS and SCRIPTALIAS directives are used to map between URLs and filesystem paths. This allows for content which is not directly under the DOCUMENTROOT served as part of the web document tree. The SCRIPTALIAS directive has the additional effect of marking the target directory as containing only CGI scripts.

The REDIRECT directives are used to instruct clients to make a new request with a different URL. They are often used when a resource has moved to a new location.

When the ALIAS, SCRIPTALIAS and REDIRECT directives are used within a <LOCATION> or <LOCATIONMATCH> section, expression syntax (p. 99) can be used to manipulate the destination path or URL.

MOD_ALIAS is designed to handle simple URL manipulation tasks. For more complicated tasks such as manipulating the query string, use the tools provided by MOD_REWRITE.

### Directives

- Alias
- AliasMatch
- Redirect
- RedirectMatch
- RedirectPermanent
- RedirectTemp
- ScriptAlias
- ScriptAliasMatch

### See also

- MOD_REWRITE
- Mapping URLs to the filesystem (p. 64)

## Order of Processing

Aliases and Redirects occurring in different contexts are processed like other directives according to standard merging rules (p. 35) . But when multiple Aliases or Redirects occur in the same context (for example, in the same <VIRTUALHOST> section) they are processed in a particular order.

First, all Redirects are processed before Aliases are processed, and therefore a request that matches a REDIRECT or REDIRECTMATCH will never have Aliases applied. Second, the Aliases and Redirects are processed in the order they appear in the configuration files, with the first match taking precedence.

For this reason, when two or more of these directives apply to the same sub-path, you must list the most specific path first in order for all the directives to have an effect. For example, the following configuration will work as expected:

```
Alias "/foo/bar" "/baz"
Alias "/foo" "/gaq"
```

But if the above two directives were reversed in order, the /foo ALIAS would always match before the /foo/bar ALIAS, so the latter directive would be ignored.

When the ALIAS, SCRIPTALIAS and REDIRECT directives are used within a <LOCATION> or <LOCATIONMATCH> section, these directives will take precedence over any globally defined ALIAS, SCRIPTALIAS and REDIRECT directives.

## Alias Directive

| | |
|---|---|
| Description: | Maps URLs to filesystem locations |
| Syntax: | `Alias [URL-path] file-path|directory-path` |
| Context: | server config, virtual host, directory |
| Status: | Base |
| Module: | mod_alias |

The ALIAS directive allows documents to be stored in the local filesystem other than under the DOCUMENTROOT. URLs with a (%-decoded) path beginning with *URL-path* will be mapped to local files beginning with *directory-path*. The *URL-path* is case-sensitive, even on case-insensitive file systems.

```
Alias "/image" "/ftp/pub/image"
```

A request for http://example.com/image/foo.gif would cause the server to return the file /ftp/pub/image/foo.gif. Only complete path segments are matched, so the above alias would not match a request for http://example.com/imagefoo.gif. For more complex matching using regular expressions, see the ALIASMATCH directive.

Note that if you include a trailing / on the *URL-path* then the server will require a trailing / in order to expand the alias. That is, if you use

```
Alias "/icons/" "/usr/local/apache/icons/"
```

then the URL /icons will not be aliased, as it lacks that trailing /. Likewise, if you omit the slash on the *URL-path* then you must also omit it from the *file-path*.

Note that you may need to specify additional <DIRECTORY> sections which cover the *destination* of aliases. Aliasing occurs before <DIRECTORY> sections are checked, so only the destination of aliases are affected. (Note however <LOCATION> sections are run through once before aliases are performed, so they will apply.)

In particular, if you are creating an Alias to a directory outside of your DOCUMENTROOT, you may need to explicitly permit access to the target directory.

```
Alias "/image" "/ftp/pub/image"
<Directory "/ftp/pub/image">
    Require all granted
</Directory>
```

Any number slashes in the *URL-path* parameter matches any number of slashes in the requested URL-path.

If the ALIAS directive is used within a <LOCATION> or <LOCATIONMATCH> section the URL-path is omitted, and the file-path is interpreted using expression syntax (p. 99) .
This syntax is available in Apache 2.4.19 and later.

```
<Location "/image">
    Alias "/ftp/pub/image"
</Location>
<LocationMatch "/error/(?<NUMBER>[0-9]+)">
    Alias "/usr/local/apache/errors/%{env:MATCH_NUMBER}.html"
</LocationMatch>
```

## AliasMatch Directive

| | |
|---|---|
| Description: | Maps URLs to filesystem locations using regular expressions |
| Syntax: | `AliasMatch regex file-path|directory-path` |
| Context: | server config, virtual host |
| Status: | Base |
| Module: | mod_alias |

This directive is equivalent to ALIAS, but makes use of regular expressions, instead of simple prefix matching. The supplied regular expression is matched against the URL-path, and if it matches, the server will substitute any parenthesized matches into the given string and use it as a filename. For example, to activate the /icons directory, one might use:

```
AliasMatch "^/icons(/|$)(.*)" "/usr/local/apache/icons$1$2"
```

The full range of regular expression power is available. For example, it is possible to construct an alias with case-insensitive matching of the URL-path:

```
AliasMatch "(?i)^/image(.*)" "/ftp/pub/image$1"
```

One subtle difference between ALIAS and ALIASMATCH is that ALIAS will automatically copy any additional part of the URI, past the part that matched, onto the end of the file path on the right side, while ALIASMATCH will not. This means that in almost all cases, you will want the regular expression to match the entire request URI from beginning to end, and to use substitution on the right side.

In other words, just changing ALIAS to ALIASMATCH will not have the same effect. At a minimum, you need to add ^ to the beginning of the regular expression and add (.*)$ to the end, and add $1 to the end of the replacement.

For example, suppose you want to replace this with AliasMatch:

```
Alias "/image/" "/ftp/pub/image/"
```

This is NOT equivalent - don't do this! This will send all requests that have /image/ anywhere in them to /ftp/pub/image/:

```
AliasMatch "/image/" "/ftp/pub/image/"
```

This is what you need to get the same effect:

```
AliasMatch "^/image/(.*)$" "/ftp/pub/image/$1"
```

Of course, there's no point in using ALIASMATCH where ALIAS would work. ALIASMATCH lets you do more complicated things. For example, you could serve different kinds of files from different directories:

```
AliasMatch "^/image/(.*)\.jpg$" "/files/jpg.images/$1.jpg"
AliasMatch "^/image/(.*)\.gif$" "/files/gif.images/$1.gif"
```

Multiple leading slashes in the requested URL are discarded by the server before directives from this module compares against the requested URL-path.

## Redirect Directive

| | |
|---|---|
| Description: | Sends an external redirect asking the client to fetch a different URL |
| Syntax: | `Redirect [status] [URL-path] URL` |
| Context: | server config, virtual host, directory, .htaccess |
| Override: | FileInfo |
| Status: | Base |
| Module: | mod_alias |

The Redirect directive maps an old URL into a new one by asking the client to refetch the resource at the new location.

The old *URL-path* is a case-sensitive (%-decoded) path beginning with a slash. A relative path is not allowed.

The new *URL* may be either an absolute URL beginning with a scheme and hostname, or a URL-path beginning with a slash. In this latter case the scheme and hostname of the current server will be added.

Then any request beginning with *URL-Path* will return a redirect request to the client at the location of the target *URL*. Additional path information beyond the matched *URL-Path* will be appended to the target URL.

```
# Redirect to a URL on a different host
Redirect "/service" "http://foo2.example.com/service"

# Redirect to a URL on the same host
Redirect "/one" "/two"
```

If the client requests `http://example.com/service/foo.txt`, it will be told to access `http://foo2.example.com/service/foo.txt` instead. This includes requests with `GET` parameters, such as `http://example.com/service/foo.pl?q=23&a=42`, it will be redirected to `http://foo2.example.com/service/foo.pl?q=23&a=42`. Note that `POST`s will be discarded.
Only complete path segments are matched, so the above example would not match a request for `http://example.com/servicefoo.txt`. For more complex matching using the expression syntax (p. 99) , omit the URL-path argument as described below. Alternatively, for matching using regular expressions, see the REDIRECTMATCH directive.

**Note**

> Redirect directives take precedence over Alias and ScriptAlias directives, irrespective of their ordering in the configuration file. Redirect directives inside a Location take precedence over Redirect and Alias directives with an URL-path.

If no *status* argument is given, the redirect will be "temporary" (HTTP status 302). This indicates to the client that the resource has moved temporarily. The *status* argument can be used to return other HTTP status codes:

**permanent** Returns a permanent redirect status (301) indicating that the resource has moved permanently.

**temp** Returns a temporary redirect status (302). This is the default.

**seeother** Returns a "See Other" status (303) indicating that the resource has been replaced.

**gone** Returns a "Gone" status (410) indicating that the resource has been permanently removed. When this status is used the *URL* argument should be omitted.

Other status codes can be returned by giving the numeric status code as the value of *status*. If the status is between 300 and 399, the *URL* argument must be present. If the status is *not* between 300 and 399, the *URL* argument must be omitted. The status must be a valid HTTP status code, known to the Apache HTTP Server (see the function `send_error_response` in http_protocol.c).

```
Redirect permanent "/one" "http://example.com/two"
Redirect 303 "/three" "http://example.com/other"
```

If the REDIRECT directive is used within a <LOCATION> or <LOCATIONMATCH> section with the URL-path omitted, then the URL parameter will be interpreted using expression syntax (p. 99).
This syntax is available in Apache 2.4.19 and later.

```
<Location "/one">
    Redirect permanent "http://example.com/two"
</Location>
<Location "/three">
    Redirect 303 "http://example.com/other"
</Location>
<LocationMatch "/error/(?<NUMBER>[0-9]+)">
    Redirect permanent "http://example.com/errors/%{env:MATCH_NUMBER}.html"
</LocationMatch>
```

## RedirectMatch Directive

| | |
|---|---|
| Description: | Sends an external redirect based on a regular expression match of the current URL |
| Syntax: | `RedirectMatch [status] regex URL` |
| Context: | server config, virtual host, directory, .htaccess |
| Override: | FileInfo |
| Status: | Base |
| Module: | mod_alias |

This directive is equivalent to REDIRECT, but makes use of regular expressions, instead of simple prefix matching. The supplied regular expression is matched against the URL-path, and if it matches, the server will substitute any parenthesized matches into the given string and use it as a filename. For example, to redirect all GIF files to like-named JPEG files on another server, one might use:

```
RedirectMatch "(.*)\.gif$" "http://other.example.com$1.jpg"
```

The considerations related to the difference between ALIAS and ALIASMATCH also apply to the difference between REDIRECT and REDIRECTMATCH. See ALIASMATCH for details.

## RedirectPermanent Directive

| | |
|---|---|
| Description: | Sends an external permanent redirect asking the client to fetch a different URL |
| Syntax: | `RedirectPermanent URL-path URL` |
| Context: | server config, virtual host, directory, .htaccess |
| Override: | FileInfo |
| Status: | Base |
| Module: | mod_alias |

This directive makes the client know that the Redirect is permanent (status 301). Exactly equivalent to `Redirect permanent`.

## RedirectTemp Directive

| | |
|---|---|
| Description: | Sends an external temporary redirect asking the client to fetch a different URL |
| Syntax: | `RedirectTemp URL-path URL` |
| Context: | server config, virtual host, directory, .htaccess |
| Override: | FileInfo |
| Status: | Base |
| Module: | mod_alias |

This directive makes the client know that the Redirect is only temporary (status 302). Exactly equivalent to `Redirect temp`.

### ScriptAlias Directive

| | |
|---|---|
| Description: | Maps a URL to a filesystem location and designates the target as a CGI script |
| Syntax: | `ScriptAlias [URL-path] file-path|directory-path` |
| Context: | server config, virtual host, directory |
| Status: | Base |
| Module: | mod_alias |

The SCRIPTALIAS directive has the same behavior as the ALIAS directive, except that in addition it marks the target directory as containing CGI scripts that will be processed by MOD_CGI's cgi-script handler. URLs with a case-sensitive (%-decoded) path beginning with *URL-path* will be mapped to scripts beginning with the second argument, which is a full pathname in the local filesystem.

```
ScriptAlias "/cgi-bin/" "/web/cgi-bin/"
```

A request for `http://example.com/cgi-bin/foo` would cause the server to run the script `/web/cgi-bin/foo`. This configuration is essentially equivalent to:

```
Alias "/cgi-bin/" "/web/cgi-bin/"
<Location "/cgi-bin">
    SetHandler cgi-script
    Options +ExecCGI
</Location>
```

SCRIPTALIAS can also be used in conjunction with a script or handler you have. For example:

```
ScriptAlias "/cgi-bin/" "/web/cgi-handler.pl"
```

In this scenario all files requested in `/cgi-bin/` will be handled by the file you have configured, this allows you to use your own custom handler. You may want to use this as a wrapper for CGI so that you can add content, or some other bespoke action.

> ⚠ It is safer to avoid placing CGI scripts under the DOCUMENTROOT in order to avoid acci-
> dentally revealing their source code if the configuration is ever changed. The SCRIPTALIAS
> makes this easy by mapping a URL and designating CGI scripts at the same time. If you do
> choose to place your CGI scripts in a directory already accessible from the web, do not use
> SCRIPTALIAS. Instead, use <DIRECTORY>, SETHANDLER, and OPTIONS as in:
>
> ```
> <Directory "/usr/local/apache2/htdocs/cgi-bin">
>     SetHandler cgi-script
>     Options ExecCGI
> </Directory>
> ```
>
> This is necessary since multiple *URL-paths* can map to the same filesystem location, potentially
> bypassing the SCRIPTALIAS and revealing the source code of the CGI scripts if they are not
> restricted by a DIRECTORY section.

If the SCRIPTALIAS directive is used within a <LOCATION> or <LOCATIONMATCH> section with the URL-path omitted, then the URL parameter will be interpreted using expression syntax (p. 99) .
This syntax is available in Apache 2.4.19 and later.

```
<Location "/cgi-bin">
    ScriptAlias "/web/cgi-bin/"
</Location>
<LocationMatch "/cgi-bin/errors/(?<NUMBER>[0-9]+)">
    ScriptAlias "/web/cgi-bin/errors/%{env:MATCH_NUMBER}.cgi"
</LocationMatch>
```

**See also**

- CGI Tutorial (p. 236)

## ScriptAliasMatch Directive

| | |
|---|---|
| Description: | Maps a URL to a filesystem location using a regular expression and designates the target as a CGI script |
| Syntax: | `ScriptAliasMatch regex file-path|directory-path` |
| Context: | server config, virtual host |
| Status: | Base |
| Module: | mod_alias |

This directive is equivalent to SCRIPTALIAS, but makes use of regular expressions, instead of simple prefix matching. The supplied regular expression is matched against the URL-path, and if it matches, the server will substitute any parenthesized matches into the given string and use it as a filename. For example, to activate the standard /cgi-bin, one might use:

```
ScriptAliasMatch "^/cgi-bin(.*)" "/usr/local/apache/cgi-bin$1"
```

As for AliasMatch, the full range of regular expression power is available. For example, it is possible to construct an alias with case-insensitive matching of the URL-path:

```
ScriptAliasMatch "(?i)^/cgi-bin(.*)" "/usr/local/apache/cgi-bin$1"
```

The considerations related to the difference between ALIAS and ALIASMATCH also apply to the difference between SCRIPTALIAS and SCRIPTALIASMATCH. See ALIASMATCH for details.

# 10.7   Apache Module mod_allowhandlers

| | |
|---|---|
| Description: | Easily restrict what HTTP handlers can be used on the server |
| Status: | Experimental |
| ModuleIdentifier: | allowhandlers_module |
| SourceFile: | mod_allowhandlers.c |

## Summary

This module makes it easy to restrict which handlers may be used for a request. A possible configuration would be:

```
<Location "/">
  AllowHandlers not server-info server-status balancer-manager ldap-status
</Location>
```

It also registers a handler named `forbidden` that simply returns 403 FORBIDDEN to the client. This can be used with directives like ADDHANDLER.

### Directives

- AllowHandlers

### See also

- SETHANDLER
- ADDHANDLER

## AllowHandlers Directive

| | |
|---|---|
| Description: | Restrict access to the listed handlers |
| Syntax: | `AllowHandlers [not] none|handler-name [none|handler-name]...` |
| Default: | `AllowHandlers all` |
| Context: | directory |
| Status: | Experimental |
| Module: | mod_allowhandlers |

The handler names are case sensitive. The special name `none` can be used to match the case where no handler has been set. The special value `all` can be used to allow all handlers again in a later config section, even if some headers were denied earlier in the configuration merge order:

```
<Location "/server-status">
  AllowHandlers all
  SetHandler server-status
</Location>
```

# 10.8  Apache Module mod_allowmethods

| | |
|---|---|
| Description: | Easily restrict what HTTP methods can be used on the server |
| Status: | Experimental |
| ModuleIdentifier: | allowmethods_module |
| SourceFile: | mod_allowmethods.c |

## Summary

This module makes it easy to restrict what HTTP methods can be used on a server. The most common configuration would be:

```
<Location "/">
   AllowMethods GET POST OPTIONS
</Location>
```

### Directives

* AllowMethods

## AllowMethods Directive

| | |
|---|---|
| Description: | Restrict access to the listed HTTP methods |
| Syntax: | AllowMethods reset\|HTTP-method [HTTP-method]... |
| Default: | AllowMethods reset |
| Context: | directory |
| Status: | Experimental |
| Module: | mod_allowmethods |

The HTTP-methods are case sensitive and are generally, as per RFC, given in upper case. The GET and HEAD methods are treated as equivalent. The `reset` keyword can be used to turn off MOD_ALLOWMETHODS in a deeper nested context:

```
<Location "/svn">
   AllowMethods reset
</Location>
```

 **Caution**
  The TRACE method cannot be denied by this module; use TRACEENABLE instead.

MOD_ALLOWMETHODS was written to replace the rather kludgy implementation of LIMIT and LIMITEXCEPT.

## 10.9    Apache Module mod_asis

| Description: | Sends files that contain their own HTTP headers |
|---|---|
| Status: | Base |
| ModuleIdentifier: | asis_module |
| SourceFile: | mod_asis.c |

## Summary

This module provides the handler `send-as-is` which causes Apache HTTP Server to send the document without adding most of the usual HTTP headers.

This can be used to send any kind of data from the server, including redirects and other special HTTP responses, without requiring a cgi-script or an nph script.

For historical reasons, this module will also process any file with the mime type `httpd/send-as-is`.

**Directives** This module provides no directives.

**See also**

- MOD_HEADERS
- MOD_CERN_META
- Apache httpd's Handler Use (p. 108)

## Usage

In the server configuration file, associate files with the `send-as-is` handler *e.g.*

```
AddHandler send-as-is asis
```

The contents of any file with a `.asis` extension will then be sent by Apache httpd to the client with almost no changes. In particular, HTTP headers are derived from the file itself according to MOD_CGI rules, so an asis file must include valid headers, and may also use the CGI `Status:` header to determine the HTTP response code. The `Content-Length:` header will automatically be inserted or, if included, corrected by httpd.

Here's an example of a file whose contents are sent *as is* so as to tell the client that a file has redirected.

```
Status:  301 Now where did I leave that URL
Location:  http://xyz.example.com/foo/bar.html
Content-type:  text/html

<html>
<head>
<title>Lame excuses'R'us</title>
</head>
<body>
<h1>Fred's exceptionally wonderful page has moved to
<a href="http://xyz.example.com/foo/bar.html">Joe's</a> site.
</h1>
</body>
</html>
```

**Notes:**

The server always adds a `Date:` and `Server:` header to the data returned to the client, so these should not be included in the file. The server does *not* add a `Last-Modified` header; it probably should.

## 10.10   Apache Module mod_auth_basic

| Description: | Basic HTTP authentication |
|---|---|
| Status: | Base |
| ModuleIdentifier: | auth_basic_module |
| SourceFile: | mod_auth_basic.c |

### Summary

This module allows the use of HTTP Basic Authentication to restrict access by looking up users in the given providers. HTTP Digest Authentication is provided by MOD_AUTH_DIGEST. This module should usually be combined with at least one authentication module such as MOD_AUTHN_FILE and one authorization module such as MOD_AUTHZ_USER.

### Directives

- AuthBasicAuthoritative
- AuthBasicFake
- AuthBasicProvider
- AuthBasicUseDigestAlgorithm

### See also

- AUTHNAME
- AUTHTYPE
- REQUIRE
- Authentication howto (p. 227)

### AuthBasicAuthoritative Directive

| Description: | Sets whether authorization and authentication are passed to lower level modules |
|---|---|
| Syntax: | AuthBasicAuthoritative On\|Off |
| Default: | AuthBasicAuthoritative On |
| Context: | directory, .htaccess |
| Override: | AuthConfig |
| Status: | Base |
| Module: | mod_auth_basic |

Normally, each authorization module listed in AUTHBASICPROVIDER will attempt to verify the user, and if the user is not found in any provider, access will be denied. Setting the AUTHBASICAUTHORITATIVE directive explicitly to Off allows for both authentication and authorization to be passed on to other non-provider-based modules if there is **no userID** or **rule** matching the supplied userID. This should only be necessary when combining MOD_AUTH_BASIC with third-party modules that are not configured with the AUTHBASICPROVIDER directive. When using such modules, the order of processing is determined in the modules' source code and is not configurable.

## AuthBasicFake Directive

| | |
|---|---|
| Description: | Fake basic authentication using the given expressions for username and password |
| Syntax: | `AuthBasicFake off|username [password]` |
| Default: | `none` |
| Context: | directory, .htaccess |
| Override: | AuthConfig |
| Status: | Base |
| Module: | mod_auth_basic |
| Compatibility: | Apache HTTP Server 2.4.5 and later |

The username and password specified are combined into an Authorization header, which is passed to the server or service behind the webserver. Both the username and password fields are interpreted using the expression parser (p. 99) , which allows both the username and password to be set based on request parameters.

If the password is not specified, the default value "password" will be used. To disable fake basic authentication for an URL space, specify "AuthBasicFake off".

In this example, we pass a fixed username and password to a backend server.

### Fixed Example

```
<Location "/demo">
    AuthBasicFake demo demopass
</Location>
```

In this example, we pass the email address extracted from a client certificate, extending the functionality of the Fake-BasicAuth option within the SSLOptions directive. Like the FakeBasicAuth option, the password is set to the fixed string "password".

### Certificate Example

```
<Location "/secure">
    AuthBasicFake "%{SSL_CLIENT_S_DN_Email}"
</Location>
```

Extending the above example, we generate a password by hashing the email address with a fixed passphrase, and passing the hash to the backend server. This can be used to gate into legacy systems that do not support client certificates.

### Password Example

```
<Location "/secure">
    AuthBasicFake "%{SSL_CLIENT_S_DN_Email}" "%{sha1:passphrase-%{SSL_CLIENT_S_DN_Ema
</Location>
```

### Exclusion Example

```
<Location "/public">
    AuthBasicFake off
</Location>
```

## AuthBasicProvider Directive

| | |
|---|---|
| Description: | Sets the authentication provider(s) for this location |
| Syntax: | `AuthBasicProvider provider-name [provider-name] ...` |
| Default: | `AuthBasicProvider file` |
| Context: | directory, .htaccess |
| Override: | AuthConfig |
| Status: | Base |
| Module: | mod_auth_basic |

The AUTHBASICPROVIDER directive sets which provider is used to authenticate the users for this location.  The default `file` provider is implemented by the MOD_AUTHN_FILE module.  Make sure that the chosen provider module is present in the server.

### Example

```
<Location "/secure">
    AuthType basic
    AuthName "private area"
    AuthBasicProvider  dbm
    AuthDBMType        SDBM
    AuthDBMUserFile    "/www/etc/dbmpasswd"
    Require            valid-user
</Location>
```

Providers are queried in order until a provider finds a match for the requested username, at which point this sole provider will attempt to check the password.  A failure to verify the password does not result in control being passed on to subsequent providers.

Providers are implemented by MOD_AUTHN_DBM, MOD_AUTHN_FILE, MOD_AUTHN_DBD, MOD_AUTHNZ_LDAP and MOD_AUTHN_SOCACHE.

## AuthBasicUseDigestAlgorithm Directive

| | |
|---|---|
| Description: | Check passwords against the authentication providers as if Digest Authentication was in force instead of Basic Authentication. |
| Syntax: | `AuthBasicUseDigestAlgorithm MD5|Off` |
| Default: | `AuthBasicUseDigestAlgorithm Off` |
| Context: | directory, .htaccess |
| Override: | AuthConfig |
| Status: | Base |
| Module: | mod_auth_basic |
| Compatibility: | Apache HTTP Server 2.4.7 and later |

Normally, when using Basic Authentication, the providers listed in AUTHBASICPROVIDER attempt to verify a user by checking their data stores for a matching username and associated password.  The stored passwords are usually encrypted, but not necessarily so; each provider may choose its own storage scheme for passwords.

When using AUTHDIGESTPROVIDER and Digest Authentication, providers perform a similar check to find a matching username in their data stores.  However, unlike in the Basic Authentication case, the value associated with each stored username must be an encrypted string composed from the username, realm name, and password. (See

RFC 2617, Section 3.2.2.2[8] for more details on the format used for this encrypted string.)

As a consequence of the difference in the stored values between Basic and Digest Authentication, converting from Digest Authentication to Basic Authentication generally requires that all users be assigned new passwords, as their

---

[8]http://tools.ietf.org/html/rfc2617#section-3.2.2.2

existing passwords cannot be recovered from the password storage scheme imposed on those providers which support Digest Authentication.

Setting the AUTHBASICUSEDIGESTALGORITHM directive to MD5 will cause the user's Basic Authentication password to be checked using the same encrypted format as for Digest Authentication. First a string composed from the username, realm name, and password is hashed with MD5; then the username and this encrypted string are passed to the providers listed in AUTHBASICPROVIDER as if AUTHTYPE was set to Digest and Digest Authentication was in force.

Through the use of AUTHBASICUSEDIGESTALGORITHM a site may switch from Digest to Basic Authentication without requiring users to be assigned new passwords.

> The inverse process of switching from Basic to Digest Authentication without assigning new passwords is generally not possible. Only if the Basic Authentication passwords have been stored in plain text or with a reversable encryption scheme will it be possible to recover them and generate a new data store following the Digest Authentication password storage scheme.

> Only providers which support Digest Authentication will be able to authenticate users when AUTHBASICUSEDIGESTALGORITHM is set to MD5. Use of other providers will result in an error response and the client will be denied access.

# 10.11    Apache Module mod_auth_digest

| | |
|---|---|
| Description: | User authentication using MD5 Digest Authentication |
| Status: | Extension |
| ModuleIdentifier: | auth_digest_module |
| SourceFile: | mod_auth_digest.c |

## Summary

This module implements HTTP Digest Authentication (RFC2617[9]), and provides an alternative to MOD_AUTH_BASIC where the password is not transmitted as cleartext. However, this does **not** lead to a significant security advantage over basic authentication. On the other hand, the password storage on the server is much less secure with digest authentication than with basic authentication. Therefore, using basic auth and encrypting the whole connection using MOD_SSL is a much better alternative.

## Directives

- AuthDigestAlgorithm
- AuthDigestDomain
- AuthDigestNcCheck
- AuthDigestNonceFormat
- AuthDigestNonceLifetime
- AuthDigestProvider
- AuthDigestQop
- AuthDigestShmemSize

## See also

- AUTHNAME
- AUTHTYPE
- REQUIRE
- Authentication howto (p. 227)

## Using Digest Authentication

To use MD5 Digest authentication, configure the location to be protected as shown in the below example:

**Example:**

```
<Location "/private/">
    AuthType Digest
    AuthName "private area"
    AuthDigestDomain "/private/" "http://mirror.my.dom/private2/"

    AuthDigestProvider file
    AuthUserFile "/web/auth/.digest_pw"
    Require valid-user
</Location>
```

---

[9]http://www.faqs.org/rfcs/rfc2617.html

AUTHDIGESTDOMAIN should list the locations that will be protected by this configuration.

The pasword file referenced in the AUTHUSERFILE directive may be created and managed using the `htdigest` tool.

**Note**

Digest authentication was intended to be more secure than basic authentication, but no longer fulfills that design goal. A man-in-the-middle attacker can trivially force the browser to downgrade to basic authentication. And even a passive eavesdropper can brute-force the password using today's graphics hardware, because the hashing algorithm used by digest authentication is too fast. Another problem is that the storage of the passwords on the server is insecure. The contents of a stolen htdigest file can be used directly for digest authentication. Therefore using MOD_SSL to encrypt the whole connection is strongly recommended.

MOD_AUTH_DIGEST only works properly on platforms where APR supports shared memory.

## AuthDigestAlgorithm Directive

| | |
|---|---|
| Description: | Selects the algorithm used to calculate the challenge and response hashes in digest authentication |
| Syntax: | `AuthDigestAlgorithm MD5|MD5-sess` |
| Default: | `AuthDigestAlgorithm MD5` |
| Context: | directory, .htaccess |
| Override: | AuthConfig |
| Status: | Extension |
| Module: | mod_auth_digest |

The AUTHDIGESTALGORITHM directive selects the algorithm used to calculate the challenge and response hashes.

`MD5-sess` is not correctly implemented yet.

## AuthDigestDomain Directive

| | |
|---|---|
| Description: | URIs that are in the same protection space for digest authentication |
| Syntax: | `AuthDigestDomain URI [URI] ...` |
| Context: | directory, .htaccess |
| Override: | AuthConfig |
| Status: | Extension |
| Module: | mod_auth_digest |

The AUTHDIGESTDOMAIN directive allows you to specify one or more URIs which are in the same protection space (*i.e.* use the same realm and username/password info). The specified URIs are prefixes; the client will assume that all URIs "below" these are also protected by the same username/password. The URIs may be either absolute URIs (*i.e.* including a scheme, host, port, etc.) or relative URIs.

This directive *should* always be specified and contain at least the (set of) root URI(s) for this space. Omitting to do so will cause the client to send the Authorization header for *every request* sent to this server. Apart from increasing the size of the request, it may also have a detrimental effect on performance if AUTHDIGESTNCCHECK is on.

The URIs specified can also point to different servers, in which case clients (which understand this) will then share username/password info across multiple servers without prompting the user each time.

## AuthDigestNcCheck Directive

| | |
|---|---|
| Description: | Enables or disables checking of the nonce-count sent by the server |
| Syntax: | `AuthDigestNcCheck On\|Off` |
| Default: | `AuthDigestNcCheck Off` |
| Context: | server config |
| Status: | Extension |
| Module: | mod_auth_digest |

⟹ Not implemented yet.

## AuthDigestNonceFormat Directive

| | |
|---|---|
| Description: | Determines how the nonce is generated |
| Syntax: | `AuthDigestNonceFormat format` |
| Context: | directory, .htaccess |
| Override: | AuthConfig |
| Status: | Extension |
| Module: | mod_auth_digest |

⟹ Not implemented yet.

## AuthDigestNonceLifetime Directive

| | |
|---|---|
| Description: | How long the server nonce is valid |
| Syntax: | `AuthDigestNonceLifetime seconds` |
| Default: | `AuthDigestNonceLifetime 300` |
| Context: | directory, .htaccess |
| Override: | AuthConfig |
| Status: | Extension |
| Module: | mod_auth_digest |

The AUTHDIGESTNONCELIFETIME directive controls how long the server nonce is valid. When the client contacts the server using an expired nonce the server will send back a 401 with `stale=true`. If *seconds* is greater than 0 then it specifies the amount of time for which the nonce is valid; this should probably never be set to less than 10 seconds. If *seconds* is less than 0 then the nonce never expires.

## AuthDigestProvider Directive

| | |
|---|---|
| Description: | Sets the authentication provider(s) for this location |
| Syntax: | `AuthDigestProvider provider-name [provider-name] ...` |
| Default: | `AuthDigestProvider file` |
| Context: | directory, .htaccess |
| Override: | AuthConfig |
| Status: | Extension |
| Module: | mod_auth_digest |

The AUTHDIGESTPROVIDER directive sets which provider is used to authenticate the users for this location. The default `file` provider is implemented by the MOD_AUTHN_FILE module. Make sure that the chosen provider module is present in the server.

See MOD_AUTHN_DBM, MOD_AUTHN_FILE, MOD_AUTHN_DBD and MOD_AUTHN_SOCACHE for providers.

## AuthDigestQop Directive

| | |
|---|---|
| Description: | Determines the quality-of-protection to use in digest authentication |
| Syntax: | `AuthDigestQop none|auth|auth-int [auth|auth-int]` |
| Default: | `AuthDigestQop auth` |
| Context: | directory, .htaccess |
| Override: | AuthConfig |
| Status: | Extension |
| Module: | mod_auth_digest |

The AUTHDIGESTQOP directive determines the *quality-of-protection* to use. `auth` will only do authentication (username/password); `auth-int` is authentication plus integrity checking (an MD5 hash of the entity is also computed and checked); `none` will cause the module to use the old RFC-2069 digest algorithm (which does not include integrity checking). Both `auth` and `auth-int` may be specified, in which the case the browser will choose which of these to use. `none` should only be used if the browser for some reason does not like the challenge it receives otherwise.

⟹ `auth-int` is not implemented yet.

## AuthDigestShmemSize Directive

| | |
|---|---|
| Description: | The amount of shared memory to allocate for keeping track of clients |
| Syntax: | `AuthDigestShmemSize size` |
| Default: | `AuthDigestShmemSize 1000` |
| Context: | server config |
| Status: | Extension |
| Module: | mod_auth_digest |

The AUTHDIGESTSHMEMSIZE directive defines the amount of shared memory, that will be allocated at the server startup for keeping track of clients. Note that the shared memory segment cannot be set less than the space that is necessary for tracking at least *one* client. This value is dependent on your system. If you want to find out the exact value, you may simply set AUTHDIGESTSHMEMSIZE to the value of 0 and read the error message after trying to start the server.

The *size* is normally expressed in Bytes, but you may follow the number with a K or an M to express your value as KBytes or MBytes. For example, the following directives are all equivalent:

```
AuthDigestShmemSize 1048576
AuthDigestShmemSize 1024K
AuthDigestShmemSize 1M
```

## 10.12   Apache Module mod_auth_form

| Description: | Form authentication |
| --- | --- |
| Status: | Base |
| ModuleIdentifier: | auth_form_module |
| SourceFile: | mod_auth_form.c |
| Compatibility: | Available in Apache 2.3 and later |

## Summary

 **Warning**
Form authentication depends on the MOD_SESSION modules, and these modules make use of
HTTP cookies, and as such can fall victim to Cross Site Scripting attacks, or expose potentially
private information to clients. Please ensure that the relevant risks have been taken into account
before enabling the session functionality on your server.

This module allows the use of an HTML login form to restrict access by looking up users in the given providers. HTML
forms require significantly more configuration than the alternatives, however an HTML login form can provide a much
friendlier experience for end users.

HTTP basic authentication is provided by MOD_AUTH_BASIC, and HTTP digest authentication is provided
by MOD_AUTH_DIGEST.   This module should be combined with at least one authentication module such as
MOD_AUTHN_FILE and one authorization module such as MOD_AUTHZ_USER.

Once the user has been successfully authenticated, the user's login details will be stored in a session provided by
MOD_SESSION.

### Directives

- AuthFormAuthoritative
- AuthFormBody
- AuthFormDisableNoStore
- AuthFormFakeBasicAuth
- AuthFormLocation
- AuthFormLoginRequiredLocation
- AuthFormLoginSuccessLocation
- AuthFormLogoutLocation
- AuthFormMethod
- AuthFormMimetype
- AuthFormPassword
- AuthFormProvider
- AuthFormSitePassphrase
- AuthFormSize
- AuthFormUsername

### See also

- MOD_SESSION

- AUTHNAME
- AUTHTYPE
- REQUIRE
- Authentication howto (p. 227)

## Basic Configuration

To protect a particular URL with MOD_AUTH_FORM, you need to decide where you will store your *session*, and you will need to decide what method you will use to authenticate. In this simple example, the login details will be stored in a session based on MOD_SESSION_COOKIE, and authentication will be attempted against a file using MOD_AUTHN_FILE. If authentication is unsuccessful, the user will be redirected to the form login page.

### Basic example

```
<Location "/admin">
    AuthFormProvider file
    AuthUserFile "conf/passwd"
    AuthType form
    AuthName "/admin"
    AuthFormLoginRequiredLocation "http://example.com/login.html"

    Session On
    SessionCookieName session path=/

    Require valid-user
</Location>
```

The directive AUTHTYPE will enable the MOD_AUTH_FORM authentication when set to the value *form*. The directives AUTHFORMPROVIDER and AUTHUSERFILE specify that usernames and passwords should be checked against the chosen file.

The directives SESSION and SESSIONCOOKIENAME session stored within an HTTP cookie on the browser. For more information on the different options for configuring a session, read the documentation for MOD_SESSION.

You can optionally add a SESSIONCRYPTOPASSPHRASE to create an encrypted session cookie. This required the additional module MOD_SESSION_CRYPTO be loaded.

In the simple example above, a URL has been protected by MOD_AUTH_FORM, but the user has yet to be given an opportunity to enter their username and password. Options for doing so include providing a dedicated standalone login page for this purpose, or for providing the login page inline.

## Standalone Login

The login form can be hosted as a standalone page, or can be provided inline on the same page.

When configuring the login as a standalone page, unsuccessful authentication attempts should be redirected to a login form created by the website for this purpose, using the AUTHFORMLOGINREQUIREDLOCATION directive. Typically this login page will contain an HTML form, asking the user to provide their usename and password.

### Example login form

```
<form method="POST" action="/dologin.html">
  Username: <input type="text" name="httpd_username" value="" />
  Password: <input type="password" name="httpd_password" value="" />
  <input type="submit" name="login" value="Login" />
</form>
```

The part that does the actual login is handled by the *form-login-handler*. The action of the form should point at this handler, which is configured within Apache httpd as follows:

**Form login handler example**

```
<Location "/dologin.html">
    SetHandler form-login-handler
    AuthFormLoginRequiredLocation "http://example.com/login.html"
    AuthFormLoginSuccessLocation "http://example.com/admin/index.html"
    AuthFormProvider file
    AuthUserFile "conf/passwd"
    AuthType form
    AuthName /admin
    Session On
    SessionCookieName session path=/
</Location>
```

The URLs specified by the AUTHFORMLOGINREQUIREDLOCATION directive will typically point to a page explaining to the user that their login attempt was unsuccessful, and they should try again. The AUTHFORMLOGINSUCCESS-LOCATION directive specifies the URL the user should be redirected to upon successful login.

Alternatively, the URL to redirect the user to on success can be embedded within the login form, as in the example below. As a result, the same *form-login-handler* can be reused for different areas of a website.

**Example login form with location**

```
<form method="POST" action="/dologin.html">
  Username: <input type="text" name="httpd_username" value="" />
  Password: <input type="password" name="httpd_password" value="" />
  <input type="submit" name="login" value="Login" />
  <input type="hidden" name="httpd_location" value="http://example.com/success.html" />
</form>
```

## Inline Login

 **Warning**
A risk exists that under certain circumstances, the login form configured using inline login may be submitted more than once, revealing login credentials to the application running underneath. The administrator must ensure that the underlying application is properly secured to prevent abuse. If in doubt, use the standalone login configuration.

As an alternative to having a dedicated login page for a website, it is possible to configure MOD_AUTH_FORM to authenticate users inline, without being redirected to another page. This allows the state of the current page to be preserved during the login attempt. This can be useful in a situation where a time limited session is in force, and the session times out in the middle of the user request. The user can be re-authenticated in place, and they can continue where they left off.

If a non-authenticated user attempts to access a page protected by MOD_AUTH_FORM that isn't configured with a AUTHFORMLOGINREQUIREDLOCATION directive, a *HTTP_UNAUTHORIZED* status code is returned to the browser indicating to the user that they are not authorized to view the page.

To configure inline authentication, the administrator overrides the error document returned by the *HTTP_UNAUTHORIZED* status code with a custom error document containing the login form, as follows:

**Basic inline example**

```
AuthFormProvider file
ErrorDocument 401 "/login.shtml"
AuthUserFile "conf/passwd"
AuthType form
AuthName /admin
AuthFormLoginRequiredLocation "http://example.com/login.html"
Session On
SessionCookieName session path=/
```

The error document page should contain a login form with an empty action property, as per the example below. This has the effect of submitting the form to the original protected URL, without the page having to know what that URL is.

**Example inline login form**

```
<form method="POST" action="">
  Username: <input type="text" name="httpd_username" value="" />
  Password: <input type="password" name="httpd_password" value="" />
  <input type="submit" name="login" value="Login" />
</form>
```

When the end user has filled in their login details, the form will make an HTTP POST request to the original password protected URL. MOD_AUTH_FORM will intercept this POST request, and if HTML fields are found present for the username and password, the user will be logged in, and the original password protected URL will be returned to the user as a GET request.

## Inline Login with Body Preservation

A limitation of the inline login technique described above is that should an HTML form POST have resulted in the request to authenticate or reauthenticate, the contents of the original form posted by the browser will be lost. Depending on the function of the website, this could present significant inconvenience for the end user.

MOD_AUTH_FORM addresses this by allowing the method and body of the original request to be embedded in the login form. If authentication is successful, the original method and body will be retried by Apache httpd, preserving the state of the original request.

To enable body preservation, add three additional fields to the login form as per the example below.

**Example with body preservation**

```
<form method="POST" action="">
  Username: <input type="text" name="httpd_username" value="" />
  Password: <input type="password" name="httpd_password" value="" />
  <input type="submit" name="login" value="Login" />
    <input type="hidden" name="httpd_method" value="POST" />
  <input type="hidden" name="httpd_mimetype" value="application/x-www-form-urlencoded
  <input type="hidden" name="httpd_body" value="name1=value1&name2=value2" />
</form>
```

How the method, mimetype and body of the original request are embedded within the login form will depend on the platform and technology being used within the website.

One option is to use the MOD_INCLUDE module along with the KEPTBODYSIZE directive, along with a suitable CGI script to embed the variables in the form.

Another option is to render the login form using a CGI script or other dynamic technology.

### CGI example

```
AuthFormProvider file
ErrorDocument 401 "/cgi-bin/login.cgi"
...
```

# Logging Out

To enable a user to log out of a particular session, configure a page to be handled by the *form-logout-handler*. Any attempt to access this URL will cause the username and password to be removed from the current session, effectively logging the user out.

By setting the AUTHFORMLOGOUTLOCATION directive, a URL can be specified that the browser will be redirected to on successful logout. This URL might explain to the user that they have been logged out, and give the user the option to log in again.

### Basic logout example

```
SetHandler form-logout-handler
AuthName realm
AuthFormLogoutLocation "http://example.com/loggedout.html"
Session On
SessionCookieName session path=/
```

Note that logging a user out does not delete the session; it merely removes the username and password from the session. If this results in an empty session, the net effect will be the removal of that session, but this is not guaranteed. If you want to guarantee the removal of a session, set the SESSIONMAXAGE directive to a small value, like 1 (setting the directive to zero would mean no session age limit).

### Basic session expiry example

```
SetHandler form-logout-handler
AuthFormLogoutLocation "http://example.com/loggedout.html"
Session On
SessionMaxAge 1
SessionCookieName session path=/
```

# Usernames and Passwords

Note that form submission involves URLEncoding the form data: in this case the username and password. You should therefore pick usernames and passwords that avoid characters that are URLencoded in form submission, or you may get unexpected results.

# AuthFormAuthoritative Directive

| | |
|---|---|
| Description: | Sets whether authorization and authentication are passed to lower level modules |
| Syntax: | `AuthFormAuthoritative On|Off` |
| Default: | `AuthFormAuthoritative On` |
| Context: | directory, .htaccess |
| Override: | AuthConfig |
| Status: | Base |
| Module: | mod_auth_form |

Normally, each authorization module listed in AUTHFORMPROVIDER will attempt to verify the user, and if the user is not found in any provider, access will be denied. Setting the AUTHFORMAUTHORITATIVE directive explicitly to Off allows for both authentication and authorization to be passed on to other non-provider-based modules if there is **no userID** or **rule** matching the supplied userID. This should only be necessary when combining MOD_AUTH_FORM with third-party modules that are not configured with the AUTHFORMPROVIDER directive. When using such modules, the order of processing is determined in the modules' source code and is not configurable.

## AuthFormBody Directive

| | |
|---|---|
| Description: | The name of a form field carrying the body of the request to attempt on successful login |
| Syntax: | AuthFormBody fieldname |
| Default: | httpd_body |
| Context: | directory |
| Status: | Base |
| Module: | mod_auth_form |
| Compatibility: | Available in Apache HTTP Server 2.3.0 and later |

The AUTHFORMMETHOD directive specifies the name of an HTML field which, if present, will contain the method of the request to to submit should login be successful.

By populating the form with fields described by AUTHFORMMETHOD, AUTHFORMMIMETYPE and AUTHFORMBODY, a website can retry a request that may have been interrupted by the login screen, or by a session timeout.

## AuthFormDisableNoStore Directive

| | |
|---|---|
| Description: | Disable the CacheControl no-store header on the login page |
| Syntax: | AuthFormDisableNoStore On|Off |
| Default: | AuthFormDisableNoStore Off |
| Context: | directory |
| Status: | Base |
| Module: | mod_auth_form |
| Compatibility: | Available in Apache HTTP Server 2.3.0 and later |

The AUTHFORMDISABLENOSTORE flag disables the sending of a Cache-Control no-store header with the error 401 page returned when the user is not yet logged in. The purpose of the header is to make it difficult for an ecmascript application to attempt to resubmit the login form, and reveal the username and password to the backend application. Disable at your own risk.

## AuthFormFakeBasicAuth Directive

| | |
|---|---|
| Description: | Fake a Basic Authentication header |
| Syntax: | AuthFormFakeBasicAuth On|Off |
| Default: | AuthFormFakeBasicAuth Off |
| Context: | directory |
| Status: | Base |
| Module: | mod_auth_form |
| Compatibility: | Available in Apache HTTP Server 2.3.0 and later |

The AUTHFORMFAKEBASICAUTH flag determines whether a Basic Authentication header will be added to the request headers. This can be used to expose the username and password to an underlying application, without the underlying application having to be aware of how the login was achieved.

## AuthFormLocation Directive

| | |
|---|---|
| Description: | The name of a form field carrying a URL to redirect to on successful login |
| Syntax: | `AuthFormLocation fieldname` |
| Default: | `httpd_location` |
| Context: | directory |
| Status: | Base |
| Module: | mod_auth_form |
| Compatibility: | Available in Apache HTTP Server 2.3.0 and later |

The AUTHFORMLOCATION directive specifies the name of an HTML field which, if present, will contain a URL to redirect the browser to should login be successful.

## AuthFormLoginRequiredLocation Directive

| | |
|---|---|
| Description: | The URL of the page to be redirected to should login be required |
| Syntax: | `AuthFormLoginRequiredLocation url` |
| Default: | `none` |
| Context: | directory |
| Status: | Base |
| Module: | mod_auth_form |
| Compatibility: | Available in Apache HTTP Server 2.3.0 and later. The use of the expression parser has been added in 2.4.4. |

The AUTHFORMLOGINREQUIREDLOCATION directive specifies the URL to redirect to should the user not be authorised to view a page. The value is parsed using the ap_expr (p. 99) parser before being sent to the client. By default, if a user is not authorised to view a page, the HTTP response code `HTTP_UNAUTHORIZED` will be returned with the page specified by the ERRORDOCUMENT directive. This directive overrides this default.

Use this directive if you have a dedicated login page to redirect users to.

## AuthFormLoginSuccessLocation Directive

| | |
|---|---|
| Description: | The URL of the page to be redirected to should login be successful |
| Syntax: | `AuthFormLoginSuccessLocation url` |
| Default: | `none` |
| Context: | directory |
| Status: | Base |
| Module: | mod_auth_form |
| Compatibility: | Available in Apache HTTP Server 2.3.0 and later. The use of the expression parser has been added in 2.4.4. |

The AUTHFORMLOGINSUCCESSLOCATION directive specifies the URL to redirect to should the user have logged in successfully. The value is parsed using the ap_expr (p. 99) parser before being sent to the client. This directive can be overridden if a form field has been defined containing another URL using the AUTHFORMLOCATION directive.

Use this directive if you have a dedicated login URL, and you have not embedded the destination page in the login form.

## AuthFormLogoutLocation Directive

| | |
|---|---|
| Description: | The URL to redirect to after a user has logged out |
| Syntax: | `AuthFormLogoutLocation uri` |
| Default: | `none` |
| Context: | directory |
| Status: | Base |
| Module: | mod_auth_form |
| Compatibility: | Available in Apache HTTP Server 2.3.0 and later. The use of the expression parser has been added in 2.4.4. |

The AUTHFORMLOGOUTLOCATION directive specifies the URL of a page on the server to redirect to should the user attempt to log out. The value is parsed using the ap_expr (p. 99) parser before being sent to the client.

When a URI is accessed that is served by the handler `form-logout-handler`, the page specified by this directive will be shown to the end user. For example:

### Example

```
<Location "/logout">
    SetHandler form-logout-handler
    AuthFormLogoutLocation "http://example.com/loggedout.html"
    Session on
    #...
</Location>
```

An attempt to access the URI */logout/* will result in the user being logged out, and the page */loggedout.html* will be displayed. Make sure that the page *loggedout.html* is not password protected, otherwise the page will not be displayed.

## AuthFormMethod Directive

| | |
|---|---|
| Description: | The name of a form field carrying the method of the request to attempt on successful login |
| Syntax: | `AuthFormMethod fieldname` |
| Default: | `httpd_method` |
| Context: | directory |
| Status: | Base |
| Module: | mod_auth_form |
| Compatibility: | Available in Apache HTTP Server 2.3.0 and later |

The AUTHFORMMETHOD directive specifies the name of an HTML field which, if present, will contain the method of the request to to submit should login be successful.

By populating the form with fields described by AUTHFORMMETHOD, AUTHFORMMIMETYPE and AUTHFORM-BODY, a website can retry a request that may have been interrupted by the login screen, or by a session timeout.

## AuthFormMimetype Directive

| | |
|---|---|
| Description: | The name of a form field carrying the mimetype of the body of the request to attempt on successful login |
| Syntax: | `AuthFormMimetype fieldname` |
| Default: | `httpd_mimetype` |
| Context: | directory |
| Status: | Base |
| Module: | mod_auth_form |
| Compatibility: | Available in Apache HTTP Server 2.3.0 and later |

The AUTHFORMMETHOD directive specifies the name of an HTML field which, if present, will contain the mimetype of the request to submit should login be successful.

By populating the form with fields described by AUTHFORMMETHOD, AUTHFORMMIMETYPE and AUTHFORM-BODY, a website can retry a request that may have been interrupted by the login screen, or by a session timeout.

## AuthFormPassword Directive

| | |
|---|---|
| Description: | The name of a form field carrying the login password |
| Syntax: | `AuthFormPassword fieldname` |
| Default: | `httpd_password` |
| Context: | directory |
| Status: | Base |
| Module: | mod_auth_form |
| Compatibility: | Available in Apache HTTP Server 2.3.0 and later |

The AUTHFORMPASSWORD directive specifies the name of an HTML field which, if present, will contain the password to be used to log in.

## AuthFormProvider Directive

| | |
|---|---|
| Description: | Sets the authentication provider(s) for this location |
| Syntax: | `AuthFormProvider provider-name [provider-name] ...` |
| Default: | `AuthFormProvider file` |
| Context: | directory, .htaccess |
| Override: | AuthConfig |
| Status: | Base |
| Module: | mod_auth_form |

The AUTHFORMPROVIDER directive sets which provider is used to authenticate the users for this location. The default `file` provider is implemented by the MOD_AUTHN_FILE module. Make sure that the chosen provider module is present in the server.

### Example

```
<Location "/secure">
    AuthType form
    AuthName "private area"
    AuthFormProvider  dbm
    AuthDBMType       SDBM
    AuthDBMUserFile   "/www/etc/dbmpasswd"
    Require           valid-user
    #...
</Location>
```

Providers are implemented by MOD_AUTHN_DBM, MOD_AUTHN_FILE, MOD_AUTHN_DBD, MOD_AUTHNZ_LDAP and MOD_AUTHN_SOCACHE.

## AuthFormSitePassphrase Directive

| | |
|---|---|
| Description: | Bypass authentication checks for high traffic sites |
| Syntax: | `AuthFormSitePassphrase secret` |
| Default: | `none` |
| Context: | directory |
| Status: | Base |
| Module: | mod_auth_form |
| Compatibility: | Available in Apache HTTP Server 2.3.0 and later |

The AUTHFORMSITEPASSPHRASE directive specifies a passphrase which, if present in the user session, causes Apache httpd to bypass authentication checks for the given URL. It can be used on high traffic websites to reduce the load induced on authentication infrastructure.

The passphrase can be inserted into a user session by adding this directive to the configuration for the *form-login-handler*. The *form-login-handler* itself will always run the authentication checks, regardless of whether a passphrase is specified or not.

 **Warning**

If the session is exposed to the user through the use of MOD_SESSION_COOKIE, and the session is not protected with MOD_SESSION_CRYPTO, the passphrase is open to potential exposure through a dictionary attack. Regardless of how the session is configured, ensure that this directive is not used within URL spaces where private user data could be exposed, or sensitive transactions can be conducted. Use at own risk.

## AuthFormSize Directive

| | |
|---|---|
| Description: | The largest size of the form in bytes that will be parsed for the login details |
| Syntax: | `AuthFormSize size` |
| Default: | `8192` |
| Context: | directory |
| Status: | Base |
| Module: | mod_auth_form |
| Compatibility: | Available in Apache HTTP Server 2.3.0 and later |

The AUTHFORMSIZE directive specifies the maximum size of the body of the request that will be parsed to find the login form.

If a login request arrives that exceeds this size, the whole request will be aborted with the HTTP response code HTTP_REQUEST_TOO_LARGE.

If you have populated the form with fields described by AUTHFORMMETHOD, AUTHFORMMIMETYPE and AUTHFORMBODY, you probably want to set this field to a similar size as the KEPTBODYSIZE directive.

## AuthFormUsername Directive

| | |
|---|---|
| Description: | The name of a form field carrying the login username |
| Syntax: | `AuthFormUsername fieldname` |
| Default: | `httpd_username` |
| Context: | directory |
| Status: | Base |
| Module: | mod_auth_form |
| Compatibility: | Available in Apache HTTP Server 2.3.0 and later |

The AUTHFORMUSERNAME directive specifies the name of an HTML field which, if present, will contain the username to be used to log in.

# 10.13 Apache Module mod_authn_anon

| | |
|---|---|
| Description: | Allows "anonymous" user access to authenticated areas |
| Status: | Extension |
| ModuleIdentifier: | authn_anon_module |
| SourceFile: | mod_authn_anon.c |

## Summary

This module provides authentication front-ends such as MOD_AUTH_BASIC to authenticate users similar to anonymous-ftp sites, *i.e.* have a 'magic' user id 'anonymous' and the email address as a password. These email addresses can be logged.

Combined with other (database) access control methods, this allows for effective user tracking and customization according to a user profile while still keeping the site open for 'unregistered' users. One advantage of using Auth-based user tracking is that, unlike magic-cookies and funny URL pre/postfixes, it is completely browser independent and it allows users to share URLs.

When using MOD_AUTH_BASIC, this module is invoked via the AUTHBASICPROVIDER directive with the anon value.

**Directives**

- Anonymous

- Anonymous_LogEmail

- Anonymous_MustGiveEmail

- Anonymous_NoUserID

- Anonymous_VerifyEmail

## Example

The example below is combined with "normal" htpasswd-file based authentication and allows users in additionally as 'guests' with the following properties:

- It insists that the user enters a userID. (ANONYMOUS_NOUSERID)

- It insists that the user enters a password. (ANONYMOUS_MUSTGIVEEMAIL)

- The password entered must be a valid email address, *i.e.* contain at least one '@' and a '.'. (ANONYMOUS_VERIFYEMAIL)

- The userID must be one of anonymous guest www test welcome and comparison is **not** case sensitive. (ANONYMOUS)

- And the Email addresses entered in the passwd field are logged to the error log file. (ANONYMOUS_LOGEMAIL)

**Example**

```
<Directory "/var/www/html/private">
    AuthName "Use 'anonymous' & Email address for guest entry"
    AuthType Basic
    AuthBasicProvider file anon
    AuthUserFile "/path/to/your/.htpasswd"

    Anonymous_NoUserID off
    Anonymous_MustGiveEmail on
    Anonymous_VerifyEmail on
    Anonymous_LogEmail on
    Anonymous anonymous guest www test welcome

    Require valid-user
</Directory>
```

## Anonymous Directive

| | |
|---|---|
| Description: | Specifies userIDs that are allowed access without password verification |
| Syntax: | `Anonymous user [user] ...` |
| Context: | directory, .htaccess |
| Override: | AuthConfig |
| Status: | Extension |
| Module: | mod_authn_anon |

A list of one or more 'magic' userIDs which are allowed access without password verification. The userIDs are space separated. It is possible to use the ' and " quotes to allow a space in a userID as well as the \escape character.

Please note that the comparison is **case-IN-sensitive**.
It's strongly recommended that the magic username 'anonymous' is always one of the allowed userIDs.

**Example:**

```
Anonymous anonymous "Not Registered" "I don't know"
```

This would allow the user to enter without password verification by using the userIDs "anonymous", "AnonyMous", "Not Registered" and "I Don't Know".

As of Apache 2.1 it is possible to specify the userID as " * ". That allows *any* supplied userID to be accepted.

## Anonymous_LogEmail Directive

| | |
|---|---|
| Description: | Sets whether the password entered will be logged in the error log |
| Syntax: | `Anonymous_LogEmail On\|Off` |
| Default: | `Anonymous_LogEmail On` |
| Context: | directory, .htaccess |
| Override: | AuthConfig |
| Status: | Extension |
| Module: | mod_authn_anon |

When set `On`, the default, the 'password' entered (which hopefully contains a sensible email address) is logged in the error log.

### Anonymous_MustGiveEmail Directive

| | |
|---|---|
| Description: | Specifies whether blank passwords are allowed |
| Syntax: | `Anonymous_MustGiveEmail On\|Off` |
| Default: | `Anonymous_MustGiveEmail On` |
| Context: | directory, .htaccess |
| Override: | AuthConfig |
| Status: | Extension |
| Module: | mod_authn_anon |

Specifies whether the user must specify an email address as the password. This prohibits blank passwords.

### Anonymous_NoUserID Directive

| | |
|---|---|
| Description: | Sets whether the userID field may be empty |
| Syntax: | `Anonymous_NoUserID On\|Off` |
| Default: | `Anonymous_NoUserID Off` |
| Context: | directory, .htaccess |
| Override: | AuthConfig |
| Status: | Extension |
| Module: | mod_authn_anon |

When set `On`, users can leave the userID (and perhaps the password field) empty. This can be very convenient for MS-Explorer users who can just hit return or click directly on the OK button; which seems a natural reaction.

### Anonymous_VerifyEmail Directive

| | |
|---|---|
| Description: | Sets whether to check the password field for a correctly formatted email address |
| Syntax: | `Anonymous_VerifyEmail On\|Off` |
| Default: | `Anonymous_VerifyEmail Off` |
| Context: | directory, .htaccess |
| Override: | AuthConfig |
| Status: | Extension |
| Module: | mod_authn_anon |

When set `On` the 'password' entered is checked for at least one '@' and a '.' to encourage users to enter valid email addresses (see the above ANONYMOUS_LOGEMAIL).

# 10.14   Apache Module mod_authn_core

| | |
|---|---|
| Description: | Core Authentication |
| Status: | Base |
| ModuleIdentifier: | authn_core_module |
| SourceFile: | mod_authn_core.c |
| Compatibility: | Available in Apache 2.3 and later |

## Summary

This module provides core authentication capabilities to allow or deny access to portions of the web site. MOD_AUTHN_CORE provides directives that are common to all authentication providers.

## Directives

- AuthName
- <AuthnProviderAlias>
- AuthType

## Creating Authentication Provider Aliases

Extended authentication providers can be created within the configuration file and assigned an alias name. The alias providers can then be referenced through the directives AUTHBASICPROVIDER or AUTHDIGESTPROVIDER in the same way as a base authentication provider. Besides the ability to create and alias an extended provider, it also allows the same extended authentication provider to be reference by multiple locations.

## Examples

This example checks for passwords in two different text files.

**Checking multiple text password files**

```
# Check here first
<AuthnProviderAlias file file1>
    AuthUserFile "/www/conf/passwords1"
</AuthnProviderAlias>

# Then check here
<AuthnProviderAlias file file2>
    AuthUserFile "/www/conf/passwords2"
</AuthnProviderAlias>

<Directory "/var/web/pages/secure">
    AuthBasicProvider file1 file2

    AuthType Basic
    AuthName "Protected Area"
    Require valid-user
</Directory>
```

The example below creates two different ldap authentication provider aliases based on the ldap provider. This allows a single authenticated location to be serviced by multiple ldap hosts:

**Checking multiple LDAP servers**

```
<AuthnProviderAlias ldap ldap-alias1>
    AuthLDAPBindDN "cn=youruser,o=ctx"
    AuthLDAPBindPassword yourpassword
    AuthLDAPURL "ldap://ldap.host/o=ctx"
</AuthnProviderAlias>
<AuthnProviderAlias ldap ldap-other-alias>
    AuthLDAPBindDN "cn=yourotheruser,o=dev"
    AuthLDAPBindPassword yourotherpassword
    AuthLDAPURL "ldap://other.ldap.host/o=dev?cn"
</AuthnProviderAlias>

Alias "/secure" "/webpages/secure"
<Directory "/webpages/secure">
    AuthBasicProvider ldap-other-alias  ldap-alias1

    AuthType Basic
    AuthName "LDAP Protected Place"
    Require valid-user
    # Note that Require ldap-* would not work here, since the
    # AuthnProviderAlias does not provide the config to authorization providers
    # that are implemented in the same module as the authentication provider.
</Directory>
```

## AuthName Directive

| | |
|---|---|
| Description: | Authorization realm for use in HTTP authentication |
| Syntax: | `AuthName auth-domain` |
| Context: | directory, .htaccess |
| Override: | AuthConfig |
| Status: | Base |
| Module: | mod_authn_core |

This directive sets the name of the authorization realm for a directory. This realm is given to the client so that the user knows which username and password to send. AUTHNAME takes a single argument; if the realm name contains spaces, it must be enclosed in quotation marks. It must be accompanied by AUTHTYPE and REQUIRE directives, and directives such as AUTHUSERFILE and AUTHGROUPFILE to work.

For example:

```
AuthName "Top Secret"
```

The string provided for the `AuthName` is what will appear in the password dialog provided by most browsers.

The expression syntax (p. 99) can be used inside the directive to produce the name dynamically.

For example:

```
AuthName "%{HTTP_HOST}"
```

**See also**

- Authentication, Authorization, and Access Control (p. 227)
- MOD_AUTHZ_CORE

## AuthnProviderAlias Directive

| | |
|---|---|
| Description: | Enclose a group of directives that represent an extension of a base authentication provider and referenced by the specified alias |
| Syntax: | `<AuthnProviderAlias baseProvider Alias> ...` `</AuthnProviderAlias>` |
| Context: | server config |
| Status: | Base |
| Module: | mod_authn_core |

`<AuthnProviderAlias>` and `</AuthnProviderAlias>` are used to enclose a group of authentication directives that can be referenced by the alias name using one of the directives AUTHBASICPROVIDER or AUTHDIGEST-PROVIDER.

 This directive has no affect on authorization, even for modules that provide both authentication and authorization.

## AuthType Directive

| | |
|---|---|
| Description: | Type of user authentication |
| Syntax: | `AuthType None|Basic|Digest|Form` |
| Context: | directory, .htaccess |
| Override: | AuthConfig |
| Status: | Base |
| Module: | mod_authn_core |

This directive selects the type of user authentication for a directory. The authentication types available are None, Basic (implemented by MOD_AUTH_BASIC), Digest (implemented by MOD_AUTH_DIGEST), and Form (implemented by MOD_AUTH_FORM).

To implement authentication, you must also use the AUTHNAME and REQUIRE directives. In addition, the server must have an authentication-provider module such as MOD_AUTHN_FILE and an authorization module such as MOD_AUTHZ_USER.

The authentication type None disables authentication. When authentication is enabled, it is normally inherited by each subsequent configuration section (p. 35) , unless a different authentication type is specified. If no authentication is desired for a subsection of an authenticated section, the authentication type None may be used; in the following example, clients may access the /www/docs/public directory without authenticating:

```
<Directory "/www/docs">
    AuthType Basic
    AuthName Documents
    AuthBasicProvider file
    AuthUserFile "/usr/local/apache/passwd/passwords"
    Require valid-user
</Directory>

<Directory "/www/docs/public">
    AuthType None
    Require all granted
</Directory>
```

From 2.4.13, expression syntax (p. 99) can be used inside the directive to specify the type dynamically.

When disabling authentication, note that clients which have already authenticated against another portion of the server's document tree will typically continue to send authentication HTTP headers or cookies with each request, regardless of whether the server actually requires authentication for every resource.

**See also**

- Authentication, Authorization, and Access Control (p. 227)

## 10.15   Apache Module mod_authn_dbd

| | |
|---|---|
| Description: | User authentication using an SQL database |
| Status: | Extension |
| ModuleIdentifier: | authn_dbd_module |
| SourceFile: | mod_authn_dbd.c |

## Summary

This module provides authentication front-ends such as MOD_AUTH_DIGEST and MOD_AUTH_BASIC to authenticate users by looking up users in SQL tables. Similar functionality is provided by, for example, MOD_AUTHN_FILE.

This module relies on MOD_DBD to specify the backend database driver and connection parameters, and manage the database connections.

When using MOD_AUTH_BASIC or MOD_AUTH_DIGEST, this module is invoked via the AUTHBASICPROVIDER or AUTHDIGESTPROVIDER with the dbd value.

### Directives

- AuthDBDUserPWQuery
- AuthDBDUserRealmQuery

### See also

- AUTHNAME
- AUTHTYPE
- AUTHBASICPROVIDER
- AUTHDIGESTPROVIDER
- DBDRIVER
- DBDPARAMS
- Password Formats (p. 371)

## Performance and Cacheing

Some users of DBD authentication in HTTPD 2.2/2.4 have reported that it imposes a problematic load on the database. This is most likely where an HTML page contains hundreds of objects (e.g. images, scripts, etc) each of which requires authentication. Users affected (or concerned) by this kind of problem should use MOD_AUTHN_SOCACHE to cache credentials and take most of the load off the database.

## Configuration Example

This simple example shows use of this module in the context of the Authentication and DBD frameworks.

```
# mod_dbd configuration
# UPDATED to include authentication cacheing
DBDriver pgsql
DBDParams "dbname=apacheauth user=apache password=xxxxxx"

DBDMin  4
```

```
DBDKeep 8
DBDMax   20
DBDExptime 300

<Directory "/usr/www/myhost/private">
  # mod_authn_core and mod_auth_basic configuration
  # for mod_authn_dbd
  AuthType Basic
  AuthName "My Server"

  # To cache credentials, put socache ahead of dbd here
  AuthBasicProvider socache dbd

  # Also required for caching: tell the cache to cache dbd lookups!
  AuthnCacheProvideFor dbd
  AuthnCacheContext my-server

  # mod_authz_core configuration
  Require valid-user

  # mod_authn_dbd SQL query to authenticate a user
  AuthDBDUserPWQuery "SELECT password FROM authn WHERE user = %s"
</Directory>
```

## Exposing Login Information

If httpd was built against APR version 1.3.0 or higher, then whenever a query is made to the database server, all column values in the first row returned by the query are placed in the environment, using environment variables with the prefix "AUTHENTICATE_".

If a database query for example returned the username, full name and telephone number of a user, a CGI program will have access to this information without the need to make a second independent database query to gather this additional information.

This has the potential to dramatically simplify the coding and configuration required in some web applications.

## Preventing SQL injections

Whether you need to care about SQL security depends on what DBD driver and backend you use. With most drivers you don't have to do anything : the statement is prepared by the database at startup, and user input is used only as data. But you may need to untaint your input. At the time of writing, the only driver that requires you to take care is FreeTDS.

Please read MOD_DBD documentation for more information about security on this scope.

## AuthDBDUserPWQuery Directive

| Description: | SQL query to look up a password for a user |
| --- | --- |
| Syntax: | `AuthDBDUserPWQuery query` |
| Context: | directory |
| Status: | Extension |
| Module: | mod_authn_dbd |

The AUTHDBDUSERPWQUERY specifies an SQL query to look up a password for a specified user. The user's ID will be passed as a single string parameter when the SQL query is executed. It may be referenced within the query statement using a %s format specifier.

```
AuthDBDUserPWQuery "SELECT password FROM authn WHERE user = %s"
```

The first column value of the first row returned by the query statement should be a string containing the encrypted password. Subsequent rows will be ignored. If no rows are returned, the user will not be authenticated through MOD_AUTHN_DBD.

If httpd was built against APR version 1.3.0 or higher, any additional column values in the first row returned by the query statement will be stored as environment variables with names of the form AUTHENTICATE_*COLUMN*.

The encrypted password format depends on which authentication frontend (e.g.     MOD_AUTH_BASIC or MOD_AUTH_DIGEST) is being used. See Password Formats (p. 371) for more information.

## AuthDBDUserRealmQuery Directive

| Description: | SQL query to look up a password hash for a user and realm. |
|---|---|
| Syntax: | AuthDBDUserRealmQuery query |
| Context: | directory |
| Status: | Extension |
| Module: | mod_authn_dbd |

The AUTHDBDUSERREALMQUERY specifies an SQL query to look up a password for a specified user and realm in a digest authentication process. The user's ID and the realm, in that order, will be passed as string parameters when the SQL query is executed. They may be referenced within the query statement using %s format specifiers.

```
AuthDBDUserRealmQuery "SELECT password FROM authn WHERE user = %s AND realm = %s"
```

The first column value of the first row returned by the query statement should be a string containing the encrypted password. Subsequent rows will be ignored. If no rows are returned, the user will not be authenticated through MOD_AUTHN_DBD.

If httpd was built against APR version 1.3.0 or higher, any additional column values in the first row returned by the query statement will be stored as environment variables with names of the form AUTHENTICATE_*COLUMN*.

The encrypted password format depends on which authentication frontend (e.g.     MOD_AUTH_BASIC or MOD_AUTH_DIGEST) is being used. See Password Formats (p. 371) for more information.

## 10.16 Apache Module mod_authn_dbm

| | |
|---|---|
| Description: | User authentication using DBM files |
| Status: | Extension |
| ModuleIdentifier: | authn_dbm_module |
| SourceFile: | mod_authn_dbm.c |

### Summary

This module provides authentication front-ends such as MOD_AUTH_DIGEST and MOD_AUTH_BASIC to authenticate users by looking up users in *dbm* password files. Similar functionality is provided by MOD_AUTHN_FILE.

When using MOD_AUTH_BASIC or MOD_AUTH_DIGEST, this module is invoked via the AUTHBASICPROVIDER or AUTHDIGESTPROVIDER with the dbm value.

### Directives

- AuthDBMType
- AuthDBMUserFile

### See also

- AUTHNAME
- AUTHTYPE
- AUTHBASICPROVIDER
- AUTHDIGESTPROVIDER
- htpasswd
- htdbm
- Password Formats (p. 371)

### AuthDBMType Directive

| | |
|---|---|
| Description: | Sets the type of database file that is used to store passwords |
| Syntax: | AuthDBMType default\|SDBM\|GDBM\|NDBM\|DB |
| Default: | AuthDBMType default |
| Context: | directory, .htaccess |
| Override: | AuthConfig |
| Status: | Extension |
| Module: | mod_authn_dbm |

Sets the type of database file that is used to store the passwords. The default database type is determined at compile time. The availability of other types of database files also depends on compile-time settings (p. 307) .

For example, in order to enable the support for Berkeley DB (correspondent to the db type) the --with-berkeley-db option needs to be added to httpd's configure to generate the necessary DSO.

It is crucial that whatever program you use to create your password files is configured to use the same type of database.

## AuthDBMUserFile Directive

| | |
|---|---|
| Description: | Sets the name of a database file containing the list of users and passwords for authentication |
| Syntax: | `AuthDBMUserFile file-path` |
| Context: | directory, .htaccess |
| Override: | AuthConfig |
| Status: | Extension |
| Module: | mod_authn_dbm |

The AUTHDBMUSERFILE directive sets the name of a DBM file containing the list of users and passwords for user authentication. *File-path* is the absolute path to the user file.

The user file is keyed on the username. The value for a user is the encrypted password, optionally followed by a colon and arbitrary data. The colon and the data following it will be ignored by the server.

 **Security:**

Make sure that the AUTHDBMUSERFILE is stored outside the document tree of the web-server; do *not* put it in the directory that it protects. Otherwise, clients will be able to download the AUTHDBMUSERFILE.

The encrypted password format depends on which authentication frontend (e.g. MOD_AUTH_BASIC or MOD_AUTH_DIGEST) is being used. See Password Formats (p. 371) for more information.

Important compatibility note: The implementation of dbmopen in the Apache modules reads the string length of the hashed values from the DBM data structures, rather than relying upon the string being NULL-appended. Some applications, such as the Netscape web server, rely upon the string being NULL-appended, so if you are having trouble using DBM files interchangeably between applications this may be a part of the problem.

A perl script called dbmmanage is included with Apache. This program can be used to create and update DBM format password files for use with this module. Another tool for maintaining the DBM files is the included program htdbm.

# 10.17  Apache Module mod_authn_file

| | |
|---|---|
| Description: | User authentication using text files |
| Status: | Base |
| ModuleIdentifier: | authn_file_module |
| SourceFile: | mod_authn_file.c |

## Summary

This module provides authentication front-ends such as MOD_AUTH_DIGEST and MOD_AUTH_BASIC to authenticate users by looking up users in plain text password files. Similar functionality is provided by MOD_AUTHN_DBM.

When using MOD_AUTH_BASIC or MOD_AUTH_DIGEST, this module is invoked via the AUTHBASICPROVIDER or AUTHDIGESTPROVIDER with the `file` value.

### Directives

- AuthUserFile

### See also

- AUTHBASICPROVIDER
- AUTHDIGESTPROVIDER
- `htpasswd`
- `htdigest`
- Password Formats (p. 371)

## AuthUserFile Directive

| | |
|---|---|
| Description: | Sets the name of a text file containing the list of users and passwords for authentication |
| Syntax: | `AuthUserFile file-path` |
| Context: | directory, .htaccess |
| Override: | AuthConfig |
| Status: | Base |
| Module: | mod_authn_file |

The AUTHUSERFILE directive sets the name of a textual file containing the list of users and passwords for user authentication. *File-path* is the path to the user file. If it is not absolute, it is treated as relative to the SERVERROOT.

Each line of the user file contains a username followed by a colon, followed by the encrypted password. If the same user ID is defined multiple times, MOD_AUTHN_FILE will use the first occurrence to verify the password.

The encrypted password format depends on which authentication frontend (e.g. MOD_AUTH_BASIC or MOD_AUTH_DIGEST) is being used. See Password Formats (p. 371) for more information.

For MOD_AUTH_BASIC, use the utility `htpasswd` which is installed as part of the binary distribution, or which can be found in `src/support`. See the man page (p. 325) for more details. In short:

Create a password file `Filename` with `username` as the initial ID. It will prompt for the password:

```
htpasswd -c Filename username
```

Add or modify `username2` in the password file `Filename`:

```
htpasswd Filename username2
```

Note that searching large text files is *very* inefficient; AuthDBMUserFile should be used instead.

For MOD_AUTH_DIGEST, use htdigest instead. Note that you cannot mix user data for Digest Authentication and Basic Authentication within the same file.

 **Security**

Make sure that the AuthUserFile is stored outside the document tree of the web-server. Do **not** put it in the directory that it protects. Otherwise, clients may be able to download the AuthUserFile.

# 10.18 Apache Module mod_authn_socache

| | |
|---|---|
| Description: | Manages a cache of authentication credentials to relieve the load on backends |
| Status: | Base |
| ModuleIdentifier: | authn_socache_module |
| SourceFile: | mod_authn_socache.c |
| Compatibility: | Version 2.3 and later |

## Summary

Maintains a cache of authentication credentials, so that a new backend lookup is not required for every authenticated request.

### Directives

- AuthnCacheContext
- AuthnCacheEnable
- AuthnCacheProvideFor
- AuthnCacheSOCache
- AuthnCacheTimeout

## Authentication Cacheing

Some users of more heavyweight authentication such as SQL database lookups (MOD_AUTHN_DBD) have reported it putting an unacceptable load on their authentication provider. A typical case in point is where an HTML page contains hundreds of objects (images, scripts, stylesheets, media, etc), and a request to the page generates hundreds of effectively-immediate requests for authenticated additional contents.

mod_authn_socache provides a solution to this problem by maintaining a cache of authentication credentials.

## Usage

The authentication cache should be used where authentication lookups impose a significant load on the server, or a backend or network. Authentication by file (MOD_AUTHN_FILE) or dbm (MOD_AUTHN_DBM) are unlikely to benefit, as these are fast and lightweight in their own right (though in some cases, such as a network-mounted file, cacheing may be worthwhile). Other providers such as SQL or LDAP based authentication are more likely to benefit, particularly where there is an observed performance issue. Amongst the standard modules, MOD_AUTHNZ_LDAP manages its own cache, so only MOD_AUTHN_DBD will usually benefit from this cache.

The basic rules to cache for a provider are:

1. Include the provider you're cacheing for in an AUTHNCACHEPROVIDEFOR directive.

2. List *socache* ahead of the provider you're cacheing for in your AUTHBASICPROVIDER or AUTHDIGEST-PROVIDER directive.

A simple usage example to accelerate MOD_AUTHN_DBD using dbm as a cache engine:

```
#AuthnCacheSOCache is optional.  If specified, it is server-wide
AuthnCacheSOCache dbm
<Directory "/usr/www/myhost/private">
```

```
    AuthType Basic
    AuthName "Cached Authentication Example"
    AuthBasicProvider socache dbd
    AuthDBDUserPWQuery "SELECT password FROM authn WHERE user = %s"
    AuthnCacheProvideFor dbd
    Require valid-user
    #Optional
    AuthnCacheContext dbd-authn-example
</Directory>
```

### Cacheing with custom modules

Module developers should note that their modules must be enabled for cacheing with mod_authn_socache. A single optional API function *ap_authn_cache_store* is provided to cache credentials a provider has just looked up or generated. Usage examples are available in r957072[10], in which three authn providers are enabled for cacheing.

### AuthnCacheContext Directive

| | |
|---|---|
| Description: | Specify a context string for use in the cache key |
| Syntax: | `AuthnCacheContext directory|server|custom-string` |
| Default: | `directory` |
| Context: | directory |
| Status: | Base |
| Module: | mod_authn_socache |

This directive specifies a string to be used along with the supplied username (and realm in the case of Digest Authentication) in constructing a cache key. This serves to disambiguate identical usernames serving different authentication areas on the server.

Two special values for this are *directory*, which uses the directory context of the request as a string, and *server* which uses the virtual host name.

The default is *directory*, which is also the most conservative setting. This is likely to be less than optimal, as it (for example) causes *$app-base*, *$app-base/images*, *$app-base/scripts* and *$app-base/media* each to have its own separate cache key. A better policy is to name the AuthnCacheContext for the password provider: for example a *htpasswd* file or database table.

Contexts can be shared across different areas of a server, where credentials are shared. However, this has potential to become a vector for cross-site or cross-application security breaches, so this directive is not permitted in *.htaccess* contexts.

### AuthnCacheEnable Directive

| | |
|---|---|
| Description: | Enable Authn caching configured anywhere |
| Syntax: | `AuthnCacheEnable` |
| Context: | server config |
| Override: | None |
| Status: | Base |
| Module: | mod_authn_socache |

This directive is not normally necessary: it is implied if authentication cacheing is enabled anywhere in *httpd.conf*. However, if it is not enabled anywhere in *httpd.conf* it will by default not be initialised, and is therefore not available in a *.htaccess* context. This directive ensures it is initialised so it can be used in *.htaccess*.

---

[10]http://svn.eu.apache.org/viewvc?view=revision&revision=957072

## AuthnCacheProvideFor Directive

| | |
|---|---|
| Description: | Specify which authn provider(s) to cache for |
| Syntax: | `AuthnCacheProvideFor authn-provider [...]` |
| Default: | `None` |
| Context: | directory, .htaccess |
| Override: | AuthConfig |
| Status: | Base |
| Module: | mod_authn_socache |

This directive specifies an authentication provider or providers to cache for. Credentials found by a provider not listed in an AuthnCacheProvideFor directive will not be cached.

For example, to cache credentials found by MOD_AUTHN_DBD or by a custom provider *myprovider*, but leave those looked up by lightweight providers like file or dbm lookup alone:

`AuthnCacheProvideFor dbd myprovider`

## AuthnCacheSOCache Directive

| | |
|---|---|
| Description: | Select socache backend provider to use |
| Syntax: | `AuthnCacheSOCache provider-name[:provider-args]` |
| Context: | server config |
| Override: | None |
| Status: | Base |
| Module: | mod_authn_socache |
| Compatibility: | Optional provider arguments are available in Apache HTTP Server 2.4.7 and later |

This is a server-wide setting to select a provider for the shared object cache (p. 114) , followed by optional arguments for that provider. Some possible values for *provider-name* are "dbm", "dc", "memcache", or "shmcb", each subject to the appropriate module being loaded. If not set, your platform's default will be used.

## AuthnCacheTimeout Directive

| | |
|---|---|
| Description: | Set a timeout for cache entries |
| Syntax: | `AuthnCacheTimeout timeout (seconds)` |
| Default: | `300 (5 minutes)` |
| Context: | directory, .htaccess |
| Override: | AuthConfig |
| Status: | Base |
| Module: | mod_authn_socache |

Cacheing authentication data can be a security issue, though short-term cacheing is unlikely to be a problem. Typically a good solution is to cache credentials for as long as it takes to relieve the load on a backend, but no longer, though if changes to your users and passwords are infrequent then a longer timeout may suit you. The default 300 seconds (5 minutes) is both cautious and ample to keep the load on a backend such as dbd (SQL database queries) down.

This should not be confused with session timeout, which is an entirely separate issue. However, you may wish to check your session-management software for whether cached credentials can "accidentally" extend a session, and bear it in mind when setting your timeout.

# 10.19   Apache Module mod_authnz_fcgi

| | |
|---|---|
| Description: | Allows a FastCGI authorizer application to handle Apache httpd authentication and authorization |
| Status: | Extension |
| ModuleIdentifier: | authnz_fcgi_module |
| SourceFile: | mod_authnz_fcgi.c |
| Compatibility: | Available in version 2.4.10 and later |

## Summary

This module allows FastCGI authorizer applications to authenticate users and authorize access to resources. It supports generic FastCGI authorizers which participate in a single phase for authentication and authorization as well as Apache httpd-specific authenticators and authorizors which participate in one or both phases.

FastCGI authorizers can authenticate using user id and password, such as for Basic authentication, or can authenticate using arbitrary mechanisms.

### Directives

- AuthnzFcgiCheckAuthnProvider
- AuthnzFcgiDefineProvider

### See also

- Authentication, Authorization, and Access Control (p. 227)
- MOD_AUTH_BASIC
- fcgistarter
- MOD_PROXY_FCGI

## Invocation modes

The invocation modes for FastCGI authorizers supported by this module are distinguished by two characteristics, *type* and auth *mechanism*.

*Type* is simply authn for authentication, authz for authorization, or authnz for combined authentication and authorization.

Auth *mechanism* refers to the Apache httpd configuration mechanisms and processing phases, and can be AuthBasicProvider, Require, or check_user_id. The first two of these correspond to the directives used to enable participation in the appropriate processing phase.

Descriptions of each mode:

**Type authn, *mechanism* AuthBasicProvider**   In this mode, FCGI_ROLE is set to AUTHORIZER and FCGI_APACHE_ROLE is set to AUTHENTICATOR. The application must be defined as provider type *authn* using AUTHNZFCGIDEFINEPROVIDER and enabled with AUTHBASICPROVIDER. When invoked, the application is expected to authenticate the client using the provided user id and password. Example application:

```
#!/usr/bin/perl
use FCGI;
my $request = FCGI::Request();
```

```
while ($request->Accept() >= 0) {
    die if $ENV{'FCGI_APACHE_ROLE'} ne "AUTHENTICATOR";
    die if $ENV{'FCGI_ROLE'}        ne "AUTHORIZER";
    die if !$ENV{'REMOTE_PASSWD'};
    die if !$ENV{'REMOTE_USER'};

    print STDERR "This text is written to the web server error log.\n";

    if ( ($ENV{'REMOTE_USER' } eq "foo" || $ENV{'REMOTE_USER'} eq "foo1") &&
        $ENV{'REMOTE_PASSWD'} eq "bar" ) {
        print "Status: 200\n";
        print "Variable-AUTHN_1: authn_01\n";
        print "Variable-AUTHN_2: authn_02\n";
        print "\n";
    }
    else {
        print "Status: 401\n\n";
    }
}
```

Example configuration:

```
AuthnzFcgiDefineProvider authn FooAuthn fcgi://localhost:10102/
<Location "/protected/">
  AuthType Basic
  AuthName "Restricted"
  AuthBasicProvider FooAuthn
  Require ...
</Location>
```

*Type* `authz`, *mechanism* `Require`  In this mode, FCGI_ROLE is set to  AUTHORIZER and FCGI_APACHE_ROLE
is set to AUTHORIZER. The application must be defined as provider type *authz* using AUTHNZFCGIDEFINE-
PROVIDER.  When invoked, the application is expected to authorize the client using the provided user id and
other request data. Example application:

```
#!/usr/bin/perl
use FCGI;
my $request = FCGI::Request();
while ($request->Accept() >= 0) {
    die if $ENV{'FCGI_APACHE_ROLE'} ne "AUTHORIZER";
    die if $ENV{'FCGI_ROLE'}        ne "AUTHORIZER";
    die if $ENV{'REMOTE_PASSWD'};

    print STDERR "This text is written to the web server error log.\n";

    if ($ENV{'REMOTE_USER'} eq "foo1") {
        print "Status: 200\n";
        print "Variable-AUTHZ_1: authz_01\n";
        print "Variable-AUTHZ_2: authz_02\n";
        print "\n";
    }
    else {
        print "Status: 403\n\n";
    }
}
```

Example configuration:

```
AuthnzFcgiDefineProvider authz FooAuthz fcgi://localhost:10103/
<Location "/protected/">
  AuthType ...
  AuthName ...
  AuthBasicProvider ...
  Require FooAuthz
</Location>
```

**Type `authnz`,** *mechanism* **`AuthBasicProvider + Require`** In this mode, which supports the web server-agnostic FastCGI AUTHORIZER protocol, FCGI_ROLE is set to AUTHORIZER and FCGI_APACHE_ROLE is not set. The application must be defined as provider type *authnz* using AUTHNZFCGIDEFINEPROVIDER. The application is expected to handle both authentication and authorization in the same invocation using the user id, password, and other request data. The invocation occurs during the Apache httpd API authentication phase. If the application returns 200 and the same provider is invoked during the authorization phase (via REQUIRE), mod_authnz_fcgi will return success for the authorization phase without invoking the application. Example application:

```
#!/usr/bin/perl
use FCGI;
my $request = FCGI::Request();
while ($request->Accept() >= 0) {
    die if $ENV{'FCGI_APACHE_ROLE'};
    die if $ENV{'FCGI_ROLE'} ne "AUTHORIZER";
    die if !$ENV{'REMOTE_PASSWD'};
    die if !$ENV{'REMOTE_USER'};

    print STDERR "This text is written to the web server error log.\n";

    if ( ($ENV{'REMOTE_USER' } eq "foo" || $ENV{'REMOTE_USER'} eq "foo1") &&
        $ENV{'REMOTE_PASSWD'} eq "bar" &&
        $ENV{'REQUEST_URI'} =~ m%/bar/.*%) {
        print "Status: 200\n";
        print "Variable-AUTHNZ_1: authnz_01\n";
        print "Variable-AUTHNZ_2: authnz_02\n";
        print "\n";
    }
    else {
        print "Status: 401\n\n";
    }
}
```

Example configuration:

```
AuthnzFcgiDefineProvider authnz FooAuthnz fcgi://localhost:10103/
<Location "/protected/">
  AuthType Basic
  AuthName "Restricted"
  AuthBasicProvider FooAuthnz
  Require FooAuthnz
</Location>
```

**Type `authn`,** *mechanism* **`check_user_id`** In this mode, FCGI_ROLE is set to AUTHORIZER and FCGI_APACHE_ROLE is set to AUTHENTICATOR. The application must be defined as provider type *authn* using AUTHNZFCGIDEFINEPROVIDER. AUTHNZFCGICHECKAUTHNPROVIDER specifies when it is called. Example application:

```perl
#!/usr/bin/perl
use FCGI;
my $request = FCGI::Request();
while ($request->Accept() >= 0) {
    die if $ENV{'FCGI_APACHE_ROLE'} ne "AUTHENTICATOR";
    die if $ENV{'FCGI_ROLE'} ne "AUTHORIZER";

    # This authorizer assumes that the RequireBasicAuth option of
    # AuthnzFcgiCheckAuthnProvider is On:
    die if !$ENV{'REMOTE_PASSWD'};
    die if !$ENV{'REMOTE_USER'};

    print STDERR "This text is written to the web server error log.\n";

    if ( ($ENV{'REMOTE_USER' } eq "foo" || $ENV{'REMOTE_USER'} eq "fool") &&
        $ENV{'REMOTE_PASSWD'} eq "bar" ) {
        print "Status: 200\n";
        print "Variable-AUTHNZ_1: authnz_01\n";
        print "Variable-AUTHNZ_2: authnz_02\n";
        print "\n";
    }
    else {
        print "Status: 401\n\n";
        # If a response body is written here, it will be returned to
        # the client.
    }
}
```

Example configuration:

```
AuthnzFcgiDefineProvider authn FooAuthn fcgi://localhost:10103/
<Location "/protected/">
  AuthType ...
  AuthName ...
  AuthnzFcgiCheckAuthnProvider FooAuthn \
                               Authoritative On \
                               RequireBasicAuth Off \
                               UserExpr "%{reqenv:REMOTE_USER}"
  Require ...
</Location>
```

## Additional examples

1. If your application supports the separate authentication and authorization roles (AUTHENTICATOR and AUTHORIZER), define separate providers as follows, even if they map to the same application:

```
AuthnzFcgiDefineProvider authn  FooAuthn  fcgi://localhost:10102/
AuthnzFcgiDefineProvider authz  FooAuthz  fcgi://localhost:10102/
```

Specify the authn provider on AUTHBASICPROVIDER and the authz provider on REQUIRE:

```
AuthType Basic
AuthName "Restricted"
AuthBasicProvider FooAuthn
Require FooAuthz
```

2. If your application supports the generic AUTHORIZER role (authentication and authorizer in one invocation), define a single provider as follows:

```
AuthnzFcgiDefineProvider authnz FooAuthnz fcgi://localhost:10103/
```

Specify the authnz provider on both AUTHBASICPROVIDER and REQUIRE:

```
AuthType Basic
AuthName "Restricted"
AuthBasicProvider FooAuthnz
Require FooAuthnz
```

## Limitations

The following are potential features which are not currently implemented:

**Apache httpd access checker**  The Apache httpd API *access check* phase is a separate phase from authentication and authorization. Some other FastCGI implementations implement this phase, which is denoted by the setting of FCGI_APACHE_ROLE to ACCESS_CHECKER.

**Local (Unix) sockets or pipes**  Only TCP sockets are currently supported.

**Support for mod_authn_socache**  mod_authn_socache interaction should be implemented for applications which participate in Apache httpd-style authentication.

**Support for digest authentication using AuthDigestProvider**  This is expected to be a permanent limitation as there is no authorizer flow for retrieving a hash.

**Application process management**  This is expected to be permanently out of scope for this module. Application processes must be controlled by other means. For example, fcgistarter can be used to start them.

**AP_AUTH_INTERNAL_PER_URI**  All providers are currently registered as AP_AUTH_INTERNAL_PER_CONF, which means that checks are not performed again for internal subrequests with the same access control configuration as the initial request.

**Protocol data charset conversion**  If mod_authn_fcgi runs in an EBCDIC compilation environment, all FastCGI protocol data is written in EBCDIC and expected to be received in EBCDIC.

**Multiple requests per connection**  Currently the connection to the FastCGI authorizer is closed after every phase of processing. For example, if the authorizer handles separate *authn* and *authz* phases then two connections will be used.

**URI Mapping**  URIs from clients can't be mapped, such as with the PROXYPASS used with FastCGI responders.

## Logging

1. Processing errors are logged at log level `error` and higher.

2. Messages written by the application are logged at log level `warn`.

3. General messages for debugging are logged at log level `debug`.

4. Environment variables passed to the application are logged at log level `trace2`. The value of the `REMOTE_PASSWD` variable will be obscured, but **any other sensitive data will be visible in the log**.

5. All I/O between the module and the FastCGI application, including all environment variables, will be logged in printable and hex format at log level `trace5`. **All sensitive data will be visible in the log.**

LOGLEVEL can be used to configure a log level specific to mod_authnz_fcgi. For example:

```
LogLevel info authnz_fcgi:trace8
```

## AuthnzFcgiCheckAuthnProvider Directive

| | |
|---|---|
| Description: | Enables a FastCGI application to handle the check_authn authentication hook. |
| Syntax: | `AuthnzFcgiCheckAuthnProvider provider-name|None option ...` |
| Default: | `none` |
| Context: | directory |
| Status: | Extension |
| Module: | mod_authnz_fcgi |

This directive is used to enable a FastCGI authorizer to handle a specific processing phase of authentication or authorization.

Some capabilities of FastCGI authorizers require enablement using this directive instead of AUTHBASICPROVIDER:

- Non-Basic authentication; generally, determining the user id of the client and returning it from the authorizer; see the `UserExpr` option below

- Selecting a custom response code; for a non-200 response from the authorizer, the code from the authorizer will be the status of the response

- Setting the body of a non-200 response; if the authorizer provides a response body with a non-200 response, that body will be returned to the client; up to 8192 bytes of text are supported

*provider-name* This is the name of a provider defined with AUTHNZFCGIDEFINEPROVIDER.

**None** Specify `None` to disable a provider enabled with this directive in an outer scope, such as in a parent directory.

*option* The following options are supported:

**Authoritative On—Off (default On)** This controls whether or not other modules are allowed to run when this module has a FastCGI authorizer configured and it fails the request.

**DefaultUser** *userid* When the authorizer returns success and `UserExpr` is configured and evaluates to an empty string (e.g., authorizer didn't return a variable), this value will be used as the user id. This is typically used when the authorizer has a concept of guest, or unauthenticated, users and guest users are mapped to some specific user id for logging and other purposes.

**RequireBasicAuth On—Off (default Off)** This controls whether or not Basic auth is required before passing the request to the authorizer. If required, the authorizer won't be invoked without a user id and password; 401 will be returned for a request without that.

**UserExpr** *expr* **(no default)**  When Basic authentication isn't provided by the client and the authorizer determines the user, this expression, evaluated after calling the authorizer, determines the user. The expression follows ap_expr syntax (p. 99) and must resolve to a string. A typical use is to reference a `Variable-XXX` setting returned by the authorizer using an option like `UserExpr "%{reqenv:XXX}"`. If this option is specified and the user id can't be retrieved using the expression after a successful authentication, the request will be rejected with a 500 error.

## AuthnzFcgiDefineProvider Directive

| | |
|---|---|
| Description: | Defines a FastCGI application as a provider for authentication and/or authorization |
| Syntax: | `AuthnzFcgiDefineProvider type provider-name backend-address` |
| Default: | `none` |
| Context: | server config |
| Status: | Extension |
| Module: | mod_authnz_fcgi |

This directive is used to define a FastCGI application as a provider for a particular phase of authentication or authorization.

*type*  This must be set to *authn* for authentication, *authz* for authorization, or *authnz* for a generic FastCGI authorizer which performs both checks.

*provider-name*  This is used to assign a name to the provider which is used in other directives such as AUTHBASICPROVIDER and REQUIRE.

*backend-address*  This specifies the address of the application, in the form *fcgi://hostname:port/*. The application process(es) must be managed independently, such as with `fcgistarter`.

# 10.20 Apache Module mod_authnz_ldap

| | |
|---|---|
| Description: | Allows an LDAP directory to be used to store the database for HTTP Basic authentication. |
| Status: | Extension |
| ModuleIdentifier: | authnz_ldap_module |
| SourceFile: | mod_authnz_ldap.c |

## Summary

This module allows authentication front-ends such as MOD_AUTH_BASIC to authenticate users through an ldap directory.

MOD_AUTHNZ_LDAP supports the following features:

- Known to support the OpenLDAP SDK[11] (both 1.x and 2.x), Novell LDAP SDK[12] and the iPlanet (Netscape)[13] SDK.

- Complex authorization policies can be implemented by representing the policy with LDAP filters.

- Uses extensive caching of LDAP operations via mod_ldap (p. 693) .

- Support for LDAP over SSL (requires the Netscape SDK) or TLS (requires the OpenLDAP 2.x SDK or Novell LDAP SDK).

When using MOD_AUTH_BASIC, this module is invoked via the AUTHBASICPROVIDER directive with the ldap value.

## Directives

- AuthLDAPAuthorizePrefix
- AuthLDAPBindAuthoritative
- AuthLDAPBindDN
- AuthLDAPBindPassword
- AuthLDAPCharsetConfig
- AuthLDAPCompareAsUser
- AuthLDAPCompareDNOnServer
- AuthLDAPDereferenceAliases
- AuthLDAPGroupAttribute
- AuthLDAPGroupAttributeIsDN
- AuthLDAPInitialBindAsUser
- AuthLDAPInitialBindPattern
- AuthLDAPMaxSubGroupDepth
- AuthLDAPRemoteUserAttribute
- AuthLDAPRemoteUserIsDN
- AuthLDAPSearchAsUser
- AuthLDAPSubGroupAttribute

---

[11] http://www.openldap.org/
[12] http://developer.novell.com/ndk/cldap.htm
[13] http://www.iplanet.com/downloads/developer/

- AuthLDAPSubGroupClass
- AuthLDAPUrl

**See also**

- MOD_LDAP
- MOD_AUTH_BASIC
- MOD_AUTHZ_USER
- MOD_AUTHZ_GROUPFILE

# Contents

- General caveats
- Operation

    - The Authentication Phase
    - The Authorization Phase

- The Require Directives

    - Require ldap-user
    - Require ldap-group
    - Require ldap-dn
    - Require ldap-attribute
    - Require ldap-filter
    - Require ldap-search

- Examples
- Using TLS
- Using SSL
- Exposing Login Information
- Using Active Directory
- Using Microsoft FrontPage with MOD_AUTHNZ_LDAP

    - How It Works
    - Caveats

# General caveats

This module caches authentication and authorization results based on the configuration of MOD_LDAP. Changes made to the backing LDAP server will not be immediately reflected on the HTTP Server, including but not limited to user lockouts/revocations, password changes, or changes to group memberships. Consult the directives in MOD_LDAP for details of the cache tunables.

## Operation

There are two phases in granting access to a user. The first phase is authentication, in which the MOD_AUTHNZ_LDAP authentication provider verifies that the user's credentials are valid. This is also called the *search/bind* phase. The second phase is authorization, in which MOD_AUTHNZ_LDAP determines if the authenticated user is allowed access to the resource in question. This is also known as the *compare* phase.

MOD_AUTHNZ_LDAP registers both an authn_ldap authentication provider and an authz_ldap authorization handler. The authn_ldap authentication provider can be enabled through the AUTHBASICPROVIDER directive using the ldap value. The authz_ldap handler extends the REQUIRE directive's authorization types by adding ldap-user, ldap-dn and ldap-group values.

### The Authentication Phase

During the authentication phase, MOD_AUTHNZ_LDAP searches for an entry in the directory that matches the username that the HTTP client passes. If a single unique match is found, then MOD_AUTHNZ_LDAP attempts to bind to the directory server using the DN of the entry plus the password provided by the HTTP client. Because it does a search, then a bind, it is often referred to as the search/bind phase. Here are the steps taken during the search/bind phase.

1. Generate a search filter by combining the attribute and filter provided in the AUTHLDAPURL directive with the username passed by the HTTP client.

2. Search the directory using the generated filter. If the search does not return exactly one entry, deny or decline access.

3. Fetch the distinguished name of the entry retrieved from the search and attempt to bind to the LDAP server using that DN and the password passed by the HTTP client. If the bind is unsuccessful, deny or decline access.

The following directives are used during the search/bind phase

| | |
|---|---|
| AUTHLDAPURL | Specifies the LDAP server, the base DN, the attribute to use in the search, as well as the extra search filter to use. |
| AUTHLDAPBINDDN | An optional DN to bind with during the search phase. |
| AUTHLDAPBINDPASSWORD | An optional password to bind with during the search phase. |

### The Authorization Phase

During the authorization phase, MOD_AUTHNZ_LDAP attempts to determine if the user is authorized to access the resource. Many of these checks require MOD_AUTHNZ_LDAP to do a compare operation on the LDAP server. This is why this phase is often referred to as the compare phase. MOD_AUTHNZ_LDAP accepts the following REQUIRE directives to determine if the credentials are acceptable:

- Grant access if there is a Require ldap-user directive, and the username in the directive matches the username passed by the client.

- Grant access if there is a Require ldap-dn directive, and the DN in the directive matches the DN fetched from the LDAP directory.

- Grant access if there is a Require ldap-group directive, and the DN fetched from the LDAP directory (or the username passed by the client) occurs in the LDAP group or, potentially, in one of its sub-groups.

- Grant access if there is a Require ldap-attribute directive, and the attribute fetched from the LDAP directory matches the given value.

- Grant access if there is a Require ldap-filter directive, and the search filter successfully finds a single user object that matches the dn of the authenticated user.

- Grant access if there is a `Require ldap-search` directive, and the search filter successfully returns a single matching object with any distinguished name.

- otherwise, deny or decline access

Other REQUIRE values may also be used which may require loading additional authorization modules.

- Grant access to all successfully authenticated users if there is a `Require valid-user` directive. (requires MOD_AUTHZ_USER)

- Grant access if there is a `Require group` directive, and MOD_AUTHZ_GROUPFILE has been loaded with the AUTHGROUPFILE directive set.

- others...

MOD_AUTHNZ_LDAP uses the following directives during the compare phase:

| | |
|---|---|
| AUTHLDAPURL | The attribute specified in the URL is used in compare operations for the `Require ldap-user` operation. |
| AUTHLDAPCOMPAREDNONSERVER | Determines the behavior of the `Require ldap-dn` directive. |
| AUTHLDAPGROUPATTRIBUTE | Determines the attribute to use for comparisons in the `Require ldap-group` directive. |
| AUTHLDAPGROUPATTRIBUTEISDN | Specifies whether to use the user DN or the username when doing comparisons for the `Require ldap-group` directive. |
| AUTHLDAPMAXSUBGROUPDEPTH | Determines the maximum depth of sub-groups that will be evaluated during comparisons in the `Require ldap-group` directive. |
| AUTHLDAPSUBGROUPATTRIBUTE | Determines the attribute to use when obtaining sub-group members of the current group during comparisons in the `Require ldap-group` directive. |
| AUTHLDAPSUBGROUPCLASS | Specifies the LDAP objectClass values used to identify if queried directory objects really are group objects (as opposed to user objects) during the `Require ldap-group` directive's sub-group processing. |

## The Require Directives

Apache's REQUIRE directives are used during the authorization phase to ensure that a user is allowed to access a resource. mod_authnz_ldap extends the authorization types with `ldap-user`, `ldap-dn`, `ldap-group`, `ldap-attribute` and `ldap-filter`. Other authorization types may also be used but may require that additional authorization modules be loaded.

Since v2.4.8, expressions (p. 99) are supported within the LDAP require directives.

### Require ldap-user

The `Require ldap-user` directive specifies what usernames can access the resource. Once MOD_AUTHNZ_LDAP has retrieved a unique DN from the directory, it does an LDAP compare operation using the username specified in the `Require ldap-user` to see if that username is part of the just-fetched LDAP entry. Multiple users can be granted access by putting multiple usernames on the line, separated with spaces. If a username has a space in it, then it must be surrounded with double quotes. Multiple users can also be granted access by using multiple `Require ldap-user` directives, with one user per line. For example, with a AUTHLDAPURL of `ldap://ldap/o=Example?cn` (i.e., cn is used for searches), the following Require directives could be used to restrict access:

```
Require ldap-user "Barbara Jenson"
Require ldap-user "Fred User"
Require ldap-user "Joe Manager"
```

Because of the way that MOD_AUTHNZ_LDAP handles this directive, Barbara Jenson could sign on as *Barbara Jenson*, *Babs Jenson* or any other cn that she has in her LDAP entry. Only the single Require ldap-user line is needed to support all values of the attribute in the user's entry.

If the uid attribute was used instead of the cn attribute in the URL above, the above three lines could be condensed to

```
Require ldap-user bjenson fuser jmanager
```

### Require ldap-group

This directive specifies an LDAP group whose members are allowed access. It takes the distinguished name of the LDAP group. Note: Do not surround the group name with quotes. For example, assume that the following entry existed in the LDAP directory:

```
dn: cn=Administrators, o=Example
objectClass: groupOfUniqueNames
uniqueMember: cn=Barbara Jenson, o=Example
uniqueMember: cn=Fred User, o=Example
```

The following directive would grant access to both Fred and Barbara:

```
Require ldap-group cn=Administrators, o=Example
```

Members can also be found within sub-groups of a specified LDAP group if AUTHLDAPMAXSUBGROUPDEPTH is set to a value greater than 0. For example, assume the following entries exist in the LDAP directory:

```
dn: cn=Employees, o=Example
objectClass: groupOfUniqueNames
uniqueMember: cn=Managers, o=Example
uniqueMember: cn=Administrators, o=Example
uniqueMember: cn=Users, o=Example

dn: cn=Managers, o=Example
objectClass: groupOfUniqueNames
uniqueMember: cn=Bob Ellis, o=Example
uniqueMember: cn=Tom Jackson, o=Example

dn: cn=Administrators, o=Example
objectClass: groupOfUniqueNames
uniqueMember: cn=Barbara Jenson, o=Example
uniqueMember: cn=Fred User, o=Example

dn: cn=Users, o=Example
objectClass: groupOfUniqueNames
uniqueMember: cn=Allan Jefferson, o=Example
uniqueMember: cn=Paul Tilley, o=Example
uniqueMember: cn=Temporary Employees, o=Example

dn: cn=Temporary Employees, o=Example
objectClass: groupOfUniqueNames
uniqueMember: cn=Jim Swenson, o=Example
uniqueMember: cn=Elliot Rhodes, o=Example
```

The following directives would allow access for Bob Ellis, Tom Jackson, Barbara Jenson, Fred User, Allan Jefferson, and Paul Tilley but would not allow access for Jim Swenson, or Elliot Rhodes (since they are at a sub-group depth of 2):

```
Require ldap-group cn=Employees, o=Example
AuthLDAPMaxSubGroupDepth 1
```

Behavior of this directive is modified by the AUTHLDAPGROUPATTRIBUTE, AUTHLDAPGROUPATTRIBUTEISDN, AUTHLDAPMAXSUBGROUPDEPTH, AUTHLDAPSUBGROUPATTRIBUTE, and AUTHLDAPSUBGROUPCLASS directives.

## Require ldap-dn

The `Require ldap-dn` directive allows the administrator to grant access based on distinguished names. It specifies a DN that must match for access to be granted. If the distinguished name that was retrieved from the directory server matches the distinguished name in the `Require ldap-dn`, then authorization is granted. Note: do not surround the distinguished name with quotes.

The following directive would grant access to a specific DN:

```
Require ldap-dn cn=Barbara Jenson, o=Example
```

Behavior of this directive is modified by the AUTHLDAPCOMPAREDNONSERVER directive.

## Require ldap-attribute

The `Require ldap-attribute` directive allows the administrator to grant access based on attributes of the authenticated user in the LDAP directory. If the attribute in the directory matches the value given in the configuration, access is granted.

The following directive would grant access to anyone with the attribute employeeType = active

```
Require ldap-attribute "employeeType=active"
```

Multiple attribute/value pairs can be specified on the same line separated by spaces or they can be specified in multiple `Require ldap-attribute` directives. The effect of listing multiple attribute/values pairs is an OR operation. Access will be granted if any of the listed attribute values match the value of the corresponding attribute in the user object. If the value of the attribute contains a space, only the value must be within double quotes.

The following directive would grant access to anyone with the city attribute equal to "San Jose" or status equal to "Active"

```
Require ldap-attribute city="San Jose" "status=active"
```

## Require ldap-filter

The `Require ldap-filter` directive allows the administrator to grant access based on a complex LDAP search filter. If the dn returned by the filter search matches the authenticated user dn, access is granted.

The following directive would grant access to anyone having a cell phone and is in the marketing department

```
Require ldap-filter "&(cell=*)(department=marketing)"
```

The difference between the `Require ldap-filter` directive and the `Require ldap-attribute` directive is that `ldap-filter` performs a search operation on the LDAP directory using the specified search filter rather than a simple attribute comparison. If a simple attribute comparison is all that is required, the comparison operation performed by `ldap-attribute` will be faster than the search operation used by `ldap-filter` especially within a large directory.

When using an expression (p. 99) within the filter, care must be taken to ensure that LDAP filters are escaped correctly to guard against LDAP injection. The ldap function can be used for this purpose.

```
<LocationMatch "^/dav/(?<SITENAME>[^/]+)/">
  Require ldap-filter "(memberOf=cn=%{ldap:%{unescape:%{env:MATCH_SITENAME}},ou=Webs
</LocationMatch>
```

### Require ldap-search

The `Require ldap-search` directive allows the administrator to grant access based on a generic LDAP search filter using an expression (p. 99) . If there is exactly one match to the search filter, regardless of the distinguished name, access is granted.

The following directive would grant access to URLs that match the given objects in the LDAP server:

```
<LocationMatch "^/dav/(?<SITENAME>[^/]+)/">
Require ldap-search "(cn=%{ldap:%{unescape:%{env:MATCH_SITENAME}} Website)"
</LocationMatch>
```

Note: care must be taken to ensure that any expressions are properly escaped to guard against LDAP injection. The **ldap** function can be used as per the example above.

## Examples

- Grant access to anyone who exists in the LDAP directory, using their UID for searches.

  ```
  AuthLDAPURL "ldap://ldap1.example.com:389/ou=People, o=Example?uid?sub?(objectCl
  Require valid-user
  ```

- The next example is the same as above; but with the fields that have useful defaults omitted. Also, note the use of a redundant LDAP server.

  ```
  AuthLDAPURL "ldap://ldap1.example.com ldap2.example.com/ou=People, o=Example"
  Require valid-user
  ```

- The next example is similar to the previous one, but it uses the common name instead of the UID. Note that this could be problematical if multiple people in the directory share the same `cn`, because a search on `cn` **must** return exactly one entry. That's why this approach is not recommended: it's a better idea to choose an attribute that is guaranteed unique in your directory, such as `uid`.

  ```
  AuthLDAPURL "ldap://ldap.example.com/ou=People, o=Example?cn"
  Require valid-user
  ```

- Grant access to anybody in the Administrators group. The users must authenticate using their UID.

  ```
  AuthLDAPURL ldap://ldap.example.com/o=Example?uid
  Require ldap-group cn=Administrators, o=Example
  ```

- Grant access to anybody in the group whose name matches the hostname of the virtual host. In this example an expression (p. 99) is used to build the filter.

```
AuthLDAPURL ldap://ldap.example.com/o=Example?uid
Require ldap-group cn=%{SERVER_NAME}, o=Example
```

- The next example assumes that everyone at Example who carries an alphanumeric pager will have an LDAP attribute of qpagePagerID. The example will grant access only to people (authenticated via their UID) who have alphanumeric pagers:

```
AuthLDAPURL ldap://ldap.example.com/o=Example?uid??(qpagePagerID=*)
Require valid-user
```

- The next example demonstrates the power of using filters to accomplish complicated administrative requirements. Without filters, it would have been necessary to create a new LDAP group and ensure that the group's members remain synchronized with the pager users. This becomes trivial with filters. The goal is to grant access to anyone who has a pager, plus grant access to Joe Manager, who doesn't have a pager, but does need to access the same resource:

```
AuthLDAPURL ldap://ldap.example.com/o=Example?uid??(|(qpagePagerID=*)(uid=jmanager))
Require valid-user
```

This last may look confusing at first, so it helps to evaluate what the search filter will look like based on who connects, as shown below. If Fred User connects as fuser, the filter would look like

```
(&(|(qpagePagerID=*)(uid=jmanager))(uid=fuser))
```

The above search will only succeed if *fuser* has a pager. When Joe Manager connects as *jmanager*, the filter looks like

```
(&(|(qpagePagerID=*)(uid=jmanager))(uid=jmanager))
```

The above search will succeed whether *jmanager* has a pager or not.

## Using TLS

To use TLS, see the MOD_LDAP directives LDAPTRUSTEDCLIENTCERT, LDAPTRUSTEDGLOBALCERT and LDAPTRUSTEDMODE.

An optional second parameter can be added to the AUTHLDAPURL to override the default connection type set by LDAPTRUSTEDMODE. This will allow the connection established by an *ldap://* Url to be upgraded to a secure connection on the same port.

## Using SSL

To use SSL, see the MOD_LDAP directives LDAPTRUSTEDCLIENTCERT, LDAPTRUSTEDGLOBALCERT and LDAPTRUSTEDMODE.

To specify a secure LDAP server, use *ldaps://* in the AUTHLDAPURL directive, instead of *ldap://*.

## Exposing Login Information

when this module performs *authentication*, ldap attributes specified in the AUTHLDAPURL directive are placed in environment variables with the prefix "AUTHENTICATE_".

when this module performs *authorization*, ldap attributes specified in the AUTHLDAPURL directive are placed in environment variables with the prefix "AUTHORIZE_".

If the attribute field contains the username, common name and telephone number of a user, a CGI program will have access to this information without the need to make a second independent LDAP query to gather this additional information.

This has the potential to dramatically simplify the coding and configuration required in some web applications.

## Using Active Directory

An Active Directory installation may support multiple domains at the same time. To distinguish users between domains, an identifier called a User Principle Name (UPN) can be added to a user's entry in the directory. This UPN usually takes the form of the user's account name, followed by the domain components of the particular domain, for example *somebody@nz.example.com*.

You may wish to configure the MOD_AUTHNZ_LDAP module to authenticate users present in any of the domains making up the Active Directory forest. In this way both *somebody@nz.example.com* and *someone@au.example.com* can be authenticated using the same query at the same time.

To make this practical, Active Directory supports the concept of a Global Catalog. This Global Catalog is a read only copy of selected attributes of all the Active Directory servers within the Active Directory forest. Querying the Global Catalog allows all the domains to be queried in a single query, without the query spanning servers over potentially slow links.

If enabled, the Global Catalog is an independent directory server that runs on port 3268 (3269 for SSL). To search for a user, do a subtree search for the attribute *userPrincipalName*, with an empty search root, like so:

```
AuthLDAPBindDN apache@example.com
AuthLDAPBindPassword password
AuthLDAPURL ldap://10.0.0.1:3268/?userPrincipalName?sub
```

Users will need to enter their User Principal Name as a login, in the form *somebody@nz.example.com*.

## Using Microsoft FrontPage with mod_authnz_ldap

Normally, FrontPage uses FrontPage-web-specific user/group files (i.e., the MOD_AUTHN_FILE and MOD_AUTHZ_GROUPFILE modules) to handle all authentication. Unfortunately, it is not possible to just change to LDAP authentication by adding the proper directives, because it will break the *Permissions* forms in the FrontPage client, which attempt to modify the standard text-based authorization files.

Once a FrontPage web has been created, adding LDAP authentication to it is a matter of adding the following directives to *every* .htaccess file that gets created in the web

```
AuthLDAPURL      "the url"
AuthGroupFile    "mygroupfile"
Require group    "mygroupfile"
```

**How It Works**

FrontPage restricts access to a web by adding the `Require valid-user` directive to the `.htaccess` files. The `Require valid-user` directive will succeed for any user who is valid *as far as LDAP is concerned*. This means that anybody who has an entry in the LDAP directory is considered a valid user, whereas FrontPage considers only those people in the local user file to be valid. By substituting the ldap-group with group file authorization, Apache is allowed to consult the local user file (which is managed by FrontPage) - instead of LDAP - when handling authorizing the user.

Once directives have been added as specified above, FrontPage users will be able to perform all management operations from the FrontPage client.

**Caveats**

- When choosing the LDAP URL, the attribute to use for authentication should be something that will also be valid for putting into a MOD_AUTHN_FILE user file. The user ID is ideal for this.

- When adding users via FrontPage, FrontPage administrators should choose usernames that already exist in the LDAP directory (for obvious reasons). Also, the password that the administrator enters into the form is ignored, since Apache will actually be authenticating against the password in the LDAP database, and not against the password in the local user file. This could cause confusion for web administrators.

- Apache must be compiled with MOD_AUTH_BASIC, MOD_AUTHN_FILE and MOD_AUTHZ_GROUPFILE in order to use FrontPage support. This is because Apache will still use the MOD_AUTHZ_GROUPFILE group file for determine the extent of a user's access to the FrontPage web.

- The directives must be put in the `.htaccess` files. Attempting to put them inside <LOCATION> or <DIRECTORY> directives won't work. This is because MOD_AUTHNZ_LDAP has to be able to grab the AUTHGROUP-FILE directive that is found in FrontPage `.htaccess` files so that it knows where to look for the valid user list. If the MOD_AUTHNZ_LDAP directives aren't in the same `.htaccess` file as the FrontPage directives, then the hack won't work, because MOD_AUTHNZ_LDAP will never get a chance to process the `.htaccess` file, and won't be able to find the FrontPage-managed user file.

## AuthLDAPAuthorizePrefix Directive

| | |
|---|---|
| Description: | Specifies the prefix for environment variables set during authorization |
| Syntax: | `AuthLDAPAuthorizePrefix prefix` |
| Default: | `AuthLDAPAuthorizePrefix AUTHORIZE_` |
| Context: | directory, .htaccess |
| Override: | AuthConfig |
| Status: | Extension |
| Module: | mod_authz_ldap |
| Compatibility: | Available in version 2.3.6 and later |

This directive allows you to override the prefix used for environment variables set during LDAP authorization. If *AUTHENTICATE_* is specified, consumers of these environment variables see the same information whether LDAP has performed authentication, authorization, or both.

**Note**

> No authorization variables are set when a user is authorized on the basis of `Require valid-user`.

## AuthLDAPBindAuthoritative Directive

| | |
|---|---|
| Description: | Determines if other authentication providers are used when a user can be mapped to a DN but the server cannot successfully bind with the user's credentials. |
| Syntax: | `AuthLDAPBindAuthoritative off|on` |
| Default: | `AuthLDAPBindAuthoritative on` |
| Context: | directory, .htaccess |
| Override: | AuthConfig |
| Status: | Extension |
| Module: | mod_authnz_ldap |

By default, subsequent authentication providers are only queried if a user cannot be mapped to a DN, but not if the user can be mapped to a DN and their password cannot be verified with an LDAP bind. If AUTHLDAPBINDAU-THORITATIVE is set to *off*, other configured authentication modules will have a chance to validate the user if the LDAP bind (with the current user's credentials) fails for any reason.

This allows users present in both LDAP and AUTHUSERFILE to authenticate when the LDAP server is available but the user's account is locked or password is otherwise unusable.

**See also**

- AUTHUSERFILE
- AUTHBASICPROVIDER

## AuthLDAPBindDN Directive

| | |
|---|---|
| Description: | Optional DN to use in binding to the LDAP server |
| Syntax: | `AuthLDAPBindDN distinguished-name` |
| Context: | directory, .htaccess |
| Override: | AuthConfig |
| Status: | Extension |
| Module: | mod_authnz_ldap |

An optional DN used to bind to the server when searching for entries. If not provided, MOD_AUTHNZ_LDAP will use an anonymous bind.

## AuthLDAPBindPassword Directive

| | |
|---|---|
| Description: | Password used in conjuction with the bind DN |
| Syntax: | `AuthLDAPBindPassword password` |
| Context: | directory, .htaccess |
| Override: | AuthConfig |
| Status: | Extension |
| Module: | mod_authnz_ldap |
| Compatibility: | *exec:* was added in 2.4.5. |

A bind password to use in conjunction with the bind DN. Note that the bind password is probably sensitive data, and should be properly protected. You should only use the AUTHLDAPBINDDN and AUTHLDAPBINDPASSWORD if you absolutely need them to search the directory.

If the value begins with exec: the resulting command will be executed and the first line returned to standard output by the program will be used as the password.

```
#Password used as-is
AuthLDAPBindPassword secret
```

```
#Run /path/to/program to get my password
AuthLDAPBindPassword exec:/path/to/program

#Run /path/to/otherProgram and provide arguments
AuthLDAPBindPassword "exec:/path/to/otherProgram argument1"
```

## AuthLDAPCharsetConfig Directive

| | |
|---|---|
| Description: | Language to charset conversion configuration file |
| Syntax: | `AuthLDAPCharsetConfig file-path` |
| Context: | server config |
| Status: | Extension |
| Module: | mod_authnz_ldap |

The AUTHLDAPCHARSETCONFIG directive sets the location of the language to charset conversion configuration file. *File-path* is relative to the SERVERROOT. This file specifies the list of language extensions to character sets. Most administrators use the provided `charset.conv` file, which associates common language extensions to character sets.

The file contains lines in the following format:

```
Language-Extension charset [Language-String] ...
```

The case of the extension does not matter. Blank lines, and lines beginning with a hash character (#) are ignored.

## AuthLDAPCompareAsUser Directive

| | |
|---|---|
| Description: | Use the authenticated user's credentials to perform authorization comparisons |
| Syntax: | `AuthLDAPCompareAsUser on\|off` |
| Default: | `AuthLDAPCompareAsUser off` |
| Context: | directory, .htaccess |
| Override: | AuthConfig |
| Status: | Extension |
| Module: | mod_authnz_ldap |
| Compatibility: | Available in version 2.3.6 and later |

When set, and MOD_AUTHNZ_LDAP has authenticated the user, LDAP comparisons for authorization use the queried distinguished name (DN) and HTTP basic authentication password of the authenticated user instead of the servers configured credentials.

The *ldap-attribute*, *ldap-user*, and *ldap-group* (single-level only) authorization checks use comparisons.

This directive only has effect on the comparisons performed during nested group processing when AUTHLDAPSEARCHASUSER is also enabled.

This directive should only be used when your LDAP server doesn't accept anonymous comparisons and you cannot use a dedicated AUTHLDAPBINDDN.

**See also**

- AUTHLDAPINITIALBINDASUSER
- AUTHLDAPSEARCHASUSER

## AuthLDAPCompareDNOnServer Directive

| | |
|---|---|
| Description: | Use the LDAP server to compare the DNs |
| Syntax: | `AuthLDAPCompareDNOnServer on\|off` |
| Default: | `AuthLDAPCompareDNOnServer on` |
| Context: | directory, .htaccess |
| Override: | AuthConfig |
| Status: | Extension |
| Module: | mod_authnz_ldap |

When set, MOD_AUTHNZ_LDAP will use the LDAP server to compare the DNs. This is the only foolproof way to compare DNs. MOD_AUTHNZ_LDAP will search the directory for the DN specified with the `Require dn` directive, then, retrieve the DN and compare it with the DN retrieved from the user entry. If this directive is not set, MOD_AUTHNZ_LDAP simply does a string comparison. It is possible to get false negatives with this approach, but it is much faster. Note the MOD_LDAP cache can speed up DN comparison in most situations.

## AuthLDAPDereferenceAliases Directive

| | |
|---|---|
| Description: | When will the module de-reference aliases |
| Syntax: | `AuthLDAPDereferenceAliases never\|searching\|finding\|always` |
| Default: | `AuthLDAPDereferenceAliases always` |
| Context: | directory, .htaccess |
| Override: | AuthConfig |
| Status: | Extension |
| Module: | mod_authnz_ldap |

This directive specifies when MOD_AUTHNZ_LDAP will de-reference aliases during LDAP operations. The default is `always`.

## AuthLDAPGroupAttribute Directive

| | |
|---|---|
| Description: | LDAP attributes used to identify the user members of groups. |
| Syntax: | `AuthLDAPGroupAttribute attribute` |
| Default: | `AuthLDAPGroupAttribute member uniquemember` |
| Context: | directory, .htaccess |
| Override: | AuthConfig |
| Status: | Extension |
| Module: | mod_authnz_ldap |

This directive specifies which LDAP attributes are used to check for user members within groups. Multiple attributes can be used by specifying this directive multiple times. If not specified, then MOD_AUTHNZ_LDAP uses the `member` and `uniquemember` attributes.

## AuthLDAPGroupAttributeIsDN Directive

| | |
|---|---|
| Description: | Use the DN of the client username when checking for group membership |
| Syntax: | `AuthLDAPGroupAttributeIsDN on\|off` |
| Default: | `AuthLDAPGroupAttributeIsDN on` |
| Context: | directory, .htaccess |
| Override: | AuthConfig |
| Status: | Extension |
| Module: | mod_authnz_ldap |

When set on, this directive says to use the distinguished name of the client username when checking for group membership.  Otherwise, the username will be used.  For example, assume that the client sent the username bjenson, which corresponds to the LDAP DN cn=Babs Jenson, o=Example.  If this directive is set, MOD_AUTHNZ_LDAP will check if the group has cn=Babs Jenson, o=Example as a member.  If this directive is not set, then MOD_AUTHNZ_LDAP will check if the group has bjenson as a member.

## AuthLDAPInitialBindAsUser Directive

| | |
|---|---|
| Description: | Determines if the server does the initial DN lookup using the basic authentication users' own username, instead of anonymously or with hard-coded credentials for the server |
| Syntax: | AuthLDAPInitialBindAsUser off\|on |
| Default: | AuthLDAPInitialBindAsUser off |
| Context: | directory, .htaccess |
| Override: | AuthConfig |
| Status: | Extension |
| Module: | mod_authnz_ldap |
| Compatibility: | Available in version 2.3.6 and later |

By default, the server either anonymously, or with a dedicated user and password, converts the basic authentication username into an LDAP distinguished name (DN). This directive forces the server to use the verbatim username and password provided by the incoming user to perform the initial DN search.

If the verbatim username can't directly bind, but needs some cosmetic transformation, see AUTHLDAPINITIALBIND-PATTERN.

This directive should only be used when your LDAP server doesn't accept anonymous searches and you cannot use a dedicated AUTHLDAPBINDDN.

 **Not available with authorization-only**
This directive can only be used if this module authenticates the user, and has no effect when this module is used exclusively for authorization.

**See also**

- AUTHLDAPINITIALBINDPATTERN
- AUTHLDAPBINDDN
- AUTHLDAPCOMPAREASUSER
- AUTHLDAPSEARCHASUSER

## AuthLDAPInitialBindPattern Directive

| | |
|---|---|
| Description: | Specifies the transformation of the basic authentication username to be used when binding to the LDAP server to perform a DN lookup |
| Syntax: | AuthLDAPInitialBindPattern regex substitution |
| Default: | AuthLDAPInitialBindPattern (.*) $1 (remote username used verbatim) |
| Context: | directory, .htaccess |
| Override: | AuthConfig |
| Status: | Extension |
| Module: | mod_authnz_ldap |
| Compatibility: | Available in version 2.3.6 and later |

If AUTHLDAPINITIALBINDASUSER is set to *ON*, the basic authentication username will be transformed according to the regular expression and substitution arguments.

The regular expression argument is compared against the current basic authentication username. The substitution argument may contain backreferences, but has no other variable interpolation.

This directive should only be used when your LDAP server doesn't accept anonymous searches and you cannot use a dedicated AUTHLDAPBINDDN.

```
AuthLDAPInitialBindPattern (.+) $1@example.com
```

```
AuthLDAPInitialBindPattern (.+) cn=$1,dc=example,dc=com
```

 **Not available with authorization-only**
This directive can only be used if this module authenticates the user, and has no effect when this module is used exclusively for authorization.

**debugging**
The substituted DN is recorded in the environment variable *LDAP_BINDASUSER*. If the regular expression does not match the input, the verbatim username is used.

**See also**

- AUTHLDAPINITIALBINDASUSER

- AUTHLDAPBINDDN

## AuthLDAPMaxSubGroupDepth Directive

| | |
|---|---|
| Description: | Specifies the maximum sub-group nesting depth that will be evaluated before the user search is discontinued. |
| Syntax: | AuthLDAPMaxSubGroupDepth Number |
| Default: | AuthLDAPMaxSubGroupDepth 0 |
| Context: | directory, .htaccess |
| Override: | AuthConfig |
| Status: | Extension |
| Module: | mod_authnz_ldap |
| Compatibility: | Available in version 2.3.0 and later, defaulted to 10 in 2.4.x and early 2.5 |

When this directive is set to a non-zero value X combined with use of the `Require ldap-group someGroupDN` directive, the provided user credentials will be searched for as a member of the `someGroupDN` directory object or of any group member of the current group up to the maximum nesting level X specified by this directive.

See the `Require ldap-group` section for a more detailed example.

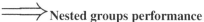 **Nested groups performance**
When AUTHLDAPSUBGROUPATTRIBUTE overlaps with AUTHLDAPGROUPATTRIBUTE (as it does by default and as required by common LDAP schemas), uncached searching for subgroups in large groups can be very slow. If you use large, non-nested groups, keep AUTHLDAPMAXSUBGROUPDEPTH set to zero.

## AuthLDAPRemoteUserAttribute Directive

| | |
|---|---|
| Description: | Use the value of the attribute returned during the user query to set the REMOTE_USER environment variable |
| Syntax: | `AuthLDAPRemoteUserAttribute uid` |
| Default: | `none` |
| Context: | directory, .htaccess |
| Override: | AuthConfig |
| Status: | Extension |
| Module: | mod_authnz_ldap |

If this directive is set, the value of the REMOTE_USER environment variable will be set to the value of the attribute specified. Make sure that this attribute is included in the list of attributes in the AuthLDAPUrl definition, otherwise this directive will have no effect. This directive, if present, takes precedence over AuthLDAPRemoteUserIsDN. This directive is useful should you want people to log into a website using an email address, but a backend application expects the username as a userid.

This directive only has effect when this module is used for authentication.

## AuthLDAPRemoteUserIsDN Directive

| | |
|---|---|
| Description: | Use the DN of the client username to set the REMOTE_USER environment variable |
| Syntax: | `AuthLDAPRemoteUserIsDN on\|off` |
| Default: | `AuthLDAPRemoteUserIsDN off` |
| Context: | directory, .htaccess |
| Override: | AuthConfig |
| Status: | Extension |
| Module: | mod_authnz_ldap |

If this directive is set to on, the value of the REMOTE_USER environment variable will be set to the full distinguished name of the authenticated user, rather than just the username that was passed by the client. It is turned off by default.

This directive only has effect when this module is used for authentication.

## AuthLDAPSearchAsUser Directive

| | |
|---|---|
| Description: | Use the authenticated user's credentials to perform authorization searches |
| Syntax: | `AuthLDAPSearchAsUser on\|off` |
| Default: | `AuthLDAPSearchAsUser off` |
| Context: | directory, .htaccess |
| Override: | AuthConfig |
| Status: | Extension |
| Module: | mod_authnz_ldap |
| Compatibility: | Available in version 2.3.6 and later |

When set, and MOD_AUTHNZ_LDAP has authenticated the user, LDAP searches for authorization use the queried distinguished name (DN) and HTTP basic authentication password of the authenticated user instead of the servers configured credentials.

The *ldap-filter* and *ldap-dn* authorization checks use searches.

This directive only has effect on the comparisons performed during nested group processing when AuthLDAPCompareAsUser is also enabled.

This directive should only be used when your LDAP server doesn't accept anonymous searches and you cannot use a dedicated AuthLDAPBindDN.

**See also**

- AUTHLDAPINITIALBINDASUSER
- AUTHLDAPCOMPAREASUSER

## AuthLDAPSubGroupAttribute Directive

| | |
|---|---|
| Description: | Specifies the attribute labels, one value per directive line, used to distinguish the members of the current group that are groups. |
| Syntax: | `AuthLDAPSubGroupAttribute attribute` |
| Default: | `AuthLDAPSubgroupAttribute member uniquemember` |
| Context: | directory, .htaccess |
| Override: | AuthConfig |
| Status: | Extension |
| Module: | mod_authnz_ldap |
| Compatibility: | Available in version 2.3.0 and later |

An LDAP group object may contain members that are users and members that are groups (called nested or sub groups). The AUTHLDAPSUBGROUPATTRIBUTE directive identifies the labels of group members and the AUTHLDAP-GROUPATTRIBUTE directive identifies the labels of the user members. Multiple attributes can be used by specifying this directive multiple times. If not specified, then MOD_AUTHNZ_LDAP uses the `member` and `uniqueMember` attributes.

## AuthLDAPSubGroupClass Directive

| | |
|---|---|
| Description: | Specifies which LDAP objectClass values identify directory objects that are groups during sub-group processing. |
| Syntax: | `AuthLDAPSubGroupClass LdapObjectClass` |
| Default: | `AuthLDAPSubGroupClass groupOfNames groupOfUniqueNames` |
| Context: | directory, .htaccess |
| Override: | AuthConfig |
| Status: | Extension |
| Module: | mod_authnz_ldap |
| Compatibility: | Available in version 2.3.0 and later |

An LDAP group object may contain members that are users and members that are groups (called nested or sub groups). The AUTHLDAPSUBGROUPATTRIBUTE directive identifies the labels of members that may be sub-groups of the current group (as opposed to user members). The AUTHLDAPSUBGROUPCLASS directive specifies the LDAP objectClass values used in verifying that these potential sub-groups are in fact group objects. Verified sub-groups can then be searched for more user or sub-group members. Multiple attributes can be used by specifying this directive multiple times. If not specified, then MOD_AUTHNZ_LDAP uses the `groupOfNames` and `groupOfUniqueNames` values.

## AuthLDAPUrl Directive

| | |
|---|---|
| Description: | URL specifying the LDAP search parameters |
| Syntax: | `AuthLDAPUrl url [NONE\|SSL\|TLS\|STARTTLS]` |
| Context: | directory, .htaccess |
| Override: | AuthConfig |
| Status: | Extension |
| Module: | mod_authnz_ldap |

An RFC 2255 URL which specifies the LDAP search parameters to use. The syntax of the URL is

```
ldap://host:port/basedn?attribute?scope?filter
```

If you want to specify more than one LDAP URL that Apache should try in turn, the syntax is:

```
AuthLDAPUrl "ldap://ldap1.example.com ldap2.example.com/dc=..."
```

***Caveat:** If you specify multiple servers, you need to enclose the entire URL string in quotes; otherwise you will get an error: "AuthLDAPURL takes one argument, URL to define LDAP connection.."* You can of course use search parameters on each of these.

**ldap** For regular ldap, use the string `ldap`. For secure LDAP, use `ldaps` instead. Secure LDAP is only available if Apache was linked to an LDAP library with SSL support.

**host:port** The name/port of the ldap server (defaults to `localhost:389` for `ldap`, and `localhost:636` for `ldaps`). To specify multiple, redundant LDAP servers, just list all servers, separated by spaces. MOD_AUTHNZ_LDAP will try connecting to each server in turn, until it makes a successful connection. If multiple ldap servers are specified, then entire LDAP URL must be encapsulated in double quotes.

Once a connection has been made to a server, that connection remains active for the life of the `httpd` process, or until the LDAP server goes down.

If the LDAP server goes down and breaks an existing connection, MOD_AUTHNZ_LDAP will attempt to reconnect, starting with the primary server, and trying each redundant server in turn. Note that this is different than a true round-robin search.

**basedn** The DN of the branch of the directory where all searches should start from. At the very least, this must be the top of your directory tree, but could also specify a subtree in the directory.

**attribute** The attribute to search for. Although RFC 2255 allows a comma-separated list of attributes, only the first attribute will be used, no matter how many are provided. If no attributes are provided, the default is to use `uid`. It's a good idea to choose an attribute that will be unique across all entries in the subtree you will be using. All attributes listed will be put into the environment with an AUTHENTICATE_ prefix for use by other modules.

**scope** The scope of the search. Can be either `one` or `sub`. Note that a scope of `base` is also supported by RFC 2255, but is not supported by this module. If the scope is not provided, or if `base` scope is specified, the default is to use a scope of `sub`.

**filter** A valid LDAP search filter. If not provided, defaults to `(objectClass=*)`, which will search for all objects in the tree. Filters are limited to approximately 8000 characters (the definition of MAX_STRING_LEN in the Apache source code). This should be more than sufficient for any application. In 2.4.10 and later, the keyword `none` disables the use of a filter; this is required by some primitive LDAP servers.

When doing searches, the attribute, filter and username passed by the HTTP client are combined to create a search filter that looks like `(&(filter)(attribute=username))`.

For example, consider an URL of `ldap://ldap.example.com/o=Example?cn?sub?(posixid=*)`. When a client attempts to connect using a username of `Babs Jenson`, the resulting search filter will be `(&(posixid=*)(cn=Babs Jenson))`.

An optional parameter can be added to allow the LDAP Url to override the connection type. This parameter can be one of the following:

**NONE** Establish an unsecure connection on the default LDAP port. This is the same as `ldap://` on port 389.

**SSL** Establish a secure connection on the default secure LDAP port. This is the same as `ldaps://`

**TLS — STARTTLS** Establish an upgraded secure connection on the default LDAP port. This connection will be initiated on port 389 by default and then upgraded to a secure connection on the same port.

See above for examples of AUTHLDAPURL URLs.

# 10.21 Apache Module mod_authz_core

| | |
|---|---|
| Description: | Core Authorization |
| Status: | Base |
| ModuleIdentifier: | authz_core_module |
| SourceFile: | mod_authz_core.c |
| Compatibility: | Available in Apache HTTPD 2.3 and later |

## Summary

This module provides core authorization capabilities so that authenticated users can be allowed or denied access to portions of the web site. MOD_AUTHZ_CORE provides the functionality to register various authorization providers. It is usually used in conjunction with an authentication provider module such as MOD_AUTHN_FILE and an authorization module such as MOD_AUTHZ_USER. It also allows for advanced logic to be applied to the authorization processing.

### Directives

- AuthMerging
- <AuthzProviderAlias>
- AuthzSendForbiddenOnFailure
- Require
- <RequireAll>
- <RequireAny>
- <RequireNone>

## Authorization Containers

The authorization container directives <REQUIREALL>, <REQUIREANY> and <REQUIRENONE> may be combined with each other and with the REQUIRE directive to express complex authorization logic.

The example below expresses the following authorization logic. In order to access the resource, the user must either be the superadmin user, or belong to both the admins group and the Administrators LDAP group and either belong to the sales group or have the LDAP dept attribute sales. Furthermore, in order to access the resource, the user must not belong to either the temps group or the LDAP group Temporary Employees.

```
<Directory "/www/mydocs">
    <RequireAll>
        <RequireAny>
            Require user superadmin
            <RequireAll>
                Require group admins
                Require ldap-group "cn=Administrators,o=Airius"
                <RequireAny>
                    Require group sales
                    Require ldap-attribute dept="sales"
                </RequireAny>
            </RequireAll>
        </RequireAny>
        <RequireNone>
            Require group temps
```

```
        Require ldap-group "cn=Temporary Employees,o=Airius"
      </RequireNone>
    </RequireAll>
</Directory>
```

## The Require Directives

MOD_AUTHZ_CORE provides some generic authorization providers which can be used with the REQUIRE directive.

### Require env

The env provider allows access to the server to be controlled based on the existence of an environment variable (p. 92) . When Require env *env-variable* is specified, then the request is allowed access if the environment variable *env-variable* exists. The server provides the ability to set environment variables in a flexible way based on characteristics of the client request using the directives provided by MOD_SETENVIF. Therefore, this directive can be used to allow access based on such factors as the clients User-Agent (browser type), Referer, or other HTTP request header fields.

```
SetEnvIf User-Agent "^KnockKnock/2\.0" let_me_in
<Directory "/docroot">
    Require env let_me_in
</Directory>
```

In this case, browsers with a user-agent string beginning with KnockKnock/2.0 will be allowed access, and all others will be denied.

When the server looks up a path via an internal subrequest such as looking for a DIRECTORYINDEX or generating a directory listing with MOD_AUTOINDEX, per-request environment variables are *not* inherited in the subrequest. Additionally, SETENVIF directives are not separately evaluated in the subrequest due to the API phases MOD_SETENVIF takes action in.

### Require all

The all provider mimics the functionality that was previously provided by the 'Allow from all' and 'Deny from all' directives. This provider can take one of two arguments which are 'granted' or 'denied'. The following examples will grant or deny access to all requests.

```
Require all granted
```

```
Require all denied
```

### Require method

The method provider allows using the HTTP method in authorization decisions. The GET and HEAD methods are treated as equivalent. The TRACE method is not available to this provider, use TRACEENABLE instead.

The following example will only allow GET, HEAD, POST, and OPTIONS requests:

```
Require method GET POST OPTIONS
```

The following example will allow GET, HEAD, POST, and OPTIONS requests without authentication, and require a valid user for all other methods:

```
<RequireAny>
    Require method GET POST OPTIONS
    Require valid-user
</RequireAny>
```

**Require expr**

The `expr` provider allows basing authorization decisions on arbitrary expressions.

```
Require expr %{TIME_HOUR} -ge 9 && %{TIME_HOUR} -le 17

<RequireAll>
    Require expr "!(%{QUERY_STRING} =~ /secret/)"
    Require expr "%{REQUEST_URI} in { '/example.cgi', '/other.cgi' }"
</RequireAll>

Require expr "!(%{QUERY_STRING} =~ /secret/) && %{REQUEST_URI} in { '/example.cgi',  '
```

The syntax is described in the ap_expr (p. 99) documentation.

Normally, the expression is evaluated before authentication. However, if the expression returns false and references the variable `%{REMOTE_USER}`, authentication will be performed and the expression will be re-evaluated.

## Creating Authorization Provider Aliases

Extended authorization providers can be created within the configuration file and assigned an alias name. The alias providers can then be referenced through the REQUIRE directive in the same way as a base authorization provider. Besides the ability to create and alias an extended provider, it also allows the same extended authorization provider to be referenced by multiple locations.

**Example**

The example below creates two different ldap authorization provider aliases based on the ldap-group authorization provider. This example allows a single authorization location to check group membership within multiple ldap hosts:

```
<AuthzProviderAlias ldap-group ldap-group-alias1 "cn=my-group,o=ctx">
    AuthLDAPBindDN "cn=youruser,o=ctx"
    AuthLDAPBindPassword yourpassword
    AuthLDAPURL "ldap://ldap.host/o=ctx"
</AuthzProviderAlias>

<AuthzProviderAlias ldap-group ldap-group-alias2 "cn=my-other-group,o=dev">
    AuthLDAPBindDN "cn=yourotheruser,o=dev"
    AuthLDAPBindPassword yourotherpassword
    AuthLDAPURL "ldap://other.ldap.host/o=dev?cn"
</AuthzProviderAlias>

Alias "/secure" "/webpages/secure"
```

```
<Directory "/webpages/secure">
    Require all granted

    AuthBasicProvider file

    AuthType Basic
    AuthName LDAP_Protected_Place

    #implied OR operation
    Require ldap-group-alias1
    Require ldap-group-alias2
</Directory>
```

## AuthMerging Directive

| | |
|---|---|
| Description: | Controls the manner in which each configuration section's authorization logic is combined with that of preceding configuration sections. |
| Syntax: | `AuthMerging Off \| And \| Or` |
| Default: | `AuthMerging Off` |
| Context: | directory, .htaccess |
| Override: | AuthConfig |
| Status: | Base |
| Module: | mod_authz_core |

When authorization is enabled, it is normally inherited by each subsequent configuration section (p. 35) , unless a different set of authorization directives is specified. This is the default action, which corresponds to an explicit setting of `AuthMerging Off`.

However, there may be circumstances in which it is desirable for a configuration section's authorization to be combined with that of its predecessor while configuration sections are being merged. Two options are available for this case, `And` and `Or`.

When a configuration section contains `AuthMerging And` or `AuthMerging Or`, its authorization logic is combined with that of the nearest predecessor (according to the overall order of configuration sections) which also contains authorization logic as if the two sections were jointly contained within a <REQUIREALL> or <REQUIREANY> directive, respectively.

⟹ The setting of AUTHMERGING is not inherited outside of the configuration section in which it appears.  In the following example, only users belonging to group `alpha` may access /www/docs.  Users belonging to either groups `alpha` or `beta` may access /www/docs/ab. However, the default `Off` setting of AUTHMERGING applies to the <DIRECTORY> configuration section for /www/docs/ab/gamma, so that section's authorization directives override those of the preceding sections.  Thus only users belong to the group `gamma` may access /www/docs/ab/gamma.

```
<Directory "/www/docs">
    AuthType Basic
    AuthName Documents
    AuthBasicProvider file
    AuthUserFile "/usr/local/apache/passwd/passwords"
    Require group alpha
</Directory>

<Directory "/www/docs/ab">
```

```
    AuthMerging Or
    Require group beta
</Directory>

<Directory "/www/docs/ab/gamma">
    Require group gamma
</Directory>
```

## AuthzProviderAlias Directive

| | |
|---|---|
| Description: | Enclose a group of directives that represent an extension of a base authorization provider and referenced by the specified alias |
| Syntax: | `<AuthzProviderAlias baseProvider Alias Require-Parameters> ... </AuthzProviderAlias>` |
| Context: | server config |
| Status: | Base |
| Module: | mod_authz_core |

<AUTHZPROVIDERALIAS> and </AuthzProviderAlias> are used to enclose a group of authorization directives that can be referenced by the alias name using the directive REQUIRE.

## AuthzSendForbiddenOnFailure Directive

| | |
|---|---|
| Description: | Send '403 FORBIDDEN' instead of '401 UNAUTHORIZED' if authentication succeeds but authorization fails |
| Syntax: | `AuthzSendForbiddenOnFailure On\|Off` |
| Default: | `AuthzSendForbiddenOnFailure Off` |
| Context: | directory, .htaccess |
| Status: | Base |
| Module: | mod_authz_core |
| Compatibility: | Available in Apache HTTPD 2.3.11 and later |

If authentication succeeds but authorization fails, Apache HTTPD will respond with an HTTP response code of '401 UNAUTHORIZED' by default. This usually causes browsers to display the password dialogue to the user again, which is not wanted in all situations. AUTHZSENDFORBIDDENONFAILURE allows to change the response code to '403 FORBIDDEN'.

 **Security Warning**

Modifying the response in case of missing authorization weakens the security of the password, because it reveals to a possible attacker, that his guessed password was right.

## Require Directive

| | |
|---|---|
| Description: | Tests whether an authenticated user is authorized by an authorization provider. |
| Syntax: | `Require [not] entity-name [entity-name] ...` |
| Context: | directory, .htaccess |
| Override: | AuthConfig |
| Status: | Base |
| Module: | mod_authz_core |

This directive tests whether an authenticated user is authorized according to a particular authorization provider and the specified restrictions. MOD_AUTHZ_CORE provides the following generic authorization providers:

**Require all granted** Access is allowed unconditionally.

**Require all denied** Access is denied unconditionally.

**Require env *env-var* [*env-var*]** ... Access is allowed only if one of the given environment variables is set.

**Require method *http-method* [*http-method*]** ... Access is allowed only for the given HTTP methods.

**Require expr *expression*** Access is allowed if *expression* evaluates to true.

Some of the allowed syntaxes provided by MOD_AUTHZ_USER, MOD_AUTHZ_HOST, and MOD_AUTHZ_GROUPFILE are:

**Require user *userid* [*userid*]** ... Only the named users can access the resource.

**Require group *group-name* [*group-name*]** ... Only users in the named groups can access the resource.

**Require valid-user** All valid users can access the resource.

**Require ip 10 172.20 192.168.2** Clients in the specified IP address ranges can access the resource.

Other authorization modules that implement require options include MOD_AUTHNZ_LDAP, MOD_AUTHZ_DBM, MOD_AUTHZ_DBD, MOD_AUTHZ_OWNER and MOD_SSL.

In most cases, for a complete authentication and authorization configuration, REQUIRE must be accompanied by AUTHNAME, AUTHTYPE and AUTHBASICPROVIDER or AUTHDIGESTPROVIDER directives, and directives such as AUTHUSERFILE and AUTHGROUPFILE (to define users and groups) in order to work correctly. Example:

```
AuthType Basic
AuthName "Restricted Resource"
AuthBasicProvider file
AuthUserFile "/web/users"
AuthGroupFile "/web/groups"
Require group admin
```

Access controls which are applied in this way are effective for **all** methods. **This is what is normally desired.** If you wish to apply access controls only to specific methods, while leaving other methods unprotected, then place the REQUIRE statement into a <LIMIT> section.

The result of the REQUIRE directive may be negated through the use of the `not` option. As with the other negated authorization directive <REQUIRENONE>, when the REQUIRE directive is negated it can only fail or return a neutral result, and therefore may never independently authorize a request.

In the following example, all users in the `alpha` and `beta` groups are authorized, except for those who are also in the `reject` group.

```
<Directory "/www/docs">
    <RequireAll>
        Require group alpha beta
        Require not group reject
    </RequireAll>
</Directory>
```

When multiple REQUIRE directives are used in a single configuration section (p. 35) and are not contained in another authorization directive like <REQUIREALL>, they are implicitly contained within a <REQUIREANY> directive. Thus the first one to authorize a user authorizes the entire request, and subsequent REQUIRE directives are ignored.

 **Security Warning**
Exercise caution when setting authorization directives in LOCATION sections that overlap with content served out of the filesystem. By default, these configuration sections (p. 35) overwrite authorization configuration in DIRECTORY, and FILES sections.
The AUTHMERGING directive can be used to control how authorization configuration sections are merged.

**See also**

- Access Control howto (p. 234)
- Authorization Containers
- MOD_AUTHN_CORE
- MOD_AUTHZ_HOST

## RequireAll Directive

| | |
|---|---|
| Description: | Enclose a group of authorization directives of which none must fail and at least one must succeed for the enclosing directive to succeed. |
| Syntax: | `<RequireAll> ... </RequireAll>` |
| Context: | directory, .htaccess |
| Override: | AuthConfig |
| Status: | Base |
| Module: | mod_authz_core |

<REQUIREALL> and </RequireAll> are used to enclose a group of authorization directives of which none must fail and at least one must succeed in order for the <REQUIREALL> directive to succeed.

If none of the directives contained within the <REQUIREALL> directive fails, and at least one succeeds, then the <REQUIREALL> directive succeeds. If none succeed and none fail, then it returns a neutral result. In all other cases, it fails.

**See also**

- Authorization Containers
- Authentication, Authorization, and Access Control (p. 227)

## RequireAny Directive

| | |
|---|---|
| Description: | Enclose a group of authorization directives of which one must succeed for the enclosing directive to succeed. |
| Syntax: | `<RequireAny> ... </RequireAny>` |
| Context: | directory, .htaccess |
| Override: | AuthConfig |
| Status: | Base |
| Module: | mod_authz_core |

<REQUIREANY> and </RequireAny> are used to enclose a group of authorization directives of which one must succeed in order for the <REQUIREANY> directive to succeed.

If one or more of the directives contained within the <REQUIREANY> directive succeed, then the <REQUIREANY> directive succeeds. If none succeed and none fail, then it returns a neutral result. In all other cases, it fails.

 Because negated authorization directives are unable to return a successful result, they can not significantly influence the result of a <REQUIREANY> directive. (At most they could cause the directive to fail in the case where they failed and all other directives returned a neutral value.) Therefore negated authorization directives are not permitted within a <REQUIRE-ANY> directive.

**See also**

- Authorization Containers
- Authentication, Authorization, and Access Control (p. 227)

## RequireNone Directive

| | |
|---|---|
| Description: | Enclose a group of authorization directives of which none must succeed for the enclosing directive to not fail. |
| Syntax: | `<RequireNone> ... </RequireNone>` |
| Context: | directory, .htaccess |
| Override: | AuthConfig |
| Status: | Base |
| Module: | mod_authz_core |

<REQUIRENONE> and </RequireNone> are used to enclose a group of authorization directives of which none must succeed in order for the <REQUIRENONE> directive to not fail.

If one or more of the directives contained within the <REQUIRENONE> directive succeed, then the <RE-QUIRENONE> directive fails. In all other cases, it returns a neutral result. Thus as with the other negated authorization directive `Require not`, it can never independently authorize a request because it can never return a successful result. It can be used, however, to restrict the set of users who are authorized to access a resource.

 Because negated authorization directives are unable to return a successful result, they can not significantly influence the result of a <REQUIRENONE> directive. Therefore negated authorization directives are not permitted within a <REQUIRENONE> directive.

**See also**

- Authorization Containers
- Authentication, Authorization, and Access Control (p. 227)

# 10.22 Apache Module mod_authz_dbd

| | |
|---|---|
| Description: | Group Authorization and Login using SQL |
| Status: | Extension |
| ModuleIdentifier: | authz_dbd_module |
| SourceFile: | mod_authz_dbd.c |
| Compatibility: | Available in Apache 2.4 and later |

## Summary

This module provides authorization capabilities so that authenticated users can be allowed or denied access to portions of the web site by group membership. Similar functionality is provided by MOD_AUTHZ_GROUPFILE and MOD_AUTHZ_DBM, with the exception that this module queries a SQL database to determine whether a user is a member of a group.

This module can also provide database-backed user login/logout capabilities. These are likely to be of most value when used in conjunction with MOD_AUTHN_DBD.

This module relies on MOD_DBD to specify the backend database driver and connection parameters, and manage the database connections.

### Directives

- AuthzDBDLoginToReferer
- AuthzDBDQuery
- AuthzDBDRedirectQuery

### See also

- REQUIRE
- AUTHDBDUSERPWQUERY
- DBDRIVER
- DBDPARAMS

## The Require Directives

Apache's REQUIRE directives are used during the authorization phase to ensure that a user is allowed to access a resource. mod_authz_dbd extends the authorization types with dbd-group, dbd-login and dbd-logout.

Since v2.4.8, expressions (p. 99) are supported within the DBD require directives.

### Require dbd-group

This directive specifies group membership that is required for the user to gain access.

```
Require dbd-group team
AuthzDBDQuery "SELECT group FROM authz WHERE user = %s"
```

**Require dbd-login**

This directive specifies a query to be run indicating the user has logged in.

```
Require dbd-login
AuthzDBDQuery "UPDATE authn SET login = 'true' WHERE user = %s"
```

**Require dbd-logout**

This directive specifies a query to be run indicating the user has logged out.

```
Require dbd-logout
AuthzDBDQuery "UPDATE authn SET login = 'false' WHERE user = %s"
```

## Database Login

In addition to the standard authorization function of checking group membership, this module can also provide server-side user session management via database-backed login/logout capabilities. Specifically, it can update a user's session status in the database whenever the user visits designated URLs (subject of course to users supplying the necessary credentials).

This works by defining two special REQUIRE types: `Require dbd-login` and `Require dbd-logout`. For usage details, see the configuration example below.

## Client Login integration

Some administrators may wish to implement client-side session management that works in concert with the server-side login/logout capabilities offered by this module, for example, by setting or unsetting an HTTP cookie or other such token when a user logs in or out.

To support such integration, MOD_AUTHZ_DBD exports an optional hook that will be run whenever a user's status is updated in the database. Other session management modules can then use the hook to implement functions that start and end client-side sessions.

## Configuration example

```
# mod_dbd configuration
DBDriver pgsql
DBDParams "dbname=apacheauth user=apache pass=xxxxxx"

DBDMin  4
DBDKeep 8
DBDMax  20
DBDExptime 300

<Directory "/usr/www/my.site/team-private/">
  # mod_authn_core and mod_auth_basic configuration
  # for mod_authn_dbd
  AuthType Basic
  AuthName Team
  AuthBasicProvider dbd
```

```
# mod_authn_dbd SQL query to authenticate a logged-in user
AuthDBDUserPWQuery \
  "SELECT password FROM authn WHERE user = %s AND login = 'true'"


# mod_authz_core configuration for mod_authz_dbd
Require dbd-group team

# mod_authz_dbd configuration
AuthzDBDQuery "SELECT group FROM authz WHERE user = %s"

# when a user fails to be authenticated or authorized,
# invite them to login; this page should provide a link
# to /team-private/login.html
ErrorDocument 401 /login-info.html

<Files "login.html">
  # don't require user to already be logged in!
  AuthDBDUserPWQuery "SELECT password FROM authn WHERE user = %s"

  # dbd-login action executes a statement to log user in
  Require dbd-login
  AuthzDBDQuery "UPDATE authn SET login = 'true' WHERE user = %s"

  # return user to referring page (if any) after
  # successful login
  AuthzDBDLoginToReferer On
</Files>

<Files "logout.html">
  # dbd-logout action executes a statement to log user out
  Require dbd-logout
  AuthzDBDQuery "UPDATE authn SET login = 'false' WHERE user = %s"
</Files>
</Directory>
```

## Preventing SQL injections

Whether you need to care about SQL security depends on what DBD driver and backend you use. With most drivers you don't have to do anything : the statement is prepared by the database at startup, and user input is used only as data. But you may need to untaint your input. At the time of writing, the only driver that requires you to take care is FreeTDS.

Please read MOD_DBD documentation for more information about security on this scope.

## AuthzDBDLoginToReferer Directive

| | |
|---|---|
| Description: | Determines whether to redirect the Client to the Referring page on successful login or logout if a `Referer` request header is present |
| Syntax: | `AuthzDBDLoginToReferer On\|Off` |
| Default: | `AuthzDBDLoginToReferer Off` |
| Context: | directory |
| Status: | Extension |
| Module: | mod_authz_dbd |

In conjunction with `Require dbd-login` or `Require dbd-logout`, this provides the option to redirect the client back to the Referring page (the URL in the `Referer` HTTP request header, if present). When there is no `Referer` header, `AuthzDBDLoginToReferer On` will be ignored.

## AuthzDBDQuery Directive

| | |
|---|---|
| Description: | Specify the SQL Query for the required operation |
| Syntax: | `AuthzDBDQuery query` |
| Context: | directory |
| Status: | Extension |
| Module: | mod_authz_dbd |

The AUTHZDBDQUERY specifies an SQL query to run. The purpose of the query depends on the REQUIRE directive in effect.

- When used with a `Require dbd-group` directive, it specifies a query to look up groups for the current user. This is the standard functionality of other authorization modules such as MOD_AUTHZ_GROUPFILE and MOD_AUTHZ_DBM. The first column value of each row returned by the query statement should be a string containing a group name. Zero, one, or more rows may be returned.

  ```
  Require dbd-group
  AuthzDBDQuery "SELECT group FROM groups WHERE user = %s"
  ```

- When used with a `Require dbd-login` or `Require dbd-logout` directive, it will never deny access, but will instead execute a SQL statement designed to log the user in or out. The user must already be authenticated with MOD_AUTHN_DBD.

  ```
  Require dbd-login
  AuthzDBDQuery "UPDATE authn SET login = 'true' WHERE user = %s"
  ```

In all cases, the user's ID will be passed as a single string parameter when the SQL query is executed. It may be referenced within the query statement using a `%s` format specifier.

## AuthzDBDRedirectQuery Directive

| | |
|---|---|
| Description: | Specify a query to look up a login page for the user |
| Syntax: | `AuthzDBDRedirectQuery query` |
| Context: | directory |
| Status: | Extension |
| Module: | mod_authz_dbd |

Specifies an optional SQL query to use after successful login (or logout) to redirect the user to a URL, which may be specific to the user. The user's ID will be passed as a single string parameter when the SQL query is executed. It may be referenced within the query statement using a `%s` format specifier.

```
AuthzDBDRedirectQuery "SELECT userpage FROM userpages WHERE user = %s"
```

The first column value of the first row returned by the query statement should be a string containing a URL to which to redirect the client. Subsequent rows will be ignored. If no rows are returned, the client will not be redirected.

Note that AUTHZDBDLOGINTOREFERER takes precedence if both are set.

## 10.23    Apache Module mod_authz_dbm

| | |
|---|---|
| Description: | Group authorization using DBM files |
| Status: | Extension |
| ModuleIdentifier: | authz_dbm_module |
| SourceFile: | mod_authz_dbm.c |

### Summary

This module provides authorization capabilities so that authenticated users can be allowed or denied access to portions of the web site by group membership. Similar functionality is provided by MOD_AUTHZ_GROUPFILE.

### Directives

- AuthDBMGroupFile
- AuthzDBMType

### See also

- REQUIRE

### The Require Directives

Apache's REQUIRE directives are used during the authorization phase to ensure that a user is allowed to access a resource. mod_authz_dbm extends the authorization types with `dbm-group`.

Since v2.4.8, expressions (p. 99) are supported within the DBM require directives.

#### Require dbm-group

This directive specifies group membership that is required for the user to gain access.

```
Require dbm-group admin
```

#### Require dbm-file-group

When this directive is specified, the user must be a member of the group assigned to the file being accessed.

```
Require dbm-file-group
```

### Example usage

*Note that using mod_authz_dbm requires you to require* `dbm-group` *instead of* `group`:

```
<Directory "/foo/bar">
  AuthType Basic
  AuthName "Secure Area"
  AuthBasicProvider dbm
  AuthDBMUserFile "site/data/users"
```

```
  AuthDBMGroupFile "site/data/users"
  Require dbm-group admin
</Directory>
```

## AuthDBMGroupFile Directive

| | |
|---|---|
| Description: | Sets the name of the database file containing the list of user groups for authorization |
| Syntax: | `AuthDBMGroupFile file-path` |
| Context: | directory, .htaccess |
| Override: | AuthConfig |
| Status: | Extension |
| Module: | mod_authz_dbm |

The AUTHDBMGROUPFILE directive sets the name of a DBM file containing the list of user groups for user authorization. *File-path* is the absolute path to the group file.

The group file is keyed on the username. The value for a user is a comma-separated list of the groups to which the users belongs. There must be no whitespace within the value, and it must never contain any colons.

 **Security**

Make sure that the AUTHDBMGROUPFILE is stored outside the document tree of the web-server. Do **not** put it in the directory that it protects. Otherwise, clients will be able to download the AUTHDBMGROUPFILE unless otherwise protected.

Combining Group and Password DBM files: In some cases it is easier to manage a single database which contains both the password and group details for each user. This simplifies any support programs that need to be written: they now only have to deal with writing to and locking a single DBM file. This can be accomplished by first setting the group and password files to point to the same DBM:

```
AuthDBMGroupFile "/www/userbase"
AuthDBMUserFile "/www/userbase"
```

The key for the single DBM is the username. The value consists of

```
Encrypted Password :  List of Groups [ :  (ignored) ]
```

The password section contains the encrypted password as before. This is followed by a colon and the comma separated list of groups. Other data may optionally be left in the DBM file after another colon; it is ignored by the authorization module. This is what www.telescope.org uses for its combined password and group database.

## AuthzDBMType Directive

| | |
|---|---|
| Description: | Sets the type of database file that is used to store list of user groups |
| Syntax: | `AuthzDBMType default\|SDBM\|GDBM\|NDBM\|DB` |
| Default: | `AuthzDBMType default` |
| Context: | directory, .htaccess |
| Override: | AuthConfig |
| Status: | Extension |
| Module: | mod_authz_dbm |

Sets the type of database file that is used to store the list of user groups. The default database type is determined at compile time. The availability of other types of database files also depends on compile-time settings (p. 22) .

It is crucial that whatever program you use to create your group files is configured to use the same type of database.

## 10.24   Apache Module mod_authz_groupfile

| Description: | Group authorization using plaintext files |
|---|---|
| Status: | Base |
| ModuleIdentifier: | authz_groupfile_module |
| SourceFile: | mod_authz_groupfile.c |

### Summary

This module provides authorization capabilities so that authenticated users can be allowed or denied access to portions of the web site by group membership. Similar functionality is provided by MOD_AUTHZ_DBM.

#### Directives

* AuthGroupFile

#### See also

* REQUIRE

### The Require Directives

Apache's REQUIRE directives are used during the authorization phase to ensure that a user is allowed to access a resource. mod_authz_groupfile extends the authorization types with `group` and `group-file`.

Since v2.4.8, expressions (p. 99) are supported within the groupfile require directives.

#### Require group

This directive specifies group membership that is required for the user to gain access.

```
Require group admin
```

#### Require file-group

When this directive is specified, the filesystem permissions on the file being accessed are consulted. The user must be a member of a group with the same name as the group that owns the file. See MOD_AUTHZ_OWNER for more details.

```
Require file-group
```

### AuthGroupFile Directive

| Description: | Sets the name of a text file containing the list of user groups for authorization |
|---|---|
| Syntax: | `AuthGroupFile file-path` |
| Context: | directory, .htaccess |
| Override: | AuthConfig |
| Status: | Base |
| Module: | mod_authz_groupfile |

The AUTHGROUPFILE directive sets the name of a textual file containing the list of user groups for user authorization. *File-path* is the path to the group file. If it is not absolute, it is treated as relative to the SERVERROOT.

Each line of the group file contains a groupname followed by a colon, followed by the member usernames separated by spaces.

---

**Example:**
```
mygroup:  bob joe anne
```

---

Note that searching large text files is *very* inefficient; AUTHDBMGROUPFILE provides a much better performance.

 **Security**

Make sure that the AUTHGROUPFILE is stored outside the document tree of the web-server; do *not* put it in the directory that it protects. Otherwise, clients may be able to download the AUTHGROUPFILE.

## 10.25   Apache Module mod_authz_host

| | |
|---|---|
| Description: | Group authorizations based on host (name or IP address) |
| Status: | Base |
| ModuleIdentifier: | authz_host_module |
| SourceFile: | mod_authz_host.c |
| Compatibility: | Available in Apache 2.3 and later |

### Summary

The authorization providers implemented by MOD_AUTHZ_HOST are registered using the REQUIRE directive. The directive can be referenced within a <DIRECTORY>, <FILES>, or <LOCATION> section as well as .htaccess (p. 380)   files to control access to particular parts of the server.   Access can be controlled based on the client hostname or IP address.

In general, access restriction directives apply to all access methods (GET, PUT, POST, etc). This is the desired behavior in most cases. However, it is possible to restrict some methods, while leaving other methods unrestricted, by enclosing the directives in a <LIMIT> section.

**Directives** This module provides no directives.

**See also**

- Authentication, Authorization, and Access Control (p. 227)
- REQUIRE

### The Require Directives

Apache's REQUIRE directive is used during the authorization phase to ensure that a user is allowed or denied access to a resource. mod_authz_host extends the authorization types with ip, host, forward-dns and local. Other authorization types may also be used but may require that additional authorization modules be loaded.

These authorization providers affect which hosts can access an area of the server. Access can be controlled by hostname, IP Address, or IP Address range.

Since v2.4.8, expressions (p. 99) are supported within the host require directives.

#### Require ip

The ip provider allows access to the server to be controlled based on the IP address of the remote client. When Require ip *ip-address* is specified, then the request is allowed access if the IP address matches.

A full IP address:

```
Require ip 10.1.2.3
Require ip 192.168.1.104 192.168.1.205
```

An IP address of a host allowed access

A partial IP address:

```
Require ip 10.1
Require ip 10 172.20 192.168.2
```

The first 1 to 3 bytes of an IP address, for subnet restriction.

A network/netmask pair:

```
Require ip 10.1.0.0/255.255.0.0
```

A network a.b.c.d, and a netmask w.x.y.z. For more fine-grained subnet restriction.

A network/nnn CIDR specification:

```
Require ip 10.1.0.0/16
```

Similar to the previous case, except the netmask consists of nnn high-order 1 bits.

Note that the last three examples above match exactly the same set of hosts.

IPv6 addresses and IPv6 subnets can be specified as shown below:

```
Require ip 2001:db8::a00:20ff:fea7:ccea
Require ip 2001:db8:1:1::a
Require ip 2001:db8:2:1::/64
Require ip 2001:db8:3::/48
```

Note: As the IP addresses are parsed on startup, expressions are not evaluated at request time.

### Require host

The `host` provider allows access to the server to be controlled based on the host name of the remote client. When `Require host host-name` is specified, then the request is allowed access if the host name matches.

A (partial) domain-name

```
Require host example.org
Require host .net example.edu
```

Hosts whose names match, or end in, this string are allowed access. Only complete components are matched, so the above example will match `foo.example.org` but it will not match `fooexample.org`. This configuration will cause Apache to perform a double reverse DNS lookup on the client IP address, regardless of the setting of the HOSTNAMELOOKUPS directive. It will do a reverse DNS lookup on the IP address to find the associated hostname, and then do a forward lookup on the hostname to assure that it matches the original IP address. Only if the forward and reverse DNS are consistent and the hostname matches will access be allowed.

### Require forward-dns

The `forward-dns` provider allows access to the server to be controlled based on simple host names. When `Require forward-dns host-name` is specified, all IP addresses corresponding to `host-name` are allowed access.

In contrast to the `host` provider, this provider does not rely on reverse DNS lookups: it simply queries the DNS for the host name and allows a client if its IP matches. As a consequence, it will only work with host names, not domain names. However, as the reverse DNS is not used, it will work with clients which use a dynamic DNS service.

```
Require forward-dns bla.example.org
```

A client the IP of which is resolved from the name `bla.example.org` will be granted access.

**Require local**

The `local` provider allows access to the server if any of the following conditions is true:

- the client address matches 127.0.0.0/8
- the client address is ::1
- both the client and the server address of the connection are the same

This allows a convenient way to match connections that originate from the local host:

```
Require local
```

**Security Note**

If you are proxying content to your server, you need to be aware that the client address will be the address of your proxy server, not the address of the client, and so using the `Require` directive in this context may not do what you mean. See MOD_REMOTEIP for one possible solution to this problem.

# 10.26 Apache Module mod_authz_owner

| | |
|---|---|
| Description: | Authorization based on file ownership |
| Status: | Extension |
| ModuleIdentifier: | authz_owner_module |
| SourceFile: | mod_authz_owner.c |

## Summary

This module authorizes access to files by comparing the userid used for HTTP authentication (the web userid) with the file-system owner or group of the requested file. The supplied username and password must be already properly verified by an authentication module, such as MOD_AUTH_BASIC or MOD_AUTH_DIGEST. MOD_AUTHZ_OWNER recognizes two arguments for the REQUIRE directive, `file-owner` and `file-group`, as follows:

**file-owner** The supplied web-username must match the system's name for the owner of the file being requested. That is, if the operating system says the requested file is owned by `jones`, then the username used to access it through the web must be `jones` as well.

**file-group** The name of the system group that owns the file must be present in a group database, which is provided, for example, by MOD_AUTHZ_GROUPFILE or MOD_AUTHZ_DBM, and the web-username must be a member of that group. For example, if the operating system says the requested file is owned by (system) group `accounts`, the group `accounts` must appear in the group database and the web-username used in the request must be a member of that group.

Note

> If MOD_AUTHZ_OWNER is used in order to authorize a resource that is not actually present in the filesystem (*i.e.* a virtual resource), it will deny the access.
> Particularly it will never authorize content negotiated "MultiViews" (p. 78) resources.

**Directives** This module provides no directives.

**See also**

- REQUIRE

## Configuration Examples

### Require file-owner

Consider a multi-user system running the Apache Web server, with each user having his or her own files in `~/public_html/private`. Assuming that there is a single AUTHDBMUSERFILE database that lists all of their web-usernames, and that these usernames match the system's usernames that actually own the files on the server, then the following stanza would allow only the user himself access to his own files. User `jones` would not be allowed to access files in `/home/smith/public_html/private` unless they were owned by `jones` instead of `smith`.

```
<Directory "/home/*/public_html/private">
    AuthType Basic
    AuthName "MyPrivateFiles"
    AuthBasicProvider dbm
    AuthDBMUserFile "/usr/local/apache2/etc/.htdbm-all"
    Require file-owner
</Directory>
```

**Require file-group**

Consider a system similar to the one described above, but with some users that share their project files in
~/public_html/project-foo. The files are owned by the system group foo and there is a single AUTHDB-
MGROUPFILE database that contains all of the web-usernames and their group membership, *i.e.* they must be at least
member of a group named foo. So if jones and smith are both member of the group foo, then both will be
authorized to access the project-foo directories of each other.

```
<Directory "/home/*/public_html/project-foo">
    AuthType Basic
    AuthName "Project Foo Files"
    AuthBasicProvider dbm

    # combined user/group database
    AuthDBMUserFile  "/usr/local/apache2/etc/.htdbm-all"
    AuthDBMGroupFile "/usr/local/apache2/etc/.htdbm-all"

    Satisfy All
    Require file-group
</Directory>
```

# 10.27 Apache Module mod_authz_user

| Description: | User Authorization |
|---|---|
| Status: | Base |
| ModuleIdentifier: | authz_user_module |
| SourceFile: | mod_authz_user.c |

## Summary

This module provides authorization capabilities so that authenticated users can be allowed or denied access to portions of the web site. MOD_AUTHZ_USER grants access if the authenticated user is listed in a `Require user` directive. Alternatively `Require valid-user` can be used to grant access to all successfully authenticated users.

**Directives** This module provides no directives.

**See also**

- REQUIRE

## The Require Directives

Apache's REQUIRE directives are used during the authorization phase to ensure that a user is allowed to access a resource. mod_authz_user extends the authorization types with `user` and `valid-user`.

Since v2.4.8, expressions (p. 99) are supported within the user require directives.

**Require user**

This directive specifies a list of users that are allowed to gain access.

```
Require user john paul george ringo
```

**Require valid-user**

When this directive is specified, any successfully authenticated user will be allowed to gain access.

```
Require valid-user
```

## 10.28   Apache Module mod_autoindex

| Description: | Generates directory indexes, automatically, similar to the Unix `ls` command or the Win32 `dir` shell command |
|---|---|
| Status: | Base |
| ModuleIdentifier: | autoindex_module |
| SourceFile: | mod_autoindex.c |

### Summary

The index of a directory can come from one of two sources:

- A file located in that directory, typically called `index.html`. The DIRECTORYINDEX directive sets the name of the file or files to be used. This is controlled by MOD_DIR.

- Otherwise, a listing generated by the server. The other directives control the format of this listing. The AD-DICON, ADDICONBYENCODING and ADDICONBYTYPE are used to set a list of icons to display for various file types; for each file listed, the first icon listed that matches the file is displayed. These are controlled by MOD_AUTOINDEX.

The two functions are separated so that you can completely remove (or replace) automatic index generation should you want to.

Automatic index generation is enabled with using `Options +Indexes`. See the OPTIONS directive for more details.

If the `FancyIndexing` option is given with the INDEXOPTIONS directive, the column headers are links that control the order of the display. If you select a header link, the listing will be regenerated, sorted by the values in that column. Selecting the same header repeatedly toggles between ascending and descending order. These column header links are suppressed with the INDEXOPTIONS directive's `SuppressColumnSorting` option.

Note that when the display is sorted by "Size", it's *actual* size of the files that's used, not the displayed value - so a 1010-byte file will always be displayed before a 1011-byte file (if in ascending order) even though they both are shown as `"1K"`.

### Directives

- AddAlt
- AddAltByEncoding
- AddAltByType
- AddDescription
- AddIcon
- AddIconByEncoding
- AddIconByType
- DefaultIcon
- HeaderName
- IndexHeadInsert
- IndexIgnore
- IndexIgnoreReset
- IndexOptions
- IndexOrderDefault

- IndexStyleSheet

- ReadmeName

## Autoindex Request Query Arguments

Various query string arguments are available to give the client some control over the ordering of the directory listing, as well as what files are listed. If you do not wish to give the client this control, the `IndexOptions IgnoreClient` option disables that functionality.

The column sorting headers themselves are self-referencing hyperlinks that add the sort query options shown below. Any option below may be added to any request for the directory resource.

- `C=N` sorts the directory by file name

- `C=M` sorts the directory by last-modified date, then file name

- `C=S` sorts the directory by size, then file name

- `C=D` sorts the directory by description, then file name

- `O=A` sorts the listing in Ascending Order

- `O=D` sorts the listing in Descending Order

- `F=0` formats the listing as a simple list (not FancyIndexed)

- `F=1` formats the listing as a FancyIndexed list

- `F=2` formats the listing as an HTMLTable FancyIndexed list

- `V=0` disables version sorting

- `V=1` enables version sorting

- `P=`*pattern* lists only files matching the given *pattern*

Note that the 'P'attern query argument is tested *after* the usual INDEXIGNORE directives are processed, and all file names are still subjected to the same criteria as any other autoindex listing. The Query Arguments parser in MOD_AUTOINDEX will stop abruptly when an unrecognized option is encountered. The Query Arguments must be well formed, according to the table above.

The simple example below, which can be clipped and saved in a header.html file, illustrates these query options. Note that the unknown "X" argument, for the submit button, is listed last to assure the arguments are all parsed before mod_autoindex encounters the X=Go input.

```
<form action="" method="get">
    Show me a <select name="F">

        <option value="0"> Plain list</option>
        <option value="1" selected="selected"> Fancy list</option>
        <option value="2"> Table list</option>

    </select>
    Sorted by <select name="C">

        <option value="N" selected="selected"> Name</option>
        <option value="M"> Date Modified</option>
        <option value="S"> Size</option>
        <option value="D"> Description</option>

    </select>
    <select name="O">

        <option value="A" selected="selected"> Ascending</option>
        <option value="D"> Descending</option>

    </select>
    <select name="V">

        <option value="0" selected="selected"> in Normal
        order</option>
        <option value="1"> in Version order</option>

    </select>
    Matching <input type="text" name="P" value="*" />
    <input type="submit" name="X" value="Go" />
</form>
```

## AddAlt Directive

| | |
|---|---|
| Description: | Alternate text to display for a file, instead of an icon selected by filename |
| Syntax: | `AddAlt string file [file] ...` |
| Context: | server config, virtual host, directory, .htaccess |
| Override: | Indexes |
| Status: | Base |
| Module: | mod_autoindex |

ADDALT provides the alternate text to display for a file, instead of an icon, for `FancyIndexing`. *File* is a file extension, partial filename, wild-card expression or full filename for files to describe. If *String* contains any whitespace, you have to enclose it in quotes (" or '). This alternate text is displayed if the client is image-incapable, has image loading disabled, or fails to retrieve the icon.

```
AddAlt "PDF file" *.pdf
AddAlt Compressed *.gz *.zip *.Z
```

## AddAltByEncoding Directive

| | |
|---|---|
| Description: | Alternate text to display for a file instead of an icon selected by MIME-encoding |
| Syntax: | `AddAltByEncoding string MIME-encoding [MIME-encoding] ...` |
| Context: | server config, virtual host, directory, .htaccess |
| Override: | Indexes |
| Status: | Base |
| Module: | mod_autoindex |

ADDALTBYENCODING provides the alternate text to display for a file, instead of an icon, for `FancyIndexing`. *MIME-encoding* is a valid content-encoding, such as `x-compress`. If *String* contains any whitespace, you have to enclose it in quotes (" or ' ). This alternate text is displayed if the client is image-incapable, has image loading disabled, or fails to retrieve the icon.

```
AddAltByEncoding gzip x-gzip
```

## AddAltByType Directive

| | |
|---|---|
| Description: | Alternate text to display for a file, instead of an icon selected by MIME content-type |
| Syntax: | `AddAltByType string MIME-type [MIME-type] ...` |
| Context: | server config, virtual host, directory, .htaccess |
| Override: | Indexes |
| Status: | Base |
| Module: | mod_autoindex |

ADDALTBYTYPE sets the alternate text to display for a file, instead of an icon, for `FancyIndexing`. *MIME-type* is a valid content-type, such as `text/html`. If *String* contains any whitespace, you have to enclose it in quotes (" or ' ). This alternate text is displayed if the client is image-incapable, has image loading disabled, or fails to retrieve the icon.

```
AddAltByType 'plain text' text/plain
```

## AddDescription Directive

| | |
|---|---|
| Description: | Description to display for a file |
| Syntax: | `AddDescription string file [file] ...` |
| Context: | server config, virtual host, directory, .htaccess |
| Override: | Indexes |
| Status: | Base |
| Module: | mod_autoindex |

This sets the description to display for a file, for `FancyIndexing`. *File* is a file extension, partial filename, wild-card expression or full filename for files to describe. *String* is enclosed in double quotes (").

```
AddDescription "The planet Mars" mars.gif
AddDescription "My friend Marshall" friends/mars.gif
```

The typical, default description field is 23 bytes wide. 6 more bytes are added by the `IndexOptions SuppressIcon` option, 7 bytes are added by the `IndexOptions SuppressSize` option, and 19 bytes are added by the `IndexOptions SuppressLastModified` option. Therefore, the widest default the description column is ever assigned is 55 bytes.

Since the *File* argument may be a partial file name, please remember that a too-short partial filename may match unintended files. For example, `le.html` will match the file `le.html` but will also match the file `example.html`. In the event that there may be ambiguity, use as complete a filename as you can, but keep in mind that the first match encountered will be used, and order your list of `AddDescription` directives accordingly.

See the DescriptionWidth INDEXOPTIONS keyword for details on overriding the size of this column, or allowing descriptions of unlimited length.

**Caution**

Descriptive text defined with ADDDESCRIPTION may contain HTML markup, such as tags and character entities. If the width of the description column should happen to truncate a tagged element (such as cutting off the end of a bolded phrase), the results may affect the rest of the directory listing.

**Arguments with path information**

Absolute paths are not currently supported and do not match anything at runtime. Arguments with relative path information, which would normally only be used in htaccess context, are implicitly prefixed with '*/' to avoid matching partial directory names.

## AddIcon Directive

| | |
|---|---|
| Description: | Icon to display for a file selected by name |
| Syntax: | `AddIcon icon name [name] ...` |
| Context: | server config, virtual host, directory, .htaccess |
| Override: | Indexes |
| Status: | Base |
| Module: | mod_autoindex |

This sets the icon to display next to a file ending in *name* for `FancyIndexing`. *Icon* is either a (%-escaped) relative URL to the icon, a fully qualified remote URL, or of the format `(alttext,url)` where *alttext* is the text tag given for an icon for non-graphical browsers.

*Name* is either `^^DIRECTORY^^` for directories, `^^BLANKICON^^` for blank lines (to format the list correctly), a file extension, a wildcard expression, a partial filename or a complete filename.

`^^BLANKICON^^` is only used for formatting, and so is unnecessary if you're using `IndexOptions HTMLTable`.

```
#Examples
AddIcon (IMG,/icons/image.png) .gif .jpg .png
AddIcon /icons/dir.png ^^DIRECTORY^^
AddIcon /icons/backup.png *~
```

ADDICONBYTYPE should be used in preference to ADDICON, when possible.

## AddIconByEncoding Directive

| | |
|---|---|
| Description: | Icon to display next to files selected by MIME content-encoding |
| Syntax: | `AddIconByEncoding icon MIME-encoding [MIME-encoding] ...` |
| Context: | server config, virtual host, directory, .htaccess |
| Override: | Indexes |
| Status: | Base |
| Module: | mod_autoindex |

This sets the icon to display next to files with `FancyIndexing`. *Icon* is either a (%-escaped) relative URL to the icon, a fully qualified remote URL, or of the format `(alttext,url)` where *alttext* is the text tag given for an icon for non-graphical browsers.

*MIME-encoding* is a valid content-encoding, such as `x-compress`.

```
AddIconByEncoding /icons/compress.png x-compress
```

## AddIconByType Directive

| | |
|---|---|
| Description: | Icon to display next to files selected by MIME content-type |
| Syntax: | `AddIconByType icon MIME-type [MIME-type] ...` |
| Context: | server config, virtual host, directory, .htaccess |
| Override: | Indexes |
| Status: | Base |
| Module: | mod_autoindex |

This sets the icon to display next to files of type *MIME-type* for `FancyIndexing`. *Icon* is either a (%-escaped) relative URL to the icon, a fully qualified remote URL, or of the format (`alttext,url`) where *alttext* is the text tag given for an icon for non-graphical browsers.

*MIME-type* is a wildcard expression matching required the mime types.

```
AddIconByType (IMG,/icons/image.png) image/*
```

## DefaultIcon Directive

| | |
|---|---|
| Description: | Icon to display for files when no specific icon is configured |
| Syntax: | `DefaultIcon url-path` |
| Context: | server config, virtual host, directory, .htaccess |
| Override: | Indexes |
| Status: | Base |
| Module: | mod_autoindex |

The DEFAULTICON directive sets the icon to display for files when no specific icon is known, for `FancyIndexing`. *Url-path* is a (%-escaped) relative URL to the icon, or a fully qualified remote URL.

```
DefaultIcon /icon/unknown.png
```

## HeaderName Directive

| | |
|---|---|
| Description: | Name of the file that will be inserted at the top of the index listing |
| Syntax: | `HeaderName filename` |
| Context: | server config, virtual host, directory, .htaccess |
| Override: | Indexes |
| Status: | Base |
| Module: | mod_autoindex |

The HEADERNAME directive sets the name of the file that will be inserted at the top of the index listing. *Filename* is the name of the file to include.

```
HeaderName HEADER.html
```

Both HeaderName and READMENAME now treat *Filename* as a URI path relative to the one used to access the directory being indexed. If *Filename* begins with a slash, it will be taken to be relative to the DOCUMENTROOT.

```
HeaderName /include/HEADER.html
```

*Filename* must resolve to a document with a major content type of text/* (*e.g.*, text/html, text/plain, etc.). This means that *filename* may refer to a CGI script if the script's actual file type (as opposed to its output) is marked as text/html such as with a directive like:

```
AddType text/html .cgi
```

Content negotiation (p. 78) will be performed if OPTIONS MultiViews is in effect. If *filename* resolves to a static text/html document (not a CGI script) and either one of the OPTIONS Includes or IncludesNOEXEC is enabled, the file will be processed for server-side includes (see the MOD_INCLUDE documentation).

If the file specified by HEADERNAME contains the beginnings of an HTML document (<html>, <head>, etc.) then you will probably want to set IndexOptions +SuppressHTMLPreamble, so that these tags are not repeated.

**See also**

- READMENAME

## IndexHeadInsert Directive

| | |
|---|---|
| Description: | Inserts text in the HEAD section of an index page. |
| Syntax: | IndexHeadInsert "markup ..." |
| Context: | server config, virtual host, directory, .htaccess |
| Override: | Indexes |
| Status: | Base |
| Module: | mod_autoindex |

The INDEXHEADINSERT directive specifies a string to insert in the *<head>* section of the HTML generated for the index page.

```
IndexHeadInsert "<link rel=\"sitemap\" href=\"/sitemap.html\">"
```

## IndexIgnore Directive

| | |
|---|---|
| Description: | Adds to the list of files to hide when listing a directory |
| Syntax: | IndexIgnore file [file] ... |
| Default: | IndexIgnore "." |
| Context: | server config, virtual host, directory, .htaccess |
| Override: | Indexes |
| Status: | Base |
| Module: | mod_autoindex |

The INDEXIGNORE directive adds to the list of files to hide when listing a directory. *File* is a shell-style wildcard expression or full filename. Multiple IndexIgnore directives add to the list, rather than replacing the list of ignored files. By default, the list contains . (the current directory).

```
IndexIgnore .??* *~ *# HEADER* README* RCS CVS *,v *,t
```

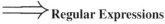

**Regular Expressions**

This directive does not currently work in configuration sections that have regular expression arguments, such as <DIRECTORYMATCH>

## IndexIgnoreReset Directive

| | |
|---|---|
| Description: | Empties the list of files to hide when listing a directory |
| Syntax: | `IndexIgnoreReset ON|OFF` |
| Context: | server config, virtual host, directory, .htaccess |
| Override: | Indexes |
| Status: | Base |
| Module: | mod_autoindex |
| Compatibility: | 2.3.10 and later |

The INDEXIGNORERESET directive removes any files ignored by INDEXIGNORE otherwise inherited from other configuration sections.

```
<Directory "/var/www">
    IndexIgnore *.bak .??* *~ *# HEADER* README* RCS CVS *,v *,t
</Directory>
<Directory "/var/www/backups">
    IndexIgnoreReset ON
    IndexIgnore .??* *# HEADER* README* RCS CVS *,v *,t
</Directory>
```

⚠ Review the default configuration for a list of patterns that you might want to explicitly ignore after using this directive.

## IndexOptions Directive

| | |
|---|---|
| Description: | Various configuration settings for directory indexing |
| Syntax: | `IndexOptions [+|-]option [[+|-]option] ...` |
| Default: | `By default, no options are enabled.` |
| Context: | server config, virtual host, directory, .htaccess |
| Override: | Indexes |
| Status: | Base |
| Module: | mod_autoindex |

The INDEXOPTIONS directive specifies the behavior of the directory indexing. *Option* can be one of

**AddAltClass** Adds an additional CSS class declaration to each row of the directory listing table when `IndexOptions HTMLTable` is in effect and an `IndexStyleSheet` is defined. Rather than the standard `even` and `odd` classes that would otherwise be applied to each row of the table, a class of `even-`*ALT* or `odd-`*ALT* where *ALT* is either the standard alt text associated with the file style (eg. *snd*, *txt*, *img*, etc) or the alt text defined by one of the various `AddAlt*` directives.

**Charset=***character-set* (*Apache HTTP Server 2.0.61 and later*) The `Charset` keyword allows you to specify the character set of the generated page. The default is `UTF-8` on Windows and Mac OS X, and `ISO-8859-1` elsewhere. (It depends on whether the underlying file system uses Unicode filenames or not.)

```
IndexOptions Charset=UTF-8
```

**DescriptionWidth=[*n* — \*]** The `DescriptionWidth` keyword allows you to specify the width of the description column in characters.

**-`DescriptionWidth` (or unset) allows** MOD_AUTOINDEX **to calculate the best width.**
> `DescriptionWidth=`*n* fixes the column width to *n* bytes wide.
>
> `DescriptionWidth=*` grows the column to the width necessary to accommodate the longest description string.
>
> **See the section on** ADDDESCRIPTION **for dangers inherent in truncating descriptions.**

**FancyIndexing** This turns on fancy indexing of directories.

**FoldersFirst** If this option is enabled, subdirectory listings will *always* appear first, followed by normal files in the directory. The listing is basically broken into two components, the files and the subdirectories, and each is sorted separately and then displayed subdirectories-first. For instance, if the sort order is descending by name, and `FoldersFirst` is enabled, subdirectory `Zed` will be listed before subdirectory `Beta`, which will be listed before normal files `Gamma` and `Alpha`. **This option only has an effect if `FancyIndexing` is also enabled.**

**HTMLTable** This option with `FancyIndexing` constructs a simple table for the fancy directory listing. It is necessary for utf-8 enabled platforms or if file names or description text will alternate between left-to-right and right-to-left reading order.

**IconsAreLinks** This makes the icons part of the anchor for the filename, for fancy indexing.

**IconHeight[=*pixels*]** Presence of this option, when used with `IconWidth`, will cause the server to include `height` and `width` attributes in the `img` tag for the file icon. This allows browser to precalculate the page layout without having to wait until all the images have been loaded. If no value is given for the option, it defaults to the standard height of the icons supplied with the Apache httpd software.

> **This option only has an effect if `FancyIndexing` is also enabled.**

**IconWidth[=*pixels*]** Presence of this option, when used with `IconHeight`, will cause the server to include `height` and `width` attributes in the `img` tag for the file icon. This allows browser to precalculate the page layout without having to wait until all the images have been loaded. If no value is given for the option, it defaults to the standard width of the icons supplied with the Apache httpd software.

**IgnoreCase** If this option is enabled, names are sorted in a case-insensitive manner. For instance, if the sort order is ascending by name, and `IgnoreCase` is enabled, file Zeta will be listed after file alfa (Note: file GAMMA will always be listed before file gamma).

**IgnoreClient** This option causes MOD_AUTOINDEX to ignore all query variables from the client, including sort order (implies `SuppressColumnSorting`.)

**NameWidth=[*n* — \*]** The `NameWidth` keyword allows you to specify the width of the filename column in bytes.
> -`NameWidth` (or unset) allows MOD_AUTOINDEX to calculate the best width, but only up to 20 bytes wide.
>
> `NameWidth=`*n* fixes the column width to *n* bytes wide.
>
> `NameWidth=*` grows the column to the necessary width.

**ScanHTMLTitles** This enables the extraction of the title from HTML documents for fancy indexing. If the file does not have a description given by ADDDESCRIPTION then httpd will read the document for the value of the `title` element. This is CPU and disk intensive.

**ShowForbidden** If specified, Apache httpd will show files normally hidden because the subrequest returned `HTTP_UNAUTHORIZED` or `HTTP_FORBIDDEN`

**SuppressColumnSorting** If specified, Apache httpd will not make the column headings in a FancyIndexed directory listing into links for sorting. The default behavior is for them to be links; selecting the column heading will sort the directory listing by the values in that column. However, query string arguments which are appended to the URL will still be honored. That behavior is controlled by `IndexOptions IgnoreClient`.

**SuppressDescription** This will suppress the file description in fancy indexing listings. By default, no file descriptions are defined, and so the use of this option will regain 23 characters of screen space to use for something else. See ADDDESCRIPTION for information about setting the file description. See also the `DescriptionWidth` index option to limit the size of the description column.

> **This option only has an effect if `FancyIndexing` is also enabled.**

**SuppressHTMLPreamble** If the directory actually contains a file specified by the HEADERNAME directive, the module usually includes the contents of the file after a standard HTML preamble (`<html>`, `<head>`, *et cetera*). The `SuppressHTMLPreamble` option disables this behaviour, causing the module to start the display with the header file contents. The header file must contain appropriate HTML instructions in this case. If there is no header file, the preamble is generated as usual. If you also specify a READMENAME, and if that file exists, The closing `</body></html>` tags are also ommitted from the output, under the assumption that you'll likely put those closing tags in that file.

**SuppressIcon** This will suppress the icon in fancy indexing listings. Combining both `SuppressIcon` and `SuppressRules` yields proper HTML 3.2 output, which by the final specification prohibits `img` and `hr` elements from the `pre` block (used to format FancyIndexed listings.)

**SuppressLastModified** This will suppress the display of the last modification date, in fancy indexing listings.

> **This option only has an effect if `FancyIndexing` is also enabled.**

**SuppressRules** This will suppress the horizontal rule lines (`hr` elements) in directory listings. Combining both `SuppressIcon` and `SuppressRules` yields proper HTML 3.2 output, which by the final specification prohibits `img` and `hr` elements from the `pre` block (used to format FancyIndexed listings.)

> **This option only has an effect if `FancyIndexing` is also enabled.**

**SuppressSize** This will suppress the file size in fancy indexing listings.

> **This option only has an effect if `FancyIndexing` is also enabled.**

**TrackModified** This returns the `Last-Modified` and `ETag` values for the listed directory in the HTTP header. It is only valid if the operating system and file system return appropriate stat() results. Some Unix systems do so, as do OS2's JFS and Win32's NTFS volumes. OS2 and Win32 FAT volumes, for example, do not. Once this feature is enabled, the client or proxy can track changes to the list of files when they perform a HEAD request. Note some operating systems correctly track new and removed files, but do not track changes for sizes or dates of the files within the directory. **Changes to the size or date stamp of an existing file will not update the `Last-Modified` header on all Unix platforms.** If this is a concern, leave this option disabled.

**Type=*MIME content-type* (*Apache HTTP Server 2.0.61 and later*)** The `Type` keyword allows you to specify the MIME content-type of the generated page. The default is *text/html*.

```
IndexOptions Type=text/plain
```

**VersionSort (*Apache HTTP Server 2.0a3 and later*)** The `VersionSort` keyword causes files containing version numbers to sort in a natural way. Strings are sorted as usual, except that substrings of digits in the name and description are compared according to their numeric value.

> **Example:**
> ```
> foo-1.7
> foo-1.7.2
> foo-1.7.12
> foo-1.8.2
> foo-1.8.2a
> foo-1.12
> ```

If the number starts with a zero, then it is considered to be a fraction:

```
foo-1.001
foo-1.002
foo-1.030
foo-1.04
```

**XHTML (*Apache HTTP Server 2.0.49 and later*)**  The XHTML keyword forces MOD_AUTOINDEX to emit XHTML 1.0 code instead of HTML 3.2. **This option only has an effect if `FancyIndexing` is also enabled.**

**Incremental IndexOptions**  Be aware of how multiple INDEXOPTIONS are handled.

- Multiple INDEXOPTIONS directives for a single directory are now merged together. The result of:

```
<Directory "/foo">
    IndexOptions HTMLTable
    IndexOptions SuppressColumnsorting
</Directory>
```

will be the equivalent of

```
IndexOptions HTMLTable SuppressColumnsorting
```

- The addition of the incremental syntax (*i.e.*, prefixing keywords with + or −).

Whenever a '+' or '-' prefixed keyword is encountered, it is applied to the current INDEXOPTIONS settings (which may have been inherited from an upper-level directory). However, whenever an unprefixed keyword is processed, it clears all inherited options and any incremental settings encountered so far. Consider the following example:

```
IndexOptions +ScanHTMLTitles -IconsAreLinks FancyIndexing
IndexOptions +SuppressSize
```

The net effect is equivalent to `IndexOptions FancyIndexing +SuppressSize`, because the unprefixed `FancyIndexing` discarded the incremental keywords before it, but allowed them to start accumulating again afterward.

To unconditionally set the INDEXOPTIONS for a particular directory, clearing the inherited settings, specify keywords without any + or − prefixes.

## IndexOrderDefault Directive

| | |
|---|---|
| Description: | Sets the default ordering of the directory index |
| Syntax: | `IndexOrderDefault Ascending|Descending Name|Date|Size|Description` |
| Default: | `IndexOrderDefault Ascending Name` |
| Context: | server config, virtual host, directory, .htaccess |
| Override: | Indexes |
| Status: | Base |
| Module: | mod_autoindex |

The INDEXORDERDEFAULT directive is used in combination with the `FancyIndexing` index option. By default, fancyindexed directory listings are displayed in ascending order by filename; the INDEXORDERDEFAULT allows you to change this initial display order.

INDEXORDERDEFAULT takes two arguments. The first must be either `Ascending` or `Descending`, indicating the direction of the sort. The second argument must be one of the keywords `Name`, `Date`, `Size`, or `Description`, and identifies the primary key. The secondary key is *always* the ascending filename.

You can, if desired, prevent the client from reordering the list by also adding the `SuppressColumnSorting` index option to remove the sort link from the top of the column, along with the `IgnoreClient` index option to prevent them from manually adding sort options to the query string in order to override your ordering preferences.

## IndexStyleSheet Directive

| | |
|---|---|
| Description: | Adds a CSS stylesheet to the directory index |
| Syntax: | `IndexStyleSheet url-path` |
| Context: | server config, virtual host, directory, .htaccess |
| Override: | Indexes |
| Status: | Base |
| Module: | mod_autoindex |

The INDEXSTYLESHEET directive sets the name of the file that will be used as the CSS for the index listing.

```
IndexStyleSheet "/css/style.css"
```

Using this directive in conjunction with `IndexOptions HTMLTable` adds a number of CSS classes to the resulting HTML. The entire table is given a CSS id of `indexlist` and the following classes are associated with the various parts of the listing:

| Class | Definition |
|---|---|
| tr.indexhead | Header row of listing |
| th.indexcolicon and td.indexcolicon | Icon column |
| th.indexcolname and td.indexcolname | File name column |
| th.indexcollastmod and td.indexcollastmod | Last modified column |
| th.indexcolsize and td.indexcolsize | File size column |
| th.indexcoldesc and td.indexcoldesc | Description column |
| tr.breakrow | Horizontal rule at the bottom of the table |
| tr.odd and tr.even | Alternating even and odd rows |

## ReadmeName Directive

| | |
|---|---|
| Description: | Name of the file that will be inserted at the end of the index listing |
| Syntax: | `ReadmeName filename` |
| Context: | server config, virtual host, directory, .htaccess |
| Override: | Indexes |
| Status: | Base |
| Module: | mod_autoindex |

The READMENAME directive sets the name of the file that will be appended to the end of the index listing. *Filename* is the name of the file to include, and is taken to be relative to the location being indexed. If *Filename* begins with a slash, as in example 2, it will be taken to be relative to the DOCUMENTROOT.

```
# Example 1
ReadmeName FOOTER.html

# Example 2
ReadmeName /include/FOOTER.html
```

See also HEADERNAME, where this behavior is described in greater detail.

# 10.29   Apache Module mod_buffer

| | |
|---|---|
| Description: | Support for request buffering |
| Status: | Extension |
| ModuleIdentifier: | buffer_module |
| SourceFile: | mod_buffer.c |
| Compatibility: | Available in Apache 2.3 and later |

## Summary

This module provides the ability to buffer the input and output filter stacks.

Under certain circumstances, content generators might create content in small chunks. In order to promote memory reuse, in memory chunks are always 8k in size, regardless of the size of the chunk itself. When many small chunks are generated by a request, this can create a large memory footprint while the request is being processed, and an unnecessarily large amount of data on the wire. The addition of a buffer collapses the response into the fewest chunks possible.

When httpd is used in front of an expensive content generator, buffering the response may allow the backend to complete processing and release resources sooner, depending on how the backend is designed.

The buffer filter may be added to either the input or the output filter stacks, as appropriate, using the SETINPUTFILTER, SETOUTPUTFILTER, ADDOUTPUTFILTER or ADDOUTPUTFILTERBYTYPE directives.

### Using buffer with mod_include

```
AddOutputFilterByType INCLUDES;BUFFER text/html
```

!  The buffer filters read the request/response into RAM and then repack the request/response into the fewest memory buckets possible, at the cost of CPU time. When the request/response is already efficiently packed, buffering the request/response could cause the request/response to be slower than not using a buffer at all. These filters should be used with care, and only where necessary.

## Directives

- BufferSize

## See also

- Filters (p. 110)

## BufferSize Directive

| | |
|---|---|
| Description: | Maximum size in bytes to buffer by the buffer filter |
| Syntax: | `BufferSize integer` |
| Default: | `BufferSize 131072` |
| Context: | server config, virtual host, directory, .htaccess |
| Status: | Extension |
| Module: | mod_buffer |

The BUFFERSIZE directive specifies the amount of data in bytes that will be buffered before being read from or written to each request. The default is 128 kilobytes.

# 10.30   Apache Module mod_cache

| | |
|---|---|
| Description: | RFC 2616 compliant HTTP caching filter. |
| Status: | Extension |
| ModuleIdentifier: | cache_module |
| SourceFile: | mod_cache.c |

## Summary

 This module should be used with care, as when the CACHEQUICKHANDLER directive is in its default value of **on**, the ALLOW and DENY directives will be circumvented. You should not enable quick handler caching for any content to which you wish to limit access by client host name, address or environment variable.

MOD_CACHE implements an RFC 2616[14] compliant **HTTP content caching filter**, with support for the caching of content negotiated responses containing the Vary header.

RFC 2616 compliant caching provides a mechanism to verify whether stale or expired content is still fresh, and can represent a significant performance boost when the origin server supports **conditional requests** by honouring the If-None-Match[15] HTTP request header. Content is only regenerated from scratch when the content has changed, and not when the cached entry expires.

As a filter, MOD_CACHE can be placed in front of content originating from any handler, including **flat files** (served from a slow disk cached on a fast disk), the output of a **CGI script** or **dynamic content generator**, or content **proxied from another server**.

In the default configuration, MOD_CACHE inserts the caching filter as far forward as possible within the filter stack, utilising the **quick handler** to bypass all per request processing when returning content to the client. In this mode of operation, MOD_CACHE may be thought of as a caching proxy server bolted to the front of the webserver, while running within the webserver itself.

When the quick handler is switched off using the CACHEQUICKHANDLER directive, it becomes possible to insert the **CACHE** filter at a point in the filter stack chosen by the administrator. This provides the opportunity to cache content before that content is personalised by the MOD_INCLUDE filter, or optionally compressed by the MOD_DEFLATE filter.

Under normal operation, MOD_CACHE will respond to and can be controlled by the Cache-Control[16] and Pragma[17] headers sent from a client in a request, or from a server within a response. Under exceptional circumstances, MOD_CACHE can be configured to override these headers and force site specific behaviour, however such behaviour will be limited to this cache only, and will not affect the operation of other caches that may exist between the client and server, and as a result is not recommended unless strictly necessary.

RFC 2616 allows for the cache to return stale data while the existing stale entry is refreshed from the origin server, and this is supported by MOD_CACHE when the CACHELOCK directive is suitably configured. Such responses will contain a Warning[18] HTTP header with a 110 response code. RFC 2616 also allows a cache to return stale data when the attempt made to refresh the stale data returns an error 500 or above, and this behaviour is supported by default by MOD_CACHE. Such responses will contain a Warning[19] HTTP header with a 111 response code.

MOD_CACHE requires the services of one or more storage management modules. The following storage management modules are included in the base Apache distribution:

---

[14]http://www.ietf.org/rfc/rfc2616.txt

[15]http://www.w3.org/Protocols/rfc2616/rfc2616-sec14.html#sec14.26

[16]http://www.w3.org/Protocols/rfc2616/rfc2616-sec14.html#sec14.9

[17]http://www.w3.org/Protocols/rfc2616/rfc2616-sec14.html#sec14.32

[18]http://www.w3.org/Protocols/rfc2616/rfc2616-sec14.html#sec14.46

[19]http://www.w3.org/Protocols/rfc2616/rfc2616-sec14.html#sec14.46

MOD_CACHE_DISK Implements a disk based storage manager. Headers and bodies are stored separately on disk, in a directory structure derived from the md5 hash of the cached URL. Multiple content negotiated responses can be stored concurrently, however the caching of partial content is not supported by this module. The `htcacheclean` tool is provided to list cached URLs, remove cached URLs, or to maintain the size of the disk cache within size and inode limits.

MOD_CACHE_SOCACHE Implements a shared object cache based storage manager. Headers and bodies are stored together beneath a single key based on the URL of the response being cached. Multiple content negotiated responses can be stored concurrently, however the caching of partial content is not supported by this module.

Further details, discussion, and examples, are provided in the Caching Guide (p. 43) .

**Directives**

- CacheDefaultExpire
- CacheDetailHeader
- CacheDisable
- CacheEnable
- CacheHeader
- CacheIgnoreCacheControl
- CacheIgnoreHeaders
- CacheIgnoreNoLastMod
- CacheIgnoreQueryString
- CacheIgnoreURLSessionIdentifiers
- CacheKeyBaseURL
- CacheLastModifiedFactor
- CacheLock
- CacheLockMaxAge
- CacheLockPath
- CacheMaxExpire
- CacheMinExpire
- CacheQuickHandler
- CacheStaleOnError
- CacheStoreExpired
- CacheStoreNoStore
- CacheStorePrivate

**See also**

- Caching Guide (p. 43)

## Related Modules and Directives

| Related Modules | Related Directives |
|---|---|
| MOD_CACHE_DISK | CACHEROOT |
| MOD_CACHE_SOCACHE | CACHEDIRLEVELS |
| | CACHEDIRLENGTH |
| | CACHEMINFILESIZE |
| | CACHEMAXFILESIZE |
| | CACHESOCACHE |
| | CACHESOCACHEMAXTIME |
| | CACHESOCACHEMINTIME |
| | CACHESOCACHEMAXSIZE |
| | CACHESOCACHEREADSIZE |
| | CACHESOCACHEREADTIME |

## Sample Configuration

**Sample httpd.conf**

```
#
# Sample Cache Configuration
#
LoadModule cache_module modules/mod_cache.so
<IfModule mod_cache.c>
    LoadModule cache_disk_module modules/mod_cache_disk.so
    <IfModule mod_cache_disk.c>
        CacheRoot c:/cacheroot
        CacheEnable disk  /
        CacheDirLevels 5
        CacheDirLength 3
    </IfModule>

    # When acting as a proxy, don't cache the list of security updates
    CacheDisable http://security.update.server/update-list/
</IfModule>
```

## Avoiding the Thundering Herd

When a cached entry becomes stale, MOD_CACHE will submit a conditional request to the backend, which is expected to confirm whether the cached entry is still fresh, and send an updated entity if not.

A small but finite amount of time exists between the time the cached entity becomes stale, and the time the stale entity is fully refreshed. On a busy server, a significant number of requests might arrive during this time, and cause a **thundering herd** of requests to strike the backend suddenly and unpredictably.

To keep the thundering herd at bay, the CACHELOCK directive can be used to define a directory in which locks are created for URLs **in flight**. The lock is used as a **hint** by other requests to either suppress an attempt to cache (someone else has gone to fetch the entity), or to indicate that a stale entry is being refreshed (stale content will be returned in the mean time).

**Initial caching of an entry**

When an entity is cached for the first time, a lock will be created for the entity until the response has been fully cached. During the lifetime of the lock, the cache will suppress the second and subsequent attempt to cache the same entity. While this doesn't hold back the thundering herd, it does stop the cache attempting to cache the same entity multiple times simultaneously.

**Refreshment of a stale entry**

When an entity reaches its freshness lifetime and becomes stale, a lock will be created for the entity until the response has either been confirmed as still fresh, or replaced by the backend. During the lifetime of the lock, the second and subsequent incoming request will cause stale data to be returned, and the thundering herd is kept at bay.

**Locks and Cache-Control: no-cache**

Locks are used as a **hint only** to enable the cache to be more gentle on backend servers, however the lock can be overridden if necessary. If the client sends a request with a Cache-Control header forcing a reload, any lock that may be present will be ignored, and the client's request will be honored immediately and the cached entry refreshed.

As a further safety mechanism, locks have a configurable maximum age. Once this age has been reached, the lock is removed, and a new request is given the opportunity to create a new lock. This maximum age can be set using the CACHELOCKMAXAGE directive, and defaults to 5 seconds.

**Example configuration**

> **Enabling the cache lock**
>
> ```
> #
> # Enable the cache lock
> #
> <IfModule mod_cache.c>
>     CacheLock on
>     CacheLockPath /tmp/mod_cache-lock
>     CacheLockMaxAge 5
> </IfModule>
> ```

# Fine Control with the CACHE Filter

Under the default mode of cache operation, the cache runs as a quick handler, short circuiting the majority of server processing and offering the highest cache performance available.

In this mode, the cache **bolts onto** the front of the server, acting as if a free standing RFC 2616 caching proxy had been placed in front of the server.

While this mode offers the best performance, the administrator may find that under certain circumstances they may want to perform further processing on the request after the request is cached, such as to inject personalisation into the cached page, or to apply authorization restrictions to the content. Under these circumstances, an administrator is often forced to place independent reverse proxy servers either behind or in front of the caching server to achieve this.

To solve this problem the CACHEQUICKHANDLER directive can be set to **off**, and the server will process all phases normally handled by a non-cached request, including the **authentication and authorization** phases.

In addition, the administrator may optionally specify the **precise point within the filter chain** where caching is to take place by adding the **CACHE** filter to the output filter chain.

For example, to cache content before applying compression to the response, place the **CACHE** filter before the **DEFLATE** filter as in the example below:

```
# Cache content before optional compression
CacheQuickHandler off
AddOutputFilterByType CACHE;DEFLATE text/plain
```

Another option is to have content cached before personalisation is applied by MOD_INCLUDE (or another content processing filter). In this example templates containing tags understood by MOD_INCLUDE are cached before being parsed:

```
# Cache content before mod_include and mod_deflate
CacheQuickHandler off
AddOutputFilterByType CACHE;INCLUDES;DEFLATE text/html
```

You may place the **CACHE** filter anywhere you wish within the filter chain. In this example, content is cached after being parsed by MOD_INCLUDE, but before being processed by MOD_DEFLATE:

```
# Cache content between mod_include and mod_deflate
CacheQuickHandler off
AddOutputFilterByType INCLUDES;CACHE;DEFLATE text/html
```

 **Warning:**
If the location of the **CACHE** filter in the filter chain is changed for any reason, you may need to **flush your cache** to ensure that your data served remains consistent. MOD_CACHE is not in a position to enforce this for you.

### Cache Status and Logging

Once MOD_CACHE has made a decision as to whether or not an entity is to be served from cache, the detailed reason for the decision is written to the subprocess environment within the request under the **cache-status** key. This reason can be logged by the LOGFORMAT directive as follows:

```
LogFormat "%{cache-status}e ..."
```

Based on the caching decision made, the reason is also written to the subprocess environment under one the following four keys, as appropriate:

**cache-hit** The response was served from cache.

**cache-revalidate** The response was stale and was successfully revalidated, then served from cache.

**cache-miss** The response was served from the upstream server.

**cache-invalidate** The cached entity was invalidated by a request method other than GET or HEAD.

This makes it possible to support conditional logging of cached requests as per the following example:

```
CustomLog "cached-requests.log" common env=cache-hit
CustomLog "uncached-requests.log" common env=cache-miss
CustomLog "revalidated-requests.log" common env=cache-revalidate
CustomLog "invalidated-requests.log" common env=cache-invalidate
```

For module authors, a hook called *cache_status* is available, allowing modules to respond to the caching outcomes above in customised ways.

## CacheDefaultExpire Directive

| | |
|---|---|
| Description: | The default duration to cache a document when no expiry date is specified. |
| Syntax: | `CacheDefaultExpire seconds` |
| Default: | `CacheDefaultExpire 3600 (one hour)` |
| Context: | server config, virtual host, directory, .htaccess |
| Status: | Extension |
| Module: | mod_cache |

The CACHEDEFAULTEXPIRE directive specifies a default time, in seconds, to cache a document if neither an expiry date nor last-modified date are provided with the document. The value specified with the CACHEMAXEXPIRE directive does *not* override this setting.

```
CacheDefaultExpire 86400
```

## CacheDetailHeader Directive

| | |
|---|---|
| Description: | Add an X-Cache-Detail header to the response. |
| Syntax: | `CacheDetailHeader on|off` |
| Default: | `CacheDetailHeader off` |
| Context: | server config, virtual host, directory, .htaccess |
| Status: | Extension |
| Module: | mod_cache |
| Compatibility: | Available in Apache 2.3.9 and later |

When the CACHEDETAILHEADER directive is switched on, an **X-Cache-Detail** header will be added to the response containing the detailed reason for a particular caching decision.

It can be useful during development of cached RESTful services to have additional information about the caching decision written to the response headers, so as to confirm whether `Cache-Control` and other headers have been correctly used by the service and client.

If the normal handler is used, this directive may appear within a <DIRECTORY> or <LOCATION> directive. If the quick handler is used, this directive must appear within a server or virtual host context, otherwise the setting will be ignored.

```
# Enable the X-Cache-Detail header
CacheDetailHeader on
```

```
X-Cache-Detail:  "conditional cache hit:  entity refreshed" from
localhost
```

## CacheDisable Directive

| | |
|---|---|
| Description: | Disable caching of specified URLs |
| Syntax: | `CacheDisable url-string | on` |
| Context: | server config, virtual host, directory, .htaccess |
| Status: | Extension |
| Module: | mod_cache |

The CACHEDISABLE directive instructs MOD_CACHE to *not* cache urls at or below *url-string*.

**Example**

```
CacheDisable /local_files
```

If used in a <LOCATION> directive, the path needs to be specified below the Location, or if the word "on" is used, caching for the whole location will be disabled.

**Example**

```
<Location "/foo">
    CacheDisable on
</Location>
```

The `no-cache` environment variable can be set to disable caching on a finer grained set of resources in versions 2.2.12 and later.

**See also**

- Environment Variables in Apache (p. 92)

## CacheEnable Directive

| | |
|---|---|
| Description: | Enable caching of specified URLs using a specified storage manager |
| Syntax: | `CacheEnable cache_type [url-string]` |
| Context: | server config, virtual host, directory |
| Status: | Extension |
| Module: | mod_cache |
| Compatibility: | A url-string of '/' applied to forward proxy content in 2.2 and earlier. |

The CACHEENABLE directive instructs MOD_CACHE to cache urls at or below *url-string*. The cache storage manager is specified with the *cache_type* argument. The CACHEENABLE directive can alternatively be placed inside either <LOCATION> or <LOCATIONMATCH> sections to indicate the content is cacheable. *cache_type* `disk` instructs MOD_CACHE to use the disk based storage manager implemented by MOD_CACHE_DISK. *cache_type* `socache` instructs MOD_CACHE to use the shared object cache based storage manager implemented by MOD_CACHE_SOCACHE.

In the event that the URL space overlaps between different CACHEENABLE directives (as in the example below), each possible storage manager will be run until the first one that actually processes the request. The order in which the storage managers are run is determined by the order of the CACHEENABLE directives in the configuration file. CACHEENABLE directives within <LOCATION> or <LOCATIONMATCH> sections are processed before globally defined CACHEENABLE directives.

When acting as a forward proxy server, *url-string* must minimally begin with a protocol for which caching should be enabled.

```
# Cache content (normal handler only)
CacheQuickHandler off
<Location "/foo">
    CacheEnable disk
</Location>

# Cache regex (normal handler only)
CacheQuickHandler off
<LocationMatch "foo$">
    CacheEnable disk
</LocationMatch>
```

```
# Cache all but forward proxy url's (normal or quick handler)
CacheEnable  disk  /

# Cache FTP-proxied url's (normal or quick handler)
CacheEnable  disk  ftp://

# Cache forward proxy content from www.example.org (normal or quick handler)
CacheEnable  disk  http://www.example.org/
```

A hostname starting with a "*" matches all hostnames with that suffix. A hostname starting with "." matches all hostnames containing the domain components that follow.

```
# Match www.example.org, and fooexample.org
CacheEnable  disk  http://*example.org/
# Match www.example.org, but not fooexample.org
CacheEnable  disk  http://.example.org/
```

The `no-cache` environment variable can be set to disable caching on a finer grained set of resources in versions 2.2.12 and later.

**See also**

- Environment Variables in Apache (p. 92)

## CacheHeader Directive

| | |
|---|---|
| Description: | Add an X-Cache header to the response. |
| Syntax: | `CacheHeader on\|off` |
| Default: | `CacheHeader off` |
| Context: | server config, virtual host, directory, .htaccess |
| Status: | Extension |
| Module: | mod_cache |
| Compatibility: | Available in Apache 2.3.9 and later |

When the CACHEHEADER directive is switched on, an **X-Cache** header will be added to the response with the cache status of this response. If the normal handler is used, this directive may appear within a <DIRECTORY> or <LO-CATION> directive. If the quick handler is used, this directive must appear within a server or virtual host context, otherwise the setting will be ignored.

**HIT** The entity was fresh, and was served from cache.

**REVALIDATE** The entity was stale, was successfully revalidated and was served from cache.

**MISS** The entity was fetched from the upstream server and was not served from cache.

```
# Enable the X-Cache header
CacheHeader on

X-Cache: HIT from localhost
```

### CacheIgnoreCacheControl Directive

| | |
|---|---|
| Description: | Ignore request to not serve cached content to client |
| Syntax: | `CacheIgnoreCacheControl On\|Off` |
| Default: | `CacheIgnoreCacheControl Off` |
| Context: | server config, virtual host |
| Status: | Extension |
| Module: | mod_cache |

Ordinarily, requests containing a Cache-Control: no-cache or Pragma: no-cache header value will not be served from the cache. The CACHEIGNORECACHECONTROL directive allows this behavior to be overridden. CACHEIGNORE-CACHECONTROL ON tells the server to attempt to serve the resource from the cache even if the request contains no-cache header values.

```
CacheIgnoreCacheControl On
```

 **Warning:**

This directive will allow serving from the cache even if the client has requested that the document not be served from the cache. This might result in stale content being served.

**See also**

- CACHESTOREPRIVATE
- CACHESTORENOSTORE

### CacheIgnoreHeaders Directive

| | |
|---|---|
| Description: | Do not store the given HTTP header(s) in the cache. |
| Syntax: | `CacheIgnoreHeaders header-string [header-string] ...` |
| Default: | `CacheIgnoreHeaders None` |
| Context: | server config, virtual host |
| Status: | Extension |
| Module: | mod_cache |

According to RFC 2616, hop-by-hop HTTP headers are not stored in the cache. The following HTTP headers are hop-by-hop headers and thus do not get stored in the cache in *any* case regardless of the setting of CACHEIGNORE-HEADERS:

- `Connection`
- `Keep-Alive`
- `Proxy-Authenticate`
- `Proxy-Authorization`
- `TE`
- `Trailers`
- `Transfer-Encoding`
- `Upgrade`

CACHEIGNOREHEADERS specifies additional HTTP headers that should not to be stored in the cache. For example, it makes sense in some cases to prevent cookies from being stored in the cache.

CACHEIGNOREHEADERS takes a space separated list of HTTP headers that should not be stored in the cache. If only hop-by-hop headers not should be stored in the cache (the RFC 2616 compliant behaviour), CACHEIGNOREHEADERS can be set to None.

**Example 1**

```
CacheIgnoreHeaders Set-Cookie
```

**Example 2**

```
CacheIgnoreHeaders None
```

 **Warning:**

If headers like Expires which are needed for proper cache management are not stored due to a CACHEIGNOREHEADERS setting, the behaviour of mod_cache is undefined.

## CacheIgnoreNoLastMod Directive

| | |
|---|---|
| Description: | Ignore the fact that a response has no Last Modified header. |
| Syntax: | CacheIgnoreNoLastMod On\|Off |
| Default: | CacheIgnoreNoLastMod Off |
| Context: | server config, virtual host, directory, .htaccess |
| Status: | Extension |
| Module: | mod_cache |

Ordinarily, documents without a last-modified date are not cached. Under some circumstances the last-modified date is removed (during MOD_INCLUDE processing for example) or not provided at all. The CACHEIGNORENOLASTMOD directive provides a way to specify that documents without last-modified dates should be considered for caching, even without a last-modified date. If neither a last-modified date nor an expiry date are provided with the document then the value specified by the CACHEDEFAULTEXPIRE directive will be used to generate an expiration date.

```
CacheIgnoreNoLastMod On
```

## CacheIgnoreQueryString Directive

| | |
|---|---|
| Description: | Ignore query string when caching |
| Syntax: | CacheIgnoreQueryString On\|Off |
| Default: | CacheIgnoreQueryString Off |
| Context: | server config, virtual host |
| Status: | Extension |
| Module: | mod_cache |

Ordinarily, requests with query string parameters are cached separately for each unique query string. This is according to RFC 2616/13.9 done only if an expiration time is specified. The CACHEIGNOREQUERYSTRING directive tells the cache to cache requests even if no expiration time is specified, and to reply with a cached reply even if the query string differs. From a caching point of view the request is treated as if having no query string when this directive is enabled.

```
CacheIgnoreQueryString On
```

## CacheIgnoreURLSessionIdentifiers Directive

| | |
|---|---|
| Description: | Ignore defined session identifiers encoded in the URL when caching |
| Syntax: | `CacheIgnoreURLSessionIdentifiers identifier [identifier] ...` |
| Default: | `CacheIgnoreURLSessionIdentifiers None` |
| Context: | server config, virtual host |
| Status: | Extension |
| Module: | mod_cache |

Sometimes applications encode the session identifier into the URL like in the following Examples:

- `/someapplication/image.gif;jsessionid=123456789`

- `/someapplication/image.gif?PHPSESSIONID=12345678`

This causes cachable resources to be stored separately for each session, which is often not desired. CACHEIGNOREURLSESSIONIDENTIFIERS lets define a list of identifiers that are removed from the key that is used to identify an entity in the cache, such that cachable resources are not stored separately for each session.

`CacheIgnoreURLSessionIdentifiers None` clears the list of ignored identifiers. Otherwise, each identifier is added to the list.

### Example 1

```
CacheIgnoreURLSessionIdentifiers jsessionid
```

### Example 2

```
CacheIgnoreURLSessionIdentifiers None
```

## CacheKeyBaseURL Directive

| | |
|---|---|
| Description: | Override the base URL of reverse proxied cache keys. |
| Syntax: | `CacheKeyBaseURL URL` |
| Default: | `CacheKeyBaseURL http://example.com` |
| Context: | server config, virtual host |
| Status: | Extension |
| Module: | mod_cache |
| Compatibility: | Available in Apache 2.3.9 and later |

When the CACHEKEYBASEURL directive is specified, the URL provided will be used as the base URL to calculate the URL of the cache keys in the reverse proxy configuration. When not specified, the scheme, hostname and port of the current virtual host is used to construct the cache key. When a cluster of machines is present, and all cached entries should be cached beneath the same cache key, a new base URL can be specified with this directive.

```
# Override the base URL of the cache key.
CacheKeyBaseURL http://www.example.com/
```

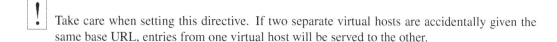 Take care when setting this directive. If two separate virtual hosts are accidentally given the same base URL, entries from one virtual host will be served to the other.

## CacheLastModifiedFactor Directive

| | |
|---|---|
| Description: | The factor used to compute an expiry date based on the LastModified date. |
| Syntax: | `CacheLastModifiedFactor float` |
| Default: | `CacheLastModifiedFactor 0.1` |
| Context: | server config, virtual host, directory, .htaccess |
| Status: | Extension |
| Module: | mod_cache |

In the event that a document does not provide an expiry date but does provide a last-modified date, an expiry date can be calculated based on the time since the document was last modified. The CACHELASTMODIFIEDFACTOR directive specifies a *factor* to be used in the generation of this expiry date according to the following formula:

```
expiry-period = time-since-last-modified-date * factor expiry-date =
current-date + expiry-period
```

For example, if the document was last modified 10 hours ago, and *factor* is 0.1 then the expiry-period will be set to 10*0.1 = 1 hour. If the current time was 3:00pm then the computed expiry-date would be 3:00pm + 1hour = 4:00pm.

If the expiry-period would be longer than that set by CACHEMAXEXPIRE, then the latter takes precedence.

```
CacheLastModifiedFactor 0.5
```

## CacheLock Directive

| | |
|---|---|
| Description: | Enable the thundering herd lock. |
| Syntax: | `CacheLock on|off` |
| Default: | `CacheLock off` |
| Context: | server config, virtual host |
| Status: | Extension |
| Module: | mod_cache |

The CACHELOCK directive enables the thundering herd lock for the given URL space.

In a minimal configuration the following directive is all that is needed to enable the thundering herd lock in the default run-time file directory.

```
# Enable cache lock
CacheLock on
```

Locks consist of empty files that only exist for stale URLs in flight, so this is significantly less resource intensive than the traditional disk cache.

## CacheLockMaxAge Directive

| | |
|---|---|
| Description: | Set the maximum possible age of a cache lock. |
| Syntax: | `CacheLockMaxAge integer` |
| Default: | `CacheLockMaxAge 5` |
| Context: | server config, virtual host |
| Status: | Extension |
| Module: | mod_cache |

The CACHELOCKMAXAGE directive specifies the maximum age of any cache lock.

A lock older than this value in seconds will be ignored, and the next incoming request will be given the opportunity to re-establish the lock. This mechanism prevents a slow client taking an excessively long time to refresh an entity.

## CacheLockPath Directive

| | |
|---|---|
| Description: | Set the lock path directory. |
| Syntax: | `CacheLockPath directory` |
| Default: | `CacheLockPath mod_cache-lock` |
| Context: | server config, virtual host |
| Status: | Extension |
| Module: | mod_cache |

The CACHELOCKPATH directive allows you to specify the directory in which the locks are created. If *directory* is not an absolute path, the location specified will be relative to the value of DEFAULTRUNTIMEDIR.

## CacheMaxExpire Directive

| | |
|---|---|
| Description: | The maximum time in seconds to cache a document |
| Syntax: | `CacheMaxExpire seconds` |
| Default: | `CacheMaxExpire 86400 (one day)` |
| Context: | server config, virtual host, directory, .htaccess |
| Status: | Extension |
| Module: | mod_cache |

The CACHEMAXEXPIRE directive specifies the maximum number of seconds for which cachable HTTP documents will be retained without checking the origin server. Thus, documents will be out of date at most this number of seconds. This maximum value is enforced even if an expiry date was supplied with the document.

```
CacheMaxExpire 604800
```

## CacheMinExpire Directive

| | |
|---|---|
| Description: | The minimum time in seconds to cache a document |
| Syntax: | `CacheMinExpire seconds` |
| Default: | `CacheMinExpire 0` |
| Context: | server config, virtual host, directory, .htaccess |
| Status: | Extension |
| Module: | mod_cache |

The CACHEMINEXPIRE directive specifies the minimum number of seconds for which cachable HTTP documents will be retained without checking the origin server. This is only used if no valid expire time was supplied with the document.

```
CacheMinExpire 3600
```

## CacheQuickHandler Directive

| | |
|---|---|
| Description: | Run the cache from the quick handler. |
| Syntax: | `CacheQuickHandler on\|off` |
| Default: | `CacheQuickHandler on` |
| Context: | server config, virtual host |
| Status: | Extension |
| Module: | mod_cache |
| Compatibility: | Apache HTTP Server 2.3.3 and later |

The CACHEQUICKHANDLER directive controls the phase in which the cache is handled.

In the default enabled configuration, the cache operates within the quick handler phase. This phase short circuits the majority of server processing, and represents the most performant mode of operation for a typical server. The cache **bolts onto** the front of the server, and the majority of server processing is avoided.

When disabled, the cache operates as a normal handler, and is subject to the full set of phases when handling a server request. While this mode is slower than the default, it allows the cache to be used in cases where full processing is required, such as when content is subject to authorization.

```
# Run cache as a normal handler
CacheQuickHandler off
```

It is also possible, when the quick handler is disabled, for the administrator to choose the precise location within the filter chain where caching is to be performed, by adding the **CACHE** filter to the chain.

```
# Cache content before mod_include and mod_deflate
CacheQuickHandler off
AddOutputFilterByType CACHE;INCLUDES;DEFLATE text/html
```

If the CACHE filter is specified more than once, the last instance will apply.


## CacheStaleOnError Directive

| | |
|---|---|
| Description: | Serve stale content in place of 5xx responses. |
| Syntax: | CacheStaleOnError on\|off |
| Default: | CacheStaleOnError on |
| Context: | server config, virtual host, directory, .htaccess |
| Status: | Extension |
| Module: | mod_cache |
| Compatibility: | Available in Apache 2.3.9 and later |

When the CACHESTALEONERROR directive is switched on, and when stale data is available in the cache, the cache will respond to 5xx responses from the backend by returning the stale data instead of the 5xx response. While the Cache-Control headers sent by clients will be respected, and the raw 5xx responses returned to the client on request, the 5xx response so returned to the client will not invalidate the content in the cache.

```
# Serve stale data on error.
CacheStaleOnError on
```


## CacheStoreExpired Directive

| | |
|---|---|
| Description: | Attempt to cache responses that the server reports as expired |
| Syntax: | CacheStoreExpired On\|Off |
| Default: | CacheStoreExpired Off |
| Context: | server config, virtual host, directory, .htaccess |
| Status: | Extension |
| Module: | mod_cache |

Since httpd 2.2.4, responses which have already expired are not stored in the cache. The CACHESTOREEXPIRED directive allows this behavior to be overridden. CACHESTOREEXPIRED On tells the server to attempt to cache the resource if it is stale. Subsequent requests would trigger an If-Modified-Since request of the origin server, and the response may be fulfilled from cache if the backend resource has not changed.

```
CacheStoreExpired On
```

## CacheStoreNoStore Directive

| | |
|---|---|
| Description: | Attempt to cache requests or responses that have been marked as no-store. |
| Syntax: | `CacheStoreNoStore On|Off` |
| Default: | `CacheStoreNoStore Off` |
| Context: | server config, virtual host, directory, .htaccess |
| Status: | Extension |
| Module: | mod_cache |

Ordinarily, requests or responses with Cache-Control: no-store header values will not be stored in the cache. The CACHESTORENOSTORE directive allows this behavior to be overridden. CACHESTORENOSTORE On tells the server to attempt to cache the resource even if it contains no-store header values.

```
CacheStoreNoStore On
```

 **Warning:**

As described in RFC 2616, the no-store directive is intended to "prevent the inadvertent release or retention of sensitive information (for example, on backup tapes)." Enabling this option could store sensitive information in the cache. You are hereby warned.

**See also**

- CACHEIGNORECACHECONTROL
- CACHESTOREPRIVATE

## CacheStorePrivate Directive

| | |
|---|---|
| Description: | Attempt to cache responses that the server has marked as private |
| Syntax: | `CacheStorePrivate On|Off` |
| Default: | `CacheStorePrivate Off` |
| Context: | server config, virtual host, directory, .htaccess |
| Status: | Extension |
| Module: | mod_cache |

Ordinarily, responses with Cache-Control: private header values will not be stored in the cache. The CACHE-STOREPRIVATE directive allows this behavior to be overridden. CACHESTOREPRIVATE On tells the server to attempt to cache the resource even if it contains private header values.

```
CacheStorePrivate On
```

 **Warning:**

This directive will allow caching even if the upstream server has requested that the resource not be cached. This directive is only ideal for a 'private' cache.

**See also**

- CACHEIGNORECACHECONTROL
- CACHESTORENOSTORE

## 10.31  Apache Module mod_cache_disk

| | |
|---|---|
| Description: | Disk based storage module for the HTTP caching filter. |
| Status: | Extension |
| ModuleIdentifier: | cache_disk_module |
| SourceFile: | mod_cache_disk.c |

### Summary

MOD_CACHE_DISK implements a disk based storage manager for MOD_CACHE.

The headers and bodies of cached responses are stored separately on disk, in a directory structure derived from the md5 hash of the cached URL.

Multiple content negotiated responses can be stored concurrently, however the caching of partial content is not yet supported by this module.

Atomic cache updates to both header and body files are achieved without the need for locking by storing the device and inode numbers of the body file within the header file. This has the side effect that cache entries manually moved into the cache will be ignored.

The htcacheclean tool is provided to list cached URLs, remove cached URLs, or to maintain the size of the disk cache within size and/or inode limits. The tool can be run on demand, or can be daemonized to offer continuous monitoring of directory sizes.

**Note:**
> MOD_CACHE_DISK requires the services of MOD_CACHE, which must be loaded before mod_cache_disk.

**Note:**
> MOD_CACHE_DISK uses the sendfile feature to serve files from the cache when supported by the platform, and when enabled with ENABLESENDFILE. However, per-directory and .htaccess configuration of ENABLESENDFILE are ignored by MOD_CACHE_DISK as the corresponding settings are not available to the module when a request is being served from the cache.

### Directives

- CacheDirLength
- CacheDirLevels
- CacheMaxFileSize
- CacheMinFileSize
- CacheReadSize
- CacheReadTime
- CacheRoot

### See also

- MOD_CACHE
- MOD_CACHE_SOCACHE
- Caching Guide (p. 43)

## CacheDirLength Directive

| | |
|---|---|
| Description: | The number of characters in subdirectory names |
| Syntax: | CacheDirLength length |
| Default: | CacheDirLength 2 |
| Context: | server config, virtual host |
| Status: | Extension |
| Module: | mod_cache_disk |

The CACHEDIRLENGTH directive sets the number of characters for each subdirectory name in the cache hierarchy. It can be used in conjunction with CACHEDIRLEVELS to determine the approximate structure of your cache hierarchy.

A high value for CACHEDIRLENGTH combined with a low value for CACHEDIRLEVELS will result in a relatively flat hierarchy, with a large number of subdirectories at each level.

⟹ The result of CACHEDIRLEVELS* CACHEDIRLENGTH must not be higher than 20.

## CacheDirLevels Directive

| | |
|---|---|
| Description: | The number of levels of subdirectories in the cache. |
| Syntax: | CacheDirLevels levels |
| Default: | CacheDirLevels 2 |
| Context: | server config, virtual host |
| Status: | Extension |
| Module: | mod_cache_disk |

The CACHEDIRLEVELS directive sets the number of subdirectory levels in the cache. Cached data will be saved this many directory levels below the CACHEROOT directory.

A high value for CACHEDIRLEVELS combined with a low value for CACHEDIRLENGTH will result in a relatively deep hierarchy, with a small number of subdirectories at each level.

⟹ The result of CACHEDIRLEVELS* CACHEDIRLENGTH must not be higher than 20.

## CacheMaxFileSize Directive

| | |
|---|---|
| Description: | The maximum size (in bytes) of a document to be placed in the cache |
| Syntax: | CacheMaxFileSize bytes |
| Default: | CacheMaxFileSize 1000000 |
| Context: | server config, virtual host, directory, .htaccess |
| Status: | Extension |
| Module: | mod_cache_disk |

The CACHEMAXFILESIZE directive sets the maximum size, in bytes, for a document to be considered for storage in the cache.

```
CacheMaxFileSize 64000
```

## CacheMinFileSize Directive

| | |
|---|---|
| Description: | The minimum size (in bytes) of a document to be placed in the cache |
| Syntax: | `CacheMinFileSize bytes` |
| Default: | `CacheMinFileSize 1` |
| Context: | server config, virtual host, directory, .htaccess |
| Status: | Extension |
| Module: | mod_cache_disk |

The CACHEMINFILESIZE directive sets the minimum size, in bytes, for a document to be considered for storage in the cache.

```
CacheMinFileSize 64
```

## CacheReadSize Directive

| | |
|---|---|
| Description: | The minimum size (in bytes) of the document to read and be cached before sending the data downstream |
| Syntax: | `CacheReadSize bytes` |
| Default: | `CacheReadSize 0` |
| Context: | server config, virtual host, directory, .htaccess |
| Status: | Extension |
| Module: | mod_cache_disk |

The CACHEREADSIZE directive sets the minimum amount of data, in bytes, to be read from the backend before the data is sent to the client. The default of zero causes all data read of any size to be passed downstream to the client immediately as it arrives. Setting this to a higher value causes the disk cache to buffer at least this amount before sending the result to the client. This can improve performance when caching content from a reverse proxy.

This directive only takes effect when the data is being saved to the cache, as opposed to data being served from the cache.

```
CacheReadSize 102400
```

## CacheReadTime Directive

| | |
|---|---|
| Description: | The minimum time (in milliseconds) that should elapse while reading before data is sent downstream |
| Syntax: | `CacheReadTime milliseconds` |
| Default: | `CacheReadTime 0` |
| Context: | server config, virtual host, directory, .htaccess |
| Status: | Extension |
| Module: | mod_cache_disk |

The CACHEREADTIME directive sets the minimum amount of elapsed time that should pass before making an attempt to send data downstream to the client. During the time period, data will be buffered before sending the result to the client. This can improve performance when caching content from a reverse proxy.

The default of zero disables this option.

This directive only takes effect when the data is being saved to the cache, as opposed to data being served from the cache. It is recommended that this option be used alongside the CACHEREADSIZE directive to ensure that the server does not buffer excessively should data arrive faster than expected.

```
CacheReadTime 1000
```

**CacheRoot Directive**

| | |
|---|---|
| Description: | The directory root under which cache files are stored |
| Syntax: | `CacheRoot directory` |
| Context: | server config, virtual host |
| Status: | Extension |
| Module: | mod_cache_disk |

The CACHEROOT directive defines the name of the directory on the disk to contain cache files.  If the
MOD_CACHE_DISK module has been loaded or compiled in to the Apache server, this directive *must* be defined. Failing to provide a value for CACHEROOT will result in a configuration file processing error. The CACHEDIRLEVELS
and CACHEDIRLENGTH directives define the structure of the directories under the specified root directory.

```
CacheRoot c:/cacheroot
```

## 10.32    Apache Module mod_cache_socache

| | |
|---|---|
| Description: | Shared object cache (socache) based storage module for the HTTP caching filter. |
| Status: | Extension |
| ModuleIdentifier: | cache_socache_module |
| SourceFile: | mod_cache_socache.c |

### Summary

MOD_CACHE_SOCACHE implements a shared object cache (socache) based storage manager for MOD_CACHE.

The headers and bodies of cached responses are combined, and stored underneath a single key in the shared object cache. A number of implementations (p. 114) of shared object caches are available to choose from.

Multiple content negotiated responses can be stored concurrently, however the caching of partial content is not yet supported by this module.

```
# Turn on caching
CacheSocache shmcb
CacheSocacheMaxSize 102400
<Location "/foo">
    CacheEnable socache
</Location>

# Fall back to the disk cache
CacheSocache shmcb
CacheSocacheMaxSize 102400
<Location "/foo">
    CacheEnable socache
    CacheEnable disk
</Location>
```

Note:

MOD_CACHE_SOCACHE requires the services of MOD_CACHE, which must be loaded before mod_cache_socache.

### Directives

- CacheSocache
- CacheSocacheMaxSize
- CacheSocacheMaxTime
- CacheSocacheMinTime
- CacheSocacheReadSize
- CacheSocacheReadTime

### See also

- MOD_CACHE
- MOD_CACHE_DISK
- Caching Guide (p. 43)

## CacheSocache Directive

| Description: | The shared object cache implementation to use |
|---|---|
| Syntax: | `CacheSocache type[:args]` |
| Context: | server config, virtual host |
| Status: | Extension |
| Module: | mod_cache_socache |
| Compatibility: | Available in Apache 2.4.5 and later |

The CACHESOCACHE directive defines the name of the shared object cache implementation to use, followed by optional arguments for that implementation. A number of implementations (p. 114) of shared object caches are available to choose from.

```
CacheSocache shmcb
```

## CacheSocacheMaxSize Directive

| Description: | The maximum size (in bytes) of an entry to be placed in the cache |
|---|---|
| Syntax: | `CacheSocacheMaxSize bytes` |
| Default: | `CacheSocacheMaxSize 102400` |
| Context: | server config, virtual host, directory, .htaccess |
| Status: | Extension |
| Module: | mod_cache_socache |
| Compatibility: | Available in Apache 2.4.5 and later |

The CACHESOCACHEMAXSIZE directive sets the maximum size, in bytes, for the combined headers and body of a document to be considered for storage in the cache. The larger the headers that are stored alongside the body, the smaller the body may be.

The MOD_CACHE_SOCACHE module will only attempt to cache responses that have an explicit content length, or that are small enough to be written in one pass. This is done to allow the MOD_CACHE_DISK module to have an opportunity to cache responses larger than those cacheable within MOD_CACHE_SOCACHE.

```
CacheSocacheMaxSize 102400
```

## CacheSocacheMaxTime Directive

| Description: | The maximum time (in seconds) for a document to be placed in the cache |
|---|---|
| Syntax: | `CacheSocacheMaxTime seconds` |
| Default: | `CacheSocacheMaxTime 86400` |
| Context: | server config, virtual host, directory, .htaccess |
| Status: | Extension |
| Module: | mod_cache_socache |
| Compatibility: | Available in Apache 2.4.5 and later |

The CACHESOCACHEMAXTIME directive sets the maximum freshness lifetime, in seconds, for a document to be stored in the cache. This value overrides the freshness lifetime defined for the document by the HTTP protocol.

```
CacheSocacheMaxTime 86400
```

## CacheSocacheMinTime Directive

| | |
|---|---|
| Description: | The minimum time (in seconds) for a document to be placed in the cache |
| Syntax: | `CacheSocacheMinTime seconds` |
| Default: | `CacheSocacheMinTime 600` |
| Context: | server config, virtual host, directory, .htaccess |
| Status: | Extension |
| Module: | mod_cache_socache |
| Compatibility: | Available in Apache 2.4.5 and later |

The CACHESOCACHEMINTIME directive sets the amount of seconds beyond the freshness lifetime of the response that the response should be cached for in the shared object cache. If a response is only stored for its freshness lifetime, there will be no opportunity to revalidate the response to make it fresh again.

```
CacheSocacheMinTime 600
```

## CacheSocacheReadSize Directive

| | |
|---|---|
| Description: | The minimum size (in bytes) of the document to read and be cached before sending the data downstream |
| Syntax: | `CacheSocacheReadSize bytes` |
| Default: | `CacheSocacheReadSize 0` |
| Context: | server config, virtual host, directory, .htaccess |
| Status: | Extension |
| Module: | mod_cache_socache |
| Compatibility: | Available in Apache 2.4.5 and later |

The CACHESOCACHEREADSIZE directive sets the minimum amount of data, in bytes, to be read from the backend before the data is sent to the client. The default of zero causes all data read of any size to be passed downstream to the client immediately as it arrives. Setting this to a higher value causes the disk cache to buffer at least this amount before sending the result to the client. This can improve performance when caching content from a slow reverse proxy.

This directive only takes effect when the data is being saved to the cache, as opposed to data being served from the cache.

```
CacheReadSize 102400
```

## CacheSocacheReadTime Directive

| | |
|---|---|
| Description: | The minimum time (in milliseconds) that should elapse while reading before data is sent downstream |
| Syntax: | `CacheSocacheReadTime milliseconds` |
| Default: | `CacheSocacheReadTime 0` |
| Context: | server config, virtual host, directory, .htaccess |
| Status: | Extension |
| Module: | mod_cache_socache |
| Compatibility: | Available in Apache 2.4.5 and later |

The CACHESOCACHEREADTIME directive sets the minimum amount of elapsed time that should pass before making an attempt to send data downstream to the client. During the time period, data will be buffered before sending the result to the client. This can improve performance when caching content from a reverse proxy.

The default of zero disables this option.

This directive only takes effect when the data is being saved to the cache, as opposed to data being served from the cache. It is recommended that this option be used alongside the CACHESOCACHEREADSIZE directive to ensure that the server does not buffer excessively should data arrive faster than expected.

```
CacheSocacheReadTime 1000
```

# 10.33   Apache Module mod_cern_meta

| Description: | CERN httpd metafile semantics |
|---|---|
| Status: | Extension |
| ModuleIdentifier: | cern_meta_module |
| SourceFile: | mod_cern_meta.c |

## Summary

Emulate the CERN HTTPD Meta file semantics. Meta files are HTTP headers that can be output in addition to the normal range of headers for each file accessed. They appear rather like the Apache .asis files, and are able to provide a crude way of influencing the Expires: header, as well as providing other curiosities. There are many ways to manage meta information, this one was chosen because there is already a large number of CERN users who can exploit this module.

More information on the CERN metafile semantics[20] is available.

### Directives

- MetaDir
- MetaFiles
- MetaSuffix

### See also

- MOD_HEADERS
- MOD_ASIS

## MetaDir Directive

| Description: | Name of the directory to find CERN-style meta information files |
|---|---|
| Syntax: | `MetaDir directory` |
| Default: | `MetaDir .web` |
| Context: | server config, virtual host, directory, .htaccess |
| Override: | Indexes |
| Status: | Extension |
| Module: | mod_cern_meta |

Specifies the name of the directory in which Apache can find meta information files. The directory is usually a 'hidden' subdirectory of the directory that contains the file being accessed. Set to " . " to look in the same directory as the file:

```
MetaDir .
```

Or, to set it to a subdirectory of the directory containing the files:

```
MetaDir .meta
```

---

[20]http://www.w3.org/pub/WWW/Daemon/User/Config/General.html#MetaDir

## MetaFiles Directive

| Description: | Activates CERN meta-file processing |
|---|---|
| Syntax: | `MetaFiles on\|off` |
| Default: | `MetaFiles off` |
| Context: | server config, virtual host, directory, .htaccess |
| Override: | Indexes |
| Status: | Extension |
| Module: | mod_cern_meta |

Turns on/off Meta file processing on a per-directory basis.

## MetaSuffix Directive

| Description: | File name suffix for the file containing CERN-style meta information |
|---|---|
| Syntax: | `MetaSuffix suffix` |
| Default: | `MetaSuffix .meta` |
| Context: | server config, virtual host, directory, .htaccess |
| Override: | Indexes |
| Status: | Extension |
| Module: | mod_cern_meta |

Specifies the file name suffix for the file containing the meta information. For example, the default values for the two directives will cause a request to `DOCUMENT_ROOT/somedir/index.html` to look in `DOCUMENT_ROOT/somedir/.web/index.html.meta` and will use its contents to generate additional MIME header information.

### Example:

```
MetaSuffix .meta
```

## 10.34   Apache Module mod_cgi

| Description: | Execution of CGI scripts |
|---|---|
| Status: | Base |
| ModuleIdentifier: | cgi_module |
| SourceFile: | mod_cgi.c |

## Summary

Any file that has the handler `cgi-script` will be treated as a CGI script, and run by the server, with its output being returned to the client. Files acquire this handler either by having a name containing an extension defined by the ADDHANDLER directive, or by being in a SCRIPTALIAS directory.

For an introduction to using CGI scripts with Apache, see our tutorial on Dynamic Content With CGI (p. 236) .

When using a multi-threaded MPM under unix, the module MOD_CGID should be used in place of this module. At the user level, the two modules are essentially identical.

For backward-compatibility, the cgi-script handler will also be activated for any file with the mime-type `application/x-httpd-cgi`. The use of the magic mime-type is deprecated.

### Directives

- ScriptLog
- ScriptLogBuffer
- ScriptLogLength

### See also

- ACCEPTPATHINFO
- OPTIONS ExecCGI
- SCRIPTALIAS
- ADDHANDLER
- Running CGI programs under different user IDs (p. 115)
- CGI Specification[21]

## CGI Environment variables

The server will set the CGI environment variables as described in the CGI specification[22], with the following provisions:

**PATH_INFO** This will not be available if the ACCEPTPATHINFO directive is explicitly set to `off`. The default behavior, if ACCEPTPATHINFO is not given, is that MOD_CGI will accept path info (trailing `/more/path/info` following the script filename in the URI), while the core server will return a 404 NOT FOUND error for requests with additional path info. Omitting the ACCEPTPATHINFO directive has the same effect as setting it `On` for MOD_CGI requests.

**REMOTE_HOST** This will only be set if HOSTNAMELOOKUPS is set to `on` (it is off by default), and if a reverse DNS lookup of the accessing host's address indeed finds a host name.

[21]http://www.ietf.org/rfc/rfc3875
[22]http://www.ietf.org/rfc/rfc3875

**REMOTE_IDENT** This will only be set if IDENTITYCHECK is set to on and the accessing host supports the ident protocol. Note that the contents of this variable cannot be relied upon because it can easily be faked, and if there is a proxy between the client and the server, it is usually totally useless.

**REMOTE_USER** This will only be set if the CGI script is subject to authentication.

This module also leverages the core functions ap_add_common_vars[23] and ap_add_cgi_vars[24] to add environment variables like:

**DOCUMENT_ROOT** Set with the content of the related DOCUMENTROOT directive.

**SERVER_NAME** The fully qualified domain name related to the request.

**SERVER_ADDR** The IP address of the Virtual Host serving the request.

**SERVER_ADMIN** Set with the content of the related SERVERADMIN directive.

For an exhaustive list it is suggested to write a basic CGI script that dumps all the environment variables passed by Apache in a convenient format.

## CGI Debugging

Debugging CGI scripts has traditionally been difficult, mainly because it has not been possible to study the output (standard output and error) for scripts which are failing to run properly. These directives provide more detailed logging of errors when they occur.

### CGI Logfile Format

When configured, the CGI error log logs any CGI which does not execute properly. Each CGI script which fails to operate causes several lines of information to be logged. The first two lines are always of the format:

```
%% [time] request-line
%% HTTP-status CGI-script-filename
```

If the error is that CGI script cannot be run, the log file will contain an extra two lines:

```
%%error
error-message
```

Alternatively, if the error is the result of the script returning incorrect header information (often due to a bug in the script), the following information is logged:

```
%request
All HTTP request headers received
POST or PUT entity (if any)
%response
All headers output by the CGI script
%stdout
CGI standard output
%stderr
CGI standard error
```

---

[23]https://ci.apache.org/projects/httpd/trunk/doxygen/group__APACHE__CORE__SCRIPT.html#ga0e81f9571a8a73f5da0e89e1f46d34b1
[24]https://ci.apache.org/projects/httpd/trunk/doxygen/group__APACHE__CORE__SCRIPT.html#ga6b975cd7ff27a338cb8752381a4cc14f

(The %stdout and %stderr parts may be missing if the script did not output anything on standard output or standard error).

## ScriptLog Directive

| | |
|---|---|
| Description: | Location of the CGI script error logfile |
| Syntax: | `ScriptLog file-path` |
| Context: | server config, virtual host |
| Status: | Base |
| Module: | MOD_CGI, MOD_CGID |

The SCRIPTLOG directive sets the CGI script error logfile. If no SCRIPTLOG is given, no error log is created. If given, any CGI errors are logged into the filename given as argument. If this is a relative file or path it is taken relative to the SERVERROOT.

### Example

```
ScriptLog logs/cgi_log
```

This log will be opened as the user the child processes run as, *i.e.* the user specified in the main USER directive. This means that either the directory the script log is in needs to be writable by that user or the file needs to be manually created and set to be writable by that user. If you place the script log in your main logs directory, do **NOT** change the directory permissions to make it writable by the user the child processes run as.

Note that script logging is meant to be a debugging feature when writing CGI scripts, and is not meant to be activated continuously on running servers. It is not optimized for speed or efficiency, and may have security problems if used in a manner other than that for which it was designed.

## ScriptLogBuffer Directive

| | |
|---|---|
| Description: | Maximum amount of PUT or POST requests that will be recorded in the scriptlog |
| Syntax: | `ScriptLogBuffer bytes` |
| Default: | `ScriptLogBuffer 1024` |
| Context: | server config, virtual host |
| Status: | Base |
| Module: | MOD_CGI, MOD_CGID |

The size of any PUT or POST entity body that is logged to the file is limited, to prevent the log file growing too big too quickly if large bodies are being received. By default, up to 1024 bytes are logged, but this can be changed with this directive.

## ScriptLogLength Directive

| | |
|---|---|
| Description: | Size limit of the CGI script logfile |
| Syntax: | `ScriptLogLength bytes` |
| Default: | `ScriptLogLength 10385760` |
| Context: | server config, virtual host |
| Status: | Base |
| Module: | MOD_CGI, MOD_CGID |

SCRIPTLOGLENGTH can be used to limit the size of the CGI script logfile. Since the logfile logs a lot of information per CGI error (all request headers, all script output) it can grow to be a big file. To prevent problems due to unbounded growth, this directive can be used to set an maximum file-size for the CGI logfile. If the file exceeds this size, no more information will be written to it.

# 10.35 Apache Module mod_cgid

| | |
|---|---|
| Description: | Execution of CGI scripts using an external CGI daemon |
| Status: | Base |
| ModuleIdentifier: | cgid_module |
| SourceFile: | mod_cgid.c |
| Compatibility: | Unix threaded MPMs only |

## Summary

Except for the optimizations and the additional SCRIPTSOCK directive noted below, MOD_CGID behaves similarly to MOD_CGI. **See the MOD_CGI summary for additional details about Apache and CGI.**

On certain unix operating systems, forking a process from a multi-threaded server is a very expensive operation because the new process will replicate all the threads of the parent process. In order to avoid incurring this expense on each CGI invocation, MOD_CGID creates an external daemon that is responsible for forking child processes to run CGI scripts. The main server communicates with this daemon using a unix domain socket.

This module is used by default instead of MOD_CGI whenever a multi-threaded MPM is selected during the compilation process. At the user level, this module is identical in configuration and operation to MOD_CGI. The only exception is the additional directive ScriptSock which gives the name of the socket to use for communication with the cgi daemon.

### Directives

- CGIDScriptTimeout
- ScriptLog (p. 582)
- ScriptLogBuffer (p. 582)
- ScriptLogLength (p. 582)
- ScriptSock

### See also

- MOD_CGI
- Running CGI programs under different user IDs (p. 115)

## CGIDScriptTimeout Directive

| | |
|---|---|
| Description: | The length of time to wait for more output from the CGI program |
| Syntax: | CGIDScriptTimeout time[s\|ms] |
| Default: | value of TIMEOUT directive when unset |
| Context: | server config, virtual host, directory, .htaccess |
| Status: | Base |
| Module: | mod_cgid |
| Compatibility: | CGIDScriptTimeout defaults to zero in releases 2.4 and earlier |

This directive limits the length of time to wait for more output from the CGI program. If the time is exceeded, the request and CGI are terminated.

### Example

```
CGIDScriptTimeout 20
```

## ScriptSock Directive

| | |
|---|---|
| Description: | The filename prefix of the socket to use for communication with the cgi daemon |
| Syntax: | `ScriptSock file-path` |
| Default: | `ScriptSock cgisock` |
| Context: | server config |
| Status: | Base |
| Module: | mod_cgid |

This directive sets the filename prefix of the socket to use for communication with the CGI daemon, an extension corresponding to the process ID of the server will be appended. The socket will be opened using the permissions of the user who starts Apache (usually root). To maintain the security of communications with CGI scripts, it is important that no other user has permission to write in the directory where the socket is located.

If *file-path* is not an absolute path, the location specified will be relative to the value of DEFAULTRUNTIMEDIR.

### Example

```
ScriptSock /var/run/cgid.sock
```

# 10.36 Apache Module mod_charset_lite

| | |
|---|---|
| Description: | Specify character set translation or recoding |
| Status: | Extension |
| ModuleIdentifier: | charset_lite_module |
| SourceFile: | mod_charset_lite.c |

## Summary

MOD_CHARSET_LITE allows the server to change the character set of responses before sending them to the client. In an EBCDIC environment, Apache always translates HTTP protocol content (e.g. response headers) from the code page of the Apache process locale to ISO-8859-1, but not the body of responses. In any environment, MOD_CHARSET_LITE can be used to specify that response bodies should be translated. For example, if files are stored in EBCDIC, then MOD_CHARSET_LITE can translate them to ISO-8859-1 before sending them to the client.

This module provides a small subset of configuration mechanisms implemented by Russian Apache and its associated mod_charset.

### Directives

- CharsetDefault
- CharsetOptions
- CharsetSourceEnc

## Common Problems

### Invalid character set names

The character set name parameters of CHARSETSOURCEENC and CHARSETDEFAULT must be acceptable to the translation mechanism used by APR on the system where MOD_CHARSET_LITE is deployed. These character set names are not standardized and are usually not the same as the corresponding values used in http headers. Currently, APR can only use iconv(3), so you can easily test your character set names using the iconv(1) program, as follows:

```
iconv -f charsetsourceenc-value -t charsetdefault-value
```

### Mismatch between character set of content and translation rules

If the translation rules don't make sense for the content, translation can fail in various ways, including:

- The translation mechanism may return a bad return code, and the connection will be aborted.
- The translation mechanism may silently place special characters (e.g., question marks) in the output buffer when it cannot translate the input buffer.

## CharsetDefault Directive

| | |
|---|---|
| Description: | Charset to translate into |
| Syntax: | `CharsetDefault charset` |
| Context: | server config, virtual host, directory, .htaccess |
| Override: | FileInfo |
| Status: | Extension |
| Module: | mod_charset_lite |

The CHARSETDEFAULT directive specifies the charset that content in the associated container should be translated to.

The value of the *charset* argument must be accepted as a valid character set name by the character set support in APR. Generally, this means that it must be supported by iconv.

### Example

```
<Directory "/export/home/trawick/apacheinst/htdocs/convert">
    CharsetSourceEnc  UTF-16BE
    CharsetDefault    ISO-8859-1
</Directory>
```

Specifying the same charset for both CHARSETSOURCEENC and CHARSETDEFAULT disables translation. The charset need not match the charset of the response, but it must be a valid charset on the system.

## CharsetOptions Directive

| | |
|---|---|
| Description: | Configures charset translation behavior |
| Syntax: | `CharsetOptions option [option] ...` |
| Default: | `CharsetOptions ImplicitAdd` |
| Context: | server config, virtual host, directory, .htaccess |
| Override: | FileInfo |
| Status: | Extension |
| Module: | mod_charset_lite |

The CHARSETOPTIONS directive configures certain behaviors of MOD_CHARSET_LITE. *Option* can be one of

**ImplicitAdd | NoImplicitAdd** The `ImplicitAdd` keyword specifies that MOD_CHARSET_LITE should implicitly insert its filter when the configuration specifies that the character set of content should be translated. If the filter chain is explicitly configured using the ADDOUTPUTFILTER directive, `NoImplicitAdd` should be specified so that MOD_CHARSET_LITE doesn't add its filter.

**TranslateAllMimeTypes | NoTranslateAllMimeTypes** Normally, MOD_CHARSET_LITE will only perform translation on a small subset of possible mimetypes. When the `TranslateAllMimeTypes` keyword is specified for a given configuration section, translation is performed without regard for mimetype.

## CharsetSourceEnc Directive

| | |
|---|---|
| Description: | Source charset of files |
| Syntax: | `CharsetSourceEnc charset` |
| Context: | server config, virtual host, directory, .htaccess |
| Override: | FileInfo |
| Status: | Extension |
| Module: | mod_charset_lite |

The CHARSETSOURCEENC directive specifies the source charset of files in the associated container.

The value of the *charset* argument must be accepted as a valid character set name by the character set support in APR. Generally, this means that it must be supported by iconv.

**Example**

```
<Directory "/export/home/trawick/apacheinst/htdocs/convert">
    CharsetSourceEnc  UTF-16BE
    CharsetDefault    ISO-8859-1
</Directory>
```

The character set names in this example work with the iconv translation support in Solaris 8.

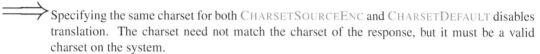 Specifying the same charset for both CHARSETSOURCEENC and CHARSETDEFAULT disables translation. The charset need not match the charset of the response, but it must be a valid charset on the system.

# 10.37   Apache Module mod_data

| | |
|---|---|
| Description: | Convert response body into an RFC2397 data URL |
| Status: | Extension |
| ModuleIdentifier: | data_module |
| SourceFile: | mod_data.c |
| Compatibility: | Available in Apache 2.3 and later |

## Summary

This module provides the ability to convert a response into an RFC2397 data URL[25].

Data URLs can be embedded inline within web pages using something like the MOD_INCLUDE module, to remove the need for clients to make separate connections to fetch what may potentially be many small images. Data URLs may also be included into pages generated by scripting languages such as PHP.

---

**An example of a data URL**

```
data:image/gif;base64,R0lGODdhMAAwAPAAAAAAAP///ywAAAAAMAAw
AAAC8IyPqcvt3wCcDkiLc7C0qwyGHhSWpjQu5yqmCYsapyuvUUlvONmOZtfzgFz
ByTB10QgxOR0TqBQejhRNzOfkVJ+5YiUqrXF5Y5lKh/DeuNcP5yLWGsEbtLiOSp
a/TPg7JpJHxyendzWTBfX0cxOnKPjgBzi4diinWGdkF8kjdfnycQZXZeYGejmJl
ZeGl9i2icVqaNVailT6F5iJ90m6mvuTS4OK05M0vDk0Q4XUtwvKOzrcd3iq9uis
F81M1OIcR7lEewwcLp7tuNNkM3uNna3F2JQFo97Vriy/Xl4/f1cf5VWzXyym7PH
hhx4dbgYKAAA7
```

---

The filter takes no parameters, and can be added to the filter stack using the SETOUTPUTFILTER directive, or any of the directives supported by the MOD_FILTER module.

### Configuring the filter

```
<Location "/data/images">
    SetOutputFilter DATA
</Location>
```

**Directives** This module provides no directives.

**See also**

- Filters (p. 110)

---

[25]http://tools.ietf.org/html/rfc2397

# 10.38 Apache Module mod_dav

| | |
|---|---|
| Description: | Distributed Authoring and Versioning (WebDAV[26]) functionality |
| Status: | Extension |
| ModuleIdentifier: | dav_module |
| SourceFile: | mod_dav.c |

## Summary

This module provides class 1 and class 2 WebDAV[27] ('Web-based Distributed Authoring and Versioning') functionality for Apache. This extension to the HTTP protocol allows creating, moving, copying, and deleting resources and collections on a remote web server.

### Directives

- Dav
- DavDepthInfinity
- DavMinTimeout

### See also

- DAVLOCKDB
- LIMITXMLREQUESTBODY
- WebDAV Resources[28]

## Enabling WebDAV

To enable MOD_DAV, add the following to a container in your `httpd.conf` file:

```
Dav On
```

This enables the DAV file system provider, which is implemented by the MOD_DAV_FS module. Therefore, that module must be compiled into the server or loaded at runtime using the LOADMODULE directive.

In addition, a location for the DAV lock database must be specified in the global section of your `httpd.conf` file using the DAVLOCKDB directive:

```
DavLockDB "/usr/local/apache2/var/DavLock"
```

The directory containing the lock database file must be writable by the USER and GROUP under which Apache is running.

You may wish to add a <LIMIT> clause inside the <LOCATION> directive to limit access to DAV-enabled locations. If you want to set the maximum amount of bytes that a DAV client can send at one request, you have to use the LIMITXMLREQUESTBODY directive. The "normal" LIMITREQUESTBODY directive has no effect on DAV requests.

---

[27]http://www.webdav.org
[28]http://www.webdav.org

**Full Example**

```
DavLockDB "/usr/local/apache2/var/DavLock"

<Directory "/usr/local/apache2/htdocs/foo">
    Require all granted
    Dav On

    AuthType Basic
    AuthName "DAV"
    AuthUserFile "user.passwd"

    <LimitExcept GET POST OPTIONS>
        Require user admin
    </LimitExcept>
</Directory>
```

## Security Issues

Since DAV access methods allow remote clients to manipulate files on the server, you must take particular care to assure that your server is secure before enabling MOD_DAV.

Any location on the server where DAV is enabled should be protected by authentication. The use of HTTP Basic Authentication is not recommended. You should use at least HTTP Digest Authentication, which is provided by the MOD_AUTH_DIGEST module. Nearly all WebDAV clients support this authentication method. An alternative is Basic Authentication over an SSL (p. 192) enabled connection.

In order for MOD_DAV to manage files, it must be able to write to the directories and files under its control using the USER and GROUP under which Apache is running. New files created will also be owned by this USER and GROUP. For this reason, it is important to control access to this account. The DAV repository is considered private to Apache; modifying files outside of Apache (for example using FTP or filesystem-level tools) should not be allowed.

MOD_DAV may be subject to various kinds of denial-of-service attacks. The LIMITXMLREQUESTBODY directive can be used to limit the amount of memory consumed in parsing large DAV requests. The DAVDEPTHINFINITY directive can be used to prevent PROPFIND requests on a very large repository from consuming large amounts of memory. Another possible denial-of-service attack involves a client simply filling up all available disk space with many large files. There is no direct way to prevent this in Apache, so you should avoid giving DAV access to untrusted users.

## Complex Configurations

One common request is to use MOD_DAV to manipulate dynamic files (PHP scripts, CGI scripts, etc). This is difficult because a GET request will always run the script, rather than downloading its contents. One way to avoid this is to map two different URLs to the content, one of which will run the script, and one of which will allow it to be downloaded and manipulated with DAV.

```
Alias "/phparea" "/home/gstein/php_files"
Alias "/php-source" "/home/gstein/php_files"
<Location "/php-source">
    Dav On
    ForceType text/plain
</Location>
```

With this setup, `http://example.com/phparea` can be used to access the output of the PHP scripts, and `http://example.com/php-source` can be used with a DAV client to manipulate them.

## Dav Directive

| | |
|---|---|
| Description: | Enable WebDAV HTTP methods |
| Syntax: | `Dav On\|Off\|provider-name` |
| Default: | `Dav Off` |
| Context: | directory |
| Status: | Extension |
| Module: | mod_dav |

Use the DAV directive to enable the WebDAV HTTP methods for the given container:

```
<Location "/foo">
    Dav On
</Location>
```

The value `On` is actually an alias for the default provider `filesystem` which is served by the MOD_DAV_FS module. Note, that once you have DAV enabled for some location, it *cannot* be disabled for sublocations. For a complete configuration example have a look at the section above.

 Do not enable WebDAV until you have secured your server. Otherwise everyone will be able to distribute files on your system.

## DavDepthInfinity Directive

| | |
|---|---|
| Description: | Allow PROPFIND, Depth: Infinity requests |
| Syntax: | `DavDepthInfinity on\|off` |
| Default: | `DavDepthInfinity off` |
| Context: | server config, virtual host, directory |
| Status: | Extension |
| Module: | mod_dav |

Use the DAVDEPTHINFINITY directive to allow the processing of PROPFIND requests containing the header 'Depth: Infinity'. Because this type of request could constitute a denial-of-service attack, by default it is not allowed.

## DavMinTimeout Directive

| | |
|---|---|
| Description: | Minimum amount of time the server holds a lock on a DAV resource |
| Syntax: | `DavMinTimeout seconds` |
| Default: | `DavMinTimeout 0` |
| Context: | server config, virtual host, directory |
| Status: | Extension |
| Module: | mod_dav |

When a client requests a DAV resource lock, it can also specify a time when the lock will be automatically removed by the server. This value is only a request, and the server can ignore it or inform the client of an arbitrary value.

Use the DAVMINTIMEOUT directive to specify, in seconds, the minimum lock timeout to return to a client. Microsoft Web Folders defaults to a timeout of 120 seconds; the DAVMINTIMEOUT can override this to a higher value (like 600 seconds) to reduce the chance of the client losing the lock due to network latency.

### Example

```
<Location "/MSWord">
    DavMinTimeout 600
</Location>
```

## 10.39   Apache Module mod_dav_fs

| | |
|---|---|
| Description: | Filesystem provider for MOD_DAV |
| Status: | Extension |
| ModuleIdentifier: | dav_fs_module |
| SourceFile: | mod_dav_fs.c |

### Summary

This module *requires* the service of MOD_DAV. It acts as a support module for MOD_DAV and provides access to resources located in the server's file system. The formal name of this provider is `filesystem`. MOD_DAV backend providers will be invoked by using the DAV directive:

#### Example

```
Dav filesystem
```

Since `filesystem` is the default provider for MOD_DAV, you may simply use the value `On` instead.

### Directives

- DavLockDB

### See also

- MOD_DAV

### DavLockDB Directive

| | |
|---|---|
| Description: | Location of the DAV lock database |
| Syntax: | `DavLockDB file-path` |
| Context: | server config, virtual host |
| Status: | Extension |
| Module: | mod_dav_fs |

Use the DAVLOCKDB directive to specify the full path to the lock database, excluding an extension. If the path is not absolute, it will be taken relative to SERVERROOT. The implementation of MOD_DAV_FS uses a SDBM database to track user locks.

#### Example

```
DavLockDB var/DavLock
```

The directory containing the lock database file must be writable by the USER and GROUP under which Apache is running. For security reasons, you should create a directory for this purpose rather than changing the permissions on an existing directory. In the above example, Apache will create files in the `var/` directory under the SERVERROOT with the base filename `DavLock` and extension name chosen by the server.

# 10.40 Apache Module mod_dav_lock

| | |
|---|---|
| Description: | Generic locking module for MOD_DAV |
| Status: | Extension |
| ModuleIdentifier: | dav_lock_module |
| SourceFile: | mod_dav_lock.c |

## Summary

This module implements a generic locking API which can be used by any backend provider of MOD_DAV. It *requires* at least the service of MOD_DAV. But without a backend provider which makes use of it, it's useless and should not be loaded into the server. A sample backend module which actually utilizes MOD_DAV_LOCK is mod_dav_svn[29], the subversion provider module.

Note that MOD_DAV_FS does *not* need this generic locking module, because it uses its own more specialized version.

In order to make MOD_DAV_LOCK functional, you just have to specify the location of the lock database using the DAVGENERICLOCKDB directive described below.

Developer's Note

> In order to retrieve the pointer to the locking provider function, you have to use the `ap_lookup_provider` API with the arguments `dav-lock`, `generic`, and `0`.

### Directives

* DavGenericLockDB

### See also

* MOD_DAV

## DavGenericLockDB Directive

| | |
|---|---|
| Description: | Location of the DAV lock database |
| Syntax: | `DavGenericLockDB file-path` |
| Context: | server config, virtual host, directory |
| Status: | Extension |
| Module: | mod_dav_lock |

Use the DAVGENERICLOCKDB directive to specify the full path to the lock database, excluding an extension. If the path is not absolute, it will be interpreted relative to SERVERROOT. The implementation of MOD_DAV_LOCK uses a SDBM database to track user locks.

#### Example

```
DavGenericLockDB var/DavLock
```

The directory containing the lock database file must be writable by the USER and GROUP under which Apache is running. For security reasons, you should create a directory for this purpose rather than changing the permissions on an existing directory. In the above example, Apache will create files in the `var/` directory under the SERVERROOT with the base filename `DavLock` and an extension added by the server.

---

[29]http://subversion.apache.org/

# 10.41   Apache Module mod_dbd

| | |
|---|---|
| Description: | Manages SQL database connections |
| Status: | Extension |
| ModuleIdentifier: | dbd_module |
| SourceFile: | mod_dbd.c |

## Summary

MOD_DBD manages SQL database connections using APR. It provides database connections on request to modules requiring SQL database functions, and takes care of managing databases with optimal efficiency and scalability for both threaded and non-threaded MPMs. For details, see the APR[30] website and this overview of the Apache DBD Framework[31] by its original developer.

**Directives**

- DBDExptime
- DBDInitSQL
- DBDKeep
- DBDMax
- DBDMin
- DBDParams
- DBDPersist
- DBDPrepareSQL
- DBDriver

**See also**

- Password Formats (p. 371)

## Connection Pooling

This module manages database connections, in a manner optimised for the platform. On non-threaded platforms, it provides a persistent connection in the manner of classic LAMP (Linux, Apache, Mysql, Perl/PHP/Python). On threaded platform, it provides an altogether more scalable and efficient *connection pool*, as described in this article at ApacheTutor[32]. Note that MOD_DBD supersedes the modules presented in that article.

## Apache DBD API

MOD_DBD exports five functions for other modules to use. The API is as follows:

```
typedef struct {
    apr_dbd_t *handle;
    apr_dbd_driver_t *driver;
    apr_hash_t *prepared;
```

---

[30]http://apr.apache.org/
[31]http://people.apache.org/~niq/dbd.html
[32]http://www.apachetutor.org/dev/reslist

```
} ap_dbd_t;

/* Export functions to access the database */

/* acquire a connection that MUST be explicitly closed.
 * Returns NULL on error
 */
AP_DECLARE(ap_dbd_t*) ap_dbd_open(apr_pool_t*, server_rec*);

/* release a connection acquired with ap_dbd_open */
AP_DECLARE(void) ap_dbd_close(server_rec*, ap_dbd_t*);

/* acquire a connection that will have the lifetime of a request
 * and MUST NOT be explicitly closed.  Return NULL on error.
 * This is the preferred function for most applications.
 */
AP_DECLARE(ap_dbd_t*) ap_dbd_acquire(request_rec*);

/* acquire a connection that will have the lifetime of a connection
 * and MUST NOT be explicitly closed.  Return NULL on error.
 */
AP_DECLARE(ap_dbd_t*) ap_dbd_cacquire(conn_rec*);

/* Prepare a statement for use by a client module */
AP_DECLARE(void) ap_dbd_prepare(server_rec*, const char*, const char*);

/* Also export them as optional functions for modules that prefer it */
APR_DECLARE_OPTIONAL_FN(ap_dbd_t*, ap_dbd_open, (apr_pool_t*, server_rec*));
APR_DECLARE_OPTIONAL_FN(void, ap_dbd_close, (server_rec*, ap_dbd_t*));
APR_DECLARE_OPTIONAL_FN(ap_dbd_t*, ap_dbd_acquire, (request_rec*));
APR_DECLARE_OPTIONAL_FN(ap_dbd_t*, ap_dbd_cacquire, (conn_rec*));
APR_DECLARE_OPTIONAL_FN(void, ap_dbd_prepare, (server_rec*, const char*, const char*
```

## SQL Prepared Statements

MOD_DBD supports SQL prepared statements on behalf of modules that may wish to use them. Each prepared statement must be assigned a name (label), and they are stored in a hash: the `prepared` field of an `ap_dbd_t`. Hash entries are of type `apr_dbd_prepared_t` and can be used in any of the apr_dbd prepared statement SQL query or select commands.

It is up to dbd user modules to use the prepared statements and document what statements can be specified in httpd.conf, or to provide their own directives and use `ap_dbd_prepare`.

 **Caveat**

When using prepared statements with a MySQL database, it is preferred to set `reconnect` to 0 in the connection string as to avoid errors that arise from the MySQL client reconnecting without properly resetting the prepared statements. If set to 1, any broken connections will be attempted fixed, but as mod_dbd is not informed, the prepared statements will be invalidated.

## SECURITY WARNING

Any web/database application needs to secure itself against SQL injection attacks. In most cases, Apache DBD is safe, because applications use prepared statements, and untrusted inputs are only ever used as data. Of course, if you use it via third-party modules, you should ascertain what precautions they may require.

However, the *FreeTDS* driver is inherently **unsafe**. The underlying library doesn't support prepared statements, so the driver emulates them, and the untrusted input is merged into the SQL statement.

It can be made safe by *untainting* all inputs: a process inspired by Perl's taint checking. Each input is matched against a regexp, and only the match is used, according to the Perl idiom:

```
$untrusted =~ /([a-z]+)/;
$trusted = $1;
```

To use this, the untainting regexps must be included in the prepared statements configured. The regexp follows immediately after the % in the prepared statement, and is enclosed in curly brackets {}. For example, if your application expects alphanumeric input, you can use:

```
"SELECT foo FROM bar WHERE input = %s"
```

with other drivers, and suffer nothing worse than a failed query. But with FreeTDS you'd need:

```
"SELECT foo FROM bar WHERE input = %{([A-Za-z0-9]+)}s"
```

Now anything that doesn't match the regexp's $1 match is discarded, so the statement is safe.

An alternative to this may be the third-party ODBC driver, which offers the security of genuine prepared statements.

## DBDExptime Directive

| | |
|---|---|
| Description: | Keepalive time for idle connections |
| Syntax: | DBDExptime time-in-seconds |
| Default: | DBDExptime 300 |
| Context: | server config, virtual host |
| Status: | Extension |
| Module: | mod_dbd |

Set the time to keep idle connections alive when the number of connections specified in DBDKeep has been exceeded (threaded platforms only).

## DBDInitSQL Directive

| | |
|---|---|
| Description: | Execute an SQL statement after connecting to a database |
| Syntax: | DBDInitSQL "SQL statement" |
| Context: | server config, virtual host |
| Status: | Extension |
| Module: | mod_dbd |

Modules, that wish it, can have one or more SQL statements executed when a connection to a database is created. Example usage could be initializing certain values or adding a log entry when a new connection is made to the database.

## DBDKeep Directive

| Description: | Maximum sustained number of connections |
|---|---|
| Syntax: | `DBDKeep number` |
| Default: | `DBDKeep 2` |
| Context: | server config, virtual host |
| Status: | Extension |
| Module: | mod_dbd |

Set the maximum number of connections per process to be sustained, other than for handling peak demand (threaded platforms only).

## DBDMax Directive

| Description: | Maximum number of connections |
|---|---|
| Syntax: | `DBDMax number` |
| Default: | `DBDMax 10` |
| Context: | server config, virtual host |
| Status: | Extension |
| Module: | mod_dbd |

Set the hard maximum number of connections per process (threaded platforms only).

## DBDMin Directive

| Description: | Minimum number of connections |
|---|---|
| Syntax: | `DBDMin number` |
| Default: | `DBDMin 1` |
| Context: | server config, virtual host |
| Status: | Extension |
| Module: | mod_dbd |

Set the minimum number of connections per process (threaded platforms only).

## DBDParams Directive

| Description: | Parameters for database connection |
|---|---|
| Syntax: | `DBDParams param1=value1[,param2=value2]` |
| Context: | server config, virtual host |
| Status: | Extension |
| Module: | mod_dbd |

As required by the underlying driver. Typically this will be used to pass whatever cannot be defaulted amongst username, password, database name, hostname and port number for connection.

Connection string parameters for current drivers include:

**FreeTDS (for MSSQL and SyBase)** username, password, appname, dbname, host, charset, lang, server

**MySQL** host, port, user, pass, dbname, sock, flags, fldsz, group, reconnect

**Oracle** user, pass, dbname, server

**PostgreSQL** The connection string is passed straight through to `PQconnectdb`

**SQLite2** The connection string is split on a colon, and `part1:part2` is used as `sqlite_open(part1, atoi(part2), NULL)`

**SQLite3** The connection string is passed straight through to `sqlite3_open`

**ODBC** datasource, user, password, connect, ctimeout, stimeout, access, txmode, bufsize

## DBDPersist Directive

| | |
|---|---|
| Description: | Whether to use persistent connections |
| Syntax: | `DBDPersist On\|Off` |
| Context: | server config, virtual host |
| Status: | Extension |
| Module: | mod_dbd |

If set to Off, persistent and pooled connections are disabled. A new database connection is opened when requested by a client, and closed immediately on release. This option is for debugging and low-usage servers.

The default is to enable a pool of persistent connections (or a single LAMP-style persistent connection in the case of a non-threaded server), and should almost always be used in operation.

Prior to version 2.2.2, this directive accepted only the values `0` and `1` instead of `Off` and `On`, respectively.

## DBDPrepareSQL Directive

| | |
|---|---|
| Description: | Define an SQL prepared statement |
| Syntax: | `DBDPrepareSQL "SQL statement" label` |
| Context: | server config, virtual host |
| Status: | Extension |
| Module: | mod_dbd |

For modules such as authentication that repeatedly use a single SQL statement, optimum performance is achieved by preparing the statement at startup rather than every time it is used. This directive prepares an SQL statement and assigns it a label.

## DBDriver Directive

| | |
|---|---|
| Description: | Specify an SQL driver |
| Syntax: | `DBDriver name` |
| Context: | server config, virtual host |
| Status: | Extension |
| Module: | mod_dbd |

Selects an apr_dbd driver by name. The driver must be installed on your system (on most systems, it will be a shared object or dll). For example, `DBDriver mysql` will select the MySQL driver in apr_dbd_mysql.so.

## 10.42 Apache Module mod_deflate

| Description: | Compress content before it is delivered to the client |
|---|---|
| Status: | Extension |
| ModuleIdentifier: | deflate_module |
| SourceFile: | mod_deflate.c |

## Summary

The MOD_DEFLATE module provides the DEFLATE output filter that allows output from your server to be compressed before being sent to the client over the network.

### Directives

- DeflateAlterETag
- DeflateBufferSize
- DeflateCompressionLevel
- DeflateFilterNote
- DeflateInflateLimitRequestBody
- DeflateInflateRatioBurst
- DeflateInflateRatioLimit
- DeflateMemLevel
- DeflateWindowSize

### See also

- Filters (p. 110)

## Supported Encodings

The gzip encoding is the only one supported to ensure complete compatibility with old browser implementations. The deflate encoding is not supported, please check the zlib's documentation[33] for a complete explanation.

## Sample Configurations

**Compression and TLS**

Some web applications are vulnerable to an information disclosure attack when a TLS connection carries deflate compressed data. For more information, review the details of the "BREACH" family of attacks.

This is a simple configuration that compresses common text-based content types.

**Compress only a few types**

```
AddOutputFilterByType DEFLATE text/html text/plain text/xml text/css text/javascript
```

---

[33]http://www.gzip.org/zlib/zlib_faq.html#faq38

## Enabling Compression

**Compression and TLS**

Some web applications are vulnerable to an information disclosure attack when a TLS connection carries deflate compressed data. For more information, review the details of the "BREACH" family of attacks.

### Output Compression

Compression is implemented by the DEFLATE filter (p. 110) . The following directive will enable compression for documents in the container where it is placed:

```
SetOutputFilter DEFLATE
SetEnvIfNoCase Request_URI \.(?:gif|jpe?g|png)$ no-gzip
```

If you want to restrict the compression to particular MIME types in general, you may use the ADDOUTPUTFILTER-BYTYPE directive. Here is an example of enabling compression only for the html files of the Apache documentation:

```
<Directory "/your-server-root/manual">
    AddOutputFilterByType DEFLATE text/html
</Directory>
```

Note

The DEFLATE filter is always inserted after RESOURCE filters like PHP or SSI. It never touches internal subrequests.

Note

There is an environment variable force-gzip, set via SETENV, which will ignore the accept-encoding setting of your browser and will send compressed output.

### Output Decompression

The MOD_DEFLATE module also provides a filter for inflating/uncompressing a gzip compressed response body. In order to activate this feature you have to insert the INFLATE filter into the output filter chain using SETOUTPUTFILTER or ADDOUTPUTFILTER, for example:

```
<Location "/dav-area">
    ProxyPass "http://example.com/"
    SetOutputFilter INFLATE
</Location>
```

This Example will uncompress gzip'ed output from example.com, so other filters can do further processing with it.

### Input Decompression

The MOD_DEFLATE module also provides a filter for decompressing a gzip compressed request body . In order to activate this feature you have to insert the DEFLATE filter into the input filter chain using SETINPUTFILTER or ADDINPUTFILTER, for example:

```
<Location "/dav-area">
    SetInputFilter DEFLATE
</Location>
```

Now if a request contains a `Content-Encoding:   gzip` header, the body will be automatically decompressed. Few browsers have the ability to gzip request bodies. However, some special applications actually do support request compression, for instance some WebDAV[34] clients.

 **Note on Content-Length**

If you evaluate the request body yourself, *don't trust the `Content-Length` header!* The Content-Length header reflects the length of the incoming data from the client and *not* the byte count of the decompressed data stream.

### Dealing with proxy servers

The MOD_DEFLATE module sends a `Vary:   Accept-Encoding` HTTP response header to alert proxies that a cached response should be sent only to clients that send the appropriate `Accept-Encoding` request header. This prevents compressed content from being sent to a client that will not understand it.

If you use some special exclusions dependent on, for example, the `User-Agent` header, you must manually configure an addition to the `Vary` header to alert proxies of the additional restrictions. For example, in a typical configuration where the addition of the `DEFLATE` filter depends on the `User-Agent`, you should add:

```
Header append Vary User-Agent
```

If your decision about compression depends on other information than request headers (*e.g.* HTTP version), you have to set the `Vary` header to the value `*`. This prevents compliant proxies from caching entirely.

#### Example

```
Header set Vary *
```

### Serving pre-compressed content

Since MOD_DEFLATE re-compresses content each time a request is made, some performance benefit can be derived by pre-compressing the content and telling mod_deflate to serve them without re-compressing them. This may be accomplished using a configuration like the following:

```
<IfModule mod_headers.c>
    # Serve gzip compressed CSS files if they exist
    # and the client accepts gzip.
    RewriteCond "%{HTTP:Accept-encoding}" "gzip"
    RewriteCond "%{REQUEST_FILENAME}\.gz" "-s"
    RewriteRule "^(.*)\.css"               "$1\.css\.gz" [QSA]

    # Serve gzip compressed JS files if they exist
    # and the client accepts gzip.
    RewriteCond "%{HTTP:Accept-encoding}" "gzip"
    RewriteCond "%{REQUEST_FILENAME}\.gz" "-s"
```

---

[34]http://www.webdav.org

```
RewriteRule "^(.*)\.js"                      "$1\.js\.gz" [QSA]


# Serve correct content types, and prevent mod_deflate double gzip.
RewriteRule "\.css\.gz$" "-" [T=text/css,E=no-gzip:1]
RewriteRule "\.js\.gz$"  "-" [T=text/javascript,E=no-gzip:1]


<FilesMatch "(\.js\.gz|\.css\.gz)$">
  # Serve correct encoding type.
  Header append Content-Encoding gzip

  # Force proxies to cache gzipped &
  # non-gzipped css/js files separately.
  Header append Vary Accept-Encoding
</FilesMatch>
</IfModule>
```

## DeflateAlterETag Directive

| | |
|---|---|
| Description: | How the outgoing ETag header should be modified during compression |
| Syntax: | `DeflateAlterETag AddSuffix|NoChange|Remove` |
| Default: | `DeflateAlterETag AddSuffix` |
| Context: | server config, virtual host |
| Status: | Extension |
| Module: | mod_deflate |

The DEFLATEALTERETAG directive specifies how the ETag hader should be altered when a response is compressed.

**AddSuffix** Append the compression method onto the end of the ETag, causing compressed and uncompressed representations to have unique ETags. This has been the default since 2.4.0, but prevents serving "HTTP Not Modified" (304) responses to conditional requests for compressed content.

**NoChange** Don't change the ETag on a compressed response. This was the default prior to 2.4.0, but does not satisfy the HTTP/1.1 property that all representations of the same resource have unique ETags.

**Remove** Remove the ETag header from compressed responses. This prevents some conditional requests from being possible, but avoids the shortcomings of the preceding options.

## DeflateBufferSize Directive

| | |
|---|---|
| Description: | Fragment size to be compressed at one time by zlib |
| Syntax: | `DeflateBufferSize value` |
| Default: | `DeflateBufferSize 8096` |
| Context: | server config, virtual host |
| Status: | Extension |
| Module: | mod_deflate |

The DEFLATEBUFFERSIZE directive specifies the size in bytes of the fragments that zlib should compress at one time. If the compressed response size is bigger than the one specified by this directive then httpd will switch to chunked encoding (HTTP header `Transfer-Encoding` set to `Chunked`), with the side effect of not setting any `Content-Length` HTTP header. This is particularly important when httpd works behind reverse caching proxies or when httpd is configured with MOD_CACHE and MOD_CACHE_DISK because HTTP responses without any `Content-Length` header might not be cached.

## DeflateCompressionLevel Directive

| | |
|---|---|
| Description: | How much compression do we apply to the output |
| Syntax: | `DeflateCompressionLevel value` |
| Default: | `Zlib's default` |
| Context: | server config, virtual host |
| Status: | Extension |
| Module: | mod_deflate |

The DEFLATECOMPRESSIONLEVEL directive specifies what level of compression should be used, the higher the value, the better the compression, but the more CPU time is required to achieve this.

The value must between 1 (less compression) and 9 (more compression).

## DeflateFilterNote Directive

| | |
|---|---|
| Description: | Places the compression ratio in a note for logging |
| Syntax: | `DeflateFilterNote [type] notename` |
| Context: | server config, virtual host |
| Status: | Extension |
| Module: | mod_deflate |

The DEFLATEFILTERNOTE directive specifies that a note about compression ratios should be attached to the request. The name of the note is the value specified for the directive. You can use that note for statistical purposes by adding the value to your access log (p. 56) .

### Example

```
DeflateFilterNote ratio

LogFormat '"%r" %b (%{ratio}n) "%{User-agent}i"' deflate
CustomLog "logs/deflate_log" deflate
```

If you want to extract more accurate values from your logs, you can use the *type* argument to specify the type of data left as a note for logging. *type* can be one of:

**Input** Store the byte count of the filter's input stream in the note.

**Output** Store the byte count of the filter's output stream in the note.

**Ratio** Store the compression ratio (`output/input * 100`) in the note. This is the default, if the *type* argument is omitted.

Thus you may log it this way:

### Accurate Logging

```
DeflateFilterNote Input instream
DeflateFilterNote Output outstream
DeflateFilterNote Ratio ratio

LogFormat '"%r" %{outstream}n/%{instream}n (%{ratio}n%%)' deflate
CustomLog "logs/deflate_log" deflate
```

### See also

- MOD_LOG_CONFIG

## DeflateInflateLimitRequestBody Directive

| | |
|---|---|
| Description: | Maximum size of inflated request bodies |
| Syntax: | `DeflateInflateLimitRequestBodyvalue` |
| Default: | `None, but LimitRequestBody applies after deflation` |
| Context: | server config, virtual host, directory, .htaccess |
| Status: | Extension |
| Module: | mod_deflate |
| Compatibility: | 2.4.10 and later |

The DEFLATEINFLATELIMITREQUESTBODY directive specifies the maximum size of an inflated request body. If it is unset, LIMITREQUESTBODY is applied to the inflated body.

## DeflateInflateRatioBurst Directive

| | |
|---|---|
| Description: | Maximum number of times the inflation ratio for request bodies can be crossed |
| Syntax: | `DeflateInflateRatioBurst value` |
| Default: | `3` |
| Context: | server config, virtual host, directory, .htaccess |
| Status: | Extension |
| Module: | mod_deflate |
| Compatibility: | 2.4.10 and later |

The DEFLATEINFLATERATIOBURST directive specifies the maximum number of times the DEFLATEINFLATERATIOLIMIT can be crossed before terminating the request.

## DeflateInflateRatioLimit Directive

| | |
|---|---|
| Description: | Maximum inflation ratio for request bodies |
| Syntax: | `DeflateInflateRatioLimit value` |
| Default: | `200` |
| Context: | server config, virtual host, directory, .htaccess |
| Status: | Extension |
| Module: | mod_deflate |
| Compatibility: | 2.4.10 and later |

The DEFLATEINFLATERATIOLIMIT directive specifies the maximum ratio of deflated to inflated size of an inflated request body. This ratio is checked as the body is streamed in, and if crossed more than DEFLATEINFLATERATIOBURST times, the request will be terminated.

## DeflateMemLevel Directive

| | |
|---|---|
| Description: | How much memory should be used by zlib for compression |
| Syntax: | `DeflateMemLevel value` |
| Default: | `DeflateMemLevel 9` |
| Context: | server config, virtual host |
| Status: | Extension |
| Module: | mod_deflate |

The DEFLATEMEMLEVEL directive specifies how much memory should be used by zlib for compression (a value between 1 and 9).

**DeflateWindowSize Directive**

| Description: | Zlib compression window size |
|---|---|
| Syntax: | `DeflateWindowSize value` |
| Default: | `DeflateWindowSize 15` |
| Context: | server config, virtual host |
| Status: | Extension |
| Module: | mod_deflate |

The DEFLATEWINDOWSIZE directive specifies the zlib compression window size (a value between 1 and 15). Generally, the higher the window size, the higher can the compression ratio be expected.

# 10.43 Apache Module mod_dialup

| | |
|---|---|
| Description: | Send static content at a bandwidth rate limit, defined by the various old modem standards |
| Status: | Experimental |
| ModuleIdentifier: | dialup_module |
| SourceFile: | mod_dialup.c |

## Summary

It is a module that sends static content at a bandwidth rate limit, defined by the various old modem standards. So, you can browse your site with a 56k V.92 modem, by adding something like this:

```
<Location "/mysite">
    ModemStandard "V.92"
</Location>
```

Previously to do bandwidth rate limiting modules would have to block an entire thread, for each client, and insert sleeps to slow the bandwidth down. Using the new suspend feature, a handler can get callback N milliseconds in the future, and it will be invoked by the Event MPM on a different thread, once the timer hits. From there the handler can continue to send data to the client.

### Directives

- ModemStandard

## ModemStandard Directive

| | |
|---|---|
| Description: | Modem standard to simulate |
| Syntax: | ModemStandard V.21\|V.26bis\|V.32\|V.34\|V.92 |
| Context: | directory |
| Status: | Experimental |
| Module: | mod_dialup |

Specify what modem standard you wish to simulate.

```
<Location "/mysite">
    ModemStandard "V.26bis"
</Location>
```

# 10.44   Apache Module mod_dir

| | |
|---|---|
| Description: | Provides for "trailing slash" redirects and serving directory index files |
| Status: | Base |
| ModuleIdentifier: | dir_module |
| SourceFile: | mod_dir.c |

## Summary

The index of a directory can come from one of two sources:

- A file written by the user, typically called `index.html`. The DIRECTORYINDEX directive sets the name of this file. This is controlled by MOD_DIR.

- Otherwise, a listing generated by the server. This is provided by MOD_AUTOINDEX.

The two functions are separated so that you can completely remove (or replace) automatic index generation should you want to.

A "trailing slash" redirect is issued when the server receives a request for a URL `http://servername/foo/dirname` where `dirname` is a directory. Directories require a trailing slash, so MOD_DIR issues a redirect to `http://servername/foo/dirname/`.

### Directives

- DirectoryCheckHandler
- DirectoryIndex
- DirectoryIndexRedirect
- DirectorySlash
- FallbackResource

## DirectoryCheckHandler Directive

| | |
|---|---|
| Description: | Toggle how this module responds when another handler is configured |
| Syntax: | `DirectoryCheckHandler On\|Off` |
| Default: | `DirectoryCheckHandler Off` |
| Context: | server config, virtual host, directory, .htaccess |
| Override: | Indexes |
| Status: | Base |
| Module: | mod_dir |
| Compatibility: | Available in 2.4.8 and later. Releases prior to 2.4 implicitly act as if "DirectoryCheckHandler ON" was specified. |

The DIRECTORYCHECKHANDLER directive determines whether MOD_DIR should check for directory indexes or add trailing slashes when some other handler has been configured for the current URL. Handlers can be set by directives such as SETHANDLER or by other modules at runtime.

In releases prior to 2.4, this module did not take any action if any other handler was configured for a URL. This allows directory indexes to be served even when a SETHANDLER directive is specified for an entire directory, but it can also result in some conflicts with other modules.

## DirectoryIndex Directive

| | |
|---|---|
| Description: | List of resources to look for when the client requests a directory |
| Syntax: | `DirectoryIndex disabled | local-url [local-url] ...` |
| Default: | `DirectoryIndex index.html` |
| Context: | server config, virtual host, directory, .htaccess |
| Override: | Indexes |
| Status: | Base |
| Module: | mod_dir |

The DIRECTORYINDEX directive sets the list of resources to look for, when the client requests an index of the directory by specifying a / at the end of the directory name. *Local-url* is the (%-encoded) URL of a document on the server relative to the requested directory; it is usually the name of a file in the directory. Several URLs may be given, in which case the server will return the first one that it finds. If none of the resources exist and the `Indexes` option is set, the server will generate its own listing of the directory.

### Example

```
DirectoryIndex index.html
```

then        a        request        for        `http://example.com/docs/`        would        return
`http://example.com/docs/index.html` if it exists, or would list the directory if it did not.

Note that the documents do not need to be relative to the directory;

```
DirectoryIndex index.html index.txt  /cgi-bin/index.pl
```

would cause the CGI script `/cgi-bin/index.pl` to be executed if neither `index.html` or `index.txt` existed in a directory.

A single argument of "disabled" prevents MOD_DIR from searching for an index. An argument of "disabled" will be interpreted literally if it has any arguments before or after it, even if they are "disabled" as well.

**Note:** Multiple DIRECTORYINDEX directives within the *same context* (p. 35) will add to the list of resources to look for rather than replace:

```
# Example A: Set index.html as an index page, then add index.php to that list as well.
<Directory "/foo">
    DirectoryIndex index.html
    DirectoryIndex index.php
</Directory>

# Example B: This is identical to example A, except it's done with a single directive.
<Directory "/foo">
    DirectoryIndex index.html index.php
</Directory>

# Example C: To replace the list, you must explicitly reset it first:
# In this example, only index.php will remain as an index resource.
<Directory "/foo">
    DirectoryIndex index.html
    DirectoryIndex disabled
    DirectoryIndex index.php
</Directory>
```

## DirectoryIndexRedirect Directive

| | |
|---|---|
| Description: | Configures an external redirect for directory indexes. |
| Syntax: | `DirectoryIndexRedirect on | off | permanent | temp | seeother | 3xx-code` |
| Default: | `DirectoryIndexRedirect off` |
| Context: | server config, virtual host, directory, .htaccess |
| Override: | Indexes |
| Status: | Base |
| Module: | mod_dir |
| Compatibility: | Available in version 2.3.14 and later |

By default, the DIRECTORYINDEX is selected and returned transparently to the client. DIRECTORYINDEXREDIRECT causes an external redirect to instead be issued.

The argument can be:

- `on`: issues a 302 redirection to the index resource.

- `off`: does not issue a redirection. This is the legacy behaviour of mod_dir.

- `permanent`: issues a 301 (permanent) redirection to the index resource.

- `temp`: this has the same effect as `on`

- `seeother`: issues a 303 redirection (also known as "See Other") to the index resource.

- *3xx-code*: issues a redirection marked by the chosen 3xx code.

### Example

```
DirectoryIndexRedirect on
```

A request for `http://example.com/docs/` would return a temporary redirect to `http://example.com/docs/index.html` if it exists.

## DirectorySlash Directive

| | |
|---|---|
| Description: | Toggle trailing slash redirects on or off |
| Syntax: | `DirectorySlash On|Off` |
| Default: | `DirectorySlash On` |
| Context: | server config, virtual host, directory, .htaccess |
| Override: | Indexes |
| Status: | Base |
| Module: | mod_dir |

The DIRECTORYSLASH directive determines whether MOD_DIR should fixup URLs pointing to a directory or not.

Typically if a user requests a resource without a trailing slash, which points to a directory, MOD_DIR redirects him to the same resource, but *with* trailing slash for some good reasons:

- The user is finally requesting the canonical URL of the resource

- MOD_AUTOINDEX works correctly. Since it doesn't emit the path in the link, it would point to the wrong path.

- DIRECTORYINDEX will be evaluated *only* for directories requested with trailing slash.

- Relative URL references inside html pages will work correctly.

If you don't want this effect *and* the reasons above don't apply to you, you can turn off the redirect as shown below. However, be aware that there are possible security implications to doing this.

```
# see security warning below!
<Location "/some/path">
    DirectorySlash Off
    SetHandler some-handler
</Location>
```

 **Security Warning**

Turning off the trailing slash redirect may result in an information disclosure.  Consider a situation where MOD_AUTOINDEX is active (`Options +Indexes`) and DIRECTORYINDEX is set to a valid resource (say, `index.html`) and there's no other special handler defined for that URL. In this case a request with a trailing slash would show the `index.html` file. **But a request without trailing slash would list the directory contents**.

Also note that some browsers may erroneously change POST requests into GET (thus discarding POST data) when a redirect is issued.

### FallbackResource Directive

| | |
|---|---|
| Description: | Define a default URL for requests that don't map to a file |
| Syntax: | `FallbackResource disabled | local-url` |
| Default: | `disabled - httpd will return 404 (Not Found)` |
| Context: | server config, virtual host, directory, .htaccess |
| Override: | Indexes |
| Status: | Base |
| Module: | mod_dir |
| Compatibility: | The `disabled` argument is available in version 2.4.4 and later |

Use this to set a handler for any URL that doesn't map to anything in your filesystem, and would otherwise return HTTP 404 (Not Found). For example

```
FallbackResource /not-404.php
```

will cause requests for non-existent files to be handled by `not-404.php`, while requests for files that exist are unaffected.

It is frequently desirable to have a single file or resource handle all requests to a particular directory, except those requests that correspond to an existing file or script. This is often referred to as a 'front controller.'

In earlier versions of httpd, this effect typically required MOD_REWRITE, and the use of the `-f` and `-d` tests for file and directory existence. This now requires only one line of configuration.

```
FallbackResource /index.php
```

Existing files, such as images, css files, and so on, will be served normally.

Use the `disabled` argument to disable that feature if inheritance from a parent directory is not desired.

In a sub-URI, such as *http://example.com/blog/* this *sub-URI* has to be supplied as *local-url*:

```
<Directory "/web/example.com/htdocs/blog">
    FallbackResource /blog/index.php
```

```
</Directory>
<Directory "/web/example.com/htdocs/blog/images">
    FallbackResource disabled
</Directory>
```

## 10.45    Apache Module mod_dumpio

| | |
|---|---|
| Description: | Dumps all I/O to error log as desired. |
| Status: | Extension |
| ModuleIdentifier: | dumpio_module |
| SourceFile: | mod_dumpio.c |

## Summary

`mod_dumpio` allows for the logging of all input received by Apache and/or all output sent by Apache to be logged (dumped) to the error.log file.

The data logging is done right after SSL decoding (for input) and right before SSL encoding (for output). As can be expected, this can produce extreme volumes of data, and should only be used when debugging problems.

### Directives

- DumpIOInput
- DumpIOOutput

## Enabling dumpio Support

To enable the module, it should be compiled and loaded in to your running Apache configuration. Logging can then be enabled or disabled separately for input and output via the below directives. Additionally, MOD_DUMPIO needs to be configured to LOGLEVEL `trace7`:

```
LogLevel dumpio:trace7
```

## DumpIOInput Directive

| | |
|---|---|
| Description: | Dump all input data to the error log |
| Syntax: | DumpIOInput On|Off |
| Default: | DumpIOInput Off |
| Context: | server config |
| Status: | Extension |
| Module: | mod_dumpio |

Enable dumping of all input.

### Example

```
DumpIOInput On
```

## DumpIOOutput Directive

| | |
|---|---|
| Description: | Dump all output data to the error log |
| Syntax: | DumpIOOutput On|Off |
| Default: | DumpIOOutput Off |
| Context: | server config |
| Status: | Extension |
| Module: | mod_dumpio |

Enable dumping of all output.

### Example

```
DumpIOOutput On
```

## 10.46   Apache Module mod_echo

| Description: | A simple echo server to illustrate protocol modules |
|---|---|
| Status: | Experimental |
| ModuleIdentifier: | echo_module |
| SourceFile: | mod_echo.c |

## Summary

This module provides an example protocol module to illustrate the concept.  It provides a simple echo server.  Telnet to it and type stuff, and it will echo it.

**Directives**

- ProtocolEcho

## ProtocolEcho Directive

| Description: | Turn the echo server on or off |
|---|---|
| Syntax: | `ProtocolEcho On|Off` |
| Default: | `ProtocolEcho Off` |
| Context: | server config, virtual host |
| Status: | Experimental |
| Module: | mod_echo |

The PROTOCOLECHO directive enables or disables the echo server.

### Example

`ProtocolEcho On`

# 10.47 Apache Module mod_env

| | |
|---|---|
| Description: | Modifies the environment which is passed to CGI scripts and SSI pages |
| Status: | Base |
| ModuleIdentifier: | env_module |
| SourceFile: | mod_env.c |

## Summary

This module allows for control of internal environment variables that are used by various Apache HTTP Server modules. These variables are also provided to CGI scripts as native system environment variables, and available for use in SSI pages. Environment variables may be passed from the shell which invoked the `httpd` process. Alternatively, environment variables may be set or unset within the configuration process.

**Directives**

- PassEnv
- SetEnv
- UnsetEnv

**See also**

- Environment Variables (p. 92)
- SETENVIF

## PassEnv Directive

| | |
|---|---|
| Description: | Passes environment variables from the shell |
| Syntax: | `PassEnv env-variable [env-variable] ...` |
| Context: | server config, virtual host, directory, .htaccess |
| Override: | FileInfo |
| Status: | Base |
| Module: | mod_env |

Specifies one or more native system environment variables to make available as internal environment variables, which are available to Apache HTTP Server modules as well as propagated to CGI scripts and SSI pages. Values come from the native OS environment of the shell which invoked the `httpd` process.

### Example

```
PassEnv LD_LIBRARY_PATH
```

## SetEnv Directive

| | |
|---|---|
| Description: | Sets environment variables |
| Syntax: | `SetEnv env-variable [value]` |
| Context: | server config, virtual host, directory, .htaccess |
| Override: | FileInfo |
| Status: | Base |
| Module: | mod_env |

Sets an internal environment variable, which is then available to Apache HTTP Server modules, and passed on to CGI scripts and SSI pages.

### Example

```
SetEnv SPECIAL_PATH /foo/bin
```

If you omit the *value* argument, the variable is set to an empty string.

 The internal environment variables set by this directive are set *after* most early request processing directives are run, such as access control and URI-to-filename mapping.  If the environment variable you're setting is meant as input into this early phase of processing such as the REWRITERULE directive, you should instead set the environment variable with SETENVIF.

**See also**

* Environment Variables (p. 92)

## UnsetEnv Directive

| | |
|---|---|
| Description: | Removes variables from the environment |
| Syntax: | `UnsetEnv env-variable [env-variable] ...` |
| Context: | server config, virtual host, directory, .htaccess |
| Override: | FileInfo |
| Status: | Base |
| Module: | mod_env |

Removes one or more internal environment variables from those passed on to CGI scripts and SSI pages.

### Example

```
UnsetEnv LD_LIBRARY_PATH
```

# 10.48  Apache Module mod_example_hooks

| | |
|---|---|
| Description: | Illustrates the Apache module API |
| Status: | Experimental |
| ModuleIdentifier: | example_hooks_module |
| SourceFile: | mod_example_hooks.c |

## Summary

The files in the `modules/examples` directory under the Apache distribution directory tree are provided as an example to those that wish to write modules that use the Apache API.

The main file is `mod_example_hooks.c`, which illustrates all the different callback mechanisms and call syntaxes. By no means does an add-on module need to include routines for all of the callbacks - quite the contrary!

The example module is an actual working module. If you link it into your server, enable the "example-hooks-handler" handler for a location, and then browse to that location, you will see a display of some of the tracing the example module did as the various callbacks were made.

### Directives

- Example

## Compiling the example_hooks module

To include the example_hooks module in your server, follow the steps below:

1. Run `configure` with `--enable-example-hooks` option.

2. Make the server (run `"make"`).

To add another module of your own:

1. `cp modules/examples/mod_example_hooks.c modules/new_module/`*`mod_myexample.c`*

2. Modify the file.

3. Create `modules/new_module/config.m4`.

   (a) Add `APACHE_MODPATH_INIT(new_module)`.
   (b) Copy `APACHE_MODULE` line with "example_hooks" from `modules/examples/config.m4`.
   (c) Replace the first argument "example_hooks" with *myexample*.
   (d) Replace the second argument with brief description of your module. It will be used in `configure --help`.
   (e) If your module needs additional C compiler flags, linker flags or libraries, add them to CFLAGS, LD-FLAGS and LIBS accordingly. See other `config.m4` files in modules directory for examples.
   (f) Add `APACHE_MODPATH_FINISH`.

4. Create `module/new_module/Makefile.in`. If your module doesn't need special build instructions, all you need to have in that file is `include $(top_srcdir)/build/special.mk`.

5. Run ./buildconf from the top-level directory.

6. Build the server with –enable-myexample

## Using the `mod_example_hooks` Module

To activate the example_hooks module, include a block similar to the following in your `httpd.conf` file:

```
<Location "/example-hooks-info">
   SetHandler example-hooks-handler
</Location>
```

As an alternative, you can put the following into a `.htaccess` (p. 380) file and then request the file "test.example" from that location:

```
AddHandler example-hooks-handler .example
```

After reloading/restarting your server, you should be able to browse to this location and see the brief display mentioned earlier.

## Example Directive

| | |
|---|---|
| Description: | Demonstration directive to illustrate the Apache module API |
| Syntax: | `Example` |
| Context: | server config, virtual host, directory, .htaccess |
| Status: | Experimental |
| Module: | mod_example_hooks |

The EXAMPLE directive just sets a demonstration flag which the example module's content handler displays. It takes no arguments. If you browse to an URL to which the example-hooks content-handler applies, you will get a display of the routines within the module and how and in what order they were called to service the document request. The effect of this directive one can observe under the point `"Example directive declared here:  YES/NO"`.

# 10.49   Apache Module mod_expires

| | |
|---|---|
| Description: | Generation of `Expires` and `Cache-Control` HTTP headers according to user-specified criteria |
| Status: | Extension |
| ModuleIdentifier: | expires_module |
| SourceFile: | mod_expires.c |

## Summary

This module controls the setting of the `Expires` HTTP header and the `max-age` directive of the `Cache-Control` HTTP header in server responses. The expiration date can set to be relative to either the time the source file was last modified, or to the time of the client access.

These HTTP headers are an instruction to the client about the document's validity and persistence. If cached, the document may be fetched from the cache rather than from the source until this time has passed. After that, the cache copy is considered "expired" and invalid, and a new copy must be obtained from the source.

To modify `Cache-Control` directives other than `max-age` (see RFC 2616 section 14.9[35]), you can use the HEADER directive.

When the `Expires` header is already part of the response generated by the server, for example when generated by a CGI script or proxied from an origin server, this module does not change or add an `Expires` or `Cache-Control` header.

### Directives

- ExpiresActive
- ExpiresByType
- ExpiresDefault

## Alternate Interval Syntax

The EXPIRESDEFAULT and EXPIRESBYTYPE directives can also be defined in a more readable syntax of the form:

```
ExpiresDefault "base  [plus num type] [num type] ..."
ExpiresByType type/encoding "base  [plus num type] [num type] ..."
```

where *base* is one of:

- `access`
- `now` (equivalent to 'access')
- `modification`

The `plus` keyword is optional. *num* should be an integer value [acceptable to `atoi()`], and *type* is one of:

- `years`
- `months`
- `weeks`

---

[35]http://www.w3.org/Protocols/rfc2616/rfc2616-sec14.html#sec14.9

- days
- hours
- minutes
- seconds

For example, any of the following directives can be used to make documents expire 1 month after being accessed, by default:

```
ExpiresDefault "access plus 1 month"
ExpiresDefault "access plus 4 weeks"
ExpiresDefault "access plus 30 days"
```

The expiry time can be fine-tuned by adding several '*num type*' clauses:

```
ExpiresByType text/html "access plus 1 month 15 days 2 hours"
ExpiresByType image/gif "modification plus 5 hours 3 minutes"
```

Note that if you use a modification date based setting, the Expires header will **not** be added to content that does not come from a file on disk. This is due to the fact that there is no modification time for such content.

## ExpiresActive Directive

| | |
|---|---|
| Description: | Enables generation of `Expires` headers |
| Syntax: | `ExpiresActive On|Off` |
| Default: | `ExpiresActive Off` |
| Context: | server config, virtual host, directory, .htaccess |
| Override: | Indexes |
| Status: | Extension |
| Module: | mod_expires |

This directive enables or disables the generation of the `Expires` and `Cache-Control` headers for the document realm in question. (That is, if found in an `.htaccess` file, for instance, it applies only to documents generated from that directory.) If set to `Off`, the headers will not be generated for any document in the realm (unless overridden at a lower level, such as an `.htaccess` file overriding a server config file). If set to `On`, the headers will be added to served documents according to the criteria defined by the EXPIRESBYTYPE and EXPIRESDEFAULT directives (*q.v.*).

Note that this directive does not guarantee that an `Expires` or `Cache-Control` header will be generated. If the criteria aren't met, no header will be sent, and the effect will be as though this directive wasn't even specified.

## ExpiresByType Directive

| | |
|---|---|
| Description: | Value of the `Expires` header configured by MIME type |
| Syntax: | `ExpiresByType MIME-type <code>seconds` |
| Context: | server config, virtual host, directory, .htaccess |
| Override: | Indexes |
| Status: | Extension |
| Module: | mod_expires |

This directive defines the value of the `Expires` header and the `max-age` directive of the `Cache-Control` header generated for documents of the specified type (*e.g.*, `text/html`). The second argument sets the number of seconds that will be added to a base time to construct the expiration date. The `Cache-Control:   max-age` is calculated by subtracting the request time from the expiration date and expressing the result in seconds.

The base time is either the last modification time of the file, or the time of the client's access to the document. Which should be used is specified by the $<code>$ field; M means that the file's last modification time should be used as the base time, and A means the client's access time should be used.

The difference in effect is subtle. If M is used, all current copies of the document in all caches will expire at the same time, which can be good for something like a weekly notice that's always found at the same URL. If A is used, the date of expiration is different for each client; this can be good for image files that don't change very often, particularly for a set of related documents that all refer to the same images (*i.e.*, the images will be accessed repeatedly within a relatively short timespan).

**Example:**

```
# enable expirations
ExpiresActive On
# expire GIF images after a month in the client's cache
ExpiresByType image/gif A2592000
# HTML documents are good for a week from the
# time they were changed
ExpiresByType text/html M604800
```

Note that this directive only has effect if ExpiresActive On has been specified. It overrides, for the specified MIME type *only*, any expiration date set by the EXPIRESDEFAULT directive.

You can also specify the expiration time calculation using an alternate syntax, described earlier in this document.

## ExpiresDefault Directive

| | |
|---|---|
| Description: | Default algorithm for calculating expiration time |
| Syntax: | ExpiresDefault <code>seconds |
| Context: | server config, virtual host, directory, .htaccess |
| Override: | Indexes |
| Status: | Extension |
| Module: | mod_expires |

This directive sets the default algorithm for calculating the expiration time for all documents in the affected realm. It can be overridden on a type-by-type basis by the EXPIRESBYTYPE directive. See the description of that directive for details about the syntax of the argument, and the alternate syntax description as well.

# 10.50   Apache Module mod_ext_filter

| | |
|---|---|
| Description: | Pass the response body through an external program before delivery to the client |
| Status: | Extension |
| ModuleIdentifier: | ext_filter_module |
| SourceFile: | mod_ext_filter.c |

## Summary

MOD_EXT_FILTER presents a simple and familiar programming model for filters (p. 110) . With this module, a program which reads from stdin and writes to stdout (i.e., a Unix-style filter command) can be a filter for Apache. This filtering mechanism is much slower than using a filter which is specially written for the Apache API and runs inside of the Apache server process, but it does have the following benefits:

- the programming model is much simpler
- any programming/scripting language can be used, provided that it allows the program to read from standard input and write to standard output
- existing programs can be used unmodified as Apache filters

Even when the performance characteristics are not suitable for production use, MOD_EXT_FILTER can be used as a prototype environment for filters.

### Directives

- ExtFilterDefine
- ExtFilterOptions

### See also

- Filters (p. 110)

## Examples

### Generating HTML from some other type of response

```
# mod_ext_filter directive to define a filter
# to HTML-ize text/c files using the external
# program /usr/bin/enscript, with the type of
# the result set to text/html
ExtFilterDefine c-to-html mode=output \
    intype=text/c outtype=text/html \
    cmd="/usr/bin/enscript --color -W html -Ec -o - -"

<Directory "/export/home/trawick/apacheinst/htdocs/c">
    # core directive to cause the new filter to
    # be run on output
    SetOutputFilter c-to-html

    # mod_mime directive to set the type of .c
    # files to text/c
    AddType text/c .c
</Directory>
```

**Implementing a content encoding filter**

Note: this gzip example is just for the purposes of illustration. Please refer to MOD_DEFLATE for a practical implementation.

```
# mod_ext_filter directive to define the external filter
ExtFilterDefine gzip mode=output cmd=/bin/gzip

<Location "/gzipped">

    # core directive to cause the gzip filter to be
    # run on output
    SetOutputFilter gzip

    # mod_headers directive to add
    # "Content-Encoding: gzip" header field
    Header set Content-Encoding gzip
</Location>
```

**Slowing down the server**

```
# mod_ext_filter directive to define a filter
# which runs everything through cat; cat doesn't
# modify anything; it just introduces extra pathlength
# and consumes more resources
ExtFilterDefine slowdown mode=output cmd=/bin/cat \
    preservescontentlength

<Location "/">
    # core directive to cause the slowdown filter to
    # be run several times on output
    #
    SetOutputFilter slowdown;slowdown;slowdown
</Location>
```

**Using sed to replace text in the response**

```
# mod_ext_filter directive to define a filter which
# replaces text in the response
#
ExtFilterDefine fixtext mode=output intype=text/html \
    cmd="/bin/sed s/verdana/arial/g"

<Location "/">
    # core directive to cause the fixtext filter to
    # be run on output
    SetOutputFilter fixtext
</Location>
```

⟹ You can do the same thing using MOD_SUBSTITUTE without invoking an external process.

**Tracing another filter**

```
# Trace the data read and written by mod_deflate
# for a particular client (IP 192.168.1.31)
# experiencing compression problems.
# This filter will trace what goes into mod_deflate.
ExtFilterDefine tracebefore \
    cmd="/bin/tracefilter.pl /tmp/tracebefore" \
    EnableEnv=trace_this_client

# This filter will trace what goes after mod_deflate.
# Note that without the ftype parameter, the default
# filter type of AP_FTYPE_RESOURCE would cause the
# filter to be placed *before* mod_deflate in the filter
# chain.  Giving it a numeric value slightly higher than
# AP_FTYPE_CONTENT_SET will ensure that it is placed
# after mod_deflate.
ExtFilterDefine traceafter \
    cmd="/bin/tracefilter.pl /tmp/traceafter" \
    EnableEnv=trace_this_client ftype=21

<Directory "/usr/local/docs">
    SetEnvIf Remote_Addr 192.168.1.31 trace_this_client
    SetOutputFilter tracebefore;deflate;traceafter
</Directory>
```

**Here is the filter which traces the data:**

```
#!/usr/local/bin/perl -w
use strict;

open(SAVE, ">$ARGV[0]")
    or die "can't open $ARGV[0]: $?";

while (<STDIN>) {
    print SAVE $_;
    print $_;
}

close(SAVE);
```

## ExtFilterDefine Directive

| Description: | Define an external filter |
| --- | --- |
| Syntax: | `ExtFilterDefine filtername parameters` |
| Context: | server config |
| Status: | Extension |
| Module: | mod_ext_filter |

The EXTFILTERDEFINE directive defines the characteristics of an external filter, including the program to run and its arguments.

*filtername* specifies the name of the filter being defined. This name can then be used in SETOUTPUTFILTER directives. It must be unique among all registered filters. *At the present time, no error is reported by the register-filter API, so a problem with duplicate names isn't reported to the user.*

Subsequent parameters can appear in any order and define the external command to run and certain other characteristics. The only required parameter is cmd=. These parameters are:

**cmd=*cmdline*** The cmd= keyword allows you to specify the external command to run. If there are arguments after the program name, the command line should be surrounded in quotation marks (*e.g.*, cmd="*/bin/mypgm arg1 arg2*".) Normal shell quoting is not necessary since the program is run directly, bypassing the shell. Program arguments are blank-delimited. A backslash can be used to escape blanks which should be part of a program argument. Any backslashes which are part of the argument must be escaped with backslash themselves. In addition to the standard CGI environment variables, DOCUMENT_URI, DOCUMENT_PATH_INFO, and QUERY_STRING_UNESCAPED will also be set for the program.

**mode=*mode*** Use mode=output (the default) for filters which process the response. Use mode=input for filters which process the request. mode=input is available in Apache 2.1 and later.

**intype=*imt*** This parameter specifies the internet media type (*i.e.*, MIME type) of documents which should be filtered. By default, all documents are filtered. If intype= is specified, the filter will be disabled for documents of other types.

**outtype=*imt*** This parameter specifies the internet media type (*i.e.*, MIME type) of filtered documents. It is useful when the filter changes the internet media type as part of the filtering operation. By default, the internet media type is unchanged.

**PreservesContentLength** The PreservesContentLength keyword specifies that the filter preserves the content length. This is not the default, as most filters change the content length. In the event that the filter doesn't modify the length, this keyword should be specified.

**ftype=*filtertype*** This parameter specifies the numeric value for filter type that the filter should be registered as. The default value, AP_FTYPE_RESOURCE, is sufficient in most cases. If the filter needs to operate at a different point in the filter chain than resource filters, then this parameter will be necessary. See the AP_FTYPE_foo definitions in util_filter.h for appropriate values.

**disableenv=*env*** This parameter specifies the name of an environment variable which, if set, will disable the filter.

**enableenv=*env*** This parameter specifies the name of an environment variable which must be set, or the filter will be disabled.

### ExtFilterOptions Directive

| | |
|---|---|
| Description: | Configure MOD_EXT_FILTER options |
| Syntax: | ExtFilterOptions option [option] ... |
| Default: | ExtFilterOptions NoLogStderr |
| Context: | directory |
| Status: | Extension |
| Module: | mod_ext_filter |

The EXTFILTEROPTIONS directive specifies special processing options for MOD_EXT_FILTER. *Option* can be one of

**LogStderr | NoLogStderr** The LogStderr keyword specifies that messages written to standard error by the external filter program will be saved in the Apache error log. NoLogStderr disables this feature.

**Onfail=[abort|remove]** Determines how to proceed if the external filter program cannot be started. With abort (the default value) the request will be aborted. With remove, the filter is removed and the request continues without it.

```
ExtFilterOptions LogStderr
```

Messages written to the filter's standard error will be stored in the Apache error log.

## 10.51    Apache Module mod_file_cache

| | |
|---|---|
| Description: | Caches a static list of files in memory |
| Status: | Experimental |
| ModuleIdentifier: | file_cache_module |
| SourceFile: | mod_file_cache.c |

## Summary

! This module should be used with care.   You can easily create a broken site using
MOD_FILE_CACHE, so read this document carefully.

*Caching* frequently requested files that change very infrequently is a technique for reducing server load.
MOD_FILE_CACHE provides two techniques for caching frequently requested *static* files.  Through configuration directives, you can direct MOD_FILE_CACHE to either open then mmap() a file, or to pre-open a file and save the file's open *file handle*. Both techniques reduce server load when processing requests for these files by doing part of the work (specifically, the file I/O) for serving the file when the server is started rather than during each request.

Notice: You cannot use this for speeding up CGI programs or other files which are served by special content handlers. It can only be used for regular files which are usually served by the Apache core content handler.

This module is an extension of and borrows heavily from the mod_mmap_static module in Apache 1.3.

### Directives

* CacheFile
* MMapFile

## Using mod_file_cache

MOD_FILE_CACHE caches a list of statically configured files via MMAPFILE or CACHEFILE directives in the main server configuration.

Not all platforms support both directives. You will receive an error message in the server error log if you attempt to use an unsupported directive. If given an unsupported directive, the server will start but the file will not be cached. On platforms that support both directives, you should experiment with both to see which works best for you.

### MMapFile Directive

The MMAPFILE directive of MOD_FILE_CACHE maps a list of statically configured files into memory through the system call mmap().  This system call is available on most modern Unix derivatives, but not on all.  There are sometimes system-specific limits on the size and number of files that can be mmap()ed, experimentation is probably the easiest way to find out.

This mmap()ing is done once at server start or restart, only.  So whenever one of the mapped files changes on the filesystem you *have* to restart the server (see the Stopping and Restarting (p. 29) documentation). To reiterate that point: if the files are modified *in place* without restarting the server you may end up serving requests that are completely bogus. You should update files by unlinking the old copy and putting a new copy in place. Most tools such as rdist and mv do this. The reason why this modules doesn't take care of changes to the files is that this check would need an extra stat() every time which is a waste and against the intent of I/O reduction.

### CacheFile Directive

The CACHEFILE directive of MOD_FILE_CACHE opens an active *handle* or *file descriptor* to the file (or files) listed in the configuration directive and places these open file handles in the cache. When the file is requested, the server retrieves the handle from the cache and passes it to the sendfile() (or TransmitFile() on Windows), socket API.

This file handle caching is done once at server start or restart, only. So whenever one of the cached files changes on the filesystem you *have* to restart the server (see the Stopping and Restarting (p. 29) documentation). To reiterate that point: if the files are modified *in place* without restarting the server you may end up serving requests that are completely bogus. You should update files by unlinking the old copy and putting a new copy in place. Most tools such as rdist and mv do this.

Note

Don't bother asking for a directive which recursively caches all the files in a directory. Try this instead... See the INCLUDE directive, and consider this command:

```
find /www/htdocs -type f -print \
| sed -e 's/.*/mmapfile &/' > /www/conf/mmap.conf
```

## CacheFile Directive

| | |
|---|---|
| Description: | Cache a list of file handles at startup time |
| Syntax: | CacheFile file-path [file-path] ... |
| Context: | server config |
| Status: | Experimental |
| Module: | mod_file_cache |

The CACHEFILE directive opens handles to one or more files (given as whitespace separated arguments) and places these handles into the cache at server startup time. Handles to cached files are automatically closed on a server shutdown. When the files have changed on the filesystem, the server should be restarted to re-cache them.

Be careful with the *file-path* arguments: They have to literally match the filesystem path Apache's URL-to-filename translation handlers create. We cannot compare inodes or other stuff to match paths through symbolic links *etc.* because that again would cost extra stat() system calls which is not acceptable. This module may or may not work with filenames rewritten by MOD_ALIAS or MOD_REWRITE.

#### Example

```
CacheFile /usr/local/apache/htdocs/index.html
```

## MMapFile Directive

| | |
|---|---|
| Description: | Map a list of files into memory at startup time |
| Syntax: | MMapFile file-path [file-path] ... |
| Context: | server config |
| Status: | Experimental |
| Module: | mod_file_cache |

The MMAPFILE directive maps one or more files (given as whitespace separated arguments) into memory at server startup time. They are automatically unmapped on a server shutdown. When the files have changed on the filesystem at least a HUP or USR1 signal should be send to the server to re-mmap() them.

Be careful with the *file-path* arguments: They have to literally match the filesystem path Apache's URL-to-filename translation handlers create.  We cannot compare inodes or other stuff to match paths through symbolic links *etc.* because that again would cost extra stat() system calls which is not acceptable. This module may or may not work with filenames rewritten by MOD_ALIAS or MOD_REWRITE.

### Example

```
MMapFile /usr/local/apache/htdocs/index.html
```

# 10.52 Apache Module mod_filter

| | |
|---|---|
| Description: | Context-sensitive smart filter configuration module |
| Status: | Base |
| ModuleIdentifier: | filter_module |
| SourceFile: | mod_filter.c |

## Summary

This module enables smart, context-sensitive configuration of output content filters. For example, apache can be configured to process different content-types through different filters, even when the content-type is not known in advance (e.g. in a proxy).

MOD_FILTER works by introducing indirection into the filter chain. Instead of inserting filters in the chain, we insert a filter harness which in turn dispatches conditionally to a filter provider. Any content filter may be used as a provider to MOD_FILTER; no change to existing filter modules is required (although it may be possible to simplify them).

## Directives

- AddOutputFilterByType

- FilterChain

- FilterDeclare

- FilterProtocol

- FilterProvider

- FilterTrace

## Smart Filtering

In the traditional filtering model, filters are inserted unconditionally using ADDOUTPUTFILTER and family. Each filter then needs to determine whether to run, and there is little flexibility available for server admins to allow the chain to be configured dynamically.

MOD_FILTER by contrast gives server administrators a great deal of flexibility in configuring the filter chain. In fact, filters can be inserted based on complex boolean expressions (p. 99) This generalises the limited flexibility offered by ADDOUTPUTFILTERBYTYPE.

**Filter Declarations, Providers and Chains**

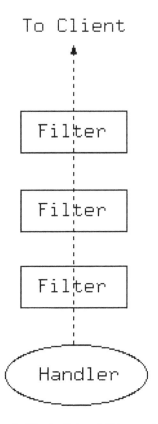

*Figure 1:* The traditional filter model

In the traditional model, output filters are a simple chain from the content generator (handler) to the client. This works well provided the filter chain can be correctly configured, but presents problems when the filters need to be configured dynamically based on the outcome of the handler.

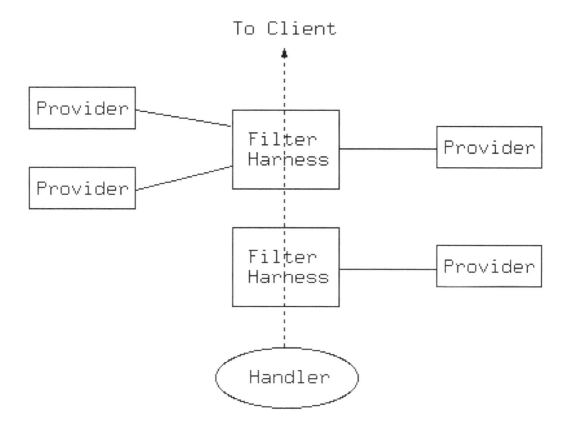

*Figure 2:* The MOD_FILTER model

MOD_FILTER works by introducing indirection into the filter chain. Instead of inserting filters in the chain, we insert a filter harness which in turn dispatches conditionally to a filter provider. Any content filter may be used as a provider to MOD_FILTER; no change to existing filter modules is required (although it may be possible to simplify them). There can be multiple providers for one filter, but no more than one provider will run for any single request.

A filter chain comprises any number of instances of the filter harness, each of which may have any number of providers. A special case is that of a single provider with unconditional dispatch: this is equivalent to inserting the provider filter directly into the chain.

## Configuring the Chain

There are three stages to configuring a filter chain with MOD_FILTER. For details of the directives, see below.

**Declare Filters** The FILTERDECLARE directive declares a filter, assigning it a name and filter type. Required only if the filter is not the default type AP_FTYPE_RESOURCE.

**Register Providers** The FILTERPROVIDER directive registers a provider with a filter. The filter may have been declared with FILTERDECLARE; if not, FilterProvider will implicitly declare it with the default type AP_FTYPE_RESOURCE. The provider must have been registered with ap_register_output_filter by some module. The final argument to FILTERPROVIDER is an expression: the provider will be selected to run for a request if and only if the expression evaluates to true. The expression may evaluate HTTP request or response headers, environment variables, or the Handler used by this request. Unlike earlier versions, mod_filter now supports complex expressions involving multiple criteria with AND / OR logic (&& / ——) and brackets. The details of the expression syntax are described in the ap_expr documentation (p. 99) .

**Configure the Chain** The above directives build components of a smart filter chain, but do not configure it to run. The FILTERCHAIN directive builds a filter chain from smart filters declared, offering the flexibility to insert filters at the beginning or end of the chain, remove a filter, or clear the chain.

### Filtering and Response Status

mod_filter normally only runs filters on responses with HTTP status 200 (OK). If you want to filter documents with other response statuses, you can set the *filter-errordocs* environment variable, and it will work on all responses regardless of status. To refine this further, you can use expression conditions with FILTERPROVIDER.

### Upgrading from Apache HTTP Server 2.2 Configuration

The FILTERPROVIDER directive has changed from httpd 2.2: the *match* and *dispatch* arguments are replaced with a single but more versatile *expression*. In general, you can convert a match/dispatch pair to the two sides of an expression, using something like:

```
"dispatch = 'match'"
```

The Request headers, Response headers and Environment variables are now interpreted from syntax %{*req:foo*}, %{*resp:foo*} and %{*env:foo*} respectively. The variables %{*HANDLER*} and %{*CONTENT_TYPE*} are also supported.

Note that the match no longer support substring matches. They can be replaced by regular expression matches.

### Examples

**Server side Includes (SSI)** A simple case of replacing ADDOUTPUTFILTERBYTYPE

```
FilterDeclare SSI
FilterProvider SSI INCLUDES "%{CONTENT_TYPE} =~ m|^text/html|"
FilterChain SSI
```

**Server side Includes (SSI)** The same as the above but dispatching on handler (classic SSI behaviour; .shtml files get processed).

```
FilterProvider SSI INCLUDES "%{HANDLER} = 'server-parsed'"
FilterChain SSI
```

**Emulating mod_gzip with mod_deflate** Insert INFLATE filter only if "gzip" is NOT in the Accept-Encoding header. This filter runs with ftype CONTENT_SET.

```
FilterDeclare gzip CONTENT_SET
FilterProvider gzip inflate "%{req:Accept-Encoding} !~ /gzip/"
FilterChain gzip
```

**Image Downsampling** Suppose we want to downsample all web images, and have filters for GIF, JPEG and PNG.

```
FilterProvider unpack jpeg_unpack "%{CONTENT_TYPE} = 'image/jpeg'"
FilterProvider unpack gif_unpack "%{CONTENT_TYPE} = 'image/gif'"
FilterProvider unpack png_unpack "%{CONTENT_TYPE} = 'image/png'"
```

```
FilterProvider downsample downsample_filter "%{CONTENT_TYPE} = m|^image/(jpeg|gi
FilterProtocol downsample "change=yes"

FilterProvider repack jpeg_pack "%{CONTENT_TYPE} = 'image/jpeg'"
FilterProvider repack gif_pack "%{CONTENT_TYPE} = 'image/gif'"
FilterProvider repack png_pack "%{CONTENT_TYPE} = 'image/png'"
<Location "/image-filter">
    FilterChain unpack downsample repack
</Location>
```

## Protocol Handling

Historically, each filter is responsible for ensuring that whatever changes it makes are correctly represented in the HTTP response headers, and that it does not run when it would make an illegal change. This imposes a burden on filter authors to re-implement some common functionality in every filter:

- Many filters will change the content, invalidating existing content tags, checksums, hashes, and lengths.
- Filters that require an entire, unbroken response in input need to ensure they don't get byteranges from a backend.
- Filters that transform output in a filter need to ensure they don't violate a `Cache-Control:` `no-transform` header from the backend.
- Filters may make responses uncacheable.

MOD_FILTER aims to offer generic handling of these details of filter implementation, reducing the complexity required of content filter modules. This is work-in-progress; the FILTERPROTOCOL implements some of this functionality for back-compatibility with Apache 2.0 modules. For httpd 2.1 and later, the `ap_register_output_filter_protocol` and `ap_filter_protocol` API enables filter modules to declare their own behaviour.

At the same time, MOD_FILTER should not interfere with a filter that wants to handle all aspects of the protocol. By default (i.e. in the absence of any FILTERPROTOCOL directives), MOD_FILTER will leave the headers untouched.

At the time of writing, this feature is largely untested, as modules in common use are designed to work with 2.0. Modules using it should test it carefully.

## AddOutputFilterByType Directive

| | |
|---|---|
| Description: | assigns an output filter to a particular media-type |
| Syntax: | `AddOutputFilterByType filter[;filter...]  media-type` `[media-type] ...` |
| Context: | server config, virtual host, directory, .htaccess |
| Override: | FileInfo |
| Status: | Base |
| Module: | mod_filter |
| Compatibility: | Had severe limitations before being moved to MOD_FILTER in version 2.3.7 |

This directive activates a particular output filter (p. 110) for a request depending on the response media-type.

The following example uses the DEFLATE filter, which is provided by MOD_DEFLATE. It will compress all output (either static or dynamic) which is labeled as `text/html` or `text/plain` before it is sent to the client.

```
AddOutputFilterByType DEFLATE text/html text/plain
```

If you want the content to be processed by more than one filter, their names have to be separated by semicolons. It's also possible to use one ADDOUTPUTFILTERBYTYPE directive for each of these filters.

The configuration below causes all script output labeled as `text/html` to be processed at first by the INCLUDES filter and then by the DEFLATE filter.

```
<Location "/cgi-bin/">
    Options Includes
    AddOutputFilterByType INCLUDES;DEFLATE text/html
</Location>
```

**See also**

- ADDOUTPUTFILTER
- SETOUTPUTFILTER
- filters (p. 110)

## FilterChain Directive

| Description: | Configure the filter chain |
|---|---|
| Syntax: | `FilterChain [+=-@!]filter-name ...` |
| Context: | server config, virtual host, directory, .htaccess |
| Override: | Options |
| Status: | Base |
| Module: | mod_filter |

This configures an actual filter chain, from declared filters. FILTERCHAIN takes any number of arguments, each optionally preceded with a single-character control that determines what to do:

**+`filter-name`** Add *filter-name* to the end of the filter chain

**@`filter-name`** Insert *filter-name* at the start of the filter chain

**-`filter-name`** Remove *filter-name* from the filter chain

**=`filter-name`** Empty the filter chain and insert *filter-name*

**!** Empty the filter chain

**`filter-name`** Equivalent to +`filter-name`

## FilterDeclare Directive

| Description: | Declare a smart filter |
|---|---|
| Syntax: | `FilterDeclare filter-name [type]` |
| Context: | server config, virtual host, directory, .htaccess |
| Override: | Options |
| Status: | Base |
| Module: | mod_filter |

This directive declares an output filter together with a header or environment variable that will determine runtime configuration. The first argument is a *filter-name* for use in FILTERPROVIDER, FILTERCHAIN and FILTERPROTOCOL directives.

The final (optional) argument is the type of filter, and takes values of `ap_filter_type` - namely RESOURCE (the default), CONTENT_SET, PROTOCOL, TRANSCODE, CONNECTION or NETWORK.

## FilterProtocol Directive

| | |
|---|---|
| Description: | Deal with correct HTTP protocol handling |
| Syntax: | `FilterProtocol filter-name [provider-name] proto-flags` |
| Context: | server config, virtual host, directory, .htaccess |
| Override: | Options |
| Status: | Base |
| Module: | mod_filter |

This directs MOD_FILTER to deal with ensuring the filter doesn't run when it shouldn't, and that the HTTP response headers are correctly set taking into account the effects of the filter.

There are two forms of this directive. With three arguments, it applies specifically to a *filter-name* and a *provider-name* for that filter. With two arguments it applies to a *filter-name* whenever the filter runs *any* provider.

Flags specified with this directive are merged with the flags that underlying providers may have registerd with MOD_FILTER. For example, a filter may internally specify the equivalent of `change=yes`, but a particular configuration of the module can override with `change=no`.

*proto-flags* is one or more of

**change=yes|no** Specifies whether the filter changes the content, including possibly the content length. The "no" argument is supported in 2.4.7 and later.

**change=1:1** The filter changes the content, but will not change the content length

**byteranges=no** The filter cannot work on byteranges and requires complete input

**proxy=no** The filter should not run in a proxy context

**proxy=transform** The filter transforms the response in a manner incompatible with the HTTP `Cache-Control: no-transform` header.

**cache=no** The filter renders the output uncacheable (eg by introducing randomised content changes)

## FilterProvider Directive

| | |
|---|---|
| Description: | Register a content filter |
| Syntax: | `FilterProvider filter-name provider-name expression` |
| Context: | server config, virtual host, directory, .htaccess |
| Override: | Options |
| Status: | Base |
| Module: | mod_filter |

This directive registers a *provider* for the smart filter. The provider will be called if and only if the *expression* declared evaluates to true when the harness is first called.

*provider-name* must have been registered by loading a module that registers the name with `ap_register_output_filter`.

*expression* is an ap_expr (p. 99) .

**See also**

- Expressions in Apache HTTP Server (p. 99) , for a complete reference and examples.

- MOD_INCLUDE

## FilterTrace Directive

| | |
|---|---|
| Description: | Get debug/diagnostic information from MOD_FILTER |
| Syntax: | `FilterTrace filter-name level` |
| Context: | server config, virtual host, directory |
| Status: | Base |
| Module: | mod_filter |

This directive generates debug information from MOD_FILTER. It is designed to help test and debug providers (filter modules), although it may also help with MOD_FILTER itself.

The debug output depends on the *level* set:

**0 (default)**  No debug information is generated.

**1**  MOD_FILTER will record buckets and brigades passing through the filter to the error log, before the provider has processed them. This is similar to the information generated by mod_diagnostics[36].

**2 (not yet implemented)**  Will dump the full data passing through to a tempfile before the provider. **For single-user debug only**; this will not support concurrent hits.

---

[36]http://apache.webthing.com/mod_diagnostics/

# 10.53   Apache Module mod_firehose

| Description: | Multiplexes all I/O to a given file or pipe. |
|---|---|
| Status: | Extension |
| ModuleIdentifier: | firehose_module |
| SourceFile: | mod_firehose.c |

## Summary

mod_firehose provides a mechanism to record data being passed between the httpd server and the client at the raw connection level to either a file or a pipe in such a way that the data can be analysed or played back to the server at a future date. It can be thought of as "tcpdump for httpd".

Connections are recorded after the SSL has been stripped, and can be used for forensic debugging.

The firehose tool can be used to demultiplex the recorded stream back into individual files for analysis, or playback using a tool like netcat.

 **WARNING**

> This module IGNORES all request level mechanisms to keep data private.  It is the responsibility of the administrator to ensure that private data is not inadvertently exposed using this module.

### Directives

- FirehoseConnectionInput
- FirehoseConnectionOutput
- FirehoseProxyConnectionInput
- FirehoseProxyConnectionOutput
- FirehoseRequestInput
- FirehoseRequestOutput

### See also

- firehose

## Enabling a Firehose

To enable the module, it should be compiled and loaded in to your running Apache configuration, and the directives below used to record the data you are interested in.

It is possible to record both incoming and outgoing data to the same filename if desired, as the direction of flow is recorded within each fragment.

It is possible to write to both normal files and fifos (pipes). In the case of fifos, mod_firehose ensures that the packet size is no larger than PIPE_BUF to ensure writes are atomic.

If a pipe is being used, something must be reading from the pipe before httpd is started for the pipe to be successfully opened for write. If the request to open the pipe fails, mod_firehose will silently stand down and not record anything, and the server will keep running as normal.

By default, all attempts to write will block the server. If the webserver has been built against APR v2.0 or later, and an optional "nonblock" parameter is specified all file writes will be non blocking, and buffer overflows will cause debugging data to be lost. In this case it is possible to prioritise the running of the server over the recording of firehose data.

**Stream Format**

The server typically serves multiple connections simultaneously, and as a result requests and responses need to be multiplexed before being written to the firehose.

The fragment format is designed as clear text, so that a firehose can be opened with and inspected by a normal text editor. Alternatively, the `firehose` tool can be used to demultiplex the firehose back into individual requests or connections.

The size of the multiplexed fragments is governed by PIPE_BUF, the maximum size of write the system is prepared to perform atomically. By keeping the multiplexed fragments below PIPE_BUF in size, the module guarantees that data from different fragments does not interleave. The size of PIPE_BUF varies on different operating systems.

The BNF for the fragment format is as follows:

```
stream = 0*(fragment)

fragment = header CRLF body CRLF

header = length SPC timestamp SPC ( request | response ) SPC uuid SPC count

length = <up to 16 byte hex fragment length>
timestamp = <up to 16 byte hex timestamp microseconds since 1970>
request = "<"
response = ">"
uuid = <formatted uuid of the connection>
count = <hex fragment number in the connection>

body = <the binary content of the fragment>

SPC = <a single space>
CRLF = <a carriage return, followed by a line feed>
```

All fragments for a connection or a request will share the same UUID, depending on whether connections or requests are being recorded. If connections are being recorded, multiple requests may appear within a connection. A fragment with a zero length indicates the end of the connection.

Fragments may go missing or be dropped if the process reading the fragments is too slow. If this happens, gaps will exist in the connection counter numbering. A warning will be logged in the error log to indicate the UUID and counter of the dropped fragment, so it can be confirmed the fragment was dropped.

It is possible that the terminating empty fragment may not appear, caused by the httpd process crashing, or being terminated ungracefully. The terminating fragment may be dropped if the process reading the fragments is not fast enough.

**FirehoseConnectionInput Directive**

| | |
|---|---|
| Description: | Capture traffic coming into the server on each connection |
| Syntax: | `FirehoseConnectionInput [ block | nonblock ] filename` |
| Default: | `none` |
| Context: | server config |
| Status: | Extension |
| Module: | mod_firehose |
| Compatibility: | FirehoseConnectionInput is only available in Apache 2.5.0 and later. |

Capture traffic coming into the server on each connection. Multiple requests will be captured within the same connection if keepalive is present.

### Example

```
FirehoseConnectionInput connection-input.firehose
```

## FirehoseConnectionOutput Directive

| | |
|---|---|
| Description: | Capture traffic going out of the server on each connection |
| Syntax: | FirehoseConnectionOutput [ block | nonblock ] filename |
| Default: | none |
| Context: | server config |
| Status: | Extension |
| Module: | mod_firehose |
| Compatibility: | FirehoseConnectionOutput is only available in Apache 2.5.0 and later. |

Capture traffic going out of the server on each connection. Multiple requests will be captured within the same connection if keepalive is present.

### Example

```
FirehoseConnectionOutput connection-output.firehose
```

## FirehoseProxyConnectionInput Directive

| | |
|---|---|
| Description: | Capture traffic coming into the back of mod_proxy |
| Syntax: | FirehoseProxyConnectionInput [ block | nonblock ] filename |
| Default: | none |
| Context: | server config |
| Status: | Extension |
| Module: | mod_firehose |
| Compatibility: | FirehoseProxyConnectionInput is only available in Apache 2.5.0 and later. |

Capture traffic being received by mod_proxy.

### Example

```
FirehoseProxyConnectionInput proxy-input.firehose
```

## FirehoseProxyConnectionOutput Directive

| | |
|---|---|
| Description: | Capture traffic sent out from the back of mod_proxy |
| Syntax: | FirehoseProxyConnectionOutput [ block | nonblock ] filename |
| Default: | none |
| Context: | server config |
| Status: | Extension |
| Module: | mod_firehose |
| Compatibility: | FirehoseProxyConnectionOutput is only available in Apache 2.5.0 and later. |

Capture traffic being sent out by mod_proxy.

**Example**

```
FirehoseProxyConnectionOutput proxy-output.firehose
```

## FirehoseRequestInput Directive

| | |
|---|---|
| Description: | Capture traffic coming into the server on each request |
| Syntax: | FirehoseRequestInput [ block \| nonblock ] filename |
| Default: | none |
| Context: | server config |
| Status: | Extension |
| Module: | mod_firehose |
| Compatibility: | FirehoseRequestInput is only available in Apache 2.5.0 and later. |

Capture traffic coming into the server on each request. Requests will be captured separately, regardless of the presence of keepalive.

**Example**

```
FirehoseRequestInput request-input.firehose
```

## FirehoseRequestOutput Directive

| | |
|---|---|
| Description: | Capture traffic going out of the server on each request |
| Syntax: | FirehoseRequestOutput [ block \| nonblock ] filename |
| Default: | none |
| Context: | server config |
| Status: | Extension |
| Module: | mod_firehose |
| Compatibility: | FirehoseRequestOutput is only available in Apache 2.5.0 and later. |

Capture traffic going out of the server on each request. Requests will be captured separately, regardless of the presence of keepalive.

**Example**

```
FirehoseRequestOutput request-output.firehose
```

# 10.54 Apache Module mod_headers

| Description: | Customization of HTTP request and response headers |
|---|---|
| Status: | Extension |
| ModuleIdentifier: | headers_module |
| SourceFile: | mod_headers.c |

## Summary

This module provides directives to control and modify HTTP request and response headers. Headers can be merged, replaced or removed.

**Directives**

- Header
- RequestHeader

## Order of Processing

The directives provided by MOD_HEADERS can occur almost anywhere within the server configuration, and can be limited in scope by enclosing them in configuration sections (p. 35) .

Order of processing is important and is affected both by the order in the configuration file and by placement in configuration sections (p. 35) . These two directives have a different effect if reversed:

```
RequestHeader append MirrorID "mirror 12"
RequestHeader unset MirrorID
```

This way round, the `MirrorID` header is not set. If reversed, the MirrorID header is set to `"mirror 12"`.

## Early and Late Processing

MOD_HEADERS can be applied either early or late in the request. The normal mode is late, when *Request* Headers are set immediately before running the content generator and *Response* Headers just as the response is sent down the wire. Always use Late mode in an operational server.

Early mode is designed as a test/debugging aid for developers. Directives defined using the `early` keyword are set right at the beginning of processing the request. This means they can be used to simulate different requests and set up test cases, but it also means that headers may be changed at any time by other modules before generating a Response.

Because early directives are processed before the request path's configuration is traversed, early headers can only be set in a main server or virtual host context. Early directives cannot depend on a request path, so they will fail in contexts such as <DIRECTORY> or <LOCATION>.

## Examples

1. Copy all request headers that begin with "TS" to the response headers:

```
Header echo ^TS
```

2. Add a header, `MyHeader`, to the response including a timestamp for when the request was received and how long it took to begin serving the request. This header can be used by the client to intuit load on the server or in isolating bottlenecks between the client and the server.

```
Header set MyHeader "%D %t"
```

results in this header being added to the response:

```
MyHeader:  D=3775428 t=991424704447256
```

3. Say hello to Joe

```
Header set MyHeader "Hello Joe. It took %D microseconds for Apache to serve this reque
```

results in this header being added to the response:

```
MyHeader:  Hello Joe.  It took D=3775428 microseconds for Apache to
serve this request.
```

4. Conditionally send `MyHeader` on the response if and only if header `MyRequestHeader` is present on the request. This is useful for constructing headers in response to some client stimulus. Note that this example requires the services of the MOD_SETENVIF module.

```
SetEnvIf MyRequestHeader myvalue HAVE_MyRequestHeader
Header set MyHeader "%D %t mytext" env=HAVE_MyRequestHeader
```

If the header `MyRequestHeader:  myvalue` is present on the HTTP request, the response will contain the following header:

```
MyHeader:  D=3775428 t=991424704447256 mytext
```

5. Enable DAV to work with Apache running HTTP through SSL hardware (problem description[37]) by replacing *https:* with *http:* in the *Destination* header:

```
RequestHeader edit Destination ^https: http: early
```

6. Set the same header value under multiple nonexclusive conditions, but do not duplicate the value in the final header. If all of the following conditions applied to a request (i.e., if the CGI, NO_CACHE and NO_STORE environment variables all existed for the request):

```
Header merge Cache-Control no-cache env=CGI
Header merge Cache-Control no-cache env=NO_CACHE
Header merge Cache-Control no-store env=NO_STORE
```

then the response would contain the following header:

```
Cache-Control:  no-cache, no-store
```

---

[37]http://svn.haxx.se/users/archive-2006-03/0549.shtml

If `append` was used instead of `merge`, then the response would contain the following header:

```
Cache-Control:  no-cache, no-cache, no-store
```

7. Set a test cookie if and only if the client didn't send us a cookie

```
Header set Set-Cookie testcookie "expr=-z %{req:Cookie}"
```

8. Append a Caching header for responses with a HTTP status code of 200

```
Header append Cache-Control s-maxage=600 "expr=%{REQUEST_STATUS} == 200"
```

## Header Directive

| | |
|---|---|
| Description: | Configure HTTP response headers |
| Syntax: | `Header [condition] add|append|echo|edit|edit*|merge|set|setifempty|unset` `header [[expr=]value [replacement] [early|env=[!]varname|expr=expression` |
| Context: | server config, virtual host, directory, .htaccess |
| Override: | FileInfo |
| Status: | Extension |
| Module: | mod_headers |
| Compatibility: | SetIfEmpty available in 2.4.7 and later, expr=value available in 2.4.10 and later |

This directive can replace, merge or remove HTTP response headers. The header is modified just after the content handler and output filters are run, allowing outgoing headers to be modified.

The optional *condition* argument determines which internal table of responses headers this directive will operate against. Despite the name, the default value of `onsuccess` does *not* limit an *action* to responses with a 2xx status code. Headers set under this condition are still used when, for example, a request is *successfully* proxied or generated by CGI, even when they have generated a failing status code.

When your action is a function of an existing header, you may need to specify a condition of `always`, depending on which internal table the original header was set in. The table that corresponds to `always` is used for locally generated error responses as well as successful responses. Note also that repeating this directive with both conditions makes sense in some scenarios because `always` is not a superset of `onsuccess` with respect to existing headers:

- You're adding a header to a locally generated non-success (non-2xx) response, such as a redirect, in which case only the table corresponding to `always` is used in the ultimate response.
- You're modifying or removing a header generated by a CGI script, in which case the CGI scripts are in the table corresponding to `always` and not in the default table.
- You're modifying or removing a header generated by some piece of the server but that header is not being found by the default `onsuccess` condition.

Separately from the *condition* parameter described above, you can limit an action based on HTTP status codes for e.g. proxied or CGI requests. See the example that uses %{REQUEST_STATUS} in the section above.

The action it performs is determined by the first argument (second argument if a *condition* is specified). This can be one of the following values:

**add** The response header is added to the existing set of headers, even if this header already exists. This can result in two (or more) headers having the same name. This can lead to unforeseen consequences, and in general `set`, `append` or `merge` should be used instead.

**append** The response header is appended to any existing header of the same name. When a new value is merged onto an existing header it is separated from the existing header with a comma. This is the HTTP standard way of giving a header multiple values.

**echo** Request headers with this name are echoed back in the response headers. *header* may be a regular expression. *value* must be omitted.

**edit**

**edit\*** If this response header exists, its value is transformed according to a regular expression search-and-replace. The *value* argument is a regular expression, and the *replacement* is a replacement string, which may contain backreferences or format specifiers. The `edit` form will match and replace exactly once in a header value, whereas the `edit*` form will replace *every* instance of the search pattern if it appears more than once.

**merge** The response header is appended to any existing header of the same name, unless the value to be appended already appears in the header's comma-delimited list of values. When a new value is merged onto an existing header it is separated from the existing header with a comma. This is the HTTP standard way of giving a header multiple values. Values are compared in a case sensitive manner, and after all format specifiers have been processed. Values in double quotes are considered different from otherwise identical unquoted values.

**set** The response header is set, replacing any previous header with this name. The *value* may be a format string.

**setifempty** The request header is set, but only if there is no previous header with this name.
Available in 2.4.7 and later.

**unset** The response header of this name is removed, if it exists. If there are multiple headers of the same name, all will be removed. *value* must be omitted.

**note** The value of the named response *header* is copied into an internal note whose name is given by *value*. This is useful if a header sent by a CGI or proxied resource is configured to be unset but should also be logged.
Available in 2.4.7 and later.

This argument is followed by a *header* name, which can include the final colon, but it is not required. Case is ignored for `set`, `append`, `merge`, `add`, `unset` and `edit`. The *header* name for `echo` is case sensitive and may be a regular expression.

For `set`, `append`, `merge` and `add` a *value* is specified as the next argument. If *value* contains spaces, it should be surrounded by double quotes. *value* may be a character string, a string containing MOD_HEADERS specific format specifiers (and character literals), or an ap_expr (p. 99) expression prefixed with *expr=*

The following format specifiers are supported in *value*:

| Format | Description |
| --- | --- |
| %% | The percent sign |
| %t | The time the request was received in Universal Coordinated Time since the epoch (Jan. 1, 1970) measured in microseconds. The value is preceded by `t=`. |
| %D | The time from when the request was received to the time the headers are sent on the wire. This is a measure of the duration of the request. The value is preceded by `D=`. The value is measured in microseconds. |
| %l | The current load averages of the actual server itself. It is designed to expose the values obtained by `getloadavg()` and this represents the current load average, the 5 minute average, and the 15 minute average. The value is preceded by `l=` with each average separated by `/`. Available in 2.4.4 and later. |
| %i | The current idle percentage of httpd (0 to 100) based on available processes and threads. The value is preceded by `i=`. Available in 2.4.4 and later. |
| %b | The current busy percentage of httpd (0 to 100) based on available processes and threads. The value is preceded by `b=`. Available in 2.4.4 and later. |
| %{VARNAME}e | The contents of the environment variable (p. 92) VARNAME. |
| %{VARNAME}s | The contents of the SSL environment variable (p. 916) VARNAME, if MOD_SSL is enabled. |

Note

> The %s format specifier is only available in Apache 2.1 and later; it can be used instead of
> %e to avoid the overhead of enabling SSLOptions +StdEnvVars. If SSLOptions
> +StdEnvVars must be enabled anyway for some other reason, %e will be more efficient
> than %s.

Note on expression values

> When the value parameter uses the ap_expr (p. 99) parser, some expression syntax will differ
> from examples that evaluate *boolean* expressions such as <If>:
>
> - The starting point of the grammar is 'string' rather than 'expr'.
>
> - Function calls use the %{funcname:arg} syntax rather than funcname(arg).
>
> - Multi-argument functions are not currently accessible from this starting point
>
> - Quote the entire parameter, such as
>
>   ```
>   Header set foo-checksum "expr=%{md5:foo}"
>   ```

For edit there is both a *value* argument which is a regular expression, and an additional *replacement* string. As of version 2.4.7 the replacement string may also contain format specifiers.

The HEADER directive may be followed by an additional argument, which may be any of:

**early** Specifies early processing.

**env=[!]*varname*** The directive is applied if and only if the environment variable (p. 92) varname exists. A ! in front of varname reverses the test, so the directive applies only if varname is unset.

**expr=*expression*** The directive is applied if and only if *expression* evaluates to true. Details of expression syntax and evaluation are documented in the ap_expr (p. 99) documentation.

```
# This delays the evaluation of the condition clause compared to <If>
Header always set CustomHeader my-value "expr=%{REQUEST_URI} =~ m#^/special_path
```

Except in early mode, the HEADER directives are processed just before the response is sent to the network. This means that it is possible to set and/or override most headers, except for some headers added by the HTTP header filter. Prior to 2.2.12, it was not possible to change the Content-Type header with this directive.

## RequestHeader Directive

| Description:   | Configure HTTP request headers |
|---|---|
| Syntax:        | RequestHeader add\|append\|edit\|edit*\|merge\|set\|setifempty\|unset header [[expr=]value [replacement] [early\|env=[!]varname\|expr=expression |
| Context:       | server config, virtual host, directory, .htaccess |
| Override:      | FileInfo |
| Status:        | Extension |
| Module:        | mod_headers |
| Compatibility: | SetIfEmpty available in 2.4.7 and later, expr=value available in 2.4.10 and later |

This directive can replace, merge, change or remove HTTP request headers. The header is modified just before the content handler is run, allowing incoming headers to be modified. The action it performs is determined by the first argument. This can be one of the following values:

**add** The request header is added to the existing set of headers, even if this header already exists. This can result in two (or more) headers having the same name. This can lead to unforeseen consequences, and in general set, append or merge should be used instead.

**append** The request header is appended to any existing header of the same name. When a new value is merged onto an existing header it is separated from the existing header with a comma. This is the HTTP standard way of giving a header multiple values.

**edit**

**edit∗** If this request header exists, its value is transformed according to a regular expression search-and-replace. The *value* argument is a regular expression, and the *replacement* is a replacement string, which may contain backreferences or format specifiers. The edit form will match and replace exactly once in a header value, whereas the edit∗ form will replace *every* instance of the search pattern if it appears more than once.

**merge** The request header is appended to any existing header of the same name, unless the value to be appended already appears in the existing header's comma-delimited list of values. When a new value is merged onto an existing header it is separated from the existing header with a comma. This is the HTTP standard way of giving a header multiple values. Values are compared in a case sensitive manner, and after all format specifiers have been processed. Values in double quotes are considered different from otherwise identical unquoted values.

**set** The request header is set, replacing any previous header with this name

**setifempty** The request header is set, but only if there is no previous header with this name. Available in 2.4.7 and later.

**unset** The request header of this name is removed, if it exists. If there are multiple headers of the same name, all will be removed. *value* must be omitted.

This argument is followed by a header name, which can include the final colon, but it is not required. Case is ignored. For set, append, merge and add a *value* is given as the third argument. If a *value* contains spaces, it should be surrounded by double quotes. For unset, no *value* should be given. *value* may be a character string, a string containing format specifiers or a combination of both. The supported format specifiers are the same as for the HEADER, please have a look there for details. For edit both a *value* and a *replacement* are required, and are a regular expression and a replacement string respectively.

The REQUESTHEADER directive may be followed by an additional argument, which may be any of:

**early** Specifies early processing.

**env=[!]varname** The directive is applied if and only if the environment variable (p. 92) varname exists. A ! in front of varname reverses the test, so the directive applies only if varname is unset.

**expr=expression** The directive is applied if and only if *expression* evaluates to true. Details of expression syntax and evaluation are documented in the ap_expr (p. 99) documentation.

Except in early mode, the REQUESTHEADER directive is processed just before the request is run by its handler in the fixup phase. This should allow headers generated by the browser, or by Apache input filters to be overridden or modified.

## 10.55 Apache Module mod_heartbeat

| Description: | Sends messages with server status to frontend proxy |
|---|---|
| Status: | Experimental |
| ModuleIdentifier: | heartbeat_module |
| SourceFile: | mod_heartbeat |
| Compatibility: | Available in Apache 2.3 and later |

### Summary

MOD_HEARTBEAT sends multicast messages to a MOD_HEARTMONITOR listener that advertises the servers current connection count. Usually, MOD_HEARTMONITOR will be running on a proxy server with MOD_LBMETHOD_HEARTBEAT loaded, which allows PROXYPASS to use the "heartbeat" *lbmethod* inside of PROXYPASS.

MOD_HEARTBEAT itself is loaded on the origin server(s) that serve requests through the proxy server(s).

> ! To use MOD_HEARTBEAT, MOD_STATUS and MOD_WATCHDOG must be either a static modules or, if a dynamic module, must be loaded before MOD_HEARTBEAT.

### Directives

- HeartbeatAddress

### Consuming mod_heartbeat Output

Every 1 second, this module generates a single multicast UDP packet, containing the number of busy and idle workers. The packet is a simple ASCII format, similar to GET query parameters in HTTP.

> **An Example Packet**
> ```
> v=1&ready=75&busy=0
> ```

Consumers should handle new variables besides busy and ready, separated by '&', being added in the future.

### HeartbeatAddress Directive

| Description: | Multicast address for heartbeat packets |
|---|---|
| Syntax: | `HeartbeatAddress addr:port` |
| Default: | `disabled` |
| Context: | server config |
| Status: | Experimental |
| Module: | mod_heartbeat |

The HEARTBEATADDRESS directive specifies the multicast address to which MOD_HEARTBEAT will send status information. This address will usually correspond to a configured HEARTBEATLISTEN on a frontend proxy system.

```
HeartbeatAddress 239.0.0.1:27999
```

## 10.56   Apache Module mod_heartmonitor

| | |
|---|---|
| Description: | Centralized monitor for mod_heartbeat origin servers |
| Status: | Experimental |
| ModuleIdentifier: | heartmonitor_module |
| SourceFile: | mod_heartmonitor.c |
| Compatibility: | Available in Apache 2.3 and later |

## Summary

MOD_HEARTMONITOR listens for server status messages generated by MOD_HEARTBEAT enabled origin servers and makes their status available to MOD_LBMETHOD_HEARTBEAT. This allows PROXYPASS to use the "heartbeat" *lb-method* inside of PROXYPASS.

This module uses the services of MOD_SLOTMEM_SHM when available instead of flat-file storage. No configuration is required to use MOD_SLOTMEM_SHM.

> [!]   To use MOD_HEARTMONITOR, MOD_STATUS and MOD_WATCHDOG must be either a static modules or, if a dynamic module, it must be loaded before MOD_HEARTMONITOR.

### Directives

- HeartbeatListen
- HeartbeatMaxServers
- HeartbeatStorage

## HeartbeatListen Directive

| | |
|---|---|
| Description: | multicast address to listen for incoming heartbeat requests |
| Syntax: | `HeartbeatListenaddr:port` |
| Default: | `disabled` |
| Context: | server config |
| Status: | Experimental |
| Module: | mod_heartmonitor |

The HEARTBEATLISTEN directive specifies the multicast address on which the server will listen for status information from MOD_HEARTBEAT-enabled servers. This address will usually correspond to a configured HEARTBEATADDRESS on an origin server.

```
HeartbeatListen 239.0.0.1:27999
```

This module is inactive until this directive is used.

## HeartbeatMaxServers Directive

| | |
|---|---|
| Description: | Specifies the maximum number of servers that will be sending heartbeat requests to this server |
| Syntax: | `HeartbeatMaxServers number-of-servers` |
| Default: | `HeartbeatMaxServers 10` |
| Context: | server config |
| Status: | Experimental |
| Module: | mod_heartmonitor |

The HEARTBEATMAXSERVERS directive specifies the maximum number of servers that will be sending requests to this monitor server. It is used to control the size of the shared memory allocated to store the heartbeat info when MOD_SLOTMEM_SHM is in use.

## HeartbeatStorage Directive

| | |
|---|---|
| Description: | Path to store heartbeat data |
| Syntax: | `HeartbeatStorage file-path` |
| Default: | `HeartbeatStorage logs/hb.dat` |
| Context: | server config |
| Status: | Experimental |
| Module: | mod_heartmonitor |

The HEARTBEATSTORAGE directive specifies the path to store heartbeat data. This flat-file is used only when MOD_SLOTMEM_SHM is not loaded.

# 10.57   Apache Module mod_http2

| Description: | Support for the HTTP/2 transport layer |
|---|---|
| Status: | Extension |
| ModuleIdentifier: | http2_module |
| SourceFile: | mod_http2.c |
| Compatibility: | Available in version 2.4.17 and later |

## Summary

This module provides HTTP/2 (RFC 7540[38]) support for the Apache HTTP Server.

This module relies on libnghttp2[39] to provide the core http/2 engine.

> **⚠ Warning**
>
> This module is experimental. Its behaviors, directives, and defaults are subject to more change
> from release to release relative to other standard modules. Users are encouraged to consult the
> "CHANGES" file for potential updates.

You must enable HTTP/2 via PROTOCOLS in order to use the functionality described in this document. The HTTP/2 protocol does not require[40] the use of encryption so two schemes are available: h2 (HTTP/2 over TLS) and h2c (HTTP/2 over TCP).

Two useful configuration schemes are:

⟹ **HTTP/2 in a VirtualHost context (TLS only)**

```
Protocols h2 http/1.1
```

Allows HTTP/2 negotiation (h2) via TLS ALPN in a secure <VIRTUALHOST>.  HTTP/2 preamble checking (Direct mode, see H2DIRECT) is disabled by default for h2.

⟹ **HTTP/2 in a Server context (TLS and cleartext)**

```
Protocols h2 h2c http/1.1
```

Allows HTTP/2 negotiation (h2) via TLS ALPN for secure <VIRTUALHOST>.  Allows HTTP/2 cleartext negotiation (h2c) upgrading from an initial HTTP/1.1 connection or via HTTP/2 preamble checking (Direct mode, see H2DIRECT).

Refer to the official HTTP/2 FAQ[41] for any doubt about the protocol.

## Directives

- H2Direct
- H2MaxSessionStreams
- H2MaxWorkerIdleSeconds
- H2MaxWorkers
- H2MinWorkers

---

[38]https://tools.ietf.org/html/rfc7540

[39]http://nghttp2.org/

[40]https://http2.github.io/faq/#does-http2-require-encryption

[41]https://http2.github.io/faq

- H2ModernTLSOnly

- H2Push

- H2PushDiarySize

- H2PushPriority

- H2SerializeHeaders

- H2SessionExtraFiles

- H2StreamMaxMemSize

- H2TLSCoolDownSecs

- H2TLSWarmUpSize

- H2Upgrade

- H2WindowSize

## How it works

### HTTP/2 Dimensioning

Enabling HTTP/2 on your Apache Server has impact on the resource consumption and if you have a busy site, you may need to consider carefully the implications.

The first noticeable thing after enabling HTTP/2 is that your server processes will start additional threads. The reason for this is that HTTP/2 gives all requests that it receives to its own *Worker* threads for processing, collects the results and streams them out to the client.

In the current implementation, these workers use a separate thread pool from the MPM workers that you might be familiar with. This is just how things are right now and not intended to be like this forever. (It might be forever for the 2.4.x release line, though.) So, HTTP/2 workers, or shorter H2Workers, will not show up in MOD_STATUS. They are also not counted against directives such as THREADSPERCHILD. However they take THREADSPERCHILD as default if you have not configured something else via H2MINWORKERS and H2MAXWORKERS.

Another thing to watch out for is is memory consumption. Since HTTP/2 keeps more state on the server to manage all the open request, priorities for and dependencies between them, it will always need more memory than HTTP/1.1 processing. There are three directives which steer the memory footprint of a HTTP/2 connection: H2MAXSESSIONSTREAMS, H2WINDOWSIZE and H2STREAMMAXMEMSIZE.

H2MAXSESSIONSTREAMS limits the number of parallel requests that a client can make on a HTTP/2 connection. It depends on your site how many you should allow. The default is 100 which is plenty and unless you run into memory problems, I would keep it this way. Most requests that browsers send are GETs without a body, so they use up only a little bit of memory until the actual processing starts.

H2WINDOWSIZE controls how much the client is allowed to send as body of a request, before it waits for the server to encourage more. Or, the other way around, it is the amount of request body data the server needs to be able to buffer. This is per request.

And last, but not least, H2STREAMMAXMEMSIZE controls how much response data shall be buffered. The request sits in a H2Worker thread and is producing data, the HTTP/2 connection tries to send this to the client. If the client does not read fast enough, the connection will buffer this amount of data and then suspend the H2Worker.

If you serve a lot of static files, H2SESSIONEXTRAFILES is of interest. This tells the server how many file handles per HTTP/2 connection it is allowed to waste for better performance. Because when a request produces a static file as the response, the file handle gets passed around and is buffered and not the file contents. That allows to serve many large files without wasting memory or copying data unnecessarily. However file handles are a limited resource for a process, and if too many are used this way, requests may fail under load as the amount of open handles has been exceeded.

**Multiple Hosts and Misdirected Requests**

Many sites use the same TLS certificate for multiple virtual hosts. The certificate either has a wildcard name, such as '*.example.org' or carries several alternate names. Browsers using HTTP/2 will recognize that and reuse an already opened connection for such hosts.

While this is great for performance, it comes at a price: such vhosts need more care in their configuration. The problem is that you will have multiple requests for multiple hosts on the same TLS connection. And that makes renegotiation impossible, in face the HTTP/2 standard forbids it.

So, if you have several virtual hosts using the same certificate and want to use HTTP/2 for them, you need to make sure that all vhosts have exactly the same SSL configuration. You need the same protocol, ciphers and settings for client verification.

If you mix things, Apache httpd will detect it and return a special response code, 421 Misdirected Request, to the client.

**Environment Variables**

This module can be configured to provide HTTP/2 related information as additional environment variables to the SSI and CGI namespace, as well as in custom log configurations (see `%{VAR_NAME}e`).

| Variable Name: | Value Type: | Description: |
|---|---|---|
| `HTTP2` | flag | HTTP/2 is being used. |
| `H2PUSH` | flag | HTTP/2 Server Push is enabled for this connection and also supported by the client. |
| `H2_PUSH` | flag | alternate name for `H2PUSH` |
| `H2_PUSHED` | string | empty or `PUSHED` for a request being pushed by the server. |
| `H2_PUSHED_ON` | number | HTTP/2 stream number that triggered the push of this request. |
| `H2_STREAM_ID` | number | HTTP/2 stream number of this request. |
| `H2_STREAM_TAG` | string | HTTP/2 process unique stream identifier, consisting of connection id and stream id separated by –. |

# H2Direct Directive

| | |
|---|---|
| Description: | H2 Direct Protocol Switch |
| Syntax: | `H2Direct on\|off` |
| Default: | `H2Direct on for h2c, off for h2 protocol` |
| Context: | server config, virtual host |
| Status: | Extension |
| Module: | mod_http2 |

This directive toggles the usage of the HTTP/2 Direct Mode. This should be used inside a <VIRTUALHOST> section to enable direct HTTP/2 communication for that virtual host.

Direct communication means that if the first bytes received by the server on a connection match the HTTP/2 preamble, the HTTP/2 protocol is switched to immediately without further negotiation. This mode is defined in RFC 7540 for the cleartext (h2c) case. Its use on TLS connections not mandated by the standard.

When a server/vhost does not have h2 or h2c enabled via PROTOCOLS, the connection is never inspected for a HTTP/2 preamble. H2DIRECT does not matter then. This is important for connections that use protocols where an initial read might hang indefinitely, such as NNTP.

For clients that have out-of-band knowledge about a server supporting h2c, direct HTTP/2 saves the client from having to perform an HTTP/1.1 upgrade, resulting in better performance and avoiding the Upgrade restrictions on request bodies.

This makes direct h2c attractive for server to server communication as well, when the connection can be trusted or is secured by other means.

### Example

```
H2Direct on
```

## H2MaxSessionStreams Directive

| | |
|---|---|
| Description: | Maximum number of active streams per HTTP/2 session. |
| Syntax: | `H2MaxSessionStreams n` |
| Default: | `H2MaxSessionStreams 100` |
| Context: | server config, virtual host |
| Status: | Extension |
| Module: | mod_http2 |

This directive sets the maximum number of active streams per HTTP/2 session (e.g. connection) that the server allows. A stream is active if it is not `idle` or `closed` according to RFC 7540.

### Example

```
H2MaxSessionStreams 20
```

## H2MaxWorkerIdleSeconds Directive

| | |
|---|---|
| Description: | Maximum number of seconds h2 workers remain idle until shut down. |
| Syntax: | `H2MaxWorkerIdleSeconds n` |
| Default: | `H2MaxWorkerIdleSeconds 600` |
| Context: | server config |
| Status: | Extension |
| Module: | mod_http2 |

This directive sets the maximum number of seconds a h2 worker may idle until it shuts itself down. This only happens while the number of h2 workers exceeds H2MINWORKERS.

### Example

```
H2MaxWorkerIdleSeconds 20
```

## H2MaxWorkers Directive

| | |
|---|---|
| Description: | Maximum number of worker threads to use per child process. |
| Syntax: | `H2MaxWorkers n` |
| Context: | server config |
| Status: | Extension |
| Module: | mod_http2 |

This directive sets the maximum number of worker threads to spawn per child process for HTTP/2 processing. If this directive is not used, MOD_HTTP2 will chose a value suitable for the mpm module loaded.

### Example

```
H2MaxWorkers 20
```

## H2MinWorkers Directive

| | |
|---|---|
| Description: | Minimal number of worker threads to use per child process. |
| Syntax: | `H2MinWorkers n` |
| Context: | server config |
| Status: | Extension |
| Module: | mod_http2 |

This directive sets the minimum number of worker threads to spawn per child process for HTTP/2 processing. If this directive is not used, MOD_HTTP2 will chose a value suitable for the mpm module loaded.

### Example

```
H2MinWorkers 10
```

## H2ModernTLSOnly Directive

| | |
|---|---|
| Description: | Require HTTP/2 connections to be "modern TLS" only |
| Syntax: | `H2ModernTLSOnly on\|off` |
| Default: | `H2ModernTLSOnly on` |
| Context: | server config, virtual host |
| Status: | Extension |
| Module: | mod_http2 |
| Compatibility: | Available in version 2.4.18 and later. |

This directive toggles the security checks on HTTP/2 connections in TLS mode (https:). This can be used server wide or for specific <VIRTUALHOST>s.

The security checks require that the TSL protocol is at least TLSv1.2 and that none of the ciphers listed in RFC 7540, Appendix A is used. These checks will be extended once new security requirements come into place.

The name stems from the Security/Server Side TLS[42] definitions at mozilla where "modern compatibility" is defined. Mozilla Firefox and other browsers require modern compatibility for HTTP/2 connections. As everything in OpSec, this is a moving target and can be expected to evolve in the future.

One purpose of having these checks in MOD_HTTP2 is to enforce this security level for all connections, not only those from browsers. The other purpose is to prevent the negotiation of HTTP/2 as a protocol should the requirements not be met.

Ultimately, the security of the TLS connection is determined by the server configuration directives for MOD_SSL.

### Example

```
H2ModernTLSOnly off
```

## H2Push Directive

| | |
|---|---|
| Description: | H2 Server Push Switch |
| Syntax: | `H2Push on\|off` |
| Default: | `H2Push on` |
| Context: | server config, virtual host |
| Status: | Extension |
| Module: | mod_http2 |
| Compatibility: | Available in version 2.4.18 and later. |

---

[42]https://wiki.mozilla.org/Security/Server_Side_TLS

This directive toggles the usage of the HTTP/2 server push protocol feature. This should be used inside a <VIRTU-ALHOST> section to enable direct HTTP/2 communication for that virtual host.

The HTTP/2 protocol allows the server to push other resources to a client when it asked for a particular one. This is helpful if those resources are connected in some way and the client can be expected to ask for it anyway. The pushing then saves the time it takes the client to ask for the resources itself. On the other hand, pushing resources the client never needs or already has is a waste of bandwidth.

Server pushes are detected by inspecting the `Link` headers of responses (see https://tools.ietf.org/html/rfc5988 for the specification). When a link thus specified has the `rel=preload` attribute, it is treated as a resource to be pushed.

Link headers in responses are either set by the application or can be configured via MOD_HEADERS as:

### mod_headers example

```
<Location /index.html>
    Header add Link "</css/site.css>;rel=preload"
    Header add Link "</images/logo.jpg>;rel=preload"
</Location>
```

As the example shows, there can be several link headers added to a response, resulting in several pushes being triggered. There are no checks in the module to avoid pushing the same resource twice or more to one client. Use with care.

HTTP/2 server pushes are enabled by default. This directive allows it to be switch off on all resources of this server/virtual host.

### Example

```
H2Push off
```

Last but not least, pushes happen only when the client signals its willingness to accept those. Most browsers do, some, like Safari 9, do not. Also, pushes also only happen for resources from the same *authority* as the original response is for.

## H2PushDiarySize Directive

| | |
|---|---|
| Description: | H2 Server Push Diary Size |
| Syntax: | H2PushDiarySize n |
| Default: | H2PushDiarySize 256 |
| Context: | server config, virtual host |
| Status: | Extension |
| Module: | mod_http2 |
| Compatibility: | Available in version 2.4.19 and later. |

This directive toggles the maximum number of HTTP/2 server pushes that are remembered per HTTP/2 connection. This can be used inside the <VIRTUALHOST> section to influence the number for all connections to that virtual host.

The push diary records a digest (currently using a 64 bit number) of pushed resources (their URL) to avoid duplicate pushes on the same connection. These value are not persisted, so clients opening a new connection will experience known pushes again. There is ongoing work to enable a client to disclose a digest of the resources it already has, so the diary maybe initialized by the client on each connection setup.

If the maximum size is reached, newer entries replace the oldest ones. A diary entry uses 8 bytes, letting a default diary with 256 entries consume around 2 KB of memory.

A size of 0 will effectively disable the push diary.

## H2PushPriority Directive

| | |
|---|---|
| Description: | H2 Server Push Priority |
| Syntax: | `H2PushPriority mime-type [after|before|interleaved] [weight]` |
| Default: | `H2PushPriority * After 16` |
| Context: | server config, virtual host |
| Status: | Extension |
| Module: | mod_http2 |
| Compatibility: | Available in version 2.4.18 and later. For having an effect, a nghttp2 library version 1.5.0 or newer is necessary. |

This directive defines the priority handling of pushed responses based on the content-type of the response. This is usually defined per server config, but may also appear in a virtual host.

HTTP/2 server pushes are always related to a client request. Each such request/response pairs, or *streams* have a dependency and a weight, together defining the *priority* of a stream.

When a stream *depends* on another, say X depends on Y, then Y gets all bandwidth before X gets any. Note that this does not mean that Y will block X. If Y has no data to send, all bandwidth allocated to Y can be used by X.

When a stream has more than one dependant, say X1 and X2 both depend on Y, the *weight* determines the bandwidth allocation. If X1 and X2 have the same weight, they both get half of the available bandwidth. If the weight of X1 is twice as large as that for X2, X1 gets twice the bandwidth of X2.

Ultimately, every stream depends on the *root* stream which gets all the bandwidth available, but never sends anything. So all its bandwidth is distributed by weight among its children. Which either have data to send or distribute the bandwidth to their own children. And so on. If none of the children have data to send, that bandwidth get distributed somewhere else according to the same rules.

The purpose of this priority system is to always make use of available bandwidth while allowing precedence and weight to be given to specific streams. Since, normally, all streams are initiated by the client, it is also the one that sets these priorities.

Only when such a stream results in a PUSH, gets the server to decide what the *initial* priority of such a pushed stream is. In the examples below, X is the client stream. It depends on Y and the server decides to PUSH streams P1 and P2 onto X.

The default priority rule is:

### Default Priority Rule

```
H2PushPriority * After 16
```

which reads as 'Send a pushed stream of any content-type depending on the client stream with weight 16'. And so P1 and P2 will be send after X and, as they have equal weight, share bandwidth equally among themselves.

### Interleaved Priority Rule

```
H2PushPriority text/css Interleaved 256
```

which reads as 'Send any CSS resource on the same dependency and weight as the client stream'. If P1 has content-type 'text/css', it will depend on Y (as does X) and its effective weight will be calculated as `P1ew = Xw * (P1w / 256)`. With P1w being 256, this will make the effective weight the same as the weight of X. If both X and P1 have data to send, bandwidth will be allocated to both equally.

With Pw specified as 512, a pushed, interleaved stream would get double the weight of X. With 128 only half as much. Note that effective weights are always capped at 256.

### Before Priority Rule

```
H2PushPriority application/json Before
```

This says that any pushed stream of content type 'application/json' should be send out *before* X. This makes P1 dependent on Y and X dependent on P1. So, X will be stalled as long as P1 has data to send. The effective weight is inherited from the client stream. Specifying a weight is not allowed.

Be aware that the effect of priority specifications is limited by the available server resources. If a server does not have workers available for pushed streams, the data for the stream may only ever arrive when other streams have been finished.

Last, but not least, there are some specifics of the syntax to be used in this directive:

1. '*' is the only special content-type that matches all others. 'image/*' will not work.

2. The default dependency is 'After'.

3. There are also default weights: for 'After' it is 16, 'interleaved' is 256.

### Shorter Priority Rules

```
H2PushPriority application/json 32          # an After rule
H2PushPriority image/jpeg before            # weight inherited
H2PushPriority text/css   interleaved       # weight 256 default
```

## H2SerializeHeaders Directive

| | |
|---|---|
| Description: | Serialize Request/Response Processing Switch |
| Syntax: | H2SerializeHeaders on\|off |
| Default: | H2SerializeHeaders off |
| Context: | server config, virtual host |
| Status: | Extension |
| Module: | mod_http2 |

This directive toggles if HTTP/2 requests shall be serialized in HTTP/1.1 format for processing by `httpd` core or if received binary data shall be passed into the `request_recs` directly.

Serialization will lower performance, but gives more backward compatibility in case custom filters/hooks need it.

### Example

```
H2SerializeHeaders on
```

## H2SessionExtraFiles Directive

| | |
|---|---|
| Description: | Number of Extra File Handles |
| Syntax: | H2SessionExtraFiles n |
| Context: | server config, virtual host |
| Status: | Extension |
| Module: | mod_http2 |

This directive sets maximum number of *extra* file handles a HTTP/2 session is allowed to use. A file handle is counted as *extra* when it is transferred from a h2 worker thread to the main HTTP/2 connection handling. This commonly happens when serving static files.

Depending on the processing model configured on the server, the number of connections times number of active streams may exceed the number of file handles for the process. On the other hand, converting every file into memory bytes early results in too many buffer writes. This option helps to mitigate that.

The number of file handles used by a server process is then in the order of:

```
(h2_connections * extra_files) + (h2_max_worker)
```

### Example

```
H2SessionExtraFiles 10
```

If nothing is configured, the module tries to make a conservative guess how many files are safe to use. This depends largely on the MPM chosen.

## H2StreamMaxMemSize Directive

| Description: | Maximum amount of output data buffered per stream. |
|---|---|
| Syntax: | H2StreamMaxMemSize bytes |
| Default: | H2StreamMaxMemSize 65536 |
| Context: | server config, virtual host |
| Status: | Extension |
| Module: | mod_http2 |

This directive sets the maximum number of outgoing data bytes buffered in memory for an active streams. This memory is not allocated per stream as such. Allocations are counted against this limit when they are about to be done. Stream processing freezes when the limit has been reached and will only continue when buffered data has been sent out to the client.

### Example

```
H2StreamMaxMemSize 128000
```

## H2TLSCoolDownSecs Directive

| Description: | |
|---|---|
| Syntax: | H2TLSCoolDownSecs seconds |
| Default: | H2TLSCoolDownSecs 1 |
| Context: | server config, virtual host |
| Status: | Extension |
| Module: | mod_http2 |
| Compatibility: | Available in version 2.4.18 and later. |

This directive sets the number of seconds of idle time on a TLS connection before the TLS write size falls back to small (~1300 bytes) length. This can be used server wide or for specific <VIRTUALHOST>s.

See H2TLSWARMUPSIZE for a description of TLS warmup. H2TLSCOOLDOWNSECS reflects the fact that connections may deteriorate over time (and TCP flow adjusts) for idle connections as well. It is beneficial to overall performance to fall back to the pre-warmup phase after a number of seconds that no data has been sent.

In deployments where connections can be considered reliable, this timer can be disabled by setting it to 0.

The following example sets the seconds to zero, effectively disabling any cool down. Warmed up TLS connections stay on maximum record size.

### Example

```
H2TLSCoolDownSecs 0
```

## H2TLSWarmUpSize Directive

| | |
|---|---|
| Description: | |
| Syntax: | `H2TLSWarmUpSize amount` |
| Default: | `H2TLSWarmUpSize 1048576` |
| Context: | server config, virtual host |
| Status: | Extension |
| Module: | mod_http2 |
| Compatibility: | Available in version 2.4.18 and later. |

This directive sets the number of bytes to be sent in small TLS records (~1300 bytes) until doing maximum sized writes (16k) on https: HTTP/2 connections. This can be used server wide or for specific <VIRTUALHOST>s.

Measurements by google performance labs[43] show that best performance on TLS connections is reached, if initial record sizes stay below the MTU level, to allow a complete record to fit into an IP packet.

While TCP adjust its flow-control and window sizes, longer TLS records can get stuck in queues or get lost and need retransmission. This is of course true for all packets. TLS however needs the whole record in order to decrypt it. Any missing bytes at the end will stall usage of the received ones.

After a sufficient number of bytes have been send successfully, the TCP state of the connection is stable and maximum TLS record sizes (16 KB) can be used for optimal performance.

In deployments where servers are reached locally or over reliable connections only, the value might be decreased with 0 disabling any warmup phase altogether.

The following example sets the size to zero, effectively disabling any warmup phase.

### Example

```
H2TLSWarmUpSize 0
```

## H2Upgrade Directive

| | |
|---|---|
| Description: | H2 Upgrade Protocol Switch |
| Syntax: | `H2Upgrade on\|off` |
| Default: | `H2Upgrade on for h2c, off for h2 protocol` |
| Context: | server config, virtual host |
| Status: | Extension |
| Module: | mod_http2 |

This directive toggles the usage of the HTTP/1.1 Upgrade method for switching to HTTP/2. This should be used inside a <VIRTUALHOST> section to enable Upgrades to HTTP/2 for that virtual host.

This method of switching protocols is defined in HTTP/1.1 and uses the "Upgrade" header (thus the name) to announce willingness to use another protocol. This may happen on any request of a HTTP/1.1 connection.

This method of protocol switching is enabled by default on cleartext (potential h2c) connections and disabled on TLS (potential h2), as mandated by RFC 7540.

Please be aware that Upgrades are only accepted for requests that carry no body. POSTs and PUTs with content will never trigger an upgrade to HTTP/2. See H2DIRECT for an alternative to Upgrade.

---

[43]https://www.igvita.com

This mode only has an effect when h2 or h2c is enabled via the PROTOCOLS.

### Example

```
H2Upgrade on
```

## H2WindowSize Directive

| | |
|---|---|
| Description: | Size of Stream Window for upstream data. |
| Syntax: | H2WindowSize bytes |
| Default: | H2WindowSize 65535 |
| Context: | server config, virtual host |
| Status: | Extension |
| Module: | mod_http2 |

This directive sets the size of the window that is used for flow control from client to server and limits the amount of data the server has to buffer. The client will stop sending on a stream once the limit has been reached until the server announces more available space (as it has processed some of the data).

This limit affects only request bodies, not its meta data such as headers. Also, it has no effect on response bodies as the window size for those are managed by the clients.

### Example

```
H2WindowSize 128000
```

# 10.58 Apache Module mod_ident

| Description: | RFC 1413 ident lookups |
|---|---|
| Status: | Extension |
| ModuleIdentifier: | ident_module |
| SourceFile: | mod_ident.c |

## Summary

This module queries an RFC 1413[44] compatible daemon on a remote host to look up the owner of a connection.

**Directives**

- IdentityCheck
- IdentityCheckTimeout

**See also**

- MOD_LOG_CONFIG

## IdentityCheck Directive

| Description: | Enables logging of the RFC 1413 identity of the remote user |
|---|---|
| Syntax: | IdentityCheck On\|Off |
| Default: | IdentityCheck Off |
| Context: | server config, virtual host, directory |
| Status: | Extension |
| Module: | mod_ident |

This directive enables RFC 1413[45]-compliant logging of the remote user name for each connection, where the client machine runs identd or something similar. This information is logged in the access log using the %...l format string (p. 705).

$\Longrightarrow$ The information should not be trusted in any way except for rudimentary usage tracking.

Note that this can cause serious latency problems accessing your server since every request requires one of these lookups to be performed. When firewalls or proxy servers are involved, each lookup might possibly fail and add a latency duration as defined by the IDENTITYCHECKTIMEOUT directive to each hit. So in general this is not very useful on public servers accessible from the Internet.

## IdentityCheckTimeout Directive

| Description: | Determines the timeout duration for ident requests |
|---|---|
| Syntax: | IdentityCheckTimeout seconds |
| Default: | IdentityCheckTimeout 30 |
| Context: | server config, virtual host, directory |
| Status: | Extension |
| Module: | mod_ident |

---

[44]http://www.ietf.org/rfc/rfc1413.txt
[45]http://www.ietf.org/rfc/rfc1413.txt

This directive specifies the timeout duration of an ident request. The default value of 30 seconds is recommended by RFC 1413[46], mainly because of possible network latency. However, you may want to adjust the timeout value according to your local network speed.

---

[46]http://www.ietf.org/rfc/rfc1413.txt

# 10.59 Apache Module mod_imagemap

| | |
|---|---|
| Description: | Server-side imagemap processing |
| Status: | Base |
| ModuleIdentifier: | imagemap_module |
| SourceFile: | mod_imagemap.c |

## Summary

This module processes `.map` files, thereby replacing the functionality of the `imagemap` CGI program. Any directory or document type configured to use the handler `imap-file` (using either ADDHANDLER or SETHANDLER) will be processed by this module.

The following directive will activate files ending with `.map` as imagemap files:

```
AddHandler imap-file map
```

Note that the following is still supported:

```
AddType application/x-httpd-imap map
```

However, we are trying to phase out "magic MIME types" so we are deprecating this method.

**Directives**

- ImapBase
- ImapDefault
- ImapMenu

## New Features

The imagemap module adds some new features that were not possible with previously distributed imagemap programs.

- URL references relative to the Referer: information.
- Default <base> assignment through a new map directive `base`.
- No need for `imagemap.conf` file.
- Point references.
- Configurable generation of imagemap menus.

## Imagemap File

The lines in the imagemap files can have one of several formats:

```
directive value [x,y ...]
directive value "Menu text" [x,y ...]
directive value x,y ...  "Menu text"
```

The directive is one of `base`, `default`, `poly`, `circle`, `rect`, or `point`. The value is an absolute or relative URL, or one of the special values listed below. The coordinates are $x$, $y$ pairs separated by whitespace. The quoted text is used as the text of the link if a imagemap menu is generated. Lines beginning with '#' are comments.

**Imagemap File Directives**

There are six directives allowed in the imagemap file. The directives can come in any order, but are processed in the order they are found in the imagemap file.

**`base` Directive** Has the effect of `<base href="value">` . The non-absolute URLs of the map-file are taken relative to this value. The `base` directive overrides IMAPBASE as set in a `.htaccess` file or in the server configuration files. In the absence of an IMAPBASE configuration directive, `base` defaults to `http://server_name/`.

> `base_uri` is synonymous with `base`. Note that a trailing slash on the URL is significant.

**`default` Directive** The action taken if the coordinates given do not fit any of the `poly`, `circle` or `rect` directives, and there are no `point` directives. Defaults to `nocontent` in the absence of an IMAPDEFAULT configuration setting, causing a status code of `204 No Content` to be returned. The client should keep the same page displayed.

**`poly` Directive** Takes three to one-hundred points, and is obeyed if the user selected coordinates fall within the polygon defined by these points.

**`circle`** Takes the center coordinates of a circle and a point on the circle. Is obeyed if the user selected point is with the circle.

**`rect` Directive** Takes the coordinates of two opposing corners of a rectangle. Obeyed if the point selected is within this rectangle.

**`point` Directive** Takes a single point. The point directive closest to the user selected point is obeyed if no other directives are satisfied. Note that `default` will not be followed if a `point` directive is present and valid coordinates are given.

**Values**

The values for each of the directives can be any of the following:

**a URL** The URL can be relative or absolute URL. Relative URLs can contain '..' syntax and will be resolved relative to the `base` value.

> `base` itself will not be resolved according to the current value. A statement `base mailto:` will work properly, though.

**`map`** Equivalent to the URL of the imagemap file itself. No coordinates are sent with this, so a menu will be generated unless IMAPMENU is set to `none`.

**`menu`** Synonymous with `map`.

**`referer`** Equivalent to the URL of the referring document. Defaults to `http://servername/` if no `Referer:` header was present.

**`nocontent`** Sends a status code of `204 No Content`, telling the client to keep the same page displayed. Valid for all but `base`.

**`error`** Fails with a `500 Server Error`. Valid for all but `base`, but sort of silly for anything but `default`.

**Coordinates**

**`0,0 200,200`** A coordinate consists of an *x* and a *y* value separated by a comma. The coordinates are separated from each other by whitespace. To accommodate the way Lynx handles imagemaps, should a user select the coordinate `0,0`, it is as if no coordinate had been selected.

**Quoted Text**

**"*Menu Text*"** After the value or after the coordinates, the line optionally may contain text within double quotes. This string is used as the text for the link if a menu is generated:

```
<a href="http://example.com/">Menu text</a>
```

If no quoted text is present, the name of the link will be used as the text:

```
<a href="http://example.com/">http://example.com</a>
```

If you want to use double quotes within this text, you have to write them as &quot;.

## Example Mapfile

```
#Comments are printed in a 'formatted' or 'semiformatted' menu.
#And can contain html tags.  <hr>
base referer
poly map "Could I have a menu, please?" 0,0 0,10 10,10 10,0
rect ..  0,0 77,27 "the directory of the referer"
circle http://www.inetnebr.example.com/lincoln/feedback/ 195,0 305,27
rect another_file "in same directory as referer" 306,0 419,27
point http://www.zyzzyva.example.com/ 100,100
point http://www.tripod.example.com/ 200,200
rect mailto:nate@tripod.example.com 100,150 200,0 "Bugs?"
```

## Referencing your mapfile

**HTML example**
```
<a href="/maps/imagemap1.map">
    <img ismap src="/images/imagemap1.gif">
</a>
```

**XHTML example**
```
<a href="/maps/imagemap1.map">
    <img ismap="ismap" src="/images/imagemap1.gif" />
</a>
```

## ImapBase Directive

| | |
|---|---|
| Description: | Default `base` for imagemap files |
| Syntax: | `ImapBase map|referer|URL` |
| Default: | `ImapBase http://servername/` |
| Context: | server config, virtual host, directory, .htaccess |
| Override: | Indexes |
| Status: | Base |
| Module: | mod_imagemap |

The IMAPBASE directive sets the default `base` used in the imagemap files. Its value is overridden by a `base` directive within the imagemap file. If not present, the `base` defaults to `http://servername/`.

**See also**

- USECANONICALNAME

## ImapDefault Directive

| | |
|---|---|
| Description: | Default action when an imagemap is called with coordinates that are not explicitly mapped |
| Syntax: | `ImapDefault error|nocontent|map|referer|URL` |
| Default: | `ImapDefault nocontent` |
| Context: | server config, virtual host, directory, .htaccess |
| Override: | Indexes |
| Status: | Base |
| Module: | mod_imagemap |

The IMAPDEFAULT directive sets the default `default` used in the imagemap files. Its value is overridden by a `default` directive within the imagemap file. If not present, the `default` action is `nocontent`, which means that a `204 No Content` is sent to the client. In this case, the client should continue to display the original page.

## ImapMenu Directive

| | |
|---|---|
| Description: | Action if no coordinates are given when calling an imagemap |
| Syntax: | `ImapMenu none|formatted|semiformatted|unformatted` |
| Default: | `ImapMenu formatted` |
| Context: | server config, virtual host, directory, .htaccess |
| Override: | Indexes |
| Status: | Base |
| Module: | mod_imagemap |

The IMAPMENU directive determines the action taken if an imagemap file is called without valid coordinates.

**none** If ImapMenu is `none`, no menu is generated, and the `default` action is performed.

**formatted** A `formatted` menu is the simplest menu. Comments in the imagemap file are ignored. A level one header is printed, then an hrule, then the links each on a separate line. The menu has a consistent, plain look close to that of a directory listing.

**semiformatted** In the `semiformatted` menu, comments are printed where they occur in the imagemap file. Blank lines are turned into HTML breaks. No header or hrule is printed, but otherwise the menu is the same as a `formatted` menu.

**unformatted** Comments are printed, blank lines are ignored. Nothing is printed that does not appear in the imagemap file. All breaks and headers must be included as comments in the imagemap file. This gives you the most flexibility over the appearance of your menus, but requires you to treat your map files as HTML instead of plaintext.

# 10.60 Apache Module mod_include

| | |
|---|---|
| Description: | Server-parsed html documents (Server Side Includes) |
| Status: | Base |
| ModuleIdentifier: | include_module |
| SourceFile: | mod_include.c |

## Summary

This module provides a filter which will process files before they are sent to the client. The processing is controlled by specially formatted SGML comments, referred to as *elements*. These elements allow conditional text, the inclusion of other files or programs, as well as the setting and printing of environment variables.

### Directives

- SSIEndTag
- SSIErrorMsg
- SSIETag
- SSILastModified
- SSILegacyExprParser
- SSIStartTag
- SSITimeFormat
- SSIUndefinedEcho
- XBitHack

### See also

- OPTIONS
- ACCEPTPATHINFO
- Filters (p. 110)
- SSI Tutorial (p. 243)

## Enabling Server-Side Includes

Server Side Includes are implemented by the INCLUDES filter (p. 110) . If documents containing server-side include directives are given the extension .shtml, the following directives will make Apache parse them and assign the resulting document the mime type of text/html:

```
AddType text/html .shtml
AddOutputFilter INCLUDES .shtml
```

The following directive must be given for the directories containing the shtml files (typically in a <DIRECTORY> section, but this directive is also valid in .htaccess files if ALLOWOVERRIDE Options is set):

```
Options +Includes
```

For backwards compatibility, the server-parsed handler (p. 108) also activates the INCLUDES filter. As well, Apache will activate the INCLUDES filter for any document with mime type text/x-server-parsed-html or text/x-server-parsed-html3 (and the resulting output will have the mime type text/html).

For more information, see our Tutorial on Server Side Includes (p. 243) .

## PATH_INFO with Server Side Includes

Files processed for server-side includes no longer accept requests with PATH_INFO (trailing pathname information) by default. You can use the AcceptPathInfo directive to configure the server to accept requests with PATH_INFO.

## Available Elements

The document is parsed as an HTML document, with special commands embedded as SGML comments. A command has the syntax:

```
<!--#element attribute=value attribute=value ...   -->
```

The value will often be enclosed in double quotes, but single quotes (') and backticks (`) are also possible. Many commands only allow a single attribute-value pair. Note that the comment terminator (-->) should be preceded by whitespace to ensure that it isn't considered part of an SSI token. Note that the leading <!--# is *one* token and may not contain any whitespaces.

The allowed elements are listed in the following table:

| Element | Description |
|---------|-------------|
| comment | SSI comment |
| config | configure output formats |
| echo | print variables |
| exec | execute external programs |
| fsize | print size of a file |
| flastmod | print last modification time of a file |
| include | include a file |
| printenv | print all available variables |
| set | set a value of a variable |

SSI elements may be defined by modules other than MOD_INCLUDE. In fact, the exec element is provided by MOD_CGI, and will only be available if this module is loaded.

### The comment Element

This command doesn't output anything. Its only use is to add comments within a file. These comments are not printed.

This syntax is available in version 2.5 and later.

```
<!--#comment Blah Blah Blah -->
```

### The config Element

This command controls various aspects of the parsing. The valid attributes are:

**echomsg** (*Apache 2.1 and later*)  The value is a message that is sent back to the client if the echo element attempts to echo an undefined variable. This overrides any SSIUndefinedEcho directives.

```
<!--#config echomsg="[Value Undefined]" -->
```

**errmsg** The value is a message that is sent back to the client if an error occurs while parsing the document. This overrides any SSIErrorMsg directives.

```
<!--#config errmsg="[Oops, something broke.]" -->
```

**sizefmt** The value sets the format to be used when displaying the size of a file. Valid values are bytes for a count in bytes, or abbrev for a count in Kb or Mb as appropriate, for example a size of 1024 bytes will be printed as "1K".

```
<!--#config sizefmt="abbrev" -->
```

**timefmt** The value is a string to be used by the strftime(3) library routine when printing dates.

```
<!--#config timefmt=""%R, %B %d, %Y"" -->
```

### The echo Element

This command prints one of the include variables defined below. If the variable is unset, the result is determined by the SSIUndefinedEcho directive. Any dates printed are subject to the currently configured timefmt.

Attributes:

**var** The value is the name of the variable to print.

**decoding** Specifies whether Apache should strip an encoding from the variable before processing the variable further. The default is none, where no decoding will be done. If set to url, then URL decoding (also known as %-encoding; this is appropriate for use within URLs in links, etc.) will be performed. If set to urlencoded, application/x-www-form-urlencoded compatible encoding (found in query strings) will be stripped. If set to base64, base64 will be decoded, and if set to entity, HTML entity encoding will be stripped. Decoding is done prior to any further encoding on the variable. Multiple encodings can be stripped by specifying more than one comma separated encoding. The decoding setting will remain in effect until the next decoding attribute is encountered, or the element ends.

The decoding attribute must *precede* the corresponding var attribute to be effective.

**encoding** Specifies how Apache should encode special characters contained in the variable before outputting them. If set to none, no encoding will be done. If set to url, then URL encoding (also known as %-encoding; this is appropriate for use within URLs in links, etc.) will be performed. If set to urlencoded, application/x-www-form-urlencoded compatible encoding will be performed instead, and should be used with query strings. If set to base64, base64 encoding will be performed. At the start of an echo element, the default is set to entity, resulting in entity encoding (which is appropriate in the context of a block-level HTML element, *e.g.* a paragraph of text). This can be changed by adding an encoding attribute, which will remain in effect until the next encoding attribute is encountered or the element ends, whichever comes first.

The encoding attribute must *precede* the corresponding var attribute to be effective.

> **!** In order to avoid cross-site scripting issues, you should *always* encode user supplied data.

**Example**
```
<!--#echo encoding="entity" var="QUERY_STRING" -->
```

**The exec Element**

The exec command executes a given shell command or CGI script. It requires MOD_CGI to be present in the server. If OPTIONS IncludesNOEXEC is set, this command is completely disabled. The valid attributes are:

**cgi** The value specifies a (%-encoded) URL-path to the CGI script. If the path does not begin with a slash (/), then it is taken to be relative to the current document. The document referenced by this path is invoked as a CGI script, even if the server would not normally recognize it as such. However, the directory containing the script must be enabled for CGI scripts (with SCRIPTALIAS or OPTIONS ExecCGI).

The CGI script is given the PATH_INFO and query string (QUERY_STRING) of the original request from the client; these *cannot* be specified in the URL path. The include variables will be available to the script in addition to the standard CGI (p. 580) environment.

> **Example**
> ```
> <!--#exec cgi="/cgi-bin/example.cgi" -->
> ```

If the script returns a Location: header instead of output, then this will be translated into an HTML anchor.

The include virtual element should be used in preference to exec cgi. In particular, if you need to pass additional arguments to a CGI program, using the query string, this cannot be done with exec cgi, but can be done with include virtual, as shown here:

> ```
> <!--#include virtual="/cgi-bin/example.cgi?argument=value" -->
> ```

**cmd** The server will execute the given string using /bin/sh. The include variables are available to the command, in addition to the usual set of CGI variables.

The use of #include virtual is almost always prefered to using either #exec cgi or #exec cmd. The former (#include virtual) uses the standard Apache sub-request mechanism to include files or scripts. It is much better tested and maintained.

In addition, on some platforms, like Win32, and on unix when using suexec (p. 115) , you cannot pass arguments to a command in an exec directive, or otherwise include spaces in the command. Thus, while the following will work under a non-suexec configuration on unix, it will not produce the desired result under Win32, or when running suexec:

> ```
> <!--#exec cmd="perl /path/to/perlscript arg1 arg2" -->
> ```

**The fsize Element**

This command prints the size of the specified file, subject to the sizefmt format specification. Attributes:

**file** The value is a path relative to the directory containing the current document being parsed.

> ```
> This file is <!--#fsize file="mod_include.html" --> bytes.
> ```

The value of file cannot start with a slash (/), nor can it contain ../ so as to refer to a file above the current directory or outside of the document root. Attempting to so will result in the error message: The given path was above the root path.

**virtual** The value is a (%-encoded) URL-path. If it does not begin with a slash (/) then it is taken to be relative to the current document. Note, that this does *not* print the size of any CGI output, but the size of the CGI script itself.

```
This file is <!--#fsize virtual="/docs/mod/mod_include.html" -->
bytes.
```

Note that in many cases these two are exactly the same thing. However, the `file` attribute doesn't respect URL-space aliases.

**The flastmod Element**

This command prints the last modification date of the specified file, subject to the `timefmt` format specification. The attributes are the same as for the `fsize` command.

**The include Element**

This command inserts the text of another document or file into the parsed file. Any included file is subject to the usual access control. If the directory containing the parsed file has Options (p. 380) `IncludesNOEXEC` set, then only documents with a text MIME-type (`text/plain`, `text/html` etc.) will be included. Otherwise CGI scripts are invoked as normal using the complete URL given in the command, including any query string.

An attribute defines the location of the document, and may appear more than once in an include element; an inclusion is done for each attribute given to the include command in turn. The valid attributes are:

**file** The value is a path relative to the directory containing the current document being parsed. It cannot contain `../`, nor can it be an absolute path. Therefore, you cannot include files that are outside of the document root, or above the current document in the directory structure. The `virtual` attribute should always be used in preference to this one.

**virtual** The value is a (%-encoded) URL-path. The URL cannot contain a scheme or hostname, only a path and an optional query string. If it does not begin with a slash (/) then it is taken to be relative to the current document.

A URL is constructed from the attribute, and the output the server would return if the URL were accessed by the client is included in the parsed output. Thus included files can be nested.

If the specified URL is a CGI program, the program will be executed and its output inserted in place of the directive in the parsed file. You may include a query string in a CGI url:

```
<!--#include virtual="/cgi-bin/example.cgi?argument=value" -->
```

`include virtual` should be used in preference to `exec cgi` to include the output of CGI programs into an HTML document.

If the KEPTBODYSIZE directive is correctly configured and valid for this included file, attempts to POST requests to the enclosing HTML document will be passed through to subrequests as POST requests as well. Without the directive, all subrequests are processed as GET requests.

**onerror** The value is a (%-encoded) URL-path which is shown should a previous attempt to include a file or virtual attribute failed. To be effective, this attribute must be specified after the file or virtual attributes being covered. If the attempt to include the onerror path fails, or if onerror is not specified, the default error message will be included.

```
# Simple example
<!--#include virtual="/not-exist.html" onerror="/error.html" -->
```

```
# Dedicated onerror paths
<!--#include virtual="/path-a.html" onerror="/error-a.html"
virtual="/path-b.html" onerror="/error-b.html" -->
```

**The printenv Element**

This prints out a plain text listing of all existing variables and their values. Special characters are entity encoded (see the `echo` element for details) before being output. There are no attributes.

**Example**
```
<pre> <!--#printenv --> </pre>
```

**The set Element**

This sets the value of a variable. Attributes:

**var** The name of the variable to set.

**value** The value to give a variable.

**decoding** Specifies whether Apache should strip an encoding from the variable before processing the variable further. The default is `none`, where no decoding will be done. If set to `url`, `urlencoded`, `base64` or `entity`, URL decoding, application/x-www-form-urlencoded decoding, base64 decoding or HTML entity decoding will be performed respectively. More than one decoding can be specified by separating with commas. The decoding setting will remain in effect until the next decoding attribute is encountered, or the element ends. The `decoding` attribute must *precede* the corresponding `var` attribute to be effective.

**encoding** Specifies how Apache should encode special characters contained in the variable before setting them. The default is `none`, where no encoding will be done. If set to `url`, `urlencoding`, `base64` or `entity`, URL encoding, application/x-www-form-urlencoded encoding, base64 encoding or HTML entity encoding will be performed respectively. More than one encoding can be specified by separating with commas. The encoding setting will remain in effect until the next encoding attribute is encountered, or the element ends. The `encoding` attribute must *precede* the corresponding `var` attribute to be effective. Encodings are applied after all decodings have been stripped.

**Example**
```
<!--#set var="category" value="help" -->
```

## Include Variables

In addition to the variables in the standard CGI environment, these are available for the `echo` command, for `if` and `elif`, and to any program invoked by the document.

**DATE_GMT** The current date in Greenwich Mean Time.

**DATE_LOCAL** The current date in the local time zone.

**DOCUMENT_ARGS** This variable contains the query string of the active SSI document, or the empty string if a query string is not included. For subrequests invoked through the `include` SSI directive, `QUERY_STRING` will represent the query string of the subrequest and `DOCUMENT_ARGS` will represent the query string of the SSI document. (Available in Apache HTTP Server 2.4.19 and later.)

**DOCUMENT_NAME** The filename (excluding directories) of the document requested by the user.

**DOCUMENT_URI** The (%-decoded) URL path of the document requested by the user. Note that in the case of nested include files, this is *not* the URL for the current document. Note also that if the URL is modified internally (e.g. by an ALIAS or DIRECTORYINDEX), the modified URL is shown.

**LAST_MODIFIED** The last modification date of the document requested by the user.

**QUERY_STRING_UNESCAPED** If a query string is present in the request for the active SSI document, this variable contains the (%-decoded) query string, which is *escaped* for shell usage (special characters like & etc. are preceded by backslashes). It is not set if a query string is not present. Use DOCUMENT_ARGS if shell escaping is not desired.

## Variable Substitution

Variable substitution is done within quoted strings in most cases where they may reasonably occur as an argument to an SSI directive. This includes the `config`, `exec`, `flastmod`, `fsize`, `include`, `echo`, and `set` directives. If SSILEGACYEXPRPARSER is set to `on`, substitution also occurs in the arguments to conditional operators. You can insert a literal dollar sign into the string using backslash quoting:

```
<!--#set var="cur" value="\$test" -->
```

If a variable reference needs to be substituted in the middle of a character sequence that might otherwise be considered a valid identifier in its own right, it can be disambiguated by enclosing the reference in braces, *a la* shell substitution:

```
<!--#set var="Zed" value="${REMOTE_HOST}_${REQUEST_METHOD}" -->
```

This will result in the `Zed` variable being set to `"X_Y"` if REMOTE_HOST is `"X"` and REQUEST_METHOD is `"Y"`.

## Flow Control Elements

The basic flow control elements are:

```
<!--#if expr="test_condition" -->
<!--#elif expr="test_condition" -->
<!--#else -->
<!--#endif -->
```

The if element works like an if statement in a programming language. The test condition is evaluated and if the result is true, then the text until the next elif, else or endif element is included in the output stream.

The elif or else statements are used to put text into the output stream if the original *test_condition* was false. These elements are optional.

The endif element ends the if element and is required.

*test_condition* is a boolean expression which follows the ap_expr (p. 99) syntax. The syntax can be changed to be compatible with Apache HTTPD 2.2.x using SSILEGACYEXPRPARSER.

The SSI variables set with the var element are exported into the request environment and can be accessed with the reqenv function. As a short-cut, the function name v is also available inside MOD_INCLUDE.

The below example will print "from local net" if client IP address belongs to the 10.0.0.0/8 subnet.

```
<!--#if expr='-R "10.0.0.0/8"' -->
   from local net
<!--#else -->
   from somewhere else
<!--#endif -->
```

The below example will print "foo is bar" if the variable foo is set to the value "bar".

```
<!--#if expr='v("foo") = "bar"' -->
   foo is bar
<!--#endif -->
```

⟹ **Reference Documentation**
See also: Expressions in Apache HTTP Server (p. 99) , for a complete reference and examples.
The *restricted* functions are not available inside MOD_INCLUDE

## Legacy expression syntax

This section describes the syntax of the #if expr element if SSILEGACYEXPRPARSER is set to on.

*string* true if *string* is not empty

**-A** *string* true if the URL represented by the string is accessible by configuration, false otherwise. This is useful where content on a page is to be hidden from users who are not authorized to view the URL, such as a link to that URL. Note that the URL is only tested for whether access would be granted, not whether the URL exists.

```
Example
<!--#if expr="-A /private" -->
   Click <a href="/private">here</a> to access private information.
<!--#endif -->
```

*string1* = *string2string1* == *string2string1* != *string2* Compare *string1* with *string2*. If *string2* has the form /*string2*/ then it is treated as a regular expression. Regular expressions are implemented by the PCRE[47] engine and have the same syntax as those in perl 5[48]. Note that == is just an alias for = and behaves exactly the same way.

---

[47]http://www.pcre.org
[48]http://www.perl.com

If you are matching positive (= or ==), you can capture grouped parts of the regular expression. The captured parts are stored in the special variables `$1` .. `$9`. The whole string matched by the regular expression is stored in the special variable `$0`

---

**Example**
```
<!--#if expr="$QUERY_STRING = /^sid=([a-zA-Z0-9]+)/" -->
    <!--#set var="session" value="$1" -->
<!--#endif -->
```

---

***string1 < string2string1 <= string2string1 > string2string1 >= string2*** Compare *string1* with *string2*. Note, that strings are compared *literally* (using `strcmp(3)`). Therefore the string `"100"` is less than `"20"`.

**( *test_condition* )** true if *test_condition* is true

**! *test_condition*** true if *test_condition* is false

***test_condition1 && test_condition2*** true if both *test_condition1* and *test_condition2* are true

***test_condition1 || test_condition2*** true if either *test_condition1* or *test_condition2* is true

`"="` and `"!="` bind more tightly than `"&&"` and `"||"`. `"!"` binds most tightly. Thus, the following are equivalent:

```
<!--#if expr="$a = test1 && $b = test2" -->
<!--#if expr="($a = test1) && ($b = test2)" -->
```

The boolean operators `&&` and `||` share the same priority. So if you want to bind such an operator more tightly, you should use parentheses.

Anything that's not recognized as a variable or an operator is treated as a string. Strings can also be quoted: `'string'`. Unquoted strings can't contain whitespace (blanks and tabs) because it is used to separate tokens such as variables. If multiple strings are found in a row, they are concatenated using blanks. So,

```
string1string2 results in string1string2
and
'string1string2' results in string1string2.
```

⟹ **Optimization of Boolean Expressions**

If the expressions become more complex and slow down processing significantly, you can try to optimize them according to the evaluation rules:

- Expressions are evaluated from left to right

- Binary boolean operators (`&&` and `||`) are short circuited wherever possible. In conclusion with the rule above that means, MOD_INCLUDE evaluates at first the left expression. If the left result is sufficient to determine the end result, processing stops here. Otherwise it evaluates the right side and computes the end result from both left and right results.

- Short circuit evaluation is turned off as long as there are regular expressions to deal with. These must be evaluated to fill in the backreference variables (`$1` .. `$9`).

If you want to look how a particular expression is handled, you can recompile MOD_INCLUDE using the `-DDEBUG_INCLUDE` compiler option. This inserts for every parsed expression tokenizer information, the parse tree and how it is evaluated into the output sent to the client.

**Escaping slashes in regex strings**

All slashes which are not intended to act as delimiters in your regex must be escaped. This is regardless of their meaning to the regex engine.

## SSIEndTag Directive

| | |
|---|---|
| Description: | String that ends an include element |
| Syntax: | SSIEndTag tag |
| Default: | SSIEndTag "-->" |
| Context: | server config, virtual host |
| Status: | Base |
| Module: | mod_include |

This directive changes the string that MOD_INCLUDE looks for to mark the end of an include element.

```
SSIEndTag "%>"
```

### See also

- SSISTARTTAG

## SSIErrorMsg Directive

| | |
|---|---|
| Description: | Error message displayed when there is an SSI error |
| Syntax: | SSIErrorMsg message |
| Default: | SSIErrorMsg "[an error occurred while processing this directive]" |
| Context: | server config, virtual host, directory, .htaccess |
| Override: | All |
| Status: | Base |
| Module: | mod_include |

The SSIERRORMSG directive changes the error message displayed when MOD_INCLUDE encounters an error. For production servers you may consider changing the default error message to "<!-- Error -->" so that the message is not presented to the user.

This directive has the same effect as the <!--#config errmsg=*message* --> element.

```
SSIErrorMsg "<!-- Error -->"
```

## SSIETag Directive

| | |
|---|---|
| Description: | Controls whether ETags are generated by the server. |
| Syntax: | SSIETag on\|off |
| Default: | SSIETag off |
| Context: | directory, .htaccess |
| Status: | Base |
| Module: | mod_include |

Under normal circumstances, a file filtered by MOD_INCLUDE may contain elements that are either dynamically generated, or that may have changed independently of the original file. As a result, by default the server is asked not to generate an ETag header for the response by adding no-etag to the request notes.

The SSIETAG directive suppresses this behaviour, and allows the server to generate an ETag header. This can be used to enable caching of the output. Note that a backend server or dynamic content generator may generate an ETag of its own, ignoring no-etag, and this ETag will be passed by MOD_INCLUDE regardless of the value of this setting. SSIETAG can take on the following values:

**off** no-etag will be added to the request notes, and the server is asked not to generate an ETag. Where a server ignores the value of no-etag and generates an ETag anyway, the ETag will be respected.

**on** Existing ETags will be respected, and ETags generated by the server will be passed on in the response.

## SSILastModified Directive

| | |
|---|---|
| Description: | Controls whether Last-Modified headers are generated by the server. |
| Syntax: | SSILastModified on\|off |
| Default: | SSILastModified off |
| Context: | directory, .htaccess |
| Status: | Base |
| Module: | mod_include |

Under normal circumstances, a file filtered by MOD_INCLUDE may contain elements that are either dynamically generated, or that may have changed independently of the original file. As a result, by default the Last-Modified header is stripped from the response.

The SSILASTMODIFIED directive overrides this behaviour, and allows the Last-Modified header to be respected if already present, or set if the header is not already present. This can be used to enable caching of the output. SSILASTMODIFIED can take on the following values:

**off** The Last-Modified header will be stripped from responses, unless the XBITHACK directive is set to full as described below.

**on** The Last-Modified header will be respected if already present in a response, and added to the response if the response is a file and the header is missing. The SSILASTMODIFIED directive takes precedence over XBITHACK.

## SSILegacyExprParser Directive

| | |
|---|---|
| Description: | Enable compatibility mode for conditional expressions. |
| Syntax: | SSILegacyExprParser on\|off |
| Default: | SSILegacyExprParser off |
| Context: | directory, .htaccess |
| Status: | Base |
| Module: | mod_include |
| Compatibility: | Available in version 2.3.13 and later. |

As of version 2.3.13, MOD_INCLUDE has switched to the new ap_expr (p. 99) syntax for conditional expressions in #if flow control elements. This directive allows to switch to the old syntax which is compatible with Apache HTTPD version 2.2.x and earlier.

## SSIStartTag Directive

| | |
|---|---|
| Description: | String that starts an include element |
| Syntax: | `SSIStartTag tag` |
| Default: | `SSIStartTag "<!--#"` |
| Context: | server config, virtual host |
| Status: | Base |
| Module: | mod_include |

This directive changes the string that MOD_INCLUDE looks for to mark an include element to process.

You may want to use this option if you have 2 servers parsing the output of a file each processing different commands (possibly at different times).

```
SSIStartTag "<%"
SSIEndTag   "%>"
```

The example given above, which also specifies a matching SSIENDTAG, will allow you to use SSI directives as shown in the example below:

> **SSI directives with alternate start and end tags**
> `<%printenv %>`

**See also**

- SSIENDTAG

## SSITimeFormat Directive

| | |
|---|---|
| Description: | Configures the format in which date strings are displayed |
| Syntax: | `SSITimeFormat formatstring` |
| Default: | `SSITimeFormat "%A, %d-%b-%Y %H:%M:%S %Z"` |
| Context: | server config, virtual host, directory, .htaccess |
| Override: | All |
| Status: | Base |
| Module: | mod_include |

This directive changes the format in which date strings are displayed when echoing DATE environment variables. The *formatstring* is as in `strftime(3)` from the C standard library.

This directive has the same effect as the `<!--#config timefmt=formatstring -->` element.

```
SSITimeFormat "%R, %B %d, %Y"
```

The above directive would cause times to be displayed in the format `"22:26, June 14, 2002"`.

## SSIUndefinedEcho Directive

| | |
|---|---|
| Description: | String displayed when an unset variable is echoed |
| Syntax: | `SSIUndefinedEcho string` |
| Default: | `SSIUndefinedEcho "(none)"` |
| Context: | server config, virtual host, directory, .htaccess |
| Override: | All |
| Status: | Base |
| Module: | mod_include |

This directive changes the string that MOD_INCLUDE displays when a variable is not set and "echoed".

```
SSIUndefinedEcho "<!-- undef -->"
```

## XBitHack Directive

| | |
|---|---|
| Description: | Parse SSI directives in files with the execute bit set |
| Syntax: | XBitHack on\|off\|full |
| Default: | XBitHack off |
| Context: | server config, virtual host, directory, .htaccess |
| Override: | Options |
| Status: | Base |
| Module: | mod_include |

The XBITHACK directive controls the parsing of ordinary html documents. This directive only affects files associated with the MIME-type text/html. XBITHACK can take on the following values:

**off** No special treatment of executable files.

**on** Any text/html file that has the user-execute bit set will be treated as a server-parsed html document.

**full** As for on but also test the group-execute bit. If it is set, then set the Last-modified date of the returned file to be the last modified time of the file. If it is not set, then no last-modified date is sent. Setting this bit allows clients and proxies to cache the result of the request.

**Note**

You would not want to use the full option, unless you assure the group-execute bit is unset for every SSI script which might #include a CGI or otherwise produces different output on each hit (or could potentially change on subsequent requests).

The SSILASTMODIFIED directive takes precedence over the XBITHACK directive when SSI-LASTMODIFIED is set to on.

# 10.61   Apache Module mod_info

| | |
|---|---|
| Description: | Provides a comprehensive overview of the server configuration |
| Status: | Extension |
| ModuleIdentifier: | info_module |
| SourceFile: | mod_info.c |

## Summary

To configure MOD_INFO, add the following to your `httpd.conf` file.

```
<Location "/server-info">
    SetHandler server-info
</Location>
```

You may wish to use MOD_AUTHZ_HOST inside the <LOCATION> directive to limit access to your server configuration information:

```
<Location "/server-info">
    SetHandler server-info
    Require host example.com
</Location>
```

Once    configured,    the    server    information    is    obtained    by    accessing
`http://your.host.example.com/server-info`

### Directives

- AddModuleInfo

## Security Issues

Once MOD_INFO is loaded into the server, its handler capability is available in *all* configuration files, including per-directory files (*e.g.*, `.htaccess`). This may have security-related ramifications for your site.

In particular, this module can leak sensitive information from the configuration directives of other Apache modules such as system paths, usernames/passwords, database names, etc.  Therefore, this module should **only** be used in a controlled environment and always with caution.

You will probably want to use MOD_AUTHZ_HOST to limit access to your server configuration information.

### Access control

```
<Location "/server-info">
    SetHandler server-info
    # Allow access from server itself
    Require ip 127.0.0.1

    # Additionally, allow access from local workstation
    Require ip 192.168.1.17
</Location>
```

### Selecting the information shown

By default, the server information includes a list of all enabled modules, and for each module, a description of the directives understood by that module, the hooks implemented by that module, and the relevant directives from the current configuration.

Other views of the configuration information are available by appending a query to the `server-info` request. For example, `http://your.host.example.com/server-info?config` will show all configuration directives.

`?<module-name>` Only information relevant to the named module

`?config` Just the configuration directives, not sorted by module

`?hooks` Only the list of Hooks each module is attached to

`?list` Only a simple list of enabled modules

`?server` Only the basic server information

### Dumping the configuration on startup

If the config define `-DDUMP_CONFIG` is set, MOD_INFO will dump the pre-parsed configuration to `stdout` during server startup. Pre-parsed means that directives like <IFDEFINE> and <IFMODULE> are evaluated and environment variables are replaced. However it does not represent the final state of the configuration. In particular, it does not represent the merging or overriding that may happen for repeated directives.

This is roughly equivalent to the `?config` query.

### Known Limitations

MOD_INFO provides its information by reading the parsed configuration, rather than reading the original configuration file. There are a few limitations as a result of the way the parsed configuration tree is created:

- Directives which are executed immediately rather than being stored in the parsed configuration are not listed. These include SERVERROOT, LOADMODULE, and LOADFILE.

- Directives which control the configuration file itself, such as INCLUDE, <IFMODULE> and <IFDEFINE> are not listed, but the included configuration directives are.

- Comments are not listed. (This may be considered a feature.)

- Configuration directives from `.htaccess` files are not listed (since they do not form part of the permanent server configuration).

- Container directives such as <DIRECTORY> are listed normally, but MOD_INFO cannot figure out the line number for the closing </DIRECTORY>.

- Directives generated by third party modules such as mod_perl[49] might not be listed.

---

[49] http://perl.apache.org

**AddModuleInfo Directive**

| | |
|---|---|
| Description: | Adds additional information to the module information displayed by the server-info handler |
| Syntax: | `AddModuleInfo module-name string` |
| Context: | server config, virtual host |
| Status: | Extension |
| Module: | mod_info |

This allows the content of *string* to be shown as HTML interpreted, **Additional Information** for the module *module-name*. Example:

```
AddModuleInfo mod_deflate.c 'See <a \
    href="http://httpd.apache.org/docs/trunk/mod/mod_deflate.html">\
    http://httpd.apache.org/docs/trunk/mod/mod_deflate.html</a>'
```

# 10.62  Apache Module mod_isapi

| | |
|---|---|
| Description: | ISAPI Extensions within Apache for Windows |
| Status: | Base |
| ModuleIdentifier: | isapi_module |
| SourceFile: | mod_isapi.c |
| Compatibility: | Win32 only |

## Summary

This module implements the Internet Server extension API. It allows Internet Server extensions (*e.g.* ISAPI .dll modules) to be served by Apache for Windows, subject to the noted restrictions.

ISAPI extension modules (.dll files) are written by third parties. The Apache Group does not author these modules, so we provide no support for them. Please contact the ISAPI's author directly if you are experiencing problems running their ISAPI extension. **Please *do not* post such problems to Apache's lists or bug reporting pages.**

### Directives

- ISAPIAppendLogToErrors
- ISAPIAppendLogToQuery
- ISAPICacheFile
- ISAPIFakeAsync
- ISAPILogNotSupported
- ISAPIReadAheadBuffer

## Usage

In the server configuration file, use the ADDHANDLER directive to associate ISAPI files with the `isapi-handler` handler, and map it to them with their file extensions. To enable any .dll file to be processed as an ISAPI extension, edit the httpd.conf file and add the following line:

```
AddHandler isapi-handler .dll
```

> In older versions of the Apache server, `isapi-isa` was the proper handler name, rather than `isapi-handler`. As of 2.3 development versions of the Apache server, `isapi-isa` is no longer valid. You will need to change your configuration to use `isapi-handler` instead.

There is no capability within the Apache server to leave a requested module loaded. However, you may preload and keep a specific module loaded by using the following syntax in your httpd.conf:

```
ISAPICacheFile c:/WebWork/Scripts/ISAPI/mytest.dll
```

Whether or not you have preloaded an ISAPI extension, all ISAPI extensions are governed by the same permissions and restrictions as CGI scripts. That is, OPTIONS `ExecCGI` must be set for the directory that contains the ISAPI .dll file.

Review the Additional Notes and the Programmer's Journal for additional details and clarification of the specific ISAPI support offered by MOD_ISAPI.

## Additional Notes

Apache's ISAPI implementation conforms to all of the ISAPI 2.0 specification, except for some "Microsoft-specific" extensions dealing with asynchronous I/O. Apache's I/O model does not allow asynchronous reading and writing in a manner that the ISAPI could access. If an ISA tries to access unsupported features, including async I/O, a message is placed in the error log to help with debugging. Since these messages can become a flood, the directive `ISAPILogNotSupported Off` exists to quiet this noise.

Some servers, like Microsoft IIS, load the ISAPI extension into the server and keep it loaded until memory usage is too high, or unless configuration options are specified. Apache currently loads and unloads the ISAPI extension each time it is requested, unless the ISAPICACHEFILE directive is specified. This is inefficient, but Apache's memory model makes this the most effective method. Many ISAPI modules are subtly incompatible with the Apache server, and unloading these modules helps to ensure the stability of the server.

Also, remember that while Apache supports ISAPI Extensions, it **does not support ISAPI Filters**. Support for filters may be added at a later date, but no support is planned at this time.

## Programmer's Journal

If you are programming Apache 2.0 MOD_ISAPI modules, you must limit your calls to `ServerSupportFunction` to the following directives:

**HSE_REQ_SEND_URL_REDIRECT_RESP** Redirect the user to another location.
> This must be a fully qualified URL (*e.g.* `http://server/location`).

**HSE_REQ_SEND_URL** Redirect the user to another location.
> This cannot be a fully qualified URL, you are not allowed to pass the protocol or a server name (*e.g.* simply `/location`).
> This redirection is handled by the server, not the browser.

> **Warning**
> In their recent documentation, Microsoft appears to have abandoned the distinction between the two `HSE_REQ_SEND_URL` functions. Apache continues to treat them as two distinct functions with different requirements and behaviors.

**HSE_REQ_SEND_RESPONSE_HEADER** Apache accepts a response body following the header if it follows the blank line (two consecutive newlines) in the headers string argument. This body cannot contain NULLs, since the headers argument is NULL terminated.

**HSE_REQ_DONE_WITH_SESSION** Apache considers this a no-op, since the session will be finished when the ISAPI returns from processing.

**HSE_REQ_MAP_URL_TO_PATH** Apache will translate a virtual name to a physical name.

**HSE_APPEND_LOG_PARAMETER** This logged message may be captured in any of the following logs:

- in the `\"%{isapi-parameter}n\"` component in a CUSTOMLOG directive
- in the `%q` log component with the ISAPIAPPENDLOGTOQUERY On directive
- in the error log with the ISAPIAPPENDLOGTOERRORS On directive

The first option, the `%{isapi-parameter}n` component, is always available and preferred.

**HSE_REQ_IS_KEEP_CONN** Will return the negotiated Keep-Alive status.

**HSE_REQ_SEND_RESPONSE_HEADER_EX** Will behave as documented, although the `fKeepConn` flag is ignored.

**HSE_REQ_IS_CONNECTED** Will report false if the request has been aborted.

Apache returns `FALSE` to any unsupported call to `ServerSupportFunction`, and sets the `GetLastError` value to `ERROR_INVALID_PARAMETER`.

`ReadClient` retrieves the request body exceeding the initial buffer (defined by ISAPIREADAHEADBUFFER). Based on the ISAPIREADAHEADBUFFER setting (number of bytes to buffer prior to calling the ISAPI handler) shorter requests are sent complete to the extension when it is invoked. If the request is longer, the ISAPI extension must use `ReadClient` to retrieve the remaining request body.

`WriteClient` is supported, but only with the `HSE_IO_SYNC` flag or no option flag (value of `0`). Any other `WriteClient` request will be rejected with a return value of `FALSE`, and a `GetLastError` value of `ERROR_INVALID_PARAMETER`.

`GetServerVariable` is supported, although extended server variables do not exist (as defined by other servers.) All the usual Apache CGI environment variables are available from `GetServerVariable`, as well as the `ALL_HTTP` and `ALL_RAW` values.

Since httpd 2.0, MOD_ISAPI supports additional features introduced in later versions of the ISAPI specification, as well as limited emulation of async I/O and the `TransmitFile` semantics. Apache httpd also supports preloading ISAPI .dlls for performance.

## ISAPIAppendLogToErrors Directive

| | |
|---|---|
| Description: | Record `HSE_APPEND_LOG_PARAMETER` requests from ISAPI extensions to the error log |
| Syntax: | `ISAPIAppendLogToErrors on|off` |
| Default: | `ISAPIAppendLogToErrors off` |
| Context: | server config, virtual host, directory, .htaccess |
| Override: | FileInfo |
| Status: | Base |
| Module: | mod_isapi |

Record `HSE_APPEND_LOG_PARAMETER` requests from ISAPI extensions to the server error log.

## ISAPIAppendLogToQuery Directive

| | |
|---|---|
| Description: | Record `HSE_APPEND_LOG_PARAMETER` requests from ISAPI extensions to the query field |
| Syntax: | `ISAPIAppendLogToQuery on|off` |
| Default: | `ISAPIAppendLogToQuery on` |
| Context: | server config, virtual host, directory, .htaccess |
| Override: | FileInfo |
| Status: | Base |
| Module: | mod_isapi |

Record `HSE_APPEND_LOG_PARAMETER` requests from ISAPI extensions to the query field (appended to the CUSTOMLOG %q component).

## ISAPICacheFile Directive

| | |
|---|---|
| Description: | ISAPI .dll files to be loaded at startup |
| Syntax: | `ISAPICacheFile file-path [file-path] ...` |
| Context: | server config, virtual host |
| Status: | Base |
| Module: | mod_isapi |

Specifies a space-separated list of file names to be loaded when the Apache server is launched, and remain loaded until the server is shut down. This directive may be repeated for every ISAPI .dll file desired. The full path name of each file should be specified. If the path name is not absolute, it will be treated relative to SERVERROOT.

## ISAPIFakeAsync Directive

| | |
|---|---|
| Description: | Fake asynchronous support for ISAPI callbacks |
| Syntax: | `ISAPIFakeAsync on\|off` |
| Default: | `ISAPIFakeAsync off` |
| Context: | server config, virtual host, directory, .htaccess |
| Override: | FileInfo |
| Status: | Base |
| Module: | mod_isapi |

While set to on, asynchronous support for ISAPI callbacks is simulated.

## ISAPILogNotSupported Directive

| | |
|---|---|
| Description: | Log unsupported feature requests from ISAPI extensions |
| Syntax: | `ISAPILogNotSupported on\|off` |
| Default: | `ISAPILogNotSupported off` |
| Context: | server config, virtual host, directory, .htaccess |
| Override: | FileInfo |
| Status: | Base |
| Module: | mod_isapi |

Logs all requests for unsupported features from ISAPI extensions in the server error log. This may help administrators to track down problems. Once set to on and all desired ISAPI modules are functioning, it should be set back to off.

## ISAPIReadAheadBuffer Directive

| | |
|---|---|
| Description: | Size of the Read Ahead Buffer sent to ISAPI extensions |
| Syntax: | `ISAPIReadAheadBuffer size` |
| Default: | `ISAPIReadAheadBuffer 49152` |
| Context: | server config, virtual host, directory, .htaccess |
| Override: | FileInfo |
| Status: | Base |
| Module: | mod_isapi |

Defines the maximum size of the Read Ahead Buffer sent to ISAPI extensions when they are initially invoked. All remaining data must be retrieved using the `ReadClient` callback; some ISAPI extensions may not support the `ReadClient` function. Refer questions to the ISAPI extension's author.

# 10.63 Apache Module mod_journald

| | |
|---|---|
| Description: | Provides "journald" ErrorLog provider |
| Status: | Extension |
| ModuleIdentifier: | journald_module |
| SourceFile: | mod_journald.c |

## Summary

This module provides "journald" ErrorLog provider. It allows logging error messages and CustomLog/TransferLog via systemd-journald(8).

**Directives** This module provides no directives.

## Structured logging

Systemd-journald allows structured logging and therefore it is possible to filter logged messages according to various variables. Currently supported variables are:

**LOG** The name of the log. For ErrorLog, the value is "error_log". For CustomLog or TransferLog, the value is the first argument of these directives.

**REQUEST_HOSTNAME** Host, as set by full URI or Host: header in the request.

**REQUEST_USER** If an authentication check was made, this gets set to the user name.

**REQUEST_USERAGENT_IP** The address that originated the request.

**REQUEST_URI** The path portion of the URI, or "/" if no path provided.

**SERVER_HOSTNAME** The hostname of server for which the log message has been generated.

These variables can be for example used to show only log messages for particular URI using `journalctl`:

```
journalctl REQUEST_URI=/index.html -a
```

For more examples, see systemd-journalctl documentation.

## Examples

Using `journald` in ErrorLog directive (see CORE) instead of a filename enables logging via systemd-journald(8) if the system supports it.

```
ErrorLog journald
```

Using `journald` as an error log provider in CustomLog directive (see MOD_LOG_CONFIG) enables logging via systemd-journald(8) if the system supports it.

```
CustomLog "journald" "%h %l %u %t \"%r\" %>s %b"
```

**Performance warning**
Currently, systemd-journald is not designed for high-throughput logging and logging access_log to systemd-journald could decrease the performance a lot.

## 10.64   Apache Module mod_lbmethod_bybusyness

| | |
|---|---|
| Description: | Pending Request Counting load balancer scheduler algorithm for MOD_PROXY_BALANCER |
| Status: | Extension |
| ModuleIdentifier: | lbmethod_bybusyness_module |
| SourceFile: | mod_lbmethod_bybusyness.c |
| Compatibility: | Split off from MOD_PROXY_BALANCER in 2.3 |

### Summary

This module does not provide any configuration directives of its own.   It requires the services of MOD_PROXY_BALANCER, and provides the bybusyness load balancing method.

**Directives** This module provides no directives.

**See also**

- MOD_PROXY
- MOD_PROXY_BALANCER

### Pending Request Counting Algorithm

Enabled via lbmethod=bybusyness, this scheduler keeps track of how many requests each worker is currently assigned at present. A new request is automatically assigned to the worker with the lowest number of active requests. This is useful in the case of workers that queue incoming requests independently of Apache, to ensure that queue length stays even and a request is always given to the worker most likely to service it the fastest and reduce latency.

In the case of multiple least-busy workers, the statistics (and weightings) used by the Request Counting method are used to break the tie. Over time, the distribution of work will come to resemble that characteristic of byrequests (as implemented by MOD_LBMETHOD_BYREQUESTS).

# 10.65 Apache Module mod_lbmethod_byrequests

| | |
|---|---|
| Description: | Request Counting load balancer scheduler algorithm for MOD_PROXY_BALANCER |
| Status: | Extension |
| ModuleIdentifier: | lbmethod_byrequests_module |
| SourceFile: | mod_lbmethod_byrequests.c |
| Compatibility: | Split off from MOD_PROXY_BALANCER in 2.3 |

## Summary

This module does not provide any configuration directives of its own. It requires the services of MOD_PROXY_BALANCER, and provides the `byrequests` load balancing method..

**Directives** This module provides no directives.

**See also**

- MOD_PROXY
- MOD_PROXY_BALANCER

## Request Counting Algorithm

Enabled via `lbmethod=byrequests`, the idea behind this scheduler is that we distribute the requests among the various workers to ensure that each gets their configured share of the number of requests. It works as follows:

*lbfactor* is *how much we expect this worker to work*, or *the workers' work quota*. This is a normalized value representing their `"share"` of the amount of work to be done.

*lbstatus* is *how urgent this worker has to work to fulfill its quota of work*.

The *worker* is a member of the load balancer, usually a remote host serving one of the supported protocols.

We distribute each worker's work quota to the worker, and then look which of them needs to work most urgently (biggest lbstatus). This worker is then selected for work, and its lbstatus reduced by the total work quota we distributed to all workers. Thus the sum of all lbstatus does not change(*) and we distribute the requests as desired.

If some workers are disabled, the others will still be scheduled correctly.

```
for each worker in workers
    worker lbstatus += worker lbfactor
    total factor    += worker lbfactor
    if worker lbstatus > candidate lbstatus
        candidate = worker

candidate lbstatus -= total factor
```

If a balancer is configured as follows:

| worker | a | b | c | d |
|---|---|---|---|---|
| **lbfactor** | 25 | 25 | 25 | 25 |
| **lbstatus** | 0 | 0 | 0 | 0 |

And *b* gets disabled, the following schedule is produced:

| worker | a |
|--------|---|
| **lbstatus** | *-50* |
| **lbstatus** | -25 |
| **lbstatus** | 0 |
| (repeat) | |

That is it schedules: *a c d a c d a c d* ... Please note that:

| worker | a | b | c | d |
|--------|---|---|---|---|
| **lbfactor** | 25 | 25 | 25 | 25 |

Has the exact same behavior as:

| worker | a | b | c | d |
|--------|---|---|---|---|
| **lbfactor** | 1 | 1 | 1 | 1 |

This is because all values of *lbfactor* are normalized with respect to the others. For:

| worker | a | b | c |
|--------|---|---|---|
| **lbfactor** | 1 | 4 | 1 |

worker *b* will, on average, get 4 times the requests that *a* and *c* will.

The following asymmetric configuration works as one would expect:

| worker | a |
|--------|---|
| **lbfactor** | 70 |
| | |
| **lbstatus** | *-30* |
| **lbstatus** | 40 |
| **lbstatus** | *10* |
| **lbstatus** | *-20* |
| **lbstatus** | *-50* |
| **lbstatus** | 20 |
| **lbstatus** | *-10* |
| **lbstatus** | *-40* |
| **lbstatus** | 30 |
| **lbstatus** | *0* |
| (repeat) | |

That is after 10 schedules, the schedule repeats and 7 *a* are selected with 3 *b* interspersed.

# 10.66 Apache Module mod_lbmethod_bytraffic

| | |
|---|---|
| Description: | Weighted Traffic Counting load balancer scheduler algorithm for MOD_PROXY_BALANCER |
| Status: | Extension |
| ModuleIdentifier: | lbmethod_bytraffic_module |
| SourceFile: | mod_lbmethod_bytraffic.c |
| Compatibility: | Split off from MOD_PROXY_BALANCER in 2.3 |

## Summary

This module does not provide any configuration directives of its own. It requires the services of MOD_PROXY_BALANCER, and provides the bytraffic load balancing method..

**Directives** This module provides no directives.

**See also**

- MOD_PROXY
- MOD_PROXY_BALANCER

## Weighted Traffic Counting Algorithm

Enabled via lbmethod=bytraffic, the idea behind this scheduler is very similar to the Request Counting method, with the following changes:

*lbfactor* is *how much traffic, in bytes, we want this worker to handle.* This is also a normalized value representing their "share" of the amount of work to be done, but instead of simply counting the number of requests, we take into account the amount of traffic this worker has either seen or produced.

If a balancer is configured as follows:

| worker | a | b | c |
|---|---|---|---|
| **lbfactor** | 1 | 2 | 1 |

Then we mean that we want *b* to process twice the amount of bytes than *a* or *c* should. It does not necessarily mean that *b* would handle twice as many requests, but it would process twice the I/O. Thus, the size of the request and response are applied to the weighting and selection algorithm.

Note: input and output bytes are weighted the same.

## 10.67   Apache Module mod_lbmethod_heartbeat

| | |
|---|---|
| Description: | Heartbeat Traffic Counting load balancer scheduler algorithm for MOD_PROXY_BALANCER |
| Status: | Experimental |
| ModuleIdentifier: | lbmethod_heartbeat_module |
| SourceFile: | mod_lbmethod_heartbeat.c |
| Compatibility: | Available in version 2.3 and later |

### Summary

lbmethod=heartbeat uses the services of MOD_HEARTMONITOR to balance between origin servers that are providing heartbeat info via the MOD_HEARTBEAT module.

This modules load balancing algorithm favors servers with more ready (idle) capacity over time, but does not select the server with the most ready capacity every time. Servers that have 0 active clients are penalized, with the assumption that they are not fully initialized.

### Directives

- HeartbeatStorage

### See also

- MOD_PROXY
- MOD_PROXY_BALANCER
- MOD_HEARTBEAT
- MOD_HEARTMONITOR

### HeartbeatStorage Directive

| | |
|---|---|
| Description: | Path to read heartbeat data |
| Syntax: | HeartbeatStorage file-path |
| Default: | HeartbeatStorage logs/hb.dat |
| Context: | server config |
| Status: | Experimental |
| Module: | mod_lbmethod_heartbeat |

The HEARTBEATSTORAGE directive specifies the path to read heartbeat data. This flat-file is used only when MOD_SLOTMEM_SHM is not loaded.

## 10.68 Apache Module mod_ldap

| | |
|---|---|
| Description: | LDAP connection pooling and result caching services for use by other LDAP modules |
| Status: | Extension |
| ModuleIdentifier: | ldap_module |
| SourceFile: | util_ldap.c |

### Summary

This module was created to improve the performance of websites relying on backend connections to LDAP servers. In addition to the functions provided by the standard LDAP libraries, this module adds an LDAP connection pool and an LDAP shared memory cache.

To enable this module, LDAP support must be compiled into apr-util. This is achieved by adding the `--with-ldap` flag to the `configure` script when building Apache.

SSL/TLS support is dependent on which LDAP toolkit has been linked to APR. As of this writing, APR-util supports: OpenLDAP SDK[50] (2.x or later), Novell LDAP SDK[51], Mozilla LDAP SDK[52], native Solaris LDAP SDK (Mozilla based) or the native Microsoft LDAP SDK. See the APR[53] website for details.

### Directives

- LDAPCacheEntries
- LDAPCacheTTL
- LDAPConnectionPoolTTL
- LDAPConnectionTimeout
- LDAPLibraryDebug
- LDAPOpCacheEntries
- LDAPOpCacheTTL
- LDAPReferralHopLimit
- LDAPReferrals
- LDAPRetries
- LDAPRetryDelay
- LDAPSharedCacheFile
- LDAPSharedCacheSize
- LDAPTimeout
- LDAPTrustedClientCert
- LDAPTrustedGlobalCert
- LDAPTrustedMode
- LDAPVerifyServerCert

---

[50]http://www.openldap.org/
[51]http://developer.novell.com/ndk/cldap.htm
[52]https://wiki.mozilla.org/LDAP_C_SDK
[53]http://apr.apache.org

## Example Configuration

The following is an example configuration that uses MOD_LDAP to increase the performance of HTTP Basic authentication provided by MOD_AUTHNZ_LDAP.

```
# Enable the LDAP connection pool and shared
# memory cache. Enable the LDAP cache status
# handler. Requires that mod_ldap and mod_authnz_ldap
# be loaded. Change the "yourdomain.example.com" to
# match your domain.

LDAPSharedCacheSize 500000
LDAPCacheEntries 1024
LDAPCacheTTL 600
LDAPOpCacheEntries 1024
LDAPOpCacheTTL 600

<Location "/ldap-status">
    SetHandler ldap-status

    Require host yourdomain.example.com

    Satisfy any
    AuthType Basic
    AuthName "LDAP Protected"
    AuthBasicProvider ldap
    AuthLDAPURL ldap://127.0.0.1/dc=example,dc=com?uid?one
    Require valid-user
</Location>
```

## LDAP Connection Pool

LDAP connections are pooled from request to request. This allows the LDAP server to remain connected and bound ready for the next request, without the need to unbind/connect/rebind. The performance advantages are similar to the effect of HTTP keepalives.

On a busy server it is possible that many requests will try and access the same LDAP server connection simultaneously. Where an LDAP connection is in use, Apache will create a new connection alongside the original one. This ensures that the connection pool does not become a bottleneck.

There is no need to manually enable connection pooling in the Apache configuration. Any module using this module for access to LDAP services will share the connection pool.

LDAP connections can keep track of the ldap client credentials used when binding to an LDAP server. These credentials can be provided to LDAP servers that do not allow anonymous binds during referral chasing. To control this feature, see the LDAPREFERRALS and LDAPREFERRALHOPLIMIT directives. By default, this feature is enabled.

## LDAP Cache

For improved performance, MOD_LDAP uses an aggressive caching strategy to minimize the number of times that the LDAP server must be contacted. Caching can easily double or triple the throughput of Apache when it is serving pages protected with mod_authnz_ldap. In addition, the load on the LDAP server will be significantly decreased.

MOD_LDAP supports two types of LDAP caching during the search/bind phase with a *search/bind cache* and during the compare phase with two *operation caches*. Each LDAP URL that is used by the server has its own set of these three caches.

### The Search/Bind Cache

The process of doing a search and then a bind is the most time-consuming aspect of LDAP operation, especially if the directory is large. The search/bind cache is used to cache all searches that resulted in successful binds. Negative results (*i.e.*, unsuccessful searches, or searches that did not result in a successful bind) are not cached. The rationale behind this decision is that connections with invalid credentials are only a tiny percentage of the total number of connections, so by not caching invalid credentials, the size of the cache is reduced.

MOD_LDAP stores the username, the DN retrieved, the password used to bind, and the time of the bind in the cache. Whenever a new connection is initiated with the same username, MOD_LDAP compares the password of the new connection with the password in the cache. If the passwords match, and if the cached entry is not too old, MOD_LDAP bypasses the search/bind phase.

The search and bind cache is controlled with the LDAPCACHEENTRIES and LDAPCACHETTL directives.

### Operation Caches

During attribute and distinguished name comparison functions, MOD_LDAP uses two operation caches to cache the compare operations. The first compare cache is used to cache the results of compares done to test for LDAP group membership. The second compare cache is used to cache the results of comparisons done between distinguished names.

Note that, when group membership is being checked, any sub-group comparison results are cached to speed future sub-group comparisons.

The behavior of both of these caches is controlled with the LDAPOPCACHEENTRIES and LDAPOPCACHETTL directives.

### Monitoring the Cache

MOD_LDAP has a content handler that allows administrators to monitor the cache performance. The name of the content handler is `ldap-status`, so the following directives could be used to access the MOD_LDAP cache information:

```
<Location "/server/cache-info">
    SetHandler ldap-status
</Location>
```

By fetching the URL `http://servername/cache-info`, the administrator can get a status report of every cache that is used by MOD_LDAP cache. Note that if Apache does not support shared memory, then each `httpd` instance has its own cache, so reloading the URL will result in different information each time, depending on which `httpd` instance processes the request.

## Using SSL/TLS

The ability to create an SSL and TLS connections to an LDAP server is defined by the directives LDAPTRUST-EDGLOBALCERT, LDAPTRUSTEDCLIENTCERT and LDAPTRUSTEDMODE. These directives specify the CA and optional client certificates to be used, as well as the type of encryption to be used on the connection (none, SSL or TLS/STARTTLS).

```
# Establish an SSL LDAP connection on port 636. Requires that
# mod_ldap and mod_authnz_ldap be loaded. Change the
# "yourdomain.example.com" to match your domain.

LDAPTrustedGlobalCert CA_DER /certs/certfile.der

<Location "/ldap-status">
    SetHandler ldap-status

    Require host yourdomain.example.com

    Satisfy any
    AuthType Basic
    AuthName "LDAP Protected"
    AuthBasicProvider ldap
    AuthLDAPURL ldaps://127.0.0.1/dc=example,dc=com?uid?one
    Require valid-user
</Location>


# Establish a TLS LDAP connection on port 389. Requires that
# mod_ldap and mod_authnz_ldap be loaded. Change the
# "yourdomain.example.com" to match your domain.

LDAPTrustedGlobalCert CA_DER /certs/certfile.der

<Location "/ldap-status">
    SetHandler ldap-status

    Require host yourdomain.example.com

    Satisfy any
    AuthType Basic
    AuthName "LDAP Protected"
    AuthBasicProvider ldap
    AuthLDAPURL ldap://127.0.0.1/dc=example,dc=com?uid?one TLS
    Require valid-user
</Location>
```

## SSL/TLS Certificates

The different LDAP SDKs have widely different methods of setting and handling both CA and client side certificates.

If you intend to use SSL or TLS, read this section CAREFULLY so as to understand the differences between configurations on the different LDAP toolkits supported.

### Netscape/Mozilla/iPlanet SDK

CA certificates are specified within a file called cert7.db. The SDK will not talk to any LDAP server whose certificate was not signed by a CA specified in this file. If client certificates are required, an optional key3.db file may be specified with an optional password. The secmod file can be specified if required. These files are in the same format as used by the Netscape Communicator or Mozilla web browsers. The easiest way to obtain these files is to grab them from your browser installation.

Client certificates are specified per connection using the LDAPTrustedClientCert directive by referring to the certificate "nickname". An optional password may be specified to unlock the certificate's private key.

The SDK supports SSL only. An attempt to use STARTTLS will cause an error when an attempt is made to contact the LDAP server at runtime.

```
# Specify a Netscape CA certificate file
LDAPTrustedGlobalCert CA_CERT7_DB /certs/cert7.db
# Specify an optional key3.db file for client certificate support
LDAPTrustedGlobalCert CERT_KEY3_DB /certs/key3.db
# Specify the secmod file if required
LDAPTrustedGlobalCert CA_SECMOD /certs/secmod
<Location "/ldap-status">
    SetHandler ldap-status

    Require host yourdomain.example.com

    Satisfy any
    AuthType Basic
    AuthName "LDAP Protected"
    AuthBasicProvider ldap
    LDAPTrustedClientCert CERT_NICKNAME <nickname> [password]
    AuthLDAPURL ldaps://127.0.0.1/dc=example,dc=com?uid?one
    Require valid-user
</Location>
```

**Novell SDK**

One or more CA certificates must be specified for the Novell SDK to work correctly. These certificates can be specified as binary DER or Base64 (PEM) encoded files.

Note: Client certificates are specified globally rather than per connection, and so must be specified with the LDAP-TrustedGlobalCert directive as below. Trying to set client certificates via the LDAPTrustedClientCert directive will cause an error to be logged when an attempt is made to connect to the LDAP server..

The SDK supports both SSL and STARTTLS, set using the LDAPTrustedMode parameter. If an ldaps:// URL is specified, SSL mode is forced, override this directive.

```
# Specify two CA certificate files
LDAPTrustedGlobalCert CA_DER /certs/cacert1.der
LDAPTrustedGlobalCert CA_BASE64 /certs/cacert2.pem
# Specify a client certificate file and key
LDAPTrustedGlobalCert CERT_BASE64 /certs/cert1.pem
LDAPTrustedGlobalCert KEY_BASE64 /certs/key1.pem [password]
# Do not use this directive, as it will throw an error
#LDAPTrustedClientCert CERT_BASE64 /certs/cert1.pem
```

**OpenLDAP SDK**

One or more CA certificates must be specified for the OpenLDAP SDK to work correctly. These certificates can be specified as binary DER or Base64 (PEM) encoded files.

Both CA and client certificates may be specified globally (LDAPTrustedGlobalCert) or per-connection (LDAPTrustedClientCert). When any settings are specified per-connection, the global settings are superceded.

The documentation for the SDK claims to support both SSL and STARTTLS, however STARTTLS does not seem to work on all versions of the SDK. The SSL/TLS mode can be set using the LDAPTrustedMode parameter. If an ldaps:// URL is specified, SSL mode is forced. The OpenLDAP documentation notes that SSL (ldaps://) support has been deprecated to be replaced with TLS, although the SSL functionality still works.

```
# Specify two CA certificate files
LDAPTrustedGlobalCert CA_DER /certs/cacert1.der
LDAPTrustedGlobalCert CA_BASE64 /certs/cacert2.pem
<Location "/ldap-status">
    SetHandler ldap-status

    Require host yourdomain.example.com

    LDAPTrustedClientCert CERT_BASE64 /certs/cert1.pem
    LDAPTrustedClientCert KEY_BASE64 /certs/key1.pem
    # CA certs respecified due to per-directory client certs
    LDAPTrustedClientCert CA_DER /certs/cacert1.der
    LDAPTrustedClientCert CA_BASE64 /certs/cacert2.pem
    Satisfy any
    AuthType Basic
    AuthName "LDAP Protected"
    AuthBasicProvider ldap
    AuthLDAPURL ldaps://127.0.0.1/dc=example,dc=com?uid?one
    Require valid-user
</Location>
```

### Solaris SDK

SSL/TLS for the native Solaris LDAP libraries is not yet supported. If required, install and use the OpenLDAP libraries instead.

### Microsoft SDK

SSL/TLS certificate configuration for the native Microsoft LDAP libraries is done inside the system registry, and no configuration directives are required.

Both SSL and TLS are supported by using the ldaps:// URL format, or by using the LDAPTrustedMode directive accordingly.

Note: The status of support for client certificates is not yet known for this toolkit.

## LDAPCacheEntries Directive

| | |
|---|---|
| Description: | Maximum number of entries in the primary LDAP cache |
| Syntax: | LDAPCacheEntries number |
| Default: | LDAPCacheEntries 1024 |
| Context: | server config |
| Status: | Extension |
| Module: | mod_ldap |

Specifies the maximum size of the primary LDAP cache. This cache contains successful search/binds. Set it to 0 to turn off search/bind caching. The default size is 1024 cached searches.

## LDAPCacheTTL Directive

| | |
|---|---|
| Description: | Time that cached items remain valid |
| Syntax: | `LDAPCacheTTL seconds` |
| Default: | `LDAPCacheTTL 600` |
| Context: | server config |
| Status: | Extension |
| Module: | mod_ldap |

Specifies the time (in seconds) that an item in the search/bind cache remains valid. The default is 600 seconds (10 minutes).

## LDAPConnectionPoolTTL Directive

| | |
|---|---|
| Description: | Discard backend connections that have been sitting in the connection pool too long |
| Syntax: | `LDAPConnectionPoolTTL n` |
| Default: | `LDAPConnectionPoolTTL -1` |
| Context: | server config, virtual host |
| Status: | Extension |
| Module: | mod_ldap |
| Compatibility: | Apache HTTP Server 2.3.12 and later |

Specifies the maximum age, in seconds, that a pooled LDAP connection can remain idle and still be available for use. Connections are cleaned up when they are next needed, not asynchronously.

A setting of 0 causes connections to never be saved in the backend connection pool. The default value of -1, and any other negative value, allows connections of any age to be reused.

For performance reasons, the reference time used by this directive is based on when the LDAP connection is returned to the pool, not the time of the last successful I/O with the LDAP server.

Since 2.4.10, new measures are in place to avoid the reference time from being inflated by cache hits or slow requests. First, the reference time is not updated if no backend LDAP conncetions were needed. Second, the reference time uses the time the HTTP request was received instead of the time the request is completed.

⟹ This timeout defaults to units of seconds, but accepts suffixes for milliseconds (ms), minutes (min), and hours (h).

## LDAPConnectionTimeout Directive

| | |
|---|---|
| Description: | Specifies the socket connection timeout in seconds |
| Syntax: | `LDAPConnectionTimeout seconds` |
| Context: | server config |
| Status: | Extension |
| Module: | mod_ldap |

This directive configures the LDAP_OPT_NETWORK_TIMEOUT (or LDAP_OPT_CONNECT_TIMEOUT) option in the underlying LDAP client library, when available. This value typically controls how long the LDAP client library will wait for the TCP connection to the LDAP server to complete.

If a connection is not successful with the timeout period, either an error will be returned or the LDAP client library will attempt to connect to a secondary LDAP server if one is specified (via a space-separated list of hostnames in the AuthLDAPURL).

The default is 10 seconds, if the LDAP client library linked with the server supports the LDAP_OPT_NETWORK_TIMEOUT option.

LDAPConnectionTimeout is only available when the LDAP client library linked with the server supports the LDAP_OPT_NETWORK_TIMEOUT (or LDAP_OPT_CONNECT_TIMEOUT) option, and the ultimate behavior is dictated entirely by the LDAP client library.

## LDAPLibraryDebug Directive

| | |
|---|---|
| Description: | Enable debugging in the LDAP SDK |
| Syntax: | `LDAPLibraryDebug 7` |
| Default: | `disabled` |
| Context: | server config |
| Status: | Extension |
| Module: | mod_ldap |

Turns on SDK-specific LDAP debug options that generally cause the LDAP SDK to log verbose trace information to the main Apache error log. The trace messages from the LDAP SDK provide gory details that can be useful during debugging of connectivity problems with backend LDAP servers

This option is only configurable when Apache HTTP Server is linked with an LDAP SDK that implements `LDAP_OPT_DEBUG` or `LDAP_OPT_DEBUG_LEVEL`, such as OpenLDAP (a value of 7 is verbose) or Tivoli Directory Server (a value of 65535 is verbose).

 The logged information will likely contain plaintext credentials being used or validated by LDAP authentication, so care should be taken in protecting and purging the error log when this directive is used.

## LDAPOpCacheEntries Directive

| | |
|---|---|
| Description: | Number of entries used to cache LDAP compare operations |
| Syntax: | `LDAPOpCacheEntries number` |
| Default: | `LDAPOpCacheEntries 1024` |
| Context: | server config |
| Status: | Extension |
| Module: | mod_ldap |

This specifies the number of entries MOD_LDAP will use to cache LDAP compare operations. The default is 1024 entries. Setting it to 0 disables operation caching.

## LDAPOpCacheTTL Directive

| | |
|---|---|
| Description: | Time that entries in the operation cache remain valid |
| Syntax: | `LDAPOpCacheTTL seconds` |
| Default: | `LDAPOpCacheTTL 600` |
| Context: | server config |
| Status: | Extension |
| Module: | mod_ldap |

Specifies the time (in seconds) that entries in the operation cache remain valid. The default is 600 seconds.

## LDAPReferralHopLimit Directive

| | |
|---|---|
| Description: | The maximum number of referral hops to chase before terminating an LDAP query. |
| Syntax: | `LDAPReferralHopLimit number` |
| Default: | `SDK dependent, typically between 5 and 10` |
| Context: | directory, .htaccess |
| Override: | AuthConfig |
| Status: | Extension |
| Module: | mod_ldap |

This directive, if enabled by the LDAPREFERRALS directive, limits the number of referral hops that are followed before terminating an LDAP query.

 Support for this tunable is uncommon in LDAP SDKs.

## LDAPReferrals Directive

| | |
|---|---|
| Description: | Enable referral chasing during queries to the LDAP server. |
| Syntax: | `LDAPReferrals On\|Off\|default` |
| Default: | `LDAPReferrals On` |
| Context: | directory, .htaccess |
| Override: | AuthConfig |
| Status: | Extension |
| Module: | mod_ldap |
| Compatibility: | The *default* parameter is available in Apache 2.4.7 and later |

Some LDAP servers divide their directory among multiple domains and use referrals to direct a client when a domain boundary is crossed. This is similar to a HTTP redirect. LDAP client libraries may or may not chase referrals by default. This directive explicitly configures the referral chasing in the underlying SDK.

LDAPREFERRALS takes the following values:

**"on"** When set to "on", the underlying SDK's referral chasing state is enabled, LDAPREFERRALHOPLIMIT is used to override the SDK's hop limit, and an LDAP rebind callback is registered.

**"off"** When set to "off", the underlying SDK's referral chasing state is disabled completely.

**"default"** When set to "default", the underlying SDK's referral chasing state is not changed, LDAPREFERRALHOPLIMIT is not used to override the SDK's hop limit, and no LDAP rebind callback is registered.

The directive LDAPREFERRALHOPLIMIT works in conjunction with this directive to limit the number of referral hops to follow before terminating the LDAP query. When referral processing is enabled by a value of "On", client credentials will be provided, via a rebind callback, for any LDAP server requiring them.

## LDAPRetries Directive

| | |
|---|---|
| Description: | Configures the number of LDAP server retries. |
| Syntax: | `LDAPRetries number-of-retries` |
| Default: | `LDAPRetries 3` |
| Context: | server config |
| Status: | Extension |
| Module: | mod_ldap |

The server will retry failed LDAP requests up to LDAPRETRIES times. Setting this directive to 0 disables retries.

LDAP errors such as timeouts and refused connections are retryable.

## LDAPRetryDelay Directive

| | |
|---|---|
| Description: | Configures the delay between LDAP server retries. |
| Syntax: | `LDAPRetryDelay seconds` |
| Default: | `LDAPRetryDelay 0` |
| Context: | server config |
| Status: | Extension |
| Module: | mod_ldap |

If LDAPRETRYDELAY is set to a non-zero value, the server will delay retrying an LDAP request for the specified amount of time. Setting this directive to 0 will result in any retry to occur without delay.

LDAP errors such as timeouts and refused connections are retryable.

## LDAPSharedCacheFile Directive

| | |
|---|---|
| Description: | Sets the shared memory cache file |
| Syntax: | `LDAPSharedCacheFile file-path` |
| Context: | server config |
| Status: | Extension |
| Module: | mod_ldap |

Specifies the path of the shared memory cache file. If not set, anonymous shared memory will be used if the platform supports it.

If *file-path* is not an absolute path, the location specified will be relative to the value of DEFAULTRUNTIMEDIR.

## LDAPSharedCacheSize Directive

| | |
|---|---|
| Description: | Size in bytes of the shared-memory cache |
| Syntax: | `LDAPSharedCacheSize bytes` |
| Default: | `LDAPSharedCacheSize 500000` |
| Context: | server config |
| Status: | Extension |
| Module: | mod_ldap |

Specifies the number of bytes to allocate for the shared memory cache. The default is 500kb. If set to 0, shared memory caching will not be used and every HTTPD process will create its own cache.

## LDAPTimeout Directive

| | |
|---|---|
| Description: | Specifies the timeout for LDAP search and bind operations, in seconds |
| Syntax: | `LDAPTimeout seconds` |
| Default: | `LDAPTimeout 60` |
| Context: | server config |
| Status: | Extension |
| Module: | mod_ldap |
| Compatibility: | Apache HTTP Server 2.3.5 and later |

This directive configures the timeout for bind and search operations, as well as the LDAP_OPT_TIMEOUT option in the underlying LDAP client library, when available.

If the timeout expires, httpd will retry in case an existing connection has been silently dropped by a firewall. However, performance will be much better if the firewall is configured to send TCP RST packets instead of silently dropping packets.

Timeouts for ldap compare operations requires an SDK with LDAP_OPT_TIMEOUT, such as OpenLDAP >= 2.4.4.

## LDAPTrustedClientCert Directive

| | |
|---|---|
| Description: | Sets the file containing or nickname referring to a per connection client certificate. Not all LDAP toolkits support per connection client certificates. |
| Syntax: | `LDAPTrustedClientCert type directory-path/filename/nickname [password]` |
| Context: | directory, .htaccess |
| Status: | Extension |
| Module: | mod_ldap |

It specifies the directory path, file name or nickname of a per connection client certificate used when establishing an SSL or TLS connection to an LDAP server. Different locations or directories may have their own independent client certificate settings. Some LDAP toolkits (notably Novell) do not support per connection client certificates, and will throw an error on LDAP server connection if you try to use this directive (Use the LDAPTrustedGlobalCert directive instead for Novell client certificates - See the SSL/TLS certificate guide above for details). The type specifies the kind of certificate parameter being set, depending on the LDAP toolkit being used. Supported types are:

- CA_DER - binary DER encoded CA certificate
- CA_BASE64 - PEM encoded CA certificate
- CERT_DER - binary DER encoded client certificate
- CERT_BASE64 - PEM encoded client certificate
- CERT_NICKNAME - Client certificate "nickname" (Netscape SDK)
- KEY_DER - binary DER encoded private key
- KEY_BASE64 - PEM encoded private key

## LDAPTrustedGlobalCert Directive

| | |
|---|---|
| Description: | Sets the file or database containing global trusted Certificate Authority or global client certificates |
| Syntax: | `LDAPTrustedGlobalCert type directory-path/filename [password]` |
| Context: | server config |
| Status: | Extension |
| Module: | mod_ldap |

It specifies the directory path and file name of the trusted CA certificates and/or system wide client certificates MOD_LDAP should use when establishing an SSL or TLS connection to an LDAP server. Note that all certificate information specified using this directive is applied globally to the entire server installation. Some LDAP toolkits (notably Novell) require all client certificates to be set globally using this directive. Most other toolkits require clients certificates to be set per Directory or per Location using LDAPTrustedClientCert. If you get this wrong, an error may be logged when an attempt is made to contact the LDAP server, or the connection may silently fail (See the SSL/TLS certificate guide above for details). The type specifies the kind of certificate parameter being set, depending on the LDAP toolkit being used. Supported types are:

- CA_DER - binary DER encoded CA certificate
- CA_BASE64 - PEM encoded CA certificate
- CA_CERT7_DB - Netscape cert7.db CA certificate database file
- CA_SECMOD - Netscape secmod database file

- CERT_DER - binary DER encoded client certificate
- CERT_BASE64 - PEM encoded client certificate
- CERT_KEY3_DB - Netscape key3.db client certificate database file
- CERT_NICKNAME - Client certificate "nickname" (Netscape SDK)
- CERT_PFX - PKCS#12 encoded client certificate (Novell SDK)
- KEY_DER - binary DER encoded private key
- KEY_BASE64 - PEM encoded private key
- KEY_PFX - PKCS#12 encoded private key (Novell SDK)

## LDAPTrustedMode Directive

| | |
|---|---|
| Description: | Specifies the SSL/TLS mode to be used when connecting to an LDAP server. |
| Syntax: | `LDAPTrustedMode type` |
| Context: | server config, virtual host |
| Status: | Extension |
| Module: | mod_ldap |

The following modes are supported:

- NONE - no encryption
- SSL - ldaps:// encryption on default port 636
- TLS - STARTTLS encryption on default port 389

Not all LDAP toolkits support all the above modes. An error message will be logged at runtime if a mode is not supported, and the connection to the LDAP server will fail.

If an ldaps:// URL is specified, the mode becomes SSL and the setting of LDAPTrustedMode is ignored.

## LDAPVerifyServerCert Directive

| | |
|---|---|
| Description: | Force server certificate verification |
| Syntax: | `LDAPVerifyServerCert On|Off` |
| Default: | `LDAPVerifyServerCert On` |
| Context: | server config |
| Status: | Extension |
| Module: | mod_ldap |

Specifies whether to force the verification of a server certificate when establishing an SSL connection to the LDAP server.

# 10.69  Apache Module mod_log_config

| | |
|---|---|
| Description: | Logging of the requests made to the server |
| Status: | Base |
| ModuleIdentifier: | log_config_module |
| SourceFile: | mod_log_config.c |

## Summary

This module provides for flexible logging of client requests. Logs are written in a customizable format, and may be written directly to a file, or to an external program. Conditional logging is provided so that individual requests may be included or excluded from the logs based on characteristics of the request.

Three directives are provided by this module: TRANSFERLOG to create a log file, LOGFORMAT to set a custom format, and CUSTOMLOG to define a log file and format in one step. The TRANSFERLOG and CUSTOMLOG directives can be used multiple times in each server to cause each request to be logged to multiple files.

### Directives

- BufferedLogs
- CustomLog
- GlobalLog
- LogFormat
- TransferLog

### See also

- Apache Log Files (p. 56)

## Custom Log Formats

The format argument to the LOGFORMAT and CUSTOMLOGdirectives is a string. This string is used to log each request to the log file. It can contain literal characters copied into the log files and the C-style control characters "\n" and "\t" to represent new-lines and tabs. Literal quotes and backslashes should be escaped with backslashes.

The characteristics of the request itself are logged by placing "%" directives in the format string, which are replaced in the log file by the values as follows:

| FormatString | Description |
|---|---|
| %% | The percent sign. |
| %a | Client IP address of the request (see the MOD_REMOTEIP module). |
| %{c}a | Underlying peer IP address of the connection (see the MOD_REMOTEIP module). |
| %A | Local IP-address. |
| %B | Size of response in bytes, excluding HTTP headers. |
| %b | Size of response in bytes, excluding HTTP headers. In CLF format, *i.e.* a '−' rather than a 0 when no bytes are sent. |
| %{VARNAME}C | The contents of cookie VARNAME in the request sent to the server. Only version 0 cookies are fully supported. |
| %D | The time taken to serve the request, in microseconds. |
| %{VARNAME}e | The contents of the environment variable VARNAME. |
| %f | Filename. |

| %h | Remote hostname. Will log the IP address if HOSTNAMELOOKUPS is set to Off, which is the default. If it logs the hostname for only a few hosts, you probably have access control directives mentioning them by name. See the Require host documentation (p. 536) . |
|---|---|
| %H | The request protocol. |
| %{VARNAME}i | The contents of VARNAME: header line(s) in the request sent to the server. Changes made by other modules (e.g. MOD_HEADERS) affect this. If you're interested in what the request header was prior to when most modules would have modified it, use MOD_SETENVIF to copy the header into an internal environment variable and log that value with the %{VARNAME}e described above. |
| %k | Number of keepalive requests handled on this connection. Interesting if KEEPALIVE is being used, so that, for example, a '1' means the first keepalive request after the initial one, '2' the second, etc...; otherwise this is always 0 (indicating the initial request). |
| %l | Remote logname (from identd, if supplied). This will return a dash unless MOD_IDENT is present and IDENTITYCHECK is set On. |
| %L | The request log ID from the error log (or '-' if nothing has been logged to the error log for this request). Look for the matching error log line to see what request caused what error. |
| %m | The request method. |
| %{VARNAME}n | The contents of note VARNAME from another module. |
| %{VARNAME}o | The contents of VARNAME : header line(s) in the reply. |
| %p | The canonical port of the server serving the request. |
| %{format}p | The canonical port of the server serving the request, or the server's actual port, or the client's actual port. Valid formats are canonical, local, or remote. |
| %P | The process ID of the child that serviced the request. |
| %{format}P | The process ID or thread ID of the child that serviced the request. Valid formats are pid, tid, and hextid. hextid requires APR 1.2.0 or higher. |
| %q | The query string (prepended with a ? if a query string exists, otherwise an empty string). |
| %r | First line of request. |
| %R | The handler generating the response (if any). |
| %s | Status. For requests that have been internally redirected, this is the status of the *original* request. Use %>s for the final status. |
| %t | Time the request was received, in the format [18/Sep/2011:19:18:28 -0400]. The last number indicates the timezone offset from GMT |
| %{format}t | The time, in the form given by format, which should be in an extended strftime(3) format (potentially localized). If the format starts with begin: (default) the time is taken at the beginning of the request processing. If it starts with end: it is the time when the log entry gets written, close to the end of the request processing. In addition to the formats supported by strftime(3), the following format tokens are supported: <table><tr><td>sec</td><td>number of seconds since the Epoch</td></tr><tr><td>msec</td><td>number of milliseconds since the Epoch</td></tr><tr><td>usec</td><td>number of microseconds since the Epoch</td></tr><tr><td>msec_frac</td><td>millisecond fraction</td></tr><tr><td>usec_frac</td><td>microsecond fraction</td></tr></table> These tokens can not be combined with each other or strftime(3) formatting in the same format string. You can use multiple %{format}t tokens instead. |
| %T | The time taken to serve the request, in seconds. |
| %{UNIT}T | The time taken to serve the request, in a time unit given by UNIT. Valid units are ms for milliseconds, us for microseconds, and s for seconds. Using s gives the same result as %T without any format; using us gives the same result as %D. Combining %T with a unit is available in 2.4.13 and later. |
| %u | Remote user if the request was authenticated. May be bogus if return status (%s) is 401 (unauthorized). |
| %U | The URL path requested, not including any query string. |
| %v | The canonical SERVERNAME of the server serving the request. |
| %V | The server name according to the USECANONICALNAME setting. |
| %X | Connection status when response is completed: <table><tr><td>X =</td><td>Connection aborted before the response completed.</td></tr><tr><td>+ =</td><td>Connection may be kept alive after the response is sent.</td></tr><tr><td>- =</td><td>Connection will be closed after the response is sent.</td></tr></table> |

| | |
|---|---|
| %I | Bytes received, including request and headers. Cannot be zero. You need to enable MOD_LOGIO to use this. |
| %O | Bytes sent, including headers. May be zero in rare cases such as when a request is aborted before a response is sent. You need to enable MOD_LOGIO to use this. |
| %S | Bytes transferred (received and sent), including request and headers, cannot be zero. This is the combination of %I and %O. You need to enable MOD_LOGIO to use this. |
| %{VARNAME}^ti | The contents of VARNAME: trailer line(s) in the request sent to the server. |
| %{VARNAME}^to | The contents of VARNAME: trailer line(s) in the response sent from the server. |

### Modifiers

Particular items can be restricted to print only for responses with specific HTTP status codes by placing a comma-separated list of status codes immediately following the "%". The status code list may be preceded by a "!" to indicate negation.

| Format String | Meaning |
|---|---|
| %400,501{User-agent}i | Logs User-agent on 400 errors and 501 errors only. For other status codes, the literal string "-" will be logged. |
| %!200,304,302{Referer}i | Logs Referer on all requests that do *not* return one of the three specified codes, "-" otherwise. |

The modifiers "<" and ">" can be used for requests that have been internally redirected to choose whether the original or final (respectively) request should be consulted. By default, the % directives %s, %U, %T, %D, and %r look at the original request while all others look at the final request. So for example, %>s can be used to record the final status of the request and %<u can be used to record the original authenticated user on a request that is internally redirected to an unauthenticated resource.

### Format Notes

For security reasons, starting with version 2.0.46, non-printable and other special characters in %r, %i and %o are escaped using \xhh sequences, where *hh* stands for the hexadecimal representation of the raw byte. Exceptions from this rule are " and \, which are escaped by prepending a backslash, and all whitespace characters, which are written in their C-style notation (\n, \t, etc). In versions prior to 2.0.46, no escaping was performed on these strings so you had to be quite careful when dealing with raw log files.

Since httpd 2.0, unlike 1.3, the %b and %B format strings do not represent the number of bytes sent to the client, but simply the size in bytes of the HTTP response (which will differ, for instance, if the connection is aborted, or if SSL is used). The %O format provided by MOD_LOGIO will log the actual number of bytes sent over the network.

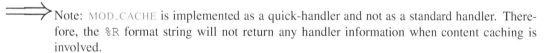

Note: MOD_CACHE is implemented as a quick-handler and not as a standard handler. Therefore, the %R format string will not return any handler information when content caching is involved.

Note: The '^' character at the start of three-character formats has no significance, but it must be the first character of any newly added three-character format to avoid potential conflicts with log formats that use literals adjacent to a format specifier, such as "%Dus".

### Examples

Some commonly used log format strings are:

**Common Log Format (CLF)** "%h %l %u %t \"%r\" %>s %b"

**Common Log Format with Virtual Host** "%v %h %l %u %t \"%r\" %>s %b"

**NCSA extended/combined log format** `"%h %l %u %t \"%r\" %>s %b \"%{Referer}i\"`
    `\"%{User-agent}i\""`

**Referer log format** `"%{Referer}i -> %U"`

**Agent (Browser) log format** `"%{User-agent}i"`

You can use the `%{format}t` directive multiple times to build up a time format using the extended format tokens like `msec_frac`:

**Timestamp including milliseconds** `"%{%d/%b/%Y %T}t.%{msec_frac}t %{%z}t"`

## Security Considerations

See the security tips (p. 364) document for details on why your security could be compromised if the directory where logfiles are stored is writable by anyone other than the user that starts the server.

## BufferedLogs Directive

| | |
|---|---|
| Description: | Buffer log entries in memory before writing to disk |
| Syntax: | `BufferedLogs On|Off` |
| Default: | `BufferedLogs Off` |
| Context: | server config |
| Status: | Base |
| Module: | mod_log_config |

The BUFFEREDLOGS directive causes MOD_LOG_CONFIG to store several log entries in memory and write them together to disk, rather than writing them after each request. On some systems, this may result in more efficient disk access and hence higher performance. It may be set only once for the entire server; it cannot be configured per virtual-host.

⟹ This directive should be used with caution as a crash might cause loss of logging data.

## CustomLog Directive

| | |
|---|---|
| Description: | Sets filename and format of log file |
| Syntax: | `CustomLog file|pipe|provider format|nickname` |
| | `[env=[!]environment-variable| expr=expression]` |
| Context: | server config, virtual host |
| Status: | Base |
| Module: | mod_log_config |

The CUSTOMLOG directive is used to log requests to the server. A log format is specified, and the logging can optionally be made conditional on request characteristics using environment variables.

The first argument, which specifies the location to which the logs will be written, can take one of the following two types of values:

*file* A filename, relative to the SERVERROOT.

*pipe* The pipe character " | ", followed by the path to a program to receive the log information on its standard input. See the notes on piped logs (p. 56) for more information.

**Security:**
If a program is used, then it will be run as the user who started `httpd`. This will be root if the server was started by root; be sure that the program is secure.

 **Note**
When entering a file path on non-Unix platforms, care should be taken to make sure that only forward slashed are used even though the platform may allow the use of back slashes. In general it is a good idea to always use forward slashes throughout the configuration files.

*provider* Modules implementing ErrorLog providers can also be used as a target for CustomLog messages. To use ErrorLog provider as a target, "provider:argument" syntax must be used. You can for example use MOD_JOURNALD or MOD_SYSLOG as a provider:

```
# CustomLog logging to journald
CustomLog "journald" "%h %l %u %t \"%r\" %>s %b"

# CustomLog logging to syslog with "user" facility
CustomLog "syslog:user" "%h %l %u %t \"%r\" %>s %b"
```

The second argument specifies what will be written to the log file. It can specify either a *nickname* defined by a previous LOGFORMAT directive, or it can be an explicit *format* string as described in the log formats section.

For example, the following two sets of directives have exactly the same effect:

```
# CustomLog with format nickname
LogFormat "%h %l %u %t \"%r\" %>s %b" common
CustomLog "logs/access_log" common

# CustomLog with explicit format string
CustomLog "logs/access_log" "%h %l %u %t \"%r\" %>s %b"
```

The third argument is optional and controls whether or not to log a particular request. The condition can be the presence or absence (in the case of a 'env=!*name*' clause) of a particular variable in the server environment (p. 92) . Alternatively, the condition can be expressed as arbitrary boolean expression (p. 99) . If the condition is not satisfied, the request will not be logged. References to HTTP headers in the expression will not cause the header names to be added to the Vary header.

Environment variables can be set on a per-request basis using the MOD_SETENVIF and/or MOD_REWRITE modules. For example, if you want to record requests for all GIF images on your server in a separate logfile but not in your main log, you can use:

```
SetEnvIf Request_URI \.gif$ gif-image
CustomLog "gif-requests.log" common env=gif-image
CustomLog "nongif-requests.log" common env=!gif-image
```

Or, to reproduce the behavior of the old RefererIgnore directive, you might use the following:

```
SetEnvIf Referer example\.com localreferer
CustomLog "referer.log" referer env=!localreferer
```

## GlobalLog Directive

| Description: | Sets filename and format of log file |
| --- | --- |
| Syntax: | `GlobalLog file|pipe|provider format|nickname`<br>`[env=[!]environment-variable| expr=expression]` |
| Context: | server config |
| Status: | Base |
| Module: | mod_log_config |
| Compatibility: | Available in Apache HTTP Server 2.4.19 and later |

The GLOBALLOG directive defines a log shared by the main server configuration and all defined virtual hosts.

The GLOBALLOG directive is identical to the CUSTOMLOG directive, apart from the following differences:

- GLOBALLOG is not valid in virtual host context.
- GLOBALLOG is used by virtual hosts that define their own CUSTOMLOG, unlike a globally specified CUSTOM-LOG.

## LogFormat Directive

| Description: | Describes a format for use in a log file |
| --- | --- |
| Syntax: | `LogFormat format|nickname [nickname]` |
| Default: | `LogFormat "%h %l %u %t \"%r\" %>s %b"` |
| Context: | server config, virtual host |
| Status: | Base |
| Module: | mod_log_config |

This directive specifies the format of the access log file.

The LOGFORMAT directive can take one of two forms. In the first form, where only one argument is specified, this directive sets the log format which will be used by logs specified in subsequent TRANSFERLOG directives. The single argument can specify an explicit *format* as discussed in the custom log formats section above. Alternatively, it can use a *nickname* to refer to a log format defined in a previous LOGFORMAT directive as described below.

The second form of the LOGFORMAT directive associates an explicit *format* with a *nickname*. This *nickname* can then be used in subsequent LOGFORMAT or CUSTOMLOG directives rather than repeating the entire format string. A LOGFORMAT directive that defines a nickname **does nothing else** – that is, it *only* defines the nickname, it doesn't actually apply the format and make it the default. Therefore, it will not affect subsequent TRANSFERLOG directives. In addition, LOGFORMAT cannot use one nickname to define another nickname. Note that the nickname should not contain percent signs (%).

### Example

```
LogFormat "%v %h %l %u %t \"%r\" %>s %b" vhost_common
```

## TransferLog Directive

| Description: | Specify location of a log file |
| --- | --- |
| Syntax: | `TransferLog file|pipe` |
| Context: | server config, virtual host |
| Status: | Base |
| Module: | mod_log_config |

This directive has exactly the same arguments and effect as the CUSTOMLOG directive, with the exception that it does not allow the log format to be specified explicitly or for conditional logging of requests. Instead, the log format is determined by the most recently specified LOGFORMAT directive which does not define a nickname. Common Log Format is used if no other format has been specified.

### Example

```
LogFormat "%h %l %u %t \"%r\" %>s %b \"%{Referer}i\" \"%{User-agent}i\""
TransferLog "logs/access_log"
```

# 10.70   Apache Module mod_log_debug

| | |
|---|---|
| Description: | Additional configurable debug logging |
| Status: | Experimental |
| ModuleIdentifier: | log_debug_module |
| SourceFile: | mod_log_debug.c |
| Compatibility: | Available in Apache 2.3.14 and later |

**Directives**

- LogMessage

## Examples

1. Log message after request to /foo/* is processed:

```
<Location "/foo/">
LogMessage "/foo/ has been requested"
</Location>
```

2. Log message if request to /foo/* is processed in a sub-request:

```
<Location "/foo/">
LogMessage "subrequest to /foo/" hook=type_checker "expr=-T %{IS_SUBREQ}"
</Location>
```

The default log_transaction hook is not executed for sub-requests, therefore we have to use a different hook.

3. Log message if an IPv6 client causes a request timeout:

```
LogMessage "IPv6 timeout from %{REMOTE_ADDR}" "expr=-T %{IPV6} && %{REQUEST_STATUS} = 4
```

Note the placing of the double quotes for the expr= argument.

4. Log the value of the "X-Foo" request environment variable in each stage of the request:

```
<Location "/">
LogMessage "%{reqenv:X-Foo}" hook=all
</Location>
```

Together with microsecond time stamps in the error log, hook=all also lets you determine the times spent in the different parts of the request processing.

## LogMessage Directive

| | |
|---|---|
| Description: | Log user-defined message to error log |
| Syntax: | LogMessage message [hook=hook] [expr=expression] |
| Default: | Unset |
| Context: | directory |
| Status: | Experimental |
| Module: | mod_log_debug |

This directive causes a user defined message to be logged to the error log. The message can use variables and functions from the ap_expr syntax (p. 99) . References to HTTP headers will not cause header names to be added to the Vary header. The messages are logged at loglevel info.

The hook specifies before which phase of request processing the message will be logged. The following hooks are supported:

| Name |
| --- |
| translate_name |
| type_checker |
| quick_handler |
| map_to_storage |
| check_access |
| check_access_ex |
| insert_filter |
| check_authn |
| check_authz |
| fixups |
| handler |
| log_transaction |

The default is log_transaction. The special value all is also supported, causing a message to be logged at each phase. Not all hooks are executed for every request.

The optional expression allows to restrict the message if a condition is met. The details of the expression syntax are described in the ap_expr documentation (p. 99) . References to HTTP headers will not cause the header names to be added to the Vary header.

# 10.71   Apache Module mod_log_forensic

| | |
|---|---|
| Description: | Forensic Logging of the requests made to the server |
| Status: | Extension |
| ModuleIdentifier: | log_forensic_module |
| SourceFile: | mod_log_forensic.c |

## Summary

This module provides for forensic logging of client requests.

Create the log file using the FORENSICLOG directive:

```
ForensicLog logs/forensic_log
```

Logging is done before and after processing a request, so the forensic log contains two log lines for each request. The forensic logger is very strict, which means:

- The format is fixed. You cannot modify the logging format at runtime.
- If it cannot write its data, the child process exits immediately and may dump core (depending on your CORE-DUMPDIRECTORY configuration).

The check_forensic script, which can be found in the distribution's support directory, processes the resulting log file to identify the requests that didn't complete.

```
check-forensic forensic_log
```

### Directives

- ForensicLog

### See also

- Apache Log Files (p. 56)
- MOD_LOG_CONFIG

## Forensic Log Format

Each request is logged two times. The first time is *before* it's processed further (that is, after receiving the headers). The second log entry is written *after* the request processing at the same time where normal logging occurs.

In order to identify each request, a unique request ID is assigned. This forensic ID can be cross logged in the normal transfer log using the %{forensic-id}n format string. If you're using MOD_UNIQUE_ID, its generated ID will be used.

The first line logs the forensic ID, the request line and all received headers, separated by pipe characters ( | ). A sample line looks like the following (all on one line):

```
+yQtJf8CoAB4AAFNXBIEAAAAA|GET /manual/de/images/down.gif
HTTP/1.1|Host:localhost%3a8080|User-Agent:Mozilla/5.0 (X11; U; Linux
i686; en-US; rv%3a1.6) Gecko/20040216 Firefox/0.8|Accept:image/png,
etc...
```

The plus character at the beginning indicates that this is the first log line of this request. The second line just contains a minus character and the ID again:

```
-yQtJf8CoAB4AAFNXBIEAAAAA
```

The `check_forensic` script takes as its argument the name of the logfile. It looks for those +/− ID pairs and complains if a request was not completed.

### Security Considerations

See the security tips (p. 364) document for details on why your security could be compromised if the directory where logfiles are stored is writable by anyone other than the user that starts the server.

The log files may contain sensitive data such as the contents of `Authorization:` headers (which can contain passwords), so they should not be readable by anyone except the user that starts the server.

### ForensicLog Directive

| Description: | Sets filename of the forensic log |
|---|---|
| Syntax: | `ForensicLog filename|pipe` |
| Context: | server config, virtual host |
| Status: | Extension |
| Module: | mod_log_forensic |

The FORENSICLOG directive is used to log requests to the server for forensic analysis. Each log entry is assigned a unique ID which can be associated with the request using the normal CUSTOMLOG directive. MOD_LOG_FORENSIC creates a token called `forensic-id`, which can be added to the transfer log using the `%{forensic-id}n` format string.

The argument, which specifies the location to which the logs will be written, can take one of the following two types of values:

*filename* A filename, relative to the SERVERROOT.

*pipe* The pipe character " | ", followed by the path to a program to receive the log information on its standard input. The program name can be specified relative to the SERVERROOT directive.

>  **Security:**
> If a program is used, then it will be run as the user who started `httpd`. This will be root if the server was started by root; be sure that the program is secure or switches to a less privileged user.

> **Note**
> When entering a file path on non-Unix platforms, care should be taken to make sure that only forward slashes are used even though the platform may allow the use of back slashes. In general it is a good idea to always use forward slashes throughout the configuration files.

## 10.72   Apache Module mod_logio

| Description: | Logging of input and output bytes per request |
|---|---|
| Status: | Extension |
| ModuleIdentifier: | logio_module |
| SourceFile: | mod_logio.c |

## Summary

This module provides the logging of input and output number of bytes received/sent per request. The numbers reflect the actual bytes as received on the network, which then takes into account the headers and bodies of requests and responses. The counting is done before SSL/TLS on input and after SSL/TLS on output, so the numbers will correctly reflect any changes made by encryption.

This module requires MOD_LOG_CONFIG.

⟹ When KeepAlive connections are used with SSL, the overhead of the SSL handshake is reflected in the byte count of the first request on the connection. When per-directory SSL renegotiation occurs, the bytes are associated with the request that triggered the renegotiation.

### Directives

- LogIOTrackTTFB

### See also

- MOD_LOG_CONFIG
- Apache Log Files (p. 56)

## Custom Log Formats

This module adds three new logging directives. The characteristics of the request itself are logged by placing "%" directives in the format string, which are replaced in the log file by the values as follows:

| FormatString | Description |
|---|---|
| %I | Bytes received, including request and headers, cannot be zero. |
| %O | Bytes sent, including headers, cannot be zero. |
| %S | Bytes transferred (received and sent), including request and headers, cannot be zero. This is the combination of %I and %O. Available in Apache 2.4.7 and later |
| %^FB | Delay in microseconds between when the request arrived and the first byte of the response headers are written. Only available if LOGIOTRACKTTFB is set to ON. Available in Apache 2.4.13 and later |

Usually, the functionality is used like this:

**Combined I/O log format:** `"%h %l %u %t \"%r\" %>s %b \"%{Referer}i\"`
    `\"%{User-agent}i\" %I %O"`

## LogIOTrackTTFB Directive

| | |
|---|---|
| Description: | Enable tracking of time to first byte (TTFB) |
| Syntax: | `LogIOTrackTTFB ON|OFF` |
| Default: | `LogIOTrackTTFB OFF` |
| Context: | server config, virtual host, directory, .htaccess |
| Override: | none |
| Status: | Extension |
| Module: | mod_logio |

This directive configures whether this module tracks the delay between the request being read and the first byte of the response headers being written. The resulting value may be logged with the `%^FB` format.

## 10.73   Apache Module mod_lua

| Description: | Provides Lua hooks into various portions of the httpd request processing |
|---|---|
| Status: | Experimental |
| ModuleIdentifier: | lua_module |
| SourceFile: | mod_lua.c |
| Compatibility: | 2.3 and later |

## Summary

This module allows the server to be extended with scripts written in the Lua programming language. The extension points (hooks) available with MOD_LUA include many of the hooks available to natively compiled Apache HTTP Server modules, such as mapping requests to files, generating dynamic responses, access control, authentication, and authorization

More information on the Lua programming language can be found at the the Lua website[54].

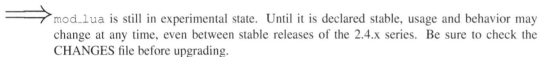mod_lua is still in experimental state.  Until it is declared stable, usage and behavior may change at any time, even between stable releases of the 2.4.x series.  Be sure to check the CHANGES file before upgrading.

! **Warning**
This module holds a great deal of power over httpd, which is both a strength and a potential security risk. It is **not** recommended that you use this module on a server that is shared with users you do not trust, as it can be abused to change the internal workings of httpd.

**Directives**

- LuaAuthzProvider
- LuaCodeCache
- LuaHookAccessChecker
- LuaHookAuthChecker
- LuaHookCheckUserID
- LuaHookFixups
- LuaHookInsertFilter
- LuaHookLog
- LuaHookMapToStorage
- LuaHookTranslateName
- LuaHookTypeChecker
- LuaInherit
- LuaInputFilter
- LuaMapHandler
- LuaOutputFilter
- LuaPackageCPath
- LuaPackagePath
- LuaQuickHandler

---

[54]http://www.lua.org/

- LuaRoot
- LuaScope

## Basic Configuration

The basic module loading directive is

```
LoadModule lua_module modules/mod_lua.so
```

mod_lua provides a handler named lua-script, which can be used with a SETHANDLER or ADDHANDLER directive:

```
<Files "*.lua">
    SetHandler lua-script
</Files>
```

This will cause mod_lua to handle requests for files ending in .lua by invoking that file's handle function.

For more flexibility, see LUAMAPHANDLER.

## Writing Handlers

In the Apache HTTP Server API, the handler is a specific kind of hook responsible for generating the response. Examples of modules that include a handler are MOD_PROXY, MOD_CGI, and MOD_STATUS.

mod_lua always looks to invoke a Lua function for the handler, rather than just evaluating a script body CGI style. A handler function looks something like this:

```
example.lua
-- example handler

require "string"

--[[
    This is the default method name for Lua handlers, see the optional
    function-name in the LuaMapHandler directive to choose a different
    entry point.
--]]
function handle(r)
    r.content_type = "text/plain"

    if r.method == 'GET' then
        r:puts("Hello Lua World!\n")
        for k, v in pairs( r:parseargs() ) do
            r:puts( string.format("%s: %s\n", k, v) )
        end
    elseif r.method == 'POST' then
        r:puts("Hello Lua World!\n")
        for k, v in pairs( r:parsebody() ) do
            r:puts( string.format("%s: %s\n", k, v) )
        end
    elseif r.method == 'PUT' then
```

```
-- use our own Error contents
        r:puts("Unsupported HTTP method " .. r.method)
        r.status = 405
        return apache2.OK
    else
-- use the ErrorDocument
        return 501
    end
    return apache2.OK
end
```

This handler function just prints out the uri or form encoded arguments to a plaintext page.

This means (and in fact encourages) that you can have multiple handlers (or hooks, or filters) in the same script.

## Writing Authorization Providers

MOD_AUTHZ_CORE provides a high-level interface to authorization that is much easier to use than using into the relevant hooks directly. The first argument to the REQUIRE directive gives the name of the responsible authorization provider. For any REQUIRE line, MOD_AUTHZ_CORE will call the authorization provider of the given name, passing the rest of the line as parameters. The provider will then check authorization and pass the result as return value.

The authz provider is normally called before authentication. If it needs to know the authenticated user name (or if the user will be authenticated at all), the provider must return apache2.AUTHZ_DENIED_NO_USER. This will cause authentication to proceed and the authz provider to be called a second time.

The following authz provider function takes two arguments, one ip address and one user name. It will allow access from the given ip address without authentication, or if the authenticated user matches the second argument:

authz_provider.lua

```
require 'apache2'

function authz_check_foo(r, ip, user)
    if r.useragent_ip == ip then
        return apache2.AUTHZ_GRANTED
    elseif r.user == nil then
        return apache2.AUTHZ_DENIED_NO_USER
    elseif r.user == user then
        return apache2.AUTHZ_GRANTED
    else
        return apache2.AUTHZ_DENIED
    end
end
```

The following configuration registers this function as provider foo and configures it for URL /:

```
LuaAuthzProvider foo authz_provider.lua authz_check_foo
<Location "/">
  Require foo 10.1.2.3 john_doe
</Location>
```

## Writing Hooks

Hook functions are how modules (and Lua scripts) participate in the processing of requests. Each type of hook exposed by the server exists for a specific purpose, such as mapping requests to the file system, performing access control, or setting mime types:

| Hook phase | mod_lua directive | Description |
|---|---|---|
| Quick handler | LUAQUICKHANDLER | This is the first hook that will be called after a request has been mapped to a host or virtual host |
| Translate name | LUAHOOKTRANSLATENAME | This phase translates the requested URI into a filename on the system. Modules such as MOD_ALIAS and MOD_REWRITE operate in this phase. |
| Map to storage | LUAHOOKMAPTOSTORAGE | This phase maps files to their physical, cached or external/proxied storage. It can be used by proxy or caching modules |
| Check Access | LUAHOOKACCESSCHECKER | This phase checks whether a client has access to a resource. This phase is run before the user is authenticated, so beware. |
| Check User ID | LUAHOOKCHECKUSERID | This phase it used to check the negotiated user ID |
| Check Authorization | LUAHOOKAUTHCHECKER or LUAAUTHZPROVIDER | This phase authorizes a user based on the negotiated credentials, such as user ID, client certificate etc. |
| Check Type | LUAHOOKTYPECHECKER | This phase checks the requested file and assigns a content type and a handler to it |
| Fixups | LUAHOOKFIXUPS | This is the final "fix anything" phase before the content handlers are run. Any last-minute changes to the request should be made here. |
| Content handler | fx. .lua files or through LUAMAPHANDLER | This is where the content is handled. Files are read, parsed, some are run, and the result is sent to the client |
| Logging | LUAHOOKLOG | Once a request has been handled, it enters several logging phases, which logs the request in either the error or access log. Mod_lua is able to hook into the start of this and control logging output. |

Hook functions are passed the request object as their only argument (except for LuaAuthzProvider, which also gets passed the arguments from the Require directive). They can return any value, depending on the hook, but most commonly they'll return OK, DONE, or DECLINED, which you can write in Lua as `apache2.OK`, `apache2.DONE`, or `apache2.DECLINED`, or else an HTTP status code.

```
translate_name.lua
-- example hook that rewrites the URI to a filesystem path.

require 'apache2'

function translate_name(r)
    if r.uri == "/translate-name" then
        r.filename = r.document_root .. "/find_me.txt"
        return apache2.OK
    end
    -- we don't care about this URL, give another module a chance
    return apache2.DECLINED
end
```

```
translate_name2.lua
--[[ example hook that rewrites one URI to another URI. It returns a
     apache2.DECLINED to give other URL mappers a chance to work on the
     substitution, including the core translate_name hook which maps based
     on the DocumentRoot.

     Note: Use the early/late flags in the directive to make it run before
           or after mod_alias.
--]]

require 'apache2'

function translate_name(r)
    if r.uri == "/translate-name" then
        r.uri = "/find_me.txt"
        return apache2.DECLINED
    end
    return apache2.DECLINED
end
```

## Data Structures

**request_rec** The request_rec is mapped in as a userdata. It has a metatable which lets you do useful things with it.
For the most part it has the same fields as the request_rec struct, many of which are writable as well as readable.
(The table fields' content can be changed, but the fields themselves cannot be set to different tables.)

| Name | Lua type | Writable | Description |
|------|----------|----------|-------------|
| `allowoverrides` | string | no | The AllowOverride options applied to the current request. |
| `ap_auth_type` | string | no | If an authentication check was made, this is set to the type of authentication (f.x. `basic`) |
| `args` | string | yes | The query string arguments extracted from the request (f.x. `foo=bar&name=johnsmith`) |
| `assbackwards` | boolean | no | Set to true if this is an HTTP/0.9 style request (e.g. `GET /foo` (with no headers) ) |
| `auth_name` | string | no | The realm name used for authorization (if applicable). |
| `banner` | string | no | The server banner, f.x. `Apache HTTP Server/2.4.3 openssl/0.9.8c` |
| `basic_auth_pw` | string | no | The basic auth password sent with this request, if any |
| `canonical_filename` | string | no | The canonical filename of the request |
| `content_encoding` | string | no | The content encoding of the current request |
| `content_type` | string | yes | The content type of the current request, as determined in the type_check phase (f.x. `image/gif` or `text/html`) |

| | | | |
|---|---|---|---|
| `context_prefix` | string | no | |
| `context_document_root` | string | no | |
| `document_root` | string | no | The document root of the host |
| `err_headers_out` | table | no | MIME header environment for the response, printed even on errors and persist across internal redirects |
| `filename` | string | yes | The file name that the request maps to, f.x. /www/example.com/foo.txt. This can be changed in the translate-name or map-to-storage phases of a request to allow the default handler (or script handlers) to serve a different file than what was requested. |
| `handler` | string | yes | The name of the handler (p. 108) that should serve this request, f.x. `lua-script` if it is to be served by mod_lua. This is typically set by the AD-DHANDLER or SETHANDLER directives, but could also be set via mod_lua to allow another handler to serve up a specific request that would otherwise not be served by it. |
| `headers_in` | table | yes | MIME header environment from the request. This contains headers such as `Host`, `User-Agent`, `Referer` and so on. |
| `headers_out` | table | yes | MIME header environment for the response. |
| `hostname` | string | no | The host name, as set by the `Host:` header or by a full URI. |
| `is_https` | boolean | no | Whether or not this request is done via HTTPS |
| `is_initial_req` | boolean | no | Whether this request is the initial request or a sub-request |
| `limit_req_body` | number | no | The size limit of the request body for this request, or 0 if no limit. |
| `log_id` | string | no | The ID to identify request in access and error log. |
| `method` | string | no | The request method, f.x. GET or POST. |
| `notes` | table | yes | A list of notes that can be passed on from one module to another. |
| `options` | string | no | The Options directive applied to the current request. |
| `path_info` | string | no | The PATH_INFO extracted from this request. |
| `port` | number | no | The server port used by the request. |

| protocol | string | no | The protocol used, f.x. `HTTP/1.1` |
|---|---|---|---|
| proxyreq | string | yes | Denotes whether this is a proxy request or not. This value is generally set in the post_read_request/translate_name phase of a request. |
| range | string | no | The contents of the `Range:` header. |
| remaining | number | no | The number of bytes remaining to be read from the request body. |
| server_built | string | no | The time the server executable was built. |
| server_name | string | no | The server name for this request. |
| some_auth_required | boolean | no | Whether some authorization is/was required for this request. |
| subprocess_env | table | yes | The environment variables set for this request. |
| started | number | no | The time the server was (re)started, in seconds since the epoch (Jan 1st, 1970) |
| status | number | yes | The (current) HTTP return code for this request, f.x. `200` or `404`. |
| the_request | string | no | The request string as sent by the client, f.x. `GET /foo/bar HTTP/1.1`. |
| unparsed_uri | string | no | The unparsed URI of the request |
| uri | string | yes | The URI after it has been parsed by httpd |
| user | string | yes | If an authentication check has been made, this is set to the name of the authenticated user. |
| useragent_ip | string | no | The IP of the user agent making the request |

## Built in functions

The request_rec object has (at least) the following methods:

```
r:flush()    -- flushes the output buffer.
             -- Returns true if the flush was successful, false otherwise.

while we_have_stuff_to_send do
    r:puts("Bla bla bla\n") -- print something to client
    r:flush() -- flush the buffer (send to client)
    r.usleep(500000) -- fake processing time for 0.5 sec. and repeat
end


r:addoutputfilter(name|function) -- add an output filter:

r:addoutputfilter("fooFilter") -- add the fooFilter to the output stream
```

```
r:sendfile(filename) -- sends an entire file to the client, using sendfile if suppor

if use_sendfile_thing then
    r:sendfile("/var/www/large_file.img")
end

r:parseargs() -- returns two tables; one standard key/value table for regular GET da
              -- and one for multi-value data (fx. foo=1&foo=2&foo=3):

local GET, GETMULTI = r:parseargs()
r:puts("Your name is: " .. GET['name'] or "Unknown")

r:parsebody([sizeLimit]) -- parse the request body as a POST and return two lua tabl
                         -- just like r:parseargs().
                         -- An optional number may be passed to specify the maximum
                         -- of bytes to parse. Default is 8192 bytes:

local POST, POSTMULTI = r:parsebody(1024*1024)
r:puts("Your name is: " .. POST['name'] or "Unknown")

r:puts("hello", " world", "!") -- print to response body, self explanatory

r:write("a single string") -- print to response body, self explanatory

r:escape_html("<html>test</html>") -- Escapes HTML code and returns the escaped resu

r:base64_encode(string) -- Encodes a string using the Base64 encoding standard:

local encoded = r:base64_encode("This is a test") -- returns VGhpcyBpcyBhIHRlc3Q=

r:base64_decode(string) -- Decodes a Base64-encoded string:

local decoded = r:base64_decode("VGhpcyBpcyBhIHRlc3Q=") -- returns 'This is a test'

r:md5(string) -- Calculates and returns the MD5 digest of a string (binary safe):

local hash = r:md5("This is a test") -- returns ce114e4501d2f4e2dcea3e17b546f339

r:sha1(string) -- Calculates and returns the SHA1 digest of a string (binary safe):

local hash = r:sha1("This is a test") -- returns a54d88e06612d820bc3be72877c74f257b5

r:escape(string) -- URL-Escapes a string:

local url = "http://foo.bar/1 2 3 & 4 + 5"
local escaped = r:escape(url) -- returns 'http%3a%2f%2ffoo.bar%2f1+2+3+%26+4+%2b+5'

r:unescape(string) -- Unescapes an URL-escaped string:

local url = "http%3a%2f%2ffoo.bar%2f1+2+3+%26+4+%2b+5"
local unescaped = r:unescape(url) -- returns 'http://foo.bar/1 2 3 & 4 + 5'
```

```
r:construct_url(string) -- Constructs an URL from an URI

local url = r:construct_url(r.uri)

r.mpm_query(number) -- Queries the server for MPM information using ap_mpm_query:

local mpm = r.mpm_query(14)
if mpm == 1 then
    r:puts("This server uses the Event MPM")
end

r:expr(string) -- Evaluates an expr string.

if r:expr("%{HTTP_HOST} =~ /^www/") then
    r:puts("This host name starts with www")
end

r:scoreboard_process(a) -- Queries the server for information about the process at position

local process = r:scoreboard_process(1)
r:puts("Server 1 has PID " .. process.pid)

r:scoreboard_worker(a, b) -- Queries for information about the worker thread, b, in process

local thread = r:scoreboard_worker(1, 1)
r:puts("Server 1's thread 1 has thread ID " .. thread.tid .. " and is in " .. thread.status

r:clock() -- Returns the current time with microsecond precision

r:requestbody(filename) -- Reads and returns the request body of a request.
                -- If 'filename' is specified, it instead saves the
                -- contents to that file:

local input = r:requestbody()
r:puts("You sent the following request body to me:\n")
r:puts(input)

r:add_input_filter(filter_name) -- Adds 'filter_name' as an input filter

r.module_info(module_name) -- Queries the server for information about a module

local mod = r.module_info("mod_lua.c")
if mod then
    for k, v in pairs(mod.commands) do
        r:puts( ("%s: %s\n"):format(k,v)) -- print out all directives accepted by this modul
    end
end

r:loaded_modules() -- Returns a list of modules loaded by httpd:

for k, module in pairs(r:loaded_modules()) do
    r:puts("I have loaded module " .. module .. "\n")
end
```

```
r:runtime_dir_relative(filename) -- Compute the name of a run-time file (e.g., share
                        -- relative to the appropriate run-time directory.


r:server_info() -- Returns a table containing server information, such as
                -- the name of the httpd executable file, mpm used etc.


r:set_document_root(file_path) -- Sets the document root for the request to file_pat


r:set_context_info(prefix, docroot) -- Sets the context prefix and context document


r:os_escape_path(file_path) -- Converts an OS path to a URL in an OS dependent way


r:escape_logitem(string) -- Escapes a string for logging


r.strcmp_match(string, pattern) -- Checks if 'string' matches 'pattern' using strcmp
                        -- fx. whether 'www.example.com' matches '*.example.com':

local match = r.strcmp_match("foobar.com", "foo*.com")
if match then
    r:puts("foobar.com matches foo*.com")
end


r:set_keepalive() -- Sets the keepalive status for a request. Returns true if possib


r:make_etag() -- Constructs and returns the etag for the current request.


r:send_interim_response(clear) -- Sends an interim (1xx) response to the client.
                        -- if 'clear' is true, available headers will be sent and cle


r:custom_response(status_code, string) -- Construct and set a custom response for a
                        -- This works much like the ErrorDocument directive:

r:custom_response(404, "Baleted!")


r.exists_config_define(string) -- Checks whether a configuration definition exists o

if r.exists_config_define("FOO") then
    r:puts("httpd was probably run with -DFOO, or it was defined in the configuratio
end


r:state_query(string) -- Queries the server for state information


r:stat(filename [,wanted]) -- Runs stat() on a file, and returns a table with file i

local info = r:stat("/var/www/foo.txt")
if info then
    r:puts("This file exists and was last modified at: " .. info.modified)
end
```

```
r:regex(string, pattern [,flags]) -- Runs a regular expression match on a string, returning

local matches = r:regex("foo bar baz", [[foo (\w+) (\S*)]])
if matches then
    r:puts("The regex matched, and the last word captured ($2) was: " .. matches[2])
end


-- Example ignoring case sensitivity:
local matches = r:regex("FOO bar BAz", [[(foo) bar]], 1)

-- Flags can be a bitwise combination of:
-- 0x01: Ignore case
-- 0x02: Multiline search


r.usleep(number_of_microseconds) -- Puts the script to sleep for a given number of microsec


r:dbacquire(dbType[, dbParams]) -- Acquires a connection to a database and returns a databa
                    -- See 'Database connectivity' for details.


r:ivm_set("key", value) -- Set an Inter-VM variable to hold a specific value.
                        -- These values persist even though the VM is gone or not being use
                        -- and so should only be used if MaxConnectionsPerChild is > 0
                        -- Values can be numbers, strings and booleans, and are stored on a
                        -- per process basis (so they won't do much good with a prefork mpm

r:ivm_get("key")        -- Fetches a variable set by ivm_set. Returns the contents of the v
                        -- if it exists or nil if no such variable exists.

-- An example getter/setter that saves a global variable outside the VM:
function handle(r)
    -- First VM to call this will get no value, and will have to create it
    local foo = r:ivm_get("cached_data")
    if not foo then
        foo = do_some_calcs() -- fake some return value
        r:ivm_set("cached_data", foo) -- set it globally
    end
    r:puts("Cached data is: ", foo)
end


r:htpassword(string [,algorithm [,cost]]) -- Creates a password hash from a string.
                                          -- algorithm: 0 = APMD5 (default), 1 = SHA, 2 = I
                                          -- cost: only valid with BCRYPT algorithm (defaul


r:mkdir(dir [,mode]) -- Creates a directory and sets mode to optional mode paramter.


r:mkrdir(dir [,mode]) -- Creates directories recursive and sets mode to optional mode param


r:rmdir(dir) -- Removes a directory.


r:touch(file [,mtime]) -- Sets the file modification time to current time or to optional mt
```

```
r:get_direntries(dir) -- Returns a table with all directory entries.

function handle(r)
  local dir = r.context_document_root
  for _, f in ipairs(r:get_direntries(dir)) do
    local info = r:stat(dir .. "/" .. f)
    if info then
      local mtime = os.date(fmt, info.mtime / 1000000)
      local ftype = (info.filetype == 2) and "[dir] " or "[file]"
      r:puts( ("%s %s %10i %s\n"):format(ftype, mtime, info.size, f) )
    end
  end
end


r.date_parse_rfc(string) -- Parses a date/time string and returns seconds since epoch

r:getcookie(key) -- Gets a HTTP cookie

r:setcookie{
  key = [key],
  value = [value],
  expires = [expiry],
  secure = [boolean],
  httponly = [boolean],
  path = [path],
  domain = [domain]
} -- Sets a HTTP cookie, for instance:

r:setcookie{
  key = "cookie1",
  value = "HDHfa9eyffh396rt",
  expires = os.time() + 86400,
  secure = true
}


r:wsupgrade() -- Upgrades a connection to WebSockets if possible (and requested):
if r:wsupgrade() then -- if we can upgrade:
    r:wswrite("Welcome to websockets!") -- write something to the client
    r:wsclose()  -- goodbye!
end


r:wsread() -- Reads a WebSocket frame from a WebSocket upgraded connection (see above

local line, isFinal = r:wsread() -- isFinal denotes whether this is the final frame.
                                 -- If it isn't, then more frames can be read
r:wswrite("You wrote: " .. line)


r:wswrite(line) -- Writes a frame to a WebSocket client:
r:wswrite("Hello, world!")


r:wsclose() -- Closes a WebSocket request and terminates it for httpd:
```

```
if r:wsupgrade() then
    r:wswrite("Write something: ")
    local line = r:wsread() or "nothing"
    r:wswrite("You wrote: " .. line);
    r:wswrite("Goodbye!")
    r:wsclose()
end

r:wspeek() -- Checks if any data is ready to be read

-- Sleep while nothing is being sent to us...
while r:wspeek() == false do
   r.usleep(50000)
end
-- We have data ready!
local line = r:wsread()

r:config() -- Get a walkable tree of the entire httpd configuration

r:activeconfig() -- Get a walkable tree of the active (virtualhost-specific) httpd configur
```

## Logging Functions

```
-- examples of logging messages
r:trace1("This is a trace log message") -- trace1 through trace8 can be used
r:debug("This is a debug log message")
r:info("This is an info log message")
r:notice("This is a notice log message")
r:warn("This is a warn log message")
r:err("This is an err log message")
r:alert("This is an alert log message")
r:crit("This is a crit log message")
r:emerg("This is an emerg log message")
```

## apache2 Package

A package named apache2 is available with (at least) the following contents.

**apache2.OK**  internal constant OK. Handlers should return this if they've handled the request.

**apache2.DECLINED**  internal constant DECLINED. Handlers should return this if they are not going to handle the request.

**apache2.DONE**  internal constant DONE.

**apache2.version**  Apache HTTP server version string

**apache2.HTTP_MOVED_TEMPORARILY**  HTTP status code

**apache2.PROXYREQ_NONE, apache2.PROXYREQ_PROXY, apache2.PROXYREQ_REVERSE, apache2.PROXYREQ_RESP** internal constants used by MOD_PROXY

**apache2.AUTHZ_DENIED, apache2.AUTHZ_GRANTED, apache2.AUTHZ_NEUTRAL, apache2.AUTHZ_GENERAL_ERROR** internal constants used by MOD_AUTHZ_CORE

(Other HTTP status codes are not yet implemented.)

## Modifying contents with Lua filters

Filter functions implemented via LUAINPUTFILTER or LUAOUTPUTFILTER are designed as three-stage non-blocking functions using coroutines to suspend and resume a function as buckets are sent down the filter chain. The core structure of such a function is:

```
function filter(r)
    -- Our first yield is to signal that we are ready to receive buckets.
    -- Before this yield, we can set up our environment, check for conditions,
    -- and, if we deem it necessary, decline filtering a request alltogether:
    if something_bad then
        return -- This would skip this filter.
    end
    -- Regardless of whether we have data to prepend, a yield MUST be called here.
    -- Note that only output filters can prepend data. Input filters must use the
    -- final stage to append data to the content.
    coroutine.yield([optional header to be prepended to the content])

    -- After we have yielded, buckets will be sent to us, one by one, and we can
    -- do whatever we want with them and then pass on the result.
    -- Buckets are stored in the global variable 'bucket', so we create a loop
    -- that checks if 'bucket' is not nil:
    while bucket ~= nil do
        local output = mangle(bucket) -- Do some stuff to the content
        coroutine.yield(output) -- Return our new content to the filter chain
    end

    -- Once the buckets are gone, 'bucket' is set to nil, which will exit the
    -- loop and land us here. Anything extra we want to append to the content
    -- can be done by doing a final yield here. Both input and output filters
    -- can append data to the content in this phase.
    coroutine.yield([optional footer to be appended to the content])
end
```

## Database connectivity

Mod_lua implements a simple database feature for querying and running commands on the most popular database engines (mySQL, PostgreSQL, FreeTDS, ODBC, SQLite, Oracle) as well as mod_dbd.

The example below shows how to acquire a database handle and return information from a table:

```
function handle(r)
    -- Acquire a database handle
    local database, err = r:dbacquire("mysql", "server=localhost,user=someuser,pass=
    if not err then
        -- Select some information from it
        local results, err = database:select(r, "SELECT `name`, `age` FROM `people`
        if not err then
            local rows = results(0) -- fetch all rows synchronously
            for k, row in pairs(rows) do
                r:puts( string.format("Name: %s, Age: %s<br/>", row[1], row[2]) )
            end
        else
```

```
            r:puts("Database query error: " .. err)
        end
        database:close()
    else
        r:puts("Could not connect to the database: " .. err)
    end
end
```

To utilize MOD_DBD, specify mod_dbd as the database type, or leave the field blank:

```
local database = r:dbacquire("mod_dbd")
```

**Database object and contained functions**

'The database object returned by dbacquire has the following methods:

**Normal select and query from a database:**

```
-- Run a statement and return the number of rows affected:
local affected, errmsg = database:query(r, "DELETE FROM `tbl` WHERE 1")

-- Run a statement and return a result set that can be used synchronously or async:
local result, errmsg = database:select(r, "SELECT * FROM `people` WHERE 1")
```

**Using prepared statements (recommended):**

```
-- Create and run a prepared statement:
local statement, errmsg = database:prepare(r, "DELETE FROM `tbl` WHERE `age` > %u")
if not errmsg then
    local result, errmsg = statement:query(20) -- run the statement with age > 20
end

-- Fetch a prepared statement from a DBDPrepareSQL directive:
local statement, errmsg = database:prepared(r, "someTag")
if not errmsg then
    local result, errmsg = statement:select("John Doe", 123) -- inject the values "John Do
end
```

**Escaping values, closing databases etc:**

```
-- Escape a value for use in a statement:
local escaped = database:escape(r, [["'|blabla]])

-- Close a database connection and free up handles:
database:close()

-- Check whether a database connection is up and running:
local connected = database:active()
```

**Working with result sets**

The result set returned by `db:select` or by the prepared statement functions created through `db:prepare` can be used to fetch rows synchronously or asynchronously, depending on the row number specified:
`result(0)` fetches all rows in a synchronous manner, returning a table of rows.
`result(-1)` fetches the next available row in the set, asynchronously.
`result(N)` fetches row number `N`, asynchronously:

```
-- fetch a result set using a regular query:
local result, err = db:select(r, "SELECT * FROM `tbl` WHERE 1")

local rows = result(0) -- Fetch ALL rows synchronously
local row = result(-1) -- Fetch the next available row, asynchronously
local row = result(1234) -- Fetch row number 1234, asynchronously
local row = result(-1, true) -- Fetch the next available row, using row names as key
```

One can construct a function that returns an iterative function to iterate over all rows in a synchronous or asynchronous way, depending on the async argument:

```
function rows(resultset, async)
    local a = 0
    local function getnext()
        a = a + 1
        local row = resultset(-1)
        return row and a or nil, row
    end
    if not async then
        return pairs(resultset(0))
    else
        return getnext, self
    end
end

local statement, err = db:prepare(r, "SELECT * FROM `tbl` WHERE `age` > %u")
if not err then
     -- fetch rows asynchronously:
    local result, err = statement:select(20)
    if not err then
        for index, row in rows(result, true) do
            ....
        end
    end

     -- fetch rows synchronously:
    local result, err = statement:select(20)
    if not err then
        for index, row in rows(result, false) do
            ....
        end
    end
end
```

**Closing a database connection**

Database handles should be closed using `database:close()` when they are no longer needed. If you do not close them manually, they will eventually be garbage collected and closed by mod_lua, but you may end up having too many unused connections to the database if you leave the closing up to mod_lua. Essentially, the following two measures are the same:

```
-- Method 1: Manually close a handle
local database = r:dbacquire("mod_dbd")
database:close() -- All done

-- Method 2: Letting the garbage collector close it
local database = r:dbacquire("mod_dbd")
database = nil -- throw away the reference
collectgarbage() -- close the handle via GC
```

**Precautions when working with databases**

Although the standard `query` and `run` functions are freely available, it is recommended that you use prepared statements whenever possible, to both optimize performance (if your db handle lives on for a long time) and to minimize the risk of SQL injection attacks. `run` and `query` should only be used when there are no variables inserted into a statement (a static statement). When using dynamic statements, use `db:prepare` or `db:prepared`.

## LuaAuthzProvider Directive

| Description: | Plug an authorization provider function into MOD_AUTHZ_CORE |
|---|---|
| Syntax: | `LuaAuthzProvider provider_name /path/to/lua/script.lua function_name` |
| Context: | server config |
| Status: | Experimental |
| Module: | mod_lua |
| Compatibility: | 2.4.3 and later |

After a lua function has been registered as authorization provider, it can be used with the REQUIRE directive:

```
LuaRoot /usr/local/apache2/lua
LuaAuthzProvider foo authz.lua authz_check_foo
<Location "/">
  Require foo johndoe
</Location>
```

```
require "apache2"
function authz_check_foo(r, who)
    if r.user ~= who then return apache2.AUTHZ_DENIED
    return apache2.AUTHZ_GRANTED
end
```

## LuaCodeCache Directive

| | |
|---|---|
| Description: | Configure the compiled code cache. |
| Syntax: | `LuaCodeCache stat\|forever\|never` |
| Default: | `LuaCodeCache stat` |
| Context: | server config, virtual host, directory, .htaccess |
| Override: | All |
| Status: | Experimental |
| Module: | mod_lua |

Specify the behavior of the in-memory code cache. The default is stat, which stats the top level script (not any included ones) each time that file is needed, and reloads it if the modified time indicates it is newer than the one it has already loaded. The other values cause it to keep the file cached forever (don't stat and replace) or to never cache the file.

In general stat or forever is good for production, and stat or never for development.

### Examples:

```
LuaCodeCache stat
LuaCodeCache forever
LuaCodeCache never
```

## LuaHookAccessChecker Directive

| | |
|---|---|
| Description: | Provide a hook for the access_checker phase of request processing |
| Syntax: | `LuaHookAccessChecker /path/to/lua/script.lua hook_function_name [early\|late]` |
| Context: | server config, virtual host, directory, .htaccess |
| Override: | All |
| Status: | Experimental |
| Module: | mod_lua |
| Compatibility: | The optional third argument is supported in 2.3.15 and later |

Add your hook to the access_checker phase. An access checker hook function usually returns OK, DECLINED, or HTTP_FORBIDDEN.

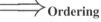**Ordering**

The optional arguments "early" or "late" control when this script runs relative to other modules.

## LuaHookAuthChecker Directive

| | |
|---|---|
| Description: | Provide a hook for the auth_checker phase of request processing |
| Syntax: | `LuaHookAuthChecker /path/to/lua/script.lua hook_function_name [early\|late]` |
| Context: | server config, virtual host, directory, .htaccess |
| Override: | All |
| Status: | Experimental |
| Module: | mod_lua |
| Compatibility: | The optional third argument is supported in 2.3.15 and later |

Invoke a lua function in the auth_checker phase of processing a request. This can be used to implement arbitrary authentication and authorization checking. A very simple example:

```
require 'apache2'

-- fake authcheck hook
-- If request has no auth info, set the response header and
-- return a 401 to ask the browser for basic auth info.
-- If request has auth info, don't actually look at it, just
-- pretend we got userid 'foo' and validated it.
-- Then check if the userid is 'foo' and accept the request.
function authcheck_hook(r)

   -- look for auth info
   auth = r.headers_in['Authorization']
   if auth ~= nil then
     -- fake the user
     r.user = 'foo'
   end

   if r.user == nil then
      r:debug("authcheck: user is nil, returning 401")
      r.err_headers_out['WWW-Authenticate'] = 'Basic realm="WallyWorld"'
      return 401
   elseif r.user == "foo" then
      r:debug('user foo: OK')
   else
      r:debug("authcheck: user='" .. r.user .. "'")
      r.err_headers_out['WWW-Authenticate'] = 'Basic realm="WallyWorld"'
      return 401
   end
   return apache2.OK
end
```

⟹ **Ordering**

The optional arguments "early" or "late" control when this script runs relative to other modules.

## LuaHookCheckUserID Directive

| | |
|---|---|
| Description: | Provide a hook for the check_user_id phase of request processing |
| Syntax: | `LuaHookCheckUserID /path/to/lua/script.lua hook_function_name` |
| Context: | server config, virtual host, directory, .htaccess |
| Override: | All |
| Status: | Experimental |
| Module: | mod_lua |

## LuaHookFixups Directive

| | |
|---|---|
| Description: | Provide a hook for the fixups phase of a request processing |
| Syntax: | `LuaHookFixups /path/to/lua/script.lua hook_function_name` |
| Context: | server config, virtual host, directory, .htaccess |
| Override: | All |
| Status: | Experimental |
| Module: | mod_lua |

Just like LuaHookTranslateName, but executed at the fixups phase

## LuaHookInsertFilter Directive

| | |
|---|---|
| Description: | Provide a hook for the insert_filter phase of request processing |
| Syntax: | `LuaHookInsertFilter /path/to/lua/script.lua hook_function_name` |
| Context: | server config, virtual host, directory, .htaccess |
| Override: | All |
| Status: | Experimental |
| Module: | mod_lua |

Not Yet Implemented

## LuaHookLog Directive

| | |
|---|---|
| Description: | Provide a hook for the access log phase of a request processing |
| Syntax: | `LuaHookLog /path/to/lua/script.lua log_function_name` |
| Context: | server config, virtual host, directory, .htaccess |
| Override: | All |
| Status: | Experimental |
| Module: | mod_lua |

This simple logging hook allows you to run a function when httpd enters the logging phase of a request. With it, you can append data to your own logs, manipulate data before the regular log is written, or prevent a log entry from being created. To prevent the usual logging from happening, simply return `apache2.DONE` in your logging handler, otherwise return `apache2.OK` to tell httpd to log as normal.

Example:

```
LuaHookLog /path/to/script.lua logger


-- /path/to/script.lua --
function logger(r)
    -- flip a coin:
    -- If 1, then we write to our own Lua log and tell httpd not to log
    -- in the main log.
    -- If 2, then we just sanitize the output a bit and tell httpd to
    -- log the sanitized bits.

    if math.random(1,2) == 1 then
        -- Log stuff ourselves and don't log in the regular log
        local f = io.open("/foo/secret.log", "a")
        if f then
            f:write("Something secret happened at " .. r.uri .. "\n")
            f:close()
        end
        return apache2.DONE -- Tell httpd not to use the regular logging functions
    else
        r.uri = r.uri:gsub("somesecretstuff", "") -- sanitize the URI
        return apache2.OK -- tell httpd to log it.
    end
end
```

## LuaHookMapToStorage Directive

| | |
|---|---|
| Description: | Provide a hook for the map_to_storage phase of request processing |
| Syntax: | `LuaHookMapToStorage /path/to/lua/script.lua hook_function_name` |
| Context: | server config, virtual host, directory, .htaccess |
| Override: | All |
| Status: | Experimental |
| Module: | mod_lua |

Like LUAHOOKTRANSLATENAME but executed at the map-to-storage phase of a request. Modules like mod_cache run at this phase, which makes for an interesting example on what to do here:

```
LuaHookMapToStorage /path/to/lua/script.lua check_cache

require"apache2"
cached_files = {}

function read_file(filename)
    local input = io.open(filename, "r")
    if input then
        local data = input:read("*a")
        cached_files[filename] = data
        file = cached_files[filename]
        input:close()
    end
    return cached_files[filename]
end

function check_cache(r)
    if r.filename:match("%.png$") then -- Only match PNG files
        local file = cached_files[r.filename] -- Check cache entries
        if not file then
            file = read_file(r.filename)  -- Read file into cache
        end
        if file then -- If file exists, write it out
            r.status = 200
            r:write(file)
            r:info(("Sent %s to client from cache"):format(r.filename))
            return apache2.DONE -- skip default handler for PNG files
        end
    end
    return apache2.DECLINED -- If we had nothing to do, let others serve this.
end
```

## LuaHookTranslateName Directive

| | |
|---|---|
| Description: | Provide a hook for the translate name phase of request processing |
| Syntax: | `LuaHookTranslateName /path/to/lua/script.lua hook_function_name [early|late]` |
| Context: | server config, virtual host |
| Override: | All |
| Status: | Experimental |
| Module: | mod_lua |
| Compatibility: | The optional third argument is supported in 2.3.15 and later |

Add a hook (at APR_HOOK_MIDDLE) to the translate name phase of request processing. The hook function receives a single argument, the request_rec, and should return a status code, which is either an HTTP error code, or the constants defined in the apache2 module: apache2.OK, apache2.DECLINED, or apache2.DONE.

For those new to hooks, basically each hook will be invoked until one of them returns apache2.OK. If your hook doesn't want to do the translation it should just return apache2.DECLINED. If the request should stop processing, then return apache2.DONE.

Example:

```
# httpd.conf
LuaHookTranslateName /scripts/conf/hooks.lua silly_mapper

-- /scripts/conf/hooks.lua --
require "apache2"
function silly_mapper(r)
    if r.uri == "/" then
        r.filename = "/var/www/home.lua"
        return apache2.OK
    else
        return apache2.DECLINED
    end
end
```

⟹ **Context**

   This directive is not valid in <DIRECTORY>, <FILES>, or htaccess context.

⟹ **Ordering**

   The optional arguments "early" or "late" control when this script runs relative to other modules.

## LuaHookTypeChecker Directive

| | |
|---|---|
| Description: | Provide a hook for the type_checker phase of request processing |
| Syntax: | `LuaHookTypeChecker /path/to/lua/script.lua hook_function_name` |
| Context: | server config, virtual host, directory, .htaccess |
| Override: | All |
| Status: | Experimental |
| Module: | mod_lua |

This directive provides a hook for the type_checker phase of the request processing. This phase is where requests are assigned a content type and a handler, and thus can be used to modify the type and handler based on input:

```
LuaHookTypeChecker /path/to/lua/script.lua type_checker

    function type_checker(r)
        if r.uri:match("%.to_gif$") then -- match foo.png.to_gif
            r.content_type = "image/gif" -- assign it the image/gif type
            r.handler = "gifWizard"      -- tell the gifWizard module to handle this
            r.filename = r.uri:gsub("%.to_gif$", "") -- fix the filename requested
            return apache2.OK
        end

        return apache2.DECLINED
    end
```

## LuaInherit Directive

| | |
|---|---|
| Description: | Controls how parent configuration sections are merged into children |
| Syntax: | `LuaInherit none|parent-first|parent-last` |
| Default: | `LuaInherit parent-first` |
| Context: | server config, virtual host, directory, .htaccess |
| Override: | All |
| Status: | Experimental |
| Module: | mod_lua |
| Compatibility: | 2.4.0 and later |

By default, if LuaHook* directives are used in overlapping Directory or Location configuration sections, the scripts defined in the more specific section are run *after* those defined in the more generic section (LuaInherit parent-first). You can reverse this order, or make the parent context not apply at all.

In previous 2.3.x releases, the default was effectively to ignore LuaHook* directives from parent configuration sections.

## LuaInputFilter Directive

| | |
|---|---|
| Description: | Provide a Lua function for content input filtering |
| Syntax: | `LuaInputFilter filter_name /path/to/lua/script.lua function_name` |
| Context: | server config |
| Status: | Experimental |
| Module: | mod_lua |
| Compatibility: | 2.4.5 and later |

Provides a means of adding a Lua function as an input filter. As with output filters, input filters work as coroutines, first yielding before buffers are sent, then yielding whenever a bucket needs to be passed down the chain, and finally (optionally) yielding anything that needs to be appended to the input data. The global variable `bucket` holds the buckets as they are passed onto the Lua script:

```
LuaInputFilter myInputFilter /www/filter.lua input_filter
<Files "*.lua">
  SetInputFilter myInputFilter
</Files>


--[[
    Example input filter that converts all POST data to uppercase.
]]--
function input_filter(r)
    print("luaInputFilter called") -- debug print
    coroutine.yield() -- Yield and wait for buckets
    while bucket do -- For each bucket, do...
        local output = string.upper(bucket) -- Convert all POST data to uppercase
        coroutine.yield(output) -- Send converted data down the chain
    end
    -- No more buckets available.
    coroutine.yield("&filterSignature=1234") -- Append signature at the end
end
```

The input filter supports denying/skipping a filter if it is deemed unwanted:

```
function input_filter(r)
    if not good then
        return -- Simply deny filtering, passing on the original content instead
    end
    coroutine.yield() -- wait for buckets
    ... -- insert filter stuff here
end
```

See "Modifying contents with Lua filters" for more information.

## LuaMapHandler Directive

| Description: | Map a path to a lua handler |
| --- | --- |
| Syntax: | `LuaMapHandler uri-pattern /path/to/lua/script.lua`<br>`[function-name]` |
| Context: | server config, virtual host, directory, .htaccess |
| Override: | All |
| Status: | Experimental |
| Module: | mod_lua |

This directive matches a uri pattern to invoke a specific handler function in a specific file. It uses PCRE regular expressions to match the uri, and supports interpolating match groups into both the file path and the function name. Be careful writing your regular expressions to avoid security issues.

### Examples:

```
LuaMapHandler /(\w+)/(\w+) /scripts/$1.lua handle_$2
```

This would match uri's such as /photos/show?id=9 to the file /scripts/photos.lua and invoke the handler function handle_show on the lua vm after loading that file.

```
LuaMapHandler /bingo /scripts/wombat.lua
```

This would invoke the "handle" function, which is the default if no specific function name is provided.

## LuaOutputFilter Directive

| Description: | Provide a Lua function for content output filtering |
| --- | --- |
| Syntax: | `LuaOutputFilter filter_name /path/to/lua/script.lua`<br>`function_name` |
| Context: | server config |
| Status: | Experimental |
| Module: | mod_lua |
| Compatibility: | 2.4.5 and later |

Provides a means of adding a Lua function as an output filter. As with input filters, output filters work as coroutines, first yielding before buffers are sent, then yielding whenever a bucket needs to be passed down the chain, and finally (optionally) yielding anything that needs to be appended to the input data. The global variable `bucket` holds the buckets as they are passed onto the Lua script:

```
LuaOutputFilter myOutputFilter /www/filter.lua output_filter
<Files "*.lua">
  SetOutputFilter myOutputFilter
</Files>
```

```
--[[
    Example output filter that escapes all HTML entities in the output
]]--
function output_filter(r)
    coroutine.yield("(Handled by myOutputFilter)<br/>\n") -- Prepend some data to the outpu
                                                          -- yield and wait for buckets.
    while bucket do -- For each bucket, do...
        local output = r:escape_html(bucket) -- Escape all output
        coroutine.yield(output) -- Send converted data down the chain
    end
    -- No more buckets available.
end
```

As with the input filter, the output filter supports denying/skipping a filter if it is deemed unwanted:

```
function output_filter(r)
    if not r.content_type:match("text/html") then
        return -- Simply deny filtering, passing on the original content instead
    end
    coroutine.yield() -- wait for buckets
    ... -- insert filter stuff here
end
```

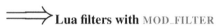**Lua filters with** MOD_FILTER

When a Lua filter is used as the underlying provider via the FILTERPROVIDER directive, filtering will only work when the *filter-name* is identical to the *provider-name*.

See "Modifying contents with Lua filters" for more information.

## LuaPackageCPath Directive

| Description: | Add a directory to lua's package.cpath |
|---|---|
| Syntax: | LuaPackageCPath /path/to/include/?.soa |
| Context: | server config, virtual host, directory, .htaccess |
| Override: | All |
| Status: | Experimental |
| Module: | mod_lua |

Add a path to lua's shared library search path. Follows the same conventions as lua. This just munges the package.cpath in the lua vms.

## LuaPackagePath Directive

| Description: | Add a directory to lua's package.path |
|---|---|
| Syntax: | LuaPackagePath /path/to/include/?.lua |
| Context: | server config, virtual host, directory, .htaccess |
| Override: | All |
| Status: | Experimental |
| Module: | mod_lua |

Add a path to lua's module search path. Follows the same conventions as lua. This just munges the package.path in the lua vms.

**Examples:**

```
LuaPackagePath /scripts/lib/?.lua
LuaPackagePath /scripts/lib/?/init.lua
```

## LuaQuickHandler Directive

| | |
|---|---|
| Description: | Provide a hook for the quick handler of request processing |
| Syntax: | `LuaQuickHandler /path/to/script.lua hook_function_name` |
| Context: | server config, virtual host |
| Override: | All |
| Status: | Experimental |
| Module: | mod_lua |

This phase is run immediately after the request has been mapped to a virtal host, and can be used to either do some request processing before the other phases kick in, or to serve a request without the need to translate, map to storage et cetera. As this phase is run before anything else, directives such as <LOCATION> or <DIRECTORY> are void in this phase, just as URIs have not been properly parsed yet.

**Context**

This directive is not valid in <DIRECTORY>, <FILES>, or htaccess context.

## LuaRoot Directive

| | |
|---|---|
| Description: | Specify the base path for resolving relative paths for mod_lua directives |
| Syntax: | `LuaRoot /path/to/a/directory` |
| Context: | server config, virtual host, directory, .htaccess |
| Override: | All |
| Status: | Experimental |
| Module: | mod_lua |

Specify the base path which will be used to evaluate all relative paths within mod_lua. If not specified they will be resolved relative to the current working directory, which may not always work well for a server.

## LuaScope Directive

| | |
|---|---|
| Description: | One of once, request, conn, thread – default is once |
| Syntax: | `LuaScope once\|request\|conn\|thread\|server [min] [max]` |
| Default: | `LuaScope once` |
| Context: | server config, virtual host, directory, .htaccess |
| Override: | All |
| Status: | Experimental |
| Module: | mod_lua |

Specify the life cycle scope of the Lua interpreter which will be used by handlers in this "Directory." The default is "once"

**once:** use the interpreter once and throw it away.

**request:** use the interpreter to handle anything based on the same file within this request, which is also request scoped.

**conn:** Same as request but attached to the connection_rec

**thread:** Use the interpreter for the lifetime of the thread handling the request (only available with threaded MPMs).

**server:** This one is different than others because the server scope is quite long lived, and multiple threads will have the same server_rec. To accommodate this, server scoped Lua states are stored in an apr resource list. The `min` and `max` arguments specify the minimum and maximum number of Lua states to keep in the pool.

Generally speaking, the `thread` and `server` scopes execute roughly 2-3 times faster than the rest, because they don't have to spawn new Lua states on every request (especially with the event MPM, as even keepalive requests will use a new thread for each request). If you are satisfied that your scripts will not have problems reusing a state, then the `thread` or `server` scopes should be used for maximum performance. While the `thread` scope will provide the fastest responses, the `server` scope will use less memory, as states are pooled, allowing f.x. 1000 threads to share only 100 Lua states, thus using only 10% of the memory required by the `thread` scope.

## 10.74 Apache Module mod_macro

| | |
|---|---|
| Description: | Provides macros within apache httpd runtime configuration files |
| Status: | Base |
| ModuleIdentifier: | macro_module |
| SourceFile: | mod_macro.c |

### Summary

Provides macros within Apache httpd runtime configuration files, to ease the process of creating numerous similar configuration blocks. When the server starts up, the macros are expanded using the provided parameters, and the result is processed as along with the rest of the configuration file.

**Directives**

- <Macro>
- UndefMacro
- Use

### Usage

Macros are defined using <MACRO> blocks, which contain the portion of your configuration that needs to be repeated, complete with variables for those parts that will need to be substituted.

For example, you might use a macro to define a <VIRTUALHOST> block, in order to define multiple similar virtual hosts:

```
<Macro VHost $name $domain>
<VirtualHost *:80>
    ServerName $domain
    ServerAlias www.$domain

    DocumentRoot "/var/www/vhosts/$name"
    ErrorLog "/var/log/httpd/$name.error_log"
    CustomLog "/var/log/httpd/$name.access_log" combined
</VirtualHost>
</Macro>
```

Macro names are case-insensitive, like httpd configuration directives. However, variable names are case sensitive.

You would then invoke this macro several times to create virtual hosts:

```
Use VHost example example.com
Use VHost myhost hostname.org
Use VHost apache apache.org

UndefMacro VHost
```

At server startup time, each of these USE invocations would be expanded into a full virtualhost, as described by the <MACRO> definition.

The UNDEFMACRO directive is used so that later macros using the same variable names don't result in conflicting definitions.

A more elaborate version of this example may be seen below in the Examples section.

## Tips

Parameter names should begin with a sigil such as $, %, or @, so that they are clearly identifiable, and also in order to help deal with interactions with other directives, such as the core DEFINE directive. Failure to do so will result in a warning. Nevertheless, you are encouraged to have a good knowledge of your entire server configuration in order to avoid reusing the same variables in different scopes, which can cause confusion.

Parameters prefixed with either $ or % are not escaped. Parameters prefixes with @ are escaped in quotes.

Avoid using a parameter which contains another parameter as a prefix, (For example, $win and $winter) as this may cause confusion at expression evaluation time. In the event of such confusion, the longest possible parameter name is used.

If you want to use a value within another string, it is useful to surround the parameter in braces, to avoid confusion:

```
<Macro DocRoot ${docroot}>
    DocumentRoot "/var/www/${docroot}/htdocs"
</Macro>
```

## Examples

### Virtual Host Definition

A common usage of MOD_MACRO is for the creation of dynamically-generated virtual hosts.

```
## Define a VHost Macro for repetitive configurations

<Macro VHost $host $port $dir>
  Listen $port
  <VirtualHost *:$port>

    ServerName $host
    DocumentRoot "$dir"

    # Public document root
    <Directory "$dir">
        Require all granted
    </Directory>

    # limit access to intranet subdir.
    <Directory "$dir/intranet">
      Require ip 10.0.0.0/8
    </Directory>
  </VirtualHost>
</Macro>

## Use of VHost with different arguments.

Use VHost www.apache.org 80 /vhosts/apache/htdocs
Use VHost example.org 8080 /vhosts/example/htdocs
Use VHost www.example.fr 1234 /vhosts/example.fr/htdocs
```

**Removal of a macro definition**

It's recommended that you undefine a macro once you've used it. This avoids confusion in a complex configuration file where there may be conflicts in variable names.

```
<Macro DirGroup $dir $group>
  <Directory "$dir">
    Require group $group
  </Directory>
</Macro>

Use DirGroup /www/apache/private private
Use DirGroup /www/apache/server  admin

UndefMacro DirGroup
```

## Macro Directive

| | |
|---|---|
| Description: | Define a configuration file macro |
| Syntax: | `<Macro name [par1 ..  parN]>` ...  `</Macro>` |
| Context: | server config, virtual host, directory |
| Status: | Base |
| Module: | mod_macro |

The <MACRO> directive controls the definition of a macro within the server runtime configuration files. The first argument is the name of the macro. Other arguments are parameters to the macro. It is good practice to prefix parameter names with any of '$%@', and not macro names with such characters.

```
<Macro LocalAccessPolicy>
    Require ip 10.2.16.0/24
</Macro>

<Macro RestrictedAccessPolicy $ipnumbers>
    Require ip $ipnumbers
</Macro>
```

## UndefMacro Directive

| | |
|---|---|
| Description: | Undefine a macro |
| Syntax: | `UndefMacro name` |
| Context: | server config, virtual host, directory |
| Status: | Base |
| Module: | mod_macro |

The UNDEFMACRO directive undefines a macro which has been defined before hand.

```
UndefMacro LocalAccessPolicy
UndefMacro RestrictedAccessPolicy
```

## Use Directive

| | |
|---|---|
| Description: | Use a macro |
| Syntax: | `Use name [value1 ...  valueN]` |
| Context: | server config, virtual host, directory |
| Status: | Base |
| Module: | mod_macro |

The USE directive controls the use of a macro. The specified macro is expanded. It must be given the same number of arguments as in the macro definition. The provided values are associated to their corresponding initial parameters and are substituted before processing.

```
Use LocalAccessPolicy
...
Use RestrictedAccessPolicy "192.54.172.0/24 192.54.148.0/24"
```

is equivalent, with the macros defined above, to:

```
Require ip 10.2.16.0/24
...
Require ip 192.54.172.0/24 192.54.148.0/24
```

# 10.75  Apache Module mod_mime

| | |
|---|---|
| Description: | Associates the requested filename's extensions with the file's behavior (handlers and filters) and content (mime-type, language, character set and encoding) |
| Status: | Base |
| ModuleIdentifier: | mime_module |
| SourceFile: | mod_mime.c |

## Summary

This module is used to assign content metadata to the content selected for an HTTP response by mapping patterns in the URI or filenames to the metadata values. For example, the filename extensions of content files often define the content's Internet media type, language, character set, and content-encoding. This information is sent in HTTP messages containing that content and used in content negotiation when selecting alternatives, such that the user's preferences are respected when choosing one of several possible contents to serve. See MOD_NEGOTIATION for more information about content negotiation (p. 78) .

The directives ADDCHARSET, ADDENCODING, ADDLANGUAGE and ADDTYPE are all used to map file extensions onto the metadata for that file. Respectively they set the character set, content-encoding, content-language, and media-type (content-type) of documents. The directive TYPESCONFIG is used to specify a file which also maps extensions onto media types.

In addition, MOD_MIME may define the handler (p. 108) and filters (p. 110) that originate and process content. The directives ADDHANDLER, ADDOUTPUTFILTER, and ADDINPUTFILTER control the modules or scripts that serve the document. The MULTIVIEWSMATCH directive allows MOD_NEGOTIATION to consider these file extensions to be included when testing Multiviews matches.

While MOD_MIME associates metadata with filename extensions, the CORE server provides directives that are used to associate all the files in a given container (*e.g.*, <LOCATION>, <DIRECTORY>, or <FILES>) with particular metadata. These directives include FORCETYPE, SETHANDLER, SETINPUTFILTER, and SETOUTPUTFILTER. The core directives override any filename extension mappings defined in MOD_MIME.

Note that changing the metadata for a file does not change the value of the Last-Modified header. Thus, previously cached copies may still be used by a client or proxy, with the previous headers. If you change the metadata (language, content type, character set or encoding) you may need to 'touch' affected files (updating their last modified date) to ensure that all visitors are receive the corrected content headers.

**Directives**

- AddCharset
- AddEncoding
- AddHandler
- AddInputFilter
- AddLanguage
- AddOutputFilter
- AddType
- DefaultLanguage
- ModMimeUsePathInfo
- MultiviewsMatch
- RemoveCharset
- RemoveEncoding

- RemoveHandler

- RemoveInputFilter

- RemoveLanguage

- RemoveOutputFilter

- RemoveType

- TypesConfig

**See also**

- MIMEMAGICFILE

- ADDDEFAULTCHARSET

- FORCETYPE

- SETHANDLER

- SETINPUTFILTER

- SETOUTPUTFILTER

## Files with Multiple Extensions

Files can have more than one extension; the order of the extensions is *normally* irrelevant. For example, if the file `welcome.html.fr` maps onto content type `text/html` and language French then the file `welcome.fr.html` will map onto exactly the same information. If more than one extension is given that maps onto the same type of meta-data, then the one to the right will be used, except for languages and content encodings. For example, if `.gif` maps to the media-type `image/gif` and `.html` maps to the media-type `text/html`, then the file `welcome.gif.html` will be associated with the media-type `text/html`.

Languages and content encodings are treated accumulative, because one can assign more than one language or encoding to a particular resource. For example, the file `welcome.html.en.de` will be delivered with `Content-Language:  en, de` and `Content-Type:  text/html`.

Care should be taken when a file with multiple extensions gets associated with both a media-type and a handler. This will usually result in the request being handled by the module associated with the handler. For example, if the `.imap` extension is mapped to the handler `imap-file` (from MOD_IMAGEMAP) and the `.html` extension is mapped to the media-type `text/html`, then the file `world.imap.html` will be associated with both the `imap-file` handler and `text/html` media-type. When it is processed, the `imap-file` handler will be used, and so it will be treated as a MOD_IMAGEMAP imagemap file.

If you would prefer only the last dot-separated part of the filename to be mapped to a particular piece of meta-data, then do not use the Add* directives. For example, if you wish to have the file `foo.html.cgi` processed as a CGI script, but not the file `bar.cgi.html`, then instead of using `AddHandler cgi-script .cgi`, use

**Configure handler based on final extension only**

```
<FilesMatch "[^.]+\.cgi$">
  SetHandler cgi-script
</FilesMatch>
```

## Content encoding

A file of a particular media-type can additionally be encoded a particular way to simplify transmission over the Internet. While this usually will refer to compression, such as `gzip`, it can also refer to encryption, such a `pgp` or to an encoding such as UUencoding, which is designed for transmitting a binary file in an ASCII (text) format.

The HTTP/1.1 RFC[55], section 14.11 puts it this way:

> The Content-Encoding entity-header field is used as a modifier to the media-type. When present, its value indicates what additional content codings have been applied to the entity-body, and thus what decoding mechanisms must be applied in order to obtain the media-type referenced by the Content-Type header field. Content-Encoding is primarily used to allow a document to be compressed without losing the identity of its underlying media type.

By using more than one file extension (see section above about multiple file extensions), you can indicate that a file is of a particular *type*, and also has a particular *encoding*.

For example, you may have a file which is a Microsoft Word document, which is pkzipped to reduce its size. If the `.doc` extension is associated with the Microsoft Word file type, and the `.zip` extension is associated with the pkzip file encoding, then the file `Resume.doc.zip` would be known to be a pkzip'ed Word document.

Apache sends a `Content-encoding` header with the resource, in order to tell the client browser about the encoding method.

```
Content-encoding: pkzip
```

## Character sets and languages

In addition to file type and the file encoding, another important piece of information is what language a particular document is in, and in what character set the file should be displayed. For example, the document might be written in the Vietnamese alphabet, or in Cyrillic, and should be displayed as such. This information, also, is transmitted in HTTP headers.

The character set, language, encoding and mime type are all used in the process of content negotiation (See MOD_NEGOTIATION) to determine which document to give to the client, when there are alternative documents in more than one character set, language, encoding or mime type. All filename extensions associations created with AD-DCHARSET, ADDENCODING, ADDLANGUAGE and ADDTYPE directives (and extensions listed in the MIMEMAG-ICFILE) participate in this select process. Filename extensions that are only associated using the ADDHANDLER, ADDINPUTFILTER or ADDOUTPUTFILTER directives may be included or excluded from matching by using the MUL-TIVIEWSMATCH directive.

### Charset

To convey this further information, Apache optionally sends a `Content-Language` header, to specify the language that the document is in, and can append additional information onto the `Content-Type` header to indicate the particular character set that should be used to correctly render the information.

```
Content-Language:  en, fr Content-Type:  text/plain;
charset=ISO-8859-1
```

The language specification is the two-letter abbreviation for the language. The `charset` is the name of the particular character set which should be used.

---

[55]http://www.ietf.org/rfc/rfc2616.txt

## AddCharset Directive

| | |
|---|---|
| Description: | Maps the given filename extensions to the specified content charset |
| Syntax: | `AddCharset charset extension [extension] ...` |
| Context: | server config, virtual host, directory, .htaccess |
| Override: | FileInfo |
| Status: | Base |
| Module: | mod_mime |

The ADDCHARSET directive maps the given filename extensions to the specified content charset (the Internet registered name for a given character encoding). *charset* is the media type's charset parameter[56] for resources with filenames containing *extension*. This mapping is added to any already in force, overriding any mappings that already exist for the same *extension*.

### Example

```
AddLanguage ja .ja
AddCharset EUC-JP .euc
AddCharset ISO-2022-JP .jis
AddCharset SHIFT_JIS .sjis
```

Then the document xxxx.ja.jis will be treated as being a Japanese document whose charset is ISO-2022-JP (as will the document xxxx.jis.ja). The ADDCHARSET directive is useful for both to inform the client about the character encoding of the document so that the document can be interpreted and displayed appropriately, and for content negotiation (p. 78) , where the server returns one from several documents based on the client's charset preference.

The *extension* argument is case-insensitive and can be specified with or without a leading dot. Filenames may have multiple extensions and the *extension* argument will be compared against each of them.

### See also

- MOD_NEGOTIATION
- ADDDEFAULTCHARSET

## AddEncoding Directive

| | |
|---|---|
| Description: | Maps the given filename extensions to the specified encoding type |
| Syntax: | `AddEncoding encoding extension [extension] ...` |
| Context: | server config, virtual host, directory, .htaccess |
| Override: | FileInfo |
| Status: | Base |
| Module: | mod_mime |

The ADDENCODING directive maps the given filename extensions to the specified HTTP content-encoding. *encoding* is the HTTP content coding to append to the value of the Content-Encoding header field for documents named with the *extension*. This mapping is added to any already in force, overriding any mappings that already exist for the same *extension*.

### Example

```
AddEncoding x-gzip .gz
AddEncoding x-compress .Z
```

---

[56]http://www.iana.org/assignments/character-sets

This will cause filenames containing the `.gz` extension to be marked as encoded using the `x-gzip` encoding, and filenames containing the `.Z` extension to be marked as encoded with `x-compress`.

Old clients expect `x-gzip` and `x-compress`, however the standard dictates that they're equivalent to `gzip` and `compress` respectively. Apache does content encoding comparisons by ignoring any leading `x-`. When responding with an encoding Apache will use whatever form (*i.e.*, `x-foo` or `foo`) the client requested. If the client didn't specifically request a particular form Apache will use the form given by the `AddEncoding` directive. To make this long story short, you should always use `x-gzip` and `x-compress` for these two specific encodings. More recent encodings, such as `deflate`, should be specified without the `x-`.

The *extension* argument is case-insensitive and can be specified with or without a leading dot. Filenames may have multiple extensions and the *extension* argument will be compared against each of them.

## AddHandler Directive

| | |
|---|---|
| Description: | Maps the filename extensions to the specified handler |
| Syntax: | `AddHandler handler-name extension [extension] ...` |
| Context: | server config, virtual host, directory, .htaccess |
| Override: | FileInfo |
| Status: | Base |
| Module: | mod_mime |

Files having the name *extension* will be served by the specified *handler-name (p. 108)* . This mapping is added to any already in force, overriding any mappings that already exist for the same *extension*. For example, to activate CGI scripts with the file extension `.cgi`, you might use:

```
AddHandler cgi-script .cgi
```

Once that has been put into your httpd.conf file, any file containing the `.cgi` extension will be treated as a CGI program.

The *extension* argument is case-insensitive and can be specified with or without a leading dot. Filenames may have multiple extensions and the *extension* argument will be compared against each of them.

**See also**

- SETHANDLER

## AddInputFilter Directive

| | |
|---|---|
| Description: | Maps filename extensions to the filters that will process client requests |
| Syntax: | `AddInputFilter filter[;filter...] extension [extension] ...` |
| Context: | server config, virtual host, directory, .htaccess |
| Override: | FileInfo |
| Status: | Base |
| Module: | mod_mime |

ADDINPUTFILTER maps the filename extension *extension* to the filters (p. 110) which will process client requests and POST input when they are received by the server. This is in addition to any filters defined elsewhere, including the SETINPUTFILTER directive. This mapping is merged over any already in force, overriding any mappings that already exist for the same *extension*.

If more than one *filter* is specified, they must be separated by semicolons in the order in which they should process the content. The *filter* is case-insensitive.

The *extension* argument is case-insensitive and can be specified with or without a leading dot. Filenames may have multiple extensions and the *extension* argument will be compared against each of them.

**See also**

- REMOVEINPUTFILTER
- SETINPUTFILTER

## AddLanguage Directive

| | |
|---|---|
| Description: | Maps the given filename extension to the specified content language |
| Syntax: | `AddLanguage language-tag extension [extension] ...` |
| Context: | server config, virtual host, directory, .htaccess |
| Override: | FileInfo |
| Status: | Base |
| Module: | mod_mime |

The ADDLANGUAGE directive maps the given filename extension to the specified content language. Files with the filename *extension* are assigned an HTTP Content-Language value of *language-tag* corresponding to the language identifiers defined by RFC 3066. This directive overrides any mappings that already exist for the same *extension*.

### Example

```
AddEncoding x-compress .Z
AddLanguage en .en
AddLanguage fr .fr
```

Then the document `xxxx.en.Z` will be treated as being a compressed English document (as will the document `xxxx.Z.en`). Although the content language is reported to the client, the browser is unlikely to use this information. The ADDLANGUAGE directive is more useful for content negotiation (p. 78) , where the server returns one from several documents based on the client's language preference.

If multiple language assignments are made for the same extension, the last one encountered is the one that is used. That is, for the case of:

```
AddLanguage en .en
AddLanguage en-gb .en
AddLanguage en-us .en
```

documents with the extension `.en` would be treated as being `en-us`.

The *extension* argument is case-insensitive and can be specified with or without a leading dot. Filenames may have multiple extensions and the *extension* argument will be compared against each of them.

**See also**

- MOD_NEGOTIATION

## AddOutputFilter Directive

| | |
|---|---|
| Description: | Maps filename extensions to the filters that will process responses from the server |
| Syntax: | `AddOutputFilter filter[;filter...] extension [extension] ...` |
| Context: | server config, virtual host, directory, .htaccess |
| Override: | FileInfo |
| Status: | Base |
| Module: | mod_mime |

The ADDOUTPUTFILTER directive maps the filename extension *extension* to the filters (p. 110) which will process responses from the server before they are sent to the client. This is in addition to any filters defined elsewhere, including SETOUTPUTFILTER and ADDOUTPUTFILTERBYTYPE directive. This mapping is merged over any already in force, overriding any mappings that already exist for the same *extension*.

For example, the following configuration will process all .shtml files for server-side includes and will then compress the output using MOD_DEFLATE.

```
AddOutputFilter INCLUDES;DEFLATE shtml
```

If more than one filter is specified, they must be separated by semicolons in the order in which they should process the content. The *filter* argument is case-insensitive.

The *extension* argument is case-insensitive and can be specified with or without a leading dot. Filenames may have multiple extensions and the *extension* argument will be compared against each of them.

Note that when defining a set of filters using the ADDOUTPUTFILTER directive, any definition made will replace any previous definition made by the ADDOUTPUTFILTER directive.

```
# Effective filter "DEFLATE"
AddOutputFilter DEFLATE shtml
<Location "/foo">
  # Effective filter "INCLUDES", replacing "DEFLATE"
  AddOutputFilter INCLUDES shtml
</Location>
<Location "/bar">
  # Effective filter "INCLUDES;DEFLATE", replacing "DEFLATE"
  AddOutputFilter INCLUDES;DEFLATE shtml
</Location>
<Location "/bar/baz">
  # Effective filter "BUFFER", replacing "INCLUDES;DEFLATE"
  AddOutputFilter BUFFER shtml
</Location>
<Location "/bar/baz/buz">
  # No effective filter, replacing "BUFFER"
  RemoveOutputFilter shtml
</Location>
```

**See also**

- REMOVEOUTPUTFILTER
- SETOUTPUTFILTER

## AddType Directive

| Description: | Maps the given filename extensions onto the specified content type |
| --- | --- |
| Syntax: | `AddType media-type extension [extension] ...` |
| Context: | server config, virtual host, directory, .htaccess |
| Override: | FileInfo |
| Status: | Base |
| Module: | mod_mime |

The ADDTYPE directive maps the given filename extensions onto the specified content type. *media-type* is the media type to use for filenames containing *extension*. This mapping is added to any already in force, overriding any mappings that already exist for the same *extension*.

It is recommended that new media types be added using the ADDTYPE directive rather than changing the TYPESCONFIG file.

### Example

```
AddType image/gif .gif
```

Or, to specify multiple file extensions in one directive:

### Example

```
AddType image/jpeg jpeg jpg jpe
```

The *extension* argument is case-insensitive and can be specified with or without a leading dot. Filenames may have multiple extensions and the *extension* argument will be compared against each of them.

A simmilar effect to MOD_NEGOTIATION's LANGUAGEPRIORITY can be achieved by qualifying a *media-type* with qs:

### Example

```
AddType application/rss+xml;qs=0.8 .xml
```

This is useful in situations, *e.g.* when a client requesting `Accept:  */*` can not actually processes the content returned by the server.

This directive primarily configures the content types generated for static files served out of the filesystem. For resources other than static files, where the generator of the response typically specifies a Content-Type, this directive has no effect.

Note

> If no handler is explicitly set for a request, the specified content type will also be used as the handler name.
> When explicit directives such as SETHANDLER or ADDHANDLER do not apply to the current request, the internal handler name normally set by those directives is instead set to the content type specified by this directive.
> This is a historical behavior that may be used by some third-party modules (such as mod_php) for taking responsibility for the matching request.
> Configurations that rely on such "synthetic" types should be avoided. Additionally, configurations that restrict access to SETHANDLER or ADDHANDLER should restrict access to this directive as well.

**See also**

- FORCETYPE
- MOD_NEGOTIATION

## DefaultLanguage Directive

| | |
|---|---|
| Description: | Defines a default language-tag to be sent in the Content-Language header field for all resources in the current context that have not been assigned a language-tag by some other means. |
| Syntax: | `DefaultLanguage language-tag` |
| Context: | server config, virtual host, directory, .htaccess |
| Override: | FileInfo |
| Status: | Base |
| Module: | mod_mime |

The DEFAULTLANGUAGE directive tells Apache that all resources in the directive's scope (*e.g.*, all resources covered by the current <DIRECTORY> container) that don't have an explicit language extension (such as .fr or .de as configured by ADDLANGUAGE) should be assigned a Content-Language of *language-tag*. This allows entire directory trees to be marked as containing Dutch content, for instance, without having to rename each file. Note that unlike using extensions to specify languages, DEFAULTLANGUAGE can only specify a single language.

If no DEFAULTLANGUAGE directive is in force and a file does not have any language extensions as configured by ADDLANGUAGE, then no Content-Language header field will be generated.

### Example

```
DefaultLanguage en
```

**See also**

- MOD_NEGOTIATION

## ModMimeUsePathInfo Directive

| | |
|---|---|
| Description: | Tells MOD_MIME to treat path_info components as part of the filename |
| Syntax: | ModMimeUsePathInfo On\|Off |
| Default: | ModMimeUsePathInfo Off |
| Context: | directory |
| Status: | Base |
| Module: | mod_mime |

The MODMIMEUSEPATHINFO directive is used to combine the filename with the path_info URL component to apply MOD_MIME's directives to the request. The default value is Off - therefore, the path_info component is ignored.

This directive is recommended when you have a virtual filesystem.

### Example

```
ModMimeUsePathInfo On
```

If you have a request for /index.php/foo.shtml MOD_MIME will now treat the incoming request as /index.php/foo.shtml and directives like AddOutputFilter INCLUDES .shtml will add the INCLUDES filter to the request. If MODMIMEUSEPATHINFO is not set, the INCLUDES filter will not be added. This will work analogously for virtual paths, such as those defined by <LOCATION>

**See also**

- ACCEPTPATHINFO

## MultiviewsMatch Directive

| | |
|---|---|
| Description: | The types of files that will be included when searching for a matching file with MultiViews |
| Syntax: | MultiviewsMatch Any\|NegotiatedOnly\|Filters\|Handlers [Handlers\|Filters] |
| Default: | MultiviewsMatch NegotiatedOnly |
| Context: | server config, virtual host, directory, .htaccess |
| Override: | FileInfo |
| Status: | Base |
| Module: | mod_mime |

MULTIVIEWSMATCH permits three different behaviors for mod_negotiation (p. 766) 's Multiviews feature. Multiviews allows a request for a file, *e.g.* `index.html`, to match any negotiated extensions following the base request, *e.g.* `index.html.en`, `index.html.fr`, or `index.html.gz`.

The `NegotiatedOnly` option provides that every extension following the base name must correlate to a recognized MOD_MIME extension for content negotiation, *e.g.* Charset, Content-Type, Language, or Encoding. This is the strictest implementation with the fewest unexpected side effects, and is the default behavior.

To include extensions associated with Handlers and/or Filters, set the MULTIVIEWSMATCH directive to either `Handlers`, `Filters`, or both option keywords. If all other factors are equal, the smallest file will be served, *e.g.* in deciding between `index.html.cgi` of 500 bytes and `index.html.pl` of 1000 bytes, the `.cgi` file would win in this example. Users of `.asis` files might prefer to use the Handler option, if `.asis` files are associated with the `asis-handler`.

You may finally allow `Any` extensions to match, even if MOD_MIME doesn't recognize the extension. This can cause unpredictable results, such as serving .old or .bak files the webmaster never expected to be served.

For example, the following configuration will allow handlers and filters to participate in Multviews, but will exclude unknown files:

```
MultiviewsMatch Handlers Filters
```

MULTIVIEWSMATCH is not allowed in a <LOCATION> or <LOCATIONMATCH> section.

**See also**

- OPTIONS
- MOD_NEGOTIATION

## RemoveCharset Directive

| Description: | Removes any character set associations for a set of file extensions |
|---|---|
| Syntax: | `RemoveCharset extension [extension] ...` |
| Context: | virtual host, directory, .htaccess |
| Override: | FileInfo |
| Status: | Base |
| Module: | mod_mime |

The REMOVECHARSET directive removes any character set associations for files with the given extensions. This allows `.htaccess` files in subdirectories to undo any associations inherited from parent directories or the server config files.

The *extension* argument is case-insensitive and can be specified with or without a leading dot.

### Example

```
RemoveCharset .html .shtml
```

## RemoveEncoding Directive

| Description: | Removes any content encoding associations for a set of file extensions |
|---|---|
| Syntax: | `RemoveEncoding extension [extension] ...` |
| Context: | virtual host, directory, .htaccess |
| Override: | FileInfo |
| Status: | Base |
| Module: | mod_mime |

The REMOVEENCODING directive removes any encoding associations for files with the given extensions. This allows .htaccess files in subdirectories to undo any associations inherited from parent directories or the server config files. An example of its use might be:

**/foo/.htaccess:**

```
AddEncoding x-gzip .gz
AddType text/plain .asc
<Files "*.gz.asc">
    RemoveEncoding .gz
</Files>
```

This will cause foo.gz to be marked as being encoded with the gzip method, but foo.gz.asc as an unencoded plaintext file.

**Note**

> REMOVEENCODING directives are processed *after* any ADDENCODING directives, so it is possible they may undo the effects of the latter if both occur within the same directory configuration.

The *extension* argument is case-insensitive and can be specified with or without a leading dot.

## RemoveHandler Directive

| | |
|---|---|
| Description: | Removes any handler associations for a set of file extensions |
| Syntax: | RemoveHandler extension [extension] ... |
| Context: | virtual host, directory, .htaccess |
| Override: | FileInfo |
| Status: | Base |
| Module: | mod_mime |

The REMOVEHANDLER directive removes any handler associations for files with the given extensions. This allows .htaccess files in subdirectories to undo any associations inherited from parent directories or the server config files. An example of its use might be:

**/foo/.htaccess:**

```
AddHandler server-parsed .html
```

**/foo/bar/.htaccess:**

```
RemoveHandler .html
```

This has the effect of returning .html files in the /foo/bar directory to being treated as normal files, rather than as candidates for parsing (see the MOD_INCLUDE module).

The *extension* argument is case-insensitive and can be specified with or without a leading dot.

## RemoveInputFilter Directive

| | |
|---|---|
| Description: | Removes any input filter associations for a set of file extensions |
| Syntax: | RemoveInputFilter extension [extension] ... |
| Context: | virtual host, directory, .htaccess |
| Override: | FileInfo |
| Status: | Base |
| Module: | mod_mime |

The REMOVEINPUTFILTER directive removes any input filter (p. 110) associations for files with the given extensions. This allows `.htaccess` files in subdirectories to undo any associations inherited from parent directories or the server config files.

The *extension* argument is case-insensitive and can be specified with or without a leading dot.

**See also**

- ADDINPUTFILTER
- SETINPUTFILTER

## RemoveLanguage Directive

| | |
|---|---|
| Description: | Removes any language associations for a set of file extensions |
| Syntax: | `RemoveLanguage extension [extension] ...` |
| Context: | virtual host, directory, .htaccess |
| Override: | FileInfo |
| Status: | Base |
| Module: | mod_mime |

The REMOVELANGUAGE directive removes any language associations for files with the given extensions. This allows `.htaccess` files in subdirectories to undo any associations inherited from parent directories or the server config files.

The *extension* argument is case-insensitive and can be specified with or without a leading dot.

## RemoveOutputFilter Directive

| | |
|---|---|
| Description: | Removes any output filter associations for a set of file extensions |
| Syntax: | `RemoveOutputFilter extension [extension] ...` |
| Context: | virtual host, directory, .htaccess |
| Override: | FileInfo |
| Status: | Base |
| Module: | mod_mime |

The REMOVEOUTPUTFILTER directive removes any output filter (p. 110) associations for files with the given extensions. This allows `.htaccess` files in subdirectories to undo any associations inherited from parent directories or the server config files.

The *extension* argument is case-insensitive and can be specified with or without a leading dot.

### Example

```
RemoveOutputFilter shtml
```

**See also**

- ADDOUTPUTFILTER

## RemoveType Directive

| | |
|---|---|
| Description: | Removes any content type associations for a set of file extensions |
| Syntax: | `RemoveType extension [extension] ...` |
| Context: | virtual host, directory, .htaccess |
| Override: | FileInfo |
| Status: | Base |
| Module: | mod_mime |

The REMOVETYPE directive removes any media type associations for files with the given extensions. This allows .htaccess files in subdirectories to undo any associations inherited from parent directories or the server config files. An example of its use might be:

**/foo/.htaccess:**

```
RemoveType .cgi
```

This will remove any special handling of .cgi files in the /foo/ directory and any beneath it, causing responses containing those files to omit the HTTP Content-Type header field.

**Note**

> REMOVETYPE directives are processed *after* any ADDTYPE directives, so it is possible they may undo the effects of the latter if both occur within the same directory configuration.

The *extension* argument is case-insensitive and can be specified with or without a leading dot.

## TypesConfig Directive

| | |
|---|---|
| Description: | The location of the mime.types file |
| Syntax: | TypesConfig file-path |
| Default: | TypesConfig conf/mime.types |
| Context: | server config |
| Status: | Base |
| Module: | mod_mime |

The TYPESCONFIG directive sets the location of the media types configuration file. *File-path* is relative to the SERVERROOT. This file sets the default list of mappings from filename extensions to content types. Most administrators use the mime.types file provided by their OS, which associates common filename extensions with the official list of IANA registered media types maintained at http://www.iana.org/assignments/media-types/index.html as well as a large number of unofficial types. This simplifies the httpd.conf file by providing the majority of media-type definitions, and may be overridden by ADDTYPE directives as needed. You should not edit the mime.types file, because it may be replaced when you upgrade your server.

The file contains lines in the format of the arguments to an ADDTYPE directive:

```
media-type [extension] ...
```

The case of the extension does not matter. Blank lines, and lines beginning with a hash character (#) are ignored. Empty lines are there for completeness (of the mime.types file). Apache httpd can still determine these types with MOD_MIME_MAGIC.

> Please do **not** send requests to the Apache HTTP Server Project to add any new entries in the distributed mime.types file unless (1) they are already registered with IANA, and (2) they use widely accepted, non-conflicting filename extensions across platforms. category/x-subtype requests will be automatically rejected, as will any new two-letter extensions as they will likely conflict later with the already crowded language and character set namespace.

**See also**

- MOD_MIME_MAGIC

# 10.76   Apache Module mod_mime_magic

| | |
|---|---|
| Description: | Determines the MIME type of a file by looking at a few bytes of its contents |
| Status: | Extension |
| ModuleIdentifier: | mime_magic_module |
| SourceFile: | mod_mime_magic.c |

## Summary

This module determines the MIME type of files in the same way the Unix `file(1)` command works: it looks at the first few bytes of the file. It is intended as a "second line of defense" for cases that MOD_MIME can't resolve.

This module is derived from a free version of the `file(1)` command for Unix, which uses "magic numbers" and other hints from a file's contents to figure out what the contents are. This module is active only if the magic file is specified by the MIMEMAGICFILE directive.

### Directives

- MimeMagicFile

## Format of the Magic File

The contents of the file are plain ASCII text in 4-5 columns. Blank lines are allowed but ignored. Commented lines use a hash mark (#). The remaining lines are parsed for the following columns:

| Column | Description | |
|---|---|---|
| 1 | byte number to begin checking from<br>">" indicates a dependency upon the previous non-">" line | |
| 2 | type of data to match | |
| | `byte` | single character |
| | `short` | machine-order 16-bit integer |
| | `long` | machine-order 32-bit integer |
| | `string` | arbitrary-length string |
| | `date` | long integer date (seconds since Unix epoch/1970) |
| | `beshort` | big-endian 16-bit integer |
| | `belong` | big-endian 32-bit integer |
| | `bedate` | big-endian 32-bit integer date |
| | `leshort` | little-endian 16-bit integer |
| | `lelong` | little-endian 32-bit integer |
| | `ledate` | little-endian 32-bit integer date |
| 3 | contents of data to match | |
| 4 | MIME type if matched | |
| 5 | MIME encoding if matched (optional) | |

For example, the following magic file lines would recognize some audio formats:

```
# Sun/NeXT audio data
0       string      .snd
>12     belong      1        audio/basic
>12     belong      2        audio/basic
>12     belong      3        audio/basic
>12     belong      4        audio/basic
>12     belong      5        audio/basic
>12     belong      6        audio/basic
>12     belong      7        audio/basic
>12     belong      23       audio/x-adpcm
```

Or these would recognize the difference between *.doc files containing Microsoft Word or FrameMaker documents. (These are incompatible file formats which use the same file suffix.)

```
# Frame
0   string  \<MakerFile        application/x-frame
0   string  \<MIFFile          application/x-frame
0   string  \<MakerDictionary  application/x-frame
0   string  \<MakerScreenFon   application/x-frame
0   string  \<MML              application/x-frame
0   string  \<Book             application/x-frame
0   string  \<Maker            application/x-frame

# MS-Word
0   string  \376\067\0\043            application/msword
0   string  \320\317\021\340\241\261  application/msword
0   string  \333\245-\0\0\0           application/msword
```

An optional MIME encoding can be included as a fifth column. For example, this can recognize gzipped files and set the encoding for them.

```
# gzip (GNU zip, not to be confused with
#       [Info-ZIP/PKWARE] zip archiver)

0   string  \037\213 application/octet-stream  x-gzip
```

## Performance Issues

This module is not for every system. If your system is barely keeping up with its load or if you're performing a web server benchmark, you may not want to enable this because the processing is not free.

However, an effort was made to improve the performance of the original file(1) code to make it fit in a busy web server. It was designed for a server where there are thousands of users who publish their own documents. This is probably very common on intranets. Many times, it's helpful if the server can make more intelligent decisions about a file's contents than the file name allows ...even if just to reduce the "why doesn't my page work" calls when users improperly name their own files. You have to decide if the extra work suits your environment.

## Notes

The following notes apply to the MOD_MIME_MAGIC module and are included here for compliance with contributors' copyright restrictions that require their acknowledgment.

mod_mime_magic: MIME type lookup via file magic numbers

Copyright (c) 1996-1997 Cisco Systems, Inc.

This software was submitted by Cisco Systems to the Apache Group in July 1997. Future revisions and derivatives of this source code must acknowledge Cisco Systems as the original contributor of this module. All other licensing and usage conditions are those of the Apache Group.

Some of this code is derived from the free version of the file command originally posted to comp.sources.unix. Copyright info for that program is included below as required.

 - Copyright (c) Ian F. Darwin, 1987. Written by Ian F. Darwin.

This software is not subject to any license of the American Telephone and Telegraph Company or of the Regents of the University of California.

Permission is granted to anyone to use this software for any purpose on any computer system, and to alter it and redistribute it freely, subject to the following restrictions:

1. The author is not responsible for the consequences of use of this software, no matter how awful, even if they arise from flaws in it.

2. The origin of this software must not be misrepresented, either by explicit claim or by omission. Since few users ever read sources, credits must appear in the documentation.

3. Altered versions must be plainly marked as such, and must not be misrepresented as being the original software. Since few users ever read sources, credits must appear in the documentation.

4. This notice may not be removed or altered.

For compliance with Mr Darwin's terms: this has been very significantly modified from the free `"file"` command.

- all-in-one file for compilation convenience when moving from one version of Apache to the next.

- Memory allocation is done through the Apache API's pool structure.

- All functions have had necessary Apache API request or server structures passed to them where necessary to call other Apache API routines. (*i.e.*, usually for logging, files, or memory allocation in itself or a called function.)

- struct magic has been converted from an array to a single-ended linked list because it only grows one record at a time, it's only accessed sequentially, and the Apache API has no equivalent of `realloc()`.

- Functions have been changed to get their parameters from the server configuration instead of globals. (It should be reentrant now but has not been tested in a threaded environment.)

- Places where it used to print results to stdout now saves them in a list where they're used to set the MIME type in the Apache request record.

- Command-line flags have been removed since they will never be used here.

## MimeMagicFile Directive

| | |
|---|---|
| Description: | Enable MIME-type determination based on file contents using the specified magic file |
| Syntax: | `MimeMagicFile file-path` |
| Context: | server config, virtual host |
| Status: | Extension |
| Module: | mod_mime_magic |

The MIMEMAGICFILE directive can be used to enable this module, the default file is distributed at `conf/magic`. Non-rooted paths are relative to the SERVERROOT. Virtual hosts will use the same file as the main server unless a more specific setting is used, in which case the more specific setting overrides the main server's file.

### Example

```
MimeMagicFile conf/magic
```

## 10.77   Apache Module mod_negotiation

| Description: | Provides for content negotiation (p. 78) |
|---|---|
| Status: | Base |
| ModuleIdentifier: | negotiation_module |
| SourceFile: | mod_negotiation.c |

### Summary

Content negotiation, or more accurately content selection, is the selection of the document that best matches the clients capabilities, from one of several available documents. There are two implementations of this.

- A type map (a file with the handler `type-map`) which explicitly lists the files containing the variants.

- A Multiviews search (enabled by the `Multiviews OPTIONS`), where the server does an implicit filename pattern match, and choose from amongst the results.

### Directives

- CacheNegotiatedDocs
- ForceLanguagePriority
- LanguagePriority

### See also

- OPTIONS
- MOD_MIME
- Content Negotiation (p. 78)
- Environment Variables (p. 92)

### Type maps

A type map has a format similar to RFC822 mail headers. It contains document descriptions separated by blank lines, with lines beginning with a hash character ('#') treated as comments. A document description consists of several header records; records may be continued on multiple lines if the continuation lines start with spaces. The leading space will be deleted and the lines concatenated. A header record consists of a keyword name, which always ends in a colon, followed by a value. Whitespace is allowed between the header name and value, and between the tokens of value. The headers allowed are:

**Content-Encoding:** The encoding of the file. Apache only recognizes encodings that are defined by an AD-DENCODING directive. This normally includes the encodings `x-compress` for compress'd files, and `x-gzip` for gzip'd files. The `x-` prefix is ignored for encoding comparisons.

**Content-Language:** The language(s) of the variant, as an Internet standard language tag (RFC 1766[57]). An example is `en`, meaning English. If the variant contains more than one language, they are separated by a comma.

**Content-Length:** The length of the file, in bytes. If this header is not present, then the actual length of the file is used.

---

[57]http://www.ietf.org/rfc/rfc1766.txt

`Content-Type:` The MIME media type of the document, with optional parameters. Parameters are separated from the media type and from one another by a semi-colon, with a syntax of `name=value`. Common parameters include:

> `level` an integer specifying the version of the media type. For `text/html` this defaults to 2, otherwise 0.
>
> `qs` a floating-point number with a value in the range 0[.000] to 1[.000], indicating the relative 'quality' of this variant compared to the other available variants, independent of the client's capabilities. For example, a jpeg file is usually of higher source quality than an ascii file if it is attempting to represent a photograph. However, if the resource being represented is ascii art, then an ascii file would have a higher source quality than a jpeg file. All `qs` values are therefore specific to a given resource.

---
**Example**
```
Content-Type:   image/jpeg; qs=0.8
```
---

`URI:` uri of the file containing the variant (of the given media type, encoded with the given content encoding). These are interpreted as URLs relative to the map file; they must be on the same server, and they must refer to files to which the client would be granted access if they were to be requested directly.

`Body:` The actual content of the resource may be included in the type-map file using the Body header. This header must contain a string that designates a delimiter for the body content. Then all following lines in the type map file will be considered part of the resource body until the delimiter string is found.

---
**Example:**
```
Body:----xyz----
<html>
<body>
<p>Content of the page.</p>
</body>
</html>
----xyz----
```
---

Consider, for example, a resource called `document.html` which is available in English, French, and German. The files for each of these are called `document.html.en`, `document.html.fr`, and `document.html.de`, respectively. The type map file will be called `document.html.var`, and will contain the following:

```
URI: document.html

Content-language:  en
Content-type:  text/html
URI: document.html.en

Content-language:  fr
Content-type:  text/html
URI: document.html.fr

Content-language:  de
Content-type:  text/html
URI: document.html.de
```

All four of these files should be placed in the same directory, and the `.var` file should be associated with the type-map handler with an ADDHANDLER directive:

```
AddHandler type-map .var
```

A request for `document.html.var` in this directory will result in choosing the variant which most closely matches the language preference specified in the user's `Accept-Language` request header.

If `Multiviews` is enabled, and MULTIVIEWSMATCH is set to `"handlers"` or `"any"`, a request to `document.html` will discover `document.html.var` and continue negotiating with the explicit type map.

Other configuration directives, such as ALIAS can be used to map `document.html` to `document.html.var`.

## Multiviews

A Multiviews search is enabled by the `Multiviews` OPTIONS. If the server receives a request for `/some/dir/foo` and `/some/dir/foo` does *not* exist, then the server reads the directory looking for all files named `foo.*`, and effectively fakes up a type map which names all those files, assigning them the same media types and content-encodings it would have if the client had asked for one of them by name. It then chooses the best match to the client's requirements, and returns that document.

The MULTIVIEWSMATCH directive configures whether Apache will consider files that do not have content negotiation meta-information assigned to them when choosing files.

## CacheNegotiatedDocs Directive

| | |
|---|---|
| Description: | Allows content-negotiated documents to be cached by proxy servers |
| Syntax: | `CacheNegotiatedDocs On|Off` |
| Default: | `CacheNegotiatedDocs Off` |
| Context: | server config, virtual host |
| Status: | Base |
| Module: | mod_negotiation |

If set, this directive allows content-negotiated documents to be cached by proxy servers. This could mean that clients behind those proxys could retrieve versions of the documents that are not the best match for their abilities, but it will make caching more efficient.

This directive only applies to requests which come from HTTP/1.0 browsers. HTTP/1.1 provides much better control over the caching of negotiated documents, and this directive has no effect in responses to HTTP/1.1 requests.

## ForceLanguagePriority Directive

| | |
|---|---|
| Description: | Action to take if a single acceptable document is not found |
| Syntax: | `ForceLanguagePriority None|Prefer|Fallback [Prefer|Fallback]` |
| Default: | `ForceLanguagePriority Prefer` |
| Context: | server config, virtual host, directory, .htaccess |
| Override: | FileInfo |
| Status: | Base |
| Module: | mod_negotiation |

The FORCELANGUAGEPRIORITY directive uses the given LANGUAGEPRIORITY to satisfy negotiation where the server could otherwise not return a single matching document.

`ForceLanguagePriority Prefer` uses `LanguagePriority` to serve a one valid result, rather than returning an HTTP result 300 (MULTIPLE CHOICES) when there are several equally valid choices. If the directives below were given, and the user's `Accept-Language` header assigned `en` and `de` each as quality `.500` (equally acceptable) then the first matching variant, `en`, will be served.

```
LanguagePriority en fr de
ForceLanguagePriority Prefer
```

ForceLanguagePriority Fallback uses LANGUAGEPRIORITY to serve a valid result, rather than returning an HTTP result 406 (NOT ACCEPTABLE). If the directives below were given, and the user's Accept-Language only permitted an es language response, but such a variant isn't found, then the first variant from the LANGUAGEPRIORITY list below will be served.

```
LanguagePriority en fr de
ForceLanguagePriority Fallback
```

Both options, Prefer and Fallback, may be specified, so either the first matching variant from LANGUAGEPRIORITY will be served if more than one variant is acceptable, or first available document will be served if none of the variants matched the client's acceptable list of languages.

**See also**

- ADDLANGUAGE

## LanguagePriority Directive

| | |
|---|---|
| Description: | The precedence of language variants for cases where the client does not express a preference |
| Syntax: | LanguagePriority MIME-lang [MIME-lang] ... |
| Context: | server config, virtual host, directory, .htaccess |
| Override: | FileInfo |
| Status: | Base |
| Module: | mod_negotiation |

The LANGUAGEPRIORITY sets the precedence of language variants for the case where the client does not express a preference, when handling a Multiviews request. The list of *MIME-lang* are in order of decreasing preference.

```
LanguagePriority en fr de
```

For a request for foo.html, where foo.html.fr and foo.html.de both existed, but the browser did not express a language preference, then foo.html.fr would be returned.

Note that this directive only has an effect if a 'best' language cannot be determined by any other means or the FORCE-LANGUAGEPRIORITY directive is not None. In general, the client determines the language preference, not the server.

**See also**

- ADDLANGUAGE

# 10.78  Apache Module mod_nw_ssl

| Description: | Enable SSL encryption for NetWare |
|---|---|
| Status: | Base |
| ModuleIdentifier: | nwssl_module |
| SourceFile: | mod_nw_ssl.c |
| Compatibility: | NetWare only |

## Summary

This module enables SSL encryption for a specified port. It takes advantage of the SSL encryption functionality that is built into the NetWare operating system.

### Directives

- NWSSLTrustedCerts
- NWSSLUpgradeable
- SecureListen

## NWSSLTrustedCerts Directive

| Description: | List of additional client certificates |
|---|---|
| Syntax: | NWSSLTrustedCerts filename [filename] ... |
| Context: | server config |
| Status: | Base |
| Module: | mod_nw_ssl |

Specifies a list of client certificate files (DER format) that are used when creating a proxied SSL connection. Each client certificate used by a server must be listed separately in its own .der file.

## NWSSLUpgradeable Directive

| Description: | Allows a connection to be upgraded to an SSL connection upon request |
|---|---|
| Syntax: | NWSSLUpgradeable [IP-address:]portnumber |
| Context: | server config |
| Status: | Base |
| Module: | mod_nw_ssl |

Allow a connection that was created on the specified address and/or port to be upgraded to an SSL connection upon request from the client. The address and/or port must have already be defined previously with a LISTEN directive.

## SecureListen Directive

| Description: | Enables SSL encryption for the specified port |
|---|---|
| Syntax: | SecureListen [IP-address:]portnumber Certificate-Name [MUTUAL] |
| Context: | server config |
| Status: | Base |
| Module: | mod_nw_ssl |

Specifies the port and the eDirectory based certificate name that will be used to enable SSL encryption. An optional third parameter also enables mutual authentication.

## 10.79  Apache Module mod_policy

| | |
|---|---|
| Description: | HTTP protocol compliance enforcement. |
| Status: | Extension |
| ModuleIdentifier: | policy_module |
| SourceFile: | mod_policy.c |

### Summary

The HTTP protocol recommends that clients should be "liberal in what they accept", and servers "strict with what they send". In some cases it can be difficult to detect when a server or an application has been misconfigured, is serving uncacheable content or is behaving suboptimally, as an HTTP client might be compensating for the server. These problems can potentially lead to excessive bandwidth consumption, or a server outage under load.

The MOD_POLICY module consists of a set of filters that test servers for HTTP protocol compliance. These tests allow the server administrator to log violations of, or outright reject responses where certain defined conditions exist.

This could be used as a way to set minimum HTTP protocol compliance criteria for a restful application. Alternatively, a reverse proxy or cache could be configured to protect itself from misconfigured origin servers or unexpectedly uncacheable content, or as a mechanism to detect configuration mistakes within the server itself.

### Directives

- PolicyConditional
- PolicyConditionalURL
- PolicyEnvironment
- PolicyFilter
- PolicyKeepalive
- PolicyKeepaliveURL
- PolicyLength
- PolicyLengthURL
- PolicyMaxage
- PolicyMaxageURL
- PolicyNocache
- PolicyNocacheURL
- PolicyType
- PolicyTypeURL
- PolicyValidation
- PolicyValidationURL
- PolicyVary
- PolicyVaryURL
- PolicyVersion
- PolicyVersionURL

### See also

- Filters (p. 110)
- HTTP Protocol Compliance (p. 71)

## Actions

If a policy is violated, one of the following actions can be taken:

**ignore** The policy check will be ignored for the given URL space, even if the filter is present.

**log** The policy check will be executed, and if a violation is detected a warning will be logged to the server error_log, and a `Warning` header added to the response for the benefit of the client.

**enforce** The policy check will be executed, and if a violation is detected an error will be logged to the server error_log, a `Warning` header added to the response, and a `502 Bad Gateway` will be returned to the client. Optional links to explanatory documentation can be added to each error message, detailing the origin of each policy.

It is also possible to selectively disable all policies for a given URL space, should the need arise, using the POLICY-FILTER directive.

Alternatively, the POLICYENVIRONMENT directive can be used to specify an environment variable, which if present, will cause the policies to be selectively downgraded or bypassed.

## Policy Tests

The following policy filters are available:

**POLICY_TYPE (p. 71) : Enforce valid content types** Content types that are syntactically invalid or blank can be detected and the request rejected. Types can be restricted to a specific list containing optional wildcards ? and *.

**POLICY_LENGTH (p. 71) : Enforce the presence of a Content-Length** The length of responses can be specified in one of three ways, by specifying an explicit length in advance, using chunked encoding to set the length, or by setting no length at all and terminating the request when complete. The absence of a specific content length can affect the cacheability of the response, and prevents the use of keepalive during HTTP/1.0 requests. This policy enforces the presence of an explicit content length on the response.

**POLICY_KEEPALIVE (p. 71) : Enforce the option to keepalive** Less restrictive than the POLICY_LENGTH test, this policy enforces the possibility that the response can be kept alive. If the response doesn't have a protocol defined zero length, and the response isn't already an error, and the response has neither a Content-Length or is declared HTTP/1.1 and lacks Content-Encoding: chunked, then this response will be rejected.

**POLICY_VARY (p. 71) : Enforce the absence of certain headers within Vary headers** If the Vary header contains any of the headers specified, this policy will reject the request. The typical case is the presence of the User-Agent within Vary, which is likely to cause a denial of service condition to a cache.

**POLICY_VALIDATION (p. 71) : Enforce the presence of Etag and/or Last-Modified** The ability for a cache to determine whether a cached entity can be refreshed is dependent on whether a valid Etag and/or Last-Modified header is present to revalidate against. The absence of both headers, or the invalid syntax of a header will cause this policy to be rejected.

**POLICY_CONDITIONAL (p. 71) : Enforce correct operation of conditional requests** When conditional headers are present in the request, a server should respond with a `304 Not Modified` or `412 Precondition Failed` response where appropriate. A server may ignore conditional headers, and this affects the efficiency of the HTTP caching mechanism. This policy rejects requests where a conditional header is present, and a 304 or 412 response code was expected, but a 2xx response was seen instead.

**POLICY_NOCACHE (p. 71) : Enforce cacheable responses** When a response is encountered that declares itself explicitly uncacheable, the request is rejected. A response is considered uncacheable if it specifies any of the following:

- `Cache-Control: no-cache`
- `Pragma: no-cache`
- `Cache-Control: no-store`
- `Cache-Control: private`

**POLICY_MAXAGE (p. 71) : Enforce a minimum maxage** When a response is encountered where the freshness lifetime is less than the given value, or the freshness lifetime is heuristic, the request is rejected. A response is checked in the following order:

- If `s-maxage` is present but too small; or
- If `max-age` is present but too small; or
- If `Expires` is present and invalid; or
- `Date` is present and invalid; or
- `Expires` minus Date is too small; or
- No `s-maxage`, `maxage`, or `Expires`/`Date` declared at all

**POLICY_VERSION (p. 71) : Enforce a minimum HTTP version within a request** When a request is encountered with an HTTP version number less than the required minimum version, the request is rejected. The following version numbers are recognised:

- `HTTP/1.1`
- `HTTP/1.0`
- `HTTP/0.9`

### Example Configuration

A typical configuration protecting a server serving static content might be as follows:

```
<Location "/">
  SetOutputFilter POLICY_TYPE;POLICY_LENGTH;POLICY_KEEPALIVE;POLICY_VARY;POLICY_VALI
    POLICY_CONDITIONAL;POLICY_NOCACHE;POLICY_MAXAGE;POLICY_VERSION

  # content type must be present and valid, but can be anything
  PolicyType enforce */*

  # reject if no explicitly declared content length
  PolicyLength enforce

  # covered by the policy length filter
  PolicyKeepalive ignore

  # reject if User-Agent appears within Vary headers
  PolicyVary enforce User-Agent

  # we want to enforce validation
  PolicyValidation enforce

  # non-functional conditional responses should be rejected
  PolicyConditional enforce

  # no-cache responses should be rejected
  PolicyNocache enforce
```

```
  # maxage must be at least a day
  PolicyMaxage enforce 86400

  # request version can be anything
  PolicyVersion ignore HTTP/1.1
</Location>

# suppress policy protection for server-status
<Location "/server-status">
  PolicyFilter off
</Location>
```

## PolicyConditional Directive

| | |
|---|---|
| Description: | Enable the conditional request policy. |
| Syntax: | `PolicyConditional ignore\|log\|enforce` |
| Default: | `ignore` |
| Context: | server config, virtual host, directory |
| Status: | Extension |
| Module: | mod_policy |
| Compatibility: | PolicyConditional is only available in Apache 2.5.0 and later. |

When logged or enforced, a response that should have been conditional but wasn't will be rejected.

### Example

```
# non-functional conditional responses should be rejected
PolicyConditional enforce
```

## PolicyConditionalURL Directive

| | |
|---|---|
| Description: | URL describing the conditional request policy. |
| Syntax: | `PolicyConditionalURL url` |
| Default: | `none` |
| Context: | server config, virtual host, directory |
| Status: | Extension |
| Module: | mod_policy |
| Compatibility: | PolicyConditionalURL is only available in Apache 2.5.0 and later. |

Specify the URL of the documentation describing the conditional request policy, to appear within error messages.

## PolicyEnvironment Directive

| | |
|---|---|
| Description: | Override policies based on an environment variable. |
| Syntax: | `PolicyEnvironment variable log-value ignore-value` |
| Default: | `none` |
| Context: | server config, virtual host, directory |
| Status: | Extension |
| Module: | mod_policy |
| Compatibility: | PolicyEnvironment is only available in Apache 2.5.0 and later. |

Downgrade policies to logging only or ignored based on the presence of an environment variable. If the given variable is present and equal to the log-value, enforced policies will be logged instead. If the given variable is present and equal to the ignore-value, all policies will be ignored.

### Example

```
# downgrade if POLICY_CONTROL was present
PolicyEnvironment POLICY_CONTROL log ignore
```

## PolicyFilter Directive

| | |
|---|---|
| Description: | Enable or disable policies for the given URL space. |
| Syntax: | `PolicyFilter on|off` |
| Default: | `on` |
| Context: | server config, virtual host, directory |
| Status: | Extension |
| Module: | mod_policy |
| Compatibility: | PolicyFilter is only available in Apache 2.5.0 and later. |

Master switch to enable or disable policies for a given URL space.

### Example

```
# enabled by default
<Location "/">
  PolicyFilter on
</Location>

# suppress policy protection for server-status
<Location "/server-status">
  PolicyFilter off
</Location>
```

## PolicyKeepalive Directive

| | |
|---|---|
| Description: | Enable the keepalive policy. |
| Syntax: | `PolicyKeepalive ignore|log|enforce` |
| Default: | `ignore` |
| Context: | server config, virtual host, directory |
| Status: | Extension |
| Module: | mod_policy |
| Compatibility: | PolicyKeepalive is only available in Apache 2.5.0 and later. |

When logged or enforced, a response that lacks both an explicit `Content-Length` header and a `Transfer-Encoding` of `chunked` will be rejected.

### Example

```
# missing Content-Length or Transfer-Encoding should be rejected
PolicyKeepalive enforce
```

### PolicyKeepaliveURL Directive

| | |
|---|---|
| Description: | URL describing the keepalive policy. |
| Syntax: | `PolicyKeepaliveURL url` |
| Default: | `none` |
| Context: | server config, virtual host, directory |
| Status: | Extension |
| Module: | mod_policy |
| Compatibility: | PolicyKeepaliveURL is only available in Apache 2.5.0 and later. |

Specify the URL of the documentation describing the keepalive policy, to appear within error messages.

### PolicyLength Directive

| | |
|---|---|
| Description: | Enable the content length policy. |
| Syntax: | `PolicyLength ignore|log|enforce` |
| Default: | `ignore` |
| Context: | server config, virtual host, directory |
| Status: | Extension |
| Module: | mod_policy |
| Compatibility: | PolicyLength is only available in Apache 2.5.0 and later. |

When logged or enforced, a response that lacks an explicit `Content-Length` header will be rejected.

#### Example

```
# missing Content-Length header should be rejected
PolicyLength enforce
```

### PolicyLengthURL Directive

| | |
|---|---|
| Description: | URL describing the content length policy. |
| Syntax: | `PolicyLengthURL url` |
| Default: | `none` |
| Context: | server config, virtual host, directory |
| Status: | Extension |
| Module: | mod_policy |
| Compatibility: | PolicyLengthURL is only available in Apache 2.5.0 and later. |

Specify the URL of the documentation describing the content length policy, to appear within error messages.

### PolicyMaxage Directive

| | |
|---|---|
| Description: | Enable the caching minimum max-age policy. |
| Syntax: | `PolicyMaxage ignore|log|enforce age` |
| Default: | `ignore` |
| Context: | server config, virtual host, directory |
| Status: | Extension |
| Module: | mod_policy |
| Compatibility: | PolicyMaxage is only available in Apache 2.5.0 and later. |

When logged or enforced, a response that lacks an explicit freshness lifetime defined with `max-age`, `s-maxage` or an `Expires` header, or where the explicit freshness lifetime is smaller than the given value, will be rejected.

**Example**

```
# reject responses with a freshness lifetime shorter than a day
PolicyMaxage enforce 86400
```

## PolicyMaxageURL Directive

| | |
|---|---|
| Description: | URL describing the caching minimum freshness lifetime policy. |
| Syntax: | `PolicyMaxageURL url` |
| Default: | `none` |
| Context: | server config, virtual host, directory |
| Status: | Extension |
| Module: | mod_policy |
| Compatibility: | PolicyMaxageURL is only available in Apache 2.5.0 and later. |

Specify the URL of the documentation describing the caching minimum freshness lifetime policy, to appear within error messages.

## PolicyNocache Directive

| | |
|---|---|
| Description: | Enable the caching no-cache policy. |
| Syntax: | `PolicyNocache ignore|log|enforce` |
| Default: | `ignore` |
| Context: | server config, virtual host, directory |
| Status: | Extension |
| Module: | mod_policy |
| Compatibility: | PolicyNocache is only available in Apache 2.5.0 and later. |

When logged or enforced, a response that defines itself uncacheable using the `Cache-Control` or `Pragma` headers will be rejected.

**Example**

```
# Cache-Control: no-cache will be rejected
PolicyNocache enforce
```

## PolicyNocacheURL Directive

| | |
|---|---|
| Description: | URL describing the caching no-cache policy. |
| Syntax: | `PolicyNocacheURL url` |
| Default: | `none` |
| Context: | server config, virtual host, directory |
| Status: | Extension |
| Module: | mod_policy |
| Compatibility: | PolicyNocacheURL is only available in Apache 2.5.0 and later. |

Specify the URL of the documentation describing the caching no-cache policy, to appear within error messages.

## PolicyType Directive

| | |
|---|---|
| Description: | Enable the content type policy. |
| Syntax: | `PolicyType ignore|log|enforce type [ type [ ... ]]` |
| Default: | `ignore` |
| Context: | server config, virtual host, directory |
| Status: | Extension |
| Module: | mod_policy |
| Compatibility: | PolicyType is only available in Apache 2.5.0 and later. |

When logged or enforced, a response that lacks a `Content-Type` header, where the `Content-Type` header is malformed, or where the header does not match the given pattern or patterns will be rejected.

### Example

```
# enforce json or XML
PolicyType enforce application/json text/xml
```

### Example

```
# malformed content type should be rejected
PolicyType enforce */*
```

## PolicyTypeURL Directive

| | |
|---|---|
| Description: | URL describing the content type policy. |
| Syntax: | `PolicyTypeURL url` |
| Default: | `none` |
| Context: | server config, virtual host, directory |
| Status: | Extension |
| Module: | mod_policy |
| Compatibility: | PolicyTypeURL is only available in Apache 2.5.0 and later. |

Specify the URL of the documentation describing the content type policy, to appear within error messages.

## PolicyValidation Directive

| | |
|---|---|
| Description: | Enable the validation policy. |
| Syntax: | `PolicyValidation ignore|log|enforce` |
| Default: | `ignore` |
| Context: | server config, virtual host, directory |
| Status: | Extension |
| Module: | mod_policy |
| Compatibility: | PolicyValidation is only available in Apache 2.5.0 and later. |

When logged or enforced, a response that lacks either a valid `ETag` header or a `Last-Modified` header, or where either header is syntactically incorrect, will be rejected.

### Example

```
# no ETag or Last-Modified will be rejected
PolicyValidation enforce
```

### PolicyValidationURL Directive

| | |
|---|---|
| Description: | URL describing the content type policy. |
| Syntax: | `PolicyValidationURL url` |
| Default: | `none` |
| Context: | server config, virtual host, directory |
| Status: | Extension |
| Module: | mod_policy |
| Compatibility: | PolicyValidationURL is only available in Apache 2.5.0 and later. |

Specify the URL of the documentation describing the validation policy, to appear within error messages.

### PolicyVary Directive

| | |
|---|---|
| Description: | Enable the Vary policy. |
| Syntax: | `PolicyVary ignore|log|enforce header [ header [ ... ]]` |
| Default: | `ignore` |
| Context: | server config, virtual host, directory |
| Status: | Extension |
| Module: | mod_policy |
| Compatibility: | PolicyVary is only available in Apache 2.5.0 and later. |

When logged or enforced, a response that contains a `Vary` header which in turn contains one of the headers listed, will be rejected.

#### Example

```
# reject reponses with "User-Agent" listed in the Vary header
PolicyVary enforce User-Agent
```

### PolicyVaryURL Directive

| | |
|---|---|
| Description: | URL describing the content type policy. |
| Syntax: | `PolicyVaryURL url` |
| Default: | `none` |
| Context: | server config, virtual host, directory |
| Status: | Extension |
| Module: | mod_policy |
| Compatibility: | PolicyVaryURL is only available in Apache 2.5.0 and later. |

Specify the URL of the documentation describing the vary policy, to appear within error messages.

### PolicyVersion Directive

| | |
|---|---|
| Description: | Enable the version policy. |
| Syntax: | `PolicyVersion ignore|log|enforce HTTP/0.9|HTTP/1.0|HTTP/1.1` |
| Default: | `ignore` |
| Context: | server config, virtual host, directory |
| Status: | Extension |
| Module: | mod_policy |
| Compatibility: | PolicyVersion is only available in Apache 2.5.0 and later. |

When logged or enforced, a request with a version lower than specified will be rejected.

**Example**

```
# reject requests with an HTTP version older than HTTP/1.1
PolicyVersion enforce HTTP/1.1
```

## PolicyVersionURL Directive

| | |
|---|---|
| Description: | URL describing the minimum request HTTP version policy. |
| Syntax: | `PolicyVersionURL url` |
| Default: | `none` |
| Context: | server config, virtual host, directory |
| Status: | Extension |
| Module: | mod_policy |
| Compatibility: | PolicyVersionURL is only available in Apache 2.5.0 and later. |

Specify the URL of the documentation describing the minimum request HTTP version policy, to appear within error messages.

# 10.80   Apache Module mod_privileges

| | |
|---|---|
| Description: | Support for Solaris privileges and for running virtual hosts under different user IDs. |
| Status: | Experimental |
| ModuleIdentifier: | privileges_module |
| SourceFile: | mod_privileges.c |
| Compatibility: | Available in Apache 2.3 and up, on Solaris 10 and OpenSolaris platforms |

## Summary

This module enables different Virtual Hosts to run with different Unix *User* and *Group* IDs, and with different Solaris Privileges[58]. In particular, it offers a solution to the problem of privilege separation between different Virtual Hosts, first promised by the abandoned perchild MPM. It also offers other security enhancements.

Unlike perchild, MOD_PRIVILEGES is not itself an MPM. It works *within* a processing model to set privileges and User/Group *per request* in a running process. It is therefore not compatible with a threaded MPM, and will refuse to run under one.

MOD_PRIVILEGES raises security issues similar to those of suexec (p. 115) . But unlike suexec, it applies not only to CGI programs but to the entire request processing cycle, including in-process applications and subprocesses. It is ideally suited to running PHP applications under **mod_php**, which is also incompatible with threaded MPMs. It is also well-suited to other in-process scripting applications such as **mod_perl**, **mod_python**, and **mod_ruby**, and to applications implemented in C as apache modules where privilege separation is an issue.

### Directives

- DTracePrivileges
- PrivilegesMode
- VHostCGIMode
- VHostCGIPrivs
- VHostGroup
- VHostPrivs
- VHostSecure
- VHostUser

## Security Considerations

MOD_PRIVILEGES introduces new security concerns in situations where **untrusted code** may be run **within the web-server process**. This applies to untrusted modules, and scripts running under modules such as mod_php or mod_perl. Scripts running externally (e.g. as CGI or in an appserver behind mod_proxy or mod_jk) are NOT affected.

The basic security concerns with mod_privileges are:

- Running as a system user introduces the same security issues as mod_suexec, and near-equivalents such as cgiwrap and suphp.
- A privileges-aware malicious user extension (module or script) could escalate its privileges to anything available to the httpd process in any virtual host. This introduces new risks if (and only if) mod_privileges is compiled with the *BIG_SECURITY_HOLE* option.

---

[58]http://sosc-dr.sun.com/bigadmin/features/articles/least_privilege.jsp

- A privileges-aware malicious user extension (module or script) could escalate privileges to set its user ID to another system user (and/or group).

The PRIVILEGESMODE directive allows you to select either *FAST* or *SECURE* mode. You can mix modes, using *FAST* mode for trusted users and fully-audited code paths, while imposing SECURE mode where an untrusted user has scope to introduce code.

Before describing the modes, we should also introduce the target use cases: Benign vs Hostile. In a benign situation, you want to separate users for their convenience, and protect them and the server against the risks posed by honest mistakes, but you trust your users are not deliberately subverting system security. In a hostile situation - e.g. commercial hosting - you may have users deliberately attacking the system or each other.

**FAST mode**  In *FAST* mode, requests are run in-process with the selected uid/gid and privileges, so the overhead is negligible. This is suitable for benign situations, but is not secure against an attacker escalating privileges with an in-process module or script.

**SECURE mode**  A request in *SECURE* mode forks a subprocess, which then drops privileges. This is a very similar case to running CGI with suexec, but for the entire request cycle, and with the benefit of fine-grained control of privileges.

You can select different PRIVILEGESMODEs for each virtual host, and even in a directory context within a virtual host. *FAST* mode is appropriate where the user(s) are trusted and/or have no privilege to load in-process code. *SECURE* mode is appropriate to cases where untrusted code might be run in-process. However, even in *SECURE* mode, there is no protection against a malicious user who is able to introduce privileges-aware code running *before the start of the request-processing cycle.*

## DTracePrivileges Directive

| | |
|---|---|
| Description: | Determines whether the privileges required by dtrace are enabled. |
| Syntax: | `DTracePrivileges On\|Off` |
| Default: | `DTracePrivileges Off` |
| Context: | server config |
| Status: | Experimental |
| Module: | mod_privileges |
| Compatibility: | Available on Solaris 10 and OpenSolaris with non-threaded MPMs (PREFORK or custom MPM). |

This server-wide directive determines whether Apache will run with the privileges[59] required to run dtrace[60]. Note that *DTracePrivileges On* will not in itself activate DTrace, but *DTracePrivileges Off* will prevent it working.

## PrivilegesMode Directive

| | |
|---|---|
| Description: | Trade off processing speed and efficiency vs security against malicious privileges-aware code. |
| Syntax: | `PrivilegesMode FAST\|SECURE\|SELECTIVE` |
| Default: | `PrivilegesMode FAST` |
| Context: | server config, virtual host, directory |
| Status: | Experimental |
| Module: | mod_privileges |
| Compatibility: | Available on Solaris 10 and OpenSolaris with non-threaded MPMs (PREFORK or custom MPM). |

---

[59]http://sosc-dr.sun.com/bigadmin/features/articles/least_privilege.jsp
[60]http://sosc-dr.sun.com/bigadmin/content/dtrace/

This directive trades off performance vs security against malicious, privileges-aware code. In *SECURE* mode, each request runs in a secure subprocess, incurring a substantial performance penalty. In *FAST* mode, the server is not protected against escalation of privileges as discussed above.

This directive differs slightly between a <Directory> context (including equivalents such as Location/Files/If) and a top-level or <VirtualHost>.

At top-level, it sets a default that will be inherited by virtualhosts. In a virtual host, FAST or SECURE mode acts on the entire HTTP request, and any settings in a <Directory> context will be **ignored**. A third pseudo-mode SELECTIVE defers the choice of FAST vs SECURE to directives in a <Directory> context.

In a <Directory> context, it is applicable only where SELECTIVE mode was set for the VirtualHost. Only FAST or SECURE can be set in this context (SELECTIVE would be meaningless).

**Warning**

Where SELECTIVE mode is selected for a virtual host, the activation of privileges must be deferred until *after* the mapping phase of request processing has determined what <Directory> context applies to the request. This might give an attacker opportunities to introduce code through a REWRITEMAP running at top-level or <VirtualHost> context *before* privileges have been dropped and userid/gid set.

## VHostCGIMode Directive

| | |
|---|---|
| Description: | Determines whether the virtualhost can run subprocesses, and the privileges available to sub-processes. |
| Syntax: | VHostCGIMode On\|Off\|Secure |
| Default: | VHostCGIMode On |
| Context: | virtual host |
| Status: | Experimental |
| Module: | mod_privileges |
| Compatibility: | Available on Solaris 10 and OpenSolaris with non-threaded MPMs (PREFORK or custom MPM). |

Determines whether the virtual host is allowed to run fork and exec, the privileges[61] required to run subprocesses. If this is set to *Off* the virtualhost is denied the privileges and will not be able to run traditional CGI programs or scripts under the traditional MOD_CGI, nor similar external programs such as those created by MOD_EXT_FILTER or REWRITEMAP *prog*. Note that it does not prevent CGI programs running under alternative process and security models such as mod_fcgid[62], which is a recommended solution in Solaris.

If set to *On* or *Secure*, the virtual host is permitted to run external programs and scripts as above. Setting VHOSTCGI-MODE *Secure* has the effect of denying privileges to the subprocesses, as described for VHOSTSECURE.

---

[61] http://sosc-dr.sun.com/bigadmin/features/articles/least_privilege.jsp
[62] https://httpd.apache.org/mod_fcgid/

## VHostCGIPrivs Directive

| | |
|---|---|
| Description: | Assign arbitrary privileges to subprocesses created by a virtual host. |
| Syntax: | `VHostPrivs [+-]?privilege-name [[+-]?privilege-name] ...` |
| Default: | `None` |
| Context: | virtual host |
| Status: | Experimental |
| Module: | mod_privileges |
| Compatibility: | Available on Solaris 10 and OpenSolaris with non-threaded MPMs (PREFORK or custom MPM) and when MOD_PRIVILEGES is compiled with the *BIG_SECURITY_HOLE* compile-time option. |

VHOSTCGIPRIVS can be used to assign arbitrary privileges[63] to subprocesses created by a virtual host, as discussed under VHOSTCGIMODE. Each *privilege-name* is the name of a Solaris privilege, such as *file_setid* or *sys_nfs*.

A *privilege-name* may optionally be prefixed by + or -, which will respectively allow or deny a privilege. If used with neither + nor -, all privileges otherwise assigned to the virtualhost will be denied. You can use this to override any of the default sets and construct your own privilege set.

**Security**
This directive can open huge security holes in apache subprocesses, up to and including running them with root-level powers. Do not use it unless you fully understand what you are doing!

## VHostGroup Directive

| | |
|---|---|
| Description: | Sets the Group ID under which a virtual host runs. |
| Syntax: | `VHostGroup unix-groupid` |
| Default: | `Inherits the group id specified in GROUP` |
| Context: | virtual host |
| Status: | Experimental |
| Module: | mod_privileges |
| Compatibility: | Available on Solaris 10 and OpenSolaris with non-threaded MPMs (PREFORK or custom MPM). |

The VHOSTGROUP directive sets the Unix group under which the server will process requests to a virtualhost. The group is set before the request is processed and reset afterwards using Solaris Privileges[64]. Since the setting applies to the *process*, this is not compatible with threaded MPMs.

*Unix-group* is one of:

**A group name** Refers to the given group by name.

**# followed by a group number.** Refers to a group by its number.

**Security**
This directive cannot be used to run apache as root! Nevertheless, it opens potential security issues similar to those discussed in the suexec (p. 115) documentation.

**See also**

- GROUP

---

[63]http://sosc-dr.sun.com/bigadmin/features/articles/least_privilege.jsp
[64]http://sosc-dr.sun.com/bigadmin/features/articles/least_privilege.jsp

- SUEXECUSERGROUP

## VHostPrivs Directive

| | |
|---|---|
| Description: | Assign arbitrary privileges to a virtual host. |
| Syntax: | `VHostPrivs [+-]?privilege-name [[+-]?privilege-name] ...` |
| Default: | `None` |
| Context: | virtual host |
| Status: | Experimental |
| Module: | mod_privileges |
| Compatibility: | Available on Solaris 10 and OpenSolaris with non-threaded MPMs (PREFORK or custom MPM) and when MOD_PRIVILEGES is compiled with the *BIG_SECURITY_HOLE* compile-time option. |

VHOSTPRIVS can be used to assign arbitrary privileges[65] to a virtual host. Each *privilege-name* is the name of a Solaris privilege, such as *file_setid* or *sys_nfs*.

A *privilege-name* may optionally be prefixed by + or -, which will respectively allow or deny a privilege. If used with neither + nor -, all privileges otherwise assigned to the virtualhost will be denied. You can use this to override any of the default sets and construct your own privilege set.

 **Security**
This directive can open huge security holes in apache, up to and including running requests with root-level powers. Do not use it unless you fully understand what you are doing!

## VHostSecure Directive

| | |
|---|---|
| Description: | Determines whether the server runs with enhanced security for the virtualhost. |
| Syntax: | `VHostSecure On|Off` |
| Default: | `VHostSecure On` |
| Context: | virtual host |
| Status: | Experimental |
| Module: | mod_privileges |
| Compatibility: | Available on Solaris 10 and OpenSolaris with non-threaded MPMs (PREFORK or custom MPM). |

Determines whether the virtual host processes requests with security enhanced by removal of Privileges[66] that are rarely needed in a webserver, but which are available by default to a normal Unix user and may therefore be required by modules and applications. It is recommended that you retain the default (On) unless it prevents an application running. Since the setting applies to the *process*, this is not compatible with threaded MPMs.

Note
If VHOSTSECURE prevents an application running, this may be a warning sign that the application should be reviewed for security.

---

[65]http://sosc-dr.sun.com/bigadmin/features/articles/least_privilege.jsp
[66]http://sosc-dr.sun.com/bigadmin/features/articles/least_privilege.jsp

**VHostUser Directive**

| | |
|---|---|
| Description: | Sets the User ID under which a virtual host runs. |
| Syntax: | `VHostUser unix-userid` |
| Default: | `Inherits the userid specified in User` |
| Context: | virtual host |
| Status: | Experimental |
| Module: | mod_privileges |
| Compatibility: | Available on Solaris 10 and OpenSolaris with non-threaded MPMs (`PREFORK` or custom MPM). |

The VHostUser directive sets the Unix userid under which the server will process requests to a virtualhost. The userid is set before the request is processed and reset afterwards using Solaris Privileges[67]. Since the setting applies to the *process*, this is not compatible with threaded MPMs.

*Unix-userid* is one of:

**A username** Refers to the given user by name.

**# followed by a user number.** Refers to a user by its number.

> **!** **Security**
> This directive cannot be used to run apache as root! Nevertheless, it opens potential security issues similar to those discussed in the suexec (p. 115) documentation.

**See also**

- USER
- SUEXECUSERGROUP

---

[67]http://sosc-dr.sun.com/bigadmin/features/articles/least_privilege.jsp

# 10.81 Apache Module mod_proxy

| | |
|---|---|
| Description: | Multi-protocol proxy/gateway server |
| Status: | Extension |
| ModuleIdentifier: | proxy_module |
| SourceFile: | mod_proxy.c |

## Summary

 **Warning**

Do not enable proxying with PROXYREQUESTS until you have secured your server. Open proxy servers are dangerous both to your network and to the Internet at large.

MOD_PROXY and related modules implement a proxy/gateway for Apache HTTP Server, supporting a number of popular protocols as well as several different load balancing algorithms. Third-party modules can add support for additional protocols and load balancing algorithms.

A set of modules must be loaded into the server to provide the necessary features. These modules can be included statically at build time or dynamically via the LOADMODULE directive). The set must include:

- MOD_PROXY, which provides basic proxy capabilities

- MOD_PROXY_BALANCER and one or more balancer modules if load balancing is required. (See MOD_PROXY_BALANCER for more information.)

- one or more proxy scheme, or protocol, modules:

| Protocol | Module |
|---|---|
| AJP13 (Apache JServe Protocol version 1.3) | MOD_PROXY_AJP |
| CONNECT (for SSL) | MOD_PROXY_CONNECT |
| FastCGI | MOD_PROXY_FCGI |
| ftp | MOD_PROXY_FTP |
| HTTP/0.9, HTTP/1.0, and HTTP/1.1 | MOD_PROXY_HTTP |
| SCGI | MOD_PROXY_SCGI |
| WS and WSS (Web-sockets) | MOD_PROXY_WSTUNNEL |

In addition, extended features are provided by other modules. Caching is provided by MOD_CACHE and related modules. The ability to contact remote servers using the SSL/TLS protocol is provided by the SSLProxy* directives of MOD_SSL. These additional modules will need to be loaded and configured to take advantage of these features.

### Directives

- BalancerGrowth
- BalancerInherit
- BalancerMember
- BalancerPersist
- NoProxy
- <Proxy>
- ProxyAddHeaders
- ProxyBadHeader
- ProxyBlock

- ProxyDomain
- ProxyErrorOverride
- ProxyIOBufferSize
- <ProxyMatch>
- ProxyMaxForwards
- ProxyPass
- ProxyPassInherit
- ProxyPassInterpolateEnv
- ProxyPassMatch
- ProxyPassReverse
- ProxyPassReverseCookieDomain
- ProxyPassReverseCookiePath
- ProxyPreserveHost
- ProxyReceiveBufferSize
- ProxyRemote
- ProxyRemoteMatch
- ProxyRequests
- ProxySet
- ProxySourceAddress
- ProxyStatus
- ProxyTimeout
- ProxyVia

**See also**

- MOD_CACHE
- MOD_PROXY_AJP
- MOD_PROXY_BALANCER
- MOD_PROXY_CONNECT
- MOD_PROXY_FCGI
- MOD_PROXY_FTP
- MOD_PROXY_HCHECK
- MOD_PROXY_HTTP
- MOD_PROXY_SCGI
- MOD_PROXY_WSTUNNEL
- MOD_SSL

## Forward Proxies and Reverse Proxies/Gateways

Apache HTTP Server can be configured in both a *forward* and *reverse* proxy (also known as *gateway*) mode.

An ordinary *forward proxy* is an intermediate server that sits between the client and the *origin server*. In order to get content from the origin server, the client sends a request to the proxy naming the origin server as the target. The proxy then requests the content from the origin server and returns it to the client. The client must be specially configured to use the forward proxy to access other sites.

A typical usage of a forward proxy is to provide Internet access to internal clients that are otherwise restricted by a firewall. The forward proxy can also use caching (as provided by MOD_CACHE) to reduce network usage.

The forward proxy is activated using the PROXYREQUESTS directive. Because forward proxies allow clients to access arbitrary sites through your server and to hide their true origin, it is essential that you secure your server so that only authorized clients can access the proxy before activating a forward proxy.

A *reverse proxy* (or *gateway*), by contrast, appears to the client just like an ordinary web server. No special configuration on the client is necessary. The client makes ordinary requests for content in the namespace of the reverse proxy. The reverse proxy then decides where to send those requests and returns the content as if it were itself the origin.

A typical usage of a reverse proxy is to provide Internet users access to a server that is behind a firewall. Reverse proxies can also be used to balance load among several back-end servers or to provide caching for a slower back-end server. In addition, reverse proxies can be used simply to bring several servers into the same URL space.

A reverse proxy is activated using the PROXYPASS directive or the [P] flag to the REWRITERULE directive. It is **not** necessary to turn PROXYREQUESTS on in order to configure a reverse proxy.

## Basic Examples

The examples below are only a very basic idea to help you get started. Please read the documentation on the individual directives.

In addition, if you wish to have caching enabled, consult the documentation from MOD_CACHE.

### Reverse Proxy

```
ProxyPass         "/foo" "http://foo.example.com/bar"
ProxyPassReverse "/foo" "http://foo.example.com/bar"
```

### Forward Proxy

```
ProxyRequests On
ProxyVia On

<Proxy *>
  Require host internal.example.com
</Proxy>
```

## Access via Handler

You can also force a request to be handled as a reverse-proxy request, by creating a suitable Handler pass-through. The example configuration below will pass all requests for PHP scripts to the specified FastCGI server using reverse proxy:

**Reverse Proxy PHP scripts**

```
<FilesMatch "\.php$">
    SetHandler  "proxy:unix:/path/to/app.sock|fcgi://localhost/"
</FilesMatch>
```

This feature is available in Apache HTTP Server 2.4.10 and later.

## Workers

The proxy manages the configuration of origin servers and their communication parameters in objects called *workers*. There are two built-in workers: the default forward proxy worker and the default reverse proxy worker. Additional workers can be configured explicitly.

The two default workers have a fixed configuration and will be used if no other worker matches the request. They do not use HTTP Keep-Alive or connection pooling. The TCP connections to the origin server will instead be opened and closed for each request.

Explicitly configured workers are identified by their URL. They are usually created and configured using PROXYPASS or PROXYPASSMATCH when used for a reverse proxy:

```
ProxyPass "/example" "http://backend.example.com" connectiontimeout=5 timeout=30
```

This will create a worker associated with the origin server URL `http://backend.example.com` that will use the given timeout values. When used in a forward proxy, workers are usually defined via the PROXYSET directive:

```
ProxySet http://backend.example.com connectiontimeout=5 timeout=30
```

or alternatively using PROXY and PROXYSET:

```
<Proxy http://backend.example.com>
  ProxySet connectiontimeout=5 timeout=30
</Proxy>
```

Using explicitly configured workers in the forward mode is not very common, because forward proxies usually communicate with many different origin servers. Creating explicit workers for some of the origin servers can still be useful if they are used very often. Explicitly configured workers have no concept of forward or reverse proxying by themselves. They encapsulate a common concept of communication with origin servers. A worker created by PROXYPASS for use in a reverse proxy will also be used for forward proxy requests whenever the URL to the origin server matches the worker URL, and vice versa.

The URL identifying a direct worker is the URL of its origin server including any path components given:

```
ProxyPass "/examples" "http://backend.example.com/examples"
ProxyPass "/docs"     "http://backend.example.com/docs"
```

This example defines two different workers, each using a separate connection pool and configuration.

**Worker Sharing**

Worker sharing happens if the worker URLs overlap, which occurs when the URL of some worker is a leading substring of the URL of another worker defined later in the configuration file. In the following example

```
ProxyPass "/apps"     "http://backend.example.com/" timeout=60
ProxyPass "/examples" "http://backend.example.com/examples" timeout=10
```

the second worker isn't actually created. Instead the first worker is used. The benefit is, that there is only one connection pool, so connections are more often reused. Note that all configuration attributes given explicitly for the later worker will be ignored. This will be logged as a warning. In the above example, the resulting timeout value for the URL /examples will be 60 instead of 10!

If you want to avoid worker sharing, sort your worker definitions by URL length, starting with the longest worker URLs. If you want to maximize worker sharing, use the reverse sort order. See also the related warning about ordering PROXYPASS directives.

Explicitly configured workers come in two flavors: *direct workers* and *(load) balancer workers*. They support many important configuration attributes which are described below in the PROXYPASS directive. The same attributes can also be set using PROXYSET.

The set of options available for a direct worker depends on the protocol which is specified in the origin server URL. Available protocols include ajp, fcgi, ftp, http and scgi.

Balancer workers are virtual workers that use direct workers known as their members to actually handle the requests. Each balancer can have multiple members. When it handles a request, it chooses a member based on the configured load balancing algorithm.

A balancer worker is created if its worker URL uses balancer as the protocol scheme. The balancer URL uniquely identifies the balancer worker. Members are added to a balancer using BALANCERMEMBER.

**DNS resolution for origin domains**

The DNS domain resolution happens when the socket to the origin server is created for the first time. When connection pooling is used, the DNS resolution is performed again only when the ttl of the connection expires (please check PROXYPASS parameters). This means that httpd does not perform any DNS resolution caching.

## Controlling Access to Your Proxy

You can control who can access your proxy via the <PROXY> control block as in the following example:

```
<Proxy *>
  Require ip 192.168.0
</Proxy>
```

For more information on access control directives, see MOD_AUTHZ_HOST.

Strictly limiting access is essential if you are using a forward proxy (using the PROXYREQUESTS directive). Otherwise, your server can be used by any client to access arbitrary hosts while hiding his or her true identity. This is dangerous both for your network and for the Internet at large. When using a reverse proxy (using the PROXYPASS directive with ProxyRequests Off), access control is less critical because clients can only contact the hosts that you have specifically configured.

**See Also** the Proxy-Chain-Auth (p. 850) environment variable.

## Slow Startup

If you're using the PROXYBLOCK directive, hostnames' IP addresses are looked up and cached during startup for later match test. This may take a few seconds (or more) depending on the speed with which the hostname lookups occur.

## Intranet Proxy

An Apache httpd proxy server situated in an intranet needs to forward external requests through the company's firewall (for this, configure the PROXYREMOTE directive to forward the respective *scheme* to the firewall proxy). However, when it has to access resources within the intranet, it can bypass the firewall when accessing hosts. The NOPROXY directive is useful for specifying which hosts belong to the intranet and should be accessed directly.

Users within an intranet tend to omit the local domain name from their WWW requests, thus requesting "http://somehost/" instead of `http://somehost.example.com/`. Some commercial proxy servers let them get away with this and simply serve the request, implying a configured local domain. When the PROXYDOMAIN directive is used and the server is configured for proxy service, Apache httpd can return a redirect response and send the client to the correct, fully qualified, server address. This is the preferred method since the user's bookmark files will then contain fully qualified hosts.

## Protocol Adjustments

For circumstances where MOD_PROXY is sending requests to an origin server that doesn't properly implement keepalives or HTTP/1.1, there are two environment variables (p. 92) that can force the request to use HTTP/1.0 with no keepalive. These are set via the SETENV directive.

These are the `force-proxy-request-1.0` and `proxy-nokeepalive` notes.

```
<Location "/buggyappserver/">
  ProxyPass "http://buggyappserver:7001/foo/"
  SetEnv force-proxy-request-1.0 1
  SetEnv proxy-nokeepalive 1
</Location>
```

## Request Bodies

Some request methods such as POST include a request body. The HTTP protocol requires that requests which include a body either use chunked transfer encoding or send a `Content-Length` request header. When passing these requests on to the origin server, MOD_PROXY_HTTP will always attempt to send the `Content-Length`. But if the body is large and the original request used chunked encoding, then chunked encoding may also be used in the upstream request. You can control this selection using environment variables (p. 92) . Setting `proxy-sendcl` ensures maximum compatibility with upstream servers by always sending the `Content-Length`, while setting `proxy-sendchunked` minimizes resource usage by using chunked encoding.

Under some circumstances, the server must spool request bodies to disk to satisfy the requested handling of request bodies. For example, this spooling will occur if the original body was sent with chunked encoding (and is large), but the administrator has asked for backend requests to be sent with Content-Length or as HTTP/1.0. This spooling can also occur if the request body already has a Content-Length header, but the server is configured to filter incoming request bodies.

LIMITREQUESTBODY only applies to request bodies that the server will spool to disk

## Reverse Proxy Request Headers

When acting in a reverse-proxy mode (using the PROXYPASS directive, for example), MOD_PROXY_HTTP adds several request headers in order to pass information to the origin server. These headers are:

**X-Forwarded-For** The IP address of the client.

**X-Forwarded-Host** The original host requested by the client in the Host HTTP request header.

**X-Forwarded-Server** The hostname of the proxy server.

Be careful when using these headers on the origin server, since they will contain more than one (comma-separated) value if the original request already contained one of these headers. For example, you can use %{X-Forwarded-For}i in the log format string of the origin server to log the original clients IP address, but you may get more than one address if the request passes through several proxies.

See also the PROXYPRESERVEHOST and PROXYVIA directives, which control other request headers.

Note: If you need to specify custom request headers to be added to the forwarded request, use the REQUESTHEADER directive.

## BalancerGrowth Directive

| | |
|---|---|
| Description: | Number of additional Balancers that can be added Post-configuration |
| Syntax: | BalancerGrowth # |
| Default: | BalancerGrowth 5 |
| Context: | server config, virtual host |
| Status: | Extension |
| Module: | mod_proxy |
| Compatibility: | BalancerGrowth is only available in Apache HTTP Server 2.3.13 and later. |

This directive allows for growth potential in the number of Balancers available for a virtualhost in addition to the number pre-configured. It only takes effect if there is at least one pre-configured Balancer.

## BalancerInherit Directive

| | |
|---|---|
| Description: | Inherit proxy Balancers/Workers defined from the main server |
| Syntax: | BalancerInherit On\|Off |
| Default: | BalancerInherit On |
| Context: | server config, virtual host |
| Status: | Extension |
| Module: | mod_proxy |
| Compatibility: | BalancerInherit is only available in Apache HTTP Server 2.4.5 and later. |

This directive will cause the current server/vhost to "inherit" Balancers and Workers defined in the main server. This can cause issues and inconsistent behavior if using the Balancer Manager for dynamic changes and so should be disabled if using that feature.

The setting in the global server defines the default for all vhosts.

Disabling PROXYPASSINHERIT also disables BalancerInherit.

## BalancerMember Directive

| | |
|---|---|
| Description: | Add a member to a load balancing group |
| Syntax: | `BalancerMember [balancerurl] url [key=value [key=value ...]]` |
| Context: | directory |
| Status: | Extension |
| Module: | mod_proxy |

This directive adds a member to a load balancing group. It can be used within a `<Proxy balancer://...>` container directive and can take any of the key value pair parameters available to PROXYPASS directives.

One additional parameter is available only to BALANCERMEMBER directives: *loadfactor*. This is the member load factor - a number between 1 (default) and 100, which defines the weighted load to be applied to the member in question.

The *balancerurl* is only needed when not within a `<Proxy balancer://...>` container directive. It corresponds to the url of a balancer defined in PROXYPASS directive.

The path component of the balancer URL in any `<Proxy balancer://...>` container directive is ignored.

Trailing slashes should typically be removed from the URL of a BALANCERMEMBER.

## BalancerPersist Directive

| | |
|---|---|
| Description: | Attempt to persist changes made by the Balancer Manager across restarts. |
| Syntax: | `BalancerPersist On\|Off` |
| Default: | `BalancerPersist Off` |
| Context: | server config, virtual host |
| Status: | Extension |
| Module: | mod_proxy |
| Compatibility: | BalancerPersist is only available in Apache HTTP Server 2.4.4 and later. |

This directive will cause the shared memory storage associated with the balancers and balancer members to be persisted across restarts. This allows these local changes to not be lost during the normal restart/graceful state transitions.

## NoProxy Directive

| | |
|---|---|
| Description: | Hosts, domains, or networks that will be connected to directly |
| Syntax: | `NoProxy host [host] ...` |
| Context: | server config, virtual host |
| Status: | Extension |
| Module: | mod_proxy |

This directive is only useful for Apache httpd proxy servers within intranets. The NOPROXY directive specifies a list of subnets, IP addresses, hosts and/or domains, separated by spaces. A request to a host which matches one or more of these is always served directly, without forwarding to the configured PROXYREMOTE proxy server(s).

### Example

```
ProxyRemote   *  http://firewall.example.com:81
NoProxy          .example.com 192.168.112.0/21
```

The *host* arguments to the NOPROXY directive are one of the following type list:

***Domain*** A *Domain* is a partially qualified DNS domain name, preceded by a period. It represents a list of hosts which logically belong to the same DNS domain or zone (*i.e.*, the suffixes of the hostnames are all ending in *Domain*).

> **Examples**
> ```
> .com .example.org.
> ```

To distinguish *Domains* from *Hostnames* (both syntactically and semantically; a DNS domain can have a DNS A record, too!), *Domains* are always written with a leading period.

**Note**

> Domain name comparisons are done without regard to the case, and *Domains* are always assumed to be anchored in the root of the DNS tree; therefore, the two domains `.ExAmple.com` and `.example.com.` (note the trailing period) are considered equal. Since a domain comparison does not involve a DNS lookup, it is much more efficient than subnet comparison.

*SubNet* A *SubNet* is a partially qualified internet address in numeric (dotted quad) form, optionally followed by a slash and the netmask, specified as the number of significant bits in the *SubNet*. It is used to represent a subnet of hosts which can be reached over a common network interface. In the absence of the explicit net mask it is assumed that omitted (or zero valued) trailing digits specify the mask. (In this case, the netmask can only be multiples of 8 bits wide.) Examples:

**192.168 or 192.168.0.0** the subnet 192.168.0.0 with an implied netmask of 16 valid bits (sometimes used in the netmask form `255.255.0.0`)

**192.168.112.0/21** the subnet `192.168.112.0/21` with a netmask of 21 valid bits (also used in the form `255.255.248.0`)

As a degenerate case, a *SubNet* with 32 valid bits is the equivalent to an *IPAddr*, while a *SubNet* with zero valid bits (*e.g.*, 0.0.0.0/0) is the same as the constant *_Default_*, matching any IP address.

*IPAddr* A *IPAddr* represents a fully qualified internet address in numeric (dotted quad) form. Usually, this address represents a host, but there need not necessarily be a DNS domain name connected with the address.

> **Example**
> ```
> 192.168.123.7
> ```

**Note**

> An *IPAddr* does not need to be resolved by the DNS system, so it can result in more effective apache performance.

*Hostname* A *Hostname* is a fully qualified DNS domain name which can be resolved to one or more *IPAddr*s via the DNS domain name service. It represents a logical host (in contrast to *Domains*, see above) and must be resolvable to at least one *IPAddr* (or often to a list of hosts with different *IPAddr*s).

> **Examples**
> ```
> prep.ai.example.edu
> www.example.org
> ```

**Note**

> In many situations, it is more effective to specify an *IPAddr* in place of a *Hostname* since a DNS lookup can be avoided. Name resolution in Apache httpd can take a remarkable deal of time when the connection to the name server uses a slow PPP link.
>
> *Hostname* comparisons are done without regard to the case, and *Hostnames* are always assumed to be anchored in the root of the DNS tree; therefore, the two hosts `WWW.ExAmple.com` and `www.example.com.` (note the trailing period) are considered equal.

**See also**

- DNS Issues (p. 121)

## Proxy Directive

| | |
|---|---|
| Description: | Container for directives applied to proxied resources |
| Syntax: | `<Proxy wildcard-url> ...</Proxy>` |
| Context: | server config, virtual host |
| Status: | Extension |
| Module: | mod_proxy |

Directives placed in <PROXY> sections apply only to matching proxied content. Shell-style wildcards are allowed.

For example, the following will allow only hosts in `yournetwork.example.com` to access content via your proxy server:

```
<Proxy *>
  Require host yournetwork.example.com
</Proxy>
```

The following example will process all files in the `foo` directory of `example.com` through the `INCLUDES` filter when they are sent through the proxy server:

```
<Proxy http://example.com/foo/*>
  SetOutputFilter INCLUDES
</Proxy>
```

The next example will allow web clients from the specified IP addresses to issue `CONNECT` requests to access the `https://www.example.com/` SSL server if MOD_PROXY_CONNECT is enabled.

```
<Proxy www.example.com:443>
  Require ip 192.168.0.0/16
</Proxy>
```

 **Differences from the Location configuration section**

A backend URL matches the configuration section if it begins with the the *wildcard-url* string, even if the last path segment in the directive only matches a prefix of the backend URL. For example, <Proxy http://example.com/foo> matches all of http://example.com/foo, http://example.com/foo/bar, and http://example.com/foobar. The matching of the final URL differs from the behavior of the <LOCATION> section, which for purposes of this note treats the final path component as if it ended in a slash.

For more control over the matching, see <PROXYMATCH>.

**See also**

- <PROXYMATCH>

## ProxyAddHeaders Directive

| | |
|---|---|
| Description: | Add proxy information in X-Forwarded-* headers |
| Syntax: | `ProxyAddHeaders Off\|On` |
| Default: | `ProxyAddHeaders On` |
| Context: | server config, virtual host, directory |
| Status: | Extension |
| Module: | mod_proxy |
| Compatibility: | Available in version 2.3.10 and later |

This directive determines whether or not proxy related information should be passed to the backend server through X-Forwarded-For, X-Forwarded-Host and X-Forwarded-Server HTTP headers.

**Effectiveness**
   This option is of use only for HTTP proxying, as handled by MOD_PROXY_HTTP.

## ProxyBadHeader Directive

| | |
|---|---|
| Description: | Determines how to handle bad header lines in a response |
| Syntax: | `ProxyBadHeader IsError\|Ignore\|StartBody` |
| Default: | `ProxyBadHeader IsError` |
| Context: | server config, virtual host |
| Status: | Extension |
| Module: | mod_proxy |

The PROXYBADHEADER directive determines the behavior of MOD_PROXY if it receives syntactically invalid response header lines (*i.e.* containing no colon) from the origin server. The following arguments are possible:

**IsError** Abort the request and end up with a 502 (Bad Gateway) response. This is the default behavior.

**Ignore** Treat bad header lines as if they weren't sent.

**StartBody** When receiving the first bad header line, finish reading the headers and treat the remainder as body. This helps to work around buggy backend servers which forget to insert an empty line between the headers and the body.

## ProxyBlock Directive

| | |
|---|---|
| Description: | Disallow proxy requests to certain hosts |
| Syntax: | `ProxyBlock *\|hostname\|partial-hostname [hostname\|partial-hostname]...` |
| Context: | server config, virtual host |
| Status: | Extension |
| Module: | mod_proxy |

The PROXYBLOCK directive can be used to block FTP or HTTP access to certain hosts via the proxy, based on a full or partial hostname match, or, if applicable, an IP address comparison.

Each of the arguments to the PROXYBLOCK directive can be either * or a alphanumeric string. At startup, the module will attempt to resolve every alphanumeric string from a DNS name to a set of IP addresses, but any DNS errors are ignored.

If an asterisk "*" argument is specified, MOD_PROXY will deny access to all FTP or HTTP sites.

Otherwise, for any request for an HTTP or FTP resource via the proxy, MOD_PROXY will check the hostname of the request URI against each specified string. If a partial string match is found, access is denied. If no matches against hostnames are found, and a remote (forward) proxy is configured using PROXYREMOTE or PROXYREMOTEMATCH, access is allowed. If no remote (forward) proxy is configured, the IP address of the hostname from the URI is compared against all resolved IP addresses determined at startup. Access is denied if any match is found.

Note that the DNS lookups may slow down the startup time of the server.

### Example

```
ProxyBlock news.example.com auctions.example.com friends.example.com
```

Note that `example` would also be sufficient to match any of these sites.

Hosts would also be matched if referenced by IP address.

Note also that

```
ProxyBlock *
```

blocks connections to all sites.

## ProxyDomain Directive

| | |
|---|---|
| Description: | Default domain name for proxied requests |
| Syntax: | `ProxyDomain Domain` |
| Context: | server config, virtual host |
| Status: | Extension |
| Module: | mod_proxy |

This directive is only useful for Apache httpd proxy servers within intranets. The PROXYDOMAIN directive specifies the default domain which the apache proxy server will belong to. If a request to a host without a domain name is encountered, a redirection response to the same host with the configured *Domain* appended will be generated.

### Example

```
ProxyRemote    "*"   "http://firewall.example.com:81"
NoProxy              ".example.com" "192.168.112.0/21"
ProxyDomain          ".example.com"
```

## ProxyErrorOverride Directive

| | |
|---|---|
| Description: | Override error pages for proxied content |
| Syntax: | `ProxyErrorOverride On|Off` |
| Default: | `ProxyErrorOverride Off` |
| Context: | server config, virtual host, directory |
| Status: | Extension |
| Module: | mod_proxy |

This directive is useful for reverse-proxy setups where you want to have a common look and feel on the error pages seen by the end user. This also allows for included files (via MOD_INCLUDE's SSI) to get the error code and act accordingly. (Default behavior would display the error page of the proxied server. Turning this on shows the SSI Error message.)

This directive does not affect the processing of informational (1xx), normal success (2xx), or redirect (3xx) responses.

## ProxyIOBufferSize Directive

| | |
|---|---|
| Description: | Determine size of internal data throughput buffer |
| Syntax: | `ProxyIOBufferSize bytes` |
| Default: | `ProxyIOBufferSize 8192` |
| Context: | server config, virtual host |
| Status: | Extension |
| Module: | mod_proxy |

The PROXYIOBUFFERSIZE directive adjusts the size of the internal buffer which is used as a scratchpad for the data between input and output. The size must be at least `512`.

In almost every case, there's no reason to change that value.

If used with AJP, this directive sets the maximum AJP packet size in bytes. Values larger than 65536 are set to 65536. If you change it from the default, you must also change the `packetSize` attribute of your AJP connector on the Tomcat side! The attribute `packetSize` is only available in Tomcat `5.5.20+` and `6.0.2+`

Normally it is not necessary to change the maximum packet size. Problems with the default value have been reported when sending certificates or certificate chains.

## ProxyMatch Directive

| | |
|---|---|
| Description: | Container for directives applied to regular-expression-matched proxied resources |
| Syntax: | `<ProxyMatch regex> ...</ProxyMatch>` |
| Context: | server config, virtual host |
| Status: | Extension |
| Module: | mod_proxy |

The <PROXYMATCH> directive is identical to the <PROXY> directive, except that it matches URLs using regular expressions.

From 2.4.8 onwards, named groups and backreferences are captured and written to the environment with the corresponding name prefixed with "MATCH_" and in upper case. This allows elements of URLs to be referenced from within expressions (p. 99) and modules like MOD_REWRITE. In order to prevent confusion, numbered (unnamed) backreferences are ignored. Use named groups instead.

```
<ProxyMatch ^http://(?<sitename>[^/]+)>
    require ldap-group cn=%{env:MATCH_SITENAME},ou=combined,o=Example
</ProxyMatch>
```

**See also**

- <PROXY>

## ProxyMaxForwards Directive

| | |
|---|---|
| Description: | Maximium number of proxies that a request can be forwarded through |
| Syntax: | `ProxyMaxForwards number` |
| Default: | `ProxyMaxForwards -1` |
| Context: | server config, virtual host |
| Status: | Extension |
| Module: | mod_proxy |

The PROXYMAXFORWARDS directive specifies the maximum number of proxies through which a request may pass if there's no `Max-Forwards` header supplied with the request. This may be set to prevent infinite proxy loops or a DoS attack.

### Example

```
ProxyMaxForwards 15
```

Note that setting PROXYMAXFORWARDS is a violation of the HTTP/1.1 protocol (RFC2616), which forbids a Proxy setting `Max-Forwards` if the Client didn't set it. Earlier Apache httpd versions would always set it. A negative PROXYMAXFORWARDS value, including the default -1, gives you protocol-compliant behavior but may leave you open to loops.

**ProxyPass Directive**

| | |
|---|---|
| Description: | Maps remote servers into the local server URL-space |
| Syntax: | `ProxyPass [path] !|url [key=value [key=value ...]]  [nocanon]` `[interpolate] [noquery]` |
| Context: | server config, virtual host, directory |
| Status: | Extension |
| Module: | mod_proxy |
| Compatibility: | Unix Domain Socket (UDS) support added in 2.4.7 |

This directive allows remote servers to be mapped into the space of the local server. The local server does not act as a proxy in the conventional sense but appears to be a mirror of the remote server. The local server is often called a *reverse proxy* or *gateway*. The *path* is the name of a local virtual path; *url* is a partial URL for the remote server and cannot include a query string.

⟹ **Note:** This directive cannot be used within a `<Directory>` context.

⚠ The PROXYREQUESTS directive should usually be set **off** when using PROXYPASS.

In 2.4.7 and later, support for using a Unix Domain Socket is available by using a target which prepends `unix:/path/lis.sock|`. For example, to proxy HTTP and target the UDS at /home/www/socket, you would use `unix:/home/www.socket|http://localhost/whatever/`. Since the socket is local, the hostname used (in this case `localhost`) is moot, but it is passed as the Host: header value of the request.

⟹ **Note:** The path associated with the `unix:` URL is DEFAULTRUNTIMEDIR aware.

⟹ **Note:** REWRITERULE requires the `[P,NE]` option to prevent the ' `|` ' character from being escaped.

When used inside a `<LOCATION>` section, the first argument is omitted and the local directory is obtained from the `<LOCATION>`. The same will occur inside a `<LOCATIONMATCH>` section; however, ProxyPass does not interpret the regexp as such, so it is necessary to use PROXYPASSMATCH in this situation instead.

Suppose the local server has address `http://example.com/`; then

```
<Location "/mirror/foo/">
    ProxyPass "http://backend.example.com/"
</Location>
```

will cause a local request for `http://example.com/mirror/foo/bar` to be internally converted into a proxy request to `http://backend.example.com/bar`.

The ProxyPass directive is not supported in `<DIRECTORY>` or `<FILES>` sections.

If you require a more flexible reverse-proxy configuration, see the REWRITERULE directive with the `[P]` flag.

The following alternative syntax is possible; however, it can carry a performance penalty when present in very large numbers. The advantage of the below syntax is that it allows for dynamic control via the Balancer Manager (p. 824) interface:

```
ProxyPass "/mirror/foo/" "http://backend.example.com/"
```

⚠ If the first argument ends with a trailing /, the second argument should also end with a trailing /, and vice versa. Otherwise, the resulting requests to the backend may miss some needed slashes and do not deliver the expected results.

The `!` directive is useful in situations where you don't want to reverse-proxy a subdirectory, *e.g.*

```
<Location "/mirror/foo/">
    ProxyPass "http://backend.example.com/"
</Location>
<Location "/mirror/foo/i">
    ProxyPass "!"
</Location>


ProxyPass "/mirror/foo/i" "!"
ProxyPass "/mirror/foo"    "http://backend.example.com"
```

will proxy all requests to /mirror/foo to backend.example.com *except* requests made to /mirror/foo/i.

 **Ordering ProxyPass Directives**
The configured PROXYPASS and PROXYPASSMATCH rules are checked in the order of configuration. The first rule that matches wins. So usually you should sort conflicting PROXYPASS rules starting with the longest URLs first. Otherwise, later rules for longer URLS will be hidden by any earlier rule which uses a leading substring of the URL. Note that there is some relation with worker sharing. In contrast, only one PROXYPASS directive can be placed in a LOCATION block, and the most specific location will take precedence.
For the same reasons, exclusions must come *before* the general PROXYPASS directives.

### ProxyPass `key=value` Parameters

In Apache HTTP Server 2.1 and later, mod_proxy supports pooled connections to a backend server. Connections created on demand can be retained in a pool for future use. Limits on the pool size and other settings can be coded on the PROXYPASS directive using key=value parameters, described in the tables below.

By default, mod_proxy will allow and retain the maximum number of connections that could be used simultaneously by that web server child process. Use the max parameter to reduce the number from the default. Use the ttl parameter to set an optional time to live; connections which have been unused for at least ttl seconds will be closed. ttl can be used to avoid using a connection which is subject to closing because of the backend server's keep-alive timeout.

The pool of connections is maintained per web server child process, and max and other settings are not coordinated among all child processes, except when only one child process is allowed by configuration or MPM design.

#### Example

```
ProxyPass "/example" "http://backend.example.com" max=20 ttl=120 retry=300
```

**BalancerMember parameters**

| Parameter | Default | Description |
| --- | --- | --- |
| min | 0 | Minimum number of connection pool entries, unrelated to the actual number of connections. This only needs to be modified from the default for special circumstances where heap memory associated with the backend connections should be preallocated or retained. |
| max | 1...n | Maximum number of connections that will be allowed to the backend server. The default for this limit is the number of threads per process in the active MPM. In the Prefork MPM, this is always 1; while with other MPMs, it is controlled by the THREADSPERCHILD directive. |

| smax | max | Retained connection pool entries above this limit are freed during certain operations if they have been unused for longer than the time to live, controlled by the `ttl` parameter. If the connection pool entry has an associated connection, it will be closed. This only needs to be modified from the default for special circumstances where connection pool entries and any associated connections which have exceeded the time to live need to be freed or closed more aggressively. |
| acquire | - | If set, this will be the maximum time to wait for a free connection in the connection pool, in milliseconds. If there are no free connections in the pool, the Apache httpd will return `SERVER_BUSY` status to the client. |
| connectiontimeout | timeout | Connect timeout in seconds. The number of seconds Apache httpd waits for the creation of a connection to the backend to complete. By adding a postfix of ms, the timeout can be also set in milliseconds. |
| disablereuse | Off | This parameter should be used when you want to force mod_proxy to immediately close a connection to the backend after being used, and thus, disable its persistent connection and pool for that backend. This helps in various situations where a firewall between Apache httpd and the backend server (regardless of protocol) tends to silently drop connections or when backends themselves may be under round- robin DNS. To disable connection pooling reuse, set this property value to `On`. |
| enablereuse | On | This is the inverse of 'disablereuse' above, provided as a convenience for scheme handlers that require opt-in for connection reuse (such as MOD_PROXY_FCGI). |
| flushpackets | off | Determines whether the proxy module will auto-flush the output brigade after each "chunk" of data. 'off' means that it will flush only when needed; 'on' means after each chunk is sent; and 'auto' means poll/wait for a period of time and flush if no input has been received for 'flushwait' milliseconds. Currently, this is in effect only for AJP. |
| flushwait | 10 | The time to wait for additional input, in milliseconds, before flushing the output brigade if 'flushpackets' is 'auto'. |
| iobuffersize | 8192 | Adjusts the size of the internal scratchpad IO buffer. This allows you to override the PROXYIOBUFFERSIZE for a specific worker. This must be at least 512 or set to 0 for the system default of 8192. |

| keepalive | Off | This parameter should be used when you have a firewall between your Apache httpd and the backend server, which tends to drop inactive connections. This flag will tell the Operating System to send KEEP_ALIVE messages on inactive connections and thus prevent the firewall from dropping the connection. To enable keepalive, set this property value to On. The frequency of initial and subsequent TCP keepalive probes depends on global OS settings, and may be as high as 2 hours. To be useful, the frequency configured in the OS must be smaller than the threshold used by the firewall. |
| lbset | 0 | Sets the load balancer cluster set that the worker is a member of. The load balancer will try all members of a lower numbered lbset before trying higher numbered ones. |
| ping | 0 | Ping property tells the webserver to "test" the connection to the backend before forwarding the request. For negative values, the test is a simple socket check; for positive values, it's a more functional check, dependent upon the protocol. For AJP, it causes MOD_PROXY_AJP to send a CPING request on the ajp13 connection (implemented on Tomcat 3.3.2+, 4.1.28+ and 5.0.13+). For HTTP, it causes MOD_PROXY_HTTP to send a 100-Continue to the backend (only valid for HTTP/1.1 - for non HTTP/1.1 backends, this property has no effect). In both cases, the parameter is the delay in seconds to wait for the reply. This feature has been added to avoid problems with hung and busy backends. This will increase the network traffic during the normal operation which could be an issue, but it will lower the traffic in case some of the cluster nodes are down or busy. By adding a postfix of ms, the delay can be also set in milliseconds. |
| receivebuffersize | 0 | Adjusts the size of the explicit (TCP/IP) network buffer size for proxied connections. This allows you to override the PROXYRECEIVEBUFFERSIZE for a specific worker. This must be at least 512 or set to 0 for the system default. |
| redirect | - | Redirection Route of the worker. This value is usually set dynamically to enable safe removal of the node from the cluster. If set, all requests without session id will be redirected to the BalancerMember that has route parameter equal to this value. |

| retry | 60 | Connection pool worker retry timeout in seconds. If the connection pool worker to the backend server is in the error state, Apache httpd will not forward any requests to that server until the timeout expires. This enables to shut down the backend server for maintenance and bring it back online later. A value of 0 means always retry workers in an error state with no timeout. |
| route | - | Route of the worker when used inside load balancer. The route is a value appended to session id. |
| status | - | Single letter value defining the initial status of this worker. |

| D | Worker is disabled and will not accept any requests; will be automatically retried. |
|---|---|
| S | Worker is administratively stopped; will not accept requests and will not be automatically retried |
| I | Worker is in ignore-errors mode and will always be considered available. |
| H | Worker is in hot-standby mode and will only be used if no other viable workers are available. |
| E | Worker is in an error state. |
| N | Worker is in drain mode and will only accept existing sticky sessions destined for itself and ignore all other requests. |

Status can be set (which is the default) by prepending with '+' or cleared by prepending with '-'. Thus, a setting of 'S-E' sets this worker to Stopped and clears the in-error flag.

| timeout | PROXYTIMEOUT | Connection timeout in seconds. The number of seconds Apache httpd waits for data sent by / to the backend. |
| ttl | - | Time to live for inactive connections and associated connection pool entries, in seconds. Once reaching this limit, a connection will not be used again; it will be closed at some later time. |

| flusher | flush | Name of the provider used by MOD_PROXY_FDPASS. See the documentation of this module for more details. |

If the Proxy directive scheme starts with the `balancer://` (eg: `balancer://cluster`, any path information is ignored), then a virtual worker that does not really communicate with the backend server will be created. Instead, it is responsible for the management of several "real" workers. In that case, the special set of parameters can be added to this virtual worker. See MOD_PROXY_BALANCER for more information about how the balancer works.

**Balancer parameters**

| Parameter | Default | Description |
|---|---|---|
| lbmethod | byrequests | Balancer load-balance method. Select the load-balancing scheduler method to use. Either `byrequests`, to perform weighted request counting; `bytraffic`, to perform weighted traffic byte count balancing; or `bybusyness`, to perform pending request balancing. The default is `byrequests`. |
| maxattempts | One less than the number of workers, or 1 with a single worker. | Maximum number of failover attempts before giving up. |
| nofailover | Off | If set to `On`, the session will break if the worker is in error state or disabled. Set this value to `On` if backend servers do not support session replication. |
| stickysession | - | Balancer sticky session name. The value is usually set to something like `JSESSIONID` or `PHPSESSIONID`, and it depends on the backend application server that support sessions. If the backend application server uses different names for cookies and url encoded id (like servlet containers), use — to separate them. The first part is for the cookie; the second is for the path. Available in Apache HTTP Server 2.4.4 and later. |
| stickysessionsep | "." | Sets the separation symbol in the session cookie. Some backend application servers do not use the '.' as the symbol. For example, the Oracle Weblogic server uses '!'. The correct symbol can be set using this option. The setting of 'Off' signifies that no symbol is used. |
| scolonpathdelim | Off | If set to `On`, the semi-colon character ';' will be used as an additional sticky session path delimiter/separator. This is mainly used to emulate mod_jk's behavior when dealing with paths such as `JSESSIONID=6736bcf34;foo=aabfa` |
| timeout | 0 | Balancer timeout in seconds. If set, this will be the maximum time to wait for a free worker. The default is to not wait. |
| failonstatus | - | A single or comma-separated list of HTTP status codes. If set, this will force the worker into error state when the backend returns any status code in the list. Worker recovery behaves the same as other worker errors. |
| failontimeout | Off | If set, an IO read timeout after a request is sent to the backend will force the worker into error state. Worker recovery behaves the same as other worker errors. Available in Apache HTTP Server 2.4.5 and later. |
| nonce | \<auto\> | The protective nonce used in the `balancer-manager` application page. The default is to use an automatically determined UUID-based nonce, to provide for further protection for the page. If set, then the nonce is set to that value. A setting of `None` disables all nonce checking. ⟹ **Note** In addition to the nonce, the `balancer-manager` page |

A sample balancer setup:

```
ProxyPass "/special-area" "http://special.example.com" smax=5 max=10
ProxyPass "/"             "balancer://mycluster/" stickysession=JSESSIONID|jsessioni
<Proxy balancer://mycluster>
    BalancerMember ajp://1.2.3.4:8009
    BalancerMember ajp://1.2.3.5:8009 loadfactor=20
    # Less powerful server, don't send as many requests there,
    BalancerMember ajp://1.2.3.6:8009 loadfactor=5
</Proxy>
```

Setting up a hot-standby that will only be used if no other members are available:

```
ProxyPass "/" "balancer://hotcluster/"
<Proxy balancer://hotcluster>
    BalancerMember ajp://1.2.3.4:8009 loadfactor=1
    BalancerMember ajp://1.2.3.5:8009 loadfactor=2
    # The server below is on hot standby
    BalancerMember ajp://1.2.3.6:8009 status=+H
    ProxySet lbmethod=bytraffic
</Proxy>
```

**Additional ProxyPass Keywords**

Normally, mod_proxy will canonicalise ProxyPassed URLs. But this may be incompatible with some backends, particularly those that make use of *PATH_INFO*. The optional *nocanon* keyword suppresses this and passes the URL path "raw" to the backend. Note that this keyword may affect the security of your backend, as it removes the normal limited protection against URL-based attacks provided by the proxy.

Normally, mod_proxy will include the query string when generating the *SCRIPT_FILENAME* environment variable. The optional *noquery* keyword (available in httpd 2.4.1 and later) prevents this.

The optional *interpolate* keyword, in combination with PROXYPASSINTERPOLATEENV, causes the ProxyPass to interpolate environment variables, using the syntax ${*VARNAME*}. Note that many of the standard CGI-derived environment variables will not exist when this interpolation happens, so you may still have to resort to MOD_REWRITE for complex rules. Also note that interpolation is not supported within the scheme portion of a URL. Dynamic determination of the scheme can be accomplished with MOD_REWRITE as in the following example.

```
RewriteEngine On

RewriteCond %{HTTPS} =off
RewriteRule . - [E=protocol:http]
RewriteCond %{HTTPS} =on
RewriteRule . - [E=protocol:https]

RewriteRule ^/mirror/foo/(.*) %{ENV:protocol}://backend.example.com/$1 [P]
ProxyPassReverse  "/mirror/foo/" "http://backend.example.com/"
ProxyPassReverse  "/mirror/foo/" "https://backend.example.com/"
```

### ProxyPassInherit Directive

| | |
|---|---|
| Description: | Inherit ProxyPass directives defined from the main server |
| Syntax: | `ProxyPassInherit On|Off` |
| Default: | `ProxyPassInherit On` |
| Context: | server config, virtual host |
| Status: | Extension |
| Module: | mod_proxy |
| Compatibility: | ProxyPassInherit is only available in Apache HTTP Server 2.4.5 and later. |

This directive will cause the current server/vhost to "inherit" PROXYPASS directives defined in the main server. This can cause issues and inconsistent behavior if using the Balancer Manager for dynamic changes and so should be disabled if using that feature.

The setting in the global server defines the default for all vhosts.

Disabling ProxyPassInherit also disables BALANCERINHERIT.

### ProxyPassInterpolateEnv Directive

| | |
|---|---|
| Description: | Enable Environment Variable interpolation in Reverse Proxy configurations |
| Syntax: | `ProxyPassInterpolateEnv On|Off` |
| Default: | `ProxyPassInterpolateEnv Off` |
| Context: | server config, virtual host, directory |
| Status: | Extension |
| Module: | mod_proxy |

This directive, together with the *interpolate* argument to PROXYPASS, PROXYPASSREVERSE, PROXYPASSREVERSECOOKIEDOMAIN, and PROXYPASSREVERSECOOKIEPATH, enables reverse proxies to be dynamically configured using environment variables which may be set by another module such as MOD_REWRITE. It affects the PROXYPASS, PROXYPASSREVERSE, PROXYPASSREVERSECOOKIEDOMAIN, and PROXYPASSREVERSECOOKIEPATH directives and causes them to substitute the value of an environment variable `varname` for the string `${varname}` in configuration directives if the *interpolate* option is set.

Keep this turned off (for server performance) unless you need it!

### ProxyPassMatch Directive

| | |
|---|---|
| Description: | Maps remote servers into the local server URL-space using regular expressions |
| Syntax: | `ProxyPassMatch [regex] !|url [key=value [key=value ...]]` |
| Context: | server config, virtual host, directory |
| Status: | Extension |
| Module: | mod_proxy |

This directive is equivalent to PROXYPASS but makes use of regular expressions instead of simple prefix matching. The supplied regular expression is matched against the *url*, and if it matches, the server will substitute any parenthesized matches into the given string and use it as a new *url*.

**Note:** This directive cannot be used within a `<Directory>` context.

Suppose the local server has address `http://example.com/`; then

```
ProxyPassMatch "^/(.*\.gif)$" "http://backend.example.com/$1"
```

will cause a local request for `http://example.com/foo/bar.gif` to be internally converted into a proxy request to `http://backend.example.com/foo/bar.gif`.

**Note**

The URL argument must be parsable as a URL *before* regexp substitutions (as well as after). This limits the matches you can use. For instance, if we had used

```
ProxyPassMatch "^(/.*\.gif)$" "http://backend.example.com:8000$1"
```

in our previous example, it would fail with a syntax error at server startup. This is a bug (PR 46665 in the ASF bugzilla), and the workaround is to reformulate the match:

```
ProxyPassMatch "^/(.*\.gif)$" "http://backend.example.com:8000/$1"
```

The ! directive is useful in situations where you don't want to reverse-proxy a subdirectory.

When used inside a <LOCATIONMATCH> section, the first argument is omitted and the regexp is obtained from the <LOCATIONMATCH>.

If you require a more flexible reverse-proxy configuration, see the REWRITERULE directive with the [P] flag.

**Default Substitution**

When the URL parameter doesn't use any backreferences into the regular expression, the original URL will be appended to the URL parameter.

**Security Warning**

Take care when constructing the target URL of the rule, considering the security impact from allowing the client influence over the set of URLs to which your server will act as a proxy. Ensure that the scheme and hostname part of the URL is either fixed or does not allow client undue influence.

## ProxyPassReverse Directive

| | |
|---|---|
| Description: | Adjusts the URL in HTTP response headers sent from a reverse proxied server |
| Syntax: | `ProxyPassReverse [path] url [interpolate]` |
| Context: | server config, virtual host, directory |
| Status: | Extension |
| Module: | mod_proxy |

This directive lets Apache httpd adjust the URL in the `Location`, `Content-Location` and `URI` headers on HTTP redirect responses. This is essential when Apache httpd is used as a reverse proxy (or gateway) to avoid bypassing the reverse proxy because of HTTP redirects on the backend servers which stay behind the reverse proxy.

Only the HTTP response headers specifically mentioned above will be rewritten. Apache httpd will not rewrite other response headers, nor will it by default rewrite URL references inside HTML pages. This means that if the proxied content contains absolute URL references, they will bypass the proxy. To rewrite HTML content to match the proxy, you must load and enable MOD_PROXY_HTML.

*path* is the name of a local virtual path; *url* is a partial URL for the remote server. These parameters are used the same way as for the PROXYPASS directive.

For example, suppose the local server has address `http://example.com/`; then

```
ProxyPass          "/mirror/foo/" "http://backend.example.com/"
ProxyPassReverse   "/mirror/foo/" "http://backend.example.com/"
ProxyPassReverseCookieDomain  backend.example.com  public.example.com
ProxyPassReverseCookiePath  "/"  "/mirror/foo/"
```

will not only cause a local request for the `http://example.com/mirror/foo/bar` to be internally converted into a proxy request to `http://backend.example.com/bar` (the functionality which `ProxyPass` provides here). It also takes care of redirects which the server `backend.example.com` sends when redirecting `http://backend.example.com/bar` to `http://backend.example.com/quux`. Apache httpd adjusts this to `http://example.com/mirror/foo/quux` before forwarding the HTTP redirect response to the client. Note that the hostname used for constructing the URL is chosen in respect to the setting of the USECANONICALNAME directive.

Note that this PROXYPASSREVERSE directive can also be used in conjunction with the proxy feature (`RewriteRule ... [P]`) from MOD_REWRITE because it doesn't depend on a corresponding PROXYPASS directive.

The optional *interpolate* keyword, used together with PROXYPASSINTERPOLATEENV, enables interpolation of environment variables specified using the format ${*VARNAME*}. Note that interpolation is not supported within the scheme portion of a URL.

When used inside a <LOCATION> section, the first argument is omitted and the local directory is obtained from the <LOCATION>. The same occurs inside a <LOCATIONMATCH> section, but will probably not work as intended, as ProxyPassReverse will interpret the regexp literally as a path; if needed in this situation, specify the ProxyPassReverse outside the section or in a separate <LOCATION> section.

This directive is not supported in <DIRECTORY> or <FILES> sections.

## ProxyPassReverseCookieDomain Directive

| | |
|---|---|
| Description: | Adjusts the Domain string in Set-Cookie headers from a reverse- proxied server |
| Syntax: | `ProxyPassReverseCookieDomain internal-domain public-domain [interpolate]` |
| Context: | server config, virtual host, directory |
| Status: | Extension |
| Module: | mod_proxy |

Usage is basically similar to PROXYPASSREVERSE, but instead of rewriting headers that are a URL, this rewrites the `domain` string in `Set-Cookie` headers.

## ProxyPassReverseCookiePath Directive

| | |
|---|---|
| Description: | Adjusts the Path string in Set-Cookie headers from a reverse- proxied server |
| Syntax: | `ProxyPassReverseCookiePath internal-path public-path [interpolate]` |
| Context: | server config, virtual host, directory |
| Status: | Extension |
| Module: | mod_proxy |

Useful in conjunction with PROXYPASSREVERSE in situations where backend URL paths are mapped to public paths on the reverse proxy. This directive rewrites the `path` string in `Set-Cookie` headers. If the beginning of the cookie path matches *internal-path*, the cookie path will be replaced with *public-path*.

In the example given with PROXYPASSREVERSE, the directive:

```
ProxyPassReverseCookiePath  "/"  "/mirror/foo/"
```

will rewrite a cookie with backend path `/` (or `/example` or, in fact, anything) to `/mirror/foo/`.

## ProxyPreserveHost Directive

| | |
|---|---|
| Description: | Use incoming Host HTTP request header for proxy request |
| Syntax: | `ProxyPreserveHost On\|Off` |
| Default: | `ProxyPreserveHost Off` |
| Context: | server config, virtual host, directory |
| Status: | Extension |
| Module: | mod_proxy |
| Compatibility: | Usable in directory context in 2.3.3 and later. |

When enabled, this option will pass the Host: line from the incoming request to the proxied host, instead of the hostname specified in the PROXYPASS line.

This option should normally be turned `Off`. It is mostly useful in special configurations like proxied mass name-based virtual hosting, where the original Host header needs to be evaluated by the backend server.

## ProxyReceiveBufferSize Directive

| | |
|---|---|
| Description: | Network buffer size for proxied HTTP and FTP connections |
| Syntax: | `ProxyReceiveBufferSize bytes` |
| Default: | `ProxyReceiveBufferSize 0` |
| Context: | server config, virtual host |
| Status: | Extension |
| Module: | mod_proxy |

The PROXYRECEIVEBUFFERSIZE directive specifies an explicit (TCP/IP) network buffer size for proxied HTTP and FTP connections, for increased throughput. It has to be greater than `512` or set to `0` to indicate that the system's default buffer size should be used.

### Example

```
ProxyReceiveBufferSize 2048
```

## ProxyRemote Directive

| | |
|---|---|
| Description: | Remote proxy used to handle certain requests |
| Syntax: | `ProxyRemote match remote-server` |
| Context: | server config, virtual host |
| Status: | Extension |
| Module: | mod_proxy |

This defines remote proxies to this proxy. *match* is either the name of a URL-scheme that the remote server supports, or a partial URL for which the remote server should be used, or * to indicate the server should be contacted for all requests. *remote-server* is a partial URL for the remote server. Syntax:

```
remote-server = scheme://hostname[:port]
```

*scheme* is effectively the protocol that should be used to communicate with the remote server; only `http` and `https` are supported by this module. When using `https`, the requests are forwarded through the remote proxy using the HTTP CONNECT method.

**Example**

```
ProxyRemote http://goodguys.example.com/ http://mirrorguys.example.com:8000
ProxyRemote * http://cleverproxy.localdomain
ProxyRemote ftp http://ftpproxy.mydomain:8080
```

In the last example, the proxy will forward FTP requests, encapsulated as yet another HTTP proxy request, to another proxy which can handle them.

This option also supports reverse proxy configuration; a backend webserver can be embedded within a virtualhost URL space even if that server is hidden by another forward proxy.

## ProxyRemoteMatch Directive

| | |
|---|---|
| Description: | Remote proxy used to handle requests matched by regular expressions |
| Syntax: | `ProxyRemoteMatch regex remote-server` |
| Context: | server config, virtual host |
| Status: | Extension |
| Module: | mod_proxy |

The PROXYREMOTEMATCH is identical to the PROXYREMOTE directive, except that the first argument is a regular expression match against the requested URL.

## ProxyRequests Directive

| | |
|---|---|
| Description: | Enables forward (standard) proxy requests |
| Syntax: | `ProxyRequests On|Off` |
| Default: | `ProxyRequests Off` |
| Context: | server config, virtual host |
| Status: | Extension |
| Module: | mod_proxy |

This allows or prevents Apache httpd from functioning as a forward proxy server. (Setting ProxyRequests to `Off` does not disable use of the PROXYPASS directive.)

In a typical reverse proxy or gateway configuration, this option should be set to `Off`.

In order to get the functionality of proxying HTTP or FTP sites, you need also MOD_PROXY_HTTP or MOD_PROXY_FTP (or both) present in the server.

In order to get the functionality of (forward) proxying HTTPS sites, you need MOD_PROXY_CONNECT enabled in the server.

 **Warning**

Do not enable proxying with PROXYREQUESTS until you have secured your server.  Open proxy servers are dangerous both to your network and to the Internet at large.

**See also**

- Forward and Reverse Proxies/Gateways

## ProxySet Directive

| Description: | Set various Proxy balancer or member parameters |
| --- | --- |
| Syntax: | `ProxySet url key=value [key=value ...]` |
| Context: | directory |
| Status: | Extension |
| Module: | mod_proxy |

This directive is used as an alternate method of setting any of the parameters available to Proxy balancers and workers normally done via the PROXYPASS directive. If used within a `<Proxy balancer url|worker url>` container directive, the *url* argument is not required. As a side effect the respective balancer or worker gets created. This can be useful when doing reverse proxying via a REWRITERULE instead of a PROXYPASS directive.

```
<Proxy balancer://hotcluster>
    BalancerMember http://www2.example.com:8080 loadfactor=1
    BalancerMember http://www3.example.com:8080 loadfactor=2
    ProxySet lbmethod=bytraffic
</Proxy>
```

```
<Proxy http://backend>
    ProxySet keepalive=On
</Proxy>
```

```
ProxySet balancer://foo lbmethod=bytraffic timeout=15
```

```
ProxySet ajp://backend:7001 timeout=15
```

> ⚠ **Warning**
>
> Keep in mind that the same parameter key can have a different meaning depending whether it is applied to a balancer or a worker, as shown by the two examples above regarding timeout.

## ProxySourceAddress Directive

| Description: | Set local IP address for outgoing proxy connections |
| --- | --- |
| Syntax: | `ProxySourceAddress address` |
| Context: | server config, virtual host |
| Status: | Extension |
| Module: | mod_proxy |
| Compatibility: | Available in version 2.3.9 and later |

This directive allows to set a specific local address to bind to when connecting to a backend server.

## ProxyStatus Directive

| Description: | Show Proxy LoadBalancer status in mod_status |
| --- | --- |
| Syntax: | `ProxyStatus Off|On|Full` |
| Default: | `ProxyStatus Off` |
| Context: | server config, virtual host |
| Status: | Extension |
| Module: | mod_proxy |

This directive determines whether or not proxy loadbalancer status data is displayed via the MOD_STATUS server-status page.

Note
**Full** is synonymous with **On**

## ProxyTimeout Directive

| | |
|---|---|
| Description: | Network timeout for proxied requests |
| Syntax: | `ProxyTimeout seconds` |
| Default: | `Value of TIMEOUT` |
| Context: | server config, virtual host |
| Status: | Extension |
| Module: | mod_proxy |

This directive allows a user to specifiy a timeout on proxy requests. This is useful when you have a slow/buggy appserver which hangs, and you would rather just return a timeout and fail gracefully instead of waiting however long it takes the server to return.

## ProxyVia Directive

| | |
|---|---|
| Description: | Information provided in the `Via` HTTP response header for proxied requests |
| Syntax: | `ProxyVia On|Off|Full|Block` |
| Default: | `ProxyVia Off` |
| Context: | server config, virtual host |
| Status: | Extension |
| Module: | mod_proxy |

This directive controls the use of the `Via:` HTTP header by the proxy. Its intended use is to control the flow of proxy requests along a chain of proxy servers. See RFC 2616[68] (HTTP/1.1), section 14.45 for an explanation of `Via:` header lines.

- If set to `Off`, which is the default, no special processing is performed. If a request or reply contains a `Via:` header, it is passed through unchanged.

- If set to `On`, each request and reply will get a `Via:` header line added for the current host.

- If set to `Full`, each generated `Via:` header line will additionally have the Apache httpd server version shown as a `Via:` comment field.

- If set to `Block`, every proxy request will have all its `Via:` header lines removed. No new `Via:` header will be generated.

---

[68]http://www.ietf.org/rfc/rfc2616.txt

## 10.82   Apache Module mod_proxy_ajp

| | |
|---|---|
| Description: | AJP support module for MOD_PROXY |
| Status: | Extension |
| ModuleIdentifier: | proxy_ajp_module |
| SourceFile: | mod_proxy_ajp.c |

### Summary

This module *requires* the service of MOD_PROXY. It provides support for the Apache JServ Protocol version 1.3 (hereafter *AJP13*).

Thus, in order to get the ability of handling AJP13 protocol, MOD_PROXY and MOD_PROXY_AJP have to be present in the server.

 **Warning**
Do not enable proxying until you have secured your server (p. 787) . Open proxy servers are dangerous both to your network and to the Internet at large.

**Directives** This module provides no directives.

**See also**

- MOD_PROXY

- Environment Variable documentation (p. 92)

### Usage

This module is used to reverse proxy to a backend application server (e.g. Apache Tomcat) using the AJP13 protocol. The usage is similar to an HTTP reverse proxy, but uses the ajp:// prefix:

#### Simple Reverse Proxy

```
ProxyPass "/app" "ajp://backend.example.com:8009/app"
```

Balancers may also be used:

#### Balancer Reverse Proxy

```
<Proxy balancer://cluster>
    BalancerMember ajp://app1.example.com:8009 loadfactor=1
    BalancerMember ajp://app2.example.com:8009 loadfactor=2
    ProxySet lbmethod=bytraffic
</Proxy>
ProxyPass "/app" "balancer://cluster/app"
```

Note that usually no PROXYPASSREVERSE directive is necessary. The AJP request includes the original host header given to the proxy, and the application server can be expected to generate self-referential headers relative to this host, so no rewriting is necessary.

The main exception is when the URL path on the proxy differs from that on the backend. In this case, a redirect header can be rewritten relative to the original host URL (not the backend ajp:// URL), for example:

### Rewriting Proxied Path

```
ProxyPass "/apps/foo" "ajp://backend.example.com:8009/foo"
ProxyPassReverse "/apps/foo" "http://www.example.com/foo"
```

However, it is usually better to deploy the application on the backend server at the same path as the proxy rather than to take this approach.

## Environment Variables

Environment variables whose names have the prefix AJP_ are forwarded to the origin server as AJP request attributes (with the AJP_ prefix removed from the name of the key).

## Overview of the protocol

The AJP13 protocol is packet-oriented. A binary format was presumably chosen over the more readable plain text for reasons of performance. The web server communicates with the servlet container over TCP connections. To cut down on the expensive process of socket creation, the web server will attempt to maintain persistent TCP connections to the servlet container, and to reuse a connection for multiple request/response cycles.

Once a connection is assigned to a particular request, it will not be used for any others until the request-handling cycle has terminated. In other words, requests are not multiplexed over connections. This makes for much simpler code at either end of the connection, although it does cause more connections to be open at once.

Once the web server has opened a connection to the servlet container, the connection can be in one of the following states:

- Idle
  No request is being handled over this connection.

- Assigned
  The connection is handling a specific request.

Once a connection is assigned to handle a particular request, the basic request information (e.g. HTTP headers, etc) is sent over the connection in a highly condensed form (e.g. common strings are encoded as integers). Details of that format are below in Request Packet Structure. If there is a body to the request (content-length > 0), that is sent in a separate packet immediately after.

At this point, the servlet container is presumably ready to start processing the request. As it does so, it can send the following messages back to the web server:

- SEND_HEADERS
  Send a set of headers back to the browser.

- SEND_BODY_CHUNK
  Send a chunk of body data back to the browser.

- GET_BODY_CHUNK
  Get further data from the request if it hasn't all been transferred yet. This is necessary because the packets have a fixed maximum size and arbitrary amounts of data can be included the body of a request (for uploaded files, for example). (Note: this is unrelated to HTTP chunked transfer).

- END_RESPONSE
  Finish the request-handling cycle.

Each message is accompanied by a differently formatted packet of data. See Response Packet Structures below for details.

## Basic Packet Structure

There is a bit of an XDR heritage to this protocol, but it differs in lots of ways (no 4 byte alignment, for example).

AJP13 uses network byte order for all data types.

There are four data types in the protocol: bytes, booleans, integers and strings.

**Byte** A single byte.

**Boolean** A single byte, `1 = true`, `0 = false`. Using other non-zero values as true (i.e. C-style) may work in some places, but it won't in others.

**Integer** A number in the range of `0 to 2^16 (32768)`. Stored in 2 bytes with the high-order byte first.

**String** A variable-sized string (length bounded by $2^{16}$). Encoded with the length packed into two bytes first, followed by the string (including the terminating '\0'). Note that the encoded length does **not** include the trailing '\0' – it is like `strlen`. This is a touch confusing on the Java side, which is littered with odd autoincrement statements to skip over these terminators. I believe the reason this was done was to allow the C code to be extra efficient when reading strings which the servlet container is sending back – with the terminating \0 character, the C code can pass around references into a single buffer, without copying. if the \0 was missing, the C code would have to copy things out in order to get its notion of a string.

### Packet Size

According to much of the code, the max packet size is `8 * 1024 bytes (8K)`. The actual length of the packet is encoded in the header.

### Packet Headers

Packets sent from the server to the container begin with `0x1234`. Packets sent from the container to the server begin with `AB` (that's the ASCII code for A followed by the ASCII code for B). After those first two bytes, there is an integer (encoded as above) with the length of the payload. Although this might suggest that the maximum payload could be as large as $2^{16}$, in fact, the code sets the maximum to be 8K.

| *Packet Format (Server->Container)* | | | | | |
|---|---|---|---|---|---|
| **Byte** | 0 | 1 | 2 | 3 | 4...(n+3) |
| **Contents** | 0x12 | 0x34 | Data Length (n) | Data | |

| *Packet Format (Container->Server)* | | | | | |
|---|---|---|---|---|---|
| **Byte** | 0 | 1 | 2 | 3 | 4...(n+3) |
| **Contents** | A | B | Data Length (n) | Data | |

For most packets, the first byte of the payload encodes the type of message. The exception is for request body packets sent from the server to the container – they are sent with a standard packet header ( `0x1234` and then length of the packet), but without any prefix code after that.

The web server can send the following messages to the servlet container:

| Code | Type of Packet | Meaning |
|------|----------------|---------|
| 2 | Forward Request | Begin the request-processing cycle with the following data |
| 7 | Shutdown | The web server asks the container to shut itself down. |
| 8 | Ping | The web server asks the container to take control (secure login phase). |
| 10 | CPing | The web server asks the container to respond quickly with a CPong. |
| none | Data | Size (2 bytes) and corresponding body data. |

To ensure some basic security, the container will only actually do the `Shutdown` if the request comes from the same machine on which it's hosted.

The first `Data` packet is send immediately after the `Forward Request` by the web server.

The servlet container can send the following types of messages to the webserver:

| Code | Type of Packet | Meaning |
|------|----------------|---------|
| 3 | Send Body Chunk | Send a chunk of the body from the servlet container to the web server (and presumably, onto the browser). |
| 4 | Send Headers | Send the response headers from the servlet container to the web server (and presumably, onto the browser). |
| 5 | End Response | Marks the end of the response (and thus the request-handling cycle). |
| 6 | Get Body Chunk | Get further data from the request if it hasn't all been transferred yet. |
| 9 | CPong Reply | The reply to a CPing request |

Each of the above messages has a different internal structure, detailed below.

## Request Packet Structure

For messages from the server to the container of type *Forward Request*:

```
AJP13_FORWARD_REQUEST :=
    prefix_code      (byte) 0x02 = JK_AJP13_FORWARD_REQUEST
    method           (byte)
    protocol         (string)
    req_uri          (string)
    remote_addr      (string)
    remote_host      (string)
    server_name      (string)
    server_port      (integer)
    is_ssl           (boolean)
    num_headers      (integer)
    request_headers *(req_header_name req_header_value)
    attributes      *(attribut_name attribute_value)
    request_terminator (byte) 0xFF
```

The `request_headers` have the following structure:

```
req_header_name :=
    sc_req_header_name | (string)  [see below for how this is parsed]

sc_req_header_name := 0xA0xx (integer)

req_header_value := (string)
```

The `attributes` are optional and have the following structure:

```
attribute_name := sc_a_name | (sc_a_req_attribute string)

attribute_value := (string)
```

Not that the all-important header is `content-length`, because it determines whether or not the container looks for another packet immediately.

**Detailed description of the elements of Forward Request**

**Request prefix**

For all requests, this will be 2. See above for details on other Prefix codes.

**Method**

The HTTP method, encoded as a single byte:

| Command Name | Code |
|---|---|
| OPTIONS | 1 |
| GET | 2 |
| HEAD | 3 |
| POST | 4 |
| PUT | 5 |
| DELETE | 6 |
| TRACE | 7 |
| PROPFIND | 8 |
| PROPPATCH | 9 |
| MKCOL | 10 |
| COPY | 11 |
| MOVE | 12 |
| LOCK | 13 |
| UNLOCK | 14 |
| ACL | 15 |
| REPORT | 16 |
| VERSION-CONTROL | 17 |
| CHECKIN | 18 |
| CHECKOUT | 19 |
| UNCHECKOUT | 20 |
| SEARCH | 21 |
| MKWORKSPACE | 22 |
| UPDATE | 23 |
| LABEL | 24 |
| MERGE | 25 |
| BASELINE_CONTROL | 26 |
| MKACTIVITY | 27 |

Later version of ajp13, will transport additional methods, even if they are not in this list.

**protocol, req_uri, remote_addr, remote_host, server_name, server_port, is_ssl**

These are all fairly self-explanatory. Each of these is required, and will be sent for every request.

### Headers

The structure of `request_headers` is the following: First, the number of headers `num_headers` is encoded. Then, a series of header name `req_header_name` / value `req_header_value` pairs follows. Common header names are encoded as integers, to save space. If the header name is not in the list of basic headers, it is encoded normally (as a string, with prefixed length). The list of common headers `sc_req_header_name` and their codes is as follows (all are case-sensitive):

| Name | Code value | Code name |
|---|---|---|
| accept | 0xA001 | SC_REQ_ACCEPT |
| accept-charset | 0xA002 | SC_REQ_ACCEPT_CHARSET |
| accept-encoding | 0xA003 | SC_REQ_ACCEPT_ENCODING |
| accept-language | 0xA004 | SC_REQ_ACCEPT_LANGUAGE |
| authorization | 0xA005 | SC_REQ_AUTHORIZATION |
| connection | 0xA006 | SC_REQ_CONNECTION |
| content-type | 0xA007 | SC_REQ_CONTENT_TYPE |
| content-length | 0xA008 | SC_REQ_CONTENT_LENGTH |
| cookie | 0xA009 | SC_REQ_COOKIE |
| cookie2 | 0xA00A | SC_REQ_COOKIE2 |
| host | 0xA00B | SC_REQ_HOST |
| pragma | 0xA00C | SC_REQ_PRAGMA |
| referer | 0xA00D | SC_REQ_REFERER |
| user-agent | 0xA00E | SC_REQ_USER_AGENT |

The Java code that reads this grabs the first two-byte integer and if it sees an '0xA0' in the most significant byte, it uses the integer in the second byte as an index into an array of header names. If the first byte is not 0xA0, it assumes that the two-byte integer is the length of a string, which is then read in.

This works on the assumption that no header names will have length greater than 0x9FFF (==0xA000 - 1), which is perfectly reasonable, though somewhat arbitrary.

**Note:**
> The `content-length` header is extremely important. If it is present and non-zero, the container assumes that the request has a body (a POST request, for example), and immediately reads a separate packet off the input stream to get that body.

### Attributes

The attributes prefixed with a ? (e.g. `?context`) are all optional. For each, there is a single byte code to indicate the type of attribute, and then its value (string or integer). They can be sent in any order (though the C code always sends them in the order listed below). A special terminating code is sent to signal the end of the list of optional attributes. The list of byte codes is:

| Information | Code Value | Type Of Value | Note |
|---|---|---|---|
| ?context | 0x01 | - | Not currently implemented |
| ?servlet_path | 0x02 | - | Not currently implemented |
| ?remote_user | 0x03 | String | |
| ?auth_type | 0x04 | String | |
| ?query_string | 0x05 | String | |
| ?jvm_route | 0x06 | String | |
| ?ssl_cert | 0x07 | String | |
| ?ssl_cipher | 0x08 | String | |
| ?ssl_session | 0x09 | String | |
| ?req_attribute | 0x0A | String | Name (the name of the attribute follows) |
| ?ssl_key_size | 0x0B | Integer | |
| are_done | 0xFF | - | request_terminator |

The `context` and `servlet_path` are not currently set by the C code, and most of the Java code completely ignores whatever is sent over for those fields (and some of it will actually break if a string is sent along after one of those codes). I don't know if this is a bug or an unimplemented feature or just vestigial code, but it's missing from both sides of the connection.

The `remote_user` and `auth_type` presumably refer to HTTP-level authentication, and communicate the remote user's username and the type of authentication used to establish their identity (e.g. Basic, Digest).

The `query_string`, `ssl_cert`, `ssl_cipher`, and `ssl_session` refer to the corresponding pieces of HTTP and HTTPS.

The `jvm_route`, is used to support sticky sessions – associating a user's sesson with a particular Tomcat instance in the presence of multiple, load-balancing servers.

Beyond this list of basic attributes, any number of other attributes can be sent via the `req_attribute` code `0x0A`. A pair of strings to represent the attribute name and value are sent immediately after each instance of that code. Environment values are passed in via this method.

Finally, after all the attributes have been sent, the attribute terminator, `0xFF`, is sent. This signals both the end of the list of attributes and also then end of the Request Packet.

## Response Packet Structure

for messages which the container can send back to the server.

```
AJP13_SEND_BODY_CHUNK :=
  prefix_code   3
  chunk_length  (integer)
  chunk         *(byte)
  chunk_terminator (byte) 0x00


AJP13_SEND_HEADERS :=
  prefix_code      4
  http_status_code  (integer)
  http_status_msg   (string)
  num_headers       (integer)
  response_headers *(res_header_name header_value)

res_header_name :=
    sc_res_header_name | (string)   [see below for how this is parsed]

sc_res_header_name := 0xA0 (byte)

header_value := (string)

AJP13_END_RESPONSE :=
  prefix_code      5
  reuse            (boolean)


AJP13_GET_BODY_CHUNK :=
  prefix_code      6
  requested_length  (integer)
```

**Details:**

**Send Body Chunk**

The chunk is basically binary data, and is sent directly back to the browser.

**Send Headers**

The status code and message are the usual HTTP things (e.g. 200 and OK). The response header names are encoded the same way the request header names are. See header_encoding above for details about how the codes are distinguished from the strings.
The codes for common headers are:

| Name | Code value |
|------|------------|
| Content-Type | 0xA001 |
| Content-Language | 0xA002 |
| Content-Length | 0xA003 |
| Date | 0xA004 |
| Last-Modified | 0xA005 |
| Location | 0xA006 |
| Set-Cookie | 0xA007 |
| Set-Cookie2 | 0xA008 |
| Servlet-Engine | 0xA009 |
| Status | 0xA00A |
| WWW-Authenticate | 0xA00B |

After the code or the string header name, the header value is immediately encoded.

**End Response**

Signals the end of this request-handling cycle. If the `reuse` flag is true (`anything other than 0 in the actual C code`), this TCP connection can now be used to handle new incoming requests. If `reuse` is false (==0), the connection should be closed.

**Get Body Chunk**

The container asks for more data from the request (If the body was too large to fit in the first packet sent over or when the request is chunked). The server will send a body packet back with an amount of data which is the minimum of the `request_length`, the maximum send body size (`8186 (8 Kbytes - 6)`), and the number of bytes actually left to send from the request body.

If there is no more data in the body (i.e. the servlet container is trying to read past the end of the body), the server will send back an *empty* packet, which is a body packet with a payload length of 0. (`0x12,0x34,0x00,0x00`)

# 10.83   Apache Module mod_proxy_balancer

| | |
|---|---|
| Description: | MOD_PROXY extension for load balancing |
| Status: | Extension |
| ModuleIdentifier: | proxy_balancer_module |
| SourceFile: | mod_proxy_balancer.c |

## Summary

This module *requires* the service of MOD_PROXY and it provides load balancing for all the supported protocols. The most important ones are:

- HTTP, using MOD_PROXY_HTTP

- FTP, using MOD_PROXY_FTP

- AJP13, using MOD_PROXY_AJP

- WebSocket, using MOD_PROXY_WSTUNNEL

The Load balancing scheduler algorithm is not provided by this module but from other ones such as:

- MOD_LBMETHOD_BYREQUESTS

- MOD_LBMETHOD_BYTRAFFIC

- MOD_LBMETHOD_BYBUSYNESS

- MOD_LBMETHOD_HEARTBEAT

Thus, in order to get the ability of load balancing, MOD_PROXY, MOD_PROXY_BALANCER and at least one of load balancing scheduler algorithm modules have to be present in the server.

 **Warning**
Do not enable proxying until you have secured your server (p. 787) . Open proxy servers are dangerous both to your network and to the Internet at large.

**Directives** This module provides no directives.

**See also**

- MOD_PROXY

## Load balancer scheduler algorithm

At present, there are 3 load balancer scheduler algorithms available for use: Request Counting, Weighted Traffic Counting and Pending Request Counting. These are controlled via the lbmethod value of the Balancer definition. See the PROXYPASS directive for more information, especially regarding how to configure the Balancer and Balancer-Members.

## Load balancer stickyness

The balancer supports stickyness. When a request is proxied to some back-end, then all following requests from the same user should be proxied to the same back-end. Many load balancers implement this feature via a table that maps client IP addresses to back-ends. This approach is transparent to clients and back-ends, but suffers from some problems: unequal load distribution if clients are themselves hidden behind proxies, stickyness errors when a client uses a dynamic IP address that changes during a session and loss of stickyness, if the mapping table overflows.

The module MOD_PROXY_BALANCER implements stickyness on top of two alternative means: cookies and URL encoding. Providing the cookie can be either done by the back-end or by the Apache web server itself. The URL encoding is usually done on the back-end.

## Examples of a balancer configuration

Before we dive into the technical details, here's an example of how you might use MOD_PROXY_BALANCER to provide load balancing between two back-end servers:

```
<Proxy balancer://mycluster>
    BalancerMember http://192.168.1.50:80
    BalancerMember http://192.168.1.51:80
</Proxy>
ProxyPass        "/test" "balancer://mycluster"
ProxyPassReverse "/test" "balancer://mycluster"
```

Another example of how to provide load balancing with stickyness using MOD_HEADERS, even if the back-end server does not set a suitable session cookie:

```
Header add Set-Cookie "ROUTEID=.%{BALANCER_WORKER_ROUTE}e; path=/" env=BALANCER_ROUTE
<Proxy balancer://mycluster>
    BalancerMember http://192.168.1.50:80 route=1
    BalancerMember http://192.168.1.51:80 route=2
    ProxySet stickysession=ROUTEID
</Proxy>
ProxyPass        "/test" "balancer://mycluster"
ProxyPassReverse "/test" "balancer://mycluster"
```

## Exported Environment Variables

At present there are 6 environment variables exported:

**BALANCER_SESSION_STICKY** This is assigned the *stickysession* value used for the current request. It is the name of the cookie or request parameter used for sticky sessions

**BALANCER_SESSION_ROUTE** This is assigned the *route* parsed from the current request.

**BALANCER_NAME** This is assigned the name of the balancer used for the current request. The value is something like `balancer://foo`.

**BALANCER_WORKER_NAME** This is assigned the name of the worker used for the current request. The value is something like `http://hostA:1234`.

**BALANCER_WORKER_ROUTE** This is assigned the *route* of the worker that will be used for the current request.

***BALANCER_ROUTE_CHANGED*** This is set to 1 if the session route does not match the worker route (BAL-ANCER_SESSION_ROUTE != BALANCER_WORKER_ROUTE) or the session does not yet have an estab-lished route. This can be used to determine when/if the client needs to be sent an updated route when sticky sessions are used.

## Enabling Balancer Manager Support

This module *requires* the service of MOD_STATUS. Balancer manager enables dynamic update of balancer members. You can use balancer manager to change the balance factor of a particular member, or put it in the off line mode.

Thus, in order to get the ability of load balancer management, MOD_STATUS and MOD_PROXY_BALANCER have to be present in the server.

To enable load balancer management for browsers from the example.com domain add this code to your `httpd.conf` configuration file

```
<Location "/balancer-manager">
    SetHandler balancer-manager
    Require host example.com
</Location>
```

You can now access load balancer manager by using a Web browser to access the page `http://your.server.name/balancer-manager`. Please note that only Balancers defined outside of `<Location ...>` containers can be dynamically controlled by the Manager.

## Details on load balancer stickyness

When using cookie based stickyness, you need to configure the name of the cookie that contains the information about which back-end to use. This is done via the *stickysession* attribute added to either PROXYPASS or PROXYSET. The name of the cookie is case-sensitive. The balancer extracts the value of the cookie and looks for a member worker with *route* equal to that value. The *route* must also be set in either PROXYPASS or PROXYSET. The cookie can either be set by the back-end, or as shown in the above example by the Apache web server itself.

Some back-ends use a slightly different form of stickyness cookie, for instance Apache Tomcat. Tomcat adds the name of the Tomcat instance to the end of its session id cookie, separated with a dot (.) from the session id. Thus if the Apache web server finds a dot in the value of the stickyness cookie, it only uses the part behind the dot to search for the route. In order to let Tomcat know about its instance name, you need to set the attribute `jvmRoute` inside the Tomcat configuration file `conf/server.xml` to the value of the *route* of the worker that connects to the respective Tomcat. The name of the session cookie used by Tomcat (and more generally by Java web applications based on servlets) is `JSESSIONID` (upper case) but can be configured to something else.

The second way of implementing stickyness is URL encoding. The web server searches for a query parameter in the URL of the request. The name of the parameter is specified again using *stickysession*. The value of the parameter is used to lookup a member worker with *route* equal to that value. Since it is not easy to extract and manipulate all URL links contained in responses, generally the work of adding the parameters to each link is done by the back-end generating the content. In some cases it might be feasible doing this via the web server using MOD_SUBSTITUTE or MOD_SED. This can have negative impact on performance though.

The Java standards implement URL encoding slightly different. They use a path info appended to the URL using a semicolon (;) as the separator and add the session id behind. As in the cookie case, Apache Tomcat can include the configured `jvmRoute` in this path info. To let Apache find this sort of path info, you neet to set `scolonpathdelim` to On in PROXYPASS or PROXYSET.

Finally you can support cookies and URL encoding at the same time, by configuring the name of the cookie and the name of the URL parameter separated by a vertical bar (|) as in the following example:

```
ProxyPass "/test" "balancer://mycluster" stickysession=JSESSIONID|jsessionid scolonp
<Proxy balancer://mycluster>
    BalancerMember http://192.168.1.50:80 route=node1
    BalancerMember http://192.168.1.51:80 route=node2
</Proxy>
```

If the cookie and the request parameter both provide routing information for the same request, the information from the request parameter is used.

### Troubleshooting load balancer stickyness

If you experience stickyness errors, e.g. users lose their application sessions and need to login again, you first want to check whether this is because the back-ends are sometimes unavailable or whether your configuration is wrong. To find out about possible stability problems with the back-ends, check your Apache error log for proxy error messages.

To verify your configuration, first check, whether the stickyness is based on a cookie or on URL encoding. Next step would be logging the appropriate data in the access log by using an enhanced LogFormat. The following fields are useful:

`%{MYCOOKIE}C` The value contained in the cookie with name `MYCOOKIE`. The name should be the same given in the *stickysession* attribute.

`%{Set-Cookie}o` This logs any cookie set by the back-end. You can track, whether the back-end sets the session cookie you expect, and to which value it is set.

`%{BALANCER_SESSION_STICKY}e` The name of the cookie or request parameter used to lookup the routing information.

`%{BALANCER_SESSION_ROUTE}e` The route information found in the request.

`%{BALANCER_WORKER_ROUTE}e` The route of the worker chosen.

`%{BALANCER_ROUTE_CHANGED}e` Set to `1` if the route in the request is different from the route of the worker, i.e. the request couldn't be handled sticky.

Common reasons for loss of session are session timeouts, which are usually configurable on the back-end server.

The balancer also logs detailed information about handling stickyness to the error log, if the log level is set to `debug` or higher. This is an easy way to troubleshoot stickyness problems, but the log volume might be to high for production servers under high load.

# 10.84    Apache Module mod_proxy_connect

| | |
|---|---|
| Description: | MOD_PROXY extension for CONNECT request handling |
| Status: | Extension |
| ModuleIdentifier: | proxy_connect_module |
| SourceFile: | mod_proxy_connect.c |

## Summary

This module *requires* the service of MOD_PROXY. It provides support for the CONNECT HTTP method. This method is mainly used to tunnel SSL requests through proxy servers.

Thus, in order to get the ability of handling CONNECT requests, MOD_PROXY and MOD_PROXY_CONNECT have to be present in the server.

CONNECT is also used when the server needs to send an HTTPS request through a forward proxy. In this case the server acts as a CONNECT client. This functionality is part of MOD_PROXY and MOD_PROXY_CONNECT is not needed in this case.

 **Warning**

Do not enable proxying until you have secured your server (p. 787) . Open proxy servers are dangerous both to your network and to the Internet at large.

### Directives

- AllowCONNECT

### See also

- MOD_PROXY

## Request notes

MOD_PROXY_CONNECT creates the following request notes for logging using the %{VARNAME}n format in LOGFOR-MAT or ERRORLOGFORMAT:

**proxy-source-port** The local port used for the connection to the backend server.

CONNECT method requests are controlled by the PROXY block as any other HTTP request going through.  SSL connections through a proxy may be filtered explicitly by specifying the target host and port, for instance:

```
<Proxy www.example.com:443>
  Require ip 192.168.0.0/16
</Proxy>
```

## AllowCONNECT Directive

| | |
|---|---|
| Description: | Ports that are allowed to CONNECT through the proxy |
| Syntax: | AllowCONNECT port[-port] [port[-port]] ... |
| Default: | AllowCONNECT 443 563 |
| Context: | server config, virtual host |
| Status: | Extension |
| Module: | mod_proxy_connect |
| Compatibility: | Moved from MOD_PROXY in Apache 2.3.5. Port ranges available since Apache 2.3.7. |

The ALLOWCONNECT directive specifies a list of port numbers or ranges to which the proxy CONNECT method may connect. Today's browsers use this method when a https connection is requested and proxy tunneling over HTTP is in effect.

By default, only the default https port (443) and the default snews port (563) are enabled. Use the ALLOWCON-NECT directive to override this default and allow connections to the listed ports only.

# 10.85   Apache Module mod_proxy_express

| Description: | Dynamic mass reverse proxy extension for MOD_PROXY |
|---|---|
| Status: | Extension |
| ModuleIdentifier: | proxy_express_module |
| SourceFile: | mod_proxy_express.c |

## Summary

This module creates dynamically configured mass reverse proxies, by mapping the Host: header of the HTTP request to a server name and backend URL stored in a DBM file. This allows for easy use of a huge number of reverse proxies with no configuration changes. It is much less feature-full than MOD_PROXY_BALANCER, which also provides dynamic growth, but is intended to handle much, much larger numbers of backends. It is ideally suited as a front-end HTTP switch.

This module *requires* the service of MOD_PROXY.

 **Warning**

Do not enable proxying until you have secured your server (p. 787) . Open proxy servers are dangerous both to your network and to the Internet at large.

Limitations

- This module is not intended to replace the dynamic capability of MOD_PROXY_BALANCER. Instead, it is intended to be mostly a lightweight and fast alternative to using MOD_REWRITE with REWRITEMAP and the [P] flag for mapped reverse proxying.

- It does not support regex or pattern matching at all.

- It emulates:

```
<VirtualHost *:80>
   ServerName front.end.server
   ProxyPass        "/" "back.end.server:port"
   ProxyPassReverse "/" "back.end.server:port"
</VirtualHost>
```

That is, the entire URL is appended to the mapped backend URL. This is in keeping with the intent of being a simple but fast reverse proxy switch.

## Directives

- ProxyExpressDBMFile

- ProxyExpressDBMType

- ProxyExpressEnable

## See also

- MOD_PROXY

### ProxyExpressDBMFile Directive

| | |
|---|---|
| Description: | Pathname to DBM file. |
| Syntax: | `ProxyExpressDBMFile <pathname>` |
| Default: | `None` |
| Context: | server config, virtual host |
| Status: | Extension |
| Module: | mod_proxy_express |
| Compatibility: | Available in Apache 2.3.13 and later |

The PROXYEXPRESSDBMFILE directive points to the location of the Express map DBM file. This file serves to map the incoming server name, obtained from the Host: header, to a backend URL.

Note

> The file is constructed from a plain text file format using the `httxt2dbm` (p. 328) utility.

---

**ProxyExpress map file**
```
##
##express-map.txt:
##
www1.example.com http://192.168.211.2:8080
www2.example.com http://192.168.211.12:8088
www3.example.com http://192.168.212.10
```

---

**Create DBM file**
```
httxt2dbm -i express-map.txt -o emap
```

---

**Configuration**
```
ProxyExpressEnable on
ProxyExpressDBMFile emap
```

---

### ProxyExpressDBMType Directive

| | |
|---|---|
| Description: | DBM type of file. |
| Syntax: | `ProxyExpressDBMFile <type>` |
| Default: | `"default"` |
| Context: | server config, virtual host |
| Status: | Extension |
| Module: | mod_proxy_express |
| Compatibility: | Available in Apache 2.3.13 and later |

The PROXYEXPRESSDBMTYPE directive controls the DBM type expected by the module. The default is the default DBM type created with `httxt2dbm` (p. 328) .

Possible values are (not all may be available at run time):

| Value | Description |
|-------|-------------|
| db | Berkeley DB files |
| gdbm | GDBM files |
| ndbm | NDBM files |
| sdbm | SDBM files (always available) |
| default | default DBM type |

## ProxyExpressEnable Directive

| | |
|---|---|
| Description: | Enable the module functionality. |
| Syntax: | ProxyExpressEnable [on\|off] |
| Default: | off |
| Context: | server config, virtual host |
| Status: | Extension |
| Module: | mod_proxy_express |
| Compatibility: | Available in Apache 2.3.13 and later |

The PROXYEXPRESSENABLE directive controls whether the module will be active.

# 10.86 Apache Module mod_proxy_fcgi

| | |
|---|---|
| Description: | FastCGI support module for MOD_PROXY |
| Status: | Extension |
| ModuleIdentifier: | proxy_fcgi_module |
| SourceFile: | mod_proxy_fcgi.c |
| Compatibility: | Available in version 2.3 and later |

## Summary

This module *requires* the service of MOD_PROXY. It provides support for the FastCGI[69] protocol.

Thus, in order to get the ability of handling the FastCGI protocol, MOD_PROXY and MOD_PROXY_FCGI have to be present in the server.

Unlike mod_fcgid[70] and mod_fastcgi[71], MOD_PROXY_FCGI has no provision for starting the application process; fcgistarter is provided (on some platforms) for that purpose. Alternatively, external launching or process management may be available in the FastCGI application framework in use.

 **Warning**
Do not enable proxying until you have secured your server (p. 787) . Open proxy servers are dangerous both to your network and to the Internet at large.

**Directives** This module provides no directives.

**See also**

- fcgistarter
- MOD_PROXY
- MOD_AUTHNZ_FCGI

## Examples

Remember, in order to make the following examples work, you have to enable MOD_PROXY and MOD_PROXY_FCGI.

### Single application instance

```
ProxyPass "/myapp/" "fcgi://localhost:4000/"
```

MOD_PROXY_FCGI disables connection reuse by default, so after a request has been completed the connection will NOT be held open by that httpd child process and won't be reused. If the FastCGI application is able to handle concurrent connections from httpd, you can opt-in to connection reuse as shown in the following example:

### Single application instance, connection reuse (2.4.11 and later)

```
ProxyPass "/myapp/" "fcgi://localhost:4000/" enablereuse=on
```

The following example passes the request URI as a filesystem path for the PHP-FPM daemon to run. The request URL is implicitly added to the 2nd parameter. The hostname and port following fcgi:// are where PHP-FPM is listening. Connection pooling is enabled.

---

[69]http://www.fastcgi.com/
[70]http://httpd.apache.org/mod_fcgid/
[71]http://www.fastcgi.com/

### PHP-FPM

```
ProxyPassMatch "^/myapp/.*\.php(/.*)?$" "fcgi://localhost:9000/var/www/" enablereuse=on
```

The following example passes the request URI as a filesystem path for the PHP-FPM daemon to run.  In this case, PHP-FPM is listening on a unix domain socket (UDS).  Requires 2.4.9 or later.  With this syntax, the hostname and optional port following fcgi:// are ignored.

### PHP-FPM with UDS

```
# UDS does not currently support connection reuse
ProxyPassMatch "^/(.*\.php(/.*)?)$" "unix:/var/run/php5-fpm.sock|fcgi://localhost/var/www/"
```

The balanced gateway needs MOD_PROXY_BALANCER and at least one load balancer algorithm module, such as MOD_LBMETHOD_BYREQUESTS, in addition to the proxy modules listed above.  MOD_LBMETHOD_BYREQUESTS is the default, and will be used for this example configuration.

### Balanced gateway to multiple application instances

```
ProxyPass "/myapp/" "balancer://myappcluster/"
<Proxy "balancer://myappcluster/">
    BalancerMember "fcgi://localhost:4000"
    BalancerMember "fcgi://localhost:4001"
</Proxy>
```

You can also force a request to be handled as a reverse-proxy request, by creating a suitable Handler pass-through. The example configuration below will pass all requests for PHP scripts to the specified FastCGI server using reverse proxy.  This feature is available in Apache HTTP Server 2.4.10 and later.  For performance reasons, you will want to define a worker (p. 787) representing the same fcgi:// backend.  The benefit of this form is that it allows the normal mapping of URI to filename to occur in the server, and the local filesystem result is passed to the backend.  When FastCGI is configured this way, the server can calculate the most accurate PATH_INFO.

### Proxy via Handler

```
<FilesMatch "\.php$">
    # Note: The only part that varies is /path/to/app.sock
    SetHandler  "proxy:unix:/path/to/app.sock|fcgi://localhost/"
</FilesMatch>

# Define a matching worker.
# The part that is matched to the SetHandler is the part that
# follows the pipe. If you need to distinguish, "localhost; can
# be anything unique.
<Proxy fcgi://localhost/ enablereuse=on max=10>
</Proxy>

<FilesMatch ...>
    SetHandler  "proxy:fcgi://localhost:9000"
</FilesMatch>

<FilesMatch ...>
    SetHandler  "proxy:balancer://myappcluster/"
</FilesMatch>
```

## Environment Variables

In addition to the configuration directives that control the behaviour of MOD_PROXY, there are a number of *environment variables* that control the FCGI protocol provider:

**proxy-fcgi-pathinfo** When configured via PROXYPASS or PROXYPASSMATCH, MOD_PROXY_FCGI will not set the *PATH_INFO* environment variable. This allows the backend FCGI server to correctly determine *SCRIPT_NAME* and *Script-URI* and be compliant with RFC 3875 section 3.3. If instead you need MOD_PROXY_FCGI to generate a "best guess" for *PATH_INFO*, set this env-var. This is a workaround for a bug in some FCGI implementations. This variable can be set to multiple values to tweak at how the best guess is chosen (In 2.4.11 and later only):

**first-dot** PATH_INFO is split from the slash following the *first* "." in the URL.

**last-dot** PATH_INFO is split from the slash following the *last* "." in the URL.

**full** PATH_INFO is calculated by an attempt to map the URL to the local filesystem.

**unescape** PATH_INFO is the path component of the URL, unescaped / decoded.

**any other value** PATH_INFO is the same as the path component of the URL. Originally, this was the only proxy-fcgi-pathinfo option.

# 10.87    Apache Module mod_proxy_fdpass

| Description: | fdpass external process support module for MOD_PROXY |
|---|---|
| Status: | Extension |
| ModuleIdentifier: | proxy_fdpass_module |
| SourceFile: | mod_proxy_fdpass.c |
| Compatibility: | Available for unix in version 2.3 and later |

## Summary

This module *requires* the service of MOD_PROXY. It provides support for the passing the socket of the client to another process.

mod_proxy_fdpass uses the ability of AF_UNIX domain sockets to pass an open file descriptor[72] to allow another process to finish handling a request.

The module has a proxy_fdpass_flusher provider interface, which allows another module to optionally send the response headers, or even the start of the response body. The default flush provider disables keep-alive, and sends the response headers, letting the external process just send a response body.

In order to use another provider, you have to set the flusher parameter in the PROXYPASS directive.

At this time the only data passed to the external process is the client socket. To receive a client socket, call recvfrom with an allocated struct cmsghdr[73]. Future versions of this module may include more data after the client socket, but this is not implemented at this time.

**Directives** This module provides no directives.

**See also**

- MOD_PROXY

---

[72]http://www.freebsd.org/cgi/man.cgi?query=recv
[73]http://www.kernel.org/doc/man-pages/online/pages/man3/cmsg.3.html

# 10.88 Apache Module mod_proxy_ftp

| | |
|---|---|
| Description: | FTP support module for MOD_PROXY |
| Status: | Extension |
| ModuleIdentifier: | proxy_ftp_module |
| SourceFile: | mod_proxy_ftp.c |

## Summary

This module *requires* the service of MOD_PROXY. It provides support for the proxying FTP sites. Note that FTP support is currently limited to the GET method.

Thus, in order to get the ability of handling FTP proxy requests, MOD_PROXY and MOD_PROXY_FTP have to be present in the server.

**Warning**
Do not enable proxying until you have secured your server (p. 787) . Open proxy servers are dangerous both to your network and to the Internet at large.

### Directives

- ProxyFtpDirCharset
- ProxyFtpEscapeWildcards
- ProxyFtpListOnWildcard

### See also

- MOD_PROXY

## Why doesn't file type *xxx* download via FTP?

You probably don't have that particular file type defined as `application/octet-stream` in your proxy's mime.types configuration file. A useful line can be

```
application/octet-stream   bin dms lha lzh exe class tgz taz
```

Alternatively you may prefer to default everything to binary:

```
ForceType application/octet-stream
```

## How can I force an FTP ASCII download of File *xxx*?

In the rare situation where you must download a specific file using the FTP `ASCII` transfer method (while the default transfer is in `binary` mode), you can override MOD_PROXY's default by suffixing the request with `;type=a` to force an ASCII transfer. (FTP Directory listings are always executed in ASCII mode, however.)

## How can I do FTP upload?

Currently, only GET is supported for FTP in mod_proxy. You can of course use HTTP upload (POST or PUT) through an Apache proxy.

## How can I access FTP files outside of my home directory?

An FTP URI is interpreted relative to the home directory of the user who is logging in. Alas, to reach higher directory levels you cannot use /../, as the dots are interpreted by the browser and not actually sent to the FTP server. To address this problem, the so called *Squid %2f hack* was implemented in the Apache FTP proxy; it is a solution which is also used by other popular proxy servers like the Squid Proxy Cache[74]. By prepending /%2f to the path of your request, you can make such a proxy change the FTP starting directory to / (instead of the home directory). For example, to retrieve the file /etc/motd, you would use the URL:

```
ftp://user@host/%2f/etc/motd
```

## How can I hide the FTP cleartext password in my browser's URL line?

To log in to an FTP server by username and password, Apache uses different strategies. In absence of a user name and password in the URL altogether, Apache sends an anonymous login to the FTP server, *i.e.*,

```
user:    anonymous
password:   apache_proxy@
```

This works for all popular FTP servers which are configured for anonymous access.

For a personal login with a specific username, you can embed the user name into the URL, like in:

```
ftp://username@host/myfile
```

If the FTP server asks for a password when given this username (which it should), then Apache will reply with a 401 (Authorization required) response, which causes the Browser to pop up the username/password dialog. Upon entering the password, the connection attempt is retried, and if successful, the requested resource is presented. The advantage of this procedure is that your browser does not display the password in cleartext (which it would if you had used

```
ftp://username:password@host/myfile
```

in the first place).

Note

> The password which is transmitted in such a way is not encrypted on its way. It travels between your browser and the Apache proxy server in a base64-encoded cleartext string, and between the Apache proxy and the FTP server as plaintext. You should therefore think twice before accessing your FTP server via HTTP (or before accessing your personal files via FTP at all!) When using insecure channels, an eavesdropper might intercept your password on its way.

---

[74]http://www.squid-cache.org/

### Why do I get a file listing when I expected a file to be downloaded?

In order to allow both browsing the directories on an FTP server and downloading files, Apache looks at the request URL. If it looks like a directory, or contains wildcard characters ("*?[{~"), then it guesses that a listing is wanted instead of a download.

You can disable the special handling of names with wildcard characters. See the PROXYFTPLISTONWILDCARD directive.

### ProxyFtpDirCharset Directive

| | |
|---|---|
| Description: | Define the character set for proxied FTP listings |
| Syntax: | ProxyFtpDirCharset character set |
| Default: | ProxyFtpDirCharset ISO-8859-1 |
| Context: | server config, virtual host, directory |
| Status: | Extension |
| Module: | mod_proxy_ftp |
| Compatibility: | Moved from MOD_PROXY in Apache 2.3.5. |

The PROXYFTPDIRCHARSET directive defines the character set to be set for FTP directory listings in HTML generated by MOD_PROXY_FTP.

### ProxyFtpEscapeWildcards Directive

| | |
|---|---|
| Description: | Whether wildcards in requested filenames are escaped when sent to the FTP server |
| Syntax: | ProxyFtpEscapeWildcards [on\|off] |
| Default: | on |
| Context: | server config, virtual host, directory |
| Status: | Extension |
| Module: | mod_proxy_ftp |
| Compatibility: | Available in Apache 2.3.3 and later |

The PROXYFTPESCAPEWILDCARDS directive controls whether wildcard characters ("*?[{~") in requested filenames are escaped with backslash before sending them to the FTP server. That is the default behavior, but many FTP servers don't know about the escaping and try to serve the literal filenames they were sent, including the backslashes in the names.

Set to "off" to allow downloading files with wildcards in their names from FTP servers that don't understand wildcard escaping.

### ProxyFtpListOnWildcard Directive

| | |
|---|---|
| Description: | Whether wildcards in requested filenames trigger a file listing |
| Syntax: | ProxyFtpListOnWildcard [on\|off] |
| Default: | on |
| Context: | server config, virtual host, directory |
| Status: | Extension |
| Module: | mod_proxy_ftp |
| Compatibility: | Available in Apache 2.3.3 and later |

The PROXYFTPLISTONWILDCARD directive controls whether wildcard characters ("*?[{~") in requested filenames cause MOD_PROXY_FTP to return a listing of files instead of downloading a file. By default (value on), they do. Set to "off" to allow downloading files even if they have wildcard characters in their names.

# 10.89   Apache Module mod_proxy_hcheck

| | |
|---|---|
| Description: | Dynamic health check of Balancer members (workers) for MOD_PROXY |
| Status: | Extension |
| ModuleIdentifier: | proxy_hcheck_module |
| SourceFile: | mod_proxy_hcheck.c |
| Compatibility: | Available in Apache 2.4.21 and later |

**Summary**

This module provides for dynamic health checking of balancer members (workers). This can be enabled on a worker-by-worker basis. The health check is done independently of the actual reverse proxy requests.

This module *requires* the service of MOD_WATCHDOG.

**Parameters**

The health check mechanism is enabled via the use of additional BalancerMember parameters, which are configured in the standard way via PROXYPASS:

A new BalancerMember status state (flag) is defined via this module: `"C"`. When the worker is taken offline due to failures as determined by the health check module, this flag is set, and can be seen (and modified) via the `balancer-manager`.

| Parameter | Default | Description |
|---|---|---|
| hcmethod | None | No dynamic health check performed. Choices are: |

| Method | Description Note |
|---|---|
| None | No dynamic health checking done |
| TCP | Check that a socket to the backend can be created: e.g. "are you up" |
| OPTIONS | Send an `HTTP` `OPTIONS` request to the backend * |
| HEAD | Send an `HTTP` `HEAD` request to the backend * |
| GET | Send an `HTTP` `GET` request to the backend * |

*: Unless `hcexpr` is used, a 2xx or 3xx HTTP status will be interpreted as *passing* the health check

| Parameter | Default | Description |
|---|---|---|
| hcpasses | 1 | Number of successful health check tests before worker is re-enabled |
| hcfails | 1 | Number of failed health check tests before worker is disabled |
| hcinterval | 30 | Period of health checks in seconds (e.g. performed every 30 seconds) |
| hcuri | | Additional URI to be appended to the worker URL for the health check. |
| hctemplate | | Name of template, created via PROXYHCTEMPLATE to use for setting health check parameters for this worker |
| hcexpr | | Name of expression, created via PROXYHCEXPR, used to check response headers for health. *If not used, 2xx thru 3xx status codes imply success* |

**Directives**

- ProxyHCExpr
- ProxyHCTemplate
- ProxyHCTPsize

**See also**

- MOD_PROXY

## Usage examples

The following example shows how one might configured health checking for various backend servers:

```
ProxyHCExpr ok234 {%{REQUEST_STATUS} =~ /^[234]/}
ProxyHCExpr gdown {%{REQUEST_STATUS} =~ /^[5]/}
ProxyHCExpr in_maint {hc('body') !~ /Under maintenance/}

<Proxy balancer://foo>
  BalancerMember http://www.example.com/  hcmethod=GET hcexpr=in_maint hcuri=/status.php
  BalancerMember http://www2.example.com/  hcmethod=HEAD hcexpr=ok234 hcinterval=10
  BalancerMember http://www3.example.com/ hcmethod=TCP hcinterval=5 hcpasses=2 hcfails=3
  BalancerMember http://www4.example.com/
</Proxy>

ProxyPass "/" "balancer://foo"
ProxyPassReverse "/" "balancer://foo"
```

In this scenario, http://www.example.com/ is health checked by sending a GET /status.php request to that server and seeing that the returned page does not include the string *Under maintenance*. If it does, that server is put in health-check fail mode, and disabled. This dynamic check is performed every 30 seconds, which is the default.

http://www2.example.com/ is checked by sending a simple HEAD request every 10 seconds and making sure that the response status is 2xx, 3xx or 4xx. http://www3.example.com/ is checked every 5 seconds by simply ensuring that the socket to that server is up. If the backend is marked as "down" and it passes 2 health check, it will be re-enabled and added back into the load balancer. It takes 3 back-to-back health check failures to disable the server and move it out of rotation. Finally, http://www4.example.com/ is not dynamically checked at all.

## ProxyHCExpr Directive

| | |
|---|---|
| Description: | Creates a named condition expression to use to determine health of the backend based on its response. |
| Syntax: | ProxyHCExpr name {ap_expr expression} |
| Context: | server config, virtual host |
| Status: | Extension |
| Module: | mod_proxy_hcheck |

The PROXYHCEXPR directive allows for creating a named condition expression that checks the response headers of the backend server to determine its health. This named condition can then be assigned to balancer members via the hcexpr parameter

### ProxyHCExpr: Allow for 2xx/3xx/4xx as passing

```
ProxyHCExpr ok234 {%{REQUEST_STATUS} =~ /^[234]/}
ProxyPass "/apps"     "http://backend.example.com/" hcexpr=ok234
```

⟹ The expression (p. 99) can use curly-parens ("{}") as quoting deliminators in addition to normal quotes.

If using a health check method (eg: GET) which results in a response body, that body itself can be checked via ap_expr using the hc() expression function, which is unique to this module.

In the following example, we send the backend a GET request and if the response body contains the phrase *Under maintenance*, we want to disable the backend.

### ProxyHCExpr: Checking response body

```
ProxyHCExpr in_maint {hc('body') !~ /Under maintenance/}
ProxyPass "/apps"     "http://backend.example.com/" hcexpr=in_maint hcmethod=get hcur
```

*NOTE:* Since response body can quite large, it is best if used against specific status pages.

## ProxyHCTemplate Directive

| | |
|---|---|
| Description: | Creates a named template for setting various health check parameters |
| Syntax: | ProxyHCTemplate name parameter=setting <...> |
| Context: | server config, virtual host |
| Status: | Extension |
| Module: | mod_proxy_hcheck |

The PROXYHCTEMPLATE directive allows for creating a named set (template) of health check parameters that can then be assigned to balancer members via the hctemplate parameter

### ProxyHCTemplate

```
ProxyHCTemplate tcp5 hcmethod=tcp hcinterval=5
ProxyPass "/apps"     "http://backend.example.com/" hctemplate=tcp5
```

## ProxyHCTPsize Directive

| | |
|---|---|
| Description: | Sets the size of the threadpool used for the health check workers. |
| Syntax: | ProxyHCTPsize <size> |
| Context: | server config, virtual host |
| Status: | Extension |
| Module: | mod_proxy_hcheck |

If Apache httpd and APR are built with thread support, the health check module will offload the work of the actual checking to a threadpool associated with the Watchdog process, allowing for parallel checks. The PROXYHCTPSIZE directive determines the size of this threadpool. If set to 0, no threadpool is used at all, resulting in serialized health checks. The default size is 16.

### ProxyHCTPsize

```
ProxyHCTPsize 32
```

# 10.90    Apache Module mod_proxy_html

| Description: | Rewrite HTML links in to ensure they are addressable from Clients' networks in a proxy context. |
|---|---|
| Status: | Base |
| ModuleIdentifier: | proxy_html_module |
| SourceFile: | mod_proxy_html.c |
| Compatibility: | Version 2.4 and later. Available as a third-party module for earlier 2.x versions |

## Summary

This module provides an output filter to rewrite HTML links in a proxy situation, to ensure that links work for users outside the proxy. It serves the same purpose as Apache's ProxyPassReverse directive does for HTTP headers, and is an essential component of a reverse proxy.

For example, if a company has an application server at `appserver.example.com` that is only visible from within the company's internal network, and a public webserver `www.example.com`, they may wish to provide a gateway to the application server at `http://www.example.com/appserver/`.  When the application server links to itself, those links need to be rewritten to work through the gateway.  mod_proxy_html serves to rewrite `<a href="http://appserver.example.com/foo/bar.html">foobar</a>` to `<a href="http://www.example.com/appserver/foo/bar.html">foobar</a>` making it accessible from outside.

mod_proxy_html was originally developed at Webÿng, whose extensive documentation[75] may be useful to users.

### Directives

- ProxyHTMLBufSize
- ProxyHTMLCharsetOut
- ProxyHTMLDocType
- ProxyHTMLEnable
- ProxyHTMLEvents
- ProxyHTMLExtended
- ProxyHTMLFixups
- ProxyHTMLInterp
- ProxyHTMLLinks
- ProxyHTMLMeta
- ProxyHTMLStripComments
- ProxyHTMLURLMap

## ProxyHTMLBufSize Directive

| Description: | Sets the buffer size increment for buffering inline scripts and stylesheets. |
|---|---|
| Syntax: | `ProxyHTMLBufSize bytes` |
| Context: | server config, virtual host, directory |
| Status: | Base |
| Module: | mod_proxy_html |
| Compatibility: | Version 2.4 and later; available as a third-party for earlier 2.x versions |

───────────
[75]http://apache.webthing.com/mod_proxy_html/

In order to parse non-HTML content (stylesheets and scripts) embedded in HTML documents, mod_proxy_html has to read the entire script or stylesheet into a buffer. This buffer will be expanded as necessary to hold the largest script or stylesheet in a page, in increments of *bytes* as set by this directive.

The default is 8192, and will work well for almost all pages. However, if you know you're proxying pages containing stylesheets and/or scripts bigger than 8K (that is, for a single script or stylesheet, NOT in total), it will be more efficient to set a larger buffer size and avoid the need to resize the buffer dynamically during a request.

## ProxyHTMLCharsetOut Directive

| Description: | Specify a charset for mod_proxy_html output. |
| --- | --- |
| Syntax: | `ProxyHTMLCharsetOut Charset | *` |
| Context: | server config, virtual host, directory |
| Status: | Base |
| Module: | mod_proxy_html |
| Compatibility: | Version 2.4 and later; available as a third-party for earlier 2.x versions |

This selects an encoding for mod_proxy_html output. It should not normally be used, as any change from the default `UTF-8` (Unicode - as used internally by libxml2) will impose an additional processing overhead. The special token `ProxyHTMLCharsetOut *` will generate output using the same encoding as the input.

Note that this relies on MOD_XML2ENC being loaded.

## ProxyHTMLDocType Directive

| Description: | Sets an HTML or XHTML document type declaration. |
| --- | --- |
| Syntax: | `ProxyHTMLDocType HTML|XHTML [Legacy]` |
| | **OR** |
| | `ProxyHTMLDocType fpi [SGML|XML]` |
| | **OR** |
| | `ProxyHTMLDocType html5` |
| | **OR** |
| | `ProxyHTMLDocType auto` |
| Default: | `ProxyHTMLDocType auto (2.5/trunk versions); no FPI (2.4.x)` |
| Context: | server config, virtual host, directory |
| Status: | Base |
| Module: | mod_proxy_html |
| Compatibility: | Version 2.4 and later; available as a third-party for earlier 2.x versions |

In the first form, documents will be declared as HTML 4.01 or XHTML 1.0 according to the option selected. This option also determines whether HTML or XHTML syntax is used for output. Note that the format of the documents coming from the backend server is immaterial: the parser will deal with it automatically. If the optional second argument is set to "Legacy", documents will be declared "Transitional", an option that may be necessary if you are proxying pre-1998 content or working with defective authoring/publishing tools.

In the second form, it will insert your own FPI. The optional second argument determines whether SGML/HTML or XML/XHTML syntax will be used.

The third form declares documents as HTML 5.

The fourth form is new in HTTPD trunk and not yet available in released versions, and uses libxml2's HTML parser to detect the doctype.

If the first form is used, mod_proxy_html will also clean up the HTML to the specified standard. It cannot fix every error, but it will strip out bogus elements and attributes. It will also optionally log other errors at LOGLEVEL Debug.

## ProxyHTMLEnable Directive

| | |
|---|---|
| Description: | Turns the proxy_html filter on or off. |
| Syntax: | `ProxyHTMLEnable On\|Off` |
| Default: | `ProxyHTMLEnable Off` |
| Context: | server config, virtual host, directory |
| Status: | Base |
| Module: | mod_proxy_html |
| Compatibility: | Version 2.4 and later; available as a third-party module for earlier 2.x versions. |

A simple switch to enable or disable the proxy_html filter. If MOD_XML2ENC is loaded it will also automatically set up internationalisation support.

Note that the proxy_html filter will only act on HTML data (Content-Type text/html or application/xhtml+xml) and when the data are proxied. You can override this (at your own risk) by setting the *PROXY_HTML_FORCE* environment variable.

## ProxyHTMLEvents Directive

| | |
|---|---|
| Description: | Specify attributes to treat as scripting events. |
| Syntax: | `ProxyHTMLEvents attribute [attribute ...]` |
| Context: | server config, virtual host, directory |
| Status: | Base |
| Module: | mod_proxy_html |
| Compatibility: | Version 2.4 and later; available as a third-party for earlier 2.x versions |

Specifies one or more attributes to treat as scripting events and apply PROXYHTMLURLMAPs to where enabled. You can specify any number of attributes in one or more ProxyHTMLEvents directives.

Normally you'll set this globally. If you set ProxyHTMLEvents in more than one scope so that one overrides the other, you'll need to specify a complete set in each of those scopes.

A default configuration is supplied in *proxy-html.conf* and defines the events in standard HTML 4 and XHTML 1.

## ProxyHTMLExtended Directive

| | |
|---|---|
| Description: | Determines whether to fix links in inline scripts, stylesheets, and scripting events. |
| Syntax: | `ProxyHTMLExtended On\|Off` |
| Default: | `ProxyHTMLExtended Off` |
| Context: | server config, virtual host, directory |
| Status: | Base |
| Module: | mod_proxy_html |
| Compatibility: | Version 2.4 and later; available as a third-party for earlier 2.x versions |

Set to `Off`, HTML links are rewritten according to the PROXYHTMLURLMAP directives, but links appearing in Javascript and CSS are ignored.

Set to `On`, all scripting events (as determined by PROXYHTMLEVENTS) and embedded scripts or stylesheets are also processed by the PROXYHTMLURLMAP rules, according to the flags set for each rule. Since this requires more parsing, performance will be best if you only enable it when strictly necessary.

You'll also need to take care over patterns matched, since the parser has no knowledge of what is a URL within an embedded script or stylesheet. In particular, extended matching of / is likely to lead to false matches.

## ProxyHTMLFixups Directive

| | |
|---|---|
| Description: | Fixes for simple HTML errors. |
| Syntax: | `ProxyHTMLFixups [lowercase] [dospath] [reset]` |
| Context: | server config, virtual host, directory |
| Status: | Base |
| Module: | mod_proxy_html |
| Compatibility: | Version 2.4 and later; available as a third-party for earlier 2.x versions |

This directive takes one to three arguments as follows:

- `lowercase` Urls are rewritten to lowercase

- `dospath` Backslashes in URLs are rewritten to forward slashes.

- `reset` Unset any options set at a higher level in the configuration.

Take care when using these. The fixes will correct certain authoring mistakes, but risk also erroneously fixing links that were correct to start with. Only use them if you know you have a broken backend server.

## ProxyHTMLInterp Directive

| | |
|---|---|
| Description: | Enables per-request interpolation of PROXYHTMLURLMAP rules. |
| Syntax: | `ProxyHTMLInterp On|Off` |
| Default: | `ProxyHTMLInterp Off` |
| Context: | server config, virtual host, directory |
| Status: | Base |
| Module: | mod_proxy_html |
| Compatibility: | Version 2.4 and later; available as a third-party for earlier 2.x versions |

This enables per-request interpolation in PROXYHTMLURLMAP to- and from- patterns.

If interpolation is not enabled, all rules are pre-compiled at startup. With interpolation, they must be re-compiled for every request, which implies an extra processing overhead. It should therefore be enabled only when necessary.

## ProxyHTMLLinks Directive

| | |
|---|---|
| Description: | Specify HTML elements that have URL attributes to be rewritten. |
| Syntax: | `ProxyHTMLLinks element attribute [attribute2 ...]` |
| Context: | server config, virtual host, directory |
| Status: | Base |
| Module: | mod_proxy_html |
| Compatibility: | Version 2.4 and later; available as a third-party for earlier 2.x versions |

Specifies elements that have URL attributes that should be rewritten using standard PROXYHTMLURLMAPs. You will need one ProxyHTMLLinks directive per element, but it can have any number of attributes.

Normally you'll set this globally. If you set ProxyHTMLLinks in more than one scope so that one overrides the other, you'll need to specify a complete set in each of those scopes.

A default configuration is supplied in *proxy-html.conf* and defines the HTML links for standard HTML 4 and XHTML 1.

## ProxyHTMLMeta Directive

| | |
|---|---|
| Description: | Turns on or off extra pre-parsing of metadata in HTML <head> sections. |
| Syntax: | `ProxyHTMLMeta On|Off` |
| Default: | `ProxyHTMLMeta Off` |
| Context: | server config, virtual host, directory |
| Status: | Base |
| Module: | mod_proxy_html |
| Compatibility: | Version 2.4 and later; available as a third-party module for earlier 2.x versions. |

This turns on or off pre-parsing of metadata in HTML <head> sections.

If not required, turning ProxyHTMLMeta Off will give a small performance boost by skipping this parse step. However, it is sometimes necessary for internationalisation to work correctly.

ProxyHTMLMeta has two effects. Firstly and most importantly it enables detection of character encodings declared in the form

```
<meta http-equiv="Content-Type" content="text/html;charset=foo">
```

or, in the case of an XHTML document, an XML declaration. It is NOT required if the charset is declared in a real HTTP header (which is always preferable) from the backend server, nor if the document is *utf-8* (unicode) or a subset such as ASCII. You may also be able to dispense with it where documents use a default declared using XML2ENCDEFAULT, but that risks propagating an incorrect declaration. A PROXYHTMLCHARSETOUT can remove that risk, but is likely to be a bigger processing overhead than enabling ProxyHTMLMeta.

The other effect of enabling ProxyHTMLMeta is to parse all <meta http-equiv=...> declarations and convert them to real HTTP headers, in keeping with the original purpose of this form of the HTML <meta> element.

## ProxyHTMLStripComments Directive

| | |
|---|---|
| Description: | Determines whether to strip HTML comments. |
| Syntax: | `ProxyHTMLStripComments On|Off` |
| Default: | `ProxyHTMLStripComments Off` |
| Context: | server config, virtual host, directory |
| Status: | Base |
| Module: | mod_proxy_html |
| Compatibility: | Version 2.4 and later; available as a third-party for earlier 2.x versions |

This directive will cause mod_proxy_html to strip HTML comments. Note that this will also kill off any scripts or styles embedded in comments (a bogosity introduced in 1995/6 with Netscape 2 for the benefit of then-older browsers, but still in use today). It may also interfere with comment-based processors such as SSI or ESI: be sure to run any of those *before* mod_proxy_html in the filter chain if stripping comments!

## ProxyHTMLURLMap Directive

| | |
|---|---|
| Description: | Defines a rule to rewrite HTML links |
| Syntax: | `ProxyHTMLURLMap from-pattern to-pattern [flags] [cond]` |
| Context: | server config, virtual host, directory |
| Status: | Base |
| Module: | mod_proxy_html |
| Compatibility: | Version 2.4 and later; available as a third-party module for earlier 2.x versions. |

This is the key directive for rewriting HTML links. When parsing a document, whenever a link target matches *from-pattern*, the matching portion will be rewritten to *to-pattern*, as modified by any flags supplied and by the PROXY-HTMLEXTENDED directive.

The optional third argument may define any of the following **Flags**. Flags are case-sensitive.

**h** Ignore HTML links (pass through unchanged)

**e** Ignore scripting events (pass through unchanged)

**c** Pass embedded script and style sections through untouched.

**L** Last-match. If this rule matches, no more rules are applied (note that this happens automatically for HTML links).

**l** Opposite to L. Overrides the one-change-only default behaviour with HTML links.

**R** Use Regular Expression matching-and-replace. `from-pattern` is a regexp, and `to-pattern` a replacement string that may be based on the regexp. Regexp memory is supported: you can use brackets () in the `from-pattern` and retrieve the matches with $1 to $9 in the `to-pattern`.

If R is not set, it will use string-literal search-and-replace. The logic is *starts-with* in HTML links, but *contains* in scripting events and embedded script and style sections.

**x** Use POSIX extended Regular Expressions. Only applicable with R.

**i** Case-insensitive matching. Only applicable with R.

**n** Disable regexp memory (for speed). Only applicable with R.

**s** Line-based regexp matching. Only applicable with R.

**^** Match at start only. This applies only to string matching (not regexps) and is irrelevant to HTML links.

**$** Match at end only. This applies only to string matching (not regexps) and is irrelevant to HTML links.

**V** Interpolate environment variables in `to-pattern`. A string of the form `${varname|default}` will be replaced by the value of environment variable `varname`. If that is unset, it is replaced by `default`. The `|default` is optional.

NOTE: interpolation will only be enabled if PROXYHTMLINTERP is *On*.

**v** Interpolate environment variables in `from-pattern`. Patterns supported are as above.

NOTE: interpolation will only be enabled if PROXYHTMLINTERP is *On*.

The optional fourth **cond** argument defines a condition that will be evaluated per Request, provided PROXYHTMLINTERP is *On*. If the condition evaluates FALSE the map will not be applied in this request. If TRUE, or if no condition is defined, the map is applied.

A **cond** is evaluated by the Expression Parser (p. 99) . In addition, the simpler syntax of conditions in mod_proxy_html 3.x for HTTPD 2.0 and 2.2 is also supported.

# 10.91    Apache Module mod_proxy_http

| | |
|---|---|
| Description: | HTTP support module for MOD_PROXY |
| Status: | Extension |
| ModuleIdentifier: | proxy_http_module |
| SourceFile: | mod_proxy_http.c |

## Summary

This module *requires* the service of MOD_PROXY. It provides the features used for proxying HTTP and HTTPS requests. MOD_PROXY_HTTP supports HTTP/0.9, HTTP/1.0 and HTTP/1.1. It does *not* provide any caching abilities. If you want to set up a caching proxy, you might want to use the additional service of the MOD_CACHE module.

Thus, in order to get the ability of handling HTTP proxy requests, MOD_PROXY and MOD_PROXY_HTTP have to be present in the server.

**Warning**

Do not enable proxying until you have secured your server (p. 787) . Open proxy servers are dangerous both to your network and to the Internet at large.

**Directives** This module provides no directives.

**See also**

- MOD_PROXY
- MOD_PROXY_CONNECT

## Environment Variables

In addition to the configuration directives that control the behaviour of MOD_PROXY, there are a number of *environment variables* that control the HTTP protocol provider. Environment variables below that don't specify specific values are enabled when set to any value.

**proxy-sendextracrlf** Causes proxy to send an extra CR-LF newline on the end of a request. This is a workaround for a bug in some browsers.

**force-proxy-request-1.0** Forces the proxy to send requests to the backend as HTTP/1.0 and disables HTTP/1.1 features.

**proxy-nokeepalive** Forces the proxy to close the backend connection after each request.

**proxy-chain-auth** If the proxy requires authentication, it will read and consume the proxy authentication credentials sent by the client. With *proxy-chain-auth* it will *also* forward the credentials to the next proxy in the chain. This may be necessary if you have a chain of proxies that share authentication information. **Security Warning:** Do not set this unless you know you need it, as it forwards sensitive information!

**proxy-sendcl** HTTP/1.0 required all HTTP requests that include a body (e.g. POST requests) to include a *Content-Length* header. This environment variable forces the Apache proxy to send this header to the backend server, regardless of what the Client sent to the proxy. It ensures compatibility when proxying for an HTTP/1.0 or unknown backend. However, it may require the entire request to be buffered by the proxy, so it becomes very inefficient for large requests.

**proxy-sendchunks or proxy-sendchunked** This is the opposite of *proxy-sendcl*. It allows request bodies to be sent to the backend using chunked transfer encoding. This allows the request to be efficiently streamed, but requires that the backend server supports HTTP/1.1.

**proxy-interim-response** This variable takes values `RFC` (the default) or `Suppress`. Earlier httpd versions would suppress HTTP interim (1xx) responses sent from the backend. This is technically a violation of the HTTP protocol. In practice, if a backend sends an interim response, it may itself be extending the protocol in a manner we know nothing about, or just broken. So this is now configurable: set `proxy-interim-response RFC` to be fully protocol compliant, or `proxy-interim-response Suppress` to suppress interim responses.

**proxy-initial-not-pooled** If this variable is set, no pooled connection will be reused if the client request is the initial request on the frontend connection. This avoids the "proxy: error reading status line from remote server" error message caused by the race condition that the backend server closed the pooled connection after the connection check by the proxy and before data sent by the proxy reached the backend. It has to be kept in mind that setting this variable downgrades performance, especially with HTTP/1.0 clients.

## Request notes

MOD_PROXY_HTTP creates the following request notes for logging using the `%{VARNAME}`n format in LOGFORMAT or ERRORLOGFORMAT:

**proxy-source-port** The local port used for the connection to the backend server.

**proxy-status** The HTTP status received from the backend server.

# 10.92   Apache Module mod_proxy_http2

| | |
|---|---|
| Description: | HTTP/2 support module for MOD_PROXY |
| Status: | Extension |
| ModuleIdentifier: | proxy_http2_module |
| SourceFile: | mod_proxy_http2.c |

## Summary

This module *requires* the service of MOD_PROXY.  It provides the features used for proxying HTTP/2 requests. MOD_PROXY_HTTP2 supports HTTP/2 only. It does *not* provide any downgrades to HTTP/1.1.

Thus, in order to get the ability of handling HTTP/2 proxy requests, MOD_PROXY and MOD_PROXY_HTTP2 have to be present in the server.

MOD_PROXY_HTTP2 works with incoming requests over HTTP/1.1 and HTTP/2 requests. If MOD_HTTP2 handles the frontend connection, requests against the same HTTP/2 backend are sent over a single connection, whenever possible.

This module relies on libnghttp2[76] to provide the core http/2 engine.

> **!  Warning**
> This module is experimental. Its behaviors, directives, and defaults are subject to more change from release to release relative to other standard modules. Users are encouraged to consult the "CHANGES" file for potential updates.

> **!  Warning**
> Do not enable proxying until you have secured your server (p. 787) . Open proxy servers are dangerous both to your network and to the Internet at large.

**Directives** This module provides no directives.

**See also**

- MOD_HTTP2
- MOD_PROXY
- MOD_PROXY_CONNECT

## Request notes

MOD_PROXY_HTTP creates the following request notes for logging using the %{VARNAME}n format in LOGFORMAT or ERRORLOGFORMAT:

**proxy-source-port** The local port used for the connection to the backend server.

**proxy-status** The HTTP/2 status received from the backend server.

---

[76]http://nghttp2.org/

# 10.93   Apache Module mod_proxy_scgi

| | |
|---|---|
| Description: | SCGI gateway module for MOD_PROXY |
| Status: | Extension |
| ModuleIdentifier: | proxy_scgi_module |
| SourceFile: | mod_proxy_scgi.c |

## Summary

This module *requires* the service of MOD_PROXY. It provides support for the SCGI protocol, version 1[77].

Thus, in order to get the ability of handling the SCGI protocol, MOD_PROXY and MOD_PROXY_SCGI have to be present in the server.

> **!** **Warning**
> Do not enable proxying until you have secured your server (p. 787) . Open proxy servers are dangerous both to your network and to the Internet at large.

## Directives

- ProxySCGIInternalRedirect
- ProxySCGISendfile

## See also

- MOD_PROXY
- MOD_PROXY_BALANCER

## Examples

Remember, in order to make the following examples work, you have to enable MOD_PROXY and MOD_PROXY_SCGI.

### Simple gateway

```
ProxyPass "/scgi-bin/" "scgi://localhost:4000/"
```

The balanced gateway needs MOD_PROXY_BALANCER and at least one load balancer algorithm module, such as MOD_LBMETHOD_BYREQUESTS, in addition to the proxy modules listed above. MOD_LBMETHOD_BYREQUESTS is the default, and will be used for this example configuration.

### Balanced gateway

```
ProxyPass "/scgi-bin/" "balancer://somecluster/"
<Proxy balancer://somecluster>
    BalancerMember scgi://localhost:4000
    BalancerMember scgi://localhost:4001
</Proxy>
```

---

[77]http://python.ca/scgi/protocol.txt

## Environment Variables

In addition to the configuration directives that control the behaviour of MOD_PROXY, an *environment variable* may also control the SCGI protocol provider:

**proxy-scgi-pathinfo** By default MOD_PROXY_SCGI will neither create nor export the *PATH_INFO* environment variable. This allows the backend SCGI server to correctly determine *SCRIPT_NAME* and *Script-URI* and be compliant with RFC 3875 section 3.3. If instead you need MOD_PROXY_SCGI to generate a "best guess" for *PATH_INFO*, set this env-var. The variable must be set before SETENV is effective. SETENVIF can be used instead: `SetEnvIf Request_URI . proxy-scgi-pathinfo`

## ProxySCGIInternalRedirect Directive

| | |
|---|---|
| Description: | Enable or disable internal redirect responses from the backend |
| Syntax: | `ProxySCGIInternalRedirect On|Off|Headername` |
| Default: | `ProxySCGIInternalRedirect On` |
| Context: | server config, virtual host, directory |
| Status: | Extension |
| Module: | mod_proxy_scgi |
| Compatibility: | The *Headername* feature is available in Apache httpd 2.4.13 and later. |

The PROXYSCGIINTERNALREDIRECT enables the backend to internally redirect the gateway to a different URL. This feature originates in MOD_CGI, which internally redirects the response if the response status is OK (200) and the response contains a `Location` (or configured alternate header) and its value starts with a slash (/). This value is interpreted as a new local URL that Apache httpd internally redirects to.

MOD_PROXY_SCGI does the same as MOD_CGI in this regard, except that you can turn off the feature or specify the use of a header other than `Location`.

### Example

```
    ProxySCGIInternalRedirect Off

# Django and some other frameworks will fully qualify "local URLs"
# set by the application, so an alternate header must be used.
<Location /django-app/>
    ProxySCGIInternalRedirect X-Location
</Location>
```

## ProxySCGISendfile Directive

| | |
|---|---|
| Description: | Enable evaluation of *X-Sendfile* pseudo response header |
| Syntax: | `ProxySCGISendfile On|Off|Headername` |
| Default: | `ProxySCGISendfile Off` |
| Context: | server config, virtual host, directory |
| Status: | Extension |
| Module: | mod_proxy_scgi |

The PROXYSCGISENDFILE directive enables the SCGI backend to let files be served directly by the gateway. This is useful for performance purposes - httpd can use `sendfile` or other optimizations, which are not possible if the file comes over the backend socket. Additionally, the file contents are not transmitted twice.

The PROXYSCGISENDFILE argument determines the gateway behaviour:

**Off** No special handling takes place.

**On** The gateway looks for a backend response header called `X-Sendfile` and interprets the value as the filename to serve. The header is removed from the final response headers. This is equivalent to `ProxySCGISendfile X-Sendfile`.

**anything else** Similar to `On`, but instead of the hardcoded header name `X-Sendfile`, the argument is used as the header name.

### Example

```
# Use the default header (X-Sendfile)
ProxySCGISendfile On

# Use a different header
ProxySCGISendfile X-Send-Static
```

## 10.94    Apache Module mod_proxy_wstunnel

| | |
|---|---|
| Description: | Websockets support module for MOD_PROXY |
| Status: | Extension |
| ModuleIdentifier: | proxy_wstunnel_module |
| SourceFile: | mod_proxy_wstunnel.c |
| Compatibility: | Available in httpd 2.4.5 and later |

### Summary

This module *requires* the service of MOD_PROXY. It provides support for the tunnelling of web socket connections to a backend websockets server. The connection is automatically upgraded to a websocket connection:

**HTTP Response**

```
Upgrade: WebSocket
Connection: Upgrade
```

Proxying requests to a websockets server like echo.websocket.org can be done using the PROXYPASS directive:

```
ProxyPass "/ws2/"  "ws://echo.websocket.org/"
ProxyPass "/wss2/" "wss://echo.websocket.org/"
```

Load balancing for multiple backends can be achieved using MOD_PROXY_BALANCER.

**Directives**

- ProxyWebsocketAsync
- ProxyWebsocketAsyncDelay
- ProxyWebsocketIdleTimeout

**See also**

- MOD_PROXY

### ProxyWebsocketAsync Directive

| | |
|---|---|
| Description: | Instructs this module to try to create an asynchronous tunnel |
| Syntax: | `ProxyWebsocketAsync ON\|OFF` |
| Context: | server config, virtual host |
| Status: | Extension |
| Module: | mod_proxy_wstunnel |

This directive instructs the server to try to create an asynchronous tunnel. If the current MPM does not support the necessary features, a synchronous tunnel is used.

**Note**

Async support is experimental and subject to change.

**ProxyWebsocketAsyncDelay Directive**

| | |
|---|---|
| Description: | Sets the amount of time the tunnel waits synchronously for data |
| Syntax: | `ProxyWebsocketAsyncDelay num[ms]` |
| Default: | `ProxyWebsocketAsyncDelay 0` |
| Context: | server config, virtual host |
| Status: | Extension |
| Module: | mod_proxy_wstunnel |

If PROXYWEBSOCKETASYNC is enabled, this directive controls how long the server synchronously waits for more data.

Note

Async support is experimental and subject to change.

**ProxyWebsocketIdleTimeout Directive**

| | |
|---|---|
| Description: | Sets the maximum amount of time to wait for data on the websockets tunnel |
| Syntax: | `ProxyWebsocketIdleTimeout num[ms]` |
| Default: | `ProxyWebsocketIdleTimeout 0` |
| Context: | server config, virtual host |
| Status: | Extension |
| Module: | mod_proxy_wstunnel |

This directive imposes a maximum amount of time for the tunnel to be left open while idle.

## 10.95    Apache Module mod_ratelimit

| Description: | Bandwidth Rate Limiting for Clients |
|---|---|
| Status: | Extension |
| ModuleIdentifier: | ratelimit_module |
| SourceFile: | mod_ratelimit.c |

## Summary

Provides a filter named RATE_LIMIT to limit client bandwidth. The connection speed to be simulated is specified, in KiB/s, using the environment variable rate-limit.

### Example Configuration

```
<Location "/downloads">
    SetOutputFilter RATE_LIMIT
    SetEnv rate-limit 400
</Location>
```

**Directives** This module provides no directives.

# 10.96 Apache Module mod_reflector

| | |
|---|---|
| Description: | Reflect a request body as a response via the output filter stack. |
| Status: | Base |
| ModuleIdentifier: | reflector_module |
| SourceFile: | mod_reflector.c |
| Compatibility: | Version 2.3 and later |

## Summary

This module allows request bodies to be reflected back to the client, in the process passing the request through the output filter stack. A suitably configured chain of filters can be used to transform the request into a response. This module can be used to turn an output filter into an HTTP service.

### Directives

- ReflectorHeader

## Examples

**Compression service** Pass the request body through the DEFLATE filter to compress the body. This request requires a Content-Encoding request header containing "gzip" for the filter to return compressed data.

```
<Location "/compress">
    SetHandler reflector
    SetOutputFilter DEFLATE
</Location>
```

**Image downsampling service** Pass the request body through an image downsampling filter, and reflect the results to the caller.

```
<Location "/downsample">
    SetHandler reflector
    SetOutputFilter DOWNSAMPLE
</Location>
```

## ReflectorHeader Directive

| | |
|---|---|
| Description: | Reflect an input header to the output headers |
| Syntax: | `ReflectorHeader inputheader [outputheader]` |
| Context: | server config, virtual host, directory, .htaccess |
| Override: | Options |
| Status: | Base |
| Module: | mod_reflector |

This directive controls the reflection of request headers to the response. The first argument is the name of the request header to copy. If the optional second argument is specified, it will be used as the name of the response header, otherwise the original request header name will be used.

# 10.97    Apache Module mod_remoteip

| | |
|---|---|
| Description: | Replaces the original client IP address for the connection with the useragent IP address list presented by a proxies or a load balancer via the request headers. |
| Status: | Base |
| ModuleIdentifier: | remoteip_module |
| SourceFile: | mod_remoteip.c |

## Summary

This module is used to treat the useragent which initiated the request as the originating useragent as identified by httpd for the purposes of authorization and logging, even where that useragent is behind a load balancer, front end server, or proxy server.

The module overrides the client IP address for the connection with the useragent IP address reported in the request header configured with the REMOTEIPHEADER directive.

Once replaced as instructed, this overridden useragent IP address is then used for the MOD_AUTHZ_HOST REQUIRE IP feature, is reported by MOD_STATUS, and is recorded by MOD_LOG_CONFIG %a and CORE %a format strings. The underlying client IP of the connection is available in the %{c}a format string.

 It is critical to only enable this behavior from intermediate hosts (proxies, etc) which are trusted by this server, since it is trivial for the remote useragent to impersonate another useragent.

### Directives

- RemoteIPHeader
- RemoteIPInternalProxy
- RemoteIPInternalProxyList
- RemoteIPProxiesHeader
- RemoteIPTrustedProxy
- RemoteIPTrustedProxyList

### See also

- MOD_AUTHZ_HOST
- MOD_STATUS
- MOD_LOG_CONFIG

## Remote IP Processing

Apache by default identifies the useragent with the connection's client_ip value, and the connection remote_host and remote_logname are derived from this value. These fields play a role in authentication, authorization and logging and other purposes by other loadable modules.

mod_remoteip overrides the client IP of the connection with the advertised useragent IP as provided by a proxy or load balancer, for the duration of the request. A load balancer might establish a long lived keepalive connection with the server, and each request will have the correct useragent IP, even though the underlying client IP address of the load balancer remains unchanged.

When multiple, comma delimited useragent IP addresses are listed in the header value, they are processed in Right-to-Left order. Processing halts when a given useragent IP address is not trusted to present the preceding IP address. The header field is updated to this remaining list of unconfirmed IP addresses, or if all IP addresses were trusted, this header is removed from the request altogether.

In overriding the client IP, the module stores the list of intermediate hosts in a remoteip-proxy-ip-list note, which MOD_LOG_CONFIG can record using the %{remoteip-proxy-ip-list}n format token. If the administrator needs to store this as an additional header, this same value can also be recording as a header using the directive REMOTEIPPROXIESHEADER.

 **IPv4-over-IPv6 Mapped Addresses**
As with httpd in general, any IPv4-over-IPv6 mapped addresses are recorded in their IPv4 representation.

 **Internal (Private) Addresses**
All internal addresses 10/8, 172.16/12, 192.168/16, 169.254/16 and 127/8 blocks (and IPv6 addresses outside of the public 2000::/3 block) are only evaluated by mod_remoteip when REMOTEIPINTERNALPROXY internal (intranet) proxies are registered.

## RemoteIPHeader Directive

| | |
|---|---|
| Description: | Declare the header field which should be parsed for useragent IP addresses |
| Syntax: | RemoteIPHeader header-field |
| Context: | server config, virtual host |
| Status: | Base |
| Module: | mod_remoteip |

The REMOTEIPHEADER directive triggers MOD_REMOTEIP to treat the value of the specified *header-field* header as the useragent IP address, or list of intermediate useragent IP addresses, subject to further configuration of the REMOTEIPINTERNALPROXY and REMOTEIPTRUSTEDPROXY directives.

 Unless these other directives are used, MOD_REMOTEIP will trust all hosts presenting a non internal address in the REMOTEIPHEADER header value.

### Internal (Load Balancer) Example

```
RemoteIPHeader X-Client-IP
```

### Proxy Example

```
RemoteIPHeader X-Forwarded-For
```

## RemoteIPInternalProxy Directive

| | |
|---|---|
| Description: | Declare client intranet IP addresses trusted to present the RemoteIPHeader value |
| Syntax: | RemoteIPInternalProxy proxy-ip\|proxy-ip/subnet\|hostname ... |
| Context: | server config, virtual host |
| Status: | Base |
| Module: | mod_remoteip |

The REMOTEIPINTERNALPROXY directive adds one or more addresses (or address blocks) to trust as presenting a valid RemoteIPHeader value of the useragent IP. Unlike the REMOTEIPTRUSTEDPROXY directive, any IP address presented in this header, including private intranet addresses, are trusted when passed from these proxies.

**Internal (Load Balancer) Example**

```
RemoteIPHeader X-Client-IP
RemoteIPInternalProxy 10.0.2.0/24
RemoteIPInternalProxy gateway.localdomain
```

## RemoteIPInternalProxyList Directive

| | |
|---|---|
| Description: | Declare client intranet IP addresses trusted to present the RemoteIPHeader value |
| Syntax: | `RemoteIPInternalProxyList filename` |
| Context: | server config, virtual host |
| Status: | Base |
| Module: | mod_remoteip |

The REMOTEIPINTERNALPROXYLIST directive specifies a file parsed at startup, and builds a list of addresses (or address blocks) to trust as presenting a valid RemoteIPHeader value of the useragent IP.

The '#' hash character designates a comment line, otherwise each whitespace or newline separated entry is processed identically to the REMOTEIPINTERNALPROXY directive.

**Internal (Load Balancer) Example**

```
RemoteIPHeader X-Client-IP
RemoteIPInternalProxyList conf/trusted-proxies.lst
```

**conf/trusted-proxies.lst contents**

```
# Our internally trusted proxies;
10.0.2.0/24        #Everyone in the testing group
gateway.localdomain #The front end balancer
```

## RemoteIPProxiesHeader Directive

| | |
|---|---|
| Description: | Declare the header field which will record all intermediate IP addresses |
| Syntax: | `RemoteIPProxiesHeader HeaderFieldName` |
| Context: | server config, virtual host |
| Status: | Base |
| Module: | mod_remoteip |

The REMOTEIPPROXIESHEADER directive specifies a header into which MOD_REMOTEIP will collect a list of all of the intermediate client IP addresses trusted to resolve the useragent IP of the request. Note that intermediate RE-MOTEIPTRUSTEDPROXY addresses are recorded in this header, while any intermediate REMOTEIPINTERNALPROXY addresses are discarded.

**Example**

```
RemoteIPHeader X-Forwarded-For
RemoteIPProxiesHeader X-Forwarded-By
```

## RemoteIPTrustedProxy Directive

| | |
|---|---|
| Description: | Restrict client IP addresses trusted to present the RemoteIPHeader value |
| Syntax: | `RemoteIPTrustedProxy proxy-ip|proxy-ip/subnet|hostname ...` |
| Context: | server config, virtual host |
| Status: | Base |
| Module: | mod_remoteip |

The REMOTEIPTRUSTEDPROXY directive restricts which peer IP addresses (or address blocks) will be trusted to present a valid RemoteIPHeader value of the useragent IP.

Unlike the REMOTEIPINTERNALPROXY directive, any intranet or private IP address reported by such proxies, including the 10/8, 172.16/12, 192.168/16, 169.254/16 and 127/8 blocks (or outside of the IPv6 public 2000::/3 block) are not trusted as the useragent IP, and are left in the REMOTEIPHEADER header's value.

 By default, MOD_REMOTEIP will trust all hosts presenting a non internal address in the RE-MOTEIPHEADER header value.

### Trusted (Load Balancer) Example

```
RemoteIPHeader X-Forwarded-For
RemoteIPTrustedProxy 10.0.2.16/28
RemoteIPTrustedProxy proxy.example.com
```

## RemoteIPTrustedProxyList Directive

| | |
|---|---|
| Description: | Restrict client IP addresses trusted to present the RemoteIPHeader value |
| Syntax: | `RemoteIPTrustedProxyList filename` |
| Context: | server config, virtual host |
| Status: | Base |
| Module: | mod_remoteip |

The REMOTEIPTRUSTEDPROXYLIST directive specifies a file parsed at startup, and builds a list of addresses (or address blocks) to trust as presenting a valid RemoteIPHeader value of the useragent IP.

The '#' hash character designates a comment line, otherwise each whitespace or newline separated entry is processed identically to the REMOTEIPTRUSTEDPROXY directive.

### Trusted (Load Balancer) Example

```
RemoteIPHeader X-Forwarded-For
RemoteIPTrustedProxyList conf/trusted-proxies.lst
```

**conf/trusted-proxies.lst contents**
```
# Identified external proxies;
192.0.2.16/28 #wap phone group of proxies
proxy.isp.example.com #some well known ISP
```

# 10.98   Apache Module mod_reqtimeout

| | |
|---|---|
| Description: | Set timeout and minimum data rate for receiving requests |
| Status: | Extension |
| ModuleIdentifier: | reqtimeout_module |
| SourceFile: | mod_reqtimeout.c |

**Directives**

- RequestReadTimeout

## Examples

1. Allow 10 seconds to receive the request including the headers and 30 seconds for receiving the request body:

   ```
   RequestReadTimeout header=10 body=30
   ```

2. Allow at least 10 seconds to receive the request body. If the client sends data, increase the timeout by 1 second for every 1000 bytes received, with no upper limit for the timeout (except for the limit given indirectly by LIMITREQUESTBODY):

   ```
   RequestReadTimeout body=10,MinRate=1000
   ```

3. Allow at least 10 seconds to receive the request including the headers. If the client sends data, increase the timeout by 1 second for every 500 bytes received. But do not allow more than 30 seconds for the request including the headers:

   ```
   RequestReadTimeout header=10-30,MinRate=500
   ```

4. Usually, a server should have both header and body timeouts configured. If a common configuration is used for http and https virtual hosts, the timeouts should not be set too low:

   ```
   RequestReadTimeout header=20-40,MinRate=500 body=20,MinRate=500
   ```

## RequestReadTimeout Directive

| | |
|---|---|
| Description: | Set timeout values for receiving request headers and body from client. |
| Syntax: | RequestReadTimeout [header=timeout[-maxtimeout][,MinRate=rate] [body=timeout[-maxtimeout][,MinRate=rate] |
| Default: | header=20-40,MinRate=500 body=20,MinRate=500 |
| Context: | server config, virtual host |
| Status: | Extension |
| Module: | mod_reqtimeout |
| Compatibility: | Defaulted to disabled in version 2.3.14 and earlier. |

This directive can set various timeouts for receiving the request headers and the request body from the client. If the client fails to send headers or body within the configured time, a 408 REQUEST TIME OUT error is sent.

For SSL virtual hosts, the header timeout values include the time needed to do the initial SSL handshake. If the user's browser is configured to query certificate revocation lists and the CRL server is not reachable, the initial SSL handshake may take a significant time until the browser gives up waiting for the CRL. Therefore the header timeout values should not be set to very low values for SSL virtual hosts. The body timeout values include the time needed for SSL renegotiation (if necessary).

When an ACCEPTFILTER is in use (usually the case on Linux and FreeBSD), the socket is not sent to the server process before at least one byte (or the whole request for `httpready`) is received. The header timeout configured with `RequestReadTimeout` is only effective after the server process has received the socket.

For each of the two timeout types (header or body), there are three ways to specify the timeout:

- **Fixed timeout value**:

```
type=timeout
```

  The time in seconds allowed for reading all of the request headers or body, respectively. A value of 0 means no limit.

- **Disable module for a vhost:**:

```
header=0 body=0
```

  This disables MOD_REQTIMEOUT completely.

- **Timeout value that is increased when data is received**:

```
type=timeout,MinRate=data_rate
```

  Same as above, but whenever data is received, the timeout value is increased according to the specified minimum data rate (in bytes per second).

- **Timeout value that is increased when data is received, with an upper bound**:

```
type=timeout-maxtimeout,MinRate=data_rate
```

  Same as above, but the timeout will not be increased above the second value of the specified timeout range.

## 10.99    Apache Module mod_request

| Description: | Filters to handle and make available HTTP request bodies |
|---|---|
| Status: | Base |
| ModuleIdentifier: | request_module |
| SourceFile: | mod_request.c |
| Compatibility: | Available in Apache 2.3 and later |

**Directives**

- KeptBodySize

### KeptBodySize Directive

| Description: | Keep the request body instead of discarding it up to the specified maximum size, for potential use by filters such as mod_include. |
|---|---|
| Syntax: | `KeptBodySize maximum size in bytes` |
| Default: | `KeptBodySize 0` |
| Context: | directory |
| Status: | Base |
| Module: | mod_request |

Under normal circumstances, request handlers such as the default handler for static files will discard the request body when it is not needed by the request handler. As a result, filters such as mod_include are limited to making `GET` requests only when including other URLs as subrequests, even if the original request was a `POST` request, as the discarded request body is no longer available once filter processing is taking place.

When this directive has a value greater than zero, request handlers that would otherwise discard request bodies will instead set the request body aside for use by filters up to the maximum size specified. In the case of the mod_include filter, an attempt to `POST` a request to the static shtml file will cause any subrequests to be `POST` requests, instead of `GET` requests as before.

This feature makes it possible to break up complex web pages and web applications into small individual components, and combine the components and the surrounding web page structure together using MOD_INCLUDE. The components can take the form of CGI programs, scripted languages, or URLs reverse proxied into the URL space from another server using MOD_PROXY.

**Note:** Each request set aside has to be set aside in temporary RAM until the request is complete. As a result, care should be taken to ensure sufficient RAM is available on the server to support the intended load. Use of this directive should be limited to where needed on targeted parts of your URL space, and with the lowest possible value that is still big enough to hold a request body.

If the request size sent by the client exceeds the maximum size allocated by this directive, the server will return `413 Request Entity Too Large`.

**See also**

- mod_include (p. 667) documentation
- mod_auth_form (p. 466) documentation

# 10.100   Apache Module mod_rewrite

| | |
|---|---|
| Description: | Provides a rule-based rewriting engine to rewrite requested URLs on the fly |
| Status: | Extension |
| ModuleIdentifier: | rewrite_module |
| SourceFile: | mod_rewrite.c |

## Summary

The MOD_REWRITE module uses a rule-based rewriting engine, based on a PCRE regular-expression parser, to rewrite requested URLs on the fly. By default, MOD_REWRITE maps a URL to a filesystem path. However, it can also be used to redirect one URL to another URL, or to invoke an internal proxy fetch.

MOD_REWRITE provides a flexible and powerful way to manipulate URLs using an unlimited number of rules. Each rule can have an unlimited number of attached rule conditions, to allow you to rewrite URL based on server variables, environment variables, HTTP headers, or time stamps.

MOD_REWRITE operates on the full URL path, including the path-info section. A rewrite rule can be invoked in `httpd.conf` or in `.htaccess`. The path generated by a rewrite rule can include a query string, or can lead to internal sub-processing, external request redirection, or internal proxy throughput.

Further details, discussion, and examples, are provided in the detailed mod_rewrite documentation (p. 146) .

### Directives

- RewriteBase
- RewriteCond
- RewriteEngine
- RewriteMap
- RewriteOptions
- RewriteRule

## Logging

MOD_REWRITE offers detailed logging of its actions at the `trace1` to `trace8` log levels. The log level can be set specifically for MOD_REWRITE using the LOGLEVEL directive: Up to level `debug`, no actions are logged, while `trace8` means that practically all actions are logged.

⟹ Using a high trace log level for MOD_REWRITE will slow down your Apache HTTP Server dramatically! Use a log level higher than `trace2` only for debugging!

### Example

```
LogLevel alert rewrite:trace3
```

⟹ **RewriteLog**

Those familiar with earlier versions of MOD_REWRITE will no doubt be looking for the `RewriteLog` and `RewriteLogLevel` directives. This functionality has been completely replaced by the new per-module logging configuration mentioned above.

To get just the MOD_REWRITE-specific log messages, pipe the log file through grep:

```
tail -f error_log|fgrep '[rewrite:'
```

## RewriteBase Directive

| | |
|---|---|
| Description: | Sets the base URL for per-directory rewrites |
| Syntax: | `RewriteBase URL-path` |
| Default: | `None` |
| Context: | directory, .htaccess |
| Override: | FileInfo |
| Status: | Extension |
| Module: | mod_rewrite |

The REWRITEBASE directive specifies the URL prefix to be used for per-directory (htaccess) REWRITERULE directives that substitute a relative path.

This directive is *required* when you use a relative path in a substitution in per-directory (htaccess) context unless either of the following conditions are true:

- The original request, and the substitution, are underneath the DOCUMENTROOT (as opposed to reachable by other means, such as ALIAS).

- The *filesystem* path to the directory containing the REWRITERULE, suffixed by the relative substitution is also valid as a URL path on the server (this is rare).

- In Apache HTTP Server 2.4.16 and later, this directive may be omitted when the request is mapped via ALIAS or MOD_USERDIR.

In the example below, REWRITEBASE is necessary to avoid rewriting to http://example.com/opt/myapp-1.2.3/welcome.html since the resource was not relative to the document root. This misconfiguration would normally cause the server to look for an "opt" directory under the document root.

```
DocumentRoot "/var/www/example.com"
AliasMatch "^/myapp" "/opt/myapp-1.2.3"
<Directory "/opt/myapp-1.2.3">
    RewriteEngine On
    RewriteBase "/myapp/"
    RewriteRule "^index\.html$"  "welcome.html"
</Directory>
```

## RewriteCond Directive

| | |
|---|---|
| Description: | Defines a condition under which rewriting will take place |
| Syntax: | `RewriteCond TestString CondPattern` |
| Context: | server config, virtual host, directory, .htaccess |
| Override: | FileInfo |
| Status: | Extension |
| Module: | mod_rewrite |

The REWRITECOND directive defines a rule condition. One or more REWRITECOND can precede a REWRITERULE directive. The following rule is then only used if both the current state of the URI matches its pattern, **and** if these conditions are met.

*TestString* is a string which can contain the following expanded constructs in addition to plain text:

- **RewriteRule backreferences**: These are backreferences of the form $N ($0 <= N <= 9$). $1 to $9 provide access to the grouped parts (in parentheses) of the pattern, from the `RewriteRule` which is subject to the current set of `RewriteCond` conditions. $0 provides access to the whole string matched by that pattern.

- **RewriteCond backreferences**: These are backreferences of the form **%N** (0 <= N <= 9). %1 to %9 provide access to the grouped parts (again, in parentheses) of the pattern, from the last matched `RewriteCond` in the current set of conditions. %0 provides access to the whole string matched by that pattern.

- **RewriteMap expansions**: These are expansions of the form **${mapname:key|default}**. See the documentation for RewriteMap for more details.

- **Server-Variables**: These are variables of the form **%{ *NAME_OF_VARIABLE* }** where *NAME_OF_VARIABLE* can be a string taken from the following list:

| HTTP headers: | connection & request: | |
|---|---|---|
| HTTP_ACCEPT | AUTH_TYPE | |
| HTTP_COOKIE | CONN_REMOTE_ADDR | |
| HTTP_FORWARDED | CONTEXT_PREFIX | |
| HTTP_HOST | CONTEXT_DOCUMENT_ROOT | |
| HTTP_PROXY_CONNECTION | IPV6 | |
| HTTP_REFERER | PATH_INFO | |
| HTTP_USER_AGENT | QUERY_STRING | |
| | REMOTE_ADDR | |
| | REMOTE_HOST | |
| | REMOTE_IDENT | |
| | REMOTE_PORT | |
| | REMOTE_USER | |
| | REQUEST_METHOD | |
| | SCRIPT_FILENAME | |
| **server internals:** | **date and time:** | **specials:** |
| DOCUMENT_ROOT | TIME_YEAR | API_VERSION |
| SCRIPT_GROUP | TIME_MON | CONN_REMOTE_ADDR |
| SCRIPT_USER | TIME_DAY | HTTPS |
| SERVER_ADDR | TIME_HOUR | IS_SUBREQ |
| SERVER_ADMIN | TIME_MIN | REMOTE_ADDR |
| SERVER_NAME | TIME_SEC | REQUEST_FILENAME |
| SERVER_PORT | TIME_WDAY | REQUEST_SCHEME |
| SERVER_PROTOCOL | TIME | REQUEST_URI |
| SERVER_SOFTWARE | | THE_REQUEST |

These variables all correspond to the similarly named HTTP MIME-headers, C variables of the Apache HTTP Server or `struct tm` fields of the Unix system. Most are documented here (p. 99) or elsewhere in the Manual or in the CGI specification.

SERVER_NAME and SERVER_PORT depend on the values of USECANONICALNAME and USECANONICAL-PHYSICALPORT respectively.

Those that are special to mod_rewrite include those below.

**API_VERSION** This is the version of the Apache httpd module API (the internal interface between server and module) in the current httpd build, as defined in include/ap_mmn.h. The module API version corresponds to the version of Apache httpd in use (in the release version of Apache httpd 1.3.14, for instance, it is 19990320:10), but is mainly of interest to module authors.

**CONN_REMOTE_ADDR** Since 2.4.8: The peer IP address of the connection (see the MOD_REMOTEIP module).

**HTTPS** Will contain the text "on" if the connection is using SSL/TLS, or "off" otherwise. (This variable can be safely used regardless of whether or not MOD_SSL is loaded).

**IS_SUBREQ** Will contain the text "true" if the request currently being processed is a sub-request, "false" otherwise. Sub-requests may be generated by modules that need to resolve additional files or URIs in order to complete their tasks.

**REMOTE_ADDR** The IP address of the remote host (see the MOD_REMOTEIP module).

**REQUEST_FILENAME** The full local filesystem path to the file or script matching the request, if this has already been determined by the server at the time REQUEST_FILENAME is referenced. Otherwise, such as when used in virtual host context, the same value as REQUEST_URI. Depending on the value of ACCEPT-PATHINFO, the server may have only used some leading components of the REQUEST_URI to map the request to a file.

**REQUEST_SCHEME** Will contain the scheme of the request (usually "http" or "https"). This value can be influenced with SERVERNAME.

**REQUEST_URI** The path component of the requested URI, such as "/index.html". This notably excludes the query string which is available as its own variable named QUERY_STRING.

**THE_REQUEST** The full HTTP request line sent by the browser to the server (e.g., "GET /index.html HTTP/1.1"). This does not include any additional headers sent by the browser. This value has not been unescaped (decoded), unlike most other variables below.

If the *TestString* has the special value expr, the *CondPattern* will be treated as an ap_expr (p. 99) . HTTP headers referenced in the expression will be added to the Vary header if the novary flag is not given.

Other things you should be aware of:

1. The variables SCRIPT_FILENAME and REQUEST_FILENAME contain the same value - the value of the filename field of the internal request_rec structure of the Apache HTTP Server. The first name is the commonly known CGI variable name while the second is the appropriate counterpart of REQUEST_URI (which contains the value of the uri field of request_rec).

   If a substitution occurred and the rewriting continues, the value of both variables will be updated accordingly.

   If used in per-server context (*i.e.*, before the request is mapped to the filesystem) SCRIPT_FILENAME and REQUEST_FILENAME cannot contain the full local filesystem path since the path is unknown at this stage of processing. Both variables will initially contain the value of REQUEST_URI in that case. In order to obtain the full local filesystem path of the request in per-server context, use an URL-based look-ahead %{LA-U:REQUEST_FILENAME} to determine the final value of REQUEST_FILENAME.

2. %{ENV:variable}, where *variable* can be any environment variable, is also available. This is looked-up via internal Apache httpd structures and (if not found there) via getenv() from the Apache httpd server process.

3. %{SSL:variable}, where *variable* is the name of an SSL environment variable (p. 916) , can be used whether or not MOD_SSL is loaded, but will always expand to the empty string if it is not. Example: %{SSL:SSL_CIPHER_USEKEYSIZE} may expand to 128. These variables are available even without setting the StdEnvVars option of the SSLOPTIONS directive.

4. %{HTTP:header}, where *header* can be any HTTP MIME-header name, can always be used to obtain the value of a header sent in the HTTP request. Example: %{HTTP:Proxy-Connection} is the value of the HTTP header "Proxy-Connection:". If a HTTP header is used in a condition this header is added to the Vary header of the response in case the condition evaluates to true for the request. It is **not** added if the condition evaluates to false for the request. Adding the HTTP header to the Vary header of the response is needed for proper caching.

   It has to be kept in mind that conditions follow a short circuit logic in the case of the '**ornext|OR**' flag so that certain conditions might not be evaluated at all.

5. %{LA-U:variable} can be used for look-aheads which perform an internal (URL-based) sub-request to determine the final value of *variable*. This can be used to access variable for rewriting which is not available at the current stage, but will be set in a later phase. For instance, to rewrite according to the REMOTE_USER variable from within the per-server context (httpd.conf file) you must use %{LA-U:REMOTE_USER} - this variable is set by the authorization phases, which come *after* the URL translation phase (during which mod_rewrite operates).

   On the other hand, because mod_rewrite implements its per-directory context (.htaccess file) via the Fixup phase of the API and because the authorization phases come *before* this phase, you just can use %{REMOTE_USER} in that context.

6. `%{LA-F:variable}` can be used to perform an internal (filename-based) sub-request, to determine the final value of *variable*. Most of the time, this is the same as LA-U above.

*CondPattern* is the condition pattern, a regular expression which is applied to the current instance of the *TestString*. *TestString* is first evaluated, before being matched against *CondPattern*.

*CondPattern* is usually a *perl compatible regular expression*, but there is additional syntax available to perform other useful tests against the *Teststring*:

1. You can prefix the pattern string with a '!' character (exclamation mark) to negate the result of the condition, no matter what kind of *CondPattern* is used.

2. You can perform lexicographical string comparisons:

   <**CondPattern** Lexicographically precedes
   Treats the *CondPattern* as a plain string and compares it lexicographically to *TestString*. True if *TestString* lexicographically precedes *CondPattern*.

   >**CondPattern** Lexicographically follows
   Treats the *CondPattern* as a plain string and compares it lexicographically to *TestString*. True if *TestString* lexicographically follows *CondPattern*.

   =**CondPattern** Lexicographically equal
   Treats the *CondPattern* as a plain string and compares it lexicographically to *TestString*. True if *TestString* is lexicographically equal to *CondPattern* (the two strings are exactly equal, character for character). If *CondPattern* is `""` (two quotation marks) this compares *TestString* to the empty string.

   <=**CondPattern** Lexicographically less than or equal to
   Treats the *CondPattern* as a plain string and compares it lexicographically to *TestString*. True if *TestString* lexicographically precedes *CondPattern*, or is equal to *CondPattern* (the two strings are equal, character for character).

   >=**CondPattern** Lexicographically greater than or equal to
   Treats the *CondPattern* as a plain string and compares it lexicographically to *TestString*. True if *TestString* lexicographically follows *CondPattern*, or is equal to *CondPattern* (the two strings are equal, character for character).

3. You can perform integer comparisons:

   **-eq** Is numerically **eq**ual to
   The *TestString* is treated as an integer, and is numerically compared to the *CondPattern*. True if the two are numerically equal.

   **-ge** Is numerically **g**reater than or **e**qual to
   The *TestString* is treated as an integer, and is numerically compared to the *CondPattern*. True if the *TestString* is numerically greater than or equal to the *CondPattern*.

   **-gt** Is numerically **g**reater **t**han
   The *TestString* is treated as an integer, and is numerically compared to the *CondPattern*. True if the *TestString* is numerically greater than the *CondPattern*.

   **-le** Is numerically **l**ess than or **e**qual to
   The *TestString* is treated as an integer, and is numerically compared to the *CondPattern*. True if the *TestString* is numerically less than or equal to the *CondPattern*. Avoid confusion with the **-l** by using the **-L** or **-h** variant.

   **-lt** Is numerically **l**ess **t**han
   The *TestString* is treated as an integer, and is numerically compared to the *CondPattern*. True if the *TestString* is numerically less than the *CondPattern*. Avoid confusion with the **-l** by using the **-L** or **-h** variant.

**-ne** Is numerically **n**ot **e**qual to

The *TestString* is treated as an integer, and is numerically compared to the *CondPattern*. True if the two are numerically different. This is equivalent to !-eq.

4. You can perform various file attribute tests:

**-d** Is **d**irectory.

Treats the *TestString* as a pathname and tests whether or not it exists, and is a directory.

**-f** Is regular **f**ile.

Treats the *TestString* as a pathname and tests whether or not it exists, and is a regular file.

**-F** Is existing file, via subrequest.

Checks whether or not *TestString* is a valid file, accessible via all the server's currently-configured access controls for that path. This uses an internal subrequest to do the check, so use it with care - it can impact your server's performance!

**-h** Is symbolic link, bash convention.

See **-l**.

**-l** Is symbolic **l**ink.

Treats the *TestString* as a pathname and tests whether or not it exists, and is a symbolic link. May also use the bash convention of **-L** or **-h** if there's a possibility of confusion such as when using the **-lt** or **-le** tests.

**-L** Is symbolic link, bash convention.

See **-l**.

**-s** Is regular file, with **s**ize.

Treats the *TestString* as a pathname and tests whether or not it exists, and is a regular file with size greater than zero.

**-U** Is existing URL, via subrequest.

Checks whether or not *TestString* is a valid URL, accessible via all the server's currently-configured access controls for that path. This uses an internal subrequest to do the check, so use it with care - it can impact your server's performance!

This flag *only* returns information about things like access control, authentication, and authorization. This flag *does not* return information about the status code the configured handler (static file, CGI, proxy, etc.) would have returned.

**-x** Has **ex**ecutable permissions.

Treats the *TestString* as a pathname and tests whether or not it exists, and has executable permissions. These permissions are determined according to the underlying OS.

For example:

```
RewriteCond /var/www/%{REQUEST_URI} !-f
RewriteRule ^(.+) /other/archive/$1 [R]
```

5. If the *TestString* has the special value expr, the *CondPattern* will be treated as an ap_expr (p. 99) .

In the below example, -strmatch is used to compare the REFERER against the site hostname, to block unwanted hotlinking.

```
RewriteCond expr "! %{HTTP_REFERER} -strmatch '*://%{HTTP_HOST}/*'"
RewriteRule "^/images" "-" [F]
```

6. You can also set special flags for *CondPattern* by appending **[*flags*]** as the third argument to the RewriteCond directive, where *flags* is a comma-separated list of any of the following flags:

- **'nocase|NC'** (**n**o **c**ase)
  This makes the test case-insensitive - differences between 'A-Z' and 'a-z' are ignored, both in the expanded *TestString* and the *CondPattern*. This flag is effective only for comparisons between *TestString* and *CondPattern*. It has no effect on filesystem and subrequest checks.

- **'ornext|OR'** (**or** next condition)
  Use this to combine rule conditions with a local OR instead of the implicit AND. Typical example:

```
RewriteCond "%{REMOTE_HOST}"  "^host1"  [OR]
RewriteCond "%{REMOTE_HOST}"  "^host2"  [OR]
RewriteCond "%{REMOTE_HOST}"  "^host3"
RewriteRule ...some special stuff for any of these hosts...
```

  Without this flag you would have to write the condition/rule pair three times.

- **'novary|NV'** (**n**o **v**ary)
  If a HTTP header is used in the condition, this flag prevents this header from being added to the Vary header of the response.
  Using this flag might break proper caching of the response if the representation of this response varies on the value of this header. So this flag should be only used if the meaning of the Vary header is well understood.

**Example:**

To rewrite the Homepage of a site according to the "`User-Agent:`" header of the request, you can use the following:

```
RewriteCond  "%{HTTP_USER_AGENT}"   "(iPhone|Blackberry|Android)"
RewriteRule  "^/$"                  "/homepage.mobile.html"  [L]

RewriteRule  "^/$"                  "/homepage.std.html"     [L]
```

Explanation: If you use a browser which identifies itself as a mobile browser (note that the example is incomplete, as there are many other mobile platforms), the mobile version of the homepage is served. Otherwise, the standard page is served.

## RewriteEngine Directive

| Description: | Enables or disables runtime rewriting engine |
|---|---|
| Syntax: | RewriteEngine on\|off |
| Default: | RewriteEngine off |
| Context: | server config, virtual host, directory, .htaccess |
| Override: | FileInfo |
| Status: | Extension |
| Module: | mod_rewrite |

The REWRITEENGINE directive enables or disables the runtime rewriting engine. If it is set to `off` this module does no runtime processing at all. It does not even update the `SCRIPT_URx` environment variables.

Use this directive to disable rules in a particular context, rather than commenting out all the REWRITERULE directives.

Note that rewrite configurations are not inherited by virtual hosts. This means that you need to have a `RewriteEngine on` directive for each virtual host in which you wish to use rewrite rules.

REWRITEMAP directives of the type `prg` are not started during server initialization if they're defined in a context that does not have REWRITEENGINE set to `on`

## RewriteMap Directive

| | |
|---|---|
| Description: | Defines a mapping function for key-lookup |
| Syntax: | `RewriteMap MapName MapType:MapSource MapTypeOptions` |
| Context: | server config, virtual host |
| Status: | Extension |
| Module: | mod_rewrite |

The REWRITEMAP directive defines a *Rewriting Map* which can be used inside rule substitution strings by the mapping-functions to insert/substitute fields through a key lookup. The source of this lookup can be of various types.

The *MapName* is the name of the map and will be used to specify a mapping-function for the substitution strings of a rewriting rule via one of the following constructs:

**$**{ *MapName* : *LookupKey* }
**$**{ *MapName* : *LookupKey* | *DefaultValue* }

When such a construct occurs, the map *MapName* is consulted and the key *LookupKey* is looked-up. If the key is found, the map-function construct is substituted by *SubstValue*. If the key is not found then it is substituted by *DefaultValue* or by the empty string if no *DefaultValue* was specified. Empty values behave as if the key was absent, therefore it is not possible to distinguish between empty-valued keys and absent keys.

For example, you might define a REWRITEMAP as:

```
RewriteMap examplemap "txt:/path/to/file/map.txt"
```

You would then be able to use this map in a REWRITERULE as follows:

```
RewriteRule "^/ex/(.*)" "${examplemap:$1}"
```

The meaning of the *MapTypeOptions* argument depends on particular *MapType*. See the Using RewriteMap (p. 166) for more information.

The following combinations for *MapType* and *MapSource* can be used:

**txt** A plain text file containing space-separated key-value pairs, one per line. (Details ... (p. 166) )

**rnd** Randomly selects an entry from a plain text file (Details ... (p. 166) )

**dbm** Looks up an entry in a dbm file containing name, value pairs. Hash is constructed from a plain text file format using the `httxt2dbm` (p. 328) utility. (Details ... (p. 166) )

**int** One of the four available internal functions provided by `RewriteMap`: toupper, tolower, escape or unescape. (Details ... (p. 166) )

**prg** Calls an external program or script to process the rewriting. (Details ... (p. 166) )

**dbd or fastdbd** A SQL SELECT statement to be performed to look up the rewrite target. (Details ... (p. 166) )

Further details, and numerous examples, may be found in the RewriteMap HowTo (p. 166)

## RewriteOptions Directive

| | |
|---|---|
| Description: | Sets some special options for the rewrite engine |
| Syntax: | `RewriteOptions Options` |
| Context: | server config, virtual host, directory, .htaccess |
| Override: | FileInfo |
| Status: | Extension |
| Module: | mod_rewrite |

The REWRITEOPTIONS directive sets some special options for the current per-server or per-directory configuration. The *Option* string can currently only be one of the following:

**Inherit** This forces the current configuration to inherit the configuration of the parent. In per-virtual-server context, this means that the maps, conditions and rules of the main server are inherited. In per-directory context this means that conditions and rules of the parent directory's .htaccess configuration or <DIRECTORY> sections are inherited. The inherited rules are virtually copied to the section where this directive is being used. If used in combination with local rules, the inherited rules are copied behind the local rules. The position of this directive - below or above of local rules - has no influence on this behavior. If local rules forced the rewriting to stop, the inherited rules won't be processed.

> [!] Rules inherited from the parent scope are applied **after** rules specified in the child scope.

**InheritBefore** Like Inherit above, but the rules from the parent scope are applied **before** rules specified in the child scope.
Available in Apache HTTP Server 2.3.10 and later.

**InheritDown** If this option is enabled, all child configurations will inherit the configuration of the current configuration. It is equivalent to specifying RewriteOptions Inherit in all child configurations. See the Inherit option for more details on how the parent-child relationships are handled.
Available in Apache HTTP Server 2.4.8 and later.

**InheritDownBefore** Like InheritDown above, but the rules from the current scope are applied **before** rules specified in any child's scope.
Available in Apache HTTP Server 2.4.8 and later.

**IgnoreInherit** This option forces the current and child configurations to ignore all rules that would be inherited from a parent specifying InheritDown or InheritDownBefore.
Available in Apache HTTP Server 2.4.8 and later.

**AllowNoSlash** By default, MOD_REWRITE will ignore URLs that map to a directory on disk but lack a trailing slash, in the expectation that the MOD_DIR module will issue the client with a redirect to the canonical URL with a trailing slash.

When the DIRECTORYSLASH directive is set to off, the AllowNoSlash option can be enabled to ensure that rewrite rules are no longer ignored. This option makes it possible to apply rewrite rules within .htaccess files that match the directory without a trailing slash, if so desired.
Available in Apache HTTP Server 2.4.0 and later.

**AllowAnyURI** When REWRITERULE is used in VirtualHost or server context with version 2.2.22 or later of httpd, MOD_REWRITE will only process the rewrite rules if the request URI is a URL-path (p. 377) . This avoids some security issues where particular rules could allow "surprising" pattern expansions (see CVE-2011-3368[78] and CVE-2011-4317[79]). To lift the restriction on matching a URL-path, the AllowAnyURI option can be enabled, and MOD_REWRITE will apply the rule set to any request URI string, regardless of whether that string matches the URL-path grammar required by the HTTP specification.
Available in Apache HTTP Server 2.4.3 and later.

> [!] **Security Warning**
>
> Enabling this option will make the server vulnerable to security issues if used with rewrite rules which are not carefully authored. It is **strongly recommended** that this option is not used. In particular, beware of input strings containing the '@' character which could change the interpretation of the transformed URI, as per the above CVE names.

---

[78] http://cve.mitre.org/cgi-bin/cvename.cgi?name=CVE-2011-3368
[79] http://cve.mitre.org/cgi-bin/cvename.cgi?name=CVE-2011-4317

**MergeBase** With this option, the value of REWRITEBASE is copied from where it's explicitly defined into any sub-directory or sub-location that doesn't define its own REWRITEBASE. This was the default behavior in 2.4.0 through 2.4.3, and the flag to restore it is available Apache HTTP Server 2.4.4 and later.

**IgnoreContextInfo** When a relative substitution is made in directory (htaccess) context and REWRITEBASE has not been set, this module uses some extended URL and filesystem context information to change the relative substitution back into a URL. Modules such as MOD_USERDIR and MOD_ALIAS supply this extended context info. Available in 2.4.16 and later.

## RewriteRule Directive

| | |
|---|---|
| Description: | Defines rules for the rewriting engine |
| Syntax: | `RewriteRule Pattern Substitution [flags]` |
| Context: | server config, virtual host, directory, .htaccess |
| Override: | FileInfo |
| Status: | Extension |
| Module: | mod_rewrite |

The REWRITERULE directive is the real rewriting workhorse. The directive can occur more than once, with each instance defining a single rewrite rule. The order in which these rules are defined is important - this is the order in which they will be applied at run-time.

*Pattern* is a perl compatible regular expression. On the first RewriteRule, it is matched against the (%-decoded) URL-path (p. 377) of the request, or, in per-directory context (see below), the URL path relative to that per-directory context. Subsequent patterns are matched against the output of the last matching RewriteRule.

 **What is matched?**

In VIRTUALHOST context, The *Pattern* will initially be matched against the part of the URL after the hostname and port, and before the query string (e.g. "/app1/index.html").

In DIRECTORY and htaccess context, the *Pattern* will initially be matched against the *filesystem* path, after removing the prefix that led the server to the current REWRITERULE (e.g. "app1/index.html" or "index.html" depending on where the directives are defined).

If you wish to match against the hostname, port, or query string, use a REWRITECOND with the %{HTTP_HOST}, %{SERVER_PORT}, or %{QUERY_STRING} variables respectively.

In any case, remember that regular expressions are substring matches. That is, you don't need the regex to describe the entire string, just the part that you wish to match. Thus, using a regex of . is often sufficient rather than .*, and the regex abc is **not** the same as ^abc$.

**Per-directory Rewrites**

- The rewrite engine may be used in .htaccess (p. 249) files and in <DIRECTORY> sections, with some additional complexity.

- To enable the rewrite engine in this context, you need to set "RewriteEngine On" **and** "Options FollowSymLinks" must be enabled. If your administrator has disabled override of FollowSymLinks for a user's directory, then you cannot use the rewrite engine. This restriction is required for security reasons.

- When using the rewrite engine in .htaccess files the per-directory prefix (which always is the same for a specific directory) is automatically *removed* for the RewriteRule pattern matching and automatically *added* after any relative (not starting with a slash or protocol name) substitution encounters the end of a rule set. See the REWRITEBASE directive for more information regarding what prefix will be added back to relative substitutions.

- If you wish to match against the full URL-path in a per-directory (htaccess) RewriteRule, use the %{REQUEST_URI} variable in a REWRITECOND.

- The removed prefix always ends with a slash, meaning the matching occurs against a string which *never* has a leading slash. Therefore, a *Pattern* with ^/ never matches in per-directory context.

- Although rewrite rules are syntactically permitted in <LOCATION> and <FILES> sections (including their regular expression counterparts), this should never be necessary and is unsupported. A likely feature to break in these contexts is relative substitutions.

For some hints on regular expressions, see the mod_rewrite Introduction (p. 147) .

In mod_rewrite, the NOT character ('!') is also available as a possible pattern prefix. This enables you to negate a pattern; to say, for instance: *"if the current URL does **NOT** match this pattern"*. This can be used for exceptional cases, where it is easier to match the negative pattern, or as a last default rule.

**Note**
> When using the NOT character to negate a pattern, you cannot include grouped wildcard parts in that pattern. This is because, when the pattern does NOT match (ie, the negation matches), there are no contents for the groups. Thus, if negated patterns are used, you cannot use $N in the substitution string!

The *Substitution* of a rewrite rule is the string that replaces the original URL-path that was matched by *Pattern*. The *Substitution* may be a:

**file-system path** Designates the location on the file-system of the resource to be delivered to the client. Substitutions are only treated as a file-system path when the rule is configured in server (virtualhost) context and the first component of the path in the substitution exists in the file-system

**URL-path** A DOCUMENTROOT-relative path to the resource to be served. Note that MOD_REWRITE tries to guess whether you have specified a file-system path or a URL-path by checking to see if the first segment of the path exists at the root of the file-system. For example, if you specify a *Substitution* string of /www/file.html, then this will be treated as a URL-path *unless* a directory named www exists at the root or your file-system (or, in the case of using rewrites in a .htaccess file, relative to your document root), in which case it will be treated as a file-system path. If you wish other URL-mapping directives (such as ALIAS) to be applied to the resulting URL-path, use the [PT] flag as described below.

**Absolute URL** If an absolute URL is specified, MOD_REWRITE checks to see whether the hostname matches the current host. If it does, the scheme and hostname are stripped out and the resulting path is treated as a URL-path. Otherwise, an external redirect is performed for the given URL. To force an external redirect back to the current host, see the [R] flag below.

**– (dash)** A dash indicates that no substitution should be performed (the existing path is passed through untouched). This is used when a flag (see below) needs to be applied without changing the path.

In addition to plain text, the *Substitution* string can include

1. back-references ($N) to the RewriteRule pattern

2. back-references (%N) to the last matched RewriteCond pattern

3. server-variables as in rule condition test-strings (%{VARNAME})

4. mapping-function calls (${mapname:key|default})

Back-references are identifiers of the form **$N** (**N**=0..9), which will be replaced by the contents of the **N**th group of the matched *Pattern*. The server-variables are the same as for the *TestString* of a RewriteCond directive. The mapping-functions come from the RewriteMap directive and are explained there. These three types of variables are expanded in the order above.

Rewrite rules are applied to the results of previous rewrite rules, in the order in which they are defined in the config file. The URL-path or file-system path (see "What is matched?", above) is **completely replaced** by the *Substitution* and the rewriting process continues until all rules have been applied, or it is explicitly terminated by an **L** flag (p. 178) , or other flag which implies immediate termination, such as **END** or **F**.

**Modifying the Query String**

By default, the query string is passed through unchanged. You can, however, create URLs in the substitution string containing a query string part. Simply use a question mark inside the substitution string to indicate that the following text should be re-injected into the query string. When you want to erase an existing query string, end the substitution string with just a question mark. To combine new and old query strings, use the [QSA] flag.

Additionally you can set special actions to be performed by appending **[*flags*]** as the third argument to the RewriteRule directive. *Flags* is a comma-separated list, surround by square brackets, of any of the flags in the following table. More details, and examples, for each flag, are available in the Rewrite Flags document (p. 178) .

| Flag and syntax | Function |
|---|---|
| B | Escape non-alphanumeric characters in backreferences *before* applying the transformation. *details ... (p. 178)* |
| backrefnoplus—BNP | If backreferences are being escaped, spaces should be escaped to %20 instead of +. Useful when the backreference will be used in the path component rather than the query string.*details ... (p. 178)* |
| chain—C | Rule is chained to the following rule. If the rule fails, the rule(s) chained to it will be skipped. *details ... (p. 178)* |
| cookie—CO=*NAME:VAL* | Sets a cookie in the client browser.  Full syntax is: CO=*NAME:VAL:domain*[:*lifetime*[:*path*[:*secure*[:*httponly*]]]] *details ... (p. 178)* |
| discardpath—DPI | Causes the PATH_INFO portion of the rewritten URI to be discarded. *details ... (p. 178)* |
| END | Stop the rewriting process immediately and don't apply any more rules.  Also prevents further execution of rewrite rules in per-directory and .htaccess context. (Available in 2.3.9 and later) *details ... (p. 178)* |
| env—E=[!]*VAR*[:*VAL*] | Causes an environment variable *VAR* to be set (to the value *VAL* if provided). The form !*VAR* causes the environment variable *VAR* to be unset. *details ... (p. 178)* |
| forbidden—F | Returns a 403 FORBIDDEN response to the client browser. *details ... (p. 178)* |

| gone—G | Returns a 410 GONE response to the client browser. *details ... (p. 178)* |
|---|---|
| Handler—H=*Content-handler* | Causes the resulting URI to be sent to the specified *Content-handler* for processing. *details ... (p. 178)* |
| last—L | Stop the rewriting process immediately and don't apply any more rules. Especially note caveats for per-directory and .htaccess context (see also the END flag). *details ... (p. 178)* |
| next—N | Re-run the rewriting process, starting again with the first rule, using the result of the ruleset so far as a starting point. *details ... (p. 178)* |
| nocase—NC | Makes the pattern comparison case-insensitive. *details ... (p. 178)* |
| noescape—NE | Prevent mod_rewrite from applying hexcode escaping of special characters in the result of the rewrite. *details ... (p. 178)* |
| nosubreq—NS | Causes a rule to be skipped if the current request is an internal sub-request. *details ... (p. 178)* |
| proxy—P | Force the substitution URL to be internally sent as a proxy request. *details ... (p. 178)* |
| passthrough—PT | Forces the resulting URI to be passed back to the URL mapping engine for processing of other URI-to-filename translators, such as `Alias` or `Redirect`. *details ... (p. 178)* |
| qsappend—QSA | Appends any query string from the original request URL to any query string created in the rewrite target.*details ... (p. 178)* |
| qsdiscard—QSD | Discard any query string attached to the incoming URI. *details ... (p. 178)* |
| qslast—QSL | Interpret the last (right-most) question mark as the query string delimiter, instead of the first (left-most) as normally used. Available in 2.4.19 and later. *details ... (p. 178)* |
| redirect—R[=*code*] | Forces an external redirect, optionally with the specified HTTP status code. *details ... (p. 178)* |
| skip—S=*num* | Tells the rewriting engine to skip the next *num* rules if the current rule matches. *details ... (p. 178)* |
| type—T=*MIME-type* | Force the MIME-type of the target file to be the specified type. *details ... (p. 178)* |

=====> **Home directory expansion**

When the substitution string begins with a string resembling "/˜user" (via explicit text or backreferences), mod_rewrite performs home directory expansion independent of the presence or configuration of MOD_USERDIR.

This expansion does not occur when the *PT* flag is used on the REWRITERULE directive.

Here are all possible substitution combinations and their meanings:

**Inside per-server configuration (`httpd.conf`)
for request "GET `/somepath/pathinfo`":**

| Given Rule | Resulting Substitution |
|---|---|
| ^/somepath(.*) otherpath$1 | invalid, not supported |
| ^/somepath(.*) otherpath$1 [R] | invalid, not supported |
| ^/somepath(.*) otherpath$1 [P] | invalid, not supported |
| ^/somepath(.*) /otherpath$1 | /otherpath/pathinfo |
| ^/somepath(.*) /otherpath$1 [R] | http://thishost/otherpath/pathinfo via external redirection |
| ^/somepath(.*) /otherpath$1 [P] | doesn't make sense, not supported |
| ^/somepath(.*) http://thishost/otherpath$1 | /otherpath/pathinfo |
| ^/somepath(.*) http://thishost/otherpath$1 [R] | http://thishost/otherpath/pathinfo via external redirection |
| ^/somepath(.*) http://thishost/otherpath$1 [P] | doesn't make sense, not supported |
| ^/somepath(.*) http://otherhost/otherpath$1 | http://otherhost/otherpath/pathinfo via external redirection |
| ^/somepath(.*) http://otherhost/otherpath$1 [R] | http://otherhost/otherpath/pathinfo via external redirection (the [R] flag is redundant) |
| ^/somepath(.*) http://otherhost/otherpath$1 [P] | http://otherhost/otherpath/pathinfo via internal proxy |

**Inside per-directory configuration for `/somepath`**
**(`/physical/path/to/somepath/.htaccess`, with `RewriteBase "/somepath"`)**
**for request "`GET /somepath/localpath/pathinfo`":**

| Given Rule | Resulting Substitution |
|---|---|
| ^localpath(.*) otherpath$1 | /somepath/otherpath/pathinfo |
| ^localpath(.*) otherpath$1 [R] | http://thishost/somepath/otherpath/pathinfo via external redirection |
| ^localpath(.*) otherpath$1 [P] | doesn't make sense, not supported |
| ^localpath(.*) /otherpath$1 | /otherpath/pathinfo |
| ^localpath(.*) /otherpath$1 [R] | http://thishost/otherpath/pathinfo via external redirection |
| ^localpath(.*) /otherpath$1 [P] | doesn't make sense, not supported |
| ^localpath(.*) http://thishost/otherpath$1 | /otherpath/pathinfo |
| ^localpath(.*) http://thishost/otherpath$1 [R] | http://thishost/otherpath/pathinfo via external redirection |
| ^localpath(.*) http://thishost/otherpath$1 [P] | doesn't make sense, not supported |
| ^localpath(.*) http://otherhost/otherpath$1 | http://otherhost/otherpath/pathinfo via external redirection |
| ^localpath(.*) http://otherhost/otherpath$1 [R] | http://otherhost/otherpath/pathinfo via external redirection (the [R] flag is redundant) |
| ^localpath(.*) http://otherhost/otherpath$1 [P] | http://otherhost/otherpath/pathinfo via internal proxy |

# 10.101 Apache Module mod_sed

| | |
|---|---|
| Description: | Filter Input (request) and Output (response) content using sed syntax |
| Status: | Experimental |
| ModuleIdentifier: | sed_module |
| SourceFile: | mod_sed.c sed0.c sed1.c regexp.c regexp.h sed.h |
| Compatibility: | Available in Apache 2.3 and later |

## Summary

MOD_SED is an in-process content filter. The MOD_SED filter implements the sed editing commands implemented by the Solaris 10 sed program as described in the manual page[80]. However, unlike sed, MOD_SED doesn't take data from standard input. Instead, the filter acts on the entity data sent between client and server. MOD_SED can be used as an input or output filter. MOD_SED is a content filter, which means that it cannot be used to modify client or server http headers.

The MOD_SED output filter accepts a chunk of data, executes the sed scripts on the data, and generates the output which is passed to the next filter in the chain.

The MOD_SED input filter reads the data from the next filter in the chain, executes the sed scripts, and returns the generated data to the caller filter in the filter chain.

Both the input and output filters only process the data if newline characters are seen in the content. At the end of the data, the rest of the data is treated as the last line.

A tutorial article on MOD_SED, and why it is more powerful than simple string or regular expression search and replace, is available on the author's blog[81].

### Directives

- InputSed
- OutputSed

## Sample Configuration

### Adding an output filter

```
# In the following example, the sed filter will change the string
# "monday" to "MON" and the string "sunday" to SUN in html documents
# before sending to the client.
<Directory "/var/www/docs/sed">
    AddOutputFilter Sed html
    OutputSed "s/monday/MON/g"
    OutputSed "s/sunday/SUN/g"
</Directory>
```

---

[80]http://www.gnu.org/software/sed/manual/sed.txt
[81]https://blogs.oracle.com/basant/entry/using_mod_sed_to_filter

**Adding an input filter**

```
# In the following example, the sed filter will change the string
# "monday" to "MON" and the string "sunday" to SUN in the POST data
# sent to PHP.
<Directory "/var/www/docs/sed">
    AddInputFilter Sed php
    InputSed "s/monday/MON/g"
    InputSed "s/sunday/SUN/g"
</Directory>
```

# Sed Commands

Complete details of the `sed` command can be found from the sed manual page[82].

**b**  Branch to the label specified (similar to goto).

**h**  Copy the current line to the hold buffer.

**H**  Append the current line to the hold buffer.

**g**  Copy the hold buffer to the current line.

**G**  Append the hold buffer to the current line.

**x**  Swap the contents of the hold buffer and the current line.

# InputSed Directive

| Description: | Sed command to filter request data (typically `POST` data) |
|---|---|
| Syntax: | `InputSed sed-command` |
| Context: | directory, .htaccess |
| Status: | Experimental |
| Module: | mod_sed |

The INPUTSED directive specifies the `sed` command to execute on the request data e.g., `POST` data.

# OutputSed Directive

| Description: | Sed command for filtering response content |
|---|---|
| Syntax: | `OutputSed sed-command` |
| Context: | directory, .htaccess |
| Status: | Experimental |
| Module: | mod_sed |

The OUTPUTSED directive specifies the `sed` command to execute on the response.

---

[82]http://www.gnu.org/software/sed/manual/sed.txt

## 10.102    Apache Module mod_session

| Description: | Session support |
|---|---|
| Status: | Extension |
| ModuleIdentifier: | session_module |
| SourceFile: | mod_session.c |
| Compatibility: | Available in Apache 2.3 and later |

### Summary

 **Warning**

The session modules make use of HTTP cookies, and as such can fall victim to Cross Site Scripting attacks, or expose potentially private information to clients. Please ensure that the relevant risks have been taken into account before enabling the session functionality on your server.

This module provides support for a server wide per user session interface. Sessions can be used for keeping track of whether a user has been logged in, or for other per user information that should be kept available across requests.

Sessions may be stored on the server, or may be stored on the browser. Sessions may also be optionally encrypted for added security. These features are divided into several modules in addition to MOD_SESSION; MOD_SESSION_CRYPTO, MOD_SESSION_COOKIE and MOD_SESSION_DBD. Depending on the server requirements, load the appropriate modules into the server (either statically at compile time or dynamically via the LOADMODULE directive).

Sessions may be manipulated from other modules that depend on the session, or the session may be read from and written to using environment variables and HTTP headers, as appropriate.

### Directives

- Session
- SessionEnv
- SessionExclude
- SessionExpiryUpdateInterval
- SessionHeader
- SessionInclude
- SessionMaxAge

### See also

- MOD_SESSION_COOKIE
- MOD_SESSION_CRYPTO
- MOD_SESSION_DBD

### What is a session?

At the core of the session interface is a table of key and value pairs that are made accessible across browser requests. These pairs can be set to any valid string, as needed by the application making use of the session.

The "session" is a **application/x-www-form-urlencoded** string containing these key value pairs, as defined by the HTML specification[83].

---

[83]http://www.w3.org/TR/html4/

The session can optionally be encrypted and base64 encoded before being written to the storage mechanism, as defined by the administrator.

## Who can use a session?

The session interface is primarily developed for the use by other server modules, such as MOD_AUTH_FORM, however CGI based applications can optionally be granted access to the contents of the session via the HTTP_SESSION environment variable. Sessions have the option to be modified and/or updated by inserting an HTTP response header containing the new session parameters.

## Keeping sessions on the server

Apache can be configured to keep track of per user sessions stored on a particular server or group of servers. This functionality is similar to the sessions available in typical application servers.

If configured, sessions are tracked through the use of a session ID that is stored inside a cookie, or extracted from the parameters embedded within the URL query string, as found in a typical GET request.

As the contents of the session are stored exclusively on the server, there is an expectation of privacy of the contents of the session. This does have performance and resource implications should a large number of sessions be present, or where a large number of webservers have to share sessions with one another.

The MOD_SESSION_DBD module allows the storage of user sessions within a SQL database via MOD_DBD.

## Keeping sessions on the browser

In high traffic environments where keeping track of a session on a server is too resource intensive or inconvenient, the option exists to store the contents of the session within a cookie on the client browser instead.

This has the advantage that minimal resources are required on the server to keep track of sessions, and multiple servers within a server farm have no need to share session information.

The contents of the session however are exposed to the client, with a corresponding risk of a loss of privacy. The MOD_SESSION_CRYPTO module can be configured to encrypt the contents of the session before writing the session to the client.

The MOD_SESSION_COOKIE allows the storage of user sessions on the browser within an HTTP cookie.

## Basic Examples

Creating a session is as simple as turning the session on, and deciding where the session will be stored. In this example, the session will be stored on the browser, in a cookie called `session`.

### Browser based session

```
Session On
SessionCookieName session path=/
```

The session is not useful unless it can be written to or read from. The following example shows how values can be injected into the session through the use of a predetermined HTTP response header called `X-Replace-Session`.

### Writing to a session

```
Session On
SessionCookieName session path=/
SessionHeader X-Replace-Session
```

The header should contain name value pairs expressed in the same format as a query string in a URL, as in the example below. Setting a key to the empty string has the effect of removing that key from the session.

### CGI to write to a session

```
#!/bin/bash
echo "Content-Type: text/plain"
echo "X-Replace-Session: key1=foo&key2=&key3=bar"
echo
env
```

If configured, the session can be read back from the HTTP_SESSION environment variable. By default, the session is kept private, so this has to be explicitly turned on with the SESSIONENV directive.

### Read from a session

```
Session On
SessionEnv On
SessionCookieName session path=/
SessionHeader X-Replace-Session
```

Once read, the CGI variable HTTP_SESSION should contain the value key1=foo&key3=bar.

## Session Privacy

Using the "show cookies" feature of your browser, you would have seen a clear text representation of the session. This could potentially be a problem should the end user need to be kept unaware of the contents of the session, or where a third party could gain unauthorised access to the data within the session.

The contents of the session can be optionally encrypted before being placed on the browser using the MOD_SESSION_CRYPTO module.

### Browser based encrypted session

```
Session On
SessionCryptoPassphrase secret
SessionCookieName session path=/
```

The session will be automatically decrypted on load, and encrypted on save by Apache, the underlying application using the session need have no knowledge that encryption is taking place.

Sessions stored on the server rather than on the browser can also be encrypted as needed, offering privacy where potentially sensitive information is being shared between webservers in a server farm using the MOD_SESSION_DBD module.

## Cookie Privacy

The HTTP cookie mechanism also offers privacy features, such as the ability to restrict cookie transport to SSL protected pages only, or to prevent browser based javascript from gaining access to the contents of the cookie.

**Warning**

Some of the HTTP cookie privacy features are either non-standard, or are not implemented consistently across browsers. The session modules allow you to set cookie parameters, but it makes no guarantee that privacy will be respected by the browser. If security is a concern, use the MOD_SESSION_CRYPTO to encrypt the contents of the session, or store the session on the server using the MOD_SESSION_DBD module.

Standard cookie parameters can be specified after the name of the cookie, as in the example below.

**Setting cookie parameters**

```
Session On
SessionCryptoPassphrase secret
SessionCookieName session path=/private;domain=example.com;httponly;secure;
```

In cases where the Apache server forms the frontend for backend origin servers, it is possible to have the session cookies removed from the incoming HTTP headers using the SESSIONCOOKIEREMOVE directive. This keeps the contents of the session cookies from becoming accessible from the backend server.

## Session Support for Authentication

As is possible within many application servers, authentication modules can use a session for storing the username and password after login. The MOD_AUTH_FORM saves the user's login name and password within the session.

**Form based authentication**

```
Session On
SessionCryptoPassphrase secret
SessionCookieName session path=/
AuthFormProvider file
AuthUserFile "conf/passwd"
AuthType form
AuthName "realm"
#...
```

See the MOD_AUTH_FORM module for documentation and complete examples.

## Integrating Sessions with External Applications

In order for sessions to be useful, it must be possible to share the contents of a session with external applications, and it must be possible for an external application to write a session of its own.

A typical example might be an application that changes a user's password set by MOD_AUTH_FORM. This application would need to read the current username and password from the session, make the required changes to the user's password, and then write the new password to the session in order to provide a seamless transition to the new password.

A second example might involve an application that registers a new user for the first time. When registration is complete, the username and password is written to the session, providing a seamless transition to being logged in.

**Apache modules**  Modules within the server that need access to the session can use the **mod_session.h** API in order to read from and write to the session. This mechanism is used by modules like MOD_AUTH_FORM.

**CGI programs and scripting languages**  Applications that run within the webserver can optionally retrieve the value of the session from the **HTTP_SESSION** environment variable. The session should be encoded as a **application/x-www-form-urlencoded** string as described by the HTML specification[84]. The environment variable is controlled by the setting of the SESSIONENV directive. The session can be written to by the script by returning a **application/x-www-form-urlencoded** response header with a name set by the SESSIONHEADER directive. In both cases, any encryption or decryption, and the reading the session from or writing the session to the chosen storage mechanism is handled by the MOD_SESSION modules and corresponding configuration.

---

[84]http://www.w3.org/TR/html4/

**Applications behind** MOD_PROXY If the SESSIONHEADER directive is used to define an HTTP request header, the session, encoded as a **application/x-www-form-urlencoded** string, will be made available to the application. If the same header is provided in the response, the value of this response header will be used to replace the session. As above, any encryption or decryption, and the reading the session from or writing the session to the chosen storage mechanism is handled by the MOD_SESSION modules and corresponding configuration.

**Standalone applications** Applications might choose to manipulate the session outside the control of the Apache HTTP server. In this case, it is the responsibility of the application to read the session from the chosen storage mechanism, decrypt the session, update the session, encrypt the session and write the session to the chosen storage mechanism, as appropriate.

### Session Directive

| | |
|---|---|
| Description: | Enables a session for the current directory or location |
| Syntax: | `Session On\|Off` |
| Default: | `Session Off` |
| Context: | server config, virtual host, directory, .htaccess |
| Override: | AuthConfig |
| Status: | Extension |
| Module: | mod_session |

The SESSION directive enables a session for the directory or location container. Further directives control where the session will be stored and how privacy is maintained.

### SessionEnv Directive

| | |
|---|---|
| Description: | Control whether the contents of the session are written to the *HTTP_SESSION* environment variable |
| Syntax: | `SessionEnv On\|Off` |
| Default: | `SessionEnv Off` |
| Context: | server config, virtual host, directory, .htaccess |
| Override: | AuthConfig |
| Status: | Extension |
| Module: | mod_session |

If set to *On*, the SESSIONENV directive causes the contents of the session to be written to a CGI environment variable called *HTTP_SESSION*.

The string is written in the URL query format, for example:

```
key1=foo&key3=bar
```

### SessionExclude Directive

| | |
|---|---|
| Description: | Define URL prefixes for which a session is ignored |
| Syntax: | `SessionExclude path` |
| Default: | `none` |
| Context: | server config, virtual host, directory, .htaccess |
| Status: | Extension |
| Module: | mod_session |

The SESSIONEXCLUDE directive allows sessions to be disabled relative to URL prefixes only. This can be used to make a website more efficient, by targeting a more precise URL space for which a session should be maintained. By default, all URLs within the directory or location are included in the session. The SESSIONEXCLUDE directive takes precedence over the SESSIONINCLUDE directive.

**Warning**

This directive has a similar purpose to the *path* attribute in HTTP cookies, but should not be confused with this attribute. This directive does not set the *path* attribute, which must be configured separately.

## SessionExpiryUpdateInterval Directive

| | |
|---|---|
| Description: | Define the number of seconds a session's expiry may change without the session being updated |
| Syntax: | `SessionExpiryUpdateInterval interval` |
| Default: | `SessionExpiryUpdateInterval 0 (always update)` |
| Context: | server config, virtual host, directory, .htaccess |
| Status: | Extension |
| Module: | mod_session |

The SESSIONEXPIRYUPDATEINTERVAL directive allows sessions to avoid the cost associated with writing the session each request when only the expiry time has changed. This can be used to make a website more efficient or reduce load on a database when using MOD_SESSION_DBD. The session is always written if the data stored in the session has changed or the expiry has changed by more than the configured interval.

Setting the interval to zero disables this directive, and the session expiry is refreshed for each request.

This directive only has an effect when combined with SESSIONMAXAGE to enable session expiry. Sessions without an expiry are only written when the data stored in the session has changed.

**Warning**

Because the session expiry may not be refreshed with each request, it's possible for sessions to expire up to *interval* seconds early. Using a small interval usually provides sufficient savings while having a minimal effect on expiry resolution.

## SessionHeader Directive

| | |
|---|---|
| Description: | Import session updates from a given HTTP response header |
| Syntax: | `SessionHeader header` |
| Default: | `none` |
| Context: | server config, virtual host, directory, .htaccess |
| Override: | AuthConfig |
| Status: | Extension |
| Module: | mod_session |

The SESSIONHEADER directive defines the name of an HTTP response header which, if present, will be parsed and written to the current session.

The header value is expected to be in the URL query format, for example:

```
key1=foo&key2=&key3=bar
```

Where a key is set to the empty string, that key will be removed from the session.

### SessionInclude Directive

| Description: | Define URL prefixes for which a session is valid |
|---|---|
| Syntax: | `SessionInclude path` |
| Default: | `all URLs` |
| Context: | server config, virtual host, directory, .htaccess |
| Override: | AuthConfig |
| Status: | Extension |
| Module: | mod_session |

The SESSIONINCLUDE directive allows sessions to be made valid for specific URL prefixes only. This can be used to make a website more efficient, by targeting a more precise URL space for which a session should be maintained. By default, all URLs within the directory or location are included in the session.

 **Warning**

This directive has a similar purpose to the *path* attribute in HTTP cookies, but should not be confused with this attribute. This directive does not set the *path* attribute, which must be configured separately.

### SessionMaxAge Directive

| Description: | Define a maximum age in seconds for a session |
|---|---|
| Syntax: | `SessionMaxAge maxage` |
| Default: | `SessionMaxAge 0` |
| Context: | server config, virtual host, directory, .htaccess |
| Override: | AuthConfig |
| Status: | Extension |
| Module: | mod_session |

The SESSIONMAXAGE directive defines a time limit for which a session will remain valid. When a session is saved, this time limit is reset and an existing session can be continued. If a session becomes older than this limit without a request to the server to refresh the session, the session will time out and be removed. Where a session is used to stored user login details, this has the effect of logging the user out automatically after the given time.

Setting the maxage to zero disables session expiry.

# 10.103    Apache Module mod_session_cookie

| Description: | Cookie based session support |
|---|---|
| Status: | Extension |
| ModuleIdentifier: | session_cookie_module |
| SourceFile: | mod_session_cookie.c |
| Compatibility: | Available in Apache 2.3 and later |

## Summary

 **Warning**
The session modules make use of HTTP cookies, and as such can fall victim to Cross Site
Scripting attacks, or expose potentially private information to clients. Please ensure that the
relevant risks have been taken into account before enabling the session functionality on your
server.

This submodule of MOD_SESSION provides support for the storage of user sessions on the remote browser within
HTTP cookies.

Using cookies to store a session removes the need for the server or a group of servers to store the session locally, or
collaborate to share a session, and can be useful for high traffic environments where a server based session might be
too resource intensive.

If session privacy is required, the MOD_SESSION_CRYPTO module can be used to encrypt the contents of the session
before writing the session to the client.

For more details on the session interface, see the documentation for the MOD_SESSION module.

### Directives

- SessionCookieName
- SessionCookieName2
- SessionCookieRemove

### See also

- MOD_SESSION
- MOD_SESSION_CRYPTO
- MOD_SESSION_DBD

## Basic Examples

To create a simple session and store it in a cookie called *session*, configure the session as follows:

**Browser based session**

```
Session On
SessionCookieName session path=/
```

For more examples on how the session can be configured to be read from and written to by a CGI application, see the
MOD_SESSION examples section.

For documentation on how the session can be used to store username and password details, see the MOD_AUTH_FORM
module.

## SessionCookieName Directive

| | |
|---|---|
| Description: | Name and attributes for the RFC2109 cookie storing the session |
| Syntax: | `SessionCookieName name attributes` |
| Default: | `none` |
| Context: | server config, virtual host, directory, .htaccess |
| Status: | Extension |
| Module: | mod_session_cookie |

The SESSIONCOOKIENAME directive specifies the name and optional attributes of an RFC2109 compliant cookie inside which the session will be stored. RFC2109 cookies are set using the `Set-Cookie` HTTP header.

An optional list of cookie attributes can be specified, as per the example below. These attributes are inserted into the cookie as is, and are not interpreted by Apache. Ensure that your attributes are defined correctly as per the cookie specification.

### Cookie with attributes

```
Session On
SessionCookieName session path=/private;domain=example.com;httponly;secure;version=1;
```

## SessionCookieName2 Directive

| | |
|---|---|
| Description: | Name and attributes for the RFC2965 cookie storing the session |
| Syntax: | `SessionCookieName2 name attributes` |
| Default: | `none` |
| Context: | server config, virtual host, directory, .htaccess |
| Status: | Extension |
| Module: | mod_session_cookie |

The SESSIONCOOKIENAME2 directive specifies the name and optional attributes of an RFC2965 compliant cookie inside which the session will be stored. RFC2965 cookies are set using the `Set-Cookie2` HTTP header.

An optional list of cookie attributes can be specified, as per the example below. These attributes are inserted into the cookie as is, and are not interpreted by Apache. Ensure that your attributes are defined correctly as per the cookie specification.

### Cookie2 with attributes

```
Session On
SessionCookieName2 session path=/private;domain=example.com;httponly;secure;version=1
```

## SessionCookieRemove Directive

| | |
|---|---|
| Description: | Control for whether session cookies should be removed from incoming HTTP headers |
| Syntax: | `SessionCookieRemove On|Off` |
| Default: | `SessionCookieRemove Off` |
| Context: | server config, virtual host, directory, .htaccess |
| Status: | Extension |
| Module: | mod_session_cookie |

The SESSIONCOOKIEREMOVE flag controls whether the cookies containing the session will be removed from the headers during request processing.

In a reverse proxy situation where the Apache server acts as a server frontend for a backend origin server, revealing the contents of the session cookie to the backend could be a potential privacy violation. When set to on, the session cookie will be removed from the incoming HTTP headers.

# 10.104 Apache Module mod_session_crypto

| Description: | Session encryption support |
|---|---|
| Status: | Experimental |
| ModuleIdentifier: | session_crypto_module |
| SourceFile: | mod_session_crypto.c |
| Compatibility: | Available in Apache 2.3 and later |

## Summary

 **Warning**

The session modules make use of HTTP cookies, and as such can fall victim to Cross Site Scripting attacks, or expose potentially private information to clients. Please ensure that the relevant risks have been taken into account before enabling the session functionality on your server.

This submodule of MOD_SESSION provides support for the encryption of user sessions before being written to a local database, or written to a remote browser via an HTTP cookie.

This can help provide privacy to user sessions where the contents of the session should be kept private from the user, or where protection is needed against the effects of cross site scripting attacks.

For more details on the session interface, see the documentation for the MOD_SESSION module.

**Directives**

- SessionCryptoCipher
- SessionCryptoDriver
- SessionCryptoPassphrase
- SessionCryptoPassphraseFile

**See also**

- MOD_SESSION
- MOD_SESSION_COOKIE
- MOD_SESSION_DBD

## Basic Usage

To create a simple encrypted session and store it in a cookie called *session*, configure the session as follows:

**Browser based encrypted session**

```
Session On
SessionCookieName session path=/
SessionCryptoPassphrase secret
```

The session will be encrypted with the given key. Different servers can be configured to share sessions by ensuring the same encryption key is used on each server.

If the encryption key is changed, sessions will be invalidated automatically.

For documentation on how the session can be used to store username and password details, see the MOD_AUTH_FORM module.

## SessionCryptoCipher Directive

| | |
|---|---|
| Description: | The crypto cipher to be used to encrypt the session |
| Syntax: | `SessionCryptoCipher name` |
| Default: | `aes256` |
| Context: | server config, virtual host, directory, .htaccess |
| Status: | Experimental |
| Module: | mod_session_crypto |
| Compatibility: | Available in Apache 2.3.0 and later |

The SESSIONCRYPTOCIPHER directive allows the cipher to be used during encryption. If not specified, the cipher defaults to `aes256`.

Possible values depend on the crypto driver in use, and could be one of:

- 3des192
- aes128
- aes192
- aes256

## SessionCryptoDriver Directive

| | |
|---|---|
| Description: | The crypto driver to be used to encrypt the session |
| Syntax: | `SessionCryptoDriver name [param[=value]]` |
| Default: | `none` |
| Context: | server config |
| Status: | Experimental |
| Module: | mod_session_crypto |
| Compatibility: | Available in Apache 2.3.0 and later |

The SESSIONCRYPTODRIVER directive specifies the name of the crypto driver to be used for encryption. If not specified, the driver defaults to the recommended driver compiled into APR-util.

The *NSS* crypto driver requires some parameters for configuration, which are specified as parameters with optional values after the driver name.

### NSS without a certificate database

```
SessionCryptoDriver nss
```

### NSS with certificate database

```
SessionCryptoDriver nss dir=certs
```

### NSS with certificate database and parameters

```
SessionCryptoDriver nss dir=certs key3=key3.db cert7=cert7.db secmod=secmod
```

### NSS with paths containing spaces

```
SessionCryptoDriver nss "dir=My Certs" key3=key3.db cert7=cert7.db secmod=secmod
```

The *NSS* crypto driver might have already been configured by another part of the server, for example from `mod_nss` or `MOD_LDAP`. If found to have already been configured, a warning will be logged, and the existing configuration will have taken affect. To avoid this warning, use the noinit parameter as follows.

### NSS with certificate database

```
SessionCryptoDriver nss noinit
```

To prevent confusion, ensure that all modules requiring NSS are configured with identical parameters.

The *openssl* crypto driver supports an optional parameter to specify the engine to be used for encryption.

### OpenSSL with engine support

```
SessionCryptoDriver openssl engine=name
```

## SessionCryptoPassphrase Directive

| | |
|---|---|
| Description: | The key used to encrypt the session |
| Syntax: | `SessionCryptoPassphrase secret [ secret ...  ]` |
| Default: | `none` |
| Context: | server config, virtual host, directory, .htaccess |
| Status: | Experimental |
| Module: | mod_session_crypto |
| Compatibility: | Available in Apache 2.3.0 and later |

The SESSIONCRYPTOPASSPHRASE directive specifies the keys to be used to enable symmetrical encryption on the contents of the session before writing the session, or decrypting the contents of the session after reading the session.

Keys are more secure when they are long, and consist of truly random characters. Changing the key on a server has the effect of invalidating all existing sessions.

Multiple keys can be specified in order to support key rotation. The first key listed will be used for encryption, while all keys listed will be attempted for decryption. To rotate keys across multiple servers over a period of time, add a new secret to the end of the list, and once rolled out completely to all servers, remove the first key from the start of the list.

As of version 2.4.7 if the value begins with *exec:* the resulting command will be executed and the first line returned to standard output by the program will be used as the key.

```
#key used as-is
SessionCryptoPassphrase secret

#Run /path/to/program to get key
SessionCryptoPassphrase exec:/path/to/program

#Run /path/to/otherProgram and provide arguments
SessionCryptoPassphrase "exec:/path/to/otherProgram argument1"
```

## SessionCryptoPassphraseFile Directive

| | |
|---|---|
| Description: | File containing keys used to encrypt the session |
| Syntax: | `SessionCryptoPassphraseFile filename` |
| Default: | `none` |
| Context: | server config, virtual host, directory |
| Status: | Experimental |
| Module: | mod_session_crypto |
| Compatibility: | Available in Apache 2.3.0 and later |

The SESSIONCRYPTOPASSPHRASEFILE directive specifies the name of a configuration file containing the keys to use for encrypting or decrypting the session, specified one per line. The file is read on server start, and a graceful restart will be necessary for httpd to pick up changes to the keys.

Unlike the SESSIONCRYPTOPASSPHRASE directive, the keys are not exposed within the httpd configuration and can be hidden by protecting the file appropriately.

Multiple keys can be specified in order to support key rotation. The first key listed will be used for encryption, while all keys listed will be attempted for decryption. To rotate keys across multiple servers over a period of time, add a new secret to the end of the list, and once rolled out completely to all servers, remove the first key from the start of the list.

# 10.105 Apache Module mod_session_dbd

| | |
|---|---|
| Description: | DBD/SQL based session support |
| Status: | Extension |
| ModuleIdentifier: | session_dbd_module |
| SourceFile: | mod_session_dbd.c |
| Compatibility: | Available in Apache 2.3 and later |

## Summary

 **Warning**

The session modules make use of HTTP cookies, and as such can fall victim to Cross Site Scripting attacks, or expose potentially private information to clients. Please ensure that the relevant risks have been taken into account before enabling the session functionality on your server.

This submodule of MOD_SESSION provides support for the storage of user sessions within a SQL database using the MOD_DBD module.

Sessions can either be **anonymous**, where the session is keyed by a unique UUID string stored on the browser in a cookie, or **per user**, where the session is keyed against the userid of the logged in user.

SQL based sessions are hidden from the browser, and so offer a measure of privacy without the need for encryption.

Different webservers within a server farm may choose to share a database, and so share sessions with one another.

For more details on the session interface, see the documentation for the MOD_SESSION module.

**Directives**

- SessionDBDCookieName
- SessionDBDCookieName2
- SessionDBDCookieRemove
- SessionDBDDeleteLabel
- SessionDBDInsertLabel
- SessionDBDPerUser
- SessionDBDSelectLabel
- SessionDBDUpdateLabel

**See also**

- MOD_SESSION
- MOD_SESSION_CRYPTO
- MOD_SESSION_COOKIE
- MOD_DBD

## DBD Configuration

Before the MOD_SESSION_DBD module can be configured to maintain a session, the MOD_DBD module must be configured to make the various database queries available to the server.

There are four queries required to keep a session maintained, to select an existing session, to update an existing session, to insert a new session, and to delete an expired or empty session. These queries are configured as per the example below.

**Sample DBD configuration**

```
DBDriver pgsql
DBDParams "dbname=apachesession user=apache password=xxxxx host=localhost"
DBDPrepareSQL "delete from session where key = %s" deletesession
DBDPrepareSQL "update session set value = %s, expiry = %lld, key = %s where key = %s" update
DBDPrepareSQL "insert into session (value, expiry, key) values (%s, %lld, %s)" insertsession
DBDPrepareSQL "select value from session where key = %s and (expiry = 0 or expiry > %lld)" s
DBDPrepareSQL "delete from session where expiry != 0 and expiry < %lld" cleansession
```

## Anonymous Sessions

Anonymous sessions are keyed against a unique UUID, and stored on the browser within an HTTP cookie. This method is similar to that used by most application servers to store session information.

To create a simple anonymous session and store it in a postgres database table called *apachesession*, and save the session ID in a cookie called *session*, configure the session as follows:

**SQL based anonymous session**

```
Session On
SessionDBDCookieName session path=/
```

For more examples on how the session can be configured to be read from and written to by a CGI application, see the MOD_SESSION examples section.

For documentation on how the session can be used to store username and password details, see the MOD_AUTH_FORM module.

## Per User Sessions

Per user sessions are keyed against the username of a successfully authenticated user. It offers the most privacy, as no external handle to the session exists outside of the authenticated realm.

Per user sessions work within a correctly configured authenticated environment, be that using basic authentication, digest authentication or SSL client certificates. Due to the limitations of who came first, the chicken or the egg, per user sessions cannot be used to store authentication credentials from a module like MOD_AUTH_FORM.

To create a simple per user session and store it in a postgres database table called *apachesession*, and with the session keyed to the userid, configure the session as follows:

**SQL based per user session**

```
Session On
SessionDBDPerUser On
```

### Database Housekeeping

Over the course of time, the database can be expected to start accumulating expired sessions. At this point, the MOD_SESSION_DBD module is not yet able to handle session expiry automatically.

 **Warning**
The administrator will need to set up an external process via cron to clean out expired sessions.

### SessionDBDCookieName Directive

| | |
|---|---|
| Description: | Name and attributes for the RFC2109 cookie storing the session ID |
| Syntax: | SessionDBDCookieName name attributes |
| Default: | none |
| Context: | server config, virtual host, directory, .htaccess |
| Status: | Extension |
| Module: | mod_session_dbd |

The SESSIONDBDCOOKIENAME directive specifies the name and optional attributes of an RFC2109 compliant cookie inside which the session ID will be stored. RFC2109 cookies are set using the Set-Cookie HTTP header.

An optional list of cookie attributes can be specified, as per the example below. These attributes are inserted into the cookie as is, and are not interpreted by Apache. Ensure that your attributes are defined correctly as per the cookie specification.

**Cookie with attributes**

```
Session On
SessionDBDCookieName session path=/private;domain=example.com;httponly;secure;version
```

### SessionDBDCookieName2 Directive

| | |
|---|---|
| Description: | Name and attributes for the RFC2965 cookie storing the session ID |
| Syntax: | SessionDBDCookieName2 name attributes |
| Default: | none |
| Context: | server config, virtual host, directory, .htaccess |
| Status: | Extension |
| Module: | mod_session_dbd |

The SESSIONDBDCOOKIENAME2 directive specifies the name and optional attributes of an RFC2965 compliant cookie inside which the session ID will be stored. RFC2965 cookies are set using the Set-Cookie2 HTTP header.

An optional list of cookie attributes can be specified, as per the example below. These attributes are inserted into the cookie as is, and are not interpreted by Apache. Ensure that your attributes are defined correctly as per the cookie specification.

**Cookie2 with attributes**

```
Session On
SessionDBDCookieName2 session path=/private;domain=example.com;httponly;secure;versio
```

## SessionDBDCookieRemove Directive

| | |
|---|---|
| Description: | Control for whether session ID cookies should be removed from incoming HTTP headers |
| Syntax: | `SessionDBDCookieRemove On|Off` |
| Default: | `SessionDBDCookieRemove On` |
| Context: | server config, virtual host, directory, .htaccess |
| Status: | Extension |
| Module: | mod_session_dbd |

The SESSIONDBDCOOKIEREMOVE flag controls whether the cookies containing the session ID will be removed from the headers during request processing.

In a reverse proxy situation where the Apache server acts as a server frontend for a backend origin server, revealing the contents of the session ID cookie to the backend could be a potential privacy violation. When set to on, the session ID cookie will be removed from the incoming HTTP headers.

## SessionDBDDeleteLabel Directive

| | |
|---|---|
| Description: | The SQL query to use to remove sessions from the database |
| Syntax: | `SessionDBDDeleteLabel label` |
| Default: | `SessionDBDDeleteLabel deletesession` |
| Context: | server config, virtual host, directory, .htaccess |
| Status: | Extension |
| Module: | mod_session_dbd |

The SESSIONDBDDELETELABEL directive sets the default delete query label to be used to delete an expired or empty session. This label must have been previously defined using the DBDPREPARESQL directive.

## SessionDBDInsertLabel Directive

| | |
|---|---|
| Description: | The SQL query to use to insert sessions into the database |
| Syntax: | `SessionDBDInsertLabel label` |
| Default: | `SessionDBDInsertLabel insertsession` |
| Context: | server config, virtual host, directory, .htaccess |
| Status: | Extension |
| Module: | mod_session_dbd |

The SESSIONDBDINSERTLABEL directive sets the default insert query label to be used to load in a session. This label must have been previously defined using the DBDPREPARESQL directive.

If an attempt to update the session affects no rows, this query will be called to insert the session into the database.

## SessionDBDPerUser Directive

| | |
|---|---|
| Description: | Enable a per user session |
| Syntax: | `SessionDBDPerUser On|Off` |
| Default: | `SessionDBDPerUser Off` |
| Context: | server config, virtual host, directory, .htaccess |
| Status: | Extension |
| Module: | mod_session_dbd |

The SESSIONDBDPERUSER flag enables a per user session keyed against the user's login name. If the user is not logged in, this directive will be ignored.

## SessionDBDSelectLabel Directive

| | |
|---|---|
| Description: | The SQL query to use to select sessions from the database |
| Syntax: | `SessionDBDSelectLabel label` |
| Default: | `SessionDBDSelectLabel selectsession` |
| Context: | server config, virtual host, directory, .htaccess |
| Status: | Extension |
| Module: | mod_session_dbd |

The SESSIONDBDSELECTLABEL directive sets the default select query label to be used to load in a session. This label must have been previously defined using the DBDPREPARESQL directive.

## SessionDBDUpdateLabel Directive

| | |
|---|---|
| Description: | The SQL query to use to update existing sessions in the database |
| Syntax: | `SessionDBDUpdateLabel label` |
| Default: | `SessionDBDUpdateLabel updatesession` |
| Context: | server config, virtual host, directory, .htaccess |
| Status: | Extension |
| Module: | mod_session_dbd |

The SESSIONDBDUPDATELABEL directive sets the default update query label to be used to load in a session. This label must have been previously defined using the DBDPREPARESQL directive.

If an attempt to update the session affects no rows, the insert query will be called to insert the session into the database. If the database supports InsertOrUpdate, override this query to perform the update in one query instead of two.

## 10.106    Apache Module mod_setenvif

| Description: | Allows the setting of environment variables based on characteristics of the request |
|---|---|
| Status: | Base |
| ModuleIdentifier: | setenvif_module |
| SourceFile: | mod_setenvif.c |

## Summary

The MOD_SETENVIF module allows you to set internal environment variables according to whether different aspects of the request match regular expressions you specify. These environment variables can be used by other parts of the server to make decisions about actions to be taken, as well as becoming available to CGI scripts and SSI pages.

The directives are considered in the order they appear in the configuration files. So more complex sequences can be used, such as this example, which sets netscape if the browser is mozilla but not MSIE.

```
BrowserMatch ^Mozilla netscape
BrowserMatch MSIE !netscape
```

When the server looks up a path via an internal subrequest such as looking for a DIRECTORYINDEX or generating a directory listing with MOD_AUTOINDEX, per-request environment variables are *not* inherited in the subrequest. Additionally, SETENVIF directives are not separately evaluated in the subrequest due to the API phases MOD_SETENVIF takes action in.

### Directives

- BrowserMatch
- BrowserMatchNoCase
- SetEnvIf
- SetEnvIfExpr
- SetEnvIfNoCase

### See also

- Environment Variables in Apache HTTP Server (p. 92)

## BrowserMatch Directive

| Description: | Sets environment variables conditional on HTTP User-Agent |
|---|---|
| Syntax: | BrowserMatch regex [!]env-variable[=value] [[!]env-variable[=value]] ... |
| Context: | server config, virtual host, directory, .htaccess |
| Override: | FileInfo |
| Status: | Base |
| Module: | mod_setenvif |

The BROWSERMATCH is a special cases of the SETENVIF directive that sets environment variables conditional on the User-Agent HTTP request header. The following two lines have the same effect:

```
BrowserMatch Robot is_a_robot
SetEnvIf User-Agent Robot is_a_robot
```

Some additional examples:

```
BrowserMatch ^Mozilla forms jpeg=yes browser=netscape
BrowserMatch "^Mozilla/[2-3]" tables agif frames javascript
BrowserMatch MSIE !javascript
```

## BrowserMatchNoCase Directive

| | |
|---|---|
| Description: | Sets environment variables conditional on User-Agent without respect to case |
| Syntax: | BrowserMatchNoCase regex [!]env-variable[=value] [[!]env-variable[=value]] ... |
| Context: | server config, virtual host, directory, .htaccess |
| Override: | FileInfo |
| Status: | Base |
| Module: | mod_setenvif |

The BROWSERMATCHNOCASE directive is semantically identical to the BROWSERMATCH directive. However, it provides for case-insensitive matching. For example:

```
BrowserMatchNoCase mac platform=macintosh
BrowserMatchNoCase win platform=windows
```

The BROWSERMATCH and BROWSERMATCHNOCASE directives are special cases of the SETENVIF and SETENV-IFNOCASE directives. The following two lines have the same effect:

```
BrowserMatchNoCase Robot is_a_robot
SetEnvIfNoCase User-Agent Robot is_a_robot
```

## SetEnvIf Directive

| | |
|---|---|
| Description: | Sets environment variables based on attributes of the request |
| Syntax: | SetEnvIf attribute regex [!]env-variable[=value] [[!]env-variable[=value]] ... |
| Context: | server config, virtual host, directory, .htaccess |
| Override: | FileInfo |
| Status: | Base |
| Module: | mod_setenvif |

The SETENVIF directive defines environment variables based on attributes of the request. The *attribute* specified in the first argument can be one of four things:

1. An HTTP request header field (see RFC2616[85] for more information about these); for example: Host, User-Agent, Referer, and Accept-Language. A regular expression may be used to specify a set of request headers.

2. One of the following aspects of the request:

   - Remote_Host - the hostname (if available) of the client making the request
   - Remote_Addr - the IP address of the client making the request
   - Server_Addr - the IP address of the server on which the request was received (only with versions later than 2.0.43)

---

[85]http://www.rfc-editor.org/rfc/rfc2616.txt

- `Request_Method` - the name of the method being used (`GET`, `POST`, *et cetera*)
- `Request_Protocol` - the name and version of the protocol with which the request was made (*e.g.*, "HTTP/0.9", "HTTP/1.1", *etc.*)
- `Request_URI` - the resource requested on the HTTP request line – generally the portion of the URL following the scheme and host portion without the query string. See the REWRITECOND directive of MOD_REWRITE for extra information on how to match your query string.

3. The name of an environment variable in the list of those associated with the request. This allows SETEN-VIF directives to test against the result of prior matches. Only those environment variables defined by earlier `SetEnvIf[NoCase]` directives are available for testing in this manner. 'Earlier' means that they were defined at a broader scope (such as server-wide) or previously in the current directive's scope. Environment variables will be considered only if there was no match among request characteristics and a regular expression was not used for the *attribute*.

The second argument (*regex*) is a regular expression. If the *regex* matches against the *attribute*, then the remainder of the arguments are evaluated.

The rest of the arguments give the names of variables to set, and optionally values to which they should be set. These take the form of

1. *varname*, or

2. `!`*varname*, or

3. *varname=value*

In the first form, the value will be set to "1". The second will remove the given variable if already defined, and the third will set the variable to the literal value given by *value*. Since version 2.0.51, Apache httpd will recognize occurrences of $1..$9 within *value* and replace them by parenthesized subexpressions of *regex*. $0 provides access to the whole string matched by that pattern.

```
SetEnvIf Request_URI "\.gif$" object_is_image=gif
SetEnvIf Request_URI "\.jpg$" object_is_image=jpg
SetEnvIf Request_URI "\.xbm$" object_is_image=xbm

SetEnvIf Referer www\.mydomain\.example\.com intra_site_referral

SetEnvIf object_is_image xbm XBIT_PROCESSING=1

SetEnvIf Request_URI "\.(.*)$" EXTENSION=$1

SetEnvIf ^TS  ^[a-z]   HAVE_TS
```

The first three will set the environment variable `object_is_image` if the request was for an image file, and the fourth sets `intra_site_referral` if the referring page was somewhere on the `www.mydomain.example.com` Web site.

The last example will set environment variable `HAVE_TS` if the request contains any headers that begin with "TS" whose values begins with any character in the set [a-z].

**See also**

- Environment Variables in Apache HTTP Server (p. 92) , for additional examples.

## SetEnvIfExpr Directive

| | |
|---|---|
| Description: | Sets environment variables based on an ap_expr expression |
| Syntax: | `SetEnvIfExpr expr [!]env-variable[=value]` `[[!]env-variable[=value]] ...` |
| Context: | server config, virtual host, directory, .htaccess |
| Override: | FileInfo |
| Status: | Base |
| Module: | mod_setenvif |

The SETENVIFEXPR directive defines environment variables based on an <IF> ap_expr. These expressions will be evaluated at runtime, and applied *env-variable* in the same fashion as SETENVIF.

```
SetEnvIfExpr "tolower(req('X-Sendfile')) == 'd:\images\very_big.iso')" iso_delivered
```

This would set the environment variable `iso_delivered` every time our application attempts to send it via `X-Sendfile`

A more useful example would be to set the variable rfc1918 if the remote IP address is a private address according to RFC 1918:

```
SetEnvIfExpr "-R '10.0.0.0/8' || -R '172.16.0.0/12' || -R '192.168.0.0/16'" rfc1918
```

**See also**

- Expressions in Apache HTTP Server (p. 99) , for a complete reference and more examples.
- <IF> can be used to achieve similar results.
- MOD_FILTER

## SetEnvIfNoCase Directive

| | |
|---|---|
| Description: | Sets environment variables based on attributes of the request without respect to case |
| Syntax: | `SetEnvIfNoCase attribute regex [!]env-variable[=value]` `[[!]env-variable[=value]] ...` |
| Context: | server config, virtual host, directory, .htaccess |
| Override: | FileInfo |
| Status: | Base |
| Module: | mod_setenvif |

The SETENVIFNOCASE is semantically identical to the SETENVIF directive, and differs only in that the regular expression matching is performed in a case-insensitive manner. For example:

```
SetEnvIfNoCase Host Example\.Org site=example
```

This will cause the `site` environment variable to be set to `"example"` if the HTTP request header field `Host:` was included and contained `Example.Org`, `example.org`, or any other combination.

# 10.107   Apache Module mod_slotmem_plain

| Description: | Slot-based shared memory provider. |
|---|---|
| Status: | Extension |
| ModuleIdentifier: | slotmem_plain_module |
| SourceFile: | mod_slotmem_plain.c |

## Summary

mod_slotmem_plain is a memory provider which provides for creation and access to a plain memory segment in which the datasets are organized in "slots."

If the memory needs to be shared between threads and processes, a better provider would be MOD_SLOTMEM_SHM.

mod_slotmem_plain provides the following API functions:

**apr_status_t doall(ap_slotmem_instance_t \*s, ap_slotmem_callback_fn_t \*func, void \*data, apr_pool_t \*pool)**
  call the callback on all worker slots

**apr_status_t create(ap_slotmem_instance_t \*\*new, const char \*name, apr_size_t item_size, unsigned int item_num, ap_slotmem_ty**
  create a new slotmem with each item size is item_size.

**apr_status_t attach(ap_slotmem_instance_t \*\*new, const char \*name, apr_size_t \*item_size, unsigned int \*item_num, apr_pool_t \***
  attach to an existing slotmem.

**apr_status_t dptr(ap_slotmem_instance_t \*s, unsigned int item_id, void\*\*mem)**  get the direct pointer to the memory associated with this worker slot.

**apr_status_t get(ap_slotmem_instance_t \*s, unsigned int item_id, unsigned char \*dest, apr_size_t dest_len)**
  get/read the memory from this slot to dest

**apr_status_t put(ap_slotmem_instance_t \*slot, unsigned int item_id, unsigned char \*src, apr_size_t src_len)**
  put/write the data from src to this slot

**unsigned int num_slots(ap_slotmem_instance_t \*s)**  return the total number of slots in the segment

**apr_size_t slot_size(ap_slotmem_instance_t \*s)**  return the total data size, in bytes, of a slot in the segment

**apr_status_t grab(ap_slotmem_instance_t \*s, unsigned int \*item_id);**  grab or allocate the first free slot and mark as in-use (does not do any data copying)

**apr_status_t fgrab(ap_slotmem_instance_t \*s, unsigned int item_id);**  forced grab or allocate the specified slot and mark as in-use (does not do any data copying)

**apr_status_t release(ap_slotmem_instance_t \*s, unsigned int item_id);**  release or free a slot and mark as not in-use (does not do any data copying)

**Directives** This module provides no directives.

# 10.108 Apache Module mod_slotmem_shm

| Description: | Slot-based shared memory provider. |
|---|---|
| Status: | Extension |
| ModuleIdentifier: | slotmem_shm_module |
| SourceFile: | mod_slotmem_shm.c |

## Summary

mod_slotmem_shm is a memory provider which provides for creation and access to a shared memory segment in which the datasets are organized in "slots."

All shared memory is cleared and cleaned with each restart, whether graceful or not. The data itself is stored and restored within a file noted by the name parameter in the create and attach calls. If not specified with an absolute path, the file will be created relative to the path specified by the DEFAULTRUNTIMEDIR directive.

mod_slotmem_shm provides the following API functions:

**apr_status_t doall(ap_slotmem_instance_t \*s, ap_slotmem_callback_fn_t \*func, void \*data, apr_pool_t \*pool)**
call the callback on all worker slots

**apr_status_t create(ap_slotmem_instance_t \*\*new, const char \*name, apr_size_t item_size, unsigned int item_num, ap_slo**
create a new slotmem with each item size is item_size. name is used to generate a filename for the persistent store of the shared memory if configured. Values are:

**"none"** Anonymous shared memory and no persistent store

**"file-name"** [DefaultRuntimeDir]/file-name

**"/absolute-file-name"** Absolute file name

**apr_status_t attach(ap_slotmem_instance_t \*\*new, const char \*name, apr_size_t \*item_size, unsigned int \*item_num, apr**
attach to an existing slotmem. See create for description of name parameter.

**apr_status_t dptr(ap_slotmem_instance_t \*s, unsigned int item_id, void\*\*mem)** get the direct pointer to the memory associated with this worker slot.

**apr_status_t get(ap_slotmem_instance_t \*s, unsigned int item_id, unsigned char \*dest, apr_size_t dest_len)**
get/read the memory from this slot to dest

**apr_status_t put(ap_slotmem_instance_t \*slot, unsigned int item_id, unsigned char \*src, apr_size_t src_len)**
put/write the data from src to this slot

**unsigned int num_slots(ap_slotmem_instance_t \*s)** return the total number of slots in the segment

**apr_size_t slot_size(ap_slotmem_instance_t \*s)** return the total data size, in bytes, of a slot in the segment

**apr_status_t grab(ap_slotmem_instance_t \*s, unsigned int \*item_id);** grab or allocate the first free slot and mark as in-use (does not do any data copying)

**apr_status_t fgrab(ap_slotmem_instance_t \*s, unsigned int item_id);** forced grab or allocate the specified slot and mark as in-use (does not do any data copying)

**apr_status_t release(ap_slotmem_instance_t \*s, unsigned int item_id);** release or free a slot and mark as not in-use (does not do any data copying)

**Directives** This module provides no directives.

## 10.109    Apache Module mod_so

| | |
|---|---|
| Description: | Loading of executable code and modules into the server at start-up or restart time |
| Status: | Extension |
| ModuleIdentifier: | so_module |
| SourceFile: | mod_so.c |
| Compatibility: | This is a Base module (always included) on Windows |

### Summary

On selected operating systems this module can be used to load modules into Apache HTTP Server at runtime via the Dynamic Shared Object (p. 68) (DSO) mechanism, rather than requiring a recompilation.

On Unix, the loaded code typically comes from shared object files (usually with `.so` extension), on Windows this may either be the `.so` or `.dll` extension.

 **Warning**
Modules built for one major version of the Apache HTTP Server will generally not work on another. (e.g. 1.3 vs. 2.0, or 2.0 vs. 2.2) There are usually API changes between one major version and another that require that modules be modified to work with the new version.

**Directives**

- LoadFile
- LoadModule

### Creating Loadable Modules for Windows

Note
On Windows, where loadable files typically have a file extension of `.dll`, Apache httpd modules are called `mod_whatever.so`, just as they are on other platforms. However, you may encounter third-party modules, such as PHP for example, that continue to use the `.dll` convention.
While `mod_so` still loads modules with `ApacheModuleFoo.dll` names, the new naming convention is preferred; if you are converting your loadable module for 2.0, please fix the name to this 2.0 convention.

The Apache httpd module API is unchanged between the Unix and Windows versions. Many modules will run on Windows with no or little change from Unix, although others rely on aspects of the Unix architecture which are not present in Windows, and will not work.

When a module does work, it can be added to the server in one of two ways. As with Unix, it can be compiled into the server. Because Apache httpd for Windows does not have the `Configure` program of Apache httpd for Unix, the module's source file must be added to the ApacheCore project file, and its symbols must be added to the `os\win32\modules.c` file.

The second way is to compile the module as a DLL, a shared library that can be loaded into the server at runtime, using the LOADMODULE directive. These module DLLs can be distributed and run on any Apache httpd for Windows installation, without recompilation of the server.

To create a module DLL, a small change is necessary to the module's source file: The module record must be exported from the DLL (which will be created later; see below). To do this, add the `AP_MODULE_DECLARE_DATA` (defined in the Apache httpd header files) to your module's module record definition. For example, if your module has:

```
module foo_module;
```

Replace the above with:

```
module AP_MODULE_DECLARE_DATA foo_module;
```

Note that this will only be activated on Windows, so the module can continue to be used, unchanged, with Unix if needed. Also, if you are familiar with `.DEF` files, you can export the module record with that method instead.

Now, create a DLL containing your module. You will need to link this against the libhttpd.lib export library that is created when the libhttpd.dll shared library is compiled. You may also have to change the compiler settings to ensure that the Apache httpd header files are correctly located. You can find this library in your server root's modules directory. It is best to grab an existing module .dsp file from the tree to assure the build environment is configured correctly, or alternately compare the compiler and link options to your .dsp.

This should create a DLL version of your module. Now simply place it in the `modules` directory of your server root, and use the LOADMODULE directive to load it.

## LoadFile Directive

| | |
|---|---|
| Description: | Link in the named object file or library |
| Syntax: | `LoadFile filename [filename] ...` |
| Context: | server config, virtual host |
| Status: | Extension |
| Module: | mod_so |

The LOADFILE directive links in the named object files or libraries when the server is started or restarted; this is used to load additional code which may be required for some module to work. *Filename* is either an absolute path or relative to ServerRoot (p. 380) .

For example:

```
LoadFile "libexec/libxmlparse.so"
```

## LoadModule Directive

| | |
|---|---|
| Description: | Links in the object file or library, and adds to the list of active modules |
| Syntax: | `LoadModule module filename` |
| Context: | server config, virtual host |
| Status: | Extension |
| Module: | mod_so |

The LOADMODULE directive links in the object file or library *filename* and adds the module structure named *module* to the list of active modules. *Module* is the name of the external variable of type `module` in the file, and is listed as the Module Identifier (p. 376) in the module documentation.

For example:

```
LoadModule status_module "modules/mod_status.so"
```

loads the named module from the modules subdirectory of the ServerRoot.

## 10.110   Apache Module mod_socache_dbm

| Description: | DBM based shared object cache provider. |
|---|---|
| Status: | Extension |
| ModuleIdentifier: | socache_dbm_module |
| SourceFile: | mod_socache_dbm.c |

### Summary

mod_socache_dbm is a shared object cache provider which provides for creation and access to a cache backed by a DBM database.

```
dbm:/path/to/datafile
```

If the path is not absolute then it is assumed to be relative to the DEFAULTRUNTIMEDIR.

Details of other shared object cache providers can be found here (p. 114) .

**Directives** This module provides no directives.

# 10.111 Apache Module mod_socache_dc

| | |
|---|---|
| Description: | Distcache based shared object cache provider. |
| Status: | Extension |
| ModuleIdentifier: | socache_dc_module |
| SourceFile: | mod_socache_dc.c |

## Summary

MOD_SOCACHE_DC is a shared object cache provider which provides for creation and access to a cache backed by the distcache[86] distributed session caching libraries.

Details of other shared object cache providers can be found here (p. 114) .

**Directives** This module provides no directives.

---

[86]http://distcache.sourceforge.net/

## 10.112  Apache Module mod_socache_memcache

| | |
|---|---|
| Description: | Memcache based shared object cache provider. |
| Status: | Extension |
| ModuleIdentifier: | socache_memcache_module |
| SourceFile: | mod_socache_memcache.c |

### Summary

mod_socache_memcache is a shared object cache provider which provides for creation and access to a cache backed by the memcached[87] high-performance, distributed memory object caching system.

This shared object cache provider's "create" method requires a comma separated list of memcached host/port specifications. If using this provider via another modules configuration (such as SSLSESSIONCACHE), provide the list of servers as the optional "arg" parameter.

```
SSLSessionCache memcache:memcache.example.com:12345,memcache2.example.com:12345
```

Details of other shared object cache providers can be found here (p. 114) .

### Directives

- MemcacheConnTTL

### MemcacheConnTTL Directive

| | |
|---|---|
| Description: | Keepalive time for idle connections |
| Syntax: | MemcacheConnTTL num[units] |
| Default: | MemcacheConnTTL 15s |
| Context: | server config, virtual host |
| Status: | Extension |
| Module: | mod_socache_memcache |
| Compatibility: | Available in Apache 2.4.17 and later |

Set the time to keep idle connections with the memcache server(s) alive (threaded platforms only).

Valid values for MEMCACHECONNTTL are times up to one hour. 0 means no timeout.

> This timeout defaults to units of seconds, but accepts suffixes for milliseconds (ms), seconds (s), minutes (min), and hours (h).

Before Apache 2.4.17, this timeout was hardcoded and its value was 600 usec. So, the closest configuration to match the legacy behaviour is to set MEMCACHECONNTTL to 1ms.

```
# Set a timeout of 10 minutes
MemcacheConnTTL 10min
# Set a timeout of 60 seconds
MemcacheConnTTL 60
```

---

[87]http://memcached.org/

## 10.113 Apache Module mod_socache_shmcb

| | |
|---|---|
| Description: | shmcb based shared object cache provider. |
| Status: | Extension |
| ModuleIdentifier: | socache_shmcb_module |
| SourceFile: | mod_socache_shmcb.c |

### Summary

`mod_socache_shmcb` is a shared object cache provider which provides for creation and access to a cache backed by a high-performance cyclic buffer inside a shared memory segment.

```
shmcb:/path/to/datafile(512000)
```

If the path is not absolute then it is assumed to be relative to the DEFAULTRUNTIMEDIR.

Details of other shared object cache providers can be found here (p. 114) .

**Directives** This module provides no directives.

# 10.114   Apache Module mod_speling

| | |
|---|---|
| Description: | Attempts to correct mistaken URLs by ignoring capitalization, or attempting to correct various minor misspellings. |
| Status: | Extension |
| ModuleIdentifier: | speling_module |
| SourceFile: | mod_speling.c |

## Summary

Requests to documents sometimes cannot be served by the core apache server because the request was misspelled or miscapitalized. This module addresses this problem by trying to find a matching document, even after all other modules gave up. It does its work by comparing each document name in the requested directory against the requested document name **without regard to case**, and allowing **up to one misspelling** (character insertion / omission / transposition or wrong character). A list is built with all document names which were matched using this strategy.

If, after scanning the directory,

- no matching document was found, Apache will proceed as usual and return a "document not found" error.

- only one document is found that "almost" matches the request, then it is returned in the form of a redirection response.

- more than one document with a close match was found, then the list of the matches is returned to the client, and the client can select the correct candidate.

### Directives

- CheckBasenameMatch

- CheckCaseOnly

- CheckSpelling

## CheckBasenameMatch Directive

| | |
|---|---|
| Description: | Also match files with differing file name extensions. |
| Syntax: | `CheckBasenameMatch on\|off` |
| Default: | `CheckBasenameMatch Off` |
| Context: | server config, virtual host, directory, .htaccess |
| Override: | Options |
| Status: | Extension |
| Module: | mod_speling |

When set, this directive extends the action of the spelling correction to the file name extension. For example a file `foo.gif` will match a request for `foo` or `foo.jpg`. This can be particulary useful in conjunction with MultiViews (p. 78).

## CheckCaseOnly Directive

| | |
|---|---|
| Description: | Limits the action of the speling module to case corrections |
| Syntax: | CheckCaseOnly on\|off |
| Default: | CheckCaseOnly Off |
| Context: | server config, virtual host, directory, .htaccess |
| Override: | Options |
| Status: | Extension |
| Module: | mod_speling |

When set, this directive limits the action of the spelling correction to lower/upper case changes. Other potential corrections are not performed, except when CHECKBASENAMEMATCH is also set.

## CheckSpelling Directive

| | |
|---|---|
| Description: | Enables the spelling module |
| Syntax: | CheckSpelling on\|off |
| Default: | CheckSpelling Off |
| Context: | server config, virtual host, directory, .htaccess |
| Override: | Options |
| Status: | Extension |
| Module: | mod_speling |

This directive enables or disables the spelling module. When enabled, keep in mind that

- the directory scan which is necessary for the spelling correction will have an impact on the server's performance when many spelling corrections have to be performed at the same time.

- the document trees should not contain sensitive files which could be matched inadvertently by a spelling "correction".

- the module is unable to correct misspelled user names (as in http://my.host/~apahce/), just file names or directory names.

- spelling corrections apply strictly to existing files, so a request for the <Location /status> may get incorrectly treated as the negotiated file "/stats.html".

mod_speling should not be enabled in DAV (p. 589) enabled directories, because it will try to "spell fix" newly created resource names against existing filenames, e.g., when trying to upload a new document doc43.html it might redirect to an existing document doc34.html, which is not what was intended.

# 10.115   Apache Module mod_ssl

| | |
|---|---|
| Description: | Strong cryptography using the Secure Sockets Layer (SSL) and Transport Layer Security (TLS) protocols |
| Status: | Extension |
| ModuleIdentifier: | ssl_module |
| SourceFile: | mod_ssl.c |

## Summary

This module provides SSL v3 and TLS v1.x support for the Apache HTTP Server. SSL v2 is no longer supported.

This module relies on OpenSSL[88] to provide the cryptography engine.

Further details, discussion, and examples are provided in the SSL documentation (p. 192) .

## Directives

- SSLCACertificateFile
- SSLCACertificatePath
- SSLCADNRequestFile
- SSLCADNRequestPath
- SSLCARevocationCheck
- SSLCARevocationFile
- SSLCARevocationPath
- SSLCertificateChainFile
- SSLCertificateFile
- SSLCertificateKeyFile
- SSLCipherSuite
- SSLCompression
- SSLCryptoDevice
- SSLEngine
- SSLFIPS
- SSLHonorCipherOrder
- SSLInsecureRenegotiation
- SSLOCSPDefaultResponder
- SSLOCSPEnable
- SSLOCSPOverrideResponder
- SSLOCSPProxyURL
- SSLOCSPResponderTimeout
- SSLOCSPResponseMaxAge
- SSLOCSPResponseTimeSkew
- SSLOCSPUseRequestNonce
- SSLOpenSSLConfCmd

---

[88]http://www.openssl.org/

- SSLOptions
- SSLPassPhraseDialog
- SSLProtocol
- SSLProxyCACertificateFile
- SSLProxyCACertificatePath
- SSLProxyCARevocationCheck
- SSLProxyCARevocationFile
- SSLProxyCARevocationPath
- SSLProxyCheckPeerCN
- SSLProxyCheckPeerExpire
- SSLProxyCheckPeerName
- SSLProxyCipherSuite
- SSLProxyEngine
- SSLProxyMachineCertificateChainFile
- SSLProxyMachineCertificateFile
- SSLProxyMachineCertificatePath
- SSLProxyProtocol
- SSLProxyVerify
- SSLProxyVerifyDepth
- SSLRandomSeed
- SSLRenegBufferSize
- SSLRequire
- SSLRequireSSL
- SSLSessionCache
- SSLSessionCacheTimeout
- SSLSessionTicketKeyFile
- SSLSessionTickets
- SSLSRPUnknownUserSeed
- SSLSRPVerifierFile
- SSLStaplingCache
- SSLStaplingErrorCacheTimeout
- SSLStaplingFakeTryLater
- SSLStaplingForceURL
- SSLStaplingResponderTimeout
- SSLStaplingResponseMaxAge
- SSLStaplingResponseTimeSkew
- SSLStaplingReturnResponderErrors
- SSLStaplingStandardCacheTimeout
- SSLStrictSNIVHostCheck
- SSLUserName
- SSLUseStapling
- SSLVerifyClient
- SSLVerifyDepth

## Environment Variables

This module can be configured to provide several items of SSL information as additional environment variables to the SSI and CGI namespace. This information is not provided by default for performance reasons. (See SSLOPTIONS StdEnvVars, below.) The generated variables are listed in the table below. For backward compatibility the information can be made available under different names, too. Look in the Compatibility (p. 202) chapter for details on the compatibility variables.

| Variable Name: | Value Type: | Description: |
| --- | --- | --- |
| HTTPS | flag | HTTPS is being used. |
| SSL_PROTOCOL | string | The SSL protocol version (SSLv3, TLSv1, TLSv1.1, TLSv1.2) |
| SSL_SESSION_ID | string | The hex-encoded SSL session id |
| SSL_SESSION_RESUMED | string | Initial or Resumed SSL Session. Note: multiple requests may be served over the same (Initial or Resumed) SSL session if HTTP KeepAlive is in use |
| SSL_SECURE_RENEG | string | `true` if secure renegotiation is supported, else `false` |
| SSL_CIPHER | string | The cipher specification name |
| SSL_CIPHER_EXPORT | string | `true` if cipher is an export cipher |
| SSL_CIPHER_USEKEYSIZE | number | Number of cipher bits (actually used) |
| SSL_CIPHER_ALGKEYSIZE | number | Number of cipher bits (possible) |
| SSL_COMPRESS_METHOD | string | SSL compression method negotiated |
| SSL_VERSION_INTERFACE | string | The mod_ssl program version |
| SSL_VERSION_LIBRARY | string | The OpenSSL program version |
| SSL_CLIENT_M_VERSION | string | The version of the client certificate |
| SSL_CLIENT_M_SERIAL | string | The serial of the client certificate |
| SSL_CLIENT_S_DN | string | Subject DN in client's certificate |
| SSL_CLIENT_S_DN_$x509$ | string | Component of client's Subject DN |
| SSL_CLIENT_SAN_Email_$n$ | string | Client certificate's subjectAltName extension entries of type rfc822Name |
| SSL_CLIENT_SAN_DNS_$n$ | string | Client certificate's subjectAltName extension entries of type dNSName |
| SSL_CLIENT_SAN_OTHER_msUPN_$n$ | string | Client certificate's subjectAltName extension entries of type otherName, Microsoft User Principal Name form (OID 1.3.6.1.4.1.311.20.2.3) |
| SSL_CLIENT_I_DN | string | Issuer DN of client's certificate |
| SSL_CLIENT_I_DN_$x509$ | string | Component of client's Issuer DN |
| SSL_CLIENT_V_START | string | Validity of client's certificate (start time) |
| SSL_CLIENT_V_END | string | Validity of client's certificate (end time) |
| SSL_CLIENT_V_REMAIN | string | Number of days until client's certificate expires |
| SSL_CLIENT_A_SIG | string | Algorithm used for the signature of client's certificate |
| SSL_CLIENT_A_KEY | string | Algorithm used for the public key of client's certificate |
| SSL_CLIENT_CERT | string | PEM-encoded client certificate |
| SSL_CLIENT_CERT_CHAIN_$n$ | string | PEM-encoded certificates in client certificate chain |
| SSL_CLIENT_CERT_RFC4523_CEA | string | Serial number and issuer of the certificate. The format matches that of the CertificateExactAssertion in RFC4523 |
| SSL_CLIENT_VERIFY | string | `NONE`, `SUCCESS`, `GENEROUS` or `FAILED`:*reason* |
| SSL_SERVER_M_VERSION | string | The version of the server certificate |
| SSL_SERVER_M_SERIAL | string | The serial of the server certificate |
| SSL_SERVER_S_DN | string | Subject DN in server's certificate |
| SSL_SERVER_SAN_Email_$n$ | string | Server certificate's subjectAltName extension entries of type rfc822Name |
| SSL_SERVER_SAN_DNS_$n$ | string | Server certificate's subjectAltName extension entries of type dNSName |
| SSL_SERVER_SAN_OTHER_dnsSRV_$n$ | string | Server certificate's subjectAltName extension entries of type otherName, SRVName form (OID 1.3.6.1.5.5.7.8.7, RFC 4985) |

| SSL_SERVER_S_DN_*x509* | string | Component of server's Subject DN |
|---|---|---|
| SSL_SERVER_I_DN | string | Issuer DN of server's certificate |
| SSL_SERVER_I_DN_*x509* | string | Component of server's Issuer DN |
| SSL_SERVER_V_START | string | Validity of server's certificate (start time) |
| SSL_SERVER_V_END | string | Validity of server's certificate (end time) |
| SSL_SERVER_A_SIG | string | Algorithm used for the signature of server's certificate |
| SSL_SERVER_A_KEY | string | Algorithm used for the public key of server's certificate |
| SSL_SERVER_CERT | string | PEM-encoded server certificate |
| SSL_SRP_USER | string | SRP username |
| SSL_SRP_USERINFO | string | SRP user info |
| SSL_TLS_SNI | string | Contents of the SNI TLS extension (if supplied with ClientHello) |

*x509* specifies a component of an X.509 DN; one of C, ST, L, O, OU, CN, T, I, G, S, D, UID, Email. In Apache 2.1 and later, *x509* may also include a numeric _n suffix. If the DN in question contains multiple attributes of the same name, this suffix is used as a zero-based index to select a particular attribute. For example, where the server certificate subject DN included two OU attributes, SSL_SERVER_S_DN_OU_0 and SSL_SERVER_S_DN_OU_1 could be used to reference each. A variable name without a _n suffix is equivalent to that name with a _0 suffix; the first (or only) attribute. When the environment table is populated using the StdEnvVars option of the SSLOPTIONS directive, the first (or only) attribute of any DN is added only under a non-suffixed name; i.e. no _0 suffixed entries are added.

The format of the *_DN* variables has changed in Apache HTTPD 2.3.11. See the LegacyDNStringFormat option for SSLOPTIONS for details.

SSL_CLIENT_V_REMAIN is only available in version 2.1 and later.

A number of additional environment variables can also be used in SSLREQUIRE expressions, or in custom log formats:

```
HTTP_USER_AGENT          PATH_INFO           AUTH_TYPE
HTTP_REFERER             QUERY_STRING        SERVER_SOFTWARE
HTTP_COOKIE              REMOTE_HOST         API_VERSION
HTTP_FORWARDED           REMOTE_IDENT        TIME_YEAR
HTTP_HOST                IS_SUBREQ           TIME_MON
HTTP_PROXY_CONNECTION    DOCUMENT_ROOT       TIME_DAY
HTTP_ACCEPT              SERVER_ADMIN        TIME_HOUR
THE_REQUEST              SERVER_NAME         TIME_MIN
REQUEST_FILENAME         SERVER_PORT         TIME_SEC
REQUEST_METHOD           SERVER_PROTOCOL     TIME_WDAY
REQUEST_SCHEME           REMOTE_ADDR         TIME
REQUEST_URI              REMOTE_USER
```

In these contexts, two special formats can also be used:

**ENV:*variablename*** This will expand to the standard environment variable *variablename*.

**HTTP:*headername*** This will expand to the value of the request header with name *headername*.

## Custom Log Formats

When MOD_SSL is built into Apache or at least loaded (under DSO situation) additional functions exist for the Custom Log Format (p. 705) of MOD_LOG_CONFIG. First there is an additional "%{*varname*}x" eXtension format function which can be used to expand any variables provided by any module, especially those provided by mod_ssl which can you find in the above table.

For backward compatibility there is additionally a special "`%{name}c`" cryptography format function provided. Information about this function is provided in the Compatibility (p. 202) chapter.

### Example

```
CustomLog "logs/ssl_request_log" "%t %h %{SSL_PROTOCOL}x %{SSL_CIPHER}x \"%r\" %b"
```

These formats even work without setting the `StdEnvVars` option of the SSLOptions directive.

## Request Notes

MOD_SSL sets "notes" for the request which can be used in logging with the `%{name}n` format string in MOD_LOG_CONFIG.

The notes supported are as follows:

**ssl-access-forbidden** This note is set to the value `1` if access was denied due to an SSLREQUIRE or SSLREQUIRESSL directive.

**ssl-secure-reneg** If MOD_SSL is built against a version of OpenSSL which supports the secure renegotiation extension, this note is set to the value `1` if SSL is in used for the current connection, and the client also supports the secure renegotiation extension. If the client does not support the secure renegotiation extension, the note is set to the value `0`. If MOD_SSL is not built against a version of OpenSSL which supports secure renegotiation, or if SSL is not in use for the current connection, the note is not set.

## Expression Parser Extension

When MOD_SSL is built into Apache or at least loaded (under DSO situation) any variables provided by MOD_SSL can be used in expressions for the ap_expr Expression Parser (p. 99) . The variables can be referenced using the syntax "`%{varname}`". Starting with version 2.4.18 one can also use the MOD_REWRITE style syntax "`%{SSL:varname}`" or the function style syntax "`ssl(varname)`".

### Example (using MOD_HEADERS)

```
Header set X-SSL-PROTOCOL "expr=%{SSL_PROTOCOL}"
Header set X-SSL-CIPHER "expr=%{SSL:SSL_CIPHER}"
```

This feature even works without setting the `StdEnvVars` option of the SSLOptions directive.

## Authorization providers for use with Require

MOD_SSL provides a few authentication providers for use with MOD_AUTHZ_CORE's REQUIRE directive.

### Require ssl

The `ssl` provider denies access if a connection is not encrypted with SSL. This is similar to the SSLREQUIRESSL directive.

```
Require ssl
```

**Require ssl-verify-client**

The `ssl` provider allows access if the user is authenticated with a valid client certificate. This is only useful if `SSLVerifyClient optional` is in effect.

The following example grants access if the user is authenticated either with a client certificate or by username and password.

```
Require ssl-verify-client
Require valid-user
```

## SSLCACertificateFile Directive

| | |
|---|---|
| Description: | File of concatenated PEM-encoded CA Certificates for Client Auth |
| Syntax: | SSLCACertificateFile file-path |
| Context: | server config, virtual host |
| Status: | Extension |
| Module: | mod_ssl |

This directive sets the *all-in-one* file where you can assemble the Certificates of Certification Authorities (CA) whose *clients* you deal with. These are used for Client Authentication. Such a file is simply the concatenation of the various PEM-encoded Certificate files, in order of preference. This can be used alternatively and/or additionally to SSLCAC-ERTIFICATEPATH.

### Example

```
SSLCACertificateFile /usr/local/apache2/conf/ssl.crt/ca-bundle-client.crt
```

## SSLCACertificatePath Directive

| | |
|---|---|
| Description: | Directory of PEM-encoded CA Certificates for Client Auth |
| Syntax: | SSLCACertificatePath directory-path |
| Context: | server config, virtual host |
| Status: | Extension |
| Module: | mod_ssl |

This directive sets the directory where you keep the Certificates of Certification Authorities (CAs) whose clients you deal with. These are used to verify the client certificate on Client Authentication.

The files in this directory have to be PEM-encoded and are accessed through hash filenames. So usually you can't just place the Certificate files there: you also have to create symbolic links named *hash-value*.N. And you should always make sure this directory contains the appropriate symbolic links.

### Example

```
SSLCACertificatePath /usr/local/apache2/conf/ssl.crt/
```

## SSLCADNRequestFile Directive

| | |
|---|---|
| Description: | File of concatenated PEM-encoded CA Certificates for defining acceptable CA names |
| Syntax: | SSLCADNRequestFile file-path |
| Context: | server config, virtual host |
| Status: | Extension |
| Module: | mod_ssl |

When a client certificate is requested by mod_ssl, a list of *acceptable Certificate Authority names* is sent to the client in the SSL handshake. These CA names can be used by the client to select an appropriate client certificate out of those it has available.

If neither of the directives SSLCADNREQUESTPATH or SSLCADNREQUESTFILE are given, then the set of acceptable CA names sent to the client is the names of all the CA certificates given by the SSLCACERTIFICATEFILE and SSLCACERTIFICATEPATH directives; in other words, the names of the CAs which will actually be used to verify the client certificate.

In some circumstances, it is useful to be able to send a set of acceptable CA names which differs from the actual CAs used to verify the client certificate - for example, if the client certificates are signed by intermediate CAs. In such cases, SSLCADNREQUESTPATH and/or SSLCADNREQUESTFILE can be used; the acceptable CA names are then taken from the complete set of certificates in the directory and/or file specified by this pair of directives.

SSLCADNREQUESTFILE must specify an *all-in-one* file containing a concatenation of PEM-encoded CA certificates.

### Example

```
SSLCADNRequestFile /usr/local/apache2/conf/ca-names.crt
```

## SSLCADNRequestPath Directive

| | |
|---|---|
| Description: | Directory of PEM-encoded CA Certificates for defining acceptable CA names |
| Syntax: | SSLCADNRequestPath directory-path |
| Context: | server config, virtual host |
| Status: | Extension |
| Module: | mod_ssl |

This optional directive can be used to specify the set of *acceptable CA names* which will be sent to the client when a client certificate is requested. See the SSLCADNREQUESTFILE directive for more details.

The files in this directory have to be PEM-encoded and are accessed through hash filenames. So usually you can't just place the Certificate files there: you also have to create symbolic links named *hash-value*.N. And you should always make sure this directory contains the appropriate symbolic links.

### Example

```
SSLCADNRequestPath /usr/local/apache2/conf/ca-names.crt/
```

## SSLCARevocationCheck Directive

| | |
|---|---|
| Description: | Enable CRL-based revocation checking |
| Syntax: | SSLCARevocationCheck chain\|leaf\|none flags |
| Default: | SSLCARevocationCheck none |
| Context: | server config, virtual host |
| Status: | Extension |
| Module: | mod_ssl |
| Compatibility: | Optional *flags* available in httpd 2.5-dev or later |

Enables certificate revocation list (CRL) checking. At least one of SSLCAREVOCATIONFILE or SSLCAREVOCATIONPATH must be configured. When set to chain (recommended setting), CRL checks are applied to all certificates in the chain, while setting it to leaf limits the checks to the end-entity cert.

The available *flags* are:

- `no_crl_for_cert_ok`

    Prior to version 2.3.15, CRL checking in mod_ssl also succeeded when no CRL(s) for the checked certificate(s) were found in any of the locations configured with SSLCAREVOCATIONFILE or SSLCAREVOCATIONPATH.

    With the introduction of SSLCAREVOCATIONFILE, the behavior has been changed: by default with `chain` or `leaf`, CRLs **must** be present for the validation to succeed - otherwise it will fail with an `"unable to get certificate CRL"` error.

    The *flag* `no_crl_for_cert_ok` allows to restore previous behaviour.

### Example

```
SSLCARevocationCheck chain
```

### Compatibility with versions 2.2

```
SSLCARevocationCheck chain no_crl_for_cert_ok
```

## SSLCARevocationFile Directive

| | |
|---|---|
| Description: | File of concatenated PEM-encoded CA CRLs for Client Auth |
| Syntax: | `SSLCARevocationFile file-path` |
| Context: | server config, virtual host |
| Status: | Extension |
| Module: | mod_ssl |

This directive sets the *all-in-one* file where you can assemble the Certificate Revocation Lists (CRL) of Certification Authorities (CA) whose *clients* you deal with. These are used for Client Authentication. Such a file is simply the concatenation of the various PEM-encoded CRL files, in order of preference. This can be used alternatively and/or additionally to SSLCAREVOCATIONPATH.

### Example

```
SSLCARevocationFile /usr/local/apache2/conf/ssl.crl/ca-bundle-client.crl
```

## SSLCARevocationPath Directive

| | |
|---|---|
| Description: | Directory of PEM-encoded CA CRLs for Client Auth |
| Syntax: | `SSLCARevocationPath directory-path` |
| Context: | server config, virtual host |
| Status: | Extension |
| Module: | mod_ssl |

This directive sets the directory where you keep the Certificate Revocation Lists (CRL) of Certification Authorities (CAs) whose clients you deal with. These are used to revoke the client certificate on Client Authentication.

The files in this directory have to be PEM-encoded and are accessed through hash filenames. So usually you have not only to place the CRL files there. Additionally you have to create symbolic links named *hash-value*.`rN`. And you should always make sure this directory contains the appropriate symbolic links.

### Example

```
SSLCARevocationPath /usr/local/apache2/conf/ssl.crl/
```

## SSLCertificateChainFile Directive

| Description: | File of PEM-encoded Server CA Certificates |
|---|---|
| Syntax: | SSLCertificateChainFile file-path |
| Context: | server config, virtual host |
| Status: | Extension |
| Module: | mod_ssl |

**⟹ SSLCertificateChainFile is deprecated**

SSLCertificateChainFile became obsolete with version 2.4.8, when SSLCERTIFI-CATEFILE was extended to also load intermediate CA certificates from the server certificate file.

This directive sets the optional *all-in-one* file where you can assemble the certificates of Certification Authorities (CA) which form the certificate chain of the server certificate. This starts with the issuing CA certificate of the server certificate and can range up to the root CA certificate. Such a file is simply the concatenation of the various PEM-encoded CA Certificate files, usually in certificate chain order.

This should be used alternatively and/or additionally to SSLCACERTIFICATEPATH for explicitly constructing the server certificate chain which is sent to the browser in addition to the server certificate. It is especially useful to avoid conflicts with CA certificates when using client authentication. Because although placing a CA certificate of the server certificate chain into SSLCACERTIFICATEPATH has the same effect for the certificate chain construction, it has the side-effect that client certificates issued by this same CA certificate are also accepted on client authentication.

But be careful: Providing the certificate chain works only if you are using a *single* RSA *or* DSA based server certificate. If you are using a coupled RSA+DSA certificate pair, this will work only if actually both certificates use the *same* certificate chain. Else the browsers will be confused in this situation.

### Example

```
SSLCertificateChainFile /usr/local/apache2/conf/ssl.crt/ca.crt
```

## SSLCertificateFile Directive

| Description: | Server PEM-encoded X.509 certificate data file |
|---|---|
| Syntax: | SSLCertificateFile file-path |
| Context: | server config, virtual host |
| Status: | Extension |
| Module: | mod_ssl |

This directive points to a file with certificate data in PEM format. At a minimum, the file must include an end-entity (leaf) certificate. The directive can be used multiple times (referencing different filenames) to support multiple algorithms for server authentication - typically RSA, DSA, and ECC. The number of supported algorithms depends on the OpenSSL version being used for mod_ssl: with version 1.0.0 or later, openssl list-public-key-algorithms will output a list of supported algorithms, see also the note below about limitations of OpenSSL versions prior to 1.0.2 and the ways to work around them.

The files may also include intermediate CA certificates, sorted from leaf to root. This is supported with version 2.4.8 and later, and obsoletes SSLCERTIFICATECHAINFILE. When running with OpenSSL 1.0.2 or later, this allows to configure the intermediate CA chain on a per-certificate basis.

Custom DH parameters and an EC curve name for ephemeral keys, can also be added to end of the first file configured using SSLCERTIFICATEFILE. This is supported in version 2.4.7 or later. Such parameters can be generated using the commands openssl dhparam and openssl ecparam. The parameters can be added as-is to the end of the first certificate file. Only the first file can be used for custom parameters, as they are applied independently of the authentication algorithm type.

Finally the end-entity certificate's private key can also be added to the certificate file instead of using a separate SSLCERTIFICATEKEYFILE directive. This practice is highly discouraged. If it is used, the certificate files using such an embedded key must be configured after the certificates using a separate key file. If the private key is encrypted, the pass phrase dialog is forced at startup time.

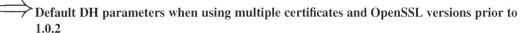

## DH parameter interoperability with primes > 1024 bit

Beginning with version 2.4.7, mod_ssl makes use of standardized DH parameters with prime lengths of 2048, 3072 and 4096 bits and with additional prime lengths of 6144 and 8192 bits beginning with version 2.4.10 (from RFC 3526[a]), and hands them out to clients based on the length of the certificate's RSA/DSA key. With Java-based clients in particular (Java 7 or earlier), this may lead to handshake failures - see this FAQ answer (p. 212) for working around such issues.

---
[a]http://www.ietf.org/rfc/rfc3526.txt

## Default DH parameters when using multiple certificates and OpenSSL versions prior to 1.0.2

When using multiple certificates to support different authentication algorithms (like RSA, DSA, but mainly ECC) and OpenSSL prior to 1.0.2, it is recommended to either use custom DH parameters (preferably) by adding them to the first certificate file (as described above), or to order the SSLCERTIFICATEFILE directives such that RSA/DSA certificates are placed **after** the ECC one.

This is due to a limitation in older versions of OpenSSL which don't let the Apache HTTP Server determine the currently selected certificate at handshake time (when the DH parameters must be sent to the peer) but instead always provide the last configured certificate. Consequently, the server may select default DH parameters based on the length of the wrong certificate's key (ECC keys are much smaller than RSA/DSA ones and their length is not relevant for selecting DH primes).

Since custom DH parameters always take precedence over the default ones, this issue can be avoided by creating and configuring them (as described above), thus using a custom/suitable length.

### Example

```
SSLCertificateFile /usr/local/apache2/conf/ssl.crt/server.crt
```

## SSLCertificateKeyFile Directive

| | |
|---|---|
| Description: | Server PEM-encoded private key file |
| Syntax: | `SSLCertificateKeyFile file-path` |
| Context: | server config, virtual host |
| Status: | Extension |
| Module: | mod_ssl |

This directive points to the PEM-encoded private key file for the server. If the contained private key is encrypted, the pass phrase dialog is forced at startup time.

The directive can be used multiple times (referencing different filenames) to support multiple algorithms for server authentication. For each SSLCERTIFICATEKEYFILE directive, there must be a matching SSLCERTIFICATEFILE directive.

The private key may also be combined with the certificate in the file given by SSLCERTIFICATEFILE, but this practice is highly discouraged. If it is used, the certificate files using such an embedded key must be configured after the certificates using a separate key file.

**Example**

```
SSLCertificateKeyFile /usr/local/apache2/conf/ssl.key/server.key
```

## SSLCipherSuite Directive

| | |
|---|---|
| Description: | Cipher Suite available for negotiation in SSL handshake |
| Syntax: | `SSLCipherSuite cipher-spec` |
| Default: | `SSLCipherSuite DEFAULT (depends on OpenSSL version)` |
| Context: | server config, virtual host, directory, .htaccess |
| Override: | AuthConfig |
| Status: | Extension |
| Module: | mod_ssl |

This complex directive uses a colon-separated *cipher-spec* string consisting of OpenSSL cipher specifications to configure the Cipher Suite the client is permitted to negotiate in the SSL handshake phase. Notice that this directive can be used both in per-server and per-directory context. In per-server context it applies to the standard SSL handshake when a connection is established. In per-directory context it forces a SSL renegotiation with the reconfigured Cipher Suite after the HTTP request was read but before the HTTP response is sent.

An SSL cipher specification in *cipher-spec* is composed of 4 major attributes plus a few extra minor ones:

- *Key Exchange Algorithm*:
  RSA, Diffie-Hellman, Elliptic Curve Diffie-Hellman, Secure Remote Password

- *Authentication Algorithm*:
  RSA, Diffie-Hellman, DSS, ECDSA, or none.

- *Cipher/Encryption Algorithm*:
  AES, DES, Triple-DES, RC4, RC2, IDEA, etc.

- *MAC Digest Algorithm*:
  MD5, SHA or SHA1, SHA256, SHA384.

An SSL cipher can also be an export cipher. SSLv2 ciphers are no longer supported. To specify which ciphers to use, one can either specify all the Ciphers, one at a time, or use aliases to specify the preference and order for the ciphers (see Table 1). The actually available ciphers and aliases depends on the used openssl version. Newer openssl versions may include additional ciphers.

| Tag | Description |
|---|---|
| *Key Exchange Algorithm:* | |
| kRSA | RSA key exchange |
| kDHr | Diffie-Hellman key exchange with RSA key |
| kDHd | Diffie-Hellman key exchange with DSA key |
| kEDH | Ephemeral (temp.key) Diffie-Hellman key exchange (no cert) |
| kSRP | Secure Remote Password (SRP) key exchange |
| *Authentication Algorithm:* | |
| aNULL | No authentication |
| aRSA | RSA authentication |
| aDSS | DSS authentication |
| aDH | Diffie-Hellman authentication |
| *Cipher Encoding Algorithm:* | |
| eNULL | No encryption |
| NULL | alias for eNULL |
| AES | AES encryption |

| DES | DES encryption |
|---|---|
| 3DES | Triple-DES encryption |
| RC4 | RC4 encryption |
| RC2 | RC2 encryption |
| IDEA | IDEA encryption |
| *MAC Digest Algorithm:* | |
| MD5 | MD5 hash function |
| SHA1 | SHA1 hash function |
| SHA | alias for SHA1 |
| SHA256 | SHA256 hash function |
| SHA384 | SHA384 hash function |
| *Aliases:* | |
| SSLv3 | all SSL version 3.0 ciphers |
| TLSv1 | all TLS version 1.0 ciphers |
| EXP | all export ciphers |
| EXPORT40 | all 40-bit export ciphers only |
| EXPORT56 | all 56-bit export ciphers only |
| LOW | all low strength ciphers (no export, single DES) |
| MEDIUM | all ciphers with 128 bit encryption |
| HIGH | all ciphers using Triple-DES |
| RSA | all ciphers using RSA key exchange |
| DH | all ciphers using Diffie-Hellman key exchange |
| EDH | all ciphers using Ephemeral Diffie-Hellman key exchange |
| ECDH | Elliptic Curve Diffie-Hellman key exchange |
| ADH | all ciphers using Anonymous Diffie-Hellman key exchange |
| AECDH | all ciphers using Anonymous Elliptic Curve Diffie-Hellman key exchange |
| SRP | all ciphers using Secure Remote Password (SRP) key exchange |
| DSS | all ciphers using DSS authentication |
| ECDSA | all ciphers using ECDSA authentication |
| aNULL | all ciphers using no authentication |

Now where this becomes interesting is that these can be put together to specify the order and ciphers you wish to use. To speed this up there are also aliases (SSLv3, TLSv1, EXP, LOW, MEDIUM, HIGH) for certain groups of ciphers. These tags can be joined together with prefixes to form the *cipher-spec*. Available prefixes are:

- none: add cipher to list
- +: move matching ciphers to the current location in list
- −: remove cipher from list (can be added later again)
- !: kill cipher from list completely (can **not** be added later again)

⟹ **aNULL, eNULL and EXP ciphers are always disabled**

> Beginning with version 2.4.7, null and export-grade ciphers are always disabled, as mod_ssl unconditionally adds !aNULL:!eNULL:!EXP to any cipher string at initialization.

A simpler way to look at all of this is to use the "openssl ciphers -v" command which provides a nice way to successively create the correct *cipher-spec* string. The default *cipher-spec* string depends on the version of the OpenSSL libraries used. Let's suppose it is "RC4-SHA:AES128-SHA:HIGH:MEDIUM:!aNULL:!MD5" which means the following: Put RC4-SHA and AES128-SHA at the beginning. We do this, because these ciphers offer a good compromise between speed and security. Next, include high and medium security ciphers. Finally, remove all ciphers which do not authenticate, i.e. for SSL the Anonymous Diffie-Hellman ciphers, as well as all ciphers which use `MD5` as hash algorithm, because it has been proven insufficient.

```
$ openssl ciphers -v 'RC4-SHA:AES128-SHA:HIGH:MEDIUM:!aNULL:!MD5'
RC4-SHA                 SSLv3 Kx=RSA     Au=RSA Enc=RC4(128)  Mac=SHA1
AES128-SHA              SSLv3 Kx=RSA     Au=RSA Enc=AES(128)  Mac=SHA1
DHE-RSA-AES256-SHA      SSLv3 Kx=DH      Au=RSA Enc=AES(256)  Mac=SHA1
...                     ...              ...    ...           ...
SEED-SHA                SSLv3 Kx=RSA     Au=RSA Enc=SEED(128) Mac=SHA1
PSK-RC4-SHA             SSLv3 Kx=PSK     Au=PSK Enc=RC4(128)  Mac=SHA1
KRB5-RC4-SHA            SSLv3 Kx=KRB5    Au=KRB5 Enc=RC4(128) Mac=SHA1
```

The complete list of particular RSA & DH ciphers for SSL is given in Table 2.

### Example

```
SSLCipherSuite RSA:!EXP:!NULL:+HIGH:+MEDIUM:-LOW
```

| Cipher-Tag | Protocol | Key Ex. | Auth. | Enc. | MAC | Type |
|---|---|---|---|---|---|---|
| *RSA Ciphers:* | | | | | | |
| DES-CBC3-SHA | SSLv3 | RSA | RSA | 3DES(168) | SHA1 | |
| IDEA-CBC-SHA | SSLv3 | RSA | RSA | IDEA(128) | SHA1 | |
| RC4-SHA | SSLv3 | RSA | RSA | RC4(128) | SHA1 | |
| RC4-MD5 | SSLv3 | RSA | RSA | RC4(128) | MD5 | |
| DES-CBC-SHA | SSLv3 | RSA | RSA | DES(56) | SHA1 | |
| EXP-DES-CBC-SHA | SSLv3 | RSA(512) | RSA | DES(40) | SHA1 | export |
| EXP-RC2-CBC-MD5 | SSLv3 | RSA(512) | RSA | RC2(40) | MD5 | export |
| EXP-RC4-MD5 | SSLv3 | RSA(512) | RSA | RC4(40) | MD5 | export |
| NULL-SHA | SSLv3 | RSA | RSA | None | SHA1 | |
| NULL-MD5 | SSLv3 | RSA | RSA | None | MD5 | |
| *Diffie-Hellman Ciphers:* | | | | | | |
| ADH-DES-CBC3-SHA | SSLv3 | DH | None | 3DES(168) | SHA1 | |
| ADH-DES-CBC-SHA | SSLv3 | DH | None | DES(56) | SHA1 | |
| ADH-RC4-MD5 | SSLv3 | DH | None | RC4(128) | MD5 | |
| EDH-RSA-DES-CBC3-SHA | SSLv3 | DH | RSA | 3DES(168) | SHA1 | |
| EDH-DSS-DES-CBC3-SHA | SSLv3 | DH | DSS | 3DES(168) | SHA1 | |
| EDH-RSA-DES-CBC-SHA | SSLv3 | DH | RSA | DES(56) | SHA1 | |
| EDH-DSS-DES-CBC-SHA | SSLv3 | DH | DSS | DES(56) | SHA1 | |
| EXP-EDH-RSA-DES-CBC-SHA | SSLv3 | DH(512) | RSA | DES(40) | SHA1 | export |
| EXP-EDH-DSS-DES-CBC-SHA | SSLv3 | DH(512) | DSS | DES(40) | SHA1 | export |
| EXP-ADH-DES-CBC-SHA | SSLv3 | DH(512) | None | DES(40) | SHA1 | export |
| EXP-ADH-RC4-MD5 | SSLv3 | DH(512) | None | RC4(40) | MD5 | export |

## SSLCompression Directive

| | |
|---|---|
| Description: | Enable compression on the SSL level |
| Syntax: | `SSLCompression on\|off` |
| Default: | `SSLCompression off` |
| Context: | server config, virtual host |
| Status: | Extension |
| Module: | mod_ssl |
| Compatibility: | Available in httpd 2.4.3 and later, if using OpenSSL 0.9.8 or later; virtual host scope available if using OpenSSL 1.0.0 or later. The default used to be `on` in version 2.4.3. |

This directive allows to enable compression on the SSL level.

! Enabling compression causes security issues in most setups (the so called CRIME attack).

## SSLCryptoDevice Directive

| | |
|---|---|
| Description: | Enable use of a cryptographic hardware accelerator |
| Syntax: | `SSLCryptoDevice engine` |
| Default: | `SSLCryptoDevice builtin` |
| Context: | server config |
| Status: | Extension |
| Module: | mod_ssl |

This directive enables use of a cryptographic hardware accelerator board to offload some of the SSL processing overhead. This directive can only be used if the SSL toolkit is built with "engine" support; OpenSSL 0.9.7 and later releases have "engine" support by default, the separate "-engine" releases of OpenSSL 0.9.6 must be used.

To discover which engine names are supported, run the command "`openssl engine`".

### Example

```
# For a Broadcom accelerator:
SSLCryptoDevice ubsec
```

## SSLEngine Directive

| | |
|---|---|
| Description: | SSL Engine Operation Switch |
| Syntax: | `SSLEngine on\|off\|optional` |
| Default: | `SSLEngine off` |
| Context: | server config, virtual host |
| Status: | Extension |
| Module: | mod_ssl |

This directive toggles the usage of the SSL/TLS Protocol Engine. This is should be used inside a <VIRTUALHOST> section to enable SSL/TLS for a that virtual host. By default the SSL/TLS Protocol Engine is disabled for both the main server and all configured virtual hosts.

### Example

```
<VirtualHost _default_:443>
SSLEngine on
#...
</VirtualHost>
```

In Apache 2.1 and later, SSLENGINE can be set to `optional`. This enables support for RFC 2817[89], Upgrading to TLS Within HTTP/1.1. At this time no web browsers support RFC 2817.

## SSLFIPS Directive

| | |
|---|---|
| Description: | SSL FIPS mode Switch |
| Syntax: | `SSLFIPS on|off` |
| Default: | `SSLFIPS off` |
| Context: | server config |
| Status: | Extension |
| Module: | mod_ssl |

This directive toggles the usage of the SSL library FIPS_mode flag. It must be set in the global server context and cannot be configured with conflicting settings (SSLFIPS on followed by SSLFIPS off or similar). The mode applies to all SSL library operations.

If httpd was compiled against an SSL library which did not support the FIPS_mode flag, `SSLFIPS on` will fail. Refer to the FIPS 140-2 Security Policy document of the SSL provider library for specific requirements to use mod_ssl in a FIPS 140-2 approved mode of operation; note that mod_ssl itself is not validated, but may be described as using FIPS 140-2 validated cryptographic module, when all components are assembled and operated under the guidelines imposed by the applicable Security Policy.

## SSLHonorCipherOrder Directive

| | |
|---|---|
| Description: | Option to prefer the server's cipher preference order |
| Syntax: | `SSLHonorCipherOrder on|off` |
| Default: | `SSLHonorCipherOrder off` |
| Context: | server config, virtual host |
| Status: | Extension |
| Module: | mod_ssl |

When choosing a cipher during an SSLv3 or TLSv1 handshake, normally the client's preference is used. If this directive is enabled, the server's preference will be used instead.

### Example

```
SSLHonorCipherOrder on
```

## SSLInsecureRenegotiation Directive

| | |
|---|---|
| Description: | Option to enable support for insecure renegotiation |
| Syntax: | `SSLInsecureRenegotiation on|off` |
| Default: | `SSLInsecureRenegotiation off` |
| Context: | server config, virtual host |
| Status: | Extension |
| Module: | mod_ssl |
| Compatibility: | Available if using OpenSSL 0.9.8m or later |

As originally specified, all versions of the SSL and TLS protocols (up to and including TLS/1.2) were vulnerable to a Man-in-the-Middle attack (CVE-2009-3555[90]) during a renegotiation. This vulnerability allowed an attacker to

---

[89]http://www.ietf.org/rfc/rfc2817.txt
[90]http://cve.mitre.org/cgi-bin/cvename.cgi?name=CAN-2009-3555

"prefix" a chosen plaintext to the HTTP request as seen by the web server. A protocol extension was developed which fixed this vulnerability if supported by both client and server.

If MOD_SSL is linked against OpenSSL version 0.9.8m or later, by default renegotiation is only supported with clients supporting the new protocol extension. If this directive is enabled, renegotiation will be allowed with old (unpatched) clients, albeit insecurely.

 **Security warning**

> If this directive is enabled, SSL connections will be vulnerable to the Man-in-the-Middle prefix attack as described in CVE-2009-3555[a].
>
> ───────────────
> [a]http://cve.mitre.org/cgi-bin/cvename.cgi?name=CAN-2009-3555

### Example

```
SSLInsecureRenegotiation on
```

The SSL_SECURE_RENEG environment variable can be used from an SSI or CGI script to determine whether secure renegotiation is supported for a given SSL connection.

## SSLOCSPDefaultResponder Directive

| | |
|---|---|
| Description: | Set the default responder URI for OCSP validation |
| Syntax: | SSLOCSDefaultResponder uri |
| Context: | server config, virtual host |
| Status: | Extension |
| Module: | mod_ssl |

This option sets the default OCSP responder to use. If SSLOCSPOVERRIDERESPONDER is not enabled, the URI given will be used only if no responder URI is specified in the certificate being verified.

## SSLOCSPEnable Directive

| | |
|---|---|
| Description: | Enable OCSP validation of the client certificate chain |
| Syntax: | SSLOCSPEnable on\|off |
| Default: | SSLOCSPEnable off |
| Context: | server config, virtual host |
| Status: | Extension |
| Module: | mod_ssl |

This option enables OCSP validation of the client certificate chain. If this option is enabled, certificates in the client's certificate chain will be validated against an OCSP responder after normal verification (including CRL checks) have taken place.

The OCSP responder used is either extracted from the certificate itself, or derived by configuration; see the SSLOC-SPDEFAULTRESPONDER and SSLOCSPOVERRIDERESPONDER directives.

### Example

```
SSLVerifyClient on
SSLOCSPEnable on
SSLOCSPDefaultResponder http://responder.example.com:8888/responder
SSLOCSPOverrideResponder on
```

## SSLOCSPOverrideResponder Directive

| | |
|---|---|
| Description: | Force use of the default responder URI for OCSP validation |
| Syntax: | `SSLOCSPOverrideResponder on\|off` |
| Default: | `SSLOCSPOverrideResponder off` |
| Context: | server config, virtual host |
| Status: | Extension |
| Module: | mod_ssl |

This option forces the configured default OCSP responder to be used during OCSP certificate validation, regardless of whether the certificate being validated references an OCSP responder.

## SSLOCSPProxyURL Directive

| | |
|---|---|
| Description: | Proxy URL to use for OCSP requests |
| Syntax: | `SSLOCSPProxyURL url` |
| Context: | server config, virtual host |
| Status: | Extension |
| Module: | mod_ssl |
| Compatibility: | Available in httpd 2.4.19 and later |

This option allows to set the URL of a HTTP proxy that should be used for all queries to OCSP responders.

## SSLOCSPResponderTimeout Directive

| | |
|---|---|
| Description: | Timeout for OCSP queries |
| Syntax: | `SSLOCSPResponderTimeout seconds` |
| Default: | `SSLOCSPResponderTimeout 10` |
| Context: | server config, virtual host |
| Status: | Extension |
| Module: | mod_ssl |

This option sets the timeout for queries to OCSP responders, when SSLOCSPEnable is turned on.

## SSLOCSPResponseMaxAge Directive

| | |
|---|---|
| Description: | Maximum allowable age for OCSP responses |
| Syntax: | `SSLOCSPResponseMaxAge seconds` |
| Default: | `SSLOCSPResponseMaxAge -1` |
| Context: | server config, virtual host |
| Status: | Extension |
| Module: | mod_ssl |

This option sets the maximum allowable age ("freshness") for OCSP responses. The default value ($-1$) does not enforce a maximum age, which means that OCSP responses are considered valid as long as their nextUpdate field is in the future.

## SSLOCSPResponseTimeSkew Directive

| | |
|---|---|
| Description: | Maximum allowable time skew for OCSP response validation |
| Syntax: | `SSLOCSPResponseTimeSkew seconds` |
| Default: | `SSLOCSPResponseTimeSkew 300` |
| Context: | server config, virtual host |
| Status: | Extension |
| Module: | mod_ssl |

This option sets the maximum allowable time skew for OCSP responses (when checking their `thisUpdate` and `nextUpdate` fields).

## SSLOCSPUseRequestNonce Directive

| | |
|---|---|
| Description: | Use a nonce within OCSP queries |
| Syntax: | `SSLOCSPUseRequestNonce on\|off` |
| Default: | `SSLOCSPUseRequestNonce on` |
| Context: | server config, virtual host |
| Status: | Extension |
| Module: | mod_ssl |
| Compatibility: | Available in httpd 2.4.10 and later |

This option determines whether queries to OCSP responders should contain a nonce or not. By default, a query nonce is always used and checked against the response's one. When the responder does not use nonces (e.g. Microsoft OCSP Responder), this option should be turned `off`.

## SSLOpenSSLConfCmd Directive

| | |
|---|---|
| Description: | Configure OpenSSL parameters through its *SSL_CONF* API |
| Syntax: | `SSLOpenSSLConfCmd command-name command-value` |
| Context: | server config, virtual host |
| Status: | Extension |
| Module: | mod_ssl |
| Compatibility: | Available in httpd 2.4.8 and later, if using OpenSSL 1.0.2 or later |

This directive exposes OpenSSL's *SSL_CONF* API to mod_ssl, allowing a flexible configuration of OpenSSL parameters without the need of implementing additional MOD_SSL directives when new features are added to OpenSSL.

The set of available SSLOPENSSLCONFCMD commands depends on the OpenSSL version being used for MOD_SSL (at least version 1.0.2 is required). For a list of supported command names, see the section *Supported configuration file commands* in the SSL_CONF_cmd(3)[91] manual page for OpenSSL.

Some of the SSLOPENSSLCONFCMD commands can be used as an alternative to existing directives (such as SSL-CIPHERSUITE or SSLPROTOCOL), though it should be noted that the syntax / allowable values for the parameters may sometimes differ.

### Examples

```
SSLOpenSSLConfCmd Options -SessionTicket,ServerPreference
SSLOpenSSLConfCmd ECDHParameters brainpoolP256r1
SSLOpenSSLConfCmd ServerInfoFile /usr/local/apache2/conf/server-info.pem
SSLOpenSSLConfCmd Protocol "-ALL, TLSv1.2"
SSLOpenSSLConfCmd SignatureAlgorithms RSA+SHA384:ECDSA+SHA256
```

---

[91]http://www.openssl.org/docs/man1.0.2/ssl/SSL_CONF_cmd.html#SUPPORTED-CONFIGURATION-FILE-COMMANDS

## SSLOptions Directive

| | |
|---|---|
| Description: | Configure various SSL engine run-time options |
| Syntax: | `SSLOptions [+|-]option ...` |
| Context: | server config, virtual host, directory, .htaccess |
| Override: | Options |
| Status: | Extension |
| Module: | mod_ssl |

This directive can be used to control various run-time options on a per-directory basis. Normally, if multiple `SSLOptions` could apply to a directory, then the most specific one is taken completely; the options are not merged. However if *all* the options on the `SSLOptions` directive are preceded by a plus (+) or minus (−) symbol, the options are merged. Any options preceded by a + are added to the options currently in force, and any options preceded by a − are removed from the options currently in force.

The available *option*s are:

- `StdEnvVars`

  When this option is enabled, the standard set of SSL related CGI/SSI environment variables are created. This per default is disabled for performance reasons, because the information extraction step is a rather expensive operation. So one usually enables this option for CGI and SSI requests only.

- `ExportCertData`

  When this option is enabled, additional CGI/SSI environment variables are created: `SSL_SERVER_CERT`, `SSL_CLIENT_CERT` and `SSL_CLIENT_CERT_CHAIN_n` (with *n* = 0,1,2,..). These contain the PEM-encoded X.509 Certificates of server and client for the current HTTPS connection and can be used by CGI scripts for deeper Certificate checking. Additionally all other certificates of the client certificate chain are provided, too. This bloats up the environment a little bit which is why you have to use this option to enable it on demand.

- `FakeBasicAuth`

  When this option is enabled, the Subject Distinguished Name (DN) of the Client X509 Certificate is translated into a HTTP Basic Authorization username. This means that the standard Apache authentication methods can be used for access control. The user name is just the Subject of the Client's X509 Certificate (can be determined by running OpenSSL's `openssl x509` command: `openssl x509 -noout -subject -in` *certificate*`.crt`). The optional SSLUSERNAME directive can be used to specify which part of the certificate Subject is embedded in the username. Note that no password is obtained from the user. Every entry in the user file needs this password: "`xxj31ZMTZzkVA`", which is the DES-encrypted version of the word '`password`". Those who live under MD5-based encryption (for instance under FreeBSD or BSD/OS, etc.) should use the following MD5 hash of the same word: "`$1$OXLyS...$Owx8s2/m9/gfkcRVXzgoE/`".

  Note that the AUTHBASICFAKE directive within MOD_AUTH_BASIC can be used as a more general mechanism for faking basic authentication, giving control over the structure of both the username and password.

- `StrictRequire`

  This *forces* forbidden access when `SSLRequireSSL` or `SSLRequire` successfully decided that access should be forbidden. Usually the default is that in the case where a "`Satisfy any`" directive is used, and other access restrictions are passed, denial of access due to `SSLRequireSSL` or `SSLRequire` is overridden (because that's how the Apache `Satisfy` mechanism should work.) But for strict access restriction you can use `SSLRequireSSL` and/or `SSLRequire` in combination with an "`SSLOptions +StrictRequire`". Then an additional "`Satisfy Any`" has no chance once mod_ssl has decided to deny access.

- `OptRenegotiate`

  This enables optimized SSL connection renegotiation handling when SSL directives are used in per-directory context. By default a strict scheme is enabled where *every* per-directory reconfiguration of SSL parameters causes a *full* SSL renegotiation handshake. When this option is used mod_ssl tries to avoid unnecessary handshakes by doing more granular (but still safe) parameter checks. Nevertheless these granular checks sometimes may not be what the user expects, so enable this on a per-directory basis only, please.

- LegacyDNStringFormat

  This option influences how values of the SSL_{CLIENT, SERVER}_{I, S}_DN variables are formatted. Since version 2.3.11, Apache HTTPD uses a RFC 2253 compatible format by default. This uses commas as delimiters between the attributes, allows the use of non-ASCII characters (which are converted to UTF8), escapes various special characters with backslashes, and sorts the attributes with the "C" attribute last.

  If LegacyDNStringFormat is set, the old format will be used which sorts the "C" attribute first, uses slashes as separators, and does not handle non-ASCII and special characters in any consistent way.

### Example

```
SSLOptions +FakeBasicAuth -StrictRequire
<Files ˜ "\.(cgi|shtml)$">
    SSLOptions +StdEnvVars -ExportCertData
</Files>
```

## SSLPassPhraseDialog Directive

| | |
|---|---|
| Description: | Type of pass phrase dialog for encrypted private keys |
| Syntax: | SSLPassPhraseDialog type |
| Default: | SSLPassPhraseDialog builtin |
| Context: | server config |
| Status: | Extension |
| Module: | mod_ssl |

When Apache starts up it has to read the various Certificate (see SSLCERTIFICATEFILE) and Private Key (see SSLCERTIFICATEKEYFILE) files of the SSL-enabled virtual servers. Because for security reasons the Private Key files are usually encrypted, mod_ssl needs to query the administrator for a Pass Phrase in order to decrypt those files. This query can be done in two ways which can be configured by *type*:

- builtin

  This is the default where an interactive terminal dialog occurs at startup time just before Apache detaches from the terminal. Here the administrator has to manually enter the Pass Phrase for each encrypted Private Key file. Because a lot of SSL-enabled virtual hosts can be configured, the following reuse-scheme is used to minimize the dialog: When a Private Key file is encrypted, all known Pass Phrases (at the beginning there are none, of course) are tried. If one of those known Pass Phrases succeeds no dialog pops up for this particular Private Key file. If none succeeded, another Pass Phrase is queried on the terminal and remembered for the next round (where it perhaps can be reused).

  This scheme allows mod_ssl to be maximally flexible (because for N encrypted Private Key files you *can* use N different Pass Phrases - but then you have to enter all of them, of course) while minimizing the terminal dialog (i.e. when you use a single Pass Phrase for all N Private Key files this Pass Phrase is queried only once).

- |/path/to/program [args...]

  This mode allows an external program to be used which acts as a pipe to a particular input device; the program is sent the standard prompt text used for the builtin mode on stdin, and is expected to write password strings on stdout. If several passwords are needed (or an incorrect password is entered), additional prompt text will be written subsequent to the first password being returned, and more passwords must then be written back.

- exec:/path/to/program

  Here an external program is configured which is called at startup for each encrypted Private Key file. It is called with one argument, a string of the form "servername:portnumber:index" (with index being a zero-based sequence number), which indicates for which server, TCP port and certificate number it has to print the corresponding Pass Phrase to `stdout`. The intent is that this external program first runs security checks to make sure that the system is not compromised by an attacker, and only when these checks were passed successfully it provides the Pass Phrase.

Both these security checks, and the way the Pass Phrase is determined, can be as complex as you like. Mod_ssl just defines the interface: an executable program which provides the Pass Phrase on `stdout`. Nothing more or less! So, if you're really paranoid about security, here is your interface. Anything else has to be left as an exercise to the administrator, because local security requirements are so different.

The reuse-algorithm above is used here, too. In other words: The external program is called only once per unique Pass Phrase.

### Example

```
SSLPassPhraseDialog exec:/usr/local/apache/sbin/pp-filter
```

## SSLProtocol Directive

| | |
|---|---|
| Description: | Configure usable SSL/TLS protocol versions |
| Syntax: | `SSLProtocol [+|-]protocol ...` |
| Default: | `SSLProtocol all -SSLv3` |
| Context: | server config, virtual host |
| Status: | Extension |
| Module: | mod_ssl |

This directive can be used to control which versions of the SSL/TLS protocol will be accepted in new connections.

The available (case-insensitive) *protocol*s are:

- `SSLv3`

  This is the Secure Sockets Layer (SSL) protocol, version 3.0, from the Netscape Corporation. It is the successor to SSLv2 and the predecessor to TLSv1, but is deprecated in RFC 7568[92].

- `TLSv1`

  This is the Transport Layer Security (TLS) protocol, version 1.0. It is the successor to SSLv3 and is defined in RFC 2246[93]. It is supported by nearly every client.

- `TLSv1.1` (when using OpenSSL 1.0.1 and later)

  A revision of the TLS 1.0 protocol, as defined in RFC 4346[94].

- `TLSv1.2` (when using OpenSSL 1.0.1 and later)

  A revision of the TLS 1.1 protocol, as defined in RFC 5246[95].

- `all`

  This is a shortcut for "+SSLv3 +TLSv1" or - when using OpenSSL 1.0.1 and later - "+SSLv3 +TLSv1 +TLSv1.1 +TLSv1.2", respectively (except for OpenSSL versions compiled with the "no-ssl3" configuration option, where `all` does not include +SSLv3).

### Example

```
SSLProtocol TLSv1
```

[92]http://www.ietf.org/rfc/rfc7568.txt
[93]http://www.ietf.org/rfc/rfc2246.txt
[94]http://www.ietf.org/rfc/rfc4346.txt
[95]http://www.ietf.org/rfc/rfc5246.txt

### SSLProxyCACertificateFile Directive

| | |
|---|---|
| Description: | File of concatenated PEM-encoded CA Certificates for Remote Server Auth |
| Syntax: | SSLProxyCACertificateFile file-path |
| Context: | server config, virtual host, proxy section |
| Override: | Not applicable |
| Status: | Extension |
| Module: | mod_ssl |

This directive sets the *all-in-one* file where you can assemble the Certificates of Certification Authorities (CA) whose *remote servers* you deal with. These are used for Remote Server Authentication. Such a file is simply the concatenation of the various PEM-encoded Certificate files, in order of preference. This can be used alternatively and/or additionally to SSLPROXYCACERTIFICATEPATH.

#### Example

```
SSLProxyCACertificateFile /usr/local/apache2/conf/ssl.crt/ca-bundle-remote-server.crt
```

### SSLProxyCACertificatePath Directive

| | |
|---|---|
| Description: | Directory of PEM-encoded CA Certificates for Remote Server Auth |
| Syntax: | SSLProxyCACertificatePath directory-path |
| Context: | server config, virtual host, proxy section |
| Override: | Not applicable |
| Status: | Extension |
| Module: | mod_ssl |

This directive sets the directory where you keep the Certificates of Certification Authorities (CAs) whose remote servers you deal with. These are used to verify the remote server certificate on Remote Server Authentication.

The files in this directory have to be PEM-encoded and are accessed through hash filenames. So usually you can't just place the Certificate files there: you also have to create symbolic links named *hash-value*.N. And you should always make sure this directory contains the appropriate symbolic links.

#### Example

```
SSLProxyCACertificatePath /usr/local/apache2/conf/ssl.crt/
```

### SSLProxyCARevocationCheck Directive

| | |
|---|---|
| Description: | Enable CRL-based revocation checking for Remote Server Auth |
| Syntax: | SSLProxyCARevocationCheck chain\|leaf\|none |
| Default: | SSLProxyCARevocationCheck none |
| Context: | server config, virtual host, proxy section |
| Override: | Not applicable |
| Status: | Extension |
| Module: | mod_ssl |

Enables certificate revocation list (CRL) checking for the *remote servers* you deal with. At least one of SSLPROXYCAREVOCATIONFILE or SSLPROXYCAREVOCATIONPATH must be configured. When set to chain (recommended setting), CRL checks are applied to all certificates in the chain, while setting it to leaf limits the checks to the end-entity cert.

⟹ **When set to `chain` or `leaf`, CRLs *must* be available for successful validation**

Prior to version 2.3.15, CRL checking in mod_ssl also succeeded when no CRL(s) were found in any of the locations configured with SSLPROXYCAREVOCATIONFILE or SSLPROXY-CAREVOCATIONPATH. With the introduction of this directive, the behavior has been changed: when checking is enabled, CRLs *must* be present for the validation to succeed - otherwise it will fail with an "`unable to get certificate CRL`" error.

### Example

```
SSLProxyCARevocationCheck chain
```

## SSLProxyCARevocationFile Directive

| | |
|---|---|
| Description: | File of concatenated PEM-encoded CA CRLs for Remote Server Auth |
| Syntax: | `SSLProxyCARevocationFile file-path` |
| Context: | server config, virtual host, proxy section |
| Override: | Not applicable |
| Status: | Extension |
| Module: | mod_ssl |

This directive sets the *all-in-one* file where you can assemble the Certificate Revocation Lists (CRL) of Certification Authorities (CA) whose *remote servers* you deal with. These are used for Remote Server Authentication. Such a file is simply the concatenation of the various PEM-encoded CRL files, in order of preference. This can be used alternatively and/or additionally to SSLPROXYCAREVOCATIONPATH.

### Example

```
SSLProxyCARevocationFile /usr/local/apache2/conf/ssl.crl/ca-bundle-remote-server.crl
```

## SSLProxyCARevocationPath Directive

| | |
|---|---|
| Description: | Directory of PEM-encoded CA CRLs for Remote Server Auth |
| Syntax: | `SSLProxyCARevocationPath directory-path` |
| Context: | server config, virtual host, proxy section |
| Override: | Not applicable |
| Status: | Extension |
| Module: | mod_ssl |

This directive sets the directory where you keep the Certificate Revocation Lists (CRL) of Certification Authorities (CAs) whose remote servers you deal with. These are used to revoke the remote server certificate on Remote Server Authentication.

The files in this directory have to be PEM-encoded and are accessed through hash filenames. So usually you have not only to place the CRL files there. Additionally you have to create symbolic links named *hash-value*`.rN`. And you should always make sure this directory contains the appropriate symbolic links.

### Example

```
SSLProxyCARevocationPath /usr/local/apache2/conf/ssl.crl/
```

### SSLProxyCheckPeerCN Directive

| | |
|---|---|
| Description: | Whether to check the remote server certificate's CN field |
| Syntax: | SSLProxyCheckPeerCN on\|off |
| Default: | SSLProxyCheckPeerCN on |
| Context: | server config, virtual host, proxy section |
| Override: | Not applicable |
| Status: | Extension |
| Module: | mod_ssl |

This directive sets whether the remote server certificate's CN field is compared against the hostname of the request URL. If both are not equal a 502 status code (Bad Gateway) is sent.

In 2.4.5 and later, SSLProxyCheckPeerCN has been superseded by SSLPROXYCHECKPEERNAME, and its setting is only taken into account when SSLProxyCheckPeerName off is specified at the same time.

#### Example

```
SSLProxyCheckPeerCN on
```

### SSLProxyCheckPeerExpire Directive

| | |
|---|---|
| Description: | Whether to check if remote server certificate is expired |
| Syntax: | SSLProxyCheckPeerExpire on\|off |
| Default: | SSLProxyCheckPeerExpire on |
| Context: | server config, virtual host, proxy section |
| Override: | Not applicable |
| Status: | Extension |
| Module: | mod_ssl |

This directive sets whether it is checked if the remote server certificate is expired or not. If the check fails a 502 status code (Bad Gateway) is sent.

#### Example

```
SSLProxyCheckPeerExpire on
```

### SSLProxyCheckPeerName Directive

| | |
|---|---|
| Description: | Configure host name checking for remote server certificates |
| Syntax: | SSLProxyCheckPeerName on\|off |
| Default: | SSLProxyCheckPeerName on |
| Context: | server config, virtual host, proxy section |
| Override: | Not applicable |
| Status: | Extension |
| Module: | mod_ssl |
| Compatibility: | Apache HTTP Server 2.4.5 and later |

This directive configures host name checking for server certificates when mod_ssl is acting as an SSL client. The check will succeed if the host name from the request URI is found in either the subjectAltName extension or (one of) the CN attribute(s) in the certificate's subject. If the check fails, the SSL request is aborted and a 502 status code (Bad Gateway) is returned. The directive supersedes SSLPROXYCHECKPEERCN, which only checks for the expected host name in the first CN attribute.

Wildcard matching is supported in one specific flavor: subjectAltName entries of type dNSName or CN attributes starting with `*.` will match for any DNS name with the same number of labels and the same suffix (i.e., `*.example.org` matches for `foo.example.org`, but not for `foo.bar.example.org`).

## SSLProxyCipherSuite Directive

| | |
|---|---|
| Description: | Cipher Suite available for negotiation in SSL proxy handshake |
| Syntax: | `SSLProxyCipherSuite cipher-spec` |
| Default: | `SSLProxyCipherSuite ALL:!ADH:RC4+RSA:+HIGH:+MEDIUM:+LOW:+EXP` |
| Context: | server config, virtual host, proxy section |
| Override: | Not applicable |
| Status: | Extension |
| Module: | mod_ssl |

Equivalent to `SSLCipherSuite`, but for the proxy connection. Please refer to SSLCIPHERSUITE for additional information.

## SSLProxyEngine Directive

| | |
|---|---|
| Description: | SSL Proxy Engine Operation Switch |
| Syntax: | `SSLProxyEngine on|off` |
| Default: | `SSLProxyEngine off` |
| Context: | server config, virtual host, proxy section |
| Override: | Not applicable |
| Status: | Extension |
| Module: | mod_ssl |

This directive toggles the usage of the SSL/TLS Protocol Engine for proxy. This is usually used inside a <VIRTUALHOST> section to enable SSL/TLS for proxy usage in a particular virtual host. By default the SSL/TLS Protocol Engine is disabled for proxy both for the main server and all configured virtual hosts.

Note that the SSLProxyEngine directive should not, in general, be included in a virtual host that will be acting as a forward proxy (using <Proxy> or <ProxyRequest> directives. SSLProxyEngine is not required to enable a forward proxy server to proxy SSL/TLS requests.

### Example

```
<VirtualHost _default_:443>
    SSLProxyEngine on
    #...
</VirtualHost>
```

## SSLProxyMachineCertificateChainFile Directive

| | |
|---|---|
| Description: | File of concatenated PEM-encoded CA certificates to be used by the proxy for choosing a certificate |
| Syntax: | `SSLProxyMachineCertificateChainFile filename` |
| Context: | server config, virtual host, proxy section |
| Override: | Not applicable |
| Status: | Extension |
| Module: | mod_ssl |

This directive sets the all-in-one file where you keep the certificate chain for all of the client certs in use. This directive will be needed if the remote server presents a list of CA certificates that are not direct signers of one of the configured client certificates.

This referenced file is simply the concatenation of the various PEM-encoded certificate files. Upon startup, each client certificate configured will be examined and a chain of trust will be constructed.

 **Security warning**
   If this directive is enabled, all of the certificates in the file will be trusted as if they were also in SSLPROXYCACERTIFICATEFILE.

### Example

```
SSLProxyMachineCertificateChainFile /usr/local/apache2/conf/ssl.crt/proxyCA.pem
```

## SSLProxyMachineCertificateFile Directive

| | |
|---|---|
| Description: | File of concatenated PEM-encoded client certificates and keys to be used by the proxy |
| Syntax: | `SSLProxyMachineCertificateFile filename` |
| Context: | server config, virtual host, proxy section |
| Override: | Not applicable |
| Status: | Extension |
| Module: | mod_ssl |

This directive sets the all-in-one file where you keep the certificates and keys used for authentication of the proxy server to remote servers.

This referenced file is simply the concatenation of the various PEM-encoded certificate files, in order of preference. Use this directive alternatively or additionally to `SSLProxyMachineCertificatePath`.

 Currently there is no support for encrypted private keys

### Example

```
SSLProxyMachineCertificateFile /usr/local/apache2/conf/ssl.crt/proxy.pem
```

## SSLProxyMachineCertificatePath Directive

| | |
|---|---|
| Description: | Directory of PEM-encoded client certificates and keys to be used by the proxy |
| Syntax: | `SSLProxyMachineCertificatePath directory` |
| Context: | server config, virtual host, proxy section |
| Override: | Not applicable |
| Status: | Extension |
| Module: | mod_ssl |

This directive sets the directory where you keep the certificates and keys used for authentication of the proxy server to remote servers.

The files in this directory must be PEM-encoded and are accessed through hash filenames. Additionally, you must create symbolic links named `hash-value.N`. And you should always make sure this directory contains the appropriate symbolic links.

Currently there is no support for encrypted private keys

**Example**

```
SSLProxyMachineCertificatePath /usr/local/apache2/conf/proxy.crt/
```

## SSLProxyProtocol Directive

| | |
|---|---|
| Description: | Configure usable SSL protocol flavors for proxy usage |
| Syntax: | SSLProxyProtocol [+\|-]protocol ... |
| Default: | SSLProxyProtocol all -SSLv3 |
| Context: | server config, virtual host, proxy section |
| Override: | Not applicable |
| Status: | Extension |
| Module: | mod_ssl |

This directive can be used to control the SSL protocol flavors mod_ssl should use when establishing its server environment for proxy . It will only connect to servers using one of the provided protocols.

Please refer to SSLPROTOCOL for additional information.

## SSLProxyVerify Directive

| | |
|---|---|
| Description: | Type of remote server Certificate verification |
| Syntax: | SSLProxyVerify level |
| Default: | SSLProxyVerify none |
| Context: | server config, virtual host, proxy section |
| Override: | Not applicable |
| Status: | Extension |
| Module: | mod_ssl |

When a proxy is configured to forward requests to a remote SSL server, this directive can be used to configure certificate verification of the remote server.

The following levels are available for *level*:

- **none**: no remote server Certificate is required at all

- **optional**: the remote server *may* present a valid Certificate

- **require**: the remote server *has to* present a valid Certificate

- **optional_no_ca**: the remote server may present a valid Certificate
  but it need not to be (successfully) verifiable.

In practice only levels **none** and **require** are really interesting, because level **optional** doesn't work with all servers and level **optional_no_ca** is actually against the idea of authentication (but can be used to establish SSL test pages, etc.)

**Example**

```
SSLProxyVerify require
```

## SSLProxyVerifyDepth Directive

| | |
|---|---|
| Description: | Maximum depth of CA Certificates in Remote Server Certificate verification |
| Syntax: | `SSLProxyVerifyDepth number` |
| Default: | `SSLProxyVerifyDepth 1` |
| Context: | server config, virtual host, proxy section |
| Override: | Not applicable |
| Status: | Extension |
| Module: | mod_ssl |

This directive sets how deeply mod_ssl should verify before deciding that the remote server does not have a valid certificate.

The depth actually is the maximum number of intermediate certificate issuers, i.e. the number of CA certificates which are max allowed to be followed while verifying the remote server certificate. A depth of 0 means that self-signed remote server certificates are accepted only, the default depth of 1 means the remote server certificate can be self-signed or has to be signed by a CA which is directly known to the server (i.e. the CA's certificate is under SSLPROXYCACERTIFICATEPATH), etc.

### Example

```
SSLProxyVerifyDepth 10
```

## SSLRandomSeed Directive

| | |
|---|---|
| Description: | Pseudo Random Number Generator (PRNG) seeding source |
| Syntax: | `SSLRandomSeed context source [bytes]` |
| Context: | server config |
| Status: | Extension |
| Module: | mod_ssl |

This configures one or more sources for seeding the Pseudo Random Number Generator (PRNG) in OpenSSL at startup time (*context* is `startup`) and/or just before a new SSL connection is established (*context* is `connect`). This directive can only be used in the global server context because the PRNG is a global facility.

The following *source* variants are available:

- `builtin` This is the always available builtin seeding source. Its usage consumes minimum CPU cycles under runtime and hence can be always used without drawbacks. The source used for seeding the PRNG contains of the current time, the current process id and (when applicable) a randomly chosen 1KB extract of the inter-process scoreboard structure of Apache. The drawback is that this is not really a strong source and at startup time (where the scoreboard is still not available) this source just produces a few bytes of entropy. So you should always, at least for the startup, use an additional seeding source.

- `file:/path/to/source`

  This variant uses an external file `/path/to/source` as the source for seeding the PRNG. When *bytes* is specified, only the first *bytes* number of bytes of the file form the entropy (and *bytes* is given to `/path/to/source` as the first argument). When *bytes* is not specified the whole file forms the entropy (and `0` is given to `/path/to/source` as the first argument). Use this especially at startup time, for instance with an available `/dev/random` and/or `/dev/urandom` devices (which usually exist on modern Unix derivatives like FreeBSD and Linux).

  *But be careful*: Usually `/dev/random` provides only as much entropy data as it actually has, i.e. when you request 512 bytes of entropy, but the device currently has only 100 bytes available two things can happen: On some platforms you receive only the 100 bytes while on other platforms the read blocks until enough bytes are available (which can take a long time). Here using an existing `/dev/urandom` is better, because it never blocks and actually gives the amount of requested data. The drawback is just that the quality of the received data may not be the best.

- `exec:/path/to/program`

  This variant uses an external executable `/path/to/program` as the source for seeding the PRNG. When *bytes* is specified, only the first *bytes* number of bytes of its `stdout` contents form the entropy. When *bytes* is not specified, the entirety of the data produced on `stdout` form the entropy. Use this only at startup time when you need a very strong seeding with the help of an external program (for instance as in the example above with the `truerand` utility you can find in the mod_ssl distribution which is based on the AT&T *truerand* library). Using this in the connection context slows down the server too dramatically, of course. So usually you should avoid using external programs in that context.

- `egd:/path/to/egd-socket` (Unix only)

  This variant uses the Unix domain socket of the external Entropy Gathering Daemon (EGD) (see http://www.lothar.com/tech /crypto/[96]) to seed the PRNG. Use this if no random device exists on your platform.

**Example**

```
SSLRandomSeed startup builtin
SSLRandomSeed startup file:/dev/random
SSLRandomSeed startup file:/dev/urandom 1024
SSLRandomSeed startup exec:/usr/local/bin/truerand 16
SSLRandomSeed connect builtin
SSLRandomSeed connect file:/dev/random
SSLRandomSeed connect file:/dev/urandom 1024
```

## SSLRenegBufferSize Directive

| | |
|---|---|
| Description: | Set the size for the SSL renegotiation buffer |
| Syntax: | `SSLRenegBufferSize bytes` |
| Default: | `SSLRenegBufferSize 131072` |
| Context: | directory, .htaccess |
| Override: | AuthConfig |
| Status: | Extension |
| Module: | mod_ssl |

If an SSL renegotiation is required in per-location context, for example, any use of SSLVERIFYCLIENT in a Directory or Location block, then MOD_SSL must buffer any HTTP request body into memory until the new SSL handshake can be performed. This directive can be used to set the amount of memory that will be used for this buffer.

 Note that in many configurations, the client sending the request body will be untrusted so a denial of service attack by consumption of memory must be considered when changing this configuration setting.

**Example**

```
SSLRenegBufferSize 262144
```

---

[96]http://www.lothar.com/tech/crypto/

## SSLRequire Directive

| | |
|---|---|
| Description: | Allow access only when an arbitrarily complex boolean expression is true |
| Syntax: | SSLRequire expression |
| Context: | directory, .htaccess |
| Override: | AuthConfig |
| Status: | Extension |
| Module: | mod_ssl |

**⟹ SSLRequire is deprecated**

SSLRequire is deprecated and should in general be replaced by Require expr (p. 519)
. The so called ap_expr (p. 99) syntax of Require expr is a superset of the syntax of
SSLRequire, with the following exception:
In SSLRequire, the comparison operators <, <=, ... are completely equivalent to the operators lt, le, ... and work in a somewhat peculiar way that first compares the length of two strings and then the lexical order. On the other hand, ap_expr (p. 99) has two sets of comparison operators: The operators <, <=, ... do lexical string comparison, while the operators -lt, -le, ... do integer comparison. For the latter, there are also aliases without the leading dashes: lt, le, ...

This directive specifies a general access requirement which has to be fulfilled in order to allow access. It is a very powerful directive because the requirement specification is an arbitrarily complex boolean expression containing any number of access checks.

The *expression* must match the following syntax (given as a BNF grammar notation):

```
expr      ::= "true" | "false"
          | "!" expr
          | expr "&&" expr
          | expr "||" expr
          | "(" expr ")"
          | comp

comp      ::= word "==" word | word "eq" word
          | word "!=" word | word "ne" word
          | word "<"  word | word "lt" word
          | word "<=" word | word "le" word
          | word ">"  word | word "gt" word
          | word ">=" word | word "ge" word
          | word "in" "{" wordlist "}"
          | word "in" "PeerExtList(" word ")"
          | word "=~" regex
          | word "!~" regex

wordlist  ::= word
          | wordlist "," word

word      ::= digit
          | cstring
          | variable
          | function

digit     ::= [0-9]+
cstring   ::= "..."
variable  ::= "%{" varname "}"
```

```
function ::= funcname "(" funcargs ")"
```

For `varname` any of the variables described in Environment Variables can be used.  For `funcname` the available functions are listed in the ap_expr documentation (p. 99) .

The *expression* is parsed into an internal machine representation when the configuration is loaded, and then evaluated during request processing.  In .htaccess context, the *expression* is both parsed and executed each time the .htaccess file is encountered during request processing.

### Example

```
SSLRequire (    %{SSL_CIPHER} !~ m/^(EXP|NULL)-/                    \
            and %{SSL_CLIENT_S_DN_O} eq "Snake Oil, Ltd."          \
            and %{SSL_CLIENT_S_DN_OU} in {"Staff", "CA", "Dev"}    \
            and %{TIME_WDAY} -ge 1 and %{TIME_WDAY} -le 5          \
            and %{TIME_HOUR} -ge 8 and %{TIME_HOUR} -le 20      ) \
            or %{REMOTE_ADDR} =~ m/^192\.76\.162\.[0-9]+$/
```

The `PeerExtList(object-ID)` function expects to find zero or more instances of the X.509 certificate extension identified by the given *object ID* (OID) in the client certificate.  The expression evaluates to true if the left-hand side string matches exactly against the value of an extension identified with this OID. (If multiple extensions with the same OID are present, at least one extension must match).

### Example

```
SSLRequire "foobar" in PeerExtList("1.2.3.4.5.6")
```

$\Longrightarrow$ **Notes on the PeerExtList function**

- The object ID can be specified either as a descriptive name recognized by the SSL library, such as `"nsComment"`, or as a numeric OID, such as `"1.2.3.4.5.6"`.
- Expressions with types known to the SSL library are rendered to a string before comparison. For an extension with a type not recognized by the SSL library, mod_ssl will parse the value if it is one of the primitive ASN.1 types UTF8String, IA5String, VisibleString, or BMPString. For an extension of one of these types, the string value will be converted to UTF-8 if necessary, then compared against the left-hand-side expression.

**See also**

- Environment Variables in Apache HTTP Server (p. 92) , for additional examples.
- Require expr (p. 519)
- Generic expression syntax in Apache HTTP Server (p. 99)

## SSLRequireSSL Directive

| | |
|---|---|
| Description: | Deny access when SSL is not used for the HTTP request |
| Syntax: | SSLRequireSSL |
| Context: | directory, .htaccess |
| Override: | AuthConfig |
| Status: | Extension |
| Module: | mod_ssl |

This directive forbids access unless HTTP over SSL (i.e. HTTPS) is enabled for the current connection. This is very handy inside the SSL-enabled virtual host or directories for defending against configuration errors that expose stuff that should be protected. When this directive is present all requests are denied which are not using SSL.

### Example

```
SSLRequireSSL
```

## SSLSessionCache Directive

| | |
|---|---|
| Description: | Type of the global/inter-process SSL Session Cache |
| Syntax: | SSLSessionCache type |
| Default: | SSLSessionCache none |
| Context: | server config |
| Status: | Extension |
| Module: | mod_ssl |

This configures the storage type of the global/inter-process SSL Session Cache. This cache is an optional facility which speeds up parallel request processing. For requests to the same server process (via HTTP keep-alive), OpenSSL already caches the SSL session information locally. But because modern clients request inlined images and other data via parallel requests (usually up to four parallel requests are common) those requests are served by *different* pre-forked server processes. Here an inter-process cache helps to avoid unnecessary session handshakes.

The following five storage *type*s are currently supported:

- `none`

  This disables the global/inter-process Session Cache. This will incur a noticeable speed penalty and may cause problems if using certain browsers, particularly if client certificates are enabled. This setting is not recommended.

- `nonenotnull`

  This disables any global/inter-process Session Cache. However it does force OpenSSL to send a non-null session ID to accommodate buggy clients that require one.

- `dbm:/path/to/datafile`

  This makes use of a DBM hashfile on the local disk to synchronize the local OpenSSL memory caches of the server processes. This session cache may suffer reliability issues under high load. To use this, ensure that MOD_SOCACHE_DBM is loaded.

- `shmcb:/path/to/datafile[(size)]`

  This makes use of a high-performance cyclic buffer (approx. *size* bytes in size) inside a shared memory segment in RAM (established via `/path/to/datafile`) to synchronize the local OpenSSL memory caches of the server processes. This is the recommended session cache. To use this, ensure that MOD_SOCACHE_SHMCB is loaded.

- `dc:UNIX:/path/to/socket`

  This makes use of the distcache[97] distributed session caching libraries. The argument should specify the location of the server or proxy to be used using the distcache address syntax; for example, `UNIX:/path/to/socket` specifies a UNIX domain socket (typically a local dc_client proxy); `IP:server.example.com:9001` specifies an IP address. To use this, ensure that MOD_SOCACHE_DC is loaded.

---

[97]http://distcache.sourceforge.net/

**Examples**

```
SSLSessionCache dbm:/usr/local/apache/logs/ssl_gcache_data
SSLSessionCache shmcb:/usr/local/apache/logs/ssl_gcache_data(512000)
```

The `ssl-cache` mutex is used to serialize access to the session cache to prevent corruption. This mutex can be configured using the MUTEX directive.

## SSLSessionCacheTimeout Directive

| | |
|---|---|
| Description: | Number of seconds before an SSL session expires in the Session Cache |
| Syntax: | `SSLSessionCacheTimeout seconds` |
| Default: | `SSLSessionCacheTimeout 300` |
| Context: | server config, virtual host |
| Status: | Extension |
| Module: | mod_ssl |
| Compatibility: | Applies also to RFC 5077 TLS session resumption in Apache 2.4.10 and later |

This directive sets the timeout in seconds for the information stored in the global/inter-process SSL Session Cache, the OpenSSL internal memory cache and for sessions resumed by TLS session resumption (RFC 5077). It can be set as low as 15 for testing, but should be set to higher values like 300 in real life.

**Example**

```
SSLSessionCacheTimeout 600
```

## SSLSessionTicketKeyFile Directive

| | |
|---|---|
| Description: | Persistent encryption/decryption key for TLS session tickets |
| Syntax: | `SSLSessionTicketKeyFile file-path` |
| Context: | server config, virtual host |
| Status: | Extension |
| Module: | mod_ssl |
| Compatibility: | Available in httpd 2.4.0 and later, if using OpenSSL 0.9.8h or later |

Optionally configures a secret key for encrypting and decrypting TLS session tickets, as defined in RFC 5077[98]. Primarily suitable for clustered environments where TLS sessions information should be shared between multiple nodes. For single-instance httpd setups, it is recommended to *not* configure a ticket key file, but to rely on (random) keys generated by mod_ssl at startup, instead.

The ticket key file must contain 48 bytes of random data, preferrably created from a high-entropy source. On a Unix-based system, a ticket key file can be created as follows:

```
dd if=/dev/random of=/path/to/file.tkey bs=1 count=48
```

Ticket keys should be rotated (replaced) on a frequent basis, as this is the only way to invalidate an existing session ticket - OpenSSL currently doesn't allow to specify a limit for ticket lifetimes. A new ticket key only gets used after restarting the web server. All existing session tickets become invalid after a restart.

! The ticket key file contains sensitive keying material and should be protected with file permissions similar to those used for SSLCERTIFICATEKEYFILE.

---

[98]http://www.ietf.org/rfc/rfc5077.txt

## SSLSessionTickets Directive

| | |
|---|---|
| Description: | Enable or disable use of TLS session tickets |
| Syntax: | SSLSessionTickets on\|off |
| Default: | SSLSessionTickets on |
| Context: | server config, virtual host |
| Status: | Extension |
| Module: | mod_ssl |
| Compatibility: | Available in httpd 2.4.11 and later, if using OpenSSL 0.9.8f or later. |

This directive allows to enable or disable the use of TLS session tickets (RFC 5077).

 TLS session tickets are enabled by default. Using them without restarting the web server with an appropriate frequency (e.g. daily) compromises perfect forward secrecy.

## SSLSRPUnknownUserSeed Directive

| | |
|---|---|
| Description: | SRP unknown user seed |
| Syntax: | SSLSRPUnknownUserSeed secret-string |
| Context: | server config, virtual host |
| Status: | Extension |
| Module: | mod_ssl |
| Compatibility: | Available in httpd 2.4.4 and later, if using OpenSSL 1.0.1 or later |

This directive sets the seed used to fake SRP user parameters for unknown users, to avoid leaking whether a given user exists. Specify a secret string. If this directive is not used, then Apache will return the UNKNOWN_PSK_IDENTITY alert to clients who specify an unknown username.

> **Example**
> ```
> SSLSRPUnknownUserSeed "secret"
> ```

## SSLSRPVerifierFile Directive

| | |
|---|---|
| Description: | Path to SRP verifier file |
| Syntax: | SSLSRPVerifierFile file-path |
| Context: | server config, virtual host |
| Status: | Extension |
| Module: | mod_ssl |
| Compatibility: | Available in httpd 2.4.4 and later, if using OpenSSL 1.0.1 or later |

This directive enables TLS-SRP and sets the path to the OpenSSL SRP (Secure Remote Password) verifier file containing TLS-SRP usernames, verifiers, salts, and group parameters.

> **Example**
> ```
> SSLSRPVerifierFile "/path/to/file.srpv"
> ```

The verifier file can be created with the `openssl` command line utility:

> **Creating the SRP verifier file**
> ```
> openssl srp -srpvfile passwd.srpv -userinfo "some info" -add username
> ```

The value given with the optional -userinfo parameter is avalable in the SSL_SRP_USERINFO request environment variable.

## SSLStaplingCache Directive

| | |
|---|---|
| Description: | Configures the OCSP stapling cache |
| Syntax: | `SSLStaplingCache type` |
| Context: | server config |
| Status: | Extension |
| Module: | mod_ssl |
| Compatibility: | Available if using OpenSSL 0.9.8h or later |

Configures the cache used to store OCSP responses which get included in the TLS handshake if SSLUSESTAPLING is enabled. Configuration of a cache is mandatory for OCSP stapling. With the exception of `none` and `nonenotnull`, the same storage types are supported as with SSLSESSIONCACHE.

## SSLStaplingErrorCacheTimeout Directive

| | |
|---|---|
| Description: | Number of seconds before expiring invalid responses in the OCSP stapling cache |
| Syntax: | `SSLStaplingErrorCacheTimeout seconds` |
| Default: | `SSLStaplingErrorCacheTimeout 600` |
| Context: | server config, virtual host |
| Status: | Extension |
| Module: | mod_ssl |
| Compatibility: | Available if using OpenSSL 0.9.8h or later |

Sets the timeout in seconds before *invalid* responses in the OCSP stapling cache (configured through SSLSTAPLING-CACHE) will expire. To set the cache timeout for valid responses, see SSLSTAPLINGSTANDARDCACHETIMEOUT.

## SSLStaplingFakeTryLater Directive

| | |
|---|---|
| Description: | Synthesize "tryLater" responses for failed OCSP stapling queries |
| Syntax: | `SSLStaplingFakeTryLater on\|off` |
| Default: | `SSLStaplingFakeTryLater on` |
| Context: | server config, virtual host |
| Status: | Extension |
| Module: | mod_ssl |
| Compatibility: | Available if using OpenSSL 0.9.8h or later |

When enabled and a query to an OCSP responder for stapling purposes fails, mod_ssl will synthesize a "tryLater" response for the client. Only effective if SSLSTAPLINGRETURNRESPONDERERRORS is also enabled.

## SSLStaplingForceURL Directive

| | |
|---|---|
| Description: | Override the OCSP responder URI specified in the certificate's AIA extension |
| Syntax: | `SSLStaplingForceURL uri` |
| Context: | server config, virtual host |
| Status: | Extension |
| Module: | mod_ssl |
| Compatibility: | Available if using OpenSSL 0.9.8h or later |

This directive overrides the URI of an OCSP responder as obtained from the authorityInfoAccess (AIA) extension of the certificate. One potential use is when a proxy is used for retrieving OCSP queries.

### SSLStaplingResponderTimeout Directive

| | |
|---|---|
| Description: | Timeout for OCSP stapling queries |
| Syntax: | `SSLStaplingResponderTimeout seconds` |
| Default: | `SSLStaplingResponderTimeout 10` |
| Context: | server config, virtual host |
| Status: | Extension |
| Module: | mod_ssl |
| Compatibility: | Available if using OpenSSL 0.9.8h or later |

This option sets the timeout for queries to OCSP responders when SSLUSESTAPLING is enabled and mod_ssl is querying a responder for OCSP stapling purposes.

### SSLStaplingResponseMaxAge Directive

| | |
|---|---|
| Description: | Maximum allowable age for OCSP stapling responses |
| Syntax: | `SSLStaplingResponseMaxAge seconds` |
| Default: | `SSLStaplingResponseMaxAge -1` |
| Context: | server config, virtual host |
| Status: | Extension |
| Module: | mod_ssl |
| Compatibility: | Available if using OpenSSL 0.9.8h or later |

This option sets the maximum allowable age ("freshness") when considering OCSP responses for stapling purposes, i.e. when SSLUSESTAPLING is turned on. The default value (-1) does not enforce a maximum age, which means that OCSP responses are considered valid as long as their `nextUpdate` field is in the future.

### SSLStaplingResponseTimeSkew Directive

| | |
|---|---|
| Description: | Maximum allowable time skew for OCSP stapling response validation |
| Syntax: | `SSLStaplingResponseTimeSkew seconds` |
| Default: | `SSLStaplingResponseTimeSkew 300` |
| Context: | server config, virtual host |
| Status: | Extension |
| Module: | mod_ssl |
| Compatibility: | Available if using OpenSSL 0.9.8h or later |

This option sets the maximum allowable time skew when mod_ssl checks the `thisUpdate` and `nextUpdate` fields of OCSP responses which get included in the TLS handshake (OCSP stapling). Only applicable if SSLUSESTAPLING is turned on.

### SSLStaplingReturnResponderErrors Directive

| | |
|---|---|
| Description: | Pass stapling related OCSP errors on to client |
| Syntax: | `SSLStaplingReturnResponderErrors on\|off` |
| Default: | `SSLStaplingReturnResponderErrors on` |
| Context: | server config, virtual host |
| Status: | Extension |
| Module: | mod_ssl |
| Compatibility: | Available if using OpenSSL 0.9.8h or later |

When enabled, mod_ssl will pass responses from unsuccessful stapling related OCSP queries (such as responses with an overall status other than "successful", responses with a certificate status other than "good", expired responses etc.)

on to the client. If set to off, only responses indicating a certificate status of "good" will be included in the TLS handshake.

## SSLStaplingStandardCacheTimeout Directive

| | |
|---|---|
| Description: | Number of seconds before expiring responses in the OCSP stapling cache |
| Syntax: | SSLStaplingStandardCacheTimeout seconds |
| Default: | SSLStaplingStandardCacheTimeout 3600 |
| Context: | server config, virtual host |
| Status: | Extension |
| Module: | mod_ssl |
| Compatibility: | Available if using OpenSSL 0.9.8h or later |

Sets the timeout in seconds before responses in the OCSP stapling cache (configured through SSLSTAPLINGCACHE) will expire. This directive applies to *valid* responses, while SSLSTAPLINGERRORCACHETIMEOUT is used for controlling the timeout for invalid/unavailable responses.

## SSLStrictSNIVHostCheck Directive

| | |
|---|---|
| Description: | Whether to allow non-SNI clients to access a name-based virtual host. |
| Syntax: | SSLStrictSNIVHostCheck on\|off |
| Default: | SSLStrictSNIVHostCheck off |
| Context: | server config, virtual host |
| Status: | Extension |
| Module: | mod_ssl |

This directive sets whether a non-SNI client is allowed to access a name-based virtual host. If set to on in the default name-based virtual host, clients that are SNI unaware will not be allowed to access *any* virtual host, belonging to this particular IP / port combination. If set to on in any other virtual host, SNI unaware clients are not allowed to access this particular virtual host.

 This option is only available if httpd was compiled against an SNI capable version of OpenSSL.

### Example

```
SSLStrictSNIVHostCheck on
```

## SSLUserName Directive

| | |
|---|---|
| Description: | Variable name to determine user name |
| Syntax: | SSLUserName varname |
| Context: | server config, directory, .htaccess |
| Override: | AuthConfig |
| Status: | Extension |
| Module: | mod_ssl |

This directive sets the "user" field in the Apache request object. This is used by lower modules to identify the user with a character string. In particular, this may cause the environment variable REMOTE_USER to be set. The *varname* can be any of the SSL environment variables.

When the FakeBasicAuth option is enabled, this directive instead controls the value of the username embedded within the basic authentication header (see SSLOptions).

**Example**

```
SSLUserName SSL_CLIENT_S_DN_CN
```

## SSLUseStapling Directive

| | |
|---|---|
| Description: | Enable stapling of OCSP responses in the TLS handshake |
| Syntax: | SSLUseStapling on\|off |
| Default: | SSLUseStapling off |
| Context: | server config, virtual host |
| Status: | Extension |
| Module: | mod_ssl |
| Compatibility: | Available if using OpenSSL 0.9.8h or later |

This option enables OCSP stapling, as defined by the "Certificate Status Request" TLS extension specified in RFC 6066. If enabled (and requested by the client), mod_ssl will include an OCSP response for its own certificate in the TLS handshake. Configuring an SSLSTAPLINGCACHE is a prerequisite for enabling OCSP stapling.

OCSP stapling relieves the client of querying the OCSP responder on its own, but it should be noted that with the RFC 6066 specification, the server's CertificateStatus reply may only include an OCSP response for a single cert. For server certificates with intermediate CA certificates in their chain (the typical case nowadays), stapling in its current implementation therefore only partially achieves the stated goal of "saving roundtrips and resources" - see also RFC 6961[99] (TLS Multiple Certificate Status Extension).

When OCSP stapling is enabled, the ssl-stapling mutex is used to control access to the OCSP stapling cache in order to prevent corruption, and the sss-stapling-refresh mutex is used to control refreshes of OCSP responses. These mutexes can be configured using the MUTEX directive.

## SSLVerifyClient Directive

| | |
|---|---|
| Description: | Type of Client Certificate verification |
| Syntax: | SSLVerifyClient level |
| Default: | SSLVerifyClient none |
| Context: | server config, virtual host, directory, .htaccess |
| Override: | AuthConfig |
| Status: | Extension |
| Module: | mod_ssl |

This directive sets the Certificate verification level for the Client Authentication. Notice that this directive can be used both in per-server and per-directory context. In per-server context it applies to the client authentication process used in the standard SSL handshake when a connection is established. In per-directory context it forces a SSL renegotiation with the reconfigured client verification level after the HTTP request was read but before the HTTP response is sent.

The following levels are available for *level*:

- **none**: no client Certificate is required at all
- **optional**: the client *may* present a valid Certificate
- **require**: the client *has to* present a valid Certificate
- **optional_no_ca**: the client may present a valid Certificate but it need not to be (successfully) verifiable.

---

[99]http://www.ietf.org/rfc/rfc6961.txt

In practice only levels **none** and **require** are really interesting, because level **optional** doesn't work with all browsers and level **optional_no_ca** is actually against the idea of authentication (but can be used to establish SSL test pages, etc.)

### Example

```
SSLVerifyClient require
```

## SSLVerifyDepth Directive

| | |
|---|---|
| Description: | Maximum depth of CA Certificates in Client Certificate verification |
| Syntax: | SSLVerifyDepth number |
| Default: | SSLVerifyDepth 1 |
| Context: | server config, virtual host, directory, .htaccess |
| Override: | AuthConfig |
| Status: | Extension |
| Module: | mod_ssl |

This directive sets how deeply mod_ssl should verify before deciding that the clients don't have a valid certificate. Notice that this directive can be used both in per-server and per-directory context. In per-server context it applies to the client authentication process used in the standard SSL handshake when a connection is established. In per-directory context it forces a SSL renegotiation with the reconfigured client verification depth after the HTTP request was read but before the HTTP response is sent.

The depth actually is the maximum number of intermediate certificate issuers, i.e. the number of CA certificates which are max allowed to be followed while verifying the client certificate. A depth of 0 means that self-signed client certificates are accepted only, the default depth of 1 means the client certificate can be self-signed or has to be signed by a CA which is directly known to the server (i.e. the CA's certificate is under SSLCACERTIFICATEPATH), etc.

### Example

```
SSLVerifyDepth 10
```

# 10.116 Apache Module mod_ssl_ct

| | |
|---|---|
| Description: | Implementation of Certificate Transparency (RFC 6962) |
| Status: | Extension |
| ModuleIdentifier: | ssl_ct_module |
| SourceFile: | mod_ssl_ct.c |

## Summary

This module provides an implementation of Certificate Transparency, in conjunction with MOD_SSL and command-line tools from the certificate-transparency[100] open source project. The goal of Certificate Transparency is to expose the use of server certificates which are trusted by browsers but were mistakenly or maliciously issued. More information about Certificate Transparency is available at http://www.certificate-transparency.org/[101]. Key terminology used in this documentation:

**Certificate log** A certificate log, referred to simply as *log* in this documentation, is a network service to which server certificates have been submitted. A user agent can confirm that the certificate of a server which it accesses has been submitted to a log which it trusts, and that the log itself has not been tampered with.

**Signed Certificate Timestamp (SCT)** This is an acknowledgement from a log that it has accepted a valid certificate. It is signed with the log's public key. One or more SCTs is passed to clients during the handshake, either in the ServerHello (TLS extension), certificate extension, or in a stapled OCSP response.

This implementation for Apache httpd provides these features for TLS servers and proxies:

- Signed Certificate Timestamps (SCTs) can be obtained from logs automatically and, in conjunction with any statically configured SCTs, sent to aware clients in the ServerHello (during the handshake).
- SCTs can be received by the proxy from origin servers in the ServerHello, in a certificate extension, and/or within stapled OCSP responses; any SCTs received can be partially validated on-line and optionally queued for off-line audit.
- The proxy can be configured to disallow communication with an origin server which does not provide an SCT which passes on-line validation.

Configuration information about logs can be defined statically in the web server configuration or maintained in a SQLite3 database. In the latter case, MOD_SSL_CT will reload the database periodically, so any site-specific infrastructure for maintaining and propagating log configuration information does not have to also restart httpd to make it take effect.

⟹ This module is experimental for the following reasons:

- Insufficient test and review
- Reliance on an unreleased version of OpenSSL (1.0.2, Beta 3 or later) for basic operation
- Incomplete off-line audit capability

Configuration mechanisms, format of data saved for off-line audit, and other characteristics are subject to change based on further feedback and testing.

### Directives

- CTAuditStorage

---

[100]https://code.google.com/p/certificate-transparency/
[101]http://www.certificate-transparency.org/

- CTLogClient
- CTLogConfigDB
- CTMaxSCTAge
- CTProxyAwareness
- CTSCTStorage
- CTServerHelloSCTLimit
- CTStaticLogConfig
- CTStaticSCTs

## Server processing overview

Servers need to send SCTs to their clients. SCTs in a certificate extension or stapled OCSP response will be sent without any special program logic. This module handles sending SCTs configured by the administrator or received from configured logs.

The number of SCTs sent in the ServerHello (i.e., not including those in a certificate extension or stapled OCSP response) can be limited by the CTSERVERHELLOSCTLIMIT directive.

For each server certificate, a daemon process maintains an SCT list to be sent in the ServerHello, created from statically configured SCTs as well as those received from logs. Logs marked as untrusted or with a maximum valid timestamp before the present time will be ignored. Periodically the daemon will submit certificates to a log as necessary (due to changed log configuration or age) and rebuild the concatenation of SCTs.

The SCT list for a server certificate will be sent to any client that indicates awareness in the ClientHello when that particular server certificate is used.

## Proxy processing overview

The proxy indicates Certificate Transparency awareness in the ClientHello by including the *signed_certificate_timestamp* extension. It can recognize SCTs received in the ServerHello, in an extension in the certificate for an origin server, or in a stapled OCSP response.

On-line verification is attempted for each received SCT:

- For any SCT, the timestamp can be checked to see if it is not yet valid based on the current time as well as any configured valid time interval for the log.
- For an SCT from a log for which a public key is configured, the server signature will be checked.

If verification fails for at least one SCT and verification was not successful for at least one SCT, the connection is aborted if CTPROXYAWARENESS is set to *require*.

Additionally, the server certificate chain and SCTs are stored for off-line verification if the CTAUDITSTORAGE directive is configured.

As an optimization, on-line verification and storing of data from the server is only performed the first time a web server child process receives the data. This saves some processing time as well as disk space. For typical reverse proxy setups, very little processing overhead will be required.

## Log configuration

Servers and proxies use different information about logs for their processing. This *log configuration* can be set in two ways:

- Create a log configuration database using `ctlogconfig`, and configure the path to that database using the CTLOGCONFIG directive. This method of configuration supports dynamic updates; MOD_SSL_CT will re-read the database at intervals. Additionally, the off-line audit program `ctauditscts` can use this configuration to find the URL of logs.

- Configure information about logs statically using the CTSTATICLOGCONFIG directive. As with all other directives, the server must be restarted in order to pick up changes to the directives.

The information that can be configured about a log using either mechanism is described below:

**log id** The log id is the SHA-256 hash of the log's public key, and is part of every SCT. This is a convenient way to identify a particular log when configuring valid timestamp ranges or certain other information.

**public key of the log** A proxy must have the public key of the log in order to check the signature in SCTs it receives which were obtained from the log.
A server must have the public key of the log in order to submit certificates to it.

**general trust/distrust setting** This is a mechanism to distrust or restore trust in a particular log, for whatever reason (including simply avoiding interaction with the log in situations where it is off-line).

**minimum and/or maximum valid timestamps** When configured, the proxy will check that timestamps from SCTs are within the valid range.

**log URL** The URL of the log (for its API) is required by a server in order to submit server certificates to the log. The server will submit each server certificate in order to obtain an SCT for each log with a configured URL, except when the log is also marked as distrusted or the current time is not within any configured valid timestamp range. The log URL is also needed by off-line auditing of SCTs received by a proxy.

Generally, only a small subset of this information is configured for a particular log. Refer to the documentation for the CTSTATICLOGCONFIG directive and the `ctlogconfig` command for more specific information.

## Storing SCTs in a form consumable by mod_ssl_ct

MOD_SSL_CT allows you to configure SCTs statically using the CTSTATICSCTS directive. These must be in binary form, ready to send to a client.

Sample code in the form of a Python script to build an SCT in the correct format from data received from a log can be found in Tom Ritter's ct-tools repository[102]. Refer to `write-sct.py`

## Logging CT status in the access log

Proxy and server modes set the `SSL_CT_PROXY_STATUS` and `SSL_CT_CLIENT_STATUS` variables, respectively, to indicate if the corresponding peer is CT-aware.

Proxy mode sets the `SSL_CT_PROXY_SCT_SOURCES` variable to indicate whether and where SCTs were obtained (ServerHello, certificate extension, etc.).

These variables can be logged with the `%{varname}e` format of MOD_LOG_CONFIG.

---

[102]https://github.com/tomrittervg/ct-tools

## Off-line audit for proxy

Experimental support for this is implemented in the `ctauditscts` command, which itself relies on the `verify_single_proof.py` tool in the *certificate-transparency* open source project. `ctauditscts` can parse data for off-line audit (enabled with the CTAUDITSTORAGE directive) and invoke `verify_single_proof.py`.

Here are rough notes for using `ctauditscts`:

- Create a *virtualenv* using the `requirements.txt` file from the *certificate-transparency* project and run the following steps with that *virtualenv* activated.
- Set `PYTHONPATH` to include the `python` directory within the *certificate-transparency* tools.
- Set `PATH` to include the `python/ct/client/tools` directory.
- Run `ctauditscts`, passing the value of the CTAUDITSTORAGE directive and, optionally, the path to the log configuration database. The latter will be used to look up log URLs by log id.

The data saved for audit can also be used by other programs; refer to the `ctauditscts` source code for details on processing the data.

## CTAuditStorage Directive

| | |
|---|---|
| Description: | Existing directory where data for off-line audit will be stored |
| Syntax: | `CTAuditStorage directory` |
| Default: | `none` |
| Context: | server config |
| Status: | Extension |
| Module: | mod_ssl_ct |

The CTAUDITSTORAGE directive sets the name of a directory where data will be stored for off-line audit. If *directory* is not absolute then it is assumed to be relative to DEFAULTRUNTIMEDIR.

If this directive is not specified, data will not be stored for off-line audit.

The directory will contain files named *PID*`.tmp` for active child processes and files named *PID*`.out` for exited child processes. These `.out` files are ready for off-line audit. The experimental command `ctauditscts` (in the httpd source tree, not currently installed) interfaces with *certificate-transparency* tools to perform the audit.

## CTLogClient Directive

| | |
|---|---|
| Description: | Location of certificate-transparency log client tool |
| Syntax: | `CTLogClient executable` |
| Default: | `none` |
| Context: | server config |
| Status: | Extension |
| Module: | mod_ssl_ct |

*executable* is the full path to the log client tool, which is normally file `cpp/client/ct` (or `ct.exe`) within the source tree of the

certificate-transparency[103] open source project.

An alternative implementation could be used to retrieve SCTs for a server certificate as long as the command-line interface is equivalent.

If this directive is not configured, server certificates cannot be submitted to logs in order to obtain SCTs; thus, only admin-managed SCTs or SCTs in certificate extensions will be provided to clients.

---

[103]https://code.google.com/p/certificate-transparency/

## CTLogConfigDB Directive

| | |
|---|---|
| Description: | Log configuration database supporting dynamic updates |
| Syntax: | `CTLogConfigDB filename` |
| Default: | `none` |
| Context: | server config |
| Status: | Extension |
| Module: | mod_ssl_ct |

The CTLOGCONFIGDB directive sets the name of a database containing configuration about known logs. If *filename* is not absolute then it is assumed to be relative to SERVERROOT.

Refer to the documentation for the `ctlogconfig` program, which manages the database.

## CTMaxSCTAge Directive

| | |
|---|---|
| Description: | Maximum age of SCT obtained from a log, before it will be refreshed |
| Syntax: | `CTMaxSCTAge num-seconds` |
| Default: | `1 day` |
| Context: | server config |
| Status: | Extension |
| Module: | mod_ssl_ct |

Server certificates with SCTs which are older than this maximum age will be resubmitted to configured logs. Generally the log will return the same SCT as before, but that is subject to log operation. SCTs will be refreshed as necessary during normal server operation, with new SCTs returned to clients as they become available.

## CTProxyAwareness Directive

| | |
|---|---|
| Description: | Level of CT awareness and enforcement for a proxy |
| Syntax: | `CTProxyAwareness oblivious|aware|require` |
| Default: | `aware` |
| Context: | server config, virtual host |
| Status: | Extension |
| Module: | mod_ssl_ct |

This directive controls awareness and checks for valid SCTs for a proxy. Several options are available:

**oblivious** The proxy will neither ask for nor examine SCTs. Certificate Transparency processing for the proxy is completely disabled.

**aware** The proxy will perform all appropriate Certificate Transparency processing, such as asking for and examining SCTs. However, the proxy will not disallow communication if the origin server does not provide any valid SCTs.

**require** The proxy will abort communication with the origin server if it does not provide at least one SCT which passes on-line validation.

## CTSCTStorage Directive

| | |
|---|---|
| Description: | Existing directory where SCTs are managed |
| Syntax: | `CTSCTStorage directory` |
| Default: | `none` |
| Context: | server config |
| Status: | Extension |
| Module: | mod_ssl_ct |

The CTSCTSTORAGE directive sets the name of a directory where SCTs and SCT lists will be stored. If *directory* is not absolute then it is assumed to be relative to DEFAULTRUNTIMEDIR.

A subdirectory for each server certificate contains information relative to that certificate; the name of the subdirectory is the SHA-256 hash of the certificate.

The certificate-specific directory contains SCTs retrieved from configured logs, SCT lists prepared from statically configured SCTs and retrieved SCTs, and other information used for managing SCTs.

## CTServerHelloSCTLimit Directive

| | |
|---|---|
| Description: | Limit on number of SCTs that can be returned in ServerHello |
| Syntax: | `CTServerHelloSCTLimit limit` |
| Default: | `100` |
| Context: | server config |
| Status: | Extension |
| Module: | mod_ssl_ct |

This directive can be used to limit the number of SCTs which can be returned by a TLS server in ServerHello, in case the number of configured logs and statically-defined SCTs is relatively high.

Typically only a few SCTs would be available, so this directive is only needed in special circumstances.

The directive does not take into account SCTs which may be provided in certificate extensions or in stapled OCSP responses.

## CTStaticLogConfig Directive

| | |
|---|---|
| Description: | Static configuration of information about a log |
| Syntax: | `CTStaticLogConfig log-id\|- public-key-file\|- 1\|0\|-`<br>`min-timestamp\|- max-timestamp\|- log-URL\|-` |
| Default: | `none` |
| Context: | server config |
| Status: | Extension |
| Module: | mod_ssl_ct |

This directive is used to configure information about a particular log. This directive is appropriate when configuration information changes rarely. If dynamic configuration updates must be supported, refer to the CTLOGCONFIGDB directive.

Each of the six fields must be specified, but usually only a small amount of information must be configured for each log; use - when no information is available for the field. For example, in support of a server-only configuration (i.e., no proxy), the administrator might configure only the log URL to be used when submitting server certificates and obtaining a Signed Certificate Timestamp.

The fields are defined as follows:

*log-id* This is the id of the log, which is the SHA-256 hash of the log's public key, provided in hexadecimal format. This string is 64 characters in length.

This field should be omitted when *public-key-file* is provided.

*public-key-file* This is the name of a file containing the **PEM** encoding of the log's public key. If the name is not absolute, then it is assumed to be relative to SERVERROOT.

*trust/distrust* Set this field to *1* to distrust this log, or to otherwise avoid using it for server certificate submission. Set this to - or *0* (the default) to treat the log normally.

*min-timestamp* and *max-timestamp* A timestamp is a time as expressed in the number of milliseconds since the epoch, ignoring leap seconds. This is the form of time used in Signed Certificate Timestamps. This must be provided as a decimal number.

Specify − for one of the timestamps if it is unknown. For example, when configuring the minimum valid timestamp for a log which remains valid, specify − for *max-timestamp*.

SCTs received from this log by the proxy are invalid if the timestamp is older than *min-timestamp* or newer than *max-timestamp*.

*log-URL* This is the URL of the log, for use in submitting server certificates and in turn obtaining an SCT to be sent to clients.

**See also**

- Log configuration contains more general information about the fields which can be configured with this directive.

## CTStaticSCTs Directive

| | |
|---|---|
| Description: | Static configuration of one or more SCTs for a server certificate |
| Syntax: | `CTStaticSCTs certificate-pem-file sct-directory` |
| Default: | `none` |
| Context: | server config |
| Status: | Extension |
| Module: | mod_ssl_ct |

This directive is used to statically define one or more SCTs corresponding to a server certificate. This mechanism can be used instead of or in addition to dynamically obtaining SCTs from configured logs. Any changes to the set of SCTs for a particular server certificate will be adopted dynamically without the need to restart the server.

*certificate-pem-file* refers to the server certificate in PEM format. If the name is not absolute, then it is assumed to be relative to SERVERROOT.

*sct-directory* should contain one or more files with extension `.sct`, representing one or more SCTs corresponding to the server certificate. If *sct-directory* is not absolute, then it is assumed to be relative to SERVERROOT.

If *sct-directory* is empty, no error will be raised.

This directive could be used to identify directories of SCTs maintained by other infrastructure, provided that they are saved in binary format with file extension *.sct*

## 10.117   Apache Module mod_status

| Description: | Provides information on server activity and performance |
|---|---|
| Status: | Base |
| ModuleIdentifier: | status_module |
| SourceFile: | mod_status.c |

### Summary

The Status module allows a server administrator to find out how well their server is performing. A HTML page is presented that gives the current server statistics in an easily readable form. If required this page can be made to automatically refresh (given a compatible browser). Another page gives a simple machine-readable list of the current server state.

The details given are:

- The number of worker serving requests
- The number of idle worker
- The status of each worker, the number of requests that worker has performed and the total number of bytes served by the worker (*)
- A total number of accesses and byte count served (*)
- The time the server was started/restarted and the time it has been running for
- Averages giving the number of requests per second, the number of bytes served per second and the average number of bytes per request (*)
- The current percentage CPU used by each worker and in total by all workers combined (*)
- The current hosts and requests being processed (*)

The lines marked "(*)" are only available if EXTENDEDSTATUS is On. In version 2.3.6, loading mod_status will toggle EXTENDEDSTATUS On by default.

**Directives** This module provides no directives.

### Enabling Status Support

To enable status reports only for browsers from the example.com domain add this code to your `httpd.conf` configuration file

```
<Location "/server-status">
    SetHandler server-status
    Require host example.com
</Location>
```

You can now access server statistics by using a Web browser to access the page `http://your.server.name/server-status`

### Automatic Updates

You can get the status page to update itself automatically if you have a browser that supports "refresh". Access the page `http://your.server.name/server-status?refresh=N` to refresh the page every N seconds.

## Machine Readable Status File

A machine-readable version of the status file is available by accessing the page `http://your.server.name/server-status?auto`. This is useful when automatically run, see the Perl program `log_server_status`, which you will find in the `/support` directory of your Apache HTTP Server installation.

> It should be noted that if MOD_STATUS is loaded into the server, its handler capability is available in *all* configuration files, including *per*-directory files (*e.g.*, `.htaccess`). This may have security-related ramifications for your site.

## Using server-status to troubleshoot

The `server-status` page may be used as a starting place for troubleshooting a situation where your server is consuming all available resources (CPU or memory), and you wish to identify which requests or clients are causing the problem.

First, ensure that you have EXTENDEDSTATUS set on, so that you can see the full request and client information for each child or thread.

Now look in your process list (using `top`, or similar process viewing utility) to identify the specific processes that are the main culprits. Order the output of `top` by CPU usage, or memory usage, depending on what problem you're trying to address.

Reload the `server-status` page, and look for those process ids, and you'll be able to see what request is being served by that process, for what client. Requests are transient, so you may need to try several times before you catch it in the act, so to speak.

This process *should* give you some idea what client, or what type of requests, are primarily responsible for your load problems. Often you will identify a particular web application that is misbehaving, or a particular client that is attacking your site.

# 10.118   Apache Module mod_substitute

| Description: | Perform search and replace operations on response bodies |
|---|---|
| Status: | Extension |
| ModuleIdentifier: | substitute_module |
| SourceFile: | mod_substitute.c |

## Summary

MOD_SUBSTITUTE provides a mechanism to perform both regular expression and fixed string substitutions on response bodies.

### Directives

- Substitute
- SubstituteInheritBefore
- SubstituteMaxLineLength

## Substitute Directive

| Description: | Pattern to filter the response content |
|---|---|
| Syntax: | `Substitute s/pattern/substitution/[infq]` |
| Context: | directory, .htaccess |
| Override: | FileInfo |
| Status: | Extension |
| Module: | mod_substitute |

The SUBSTITUTE directive specifies a search and replace pattern to apply to the response body.

The meaning of the pattern can be modified by using any combination of these flags:

**i** Perform a case-insensitive match.

**n** By default the pattern is treated as a regular expression. Using the n flag forces the pattern to be treated as a fixed string.

**f** The f flag causes `mod_substitute` to flatten the result of a substitution allowing for later substitutions to take place on the boundary of this one. This is the default.

**q** The q flag causes `mod_substitute` to not flatten the buckets after each substitution. This can result in much faster response and a decrease in memory utilization, but should only be used if there is no possibility that the result of one substitution will ever match a pattern or regex of a subsequent one.

### Example

```
<Location "/">
    AddOutputFilterByType SUBSTITUTE text/html
    Substitute "s/foo/bar/ni"
</Location>
```

If either the pattern or the substitution contain a slash character then an alternative delimiter should be used:

**Example of using an alternate delimiter**

```
<Location "/">
    AddOutputFilterByType SUBSTITUTE text/html
    Substitute "s|<BR */?>|<br />|i"
</Location>
```

Backreferences can be used in the comparison and in the substitution, when regular expressions are used, as illustrated in the following example:

**Example of using backreferences and captures**

```
<Location "/">
    AddOutputFilterByType SUBSTITUTE text/html
    # "foo=k,bar=k" -> "foo/bar=k"
    Substitute "s|foo=(\w+),bar=\1|foo/bar=$1"
</Location>
```

A common use scenario for `mod_substitute` is the situation in which a front-end server proxies requests to a back-end server which returns HTML with hard-coded embedded URLs that refer to the back-end server. These URLs don't work for the end-user, since the back-end server is unreachable.

In this case, `mod_substitute` can be used to rewrite those URLs into something that will work from the front end:

**Rewriting URLs embedded in proxied content**

```
ProxyPass         "/blog/" "http://internal.blog.example.com"
ProxyPassReverse "/blog/" "http://internal.blog.example.com/"

Substitute "s|http://internal.blog.example.com/|http://www.example.com/blog/|i"
```

PROXYPASSREVERSE modifies any Location (redirect) headers that are sent by the back-end server, and, in this example, SUBSTITUTE takes care of the rest of the problem by fixing up the HTML response as well.

## SubstituteInheritBefore Directive

| | |
|---|---|
| Description: | Change the merge order of inherited patterns |
| Syntax: | `SubstituteInheritBefore on|off` |
| Default: | `SubstituteInheritBefore on` |
| Context: | directory, .htaccess |
| Override: | FileInfo |
| Status: | Extension |
| Module: | mod_substitute |
| Compatibility: | Available in httpd 2.4.17 and later |

Whether to apply the inherited SUBSTITUTE patterns first (`on`), or after the ones of the current context (`off`). The latter was the default in versions 2.4 and earlier, but changed starting with 2.5, hence SUBSTITUTEINHERITBEFORE set to `off` allows to restore the legacy behaviour. SUBSTITUTEINHERITBEFORE is itself inherited, hence contexts that inherit it (those that don't specify their own SUBSTITUTEINHERITBEFORE value) will apply the closest defined merge order.

## SubstituteMaxLineLength Directive

| | |
|---|---|
| Description: | Set the maximum line size |
| Syntax: | SubstituteMaxLineLength bytes(b\|B\|k\|K\|m\|M\|g\|G) |
| Default: | SubstituteMaxLineLength 1m |
| Context: | directory, .htaccess |
| Override: | FileInfo |
| Status: | Extension |
| Module: | mod_substitute |
| Compatibility: | Available in httpd 2.4.11 and later |

The maximum line size handled by MOD_SUBSTITUTE is limited to restrict memory use. The limit can be configured using SUBSTITUTEMAXLINELENGTH. The value can be given as the number of bytes and can be suffixed with a single letter b, B, k, K, m, M, g, G to provide the size in bytes, kilobytes, megabytes or gigabytes respectively.

### Example

```
<Location "/">
    AddOutputFilterByType SUBSTITUTE text/html
    SubstituteMaxLineLength 10m
    Substitute "s/foo/bar/ni"
</Location>
```

# 10.119 Apache Module mod_suexec

| | |
|---|---|
| Description: | Allows CGI scripts to run as a specified user and Group |
| Status: | Extension |
| ModuleIdentifier: | suexec_module |
| SourceFile: | mod_suexec.c |

## Summary

This module, in combination with the `suexec` support program allows CGI scripts to run as a specified user and Group.

### Directives

- SuexecUserGroup

### See also

- SuEXEC support (p. 115)

## SuexecUserGroup Directive

| | |
|---|---|
| Description: | User and group for CGI programs to run as |
| Syntax: | `SuexecUserGroup User Group` |
| Context: | server config, virtual host |
| Status: | Extension |
| Module: | mod_suexec |

The SUEXECUSERGROUP directive allows you to specify a user and group for CGI programs to run as. Non-CGI requests are still processed with the user specified in the USER directive.

### Example

```
SuexecUserGroup nobody nogroup
```

Startup will fail if this directive is specified but the suEXEC feature is disabled.

### See also

- SUEXEC

## 10.120   Apache Module mod_syslog

| Description: | Provides "syslog" ErrorLog provider |
|---|---|
| Status: | Extension |
| ModuleIdentifier: | syslog_module |
| SourceFile: | mod_syslog.c |

### Summary

This module provides "syslog" ErrorLog provider. It allows logging error messages via syslogd(8).

**Directives** This module provides no directives.

### Examples

Using `syslog` in ErrorLog directive (see CORE) instead of a filename enables logging via syslogd(8) if the system supports it. The default is to use syslog facility `local7`, but you can override this by using the `syslog:`*facility* syntax where *facility* can be one of the names usually documented in syslog(1). The facility is effectively global, and if it is changed in individual virtual hosts, the final facility specified affects the entire server.

```
ErrorLog syslog:user
```

# 10.121 Apache Module mod_systemd

| | |
|---|---|
| Description: | Provides better support for systemd integration |
| Status: | Extension |
| ModuleIdentifier: | systemd_module |
| SourceFile: | mod_systemd.c |

## Summary

This module provides support for systemd integration. It allows starting httpd as a service with systemd Type=notify (see systemd.service(5) manual page for more information). It also provides statistics in systemctl status output and adds various directives useful for systemd integration.

**Directives**

- IdleShutdown

## IdleShutdown Directive

| | |
|---|---|
| Description: | Enable shutting down the httpd when it is idle for some time. |
| Syntax: | IdleShutdown seconds |
| Default: | IdleShutdown 0 |
| Context: | server config |
| Status: | Extension |
| Module: | mod_systemd |

The IDLESHUTDOWN directive enables shutting down the httpd when it is idle for some time. The idleness is based on bytes served, so if there are no bytes sent for some time defined by this directive, httpd will shutdown. By default, IdleShutdown is set to 0 meaning this feature is disabled.

This feature is useful in a combination with systemd socket activation (see systemd.socket(5) manual page). When httpd is started by systemd on some request, using this directive you can stop the httpd automatically when all the requests are served.

**Implementation warning**
Because of implementation details, idleness is checked only every 10 seconds. That means that if you specify IdleShutdown 14, httpd will stop itself after 20 seconds of idleness.

# 10.122   Apache Module mod_unique_id

| Description: | Provides an environment variable with a unique identifier for each request |
|---|---|
| Status: | Extension |
| ModuleIdentifier: | unique_id_module |
| SourceFile: | mod_unique_id.c |

## Summary

This module provides a magic token for each request which is guaranteed to be unique across "all" requests under very specific conditions. The unique identifier is even unique across multiple machines in a properly configured cluster of machines. The environment variable UNIQUE_ID is set to the identifier for each request. Unique identifiers are useful for various reasons which are beyond the scope of this document.

**Directives** This module provides no directives.

## Theory

First a brief recap of how the Apache server works on Unix machines. This feature currently isn't supported on Windows NT. On Unix machines, Apache creates several children, the children process requests one at a time. Each child can serve multiple requests in its lifetime. For the purpose of this discussion, the children don't share any data with each other. We'll refer to the children as *httpd processes*.

Your website has one or more machines under your administrative control, together we'll call them a cluster of machines. Each machine can possibly run multiple instances of Apache. All of these collectively are considered "the universe", and with certain assumptions we'll show that in this universe we can generate unique identifiers for each request, without extensive communication between machines in the cluster.

The machines in your cluster should satisfy these requirements. (Even if you have only one machine you should synchronize its clock with NTP.)

- The machines' times are synchronized via NTP or other network time protocol.
- The machines' hostnames all differ, such that the module can do a hostname lookup on the hostname and receive a different IP address for each machine in the cluster.

As far as operating system assumptions go, we assume that pids (process ids) fit in 32-bits. If the operating system uses more than 32-bits for a pid, the fix is trivial but must be performed in the code.

Given those assumptions, at a single point in time we can identify any httpd process on any machine in the cluster from all other httpd processes. The machine's IP address and the pid of the httpd process are sufficient to do this. A httpd process can handle multiple requests simultaneously if you use a multi-threaded MPM. In order to identify threads, we use a thread index Apache httpd uses internally. So in order to generate unique identifiers for requests we need only distinguish between different points in time.

To distinguish time we will use a Unix timestamp (seconds since January 1, 1970 UTC), and a 16-bit counter. The timestamp has only one second granularity, so the counter is used to represent up to 65536 values during a single second. The quadruple ( *ip_addr, pid, time_stamp, counter* ) is sufficient to enumerate 65536 requests per second per httpd process. There are issues however with pid reuse over time, and the counter is used to alleviate this issue.

When an httpd child is created, the counter is initialized with ( current microseconds divided by 10 ) modulo 65536 (this formula was chosen to eliminate some variance problems with the low order bits of the microsecond timers on some systems). When a unique identifier is generated, the time stamp used is the time the request arrived at the web server. The counter is incremented every time an identifier is generated (and allowed to roll over).

The kernel generates a pid for each process as it forks the process, and pids are allowed to roll over (they're 16-bits on many Unixes, but newer systems have expanded to 32-bits). So over time the same pid will be reused. However unless it is reused within the same second, it does not destroy the uniqueness of our quadruple. That is, we assume the system does not spawn 65536 processes in a one second interval (it may even be 32768 processes on some Unixes, but even this isn't likely to happen).

Suppose that time repeats itself for some reason. That is, suppose that the system's clock is screwed up and it revisits a past time (or it is too far forward, is reset correctly, and then revisits the future time). In this case we can easily show that we can get pid and time stamp reuse. The choice of initializer for the counter is intended to help defeat this. Note that we really want a random number to initialize the counter, but there aren't any readily available numbers on most systems (*i.e.*, you can't use rand() because you need to seed the generator, and can't seed it with the time because time, at least at one second resolution, has repeated itself). This is not a perfect defense.

How good a defense is it? Suppose that one of your machines serves at most 500 requests per second (which is a very reasonable upper bound at this writing, because systems generally do more than just shovel out static files). To do that it will require a number of children which depends on how many concurrent clients you have. But we'll be pessimistic and suppose that a single child is able to serve 500 requests per second. There are 1000 possible starting counter values such that two sequences of 500 requests overlap. So there is a 1.5% chance that if time (at one second resolution) repeats itself this child will repeat a counter value, and uniqueness will be broken. This was a very pessimistic example, and with real world values it's even less likely to occur. If your system is such that it's still likely to occur, then perhaps you should make the counter 32 bits (by editing the code).

You may be concerned about the clock being "set back" during summer daylight savings. However this isn't an issue because the times used here are UTC, which "always" go forward. Note that x86 based Unixes may need proper configuration for this to be true – they should be configured to assume that the motherboard clock is on UTC and compensate appropriately. But even still, if you're running NTP then your UTC time will be correct very shortly after reboot.

The UNIQUE_ID environment variable is constructed by encoding the 144-bit (32-bit IP address, 32 bit pid, 32 bit time stamp, 16 bit counter, 32 bit thread index) quadruple using the alphabet [A-Za-z0-9@-] in a manner similar to MIME base64 encoding, producing 24 characters. The MIME base64 alphabet is actually [A-Za-z0-9+/] however + and / need to be specially encoded in URLs, which makes them less desirable. All values are encoded in network byte ordering so that the encoding is comparable across architectures of different byte ordering. The actual ordering of the encoding is: time stamp, IP address, pid, counter. This ordering has a purpose, but it should be emphasized that applications should not dissect the encoding. Applications should treat the entire encoded UNIQUE_ID as an opaque token, which can be compared against other UNIQUE_IDs for equality only.

The ordering was chosen such that it's possible to change the encoding in the future without worrying about collision with an existing database of UNIQUE_IDs. The new encodings should also keep the time stamp as the first element, and can otherwise use the same alphabet and bit length. Since the time stamps are essentially an increasing sequence, it's sufficient to have a *flag second* in which all machines in the cluster stop serving any request, and stop using the old encoding format. Afterwards they can resume requests and begin issuing the new encodings.

This we believe is a relatively portable solution to this problem. The identifiers generated have essentially an infinite life-time because future identifiers can be made longer as required. Essentially no communication is required between machines in the cluster (only NTP synchronization is required, which is low overhead), and no communication between httpd processes is required (the communication is implicit in the pid value assigned by the kernel). In very specific situations the identifier can be shortened, but more information needs to be assumed (for example the 32-bit IP address is overkill for any site, but there is no portable shorter replacement for it).

# 10.123   Apache Module mod_unixd

| | |
|---|---|
| Description: | Basic (required) security for Unix-family platforms. |
| Status: | Base |
| ModuleIdentifier: | unixd_module |
| SourceFile: | mod_unixd.c |

**Directives**

- ChrootDir
- Group
- Suexec
- User

**See also**

- suEXEC support (p. 115)

## ChrootDir Directive

| | |
|---|---|
| Description: | Directory for apache to run chroot(8) after startup. |
| Syntax: | `ChrootDir /path/to/directory` |
| Default: | `none` |
| Context: | server config |
| Status: | Base |
| Module: | MOD_UNIXD |

This directive tells the server to *chroot(8)* to the specified directory after startup, but before accepting requests over the 'net.

Note that running the server under chroot is not simple, and requires additional setup, particularly if you are running scripts such as CGI or PHP. Please make sure you are properly familiar with the operation of chroot before attempting to use this feature.

## Group Directive

| | |
|---|---|
| Description: | Group under which the server will answer requests |
| Syntax: | `Group unix-group` |
| Default: | `Group #-1` |
| Context: | server config |
| Status: | Base |
| Module: | mod_unixd |

The GROUP directive sets the group under which the server will answer requests. In order to use this directive, the server must be run initially as `root`. If you start the server as a non-root user, it will fail to change to the specified group, and will instead continue to run as the group of the original user. *Unix-group* is one of:

**A group name** Refers to the given group by name.

**# followed by a group number.** Refers to a group by its number.

**Example**

```
Group www-group
```

It is recommended that you set up a new group specifically for running the server. Some admins use user `nobody`, but this is not always possible or desirable.

 **Security**

Don't set GROUP (or USER) to `root` unless you know exactly what you are doing, and what the dangers are.

**See also**

- VHostGroup
- SuexecUserGroup

## Suexec Directive

| | |
|---|---|
| Description: | Enable or disable the suEXEC feature |
| Syntax: | Suexec On\|Off |
| Default: | On if suexec binary exists with proper owner and mode, Off otherwise |
| Context: | server config |
| Status: | Base |
| Module: | mod_unixd |

When On, startup will fail if the suexec binary doesn't exist or has an invalid owner or file mode.

When Off, suEXEC will be disabled even if the suexec binary exists and has a valid owner and file mode.

## User Directive

| | |
|---|---|
| Description: | The userid under which the server will answer requests |
| Syntax: | User unix-userid |
| Default: | User #-1 |
| Context: | server config |
| Status: | Base |
| Module: | mod_unixd |

The USER directive sets the user ID as which the server will answer requests. In order to use this directive, the server must be run initially as `root`. If you start the server as a non-root user, it will fail to change to the lesser privileged user, and will instead continue to run as that original user. If you do start the server as `root`, then it is normal for the parent process to remain running as root. *Unix-userid* is one of:

**A username** Refers to the given user by name.

**# followed by a user number.** Refers to a user by its number.

The user should have no privileges that result in it being able to access files that are not intended to be visible to the outside world, and similarly, the user should not be able to execute code that is not meant for HTTP requests. It is recommended that you set up a new user and group specifically for running the server. Some admins use user `nobody`, but this is not always desirable, since the `nobody` user can have other uses on the system.

**Security**
Don't set USER (or GROUP) to `root` unless you know exactly what you are doing, and what
the dangers are.

**See also**

- VHostUser
- SuexecUserGroup

# 10.124   Apache Module mod_userdir

| | |
|---|---|
| Description: | User-specific directories |
| Status: | Base |
| ModuleIdentifier: | userdir_module |
| SourceFile: | mod_userdir.c |

## Summary

This module allows user-specific directories to be accessed using the `http://example.com/~user/` syntax.

**Directives**

- UserDir

**See also**

- Mapping URLs to the Filesystem (p. 64)
- public_html tutorial (p. 258)

## UserDir Directive

| | |
|---|---|
| Description: | Location of the user-specific directories |
| Syntax: | `UserDir directory-filename [directory-filename] ...` |
| Context: | server config, virtual host |
| Status: | Base |
| Module: | mod_userdir |

The USERDIR directive sets the real directory in a user's home directory to use when a request for a document for a user is received. *Directory-filename* is one of the following:

- The name of a directory or a pattern such as those shown below.
- The keyword `disabled`. This turns off *all* username-to-directory translations except those explicitly named with the `enabled` keyword (see below).
- The keyword `disabled` followed by a space-delimited list of usernames. Usernames that appear in such a list will *never* have directory translation performed, even if they appear in an `enabled` clause.
- The keyword `enabled` followed by a space-delimited list of usernames. These usernames will have directory translation performed even if a global disable is in effect, but not if they also appear in a `disabled` clause.

If neither the `enabled` nor the `disabled` keywords appear in the USERDIR directive, the argument is treated as a filename pattern, and is used to turn the name into a directory specification. A request for `http://www.example.com/~bob/one/two.html` will be translated to:

| UserDir directive used | Translated path |
|---|---|
| UserDir public_html | ~bob/public_html/one/two.html |
| UserDir /usr/web | /usr/web/bob/one/two.html |
| UserDir /home/*/www | /home/bob/www/one/two.html |

The following directives will send redirects to the client:

| UserDir directive used | Translated path |
|---|---|
| UserDir http://www.example.com/users | http://www.example.com/users/bob/one/two.html |
| UserDir http://www.example.com/*/usr | http://www.example.com/bob/usr/one/two.html |
| UserDir http://www.example.com/~*/ | http://www.example.com/~bob/one/two.html |

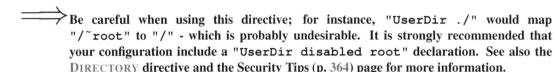 Be careful when using this directive; for instance, "UserDir ./" would map "/~root" to "/" - which is probably undesirable. It is strongly recommended that your configuration include a "UserDir disabled root" declaration. See also the DIRECTORY directive and the Security Tips (p. 364) page for more information.

Additional examples:

To allow a few users to have `UserDir` directories, but not anyone else, use the following:

```
UserDir disabled
UserDir enabled user1 user2 user3
```

To allow most users to have `UserDir` directories, but deny this to a few, use the following:

```
UserDir disabled user4 user5 user6
```

It is also possible to specify alternative user directories. If you use a command like:

```
UserDir "public_html" "/usr/web" "http://www.example.com/"
```

With a request for `http://www.example.com/~bob/one/two.html`, will try to find the page at `~bob/public_html/one/two.html` first, then `/usr/web/bob/one/two.html`, and finally it will send a redirect to `http://www.example.com/bob/one/two.html`.

If you add a redirect, it must be the last alternative in the list. Apache httpd cannot determine if the redirect succeeded or not, so if you have the redirect earlier in the list, that will always be the alternative that is used.

User directory substitution is not active by default in versions 2.1.4 and later. In earlier versions, `UserDir public_html` was assumed if no USERDIR directive was present.

 **Merging details**

    Lists of specific enabled and disabled users are replaced, not merged, from global to virtual host scope

**See also**

- Per-user web directories tutorial (p. 258)

# 10.125 Apache Module mod_usertrack

| | |
|---|---|
| Description: | *Clickstream* logging of user activity on a site |
| Status: | Extension |
| ModuleIdentifier: | usertrack_module |
| SourceFile: | mod_usertrack.c |

## Summary

Provides tracking of a user through your website via browser cookies.

### Directives

- CookieDomain
- CookieExpires
- CookieName
- CookieStyle
- CookieTracking

## Logging

MOD_USERTRACK sets a cookie which can be logged via MOD_LOG_CONFIG configurable logging formats:

```
LogFormat "%{Apache}n %r %t" usertrack
CustomLog "logs/clickstream.log" usertrack
```

## CookieDomain Directive

| | |
|---|---|
| Description: | The domain to which the tracking cookie applies |
| Syntax: | CookieDomain domain |
| Context: | server config, virtual host, directory, .htaccess |
| Override: | FileInfo |
| Status: | Extension |
| Module: | mod_usertrack |

This directive controls the setting of the domain to which the tracking cookie applies. If not present, no domain is included in the cookie header field.

The domain string **must** begin with a dot, and **must** include at least one embedded dot. That is, .example.com is legal, but www.example.com and .com are not.

⟹ Most browsers in use today will not allow cookies to be set for a two-part top level domain, such as .co.uk, although such a domain ostensibly fulfills the requirements above.

These domains are equivalent to top level domains such as .com, and allowing such cookies may be a security risk. Thus, if you are under a two-part top level domain, you should still use your actual domain, as you would with any other top level domain (for example .example.co.uk).

```
CookieDomain .example.com
```

## CookieExpires Directive

| | |
|---|---|
| Description: | Expiry time for the tracking cookie |
| Syntax: | `CookieExpires expiry-period` |
| Context: | server config, virtual host, directory, .htaccess |
| Override: | FileInfo |
| Status: | Extension |
| Module: | mod_usertrack |

When used, this directive sets an expiry time on the cookie generated by the usertrack module. The *expiry-period* can be given either as a number of seconds, or in the format such as "2 weeks 3 days 7 hours". Valid denominations are: years, months, weeks, days, hours, minutes and seconds. If the expiry time is in any format other than one number indicating the number of seconds, it must be enclosed by double quotes.

If this directive is not used, cookies last only for the current browser session.

```
CookieExpires "3 weeks"
```

## CookieName Directive

| | |
|---|---|
| Description: | Name of the tracking cookie |
| Syntax: | `CookieName token` |
| Default: | `CookieName Apache` |
| Context: | server config, virtual host, directory, .htaccess |
| Override: | FileInfo |
| Status: | Extension |
| Module: | mod_usertrack |

This directive allows you to change the name of the cookie this module uses for its tracking purposes. By default the cookie is named `"Apache"`.

You must specify a valid cookie name; results are unpredictable if you use a name containing unusual characters. Valid characters include A-Z, a-z, 0-9, `"_"`, and `"-"`.

```
CookieName clicktrack
```

## CookieStyle Directive

| | |
|---|---|
| Description: | Format of the cookie header field |
| Syntax: | `CookieStyle Netscape|Cookie|Cookie2|RFC2109|RFC2965` |
| Default: | `CookieStyle Netscape` |
| Context: | server config, virtual host, directory, .htaccess |
| Override: | FileInfo |
| Status: | Extension |
| Module: | mod_usertrack |

This directive controls the format of the cookie header field. The three formats allowed are:

- **Netscape**, which is the original but now deprecated syntax. This is the default, and the syntax Apache has historically used.

- **Cookie** or **RFC2109**, which is the syntax that superseded the Netscape syntax.

- **Cookie2** or **RFC2965**, which is the most current cookie syntax.

Not all clients can understand all of these formats, but you should use the newest one that is generally acceptable to your users' browsers. At the time of writing, most browsers support all three of these formats, with `Cookie2` being the preferred format.

```
CookieStyle Cookie2
```

## CookieTracking Directive

| | |
|---|---|
| Description: | Enables tracking cookie |
| Syntax: | `CookieTracking on\|off` |
| Default: | `CookieTracking off` |
| Context: | server config, virtual host, directory, .htaccess |
| Override: | FileInfo |
| Status: | Extension |
| Module: | mod_usertrack |

When MOD_USERTRACK is loaded, and `CookieTracking on` is set, Apache will send a user-tracking cookie for all new requests. This directive can be used to turn this behavior on or off on a per-server or per-directory basis. By default, enabling MOD_USERTRACK will **not** activate cookies.

```
CookieTracking on
```

# 10.126   Apache Module mod_version

| | |
|---|---|
| Description: | Version dependent configuration |
| Status: | Extension |
| ModuleIdentifier: | version_module |
| SourceFile: | mod_version.c |

## Summary

This module is designed for the use in test suites and large networks which have to deal with different httpd versions and different configurations. It provides a new container – <IFVERSION>, which allows a flexible version checking including numeric comparisons and regular expressions.

### Examples

```
<IfVersion 2.4.2>
    # current httpd version is exactly 2.4.2
</IfVersion>

<IfVersion >= 2.5>
    # use really new features :-)
</IfVersion>
```

See below for further possibilities.

### Directives

* <IfVersion>

## IfVersion Directive

| | |
|---|---|
| Description: | contains version dependent configuration |
| Syntax: | <IfVersion [[!]operator] version> ... </IfVersion> |
| Context: | server config, virtual host, directory, .htaccess |
| Override: | All |
| Status: | Extension |
| Module: | mod_version |

The <IFVERSION> section encloses configuration directives which are executed only if the httpd version matches the desired criteria. For normal (numeric) comparisons the *version* argument has the format major[.minor[.patch]], e.g. 2.1.0 or 2.2. *minor* and *patch* are optional. If these numbers are omitted, they are assumed to be zero. The following numerical *operator*s are possible:

| *operator* | description |
|---|---|
| = or == | httpd version is equal |
| > | httpd version is greater than |
| >= | httpd version is greater or equal |
| < | httpd version is less than |
| <= | httpd version is less or equal |

### Example

```
<IfVersion >= 2.3>
    # this happens only in versions greater or
    # equal 2.3.0.
</IfVersion>
```

Besides the numerical comparison it is possible to match a regular expression against the httpd version. There are two ways to write it:

| operator | description |
|---|---|
| = or == | *version* has the form /`regex`/ |
| ~ | *version* has the form `regex` |

### Example

```
<IfVersion = /^2.4.[01234]$/>
    # e.g. workaround for buggy versions
</IfVersion>
```

In order to reverse the meaning, all operators can be preceded by an exclamation mark ( ! ):

```
<IfVersion !~ ^2.4.[01234]$>
    # not for those versions
</IfVersion>
```

If the *operator* is omitted, it is assumed to be =.

# 10.127   Apache Module mod_vhost_alias

| Description: | Provides for dynamically configured mass virtual hosting |
|---|---|
| Status: | Extension |
| ModuleIdentifier: | vhost_alias_module |
| SourceFile: | mod_vhost_alias.c |

## Summary

This module creates dynamically configured virtual hosts, by allowing the IP address and/or the Host: header of the
HTTP request to be used as part of the pathname to determine what files to serve. This allows for easy use of a huge
number of virtual hosts with similar configurations.

Note

> If MOD_ALIAS or MOD_USERDIR are used for translating URIs to filenames,
> they will override the directives of MOD_VHOST_ALIAS described below. For
> example, the following configuration will map /cgi-bin/script.pl to
> /usr/local/apache2/cgi-bin/script.pl in all cases:
>
> ScriptAlias "/cgi-bin/" "/usr/local/apache2/cgi-bin/"
> VirtualScriptAlias "/never/found/%0/cgi-bin/"

### Directives

- VirtualDocumentRoot
- VirtualDocumentRootIP
- VirtualScriptAlias
- VirtualScriptAliasIP

### See also

- USECANONICALNAME
- Dynamically configured mass virtual hosting (p. 130)

## Directory Name Interpolation

All the directives in this module interpolate a string into a pathname. The interpolated string (henceforth called
the "name") may be either the server name (see the USECANONICALNAME directive for details on how this is
determined) or the IP address of the virtual host on the server in dotted-quad format. The interpolation is controlled
by specifiers inspired by printf which have a number of formats:

| %% | insert a % |
|---|---|
| %p | insert the port number of the virtual host |
| %N.M | insert (part of) the name |

N and M are used to specify substrings of the name. N selects from the dot-separated components of the name, and M
selects characters within whatever N has selected. M is optional and defaults to zero if it isn't present; the dot must be
present if and only if M is present. The interpretation is as follows:

| | |
|---|---|
| 0 | the whole name |
| 1 | the first part |
| 2 | the second part |
| −1 | the last part |
| −2 | the penultimate part |
| 2+ | the second and all subsequent parts |
| −2+ | the penultimate and all preceding parts |
| 1+ and −1+ | the same as 0 |

If N or M is greater than the number of parts available a single underscore is interpolated.

## Examples

For simple name-based virtual hosts you might use the following directives in your server configuration file:

```
UseCanonicalName    Off
VirtualDocumentRoot "/usr/local/apache/vhosts/%0"
```

A request for `http://www.example.com/directory/file.html` will be satisfied by the file `/usr/local/apache/vhosts/www.example.com/directory/file.html`.

For a very large number of virtual hosts it is a good idea to arrange the files to reduce the size of the `vhosts` directory. To do this you might use the following in your configuration file:

```
UseCanonicalName    Off
VirtualDocumentRoot "/usr/local/apache/vhosts/%3+/%2.1/%2.2/%2.3/%2"
```

A request for `http://www.domain.example.com/directory/file.html` will be satisfied by the file `/usr/local/apache/vhosts/example.com/d/o/m/domain/directory/file.html`.

A more even spread of files can be achieved by hashing from the end of the name, for example:

```
VirtualDocumentRoot "/usr/local/apache/vhosts/%3+/%2.-1/%2.-2/%2.-3/%2"
```

The example request would come from `/usr/local/apache/vhosts/example.com/n/i/a/domain/director`

Alternatively you might use:

```
VirtualDocumentRoot "/usr/local/apache/vhosts/%3+/%2.1/%2.2/%2.3/%2.4+"
```

The example request would come from `/usr/local/apache/vhosts/example.com/d/o/m/ain/directory/f`

A very common request by users is the ability to point multiple domains to multiple document roots without having to worry about the length or number of parts of the hostname being requested. If the requested hostname is `sub.www.domain.example.com` instead of simply `www.domain.example.com`, then using %3+ will result in the document root being `/usr/local/apache/vhosts/domain.example.com/...` instead of the intended `example.com` directory. In such cases, it can be beneficial to use the combination `%-2.0.%-1.0`, which will always yield the domain name and the tld, for example `example.com` regardless of the number of subdomains appended to the hostname. As such, one can make a configuration that will direct all first, second or third level subdomains to the same directory:

```
VirtualDocumentRoot "/usr/local/apache/vhosts/%-2.0.%-1.0"
```

In the example above, both `www.example.com` as well as `www.sub.example.com` or `example.com` will all point to `/usr/local/apache/vhosts/example.com`.

For IP-based virtual hosting you might use the following in your configuration file:

```
UseCanonicalName DNS
VirtualDocumentRootIP "/usr/local/apache/vhosts/%1/%2/%3/%4/docs"
VirtualScriptAliasIP  "/usr/local/apache/vhosts/%1/%2/%3/%4/cgi-bin"
```

A request for `http://www.domain.example.com/directory/file.html` would be satisfied by the file `/usr/local/apache/vhosts/10/20/30/40/docs/directory/file.html` if the IP address of `www.domain.example.com` were 10.20.30.40. A request for `http://www.domain.example.com/cgi-bin/script.pl` would be satisfied by executing the program `/usr/local/apache/vhosts/10/20/30/40/cgi-bin/script.pl`.

If you want to include the `.` character in a `VirtualDocumentRoot` directive, but it clashes with a `%` directive, you can work around the problem in the following way:

```
VirtualDocumentRoot "/usr/local/apache/vhosts/%2.0.%3.0"
```

A request for `http://www.domain.example.com/directory/file.html` will be satisfied by the file `/usr/local/apache/vhosts/domain.example/directory/file.html`.

The LOGFORMAT directives `%V` and `%A` are useful in conjunction with this module.

## VirtualDocumentRoot Directive

| | |
|---|---|
| Description: | Dynamically configure the location of the document root for a given virtual host |
| Syntax: | `VirtualDocumentRoot interpolated-directory|none` |
| Default: | `VirtualDocumentRoot none` |
| Context: | server config, virtual host |
| Status: | Extension |
| Module: | mod_vhost_alias |

The VIRTUALDOCUMENTROOT directive allows you to determine where Apache HTTP Server will find your documents based on the value of the server name. The result of expanding *interpolated-directory* is used as the root of the document tree in a similar manner to the DOCUMENTROOT directive's argument. If *interpolated-directory* is `none` then VIRTUALDOCUMENTROOT is turned off. This directive cannot be used in the same context as VIRTUALDOCUMENTROOTIP.

**Note**

VIRTUALDOCUMENTROOT will override any DOCUMENTROOT directives you may have put in the same context or child contexts. Putting a VIRTUALDOCUMENTROOT in the global server scope will effectively override DOCUMENTROOT directives in any virtual hosts defined later on, unless you set VIRTUALDOCUMENTROOT to `None` in each virtual host.

## VirtualDocumentRootIP Directive

| | |
|---|---|
| Description: | Dynamically configure the location of the document root for a given virtual host |
| Syntax: | `VirtualDocumentRootIP interpolated-directory|none` |
| Default: | `VirtualDocumentRootIP none` |
| Context: | server config, virtual host |
| Status: | Extension |
| Module: | mod_vhost_alias |

The VIRTUALDOCUMENTROOTIP directive is like the VIRTUALDOCUMENTROOT directive, except that it uses the IP address of the server end of the connection for directory interpolation instead of the server name.

## VirtualScriptAlias Directive

| | |
|---|---|
| Description: | Dynamically configure the location of the CGI directory for a given virtual host |
| Syntax: | `VirtualScriptAlias interpolated-directory|none` |
| Default: | `VirtualScriptAlias none` |
| Context: | server config, virtual host |
| Status: | Extension |
| Module: | mod_vhost_alias |

The VIRTUALSCRIPTALIAS directive allows you to determine where Apache httpd will find CGI scripts in a similar manner to VIRTUALDOCUMENTROOT does for other documents. It matches requests for URIs starting `/cgi-bin/`, much like SCRIPTALIAS `/cgi-bin/` would.

## VirtualScriptAliasIP Directive

| | |
|---|---|
| Description: | Dynamically configure the location of the CGI directory for a given virtual host |
| Syntax: | `VirtualScriptAliasIP interpolated-directory|none` |
| Default: | `VirtualScriptAliasIP none` |
| Context: | server config, virtual host |
| Status: | Extension |
| Module: | mod_vhost_alias |

The VIRTUALSCRIPTALIASIP directive is like the VIRTUALSCRIPTALIAS directive, except that it uses the IP address of the server end of the connection for directory interpolation instead of the server name.

# 10.128   Apache Module mod_watchdog

| | |
|---|---|
| Description: | provides infrastructure for other modules to periodically run tasks |
| Status: | Base |
| ModuleIdentifier: | watchdog_module |
| SourceFile: | mod_watchdog.c |
| Compatibility: | Available in Apache 2.3 and later |

## Summary

MOD_WATCHDOG defines programmatic hooks for other modules to periodically run tasks. These modules can register handlers for MOD_WATCHDOG hooks. Currently, the following modules in the Apache distribution use this functionality:

- MOD_HEARTBEAT
- MOD_HEARTMONITOR

! To allow a module to use MOD_WATCHDOG functionality, MOD_WATCHDOG itself must be statically linked to the server core or, if a dynamic module, be loaded before the calling module.

**Directives**

- WatchdogInterval

## WatchdogInterval Directive

| | |
|---|---|
| Description: | Watchdog interval in seconds |
| Syntax: | `WatchdogInterval number-of-seconds` |
| Default: | `WatchdogInterval 1` |
| Context: | server config |
| Status: | Base |
| Module: | mod_watchdog |

Sets the interval at which the watchdog_step hook runs. Default is to run every second.

## 10.129 Apache Module mod_xml2enc

| | |
|---|---|
| Description: | Enhanced charset/internationalisation support for libxml2-based filter modules |
| Status: | Base |
| ModuleIdentifier: | xml2enc_module |
| SourceFile: | mod_xml2enc.c |
| Compatibility: | Version 2.4 and later. Available as a third-party module for 2.2.x versions |

### Summary

This module provides enhanced internationalisation support for markup-aware filter modules such as MOD_PROXY_HTML. It can automatically detect the encoding of input data and ensure they are correctly processed by the libxml2[104] parser, including converting to Unicode (UTF-8) where necessary. It can also convert data to an encoding of choice after markup processing, and will ensure the correct *charset* value is set in the HTTP *Content-Type* header.

### Directives

- xml2EncAlias
- xml2EncDefault
- xml2StartParse

### Usage

There are two usage scenarios: with modules programmed to work with mod_xml2enc, and with those that are not aware of it:

**Filter modules enabled for mod_xml2enc** Modules such as MOD_PROXY_HTML version 3.1 and up use the `xml2enc_charset` optional function to retrieve the charset argument to pass to the libxml2 parser, and may use the `xml2enc_filter` optional function to postprocess to another encoding. Using mod_xml2enc with an enabled module, no configuration is necessary: the other module will configure mod_xml2enc for you (though you may still want to customise it using the configuration directives below).

**Non-enabled modules** To use it with a libxml2-based module that isn't explicitly enabled for mod_xml2enc, you will have to configure the filter chain yourself. So to use it with a filter foo provided by a module mod_foo to improve the latter's i18n support with HTML and XML, you could use

```
FilterProvider iconv    xml2enc Content-Type $text/html
FilterProvider iconv    xml2enc Content-Type $xml
FilterProvider markup   foo Content-Type $text/html
FilterProvider markup   foo Content-Type $xml
FilterChain     iconv markup
```

mod_foo will now support any character set supported by either (or both) of libxml2 or apr_xlate/iconv.

### Programming API

Programmers writing libxml2-based filter modules are encouraged to enable them for mod_xml2enc, to provide strong i18n support for your users without reinventing the wheel. The programming API is exposed in *mod_xml2enc.h*, and a usage example is MOD_PROXY_HTML.

---

[104]http://xmlsoft.org/

## Detecting an Encoding

Unlike MOD_CHARSET_LITE, mod_xml2enc is designed to work with data whose encoding cannot be known in advance and thus configured. It therefore uses 'sniffing' techniques to detect the encoding of HTTP data as follows:

1. If the HTTP *Content-Type* header includes a *charset* parameter, that is used.

2. If the data start with an XML Byte Order Mark (BOM) or an XML encoding declaration, that is used.

3. If an encoding is declared in an HTML <META> element, that is used.

4. If none of the above match, the default value set by XML2ENCDEFAULT is used.

The rules are applied in order. As soon as a match is found, it is used and detection is stopped.

## Output Encoding

libxml2[105] always uses UTF-8 (Unicode) internally, and libxml2-based filter modules will output that by default. mod_xml2enc can change the output encoding through the API, but there is currently no way to configure that directly.

Changing the output encoding should (in theory, at least) never be necessary, and is not recommended due to the extra processing load on the server of an unnecessary conversion.

## Unsupported Encodings

If you are working with encodings that are not supported by any of the conversion methods available on your platform, you can still alias them to a supported encoding using XML2ENCALIAS.

## xml2EncAlias Directive

| | |
|---|---|
| Description: | Recognise Aliases for encoding values |
| Syntax: | xml2EncAlias charset alias [alias ...] |
| Context: | server config |
| Status: | Base |
| Module: | mod_xml2enc |

This server-wide directive aliases one or more encoding to another encoding. This enables encodings not recognised by libxml2 to be handled internally by libxml2's encoding support using the translation table for a recognised encoding. This serves two purposes: to support character sets (or names) not recognised either by libxml2 or iconv, and to skip conversion for an encoding where it is known to be unnecessary.

## xml2EncDefault Directive

| | |
|---|---|
| Description: | Sets a default encoding to assume when absolutely no information can be automatically detected |
| Syntax: | xml2EncDefault name |
| Context: | server config, virtual host, directory, .htaccess |
| Status: | Base |
| Module: | mod_xml2enc |
| Compatibility: | Version 2.4.0 and later; available as a third-party module for earlier versions. |

---

[105]http://xmlsoft.org/

If you are processing data with known encoding but no encoding information, you can set this default to help mod_xml2enc process the data correctly. For example, to work with the default value of Latin1 (*iso-8859-1* specified in HTTP/1.0, use

```
xml2EncDefault iso-8859-1
```

### xml2StartParse Directive

| | |
|---|---|
| Description: | Advise the parser to skip leading junk. |
| Syntax: | `xml2StartParse element [element ...]` |
| Context: | server config, virtual host, directory, .htaccess |
| Status: | Base |
| Module: | mod_xml2enc |

Specify that the markup parser should start at the first instance of any of the elements specified. This can be used as a workaround where a broken backend inserts leading junk that messes up the parser (example here[106]).

It should never be used for XML, nor well-formed HTML.

---

[106]http://bahumbug.wordpress.com/2006/10/12/mod_proxy_html-revisited/

# 10.130   Apache Module mpm_common

| Description: | A collection of directives that are implemented by more than one multi-processing module (MPM) |
|---|---|
| Status: | MPM |

**Directives**

- CoreDumpDirectory
- EnableExceptionHook
- GracefulShutdownTimeout
- Listen
- ListenBackLog
- ListenCoresBucketsRatio
- MaxConnectionsPerChild
- MaxMemFree
- MaxRequestWorkers
- MaxSpareThreads
- MinSpareThreads
- PidFile
- ReceiveBufferSize
- ScoreBoardFile
- SendBufferSize
- ServerLimit
- StartServers
- StartThreads
- ThreadLimit
- ThreadsPerChild
- ThreadStackSize

## CoreDumpDirectory Directive

| Description: | Directory where Apache HTTP Server attempts to switch before dumping core |
|---|---|
| Syntax: | `CoreDumpDirectory directory` |
| Default: | `See usage for the default setting` |
| Context: | server config |
| Status: | MPM |
| Module: | EVENT, WORKER, PREFORK |

This controls the directory to which Apache httpd attempts to switch before dumping core. If your operating system is configured to create core files in the working directory of the crashing process, CoreDumpDirectory is necessary to change working directory from the default ServerRoot directory, which should not be writable by the user the server runs as.

If you want a core dump for debugging, you can use this directive to place it in a different location. This directive has no effect if your operating system is not configured to write core files to the working directory of the crashing processes.

**Core Dumps on Linux**

If Apache httpd starts as root and switches to another user, the Linux kernel *disables* core dumps even if the directory is writable for the process. Apache httpd (2.0.46 and later) reenables core dumps on Linux 2.4 and beyond, but only if you explicitly configure a CORE-DUMPDIRECTORY.

**Core Dumps on BSD**

To enable core-dumping of suid-executables on BSD-systems (such as FreeBSD), set `kern.sugid_coredump` to 1.

**Specific signals**

COREDUMPDIRECTORY processing only occurs for a select set of fatal signals: SIGFPE, SIGILL, SIGABORT, SIGSEGV, and SIGBUS.

On some operating systems, SIGQUIT also results in a core dump but does not go through COREDUMPDIRECTORY or ENABLEEXCEPTIONHOOK processing, so the core location is dictated entirely by the operating system.

## EnableExceptionHook Directive

| | |
|---|---|
| Description: | Enables a hook that runs exception handlers after a crash |
| Syntax: | `EnableExceptionHook On|Off` |
| Default: | `EnableExceptionHook Off` |
| Context: | server config |
| Status: | MPM |
| Module: | EVENT, WORKER, PREFORK |

For safety reasons this directive is only available if the server was configured with the `--enable-exception-hook` option. It enables a hook that allows external modules to plug in and do something after a child crashed.

There are already two modules, `mod_whatkilledus` and `mod_backtrace` that make use of this hook. Please have a look at Jeff Trawick's EnableExceptionHook site[107] for more information about these.

## GracefulShutdownTimeout Directive

| | |
|---|---|
| Description: | Specify a timeout after which a gracefully shutdown server will exit. |
| Syntax: | `GracefulShutdownTimeout seconds` |
| Default: | `GracefulShutdownTimeout 0` |
| Context: | server config |
| Status: | MPM |
| Module: | EVENT, WORKER, PREFORK |

The GRACEFULSHUTDOWNTIMEOUT specifies how many seconds after receiving a "graceful-stop" signal, a server should continue to run, handling the existing connections.

Setting this value to zero means that the server will wait indefinitely until all remaining requests have been fully served.

---

[107]http://people.apache.org/~trawick/exception_hook.html

## Listen Directive

| | |
|---|---|
| Description: | IP addresses and ports that the server listens to |
| Syntax: | `Listen [IP-address:]portnumber [protocol]` |
| Context: | server config |
| Status: | MPM |
| Module: | EVENT, WORKER, PREFORK, MPM_WINNT, MPM_NETWARE, MPMT_OS2 |

The LISTEN directive instructs Apache httpd to listen to only specific IP addresses or ports; by default it responds to requests on all IP interfaces. LISTEN is now a required directive. If it is not in the config file, the server will fail to start. This is a change from previous versions of Apache httpd.

The LISTEN directive tells the server to accept incoming requests on the specified port or address-and-port combination. If only a port number is specified, the server listens to the given port on all interfaces. If an IP address is given as well as a port, the server will listen on the given port and interface.

Multiple LISTEN directives may be used to specify a number of addresses and ports to listen to. The server will respond to requests from any of the listed addresses and ports.

For example, to make the server accept connections on both port 80 and port 8000, use:

```
Listen 80
Listen 8000
```

To make the server accept connections on two specified interfaces and port numbers, use

```
Listen 192.170.2.1:80
Listen 192.170.2.5:8000
```

IPv6 addresses must be surrounded in square brackets, as in the following example:

```
Listen [2001:db8::a00:20ff:fea7:ccea]:80
```

The optional *protocol* argument is not required for most configurations. If not specified, `https` is the default for port 443 and `http` the default for all other ports. The protocol is used to determine which module should handle a request, and to apply protocol specific optimizations with the ACCEPTFILTER directive.

You only need to set the protocol if you are running on non-standard ports. For example, running an `https` site on port 8443:

```
Listen 192.170.2.1:8443 https
```

**Error condition**

Multiple LISTEN directives for the same ip address and port will result in an `Address already in use` error message.

**See also**

- DNS Issues (p. 121)
- Setting which addresses and ports Apache HTTP Server uses (p. 88)
- Further discussion of the `Address already in use` error message, including other causes.[108]

---

[108]http://wiki.apache.org/httpd/CouldNotBindToAddress

## ListenBackLog Directive

| Description: | Maximum length of the queue of pending connections |
|---|---|
| Syntax: | `ListenBacklog backlog` |
| Default: | `ListenBacklog 511` |
| Context: | server config |
| Status: | MPM |
| Module: | EVENT, WORKER, PREFORK, MPM_WINNT, MPM_NETWARE, MPMT_OS2 |

The maximum length of the queue of pending connections. Generally no tuning is needed or desired, however on some systems it is desirable to increase this when under a TCP SYN flood attack. See the backlog parameter to the `listen(2)` system call.

This will often be limited to a smaller number by the operating system. This varies from OS to OS. Also note that many OSes do not use exactly what is specified as the backlog, but use a number based on (but normally larger than) what is set.

## ListenCoresBucketsRatio Directive

| Description: | Ratio between the number of CPU cores (online) and the number of listeners' buckets |
|---|---|
| Syntax: | `ListenCoresBucketsRatio ratio` |
| Default: | `ListenCoresBucketsRatio 0 (disabled)` |
| Context: | server config |
| Status: | MPM |
| Module: | EVENT, WORKER, PREFORK |
| Compatibility: | Available in Apache HTTP Server 2.4.17, with a kernel supporting the socket option SO_REUSEPORT and distributing new connections evenly accross listening processes' (or threads') sockets using it (eg. Linux 3.9 and later, but not the current implementations of SO_REUSEPORT in *BSDs. |

A *ratio* between the number of (online) CPU cores and the number of listeners' buckets can be used to make Apache HTTP Server create `num_cpu_cores / ratio` listening buckets, each containing its own LISTEN-ing socket(s) on the same port(s), and then make each child handle a single bucket (with round-robin distribution of the buckets at children creation time).

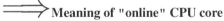

**Meaning of "online" CPU core**
On Linux (and also BSD) a CPU core can be turned on/off if Hotplug[a] is configured, therefore LISTENCORESBUCKETSRATIO needs to take this parameter into account while calculating the number of buckets to create.

[a]https://www.kernel.org/doc/Documentation/cpu-hotplug.txt

LISTENCORESBUCKETSRATIO can improve the scalability when accepting new connections is/becomes the bottleneck. On systems with a large number of CPU cores, enabling this feature has been tested to show significant performances improvement and shorter responses time.

There must be at least twice the number of CPU cores than the configured *ratio* for this to be active. The recommended *ratio* is 8, hence at least 16 cores should be available at runtime when this value is used. The right *ratio* to obtain maximum performance needs to be calculated for each target system, testing multiple values and observing the variations in your key performance metrics.

## MaxConnectionsPerChild Directive

| | |
|---|---|
| Description: | Limit on the number of connections that an individual child server will handle during its life |
| Syntax: | `MaxConnectionsPerChild number` |
| Default: | `MaxConnectionsPerChild 0` |
| Context: | server config |
| Status: | MPM |
| Module: | EVENT, WORKER, PREFORK, MPM_WINNT, MPM_NETWARE, MPMT_OS2 |
| Compatibility: | Available Apache HTTP Server 2.3.9 and later. The old name `MaxRequestsPerChild` is still supported. |

The MAXCONNECTIONSPERCHILD directive sets the limit on the number of connections that an individual child server process will handle. After MAXCONNECTIONSPERCHILD connections, the child process will die. If MAX-CONNECTIONSPERCHILD is 0, then the process will never expire.

Setting MAXCONNECTIONSPERCHILD to a non-zero value limits the amount of memory that process can consume by (accidental) memory leakage.

## MaxMemFree Directive

| | |
|---|---|
| Description: | Maximum amount of memory that the main allocator is allowed to hold without calling `free()` |
| Syntax: | `MaxMemFree KBytes` |
| Default: | `MaxMemFree 2048` |
| Context: | server config |
| Status: | MPM |
| Module: | EVENT, WORKER, PREFORK, MPM_WINNT, MPM_NETWARE |

The MAXMEMFREE directive sets the maximum number of free Kbytes that every allocator is allowed to hold without calling `free()`. In threaded MPMs, every thread has its own allocator. When set to zero, the threshold will be set to unlimited.

## MaxRequestWorkers Directive

| | |
|---|---|
| Description: | Maximum number of connections that will be processed simultaneously |
| Syntax: | `MaxRequestWorkers number` |
| Default: | `See usage for details` |
| Context: | server config |
| Status: | MPM |
| Module: | EVENT, WORKER, PREFORK |

The MAXREQUESTWORKERS directive sets the limit on the number of simultaneous requests that will be served. Any connection attempts over the MAXREQUESTWORKERS limit will normally be queued, up to a number based on the LISTENBACKLOG directive. Once a child process is freed at the end of a different request, the connection will then be serviced.

For non-threaded servers (*i.e.*, PREFORK), MAXREQUESTWORKERS translates into the maximum number of child processes that will be launched to serve requests. The default value is 256; to increase it, you must also raise SERVER-LIMIT.

For threaded and hybrid servers (*e.g.* EVENT or WORKER) MAXREQUESTWORKERS restricts the total number of threads that will be available to serve clients. For hybrid MPMs the default value is 16 (SERVERLIMIT) multiplied by the value of 25 (THREADSPERCHILD). Therefore, to increase MAXREQUESTWORKERS to a value that requires more than 16 processes, you must also raise SERVERLIMIT.

MAXREQUESTWORKERS was called MAXCLIENTS before version 2.3.13. The old name is still supported.

## MaxSpareThreads Directive

| | |
|---|---|
| Description: | Maximum number of idle threads |
| Syntax: | MaxSpareThreads number |
| Default: | See usage for details |
| Context: | server config |
| Status: | MPM |
| Module: | EVENT, WORKER, MPM_NETWARE, MPMT_OS2 |

Maximum number of idle threads. Different MPMs deal with this directive differently.

For WORKER and EVENT, the default is MaxSpareThreads 250. These MPMs deal with idle threads on a server-wide basis. If there are too many idle threads in the server then child processes are killed until the number of idle threads is less than this number.

For MPM_NETWARE the default is MaxSpareThreads 100. Since this MPM runs a single-process, the spare thread count is also server-wide.

MPMT_OS2 works similar to MPM_NETWARE. For MPMT_OS2 the default value is 10.

**Restrictions**

> The range of the MAXSPARETHREADS value is restricted. Apache httpd will correct the given value automatically according to the following rules:
>
> - MPM_NETWARE wants the value to be greater than MINSPARETHREADS.
> - For WORKER and EVENT, the value must be greater or equal to the sum of MINSPARETHREADS and THREADSPERCHILD.

**See also**

- MINSPARETHREADS
- STARTSERVERS
- MAXSPARESERVERS

## MinSpareThreads Directive

| | |
|---|---|
| Description: | Minimum number of idle threads available to handle request spikes |
| Syntax: | MinSpareThreads number |
| Default: | See usage for details |
| Context: | server config |
| Status: | MPM |
| Module: | EVENT, WORKER, MPM_NETWARE, MPMT_OS2 |

Minimum number of idle threads to handle request spikes. Different MPMs deal with this directive differently.

WORKER and EVENT use a default of MinSpareThreads 75 and deal with idle threads on a server-wide basis. If there aren't enough idle threads in the server then child processes are created until the number of idle threads is greater than *number*. Please also note that additional processes/threads might be created if LISTENCORESBUCKETSRATIO is enabled.

MPM_NETWARE uses a default of MinSpareThreads 10 and, since it is a single-process MPM, tracks this on a server-wide bases.

MPMT_OS2 works similar to MPM_NETWARE. For MPMT_OS2 the default value is 5.

**See also**

- MAXSPARETHREADS

- STARTSERVERS
- MINSPARESERVERS

## PidFile Directive

| | |
|---|---|
| Description: | File where the server records the process ID of the daemon |
| Syntax: | PidFile filename |
| Default: | PidFile httpd.pid |
| Context: | server config |
| Status: | MPM |
| Module: | EVENT, WORKER, PREFORK, MPM_WINNT, MPMT_OS2 |

The PIDFILE directive sets the file to which the server records the process id of the daemon.  If the filename is not absolute then it is assumed to be relative to the DEFAULTRUNTIMEDIR.

### Example

```
PidFile /var/run/apache.pid
```

It is often useful to be able to send the server a signal, so that it closes and then re-opens its ERRORLOG and TRANS-FERLOG, and re-reads its configuration files. This is done by sending a SIGHUP (kill -1) signal to the process id listed in the PIDFILE.

The PIDFILE is subject to the same warnings about log file placement and security (p. 364) .

Note

As of Apache HTTP Server 2, we recommended that you only use the  apachectl script, or the init script that your OS provides, for (re-)starting or stopping the server.

## ReceiveBufferSize Directive

| | |
|---|---|
| Description: | TCP receive buffer size |
| Syntax: | ReceiveBufferSize bytes |
| Default: | ReceiveBufferSize 0 |
| Context: | server config |
| Status: | MPM |
| Module: | EVENT, WORKER, PREFORK, MPM_WINNT, MPM_NETWARE, MPMT_OS2 |

The server will set the TCP receive buffer size to the number of bytes specified.

If set to the value of 0, the server will use the OS default.

## ScoreBoardFile Directive

| | |
|---|---|
| Description: | Location of the file used to store coordination data for the child processes |
| Syntax: | ScoreBoardFile file-path |
| Default: | ScoreBoardFile apache_runtime_status |
| Context: | server config |
| Status: | MPM |
| Module: | EVENT, WORKER, PREFORK, MPM_WINNT |

Apache HTTP Server uses a scoreboard to communicate between its parent and child processes. Some architectures require a file to facilitate this communication. If the file is left unspecified, Apache httpd first attempts to create the scoreboard entirely in memory (using anonymous shared memory) and, failing that, will attempt to create the file on disk (using file-based shared memory). Specifying this directive causes Apache httpd to always create the file on the disk.

If *file-path* is not an absolute path, the location specified will be relative to the value of DEFAULTRUNTIMEDIR.

### Example

```
ScoreBoardFile /var/run/apache_runtime_status
```

File-based shared memory is useful for third-party applications that require direct access to the scoreboard.

If you use a SCOREBOARDFILE then you may see improved speed by placing it on a RAM disk. But be careful that you heed the same warnings about log file placement and security (p. 364) .

**See also**

- Stopping and Restarting Apache HTTP Server (p. 29)

## SendBufferSize Directive

| Description: | TCP buffer size |
|---|---|
| Syntax: | SendBufferSize bytes |
| Default: | SendBufferSize 0 |
| Context: | server config |
| Status: | MPM |
| Module: | EVENT, WORKER, PREFORK, MPM_WINNT, MPM_NETWARE, MPMT_OS2 |

Sets the server's TCP send buffer size to the number of bytes specified. It is often useful to set this past the OS's standard default value on high speed, high latency connections (*i.e.*, 100ms or so, such as transcontinental fast pipes).

If set to the value of 0, the server will use the default value provided by your OS.

Further configuration of your operating system may be required to elicit better performance on high speed, high latency connections.

On some operating systems, changes in TCP behavior resulting from a larger SENDBUFFER-SIZE may not be seen unless ENABLESENDFILE is set to OFF. This interaction applies only to static files.

## ServerLimit Directive

| Description: | Upper limit on configurable number of processes |
|---|---|
| Syntax: | ServerLimit number |
| Default: | See usage for details |
| Context: | server config |
| Status: | MPM |
| Module: | EVENT, WORKER, PREFORK |

For the PREFORK MPM, this directive sets the maximum configured value for MAXREQUESTWORKERS for the lifetime of the Apache httpd process. For the WORKER and EVENT MPMs, this directive in combination with THREADLIMIT sets the maximum configured value for MAXREQUESTWORKERS for the lifetime of the Apache httpd process. Any attempts to change this directive during a restart will be ignored, but MAXREQUESTWORKERS can be modified during a restart.

Special care must be taken when using this directive. If SERVERLIMIT is set to a value much higher than necessary, extra, unused shared memory will be allocated. If both SERVERLIMIT and MAXREQUESTWORKERS are set to values higher than the system can handle, Apache httpd may not start or the system may become unstable.

With the PREFORK MPM, use this directive only if you need to set MAXREQUESTWORKERS higher than 256 (default). Do not set the value of this directive any higher than what you might want to set MAXREQUESTWORKERS to.

With WORKER and EVENT, use this directive only if your MAXREQUESTWORKERS and THREADSPERCHILD settings require more than 16 server processes (default). Do not set the value of this directive any higher than the number of server processes required by what you may want for MAXREQUESTWORKERS and THREADSPERCHILD.

**Note**

There is a hard limit of `ServerLimit 20000` compiled into the server (for the PREFORK MPM 200000). This is intended to avoid nasty effects caused by typos. To increase it even further past this limit, you will need to modify the value of MAX_SERVER_LIMIT in the mpm source file and rebuild the server.

**See also**

- Stopping and Restarting Apache HTTP Server (p. 29)

## StartServers Directive

| | |
|---|---|
| Description: | Number of child server processes created at startup |
| Syntax: | `StartServers number` |
| Default: | `See usage for details` |
| Context: | server config |
| Status: | **MPM** |
| Module: | EVENT, WORKER, PREFORK, MPMT_OS2 |

The STARTSERVERS directive sets the number of child server processes created on startup. As the number of processes is dynamically controlled depending on the load, (see MINSPARETHREADS, MAXSPARETHREADS, MINSPARESERVERS, MAXSPARESERVERS) there is usually little reason to adjust this parameter.

The default value differs from MPM to MPM. WORKER and EVENT default to `StartServers 3`; PREFORK defaults to 5; MPMT_OS2 defaults to 2.

## StartThreads Directive

| | |
|---|---|
| Description: | Number of threads created on startup |
| Syntax: | `StartThreads number` |
| Default: | `See usage for details` |
| Context: | server config |
| Status: | **MPM** |
| Module: | MPM_NETWARE |

Number of threads created on startup. As the number of threads is dynamically controlled depending on the load, (see MINSPARETHREADS, MAXSPARETHREADS, MINSPARESERVERS, MAXSPARESERVERS) there is usually little reason to adjust this parameter.

For MPM_NETWARE the default is `StartThreads 50` and, since there is only a single process, this is the total number of threads created at startup to serve requests.

## ThreadLimit Directive

| | |
|---|---|
| Description: | Sets the upper limit on the configurable number of threads per child process |
| Syntax: | `ThreadLimit number` |
| Default: | `See usage for details` |
| Context: | server config |
| Status: | MPM |
| Module: | EVENT, WORKER, MPM_WINNT |

This directive sets the maximum configured value for THREADSPERCHILD for the lifetime of the Apache httpd process. Any attempts to change this directive during a restart will be ignored, but THREADSPERCHILD can be modified during a restart up to the value of this directive.

Special care must be taken when using this directive. If THREADLIMIT is set to a value much higher than THREADSPERCHILD, extra unused shared memory will be allocated. If both THREADLIMIT and THREADSPER-CHILD are set to values higher than the system can handle, Apache httpd may not start or the system may become unstable. Do not set the value of this directive any higher than your greatest predicted setting of THREADSPERCHILD for the current run of Apache httpd.

The default value for THREADLIMIT is `1920` when used with MPM_WINNT and `64` when used with the others.

Note

> There is a hard limit of `ThreadLimit 20000` (or `ThreadLimit 100000` with EVENT, `ThreadLimit 15000` with MPM_WINNT) compiled into the server. This is intended to avoid nasty effects caused by typos. To increase it even further past this limit, you will need to modify the value of MAX_THREAD_LIMIT in the mpm source file and rebuild the server.

## ThreadsPerChild Directive

| | |
|---|---|
| Description: | Number of threads created by each child process |
| Syntax: | `ThreadsPerChild number` |
| Default: | `See usage for details` |
| Context: | server config |
| Status: | MPM |
| Module: | EVENT, WORKER, MPM_WINNT |

This directive sets the number of threads created by each child process. The child creates these threads at startup and never creates more. If using an MPM like MPM_WINNT, where there is only one child process, this number should be high enough to handle the entire load of the server. If using an MPM like WORKER, where there are multiple child processes, the *total* number of threads should be high enough to handle the common load on the server.

The default value for THREADSPERCHILD is `64` when used with MPM_WINNT and `25` when used with the others.

## ThreadStackSize Directive

| | |
|---|---|
| Description: | The size in bytes of the stack used by threads handling client connections |
| Syntax: | `ThreadStackSize size` |
| Default: | `65536 on NetWare; varies on other operating systems` |
| Context: | server config |
| Status: | MPM |
| Module: | EVENT, WORKER, MPM_WINNT, MPM_NETWARE, MPMT_OS2 |

The THREADSTACKSIZE directive sets the size of the stack (for autodata) of threads which handle client connections and call modules to help process those connections. In most cases the operating system default for stack size is reasonable, but there are some conditions where it may need to be adjusted:

- On platforms with a relatively small default thread stack size (e.g., HP-UX), Apache httpd may crash when using some third-party modules which use a relatively large amount of autodata storage. Those same modules may have worked fine on other platforms where the default thread stack size is larger. This type of crash is resolved by setting THREADSTACKSIZE to a value higher than the operating system default. This type of adjustment is necessary only if the provider of the third-party module specifies that it is required, or if diagnosis of an Apache httpd crash indicates that the thread stack size was too small.

- On platforms where the default thread stack size is significantly larger than necessary for the web server config-uration, a higher number of threads per child process will be achievable if THREADSTACKSIZE is set to a value lower than the operating system default. This type of adjustment should only be made in a test environment which allows the full set of web server processing can be exercised, as there may be infrequent requests which require more stack to process. The minimum required stack size strongly depends on the modules used, but any change in the web server configuration can invalidate the current THREADSTACKSIZE setting.

- On Linux, this directive can only be used to increase the default stack size, as the underlying system call uses the value as a *minimum* stack size. The (often large) soft limit for `ulimit -s` (8MB if unlimited) is used as the default stack size.

It is recommended to not reduce THREADSTACKSIZE unless a high number of threads per child process is needed. On some platforms (including Linux), a setting of 128000 is already too low and causes crashes with some common modules.

# 10.131  Apache Module event

| | |
|---|---|
| Description: | A variant of the WORKER MPM with the goal of consuming threads only for connections with active processing |
| Status: | MPM |
| ModuleIdentifier: | mpm_event_module |
| SourceFile: | event.c |

## Summary

The EVENT Multi-Processing Module (MPM) is, as its name implies, an asynchronous, event-based implementation designed to allow more requests to be served simultaneously by passing off some processing work to the listeners threads, freeing up the worker threads to serve new requests.

To use the EVENT MPM, add `--with-mpm=event` to the `configure` script's arguments when building the `httpd`.

**Directives**

- AsyncRequestWorkerFactor
- CoreDumpDirectory (p. 990)
- EnableExceptionHook (p. 991)
- Group (p. 972)
- Listen (p. 992)
- ListenBacklog (p. 993)
- MaxConnectionsPerChild (p. 994)
- MaxMemFree (p. 994)
- MaxRequestWorkers (p. 994)
- MaxSpareThreads (p. 995)
- MinSpareThreads (p. 995)
- PidFile (p. 996)
- ScoreBoardFile (p. 996)
- SendBufferSize (p. 997)
- ServerLimit (p. 997)
- StartServers (p. 998)
- ThreadLimit (p. 999)
- ThreadsPerChild (p. 999)
- ThreadStackSize (p. 999)
- User (p. 973)

**See also**

- The worker MPM (p. 1014)

## Relationship with the Worker MPM

EVENT is based on the WORKER MPM, which implements a hybrid multi-process multi-threaded server. A single control process (the parent) is responsible for launching child processes. Each child process creates a fixed number of server threads as specified in the THREADSPERCHILD directive, as well as a listener thread which listens for connections and passes them to a worker thread for processing when they arrive.

Run-time configuration directives are identical to those provided by WORKER, with the only addition of the ASYN-CREQUESTWORKERFACTOR.

## How it Works

This original goal of this MPM was to fix the 'keep alive problem' in HTTP. After a client completes the first request, it can keep the connection open, sending further requests using the same socket and saving significant overhead in creating TCP connections. However, Apache HTTP Server traditionally keeps an entire child process/thread waiting for data from the client, which brings its own disadvantages. To solve this problem, this MPM uses a dedicated listener thread for each process along with a pool of worker threads, sharing queues specific for those requests in keep-alive mode (or, more simply, "readable"), those in write- completion mode, and those in the process of shutting down ("closing"). An event loop, triggered on the status of the socket's availability, adjusts these queues and pushes work to the worker pool.

This new architecture, leveraging non-blocking sockets and modern kernel features exposed by APR (like Linux's epoll), no longer requires the `mpm-accept` MUTEX configured to avoid the thundering herd problem.

The total amount of connections that a single process/threads block can handle is regulated by the ASYNCREQUEST-WORKERFACTOR directive.

### Async connections

Async connections would need a fixed dedicated worker thread with the previous MPMs but not with event. The status page of MOD_STATUS shows new columns under the Async connections section:

**Writing** While sending the response to the client, it might happen that the TCP write buffer fills up because the connection is too slow. Usually in this case a `write()` to the socket returns EWOULDBLOCK or EAGAIN, to become writable again after an idle time. The worker holding the socket might be able to offload the waiting task to the listener thread, that in turn will re-assign it to the first idle worker thread available once an event will be raised for the socket (for example, "the socket is now writable"). Please check the Limitations section for more information.

**Keep-alive** Keep Alive handling is the most basic improvement from the worker MPM. Once a worker thread finishes to flush the response to the client, it can offload the socket handling to the listener thread, that in turns will wait for any event from the OS, like "the socket is readable". If any new request comes from the client, then the listener will forward it to the first worker thread available. Conversely, if the KEEPALIVETIMEOUT occurs then the socket will be closed by the listener. In this way the worker threads are not responsible for idle sockets and they can be re-used to serve other requests.

**Closing** Sometimes the MPM needs to perform a lingering close, namely sending back an early error to the client while it is still transmitting data to httpd. Sending the response and then closing the connection immediately is not the correct thing to do since the client (still trying to send the rest of the request) would get a connection reset and could not read the httpd's response. So in such cases, httpd tries to read the rest of the request to allow the client to consume the response. The lingering close is time bounded but it can take relatively long time, so a worker thread can offload this work to the listener.

These improvements are valid for both HTTP/HTTPS connections.

**Limitations**

The improved connection handling may not work for certain connection filters that have declared themselves as incompatible with event. In these cases, this MPM will fall back to the behaviour of the WORKER MPM and reserve one worker thread per connection. All modules shipped with the server are compatible with the event MPM.

A similar restriction is currently present for requests involving an output filter that needs to read and/or modify the whole response body. If the connection to the client blocks while the filter is processing the data, and the amount of data produced by the filter is too big to be buffered in memory, the thread used for the request is not freed while httpd waits until the pending data is sent to the client.

To illustrate this point we can think about the following two situations: serving a static asset (like a CSS file) versus serving content retrieved from FCGI/CGI or a proxied server. The former is predictable, namely the event MPM has full visibility on the end of the content and it can use events: the worker thread serving the response content can flush the first bytes until EWOULDBLOCK or EAGAIN is returned, delegating the rest to the listener. This one in turn waits for an event on the socket, and delegates the work to flush the rest of the content to the first idle worker thread. Meanwhile in the latter example (FCGI/CGI/proxied content) the MPM can't predict the end of the response and a worker thread has to finish its work before returning the control to the listener. The only alternative is to buffer the response in memory, but it wouldn't be the safest option for the sake of the server's stability and memory footprint.

**Background material**

The event model was made possible by the introduction of new APIs into the supported operating systems:

- epoll (Linux)
- kqueue (BSD)
- event ports (Solaris)

Before these new APIs where made available, the traditional select and poll APIs had to be used. Those APIs get slow if used to handle many connections or if the set of connections rate of change is high. The new APIs allow to monitor much more connections and they perform way better when the set of connections to monitor changes frequently. So these APIs made it possible to write the event MPM, that scales much better with the typical HTTP pattern of many idle connections.

The MPM assumes that the underlying apr_pollset implementation is reasonably threadsafe. This enables the MPM to avoid excessive high level locking, or having to wake up the listener thread in order to send it a keep-alive socket. This is currently only compatible with KQueue and EPoll.

## Requirements

This MPM depends on APR's atomic compare-and-swap operations for thread synchronization. If you are compiling for an x86 target and you don't need to support 386s, or you are compiling for a SPARC and you don't need to run on pre-UltraSPARC chips, add --enable-nonportable-atomics=yes to the configure script's arguments. This will cause APR to implement atomic operations using efficient opcodes not available in older CPUs.

This MPM does not perform well on older platforms which lack good threading, but the requirement for EPoll or KQueue makes this moot.

- To use this MPM on FreeBSD, FreeBSD 5.3 or higher is recommended. However, it is possible to run this MPM on FreeBSD 5.2.1, if you use libkse (see man libmap.conf).
- For NetBSD, at least version 2.0 is recommended.
- For Linux, a 2.6 kernel is recommended. It is also necessary to ensure that your version of glibc has been compiled with support for EPoll.

## AsyncRequestWorkerFactor Directive

| | |
|---|---|
| Description: | Limit concurrent connections per process |
| Syntax: | `AsyncRequestWorkerFactor factor` |
| Default: | `2` |
| Context: | server config |
| Status: | MPM |
| Module: | event |
| Compatibility: | Available in version 2.3.13 and later |

The event MPM handles some connections in an asynchronous way, where request worker threads are only allocated for short periods of time as needed, and other connections with one request worker thread reserved per connection. This can lead to situations where all workers are tied up and no worker thread is available to handle new work on established async connections.

To mitigate this problem, the event MPM does two things:

- it limits the number of connections accepted per process, depending on the number of idle request workers;

- if all workers are busy, it will close connections in keep-alive state even if the keep-alive timeout has not expired. This allows the respective clients to reconnect to a different process which may still have worker threads available.

This directive can be used to fine-tune the per-process connection limit. A **process** will only accept new connections if the current number of connections (not counting connections in the "closing" state) is lower than:

THREADSPERCHILD + (ASYNCREQUESTWORKERFACTOR * *number of idle workers*)

An estimation of the maximum concurrent connections across all the processes given an average value of idle worker threads can be calculated with:

(THREADSPERCHILD + (ASYNCREQUESTWORKERFACTOR * *number of idle workers*)) * SERVERLIMIT

**Example**

```
ThreadsPerChild = 10
ServerLimit = 4
AsyncRequestWorkerFactor = 2
MaxRequestWorkers = 40

idle_workers = 4 (average for all the processes to keep it simple)

max_connections = (ThreadsPerChild + (AsyncRequestWorkerFactor * idle_workers)) * Se
                = (10 + (2 * 4)) * 4 = 72
```

When all the worker threads are idle, then absolute maximum numbers of concurrent connections can be calculared in a simpler way:

(ASYNCREQUESTWORKERFACTOR + 1) * MAXREQUESTWORKERS

**Example**

```
ThreadsPerChild = 10
ServerLimit = 4
MaxRequestWorkers = 40
AsyncRequestWorkerFactor = 2
```

If all the processes have all threads idle then:

```
idle_workers = 10
```

We can calculate the absolute maximum numbers of concurrent connections in two ways:

```
max_connections = (ThreadsPerChild + (AsyncRequestWorkerFactor * idle_workers)
                = (10 + (2 * 10)) * 4 = 120

max_connections = (AsyncRequestWorkerFactor + 1) * MaxRequestWorkers
                = (2 + 1) * 40 = 120
```

Tuning ASYNCREQUESTWORKERFACTOR requires knowledge about the traffic handled by httpd in each specific use case, so changing the default value requires extensive testing and data gathering from MOD_STATUS.

MAXREQUESTWORKERS was called MAXCLIENTS prior to version 2.3.13. The above value shows that the old name did not accurately describe its meaning for the event MPM.

ASYNCREQUESTWORKERFACTOR can take non-integer arguments, e.g "1.5".

## 10.132   Apache Module mpm_netware

| | |
|---|---|
| Description: | Multi-Processing Module implementing an exclusively threaded web server optimized for Novell NetWare |
| Status: | MPM |
| ModuleIdentifier: | mpm_netware_module |
| SourceFile: | mpm_netware.c |

### Summary

This Multi-Processing Module (MPM) implements an exclusively threaded web server that has been optimized for Novell NetWare.

The main thread is responsible for launching child worker threads which listen for connections and serve them when they arrive. Apache HTTP Server always tries to maintain several *spare* or idle worker threads, which stand ready to serve incoming requests. In this way, clients do not need to wait for a new child threads to be spawned before their requests can be served.

The STARTTHREADS, MINSPARETHREADS, MAXSPARETHREADS, and MAXTHREADS regulate how the main thread creates worker threads to serve requests. In general, Apache httpd is very self-regulating, so most sites do not need to adjust these directives from their default values. Sites with limited memory may need to decrease MAX-THREADS to keep the server from thrashing (spawning and terminating idle threads). More information about tuning process creation is provided in the performance hints (p. 339) documentation.

MAXCONNECTIONSPERCHILD controls how frequently the server recycles processes by killing old ones and launching new ones. On the NetWare OS it is highly recommended that this directive remain set to 0. This allows worker threads to continue servicing requests indefinitely.

### Directives

- Listen (p. 992)

- ListenBacklog (p. 993)

- MaxConnectionsPerChild (p. 994)

- MaxMemFree (p. 994)

- MaxSpareThreads (p. 995)

- MaxThreads

- MinSpareThreads (p. 995)

- ReceiveBufferSize (p. 996)

- SendBufferSize (p. 997)

- StartThreads (p. 998)

- ThreadStackSize (p. 999)

### See also

- Setting which addresses and ports Apache httpd uses (p. 88)

## MaxThreads Directive

| | |
|---|---|
| Description: | Set the maximum number of worker threads |
| Syntax: | `MaxThreads number` |
| Default: | `MaxThreads 2048` |
| Context: | server config |
| Status: | MPM |
| Module: | mpm_netware |

The MAXTHREADS directive sets the desired maximum number worker threads allowable. The default value is also the compiled in hard limit. Therefore it can only be lowered, for example:

```
MaxThreads 512
```

## 10.133    Apache Module mpmt_os2

| | |
|---|---|
| Description: | Hybrid multi-process, multi-threaded MPM for OS/2 |
| Status: | MPM |
| ModuleIdentifier: | mpm_mpmt_os2_module |
| SourceFile: | mpmt_os2.c |

### Summary

The Server consists of a main, parent process and a small, static number of child processes.

The parent process' job is to manage the child processes. This involves spawning children as required to ensure there are always STARTSERVERS processes accepting connections.

Each child process consists of a pool of worker threads and a main thread that accepts connections and passes them to the workers via a work queue. The worker thread pool is dynamic, managed by a maintenance thread so that the number of idle threads is kept between MINSPARETHREADS and MAXSPARETHREADS.

### Directives

- Group (p. 972)
- Listen (p. 992)
- ListenBacklog (p. 993)
- MaxConnectionsPerChild (p. 994)
- MaxSpareThreads (p. 995)
- MinSpareThreads (p. 995)
- PidFile (p. 996)
- ReceiveBufferSize (p. 996)
- SendBufferSize (p. 997)
- StartServers (p. 998)
- User (p. 973)

### See also

- Setting which addresses and ports Apache uses (p. 88)

# 10.134 Apache Module prefork

| | |
|---|---|
| Description: | Implements a non-threaded, pre-forking web server |
| Status: | MPM |
| ModuleIdentifier: | mpm_prefork_module |
| SourceFile: | prefork.c |

## Summary

This Multi-Processing Module (MPM) implements a non-threaded, pre-forking web server. Each server process may answer incoming requests, and a parent process manages the size of the server pool. It is appropriate for sites that need to avoid threading for compatibility with non-thread-safe libraries. It is also the best MPM for isolating each request, so that a problem with a single request will not affect any other.

This MPM is very self-regulating, so it is rarely necessary to adjust its configuration directives. Most important is that MAXREQUESTWORKERS be big enough to handle as many simultaneous requests as you expect to receive, but small enough to assure that there is enough physical RAM for all processes.

## Directives

- CoreDumpDirectory (p. 990)
- EnableExceptionHook (p. 991)
- Group (p. 972)
- Listen (p. 992)
- ListenBacklog (p. 993)
- MaxConnectionsPerChild (p. 994)
- MaxMemFree (p. 994)
- MaxRequestWorkers (p. 994)
- MaxSpareServers
- MinSpareServers
- PidFile (p. 996)
- ReceiveBufferSize (p. 996)
- ScoreBoardFile (p. 996)
- SendBufferSize (p. 997)
- ServerLimit (p. 997)
- StartServers (p. 998)
- User (p. 973)

## See also

- Setting which addresses and ports Apache HTTP Server uses (p. 88)

## How it Works

A single control process is responsible for launching child processes which listen for connections and serve them when they arrive. Apache httpd always tries to maintain several *spare* or idle server processes, which stand ready to serve incoming requests. In this way, clients do not need to wait for a new child processes to be forked before their requests can be served.

The STARTSERVERS, MINSPARESERVERS, MAXSPARESERVERS, and MAXREQUESTWORKERS regulate how the parent process creates children to serve requests. In general, Apache httpd is very self-regulating, so most sites do not need to adjust these directives from their default values. Sites which need to serve more than 256 simultaneous requests may need to increase MAXREQUESTWORKERS, while sites with limited memory may need to decrease MAXREQUESTWORKERS to keep the server from thrashing (swapping memory to disk and back). More information about tuning process creation is provided in the performance hints (p. 339) documentation.

While the parent process is usually started as root under Unix in order to bind to port 80, the child processes are launched by Apache httpd as a less-privileged user. The USER and GROUP directives are used to set the privileges of the Apache httpd child processes. The child processes must be able to read all the content that will be served, but should have as few privileges beyond that as possible.

MAXCONNECTIONSPERCHILD controls how frequently the server recycles processes by killing old ones and launching new ones.

This MPM uses the mpm-accept mutex to serialize access to incoming connections when subject to the thundering herd problem (generally, when there are multiple listening sockets). The implementation aspects of this mutex can be configured with the MUTEX directive. The performance hints (p. 339) documentation has additional information about this mutex.

## MaxSpareServers Directive

| | |
|---|---|
| Description: | Maximum number of idle child server processes |
| Syntax: | MaxSpareServers number |
| Default: | MaxSpareServers 10 |
| Context: | server config |
| Status: | MPM |
| Module: | prefork |

The MAXSPARESERVERS directive sets the desired maximum number of *idle* child server processes. An idle process is one which is not handling a request. If there are more than MAXSPARESERVERS idle, then the parent process will kill off the excess processes.

Tuning of this parameter should only be necessary on very busy sites. Setting this parameter to a large number is almost always a bad idea. If you are trying to set the value equal to or lower than MINSPARESERVERS, Apache HTTP Server will automatically adjust it to MINSPARESERVERS + 1.

**See also**

- MINSPARESERVERS
- STARTSERVERS
- MAXSPARETHREADS

## MinSpareServers Directive

| | |
|---|---|
| Description: | Minimum number of idle child server processes |
| Syntax: | MinSpareServers number |
| Default: | MinSpareServers 5 |
| Context: | server config |
| Status: | MPM |
| Module: | prefork |

The MINSPARESERVERS directive sets the desired minimum number of *idle* child server processes. An idle process is one which is not handling a request. If there are fewer than MINSPARESERVERS idle, then the parent process creates new children: It will spawn one, wait a second, then spawn two, wait a second, then spawn four, and it will continue exponentially until it is spawning 32 children per second. It will stop whenever it satisfies the MINSPARESERVERS setting.

Tuning of this parameter should only be necessary on very busy sites. Setting this parameter to a large number is almost always a bad idea.

**See also**

- MAXSPARESERVERS
- STARTSERVERS
- MINSPARETHREADS

## 10.135   Apache Module mpm_winnt

| | |
|---|---|
| Description: | Multi-Processing Module optimized for Windows NT. |
| Status: | MPM |
| ModuleIdentifier: | mpm_winnt_module |
| SourceFile: | mpm_winnt.c |

### Summary

This Multi-Processing Module (MPM) is the default for the Windows NT operating systems. It uses a single control process which launches a single child process which in turn creates threads to handle requests

Capacity is configured using the THREADSPERCHILD directive, which sets the maximum number of concurrent client connections.

By default, this MPM uses advanced Windows APIs for accepting new client connections. In some configurations, third-party products may interfere with this implementation, with the following messages written to the web server log:

```
Child:  Encountered too many AcceptEx faults accepting client
connections.
winnt_mpm:  falling back to 'AcceptFilter none'.
```

The MPM falls back to a safer implementation, but some client requests were not processed correctly. In order to avoid this error, use ACCEPTFILTER with accept filter none.

```
AcceptFilter http none
AcceptFilter https none
```

*In Apache httpd 2.0 and 2.2,* WIN32DISABLEACCEPTEX *was used for this purpose.*

The WinNT MPM differs from the Unix MPMs such as worker and event in several areas:

- When a child process is exiting due to shutdown, restart, or MAXCONNECTIONSPERCHILD, active requests in the exiting process have TIMEOUT seconds to finish before processing is aborted. Alternate types of restart and shutdown are not implemented.

- New child processes read the configuration files instead of inheriting the configuration from the parent. The behavior will be the same as on Unix if the child process is created at startup or restart, but if a child process is created because the prior one crashed or reached MAXCONNECTIONSPERCHILD, any pending changes to the configuration will become active in the child at that point, and the parent and child will be using a different configuration. If planned configuration changes have been partially implemented and the current configuration cannot be parsed, the replacement child process cannot start up and the server will halt. Because of this behavior, configuration files should not be changed until the time of a server restart.

- The `monitor` and `fatal_exception` hooks are not currently implemented.

- ACCEPTFILTER is implemented in the MPM and has a different type of control over handling of new connections. (Refer to the ACCEPTFILTER documentation for details.)

### Directives

- AcceptFilter (p. 382)

- CoreDumpDirectory (p. 990)

- Listen (p. 992)
- ListenBacklog (p. 993)
- MaxConnectionsPerChild (p. 994)
- MaxMemFree (p. 994)
- PidFile (p. 996)
- ReceiveBufferSize (p. 996)
- ScoreBoardFile (p. 996)
- SendBufferSize (p. 997)
- ThreadLimit (p. 999)
- ThreadsPerChild (p. 999)
- ThreadStackSize (p. 999)

**See also**

- Using Apache HTTP Server on Microsoft Windows (p. 267)

# 10.136 Apache Module worker

| Description: | Multi-Processing Module implementing a hybrid multi-threaded multi-process web server |
|---|---|
| Status: | MPM |
| ModuleIdentifier: | mpm_worker_module |
| SourceFile: | worker.c |

## Summary

This Multi-Processing Module (MPM) implements a hybrid multi-process multi-threaded server. By using threads to serve requests, it is able to serve a large number of requests with fewer system resources than a process-based server. However, it retains much of the stability of a process-based server by keeping multiple processes available, each with many threads.

The most important directives used to control this MPM are THREADSPERCHILD, which controls the number of threads deployed by each child process and MAXREQUESTWORKERS, which controls the maximum total number of threads that may be launched.

### Directives

- CoreDumpDirectory (p. 990)
- EnableExceptionHook (p. 991)
- Group (p. 972)
- Listen (p. 992)
- ListenBacklog (p. 993)
- MaxConnectionsPerChild (p. 994)
- MaxMemFree (p. 994)
- MaxRequestWorkers (p. 994)
- MaxSpareThreads (p. 995)
- MinSpareThreads (p. 995)
- PidFile (p. 996)
- ReceiveBufferSize (p. 996)
- ScoreBoardFile (p. 996)
- SendBufferSize (p. 997)
- ServerLimit (p. 997)
- StartServers (p. 998)
- ThreadLimit (p. 999)
- ThreadsPerChild (p. 999)
- ThreadStackSize (p. 999)
- User (p. 973)

### See also

- Setting which addresses and ports Apache HTTP Server uses (p. 88)

## How it Works

A single control process (the parent) is responsible for launching child processes. Each child process creates a fixed number of server threads as specified in the THREADSPERCHILD directive, as well as a listener thread which listens for connections and passes them to a server thread for processing when they arrive.

Apache HTTP Server always tries to maintain a pool of *spare* or idle server threads, which stand ready to serve incoming requests. In this way, clients do not need to wait for a new threads or processes to be created before their requests can be served. The number of processes that will initially launch is set by the STARTSERVERS directive. During operation, the server assesses the total number of idle threads in all processes, and forks or kills processes to keep this number within the boundaries specified by MINSPARETHREADS and MAXSPARETHREADS. Since this process is very self-regulating, it is rarely necessary to modify these directives from their default values. The maximum number of clients that may be served simultaneously (i.e., the maximum total number of threads in all processes) is determined by the MAXREQUESTWORKERS directive. The maximum number of active child processes is determined by the MAXREQUESTWORKERS directive divided by the THREADSPERCHILD directive.

Two directives set hard limits on the number of active child processes and the number of server threads in a child process, and can only be changed by fully stopping the server and then starting it again. SERVERLIMIT is a hard limit on the number of active child processes, and must be greater than or equal to the MAXREQUESTWORKERS directive divided by the THREADSPERCHILD directive. THREADLIMIT is a hard limit of the number of server threads, and must be greater than or equal to the THREADSPERCHILD directive.

In addition to the set of active child processes, there may be additional child processes which are terminating, but where at least one server thread is still handling an existing client connection. Up to MAXREQUESTWORKERS terminating processes may be present, though the actual number can be expected to be much smaller. This behavior can be avoided by disabling the termination of individual child processes, which is achieved using the following:

- set the value of MAXCONNECTIONSPERCHILD to zero
- set the value of MAXSPARETHREADS to the same value as MAXREQUESTWORKERS

A typical configuration of the process-thread controls in the WORKER MPM could look as follows:

```
ServerLimit         16
StartServers         2
MaxRequestWorkers  150
MinSpareThreads     25
MaxSpareThreads     75
ThreadsPerChild     25
```

While the parent process is usually started as `root` under Unix in order to bind to port 80, the child processes and threads are launched by the server as a less-privileged user. The USER and GROUP directives are used to set the privileges of the Apache HTTP Server child processes. The child processes must be able to read all the content that will be served, but should have as few privileges beyond that as possible. In addition, unless `suexec` is used, these directives also set the privileges which will be inherited by CGI scripts.

MAXCONNECTIONSPERCHILD controls how frequently the server recycles processes by killing old ones and launching new ones.

This MPM uses the `mpm-accept` mutex to serialize access to incoming connections when subject to the thundering herd problem (generally, when there are multiple listening sockets). The implementation aspects of this mutex can be configured with the MUTEX directive. The performance hints (p. 339) documentation has additional information about this mutex.

# Chapter 11

# Developer Documentation

# 11.1   Developer Documentation for the Apache HTTP Server 2.4

 **Warning**

Many of the documents listed here are in need of update. They are in different stages of progress. Please be patient and follow this link[a] to propose a fix or point out any error/discrepancy.

---

[a]https://httpd.apache.org/docs-project/

## 2.4 development documents

- Developing modules for the Apache HTTP Server 2.4 (p. 1042)
- Hook Functions in 2.4 (p. 1071)
- Request Processing in 2.4 (p. 1078)
- How filters work in 2.4 (p. 1081)
- Guidelines for output filters in 2.4 (p. 1084)
- Documenting code in 2.4 (p. 1070)
- Thread Safety Issues in 2.4 (p. 1091)

## Upgrading to 2.4

- API changes in 2.3/2.4 (p. 1035)
- Converting Modules from 1.3 to 2.x (p. 1074)

## External Resources

- Autogenerated Apache HTTP Server (trunk) code documentation[1] (the link is built by this job[2]).
- Developer articles at apachetutor[3] include:

  - Request Processing[4]
  - Configuration for Modules[5]
  - Resource Management[6]
  - Connection Pooling[7]
  - Introduction to Buckets and Brigades[8]

---

[1]http://ci.apache.org/projects/httpd/trunk/doxygen/
[2]https://ci.apache.org/builders/httpd-doxygen-nightly
[3]http://www.apachetutor.org/
[4]http://www.apachetutor.org/dev/request
[5]http://www.apachetutor.org/dev/config
[6]http://www.apachetutor.org/dev/pools
[7]http://www.apachetutor.org/dev/reslist
[8]http://www.apachetutor.org/dev/brigades

## 11.2 Apache 1.3 API notes

 **Warning**

This document has not been updated to take into account changes made in the 2.0 version of the Apache HTTP Server. Some of the information may still be relevant, but please use it with care.

These are some notes on the Apache API and the data structures you have to deal with, *etc.* They are not yet nearly complete, but hopefully, they will help you get your bearings. Keep in mind that the API is still subject to change as we gain experience with it. (See the TODO file for what *might* be coming). However, it will be easy to adapt modules to any changes that are made. (We have more modules to adapt than you do).

A few notes on general pedagogical style here. In the interest of conciseness, all structure declarations here are incomplete – the real ones have more slots that I'm not telling you about. For the most part, these are reserved to one component of the server core or another, and should be altered by modules with caution. However, in some cases, they really are things I just haven't gotten around to yet. Welcome to the bleeding edge.

Finally, here's an outline, to give you some bare idea of what's coming up, and in what order:

- Basic concepts.

    - Handlers, Modules, and Requests
    - A brief tour of a module

- How handlers work

    - A brief tour of the `request_rec`
    - Where request_rec structures come from
    - Handling requests, declining, and returning error codes
    - Special considerations for response handlers
    - Special considerations for authentication handlers
    - Special considerations for logging handlers

- Resource allocation and resource pools
- Configuration, commands and the like

    - Per-directory configuration structures
    - Command handling
    - Side notes — per-server configuration, virtual servers, *etc.*

### Basic concepts

We begin with an overview of the basic concepts behind the API, and how they are manifested in the code.

#### Handlers, Modules, and Requests

Apache breaks down request handling into a series of steps, more or less the same way the Netscape server API does (although this API has a few more stages than NetSite does, as hooks for stuff I thought might be useful in the future). These are:

- URI -> Filename translation

- Auth ID checking [is the user who they say they are?]
- Auth access checking [is the user authorized *here*?]
- Access checking other than auth
- Determining MIME type of the object requested
- 'Fixups' – there aren't any of these yet, but the phase is intended as a hook for possible extensions like SETENV, which don't really fit well elsewhere.
- Actually sending a response back to the client.
- Logging the request

These phases are handled by looking at each of a succession of *modules*, looking to see if each of them has a handler for the phase, and attempting invoking it if so. The handler can typically do one of three things:

- *Handle* the request, and indicate that it has done so by returning the magic constant OK.
- *Decline* to handle the request, by returning the magic integer constant DECLINED. In this case, the server behaves in all respects as if the handler simply hadn't been there.
- Signal an error, by returning one of the HTTP error codes. This terminates normal handling of the request, although an ErrorDocument may be invoked to try to mop up, and it will be logged in any case.

Most phases are terminated by the first module that handles them; however, for logging, 'fixups', and non-access authentication checking, all handlers always run (barring an error). Also, the response phase is unique in that modules may declare multiple handlers for it, via a dispatch table keyed on the MIME type of the requested object. Modules may declare a response-phase handler which can handle *any* request, by giving it the key */* (*i.e.*, a wildcard MIME type specification). However, wildcard handlers are only invoked if the server has already tried and failed to find a more specific response handler for the MIME type of the requested object (either none existed, or they all declined).

The handlers themselves are functions of one argument (a request_rec structure. vide infra), which returns an integer, as above.

**A brief tour of a module**

At this point, we need to explain the structure of a module. Our candidate will be one of the messier ones, the CGI module – this handles both CGI scripts and the SCRIPTALIAS config file command. It's actually a great deal more complicated than most modules, but if we're going to have only one example, it might as well be the one with its fingers in every place.

Let's begin with handlers. In order to handle the CGI scripts, the module declares a response handler for them. Because of SCRIPTALIAS, it also has handlers for the name translation phase (to recognize SCRIPTALIASed URIs), the type-checking phase (any SCRIPTALIASed request is typed as a CGI script).

The module needs to maintain some per (virtual) server information, namely, the SCRIPTALIASes in effect; the module structure therefore contains pointers to a functions which builds these structures, and to another which combines two of them (in case the main server and a virtual server both have SCRIPTALIASes declared).

Finally, this module contains code to handle the SCRIPTALIAS command itself. This particular module only declares one command, but there could be more, so modules have *command tables* which declare their commands, and describe where they are permitted, and how they are to be invoked.

A final note on the declared types of the arguments of some of these commands: a pool is a pointer to a *resource pool* structure; these are used by the server to keep track of the memory which has been allocated, files opened, *etc.*, either to service a particular request, or to handle the process of configuring itself. That way, when the request is over (or, for the configuration pool, when the server is restarting), the memory can be freed, and the files closed, *en masse*, without anyone having to write explicit code to track them all down and dispose of them. Also, a cmd_parms structure contains various information about the config file being read, and other status information, which is sometimes of use to the function which processes a config-file command (such as SCRIPTALIAS). With no further ado, the module itself:

```
/* Declarations of handlers.  */
int translate_scriptalias (request_rec *);
int type_scriptalias (request_rec *);
int cgi_handler (request_rec *);
/* Subsidiary dispatch table for response-phase
* handlers, by MIME type */
handler_rec cgi_handlers[] = {
    { "application/x-httpd-cgi", cgi_handler },
    { NULL }
};
/* Declarations of routines to manipulate the
* module's configuration info.  Note that these are
* returned, and passed in, as void *'s; the server
* core keeps track of them, but it doesn't, and can't,
* know their internal structure.
*/
void *make_cgi_server_config (pool *);
void *merge_cgi_server_config (pool *, void *, void *);
/* Declarations of routines to handle config-file commands */
extern char *script_alias(cmd_parms *, void *per_dir_config, char
*fake, char *real);
command_rec cgi_cmds[] = {
    { "ScriptAlias", script_alias, NULL, RSRC_CONF, TAKE2,
        "a fakename and a realname"},
    { NULL }
};
module cgi_module = {
  STANDARD_MODULE_STUFF,
  NULL,                      /* initializer */
  NULL,                      /* dir config creator */
  NULL,                      /* dir merger */
  make_cgi_server_config,    /* server config */
  merge_cgi_server_config,   /* merge server config */
  cgi_cmds,                  /* command table */
  cgi_handlers,              /* handlers */
  translate_scriptalias,     /* filename translation */
  NULL,                      /* check_user_id */
  NULL,                      /* check auth */
  NULL,                      /* check access */
  type_scriptalias,          /* type_checker */
  NULL,                      /* fixups */
  NULL,                      /* logger */
  NULL                       /* header parser */
};
```

## How handlers work

The sole argument to handlers is a `request_rec` structure. This structure describes a particular request which has been made to the server, on behalf of a client. In most cases, each connection to the client generates only one `request_rec` structure.

### A brief tour of the request_rec

The `request_rec` contains pointers to a resource pool which will be cleared when the server is finished handling the request; to structures containing per-server and per-connection information, and most importantly, information on the request itself.

The most important such information is a small set of character strings describing attributes of the object being requested, including its URI, filename, content-type and content-encoding (these being filled in by the translation and type-check handlers which handle the request, respectively).

Other commonly used data items are tables giving the MIME headers on the client's original request, MIME headers to be sent back with the response (which modules can add to at will), and environment variables for any subprocesses which are spawned off in the course of servicing the request. These tables are manipulated using the `ap_table_get` and `ap_table_set` routines.

Note that the `Content-type` header value *cannot* be set by module content-handlers using the `ap_table_*()` routines. Rather, it is set by pointing the `content_type` field in the `request_rec` structure to an appropriate string. *e.g.*,

```
r->content_type = "text/html";
```

Finally, there are pointers to two data structures which, in turn, point to per-module configuration structures. Specifically, these hold pointers to the data structures which the module has built to describe the way it has been configured to operate in a given directory (via `.htaccess` files or <DIRECTORY> sections), for private data it has built in the course of servicing the request (so modules' handlers for one phase can pass 'notes' to their handlers for other phases). There is another such configuration vector in the `server_rec` data structure pointed to by the `request_rec`, which contains per (virtual) server configuration data.

Here is an abridged declaration, giving the fields most commonly used:

```
struct request_rec {

pool *pool;
conn_rec *connection;
server_rec *server;

/* What object is being requested */

char *uri;
char *filename;
char *path_info;

char *args;           /* QUERY_ARGS, if any */
struct stat finfo;    /* Set by server core;
                       * st_mode set to zero if no such file */

char *content_type;
char *content_encoding;

/* MIME header environments, in and out.  Also,
 * an array containing environment variables to
 * be passed to subprocesses, so people can write
 * modules to add to that environment.
 *
 * The difference between headers_out and
 * err_headers_out is that the latter are printed
 * even on error, and persist across internal
 * redirects (so the headers printed for
 * ERRORDOCUMENT handlers will have them).
 */

table *headers_in;
table *headers_out;
table *err_headers_out;
table *subprocess_env;

/* Info about the request itself...  */

int header_only;     /* HEAD request, as opposed to GET */
char *protocol;      /* Protocol, as given to us, or HTTP/0.9 */
char *method;        /* GET, HEAD, POST, etc. */
int method_number;   /* M_GET, M_POST, etc. */

/* Info for logging */

char *the_request;
int bytes_sent;

/* A flag which modules can set, to indicate that
 * the data being returned is volatile, and clients
 * should be told not to cache it.
 */

int no_cache;

/* Various other config info which may change
 * with .htaccess files
 * These are config vectors, with one void*
 * pointer for each module (the thing pointed
 * to being the module's business).
 */

void *per_dir_config;   /* Options set in config files, etc. */
void *request_config;   /* Notes on *this* request */

};
```

**Where request_rec structures come from**

Most `request_rec` structures are built by reading an HTTP request from a client, and filling in the fields. However, there are a few exceptions:

- If the request is to an imagemap, a type map (*i.e.*, a `*.var` file), or a CGI script which returned a local 'Location:', then the resource which the user requested is going to be ultimately located by some URI other than what the client originally supplied. In this case, the server does an *internal redirect*, constructing a new `request_rec` for the new URI, and processing it almost exactly as if the client had requested the new URI directly.

- If some handler signaled an error, and an `ErrorDocument` is in scope, the same internal redirect machinery comes into play.

- Finally, a handler occasionally needs to investigate 'what would happen if' some other request were run. For instance, the directory indexing module needs to know what MIME type would be assigned to a request for each directory entry, in order to figure out what icon to use.

  Such handlers can construct a *sub-request*, using the functions `ap_sub_req_lookup_file`, `ap_sub_req_lookup_uri`, and `ap_sub_req_method_uri`; these construct a new `request_rec` structure and processes it as you would expect, up to but not including the point of actually sending a response. (These functions skip over the access checks if the sub-request is for a file in the same directory as the original request).

  (Server-side includes work by building sub-requests and then actually invoking the response handler for them, via the function `ap_run_sub_req`).

**Handling requests, declining, and returning error codes**

As discussed above, each handler, when invoked to handle a particular `request_rec`, has to return an `int` to indicate what happened. That can either be

- `OK` – the request was handled successfully. This may or may not terminate the phase.

- `DECLINED` – no erroneous condition exists, but the module declines to handle the phase; the server tries to find another.

- an HTTP error code, which aborts handling of the request.

Note that if the error code returned is `REDIRECT`, then the module should put a `Location` in the request's `headers_out`, to indicate where the client should be redirected *to*.

**Special considerations for response handlers**

Handlers for most phases do their work by simply setting a few fields in the `request_rec` structure (or, in the case of access checkers, simply by returning the correct error code). However, response handlers have to actually send a request back to the client.

They should begin by sending an HTTP response header, using the function `ap_send_http_header`. (You don't have to do anything special to skip sending the header for HTTP/0.9 requests; the function figures out on its own that it shouldn't do anything). If the request is marked `header_only`, that's all they should do; they should return after that, without attempting any further output.

Otherwise, they should produce a request body which responds to the client as appropriate. The primitives for this are `ap_rputc` and `ap_rprintf`, for internally generated output, and `ap_send_fd`, to copy the contents of some `FILE *` straight to the client.

At this point, you should more or less understand the following piece of code, which is the handler which handles GET requests which have no more specific handler; it also shows how conditional GETs can be handled, if it's desirable to do so in a particular response handler – ap_set_last_modified checks against the If-modified-since value supplied by the client, if any, and returns an appropriate code (which will, if nonzero, be USE_LOCAL_COPY). No similar considerations apply for ap_set_content_length, but it returns an error code for symmetry.

```
int default_handler (request_rec *r)
{
    int errstatus;
    FILE *f;

    if (r->method_number != M_GET) return DECLINED;
    if (r->finfo.st_mode == 0) return NOT_FOUND;

    if ((errstatus = ap_set_content_length (r, r->finfo.st_size))
    || (errstatus = ap_set_last_modified (r, r->finfo.st_mtime)))
    return errstatus;

    f = fopen (r->filename, "r");

    if (f == NULL) {
        log_reason("file permissions deny server access", r->filename,
        r);
        return FORBIDDEN;
    }

    register_timeout ("send", r);
    ap_send_http_header (r);

    if (!r->header_only) send_fd (f, r);
    ap_pfclose (r->pool, f);
    return OK;

}
```

Finally, if all of this is too much of a challenge, there are a few ways out of it. First off, as shown above, a response handler which has not yet produced any output can simply return an error code, in which case the server will automatically produce an error response. Secondly, it can punt to some other handler by invoking ap_internal_redirect, which is how the internal redirection machinery discussed above is invoked. A response handler which has internally redirected should always return OK.

(Invoking ap_internal_redirect from handlers which are *not* response handlers will lead to serious confusion).

**Special considerations for authentication handlers**

Stuff that should be discussed here in detail:

- Authentication-phase handlers not invoked unless auth is configured for the directory.

- Common auth configuration stored in the core per-dir configuration; it has accessors ap_auth_type, ap_auth_name, and ap_requires.

- Common routines, to handle the protocol end of things, at least for HTTP basic authentication (ap_get_basic_auth_pw, which sets the connection->user structure field automatically, and ap_note_basic_auth_failure, which arranges for the proper WWW-Authenticate: header to be sent back).

**Special considerations for logging handlers**

When a request has internally redirected, there is the question of what to log. Apache handles this by bundling the entire chain of redirects into a list of `request_rec` structures which are threaded through the `r->prev` and `r->next` pointers. The `request_rec` which is passed to the logging handlers in such cases is the one which was originally built for the initial request from the client; note that the `bytes_sent` field will only be correct in the last request in the chain (the one for which a response was actually sent).

# Resource allocation and resource pools

One of the problems of writing and designing a server-pool server is that of preventing leakage, that is, allocating resources (memory, open files, *etc.*), without subsequently releasing them. The resource pool machinery is designed to make it easy to prevent this from happening, by allowing resource to be allocated in such a way that they are *automatically* released when the server is done with them.

The way this works is as follows: the memory which is allocated, file opened, *etc.*, to deal with a particular request are tied to a *resource pool* which is allocated for the request. The pool is a data structure which itself tracks the resources in question.

When the request has been processed, the pool is *cleared*. At that point, all the memory associated with it is released for reuse, all files associated with it are closed, and any other clean-up functions which are associated with the pool are run. When this is over, we can be confident that all the resource tied to the pool have been released, and that none of them have leaked.

Server restarts, and allocation of memory and resources for per-server configuration, are handled in a similar way. There is a *configuration pool*, which keeps track of resources which were allocated while reading the server configuration files, and handling the commands therein (for instance, the memory that was allocated for per-server module configuration, log files and other files that were opened, and so forth). When the server restarts, and has to reread the configuration files, the configuration pool is cleared, and so the memory and file descriptors which were taken up by reading them the last time are made available for reuse.

It should be noted that use of the pool machinery isn't generally obligatory, except for situations like logging handlers, where you really need to register cleanups to make sure that the log file gets closed when the server restarts (this is most easily done by using the function `ap_pfopen`, which also arranges for the underlying file descriptor to be closed before any child processes, such as for CGI scripts, are `exec`ed), or in case you are using the timeout machinery (which isn't yet even documented here). However, there are two benefits to using it: resources allocated to a pool never leak (even if you allocate a scratch string, and just forget about it); also, for memory allocation, `ap_palloc` is generally faster than `malloc`.

We begin here by describing how memory is allocated to pools, and then discuss how other resources are tracked by the resource pool machinery.

**Allocation of memory in pools**

Memory is allocated to pools by calling the function `ap_palloc`, which takes two arguments, one being a pointer to a resource pool structure, and the other being the amount of memory to allocate (in `char`s). Within handlers for handling requests, the most common way of getting a resource pool structure is by looking at the `pool` slot of the relevant `request_rec`; hence the repeated appearance of the following idiom in module code:

```
int my_handler(request_rec *r)
{
    struct my_structure *foo;
    ...
    foo = (foo *)ap_palloc (r->pool, sizeof(my_structure));
}
```

Note that *there is no ap_pfree* – ap_palloced memory is freed only when the associated resource pool is cleared. This means that ap_palloc does not have to do as much accounting as malloc(); all it does in the typical case is to round up the size, bump a pointer, and do a range check.

(It also raises the possibility that heavy use of ap_palloc could cause a server process to grow excessively large. There are two ways to deal with this, which are dealt with below; briefly, you can use malloc, and try to be sure that all of the memory gets explicitly freed, or you can allocate a sub-pool of the main pool, allocate your memory in the sub-pool, and clear it out periodically. The latter technique is discussed in the section on sub-pools below, and is used in the directory-indexing code, in order to avoid excessive storage allocation when listing directories with thousands of files).

### Allocating initialized memory

There are functions which allocate initialized memory, and are frequently useful. The function ap_pcalloc has the same interface as ap_palloc, but clears out the memory it allocates before it returns it. The function ap_pstrdup takes a resource pool and a char * as arguments, and allocates memory for a copy of the string the pointer points to, returning a pointer to the copy. Finally ap_pstrcat is a varargs-style function, which takes a pointer to a resource pool, and at least two char * arguments, the last of which must be NULL. It allocates enough memory to fit copies of each of the strings, as a unit; for instance:

```
ap_pstrcat (r->pool, "foo", "/", "bar", NULL);
```

returns a pointer to 8 bytes worth of memory, initialized to "foo/bar".

### Commonly-used pools in the Apache Web server

A pool is really defined by its lifetime more than anything else. There are some static pools in http_main which are passed to various non-http_main functions as arguments at opportune times. Here they are:

**permanent_pool** never passed to anything else, this is the ancestor of all pools

**pconf**
- subpool of permanent_pool
- created at the beginning of a config "cycle"; exists until the server is terminated or restarts; passed to all config-time routines, either via cmd->pool, or as the "pool *p" argument on those which don't take pools
- passed to the module init() functions

**ptemp**
- sorry I lie, this pool isn't called this currently in 1.3, I renamed it this in my pthreads development. I'm referring to the use of ptrans in the parent... contrast this with the later definition of ptrans in the child.
- subpool of permanent_pool
- created at the beginning of a config "cycle"; exists until the end of config parsing; passed to config-time routines *via* cmd->temp_pool. Somewhat of a "bastard child" because it isn't available everywhere. Used for temporary scratch space which may be needed by some config routines but which is deleted at the end of config.

`pchild`   • subpool of permanent_pool
   • created when a child is spawned (or a thread is created); lives until that child (thread) is destroyed
   • passed to the module child_init functions
   • destruction happens right after the child_exit functions are called... (which may explain why I think child_exit is redundant and unneeded)

`ptrans`   • should be a subpool of pchild, but currently is a subpool of permanent_pool, see above
   • cleared by the child before going into the accept() loop to receive a connection
   • used as connection->pool

`r->pool`   • for the main request this is a subpool of connection->pool; for subrequests it is a subpool of the parent request's pool.
   • exists until the end of the request (*i.e.*, ap_destroy_sub_req, or in child_main after process_request has finished)
   • note that r itself is allocated from r->pool; *i.e.*, r->pool is first created and then r is the first thing palloc()d from it

For almost everything folks do, `r->pool` is the pool to use. But you can see how other lifetimes, such as pchild, are useful to some modules... such as modules that need to open a database connection once per child, and wish to clean it up when the child dies.

You can also see how some bugs have manifested themself, such as setting `connection->user` to a value from `r->pool` – in this case connection exists for the lifetime of `ptrans`, which is longer than `r->pool` (especially if `r->pool` is a subrequest!). So the correct thing to do is to allocate from `connection->pool`.

And there was another interesting bug in MOD_INCLUDE / MOD_CGI. You'll see in those that they do this test to decide if they should use `r->pool` or `r->main->pool`. In this case the resource that they are registering for cleanup is a child process. If it were registered in `r->pool`, then the code would `wait()` for the child when the subrequest finishes. With MOD_INCLUDE this could be any old `#include`, and the delay can be up to 3 seconds... and happened quite frequently. Instead the subprocess is registered in `r->main->pool` which causes it to be cleaned up when the entire request is done – *i.e.*, after the output has been sent to the client and logging has happened.

**Tracking open files, etc.**

As indicated above, resource pools are also used to track other sorts of resources besides memory. The most common are open files. The routine which is typically used for this is `ap_pfopen`, which takes a resource pool and two strings as arguments; the strings are the same as the typical arguments to `fopen`, *e.g.*,

```
...
FILE *f = ap_pfopen (r->pool, r->filename, "r");
if (f == NULL) { ... } else { ... }
```

There is also a `ap_popenf` routine, which parallels the lower-level `open` system call. Both of these routines arrange for the file to be closed when the resource pool in question is cleared.

Unlike the case for memory, there *are* functions to close files allocated with `ap_pfopen`, and `ap_popenf`, namely `ap_pfclose` and `ap_pclosef`. (This is because, on many systems, the number of files which a single process can have open is quite limited). It is important to use these functions to close files allocated with `ap_pfopen` and `ap_popenf`, since to do otherwise could cause fatal errors on systems such as Linux, which react badly if the same `FILE*` is closed more than once.

(Using the `close` functions is not mandatory, since the file will eventually be closed regardless, but you should consider it in cases where your module is opening, or could open, a lot of files).

**Other sorts of resources – cleanup functions**

More text goes here. Describe the cleanup primitives in terms of which the file stuff is implemented; also, `spawn_process`.

Pool cleanups live until `clear_pool()` is called: `clear_pool(a)` recursively calls `destroy_pool()` on all subpools of a; then calls all the cleanups for a; then releases all the memory for a. `destroy_pool(a)` calls `clear_pool(a)` and then releases the pool structure itself. *i.e.*, `clear_pool(a)` doesn't delete a, it just frees up all the resources and you can start using it again immediately.

**Fine control – creating and dealing with sub-pools, with a note on sub-requests**

On rare occasions, too-free use of `ap_palloc()` and the associated primitives may result in undesirably profligate resource allocation. You can deal with such a case by creating a *sub-pool*, allocating within the sub-pool rather than the main pool, and clearing or destroying the sub-pool, which releases the resources which were associated with it. (This really *is* a rare situation; the only case in which it comes up in the standard module set is in case of listing directories, and then only with *very* large directories. Unnecessary use of the primitives discussed here can hair up your code quite a bit, with very little gain).

The primitive for creating a sub-pool is `ap_make_sub_pool`, which takes another pool (the parent pool) as an argument. When the main is cleared, the sub-pool will be destroyed. The sub-pool may also be cleared or destroyed at any time, by calling the functions `ap_clear_pool` and `ap_destroy_pool`, respectively. (The difference is that `ap_clear_pool` frees resources associated with the pool, while `ap_destroy_pool` also deallocates the pool itself. In the former case, you can allocate new resources within the pool, and clear it again, and so forth; in the latter case, it is simply gone).

One final note – sub-requests have their own resource pools, which are sub-pools of the resource pool for the main request. The polite way to reclaim the resources associated with a sub request which you have allocated (using the `ap_sub_req...` functions) is `ap_destroy_sub_req`, which frees the resource pool. Before calling this function, be sure to copy anything that you care about which might be allocated in the sub-request's resource pool into someplace a little less volatile (for instance, the filename in its `request_rec` structure).

(Again, under most circumstances, you shouldn't feel obliged to call this function; only 2K of memory or so are allocated for a typical sub request, and it will be freed anyway when the main request pool is cleared. It is only when you are allocating many, many sub-requests for a single main request that you should seriously consider the `ap_destroy_...` functions).

## Configuration, commands and the like

One of the design goals for this server was to maintain external compatibility with the NCSA 1.3 server — that is, to read the same configuration files, to process all the directives therein correctly, and in general to be a drop-in replacement for NCSA. On the other hand, another design goal was to move as much of the server's functionality into modules which have as little as possible to do with the monolithic server core. The only way to reconcile these goals is to move the handling of most commands from the central server into the modules.

However, just giving the modules command tables is not enough to divorce them completely from the server core. The server has to remember the commands in order to act on them later. That involves maintaining data which is private to the modules, and which can be either per-server, or per-directory. Most things are per-directory, including in particular access control and authorization information, but also information on how to determine file types from suffixes, which can be modified by ADDTYPE and FORCETYPE directives, and so forth. In general, the governing philosophy is that anything which *can* be made configurable by directory should be; per-server information is generally used in the standard set of modules for information like ALIASes and REDIRECTs which come into play before the request is tied to a particular place in the underlying file system.

Another requirement for emulating the NCSA server is being able to handle the per-directory configuration files, generally called .htaccess files, though even in the NCSA server they can contain directives which have nothing at all to do with access control. Accordingly, after URI -> filename translation, but before performing any other phase, the server walks down the directory hierarchy of the underlying filesystem, following the translated pathname, to read any .htaccess files which might be present. The information which is read in then has to be *merged* with the applicable information from the server's own config files (either from the <DIRECTORY> sections in access.conf, or from defaults in srm.conf, which actually behaves for most purposes almost exactly like <Directory />).

Finally, after having served a request which involved reading .htaccess files, we need to discard the storage allocated for handling them. That is solved the same way it is solved wherever else similar problems come up, by tying those structures to the per-transaction resource pool.

**Per-directory configuration structures**

Let's look out how all of this plays out in mod_mime.c, which defines the file typing handler which emulates the NCSA server's behavior of determining file types from suffixes. What we'll be looking at, here, is the code which implements the ADDTYPE and ADDENCODING commands. These commands can appear in .htaccess files, so they must be handled in the module's private per-directory data, which in fact, consists of two separate tables for MIME types and encoding information, and is declared as follows:

```
typedef struct {
    table *forced_types;     /* Additional AddTyped stuff */
    table *encoding_types;   /* Added with AddEncoding... */
} mime_dir_config;
```

When the server is reading a configuration file, or <DIRECTORY> section, which includes one of the MIME module's commands, it needs to create a mime_dir_config structure, so those commands have something to act on. It does this by invoking the function it finds in the module's 'create per-dir config slot', with two arguments: the name of the directory to which this configuration information applies (or NULL for srm.conf), and a pointer to a resource pool in which the allocation should happen.

(If we are reading a .htaccess file, that resource pool is the per-request resource pool for the request; otherwise it is a resource pool which is used for configuration data, and cleared on restarts. Either way, it is important for the structure being created to vanish when the pool is cleared, by registering a cleanup on the pool if necessary).

For the MIME module, the per-dir config creation function just ap_pallocs the structure above, and a creates a couple of tables to fill it. That looks like this:

```
void *create_mime_dir_config (pool *p, char *dummy)
{
    mime_dir_config *new =
        (mime_dir_config *) ap_palloc (p, sizeof(mime_dir_config));

    new->forced_types = ap_make_table (p, 4);
    new->encoding_types = ap_make_table (p, 4);

    return new;
}
```

Now, suppose we've just read in a .htaccess file. We already have the per-directory configuration structure for the next directory up in the hierarchy. If the .htaccess file we just read in didn't have any ADDTYPE or ADDENCODING commands, its per-directory config structure for the MIME module is still valid, and we can just use it. Otherwise, we need to merge the two structures somehow.

To do that, the server invokes the module's per-directory config merge function, if one is present. That function takes three arguments: the two structures being merged, and a resource pool in which to allocate the result. For the MIME module, all that needs to be done is overlay the tables from the new per-directory config structure with those from the parent:

```
void *merge_mime_dir_configs (pool *p, void *parent_dirv, void
*subdirv)
{
    mime_dir_config *parent_dir = (mime_dir_config *)parent_dirv;
    mime_dir_config *subdir = (mime_dir_config *)subdirv;
    mime_dir_config *new =
        (mime_dir_config *)ap_palloc (p, sizeof(mime_dir_config));

    new->forced_types = ap_overlay_tables (p, subdir->forced_types,
        parent_dir->forced_types);

    new->encoding_types = ap_overlay_tables (p, subdir->encoding_types,
        parent_dir->encoding_types);

    return new;
}
```

As a note – if there is no per-directory merge function present, the server will just use the subdirectory's configuration info, and ignore the parent's. For some modules, that works just fine (*e.g.*, for the includes module, whose per-directory configuration information consists solely of the state of the XBITHACK), and for those modules, you can just not declare one, and leave the corresponding structure slot in the module itself NULL.

**Command handling**

Now that we have these structures, we need to be able to figure out how to fill them. That involves processing the actual ADDTYPE and ADDENCODING commands. To find commands, the server looks in the module's command table. That table contains information on how many arguments the commands take, and in what formats, where it is permitted, and so forth. That information is sufficient to allow the server to invoke most command-handling functions with pre-parsed arguments. Without further ado, let's look at the ADDTYPE command handler, which looks like this (the ADDENCODING command looks basically the same, and won't be shown here):

```
char *add_type(cmd_parms *cmd, mime_dir_config *m, char *ct, char *ext)
{
    if (*ext == '.')  ++ext;
    ap_table_set (m->forced_types, ext, ct);
    return NULL;
}
```

This command handler is unusually simple. As you can see, it takes four arguments, two of which are pre-parsed arguments, the third being the per-directory configuration structure for the module in question, and the fourth being a pointer to a cmd_parms structure. That structure contains a bunch of arguments which are frequently of use to some, but not all, commands, including a resource pool (from which memory can be allocated, and to which cleanups should be tied), and the (virtual) server being configured, from which the module's per-server configuration data can be obtained if required.

Another way in which this particular command handler is unusually simple is that there are no error conditions which it can encounter. If there were, it could return an error message instead of NULL; this causes an error to be printed out on the server's `stderr`, followed by a quick exit, if it is in the main config files; for a `.htaccess` file, the syntax error is logged in the server error log (along with an indication of where it came from), and the request is bounced with a server error response (HTTP error status, code 500).

The MIME module's command table has entries for these commands, which look like this:

```
command_rec mime_cmds[] = {
    { "AddType", add_type, NULL, OR_FILEINFO, TAKE2,
        "a mime type followed by a file extension" },
    { "AddEncoding", add_encoding, NULL, OR_FILEINFO, TAKE2,
        "an encoding (e.g., gzip), followed by a file extension" },
    { NULL }
};
```

The entries in these tables are:

- The name of the command

- The function which handles it

- a (`void *`) pointer, which is passed in the `cmd_parms` structure to the command handler — this is useful in case many similar commands are handled by the same function.

- A bit mask indicating where the command may appear. There are mask bits corresponding to each `AllowOverride` option, and an additional mask bit, `RSRC_CONF`, indicating that the command may appear in the server's own config files, but *not* in any `.htaccess` file.

- A flag indicating how many arguments the command handler wants pre-parsed, and how they should be passed in. `TAKE2` indicates two pre-parsed arguments. Other options are `TAKE1`, which indicates one pre-parsed argument, `FLAG`, which indicates that the argument should be `On` or `Off`, and is passed in as a boolean flag, `RAW_ARGS`, which causes the server to give the command the raw, unparsed arguments (everything but the command name itself). There is also `ITERATE`, which means that the handler looks the same as `TAKE1`, but that if multiple arguments are present, it should be called multiple times, and finally `ITERATE2`, which indicates that the command handler looks like a `TAKE2`, but if more arguments are present, then it should be called multiple times, holding the first argument constant.

- Finally, we have a string which describes the arguments that should be present. If the arguments in the actual config file are not as required, this string will be used to help give a more specific error message. (You can safely leave this `NULL`).

Finally, having set this all up, we have to use it. This is ultimately done in the module's handlers, specifically for its file-typing handler, which looks more or less like this; note that the per-directory configuration structure is extracted from the `request_rec`'s per-directory configuration vector by using the `ap_get_module_config` function.

```
int find_ct(request_rec *r)
{
    int i;
    char *fn = ap_pstrdup (r->pool, r->filename);
    mime_dir_config *conf = (mime_dir_config *)
        ap_get_module_config(r->per_dir_config, &mime_module);
    char *type;
    if (S_ISDIR(r->finfo.st_mode)) {
        r->content_type = DIR_MAGIC_TYPE;
        return OK;
    }
    if((i=ap_rind(fn,'.'))  < 0) return DECLINED;
    ++i;
    if ((type = ap_table_get (conf->encoding_types, &fn[i])))
    {
        r->content_encoding = type;
        /* go back to previous extension to try to use it as a type */
        fn[i-1] = '\0';
        if((i=ap_rind(fn,'.'))  < 0) return OK;
        ++i;
    }
    if ((type = ap_table_get (conf->forced_types, &fn[i])))
    {
        r->content_type = type;
    }
    return OK;
}
```

**Side notes – per-server configuration, virtual servers, *etc*.**

The basic ideas behind per-server module configuration are basically the same as those for per-directory configuration; there is a creation function and a merge function, the latter being invoked where a virtual server has partially overridden the base server configuration, and a combined structure must be computed. (As with per-directory configuration, the default if no merge function is specified, and a module is configured in some virtual server, is that the base configuration is simply ignored).

The only substantial difference is that when a command needs to configure the per-server private module data, it needs to go to the cmd_parms data to get at it. Here's an example, from the alias module, which also indicates how a syntax error can be returned (note that the per-directory configuration argument to the command handler is declared as a dummy, since the module doesn't actually have per-directory config data):

```
char *add_redirect(cmd_parms *cmd, void *dummy, char *f, char *url)
{
    server_rec *s = cmd->server;
    alias_server_conf *conf = (alias_server_conf *)
        ap_get_module_config(s->module_config,&alias_module);
    alias_entry *new = ap_push_array (conf->redirects);
    if (!ap_is_url (url)) return "Redirect to non-URL";
    new->fake = f; new->real = url;
    return NULL;
}
```

# 11.3 API Changes in Apache HTTP Server 2.4 since 2.2

This document describes changes to the Apache HTTPD API from version 2.2 to 2.4, that may be of interest to module/application developers and core hacks. As of the first GA release of the 2.4 branch API compatibility is preserved for the life of the 2.4 branch. (The VERSIONING[9] description for the 2.4 release provides more information about API compatibility.)

API changes fall into two categories: APIs that are altogether new, and existing APIs that are expanded or changed. The latter are further divided into those where all changes are backwards-compatible (so existing modules can ignore them), and those that might require attention by maintainers. As with the transition from HTTPD 2.0 to 2.2, existing modules and applications will require recompiling and may call for some attention, but most should not require any substantial updating (although some may be able to take advantage of API changes to offer significant improvements).

For the purpose of this document, the API is split according to the public header files. These headers are themselves the reference documentation, and can be used to generate a browsable HTML reference with `make docs`.

## Changed APIs

### ap_expr (NEW!)

Introduces a new API to parse and evaluate boolean and algebraic expressions, including provision for a standard syntax and customised variants.

### ap_listen (changed; backwards-compatible)

Introduces a new API to enable httpd child processes to serve different purposes.

### ap_mpm (changed)

`ap_mpm_run` is replaced by a new `mpm` hook.    Also `ap_graceful_stop_signalled` is lost, and `ap_mpm_register_timed_callback` is new.

### ap_regex (changed)

In addition to the existing regexp wrapper, a new higher-level API `ap_rxplus` is now provided. This provides the capability to compile Perl-style expressions like `s/regexp/replacement/flags` and to execute them against arbitrary strings. Support for regexp backreferences is also added.

### ap_slotmem (NEW!)

Introduces an API for modules to allocate and manage memory slots, most commonly for shared memory.

### ap_socache (NEW!)

API to manage a shared object cache.

### heartbeat (NEW!)

common structures for heartbeat modules

---

[9]http://svn.apache.org/repos/asf/httpd/httpd/branches/2.4.x/VERSIONING

**ap_parse_htaccess (changed)**

The function signature for `ap_parse_htaccess` has been changed. A `apr_table_t` of individual directives allowed for override must now be passed (override remains).

**http_config (changed)**

- Introduces per-module, per-directory loglevels, including macro wrappers.
- New `AP_DECLARE_MODULE` macro to declare all modules.
- New `APLOG_USE_MODULE` macro necessary for per-module loglevels in multi-file modules.
- New API to retain data across module unload/load
- New `check_config` hook
- New `ap_process_fnmatch_configs()` function to process wildcards
- Change `ap_configfile_t`, `ap_cfg_getline()`, `ap_cfg_getc()` to return error codes, and add `ap_pcfg_strerror()` for retrieving an error description.
- Any config directive permitted in ACCESS_CONF context must now correctly handle being called from an .htaccess file via the new ALLOWOVERRIDELIST directive. ap_check_cmd_context() accepts a new flag NOT_IN_HTACCESS to detect this case.

**http_core (changed)**

- REMOVED `ap_default_type`, `ap_requires`, all 2.2 authnz API
- Introduces Optional Functions for logio and authnz
- New function `ap_get_server_name_for_url` to support IPv6 literals.
- New function `ap_register_errorlog_handler` to register error log format string handlers.
- Arguments of `error_log` hook have changed. Declaration has moved to `http_core.h`.
- New function `ap_state_query` to determine if the server is in the initial configuration preflight phase or not. This is both easier to use and more correct than the old method of creating a pool userdata entry in the process pool.
- New function `ap_get_conn_socket` to get the socket descriptor for a connection. This should be used instead of accessing the core connection config directly.

**httpd (changed)**

- Introduce per-directory, per-module loglevel
- New loglevels `APLOG_TRACEn`
- Introduce errorlog ids for requests and connections
- Support for mod_request kept_body
- Support buffering filter data for async requests
- New `CONN_STATE` values
- Function changes: `ap_escape_html` updated; `ap_unescape_all`, `ap_escape_path_segment_buffer`
- Modules that load other modules later than the `EXEC_ON_READ` config reading stage need to call `ap_reserve_module_slots()` or `ap_reserve_module_slots_directive()` in their `pre_config` hook.

- The useragent IP address per request can now be tracked independently of the client IP address of the connection, for support of deployments with load balancers.

### http_log (changed)

- Introduce per-directory, per-module loglevel
- New loglevels `APLOG_TRACEn`
- `ap_log_*error` become macro wrappers (backwards-compatible if `APLOG_MARK` macro is used, except that is no longer possible to use `#ifdef` inside the argument list)
- piped logging revamped
- `module_index` added to error_log hook
- new function: `ap_log_command_line`

### http_request (changed)

- New auth_internal API and auth_provider API
- New `EOR` bucket type
- New function `ap_process_async_request`
- New flags `AP_AUTH_INTERNAL_PER_CONF` and `AP_AUTH_INTERNAL_PER_URI`
- New `access_checker_ex` hook to apply additional access control and/or bypass authentication.
- New functions `ap_hook_check_access_ex`, `ap_hook_check_access`, `ap_hook_check_authn`, `ap_hook_check_authz` which accept `AP_AUTH_INTERNAL_PER_*` flags
- DEPRECATED direct use of `ap_hook_access_checker`, `access_checker_ex`, `ap_hook_check_user_id`, `ap_hook_auth_checker`

When possible, registering all access control hooks (including authentication and authorization hooks) using `AP_AUTH_INTERNAL_PER_CONF` is recommended. If all modules' access control hooks are registered with this flag, then whenever the server handles an internal sub-request that matches the same set of access control configuration directives as the initial request (which is the common case), it can avoid invoking the access control hooks another time.

If your module requires the old behavior and must perform access control checks on every sub-request with a different URI from the initial request, even if that URI matches the same set of access control configuration directives, then use `AP_AUTH_INTERNAL_PER_URI`.

### mod_auth (NEW!)

Introduces the new provider framework for authn and authz

### mod_cache (changed)

Introduces a `commit_entity()` function to the cache provider interface, allowing atomic writes to cache. Add a `cache_status()` hook to report the cache decision. All private structures and functions were removed.

### mod_core (NEW!)

This introduces low-level APIs to send arbitrary headers, and exposes functions to handle HTTP OPTIONS and TRACE.

**mod_cache_disk (changed)**

Changes the disk format of the disk cache to support atomic cache updates without locking. The device/inode pair of the body file is embedded in the header file, allowing confirmation that the header and body belong to one another.

**mod_disk_cache (renamed)**

The mod_disk_cache module has been renamed to mod_cache_disk in order to be consistent with the naming of other modules within the server.

**mod_request (NEW!)**

The API for MOD_REQUEST, to make input data available to multiple application/handler modules where required, and to parse HTML form data.

**mpm_common (changed)**

- REMOVES: `accept`, `lockfile`, `lock_mech`, `set_scoreboard` (locking uses the new ap_mutex API)
- NEW API to drop privileges (delegates this platform-dependent function to modules)
- NEW Hooks: `mpm_query`, `timed_callback`, and `get_name`
- CHANGED interfaces: `monitor` hook, `ap_reclaim_child_processes`, `ap_relieve_child_processes`

**scoreboard (changed)**

`ap_get_scoreboard_worker` is made non-backwards-compatible as an alternative version is introduced. Additional proxy_balancer support. Child status stuff revamped.

**util_cookies (NEW!)**

Introduces a new API for managing HTTP Cookies.

**util_ldap (changed)**

*no description available*

**util_mutex (NEW!)**

A wrapper for APR proc and global mutexes in httpd, providing common configuration for the underlying mechanism and location of lock files.

**util_script (changed)**

NEW: `ap_args_to_table`

**util_time (changed)**

NEW: `ap_recent_ctime_ex`

## Specific information on upgrading modules from 2.2

### Logging

In order to take advantage of per-module loglevel configuration, any source file that calls the `ap_log_*` functions should declare which module it belongs to. If the module's module_struct is called `foo_module`, the following code can be used to remain backward compatible with HTTPD 2.0 and 2.2:

```
#include <http_log.h>
#ifdef APLOG_USE_MODULE
APLOG_USE_MODULE(foo);
#endif
```

Note: This is absolutely required for C++-language modules. It can be skipped for C-language modules, though that breaks module-specific log level support for files without it.

The number of parameters of the `ap_log_*` functions and the definition of `APLOG_MARK` has changed. Normally, the change is completely transparent. However, changes are required if a module uses `APLOG_MARK` as a parameter to its own functions or if a module calls `ap_log_*` without passing `APLOG_MARK`. A module which uses wrappers around `ap_log_*` typically uses both of these constructs.

The easiest way to change code which passes `APLOG_MARK` to its own functions is to define and use a different macro that expands to the parameters required by those functions, as `APLOG_MARK` should only be used when calling `ap_log_*` directly. In this way, the code will remain compatible with HTTPD 2.0 and 2.2.

Code which calls `ap_log_*` without passing `APLOG_MARK` will necessarily differ between 2.4 and earlier releases, as 2.4 requires a new third argument, `APLOG_MODULE_INDEX`.

```
/* code for httpd 2.0/2.2 */
ap_log_perror(file, line, APLOG_ERR, 0, p, "Failed to allocate dynamic
lock structure");
/* code for httpd 2.4 */
ap_log_perror(file, line, APLOG_MODULE_INDEX, APLOG_ERR, 0, p, "Failed
to allocate dynamic lock structure");
```

`ap_log_*error` are now implemented as macros. This means that it is no longer possible to use `#ifdef` inside the argument list of `ap_log_*error`, as this would cause undefined behavior according to C99.

A `server_rec` pointer must be passed to `ap_log_error()` when called after startup. This was always appropriate, but there are even more limitations with a `NULL` `server_rec` in 2.4 than in previous releases. Beginning with 2.3.12, the global variable `ap_server_conf` can always be used as the `server_rec` parameter, as it will be `NULL` only when it is valid to pass `NULL` to `ap_log_error()`. `ap_server_conf` should be used only when a more appropriate `server_rec` is not available.

Consider the following changes to take advantage of the new `APLOG_TRACE1..8` log levels:

- Check current use of `APLOG_DEBUG` and consider if one of the `APLOG_TRACEn` levels is more appropriate.

- If your module currently has a mechanism for configuring the amount of debug logging which is performed, consider eliminating that mechanism and relying on the use of different APLOG_TRACE*n* levels. If expensive trace processing needs to be bypassed depending on the configured log level, use the APLOGtrace*n* and APLOGrtrace*n* macros to first check if tracing is enabled.

Modules sometimes add process id and/or thread id to their log messages. These ids are now logged by default, so it may not be necessary for the module to log them explicitly. (Users may remove them from the error log format, but they can be instructed to add it back if necessary for problem diagnosis.)

**If your module uses these existing APIs...**

**ap_default_type()** This is no longer available; Content-Type must be configured explicitly or added by the application.

**ap_get_server_name()** If the returned server name is used in a URL, use ap_get_server_name_for_url() instead. This new function handles the odd case where the server name is an IPv6 literal address.

**ap_get_server_version()** For logging purposes, where detailed information is appropriate, use ap_get_server_description(). When generating output, where the amount of information should be configurable by ServerTokens, use ap_get_server_banner().

**ap_graceful_stop_signalled()** Replace with a call to ap_mpm_query(AP_MPMQ_MPM_STATE) and checking for state AP_MPMQ_STOPPING.

**ap_max_daemons_limit, ap_my_generation, and ap_threads_per_child** Use ap_mpm_query() query codes AP_MPMQ_MAX_DAEMON_USED, AP_MPMQ_GENERATION, and AP_MPMQ_MAX_THREADS, respectively.

**ap_mpm_query()** Ensure that it is not used until after the register-hooks hook has completed. Otherwise, an MPM built as a DSO would not have had a chance to enable support for this function.

**ap_requires()** The core server now provides better infrastructure for handling REQUIRE configuration. Register an auth provider function for each supported entity using ap_register_auth_provider(). The function will be called as necessary during REQUIRE processing. (Consult bundled modules for detailed examples.)

**ap_server_conf->process->pool userdata** Optional:

  - If your module uses this to determine which pass of the startup hooks is being run, use ap_state_query(AP_SQ_MAIN_STATE).
  - If your module uses this to maintain data across the unloading and reloading of your module, use ap_retained_data_create() and ap_retained_data_get().

**apr_global_mutex_create(), apr_proc_mutex_create()** Optional: See ap_mutex_register(), ap_global_mutex_create(), and ap_proc_mutex_create(); these allow your mutexes to be configurable with the MUTEX directive; you can also remove any configuration mechanisms in your module for such mutexes

**CORE_PRIVATE** This is now unnecessary and ignored.

**dav_new_error() and dav_new_error_tag()** Previously, these assumed that errno contained information describing the failure. Now, an apr_status_t parameter must be provided. Pass 0/APR_SUCCESS if there is no such error information, or a valid apr_status_t value otherwise.

**mpm_default.h, DEFAULT_LOCKFILE, DEFAULT_THREAD_LIMIT, DEFAULT_PIDLOG, etc.** The header file and most of the default configuration values set in it are no longer visible to modules. (Most can still be overridden at build time.) DEFAULT_PIDLOG and DEFAULT_REL_RUNTIMEDIR are now universally available via ap_config.h.

`unixd_config` This has been renamed to ap_unixd_config.

`conn_rec->remote_ip and conn_rec->remote_addr` These fields have been renamed in order to distinguish between the client IP address of the connection and the useragent IP address of the request (potentially overridden by a load balancer or proxy). References to either of these fields must be updated with one of the following options, as appropriate for the module:

- When you require the IP address of the user agent, which might be connected directly to the server, or might optionally be separated from the server by a transparent load balancer or proxy, use `request_rec->useragent_ip` and `request_rec->useragent_addr`.
- When you require the IP address of the client that is connected directly to the server, which might be the useragent or might be the load balancer or proxy itself, use `conn_rec->client_ip` and `conn_rec->client_addr`.

**If your module interfaces with this feature...**

**suEXEC** Optional: If your module logs an error when `ap_unixd_config.suexec_enabled` is 0, also log the value of the new field `suexec_disabled_reason`, which contains an explanation of why it is not available.

**Extended status data in the scoreboard** In previous releases, `ExtendedStatus` had to be set to `On`, which in turn required that mod_status was loaded. In 2.4, just set `ap_extended_status` to 1 in a pre-config hook and the extended status data will be available.

**Does your module...**

**Parse query args** Consider if `ap_args_to_table()` would be helpful.

**Parse form data...** Use `ap_parse_form_data()`.

**Check for request header fields** `Content-Length` **and** `Transfer-Encoding` **to see if a body was specified** Use `ap_request_has_body()`.

**Implement cleanups which clear pointer variables** Use `ap_pool_cleanup_set_null()`.

**Create run-time files such as shared memory files, pid files, etc.** Use `ap_runtime_dir_relative()` so that the global configuration for the location of such files, either by the DEFAULT_REL_RUNTIMEDIR compile setting or the DEFAULTRUNTIMEDIR directive, will be respected. *Apache httpd 2.4.2 and above.*

## 11.4 Developing modules for the Apache HTTP Server 2.4

This document explains how you can develop modules for the Apache HTTP Server 2.4

**See also**

- Request Processing in Apache 2.4 (p. 1078)

- Apache 2.x Hook Functions (p. 1071)

### Introduction

#### What we will be discussing in this document

This document will discuss how you can create modules for the Apache HTTP Server 2.4, by exploring an example module called `mod_example`. In the first part of this document, the purpose of this module will be to calculate and print out various digest values for existing files on your web server, whenever we access the URL `http://hostname/filename.sum`. For instance, if we want to know the MD5 digest value of the file located at `http://www.example.com/index.html`, we would visit `http://www.example.com/index.html.sum`.

In the second part of this document, which deals with configuration directive and context awareness, we will be looking at a module that simply writes out its own configuration to the client.

#### Prerequisites

First and foremost, you are expected to have a basic knowledge of how the C programming language works. In most cases, we will try to be as pedagogical as possible and link to documents describing the functions used in the examples, but there are also many cases where it is necessary to either just assume that "it works" or do some digging yourself into what the hows and whys of various function calls.

Lastly, you will need to have a basic understanding of how modules are loaded and configured in the Apache HTTP Server, as well as how to get the headers for Apache if you do not have them already, as these are needed for compiling new modules.

#### Compiling your module

To compile the source code we are building in this document, we will be using APXS (p. 303) . Assuming your source file is called mod_example.c, compiling, installing and activating the module is as simple as:

```
apxs -i -a -c mod_example.c
```

## Defining a module

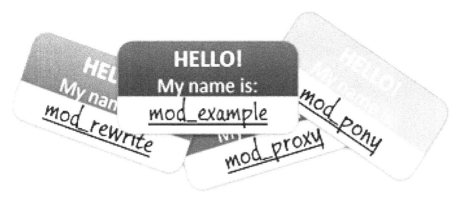

Every module starts with the same declaration, or name tag if you will, that defines a module as *a separate entity within Apache*:

```
module AP_MODULE_DECLARE_DATA    example_module =
{
    STANDARD20_MODULE_STUFF,
    create_dir_conf, /* Per-directory configuration handler */
    merge_dir_conf,  /* Merge handler for per-directory configurations */
    create_svr_conf, /* Per-server configuration handler */
    merge_svr_conf,  /* Merge handler for per-server configurations */
    directives,      /* Any directives we may have for httpd */
    register_hooks   /* Our hook registering function */
};
```

This bit of code lets the server know that we have now registered a new module in the system, and that its name is example_module. The name of the module is used primarily for two things:

- Letting the server know how to load the module using the LoadModule
- Setting up a namespace for the module to use in configurations

For now, we're only concerned with the first purpose of the module name, which comes into play when we need to load the module:

```
LoadModule example_module "modules/mod_example.so"
```

In essence, this tells the server to open up mod_example.so and look for a module called example_module.

Within this name tag of ours is also a bunch of references to how we would like to handle things: Which directives do we respond to in a configuration file or .htaccess, how do we operate within specific contexts, and what handlers are we interested in registering with the Apache HTTP service. We'll return to all these elements later in this document.

## Getting started: Hooking into the server

### An introduction to hooks

When handling requests in Apache HTTP Server 2.4, the first thing you will need to do is create a hook into the request handling process. A hook is essentially a message telling the server that you are willing to either serve or at least take a glance at certain requests given by clients. All handlers, whether it's mod_rewrite, mod_authn_*, mod_proxy and so on, are hooked into specific parts of the request process. As you are probably aware, modules serve different purposes; Some are authentication/authorization handlers, others are file or script handlers while some third modules rewrite URIs or proxies content. Furthermore, in the end, it is up to the user of the server how and when each module will come into place. Thus, the server itself does not presume to know which module is responsible for handling a specific request, and will ask each module whether they have an interest in a given request or not. It is then up to each module to either gently decline serving a request, accept serving it or flat out deny the request from being served, as authentication/authorization modules do:

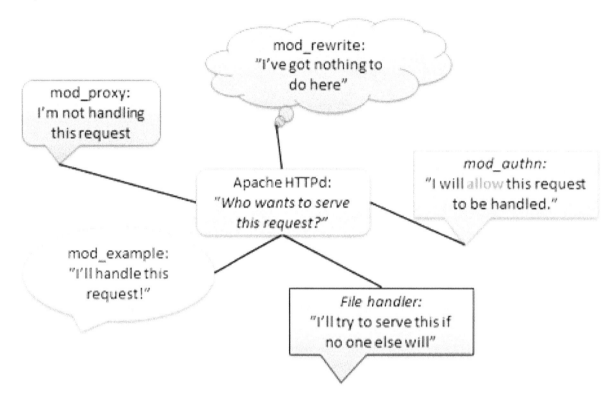

To make it a bit easier for handlers such as our mod_example to know whether the client is requesting content we should handle or not, the server has directives for hinting to modules whether their assistance is needed or not. Two of these are ADDHANDLER and SETHANDLER. Let's take a look at an example using ADDHANDLER. In our example case, we want every request ending with .sum to be served by mod_example, so we'll add a configuration directive that tells the server to do just that:

```
AddHandler example-handler ".sum"
```

What this tells the server is the following: *Whenever we receive a request for a URI ending in .sum, we are to let all modules know that we are looking for whoever goes by the name of "example-handler"* . Thus, when a request is being served that ends in .sum, the server will let all modules know, that this request should be served by "example-handler". As you will see later, when we start building mod_example, we will check for this handler tag relayed by AddHandler and reply to the server based on the value of this tag.

**Hooking into httpd**

To begin with, we only want to create a simple handler, that replies to the client browser when a specific URL is requested, so we won't bother setting up configuration handlers and directives just yet. Our initial module definition will look like this:

```
module AP_MODULE_DECLARE_DATA    example_module =
```

```
{
    STANDARD20_MODULE_STUFF,
    NULL,
    NULL,
    NULL,
    NULL,
    NULL,
    register_hooks    /* Our hook registering function */
};
```

This lets the server know that we are not interested in anything fancy, we just want to hook onto the requests and possibly handle some of them.

The reference in our example declaration, `register_hooks` is the name of a function we will create to manage how we hook onto the request process. In this example module, the function has just one purpose; To create a simple hook that gets called after all the rewrites, access control etc has been handled. Thus, we will let the server know, that we want to hook into its process as one of the last modules:

```
static void register_hooks(apr_pool_t *pool)
{
    /* Create a hook in the request handler, so we get called when a request arrives
    ap_hook_handler(example_handler, NULL, NULL, APR_HOOK_LAST);
}
```

The `example_handler` reference is the function that will handle the request. We will discuss how to create a handler in the next chapter.

### Other useful hooks

Hooking into the request handling phase is but one of many hooks that you can create. Some other ways of hooking are:

- `ap_hook_child_init`: Place a hook that executes when a child process is spawned (commonly used for initializing modules after the server has forked)
- `ap_hook_pre_config`: Place a hook that executes before any configuration data has been read (very early hook)
- `ap_hook_post_config`: Place a hook that executes after configuration has been parsed, but before the server has forked
- `ap_hook_translate_name`: Place a hook that executes when a URI needs to be translated into a filename on the server (think `mod_rewrite`)
- `ap_hook_quick_handler`: Similar to `ap_hook_handler`, except it is run before any other request hooks (translation, auth, fixups etc)
- `ap_hook_log_transaction`: Place a hook that executes when the server is about to add a log entry of the current request

### Building a handler

A handler is essentially a function that receives a callback when a request to the server is made. It is passed a record of the current request (how it was made, which headers and requests were passed along, who's giving the request and so on), and is put in charge of either telling the server that it's not interested in the request or handle the request with the tools provided.

**A simple "Hello, world!" handler**

Let's start off by making a very simple request handler that does the following:

1. Check that this is a request that should be served by "example-handler"

2. Set the content type of our output to text/html

3. Write "Hello, world!" back to the client browser

4. Let the server know that we took care of this request and everything went fine

In C code, our example handler will now look like this:

```
static int example_handler(request_rec *r)
{
    /* First off, we need to check if this is a call for the "example-handler" handler.
     * If it is, we accept it and do our things, if not, we simply return DECLINED,
     * and the server will try somewhere else.
     */
    if (!r->handler || strcmp(r->handler, "example-handler")) return (DECLINED);

    /* Now that we are handling this request, we'll write out "Hello, world!" to the client
     * To do so, we must first set the appropriate content type, followed by our output.
     */
    ap_set_content_type(r, "text/html");
    ap_rprintf(r, "Hello, world!");

    /* Lastly, we must tell the server that we took care of this request and everything wer
     * We do so by simply returning the value OK to the server.
     */
    return OK;
}
```

Now, we put all we have learned together and end up with a program that looks like mod_example_1.c[10] . The functions used in this example will be explained later in the section "Some useful functions you should know".

**The request_rec structure**

The most essential part of any request is the *request record* . In a call to a handler function, this is represented by the request_rec* structure passed along with every call that is made. This struct, typically just referred to as r in modules, contains all the information you need for your module to fully process any HTTP request and respond accordingly.

Some key elements of the request_rec structure are:

- r->handler (char*) : Contains the name of the handler the server is currently asking to do the handling of this request

- r->method (char*) : Contains the HTTP method being used, f.x. GET or POST

- r->filename (char*) : Contains the translated filename the client is requesting

- r->args (char*) : Contains the query string of the request, if any

---

[10]http://people.apache.org/~humbedooh/mods/examples/mod_example_1.c

- `r->headers_in (apr_table_t*)`: Contains all the headers sent by the client
- `r->connection (conn_rec*)`: A record containing information about the current connection
- `r->user (char*)`: If the URI requires authentication, this is set to the username provided
- `r->useragent_ip (char*)`: The IP address of the client connecting to us
- `r->pool (apr_pool_t*)`: The memory pool of this request. We'll discuss this in the "Memory management" chapter.

A complete list of all the values contained within the `request_rec` structure can be found in the `httpd.h`[11] header file or at http://ci.apache.org/projects/httpd/trunk/doxygen/structrequest_rec.html.

Let's try out some of these variables in another example handler:

```
static int example_handler(request_rec *r)
{
    /* Set the appropriate content type */
    ap_set_content_type(r, "text/html");

    /* Print out the IP address of the client connecting to us: */
    ap_rprintf(r, "<h2>Hello, %s!</h2>", r->useragent_ip);

    /* If we were reached through a GET or a POST request, be happy, else sad. */
    if ( !strcmp(r->method, "POST") || !strcmp(r->method, "GET") ) {
        ap_rputs("You used a GET or a POST method, that makes us happy!<br/>", r);
    }
    else {
        ap_rputs("You did not use POST or GET, that makes us sad :(<br/>", r);
    }

    /* Lastly, if there was a query string, let's print that too! */
    if (r->args) {
        ap_rprintf(r, "Your query string was: %s", r->args);
    }
    return OK;
}
```

**Return values**

Apache relies on return values from handlers to signify whether a request was handled or not, and if so, whether the request went well or not. If a module is not interested in handling a specific request, it should always return the value `DECLINED`. If it is handling a request, it should either return the generic value `OK`, or a specific HTTP status code, for example:

```
static int example_handler(request_rec *r)
{
    /* Return 404: Not found */
    return HTTP_NOT_FOUND;
}
```

Returning `OK` or a HTTP status code does not necessarily mean that the request will end. The server may still have other handlers that are interested in this request, for instance the logging modules which, upon a successful request,

---

[11]http://svn.apache.org/repos/asf/httpd/httpd/trunk/include/httpd.h

will write down a summary of what was requested and how it went. To do a full stop and prevent any further processing after your module is done, you can return the value DONE to let the server know that it should cease all activity on this request and carry on with the next, without informing other handlers.

**General response codes:**

- DECLINED: We are not handling this request

- OK: We handled this request and it went well

- DONE: We handled this request and the server should just close this thread without further processing

**HTTP specific return codes (excerpt):**

- HTTP_OK (200): Request was okay

- HTTP_MOVED_PERMANENTLY (301): The resource has moved to a new URL

- HTTP_UNAUTHORIZED (401): Client is not authorized to visit this page

- HTTP_FORBIDDEN (403): Permission denied

- HTTP_NOT_FOUND (404): File not found

- HTTP_INTERNAL_SERVER_ERROR (500): Internal server error (self explanatory)

**Some useful functions you should know**

- ap_rputs(const char *string, request_rec *r):
  Sends a string of text to the client. This is a shorthand version of ap_rwrite[12].

  ```
  ap_rputs("Hello, world!", r);
  ```

- ap_rprintf[13]:
  This function works just like printf, except it sends the result to the client.

  ```
  ap_rprintf(r, "Hello, %s!", r->useragent_ip);
  ```

- ap_set_content_type[14](request_rec *r, const char *type):
  Sets the content type of the output you are sending.

  ```
  ap_set_content_type(r, "text/plain"); /* force a raw text output */
  ```

**Memory management**

Managing your resources in Apache HTTP Server 2.4 is quite easy, thanks to the memory pool system. In essence, each server, connection and request have their own memory pool that gets cleaned up when its scope ends, e.g. when a request is done or when a server process shuts down. All your module needs to do is latch onto this memory pool, and you won't have to worry about having to clean up after yourself - pretty neat, huh?

In our module, we will primarily be allocating memory for each request, so it's appropriate to use the r->pool reference when creating new objects. A few of the functions for allocating memory within a pool are:

---

[12]http://ci.apache.org/projects/httpd/trunk/doxygen/group__APACHE__CORE__PROTO.html#gac827cd0537d2b6213a7c06d7c26cc36e

[13]http://ci.apache.org/projects/httpd/trunk/doxygen/group__APACHE__CORE__PROTO.html#ga5e91eb6ca777c9a427b2e82bf1eeb81d

[14]http://ci.apache.org/projects/httpd/trunk/doxygen/group__APACHE__CORE__PROTO.html#gaa2f8412c400197338ec509f4a45e4579

- `void* apr_palloc`[15]`( apr_pool_t *p, apr_size_t size)`: Allocates `size` number of bytes in the pool for you

- `void* apr_pcalloc`[16]`( apr_pool_t *p, apr_size_t size)`: Allocates `size` number of bytes in the pool for you and sets all bytes to 0

- `char* apr_pstrdup`[17]`( apr_pool_t *p, const char *s)`: Creates a duplicate of the string `s`. This is useful for copying constant values so you can edit them

- `char* apr_psprintf`[18]`( apr_pool_t *p, const char *fmt, ...)`: Similar to `sprintf`, except the server supplies you with an appropriately allocated target variable

Let's put these functions into an example handler:

```
static int example_handler(request_rec *r)
{
    const char *original = "You can't edit this!";
    char *copy;
    int *integers;

    /* Allocate space for 10 integer values and set them all to zero. */
    integers = apr_pcalloc(r->pool, sizeof(int)*10);

    /* Create a copy of the 'original' variable that we can edit. */
    copy = apr_pstrdup(r->pool, original);
    return OK;
}
```

This is all well and good for our module, which won't need any pre-initialized variables or structures. However, if we wanted to initialize something early on, before the requests come rolling in, we could simply add a call to a function in our `register_hooks` function to sort it out:

```
static void register_hooks(apr_pool_t *pool)
{
    /* Call a function that initializes some stuff */
    example_init_function(pool);
    /* Create a hook in the request handler, so we get called when a request arrives
    ap_hook_handler(example_handler, NULL, NULL, APR_HOOK_LAST);
}
```

In this pre-request initialization function we would not be using the same pool as we did when allocating resources for request-based functions. Instead, we would use the pool given to us by the server for allocating memory on a per-process based level.

**Parsing request data**

In our example module, we would like to add a feature, that checks which type of digest, MD5 or SHA1 the client would like to see. This could be solved by adding a query string to the request. A query string is typically comprised of several keys and values put together in a string, for instance `valueA=yes&valueB=no&valueC=maybe`. It is

---

[15] http://apr.apache.org/docs/apr/1.4/group__apr__pools.html#ga85f1e193c31d109affda72f9a92c6915

[16] http://apr.apache.org/docs/apr/1.4/group__apr__pools.html#gaf61c098ad258069d64cdf8c0a9369f9e

[17] http://apr.apache.org/docs/apr/1.4/group__apr__strings.html#gabc79e99ff19abbd7cfd18308c5f85d47

[18] http://apr.apache.org/docs/apr/1.4/group__apr__strings.html#ga3eca76b8d293c5c3f8021e45eda813d8

up to the module itself to parse these and get the data it requires.  In our example, we'll be looking for a key called digest, and if set to md5, we'll produce an MD5 digest, otherwise we'll produce a SHA1 digest.

Since the introduction of Apache HTTP Server 2.4, parsing request data from GET and POST requests have never been easier.  All we require to parse both GET and POST data is four simple lines:

```
apr_table_t *GET;
apr_array_header_t*POST;



ap_args_to_table(r, &GET);

ap_parse_form_data(r, NULL, &POST, -1, 8192);
```

In our specific example module, we're looking for the digest value from the query string, which now resides inside a table called GET.  To extract this value, we need only perform a simple operation:

```
/* Get the "digest" key from the query string, if any. */
const char *digestType = apr_table_get(GET, "digest");

/* If no key was returned, we will set a default value instead. */
if (!digestType) digestType = "sha1";
```

The structures used for the POST and GET data are not exactly the same, so if we were to fetch a value from POST data instead of the query string, we would have to resort to a few more lines, as outlined in this example in the last chapter of this document.

**Making an advanced handler**

Now that we have learned how to parse form data and manage our resources, we can move on to creating an advanced version of our module, that spits out the MD5 or SHA1 digest of files:

```
static int example_handler(request_rec *r)
{
    int rc, exists;
    apr_finfo_t finfo;
    apr_file_t *file;
    char *filename;
    char buffer[256];
    apr_size_t readBytes;
    int n;
    apr_table_t *GET;
    apr_array_header_t *POST;
    const char *digestType;


    /* Check that the "example-handler" handler is being called. */
    if (!r->handler || strcmp(r->handler, "example-handler")) return (DECLINED);

    /* Figure out which file is being requested by removing the .sum from it */
    filename = apr_pstrdup(r->pool, r->filename);
```

```
filename[strlen(filename)-4] = 0; /* Cut off the last 4 characters. */

/* Figure out if the file we request a sum on exists and isn't a directory */
rc = apr_stat(&finfo, filename, APR_FINFO_MIN, r->pool);
if (rc == APR_SUCCESS) {
    exists =
    (
        (finfo.filetype != APR_NOFILE)
    &&  !(finfo.filetype & APR_DIR)
    );
    if (!exists) return HTTP_NOT_FOUND; /* Return a 404 if not found. */
}
/* If apr_stat failed, we're probably not allowed to check this file. */
else return HTTP_FORBIDDEN;

/* Parse the GET and, optionally, the POST data sent to us */

ap_args_to_table(r, &GET);
ap_parse_form_data(r, NULL, &POST, -1, 8192);

/* Set the appropriate content type */
ap_set_content_type(r, "text/html");

/* Print a title and some general information */
ap_rprintf(r, "<h2>Information on %s:</h2>", filename);
ap_rprintf(r, "<b>Size:</b> %u bytes<br/>", finfo.size);

/* Get the digest type the client wants to see */
digestType = apr_table_get(GET, "digest");
if (!digestType) digestType = "MD5";


rc = apr_file_open(&file, filename, APR_READ, APR_OS_DEFAULT, r->pool);
if (rc == APR_SUCCESS) {

    /* Are we trying to calculate the MD5 or the SHA1 digest? */
    if (!strcasecmp(digestType, "md5")) {
        /* Calculate the MD5 sum of the file */
        union {
            char      chr[16];
            uint32_t  num[4];
        } digest;
        apr_md5_ctx_t md5;
        apr_md5_init(&md5);
        readBytes = 256;
        while ( apr_file_read(file, buffer, &readBytes) == APR_SUCCESS ) {
            apr_md5_update(&md5, buffer, readBytes);
        }
        apr_md5_final(digest.chr, &md5);

        /* Print out the MD5 digest */
        ap_rputs("<b>MD5: </b><code>", r);
        for (n = 0; n < APR_MD5_DIGESTSIZE/4; n++) {
```

```
            ap_rprintf(r, "%08x", digest.num[n]);
        }
        ap_rputs("</code>", r);
        /* Print a link to the SHA1 version */
        ap_rputs("<br/><a href='?digest=sha1'>View the SHA1 hash instead</a>", r);
    }
    else {
        /* Calculate the SHA1 sum of the file */
        union {
            char      chr[20];
            uint32_t  num[5];
        } digest;
        apr_sha1_ctx_t sha1;
        apr_sha1_init(&sha1);
        readBytes = 256;
        while ( apr_file_read(file, buffer, &readBytes) == APR_SUCCESS ) {
            apr_sha1_update(&sha1, buffer, readBytes);
        }
        apr_sha1_final(digest.chr, &sha1);

        /* Print out the SHA1 digest */
        ap_rputs("<b>SHA1: </b><code>", r);
        for (n = 0; n < APR_SHA1_DIGESTSIZE/4; n++) {
            ap_rprintf(r, "%08x", digest.num[n]);
        }
        ap_rputs("</code>", r);

        /* Print a link to the MD5 version */
        ap_rputs("<br/><a href='?digest=md5'>View the MD5 hash instead</a>", r);
    }
    apr_file_close(file);

    }
    /* Let the server know that we responded to this request. */
    return OK;
}
```

This version in its entirety can be found here: mod_example_2.c[19].


## Adding configuration options

In this next segment of this document, we will turn our eyes away from the digest module and create a new example
module, whose only function is to write out its own configuration. The purpose of this is to examine how the server
works with configuration, and what happens when you start writing advanced configurations for your modules.


### An introduction to configuration directives

If you are reading this, then you probably already know what a configuration directive is. Simply put, a directive
is a way of telling an individual module (or a set of modules) how to behave, such as these directives control how
mod_rewrite works:

---

[19]http://people.apache.org/~humbedooh/mods/examples/mod_example_2.c

```
RewriteEngine On
RewriteCond "%{REQUEST_URI}"  "^/foo/bar"
RewriteRule "^/foo/bar/(.*)$" "/foobar?page=$1"
```

Each of these configuration directives are handled by a separate function, that parses the parameters given and sets up a configuration accordingly.

### Making an example configuration

To begin with, we'll create a basic configuration in C-space:

```
typedef struct {
    int         enabled;      /* Enable or disable our module */
    const char *path;         /* Some path to...something */
    int         typeOfAction; /* 1 means action A, 2 means action B and so on */
} example_config;
```

Now, let's put this into perspective by creating a very small module that just prints out a hard-coded configuration. You'll notice that we use the `register_hooks` function for initializing the configuration values to their defaults:

```
typedef struct {
    int         enabled;      /* Enable or disable our module */
    const char *path;         /* Some path to...something */
    int         typeOfAction; /* 1 means action A, 2 means action B and so on */
} example_config;

static example_config config;

static int example_handler(request_rec *r)
{
    if (!r->handler || strcmp(r->handler, "example-handler")) return(DECLINED);
    ap_set_content_type(r, "text/plain");
    ap_rprintf(r, "Enabled: %u\n", config.enabled);
    ap_rprintf(r, "Path: %s\n", config.path);
    ap_rprintf(r, "TypeOfAction: %x\n", config.typeOfAction);
    return OK;
}

static void register_hooks(apr_pool_t *pool)
{
    config.enabled = 1;
    config.path = "/foo/bar";
    config.typeOfAction = 0x00;
    ap_hook_handler(example_handler, NULL, NULL, APR_HOOK_LAST);
}

/* Define our module as an entity and assign a function for registering hooks  */

module AP_MODULE_DECLARE_DATA   example_module =
{
    STANDARD20_MODULE_STUFF,
    NULL,               /* Per-directory configuration handler */
```

```
    NULL,              /* Merge handler for per-directory configurations */
    NULL,              /* Per-server configuration handler */
    NULL,              /* Merge handler for per-server configurations */
    NULL,              /* Any directives we may have for httpd */
    register_hooks     /* Our hook registering function */
};
```

So far so good. To access our new handler, we could add the following to our configuration:

```
<Location "/example">
    SetHandler example-handler
</Location>
```

When we visit, we'll see our current configuration being spit out by our module.

### Registering directives with the server

What if we want to change our configuration, not by hard-coding new values into the module, but by using either the
httpd.conf file or possibly a .htaccess file? It's time to let the server know that we want this to be possible. To do so,
we must first change our *name tag* to include a reference to the configuration directives we want to register with the
server:

```
module AP_MODULE_DECLARE_DATA   example_module =
{
    STANDARD20_MODULE_STUFF,
    NULL,                 /* Per-directory configuration handler */
    NULL,                 /* Merge handler for per-directory configurations */
    NULL,                 /* Per-server configuration handler */
    NULL,                 /* Merge handler for per-server configurations */
    example_directives, /* Any directives we may have for httpd */
    register_hooks        /* Our hook registering function */
};
```

This will tell the server that we are now accepting directives from the configuration files, and that the structure called
example_directives   holds information on what our directives are and how they work. Since we have three
different variables in our module configuration, we will add a structure with three directives and a NULL at the end:

```
static const command_rec        example_directives[] =
{
    AP_INIT_TAKE1("exampleEnabled", example_set_enabled, NULL, RSRC_CONF, "Enable or disab
    AP_INIT_TAKE1("examplePath", example_set_path, NULL, RSRC_CONF, "The path to whatever"
    AP_INIT_TAKE2("exampleAction", example_set_action, NULL, RSRC_CONF, "Special action va
    { NULL }
};
```

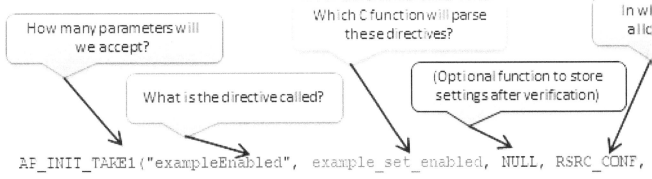

```
AP_INIT_TAKE1("exampleEnabled", example_set_enabled, NULL, RSRC_CONF,
```

As you can see, each directive needs at least 5 parameters set:

1. AP_INIT_TAKE1[20]: This is a macro that tells the server that this directive takes one and only one argument. If we required two arguments, we could use the macro AP_INIT_TAKE2[21] and so on (refer to httpd_conf.h for more macros).

2. exampleEnabled: This is the name of our directive. More precisely, it is what the user must put in his/her configuration in order to invoke a configuration change in our module.

3. example_set_enabled: This is a reference to a C function that parses the directive and sets the configuration accordingly. We will discuss how to make this in the following paragraph.

4. RSRC_CONF: This tells the server where the directive is permitted. We'll go into details on this value in the later chapters, but for now, RSRC_CONF means that the server will only accept these directives in a server context.

5. "Enable or disable....": This is simply a brief description of what the directive does.

*(The "missing" parameter in our definition, which is usually set to NULL, is an optional function that can be run after the initial function to parse the arguments have been run. This is usually omitted, as the function for verifying arguments might as well be used to set them.)*

**The directive handler function**

Now that we have told the server to expect some directives for our module, it's time to make a few functions for handling these. What the server reads in the configuration file(s) is text, and so naturally, what it passes along to our directive handler is one or more strings, that we ourselves need to recognize and act upon. You'll notice, that since we set our exampleAction directive to accept two arguments, its C function also has an additional parameter defined:

```
/* Handler for the "exampleEnabled" directive */
const char *example_set_enabled(cmd_parms *cmd, void *cfg, const char *arg)
{
    if(!strcasecmp(arg, "on")) config.enabled = 1;
    else config.enabled = 0;
    return NULL;
}

/* Handler for the "examplePath" directive */
const char *example_set_path(cmd_parms *cmd, void *cfg, const char *arg)
{
```

---

[20]http://ci.apache.org/projects/httpd/trunk/doxygen/group__APACHE__CORE__CONFIG.html#ga07c7d22ae17805e61204463326cf9c34
[21]http://ci.apache.org/projects/httpd/trunk/doxygen/group__APACHE__CORE__CONFIG.html#gafaec43534fcf200f37d9fecbf9247c21

```
    config.path = arg;
    return NULL;
}


/* Handler for the "exampleAction" directive */
/* Let's pretend this one takes one argument (file or db), and a second (deny or allow), */
/* and we store it in a bit-wise manner. */
const char *example_set_action(cmd_parms *cmd, void *cfg, const char *arg1, const char *arg
{
    if(!strcasecmp(arg1, "file")) config.typeOfAction = 0x01;
    else config.typeOfAction = 0x02;

    if(!strcasecmp(arg2, "deny")) config.typeOfAction += 0x10;
    else config.typeOfAction += 0x20;
    return NULL;
}
```

**Putting it all together**

Now that we have our directives set up, and handlers configured for them, we can assemble our module into one big file:

```
/* mod_example_config_simple.c: */
#include <stdio.h>
#include "apr_hash.h"
#include "ap_config.h"
#include "ap_provider.h"
#include "httpd.h"
#include "http_core.h"
#include "http_config.h"
#include "http_log.h"
#include "http_protocol.h"
#include "http_request.h"

/*
 ==========================================================================
 Our configuration prototype and declaration:
 ==========================================================================
 */
typedef struct {
    int         enabled;      /* Enable or disable our module */
    const char *path;         /* Some path to...something */
    int         typeOfAction; /* 1 means action A, 2 means action B and so on */
} example_config;

static example_config config;

/*
 ==========================================================================
 Our directive handlers:
 ==========================================================================
 */
/* Handler for the "exampleEnabled" directive */
```

```
const char *example_set_enabled(cmd_parms *cmd, void *cfg, const char *arg)
{
    if(!strcasecmp(arg, "on")) config.enabled = 1;
    else config.enabled = 0;
    return NULL;
}

/* Handler for the "examplePath" directive */
const char *example_set_path(cmd_parms *cmd, void *cfg, const char *arg)
{
    config.path = arg;
    return NULL;
}

/* Handler for the "exampleAction" directive */
/* Let's pretend this one takes one argument (file or db), and a second (deny or allo
/* and we store it in a bit-wise manner. */
const char *example_set_action(cmd_parms *cmd, void *cfg, const char *arg1, const cha
{
    if(!strcasecmp(arg1, "file")) config.typeOfAction = 0x01;
    else config.typeOfAction = 0x02;

    if(!strcasecmp(arg2, "deny")) config.typeOfAction += 0x10;
    else config.typeOfAction += 0x20;
    return NULL;
}

/*
 ==============================================================================
 The directive structure for our name tag:
 ==============================================================================
 */
static const command_rec       example_directives[] =
{
    AP_INIT_TAKE1("exampleEnabled", example_set_enabled, NULL, RSRC_CONF, "Enable or
    AP_INIT_TAKE1("examplePath", example_set_path, NULL, RSRC_CONF, "The path to what
    AP_INIT_TAKE2("exampleAction", example_set_action, NULL, RSRC_CONF, "Special act:
    { NULL }
};
/*
 ==============================================================================
 Our module handler:
 ==============================================================================
 */
static int example_handler(request_rec *r)
{
    if(!r->handler || strcmp(r->handler, "example-handler")) return(DECLINED);
    ap_set_content_type(r, "text/plain");
    ap_rprintf(r, "Enabled: %u\n", config.enabled);
    ap_rprintf(r, "Path: %s\n", config.path);
    ap_rprintf(r, "TypeOfAction: %x\n", config.typeOfAction);
    return OK;
}
```

```
/*
  ======================================================================
  The hook registration function (also initializes the default config values):
  ======================================================================
 */
static void register_hooks(apr_pool_t *pool)
{
    config.enabled = 1;
    config.path = "/foo/bar";
    config.typeOfAction = 3;
    ap_hook_handler(example_handler, NULL, NULL, APR_HOOK_LAST);
}
/*
  ======================================================================
  Our module name tag:
  ======================================================================
 */
module AP_MODULE_DECLARE_DATA   example_module =
{
    STANDARD20_MODULE_STUFF,
    NULL,                 /* Per-directory configuration handler */
    NULL,                 /* Merge handler for per-directory configurations */
    NULL,                 /* Per-server configuration handler */
    NULL,                 /* Merge handler for per-server configurations */
    example_directives, /* Any directives we may have for httpd */
    register_hooks      /* Our hook registering function */
};
```

In our httpd.conf file, we can now change the hard-coded configuration by adding a few lines:

```
ExampleEnabled On
ExamplePath "/usr/bin/foo"
ExampleAction file allow
```

And thus we apply the configuration, visit /example on our web site, and we see the configuration has adapted to what we wrote in our configuration file.


## Context aware configurations

### Introduction to context aware configurations

In Apache HTTP Server 2.4, different URLs, virtual hosts, directories etc can have very different meanings to the user of the server, and thus different contexts within which modules must operate. For example, let's assume you have this configuration set up for mod_rewrite:

```
<Directory "/var/www">
    RewriteCond "%{HTTP_HOST}" "^example.com$"
    RewriteRule "(.*)"         "http://www.example.com/$1"
</Directory>
<Directory "/var/www/sub">
    RewriteRule "^foobar$" "index.php?foobar=true"
</Directory>
```

In this example, you will have set up two different contexts for mod_rewrite:

1. Inside `/var/www`, all requests for `http://example.com` must go to `http://www.example.com`

2. Inside `/var/www/sub`, all requests for `foobar` must go to `index.php?foobar=true`

If mod_rewrite (or the entire server for that matter) wasn't context aware, then these rewrite rules would just apply to every and any request made, regardless of where and how they were made, but since the module can pull the context specific configuration straight from the server, it does not need to know itself, which of the directives are valid in this context, since the server takes care of this.

So how does a module get the specific configuration for the server, directory or location in question? It does so by making one simple call:

```
example_config *config = (example_config*) ap_get_module_config(r->per_dir_config, &
```

That's it! Of course, a whole lot goes on behind the scenes, which we will discuss in this chapter, starting with how the server came to know what our configuration looks like, and how it came to be set up as it is in the specific context.

### Our basic configuration setup

In this chapter, we will be working with a slightly modified version of our previous context structure. We will set a `context` variable that we can use to track which context configuration is being used by the server in various places:

```
typedef struct {
    char        context[256];
    char        path[256];
    int         typeOfAction;
    int         enabled;
} example_config;
```

Our handler for requests will also be modified, yet still very simple:

```
static int example_handler(request_rec *r)
{
    if(!r->handler || strcmp(r->handler, "example-handler")) return(DECLINED);
    example_config *config = (example_config*) ap_get_module_config(r->per_dir_confi
    ap_set_content_type(r, "text/plain");
    ap_rprintf("Enabled: %u\n", config->enabled);
    ap_rprintf("Path: %s\n", config->path);
    ap_rprintf("TypeOfAction: %x\n", config->typeOfAction);
    ap_rprintf("Context: %s\n", config->context);
    return OK;
}
```

### Choosing a context

Before we can start making our module context aware, we must first define, which contexts we will accept. As we saw in the previous chapter, defining a directive required five elements be set:

```
AP_INIT_TAKE1("exampleEnabled", example_set_enabled, NULL, RSRC_CONF, "Enable or dis
```

The RSRC_CONF definition told the server that we would only allow this directive in a global server context, but since we are now trying out a context aware version of our module, we should set this to something more lenient, namely the value ACCESS_CONF, which lets us use the directive inside <Directory> and <Location> blocks. For more control over the placement of your directives, you can combine the following restrictions together to form a specific rule:

- RSRC_CONF: Allow in .conf files (not .htaccess) outside <Directory> or <Location>
- ACCESS_CONF: Allow in .conf files (not .htaccess) inside <Directory> or <Location>
- OR_OPTIONS: Allow in .conf files and .htaccess when AllowOverride Options is set
- OR_FILEINFO: Allow in .conf files and .htaccess when AllowOverride FileInfo is set
- OR_AUTHCFG: Allow in .conf files and .htaccess when AllowOverride AuthConfig is set
- OR_INDEXES: Allow in .conf files and .htaccess when AllowOverride Indexes is set
- OR_ALL: Allow anywhere in .conf files and .htaccess

**Using the server to allocate configuration slots**

A much smarter way to manage your configurations is by letting the server help you create them. To do so, we must first start off by changing our *name tag* to let the server know, that it should assist us in creating and managing our configurations. Since we have chosen the per-directory (or per-location) context for our module configurations, we'll add a per-directory creator and merger function reference in our tag:

```
module AP_MODULE_DECLARE_DATA    example_module =
{
    STANDARD20_MODULE_STUFF,
    create_dir_conf, /* Per-directory configuration handler */
    merge_dir_conf,  /* Merge handler for per-directory configurations */
    NULL,            /* Per-server configuration handler */
    NULL,            /* Merge handler for per-server configurations */
    directives,      /* Any directives we may have for httpd */
    register_hooks   /* Our hook registering function */
};
```

**Creating new context configurations**

Now that we have told the server to help us create and manage configurations, our first step is to make a function for creating new, blank configurations. We do so by creating the function we just referenced in our name tag as the Per-directory configuration handler:

```
void *create_dir_conf(apr_pool_t *pool, char *context) {
    context = context ? context : "(undefined context)";
    example_config *cfg = apr_pcalloc(pool, sizeof(example_config));
    if(cfg) {
        /* Set some default values */
        strcpy(cfg->context, context);
        cfg->enabled = 0;
        cfg->path = "/foo/bar";
        cfg->typeOfAction = 0x11;
    }
    return cfg;
}
```

**Merging configurations**

Our next step in creating a context aware configuration is merging configurations. This part of the process particularly applies to scenarios where you have a parent configuration and a child, such as the following:

```
<Directory "/var/www">
    ExampleEnabled On
    ExamplePath "/foo/bar"
    ExampleAction file allow
</Directory>
<Directory "/var/www/subdir">
    ExampleAction file deny
</Directory>
```

In this example, it is natural to assume that the directory `/var/www/subdir` should inherit the values set for the `/var/www` directory, as we did not specify an `ExampleEnabled` nor an `ExamplePath` for this directory. The server does not presume to know if this is true, but cleverly does the following:

1. Creates a new configuration for `/var/www`

2. Sets the configuration values according to the directives given for `/var/www`

3. Creates a new configuration for `/var/www/subdir`

4. Sets the configuration values according to the directives given for `/var/www/subdir`

5. **Proposes a merge** of the two configurations into a new configuration for `/var/www/subdir`

This proposal is handled by the `merge_dir_conf` function we referenced in our name tag. The purpose of this function is to assess the two configurations and decide how they are to be merged:

```
void *merge_dir_conf(apr_pool_t *pool, void *BASE, void *ADD) {
    example_config *base = (example_config *) BASE ; /* This is what was set in the ｜
    example_config *add = (example_config *) ADD ;   /* This is what is set in the ne
    example_config *conf = (example_config *) create_dir_conf(pool, "Merged configura

    /* Merge configurations */
    conf->enabled = ( add->enabled == 0 ) ? base->enabled : add->enabled ;
    conf->typeOfAction = add->typeOfAction ? add->typeOfAction : base->typeOfAction;
    strcpy(conf->path, strlen(add->path) ? add->path : base->path);

    return conf ;
}
```

**Trying out our new context aware configurations**

Now, let's try putting it all together to create a new module that is context aware. First off, we'll create a configuration that lets us test how the module works:

```
<Location "/a">
    SetHandler example-handler
    ExampleEnabled on
    ExamplePath "/foo/bar"
```

```
        ExampleAction file allow
</Location>

<Location "/a/b">
        ExampleAction file deny
        ExampleEnabled off
</Location>

<Location "/a/b/c">
        ExampleAction db deny
        ExamplePath "/foo/bar/baz"
        ExampleEnabled on
</Location>
```

Then we'll assemble our module code. Note, that since we are now using our name tag as reference when fetching configurations in our handler, I have added some prototypes to keep the compiler happy:

```
/*$6
 +++++++++++++++++++++++++++++++++++++++++++++++++++++++++++++++++++++++++++++++++++
 * mod_example_config.c
 +++++++++++++++++++++++++++++++++++++++++++++++++++++++++++++++++++++++++++++++++++
 */


#include <stdio.h>
#include "apr_hash.h"
#include "ap_config.h"
#include "ap_provider.h"
#include "httpd.h"
#include "http_core.h"
#include "http_config.h"
#include "http_log.h"
#include "http_protocol.h"
#include "http_request.h"

/*$1
 ~~~~~~~~~~~~~~~~~~~~~~~~~~~~~~~~~~~~~~~~~~~~~~~~~~~~~~~~~~~~~~~~~~~~~~~~~~~~~~~~~~~~~
    Configuration structure
 ~~~~~~~~~~~~~~~~~~~~~~~~~~~~~~~~~~~~~~~~~~~~~~~~~~~~~~~~~~~~~~~~~~~~~~~~~~~~~~~~~~~~~
 */

typedef struct
{
    char    context[256];
    char    path[256];
    int     typeOfAction;
    int     enabled;
} example_config;

/*$1
 ~~~~~~~~~~~~~~~~~~~~~~~~~~~~~~~~~~~~~~~~~~~~~~~~~~~~~~~~~~~~~~~~~~~~~~~~~~~~~~~~~~~~~
    Prototypes
 ~~~~~~~~~~~~~~~~~~~~~~~~~~~~~~~~~~~~~~~~~~~~~~~~~~~~~~~~~~~~~~~~~~~~~~~~~~~~~~~~~~~~~
```

```
 */

static int     example_handler(request_rec *r);
const char     *example_set_enabled(cmd_parms *cmd, void *cfg, const char *arg);
const char     *example_set_path(cmd_parms *cmd, void *cfg, const char *arg);
const char     *example_set_action(cmd_parms *cmd, void *cfg, const char *arg1, const
void           *create_dir_conf(apr_pool_t *pool, char *context);
void           *merge_dir_conf(apr_pool_t *pool, void *BASE, void *ADD);
static void    register_hooks(apr_pool_t *pool);

/*$1
 ~~~~~~~~~~~~~~~~~~~~~~~~~~~~~~~~~~~~~~~~~~~~~~~~~~~~~~~~~~~~~~~~~~~~~~~~~~~~~~~~~~~~~~~~
    Configuration directives
 ~~~~~~~~~~~~~~~~~~~~~~~~~~~~~~~~~~~~~~~~~~~~~~~~~~~~~~~~~~~~~~~~~~~~~~~~~~~~~~~~~~~~~~~~
 */

static const command_rec    directives[] =
{
    AP_INIT_TAKE1("exampleEnabled", example_set_enabled, NULL, ACCESS_CONF, "Enable
    AP_INIT_TAKE1("examplePath", example_set_path, NULL, ACCESS_CONF, "The path to w
    AP_INIT_TAKE2("exampleAction", example_set_action, NULL, ACCESS_CONF, "Special a
    { NULL }
};

/*$1
 ~~~~~~~~~~~~~~~~~~~~~~~~~~~~~~~~~~~~~~~~~~~~~~~~~~~~~~~~~~~~~~~~~~~~~~~~~~~~~~~~~~~~~~~~
    Our name tag
 ~~~~~~~~~~~~~~~~~~~~~~~~~~~~~~~~~~~~~~~~~~~~~~~~~~~~~~~~~~~~~~~~~~~~~~~~~~~~~~~~~~~~~~~~
 */

module AP_MODULE_DECLARE_DATA    example_module =
{
    STANDARD20_MODULE_STUFF,
    create_dir_conf,    /* Per-directory configuration handler */
    merge_dir_conf,     /* Merge handler for per-directory configurations */
    NULL,               /* Per-server configuration handler */
    NULL,               /* Merge handler for per-server configurations */
    directives,         /* Any directives we may have for httpd */
    register_hooks      /* Our hook registering function */
};

/*
 ====================================================================================
    Hook registration function
 ====================================================================================
 */
static void register_hooks(apr_pool_t *pool)
{
    ap_hook_handler(example_handler, NULL, NULL, APR_HOOK_LAST);
}

/*
 ====================================================================================
```

```
    Our example web service handler
 =============================================================================
 */
static int example_handler(request_rec *r)
{
    if(!r->handler || strcmp(r->handler, "example-handler")) return(DECLINED);

    /*~~~~~~~~~~~~~~~~~~~~~~~~~~~~~~~~~~~~~~~~~~~~~~~~~~~~~~~~~~~~~~~~~~~~~~~~~~~
    example_config    *config = (example_config *) ap_get_module_config(r->per_dir_config,
    /*~~~~~~~~~~~~~~~~~~~~~~~~~~~~~~~~~~~~~~~~~~~~~~~~~~~~~~~~~~~~~~~~~~~~~~~~~~~

    ap_set_content_type(r, "text/plain");
    ap_rprintf(r, "Enabled: %u\n", config->enabled);
    ap_rprintf(r, "Path: %s\n", config->path);
    ap_rprintf(r, "TypeOfAction: %x\n", config->typeOfAction);
    ap_rprintf(r, "Context: %s\n", config->context);
    return OK;
}


/*
 =============================================================================
    Handler for the "exampleEnabled" directive
 =============================================================================
 */
const char *example_set_enabled(cmd_parms *cmd, void *cfg, const char *arg)
{
    /*~~~~~~~~~~~~~~~~~~~~~~~~~~~~~~~~~~~~~~~~~~~~~~~*/
    example_config    *conf = (example_config *) cfg;
    /*~~~~~~~~~~~~~~~~~~~~~~~~~~~~~~~~~~~~~~~~~~~~~~~*/

    if(conf)
    {
        if(!strcasecmp(arg, "on"))
            conf->enabled = 1;
        else
            conf->enabled = 0;
    }

    return NULL;
}


/*
 =============================================================================
    Handler for the "examplePath" directive
 =============================================================================
 */
const char *example_set_path(cmd_parms *cmd, void *cfg, const char *arg)
{
    /*~~~~~~~~~~~~~~~~~~~~~~~~~~~~~~~~~~~~~~~~~~~~~~~*/
    example_config    *conf = (example_config *) cfg;
    /*~~~~~~~~~~~~~~~~~~~~~~~~~~~~~~~~~~~~~~~~~~~~~~~*/

    if(conf)
```

```
    {
        strcpy(conf->path, arg);
    }

    return NULL;
}

/*
 ===============================================================================
    Handler for the "exampleAction" directive ;
    Let's pretend this one takes one argument (file or db), and a second (deny or al
    and we store it in a bit-wise manner.
 ===============================================================================
 */
const char *example_set_action(cmd_parms *cmd, void *cfg, const char *arg1, const cha
{
    /*~~~~~~~~~~~~~~~~~~~~~~~~~~~~~~~~~~~~~~~~~~~~~*/
    example_config    *conf = (example_config *) cfg;
    /*~~~~~~~~~~~~~~~~~~~~~~~~~~~~~~~~~~~~~~~~~~~~~*/

    if(conf)
    {
        {
            if(!strcasecmp(arg1, "file"))
                conf->typeOfAction = 0x01;
            else
                conf->typeOfAction = 0x02;
            if(!strcasecmp(arg2, "deny"))
                conf->typeOfAction += 0x10;
            else
                conf->typeOfAction += 0x20;
        }
    }

    return NULL;
}

/*
 ===============================================================================
    Function for creating new configurations for per-directory contexts
 ===============================================================================
 */
void *create_dir_conf(apr_pool_t *pool, char *context)
{
    context = context ? context : "Newly created configuration";

    /*~~~~~~~~~~~~~~~~~~~~~~~~~~~~~~~~~~~~~~~~~~~~~~~~~~~~~~~~~~~~~~~~~*/
    example_config    *cfg = apr_pcalloc(pool, sizeof(example_config));
    /*~~~~~~~~~~~~~~~~~~~~~~~~~~~~~~~~~~~~~~~~~~~~~~~~~~~~~~~~~~~~~~~~~*/

    if(cfg)
    {
        {
```

```
            /* Set some default values */
            strcpy(cfg->context, context);
            cfg->enabled = 0;
            memset(cfg->path, 0, 256);
            cfg->typeOfAction = 0x00;
        }
    }

    return cfg;
}

/*
 ========================================================================================
    Merging function for configurations
 ========================================================================================
 */
void *merge_dir_conf(apr_pool_t *pool, void *BASE, void *ADD)
{
    /*~~~~~~~~~~~~~~~~~~~~~~~~~~~~~~~~~~~~~~~~~~~~~~~~~~~~~~~~~~~~~~~~~~~~~~~*/
    example_config    *base = (example_config *) BASE;
    example_config    *add = (example_config *) ADD;
    example_config    *conf = (example_config *) create_dir_conf(pool, "Merged configurati(
    /*~~~~~~~~~~~~~~~~~~~~~~~~~~~~~~~~~~~~~~~~~~~~~~~~~~~~~~~~~~~~~~~~~~~~~~~*/

    conf->enabled = (add->enabled == 0) ? base->enabled : add->enabled;
    conf->typeOfAction = add->typeOfAction ? add->typeOfAction : base->typeOfAction;
    strcpy(conf->path, strlen(add->path) ? add->path : base->path);
    return conf;
}
```

## Summing up

We have now looked at how to create simple modules for Apache HTTP Server 2.4 and configuring them. What you do next is entirely up to you, but it is my hope that something valuable has come out of reading this documentation. If you have questions on how to further develop modules, you are welcome to join our mailing lists[22] or check out the rest of our documentation for further tips.

## Some useful snippets of code

### Retrieve variables from POST form data

```
typedef struct {
    const char *key;
    const char *value;
} keyValuePair;

keyValuePair *readPost(request_rec *r) {
    apr_array_header_t *pairs = NULL;
    apr_off_t len;
    apr_size_t size;
```

---

[22]http://httpd.apache.org/lists.html

```
    int res;
    int i = 0;
    char *buffer;
    keyValuePair *kvp;

    res = ap_parse_form_data(r, NULL, &pairs, -1, HUGE_STRING_LEN);
    if (res != OK || !pairs) return NULL; /* Return NULL if we failed or if there ar
    kvp = apr_pcalloc(r->pool, sizeof(keyValuePair) * (pairs->nelts + 1));
    while (pairs && !apr_is_empty_array(pairs)) {
        ap_form_pair_t *pair = (ap_form_pair_t *) apr_array_pop(pairs);
        apr_brigade_length(pair->value, 1, &len);
        size = (apr_size_t) len;
        buffer = apr_palloc(r->pool, size + 1);
        apr_brigade_flatten(pair->value, buffer, &size);
        buffer[len] = 0;
        kvp[i].key = apr_pstrdup(r->pool, pair->name);
        kvp[i].value = buffer;
        i++;
    }
    return kvp;
}

static int example_handler(request_rec *r)
{
    /*~~~~~~~~~~~~~~~~~~~~~~~~*/
    keyValuePair *formData;
    /*~~~~~~~~~~~~~~~~~~~~~~~~*/

    formData = readPost(r);
    if (formData) {
        int i;
        for (i = 0; &formData[i]; i++) {
            if (formData[i].key && formData[i].value) {
                ap_rprintf(r, "%s = %s\n", formData[i].key, formData[i].value);
            } else if (formData[i].key) {
                ap_rprintf(r, "%s\n", formData[i].key);
            } else if (formData[i].value) {
                ap_rprintf(r, "= %s\n", formData[i].value);
            } else {
                break;
            }
        }
    }
    return OK;
}
```

**Printing out every HTTP header received**

```
static int example_handler(request_rec *r)
{
    /*~~~~~~~~~~~~~~~~~~~~~~~~~~~~~~~~~~~~~~~~~*/
    const apr_array_header_t    *fields;
    int                         i;
```

```
    apr_table_entry_t               *e = 0;
    /*~~~~~~~~~~~~~~~~~~~~~~~~~~~~~~~~~~~~~~*/

    fields = apr_table_elts(r->headers_in);
    e = (apr_table_entry_t *) fields->elts;
    for(i = 0; i < fields->nelts; i++) {
        ap_rprintf(r, "%s: %s\n", e[i].key, e[i].val);
    }
    return OK;
}
```

**Reading the request body into memory**

```
static int util_read(request_rec *r, const char **rbuf, apr_off_t *size)
{
    /*~~~~~~~~~*/
    int rc = OK;
    /*~~~~~~~~~*/

    if((rc = ap_setup_client_block(r, REQUEST_CHUNKED_ERROR))) {
        return(rc);
    }

    if(ap_should_client_block(r)) {

        /*~~~~~~~~~~~~~~~~~~~~~~~~~~~~~~~~~~~~~~~*/
        char          argsbuffer[HUGE_STRING_LEN];
        apr_off_t     rsize, len_read, rpos = 0;
        apr_off_t length = r->remaining;
        /*~~~~~~~~~~~~~~~~~~~~~~~~~~~~~~~~~~~~~~~*/

        *rbuf = (const char *) apr_pcalloc(r->pool, (apr_size_t) (length + 1));
        *size = length;
        while((len_read = ap_get_client_block(r, argsbuffer, sizeof(argsbuffer))) > 0) {
            if((rpos + len_read) > length) {
                rsize = length - rpos;
            }
            else {
                rsize = len_read;
            }

            memcpy((char *) *rbuf + rpos, argsbuffer, (size_t) rsize);
            rpos += rsize;
        }
    }
    return(rc);
}

static int example_handler(request_rec *r)
{
    /*~~~~~~~~~~~~~~~~~~*/
    apr_off_t   size;
    const char  *buffer;
```

```
    /*~~~~~~~~~~~~~~~~~*/

    if(util_read(r, &buffer, &size) == OK) {
        ap_rprintf(r, "We read a request body that was %" APR_OFF_T_FMT " bytes long
    }
    return OK;
}
```

## 11.5 Documenting code in Apache 2.4

Apache 2.4 uses Doxygen[23] to document the APIs and global variables in the code. This will explain the basics of how to document using Doxygen.

### Brief Description

To start a documentation block, use /**
To end a documentation block, use */

In the middle of the block, there are multiple tags we can use:

```
Description of this functions purpose
@param parameter_name description
@return description
@deffunc signature of the function
```

The deffunc is not always necessary. DoxyGen does not have a full parser in it, so any prototype that use a macro in the return type declaration is too complex for scandoc. Those functions require a deffunc. An example (using &gt; rather than >):

```
/**
 * return the final element of the pathname
 * @param pathname The path to get the final element of
 * @return the final element of the path
 * @tip Examples:
 * <pre>
 * "/foo/bar/gum" -&gt; "gum"
 * "/foo/bar/gum/" -&gt; ""
 * "gum" -&gt; "gum"
 * "wi\\n32\\stuff" -&gt; "stuff"
 * </pre>
 * @deffunc const char * ap_filename_of_pathname(const char *pathname)
 */
```

At the top of the header file, always include:

```
/**
 * @package Name of library header
 */
```

Doxygen uses a new HTML file for each package. The HTML files are named {Name_of_library_header}.html, so try to be concise with your names.

For a further discussion of the possibilities please refer to the Doxygen site[24].

---

[23] http://www.doxygen.org/
[24] http://www.doxygen.org/

## 11.6 Hook Functions in the Apache HTTP Server 2.x

 **Warning**
This document is still in development and may be partially out of date.

In general, a hook function is one that the Apache HTTP Server will call at some point during the processing of a request. Modules can provide functions that are called, and specify when they get called in comparison to other modules.

### Core Hooks

The httpd's core modules offer a predefinined list of hooks used during the standard request processing (p. 1078) phase. Creating a new hook will expose a function that implements it (see sections below) but it is essential to undestand that you will not extend the httpd's core hooks. Their presence and order in the request processing is in fact a consequence of how they are called in `server/request.c` (check this section (p. 1042) for an overview). The core hooks are listed in the doxygen documentation[25].

Reading guide for developing modules (p. 1042) and request processing (p. 1078) before proceeding is highly recomended.

### Creating a hook function

In order to create a new hook, four things need to be done:

#### Declare the hook function

Use the `AP_DECLARE_HOOK` macro, which needs to be given the return type of the hook function, the name of the hook, and the arguments. For example, if the hook returns an `int` and takes a `request_rec *` and an `int` and is called `do_something`, then declare it like this:

```
AP_DECLARE_HOOK(int, do_something, (request_rec *r, int n))
```

This should go in a header which modules will include if they want to use the hook.

#### Create the hook structure

Each source file that exports a hook has a private structure which is used to record the module functions that use the hook. This is declared as follows:

```
APR_HOOK_STRUCT(
  APR_HOOK_LINK(do_something)
  ...
)
```

#### Implement the hook caller

The source file that exports the hook has to implement a function that will call the hook. There are currently three possible ways to do this. In all cases, the calling function is called `ap_run_hookname()`.

---

[25]https://ci.apache.org/projects/httpd/trunk/doxygen/group__hooks.html

**Void hooks**

If the return value of a hook is `void`, then all the hooks are called, and the caller is implemented like this:

```
AP_IMPLEMENT_HOOK_VOID(do_something, (request_rec *r, int n), (r, n))
```

The second and third arguments are the dummy argument declaration and the dummy arguments as they will be used when calling the hook. In other words, this macro expands to something like this:

```
void ap_run_do_something(request_rec *r, int n)
{
    ...
    do_something(r, n);
}
```

**Hooks that return a value**

If the hook returns a value, then it can either be run until the first hook that does something interesting, like so:

```
AP_IMPLEMENT_HOOK_RUN_FIRST(int, do_something, (request_rec *r, int n), (r, n), DECLINED)
```

The first hook that does *not* return `DECLINED` stops the loop and its return value is returned from the hook caller. Note that `DECLINED` is the traditional hook return value meaning "I didn't do anything", but it can be whatever suits you.

Alternatively, all hooks can be run until an error occurs. This boils down to permitting *two* return values, one of which means "I did something, and it was OK" and the other meaning "I did nothing". The first function that returns a value other than one of those two stops the loop, and its return is the return value. Declare these like so:

```
AP_IMPLEMENT_HOOK_RUN_ALL(int, do_something, (request_rec *r, int n), (r, n), OK, DECLINED)
```

Again, `OK` and `DECLINED` are the traditional values. You can use what you want.

**Call the hook callers**

At appropriate moments in the code, call the hook caller, like so:

```
int n, ret;
request_rec *r;

ret=ap_run_do_something(r, n);
```

## Hooking the hook

A module that wants a hook to be called needs to do two things.

**Implement the hook function**

Include the appropriate header, and define a static function of the correct type:

```
static int my_something_doer(request_rec *r, int n)
{
    ...
    return OK;
}
```

**Add a hook registering function**

During initialisation, the server will call each modules hook registering function, which is included in the module structure:

```
static void my_register_hooks()
{
    ap_hook_do_something(my_something_doer, NULL, NULL, APR_HOOK_MIDDLE);
}

mode MODULE_VAR_EXPORT my_module =
{
    ...
    my_register_hooks       /* register hooks */
};
```

**Controlling hook calling order**

In the example above, we didn't use the three arguments in the hook registration function that control calling order of all the functions registered within the hook. There are two mechanisms for doing this. The first, rather crude, method, allows us to specify roughly where the hook is run relative to other modules. The final argument control this. There are three possible values: APR_HOOK_FIRST, APR_HOOK_MIDDLE and APR_HOOK_LAST.

All modules using any particular value may be run in any order relative to each other, but, of course, all modules using APR_HOOK_FIRST will be run before APR_HOOK_MIDDLE which are before APR_HOOK_LAST. Modules that don't care when they are run should use APR_HOOK_MIDDLE. *These values are spaced out, so that positions like APR_HOOK_FIRST-2 are possible to hook slightly earlier than other functions.*

Note that there are two more values, APR_HOOK_REALLY_FIRST and APR_HOOK_REALLY_LAST. These should only be used by the hook exporter.

The other method allows finer control. When a module knows that it must be run before (or after) some other modules, it can specify them by name. The second (third) argument is a NULL-terminated array of strings consisting of the names of modules that must be run before (after) the current module. For example, suppose we want "mod_xyz.c" and "mod_abc.c" to run before we do, then we'd hook as follows:

```
static void register_hooks()
{
    static const char * const aszPre[] = { "mod_xyz.c", "mod_abc.c", NULL };

    ap_hook_do_something(my_something_doer, aszPre, NULL, APR_HOOK_MIDDLE);
}
```

Note that the sort used to achieve this is stable, so ordering set by APR_HOOK_ORDER is preserved, as far as is possible.

# 11.7   Converting Modules from Apache 1.3 to Apache 2.0

This is a first attempt at writing the lessons I learned when trying to convert the `mod_mmap_static` module to Apache 2.0. It's by no means definitive and probably won't even be correct in some ways, but it's a start.

## The easier changes ...

### Cleanup Routines

These now need to be of type `apr_status_t` and return a value of that type. Normally the return value will be `APR_SUCCESS` unless there is some need to signal an error in the cleanup. Be aware that even though you signal an error not all code yet checks and acts upon the error.

### Initialisation Routines

These should now be renamed to better signify where they sit in the overall process. So the name gets a small change from `mmap_init` to `mmap_post_config`. The arguments passed have undergone a radical change and now look like

- `apr_pool_t *p`
- `apr_pool_t *plog`
- `apr_pool_t *ptemp`
- `server_rec *s`

### Data Types

A lot of the data types have been moved into the APR[26]. This means that some have had a name change, such as the one shown above. The following is a brief list of some of the changes that you are likely to have to make.

- `pool` becomes `apr_pool_t`
- `table` becomes `apr_table_t`

## The messier changes...

### Register Hooks

The new architecture uses a series of hooks to provide for calling your functions. These you'll need to add to your module by way of a new function, `static void register_hooks(void)`. The function is really reasonably straightforward once you understand what needs to be done. Each function that needs calling at some stage in the processing of a request needs to be registered, handlers do not. There are a number of phases where functions can be added, and for each you can specify with a high degree of control the relative order that the function will be called in.

This is the code that was added to `mod_mmap_static`:

---

[26]http://apr.apache.org/

```
static void register_hooks(void)
{
    static const char * const aszPre[]={ "http_core.c",NULL };
    ap_hook_post_config(mmap_post_config,NULL,NULL,HOOK_MIDDLE);
    ap_hook_translate_name(mmap_static_xlat,aszPre,NULL,HOOK_LAST);
};
```

This registers 2 functions that need to be called, one in the `post_config` stage (virtually every module will need this one) and one for the `translate_name` phase. note that while there are different function names the format of each is identical. So what is the format?

```
ap_hook_phase_name(function_name, predecessors, successors, position);
```

There are 3 hook positions defined...

- HOOK_FIRST
- HOOK_MIDDLE
- HOOK_LAST

To define the position you use the position and then modify it with the predecessors and successors. Each of the modifiers can be a list of functions that should be called, either before the function is run (predecessors) or after the function has run (successors).

In the `mod_mmap_static` case I didn't care about the `post_config` stage, but the `mmap_static_xlat` **must** be called after the core module had done its name translation, hence the use of the aszPre to define a modifier to the position HOOK_LAST.

**Module Definition**

There are now a lot fewer stages to worry about when creating your module definition. The old definition looked like

```
module MODULE_VAR_EXPORT module_name_module =
{
    STANDARD_MODULE_STUFF,
    /* initializer */
    /* dir config creater */
    /* dir merger --- default is to override */
    /* server config */
    /* merge server config */
    /* command handlers */
    /* handlers */
    /* filename translation */
    /* check_user_id */
    /* check auth */
    /* check access */
    /* type_checker */
    /* fixups */
    /* logger */
    /* header parser */
    /* child_init */
    /* child_exit */
    /* post read-request */
};
```

The new structure is a great deal simpler...

```
module MODULE_VAR_EXPORT module_name_module =
{
    STANDARD20_MODULE_STUFF,
    /* create per-directory config structures */
    /* merge per-directory config structures  */
    /* create per-server config structures    */
    /* merge per-server config structures      */
    /* command handlers */
    /* handlers */
    /* register hooks */
};
```

Some of these read directly across, some don't. I'll try to summarise what should be done below.

The stages that read directly across :

**/\* dir config creater \*/** /\* create per-directory config structures \*/

**/\* server config \*/** /\* create per-server config structures \*/

**/\* dir merger \*/** /\* merge per-directory config structures \*/

**/\* merge server config \*/** /\* merge per-server config structures \*/

**/\* command table \*/** /\* command apr_table_t \*/

**/\* handlers \*/** /\* handlers \*/

The remainder of the old functions should be registered as hooks. There are the following hook stages defined so far...

**ap_hook_pre_config** do any setup required prior to processing configuration directives

**ap_hook_check_config** review configuration directive interdependencies

**ap_hook_test_config** executes only with -t option

**ap_hook_open_logs** open any specified logs

**ap_hook_post_config** this is where the old _init routines get registered

**ap_hook_http_method** retrieve the http method from a request. (legacy)

**ap_hook_auth_checker** check if the resource requires authorization

**ap_hook_access_checker** check for module-specific restrictions

**ap_hook_check_user_id** check the user-id and password

**ap_hook_default_port** retrieve the default port for the server

**ap_hook_pre_connection** do any setup required just before processing, but after accepting

**ap_hook_process_connection** run the correct protocol

**ap_hook_child_init** call as soon as the child is started

**ap_hook_create_request** ??

**ap_hook_fixups** last chance to modify things before generating content

**ap_hook_handler** generate the content

**ap_hook_header_parser** lets modules look at the headers, not used by most modules, because they use `post_read_request` for this

**ap_hook_insert_filter** to insert filters into the filter chain

**ap_hook_log_transaction** log information about the request

**ap_hook_optional_fn_retrieve** retrieve any functions registered as optional

**ap_hook_post_read_request** called after reading the request, before any other phase

**ap_hook_quick_handler** called before any request processing, used by cache modules.

**ap_hook_translate_name** translate the URI into a filename

**ap_hook_type_checker** determine and/or set the doc type

## 11.8   Request Processing in the Apache HTTP Server 2.x

> ⚠ **Warning**
> Warning - this is a first (fast) draft that needs further revision!

Several changes in 2.0 and above affect the internal request processing mechanics. Module authors need to be aware of these changes so they may take advantage of the optimizations and security enhancements.

The first major change is to the subrequest and redirect mechanisms. There were a number of different code paths in the Apache HTTP Server 1.3 to attempt to optimize subrequest or redirect behavior. As patches were introduced to 2.0, these optimizations (and the server behavior) were quickly broken due to this duplication of code. All duplicate code has been folded back into `ap_process_request_internal()` to prevent the code from falling out of sync again.

This means that much of the existing code was 'unoptimized'. It is the Apache HTTP Project's first goal to create a robust and correct implementation of the HTTP server RFC. Additional goals include security, scalability and optimization. New methods were sought to optimize the server (beyond the performance of 1.3) without introducing fragile or insecure code.

### The Request Processing Cycle

All requests pass through `ap_process_request_internal()` in `server/request.c`, including subrequests and redirects. If a module doesn't pass generated requests through this code, the author is cautioned that the module may be broken by future changes to request processing.

To streamline requests, the module author can take advantage of the hooks offered (p. 1042) to drop out of the request cycle early, or to bypass core hooks which are irrelevant (and costly in terms of CPU.)

### The Request Parsing Phase

#### Unescapes the URL

The request's `parsed_uri` path is unescaped, once and only once, at the beginning of internal request processing.

This step is bypassed if the proxyreq flag is set, or the `parsed_uri.path` element is unset. The module has no further control of this one-time unescape operation, either failing to unescape or multiply unescaping the URL leads to security repercussions.

#### Strips Parent and This Elements from the URI

All `/../` and `/./` elements are removed by `ap_getparents()`. This helps to ensure the path is (nearly) absolute before the request processing continues.

This step cannot be bypassed.

#### Initial URI Location Walk

Every request is subject to an `ap_location_walk()` call. This ensures that <Location> sections are consistently enforced for all requests. If the request is an internal redirect or a sub-request, it may borrow some or all of the processing from the previous or parent request's ap_location_walk, so this step is generally very efficient after processing the main request.

**translate_name**

Modules can determine the file name, or alter the given URI in this step. For example, MOD_VHOST_ALIAS will translate the URI's path into the configured virtual host, MOD_ALIAS will translate the path to an alias path, and if the request falls back on the core, the DOCUMENTROOT is prepended to the request resource.

If all modules DECLINE this phase, an error 500 is returned to the browser, and a "couldn't translate name" error is logged automatically.

**Hook: map_to_storage**

After the file or correct URI was determined, the appropriate per-dir configurations are merged together. For example, MOD_PROXY compares and merges the appropriate <PROXY> sections. If the URI is nothing more than a local (non-proxy) TRACE request, the core handles the request and returns DONE. If no module answers this hook with OK or DONE, the core will run the request filename against the <DIRECTORY> and <FILES> sections. If the request 'filename' isn't an absolute, legal filename, a note is set for later termination.

**URI Location Walk**

Every request is hardened by a second ap_location_walk() call. This reassures that a translated request is still subjected to the configured <LOCATION> sections. The request again borrows some or all of the processing from its previous location_walk above, so this step is almost always very efficient unless the translated URI mapped to a substantially different path or Virtual Host.

**Hook: header_parser**

The main request then parses the client's headers. This prepares the remaining request processing steps to better serve the client's request.

## The Security Phase

Needs Documentation. Code is:

```
if ((access_status = ap_run_access_checker(r)) != 0) {
    return decl_die(access_status, "check access", r);
}

if ((access_status = ap_run_check_user_id(r)) != 0) {
    return decl_die(access_status, "check user", r);
}

if ((access_status = ap_run_auth_checker(r)) != 0) {
    return decl_die(access_status, "check authorization", r);
}
```

## The Preparation Phase

**Hook: type_checker**

The modules have an opportunity to test the URI or filename against the target resource, and set mime information for the request. Both MOD_MIME and MOD_MIME_MAGIC use this phase to compare the file name or contents against the administrator's configuration and set the content type, language, character set and request handler. Some modules may set up their filters or other request handling parameters at this time.

If all modules `DECLINE` this phase, an error 500 is returned to the browser, and a "couldn't find types" error is logged automatically.

**Hook: fixups**

Many modules are 'trounced' by some phase above. The fixups phase is used by modules to 'reassert' their ownership or force the request's fields to their appropriate values. It isn't always the cleanest mechanism, but occasionally it's the only option.

## The Handler Phase

This phase is **not** part of the processing in `ap_process_request_internal()`. Many modules prepare one or more subrequests prior to creating any content at all. After the core, or a module calls `ap_process_request_internal()` it then calls `ap_invoke_handler()` to generate the request.

**Hook: insert_filter**

Modules that transform the content in some way can insert their values and override existing filters, such that if the user configured a more advanced filter out-of-order, then the module can move its order as need be. There is no result code, so actions in this hook better be trusted to always succeed.

**Hook: handler**

The module finally has a chance to serve the request in its handler hook. Note that not every prepared request is sent to the handler hook. Many modules, such as MOD_AUTOINDEX, will create subrequests for a given URI, and then never serve the subrequest, but simply lists it for the user. Remember not to put required teardown from the hooks above into this module, but register pool cleanups against the request pool to free resources as required.

## 11.9 How filters work in Apache 2.0

 **Warning**
This is a cut 'n paste job from an email (<022501c1c529$f63a9550$7f00000a@KOJ>) and only reformatted for better readability. It's not up to date but may be a good start for further research.

### Filter Types

There are three basic filter types (each of these is actually broken down into two categories, but that comes later).

**CONNECTION** Filters of this type are valid for the lifetime of this connection. (AP_FTYPE_CONNECTION, AP_FTYPE_NETWORK)

**PROTOCOL** Filters of this type are valid for the lifetime of this request from the point of view of the client, this means that the request is valid from the time that the request is sent until the time that the response is received. (AP_FTYPE_PROTOCOL, AP_FTYPE_TRANSCODE)

**RESOURCE** Filters of this type are valid for the time that this content is used to satisfy a request. For simple requests, this is identical to PROTOCOL, but internal redirects and sub-requests can change the content without ending the request. (AP_FTYPE_RESOURCE, AP_FTYPE_CONTENT_SET)

It is important to make the distinction between a protocol and a resource filter. A resource filter is tied to a specific resource, it may also be tied to header information, but the main binding is to a resource. If you are writing a filter and you want to know if it is resource or protocol, the correct question to ask is: "Can this filter be removed if the request is redirected to a different resource?" If the answer is yes, then it is a resource filter. If it is no, then it is most likely a protocol or connection filter. I won't go into connection filters, because they seem to be well understood. With this definition, a few examples might help:

**Byterange** We have coded it to be inserted for all requests, and it is removed if not used. Because this filter is active at the beginning of all requests, it can not be removed if it is redirected, so this is a protocol filter.

**http_header** This filter actually writes the headers to the network. This is obviously a required filter (except in the asis case which is special and will be dealt with below) and so it is a protocol filter.

**Deflate** The administrator configures this filter based on which file has been requested. If we do an internal redirect from an autoindex page to an index.html page, the deflate filter may be added or removed based on config, so this is a resource filter.

The further breakdown of each category into two more filter types is strictly for ordering. We could remove it, and only allow for one filter type, but the order would tend to be wrong, and we would need to hack things to make it work. Currently, the RESOURCE filters only have one filter type, but that should change.

### How are filters inserted?

This is actually rather simple in theory, but the code is complex. First of all, it is important that everybody realize that there are three filter lists for each request, but they are all concatenated together:

- r->output_filters (corresponds to RESOURCE)
- r->proto_output_filters (corresponds to PROTOCOL)

- `r->connection->output_filters` (corresponds to CONNECTION)

The problem previously, was that we used a singly linked list to create the filter stack, and we started from the "correct" location. This means that if I had a RESOURCE filter on the stack, and I added a CONNECTION filter, the CONNECTION filter would be ignored. This should make sense, because we would insert the connection filter at the top of the `c->output_filters` list, but the end of `r->output_filters` pointed to the filter that used to be at the front of `c->output_filters`. This is obviously wrong. The new insertion code uses a doubly linked list. This has the advantage that we never lose a filter that has been inserted. Unfortunately, it comes with a separate set of headaches.

The problem is that we have two different cases were we use subrequests. The first is to insert more data into a response. The second is to replace the existing response with an internal redirect. These are two different cases and need to be treated as such.

In the first case, we are creating the subrequest from within a handler or filter. This means that the next filter should be passed to `make_sub_request` function, and the last resource filter in the sub-request will point to the next filter in the main request. This makes sense, because the sub-request's data needs to flow through the same set of filters as the main request. A graphical representation might help:

```
Default_handler --> includes_filter --> byterange --> ...
```

If the includes filter creates a sub request, then we don't want the data from that sub-request to go through the includes filter, because it might not be SSI data. So, the subrequest adds the following:

```
Default_handler --> includes_filter -/-> byterange --> ...
                                     /
Default_handler --> sub_request_core
```

What happens if the subrequest is SSI data? Well, that's easy, the `includes_filter` is a resource filter, so it will be added to the sub request in between the `Default_handler` and the `sub_request_core` filter.

The second case for sub-requests is when one sub-request is going to become the real request. This happens whenever a sub-request is created outside of a handler or filter, and NULL is passed as the next filter to the `make_sub_request` function.

In this case, the resource filters no longer make sense for the new request, because the resource has changed. So, instead of starting from scratch, we simply point the front of the resource filters for the sub-request to the front of the protocol filters for the old request. This means that we won't lose any of the protocol filters, neither will we try to send this data through a filter that shouldn't see it.

The problem is that we are using a doubly-linked list for our filter stacks now. But, you should notice that it is possible for two lists to intersect in this model. So, you do you handle the previous pointer? This is a very difficult question to answer, because there is no "right" answer, either method is equally valid. I looked at why we use the previous pointer. The only reason for it is to allow for easier addition of new servers. With that being said, the solution I chose was to make the previous pointer always stay on the original request.

This causes some more complex logic, but it works for all cases. My concern in having it move to the sub-request, is that for the more common case (where a sub-request is used to add data to a response), the main filter chain would be wrong. That didn't seem like a good idea to me.

## Asis

The final topic. :-) Mod_Asis is a bit of a hack, but the handler needs to remove all filters except for connection filters, and send the data. If you are using MOD_ASIS, all other bets are off.

## Explanations

The absolutely last point is that the reason this code was so hard to get right, was because we had hacked so much to force it to work. I wrote most of the hacks originally, so I am very much to blame. However, now that the code is right, I have started to remove some hacks. Most people should have seen that the `reset_filters` and `add_required_filters` functions are gone. Those inserted protocol level filters for error conditions, in fact, both functions did the same thing, one after the other, it was really strange. Because we don't lose protocol filters for error cases any more, those hacks went away. The `HTTP_HEADER`, `Content-length`, and `Byterange` filters are all added in the `insert_filters` phase, because if they were added earlier, we had some interesting interactions. Now, those could all be moved to be inserted with the `HTTP_IN`, `CORE`, and `CORE_IN` filters. That would make the code easier to follow.

# 11.10  Guide to writing output filters

There are a number of common pitfalls encountered when writing output filters; this page aims to document best practice for authors of new or existing filters.

This document is applicable to both version 2.0 and version 2.2 of the Apache HTTP Server; it specifically targets `RESOURCE`-level or `CONTENT_SET`-level filters though some advice is generic to all types of filter.

### Filters and bucket brigades

Each time a filter is invoked, it is passed a *bucket brigade*, containing a sequence of *buckets* which represent both data content and metadata. Every bucket has a *bucket type*; a number of bucket types are defined and used by the `httpd` core modules (and the `apr-util` library which provides the bucket brigade interface), but modules are free to define their own types.

⟹ Output filters must be prepared to process buckets of non-standard types; with a few exceptions, a filter need not care about the types of buckets being filtered.

A filter can tell whether a bucket represents either data or metadata using the `APR_BUCKET_IS_METADATA` macro. Generally, all metadata buckets should be passed down the filter chain by an output filter. Filters may transform, delete, and insert data buckets as appropriate.

There are two metadata bucket types which all filters must pay attention to: the `EOS` bucket type, and the `FLUSH` bucket type. An `EOS` bucket indicates that the end of the response has been reached and no further buckets need be processed. A `FLUSH` bucket indicates that the filter should flush any buffered buckets (if applicable) down the filter chain immediately.

⟹ `FLUSH` buckets are sent when the content generator (or an upstream filter) knows that there may be a delay before more content can be sent. By passing `FLUSH` buckets down the filter chain immediately, filters ensure that the client is not kept waiting for pending data longer than necessary.

Filters can create `FLUSH` buckets and pass these down the filter chain if desired. Generating `FLUSH` buckets unnecessarily, or too frequently, can harm network utilisation since it may force large numbers of small packets to be sent, rather than a small number of larger packets. The section on Non-blocking bucket reads covers a case where filters are encouraged to generate `FLUSH` buckets.

> **Example bucket brigade**
> `HEAP FLUSH FILE EOS`

This shows a bucket brigade which may be passed to a filter; it contains two metadata buckets (`FLUSH` and `EOS`), and two data buckets (`HEAP` and `FILE`).

### Filter invocation

For any given request, an output filter might be invoked only once and be given a single brigade representing the entire response. It is also possible that the number of times a filter is invoked for a single response is proportional to the size of the content being filtered, with the filter being passed a brigade containing a single bucket each time. Filters must operate correctly in either case.

⚠ An output filter which allocates long-lived memory every time it is invoked may consume memory proportional to response size. Output filters which need to allocate memory should do so once per response; see Maintaining state below.

An output filter can distinguish the final invocation for a given response by the presence of an `EOS` bucket in the brigade. Any buckets in the brigade after an EOS should be ignored.

An output filter should never pass an empty brigade down the filter chain. To be defensive, filters should be prepared to accept an empty brigade, and should return success without passing this brigade on down the filter chain. The handling of an empty brigade should have no side effects (such as changing any state private to the filter).

**How to handle an empty brigade**

```
apr_status_t dummy_filter(ap_filter_t *f, apr_bucket_brigade *bb)
{
    if (APR_BRIGADE_EMPTY(bb)) {
        return APR_SUCCESS;
    }
    ...
```

## Brigade structure

A bucket brigade is a doubly-linked list of buckets. The list is terminated (at both ends) by a *sentinel* which can be distinguished from a normal bucket by comparing it with the pointer returned by `APR_BRIGADE_SENTINEL`. The list sentinel is in fact not a valid bucket structure; any attempt to call normal bucket functions (such as `apr_bucket_read`) on the sentinel will have undefined behaviour (i.e. will crash the process).

There are a variety of functions and macros for traversing and manipulating bucket brigades; see the apr_buckets.h[27] header for complete coverage. Commonly used macros include:

**APR_BRIGADE_FIRST(bb)**  returns the first bucket in brigade bb

**APR_BRIGADE_LAST(bb)**  returns the last bucket in brigade bb

**APR_BUCKET_NEXT(e)**  gives the next bucket after bucket e

**APR_BUCKET_PREV(e)**  gives the bucket before bucket e

The `apr_bucket_brigade` structure itself is allocated out of a pool, so if a filter creates a new brigade, it must ensure that memory use is correctly bounded. A filter which allocates a new brigade out of the request pool (`r->pool`) on every invocation, for example, will fall foul of the warning above concerning memory use. Such a filter should instead create a brigade on the first invocation per request, and store that brigade in its state structure.

! It is generally never advisable to use `apr_brigade_destroy` to "destroy" a brigade unless you know for certain that the brigade will never be used again, even then, it should be used rarely. The memory used by the brigade structure will not be released by calling this function (since it comes from a pool), but the associated pool cleanup is unregistered. Using `apr_brigade_destroy` can in fact cause memory leaks; if a "destroyed" brigade contains buckets when its containing pool is destroyed, those buckets will *not* be immediately destroyed. In general, filters should use `apr_brigade_cleanup` in preference to `apr_brigade_destroy`.

---

[27]http://apr.apache.org/docs/apr-util/trunk/group__a_p_r__util__bucket__brigades.html

## Processing buckets

When dealing with non-metadata buckets, it is important to understand that the "apr_bucket *" object is an abstract *representation* of data:

1. The amount of data represented by the bucket may or may not have a determinate length; for a bucket which represents data of indeterminate length, the ->length field is set to the value (apr_size_t)-1. For example, buckets of the PIPE bucket type have an indeterminate length; they represent the output from a pipe.

2. The data represented by a bucket may or may not be mapped into memory. The FILE bucket type, for example, represents data stored in a file on disk.

Filters read the data from a bucket using the apr_bucket_read function. When this function is invoked, the bucket may *morph* into a different bucket type, and may also insert a new bucket into the bucket brigade. This must happen for buckets which represent data not mapped into memory.

To give an example; consider a bucket brigade containing a single FILE bucket representing an entire file, 24 kilobytes in size:

```
FILE(0K-24K)
```

When this bucket is read, it will read a block of data from the file, morph into a HEAP bucket to represent that data, and return the data to the caller. It also inserts a new FILE bucket representing the remainder of the file; after the apr_bucket_read call, the brigade looks like:

```
HEAP(8K) FILE(8K-24K)
```

## Filtering brigades

The basic function of any output filter will be to iterate through the passed-in brigade and transform (or simply examine) the content in some manner. The implementation of the iteration loop is critical to producing a well-behaved output filter.

Taking an example which loops through the entire brigade as follows:

**Bad output filter – do not imitate!**

```
apr_bucket *e = APR_BRIGADE_FIRST(bb);
const char *data;
apr_size_t length;

while (e != APR_BRIGADE_SENTINEL(bb)) {
    apr_bucket_read(e, &data, &length, APR_BLOCK_READ);
    e = APR_BUCKET_NEXT(e);
}

return ap_pass_brigade(bb);
```

The above implementation would consume memory proportional to content size. If passed a FILE bucket, for example, the entire file contents would be read into memory as each apr_bucket_read call morphed a FILE bucket into a HEAP bucket.

In contrast, the implementation below will consume a fixed amount of memory to filter any brigade; a temporary brigade is needed and must be allocated only once per response, see the Maintaining state section.

### Better output filter

```
apr_bucket *e;
const char *data;
apr_size_t length;

while ((e = APR_BRIGADE_FIRST(bb)) != APR_BRIGADE_SENTINEL(bb)) {
    rv = apr_bucket_read(e, &data, &length, APR_BLOCK_READ);
    if (rv) ...;
    /* Remove bucket e from bb. */
    APR_BUCKET_REMOVE(e);
    /* Insert it into  temporary brigade. */
    APR_BRIGADE_INSERT_HEAD(tmpbb, e);
    /* Pass brigade downstream. */
    rv = ap_pass_brigade(f->next, tmpbb);
    if (rv) ...;
    apr_brigade_cleanup(tmpbb);
}
```

## Maintaining state

A filter which needs to maintain state over multiple invocations per response can use the `->ctx` field of its `ap_filter_t` structure. It is typical to store a temporary brigade in such a structure, to avoid having to allocate a new brigade per invocation as described in the Brigade structure section.

### Example code to maintain filter state

```
struct dummy_state {
    apr_bucket_brigade *tmpbb;
    int filter_state;
    ...
};

apr_status_t dummy_filter(ap_filter_t *f, apr_bucket_brigade *bb)
{
    struct dummy_state *state;

    state = f->ctx;
    if (state == NULL) {

        /* First invocation for this response: initialise state structure.
         */
        f->ctx = state = apr_palloc(f->r->pool, sizeof *state);

        state->tmpbb = apr_brigade_create(f->r->pool, f->c->bucket_alloc);
        state->filter_state = ...;
    }
    ...
```

## Buffering buckets

If a filter decides to store buckets beyond the duration of a single filter function invocation (for example storing them in its `->ctx` state structure), those buckets must be *set aside*. This is necessary because some bucket types provide buckets which represent temporary resources (such as stack memory) which will fall out of scope as soon as the filter chain completes processing the brigade.

To setaside a bucket, the `apr_bucket_setaside` function can be called. Not all bucket types can be setaside, but if successful, the bucket will have morphed to ensure it has a lifetime at least as long as the pool given as an argument to the `apr_bucket_setaside` function.

Alternatively, the `ap_save_brigade` function can be used, which will move all the buckets into a separate brigade containing buckets with a lifetime as long as the given pool argument. This function must be used with care, taking into account the following points:

1. On return, `ap_save_brigade` guarantees that all the buckets in the returned brigade will represent data mapped into memory. If given an input brigade containing, for example, a `PIPE` bucket, `ap_save_brigade` will consume an arbitrary amount of memory to store the entire output of the pipe.

2. When `ap_save_brigade` reads from buckets which cannot be setaside, it will always perform blocking reads, removing the opportunity to use Non-blocking bucket reads.

3. If `ap_save_brigade` is used without passing a non-NULL `"saveto"` (destination) brigade parameter, the function will create a new brigade, which may cause memory use to be proportional to content size as described in the Brigade structure section.

> **!** Filters must ensure that any buffered data is processed and passed down the filter chain during the last invocation for a given response (a brigade containing an EOS bucket). Otherwise such data will be lost.

## Non-blocking bucket reads

The `apr_bucket_read` function takes an `apr_read_type_e` argument which determines whether a *blocking* or *non-blocking* read will be performed from the data source. A good filter will first attempt to read from every data bucket using a non-blocking read; if that fails with `APR_EAGAIN`, then send a `FLUSH` bucket down the filter chain, and retry using a blocking read.

This mode of operation ensures that any filters further down the filter chain will flush any buffered buckets if a slow content source is being used.

A CGI script is an example of a slow content source which is implemented as a bucket type. MOD_CGI will send `PIPE` buckets which represent the output from a CGI script; reading from such a bucket will block when waiting for the CGI script to produce more output.

**Example code using non-blocking bucket reads**

```
apr_bucket *e;
apr_read_type_e mode = APR_NONBLOCK_READ;

while ((e = APR_BRIGADE_FIRST(bb)) != APR_BRIGADE_SENTINEL(bb)) {
    apr_status_t rv;

    rv = apr_bucket_read(e, &data, &length, mode);
    if (rv == APR_EAGAIN && mode == APR_NONBLOCK_READ) {

        /* Pass down a brigade containing a flush bucket: */
        APR_BRIGADE_INSERT_TAIL(tmpbb, apr_bucket_flush_create(...));
        rv = ap_pass_brigade(f->next, tmpbb);
        apr_brigade_cleanup(tmpbb);
        if (rv != APR_SUCCESS) return rv;

        /* Retry, using a blocking read. */
        mode = APR_BLOCK_READ;
        continue;
    }
    else if (rv != APR_SUCCESS) {
        /* handle errors */
    }

    /* Next time, try a non-blocking read first. */
    mode = APR_NONBLOCK_READ;
    ...
}
```

## Ten rules for output filters

In summary, here is a set of rules for all output filters to follow:

1. Output filters should not pass empty brigades down the filter chain, but should be tolerant of being passed empty brigades.

2. Output filters must pass all metadata buckets down the filter chain; FLUSH buckets should be respected by passing any pending or buffered buckets down the filter chain.

3. Output filters should ignore any buckets following an EOS bucket.

4. Output filters must process a fixed amount of data at a time, to ensure that memory consumption is not proportional to the size of the content being filtered.

5. Output filters should be agnostic with respect to bucket types, and must be able to process buckets of unfamiliar type.

6. After calling ap_pass_brigade to pass a brigade down the filter chain, output filters should call apr_brigade_cleanup to ensure the brigade is empty before reusing that brigade structure; output filters should never use apr_brigade_destroy to "destroy" brigades.

7. Output filters must *setaside* any buckets which are preserved beyond the duration of the filter function.

8. Output filters must not ignore the return value of ap_pass_brigade, and must return appropriate errors back up the filter chain.

9. Output filters must only create a fixed number of bucket brigades for each response, rather than one per invocation.

10. Output filters should first attempt non-blocking reads from each data bucket, and send a `FLUSH` bucket down the filter chain if the read blocks, before retrying with a blocking read.

# 11.11 Apache HTTP Server 2.x Thread Safety Issues

When using any of the threaded mpms in the Apache HTTP Server 2.x it is important that every function called from Apache be thread safe. When linking in 3rd party extensions it can be difficult to determine whether the resulting server will be thread safe. Casual testing generally won't tell you this either as thread safety problems can lead to subtle race conditions that may only show up in certain conditions under heavy load.

### Global and static variables

When writing your module or when trying to determine if a module or 3rd party library is thread safe there are some common things to keep in mind.

First, you need to recognize that in a threaded model each individual thread has its own program counter, stack and registers. Local variables live on the stack, so those are fine. You need to watch out for any static or global variables. This doesn't mean that you are absolutely not allowed to use static or global variables. There are times when you actually want something to affect all threads, but generally you need to avoid using them if you want your code to be thread safe.

In the case where you have a global variable that needs to be global and accessed by all threads, be very careful when you update it. If, for example, it is an incrementing counter, you need to atomically increment it to avoid race conditions with other threads. You do this using a mutex (mutual exclusion). Lock the mutex, read the current value, increment it and write it back and then unlock the mutex. Any other thread that wants to modify the value has to first check the mutex and block until it is cleared.

If you are using APR[28], have a look at the `apr_atomic_*` functions and the `apr_thread_mutex_*` functions.

### errno

This is a common global variable that holds the error number of the last error that occurred. If one thread calls a low-level function that sets errno and then another thread checks it, we are bleeding error numbers from one thread into another. To solve this, make sure your module or library defines _REENTRANT or is compiled with -D_REENTRANT. This will make errno a per-thread variable and should hopefully be transparent to the code. It does this by doing something like this:

```
#define errno (*(__errno_location()))
```

which means that accessing errno will call `__errno_location()` which is provided by the libc. Setting _REENTRANT also forces redefinition of some other functions to their `*_r` equivalents and sometimes changes the common `getc`/`putc` macros into safer function calls. Check your libc documentation for specifics. Instead of, or in addition to _REENTRANT the symbols that may affect this are _POSIX_C_SOURCE, _THREAD_SAFE, _SVID_SOURCE, and _BSD_SOURCE.

### Common standard troublesome functions

Not only do things have to be thread safe, but they also have to be reentrant. `strtok()` is an obvious one. You call it the first time with your delimiter which it then remembers and on each subsequent call it returns the next token. Obviously if multiple threads are calling it you will have a problem. Most systems have a reentrant version of the function called `strtok_r()` where you pass in an extra argument which contains an allocated `char *` which the function will use instead of its own static storage for maintaining the tokenizing state. If you are using APR[29] you can use `apr_strtok()`.

---

[28]http://apr.apache.org/
[29]http://apr.apache.org/

`crypt()` is another function that tends to not be reentrant, so if you run across calls to that function in a library, watch out. On some systems it is reentrant though, so it is not always a problem. If your system has `crypt_r()` chances are you should be using that, or if possible simply avoid the whole mess by using md5 instead.

## Common 3rd Party Libraries

The following is a list of common libraries that are used by 3rd party Apache modules. You can check to see if your module is using a potentially unsafe library by using tools such as `ldd(1)` and `nm(1)`. For PHP[30], for example, try this:

```
% ldd libphp4.so
libsablot.so.0 => /usr/local/lib/libsablot.so.0 (0x401f6000)
libexpat.so.0 => /usr/lib/libexpat.so.0 (0x402da000)
libsnmp.so.0 => /usr/lib/libsnmp.so.0 (0x402f9000)
libpdf.so.1 => /usr/local/lib/libpdf.so.1 (0x40353000)
libz.so.1 => /usr/lib/libz.so.1 (0x403e2000)
libpng.so.2 => /usr/lib/libpng.so.2 (0x403f0000)
libmysqlclient.so.11 => /usr/lib/libmysqlclient.so.11 (0x40411000)
libming.so => /usr/lib/libming.so (0x40449000)
libm.so.6 => /lib/libm.so.6 (0x40487000)
libfreetype.so.6 => /usr/lib/libfreetype.so.6 (0x404a8000)
libjpeg.so.62 => /usr/lib/libjpeg.so.62 (0x404e7000)
libcrypt.so.1 => /lib/libcrypt.so.1 (0x40505000)
libssl.so.2 => /lib/libssl.so.2 (0x40532000)
libcrypto.so.2 => /lib/libcrypto.so.2 (0x40560000)
libresolv.so.2 => /lib/libresolv.so.2 (0x40624000)
libdl.so.2 => /lib/libdl.so.2 (0x40634000)
libnsl.so.1 => /lib/libnsl.so.1 (0x40637000)
libc.so.6 => /lib/libc.so.6 (0x4064b000)
/lib/ld-linux.so.2 -> /lib/ld linux.so.2 (0x80000000)
```

In addition to these libraries you will need to have a look at any libraries linked statically into the module. You can use `nm(1)` to look for individual symbols in the module.

## Library List

Please drop a note to dev@httpd.apache.org[31] if you have additions or corrections to this list.

| Library | Version | Thread Safe? | Notes |
|---------|---------|--------------|-------|
| ASpell/PSpell[a]<br><br>[a]http://aspell.sourceforge.net/ | | ? | |
| Berkeley DB[a]<br><br>[a]http://www.sleepycat.com/ | 3.x, 4.x | Yes | Be careful about sharing a connection across threads. |
| bzip2[a]<br><br>[a]http://sources.redhat.com/bzip2/index.html | | Yes | Both low-level and high-level APIs are thread-safe. However, high-level API requires thread-safe access to errno. |
| cdb[a]<br><br>[a]http://cr.yp.to/cdb.html | | ? | |

---

[30]http://www.php.net/
[31]http://httpd.apache.org/lists.html#http-dev

| C-Client[a] | | Perhaps | c-client uses `strtok()` and `gethostbyname()` which are not thread-safe on most C library implementations. c-client's static data is meant to be shared across threads. If `strtok()` and `gethostbyname()` are thread-safe on your OS, c-client *may* be thread-safe. |
|---|---|---|---|
| [a]http://www.washington.edu/imap/ | | | |
| libcrypt[a] | | ? | |
| [a]http://www.ijg.org/files/ | | | |
| Expat[a] | | Yes | Need a separate parser instance per thread |
| [a]http://expat.sourceforge.net/ | | | |
| FreeTDS[a] | | ? | |
| [a]http://www.freetds.org/ | | | |
| FreeType[a] | | ? | |
| [a]http://www.freetype.org/ | | | |
| GD 1.8.x[a] | | ? | |
| [a]http://www.boutell.com/gd/ | | | |
| GD 2.0.x[a] | | ? | |
| [a]http://www.boutell.com/gd/ | | | |
| gdbm[a] | | No | Errors returned via a static `gdbm_error` variable |
| [a]http://www.gnu.org/software/gdbm/gdbm.html | | | |
| ImageMagick[a] | 5.2.2 | Yes | ImageMagick docs claim it is thread safe since version 5.2.2 (see Change log[a]). [a]http://www.imagemagick.com/www |
| [a]http://www.imagemagick.org/ | | | |
| Imlib2[a] | | ? | |
| [a]http://www.enlightenment.org/p.php?p=about/efl&l=en | | | |
| libjpeg[a] | v6b | ? | |
| [a]http://www.ijg.org/files/ | | | |
| libmysqlclient[a] | | Yes | Use mysqlclient_r library variant to ensure thread-safety. For more information, please read http://dev.mysql.com/doc/mysql/en/ |
| [a]http://mysql.com | | | |
| Ming[a] | 0.2a | ? | |
| [a]http://www.opaque.net/ming/ | | | |
| Net-SNMP[a] | 5.0.x | ? | |
| [a]http://net-snmp.sourceforge.net/ | | | |
| OpenLDAP[a] | 2.1.x | Yes | Use `ldap_r` library variant to ensure thread-safety. |
| [a]http://www.openldap.org/ | | | |
| OpenSSL[a] | 0.9.6g | Yes | Requires proper usage of `CRYPTO_num_locks`, `CRYPTO_set_locking_callba` `CRYPTO_set_id_callback` |
| [a]http://www.openssl.org/ | | | |
| liboci8 (Oracle 8+)[a] | 8.x,9.x | ? | |
| [a]http://www.oracle.com/ | | | |

| pdflib[a]  [a]http://pdflib.com/ | 5.0.x | Yes | PDFLib docs claim it is thread safe; changes.txt indicates it has been partially thread-safe since V1.91: http://www.pdflib.com/products/pdflib-family/pdflib/. |
|---|---|---|---|
| libpng[a]  [a]http://www.libpng.org/pub/png/libpng.html | 1.0.x | ? | |
| libpng[a]  [a]http://www.libpng.org/pub/png/libpng.html | 1.2.x | ? | |
| libpq (PostgreSQL)[a]  [a]http://www.postgresql.org/docs/8.4/static/libpq-threading.html | 8.x | Yes | Don't share connections across threads and watch out for `crypt()` calls |
| Sablotron[a]  [a]http://www.gingerall.com/charlie/ga/xml/p_sab.xml | 0.95 | ? | |
| zlib[a]  [a]http://www.gzip.org/zlib/ | 1.1.4 | Yes | Relies upon thread-safe zalloc and zfree functions Default is to use libc's calloc/free which are thread-safe. |

# Chapter 12

# Glossary and Index

## 12.1   Glossary

This glossary defines some of the common terminology related to Apache in particular, and web serving in general. More information on each concept is provided in the links.

### Definitions

**Access Control**  The restriction of access to network realms. In an Apache context usually the restriction of access to certain *URLs*.
See: Authentication, Authorization, and Access Control (p. 227)

**Algorithm**  An unambiguous formula or set of rules for solving a problem in a finite number of steps. Algorithms for encryption are usually called *Ciphers*.

**APache eXtension Tool (apxs)**  A perl script that aids in compiling module sources into Dynamic Shared Objects (DSOs) and helps install them in the Apache Web server.
See: Manual Page: `apxs`

**Apache Portable Runtime (APR)**  A set of libraries providing many of the basic interfaces between the server and the operating system. APR is developed parallel to the Apache HTTP Server as an independent project.
See: Apache Portable Runtime Project[1]

**Authentication**  The positive identification of a network entity such as a server, a client, or a user.
See: Authentication, Authorization, and Access Control (p. 227)

**Certificate**  A data record used for authenticating network entities such as a server or a client. A certificate contains X.509 information pieces about its owner (called the subject) and the signing Certification Authority (called the issuer), plus the owner's public key and the signature made by the CA. Network entities verify these signatures using CA certificates.
See: SSL/TLS Encryption (p. 192)

**Certificate Signing Request (CSR)**  An unsigned certificate for submission to a Certification Authority, which signs it with the Private Key of their CA *Certificate*. Once the CSR is signed, it becomes a real certificate.
See: SSL/TLS Encryption (p. 192)

**Certification Authority (CA)**  A trusted third party whose purpose is to sign certificates for network entities it has authenticated using secure means.  Other network entities can check the signature to verify that a CA has authenticated the bearer of a certificate.
See: SSL/TLS Encryption (p. 192)

**Cipher**  An algorithm or system for data encryption. Examples are DES, IDEA, RC4, etc.
See: SSL/TLS Encryption (p. 192)

**Ciphertext**  The result after Plaintext is passed through a Cipher.
See: SSL/TLS Encryption (p. 192)

**Common Gateway Interface (CGI)**  A standard definition for an interface between a web server and an external program that allows the external program to service requests. There is an Informational RFC[2] which covers the specifics.
See: Dynamic Content with CGI (p. 236)

**Configuration Directive**  See: Directive

**Configuration File**  A text file containing Directives that control the configuration of Apache.
See: Configuration Files (p. 32)

---

[1] http://apr.apache.org/
[2] http://www.ietf.org/rfc/rfc3875

**CONNECT** An HTTP method for proxying raw data channels over HTTP. It can be used to encapsulate other protocols, such as the SSL protocol.

**Context** An area in the configuration files where certain types of directives are allowed.
See: Terms Used to Describe Apache Directives (p. 377)

**Digital Signature** An encrypted text block that validates a certificate or other file. A Certification Authority creates a signature by generating a hash of the *Public Key* embedded in a *Certificate*, then encrypting the hash with its own *Private Key*. Only the CA's public key can decrypt the signature, verifying that the CA has authenticated the network entity that owns the *Certificate*.
See: SSL/TLS Encryption (p. 192)

**Directive** A configuration command that controls one or more aspects of Apache's behavior. Directives are placed in the Configuration File
See: Directive Index (p. 1106)

**Dynamic Shared Object (DSO)** Modules compiled separately from the Apache `httpd` binary that can be loaded on-demand.
See: Dynamic Shared Object Support (p. 68)

**Environment Variable (env-variable)** Named variables managed by the operating system shell and used to store information and communicate between programs. Apache also contains internal variables that are referred to as environment variables, but are stored in internal Apache structures, rather than in the shell environment.
See: Environment Variables in Apache (p. 92)

**Export-Crippled** Diminished in cryptographic strength (and security) in order to comply with the United States' Export Administration Regulations (EAR). Export-crippled cryptographic software is limited to a small key size, resulting in *Ciphertext* which usually can be decrypted by brute force.
See: SSL/TLS Encryption (p. 192)

**Filter** A process that is applied to data that is sent or received by the server. Input filters process data sent by the client to the server, while output filters process documents on the server before they are sent to the client. For example, the `INCLUDES` output filter processes documents for Server Side Includes.
See: Filters (p. 110)

**Fully-Qualified Domain-Name (FQDN)** The unique name of a network entity, consisting of a hostname and a domain name that can resolve to an IP address. For example, `www` is a hostname, `example.com` is a domain name, and `www.example.com` is a fully-qualified domain name.

**Handler** An internal Apache representation of the action to be performed when a file is called. Generally, files have implicit handlers, based on the file type. Normally, all files are simply served by the server, but certain file types are "handled" separately. For example, the `cgi-script` handler designates files to be processed as CGIs.
See: Apache's Handler Use (p. 108)

**Hash** A mathematical one-way, irreversible algorithm generating a string with fixed-length from another string of any length. Different input strings will usually produce different hashes (depending on the hash function).

**Header** The part of the HTTP request and response that is sent before the actual content, and that contains meta-information describing the content.

**.htaccess** A configuration file that is placed inside the web tree and applies configuration directives to the directory where it is placed and all sub-directories. Despite its name, this file can hold almost any type of directive, not just access-control directives.
See: Configuration Files (p. 32)

**httpd.conf** The main Apache configuration file. The default location is `/usr/local/apache2/conf/httpd.conf`, but it may be moved using run-time or compile-time configuration.
See: Configuration Files (p. 32)

**HyperText Transfer Protocol (HTTP)**  The standard transmission protocol used on the World Wide Web.  Apache implements version 1.1 of the protocol, referred to as HTTP/1.1 and defined by RFC 2616[3].

**HTTPS**  The HyperText Transfer Protocol (Secure), the standard encrypted communication mechanism on the World Wide Web. This is actually just HTTP over SSL.
   See: SSL/TLS Encryption (p. 192)

**Method**  In the context of HTTP, an action to perform on a resource, specified on the request line by the client. Some of the methods available in HTTP are `GET`, `POST`, and `PUT`.

**Message Digest**  A hash of a message, which can be used to verify that the contents of the message have not been altered in transit.
   See: SSL/TLS Encryption (p. 192)

**MIME-type**  A way to describe the kind of document being transmitted. Its name comes from that fact that its format is borrowed from the Multipurpose Internet Mail Extensions.  It consists of a major type and a minor type, separated by a slash. Some examples are `text/html`, `image/gif`, and `application/octet-stream`. In HTTP, the MIME-type is transmitted in the `Content-Type` header.
   See: mod_mime (p. 749)

**Module**  An independent part of a program.  Much of Apache's functionality is contained in modules that you can choose to include or exclude.  Modules that are compiled into the Apache `httpd` binary are called *static modules*, while modules that are stored separately and can be optionally loaded at run-time are called *dynamic modules* or DSOs. Modules that are included by default are called *base modules*. Many modules are available for Apache that are not distributed as part of the Apache HTTP Server tarball. These are referred to as *third-party modules*.
   See: Module Index (p. 1101)

**Module Magic Number (MMN)**  Module Magic Number is a constant defined in the Apache source code that is associated with binary compatibility of modules. It is changed when internal Apache structures, function calls and other significant parts of API change in such a way that binary compatibility cannot be guaranteed any more. On MMN change, all third party modules have to be at least recompiled, sometimes even slightly changed in order to work with the new version of Apache.

**OpenSSL**  The Open Source toolkit for SSL/TLS
   See http://www.openssl.org/#

**Pass Phrase**  The word or phrase that protects private key files. It prevents unauthorized users from encrypting them. Usually it's just the secret encryption/decryption key used for Ciphers.
   See: SSL/TLS Encryption (p. 192)

**Plaintext**  The unencrypted text.

**Private Key**  The secret key in a Public Key Cryptography system, used to decrypt incoming messages and sign outgoing ones.
   See: SSL/TLS Encryption (p. 192)

**Proxy**  An intermediate server that sits between the client and the *origin server*.  It accepts requests from clients, transmits those requests on to the origin server, and then returns the response from the origin server to the client. If several clients request the same content, the proxy can deliver that content from its cache, rather than requesting it from the origin server each time, thereby reducing response time.
   See: mod_proxy (p. 787)

**Public Key**  The publicly available key in a Public Key Cryptography system, used to encrypt messages bound for its owner and to decrypt signatures made by its owner.
   See: SSL/TLS Encryption (p. 192)

---

[3]http://ietf.org/rfc/rfc2616.txt

**Public Key Cryptography** The study and application of asymmetric encryption systems, which use one key for encryption and another for decryption. A corresponding pair of such keys constitutes a key pair. Also called Asymmetric Cryptography.
See: SSL/TLS Encryption (p. 192)

**Regular Expression (Regex)** A way of describing a pattern in text - for example, "all the words that begin with the letter A" or "every 10-digit phone number" or even "Every sentence with two commas in it, and no capital letter Q". Regular expressions are useful in Apache because they let you apply certain attributes against collections of files or resources in very flexible ways - for example, all .gif and .jpg files under any "images" directory could be written as "/images/.*(jpg|gif)$". In places where regular expressions are used to replace strings, the special variables $1 ... $9 contain backreferences to the grouped parts (in parentheses) of the matched expression. The special variable $0 contains a backreference to the whole matched expression. To write a literal dollar sign in a replacement string, it can be escaped with a backslash. Historically, the variable & could be used as alias for $0 in some places. This is no longer possible since version 2.3.6. Apache uses Perl Compatible Regular Expressions provided by the PCRE[4] library. You can find more documentation about PCRE's regular expression syntax at that site, or at Wikipedia[5].

**Reverse Proxy** A proxy server that appears to the client as if it is an *origin server*. This is useful to hide the real origin server from the client for security reasons, or to load balance.

**Secure Sockets Layer (SSL)** A protocol created by Netscape Communications Corporation for general communication authentication and encryption over TCP/IP networks. The most popular usage is *HTTPS*, i.e. the HyperText Transfer Protocol (HTTP) over SSL.
See: SSL/TLS Encryption (p. 192)

**Server Name Indication (SNI)** An SSL function that allows passing the desired server hostname in the initial SSL handshake message, so that the web server can select the correct virtual host configuration to use in processing the SSL handshake. It was added to SSL starting with the TLS extensions, RFC 3546.
See: the SSL FAQ (p. 212) and RFC 3546[6]

**Server Side Includes (SSI)** A technique for embedding processing directives inside HTML files.
See: Introduction to Server Side Includes (p. 243)

**Session** The context information of a communication in general.

**SSLeay** The original SSL/TLS implementation library developed by Eric A. Young

**Subrequest** Apache provides a subrequest API to modules that allows other filesystem or URL paths to be partially or fully evaluated by the server. Example consumers of this API are DIRECTORYINDEX, MOD_AUTOINDEX, and MOD_INCLUDE.

**Symmetric Cryptography** The study and application of *Ciphers* that use a single secret key for both encryption and decryption operations.
See: SSL/TLS Encryption (p. 192)

**Tarball** A package of files gathered together using the `tar` utility. Apache distributions are stored in compressed tar archives or using pkzip.

**Transport Layer Security (TLS)** The successor protocol to SSL, created by the Internet Engineering Task Force (IETF) for general communication authentication and encryption over TCP/IP networks. TLS version 1 is nearly identical with SSL version 3.
See: SSL/TLS Encryption (p. 192)

---

[4] http://www.pcre.org/
[5] http://en.wikipedia.org/wiki/PCRE
[6] http://www.ietf.org/rfc/rfc3546.txt

**Uniform Resource Locator (URL)** The name/address of a resource on the Internet.  This is the common informal term for what is formally called a Uniform Resource Identifier.  URLs are usually made up of a scheme, like `http` or `https`, a hostname, and a path.  A URL for this page might be `http://httpd.apache.org/docs/trunk/glossary.html`.

**Uniform Resource Identifier (URI)** A compact string of characters for identifying an abstract or physical resource. It is formally defined by RFC 2396[7]. URIs used on the world-wide web are commonly referred to as URLs.

**Virtual Hosting** Serving multiple websites using a single instance of Apache. *IP virtual hosting* differentiates between websites based on their IP address, while *name-based virtual hosting* uses only the name of the host and can therefore host many sites on the same IP address.
See: Apache Virtual Host documentation (p. 124)

**X.509** An authentication certificate scheme recommended by the International Telecommunication Union (ITU-T) which is used for SSL/TLS authentication.
See: SSL/TLS Encryption (p. 192)

---

[7]http://www.ietf.org/rfc/rfc2396.txt

## 12.2 Module Index

Below is a list of all of the modules that come as part of the Apache HTTP Server distribution. See also the complete alphabetical list of all Apache HTTP Server directives (p. 1106) .

**See also**

- Multi-Processing Modules (MPMs) (p. 90)
- Directive Quick Reference (p. 1106)

### Core Features and Multi-Processing Modules

**core** (p. 380) Core Apache HTTP Server features that are always available

**mpm_common** (p. 990) A collection of directives that are implemented by more than one multi-processing module (MPM)

**event** (p. 1001) A variant of the WORKER MPM with the goal of consuming threads only for connections with active processing

**mpm_netware** (p. 1006) Multi-Processing Module implementing an exclusively threaded web server optimized for Novell NetWare

**mpmt_os2** (p. 1008) Hybrid multi-process, multi-threaded MPM for OS/2

**prefork** (p. 1009) Implements a non-threaded, pre-forking web server

**mpm_winnt** (p. 1012) Multi-Processing Module optimized for Windows NT.

**worker** (p. 1014) Multi-Processing Module implementing a hybrid multi-threaded multi-process web server

### Other Modules

**mod_access_compat** (p. 440) Group authorizations based on host (name or IP address)

**mod_actions** (p. 445) Execute CGI scripts based on media type or request method.

**mod_alias** (p. 447) Provides for mapping different parts of the host filesystem in the document tree and for URL redirection

**mod_allowhandlers** (p. 454) Easily restrict what HTTP handlers can be used on the server

**mod_allowmethods** (p. 455) Easily restrict what HTTP methods can be used on the server

**mod_asis** (p. 456) Sends files that contain their own HTTP headers

**mod_auth_basic** (p. 458) Basic HTTP authentication

**mod_auth_digest** (p. 462) User authentication using MD5 Digest Authentication

**mod_auth_form** (p. 466) Form authentication

**mod_authn_anon** (p. 477) Allows "anonymous" user access to authenticated areas,

**mod_authn_core** (p. 480) Core Authentication

**mod_authn_dbd** (p. 484) User authentication using an SQL database

**mod_authn_dbm**  (p. 487) User authentication using DBM files

**mod_authn_file**  (p. 489) User authentication using text files

**mod_authn_socache**  (p. 491) Manages a cache of authentication credentials to relieve the load on backends

**mod_authnz_fcgi**  (p. 494) Allows a FastCGI authorizer application to handle Apache httpd authentication and authorization

**mod_authnz_ldap**  (p. 501) Allows an LDAP directory to be used to store the database for HTTP Basic authentication.

**mod_authz_core**  (p. 519) Core Authorization

**mod_authz_dbd**  (p. 527) Group Authorization and Login using SQL

**mod_authz_dbm**  (p. 532) Group authorization using DBM files

**mod_authz_groupfile**  (p. 534) Group authorization using plaintext files

**mod_authz_host**  (p. 536) Group authorizations based on host (name or IP address)

**mod_authz_owner**  (p. 539) Authorization based on file ownership

**mod_authz_user**  (p. 541) User Authorization

**mod_autoindex**  (p. 542) Generates directory indexes, automatically, similar to the Unix ls command or the Win32 dir shell command

**mod_buffer**  (p. 554) Support for request buffering

**mod_cache**  (p. 555) RFC 2616 compliant HTTP caching filter.

**mod_cache_disk**  (p. 570) Disk based storage module for the HTTP caching filter.

**mod_cache_socache**  (p. 574) Shared object cache (socache) based storage module for the HTTP caching filter.

**mod_cern_meta**  (p. 578) CERN httpd metafile semantics

**mod_cgi**  (p. 580) Execution of CGI scripts

**mod_cgid**  (p. 583) Execution of CGI scripts using an external CGI daemon

**mod_charset_lite**  (p. 585) Specify character set translation or recoding

**mod_data**  (p. 588) Convert response body into an RFC2397 data URL

**mod_dav**  (p. 589) Distributed Authoring and Versioning (WebDAV[8]) functionality

**mod_dav_fs**  (p. 592) Filesystem provider for MOD_DAV

**mod_dav_lock**  (p. 593) Generic locking module for MOD_DAV

**mod_dbd**  (p. 594) Manages SQL database connections

**mod_deflate**  (p. 599) Compress content before it is delivered to the client

**mod_dialup**  (p. 606) Send static content at a bandwidth rate limit, defined by the various old modem standards

**mod_dir**  (p. 607) Provides for "trailing slash" redirects and serving directory index files

**mod_dumpio**  (p. 612) Dumps all I/O to error log as desired.

**mod_echo**  (p. 614) A simple echo server to illustrate protocol modules

---

[8]http://www.webdav.org/

**mod_mime_magic**  (p. 762) Determines the MIME type of a file by looking at a few bytes of its contents

**mod_negotiation**  (p. 766) Provides for content negotiation (p. 78)

**mod_nw_ssl**  (p. 770) Enable SSL encryption for NetWare

**mod_policy**  (p. 771) HTTP protocol compliance enforcement.

**mod_privileges**  (p. 781) Support for Solaris privileges and for running virtual hosts under different user IDs.

**mod_proxy**  (p. 787) Multi-protocol proxy/gateway server

**mod_proxy_ajp**  (p. 815) AJP support module for MOD_PROXY

**mod_proxy_balancer**  (p. 824) MOD_PROXY extension for load balancing

**mod_proxy_connect**  (p. 828) MOD_PROXY extension for CONNECT request handling

**mod_proxy_express**  (p. 830) Dynamic mass reverse proxy extension for MOD_PROXY

**mod_proxy_fcgi**  (p. 833) FastCGI support module for MOD_PROXY

**mod_proxy_fdpass**  (p. 836) fdpass external process support module for MOD_PROXY

**mod_proxy_ftp**  (p. 837) FTP support module for MOD_PROXY

**mod_proxy_hcheck**  (p. 840) Dynamic health check of Balancer members (workers) for MOD_PROXY

**mod_proxy_html**  (p. 844) Rewrite HTML links in to ensure they are addressable from Clients' networks in a proxy context.

**mod_proxy_http**  (p. 850) HTTP support module for MOD_PROXY

**mod_proxy_http2**  (p. 852) HTTP/2 support module for MOD_PROXY

**mod_proxy_scgi**  (p. 853) SCGI gateway module for MOD_PROXY

**mod_proxy_wstunnel**  (p. 856) Websockets support module for MOD_PROXY

**mod_ratelimit**  (p. 858) Bandwidth Rate Limiting for Clients

**mod_reflector**  (p. 859) Reflect a request body as a response via the output filter stack.

**mod_remoteip**  (p. 860) Replaces the original client IP address for the connection with the useragent IP address list presented by a proxies or a load balancer via the request headers.

**mod_reqtimeout**  (p. 864) Set timeout and minimum data rate for receiving requests

**mod_request**  (p. 866) Filters to handle and make available HTTP request bodies

**mod_rewrite**  (p. 867) Provides a rule-based rewriting engine to rewrite requested URLs on the fly

**mod_sed**  (p. 881) Filter Input (request) and Output (response) content using sed syntax

**mod_session**  (p. 883) Session support

**mod_session_cookie**  (p. 890) Cookie based session support

**mod_session_crypto**  (p. 893) Session encryption support

**mod_session_dbd**  (p. 897) DBD/SQL based session support

**mod_setenvif**  (p. 902) Allows the setting of environment variables based on characteristics of the request

**mod_slotmem_plain** (p. 906) Slot-based shared memory provider.

**mod_slotmem_shm** (p. 907) Slot-based shared memory provider.

**mod_so** (p. 908) Loading of executable code and modules into the server at start-up or restart time

**mod_socache_dbm** (p. 910) DBM based shared object cache provider.

**mod_socache_dc** (p. 911) Distcache based shared object cache provider.

**mod_socache_memcache** (p. 912) Memcache based shared object cache provider.

**mod_socache_shmcb** (p. 913) shmcb based shared object cache provider.

**mod_speling** (p. 914) Attempts to correct mistaken URLs by ignoring capitalization, or attempting to correct various minor misspellings.

**mod_ssl** (p. 916) Strong cryptography using the Secure Sockets Layer (SSL) and Transport Layer Security (TLS) protocols

**mod_ssl_ct** (p. 955) Implementation of Certificate Transparency (RFC 6962)

**mod_status** (p. 962) Provides information on server activity and performance

**mod_substitute** (p. 964) Perform search and replace operations on response bodies

**mod_suexec** (p. 967) Allows CGI scripts to run as a specified user and Group

**mod_syslog** (p. 968) Provides "syslog" ErrorLog provider

**mod_systemd** (p. 969) Provides better support for systemd integration

**mod_unique_id** (p. 970) Provides an environment variable with a unique identifier for each request

**mod_unixd** (p. 972) Basic (required) security for Unix-family platforms.

**mod_userdir** (p. 975) User-specific directories

**mod_usertrack** (p. 977) *Clickstream* logging of user activity on a site

**mod_version** (p. 980) Version dependent configuration

**mod_vhost_alias** (p. 982) Provides for dynamically configured mass virtual hosting

**mod_watchdog** (p. 986) provides infrastructure for other modules to periodically run tasks

**mod_xml2enc** (p. 987) Enhanced charset/internationalisation support for libxml2-based filter modules

## 12.3   Directive Quick Reference

The directive quick reference shows the usage, default, status, and context of each Apache configuration directive. For more information about each of these, see the Directive Dictionary (p. 377) .

The first column gives the directive name and usage. The second column shows the default value of the directive, if a default exists. If the default is too large to display, it will be truncated and followed by "+".

The third and fourth columns list the contexts where the directive is allowed and the status of the directive according to the legend tables below.

| | | | |
|---|---|---|---|
| `/AcceptFilter protocol accept_filter`<br>Configures optimizations for a Protocol's Listener Sockets | | s<br>p. 382 | C |
| `AcceptPathInfo On\|Off\|Default`<br>Resources accept trailing pathname information | Default | svdh<br>p. 383 | C |
| `AccessFileName filename [filename] ...`<br>Name of the distributed configuration file | .htaccess | sv<br>p. 384 | C |
| `Action action-type cgi-script [virtual]`<br>Activates a CGI script for a particular handler or content-type | | svdh<br>p. 445 | B |
| `AddAlt string file [file] ...`<br>Alternate text to display for a file, instead of an icon selected by filename | | svdh<br>p. 544 | B |
| `AddAltByEncoding string MIME-encoding [MIME-encoding] ...`<br>Alternate text to display for a file instead of an icon selected by MIME-encoding | | svdh<br>p. 544 | B |
| `AddAltByType string MIME-type [MIME-type] ...`<br>Alternate text to display for a file, instead of an icon selected by MIME content-type | | svdh<br>p. 545 | B |
| `AddCharset charset extension [extension] ...`<br>Maps the given filename extensions to the specified content charset | | svdh<br>p. 752 | B |
| `AddDefaultCharset On\|Off\|charset`<br>Default charset parameter to be added when a response content-type is `text/plain` or `text/html` | Off | svdh<br>p. 384 | C |
| `AddDescription string file [file] ...`<br>Description to display for a file | | svdh<br>p. 545 | B |
| `AddEncoding encoding extension [extension] ...`<br>Maps the given filename extensions to the specified encoding type | | svdh<br>p. 752 | B |
| `AddHandler handler-name extension [extension] ...`<br>Maps the filename extensions to the specified handler | | svdh<br>p. 753 | B |
| `AddIcon icon name [name] ...`<br>Icon to display for a file selected by name | | svdh<br>p. 546 | B |
| `AddIconByEncoding icon MIME-encoding [MIME-encoding] ...`<br>Icon to display next to files selected by MIME content-encoding | | svdh<br>p. 546 | B |
| `AddIconByType icon MIME-type [MIME-type] ...`<br>Icon to display next to files selected by MIME content-type | | svdh<br>p. 547 | B |
| `AddInputFilter filter[;filter...] extension [extension] ...`<br>Maps filename extensions to the filters that will process client requests | | svdh<br>p. 753 | B |
| `AddLanguage language-tag extension [extension] ...`<br>Maps the given filename extension to the specified content language | | svdh<br>p. 754 | B |
| `AddModuleInfo module-name string`<br>Adds additional information to the module information displayed by the server-info handler | | sv<br>p. 682 | E |
| `AddOutputFilter filter[;filter...] extension [extension] ...`<br>Maps filename extensions to the filters that will process responses from the server | | svdh<br>p. 754 | B |
| `AddOutputFilterByType filter[;filter...] media-type [media-type] ...`<br>assigns an output filter to a particular media-type | | svdh<br>p. 633 | B |
| `AddType media-type extension [extension] ...`<br>Maps the given filename extensions onto the specified content type | | svdh<br>p. 755 | B |
| `Alias [URL-path] file-path\|directory-path`<br>Maps URLs to filesystem locations | | svd<br>p. 448 | B |
| `AliasMatch regex file-path\|directory-path`<br>Maps URLs to filesystem locations using regular expressions | | sv<br>p. 449 | B |
| `Allow from all\|host\|env=[!]env-variable [host\|env=[!]env-variable] ...`<br>Controls which hosts can access an area of the server | | dh<br>p. 441 | E |
| `AllowCONNECT port[-port] [port[-port]] ...`<br>Ports that are allowed to CONNECT through the proxy | 443 563 | sv<br>p. 829 | E |

| | | | |
|---|---|---|---|
| `AllowEncodedSlashes On|Off|NoDecode` | Off | sv | C |
| Determines whether encoded path separators in URLs are allowed to be passed through | | p. 385 | |
| `AllowHandlers [not] none|handler-name` | all | d | X |
| `[none|handler-name]...` | | | |
| Restrict access to the listed handlers | | p. 454 | |
| `AllowMethods reset|HTTP-method [HTTP-method]...` | reset | d | X |
| Restrict access to the listed HTTP methods | | p. 455 | |
| `AllowOverride All|None|directive-type [directive-type] ...` | None (2.3.9 and lat + | d | C |
| Types of directives that are allowed in `.htaccess` files | | p. 386 | |
| `AllowOverrideList None|directive [directive-type] ...` | None | d | C |
| Individual directives that are allowed in `.htaccess` files | | p. 387 | |
| `Anonymous user [user] ...` | | dh | E |
| Specifies userIDs that are allowed access without password verification | | p. 478 | |
| `Anonymous_LogEmail On|Off` | On | dh | E |
| Sets whether the password entered will be logged in the error log | | p. 478 | |
| `Anonymous_MustGiveEmail On|Off` | On | dh | E |
| Specifies whether blank passwords are allowed | | p. 479 | |
| `Anonymous_NoUserID On|Off` | Off | dh | E |
| Sets whether the userID field may be empty | | p. 479 | |
| `Anonymous_VerifyEmail On|Off` | Off | dh | E |
| Sets whether to check the password field for a correctly formatted email address | | p. 479 | |
| `AsyncFilter request|connection|network` | request | sv | C |
| Set the minimum filter type eligible for asynchronous handling | | p. 388 | |
| `AsyncRequestWorkerFactor factor` | | s | M |
| Limit concurrent connections per process | | p. 1004 | |
| `AuthBasicAuthoritative On|Off` | On | dh | B |
| Sets whether authorization and authentication are passed to lower level modules | | p. 458 | |
| `AuthBasicFake off|username [password]` | | dh | B |
| Fake basic authentication using the given expressions for username and password | | p. 459 | |
| `AuthBasicProvider provider-name [provider-name] ...` | file | dh | B |
| Sets the authentication provider(s) for this location | | p. 460 | |
| `AuthBasicUseDigestAlgorithm MD5|Off` | Off | dh | B |
| Check passwords against the authentication providers as if Digest Authentication was in force instead of Basic Authentication. | | p. 460 | |
| `AuthDBDUserPWQuery query` | | d | E |
| SQL query to look up a password for a user | | p. 485 | |
| `AuthDBDUserRealmQuery query` | | d | E |
| SQL query to look up a password hash for a user and realm. | | p. 486 | |
| `AuthDBMGroupFile file-path` | | dh | E |
| Sets the name of the database file containing the list of user groups for authorization | | p. 533 | |
| `AuthDBMType default|SDBM|GDBM|NDBM|DB` | default | dh | E |
| Sets the type of database file that is used to store passwords | | p. 487 | |
| `AuthDBMUserFile file-path` | | dh | E |
| Sets the name of a database file containing the list of users and passwords for authentication | | p. 488 | |
| `AuthDigestAlgorithm MD5|MD5-sess` | MD5 | dh | E |
| Selects the algorithm used to calculate the challenge and response hashes in digest authentication | | p. 463 | |
| `AuthDigestDomain URI [URI] ...` | | dh | E |
| URIs that are in the same protection space for digest authentication | | p. 463 | |
| `AuthDigestNcCheck On|Off` | Off | s | E |
| Enables or disables checking of the nonce-count sent by the server | | p. 464 | |
| `AuthDigestNonceFormat format` | | dh | E |
| Determines how the nonce is generated | | p. 464 | |
| `AuthDigestNonceLifetime seconds` | 300 | dh | E |
| How long the server nonce is valid | | p. 464 | |
| `AuthDigestProvider provider-name [provider-name] ...` | file | dh | E |
| Sets the authentication provider(s) for this location | | p. 464 | |
| `AuthDigestQop none|auth|auth-int [auth|auth-int]` | auth | dh | E |
| Determines the quality-of-protection to use in digest authentication | | p. 465 | |
| `AuthDigestShmemSize size` | 1000 | s | E |
| The amount of shared memory to allocate for keeping track of clients | | p. 465 | |
| `AuthFormAuthoritative On|Off` | On | dh | B |
| Sets whether authorization and authentication are passed to lower level modules | | p. 470 | |
| `AuthFormBody fieldname` | | d | B |
| The name of a form field carrying the body of the request to attempt on successful login | | p. 471 | |
| `AuthFormDisableNoStore On|Off` | Off | d | B |
| Disable the CacheControl no-store header on the login page | | p. 471 | |

| Directive / Description | Default | Ctx | Mod | Page |
|---|---|---|---|---|
| `AuthFormFakeBasicAuth On\|Off`<br>Fake a Basic Authentication header | Off | d | B | p. 471 |
| `AuthFormLocation fieldname`<br>The name of a form field carrying a URL to redirect to on successful login | | d | B | p. 472 |
| `AuthFormLoginRequiredLocation url`<br>The URL of the page to be redirected to should login be required | | d | B | p. 472 |
| `AuthFormLoginSuccessLocation url`<br>The URL of the page to be redirected to should login be successful | | d | B | p. 472 |
| `AuthFormLogoutLocation uri`<br>The URL to redirect to after a user has logged out | | d | B | p. 473 |
| `AuthFormMethod fieldname`<br>The name of a form field carrying the method of the request to attempt on successful login | | d | B | p. 473 |
| `AuthFormMimetype fieldname`<br>The name of a form field carrying the mimetype of the body of the request to attempt on successful login | | d | B | p. 473 |
| `AuthFormPassword fieldname`<br>The name of a form field carrying the login password | | d | B | p. 474 |
| `AuthFormProvider provider-name [provider-name] ...`<br>Sets the authentication provider(s) for this location | file | dh | B | p. 474 |
| `AuthFormSitePassphrase secret`<br>Bypass authentication checks for high traffic sites | | d | B | p. 475 |
| `AuthFormSize size`<br>The largest size of the form in bytes that will be parsed for the login details | | d | B | p. 475 |
| `AuthFormUsername fieldname`<br>The name of a form field carrying the login username | | d | B | p. 475 |
| `AuthGroupFile file-path`<br>Sets the name of a text file containing the list of user groups for authorization | | dh | B | p. 534 |
| `AuthLDAPAuthorizePrefix prefix`<br>Specifies the prefix for environment variables set during authorization | AUTHORIZE_ | dh | E | p. 510 |
| `AuthLDAPBindAuthoritative off\|on`<br>Determines if other authentication providers are used when a user can be mapped to a DN but the server cannot successfully bind with the user's credentials. | on | dh | E | p. 511 |
| `AuthLDAPBindDN distinguished-name`<br>Optional DN to use in binding to the LDAP server | | dh | E | p. 511 |
| `AuthLDAPBindPassword password`<br>Password used in conjuction with the bind DN | | dh | E | p. 511 |
| `AuthLDAPCharsetConfig file-path`<br>Language to charset conversion configuration file | | s | E | p. 512 |
| `AuthLDAPCompareAsUser on\|off`<br>Use the authenticated user's credentials to perform authorization comparisons | off | dh | E | p. 512 |
| `AuthLDAPCompareDNOnServer on\|off`<br>Use the LDAP server to compare the DNs | on | dh | E | p. 513 |
| `AuthLDAPDereferenceAliases never\|searching\|finding\|always`<br>When will the module de-reference aliases | always | dh | E | p. 513 |
| `AuthLDAPGroupAttribute attribute`<br>LDAP attributes used to identify the user members of groups. | member uniquemember + | dh | E | p. 513 |
| `AuthLDAPGroupAttributeIsDN on\|off`<br>Use the DN of the client username when checking for group membership | on | dh | E | p. 513 |
| `AuthLDAPInitialBindAsUser off\|on`<br>Determines if the server does the initial DN lookup using the basic authentication users' own username, instead of anonymously or with hard-coded credentials for the server | off | dh | E | p. 514 |
| `AuthLDAPInitialBindPattern regex substitution`<br>Specifies the transformation of the basic authentication username to be used when binding to the LDAP server to perform a DN lookup | (.*) $1 (remote use + | dh | E | p. 514 |
| `AuthLDAPMaxSubGroupDepth Number`<br>Specifies the maximum sub-group nesting depth that will be evaluated before the user search is discontinued. | 0 | dh | E | p. 515 |
| `AuthLDAPRemoteUserAttribute uid`<br>Use the value of the attribute returned during the user query to set the REMOTE_USER environment variable | | dh | E | p. 516 |
| `AuthLDAPRemoteUserIsDN on\|off`<br>Use the DN of the client username to set the REMOTE_USER environment variable | off | dh | E | p. 516 |
| `AuthLDAPSearchAsUser on\|off`<br>Use the authenticated user's credentials to perform authorization searches | off | dh | E | p. 516 |
| `AuthLDAPSubGroupAttribute attribute`<br>Specifies the attribute labels, one value per directive line, used to distinguish the members of the current group that are groups. | | dh | E | p. 517 |
| `AuthLDAPSubGroupClass LdapObjectClass`<br>Specifies which LDAP objectClass values identify directory objects that are groups during sub-group processing. | groupOfNames groupO + | dh | E | p. 517 |

| | | | |
|---|---|---|---|
| `AuthLDAPUrl url [NONE|SSL|TLS|STARTTLS]` | | dh | E |
| URL specifying the LDAP search parameters | | p. 517 | |
| `AuthMerging Off | And | Or` | Off | dh | B |
| Controls the manner in which each configuration section's authorization logic is combined with that of preceding configuration sections. p. 522 | | | |
| `AuthName auth-domain` | | dh | B |
| Authorization realm for use in HTTP authentication | | p. 481 | |
| `AuthnCacheContext directory|server|custom-string` | | d | B |
| Specify a context string for use in the cache key | | p. 492 | |
| `AuthnCacheEnable` | | s | B |
| Enable Authn caching configured anywhere | | p. 492 | |
| `AuthnCacheProvideFor authn-provider [...]` | | dh | B |
| Specify which authn provider(s) to cache for | | p. 493 | |
| `AuthnCacheSOCache provider-name[:provider-args]` | | s | B |
| Select socache backend provider to use | | p. 493 | |
| `AuthnCacheTimeout timeout (seconds)` | | dh | B |
| Set a timeout for cache entries | | p. 493 | |
| `<AuthnProviderAlias baseProvider Alias> ...` `</AuthnProviderAlias>` | | s | B |
| Enclose a group of directives that represent an extension of a base authentication provider and referenced by the specified alias | | p. 482 | |
| `AuthnzFcgiCheckAuthnProvider provider-name|None option ...` | | d | E |
| Enables a FastCGI application to handle the check_authn authentication hook. | | p. 499 | |
| `AuthnzFcgiDefineProvider type provider-name` `backend-address` | | s | E |
| Defines a FastCGI application as a provider for authentication and/or authorization | | p. 500 | |
| `AuthType None|Basic|Digest|Form` | | dh | B |
| Type of user authentication | | p. 482 | |
| `AuthUserFile file-path` | | dh | B |
| Sets the name of a text file containing the list of users and passwords for authentication | | p. 489 | |
| `AuthzDBDLoginToReferer On|Off` | Off | d | E |
| Determines whether to redirect the Client to the Referring page on successful login or logout if a `Referer` request header is present | p. 530 | |
| `AuthzDBDQuery query` | | d | E |
| Specify the SQL Query for the required operation | | p. 530 | |
| `AuthzDBDRedirectQuery query` | | d | E |
| Specify a query to look up a login page for the user | | p. 530 | |
| `AuthzDBMType default|SDBM|GDBM|NDBM|DB` | default | dh | E |
| Sets the type of database file that is used to store list of user groups | | p. 533 | |
| `<AuthzProviderAlias baseProvider Alias` `Require-Parameters> ... </AuthzProviderAlias>` | | s | B |
| Enclose a group of directives that represent an extension of a base authorization provider and referenced by the specified alias | | p. 523 | |
| `AuthzSendForbiddenOnFailure On|Off` | Off | dh | B |
| Send '403 FORBIDDEN' instead of '401 UNAUTHORIZED' if authentication succeeds but authorization fails | | p. 523 | |
| `BalancerGrowth #` | 5 | sv | E |
| Number of additional Balancers that can be added Post-configuration | | p. 793 | |
| `BalancerInherit On|Off` | On | sv | E |
| Inherit proxy Balancers/Workers defined from the main server | | p. 793 | |
| `BalancerMember [balancerurl] url [key=value [key=value ...]]` | | d | E |
| Add a member to a load balancing group | | p. 794 | |
| `BalancerPersist On|Off` | Off | sv | E |
| Attempt to persist changes made by the Balancer Manager across restarts. | | p. 794 | |
| `BrowserMatch regex [!]env-variable[=value]` `[[!]env-variable[=value]] ...` | | svdh | B |
| Sets environment variables conditional on HTTP User-Agent | | p. 902 | |
| `BrowserMatchNoCase regex [!]env-variable[=value]` `[[!]env-variable[=value]] ...` | | svdh | B |
| Sets environment variables conditional on User-Agent without respect to case | | p. 903 | |
| `BufferedLogs On|Off` | Off | s | B |
| Buffer log entries in memory before writing to disk | | p. 708 | |
| `BufferSize integer` | 131072 | svdh | E |
| Maximum size in bytes to buffer by the buffer filter | | p. 554 | |
| `CacheDefaultExpire seconds` | 3600 (one hour) | svdh | E |
| The default duration to cache a document when no expiry date is specified. | | p. 560 | |
| `CacheDetailHeader on|off` | off | svdh | E |
| Add an X-Cache-Detail header to the response. | | p. 560 | |

| | | | |
|---|---|---|---|
| `CacheStoreExpired On|Off`<br>Attempt to cache responses that the server reports as expired | Off | svdh<br>p. 568 | E |
| `CacheStoreNoStore On|Off`<br>Attempt to cache requests or responses that have been marked as no-store. | Off | svdh<br>p. 569 | E |
| `CacheStorePrivate On|Off`<br>Attempt to cache responses that the server has marked as private | Off | svdh<br>p. 569 | E |
| `CGIDScriptTimeout time[s|ms]`<br>The length of time to wait for more output from the CGI program | | svdh<br>p. 583 | B |
| `CGIMapExtension cgi-path .extension`<br>Technique for locating the interpreter for CGI scripts | | dh<br>p. 388 | C |
| `CGIPassAuth On|Off`<br>Enables passing HTTP authorization headers to scripts as CGI variables | Off | dh<br>p. 389 | C |
| `CGIVar variable rule`<br>Controls how some CGI variables are set | | dh<br>p. 389 | C |
| `CharsetDefault charset`<br>Charset to translate into | | svdh<br>p. 586 | E |
| `CharsetOptions option [option] ...`<br>Configures charset translation behavior | ImplicitAdd | svdh<br>p. 586 | E |
| `CharsetSourceEnc charset`<br>Source charset of files | | svdh<br>p. 586 | E |
| `CheckBasenameMatch on|off`<br>Also match files with differing file name extensions. | Off | svdh<br>p. 914 | E |
| `CheckCaseOnly on|off`<br>Limits the action of the speling module to case corrections | Off | svdh<br>p. 915 | E |
| `CheckSpelling on|off`<br>Enables the spelling module | Off | svdh<br>p. 915 | E |
| `ChrootDir /path/to/directory`<br>Directory for apache to run chroot(8) after startup. | | s<br>p. 972 | B |
| `ContentDigest On|Off`<br>Enables the generation of `Content-MD5` HTTP Response headers | Off | svdh<br>p. 389 | C |
| `CookieDomain domain`<br>The domain to which the tracking cookie applies | | svdh<br>p. 977 | E |
| `CookieExpires expiry-period`<br>Expiry time for the tracking cookie | | svdh<br>p. 978 | E |
| `CookieName token`<br>Name of the tracking cookie | Apache | svdh<br>p. 978 | E |
| `CookieStyle Netscape|Cookie|Cookie2|RFC2109|RFC2965`<br>Format of the cookie header field | Netscape | svdh<br>p. 978 | E |
| `CookieTracking on|off`<br>Enables tracking cookie | off | svdh<br>p. 979 | E |
| `CoreDumpDirectory directory`<br>Directory where Apache HTTP Server attempts to switch before dumping core | | s<br>p. 990 | M |
| `CTAuditStorage directory`<br>Existing directory where data for off-line audit will be stored | | s<br>p. 958 | E |
| `CTLogClient executable`<br>Location of certificate-transparency log client tool | | s<br>p. 958 | E |
| `CTLogConfigDB filename`<br>Log configuration database supporting dynamic updates | | s<br>p. 959 | E |
| `CTMaxSCTAge num-seconds`<br>Maximum age of SCT obtained from a log, before it will be refreshed | | s<br>p. 959 | E |
| `CTProxyAwareness oblivious|aware|require`<br>Level of CT awareness and enforcement for a proxy | | sv<br>p. 959 | E |
| `CTSCTStorage directory`<br>Existing directory where SCTs are managed | | s<br>p. 960 | E |
| `CTServerHelloSCTLimit limit`<br>Limit on number of SCTs that can be returned in ServerHello | | s<br>p. 960 | E |
| `CTStaticLogConfig log-id|- public-key-file|- 1|0|-`<br>`min-timestamp|- max-timestamp|- log-URL|-`<br>Static configuration of information about a log | | s<br><br>p. 960 | E |
| `CTStaticSCTs certificate-pem-file sct-directory`<br>Static configuration of one or more SCTs for a server certificate | | s<br>p. 961 | E |
| `CustomLog file|pipe|provider format|nickname`<br>`[env=[!]environment-variable| expr=expression]`<br>Sets filename and format of log file | | sv<br><br>p. 708 | B |

| | | | |
|---|---|---|---|
| `Dav On\|Off\|provider-name`<br>Enable WebDAV HTTP methods | Off | d<br>p. 591 | E |
| `DavDepthInfinity on\|off`<br>Allow PROPFIND, Depth: Infinity requests | off | svd<br>p. 591 | E |
| `DavGenericLockDB file-path`<br>Location of the DAV lock database | | svd<br>p. 593 | E |
| `DavLockDB file-path`<br>Location of the DAV lock database | | sv<br>p. 592 | E |
| `DavMinTimeout seconds`<br>Minimum amount of time the server holds a lock on a DAV resource | 0 | svd<br>p. 591 | E |
| `DBDExptime time-in-seconds`<br>Keepalive time for idle connections | 300 | sv<br>p. 596 | E |
| `DBDInitSQL "SQL statement"`<br>Execute an SQL statement after connecting to a database | | sv<br>p. 596 | E |
| `DBDKeep number`<br>Maximum sustained number of connections | 2 | sv<br>p. 597 | E |
| `DBDMax number`<br>Maximum number of connections | 10 | sv<br>p. 597 | E |
| `DBDMin number`<br>Minimum number of connections | 1 | sv<br>p. 597 | E |
| `DBDParams param1=value1[,param2=value2]`<br>Parameters for database connection | | sv<br>p. 597 | E |
| `DBDPersist On\|Off`<br>Whether to use persistent connections | | sv<br>p. 598 | E |
| `DBDPrepareSQL "SQL statement" label`<br>Define an SQL prepared statement | | sv<br>p. 598 | E |
| `DBDriver name`<br>Specify an SQL driver | | sv<br>p. 598 | E |
| `DefaultIcon url-path`<br>Icon to display for files when no specific icon is configured | | svdh<br>p. 547 | B |
| `DefaultLanguage language-tag`<br>Defines a default language-tag to be sent in the Content-Language header field for all resources in the current context that have not been assigned a language-tag by some other means. | | svdh<br>p. 756 | B |
| `DefaultRuntimeDir directory-path`<br>Base directory for the server run-time files | DEFAULT_REL_RUNTIME + | s<br>p. 390 | C |
| `DefaultType media-type\|none`<br>This directive has no effect other than to emit warnings if the value is not none. In prior versions, DefaultType would specify a default media type to assign to response content for which no other media type configuration could be found. | none | svdh<br>p. 390 | C |
| `Define parameter-name [parameter-value]`<br>Define a variable | | sv<br>p. 391 | C |
| `DeflateAlterETag AddSuffix\|NoChange\|Remove`<br>How the outgoing ETag header should be modified during compression | AddSuffix | sv<br>p. 602 | E |
| `DeflateBufferSize value`<br>Fragment size to be compressed at one time by zlib | 8096 | sv<br>p. 602 | E |
| `DeflateCompressionLevel value`<br>How much compression do we apply to the output | | sv<br>p. 603 | E |
| `DeflateFilterNote [type] notename`<br>Places the compression ratio in a note for logging | | sv<br>p. 603 | E |
| `DeflateInflateLimitRequestBody value`<br>Maximum size of inflated request bodies | | svdh<br>p. 604 | E |
| `DeflateInflateRatioBurst value`<br>Maximum number of times the inflation ratio for request bodies can be crossed | | svdh<br>p. 604 | E |
| `DeflateInflateRatioLimit value`<br>Maximum inflation ratio for request bodies | | svdh<br>p. 604 | E |
| `DeflateMemLevel value`<br>How much memory should be used by zlib for compression | 9 | sv<br>p. 604 | E |
| `DeflateWindowSize value`<br>Zlib compression window size | 15 | sv<br>p. 605 | E |
| `Deny from all\|host\|env=[!]env-variable`<br>`[host\|env=[!]env-variable] ...`<br>Controls which hosts are denied access to the server | | dh<br>p. 442 | E |
| `<Directory directory-path> ... </Directory>`<br>Enclose a group of directives that apply only to the named file-system directory, sub-directories, and their contents. | | sv<br>p. 391 | C |
| `DirectoryCheckHandler On\|Off`<br>Toggle how this module responds when another handler is configured | Off | svdh<br>p. 607 | B |

| | | | |
|---|---|---|---|
| `DirectoryIndex disabled | local-url [local-url] ...`<br>List of resources to look for when the client requests a directory | index.html | svdh<br>p. 608 | B |
| `DirectoryIndexRedirect on | off | permanent | temp |`<br>`seeother | 3xx-code`<br>Configures an external redirect for directory indexes. | off | svdh<br>p. 609 | B |
| `<DirectoryMatch regex> ... </DirectoryMatch>`<br>Enclose directives that apply to the contents of file-system directories matching a regular expression. | | sv<br>p. 393 | C |
| `DirectorySlash On|Off`<br>Toggle trailing slash redirects on or off | On | svdh<br>p. 609 | B |
| `DocumentRoot directory-path`<br>Directory that forms the main document tree visible from the web | /usr/local/apache/h + | sv<br>p. 394 | C |
| `DTracePrivileges On|Off`<br>Determines whether the privileges required by dtrace are enabled. | Off | s<br>p. 782 | X |
| `DumpIOInput On|Off`<br>Dump all input data to the error log | Off | s<br>p. 612 | E |
| `DumpIOOutput On|Off`<br>Dump all output data to the error log | Off | s<br>p. 612 | E |
| `<Else> ... </Else>`<br>Contains directives that apply only if the condition of a previous <IF> or <ELSEIF> section is not satisfied by a request at runtime | | svdh<br>p. 394 | C |
| `<ElseIf expression> ... </ElseIf>`<br>Contains directives that apply only if a condition is satisfied by a request at runtime while the condition of a previous <IF> or <ELSEIF> section is not satisfied | | svdh<br>p. 395 | C |
| `EnableExceptionHook On|Off`<br>Enables a hook that runs exception handlers after a crash | Off | s<br>p. 991 | M |
| `EnableMMAP On|Off`<br>Use memory-mapping to read files during delivery | On | svdh<br>p. 395 | C |
| `EnableSendfile On|Off`<br>Use the kernel sendfile support to deliver files to the client | Off | svdh<br>p. 396 | C |
| `Error message`<br>Abort configuration parsing with a custom error message | | svdh<br>p. 397 | C |
| `ErrorDocument error-code document`<br>What the server will return to the client in case of an error | | svdh<br>p. 397 | C |
| `ErrorLog file-path|syslog[:facility]`<br>Location where the server will log errors | logs/error_log (Uni + | sv<br>p. 399 | C |
| `ErrorLogFormat [connection|request] format`<br>Format specification for error log entries | | sv<br>p. 399 | C |
| `Example`<br>Demonstration directive to illustrate the Apache module API | | svdh<br>p. 618 | X |
| `ExpiresActive On|Off`<br>Enables generation of Expires headers | Off | svdh<br>p. 620 | E |
| `ExpiresByType MIME-type <code>seconds`<br>Value of the Expires header configured by MIME type | | svdh<br>p. 620 | E |
| `ExpiresDefault <code>seconds`<br>Default algorithm for calculating expiration time | | svdh<br>p. 621 | E |
| `ExtendedStatus On|Off`<br>Keep track of extended status information for each request | Off[*] | s<br>p. 401 | C |
| `ExtFilterDefine filtername parameters`<br>Define an external filter | | s<br>p. 624 | E |
| `ExtFilterOptions option [option] ...`<br>Configure MOD_EXT_FILTER options | NoLogStderr | d<br>p. 625 | E |
| `FallbackResource disabled | local-url`<br>Define a default URL for requests that don't map to a file | | svdh<br>p. 610 | B |
| `FileETag component ...`<br>File attributes used to create the ETag HTTP response header for static files | MTime Size | svdh<br>p. 402 | C |
| `<Files filename> ... </Files>`<br>Contains directives that apply to matched filenames | | svdh<br>p. 403 | C |
| `<FilesMatch regex> ... </FilesMatch>`<br>Contains directives that apply to regular-expression matched filenames | | svdh<br>p. 403 | C |
| `FilterChain [+=-@!]filter-name ...`<br>Configure the filter chain | | svdh<br>p. 634 | B |
| `FilterDeclare filter-name [type]`<br>Declare a smart filter | | svdh<br>p. 634 | B |
| `FilterProtocol filter-name [provider-name] proto-flags`<br>Deal with correct HTTP protocol handling | | svdh<br>p. 635 | B |

| | | | |
|---|---|---|---|
| `FilterProvider filter-name provider-name expression`<br>Register a content filter | | svdh<br>p. 635 | B |
| `FilterTrace filter-name level`<br>Get debug/diagnostic information from MOD_FILTER | | svd<br>p. 636 | B |
| `FirehoseConnectionInput [ block | nonblock ] filename`<br>Capture traffic coming into the server on each connection | | s<br>p. 638 | E |
| `FirehoseConnectionOutput [ block | nonblock ] filename`<br>Capture traffic going out of the server on each connection | | s<br>p. 639 | E |
| `FirehoseProxyConnectionInput [ block | nonblock ] filename`<br>Capture traffic coming into the back of mod_proxy | | s<br>p. 639 | E |
| `FirehoseProxyConnectionOutput [ block | nonblock ]`<br>`filename`<br>Capture traffic sent out from the back of mod_proxy | | s<br>p. 639 | E |
| `FirehoseRequestInput [ block | nonblock ] filename`<br>Capture traffic coming into the server on each request | | s<br>p. 640 | E |
| `FirehoseRequestOutput [ block | nonblock ] filename`<br>Capture traffic going out of the server on each request | | s<br>p. 640 | E |
| `ForceLanguagePriority None|Prefer|Fallback`<br>`[Prefer|Fallback]`<br>Action to take if a single acceptable document is not found | Prefer | svdh<br>p. 768 | B |
| `ForceType media-type|None`<br>Forces all matching files to be served with the specified media type in the HTTP Content-Type header field | | dh<br>p. 404 | C |
| `ForensicLog filename|pipe`<br>Sets filename of the forensic log | | sv<br>p. 715 | E |
| `GlobalLog file|pipe|provider format|nickname`<br>`[env=[!]environment-variable| expr=expression]`<br>Sets filename and format of log file | | s<br>p. 710 | B |
| `GprofDir /tmp/gprof/|/tmp/gprof/%`<br>Directory to write gmon.out profiling data to. | | sv<br>p. 405 | C |
| `GracefulShutdownTimeout seconds`<br>Specify a timeout after which a gracefully shutdown server will exit. | 0 | s<br>p. 991 | M |
| `Group unix-group`<br>Group under which the server will answer requests | #-1 | s<br>p. 972 | B |
| `H2Direct on|off`<br>H2 Direct Protocol Switch | on for h2c, off for + | sv<br>p. 652 | E |
| `H2MaxSessionStreams n`<br>Maximum number of active streams per HTTP/2 session. | 100 | sv<br>p. 653 | E |
| `H2MaxWorkerIdleSeconds n`<br>Maximum number of seconds h2 workers remain idle until shut down. | 600 | s<br>p. 653 | E |
| `H2MaxWorkers n`<br>Maximum number of worker threads to use per child process. | | s<br>p. 653 | E |
| `H2MinWorkers n`<br>Minimal number of worker threads to use per child process. | | s<br>p. 654 | E |
| `H2ModernTLSOnly on|off`<br>Require HTTP/2 connections to be "modern TLS" only | on | sv<br>p. 654 | E |
| `H2Push on|off`<br>H2 Server Push Switch | on | sv<br>p. 654 | E |
| `H2PushDiarySize n`<br>H2 Server Push Diary Size | 256 | sv<br>p. 655 | E |
| `H2PushPriority mime-type [after|before|interleaved]`<br>`[weight]`<br>H2 Server Push Priority | * After 16 | sv<br>p. 656 | E |
| `H2SerializeHeaders on|off`<br>Serialize Request/Response Processing Switch | off | sv<br>p. 657 | E |
| `H2SessionExtraFiles n`<br>Number of Extra File Handles | | sv<br>p. 657 | E |
| `H2StreamMaxMemSize bytes`<br>Maximum amount of output data buffered per stream. | 65536 | sv<br>p. 658 | E |
| `H2TLSCoolDownSecs seconds`<br>- | 1 | sv<br>p. 658 | E |
| `H2TLSWarmUpSize amount`<br>- | 1048576 | sv<br>p. 659 | E |
| `H2Upgrade on|off`<br>H2 Upgrade Protocol Switch | on for h2c, off for + | sv<br>p. 659 | E |

| | | | |
|---|---|---|---|
| `H2WindowSize bytes` | 65535 | sv | E |
| Size of Stream Window for upstream data. | | p. 660 | |
| `Header [condition] add|append|echo|edit|edit*|merge|set|setifempty|unset|note header [[expr=]value [replacement] [early|env=[!]varname|expr=expression]]` | | svdh | E |
| Configure HTTP response headers | | p. 643 | |
| `HeaderName filename` | | svdh | B |
| Name of the file that will be inserted at the top of the index listing | | p. 547 | |
| `HeartbeatAddress addr:port` | | s | X |
| Multicast address for heartbeat packets | | p. 647 | |
| `HeartbeatListenaddr:port` | | s | X |
| multicast address to listen for incoming heartbeat requests | | p. 648 | |
| `HeartbeatMaxServers number-of-servers` | 10 | s | X |
| Specifies the maximum number of servers that will be sending heartbeat requests to this server | | p. 648 | |
| `HeartbeatStorage file-path` | logs/hb.dat | s | X |
| Path to store heartbeat data | | p. 649 | |
| `HeartbeatStorage file-path` | logs/hb.dat | s | X |
| Path to read heartbeat data | | p. 692 | |
| `HostnameLookups On|Off|Double` | Off | svd | C |
| Enables DNS lookups on client IP addresses | | p. 405 | |
| `IdentityCheck On|Off` | Off | svd | E |
| Enables logging of the RFC 1413 identity of the remote user | | p. 661 | |
| `IdentityCheckTimeout seconds` | 30 | svd | E |
| Determines the timeout duration for ident requests | | p. 661 | |
| `IdleShutdown seconds` | 0 | s | E |
| Enable shutting down the httpd when it is idle for some time. | | p. 969 | |
| `<If expression> ... </If>` | | svdh | C |
| Contains directives that apply only if a condition is satisfied by a request at runtime | | p. 406 | |
| `<IfDefine [!]parameter-name> ... </IfDefine>` | | svdh | C |
| Encloses directives that will be processed only if a test is true at startup | | p. 406 | |
| `<IfModule [!]module-file|module-identifier> ... </IfModule>` | | svdh | C |
| Encloses directives that are processed conditional on the presence or absence of a specific module | | p. 407 | |
| `<IfVersion [[!]operator] version> ... </IfVersion>` | | svdh | E |
| contains version dependent configuration | | p. 980 | |
| `ImapBase map|referer|URL` | http://servername/ | svdh | B |
| Default `base` for imagemap files | | p. 665 | |
| `ImapDefault error|nocontent|map|referer|URL` | nocontent | svdh | B |
| Default action when an imagemap is called with coordinates that are not explicitly mapped | | p. 666 | |
| `ImapMenu none|formatted|semiformatted|unformatted` | formatted | svdh | B |
| Action if no coordinates are given when calling an imagemap | | p. 666 | |
| `Include file-path|directory-path|wildcard` | | svd | C |
| Includes other configuration files from within the server configuration files | | p. 408 | |
| `IncludeOptional file-path|directory-path|wildcard` | | svd | C |
| Includes other configuration files from within the server configuration files | | p. 409 | |
| `IndexHeadInsert "markup ..."` | | svdh | B |
| Inserts text in the HEAD section of an index page. | | p. 548 | |
| `IndexIgnore file [file] ...` | "." | svdh | B |
| Adds to the list of files to hide when listing a directory | | p. 548 | |
| `IndexIgnoreReset ON|OFF` | | svdh | B |
| Empties the list of files to hide when listing a directory | | p. 549 | |
| `IndexOptions [+|-]option [[+|-]option] ...` | | svdh | B |
| Various configuration settings for directory indexing | | p. 549 | |
| `IndexOrderDefault Ascending|Descending Name|Date|Size|Description` | Ascending Name | svdh | B |
| Sets the default ordering of the directory index | | p. 552 | |
| `IndexStyleSheet url-path` | | svdh | B |
| Adds a CSS stylesheet to the directory index | | p. 553 | |
| `InputSed sed-command` | | dh | X |
| Sed command to filter request data (typically POST data) | | p. 882 | |
| `ISAPIAppendLogToErrors on|off` | off | svdh | B |
| Record HSE_APPEND_LOG_PARAMETER requests from ISAPI extensions to the error log | | p. 685 | |
| `ISAPIAppendLogToQuery on|off` | on | svdh | B |
| Record HSE_APPEND_LOG_PARAMETER requests from ISAPI extensions to the query field | | p. 685 | |
| `ISAPICacheFile file-path [file-path] ...` | | sv | B |
| ISAPI .dll files to be loaded at startup | | p. 685 | |

| Directive | Default | Context | Module | Page |
|---|---|---|---|---|
| `ISAPIFakeAsync on|off`<br>Fake asynchronous support for ISAPI callbacks | off | svdh | B | p. 686 |
| `ISAPILogNotSupported on|off`<br>Log unsupported feature requests from ISAPI extensions | off | svdh | B | p. 686 |
| `ISAPIReadAheadBuffer size`<br>Size of the Read Ahead Buffer sent to ISAPI extensions | 49152 | svdh | B | p. 686 |
| `KeepAlive On|Off`<br>Enables HTTP persistent connections | On | sv | C | p. 409 |
| `KeepAliveTimeout num[ms]`<br>Amount of time the server will wait for subsequent requests on a persistent connection | 5 | sv | C | p. 410 |
| `KeptBodySize maximum size in bytes`<br>Keep the request body instead of discarding it up to the specified maximum size, for potential use by filters such as mod_include. | 0 | d | B | p. 866 |
| `LanguagePriority MIME-lang [MIME-lang] ...`<br>The precendence of language variants for cases where the client does not express a preference | | svdh | B | p. 769 |
| `LDAPCacheEntries number`<br>Maximum number of entries in the primary LDAP cache | 1024 | s | E | p. 698 |
| `LDAPCacheTTL seconds`<br>Time that cached items remain valid | 600 | s | E | p. 699 |
| `LDAPConnectionPoolTTL n`<br>Discard backend connections that have been sitting in the connection pool too long | -1 | sv | E | p. 699 |
| `LDAPConnectionTimeout seconds`<br>Specifies the socket connection timeout in seconds | | s | E | p. 699 |
| `LDAPLibraryDebug 7`<br>Enable debugging in the LDAP SDK | | s | E | p. 700 |
| `LDAPOpCacheEntries number`<br>Number of entries used to cache LDAP compare operations | 1024 | s | E | p. 700 |
| `LDAPOpCacheTTL seconds`<br>Time that entries in the operation cache remain valid | 600 | s | E | p. 700 |
| `LDAPReferralHopLimit number`<br>The maximum number of referral hops to chase before terminating an LDAP query. | | dh | E | p. 701 |
| `LDAPReferrals On|Off|default`<br>Enable referral chasing during queries to the LDAP server. | On | dh | E | p. 701 |
| `LDAPRetries number-of-retries`<br>Configures the number of LDAP server retries. | 3 | s | E | p. 701 |
| `LDAPRetryDelay seconds`<br>Configures the delay between LDAP server retries. | 0 | s | E | p. 702 |
| `LDAPSharedCacheFile file-path`<br>Sets the shared memory cache file | | s | E | p. 702 |
| `LDAPSharedCacheSize bytes`<br>Size in bytes of the shared-memory cache | 500000 | s | E | p. 702 |
| `LDAPTimeout seconds`<br>Specifies the timeout for LDAP search and bind operations, in seconds | 60 | s | E | p. 702 |
| `LDAPTrustedClientCert type directory-path/filename/nickname [password]`<br>Sets the file containing or nickname referring to a per connection client certificate. Not all LDAP toolkits support per connection client certificates. | | dh | E | p. 703 |
| `LDAPTrustedGlobalCert type directory-path/filename [password]`<br>Sets the file or database containing global trusted Certificate Authority or global client certificates | | s | E | p. 703 |
| `LDAPTrustedMode type`<br>Specifies the SSL/TLS mode to be used when connecting to an LDAP server. | | sv | E | p. 704 |
| `LDAPVerifyServerCert On|Off`<br>Force server certificate verification | On | s | E | p. 704 |
| `<Limit method [method] ... > ... </Limit>`<br>Restrict enclosed access controls to only certain HTTP methods | | dh | C | p. 410 |
| `<LimitExcept method [method] ... > ... </LimitExcept>`<br>Restrict access controls to all HTTP methods except the named ones | | dh | C | p. 411 |
| `LimitInternalRecursion number [number]`<br>Determine maximum number of internal redirects and nested subrequests | 10 | sv | C | p. 411 |
| `LimitRequestBody bytes`<br>Restricts the total size of the HTTP request body sent from the client | 0 | svdh | C | p. 412 |
| `LimitRequestFields number`<br>Limits the number of HTTP request header fields that will be accepted from the client | 100 | sv | C | p. 412 |
| `LimitRequestFieldSize bytes`<br>Limits the size of the HTTP request header allowed from the client | 8190 | sv | C | p. 413 |

| | | | |
|---|---|---|---|
| `LimitRequestLine bytes`<br>Limit the size of the HTTP request line that will be accepted from the client | 8190 | sv<br>p. 413 | C |
| `LimitXMLRequestBody bytes`<br>Limits the size of an XML-based request body | 1000000 | svdh<br>p. 414 | C |
| `Listen [IP-address:]portnumber [protocol]`<br>IP addresses and ports that the server listens to | | s<br>p. 992 | M |
| `ListenBacklog backlog`<br>Maximum length of the queue of pending connections | | s<br>p. 993 | M |
| `ListenCoresBucketsRatio ratio`<br>Ratio between the number of CPU cores (online) and the number of listeners' buckets | 0 (disabled) | s<br>p. 993 | M |
| `LoadFile filename [filename] ...`<br>Link in the named object file or library | | sv<br>p. 909 | E |
| `LoadModule module filename`<br>Links in the object file or library, and adds to the list of active modules | | sv<br>p. 909 | E |
| `<Location URL-path\|URL> ... </Location>`<br>Applies the enclosed directives only to matching URLs | | sv<br>p. 414 | C |
| `<LocationMatch regex> ... </LocationMatch>`<br>Applies the enclosed directives only to regular-expression matching URLs | | sv<br>p. 416 | C |
| `LogFormat format\|nickname [nickname]`<br>Describes a format for use in a log file | `"%h %l %u %t \"%r\" +` | sv<br>p. 710 | B |
| `LogIOTrackTTFB ON\|OFF`<br>Enable tracking of time to first byte (TTFB) | OFF | svdh<br>p. 717 | E |
| `LogLevel [module:]level [module:level] ...`<br>Controls the verbosity of the ErrorLog | warn | svd<br>p. 416 | C |
| `LogLevel ipaddress[/prefixlen] [module:]level`<br>`[module:level] ...`<br>Override the verbosity of the ErrorLog for certain clients | | sv<br>p. 418 | C |
| `LogMessage message [hook=hook] [expr=expression]`<br>Log user-defined message to error log | | d<br>p. 712 | X |
| `LuaAuthzProvider provider_name /path/to/lua/script.lua`<br>`function_name`<br>Plug an authorization provider function into MOD_AUTHZ_CORE | | s<br>p. 734 | X |
| `LuaCodeCache stat\|forever\|never`<br>Configure the compiled code cache. | stat | svdh<br>p. 735 | X |
| `LuaHookAccessChecker /path/to/lua/script.lua`<br>`hook_function_name [early\|late]`<br>Provide a hook for the access_checker phase of request processing | | svdh<br>p. 735 | X |
| `LuaHookAuthChecker /path/to/lua/script.lua`<br>`hook_function_name [early\|late]`<br>Provide a hook for the auth_checker phase of request processing | | svdh<br>p. 735 | X |
| `LuaHookCheckUserID /path/to/lua/script.lua`<br>`hook_function_name`<br>Provide a hook for the check_user_id phase of request processing | | svdh<br>p. 736 | X |
| `LuaHookFixups /path/to/lua/script.lua hook_function_name`<br>Provide a hook for the fixups phase of a request processing | | svdh<br>p. 736 | X |
| `LuaHookInsertFilter /path/to/lua/script.lua`<br>`hook_function_name`<br>Provide a hook for the insert_filter phase of request processing | | svdh<br>p. 737 | X |
| `LuaHookLog /path/to/lua/script.lua log_function_name`<br>Provide a hook for the access log phase of a request processing | | svdh<br>p. 737 | X |
| `LuaHookMapToStorage /path/to/lua/script.lua`<br>`hook_function_name`<br>Provide a hook for the map_to_storage phase of request processing | | svdh<br>p. 738 | X |
| `LuaHookTranslateName /path/to/lua/script.lua`<br>`hook_function_name [early\|late]`<br>Provide a hook for the translate name phase of request processing | | sv<br>p. 738 | X |
| `LuaHookTypeChecker /path/to/lua/script.lua`<br>`hook_function_name`<br>Provide a hook for the type_checker phase of request processing | | svdh<br>p. 739 | X |
| `LuaInherit none\|parent-first\|parent-last`<br>Controls how parent configuration sections are merged into children | parent-first | svdh<br>p. 740 | X |
| `LuaInputFilter filter_name /path/to/lua/script.lua`<br>`function_name`<br>Provide a Lua function for content input filtering | | s<br>p. 740 | X |

| | | | |
|---|---|---|---|
| `LuaMapHandler uri-pattern /path/to/lua/script.lua [function-name]` | | svdh | X |
| Map a path to a lua handler | | p. 741 | |
| `LuaOutputFilter filter_name /path/to/lua/script.lua function_name` | | s | X |
| Provide a Lua function for content output filtering | | p. 741 | |
| `LuaPackageCPath /path/to/include/?.soa` | | svdh | X |
| Add a directory to lua's package.cpath | | p. 742 | |
| `LuaPackagePath /path/to/include/?.lua` | | svdh | X |
| Add a directory to lua's package.path | | p. 742 | |
| `LuaQuickHandler /path/to/script.lua hook_function_name` | | sv | X |
| Provide a hook for the quick handler of request processing | | p. 743 | |
| `LuaRoot /path/to/a/directory` | | svdh | X |
| Specify the base path for resolving relative paths for mod_lua directives | | p. 743 | |
| `LuaScope once\|request\|conn\|thread\|server [min] [max]` | once | svdh | X |
| One of once, request, conn, thread – default is once | | p. 743 | |
| `<Macro name [par1 .. parN]> ... </Macro>` | | svd | B |
| Define a configuration file macro | | p. 747 | |
| `MaxConnectionsPerChild number` | 0 | s | M |
| Limit on the number of connections that an individual child server will handle during its life | | p. 994 | |
| `MaxKeepAliveRequests number` | 100 | sv | C |
| Number of requests allowed on a persistent connection | | p. 418 | |
| `MaxMemFree KBytes` | 2048 | s | M |
| Maximum amount of memory that the main allocator is allowed to hold without calling `free()` | | p. 994 | |
| `MaxRangeOverlaps default \| unlimited \| none \| number-of-ranges` | 20 | svd | C |
| Number of overlapping ranges (eg: `100-200,150-300`) allowed before returning the complete resource | | p. 419 | |
| `MaxRangeReversals default \| unlimited \| none \| number-of-ranges` | 20 | svd | C |
| Number of range reversals (eg: `100-200,50-70`) allowed before returning the complete resource | | p. 419 | |
| `MaxRanges default \| unlimited \| none \| number-of-ranges` | 200 | svd | C |
| Number of ranges allowed before returning the complete resource | | p. 419 | |
| `MaxRequestWorkers number` | | s | M |
| Maximum number of connections that will be processed simultaneously | | p. 994 | |
| `MaxSpareServers number` | 10 | s | M |
| Maximum number of idle child server processes | | p. 1010 | |
| `MaxSpareThreads number` | | s | M |
| Maximum number of idle threads | | p. 995 | |
| `MaxThreads number` | 2048 | s | M |
| Set the maximum number of worker threads | | p. 1007 | |
| `MemcacheConnTTL num[units]` | 15s | sv | E |
| Keepalive time for idle connections | | p. 912 | |
| `MergeTrailers [on\|off]` | off | sv | C |
| Determines whether trailers are merged into headers | | p. 420 | |
| `MetaDir directory` | .web | svdh | E |
| Name of the directory to find CERN-style meta information files | | p. 578 | |
| `MetaFiles on\|off` | off | svdh | E |
| Activates CERN meta-file processing | | p. 579 | |
| `MetaSuffix suffix` | .meta | svdh | E |
| File name suffix for the file containing CERN-style meta information | | p. 579 | |
| `MimeMagicFile file-path` | | sv | E |
| Enable MIME-type determination based on file contents using the specified magic file | | p. 765 | |
| `MinSpareServers number` | 5 | s | M |
| Minimum number of idle child server processes | | p. 1010 | |
| `MinSpareThreads number` | | s | M |
| Minimum number of idle threads available to handle request spikes | | p. 995 | |
| `MMapFile file-path [file-path] ...` | | s | X |
| Map a list of files into memory at startup time | | p. 627 | |
| `ModemStandard V.21\|V.26bis\|V.32\|V.34\|V.92` | | d | X |
| Modem standard to simulate | | p. 606 | |
| `ModMimeUsePathInfo On\|Off` | Off | d | B |
| Tells MOD_MIME to treat path_info components as part of the filename | | p. 757 | |
| `MultiviewsMatch Any\|NegotiatedOnly\|Filters\|Handlers [Handlers\|Filters]` | NegotiatedOnly | svdh | B |
| The types of files that will be included when searching for a matching file with MultiViews | | p. 757 | |

| | | | |
|---|---|---|---|
| `Mutex mechanism [default\|mutex-name] ...  [OmitPID]` | default | s | C |
| Configures mutex mechanism and lock file directory for all or specified mutexes | | p. 420 | |
| `NameVirtualHost addr[:port]` | | s | C |
| DEPRECATED: Designates an IP address for name-virtual hosting | | p. 422 | |
| `NoProxy host [host] ...` | | sv | E |
| Hosts, domains, or networks that will be connected to directly | | p. 794 | |
| `NWSSLTrustedCerts filename [filename] ...` | | s | B |
| List of additional client certificates | | p. 770 | |
| `NWSSLUpgradeable [IP-address:]portnumber` | | s | B |
| Allows a connection to be upgraded to an SSL connection upon request | | p. 770 | |
| `Options [+\|-]option [[+\|-]option] ...` | FollowSymlinks | svdh | C |
| Configures what features are available in a particular directory | | p. 423 | |
| `Order ordering` | Deny,Allow | dh | E |
| Controls the default access state and the order in which ALLOW and DENY are evaluated. | | p. 442 | |
| `OutputSed sed-command` | | dh | X |
| Sed command for filtering response content | | p. 882 | |
| `PassEnv env-variable [env-variable] ...` | | svdh | B |
| Passes environment variables from the shell | | p. 615 | |
| `PidFile filename` | httpd.pid | s | M |
| File where the server records the process ID of the daemon | | p. 996 | |
| `PolicyConditional ignore\|log\|enforce` | | svd | E |
| Enable the conditional request policy. | | p. 774 | |
| `PolicyConditionalURL url` | | svd | E |
| URL describing the conditional request policy. | | p. 774 | |
| `PolicyEnvironment variable log-value ignore-value` | | svd | E |
| Override policies based on an environment variable. | | p. 774 | |
| `PolicyFilter on\|off` | | svd | E |
| Enable or disable policies for the given URL space. | | p. 775 | |
| `PolicyKeepalive ignore\|log\|enforce` | | svd | E |
| Enable the keepalive policy. | | p. 775 | |
| `PolicyKeepaliveURL url` | | svd | E |
| URL describing the keepalive policy. | | p. 776 | |
| `PolicyLength ignore\|log\|enforce` | | svd | E |
| Enable the content length policy. | | p. 776 | |
| `PolicyLengthURL url` | | svd | E |
| URL describing the content length policy. | | p. 776 | |
| `PolicyMaxage ignore\|log\|enforce age` | | svd | E |
| Enable the caching minimum max-age policy. | | p. 776 | |
| `PolicyMaxageURL url` | | svd | E |
| URL describing the caching minimum freshness lifetime policy. | | p. 777 | |
| `PolicyNocache ignore\|log\|enforce` | | svd | E |
| Enable the caching no-cache policy. | | p. 777 | |
| `PolicyNocacheURL url` | | svd | E |
| URL describing the caching no-cache policy. | | p. 777 | |
| `PolicyType ignore\|log\|enforce type [ type [ ... ]]` | | svd | E |
| Enable the content type policy. | | p. 778 | |
| `PolicyTypeURL url` | | svd | E |
| URL describing the content type policy. | | p. 778 | |
| `PolicyValidation ignore\|log\|enforce` | | svd | E |
| Enable the validation policy. | | p. 778 | |
| `PolicyValidationURL url` | | svd | E |
| URL describing the content type policy. | | p. 779 | |
| `PolicyVary ignore\|log\|enforce header [ header [ ... ]]` | | svd | E |
| Enable the Vary policy. | | p. 779 | |
| `PolicyVaryURL url` | | svd | E |
| URL describing the content type policy. | | p. 779 | |
| `PolicyVersion ignore\|log\|enforce HTTP/0.9\|HTTP/1.0\|HTTP/1.1` | | svd | E |
| Enable the version policy. | | p. 779 | |
| `PolicyVersionURL url` | | svd | E |
| URL describing the minimum request HTTP version policy. | | p. 780 | |
| `PrivilegesMode FAST\|SECURE\|SELECTIVE` | FAST | svd | X |
| Trade off processing speed and efficiency vs security against malicious privileges-aware code. | | p. 782 | |
| `Protocol protocol` | | sv | C |
| Protocol for a listening socket | | p. 424 | |

| | | | |
|---|---|---|---|
| `ProxyHTMLURLMap from-pattern to-pattern [flags] [cond]` Defines a rule to rewrite HTML links | | svd p. 848 | B |
| `ProxyIOBufferSize bytes` Determine size of internal data throughput buffer | 8192 | sv p. 798 | E |
| `<ProxyMatch regex> ...</ProxyMatch>` Container for directives applied to regular-expression-matched proxied resources | | sv p. 799 | E |
| `ProxyMaxForwards number` Maximum number of proxies that a request can be forwarded through | -1 | sv p. 799 | E |
| `ProxyPass [path] !\|url [key=value [key=value ...]]` `[nocanon] [interpolate] [noquery]` Maps remote servers into the local server URL-space | | svd p. 800 | E |
| `ProxyPassInherit On\|Off` Inherit ProxyPass directives defined from the main server | On | sv p. 808 | E |
| `ProxyPassInterpolateEnv On\|Off` Enable Environment Variable interpolation in Reverse Proxy configurations | Off | svd p. 808 | E |
| `ProxyPassMatch [regex] !\|url [key=value [key=value ...]]` Maps remote servers into the local server URL-space using regular expressions | | svd p. 808 | E |
| `ProxyPassReverse [path] url [interpolate]` Adjusts the URL in HTTP response headers sent from a reverse proxied server | | svd p. 809 | E |
| `ProxyPassReverseCookieDomain internal-domain public-domain` `[interpolate]` Adjusts the Domain string in Set-Cookie headers from a reverse- proxied server | | svd p. 810 | E |
| `ProxyPassReverseCookiePath internal-path public-path` `[interpolate]` Adjusts the Path string in Set-Cookie headers from a reverse- proxied server | | svd p. 810 | E |
| `ProxyPreserveHost On\|Off` Use incoming Host HTTP request header for proxy request | Off | svd p. 811 | E |
| `ProxyReceiveBufferSize bytes` Network buffer size for proxied HTTP and FTP connections | 0 | sv p. 811 | E |
| `ProxyRemote match remote-server` Remote proxy used to handle certain requests | | sv p. 811 | E |
| `ProxyRemoteMatch regex remote-server` Remote proxy used to handle requests matched by regular expressions | | sv p. 812 | E |
| `ProxyRequests On\|Off` Enables forward (standard) proxy requests | Off | sv p. 812 | E |
| `ProxySCGIInternalRedirect On\|Off\|Headername` Enable or disable internal redirect responses from the backend | On | svd p. 854 | E |
| `ProxySCGISendfile On\|Off\|Headername` Enable evaluation of *X-Sendfile* pseudo response header | Off | svd p. 854 | E |
| `ProxySet url key=value [key=value ...]` Set various Proxy balancer or member parameters | | d p. 813 | E |
| `ProxySourceAddress address` Set local IP address for outgoing proxy connections | | sv p. 813 | E |
| `ProxyStatus Off\|On\|Full` Show Proxy LoadBalancer status in mod_status | Off | sv p. 813 | E |
| `ProxyTimeout seconds` Network timeout for proxied requests | | sv p. 814 | E |
| `ProxyVia On\|Off\|Full\|Block` Information provided in the `Via` HTTP response header for proxied requests | Off | sv p. 814 | E |
| `ProxyWebsocketAsync ON\|OFF` Instructs this module to try to create an asynchronous tunnel | | sv p. 856 | E |
| `ProxyWebsocketAsyncDelay num[ms]` Sets the amount of time the tunnel waits synchronously for data | 0 | sv p. 857 | E |
| `ProxyWebsocketIdleTimeout num[ms]` Sets the maximum amount of time to wait for data on the websockets tunnel | 0 | sv p. 857 | E |
| `QualifyRedirectURL ON\|OFF` Controls whether the REDIRECT_URL environment variable is fully qualified | OFF | svd p. 426 | C |
| `ReadmeName filename` Name of the file that will be inserted at the end of the index listing | | svdh p. 553 | B |
| `ReceiveBufferSize bytes` TCP receive buffer size | 0 | s p. 996 | M |
| `Redirect [status] [URL-path] URL` Sends an external redirect asking the client to fetch a different URL | | svdh p. 450 | B |
| `RedirectMatch [status] regex URL` Sends an external redirect based on a regular expression match of the current URL | | svdh p. 451 | B |

| | | | |
|---|---|---|---|
| `RLimitMEM bytes|max [bytes|max]` | | svdh | C |
| Limits the memory consumption of processes launched by Apache httpd children | | p. 427 | |
| `RLimitNPROC number|max [number|max]` | | svdh | C |
| Limits the number of processes that can be launched by processes launched by Apache httpd children | | p. 427 | |
| `Satisfy Any|All` | All | dh | E |
| Interaction between host-level access control and user authentication | | p. 444 | |
| `ScoreBoardFile file-path` | apache_runtime_stat + | s | M |
| Location of the file used to store coordination data for the child processes | | p. 996 | |
| `Script method cgi-script` | | svd | B |
| Activates a CGI script for a particular request method. | | p. 446 | |
| `ScriptAlias [URL-path] file-path|directory-path` | | svd | B |
| Maps a URL to a filesystem location and designates the target as a CGI script | | p. 452 | |
| `ScriptAliasMatch regex file-path|directory-path` | | sv | B |
| Maps a URL to a filesystem location using a regular expression and designates the target as a CGI script | | p. 453 | |
| `ScriptInterpreterSource Registry|Registry-Strict|Script` | Script | svdh | C |
| Technique for locating the interpreter for CGI scripts | | p. 428 | |
| `ScriptLog file-path` | | sv | B |
| Location of the CGI script error logfile | | p. 582 | |
| `ScriptLogBuffer bytes` | 1024 | sv | B |
| Maximum amount of PUT or POST requests that will be recorded in the scriptlog | | p. 582 | |
| `ScriptLogLength bytes` | 10385760 | sv | B |
| Size limit of the CGI script logfile | | p. 582 | |
| `ScriptSock file-path` | cgisock | s | B |
| The filename prefix of the socket to use for communication with the cgi daemon | | p. 584 | |
| `SecureListen [IP-address:]portnumber Certificate-Name [MUTUAL]` | | s | B |
| Enables SSL encryption for the specified port | | p. 770 | |
| `SeeRequestTail On|Off` | Off | s | C |
| Determine if mod_status displays the first 63 characters of a request or the last 63, assuming the request itself is greater than 63 chars. | | p. 428 | |
| `SendBufferSize bytes` | 0 | s | M |
| TCP buffer size | | p. 997 | |
| `ServerAdmin email-address|URL` | | sv | C |
| Email address that the server includes in error messages sent to the client | | p. 429 | |
| `ServerAlias hostname [hostname] ...` | | v | C |
| Alternate names for a host used when matching requests to name-virtual hosts | | p. 429 | |
| `ServerLimit number` | | s | M |
| Upper limit on configurable number of processes | | p. 997 | |
| `ServerName [scheme://]domain-name|ip-address[:port]` | | sv | C |
| Hostname and port that the server uses to identify itself | | p. 430 | |
| `ServerPath URL-path` | | v | C |
| Legacy URL pathname for a name-based virtual host that is accessed by an incompatible browser | | p. 431 | |
| `ServerRoot directory-path` | /usr/local/apache | s | C |
| Base directory for the server installation | | p. 431 | |
| `ServerSignature On|Off|EMail` | Off | svdh | C |
| Configures the footer on server-generated documents | | p. 431 | |
| `ServerTokens Major|Minor|Min[imal]|Prod[uctOnly]|OS|Full` | Full | s | C |
| Configures the `Server` HTTP response header | | p. 432 | |
| `Session On|Off` | Off | svdh | E |
| Enables a session for the current directory or location | | p. 887 | |
| `SessionCookieName name attributes` | | svdh | E |
| Name and attributes for the RFC2109 cookie storing the session | | p. 891 | |
| `SessionCookieName2 name attributes` | | svdh | E |
| Name and attributes for the RFC2965 cookie storing the session | | p. 891 | |
| `SessionCookieRemove On|Off` | Off | svdh | E |
| Control for whether session cookies should be removed from incoming HTTP headers | | p. 891 | |
| `SessionCryptoCipher name` | | svdh | X |
| The crypto cipher to be used to encrypt the session | | p. 894 | |
| `SessionCryptoDriver name [param[=value]]` | | s | X |
| The crypto driver to be used to encrypt the session | | p. 894 | |
| `SessionCryptoPassphrase secret [ secret ... ]` | | svdh | X |
| The key used to encrypt the session | | p. 895 | |
| `SessionCryptoPassphraseFile filename` | | svd | X |
| File containing keys used to encrypt the session | | p. 896 | |
| `SessionDBDCookieName name attributes` | | svdh | E |
| Name and attributes for the RFC2109 cookie storing the session ID | | p. 899 | |

| | | | |
|---|---|---|---|
| `SSLCADNRequestPath directory-path` | | sv | E |
| Directory of PEM-encoded CA Certificates for defining acceptable CA names | | p. 922 | |
| `SSLCARevocationCheck chain\|leaf\|none flags` | none | sv | E |
| Enable CRL-based revocation checking | | p. 922 | |
| `SSLCARevocationFile file-path` | | sv | E |
| File of concatenated PEM-encoded CA CRLs for Client Auth | | p. 923 | |
| `SSLCARevocationPath directory-path` | | sv | E |
| Directory of PEM-encoded CA CRLs for Client Auth | | p. 923 | |
| `SSLCertificateChainFile file-path` | | sv | E |
| File of PEM-encoded Server CA Certificates | | p. 924 | |
| `SSLCertificateFile file-path` | | sv | E |
| Server PEM-encoded X.509 certificate data file | | p. 924 | |
| `SSLCertificateKeyFile file-path` | | sv | E |
| Server PEM-encoded private key file | | p. 925 | |
| `SSLCipherSuite cipher-spec` | DEFAULT (depends on + | svdh | E |
| Cipher Suite available for negotiation in SSL handshake | | p. 926 | |
| `SSLCompression on\|off` | off | sv | E |
| Enable compression on the SSL level | | p. 929 | |
| `SSLCryptoDevice engine` | builtin | s | E |
| Enable use of a cryptographic hardware accelerator | | p. 929 | |
| `SSLEngine on\|off\|optional` | off | sv | E |
| SSL Engine Operation Switch | | p. 929 | |
| `SSLFIPS on\|off` | off | s | E |
| SSL FIPS mode Switch | | p. 930 | |
| `SSLHonorCipherOrder on\|off` | off | sv | E |
| Option to prefer the server's cipher preference order | | p. 930 | |
| `SSLInsecureRenegotiation on\|off` | off | sv | E |
| Option to enable support for insecure renegotiation | | p. 930 | |
| `SSLOCSDefaultResponder uri` | | sv | E |
| Set the default responder URI for OCSP validation | | p. 931 | |
| `SSLOCSPEnable on\|off` | off | sv | E |
| Enable OCSP validation of the client certificate chain | | p. 931 | |
| `SSLOCSPOverrideResponder on\|off` | off | sv | E |
| Force use of the default responder URI for OCSP validation | | p. 932 | |
| `SSLOCSPProxyURL url` | | sv | E |
| Proxy URL to use for OCSP requests | | p. 932 | |
| `SSLOCSPResponderTimeout seconds` | 10 | sv | E |
| Timeout for OCSP queries | | p. 932 | |
| `SSLOCSPResponseMaxAge seconds` | -1 | sv | E |
| Maximum allowable age for OCSP responses | | p. 932 | |
| `SSLOCSPResponseTimeSkew seconds` | 300 | sv | E |
| Maximum allowable time skew for OCSP response validation | | p. 933 | |
| `SSLOCSPUseRequestNonce on\|off` | on | sv | E |
| Use a nonce within OCSP queries | | p. 933 | |
| `SSLOpenSSLConfCmd command-name command-value` | | sv | E |
| Configure OpenSSL parameters through its *SSL_CONF* API | | p. 933 | |
| `SSLOptions [+\|-]option ...` | | svdh | E |
| Configure various SSL engine run-time options | | p. 934 | |
| `SSLPassPhraseDialog type` | builtin | s | E |
| Type of pass phrase dialog for encrypted private keys | | p. 935 | |
| `SSLProtocol [+\|-]protocol ...` | all -SSLv3 | sv | E |
| Configure usable SSL/TLS protocol versions | | p. 936 | |
| `SSLProxyCACertificateFile file-path` | | svp | E |
| File of concatenated PEM-encoded CA Certificates for Remote Server Auth | | p. 937 | |
| `SSLProxyCACertificatePath directory-path` | | svp | E |
| Directory of PEM-encoded CA Certificates for Remote Server Auth | | p. 937 | |
| `SSLProxyCARevocationCheck chain\|leaf\|none` | none | svp | E |
| Enable CRL-based revocation checking for Remote Server Auth | | p. 937 | |
| `SSLProxyCARevocationFile file-path` | | svp | E |
| File of concatenated PEM-encoded CA CRLs for Remote Server Auth | | p. 938 | |
| `SSLProxyCARevocationPath directory-path` | | svp | E |
| Directory of PEM-encoded CA CRLs for Remote Server Auth | | p. 938 | |
| `SSLProxyCheckPeerCN on\|off` | on | svp | E |
| Whether to check the remote server certificate's CN field | | p. 939 | |

| Directive | Default | Context | E |
|---|---|---|---|
| `SSLProxyCheckPeerExpire on\|off` <br> Whether to check if remote server certificate is expired | on | svp <br> p. 939 | E |
| `SSLProxyCheckPeerName on\|off` <br> Configure host name checking for remote server certificates | on | svp <br> p. 939 | E |
| `SSLProxyCipherSuite cipher-spec` <br> Cipher Suite available for negotiation in SSL proxy handshake | ALL:!ADH:RC4+RSA:+H + | svp <br> p. 940 | E |
| `SSLProxyEngine on\|off` <br> SSL Proxy Engine Operation Switch | off | svp <br> p. 940 | E |
| `SSLProxyMachineCertificateChainFile filename` <br> File of concatenated PEM-encoded CA certificates to be used by the proxy for choosing a certificate | | svp <br> p. 940 | E |
| `SSLProxyMachineCertificateFile filename` <br> File of concatenated PEM-encoded client certificates and keys to be used by the proxy | | svp <br> p. 941 | E |
| `SSLProxyMachineCertificatePath directory` <br> Directory of PEM-encoded client certificates and keys to be used by the proxy | | svp <br> p. 941 | E |
| `SSLProxyProtocol [+\|-]protocol ...` <br> Configure usable SSL protocol flavors for proxy usage | all -SSLv3 | svp <br> p. 942 | E |
| `SSLProxyVerify level` <br> Type of remote server Certificate verification | none | svp <br> p. 942 | E |
| `SSLProxyVerifyDepth number` <br> Maximum depth of CA Certificates in Remote Server Certificate verification | 1 | svp <br> p. 943 | E |
| `SSLRandomSeed context source [bytes]` <br> Pseudo Random Number Generator (PRNG) seeding source | | s <br> p. 943 | E |
| `SSLRenegBufferSize bytes` <br> Set the size for the SSL renegotiation buffer | 131072 | dh <br> p. 944 | E |
| `SSLRequire expression` <br> Allow access only when an arbitrarily complex boolean expression is true | | dh <br> p. 945 | E |
| `SSLRequireSSL` <br> Deny access when SSL is not used for the HTTP request | | dh <br> p. 946 | E |
| `SSLSessionCache type` <br> Type of the global/inter-process SSL Session Cache | none | s <br> p. 947 | E |
| `SSLSessionCacheTimeout seconds` <br> Number of seconds before an SSL session expires in the Session Cache | 300 | sv <br> p. 948 | E |
| `SSLSessionTicketKeyFile file-path` <br> Persistent encryption/decryption key for TLS session tickets | | sv <br> p. 948 | E |
| `SSLSessionTickets on\|off` <br> Enable or disable use of TLS session tickets | on | sv <br> p. 949 | E |
| `SSLSRPUnknownUserSeed secret-string` <br> SRP unknown user seed | | sv <br> p. 949 | E |
| `SSLSRPVerifierFile file-path` <br> Path to SRP verifier file | | sv <br> p. 949 | E |
| `SSLStaplingCache type` <br> Configures the OCSP stapling cache | | s <br> p. 950 | E |
| `SSLStaplingErrorCacheTimeout seconds` <br> Number of seconds before expiring invalid responses in the OCSP stapling cache | 600 | sv <br> p. 950 | E |
| `SSLStaplingFakeTryLater on\|off` <br> Synthesize "tryLater" responses for failed OCSP stapling queries | on | sv <br> p. 950 | E |
| `SSLStaplingForceURL uri` <br> Override the OCSP responder URI specified in the certificate's AIA extension | | sv <br> p. 950 | E |
| `SSLStaplingResponderTimeout seconds` <br> Timeout for OCSP stapling queries | 10 | sv <br> p. 951 | E |
| `SSLStaplingResponseMaxAge seconds` <br> Maximum allowable age for OCSP stapling responses | -1 | sv <br> p. 951 | E |
| `SSLStaplingResponseTimeSkew seconds` <br> Maximum allowable time skew for OCSP stapling response validation | 300 | sv <br> p. 951 | E |
| `SSLStaplingReturnResponderErrors on\|off` <br> Pass stapling related OCSP errors on to client | on | sv <br> p. 951 | E |
| `SSLStaplingStandardCacheTimeout seconds` <br> Number of seconds before expiring responses in the OCSP stapling cache | 3600 | sv <br> p. 952 | E |
| `SSLStrictSNIVHostCheck on\|off` <br> Whether to allow non-SNI clients to access a name-based virtual host. | off | sv <br> p. 952 | E |
| `SSLUserName varname` <br> Variable name to determine user name | | sdh <br> p. 952 | E |
| `SSLUseStapling on\|off` <br> Enable stapling of OCSP responses in the TLS handshake | off | sv <br> p. 953 | E |

| | | | |
|---|---|---|---|
| `SSLVerifyClient level` <br> Type of Client Certificate verification | none | svdh <br> p. 953 | E |
| `SSLVerifyDepth number` <br> Maximum depth of CA Certificates in Client Certificate verification | 1 | svdh <br> p. 954 | E |
| `StartServers number` <br> Number of child server processes created at startup | | s <br> p. 998 | M |
| `StartThreads number` <br> Number of threads created on startup | | s <br> p. 998 | M |
| `Substitute s/pattern/substitution/[infq]` <br> Pattern to filter the response content | | dh <br> p. 964 | E |
| `SubstituteInheritBefore on\|off` <br> Change the merge order of inherited patterns | on | dh <br> p. 965 | E |
| `SubstituteMaxLineLength bytes(b\|B\|k\|K\|m\|M\|g\|G)` <br> Set the maximum line size | 1m | dh <br> p. 966 | E |
| `Suexec On\|Off` <br> Enable or disable the suEXEC feature | | s <br> p. 973 | B |
| `SuexecUserGroup User Group` <br> User and group for CGI programs to run as | | sv <br> p. 967 | E |
| `ThreadLimit number` <br> Sets the upper limit on the configurable number of threads per child process | | s <br> p. 999 | M |
| `ThreadsPerChild number` <br> Number of threads created by each child process | | s <br> p. 999 | M |
| `ThreadStackSize size` <br> The size in bytes of the stack used by threads handling client connections | | s <br> p. 999 | M |
| `TimeOut seconds` <br> Amount of time the server will wait for certain events before failing a request | 60 | sv <br> p. 434 | C |
| `TraceEnable [on\|off\|extended]` <br> Determines the behavior on TRACE requests | on | sv <br> p. 435 | C |
| `TransferLog file\|pipe` <br> Specify location of a log file | | sv <br> p. 710 | B |
| `TypesConfig file-path` <br> The location of the `mime.types` file | conf/mime.types | s <br> p. 761 | B |
| `UnDefine parameter-name` <br> Undefine the existence of a variable | | sv <br> p. 435 | C |
| `UndefMacro name` <br> Undefine a macro | | svd <br> p. 747 | B |
| `UnsetEnv env-variable [env-variable] ...` <br> Removes variables from the environment | | svdh <br> p. 616 | B |
| `Use name [value1 ...  valueN]` <br> Use a macro | | svd <br> p. 748 | B |
| `UseCanonicalName On\|Off\|DNS` <br> Configures how the server determines its own name and port | Off | svd <br> p. 435 | C |
| `UseCanonicalPhysicalPort On\|Off` <br> Configures how the server determines its own port | Off | svd <br> p. 436 | C |
| `User unix-userid` <br> The userid under which the server will answer requests | #-1 | s <br> p. 973 | B |
| `UserDir directory-filename [directory-filename] ...` <br> Location of the user-specific directories | | sv <br> p. 975 | B |
| `VHostCGIMode On\|Off\|Secure` <br> Determines whether the virtualhost can run subprocesses, and the privileges available to subprocesses. | On | v <br> p. 783 | X |
| `VHostPrivs [+-]?privilege-name [[+-]?privilege-name] ...` <br> Assign arbitrary privileges to subprocesses created by a virtual host. | | v <br> p. 784 | X |
| `VHostGroup unix-groupid` <br> Sets the Group ID under which a virtual host runs. | | v <br> p. 784 | X |
| `VHostPrivs [+-]?privilege-name [[+-]?privilege-name] ...` <br> Assign arbitrary privileges to a virtual host. | | v <br> p. 785 | X |
| `VHostSecure On\|Off` <br> Determines whether the server runs with enhanced security for the virtualhost. | On | v <br> p. 785 | X |
| `VHostUser unix-userid` <br> Sets the User ID under which a virtual host runs. | | v <br> p. 786 | X |
| `VirtualDocumentRoot interpolated-directory\|none` <br> Dynamically configure the location of the document root for a given virtual host | none | sv <br> p. 984 | E |
| `VirtualDocumentRootIP interpolated-directory\|none` <br> Dynamically configure the location of the document root for a given virtual host | none | sv <br> p. 984 | E |

| | | | |
|---|---|---|---|
| `<VirtualHost addr[:port] [addr[:port]] ...> ...`<br>`</VirtualHost>`<br>Contains directives that apply only to a specific hostname or IP address | | s<br>p. 437 | C |
| `VirtualScriptAlias interpolated-directory\|none`<br>Dynamically configure the location of the CGI directory for a given virtual host | none | sv<br>p. 985 | E |
| `VirtualScriptAliasIP interpolated-directory\|none`<br>Dynamically configure the location of the CGI directory for a given virtual host | none | sv<br>p. 985 | E |
| `Warning message`<br>Warn from configuration parsing with a custom message | | svdh<br>p. 438 | C |
| `WatchdogInterval number-of-seconds`<br>Watchdog interval in seconds | 1 | s<br>p. 986 | B |
| `XBitHack on\|off\|full`<br>Parse SSI directives in files with the execute bit set | off | svdh<br>p. 679 | B |
| `xml2EncAlias charset alias [alias ...]`<br>Recognise Aliases for encoding values | | s<br>p. 988 | B |
| `xml2EncDefault name`<br>Sets a default encoding to assume when absolutely no information can be automatically detected | | svdh<br>p. 988 | B |
| `xml2StartParse element [element ...]`<br>Advise the parser to skip leading junk. | | svdh<br>p. 989 | B |

www.ingramcontent.com/pod-product-compliance
Lightning Source LLC
Chambersburg PA
CBHW081446050326
40690CB00015B/2700